3D GAME PROGRAMMING
USING DIRECTX 10 AND OPENGL

Pierre Rautenbach

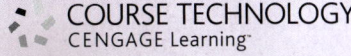

COURSE TECHNOLOGY
CENGAGE Learning™

Australia • Brazil • Japan • Korea • Mexico • Singapore • Spain • United Kingdom • United States

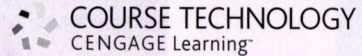

COURSE TECHNOLOGY
CENGAGE Learning

3DGAME PROGRAMMING
Pierre Rautenbach

Publishing Director: John Yates

Publisher: Patrick Bond

Development Editor: Matthew Lane

Content Project Editor: Jamina Ward

Manufacturing Manager: Helen Mason

Senior Production Controller: Maeve Healy

Marketing Manager: Tally Judge

Typesetter: ICC Macmillan Inc.

Cover design: Design Deluxe, Bath, UK

Text design: Design Deluxe, Bath, UK

For product information and technology assistance,
contact **emea.info@cengage.com**

For permission to use material from this text or product,
and for permissions queries,
email **clsuk.permissions@cengage.com**

British Library Cataloguing-in-Publication Data A catalogue record for this book is available from the British Library.

ISBN-13: 978-1-84480-877-9

Cengage Learning EMEA
High Holborn House, 50-51 Bedford Row
London WC1R4LR

Cengage Learning products are represented in Canada by Nelson Education, Ltd.

For your lifelong learning solutions, visit **www.cengage.co.uk**

Visit our corporate website at **cengage.com**

Printed by C & C Offset, China
1 2 3 4 5 6 7 8 9 10–10 09 08

BRIEF CONTENTS

Acknowledgments xiii
Preface xiv

1   Introduction to Game Development 1

2   OpenGL vs. DirectX as API 37

3   The Component Object Model and DirectX 67

4   Window Creation and Control 85

5   Input Control 141

6   Rendering: Direct3D and OpenGL 192

7   Viewing and Transformations 268

8   Color and Texture Mapping 309

9   Lighting 358

10   Alpha Blending and Fog 403

11   Shadows 431

12   Height Maps, Hidden Surface Removal, Clipping and Level of Detail Algorithms 464

13   Polygonal Meshes and Animation 513

14   Physics Modeling 539

15   Artificial Intelligence 567

16   Audio 592

17   Creating an Interactive 3D Environment 623

Bibliography 659
Index 665

CONTENTS

Acknowledgments xiii
Preface xiv

1 Introduction to Game Development 1

1.1 Introduction to Game Development 2
    1.1.1 History 4
    1.1.2 Elements of Game Programming 8
    1.1.3 A Short Introduction to Operating System Architecture 12
1.2 Game Development Techniques and Methodologies 15
    1.2.1 Sequential Software Development: The Waterfall Model 16
    1.2.2 Iterative Software Development: The Rational Unified Process 17
    1.2.3 Agile Software Development: Extreme Programming 21
1.3 Introduction to the Unified Modeling Language (UML) 23
    1.3.1 Class Diagrams 23
        1.3.1.1 Representing Classes 25
        1.3.1.2 Representing Associations 25
        1.3.1.3 Representing Generalizations 27
        1.3.1.4 Aggregation 27
        1.3.1.5 Interfaces 28
    1.3.2 Instance Diagrams 28
1.4 Game Development Tools 29
1.5 Summary 35
1.6 Further Reading 35
1.7 Exercises 36

2 OpenGL vs. DirectX as API 37

2.1 Application Programming Interfaces 38
2.2 OpenGL: A Standard for Cross-Platform High Performance Graphics 40
    2.2.1 A Very Basic OpenGL Program 41
2.3 The OpenGL Utility Toolkit (GLUT) 44
    2.3.1 A Very Simple GLUT Program 48
2.4 DirectX Foundation Classes 52
    2.4.1 A Very Simple Direct3D 10 Program 54

2.5 Summary 65
2.6 Further Reading 65
2.7 Exercises 66

3   The Component Object Model and DirectX 67

3.1 The Component Object Model 68
    3.1.1 The COM Object and Interfaces 69
    3.1.2 GUIDs and IIDs 70
    3.1.3 Defining a COM Object 71
    3.1.4 A Comprehensive COM Program 74
3.2 DirectX and the Component Object Model 79
    3.2.1 DirectX's HRESULT Values 80
    3.2.2 DirectX Interface Creation and Queries 80
3.3 Summary 83
3.4 Further Reading 83
3.5 Exercises 83

4   Window Creation and Control 85

4.1 The Graphics System 86
    4.1.1 Input Devices 86
    4.1.2 Output Devices 88
    4.1.3 Frame Buffer 89
4.2 Elements of a 3D Environment 90
4.3 The Graphics Pipeline Architecture 92
    4.3.1 Vertex Processing 93
    4.3.2 Clipping and Culling 94
    4.3.3 Rasterization and Fragment Processing 95
    4.3.4 Programmable Pipelines 95
        4.3.4.1 The Direct3D 10 Processing Pipeline 96
        4.3.4.2 The OpenGL Processing Pipeline 108
4.4 The Programming Interface 114
    4.4.1 OpenGL/GLUT 114
    4.4.2 DirectX 117
4.5 Window Creation and Control 119
    4.5.1 Setting up a Window and the Main Message Loop 119
    4.5.2 Initializing Direct3D/OpenGL and Generating Output 126
4.6 Summary 138
4.7 Further Reading 138
4.8 Exercises 139

5   Input Control 141

5.1 Input Devices 142
5.2 Six Classes of Input 144

5.3 DirectInput 145
    5.3.1 DirectInput Device Setup (Keyboard, Mouse, or Joystick) 147
        5.3.1.1 Creating a DirectInput Object 147
        5.3.1.2 Creating a DirectInput Device 149
        5.3.1.3 Setting the Data Format of a DirectInput Device 153
        5.3.1.4 Setting the Cooperative Level of a DirectInput Device 155
        5.3.1.5 Acquiring the DirectInput Device 161
        5.3.1.6 Reading Data from a DirectInput Device 162
    5.3.2 Device Data 168
        5.3.2.1 Buffered as an Alternative to Immediate Keyboard Data 168
        5.3.2.2 Buffered as an Alternative to Immediate Mouse Data 171
        5.3.2.3 Buffered as an Alternative to Immediate Joystick Data 171
    5.3.3 Action Mapping 172
        5.3.3.1 Specifying the Actions 173
        5.3.3.2 Setting up the Action Map 173
        5.3.3.3 Applying an Action Map to Physical Devices 177
        5.3.3.4 Applying the Action Map to a Device 178
        5.3.3.5 Retrieving Action Map Data 179
    5.3.4 Force Feedback 179
        5.3.4.1 Setting up a Force Feedback Device 180
        5.3.4.2 Using Effects 182
5.4 XInput 188
5.5 Summary 189
5.6 Further Reading 190
5.7 Exercises 190

6   Rendering: Direct3D and OpenGL 192

6.1 Introduction: Primitives and Polygons 193
    6.1.1 Primitive and Polygon Types 194
    6.1.2 Rendering Stroke and Raster Text 200
6.2 Drawing: Primitives and Polygons 203
6.3 Direct3D Render States 212
    6.3.1 The Rasterizer State Object 212
    6.3.2 The Input-Layout State Object 213
    6.3.3 The Depth Stencil State Object 214
    6.3.4 The Blend State Object 214
    6.3.5 The Sample State Object 216
6.4 The DXUT Framework 216
6.5 Shaders 227
    6.5.1 The Hardware Graphics Pipeline Revisited 229
    6.5.2 The Programmable Graphics Pipeline Revisited 232
    6.5.3 Cg: C for Graphics (Direct3D & OpenGL) 236
        6.5.3.1 Cg Language Profiles 236
        6.5.3.2 The Cg Compiler 238
        6.5.3.3 The Cg Runtime 238

6.5.3.4 Initializing Cg 238

6.5.3.5 Creating a Vertex Program 242

6.5.3.6 Creating a Fragment Program 249

6.5.4 High Level Shader Language (HLSL) 252

6.5.4.1 The HLSL Compiler 253

6.5.4.2 Initializing the High Level Shader Language 254

6.5.4.3 Creating HLSL Shaders 258

6.5.4.4 Common HLSL Data Types 260

6.5.4.5 Utilizing a Created HLSL Effect 261

6.6 Summary 265

6.7 Further Reading 266

6.8 Exercises 266

7   Viewing and Transformations 268

7.1 3D Cartesian Coordinate Systems 269

7.2 The Synthetic-Camera Model 271

7.3 The Viewing System 272

7.3.1 The View Volume 272

7.3.2 Culling 272

7.3.3 Clipping 275

7.4 Changing Coordinate Systems 275

7.4.1 Viewing Transformation 276

7.4.2 Modeling Transformation 276

7.4.3 Projection Transformation 278

7.4.4 Viewport Transformation 281

7.5 Spatial Transformations 282

7.5.1 Translation 283

7.5.2 Rotation 285

7.5.2.1 Rotation About the Coordinate Axes 286

7.5.2.2 Rotation About an Arbitrary Fixed Point 288

7.5.3 Scaling 290

7.6 Examples 291

7.6.1 Rendering a Triangle Without Any Transformations 291

7.6.2 Rendering a Triangle Translated 299

7.6.3 Rendering a Triangle Rotated 301

7.6.4 Rendering a Scaled Triangle 303

7.7 Summary 306

7.8 Further Reading 306

7.9 Exercises 307

8   Color and Texture Mapping 309

8.1 Color 310

8.2 Texturing 315

8.2.1 Texture Filtering 318

8.2.1.1 Mipmapping 318

8.2.1.2 Nearest Point Interpolation 319

8.2.1.3 Bilinear Filtering 320

8.2.1.4 Trilinear Filtering 320

8.2.1.5 Anisotropic Filtering 321

8.2.2 Basic Texture Mapping 321

8.2.3 Bump Mapping 338

8.2.3.1 Implementing Bump Mapping 340

8.2.4 Cube Mapping 346

8.2.4.1 Implementing Cube Mapping 346

8.3 Summary 355

8.4 Further Reading 356

8.5 Exercises 356

9   Lighting 358

9.1 Light Sources 359

9.1.1 Point Lights 361

9.1.2 Spotlights 362

9.1.3 Ambient Lights 362

9.1.4 Parallel Lights 363

9.1.5 Emissive Light 363

9.2 Reflection Models 364

9.2.1 Ambient Reflection Model 364

9.2.2 Specular Reflection Model 365

9.2.3 Diffuse Reflection Model 367

9.2.4 The Phong Reflection Model 368

9.3 Vectors 370

9.3.1 Vector Length 370

9.3.2 Vector Addition (Head-to-Tail Rule) 371

9.3.3 Scalar Multiplication 372

9.3.4 Cross Product (Normal Vectors) 373

9.3.5 Unit Vectors 373

9.3.6 Direct3D Extension Vector Functions 374

9.4 Implementing Local Illumination 376

9.5 Reflection and Refraction 386

9.5.1 Refraction 387

9.5.2 Reflection and Refraction Extended 390

9.6 High Dynamic Range (HDR) Lighting 395

9.7 Summary 400

9.8 Further Reading 401

9.9 Exercises 401

10   Alpha Blending and Fog 403

10.1 Alpha Blending 404

10.1.1 Implementing Blending 406

10.1.2 Implementing Blending using Shaders 411

10.1.3 Alpha Testing 413

10.2 Fog 417
    10.2.1 The Physics of Fog 419
    10.2.2 Implementing Fog 421
10.3 Summary 429
10.4 Further Reading 429
10.5 Exercises 429

11 Shadows 431

11.1 Shadow Rendering Algorithms 432
    11.1.1 Blinn's Shadow Polygons 433
    11.1.2 Scan-Line Polygon Projection 435
    11.1.3 Shadow Mapping 435
    11.1.4 Shadow Volumes 437
        11.1.4.1 Depth-pass 439
        11.1.4.2 Depth-fail 439
        11.1.4.3 Soft-edged Shadows using Penumbra Wedges 440
11.2 The Stencil Buffer 442
    11.2.1 Enabling Depth Stencil Testing 443
11.3 Implementing Stencil Shadow Volumes 454
11.4 Summary 461
11.5 Further Reading 461
11.6 Exercises 462

12 Height Maps, Hidden Surface Removal, Clipping and Level of Detail Algorithms 464

12.1 Height Maps 465
    12.1.1 Creating and Rendering a Height Map 466
12.2 Hidden Surface Removal 475
    12.2.1 The Z-Buffer Algorithm 478
    12.2.2 The Painter's Algorithm 483
12.3 Clipping 484
    12.3.1 Two-Dimensional Line Clipping 485
        12.3.1.1 Cohen-Sutherland Clipping 489
        12.3.1.2 Introduction to Liang-Barsky Clipping 498
    12.3.2 Clipping Polygons 500
    12.3.3 Three-Dimensional Clipping 501
12.4 Introduction to Level of Detail (LOD) Algorithms 505
12.5 Summary 511
12.6 Further Reading 511
12.7 Exercises 511

13 Polygonal Meshes and Animation 513

13.1 Polygonal Meshes 514
    13.1.1 Representing a Mesh 515
    13.1.2 Connecting Rigid Parts of Objects Using Joints 525

13.2 Animation 526

    13.2.1 Introduction to Computer Animation Techniques 528

        13.2.1.1 Animation of Rigid Bodies 529

        13.2.1.2 Animation of Particles 530

        13.2.1.3 Animation via the Laws of Physics 531

        13.2.1.4 Animation of Articulated Objects 531

        13.2.1.5 Behavioural Animation of Objects 532

13.3 Loading and Rendering Meshes in Direct3D 10 534

13.4 Summary 537

13.5 Further Reading 537

13.6 Exercises 537

14 Physics Modeling 539

14.1 Fundamentals of Physics 540

    14.1.1 Time 541

    14.1.2 Position 541

    14.1.3 Mass and Weight 542

    14.1.4 Velocity 543

    14.1.5 Acceleration 543

    14.1.6 Force 544

    14.1.7 Momentum 545

14.2 Physics Modeling and Implementation 546

    14.2.1 Linear Momentum 547

    14.2.2 Gravitational Pull 549

    14.2.3 Trajectory Paths 552

    14.2.4 Friction 553

    14.2.5 Introduction to Object Collisions 555

14.3 Particle Systems 560

    14.3.1 Implementing a Particle System 561

14.4 Summary 565

14.5 Further Reading 566

14.6 Exercises 566

15 Artificial Intelligence 567

15.1 History of AI in Games 568

15.2 Pre-Programmed AI 570

15.3 Scripting 574

15.4 Modeling AI by Means of Finite State Machines 576

15.5 Autonomous Behaviour: Memory and Planning 578

15.6 Pathfinding 582

    15.6.1 The A* Algorithm 583

    15.6.2 Depth-First Search 585

    15.6.3 Breadth-First Search 585

    15.6.4 Waypoint Pathfinding 586

15.7 Introduction to More Advanced AI: Neural Networks, Expert Systems and Genetic Algorithms 588

15.8 Summary 590

15.9 Further Reading 591

15.10 Exercises 591

16   Audio 592

16.1 Introduction to Sound 593

16.2 DirectX Audio 597

    16.2.1 DirectSound 597

    16.2.2 XACT 611

    16.2.3 XAudio2 617

16.3 Summary 621

16.4 Further Reading 622

16.5 Exercises 622

17   Creating an Interactive 3D Environment 623

17.1 Game Engine Architecture 624

    17.1.1 Initialization and Shutdown 627

    17.1.2 The Game Loop 628

17.2 Creating an Interactive DirectX 10 3D Environment 630

17.3 Creating an Interactive OpenGL 3D Environment 643

17.4 Summary 657

17.5 Further Reading 658

17.6 Exercises 658

Bibliography 659

Index 665

ACKNOWLEDGMENTS

The author would like to thank the following:

- My eternal gratitude to Professor Judith Bishop and Gaynor Redvers-Mutton, two people without whom this project never would have been. Special thanks to Gaynor for all her support, encouragement, input and hard work as editor throughout production of this book; it has truly been a privilege.

- Special thanks to Anton Spalovsky for creating the awesome 'cyber dog' 3D mesh used for the front cover image – here is to all the matchless models and animations to come!

- It has been a tremendous pleasure working with Matthew Lane and Jamina Ward at Cengage Learning (EMEA). My thanks and appreciation for all their support, effort and care with the manuscript. I'd also like to give special thanks to Helen Parry for all her effort as copy-editor and David Stone as proofreader.

- Also, special thanks to the entire Cengage production staff and to Cengage Learning EMEA for their hard work and support, and for believing in the project.

- My endless respect to industry pioneers like Mark Kilgard (NVIDIA), John Carmack (id Software) and Tim Sweeney (Epic Games) for everlasting inspiration, groundbreaking research and ceaseless innovation.

- Last but not least, special thanks to my family and friends for their love and encouragement, especially Kepler Engelbrecht for all his advice through the years; Deon Pienaar for being a great sounding board; the original Itlit Software team (Kevin Francis, Alex Liebman, Deon Lee and Andre Viljoen) for sharing my dream of making games; Jeanri Pellissier for sparking my interest in programming; Professor Derrick Kourie, Vreda Pieterse and Morkel Theunissen at the University of Pretoria for their guidance and inspiration; Nikki Fellinger for her encouragement and making me laugh on a daily basis; Anna Rakitianskaia for always listening and tolerating my mindless chatter; and, finally, my mom, Wilna, and dad, Ig, for their incessant encouragement and support through the years.

PREFACE ACKNOWLEDGMENTS

Welcome to *3D Game Programming using DirectX 10 and OpenGL*, a truly unique book that combines various elements of game development and game programming with the in-depth coverage of DirectX 10 and OpenGL to provide you with an unprecedented tome for 3D game programming.

The book starts off with an introduction to game development. This is followed by an introductory comparison highlighting the common ground and disparities between the OpenGL and the DirectX 10 Application Programming Interfaces. Next it examines Microsoft's Component Object Model (COM), including how DirectX and COM fit together. The book subsequently deals with window creation and control, the graphics pipeline architecture, input control (using GLUT, DirectInput and XInput) and the representation and drawing of geometric primitives as well as more complex polygonal types. Following this, it investigates the DXUT framework, Direct3D render states, the usage and programming of shaders (via NVIDIA's Cg and Microsoft's High Level Shader Language) and the specification of effects. Building on this, the book focuses on the mathematical representation of objects in a three-dimensional environment including the definition of the virtual camera model essential for perspective and ortho-graphic projections and the mechanisms used for changing coordinate systems, as well as various transformation techniques such as rotation, translation, and scaling.

The book proceeds with the in-depth coverage of texturing, including a number of texture filtering techniques such as mipmapping and the implementation of advanced texturing effects, for instance, bump and environmental mapping. Next it deals with lighting by focusing on a number of different light source types and various reflection models, the implementation of local illumination, reflection and refraction and High Dynamic Range lighting. Building on this, the book investigates alpha blending and fog, shadow rendering algorithms such as shadow mapping and stencil shadow volumes, terrain rendering using heightmaps, hidden surface removal, clipping and level of detail algorithms. Additional topics looked at include the representation and rendering of meshes, bounding volumes and a number of computer animation techniques.

Subsequent chapters deal with the foundational principles and implementation of basic physics as required by games. Elements focused on, from both a theoretical and practical perspective, include the laws of physics and the modeling and implementation of gravity, friction, trajectory paths, momentum, acceleration, force and collisions. This is followed by chapters dealing with artificial intelligence and audio playback. The final chapter combines the knowledge and several of the techniques presented throughout the book. It starts off by outlining the general design of a game engine. Focus then shifts to the implementation of two interactive 3D environments.

INTENDED AUDIENCE

This book is aimed at both advanced and novice readers as well as undergraduate students in game development, engineering and graphics/game programming courses. The book will also serve as a useful reference guide to many professionals – or anyone interested in creating his or her own next-generation 3D game engine with support for vertex and pixel-shading GPU techniques, dynamic lighting and shadowing, geometric meshes, audio, artificial intelligence, physics, environmental reflections, refraction and advanced lighting techniques such as High Dynamic Range lighting.

A prerequisite for the book is familiarity with programming language concepts. The book's website includes an ancillary C++ primer for students new to the world of programming and all the code samples are fully explained and commented. The discussion of concepts such as data structures (lists, trees, etc.) and rudimentary linear algebra and trigonometry, forming an integral part of graphics programming, is integrated into the text.

SUPPORT MATERIALS

Support material, available from the book's website, *www.cengage.co.uk/rautenbach*, includes:

■ instructor's PowerPoint slides

■ solutions to each chapter's exercise questions

■ program code

■ compiler setup and DirectX/OpenGL setup instructions

■ ancillary material on coding conventions, specifically focusing on the hungarian Notation

■ chapter on C++

■ chapter on XNA.

CHAPTER 1

Introduction to Game Development

LEARNING OBJECTIVES

In this chapter you will learn about:

- The game development process
- The history of game development
- Elements of game programming
- Operating system architecture
- Game development techniques and methodologies
- Sequential software development: the waterfall model
- Iterative software development: the Rational Unified Process
- Agile software development: Extreme Programming
- The Unified Modeling Language (UML)
- Class diagrams
- Representing classes
- Representing associations
- Representing generalizations
- Aggregation
- Interfaces
- Instance diagrams
- Game development tools

INTRODUCTION

Chapter 1 introduces the reader to game development as a multifaceted discipline consisting of several phases. The chapter starts off by looking at the evolution of game development and the interaction considerations necessary when programming real-time games as opposed to general applications. Following this, the chapter features a short introduction to operating system fundamentals. It subsequently looks at game development techniques and methodologies to highlight the design considerations necessary for the development of games. This is followed by an introduction to the Unified Modeling Language. The chapter closes by considering a number of game development tools.

1.1   INTRODUCTION TO GAME DEVELOPMENT

Game development is a multifaceted discipline concerned with the production of video games. This discipline is practiced by both individuals and teams of people and the development of one video game often takes several years to complete (depending on the complexity of the title). A *video game* is, in its most basic form, a game where the player interacts with some virtually represented environment via a particular controller or input device. Input generated by the player leads to changes in this virtual environment and some basic goal or reward system is often present, encouraging the changes. Video games often make use of a wide array of player-system feedback, such as audio playback and tactile response via force feedback devices.

Game developers target a series of platforms, with the personal computer being perhaps the most accessible and popular due to its widespread use. Other platforms include *console systems* which are commonly connected to television systems or a standalone video monitor, Java and BREW enabled mobile phones, *handheld devices* such as Pocket PCs, dedicated *portable gaming systems* such as Nintendo's DS and Game Boy Advance and *arcade systems* which are often dedicated to playing only one specific game.

The game development process is often defined by combining some software engineering methodology with a project management process. *Software engineering* deals with the design, implementation and maintenance of software. *Project management* deals with the administration of resources so that some project can be completed within a predefined timeframe, budget and scope. There are numerous software engineering methodologies and project management methods, and these practices will differ from team to team; however, any game development effort will at least include a pre-production phase, a mainstream production phase, project milestones, testing, release to manufacturing, and patch-based maintenance.

The *pre-production* phase consists of the general game idea or design, the backstory, concept artwork, storyboards, gameplay elements and often a working prototype demonstrating key game features. The pre-production phase is critical for securing project approval and is often the first step in publisher/developer negotiations. For independent commercial game development companies this phase also frequently includes a game demo or running framework. Most of these pre-production elements are combined into a constantly revised *game design document* giving the development team a clear sense of direction and vision. The *pre-production* phase comes to a close with a group of developers doing preliminary development on some of the proposed features.

The *mainstream production* phase constitutes the greatest part of the development process with software developers designing and implementing the game engine, sound engine, 3D engine, networking components, input control, etc. (with implementation details differing depending on whether a third-party game engine has been licensed or not). The artists, animators and 3D modelers are responsible for creating the game assets such as textures, interface elements, and 3D models. The project's level designers design and construct the interactive environment's levels with script writers adding game-play elements to these levels and writers creating the cut-scene and in-game dialog. The game's audio components are also produced during this phase. The mainstream production phase is highly dynamic and not all elements produced will end up in the finished title. The primary person responsible for this decision is the game designer and the decision of cutting elements from the game is based on the constantly changing design document and external or internal time/money/scope constraints. Testing is always conducted to verify software component interaction and that all the requirements were properly implemented during the production phase.

A project *milestone* is analogous to a deadline and it is a very important element of the game development process. Every project milestone focuses on the completion of a development goal. These goals can range from single levels to the completed game. Milestones are set by both the development team and external stakeholders with various (often negative) consequences when they are not met. For example, game publishing companies will often require the payment of a penalty when a milestone is not met. Missing a game's release date also has its own public relations, credibility-related and financial consequences.

- The first big milestone is known as the *pre-alpha* version. This milestone usually includes some functionality and content that will end up in the finished title but a lot of functional and asset/content-based decisions still have to be made.

- The *alpha* version is the next milestone. This release version satisfies most of the project goals and requirements while still requiring extensive testing and debugging. Following this milestone the team has to implement all the remaining requirements and features, leading to the *beta* version of the game.

- The beta version generally has numerous bugs, stability and compatibility issues to sort out and are often only released to a selected group (*closed beta*) as opposed to a larger community group (*open beta*).

- The final milestone is often the release candidate. The *release candidate* version is very close to the final game release version but still has to undergo some extensive testing to ensure that no fatal bugs are present.

Figure 1-1 shows the relation between these various release stages.

Testing is the one element of game and software development that contributes heavily towards the quality of the finished product but that is often cut short to meet the release date. Testing verifies software component interaction and that all the requirements were properly implemented during the production phases. The testing process is commonly divided into unit testing, functional testing and automated testing.

- *Unit testing* is primarily done by the programmers themselves and is used to determine whether a particular section of source code is functioning as expected. Unit tests are conducted via programming units called *test cases*. These test cases are written for all the member functions and methods the programmer desires to test. Test cases will quickly, via a series of inputs and expected outputs, identify a portion of the program not conforming to the functional requirements, should it exist. Unit tests, as the name suggests, operate on isolated portions of the program; quickly identifying an incorrect section (the focus being on functionality only). Extreme Programming makes use of unit testing for white box testing – i.e. checking the outputs of a program against certain inputs with the knowledge of the underlying code in mind.

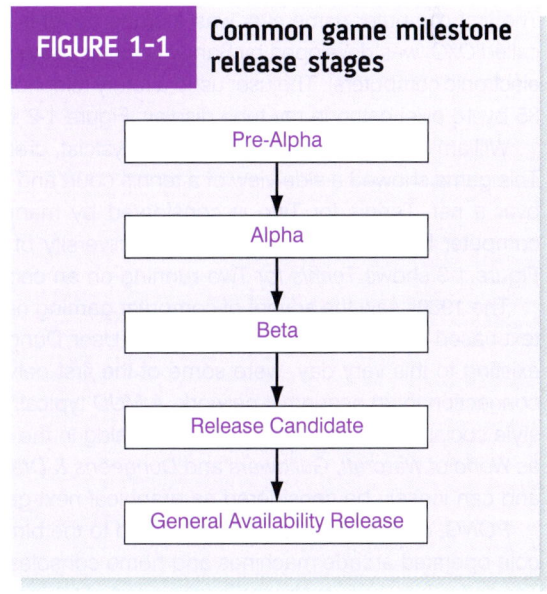

FIGURE 1-1 Common game milestone release stages

Pre-Alpha

↓

Alpha

↓

Beta

↓

Release Candidate

↓

General Availability Release

- *Functional testing* is based on scripts targeted at groups of classes – the focus is on user requirements and performance constraints. Functional tests are aimed at the gameplayer rather than the developers because the players will be able to give exact feedback regarding the current state of the game.

- *Automated testing* focuses on the generation of test units reflecting the existing programming units. Testing is conducted concurrently throughout the implementation phase. Following successful testing and quality assurance the game is released to manufacturing. Such a release is referred to as the *gold* or *general availability release* version. Game companies often announce that their title has 'gone gold', thus indicating that the game has been completed with the general availability release version sent off to manufacturing and that retail copies will soon be available. Smaller, less well-funded, or hobbyist game development teams will rather do a direct-to-public release via the internet.

Despite extensive testing, no software product will ever be 100 percent bug-free. It is also impossible to test every possible hardware combination a game will be run on and incompatibility issues often remain hidden until after release. These issues can, however, be rectified via the release of software patches. Patching is the most common form of maintaining and updating computer games, but care should be taken to ensure that *software regression* (the introduction of bugs affecting a previously functioning component) doesn't occur when a patch is released. Patches are not, however, solely used for the correction of bugs and are often released to improve or change some gameplay element. For example, multiplayer games are frequently patched to resolve certain gameplay exploitations that negatively affect the overall game experience. Many Massively Multiplayer Online Games (MMOGs) go beyond simple patching with regard to maintenance, with new gameplay elements and objects constantly being added dynamically while the game is being played – this could also be used for in-game advertisement streaming and product placements.

The above described game development process is by no means inflexible and the exact development methodology implemented varies from team to team. The software engineering and game development processes implemented are mostly dependent on the nature of the development team, their background, work environment and project requirements. We will now investigate game development by briefly focusing on its historical background, the elements of game programming, core operating system architecture with the aim of understanding event-driven programming and some general game programming techniques, conventions, and methodologies.

1.1.1 History

The first computer game ever was a crude noughts and crosses simulation written in 1952. This game, called *OXO,* was developed by Sandy Douglas using an EDSAC computer (one of the first stored program electronic computers). The user used a rotary telephone dial for input with the output being generated on a 35 by 16 pixel cathode ray tube display. Figure 1-2 shows an emulation of the original program.

William Higinbotham, an American physicist, created *Tennis for Two* in 1958 using an oscilloscope. This game showed a side view of a tennis court and the player was required to hit a gravity affected ball over a net. Tennis for Two is considered by many as the first computer game due to the EDSAC computer being mainly limited to the University of Cambridge Mathematical Laboratory in England. Figure 1-3 shows *Tennis for Two* running on an oscilloscope.

The 1960s saw the advent of computer gaming on mainframe computers. Most of these games were text-based adventures with MUDs (Multi-User Dungeons) appearing in the late 1970s. These MUDs, existing to this very day, were some of the first networked games, with the original MUDs requiring a connection to an academic network. A *MUD* typically combines elements of role playing and chatroom style social interaction. All actions and dialog in the environment are text driven. Modern MMOGs such as *World of Warcraft, Guildwars* and *Dungeons & Dragons Online* have several similarities to early MUDs and can loosely be considered as graphical next-generation MUDs.

PONG, designed by Nolan Busnell, led to the birth of Atari Interactive and was mainly distributed via coin-operated arcade machines and home consoles. The original PONG was related to Higinbotham's *Tennis for Two,* but was based on the sport of table tennis and had a top-down view. *PONG* made use of

FIGURE 1-2	A screenshot of the game OXO

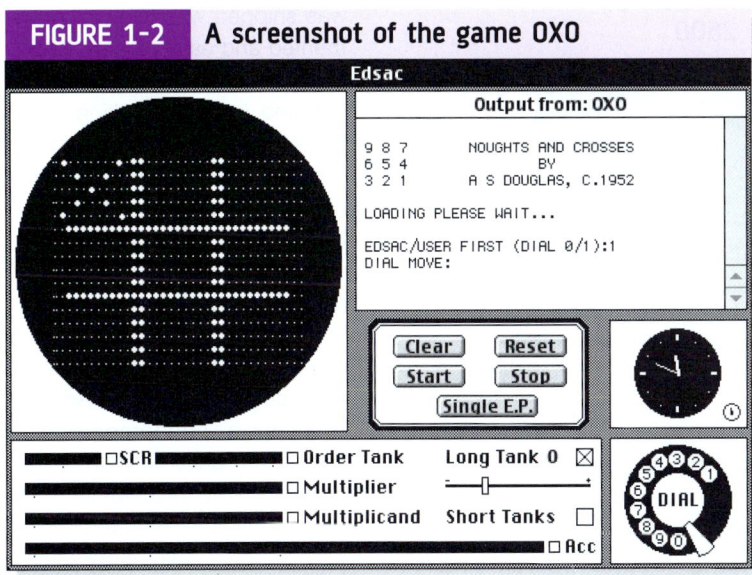

FIGURE 1-3	A photograph of the game Tennis for Two

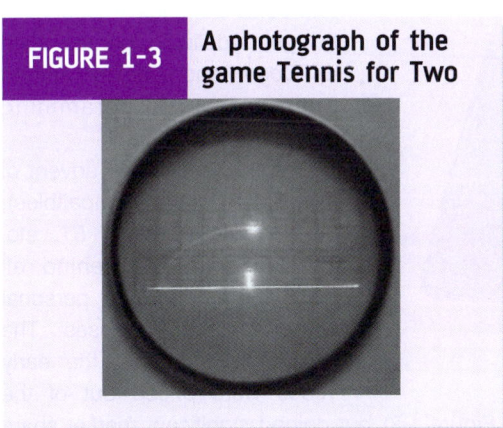

FIGURE 1-4	A PONG clone

solid lines to represent paddles, a dotted line to represent the net and a square to represent the ball. Many versions of the original Atari classic have been made over the years and the entire genre of ball-and-bat video games have become known as *Pong* games (note the lower case spelling). Figure 1-4 shows a clone of the original classic using DirectDraw.

The Atari 2600 (Figure 1-5), released in 1977, allowed for the use of plug-in cartridges. Dedicated consoles offering one or two games were the norm before then and having one console supporting a theoretically unlimited number of games, such as *Breakout, Donkey Kong, Pac-Man* and *Space Invaders,* was extremely popular with the buying market and contributed heavily towards the growth of computer gaming.

The term *personal computer game* or *PC game* surfaced with the release of the *Apple II* (see Figure 1-6) in 1977. Although the Apple II offered some productivity and business applications such as a spreadsheet and word processor, it was designed specifically with educational and personal use in mind. The Apple II

FIGURE 1-5   **The Atari 2600**

FIGURE 1-6   **One of the first Apple II computers**

was shipped with two well-documented and easy to learn BASIC programming languages, *Applesoft* and *Integer,* resulting in the Apple II being used by many computer enthusiasts learning how to program. Applesoft BASIC, created by Microsoft, supported floating point arithmetic and was initially offered as an upgrade to Integer BASIC and later included with the release of the *Apple II Plus*. The Apple II enjoyed a phenomenal user base and grew into the most popular game development platform of the time with hundreds of titles shipped. Two of the world's most respected and prolific game developers, *John Romero* and *John Carmack* (responsible for genre-defining games such as *Doom* and *Quake*), started their careers programming games for the Apple II.

The 1980s saw the advent of the IBM PC (and compatibles), *Commodore 64, Atari ST,* etc. The general idea behind all these systems was 'a personal computer for the masses'. The original IBM PCs of the early 1980s were priced out of the reach of most home users (an example is shown in Figure 1-7) but gained significant market share in the business sector. IBM PCs featured Microsoft BASIC as programming language and an open architecture allowing other manufacturers to develop both peripherals and software for it. This open architecture is the primary reason for the popularity of the PC today. The Commodore 64 featured impressive graphics and sound capabilities compared to the Apple II and IBM PCs of the time. It was also priced much more aggressively than its counterparts. The Commodore 64 also competed against video game consoles such as the Atari 2600 by allowing direct connectivity with a television set. The 'video game crash of 1983' led to the bankruptcy of numerous video game, console and home computer manufacturers. This industry crash was the direct result of the video game market being swamped by a large number of sub-quality games and the availability of competitively priced personal computer systems fulfilling multiple educational, business and entertainment roles. With video game console companies collapsing, PC games quickly took the place of their console counterparts.

The Atari ST (see Figure 1-8) was released in 1985 and was especially suited for PC gaming due to its colorful graphics, good sound, fast performance and good price. 3D computer games such as *Dungeon Master* and notable classics such as *Peter Molyneux's Populous* (also released on the PC and various other platforms) were created for it. The PC, although lagging behind at the beginning of the 1980s, slowly gained popularity due to its open architecture, dropping price, easy upgrading and usefulness as a business tool. The IBM PC compatible was at the forefront of the personal computer race at the start of the 1990s, and the release of Windows 3.0 in May 1990 in particular led to the PC becoming the computing platform of choice to this very day.

FIGURE 1-7   The IBM PC Junior released in 1983

The introduction of high quality soundcards, high resolution displays and peripherals such as the computer mouse and joystick really drove the adoption of computer gaming but it wasn't until 1992 that the real power of the PC as a gaming platform was realized. The main game responsible for this was id Software's shareware mega-hit *Wolfenstein 3D*. *Wolfenstein 3D* popularized the first-person shooter genre and the PC as a gaming platform by allowing the player to interact with a virtual environment from a first-person perspective. *Wolfenstein 3D* was of course not the first 3D computer game for the PC with id Software employing and refining the technology that would become *Wolfenstein 3D* in *Hovertank 3D* and *Catacomb 3D* during 1991. Other older PC games such as *Elite* also featured 3D environments but never achieved the level of technical complexity of *Wolfenstein 3D* nor its cultural and industry impact. Another breakthrough in the graphics of 3D games came with id Software's release of *Doom* in 1993.

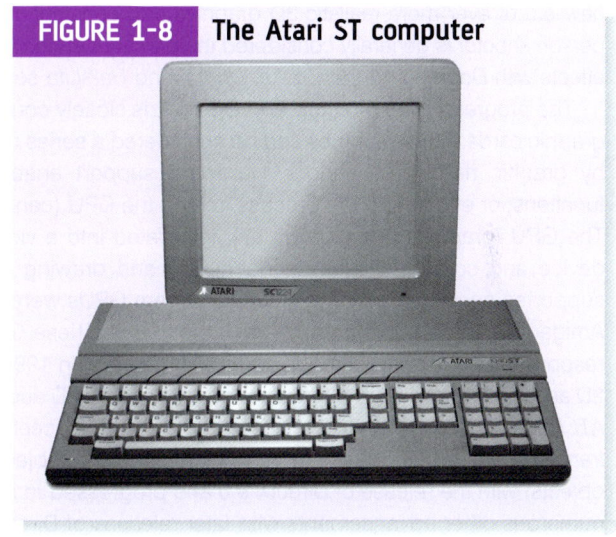

FIGURE 1-8   The Atari ST computer

Doom, a screenshot of which is shown in Figure 1-9, really revolutionized the gaming industry with its fast paced network play and immersive graphics and companies like Microsoft started spending millions of dollars on research and development to migrate gaming from *MS-DOS* to their Windows platform. This research and development culminated in the *DirectX* Application Programming Interface (API).

Following the release of *Doom,* Microsoft wanted to establish *Windows 95* as the gaming platform of choice, as opposed to MS-DOS still being used by the majority of games throughout 1995 and 1996. During a Microsoft Halloween media event at the end of 1995, called *Judgement Day,* a 32-bit port of *Doom* was showcased featuring a video address by *Bill Gates* superimposed inside the game proclaiming Windows 95, using the DirectX API, as 'the game platform'. Initial DirectX versions weren't

FIGURE 1-9 id Software's Doom released in 1993

precisely successful products but were none the less important as technological building blocks. Most of the issues associated with these initial DirectX releases were, however, resolved with the release of DirectX 5.0 in 1997: the era of MS-DOS based games was officially over. There were also a number of developers using OpenGL due to it being a cross-platform graphics API, unlike Microsoft's Direct3D. OpenGL has since had a strong footing in the science and gaming's first-person shooter genre, not only because of its cross-platform nature but also due to its minimalist design, in contrast to Direct3D's perceived complexity. Direct3D's (DirectX's graphics library) inception and the standardization of its competitor, OpenGL, together with the advent of mainstream 3D accelerated graphics hardware revolutionized computer gaming and led to a new era of ever more realistic 3D graphics and constant improvements in graphics hardware. The first-person shooter is generally considered the primary benchmark for graphics complexity, realism and visual effects with *Doom3* and the *Quake, Unreal* and *Half-Life* series often setting the standard for other titles.

The progression of Direct3D and OpenGL is closely coupled with the development of 3D accelerated graphic cards. These libraries can be considered a series of specifications that requires implementation by graphic hardware vendors. Hardware support enables the rapid execution of graphics calls, functions, or effects – in the process freeing the CPU (central processing unit) to do other calculations. The GPU (graphics processing unit), integrated into a video card, is a dedicated graphics rendering device and controls the rendering quality and drawing performance depending on the number of supported specifications. The first mainstream GPUs were released with the Atari ST, the Commodore Amiga and some home computers of the 1980s. These GPUs were nothing more than simple *blitters* responsible for moving bitmaps around in memory. In 1991 S3 Graphics launched the first mainstream 2D accelerator for the PC and was soon followed by 2D accelerators with added 3D features such as the *ATI Rage* and the *S3 ViRGE*. These basic graphics accelerators soon evolved to include support for *transform* and *lighting* (translating three-dimensional objects and calculating the effects of lighting on objects) with the release of DirectX 5.0 and progressed to include programmable shaders in addition to numerous other advancements with later releases of DirectX and OpenGL.

1.1.2 Elements of Game Programming

Game programming is concerned with the software engineering elements of computer, console and arcade games. Most game programming endeavors begin during the game design phase. The programming effort can commence by implementing a series of loose ideas and concepts or by laying down a structured framework. The programming team will often start by defining and designing the various networking, interface, AI, scripting and graphics components needed to fulfill the game's requirements in cases where a 3D engine and related technologies need to be developed from scratch. The team will also evaluate whether all game design requirements are programmatically fulfilled, determining the lacking components, in cases where a third-party game engine such as *RenderWare* or the *Doom3 engine* are used.

The primary difference between game programming and general application programming is the real-time nature of games. Normal applications rely on sequential or event-driven input, only initiating or performing a task once the user has executed some action. Computer programs were traditionally written using a flow-driven or procedural programming paradigm. *Flow-driven* program execution is based on a predefined control flow pattern specified within the program. The program's flow can change when certain conditions are met but the program does not respond to any external events. Modern-day programs generally make use of the *event-driven* programming model. This model enables program control based on external events such as user input, or information from other programs via the use of an event loop and trigger function. The *event loop* continuously monitors system input ranging from file accesses, to keyboard and mouse events, to program events. Once some event has occurred, it is processed by calling a *trigger function*. There are numerous trigger functions defined by the operating system and it is the application programmer's job to rewrite these default trigger functions for use with the application.

Events can be monitored either using *polling* (continuously monitoring the status of some external device) coupled with an event loop, or via the use of interrupt handlers responding to hardware changes. *Interrupt handlers* are the routines built into the operating system or a device driver dealing with generated hardware signal variations known as interrupts. Interrupt handling can be divided into two levels: top-half interrupts and bottom-half interrupts. *Top-half interrupts,* also known as fast-interrupts, quickly deal with any platform specific interrupt when it is generated. The system responds to the interrupt, saves the current CPU state, loads and processes the code for the interrupt and restores the saved CPU state. *Bottom-half* interrupts, commonly referred to as slow interrupt handlers, are concerned with more complex, time-consuming interrupt processing tasks. These interrupts are often generated by software and are similar to processes with regard to the amount of processing time required.

Games on the other hand require a more independent execution approach. This is accomplished via the implementation of a game loop. The *game loop* allows uninterrupted execution of the game, independent of the user's input. One problem with defining a game event loop is that it must run within the constraints imposed by the operating system – specifically the operating system's process scheduler. The *process scheduler* is a key part of any multiprocessing operating system, governing the execution of applications by assigning an execution priority to these processes. An instance of an application is called a *process* with subsets of a process known as *threads*. Game loops will normally create multiple threads for execution, each thread dealing with some subset of the game loop. A standard game loop, as shown in Figure 1-10, generally consists of the following elements:

1 Initialization and memory allocation.

2 Input monitoring.

3 Execution of artificial intelligence (AI) and physics routines.

4 Sound and music output.

5 Execution of game logic.

6 Rendering of the scene based on the input from the user and other subsystems.

7 Display synchronization.

8 Shutdown of the game if the user wishes to terminate the program.

The initialization and memory allocation of the game actually occurs before the game loop and is required for setting up the environment by assigning resources and loading game data and assets. The

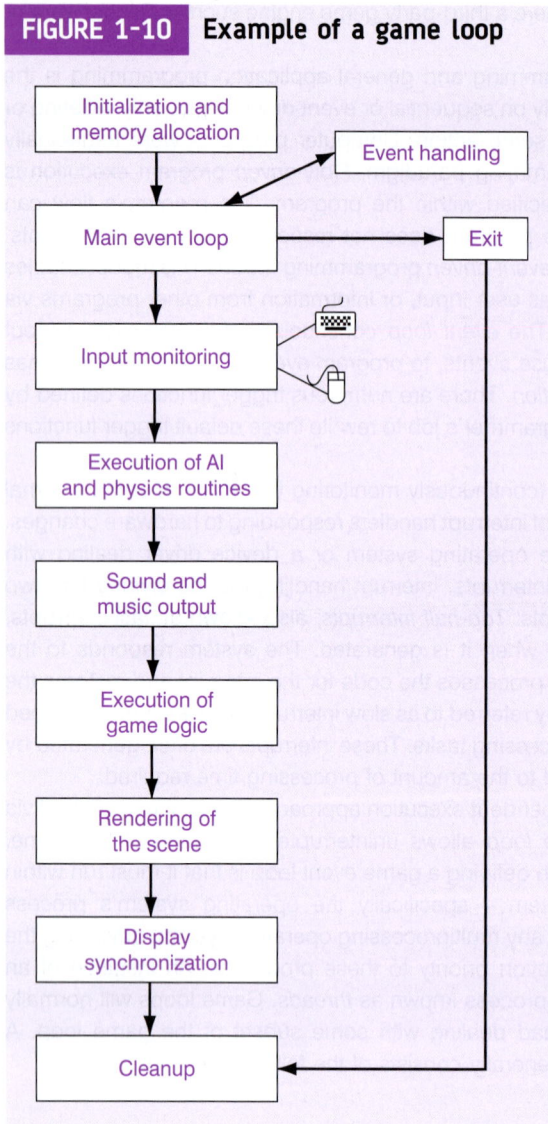

FIGURE 1-10 **Example of a game loop**

game loop is entered following this initialization and only termination from the user can cause the loop to exit. Once executed, the game loop controls all of the game's subsystems including input, AI, sound and graphics. After the scene has been rendered it is important to synchronise the display by avoiding an erratic frame rate due to varying processor load via the use of timing and wait calls. When the main body of the loop is terminated, the user has selected to end the game and return to the operating system. The final action of the loop will be to release all used system memory and resources. The code sample below illustrates the structure of a simple game event loop.

We start by defining the possible game states (using the '#define' pre-processor directive to specify a symbolic constant which is in essence a simple text substitution where the pre-processor accesses the value correlating with the symbolic constant):

```
#define INIT_STATE       0
#define MENU_STATE       1
#define CONSOLE_STATE    2
#define LOADING_STATE    3
#define RUN_STATE        4
#define EXIT_STATE       5
```

Next we set the initial game state:

```
int current_game_state = INIT_STATE;
```

We now implement the game event loop within the program's main section – with main a *function* required by every C++ program. From this function at least one of our other functions is called (assuming their definition). A *function* is just a grouping of code performing one or more actions. The main function is always called, no matter what:

```
int main()
{
```

Looping is an essential part of most programs. A group of instructions executed repeatedly are referred to as a *loop*. The whole looping structure is a repetition structure used to repeat a sequence of statements or actions. This sequence of statements is repeated infinitely, or until the *starting condition* becomes false (current_game_state in this case). The game event loop only terminates when the exit state is reached (we check for this state using the Boolean not-equals != operator):

```
while(current_game_state != EXIT_STATE)
{
```

The switch multiple-selection structure allows us to branch on several different values. Switch structures normally consist of a number of case labels, breaks and one default case. The structure starts to execute at the case statement corresponding to the switch statement's starting condition. It subsequently stops at the first break. The next case statement will also execute in the event where the break statement has been left out. The default case can be left out but its inclusion generally ensures the handling of incorrect input. Using a simple switch statement, we can react to the different game states:

```
switch (current_game_state)
{
```

The initialization state allocates memory, resources, etc.:

```
case INIT_STATE:
{
    AcquireResources ();
    AllocMem ();
    InitGame ();
}
break;
```

The menu state executes some function, DisplayMenu, responsible for displaying the game's menu. This state also halts the game, using the PauseGame function, while the menu is being displayed:

```
case MENU_STATE:
{
    PauseGame ();
    DisplayMenu ();
}
break;
```

The console state displays the game's debug console using some function, DisplayConsole:

```
case CONSOLE_STATE:
{
    DisplayConsole ();
}
break;
```

The loading state does the final initialization before the actual gameplay starts. Once this final initialization stage is complete, the program switches to the run state:

```
case LOADING_STATE:
{
    DoFinalSetup ();
    current_game_state = RUN_STATE;
}
break;
```

The run state, which can only be terminated through user or system intervention, executes all the game logic and game subsystems, for example:

```
case RUN_STATE:
{
    InputHandling ();
```

1

```
            InitPhysics ();
            InitSound ();
            InitGraphicsSystem ();
            InitNetworking ();
            InitAI ();
            //...etc
        }
        break;
```

All devices and resources are released and final program cleanup is done during the exit state. The program falls out of the main while loop after this stage has been completed:

```
        case EXIT_STATE:
        {
            Cleanup ();
        }
        break;
        default: break;
    }
  }
}
```

The transition between the various states of the game loop is illustrated in Figure 1-11. This representation is given as a simplified *finite state machine* (also known as a *finite state automaton*) which is simply a model used to depict various states as well as the transition between those states due to the occurrence of certain actions.

1.1.3 A Short Introduction to Operating System Architecture

It is important to understand the underlying architecture of modern Windows and Unix-based operating systems when developing games for these platforms. The primary rationale behind this is proper resource acquisition, thread/process creation and termination, as well as memory allocation. Basic operating system architecture depends on the design of a central component known as the kernel. The operating system *kernel* is responsible for managing system resources and controlling communication between an application and the system's hardware. Three types of kernels are generally employed today: monolithic kernels, micro kernels and hybrid kernels.

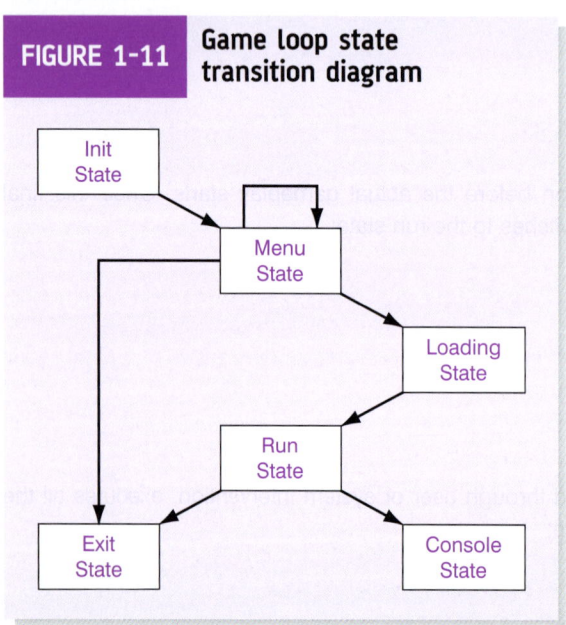

FIGURE 1-11 Game loop state transition diagram

- A *monolithic kernel* (used by Linux and all the UNIX variants), controls process management, memory management, networking, system devices, scheduling, etc. Such a kernel is implemented as a single process sharing a single address space.

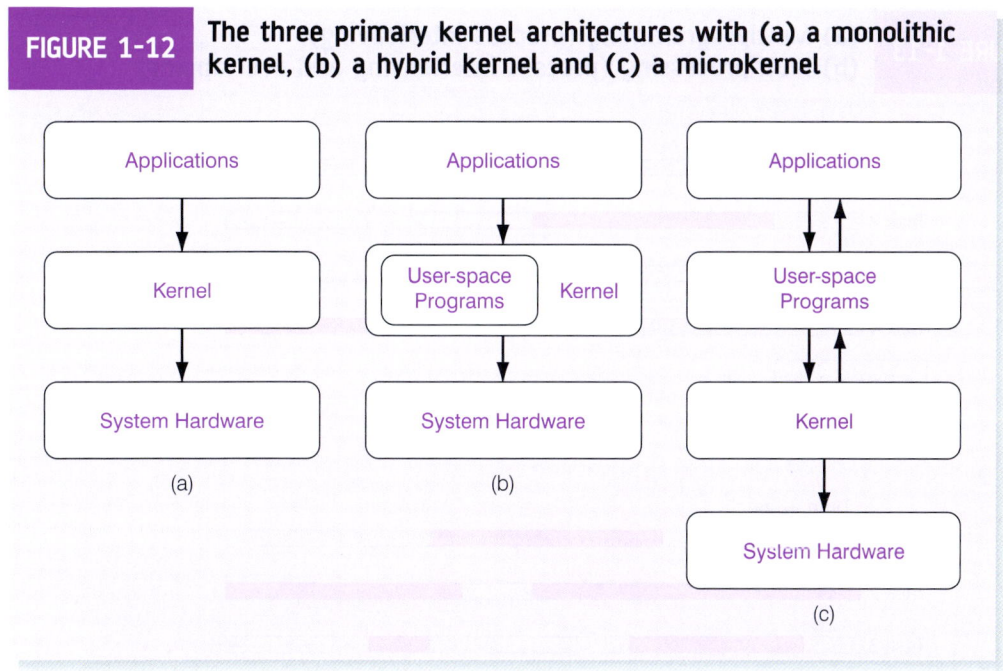

FIGURE 1-12 The three primary kernel architectures with (a) a monolithic kernel, (b) a hybrid kernel and (c) a microkernel

- *Microkernel* architecture (employed by operating systems such as *Minix*) supports only basic service requests from the operating system and a few additional functions such as interprocess communication and simple scheduling with additional operating system services being executed as user-space programs (also referred to as servers). These user-space programs are treated just like normal application processes.

- A *hybrid kernel,* as found in Windows 2000/XP/Vista, combines elements of both the microkernel and monolithic kernel architectures. This kernel architecture is, however, much more similar to monolithic kernel design than microkernels, with nearly all services running in kernel space but with the additional benefit of executing services as user-space programs.

Figure 1-12 illustrates these different kernel architectures.

One operating system element crucial for efficient game execution is *multithreading* – the technique of dividing a process into multiple threads that can be executed concurrently. We previously described a thread as a subset of a process; however, it is also important to note that threads are interruptible, thus allowing the processor the freedom of executing whichever threads are required with multiple threads often being executed in parallel. For example, a game's general logic can be executed as a thread running in parallel with an AI subroutine thread.

A related feature to multithreading provided by modern-day operating systems is *multitasking* (the simultaneous execution of multiple processes or applications). When a computer has only one CPU, then only one process can execute at any given instance. Multitasking schedules the execution of tasks by queuing and switching processes, in this way creating the illusion of numerous tasks being executed in parallel. Multitasking is also required for *multiprocessor* machines (computers with multiple CPUs), allowing the execution of many more processes than the available number of CPUs. Single CPU-based computers make use of a multitasking technique called multiprogramming, with multiprocessor computers making use of multiprocessing. *Multiprogramming* involves the execution of only one task at any given moment while all the other tasks are queued for execution. *Multiprocessing* allows more than one tasks to run in parallel, each on a distinct processor. Multiprogramming and multiprocessing are illustrated in Figure 1-13.

1

FIGURE 1-13 **(a) Multiprogramming (process interleaving).**
(b) Multiprocessing (process interleaving and overlapping)

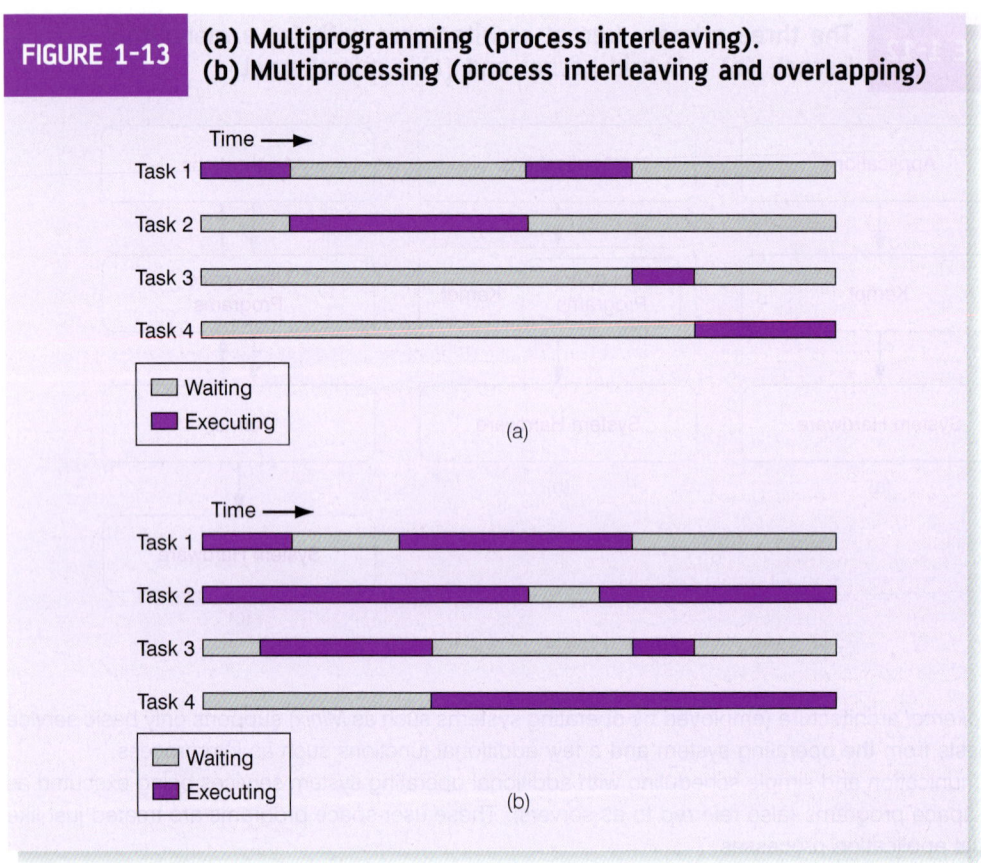

The only problem with multiprogramming is that it lacks any guarantee of timely process execution. For example, if the first executing task doesn't require any peripheral access, user input, or other system resource it can execute indefinitely, thus blocking the execution of all other queued processes. This issue led to the development of cooperative multitasking (as seen in Windows 3.1, for example).

■ *Cooperative multitasking* is based on the principle that any executing task must, at some point, release the CPU either voluntarily or after some system interrupt has been issued. However, cooperative multitasking is vulnerable to badly designed processes which cause the system to 'hang' indefinitely when two or more processes try to access the same resource simultaneously (known as *deadlock*). As a result, the more advanced technique of pre-emptive multitasking was implemented with the release of Windows 95, Mac OS X, Linux and AmigaOS.

■ *Pre-emptive multitasking* is based on the use of a system interrupt mechanism coupled with a scheduler ensuring that all active processes can gain access to the CPU at any given time, thus creating a more reliable operating environment where each and every process are guaranteed some CPU time. Pre-emptive multitasking group processes into two categories: I/O bound and CPU bound. *I/O-bound processes* are all waiting for user input or to generate some output with *CPU-bound processes* waiting for CPU access. I/O-bound processes are blocked pending the availability of needed resources or data, enabling the execution of CPU-bound processes.

An issue arising with multiple processes sharing system memory is one process writing to a memory area used by another process. The operating system prevents this scenario by assigning a specific memory range to a running process and terminating the process immediately in the event that it tries to write to memory outside of its assigned range. Operating systems also allow the assignment of more memory than physically available. This is achieved through the use of virtual memory and swapping. *Virtual memory* allows the extension of the system's random access memory (RAM) through the use of secondary memory, specifically hard drive space in the form of a file or partition. There are two modes of addressing memory: virtual mode addressing and real mode addressing.

■ *Virtual mode addressing* divides memory into blocks known as *pages.* The size of these pages can vary from large to small, with larger page sizes often leading to some overhead due to the operating system keeping track of each and every page. Increasing the page size can reduce this overhead and writing a large page to virtual memory can free a substantial amount of system memory. Microsoft Windows (since 1990) makes use of a physical file to implement a virtual memory strategy with Linux and UNIX variants utilizing a hard drive swap partition.

■ *Real mode addressing* describes a memory addressing mode supported by all x86-compatible CPUs. It contrasts virtual memory by limiting the execution of processes to the main memory. Real mode memory addressing was introduced in 1978 with the release of Intel's 16-bit 8086 processor. Only 1MB of system memory can be addressed using this mode. Unlike virtual addressing, real mode doesn't support any multitasking nor does it prevent a process from accessing memory outside the segment allocated to it.

Most of the operating system fundamentals discussed here are transparent to the game programmer; however, having some understanding and appreciation for the complexity of the underlying operating system can greatly contribute to writing not only portable code, but also ensures that the developer is equipped for exploiting advancements in operating system architecture. An example of such advancement would be the use of object-orientated technologies in operating system design. *Object-orientated operating system design* is based on the process of extending the kernel modularly, allowing programmers to customize the operating system without affecting the overall system reliability or functionality.

1.2   GAME DEVELOPMENT TECHNIQUES AND METHODOLOGIES

Game programming is an extremely involved process due to the synergy required among a large number of independently developed systems. Only through the adaptation of several programming conventions and methodologies can these subsystems work together in a seamless fashion. Performance is also of paramount importance due to the high memory and processing requirements imposed by the ever increasing realism, immersion and real-time nature of video games. Commercial games are developed by large teams ranging from twenty-five to over a hundred developers. Large team sizes and asset requirements often lead to cohesion problems when proper design techniques are not utilized.

Traditional game development methodologies focus on the specification and design of the game and its required functionality, leading to the linear or stepwise implementation of these requirements. One such traditional methodology is called the *waterfall model* due to progress 'flowing' from top to bottom, similar to a waterfall. Designing a game in this stepwise manner results in the developers never realizing the full impact of design decisions made previously. This overall impact can only be accessed when the waterfall model comes full circle. Simply being able to analyze the full influence of design decisions at a later stage often results in features mismatching original requirements – generally impacting on the game's overall level of quality.

Problems associated with the waterfall model are bridged quite easily with the implementation of alternate project and process management methodologies. Such methodologies include the Agile

Software Development Conceptual Framework (specifically the Extreme Programming methodology), Scrum, iterative software development (specifically IBM's Rational Unified Process), and the Spiral model.

1.2.1 Sequential Software Development: The Waterfall Model

The waterfall model is a sequential software engineering methodology where the system's requirements specification, design, implementation, testing, integration and maintenance phases are conducted in a linear, top-down fashion. The waterfall model is generally considered a risky and failure prone methodology not fit for real world implementations. This is mainly due to its sequential and inflexible nature resulting from the feedback of later development stages having no effect on earlier phases.

The waterfall model, illustrated in Figure 1-14, consists of the following stages (each stage is initiated and completed in a linear fashion before continuing to the next):

1 *Requirements analysis and specification* deal with the overall project goals and requirements proposed by the various project stakeholders (developers, the game's publisher(s), users, etc.). All project requirements must be quantifiable and testable. The length of the requirements analysis phase varies depending on the size of the project; however, this phase is generally a stretched out and arduous process consisting of the creation of requirements lists, focus group meetings, prototyping (creating a bare-bone working system to illustrate certain features) and use cases

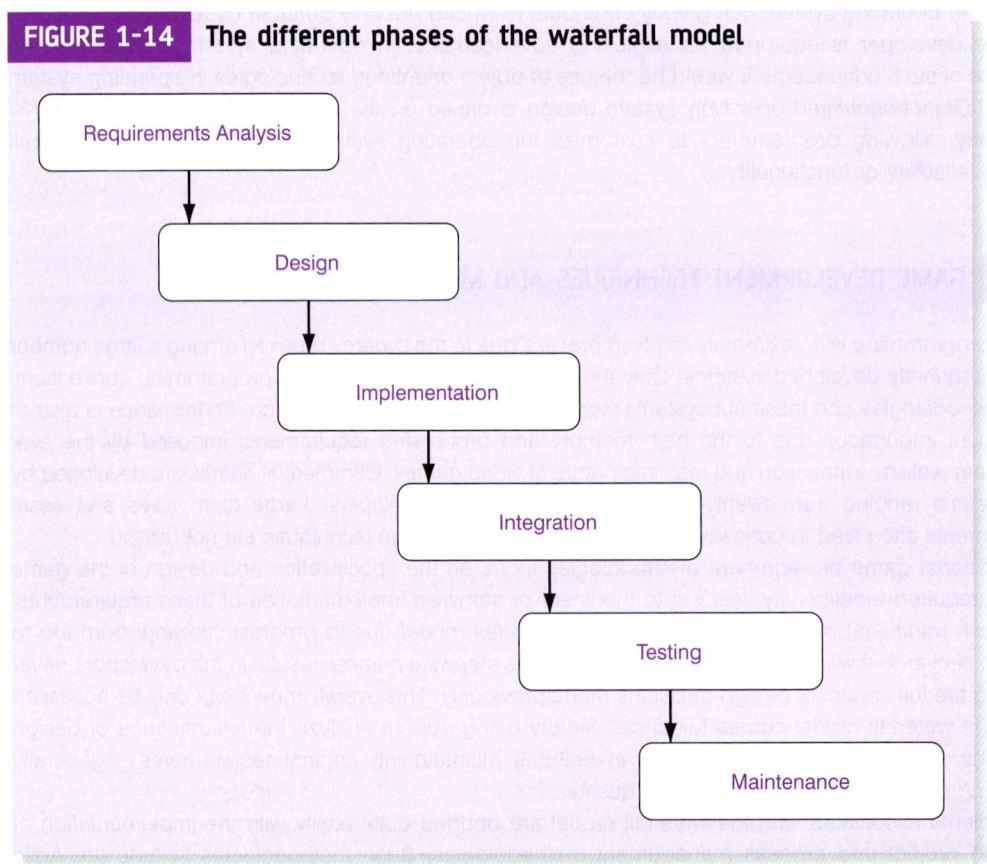

FIGURE 1-14   The different phases of the waterfall model

(a method based on the specification of usage scenarios dealing with how a user will interact with the given system to achieve a specific goal).

2   *Design* is concerned with the technical implementation details of the various requirements generated during the previous phase. This phase normally includes the generation of the design document and storyboards. A game's design document will normally detail each and every detail about the game, its levels, characters, story, concept art and gameplay. On the programming side it will at least consist of four documents, namely: the data design document, the architecture design document, the procedural design document and the interface design document.

   - The *data design document* details the relationships between various data objects, specifying the use and interaction between various data structures.
   - The *architecture design document* presents various data flow diagrams illustrating input and output control, data processing and all other possible forms of program flow based on both internal system events and user interaction.
   - The *procedural design document* is concerned with all procedural elements of the implementation, forming the foundation for all successive design work.
   - The *interface design document* details the overall look and feel of the user interface; it also describes the program interfaces and general process flow within the system.

3   *Implementation* is the physical development work and execution of the design document and realization of the defined requirements. This phase includes the programming of all the game subsystems, and the creation of all art assets and 3D models, narrative elements, sound recording and music composition, etc.

4   *Integration* is not really applicable to game development since it mainly deals with the process of integrating a new software system into an existing enterprise environment. This phase does, however, come into play when developing an update/patch for a game or an expansion pack requiring the original version.

5   *Testing* to ensure that the original desired level of functionality, quality and totality has been met.

6   *Installation and maintenance* deal with the release, deployment and the resolution of any defects that might arise following release of the package.

1.2.2 Iterative Software Development: The Rational Unified Process

The Rational Unified Process (RUP) is an iterative, comprehensive software development process designed by a division of IBM to deal with all foreseeable aspects of and changes throughout the software development cycle. This methodology was conceived by looking at various failed software development projects and identifying the perceivable causes of these failures. The Rational Unified Process was originally designed with big teams in mind resulting in the methodology's widespread focus on design, engineering and tangible development aspects. It was conceived with the aim of encapsulating all the best practices of modern development methodologies. Although RUP emphasizes the iterative software development process, it differs from most methodologies by not being a solitary rigid process. RUP can be accurately described as a framework because it focuses on the software development process via established guidelines.

RUP is primarily concerned with object-orientated techniques and is heavily dependent on the use of Unified Modeling Language (UML) diagrams during the design process. RUP's secondary concern is the assignment of responsibilities and tasks within the development and conception environment.

1

The Rational Unified Process is actually a framework provided by means of a product (IBM's Rational Method Compiler). This *Rational Method Compiler* is basically an integrated collection of software design and development tools which allows the developer to customize the RUP. This customizable software development framework is employed via the development team's Intranet – serving as a constant source of process control.

In RUP, software lifecycles are decomposed into stand-alone development cycles which are in turn broken down into phases. RUP consists of four phases: the inception phase, the elaboration phase, the construction phase and the transition phase. RUP covers the core facets of the software development process – both the organizational and work areas as designated by any software development project.

The basic RUP framework consists of a process content library, capability patterns, and out-of-the-box delivery processes. The best practices, identifiably linked to successful projects, are outlined by the process content library and allow developers to influence their designs based on what worked for other successful developers and what didn't. Capability patterns deal with reusable process segments. These process segments are also based on past project successes and are aimed at helping project managers solve common problems. Out-of-the-box delivery processes serve as a starting point for project initialization and planning. The term out-of-the-box emphasizes the template nature of the process, providing design templates and milestones that should be met by the project based on resources made available to the team.

■ The *inception phase* is used for project objective definition and to define the project business case. A *business case* contains factors such as expected project revenue, market share and market acceptance. Accompanying this business case is a *use case model* used for capturing the requirements of the new software system, a project plan, the project description and risk assessments. The inception phase is all about testing the project's viability, if the project fails to pass the inception phase it can be canceled without any resource wastage. Figure 1-15 compares the resources usage vs. phase duration for the inception – and three subsequent phases.

■ The *elaboration phase* deals with the creation and validation of the software system's architectural requirements. It also deals with the final planning and assessment of the project. It is during this phase that the project becomes more than just a concept. The business case and risk analysis are revised and a development plan for the entire project is composed. If the project fails to pass the elaboration phase it can be canceled with only minimal resource wastage.

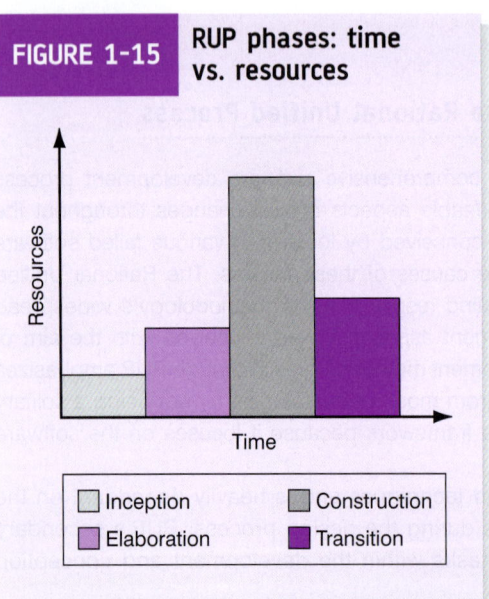

FIGURE 1-15 RUP phases: time vs. resources

■ The system is finally implemented during the *construction phase*. The implementation is based on the architecture defined during the elaboration phase. During this phase the developers focus on the game's development, leading to the first internal release of the developed game.

■ The *transition phase* consists of beta testing and preparing the release candidates. During this phase the software moves from the developer to the users. This phase also includes a quality check against the original quality level defined during the inception phase. If the software fails the quality check the entire phase cycle is repeated else the development cycle has successfully come to an end.

RUP is an artifact-heavy and process-expensive framework to implement. IBM developed the Rational Method Composer for this very reason; helping software developers easily customize the standard defined Rational Unified Process to suit their specific needs. RUP is not an agile process and this is perhaps its biggest weakness, while at the same time being its biggest strength. Where agile software development methodologies are most suited for small to medium-sized teams, RUP is targeted at enterprise groups where agile methodologies often suffer lack of cohesion. RUP is, however, adaptable to smaller projects teams (2 to 25 developers) by selecting a number of RUP's 80 artefacts, 150 activities and 40 roles to suit these smaller projects. RUP is a management-heavy and high-cost method when considered for small teams. It must, however, be noted that RUP was never intended for use outside the enterprise environment.

1.2.3 Agile Software Development: Extreme Programming

Extreme Programming is rapidly becoming more than just a viable software engineering methodology. With its focus on small to medium-sized teams, extreme programming is finding its way into many diverse software development environments, including game development. The primary motivation for this rapid adaptation lies with extreme programming's core purpose – the promotion of an efficiently structured software development process.

Kent Beck, Ward Cunningham and Ron Jefferies conceptualized the extreme programming methodology while working on the Chrysler Comprehensive Compensation System – a project aimed at replacing numerous stand-alone payroll applications. Beck's original goal was to create a software development methodology aimed at small and organized teams developing software plagued by constant fluctuating requirements. In his book he outlines that a project's ever-changing requirements could be effectively dealt with via good communication and dedicated team work.

Extreme programming promotes not only good communication between team members but emphasizes the involvement of the various stakeholders – by doing so, it facilitates quick feedback, resulting in better customer satisfaction, and outcome-focused developers. Extreme programming has a series of practices, ranging from continuous integration and evolutionary design to pair programming, refactoring, and testing.

- *Continuous integration* is the integration of new untested source code into a well-tested code base. This new code base, consisting of both tested and untested code, is then thoroughly tested again via testing techniques as defined by the extreme programming paradigm. This process results in a continually, dynamically tested code base, enforcing release candidacy only after thorough and successful testing.

- *Evolutionary design* is all about making minute-based iterations, quite the contrary to other design paradigms with their day-based iteration cycles. A problem is defined and implemented in terms of iterations. *Implementation iteration* is normally defined as trial-and-error to successfully solve a given problem. For example, when implementing the search algorithm for finding hosts connected to a game server one iteration could be to 'flood-search' the entire network – from node to node with the next iteration making use of a hashing function, hence improving on the initial brute-force approach.

- *Pair programming* is perhaps the most controversial aspect of extreme programming. This is not because it lacks effectiveness, far from it; pair programming's successes in the software engineering industry are well known and documented. Some of these successes include benefits to new programmers joining a project and through pair programming rapidly becoming familiar with an existing code base, the sharing of work in pairs and developers learning from each other. The danger of being a 'lone-wolf' programmer is normally the programmer's inability to find multiple solutions to a problem – a scenario avoidable by having two programmers collaborate on some specific problem. *Pair programming* is the activity of having two programmers co-develop a programming unit while

1

sharing the same workstation. Pair programming has been criticized for being vulnerable to one-sided input; however, when both programmers are equally experienced, the arrangement works quite well. It has been found that code developed in a pair-programming environment is often robust, defect-free and frequently shorter, but these benefits are often clouded by the possible loss of productivity.

■ *Refactoring* is defined as the process of continuously redesigning a program by taking programming techniques and methodologies such as object-orientated design and design patters into account. The aim is the creation of more efficient, simpler, and more user-friendly programs. As mentioned, because refactoring is a continuous process, it can occur at any time during the development process. For example, when a developer has implemented a certain subsystem but finds relatively similar functionality in another class, the programmer would refactor these two classes into one.

■ Extreme Programming's *testing* process is divided into unit testing, functional testing and automated testing. These various testing techniques are discussed in section 1.1.

Five Extreme Programming values are identifiable; four of these values were initially introduced by Kent Beck in 1999 (*Extreme Programming Explained: Embrace Change*) and a fifth, respect, later added. These five values are communication, simplicity, feedback, courage, and respect.

1 *Communication* refers to the process of relating the program's requirements to the developers. Communication ensures that the same understanding of the system's requirements and functionality are shared by both the software developers and all other stakeholders. According to Beck, communication is only effective when frequently done by relating design requirements with high-quality feedback.

2 *Simplicity* is concerned with the implemented solution. Extreme Programming promotes the concept of initially starting with a straightforward solution, then progressing to more advanced implementations. For example, say you're involved in the development of a peer-to-peer networked game, your first aim could be a fully distributed network but time constrains and a nearing release date would urge the development team to rather opt for a kind of hybrid system where a server is used to cache nodes and files shared to facilitate the easy locating of nodes. This solution could now be refactored into a fully distributed network for the next version.

3 Three forms of feedback are common in the Extreme Programming methodology. The first form, *system feedback,* is generated by running unit tests on various implemented subsystems with the feedback being instantaneous. The second form of feedback, *customer feedback,* deals with functional tests developed by both stakeholders and testers. Using these functional tests, the stakeholders and testers will be able to give exact feedback regarding the current state of the system. The last form of feedback, *team feedback,* deals with time estimates for the implementation cycle from the development team to the game's public release.

4 The first practice encompassed by *courage* is to develop software for today and not tomorrow–doing this will avoid being caught up in the design and missing one deadline after another. Courage promotes the freedom to cancel the implementation of various components should the developer later find them irrelevant or overly complicated.

5 *Respect* primarily deals with the development team and focuses on, not only personal respect, but also respect for developed subsystems and components. A programmer must never do something that will affect the functionality of someone else's work. Respect further manifests in the quality of an implementation – constantly reminding programmers that less is in fact more.

When considering Extreme Programming's set of day-to-day practices one might be fooled into thinking that it leaves no room for other methodologies – this simply is not the case. These practices are only there to guide the software development process, placing a higher value on adaptability than predictability.

This value shift categorizes Extreme Programming as an agile software development process. Extreme Programming, as an agile software development process, emphasizes that changes during a project's development life cycle is much better than strictly defining requirements at the beginning. Extreme Programming is also every so often updated with the newest industry trends. Some controversial aspects have been identified, such as conflicts arising between clashing personalities of programmers – leading to friction when utilizing the concept of pair programming. Another rather huge issue is the lack of any big documentation set on the outset of the project. Although Extreme Programming proponents shun this, it must be considered that the possibility exists for a lot of unnecessary refactoring, something completely avoidable, were the original system requirements well documented and thoroughly outlined. These criticisms don't, however, carry much weight since Extreme Programming, by its very nature, is but one solution to the criticism of other development methodologies.

Although it was originally advocated that Extreme Programming should be applied in its entirety, software developers have found it useful to implement only some of the practices, for example, using pair programming to accelerate the learning curve of new team members joining a project midway through its development.

1.3   INTRODUCTION TO THE UNIFIED MODELING LANGUAGE (UML)

The Unified Modeling Language (UML) is a graphical modeling language developed in the mid 1990s for the visual representation of object-orientated software. UML is actually the 'unification' between three independently developed modeling languages. These three original modeling languages were separately developed by James Rumbaugh, Grady Booch and Ivar Jacobson and later united into the Unified Modeling Language by combining the best features of each, resulting in support for a great number of diagram types. A complete discussion of these diagram types could, however, easily fill up an entire textbook and we will for this reason rather focus just on the essentials of UML modeling in the coming subsections.

Table 1-1 lists UML's primary diagram types and their purpose.

UML provides a standardized method for modeling object-orientated software. Object-oriented software is based on the paradigm of defining objects to create computer software. These objects operate as a collective, with each object either processing data or sending messages to and receiving messages from other objects. With object orientation everything is thought of in terms of objects. All the instructions and procedures are seen as objects with stand-alone entities functioning as user created types. Object-orientation is used to design programs through the definition of objects, their relationships and their properties and it is a widely embraced programming paradigm (a typical style of programming and software engineering). Developing programs using object-orientation (known as object-orientated programming (OOP)) has the advantage of easy maintenance and facilitates the easy implementation of both complex methods and types. These methods and types may not always be clearly understood or implemented when using a purely procedural language such as C. Object-orientated programming increases software productivity, reusability, and the quality of the software produced. Object-orientated programming concepts are fully explained in the ancillary C++ chapter available on the book's companion website.

1.3.1 Class Diagrams

Class diagrams convey the software system's overall structure by describing classes and all inter-class relationships. Class diagrams make use of a number of symbols to represent the software system's

TABLE 1-1	UML diagram types
Diagram type	**Purpose**
Activity diagrams	Illustrates the software system's overall flow of control.
Class diagrams	Describes the program's classes and all inter-class relationships.
Communication diagrams	Models object interaction via sequence messages and can be considered a simplified collaboration diagram combining data from class and sequence diagrams to illustrate the physical structure and dynamic behavior of the software system.
Component diagrams	Illustrates the logical and physical arrangements of the software system's components.
Composite structure diagrams	Describes a class's internal structure via parts, ports and connectors. *Parts* are the internal class components with *ports* indicating the connections through which the internal class components interact with each other. *Connectors* illustrate the links between *parts* and *ports*.
Deployment diagrams	Describes the software system's hardware usage, its hardware deployment and the relations between the various hardware components.
Interaction diagrams	Illustrates the behavior of the software system with regard to object interaction. There are two types of interaction diagrams: sequence diagrams and collaboration diagrams.
Interaction overview diagrams	Depicts the flow of control for all possible interactions where messages are hidden. The interaction overview diagram is a variant of the activity diagram.
Object diagrams	Details the structure, object instances and attributes of a software system at some specific instance. These diagrams can be considered more detailed class diagrams.
Package diagrams	Illustrates a software system's high-level logical components and the dependencies among these components.
Sequence diagrams	Illustrates the series of messages exchanged by a number of objects.
State diagrams	Describes the internal system behavior.
Timing diagrams	Describes object behavior over a specific time period.
Use case diagrams	Illustrates the relationships among a series of actors and use cases to convey the overall high-level functionality of the software system.

classes, the attributes found in these classes, the inter-class relationships or inter-class associations, the operations performed by these classes and generalizations leading to inheritance hierarchies. These symbols are only the main ones shown on class diagrams with UML supporting several others. They are, however, more than sufficient for mapping out any of the book's example programs, including the complex interactive environment presented in Chapter 17. We will now discuss these four UML class diagram symbols and their usage.

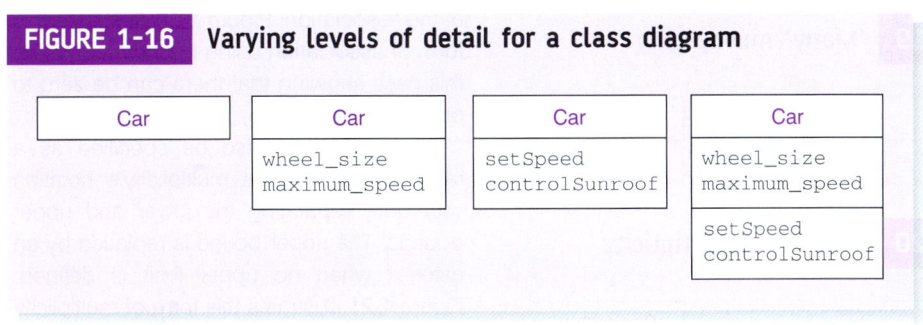

FIGURE 1-16   **Varying levels of detail for a class diagram**

1.3.1.1 Representing Classes

A class is represented using a rectangle with the name of the class starting with a capital letter and written in boldface. This is a class diagram in its purest form, stating that a class with the given name is present in the software system. Class diagrams also often contain extra information such as the class's attributes (for example, data types such as integers used for the storing of values) and the operations or functions performed by the class. This supplementary information is represented using an additional two rectangles affixed to the rectangle containing the class name. The class attributes are contained within the second rectangle with the bottom rectangle listing the operations performed by the class. Class diagrams can show only the class name, the class name and class attributes, the class name and class operations, or the class name and both the attributes and operations depending on the level of detail required. Figure 1-16 illustrates this varying level of detail for a class Car with attributes wheel_size and maximum_speed, and two functions: setSpeed used for controlling the vehicle's cruise control system and controlSunroof used to open or close the vehicle's sunroof.

A class diagram can also contain information about the type of an attribute (int, float, double, char, etc.) and the parameter types and return type of an operation. This return type and parameter types are referred to as the signature of the operation or function and this is specified via the notation illustrated in Figure 1-17.

functionName(parameterName: type, ...): returnType

1.3.1.2 Representing Associations

An association shows the relationship between two classes as a drawn line. Inter-class relationships are closely related to multiplicity. *Multiplicity* shows the number of instances of one class linkable to an instance of another class – it is given at each end of the association. Multiplicity is by default set to 'one' specifying that only one instance is to be linked to each object at the other side of the association. This form of multiplicity, illustrated in Figure 1-18, is denoted by drawing a simple line between two classes.

The next form of multiplicity, called 'many', specifies that many instances can be linked to each object at the other side of the association. In Figure 1-19, for example, an asterisk indicates that many Cars can be linked to one Dealership.

Another form of multiplicity, called 'optional', occurs when zero to one object can be linked to an object at the other side

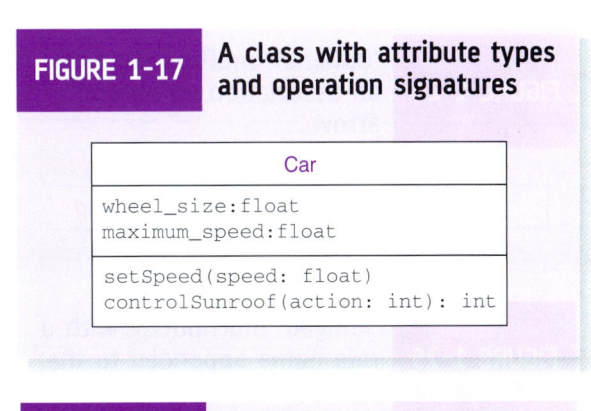

FIGURE 1-17   **A class with attribute types and operation signatures**

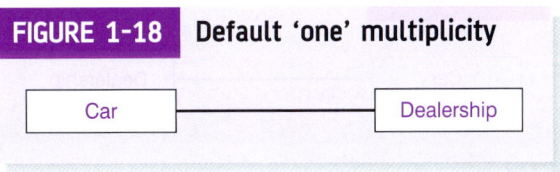

FIGURE 1-18   **Default 'one' multiplicity**

1

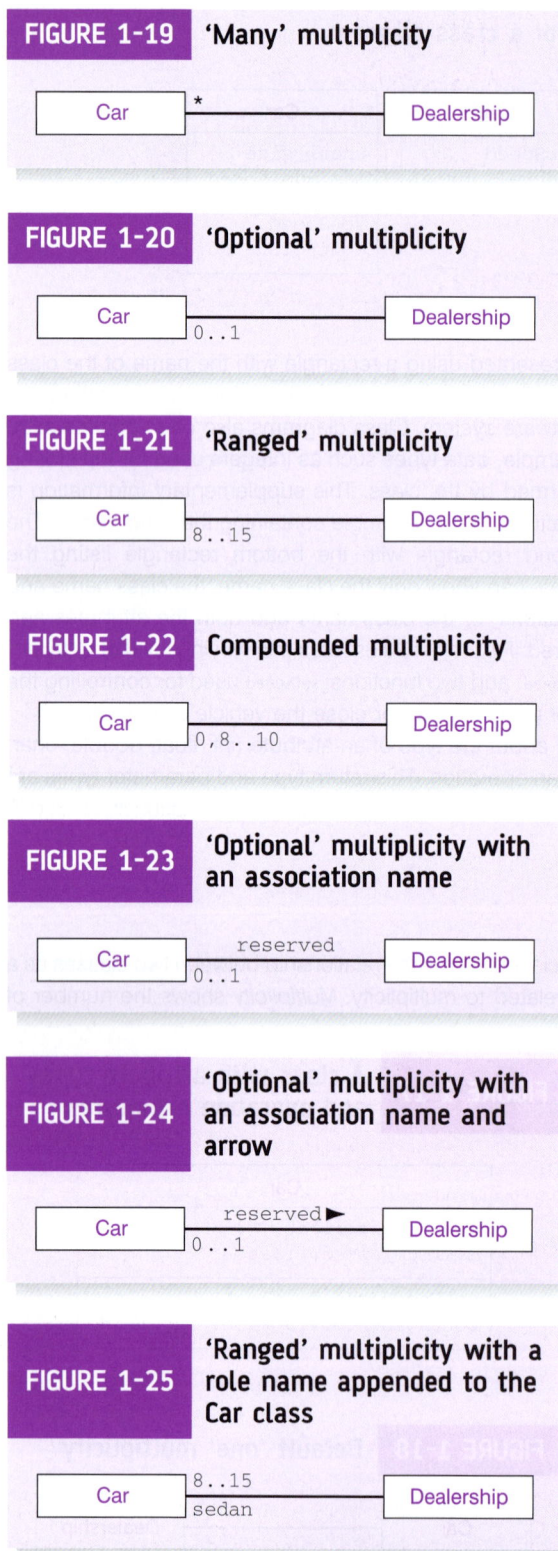

FIGURE 1-19 'Many' multiplicity

FIGURE 1-20 'Optional' multiplicity

FIGURE 1-21 'Ranged' multiplicity

FIGURE 1-22 Compounded multiplicity

FIGURE 1-23 'Optional' multiplicity with an association name

FIGURE 1-24 'Optional' multiplicity with an association name and arrow

FIGURE 1-25 'Ranged' multiplicity with a role name appended to the Car class

of the association. Figure 1-20 illustrates this form of association using the notation 0..1, in this case showing that there can be zero to one Car per Dealership.

Multiplicity can also be specified as a range using optional multiplicity's notation with dots separating the lower and upper bounds. The upper bound is replaced by an asterisk when no upper limit is defined. Figure 1-21 illustrates this form of multiplicity where there can be 8 to 15 Cars per Dealership.

Several multiplicity values and/or ranges can also be specified by separating these values with commas. For example, Figure 1-22 depicts the situation where there can be either zero Cars, or between 8 and 10 Cars at a Dealership.

Associations are also often labeled using association names and role names to make clear their purpose. An *association name* is positioned above the line connecting two classes, stressing the relationship between one class and another (an arrow is generally added next to the association name for the sake of clarity). Figure 1-23 illustrates optional multiplicity with an association name added to it – in this case indicating that a Car is reserved by a Dealership (Figure 1-24 shows this same association with the optional arrow next to the association name).

Role names are written next to a class to specify an alternate name for the attached class. Role names can be added to either or both ends of the association, serving to clarify the meaning of the class attached to it. Figure 1-25 shows a ranged multiplicity with the role name sedan describing the Cars stocked by the Dealership.

It is often necessary to limit the direction-ality of an association through the use of an arrow at one side of the interconnection. For example, say we have a class, Level, and another, Monster, and that any number of monsters can be associated with a given level. This leads to class Level being associated with Monster; however, not all instances of class Monster might necessarily be linked to a specific Level resulting in a one-directional association as illustrated in Figure 1-26.

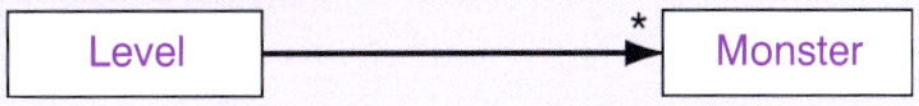

1.3.1.3 Representing Generalizations Generalization, more commonly called *inheritance,* enables one class access to the members of some other class, in the process allowing the extension of pre-defined classes into new classes. Generalization has become pivotal to modern program design and is one of the most important features of object-orientated programming.

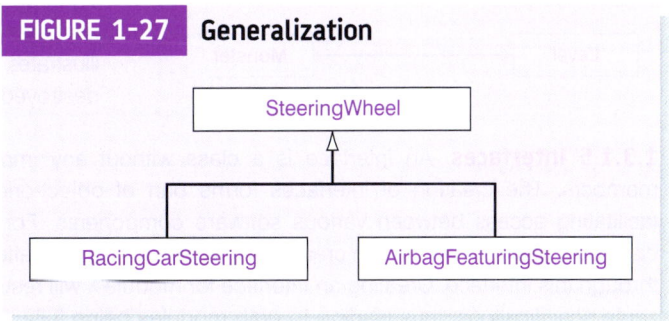

FIGURE 1-26 A one-directional association

Level ⟶ * Monster

Inheritance is based on a 'is a' relationship due to the hierarchical structure between classes and objects. Let's look at a general example in everyday life. Say we have a car, this car has many components, including a steering wheel and four tires, each necessary for the vehicle's operation. Now, the previous paragraph stated that inheritance provides a way for us to create new classes from existing classes. Thus, in the case of our car example, car is a generalization of the vehicle's make. So car is a generalization of BMW, VW, etc. But because BMW is a car, it inherits all these common components a car is made up of (the steering wheel, the four tires, etc.).

FIGURE 1-27 **Generalization**

SteeringWheel

RacingCarSteering   AirbagFeaturingSteering

FIGURE 1-28 **Generalization using a discriminator**

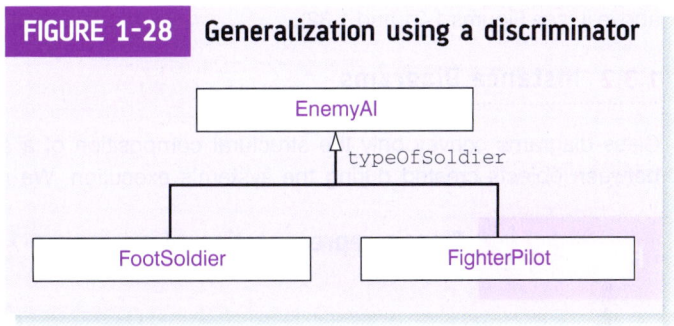

EnemyAI

typeOfSoldier

FootSoldier   FighterPilot

Our trivial example illustrates the importance of inheritance – the complexity of a program can be reduced by avoiding the redefinition of classes and member functions already defined. In essence, one class shares code already defined in another class. The class where the code is shared from is known as the *base class* with the class inheriting this code and attributes being called the *derived class*.

Basic generalization is indicated by an arrow pointing from the derived class or classes to the base class; for example, for our car example we can have a SteeringWheel base class defining a basic steering wheel and two specialization derived classes, RacingCarSteering and AirbagFeaturingSteering, used for defining more advanced or feature rich steering wheels. Figure 1-27 illustrates this class hierarchy.

We can further specify the generalization criteria used for the specialization of a base class via the use of a discriminator. A *discriminator* is simply a label written next to the generalization arrow used for describing the specialization criteria and it is similar to an attribute in the sense that it will have a different value for each of the derived classes. Figure 1-28 illustrates the use of a discriminator, typeOfSoldier, to generate two subclasses, FootSoldier and FighterPilot, from a game's basic enemy AI logic class, EnemyAI.

1.3.1.4 Aggregation An *aggregation* is a form of association between two classes where a 'has a' relationship is expressed. Aggregations are indicated using a clear diamond symbol placed next to the

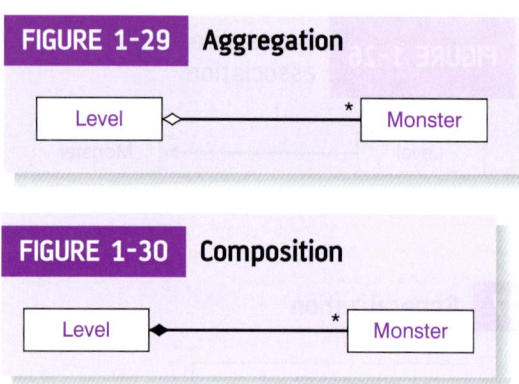

FIGURE 1-29   Aggregation

FIGURE 1-30   Composition

base class (also referred to as the *aggregate* or *assembly*). This diamond symbol basically denotes 'is part of' or 'has a', relationship. For example, in Figure 1-29 we have an aggregation where a Level 'has a' Monster.

A stronger form of aggregation is called composition. *Composition* is indicated using a solid diamond symbol and it denotes that if the aggregate is destroyed, then all its related attributes are destroyed as well. Figure 1-30 illustrates composition where all monsters are destroyed in the event that the level is destroyed.

1.3.1.5 Interfaces An interface is a class without any implemented member functions or data members. The creation of interfaces forms part of object-orientated programming, their presence facilitating access between various software components. For example, say we have two software classes, *X* and *Y*. Then we can create an interface for class *X*, effectively forcing all interaction of class *Y* through this interface. Creating an interface for module *X* will result in module *X* and *Y* having exactly the same specifications, thus leading to both modules being fully compatible with each other.

Interfaces are represented in UML notation as either a rectangle with the expression «interface» positioned above the interface name or as a little circle, called a lollipop, with the interface name written above it (see Figures 1-31 and 1-32).

1.3.2 Instance Diagrams

Class diagrams convey only the structural composition of a software system, not the associations between objects created during the system's execution. We make use of instance diagrams (also

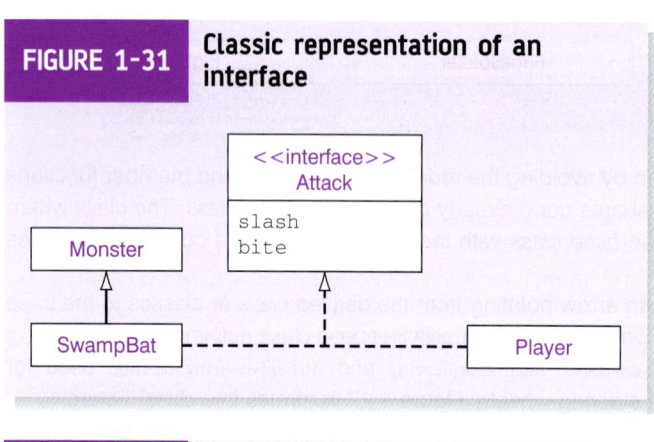

FIGURE 1-31   Classic representation of an interface

called object diagrams) to visualize these inter-object relationships. Instance diagrams are typically generated from class diagrams via the use of some UML modeling tool such as Umbrello UML Modeler or Microsoft Visio. The term 'instance' is used due to these diagrams focusing on the object instances and attributes of a software system at a particular moment in time. Instance diagrams make use of rectangles to represent objects containing the instance name followed by a colon and the name of the class. Either the instance name or the name of the class can be omitted if the context is apparent with all object instances connected using straight lines. Figure 1-33 shows an instance diagram generated from the class diagram in Figure 1-28.

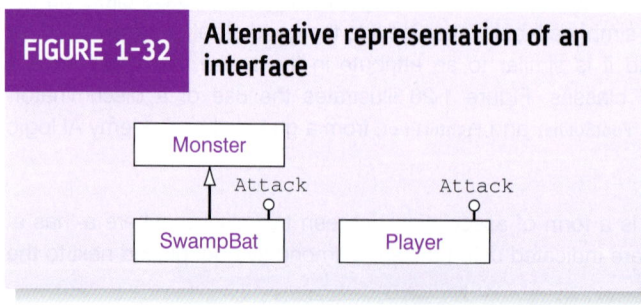

FIGURE 1-32   Alternative representation of an interface

FIGURE 1-33   **Instance diagram**

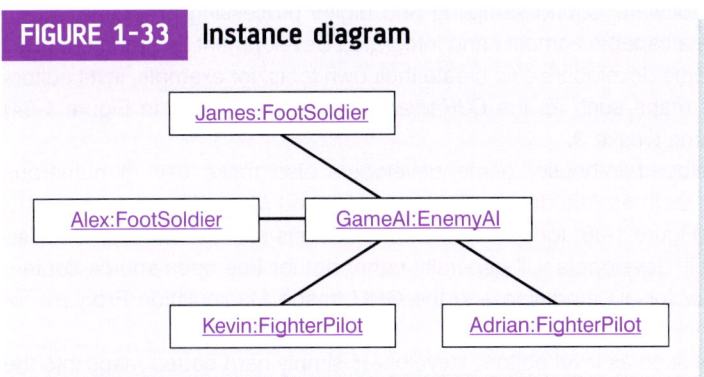

1.4   GAME DEVELOPMENT TOOLS

Creating a game as part of a development team allows each individual to focus on their field of expertise; however, creating a game as an individual (as often the case during the early stages of an aspirant game developer's career) requires proficiency in the use of multiple asset creation tools such

FIGURE 1-34   **A screenshot of Quake 3's level editor, Q3Radiant**

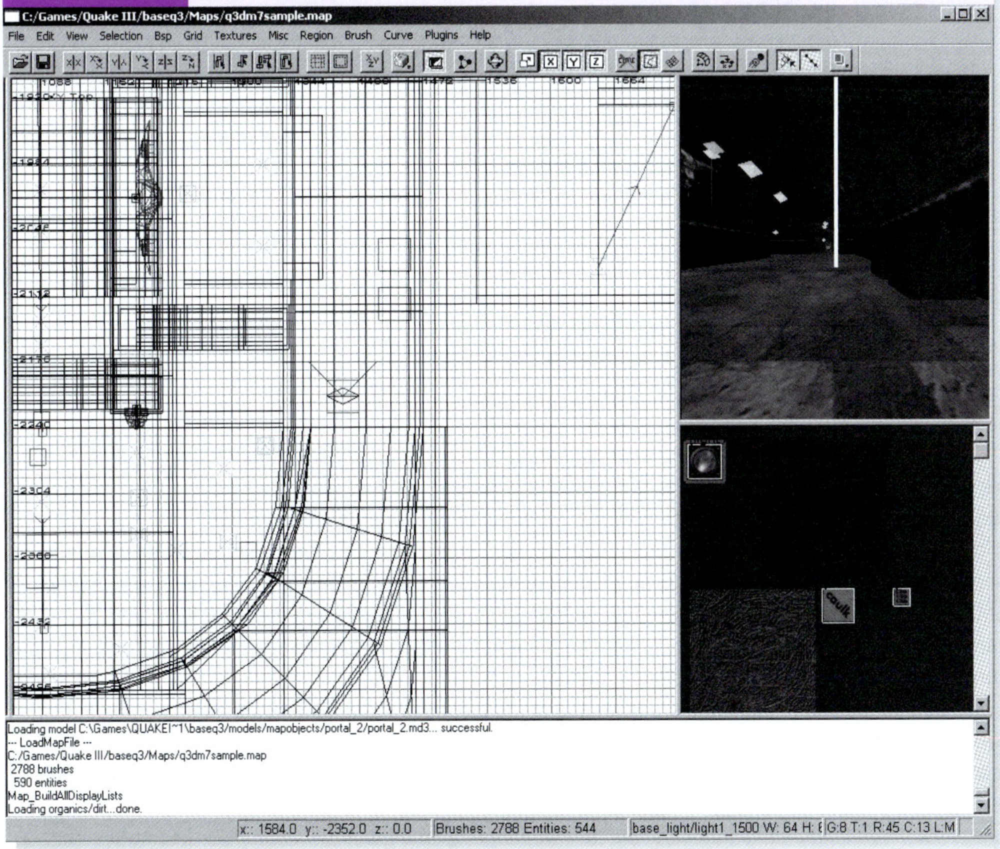

1

as 3D modeling software, 2D art software, sound sampling and digital processing programs, music sequencing software and of course a capable compiler and Integrated Development Environment (IDE) such as Microsoft Visual Studio. Game developers also create their own tools, for example, level editors used for the interactive design of maps such as the *Q3Radiant* map editor (shown in Figure 1-34) created by id Software for their game *Quake 3*.

Although most tools are developed in-house, game developers also make use of numerous commercial off-the-shelf packages such as Autodesk's *3D Studio Max* and *Maya* (Figure 1-35) for 3D modeling, and *Adobe Photoshop* (Figure 1-36) for the creation of art assets such as textures. Smaller, less well-funded teams or 'lone wolf' developers will generally rather opt for free open-source content creation packages such as *Blender* for 3D modeling and the GNU Image Manipulation Program, or *GIMP,* for graphics editing.

Before the advent of game tools such as level editors, developers simply hard-coded maps into the source code of the game. For example, the game shown in Figure 1-37, taken from the ancillary C++ chapter available on the book's website, makes use of hard-coded maps in the form of multidimensional arrays.

The in-game map shown in Figure 1-37 is represented programmatically as follows:

```
int map[ROWS][COLUMNS] =
          {{1, 1, 1, 1, 1, 1, 1, 1, 1, 1, 1, 1, 1, 1, 1, 1, 1, 1, 1},
           {1, 0, 0, 0, 1, 0, 0, 0, 0, 0, 0, 1, 1, 1, 1, 1, 1, 1, 1},
           {0, 0, 1, 0, 1, 0, 1, 1, 1, 1, 0, 1, 1, 1, 1, 1, 1, 1, 1},
           {1, 1, 1, 0, 1, 0, 0, 0, 0, 1, 0, 1, 1, 1, 1, 1, 1, 1, 1},
           {1, 0, 0, 0, 0, 1, 1, 1, 0, 1, 0, 0, 0, 0, 0, 0, 0, 0, 1},
           {1, 1, 1, 1, 0, 1, 0, 1, 0, 1, 0, 1, 0, 0, 1, 1, 1, 1, 1},
           {1, 0, 0, 1, 0, 1, 0, 1, 0, 1, 0, 1, 0, 0, 1, 1, 1, 1, 1},
           {1, 1, 0, 1, 0, 1, 0, 1, 0, 1, 0, 1, 1, 1, 1, 1, 1, 1, 1},
           {1, 0, 0, 0, 0, 0, 0, 0, 0, 0, 1, 0, 1, 1, 0, 0, 0, 1, 1, 1},
           {1, 1, 1, 1, 1, 1, 0, 1, 1, 1, 0, 1, 1, 0, 0, 0, 1, 1, 1},
           {1, 0, 0, 0, 0, 0, 0, 1, 0, 0, 0, 1, 1, 0, 0, 0, 1, 1, 1},
           {1, 1, 1, 1, 1, 1, 1, 1, 1, 1, 0, 0, 0, 0, 1, 0, 1, 1, 1},
           {1, 1, 1, 1, 1, 1, 1, 1, 1, 1, 1, 1, 1, 0, 1, 0, 1, 1, 1},
           {1, 1, 1, 1, 1, 1, 1, 1, 1, 1, 1, 1, 1, 1, 0, 1, 0, 0, 0, 1},
           {1, 1, 1, 1, 1, 1, 1, 1, 1, 1, 1, 1, 1, 1, 0, 1, 0, 0, 1, 1},
           {1, 1, 1, 1, 1, 1, 1, 1, 1, 1, 1, 1, 1, 1, 0, 1, 1, 0, 1, 1},
           {1, 1, 1, 1, 1, 1, 1, 1, 1, 1, 0, 0, 0, 0, 1, 1, 1, 1, 1},
           {1, 1, 1, 1, 1, 1, 1, 1, 1, 1, 0, 0, 1, 1, 1, 1, 1, 1, 1},
           {1, 1, 1, 1, 1, 1, 1, 1, 1, 1, 0, 0, 1, 1, 1, 1, 1, 1, 1}};
```

This two-dimensional array, `map`, is the 'level' the player gets to walk around in. All the ones '1' represent solid unsurpassable objects with the zeros '0' representing the corridors.

As games got more complicated the necessity for tools such as level editors became apparent. Teams soon developed these tools to speed up production time and to transfer the responsibility of content creation from the programmer to artists and game designers not familiar with low-level programming. Tool development also grew into a career, with many development teams employing a programmer specifically dedicated to the creation of tools.

In addition to in-house content creation tools, developers also frequently make use of utilities created by companies like NVIDIA and Microsoft to debug and tweak the performance of their applications. One such useful tool, targeted at both OpenGL and Direct3D applications, is the *NVIDIA*

FIGURE 1-35	A screenshot of Autodesk's high-end 3D modeling package, Maya

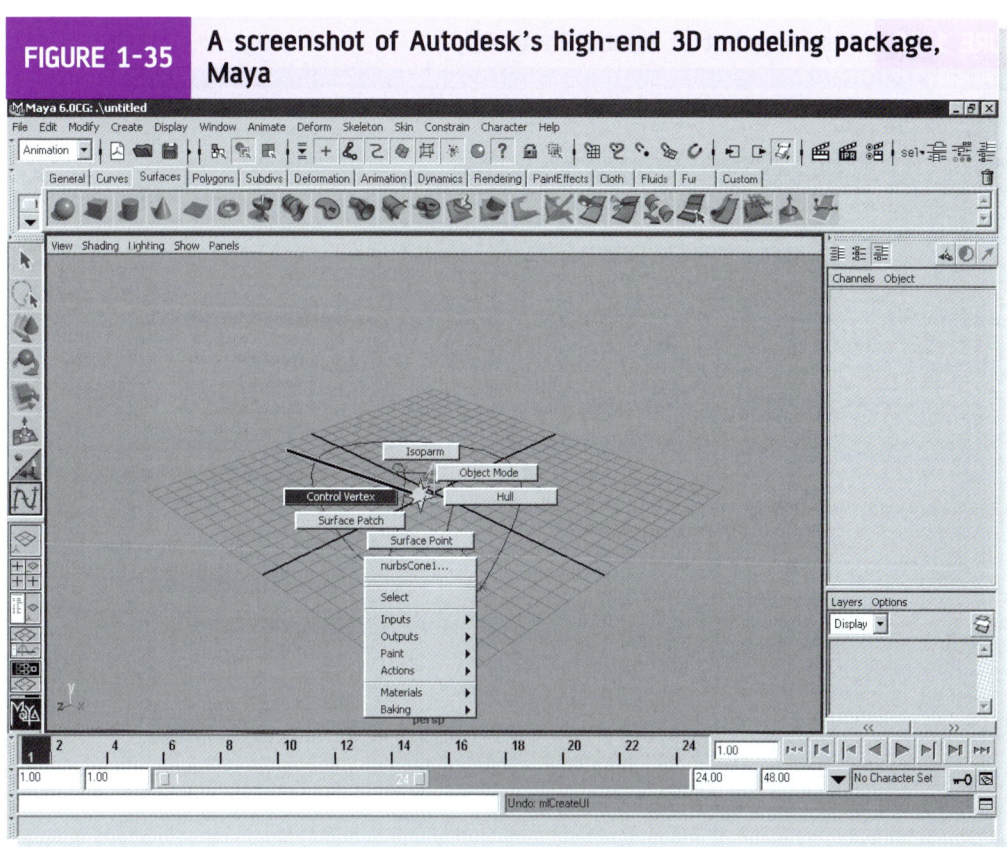

PerfKit. The NVPerfKit is actually a collection of performance monitoring, debugging and profiling utilities focused on accessing the low-level performance indicating components of the graphics driver and the GPU itself (assuming an NVIDIA GPU is being used). These low-level components are known as *performance counters,* and gives information on the application's overall frames per second rendering, the video memory used in MB, the graphics driver's sleep time, the polygon count, etc. Using the NVPerfKit, we are thus able to profile the application in terms of its GPU, driver and memory usage. A useful component of NVPerfKit is called *PerfHUD,* a real-time Direct3D and OpenGL application profiler that generates its output in the form of a heads-up display (shown in Figure 1-38).

Another useful tool, also freely available from NVIDIA, is the *FX Composer*. The FX Composer is practically an IDE for the real-time creation and testing of shaders (see Chapter 6). The IDE supports both the DirectX High Level Shader Language and NVIDIA's Cg shader language as presented in subsequent chapters. It also supports various other formats, such as Microsoft's '.x' file format and 3D Studio Max's '.3ds' file format. The FX Composer features a shader creation wizard, a high-quality code editor, detailed tweaking of shader parameters, material property management, full scene management, etc. Figure 1-39 shows the FX Composer Integrated Development Environment with its real-time shader creation.

A number of tools are also distributed in the form of plugins. A *plug-in* is basically an add-on to a host application such as Adobe Photoshop or Maya. These plug-ins provide third-party developers with the

FIGURE 1-36   A screenshot of Adobe Photoshop

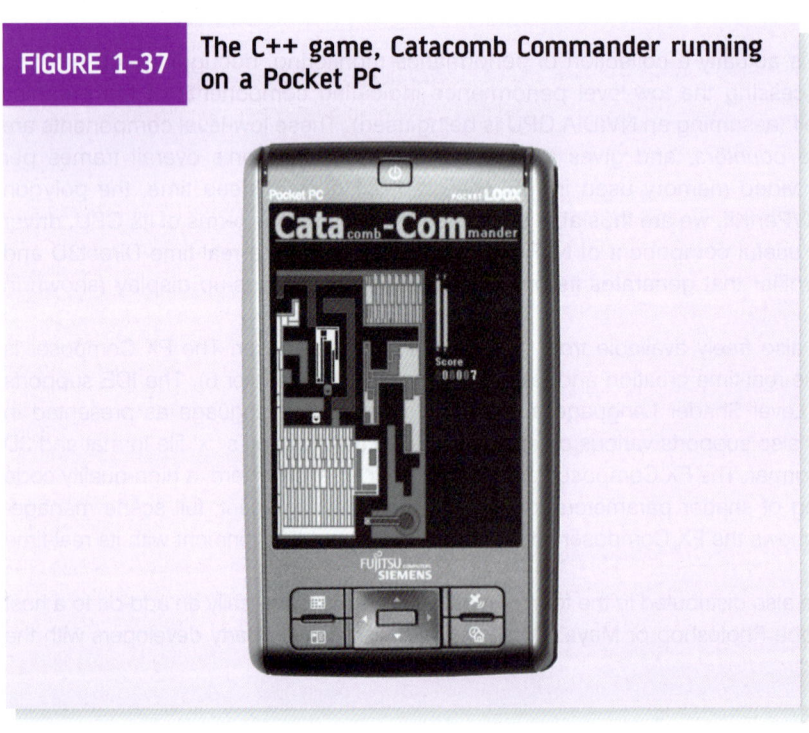

FIGURE 1-37   The C++ game, Catacomb Commander running on a Pocket PC

FIGURE 1-38   **NVIDIA's PerfHUD**

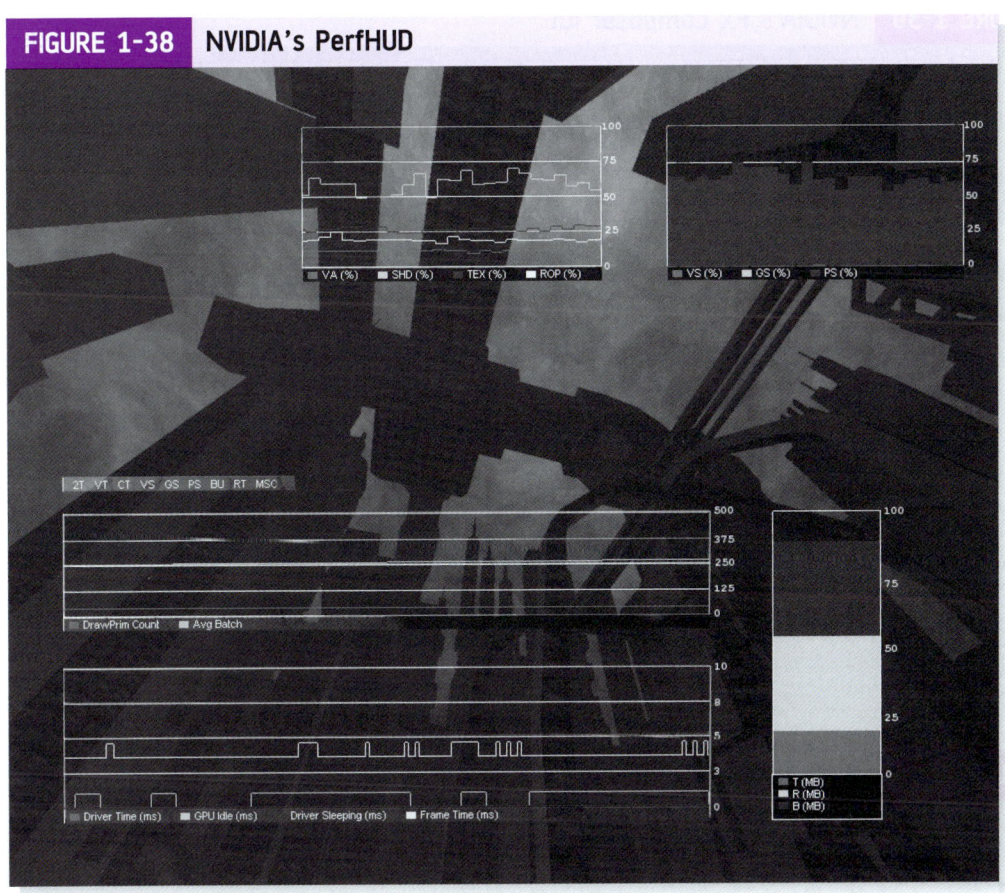

means to create a tool that extends the existing functionality of an application in some specific way. NVIDIA's Adobe Photoshop Normal Map plug-in is an example of one such a tool. This plug-in creates normal maps from texture maps. The generated normal maps can then subsequently be used for per-pixel rendering. An alternative to this plug-in is to use the GIMP normal map plug-in (a plug-in for the GNU Image Manipulation Program). The generation and use of normal maps are discussed in Chapter 8.

One final tool worth mentioning is concerned with the programming side of game development (or programming in general). This tool, called an *integrated development environment,* is normally made up of a text editor with special source code highlighting (called *syntax highlighting*), a compiler used for the translation of human readable to executable machine or object code and a debugger for testing and tracking down program errors and bugs. Numerous commercial and freely downloadable IDEs are available, with most providing an uncluttered and aesthetically pleasing environment to work in. The majority of IDEs also provide tools to aid in the detection of memory leaks and performance profiling. The most common IDE in both the game development and business software industry is by far *Microsoft Visual Studio*. Visual Studio supports application development using traditional programming languages such as C++ as well as rapid application development via Microsoft's .NET framework (including languages such as C#, J#, ASP.NET, etc). Alternative IDEs include Apple's Xcode, Sun Microsystems's NetBeans (traditionally a Java IDE but extended to support C/C++ development via the NetBeans C/C++ Pack), and MinGW Developer Studio (a freeware IDE for C and C++ development). Figure 1-40 shows the Microsoft Visual Studio 2005 IDE front-end.

FIGURE 1-39   NVIDIA's FX Composer IDE

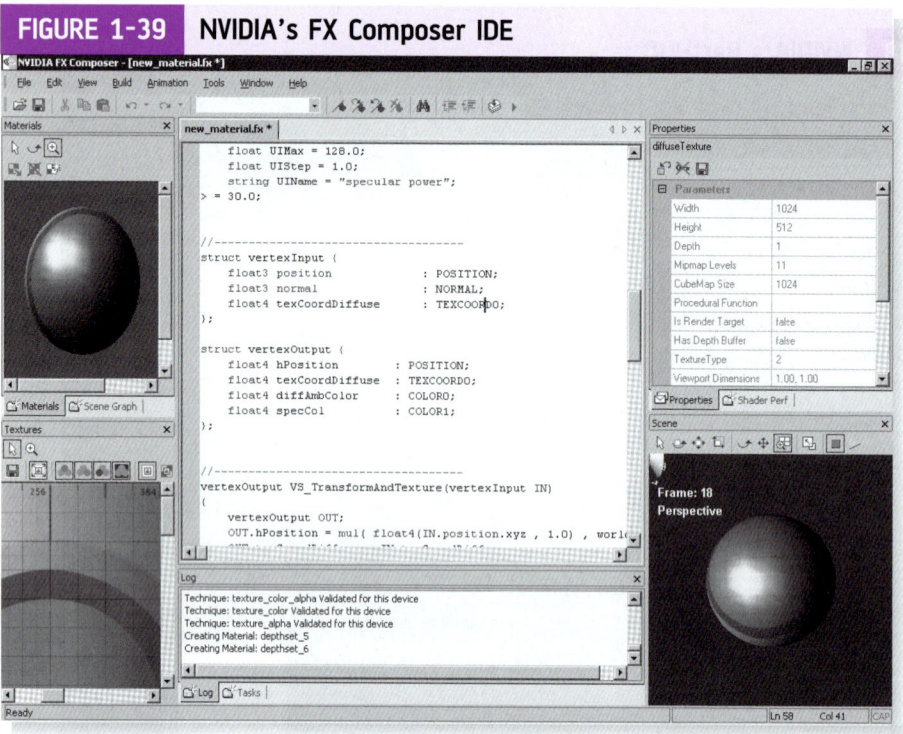

FIGURE 1-40   Basic Visual Studio 2005 interface

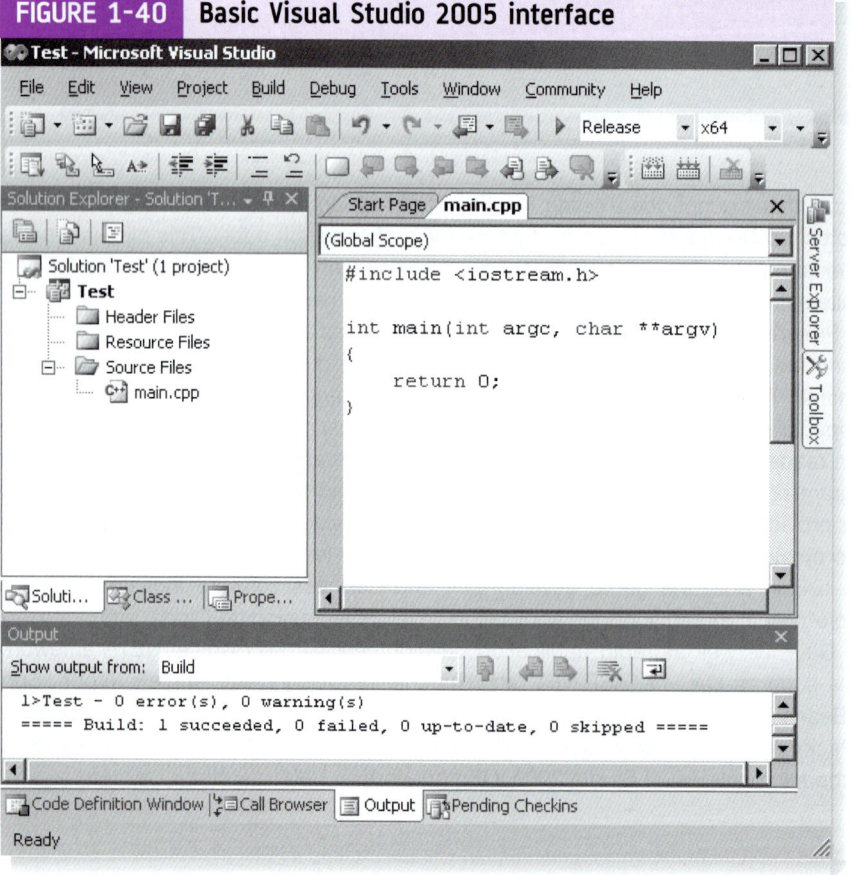

1.5　SUMMARY

One can easily feel overwhelmed when first breaking into the world of game development. This is mostly due to the game development industry's coming of age – i.e. evolving from small 'garage-based' operations in the 1980s to multinational corporations where titles take a number of years and significant funding to complete. The size of the industry, however, places no constraint on entering it. An example of a logical place to start, from both a startup company/business and personal learning perspective, would be to create online-released casual games. Casual games are targeted at a mass audience and don't require extremely long development cycles. Progressing from casual games to more high-profile games such as first-person shooters or real-time strategy titles is also more intuitive than 'biting off more than you can chew'.

In this chapter, we started by looking at game development as a multifaceted discipline. We defined the game development process as the combination of a software engineering methodology and a project management process. Building on this we defined game development through a number of phases, namely, pre-production, mainstream production, project milestones, testing, release to manufacturing, and patch-based maintenance. Following this introduction we considered the history of game development and how continuous technological advancements led to technologies such as 3D accelerators and APIs such as OpenGL and DirectX.

Next we considered the elements of game programming, noting the difference between game programming and general application programming. This difference was specifically concerned with the sequential or event-driven input of normal applications as opposed to the real-time execution of games. The real-time execution of games was discussed via the implementation of a game loop.

We then investigated general operating system architecture to understand the need for proper resource acquisition, thread/process creation and termination, and memory allocation, as well as managing system resources and controlling communication between an application and the system's hardware.

The remainder of the chapter focused on game development techniques and methodologies such as sequential software development via the waterfall model, iterative software development using the Rational Unified Process and agile software development via Extreme Programming. The discussion of these methodologies was followed by an introduction to the Unified Modeling Language, specifically dealing with the representation of classes, associations, generalizations, aggregation, and interfaces.

At this point, we have introduced game development in a general sense. The next chapter provides a more in-depth look at game programming and deals with the OpenGL and DirectX 10 Application Programming Interfaces on an introductory level.

1.6　FURTHER READING

There are several good books focusing on game design, development, production, the game development industry and the use of tools. One such book reviewing all aspects of the theory and practice of game development, design and production is *Steve Rabin's Introduction to Game Development* (ISBN: 1584503777). Also, the specifics of game programming are nicely laid out in *Jonathan S. Harbour's Game Programming All in One* (ISBN: 1598632892).

Software engineering is also a very big field with each methodology characterized by at least one landmark title. A very nice game-orientated software engineering book is *John P. Flynt and Omar Salen's Software Engineering for Game Developers* (ISBN: 1592001556).

Kent Beck's Extreme Programming Explained: Embrace Change (ISBN: 0201616416) and *Refactoring: Improving the Design of Existing Code* by Martin Fowler et al. (ISBN: 0201485672) are two great books for more information on Extreme Programming. For more on the waterfall sequential software development model, see *Winston Royce's* 1970 *IEEE WESCON 26* article, *'Managing the Development of Large Software Systems'*. The Rational Unified

1

Process is very nicely presented in *Philippe Kruchten's The Rational Unified Process: An Introduction* (ISBN: 0321197704) as well as *Ivar Jacobsen, Grady Booch and James Rumbaugh's The Unified Software Development Process* (ISBN: 0201571692).

Many resources focusing solely on the Unified Modeling Language exist. One such a book is *Dan Pilone and Neil Pitman's UML 2.0 in a Nutshell* (ISBN: 0596007957). The Object Management Group (a consortium that defines standards such as UML) also provides the most recent UML specification for free from their website (www.uml.org).

1.7   EXERCISES

1   Identify the key differences between a pre-alpha project milestone and a beta release.

2   What is the main difference between unit testing, functional testing and automated testing?

3   What industry development accelerated the development and subsequent adaptation of Direct3D and OpenGL?

4   Describe two techniques used for the monitoring of events.

5   List the main purpose of top-half and bottom-half interrupts.

6   How would one ensure uninterrupted execution of a game?

7   Describe the main difference between multithreading, multiprogramming and multitasking.

8   Why are game development techniques and methodologies important?

9   List and describe the main phases of the waterfall model.

10   What seems to be the main weakness of sequential software development?

11   Describe the general idea behind iterative software development and out-of-the-box delivery.

12   What is the rationale behind RUP's component-based architecture?

13   List and briefly explain each of RUP's nine disciplines.

14   What is agile software development?

15   Describe Extreme Programming by focusing on its main practices.

16   What is the purpose of the Unified Modeling Language?

17   Consider Figure 1-41.
     Explain in common English the relationship between the two classes.

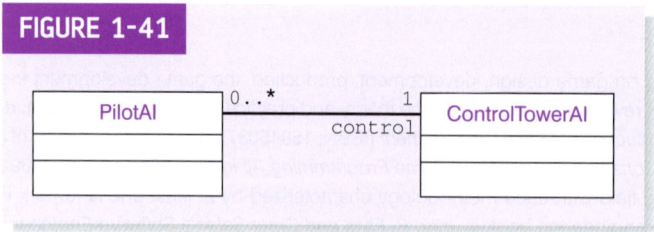

FIGURE 1-41

18   How can we get a stronger form of aggregation?

19   Why are instance diagrams needed?

20   Why would a development team require in-house game tools?

CHAPTER 2

OpenGL vs. DirectX as API

LEARNING OBJECTIVES

In this chapter you will learn about:

- Application programming interfaces
- OpenGL: a standard for cross-platform high performance graphics
- The OpenGL Utility Toolkit (GLUT)
- DirectX foundation classes and Direct3D 10

INTRODUCTION

Chapter 2 provides an introductory comparison between OpenGL, GLUT, and the DirectX 10 application programming interfaces, highlighting the common ground and disparities between them. The chapter starts by looking at application programming interfaces in general, after which it introduces the reader to OpenGL, the OpenGL Utility Toolkit, and DirectX 10. The chapter features three short programs illustrating the implementation of each API.

2

2.1   APPLICATION PROGRAMMING INTERFACES

An *application programming interface*, or API, is a programmatically implemented interface provided in the form of a library. This interface provides a certain number of services for use by an application program. APIs are specified in terms of a programming language, thus resulting in the API being compiled together with the application. API libraries are loaded at run-time and can either be shipped with the application or pre-installed on the system executing the application.

An API is thus a unified interface featuring a number of classes/structures, constants and functions. Examples of common APIs include Microsoft's Win32 API, Sun Microsystems's Java Platform, the OpenGL graphics API, Microsoft's DirectX API (consisting of several APIs providing interfaces for sound, input control, graphics, etc.), the Simple DirectMedia Layer, and the Single UNIX Specification.

Graphics interfaces, such as OpenGL and Direct3D, can be investigated using a black-box approach. A *blackbox* is a system described through its inputs and outputs without any consideration of its internal workings. OpenGL can thus be thought of as a system with inputs in the form of user program function calls and its outputs being the graphics (primitives) displayed on the output device, as shown in Figure 2-1.

Application programming interfaces can be described through the functions contained in their libraries. These functions can be divided into the following main categories:

1   Attribute functions.

2   Primitive functions.

3   Viewing functions.

4   Transformation functions.

5   Query functions.

6   Control functions.

7   Input functions.

Figure 2-2 shows the interaction between these library functions.

- *Attribute functions* focus on the properties of primitives, for example, allowing the application programmer to specify a polygon's fill pattern or the color of a line segment. Attribute functions are normally closely coupled with primitive functions – controlling the appearance of objects defined by these functions.

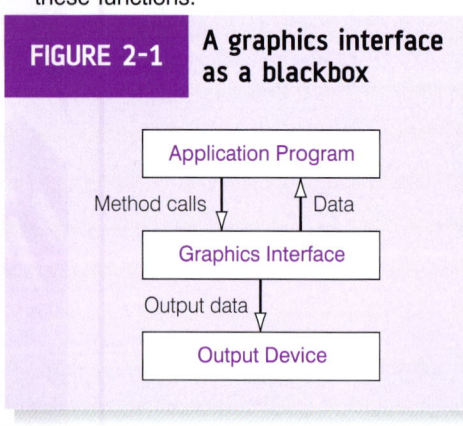

FIGURE 2-1   A graphics interface as a blackbox

- *Primitive functions* facilitate the definition of low-level geometric objects such as points, lines, triangles, text and various other primitives and surfaces. These functions specify the building blocks of geometric objects; for example, a soccer ball can be defined using nothing more than a collection of triangles arranged in the shape of a sphere.

- *Viewing functions* are used to describe the position, orientation and field of view of the camera used to view the scene. These functions also allow us to define a clipping volume to block

FIGURE 2-2   **The interaction of the main functions of an API**

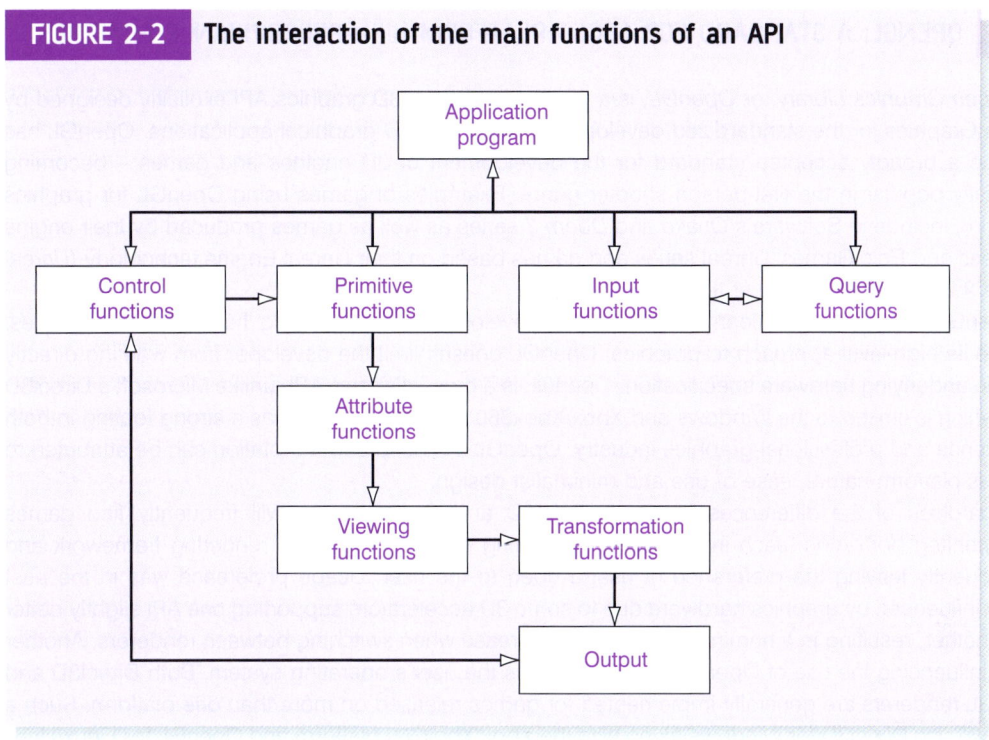

out objects not visible to the viewer. All objects and portions of objects falling outside this clipping volume are clipped out, and thus do not appear in the viewable image.

- *Transformation functions* allow us to perform various transformation techniques such as rotation, translation, and scaling. These transformations are simply the process of switching between different coordinate systems. Coordinate system changes are represented by matrices, with a transformation matrix representing a series of translations, rotations and/or scaling operations. Chapter 7 deals with transformations in detail.

- APIs should also be able to query devices to determine both the device type and its supported feature set. For example, a graphics card might be queried for its maximum supported resolution or a joystick device could be queried to establish its current state (pressed buttons, the stick's angle of rotation, etc.). This device data is acquired through a collection of *query functions*.

- *Control functions* are used for window creation, program initialization, control and error handling. These functions communicate with the underlying window system (such as the X Window System display protocol used with Linux and Unix-like operating systems), the network subsystem and the underlying graphics and system hardware.

- It is one thing to render an image to a screen but interaction with this image must also be possible. Our graphical applications require some way to perform this system level input control and interaction, thus at the most basic level necessitating some form of keyboard and mouse input handling. This is the purpose of *input functions*. Chapter 5 focuses on input and interaction control by means of DirectInput and the Xbox 360's XInput API.

2.2 OPENGL: A STANDARD FOR CROSS-PLATFORM HIGH PERFORMANCE GRAPHICS

2

The *Open Graphics Library*, or *OpenGL*, is a procedural-based 3D graphics API explicitly designed by Silicon Graphics for the standardized development of 3D and 2D graphical applications. OpenGL has become a broadly accepted standard for the development of 3D engines and games – becoming especially popular in the first-person shooter genre. Examples of games using OpenGL for graphics rendering include id Software's *Quake* and *Doom 3* series as well as games produced by their engine licensees and Epic Games' Unreal series and games based on their Unreal Engine technology (*Unreal Engine 3* is the latest release at the time of writing).

OpenGL is very easy to learn and frees the developer from underlying hardware technicalities. Despite its high-level approach to graphics, OpenGL doesn't limit the developer from working directly with the underlying hardware specification. OpenGL is a cross-platform API, unlike Microsoft's Direct3D API, (which is limited to the Windows and Xbox/Xbox360 platforms), and it has a strong footing in both the science and professional graphics industry. OpenGL's widespread adaptation can be attributed to its cross-platform nature, ease of use and minimalist design.

Regardless of the differences between Direct3D and OpenGL, one will frequently find games implementing both APIs; each implementation forming part of the game's rendering framework and subsequently leaving the preference of usage open to the user. Usage preference was in the past mainly influenced by graphics hardware due to some 3D accelerators supporting one API slightly better than another, resulting in a nominal performance increase when switching between renderers. Another factor influencing the use of OpenGL and Direct3D is the user's operating system. Both Direct3D and OpenGL renderers are generally implemented for games released on more than one platform. Such a game will use Direct3D for Windows along with the Xbox/Xbox360 platform and OpenGL for Linux/Unix/Solaris/MacOS X and the PlayStation3. OpenGL has an extremely far reaching following and loyal user base in the field of computer-aided design (CAD), virtual reality simulations, science, gaming and information visualization. That said, it is important to remember that both Direct3D and OpenGL support similar functionality at their respective higher levels.

OpenGL is, at the lowest level, nothing more than a specification periodically updated and/or revised by the OpenGL Architecture Review Board (ARB). This specification is simply a document outlining all its functions, including the actions that should be performed by each function. The OpenGL specification document serves as a reference for hardware vendors such as NVIDIA and ATI when creating OpenGL implementations in the form of libraries and hardware components. All OpenGL hardware and software implementations created for MacOS X, Windows, Linux, the PlayStation3, and flavors of UNIX must be put through some testing to guarantee compliance with the OpenGL specification.

The Architecture Review Board was founded in 1992 by a group of companies sharing the common goal of defining a consistent and platform independent graphics application programming interface. Companies, past and/or present, include 3Dlabs, Apple Computer, ATI, Dell, IBM, Intel, Microsoft Corporation, NVIDIA, SGI, and Sun Microsystems. Microsoft left the ARB in 2003 and it was subsequently announced that control of the OpenGL specification would be assigned to the Khronos Group to improve the marketing of the API. Some of the current members of the Khronos Group include AMD, Intel, Creative Labs, NVIDIA, Sony Computer Entertainment, Sun Microsystems and Texas Instruments – companies whose varying interests ensure the specification of a general purpose graphics API.

From a design standpoint OpenGL has two main goals. Its first goal is seamless interaction with a vast array of 3D accelerators. This is accomplished by hiding the underlying interfacing complexities from the programmer. The second goal is to offer the same capabilities on a number of computing platforms. This is done by each supporting platform implementing the full OpenGL feature set regardless of the availability of hardware acceleration (thus using software emulation if needed).

The OpenGL API is also designed for the creation and execution of graphical applications over a networked computing environment. For example, an OpenGL program might be created on a system incapable of displaying 3D graphics and then executed on another computer connected via a network. This is called a *client-server model*, and the main idea behind this concept is to issue OpenGL commands from a computer to a server. The server is then responsible for executing these drawing commands. Today this model is more commonly used to represent the computer as the client and the graphics processing unit (GPU) as the server.

In addition to being based on this client-server architecture, OpenGL is also modeled as a state machine. This state-based design is carried over to the OpenGL Shading Language, a high-level shading language based on the C programming language, used for programming the graphics pipeline (similar to the High Level Shader Language and NVIDIA's Cg discussed in Chapter 6). *State-based* simply means that the application programmer has to put OpenGL into a specific state, in which it stays until the programmer explicitly alters this state. For example, we can specify a state in which OpenGL always draws a line whenever it receives two vertices as input.

The OpenGL programming interface is provided as a library specifying a set of drawing functions and commands. When writing an OpenGL program we will only interact with the API. All of OpenGL's rendering functionality is dependent on the level of support offered by the graphics card's manufacturer (or software emulation layer such as the *Mesa* graphics library) and are shielded from visibility by the card's device drivers. The OpenGL API is thus responsible for hiding the intricacy of communicating with various graphics accelerators.

OpenGL is closely integrated with the graphics pipeline and each of its operations either feeds primitives (points, lines, polygons) into the pipeline or controls the processing of these primitives by configuring or programming the pipeline stages. Chapter 4 deals with the graphics pipeline in detail while Chapter 6 focuses on the programmable graphics pipeline.

The OpenGL interface consists of over 120 commands, with the letters 'gl' preceding each, for example: glColor, glVertex, glBegin, glDisable, glBitmap. These commands, or functions, are used to define a scene's geometry, lighting, atmospheric elements such as fog, and material properties – all the elements needed to create interactive three-dimensional scenes. OpenGL constants are in turn preceded by the character sequence 'GL_', for example: GL_POINTS, GL_POLYGON, GL_SCISSOR_TEST. OpenGL also has a series of predefined types such as GLint, GLfloat, GLsizei, GLboolean. These types are simply ANSI C implementations of common C/C++ types such as int, float, long and bool.

OpenGL doesn't offer any high-level commands to describe complex models or three-dimensional objects. It rather provides the programmer with a set of commands that can be used to define basic geometry such as triangles, points and lines. These geometric primitives can in turn be used to create complicated geometry meshes. The OpenGL library, thus, features all the commands needed to define any two- and three-dimensional object or environment conceivable. Additional functions for the specification of common objects (such as spheres, cones, cylinders) are provided by the OpenGL Utility Library included with all versions of OpenGL. Figure 2-3 shows a series of screenshots taken within a scene created using only the most basic OpenGL drawing commands.

2.2.1 A Very Basic OpenGL Program

We will now look at the basic structure of an OpenGL program. This program creates a simple triangle via the specification of three spatial points, subsequently initializing certain OpenGL states to control the manner in which these points are connected and the final object rendered.

OpenGL, as mentioned, constructs objects or models from geometric primitives such as points (also called vertices), lines and polygons (such as a triangle or other flat surfaces). The final object is displayed, or rendered, on a monitor in the form of pixels (picture elements or dots on the monitor).

2

FIGURE 2-3	A scene created using the most basic OpenGL drawing functions

Chapter 4 and 6 deal with this conversion process in much more detail. For now, just know that OpenGL processes a number of input parameters using the graphics pipeline, subsequently outputting the final image consisting of pixels to the monitor.

Our program starts with a number of 'include' directives:

```
#include <GL/gl.h>    //default OpenGL API header file
#include "basicIO.h"    //a user created header file
and so on.
```

The include directive, written as 'include', is used for the inclusion of header files. This time we included gl.h. The hash sign, '#', signals the C/C++ pre-processor (active during the compilation process) to include the specified file – generally header files. The *pre-processor* is a program run during the compilation cycle and it is responsible for the translation of source code prior to the actual compilation phase. Header files are saved with the dot-h, '.h', file extension (adding the dot-h file extension to default headers such as iostream have been deprecated in C++). In short, the include directive is used whenever we want to access source code stored in another file.

Just a note on the angular brackets, '< >', following the include directive – whenever the pre-processor reads an angular bracket, it looks for the file in our compiler's default or user specified include directories. User-created header files are included with standard quotation marks, '" "'. This inclusion process is a little bit different when working with templates (discussed in the C++ documentation available from the book's website).

2

The entry point of this program is specified using the main function. This function is required by every C/C++ program (the WinMain function serves as such an initial entry point for Win32-based applications). This function is used to call at least one of our other functions (should we have any) and it's the first function called upon execution of the application. A function is just a grouping of code performing one or more actions. Our main function rendering a red triangle on a white background is defined as follows:

```
int main()
{
    /* call some routine to create the window */
    SomeWindowCreationRoutine();

    /* set the clear color – red, green, blue, alpha*/
    glClearColor (1.0, 1.0, 1.0, 0.0);

    /* clear frame buffer */
    glColor (GL_COLOR_BUFFER_BIT);

    /* set color to red */
    glColor3f(1.0, 0.0, 0.0);

    /* glBegin composes the group of vertices below as a
       polygon */
    glBegin (GL_POLYGON);
        glVertex3f(0.0, –10.0, –6.0); //x = 0, y = –10, z = –6
        glVertex3f(–10.0, 0.0, 6.0); //x = –10, y = 0, z = 6
        glVertex3f(10.0, 0.0, 6.0); //x = 10, y = 0, z = 6
    /* glEnd indicates the end of the rendering group */
    glEnd();

    /* make sure all previously issued commands are
       completed */
    glFlush ();

    /* call a routine to keep the window active – allowing
       the triangle to be shown */
    KeepTheWindowActive();

    /* exit the application*/
    return 0;
}
```

The main function is responsible for rendering a red triangle on a white background (Figure 2-4). Its first function call, glClearColor, sets the color value with which to clear the back buffer (i.e. the background color). This function takes four parameters, namely the clear color's level of red (0 to 1), level of green (0 to 1), level of blue (0 to 1)

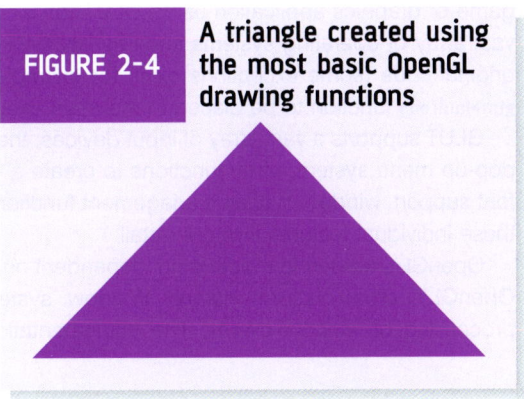

FIGURE 2-4   **A triangle created using the most basic OpenGL drawing functions**

and the alpha value controlling the level of transparency (0 to 1). We set this clear color to white by setting the red, green and blue components to their maximum values. Following this we call the glClear function. This function clears the buffers specified by its parameters, in our case clearing the frame buffer. Chapter 4 deals with the frame buffer in detail.

The glColor3f function specifies the red, green and blue color components by setting the color value of each parameter to a floating-point value ranging from 0 to 1 (in our case setting the object's fill color to red) – see Chapter 8.

To define a geometric object, OpenGL makes use of multiple vertex function calls arranged in sequence, located between a glBegin and glEnd call respectively. The glBegin call serves as rendering starting point for a group of primitives (in our case connecting the three vertices and filling the enclosed area to form a triangle using the GL_POLYGON primitive type specification). Chapter 6 examines these concepts in much more detail.

To define an object we must make use of multiple vertex function calls arranged in sequence (located between a glBegin and glEnd function call). Each glVertex3f function draws a vertex at the specified x-, y- and z-coordinates. We specify three independent vertices with the GL_POLYGON type specification leading to the rendering of a closed, filled surface. Each of these vertices corresponds to a corner of the triangle.

Finally, the glFlush function is called to force the execution of all previously defined OpenGL calls. The KeepTheWindowActive placeholder function keeps the window active, allowing the triangle to be shown. This routine, along with the SomeWindowCreationRoutine function, is needed due to OpenGL only being concerned with graphical elements and not providing functions for window creation and control. It is thus one thing to render an image to a screen but interaction with this image must also be possible. Our OpenGL programs will make use of the OpenGL Utility Toolkit (GLUT) to perform this system level input control and interaction. GLUT is very powerful yet easy to use and allows both keyboard and mouse input handling. It is also used for window creation and control. There are of course numerous other ways to achieve input interaction; when using Windows for example, we can make use of Microsoft's DirectInput.

2.3   THE OPENGL UTILITY TOOLKIT (GLUT)

The *OpenGL Utility Toolkit*, or *GLUT*, is a utility library for OpenGL applications. GLUT, as a programming interface, provides functions for system-level control and initialization – in essence window creation and control. GLUT was created to hide all the complexities related to window creation and manipulation, menu and GUI creation and interaction, as well as mouse, keyboard and joystick Input/Output, while at the same time facilitating the creation of cross-platform applications. An OpenGL game or graphics application using GLUT for window creation and input control can be run across a vast array of operating systems such as UNIX, Linux, and Windows, without any modifications to the original code (some exceptions exist: for example, the MacOS X GLUT implementation requires the glutMainLoop function to be placed in the main execution thread – but more on this later).

GLUT supports a vast array of input devices, the creation of multiple OpenGL windows, a cascading pop-up menu system, utility functions to create a variety of geometric objects, stroke text and bitmap font support, window overlay management functions, event timing, etc. Subsequent chapters deal with these individual features in more detail.

OpenGL's rendering model is not dependent on the underlying window system. This is the reason for OpenGL's cross-platform nature. Window system operations include window creation and the processing of window events. The implementation details concerning these operations differ from operating system to operating system. For example, creating a window within, say, Microsoft Windows Vista, differs substantially from how we might go about this when creating a window using the X Windows System under Linux. The manner in which OpenGL interacts with an underlying window system is separated from the OpenGL specification. The lack of a window system interface allows the OpenGL graphics system to run across a vast array of systems. GLUT provides OpenGL applications with an independent window creation and control programming interface – eliminating the daunting task of directly working with the X Window System (a standardized toolkit/protocol to build graphical user interfaces), Motif (a toolkit for building graphical user interfaces under UNIX), or Microsoft's WINAPI (Microsoft's core set of application programming interfaces).

GLUT functions are arranged into the following API categories based on their respective area of functionality:

1 Callback creation and registration functions.

2 Event processing initialization.

3 Font rendering functions.

4 Initialization functions.

5 Menu creation and control functions.

6 Model rendering functions.

7 State retrieval functions.

8 Window color-map manipulation functions.

9 Window creation and control functions.

10 Window overlay specification and control functions.

Callback creation and registration functions register the callbacks called by GLUT's main event processing loop. A callback function is basically a software routine passed as an argument. These callbacks are registered to be invoked when some event occurs (see Chapter 4). Three types of callbacks are supported by GLUT: menu callbacks, window callbacks and global callbacks. A *menu callback* is a function called whenever the user selects a menu entry. *Window callback* functions handle window resize and redisplay events, for example, when the user minimizes the window or when the rendered image needs to be updated. *Global callback* functions deal with everything from menu control to timer events. Examples of callback registration functions include the following:

- glutDisplayFunc (sets the display callback for a window).

- glutKeyboardFunc (sets the keyboard callback for a window).

- glutMouseFunc (sets the mouse callback for a window).

- glutMenuStatusFunc (sets the global menu status callback).

- glutIdleFunc (sets the global idle callback).

Event processing is initialized using one GLUT function call following the initial GLUT setup. The glutMainLoop function serves as entry point to the GLUT event processing loop, dealing with any event callback being generated. This function is only called once for any GLUT program and the entered event processing loop will not return at any stage during the application's execution.

Font rendering functions facilitate the rendering of both stroke and bitmap text (see Chapter 6). Stroke text is based on geometric shapes while bitmap text are defined using a bitmap image for each character. The following GLUT functions deal with font rendering:

- glutBitmapCharacter (renders a bitmap character via OpenGL).
- glutBitmapWidth (determines the width of the bitmap character to use).
- glutStrokeCharacter (renders a stroke character via OpenGL).
- glutStrokeWidth (determines the width of the stroke character to use).

Initialization functions deal with the initialization and creation of the window system as well as the GLUT state. This API subgroup also includes command line processing. All these functions begin with the glutInit prefix. Four initialization functions are provided by the GLUT API:

- glutInit (initializes the GLUT library).
- glutInitWindowPosition (sets the initial window position in terms of *x*- and *y*- pixel coordinates).
- glutInitWindowSize (sets the window's size by specifying the window width and height in pixels).
- glutInitDisplayMode (sets the initial display mode, in particular the specification of supported modes such as the use of double buffering, multi-sampling, etc. – concepts discussed in subsequent chapters).

A menu interface is a crucial part of any application as it allows the execution of certain functions or the setting of certain states. We can, for example, make use of menu interfaces to control lights and shadows, or to activate some external force such as wind or fog. GLUT has a very usable menu pop-up system that, for instance, allows the user access to the menu by either left–or right-clicking in the graphics application's window area. *Menu creation and control functions* are concerned with the specification and control of this built-in pop-up menu system. Examples of GLUT menu management functions include:

- glutCreateMenu (creates a new pop-up menu).
- glutSetMenu (sets the active menu).
- glutGetMenu (returns the ID of the active menu).
- glutDestroyMenu (destroys the identified menu).
- glutAddMenuEntry (adds menu items to the bottom of the current menu).
- glutAddSubMenu (adds submenu entries to the bottom of the current menu).
- glutChangeToMenuEntry (changes a menu item to a menu entry).
- glutChangeToSubMenu (changes a menu item to a submenu entry).
- glutRemoveMenuItem (removes the specified menu item).
- glutAttachMenu (attaches a mouse button for menu selection).
- glutDetachMenu (detaches an attached mouse button that was used for menu selection).

Model rendering functions make it easier to quickly render commonly used 3D geometric objects such as cylinders, spheres, cones and teapots. All 3D objects can be rendered in either solid or wire-frame form. These routines render geometric objects using pure OpenGL primitives. Examples of GLUT geometric object rendering functions include:

- glutSolidSphere (renders a solid sphere).

- glutWireSphere (renders a wire-frame sphere).

- glutSolidCube (renders a solid cube).

- glutWireCube (renders a wire-frame cube).

- glutSolidCone (renders a solid cone).

- glutWireCone (renders a wire-frame cone).

- glutSolidTorus (renders a solid torus/doughnut).

- glutWireTorus (renders a wire-frime torus/doughnut).

- glutSolidTeapot (renders a solid Utah teapot).

- glutWireTeapot (renders a wire-frame Utah teapot).

State retrieval functions allow graphics applications to retrieve state information from the GLUT subsystem. State information includes information about the height and width of the current window, width and height of the screen in pixels, query data pertaining to whether a specific OpenGL extension is supported, and modifier key states returned when certain callbacks are generated (such as when the Alt-key is pressed). GLUT state retrieval functions include the following:

- glutGet (to retrieve a simple GLUT state such as a window's spawn position, its width, etc.).

- glutLayerGet (to retrieve the GLUT state relevant to one of the layers of the current window – for example to determine whether an overlay could be established for the current window).

- glutDeviceGet (to retrieve device specific information, for example to determine whether a keyboard or mouse is available for input).

- glutGetModifiers (to query for certain callbacks generated by modifier keys such as 'Ctrl', 'Alt', 'Shift' and 'Caps Lock').

- glutExtensionSupported (to determine whether a specific OpenGL extension is supported).

Window color-map manipulation functions are used to manipulate index color-maps defined for each created window. APIs such as OpenGL and Direct3D support two types of color modes: indexed and red–green–blue–alpha color. Indexed color is a type of color management system where each image is assigned a table of color values pertaining to each of its pixels (called a color-map). The red–green–blue–alpha color mode is much more common and greatly replaced indexed color (more frequently utilized when working with older graphics cards). Chapter 8 discusses color and color models in more detail. The following GLUT functions deal with color-map management:

- glutSetColor (sets the entries in a color table for each window on the screen).

- glutGetColor (retrieves the red, green, or blue color component of a given color index entry).

- glutCopyColormap (copies the color-map from some specified window for use with the active window).

Window creation and control functions, responsible for the creation and control of windows, are perhaps the most valuable of all the functions provided by the GLUT interface. Two types of windows, namely top-level and sub-level windows are supported by GLUT. A top-level window can be considered the main 'parent' window, with all the sublevel windows as 'child' windows. Window management functions include the following:

- glutCreateWindow (creates a top-level window with a caption).

- glutCreateSubWindow (creates a sublevel window with an identifier to this new window's parent window).

- glutSetWindow (sets the specified window as active).

- glutGetWindow (returns the identifier of the current active window).

- glutDestroyWindow (destroys a particular window, performing the necessary cleanup and releasing all of its resources).

- glutPostRedisplay (indicates that the current window is to be repainted by the window's display callback during the next main loop iteration).

- glutSwapBuffers (swaps one buffer with another when using double buffering – more specifically, the back buffer is used for redrawing the image while the front buffer is concerned with displaying the redrawn image. We thus swap these buffers throughout the execution of the program to give the perception of a still image – see Chapter 4).

- glutPositionWindow (repositions the window based on some new *x*- and *y*-coordinate values).

- glutReshapeWindow (resizes the window based on some new width and height values).

- glutFullScreen (switches to full-screen mode).

- glutPopWindow (pops a window on top of one of its 'sibling' windows).

- glutPushWindow (pushes a window beneath one of its 'sibling' windows).

- glutShowWindow (sets the current top-level window as visible).

- glutHideWindow (hides the current top-level window).

- glutIconifyWindow (adds an icon to the current top-level window).

- glutSetWindowTitle (alters the current top-level window title).

- glutSetIconTitle (alters the current top-level window's icon title).

- glutSetCursor (sets the mouse cursor image used with the current window).

2.3.1 A Very Simple GLUT Program

We will now look at the basic structure of an OpenGL program utilizing the GLUT utility library. This program focuses on window initialization, control and menu interaction via the mouse. Window creation and control are discussed in Chapter 4 with Chapter 5 focusing on input control. The following program will not draw any image on the screen; it instead only illustrates event-driven menu interaction via the mouse. In short, a menu is accessible by clicking the right mouse button anywhere in the window. A menu item is selected by clicking on it with the left mouse button. Each time a menu item is selected the corresponding output is printed in the command prompt window.

Our program once again starts with a number of 'include' directives:

```
#include <GL/glut.h> //glut library, it imports gl.h, glu.h
#include <iostream>  //standard IO
```

The first header file, "glut.h", includes the GLUT library which in turn imports the OpenGL headers, 'gl.h' and 'glu.h'. Without the inclusion of 'iostream' we would not be able to use the standard output stream or the related 'cout' routine. The header file, iostream.h, provides the default Input Output Stream to C++ programs; don't expect to see it that much outside the terminal environment though.

The following function, display, is responsible for rendering the output to the screen. Such a function will normally call OpenGL routines to initialize the screen for rendering. Following this initialization, we can display the rendered image by swapping the front buffer with the back buffer using the glutSwapBuffers function (as discussed in Chapter 4):

```
void display(void)
{
    //...some OpenGL initialization functions

    /* contents of back buffer are set to become that of
       front buffer (double buffering)*/
    glutSwapBuffers ();
}
```

The next function, controlMenu, prints the text 'First item selected' when the user selects the first menu item and 'Second item selected' when the second menu item is selected. The application terminates when the third menu item is chosen. This function is passed as parameter to the glutCreateMenu function when creating the new pop-up menu:

```
void controlMenu(int x)
{
    /* basic switch control structure, prints the text
       corresponding to the selected action in the command
       prompt window */
    switch(x)
    {
        case 1: cout << "First item selected" << endl;
            break;
        case 2: cout << "Second item selected" << endl;
            break;
        case 3: exit(0); //terminate the application
    }

    /* set the current window for redisplay */
    glutPostRedisplay();
}
```

The line, 'cout << "First item selected" << endl', outputs the phrase 'First item selected' to the command prompt window. The output redirection operator '<<' is used, as its name suggests, to direct output. In this case it directs output to the screen. There can be quite a number of these redirection operators in a cout statement; the second one, in this case, directs a new-line to the screen. The end-line 'endl' statement is similar to the C programming language's new-line escape sequence '\n'. This end-line statement ensures that the following printed character or string is positioned on a new-line and thus not next to this string. Omitting the end-line iostream manipulator would cause any following output to be placed right next to this 'First item selected' string.

The glutCreateMenu function takes the callback function for the menu that is called whenever a menu entry is selected as parameter. The value of the selected menu item is then sent to the callback which is in turn tasked with the processing of this event. We also call the glutPostRedisplay function to redisplay the window after printing the text corresponding to the selected action.

Following the controlMenu function, we define a function containing the mouse menu's GLUT routines:

```
void menu()
{
    /* create a new pop-up menu */
    glutCreateMenu(controlMenu);

    /* add menu entries to the bottom of the current menu */
    glutAddMenuEntry("First Item",1);
    glutAddMenuEntry("Second Item",2);
    glutAddMenuEntry("Quit",3);

    /* attach the right mouse button for menu selection */
    glutAttachMenu(GLUT_RIGHT_BUTTON);
}
```

The first function call, glutCreateMenu, creates the pop-up menu, linking it with the menu callback – controlMenu. The glutCreateMenu function returns an integer identifier (starting at '1'). This identifier is then passed to the callback function for processing.

Each glutAddMenuEntry function call adds a menu entry to the current menu. This function takes two parameters: an ASCII character string containing the menu entry's name, and the identifier to return to the menu callback when the entry is selected.

The glutAttachMenu function attaches the specified mouse button for menu selection. We attach the right mouse button by passing the GLUT_RIGHT_BUTTON flag as parameter to this function (alternative flags include GLUT_LEFT_BUTTON and GLUT_MIDDLE_BUTTON).

Moving on to the main function, we start by calling the glutInit routine:

```
int main(int argc, char** argv)
{
    /* initialize the GLUT library. */
    glutInit(&argc, argv);

    /* set the initial display mode: double buffering and a
       depth buffer. */
    glutInitDisplayMode(GLUT_DOUBLE | GLUT_RGB | GLUT_DEPTH);

    /* set default window size */
    glutInitWindowSize(300, 200);
```

2

```
/* create a top-level window with a caption */
glutCreateWindow("...event-driven mouse input...");

/* display our contents in the window */
glutDisplayFunc(display);

/* call our menu function */
menu();

/* enter the GLUT event processing loop - will handle
   any callback */
glutMainLoop();

return 0;
}
```

The first function, glutInit, initializes the GLUT library. It takes the command line arguments (passed to the main function at the start of the program's execution) as parameters. Next we set the initial display mode using the glutInitDisplayMode function. We specify its parameters so that double buffering (GLUT_DOUBLE), nonindexed color mode (GLUT_RGB) as well as the depth buffer (GLUT_DEPTH) are supported. These display mode parameters are discussed in later chapters.

With the display mode set, we can define the dimension of the output window using the glutInitWindowSize function. This function takes two parameters, namely, the width and height of the window, respectively. We create the top-level window using the glutCreateWindow function. This function takes an ASCII character string containing the window caption as parameter.

The display callback function, display, is now set using the glutDisplayFunc function. The display callback is called without any parameters. GLUT triggers this display callback function either explicitly through a glutPostRedisplay function call or implicitly when some window change is reported by the underlying window system. Hence, the glutDisplayFunc function displays the contents of our display function in the newly created window.

Following the glutDisplayFunc call we can invoke the menu function containing the mouse menu's GLUT routines. The final function call, glutMainLoop, serves as entry point to the GLUT event processing loop, dealing with any event callback being generated (Chapter 4). Figure 2-5 shows the created GLUT window and interaction with its pop-up menu system.

Despite GLUTs notable window creation, window control, input device monitoring and simplicity, it does suffer from some limitations. These limitations are mostly due to original design considerations.

The first common problem is the result of the GLUT library requiring the invocation of the glutMainLoop routine. This leads to problems when integrating GLUT into an application that specifies its own event loop. GLUT's event loop can be run in a separate thread when integrating GLUT into a program that already has its own event loop. This workaround is easy enough to implement; however, it might lead to synchronization issues and other problems such as when the operating system requires the glutMainLoop routine to be run in the main thread (as is the case with MacOS X).

The GLUT library also terminates all processes associated with a window when the window is destroyed. There is no real workaround for this except a number of nonofficial patches and an extra callback, namely, glutWMCloseFunc, provided by the freeglut implementation (a fairly exact clone of GLUT with an additional number of workarounds in the form of new functions).

GLUT programs also suffer from the inability to exit the main event loop due to the glutMainLoop routine never returning. This is also rectified through the use of an additional freeglut function, namely, glutLeaveMainLoop. Calling this function leads to a forced exit from the main loop.

FIGURE 2-5 **(a) GLUT pop-up menu system with related output after selection of the first item. (b) The same pop-up menu system with associated output following multiple menu element selections**

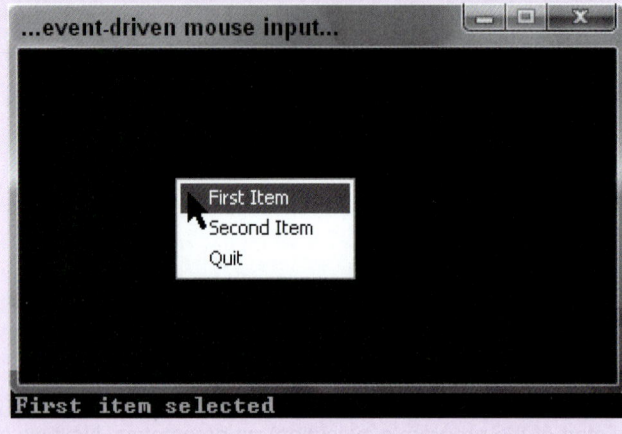

(a)

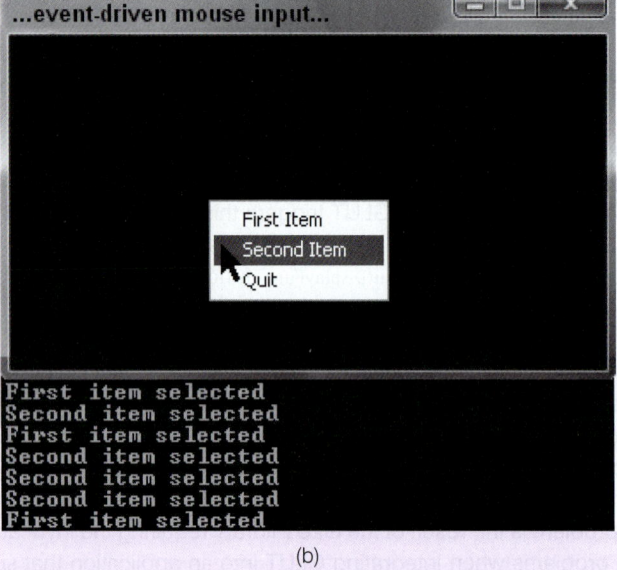

(b)

2.4   DIRECTX FOUNDATION CLASSES

Microsoft DirectX is, as presented in Chapter 4, an all encompassing description for a number of game-programming-centric APIs. These APIs are also used outside the game development sphere for tasks such as video editing, video playback, input control, 3D rendering, and sound and music playback. DirectX is targeted at the Windows and Xbox/Xbox 360 platforms, with DirectX 10, the version covered by this book, completely exclusive to Microsoft Windows Vista. Direct3D allows for the quick rendering of high-quality three-dimensional graphics and is, just like its main competitor,

OpenGL, used throughout the gaming, animation, science, simulation, and CAD (computer aided design) industries.

DirectX is released as both a runtime and software development kit (SDK), constantly updated and available from Microsoft's DirectX website. The DirectX SDK allows developers to utilize each of the DirectX APIs and it includes a number of tools and utilities such as the Microsoft cross-platform audio creation tool. The SDK also features tutorials, documentation, the DirectX runtime, headers, libraries and code samples. When installing a DirectX-based game, the user will often be prompted to install the latest DirectX runtime. The newest runtime version at the time of release is included with the game to ensure overall functionality of the game software. The DirectX end-user runtime library is thus required to execute a program utilizing one of the DirectX APIs. DirectX 10 is currently the latest version of DirectX and isn't backwards-compatible with older versions of Microsoft Windows due to architectural changes made to Windows Vista's Windows Display Driver Model (WDDM) (discussed in Chapter 4).

The DirectX API consists of the following main technologies, each of which is linked as a library during the application's compilation and execution process:

- *DirectX Graphics* (actually containing three versions of Direct3D for the sake of backwards compatibility):
  - *Direct3D 9*
    - The latest release of the Direct3D 3D graphics rendering API for Windows XP and Windows 2000 based computers (not taking advantage of the Windows Vista Display Driver Model).
  - *Direct3D 9Ex* (also called DirectX 9 for Windows Vista)
    - An extended version of the Direct3D 9 API, providing additional access to Windows Vista specific extensions for the rendering of 3D graphics. The Windows Aero graphical user interface utilizes this API, for example.
  - *Direct3D 10*
    - The newest API for the rendering of two– and three-dimensional graphics targeted at Windows Vista's Display Driver Model. Also the only API supporting Shader Model 4 (see Chapter 6).
  - *DirectDraw* (deprecated)
    - An API for the rendering of 2D graphics (can use software or hardware acceleration depending on availability).
    - DirectDraw never supported the rendering of 3D graphics and have been deprecated since the release of DirectX 8. A number of crucial 2D DirectDraw rendering calls remains and are available via the Direct3D API.

- *DirectX Audio:*
  - *Cross-Platform Audio Creation (XACT)*
    - A high-level audio library and engine for the playback and recording of digital audio using the Xbox 360's compressed audio format (XAudio) and DirectSound on Windows.
    - Also features the XACT Audio Creation Tool that arranges audio files into so called wave banks (a single audio file made up of multiple audio files).
    - XACT also supports 5.1 surround sound configurations.
  - *DirectSound*
    - An API for the playback and recording of digital audio – allowing a single audio playback/recording implementation regardless of the audio hardware being used.
    - Following the architectural changes in Windows Vista, DirectSound no longer has direct communication with the underlying hardware, rather using an emulation layer – there is thus no longer any DirectSound hardware acceleration.
    - At the time of writing, this API is expected to be replaced by XAudio2, a cross-platform, low-level API that will be used in unison with Windows XP, Vista and the Xbox 360 console.

■ *DirectSound3D*
  — An extension of the DirectSound API to facilitate the playback of 3D audio (a sequence of sound effects expanding the listener's awareness from pure stereo to a spatial environment).
  — Integrated into the DirectSound API for the DirectX 10 SDK release.
■ *DirectMusic*
  — Not strictly speaking an API; DirectMusic can rather be considered a high-level set of objects utilizing the DirectSound API.
  — It provides high-level functions for the playback of sounds and music.
  — Provides support for the playback of MIDI, Wav, playback using the Microsoft Software Synthesizer when hardware synthesis is not available, the control of playback tempo and pitch, the simultaneous playback from several sounds sources and numerous other capabilities.
  — DirectMusic, although remaining unchanged, has now mostly been integrated into the DirectSound subsystem since the DirectX 10 SDK release.

■ *DirectX Input:*
  ■ *XInput*
    — An API allowing input control using an Xbox 360 Controller connected to a Microsoft Windows-based computer.
  ■ *DirectInput*
    — An API for input control via input devices such as the mouse, keyboard or game controllers.
    — This API was last updated with the release of DirectX 8.

■ *DirectX Networking:*
  ■ *DirectPlay (deprecated)*
    — This API facilitates easy network programming for connecting games and other kinds of applications over a dial-up connection, within a LAN environment as well as via the Internet.
    — In short DirectPlay only sends and receives packets – the network architecture remains the responsibility of the programmer.
    — DirectPlay was deprecated in 2004, the last release being part of the DirectX 8 SDK.

■ *DirectX Media (completely phased out)*
  ■ *DirectAnimation, DirectShow* and some DirectX plug-ins
    — An API dealing with multimedia functions such as 2D animation for websites (DirectAnimation), audio processing, video acceleration and the streaming of media (*DirectShow*).
    — DirectShow was integrated into Microsoft's Platform SDK with most of the other components completely deprecated and replaced by newer Microsoft technologies.

A useful utility coupled with each release of the DirectX runtime is the *DxDiag* (DirectX Diagnostic) application. This utility is useful when diagnosing problems related to DirectX functionality. It reveals details about the installed version of DirectX, system specifications, detailed versions of each installed DirectX file, a section to diagnose problems related to Direct3D, etc. DxDiag.exe is generally located in Window's 'System32' folder and can be accessed either directly from this location or via the run command (by simply typing dxdiag in the run command's text box). Figure 2-6 shows DxDiag running in Windows Vista.

2.4.1 A Very Simple Direct3D 10 Program

The following program illustrates the basic structure of a Direct3D program. As with the OpenGL version, this program creates a simple colored triangle. Identical to OpenGL, Direct3D creates geometric objects from primitives such as points, lines, and polygons. This program will create a red

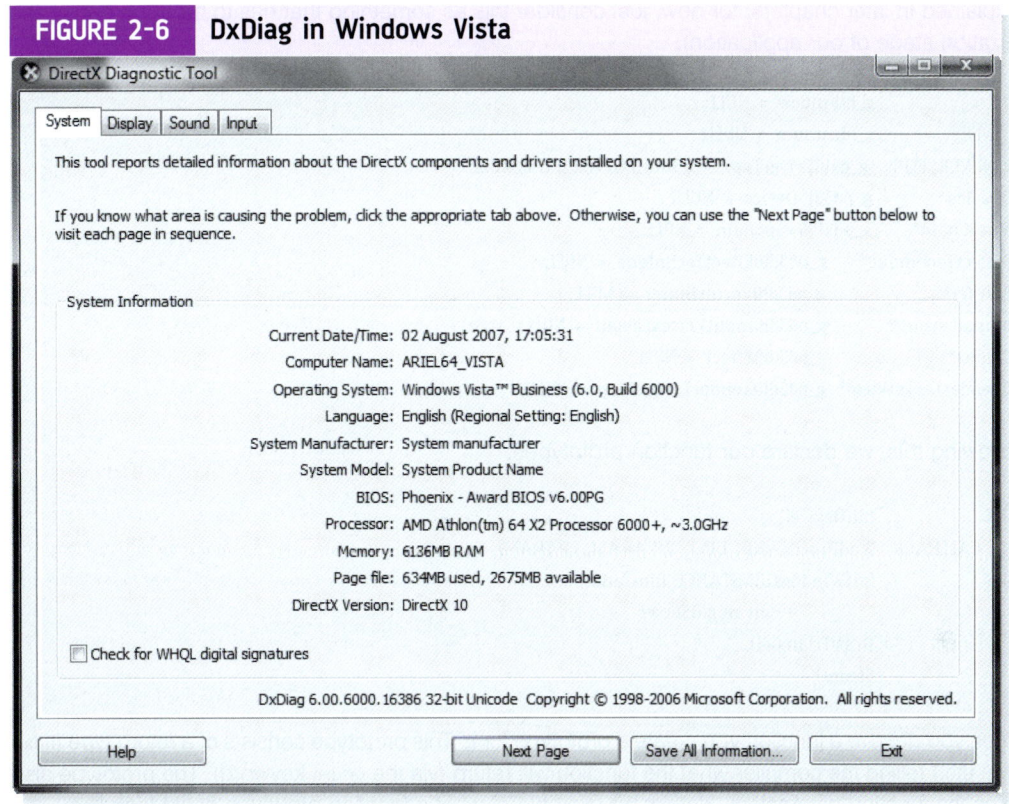

FIGURE 2-6 DxDiag in Windows Vista

triangle consisting of three vertices by connecting the vertices and forming a closed surface which is then filled with a single color.

Our program starts with the inclusion of the standard Windows and DirectX 10 headers:

```
#include <windows.h>
#include <d3d10.h>
#include <d3dx10.h>
```

The first step is to create a structure to store our triangle's vertex coordinates. The D3DXVECTOR3 type is a standard D3DX (a high-level library layered on top of Direct3D) structure holding an *x*-, *y*- and *z*-component of a three-dimensional vector:

```
struct TriangleVertex
{
    D3DXVECTOR3 Coordinate;
};
```

Next we have to initialize the instance handle, g_hInstance, the handle to the window, g_hWindow, the DirectX 10 device driver type (g_dx10DriverType) and the ID3D10Device interface, g_pd3d10Device, used for DrawPrimitive-based rendering. We also have to set the IDXGISwapChain, ID3D10RenderTargetView, ID3D10Effect, ID3D10EffectTechnique, ID3D10InputLayout and ID3D10Buffer interfaces (these interfaces, structures and handles

2

are explained in later chapters, for now, just consider this as something that has to be done during the initialization stage of our application):

```
HWND                    g_hWindow = NULL;
HINSTANCE               g_hInstance = NULL;
D3D10_DRIVER_TYPE   g_dx10DriverType = D3D10_DRIVER_TYPE_NULL;
ID3D10Device*           g_pd3d10Device = NULL;
IDXGISwapChain*         g_pdx10SwapChain = NULL;
ID3D10EffectTechnique*    g_pd3d10EffectTechnique = NULL;
ID3D10Buffer*             g_pd3d10VertexBuffer = NULL;
ID3D10InputLayout*        g_pd3d10InputVertexLayout = NULL;
ID3D10Effect*             g_pd3d10Effect = NULL;
ID3D10RenderTargetView* g_pd3d10RenderTargetView = NULL;
```

Following this, we declare our function prototypes:

```
HRESULT             InitDevice();
LRESULT CALLBACK  WndProc(HWND, UINT, WPARAM, LPARAM);
HRESULT             InitWindow(HINSTANCE hInstance,
                              int nCmdShow);
void                DrawTriangle();
void                Clean();
```

When you declare a function you create a prototype for it. This prototype consists of a return type (float, int, void, etc.) telling the compiler what the function will return (via the return keyword). The prototype also contains the function parameters. Here is an example of what a function prototype could look like:

```
int FunctionOne(string str);
```

This declaration communicates to the compiler what it is dealing with. The above statement starts with int. This return type indicates the return of an integer value. The second item in the declaration is FunctionOne – the function name. Notice we start this name with a capital; that is just a convention for function names. The function name is used whenever we call the function, either from within itself when using recursion, or from another function, be it the main function. The function name is followed by brackets '()'. Function parameters are contained within them. Function parameters specify the values passed to the function when it is called.

Back to our example, we initialize the message processing loop elements and the idle time required for the rendering of our triangle via winMain, the entry point of our application. This function starts with a call to the InitWindow and InitDevice functions (used to create the window as well as define and render the triangle). The WinMain function is set to listen for any event messages via the specification of the main event loop. This event loop consists of a while loop that executes as long as the value returned by PeekMessage is not equal to 0. The PeekMessage function simply fetches the next message from the event queue for processing. We also call the function responsible for the rendering of triangle (DrawTriangle) from within this main event loop. Chapter 4 deals with WinMain and event loop message processing, including functions such as PeekMessage, and TranslateMessage in detail:

```
int WINAPI wWinMain(HINSTANCE hInstance, HINSTANCE
                    hPrevInstance, LPWSTR lpCmdLine,
                    int nCmdShow)
```

2

```
{
    if((FAILED(InitDevice()))||(FAILED(InitWindow(hInstance,
            nCmdShow))))
    {
        Clean(); //do device cleanup – freeing resources
        return 0;
    }
    MSG msg = {0};
    while(WM_QUIT != msg.message)
    {
        if(PeekMessage(&msg, NULL, 0, 0, PM_REMOVE))
        {
            TranslateMessage(&msg);
            DispatchMessage(&msg);
        }
        else
        {
            DrawTriangle(); //render our triangle
        }
    }
    Clean();
    return (int)msg.wParam;
}
```

With the application's entry point declared we need to register the class and create the output window as detailed in Chapter 4. This is all done in the InitWindow function. We will not concern ourselves too much with the WNDCLASSEX structure at this time, simply taking note of that fact that, before we can even start thinking about initializing any of the DirectX components, we have to set up a window. We create the window using the AdjustWindowRect and CreateWindow functions. The ShowWindow function is called to make the window visible (see Chapter 4 for a full discussion):

```
HRESULT InitWindow(HINSTANCE hInstance, int nCmdShow)
{

    /* register the window class */
    ///////////////////////////////
    WNDCLASSEX wndcex;

    wndcex.cbSize           = sizeof(WNDCLASSEX);
    wndcex.style            = CS_HREDRAW | CS_VREDRAW;
    wndcex.lpfnWndProc      = WndProc;
    wndcex.cbClsExtra       = 0;
    wndcex.cbWndExtra       = 0;
    wndcex.hInstance        = hInstance;
    wndcex.hIcon            = LoadIcon(hInstance,
                                    (LPCTSTR) IDI_PROG1);
    wndcex.hCursor          = LoadCursor(NULL, IDC_ARROW);
    wndcex.hbrBackground    = (HBRUSH)(COLOR_WINDOW+1);
    wndcex.lpszMenuName     = NULL;
```

```
wndcex.lpszClassName    = L"StaticTriangle";
wndcex.hIconSm          = LoadIcon(wndcex.hInstance,
                                (LPCTSTR) IDI_PROG1);
if(!RegisterClassEx(&wndcex))
   return E_FAIL;
/* create the window */
/////////////////////////////
g_hInstance = hInstance;

RECT rectangle = {0, 0, 800, 600};
AdjustWindowRect(&rectangle, WS_OVERLAPPEDWINDOW, FALSE);

g_hWindow = CreateWindow(
              L"StaticTriangle",
              L"Rendering a triangle without any transformations",
              WS_OVERLAPPEDWINDOW,
              CW_USEDEFAULT, CW_USEDEFAULT,
              rectangle.right - rectangle.left,
              rectangle.bottom - rectangle.top,
              NULL, NULL, hInstance, NULL);
if(!g_hWindow)
   return E_FAIL;

ShowWindow(g_hWindow, nCmdShow);

return S_OK;
}
```

Next we create the Direct3D device and swap chain as presented in Chapter 4. The swap chain is used to display the contents of either the front or back buffer. We also set the client rectangle's width and height, the Direct3D 10 drivers to use, the render target view (in our case the surface being rendered to), the viewport (a window located inside a viewing volume), the shader effect specifying our triangle's color, and the triangle's vertices. The function closes with the setup of the vertex buffer (responsible for feeding the vertex data comprising our triangle to the pipeline) and binding of the primitive type and data order information to a triangle list. All these concepts and related function calls are dealt with in subsequent chapters:

```
HRESULT InitDevice()
{
   HRESULT hresult_ = S_OK;

   /* setup client rectangle width and height */
   /////////////////////////////////////////////
   RECT rectangle;
   GetClientRect(g_hWindow, &rectangle);

   int rectangle_width = rectangle.right - rectangle.left;
   int rectangle_height = rectangle.bottom - rectangle.top;
   int deviceFlags = 0;
```

```
/* specify D3D10 drivers to use */
//////////////////////////////
D3D10_DRIVER_TYPE d3d10drivers[] =
{
    D3D10_DRIVER_TYPE_HARDWARE,
    D3D10_DRIVER_TYPE_REFERENCE,
};

int numberDrivers =
            sizeof(d3d10drivers)/sizeof(d3d10drivers[0]);

/* create the swap chain */
////////////////////////
DXGI_SWAP_CHAIN_DESC swapchain;
SecureZeroMemory(&swapchain, sizeof(swapchain));

swapchain.BufferCount = 1;
swapchain.BufferDesc.Width = rectangle_width;
swapchain.BufferDesc.Height = rectangle_height;
swapchain.BufferDesc.Format = DXGI_FORMAT_R8G8B8A8_UNORM;
swapchain.BufferDesc.RefreshRate.Numerator = 30;
swapchain.BufferDesc.RefreshRate.Denominator = 1;
swapchain.BufferUsage = DXGI_USAGE_RENDER_TARGET_OUTPUT;
swapchain.OutputWindow = g_hWindow;
swapchain.SampleDesc.Count = 1;
swapchain.SampleDesc.Quality = 0;
swapchain.Windowed = TRUE;

for(int d3d10DriverCount = 0; d3d10DriverCount <
    numberDrivers; d3d10DriverCount++)
{
    g_dxl0DriverType = d3d10drivers[d3d10DriverCount];
    hresult_ = D3D10CreateDeviceAndSwapChain(
            NULL, g_dxl0DriverType, NULL,
            deviceFlags, D3D10_SDK_VERSION,
            &swapchain, &g_pdxl0SwapChain,
            &g_pd3d10Device);

    if(SUCCEEDED(hresult_))
        break;
}

if(FAILED(hresult_))
    return hresult_;
/* specify the render target view */
//////////////////////////////////
ID3D10Texture2D *pBuffer;
hresult_ = g_pdxl0SwapChain->
            GetBuffer(NULL, __uuidof(ID3D10Texture2D),
                (LPVOID*) &pBuffer);
```

2

```
if(FAILED(hresult_))
    return hresult_;

hresult_ = g_pd3d10Device->
            CreateRenderTargetView(pBuffer, NULL,
                        &g_pd3d10RenderTargetView);

pBuffer->Release();

if(FAILED(hresult_))
    return hresult_;

g_pd3d10Device->OMSetRenderTargets(
                    1, &g_pd3d10RenderTargetView, NULL);

/* create the viewport */
//////////////////////////
D3D10_VIEWPORT viewport;
viewport.TopLeftX     = 0;
viewport.TopLeftY     = 0;
viewport.Width        = rectangle_width;
viewport.Height       = rectangle_height;
viewport.MinDepth     = 0.0f;
viewport.MaxDepth     = 1.0f;

g_pd3d10Device->RSSetViewports(1, &viewport);

/* load the effect file specifying our triangle's color*/
////////////////////////////////////////////////////////
hresult_ = D3DX10CreateEffectFromFile(
                    L"effect.fx", NULL, NULL,
                    D3D10_SHADER_ENABLE_STRICTNESS, 0,
                    g_pd3d10Device, NULL, NULL, &g_pd3d10Effect,
                    NULL);

/* if the effect file is missing */
///////////////////////////////////
if(FAILED(hresult_))
{
    return hresult_;
}

/* set the effect technique and input layout */
////////////////////////////////////////////////
g_pd3d10EffectTechnique = g_pd3d10Effect->
                    GetTechniqueByName("Triangle");

D3D10_INPUT_ELEMENT_DESC inputlayout[] =
{
```

2

```
        {"POSITION", 0, DXGI_FORMAT_R32G32B32_FLOAT, 0, 0,
            D3D10_INPUT_PER_VERTEX_DATA, 0},
};

int numberOfElements = sizeof(inputlayout) /
                          sizeof(inputlayout[0]);

D3D10_PASS_DESC PassDescription;
g_pd3d10EffectTechnique->
        GetPassByIndex(0)->GetDesc(&PassDescription);

hresult_ = g_pd3d10Device->CreateInputLayout(
                            inputlayout, numberOfElements,
                            PassDescription.pIAInputSignature,
                            PassDescription.IAInputSignatureSize,
                            &g_pd3d10InputVertexLayout);

if(FAILED(hresult_))
    return hresult_;

g_pd3d10Device->IASetInputLayout(
                g_pd3d10InputVertexLayout);

/* specify our triangle's vertices */
///////////////////////////////////////
TriangleVertex vertices[] =
{
    D3DXVECTOR3(0.0f, 1.0f, 1.0f),
    D3DXVECTOR3(1.0f, -1.0f, 1.0f),
    D3DXVECTOR3(-1.0f, -1.0f, 1.0f),
};

/* setup the buffer resource */
///////////////////////////////////////
D3D10_BUFFER_DESC bufferdesc;
bufferdesc.Usage          = D3D10_USAGE_DEFAULT;
bufferdesc.BindFlags      = D3D10_BIND_VERTEX_BUFFER;
bufferdesc.CPUAccessFlags = 0;
bufferdesc.MiscFlags      = 0;
bufferdesc.ByteWidth      = sizeof(TriangleVertex)*3;

/* initialize resource */
////////////////////////////////
D3D10_SUBRESOURCE_DATA ResourceData;
ResourceData.pSysMem = vertices;

hresult_ = g_pd3d10Device->CreateBuffer(
                            &bufferdesc, &ResourceData,
                            &g_pd3d10VertexBuffer);
```

```
if(FAILED(hresult_))
    return hresult_;

/* setup the vertex buffer */
///////////////////////////
int elementstride = sizeof(TriangleVertex);

int bufferoffset = 0;
g_pd3d10Device->IASetVertexBuffers(
                0, 1, &g_pd3d10VertexBuffer,
                &elementstride, &bufferoffset);

/* bind the primitive type and data order information to a
   triangle list */
g_pd3d10Device->IASetPrimitiveTopology(
                D3D10_PRIMITIVE_TOPOLOGY_TRIANGLELIST);

return S_OK;
}
```

This sample utilizes DirectX's effect system (shaders). It thus uses a pixel shader to return the color of the triangle. Pixel shaders perform per-pixel processing; operating on the discrete pixels of a primitive, applying some effect to a primitive (such as bump mapping, shadowing, and fog). We use such a shader to color the pixels of our triangle. The physical file, effect.fx, is loaded in the above defined function via the D3DX10CreateEffectFromFile D3DX function. This file contains the following shader model 4 pixel shader and its related technique, Triangle (Chapter 6 discusses HLSL and Cg shaders in detail):

```
float4 PixelShader(float4 Pos : SV_POSITION) : SV_Target
{
    /* set the pixel color to red */
    return float4(1.0f, 0.0f, 0.0f, 1.0f);
}


technique10 Triangle
{
    pass P0
    {
        SetGeometryShader(NULL);
        SetPixelShader(CompileShader(ps_4_0, PixelShader()));
    }
}
```

Following the InitDevice function declaration, we setup our WndProc callback. This callback function is called whenever an event occurs. The number of events that can be handled by this callback function depends on the implementation. All the events not handled are simply passed on to Windows. This WndProc function receives messages from the main event loop whenever an event occurs. These events are either generated by the user or Windows and are read into the main event queue. The callback function given here handles events where a message is generated when a window needs to be redrawn

(WM.PAINT) or when the window is about to be destroyed (WM_DESTROY). It calls the DefWindowProc function for all other event messages sent to it. This DefWindowProc function simply sends all other unprocessed messages to the default window procedure for default processing (discussed in Chapter 4):

```
LRESULT CALLBACK WndProc(HWND hWindow, UINT msg, WPARAM
                          wParam, LPARAM lParam)
{
    HDC devicecontext;
    PAINTSTRUCT paintstructure;

    switch(msg)
    {
        case WM_DESTROY:
            PostQuitMessage(0);
            break;

        case WM PAINT:
            devicecontext = BeginPaint (hWindow,
                                         &paintstructure);
            EndPaint(hWindow, &paintstructure);
            break;

        default:
            return DefWindowProc(hWindow, message, wParam,
                                  lParam);
    }
    return 0;
}
```

Our second last function, Clean, checks whether an object has been created, and if it has, it deallocates it – freeing the resources for use by other applications. This function is called from the wWinMain function just before complete program termination. The ClearState function resets the device to its original settings with the Release function decrementing the COM reference count when an object is destroyed (as discussed in Chapter 3):

```
void Clean()
{
    if(g_pd3d10Device)
        g_pd3d10Device->ClearState();

    if(g_pd3d10InputVertexLayout)
        g_pd3d10InputVertexLayout->Release();

    if(g_pd3d10VertexBuffer)
        g_pd3d10VertexBuffer->Release();

    if(g_pd3d10RenderTargetView)
        g_pd3d10RenderTargetView->Release();
```

```
if(g_pd3d10Effect)
    g_pd3d10Effect->Release();

if(g_pd3d10Device)
    g_pd3d10Device->Release();

if(g_pdx10SwapChain)
    g_pdx10SwapChain->Release();
}
```

The DrawTriangle function is responsible for the actual triangle rendering. We start by clearing the backbuffer using the ClearRenderTargetView method. Next we invoke the GetDesc ID3D10EffectTechnique function on the previously defined technique object that will store the returned D3D10_TECHNIQUE_DESC structure describing the technique. We draw the triangle by looping over this number of passes, with the GetPassByIndex method being called for each pass, returning the pass object. This pass object is then applied by the effect system binding all related render states and shaders to the graphics pipeline using

the Apply ID3D10EffectPass method. This is followed by a call to the Draw ID3D10Device function. This function instructs the GPU to render the contents defined in the vertex buffer based on the specified vertex layout and primitive type. The Draw function's first parameter is the number of vertices to render, with the second parameter indicating the first vertex in this set – this effect technique sets the pixel color of the rendered triangle. Finally, the IDXGISwapChain Present function is called to display this processed triangle (shown in Figure 2-7):

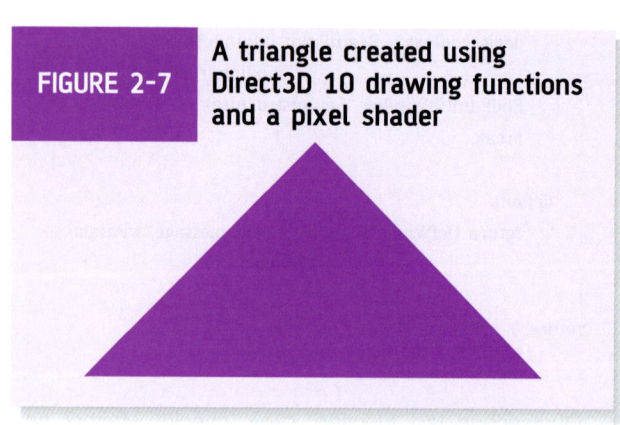

FIGURE 2-7   A triangle created using Direct3D 10 drawing functions and a pixel shader

```
void DrawTriangle()
{
    /* start by clearing the back-buffer with the color white
    */
    float ClearBufferColour[4] = {1.0f, 1.0f, 1.0f, 1.0f};
    g_pd3d10Device->ClearRenderTargetView(
                        g_pd3d10RenderTargetView,
                        ClearBufferColour);

    /* obtain the D3D10_TECHNIQUE_DESC effect-variable
       description */
    D3D10_TECHNIQUE_DESC technique;
    g_pd3d10EffectTechnique->GetDesc(&technique);

    /* render by looping over the number of technique passes */
    for(int i = 0; i < technique.Passes; ++i)
    {
        g_pd3d10EffectTechnique->GetPassByIndex(i)->Apply(0);
        g_pd3d10Device->Draw(3, 0);
    }
```

```
/* switch the back- and front-buffer and display the
    triangle */
g_pdxl0SwapChain->Present(0,0);
}
```

As can be seen from this example, Direct3D is quite a bit more involved than OpenGL, however, a lot of the code in this program sample deals with event processing and window creation and control elements intuitively handled by GLUT. Our OpenGL programs thus seem much simpler than their native Windows Direct3D 10 counterparts; however, this is only due to the GLUT library hiding system-specific windowing API calls from the programmer. Also, this program gives a feel for many of the concepts that will be discussed in subsequent chapters, which, even though because we have not discussed them at this point, the program sections of the code remain unclear, results in questions which will lead to a sense of familiarity when these concepts are discussed in upcoming chapters.

2.5 SUMMARY

In this chapter, we have set the stage for the development of computer games; outlining the main technologies, specifically DirectX, GLUT, and OpenGL, vital to the development of modern games and graphical applications. The chapter started by looking at application programming interfaces in general, subsequently presenting an API as a unified interface featuring a number of classes/structures, constants and functions. Building on this, we defined the functions provided by APIs into a number of categories.

Next we introduced the OpenGL graphics, API specification, specifically looking at the reasons responsible for its widespread adaptation and its main goals from a design standpoint. We then considered OpenGL as an interface consisting of over 120 functions, a number of constants and a series of predefined types. This section concluded with a very basic example illustrating the basic structure of an OpenGL program.

Following this we looked at the OpenGL Utility Toolkit, or GLUT, as an add-on to OpenGL for window creation and control. We also described the main GLUT functions arranged into a number of API categories followed by a simple GLUT program illustrating event-driven menu interaction via the mouse.

The remainder of the chapter focused on the DirectX foundation classes, providing an introduction to the DirectX APIs concerned with graphics, audio, input, networking, and media. The chapter closed with a program example illustrating the basic structure of a Direct3D application. As with the OpenGL version, this program created a simple colored triangle.

The next chapter provides a detailed look at Microsoft's Component Object Model, including how DirectX and COM fit together – ensuring a thorough understanding of the technology DirectX is built on.

2.6 FURTHER READING

There are plenty of books dealing with the Microsoft Windows API, with the official Microsoft documentation being available from Microsoft's msdn2.microsoft.com website. *Win32 Programming by Brent E. Rector and Joseph M. Newcomer* (ISBN: 0201634929) is also an excellent resource for Win32 C programming. *The X Window System: Programming and Applications with XT, OSF/Motif by Douglas A. Young* (ISBN: 0131238035) is a great book that deals with the development of X Window System applications.

The OpenGL Programming Guide: The Official Guide to Learning OpenGL (6th edition) by the OpenGL Architecture Review Board, Dave Shreiner, Mason Woo, Jackie Neider and Tom Davis, (ISBN: 0321481003), the *OpenGL Reference Manual: The Official Reference Document to OpenGL, Version 1.4 by the OpenGL Architecture Review*

Board and Dave Shreiner (ISBN: 032117383X), and *The OpenGL Graphics System: A Specification by Mark Segal* are all excellent resources for OpenGL with previous editions freely available from the OpenGL website ⟨www.opengl. org⟩. The OpenGL Reference Pages ⟨http://www.opengl.org/sdk/docs/man/⟩ are also very useful. The official GLUT documentation is also available from the OpenGL website ⟨http://www.opengl.org/documentation/specs/glut/⟩.

Documentation for the DirectX application programming interface is provided with each SDK distribution and available from Microsoft's msdn2.microsoft.com website.

2.7 EXERCISES

1 What is the primary purpose of application programming interfaces?

2 How would one go about creating complex models or three-dimensional objects using OpenGL's low-level functions?

3 What is the relationship between OpenGL and the graphics pipeline?

4 Extend the following code snippet to draw a rectangle instead of a triangle:

```
glBegin(GL_POLYGON);
    glVertex3f(0.0, 1.0, 1.0);
    glVertex3f(1.0, -1.0, 1.0);
    glVertex3f(-1.0, -1.0, 1.0);
glEnd();
```

5 For OpenGL programs, is it always necessary to call the glFlush function? (Tip: think about the real-time nature of games.)

6 What is the purpose of the OpenGL Utility Toolkit?

7 Describe the use of Callback creation and registration functions.

8 Why are GLUT state retrieval functions needed?

9 Modify section 2.3.1's GLUT program to use the left mouse button, instead of the right mouse button, for menu selection.

10 Why does GLUT have an event processing loop? Also discuss the problems and workarounds related to this event loop.

11 Describe the differences between DirectX, Direct3D and OpenGL.

12 How did the architectural changes in Windows Vista affect the DirectX API?

13 Consider the following code sample:

```
TriangleVertex vertices[] =
{
    D3DXVECTOR3(0.0f, 1.0f, 1.0f),
    D3DXVECTOR3(1.0f, -1.0f, 1.0f),
    D3DXVECTOR3(-1.0f, -1.0f, 1.0f),
};
```

Now, modify this vertex array to represent a three-dimensional pyramid.

CHAPTER 3

The Component Object Model and DirectX

LEARNING OBJECTIVES

In this chapter you will learn about:

- The Component Object Model
- COM objects and interfaces
- GUIDs and IIDs
- Writing a comprehensive COM program
- DirectX and the Component Object Model
- DirectX's HRESULT value
- DirectX interface creation and queries

INTRODUCTION

Chapter 3 provides a detailed look at Microsoft's Component Object Model (COM), specifically focusing on the fundamental elementals constituting this technology. Following this, the focus shifts to highlight the relationship between DirectX and COM. The chapter also features a working COM implementation.

3.1   THE COMPONENT OBJECT MODEL

The *Component Object Model* (COM) is an object-oriented programming model used for inter-object-process interaction. Looking at COM from a higher level reveals it as a software paradigm revolving around the idea that different software components should be pluggable and interchangeable. COM is thus based on the idea of *software componentry*, that is, the idea that software components should be defined in an interchangeable manner. Microsoft developed the Component Object Model as a platform for software componentry in 1993. It was based on their *Dynamic Data Exchange* (DDE) technology which allowed for interapplication communication. This technology formed the base of *Object Linking and Embedding* (OLE) which allowed custom user interface elements and the embedding of one type of document within another (for example, a spreadsheet embedded in a word document). OLE was one of the primary technologies showcased with the release of Windows 3.0. OLE was, however, quickly replaced by an updated version, namely OLE2, with the release of Windows 3.1. The reason for this was the introduction of the Component Object Model – OLE2 offered an extended level of object embedding and linking by being re-implemented on top of the Component Object Model. New features included drag-and-drop, structured storage, and automation. OLE2 also focused more on the integration of software components, as opposed to its predecessor mainly focusing on embedded documents.

COM was developed so that objects could be created in a language neutral fashion. Language neutral objects have the benefit that they can be deployed in a vast array of environments. COM also permits the reuse of objects without any concern for the specific implementation of these objects. Components thus require properly defined, stand-alone interfaces that can be accessed independently from their implementations.

COM objects are language neutral due to the objects themselves being in charge of their own creation and destruction. COM features a function, `QueryInterface`, which is responsible for casting between the different interfaces of an object – thus giving the client access to specified interfaces. This function is part of the basic interface all other interfaces are derived from – `IUnknown`. For now, just know that the `QueryInterface` function is the key to the Component Object Model and that it allows an interface user access to another interface. COM also allows inheritance within itself by assigning method calls to so-called subobjects.

Another interesting feature of COM objects is that new features can be added to a COM object without the functionality of the old object being impaired in the process. Furthermore, COM objects can be replaced without the need to recompile the application program. For example, say we have an application making use of four COM objects: one for implementing a renderer in OpenGL, one for network support, one for 3D audio, and another to handle input control. Now, say we want to change the renderer to a Direct3D version, then we can simply replace the OpenGL COM object with this version and the application will use it automatically without ever knowing the difference. COM objects are normally contained as Dynamic-link Libraries (DLLs). DLLs are based on Microsoft's shared library concept and can contain source code, data and resources. These libraries are generally loaded at run-time, a process referred to as *run-time dynamic linking* – thus allowing us to replace DLLs without recompiling the main executable. Not all DLLs are COM objects though; the Component Object Model rather extends DLLs to object-orientated programming. The original DLL concept was introduced by Microsoft for the preservation of disk space and memory – i.e. code shared by multiple applications can be separated into a DLL stored at some generic location, such as in the 'system' folder under Windows. This DLL is then loaded once into system memory, thus not only resulting in smaller executables, but also better memory management.

COM was, before the advent of .NET, a major Microsoft software development platform and as a consequence a number of technologies were built on it. One such technology is the DirectX Application

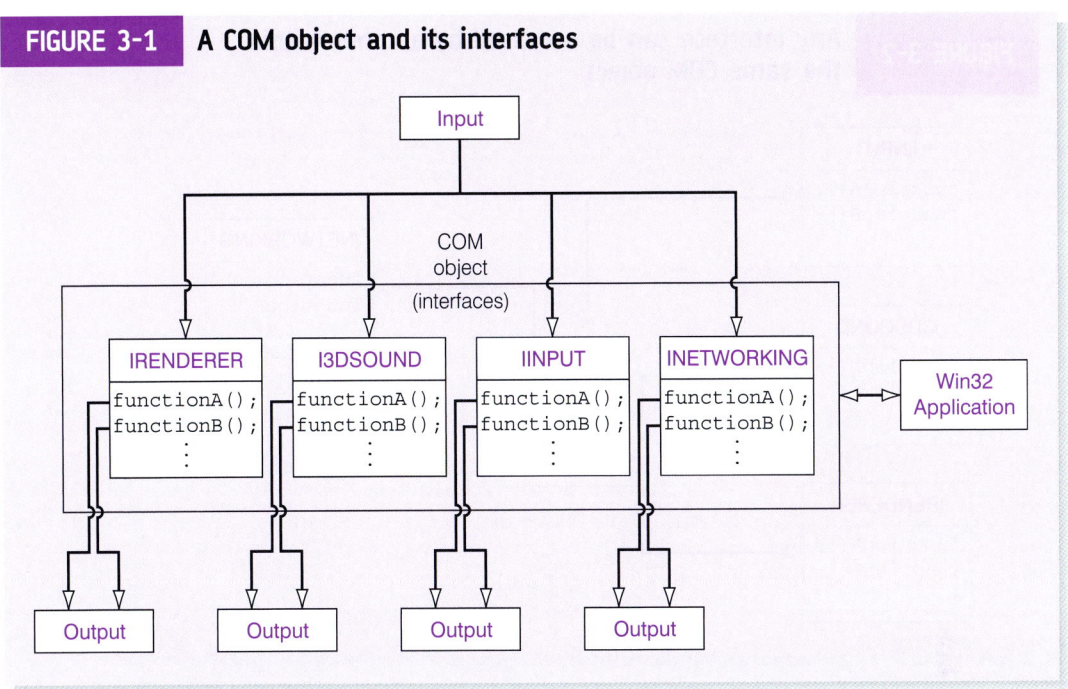

FIGURE 3-1   A COM object and its interfaces

Programming Interface. More specifically, all the DirectX components are built on top of the Component Object Model. The DirectX runtime is thus in the form of COM objects – requiring some understanding of COM's underlying principles and usage conventions.

Please note, this chapter assumes familiarity with the C++ programming language – especially the concept of interfaces, multiple inheritance and instancing. So, please refer to the C++ documentation available on the book's website if any of the code snippets or examples are unclear.

3.1.1 The COM Object and Interfaces

A *COM object* can be described as either one or more C++ classes implementing a series of interfaces. Each interface is basically a collection of functions, and interfaces are used to communicate with COM objects. COM interfaces can be linked to programs written in a number of languages such as C, C++ and Visual Basic. COM-utilizing components can be accessed via the functions contained in these interfaces – thus facilitating inter-process communication. Figure 3-1 shows a COM object with four interfaces named IRENDERER, I3DSOUND, IINPUT and INETWORKING.

As can be seen from the figure, a COM object can contain any number of interfaces, with each interface defining a number of functions. There is also no limit on the number of COM objects that can be used by an application. All COM components are required to implement the standard IUnknown interface (every COM interface is thus derived from IUnknown). The IUnknown interface can thus be described as the foundation of any interface being created.

The IUnknown interface defines three functions: QueryInterface, Release and AddRef. The QueryInterface function allows the retrieval of references to the various interfaces implemented by a COM component. This function, returning a pointer to the specified interface, takes two parameters, namely the queried interface's identifier (a 128-bit long unique number) and the address of a pointer to the variable used for storing the returned pointer. The AddRef function increments the reference count whenever a COM object

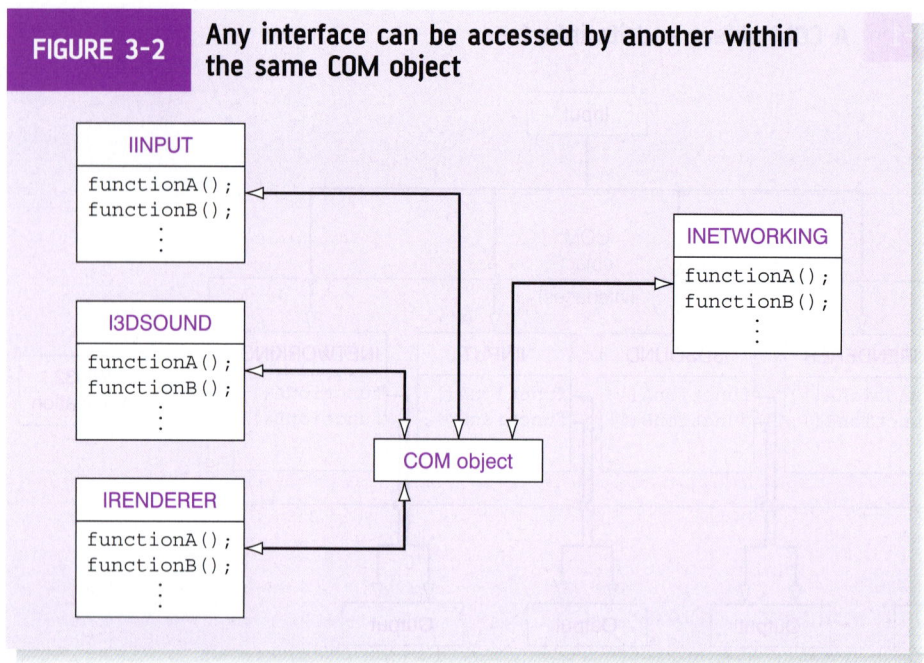

FIGURE 3-2   Any interface can be accessed by another within the same COM object

is created. *Reference counting* is a technique used by COM objects to keep track of an object's life (due to COM objects being responsible for their own creation and destruction). Thus, the AddRef function is called the moment a COM object is created. This function is also called when interfaces are created – in this case keeping count of the number of references to objects. The third function, Release, decrements the reference count when an object is destroyed. All interfaces derived from the IUnknown interface must implement these three virtual functions.

COM interfaces are reflective, transitive and symmetric. Being *symmetric* means that when we use, say, an interface X to retrieve an interface Y (using the QueryInterface function), then interface X should also be retrievable from interface Y. Also, the QueryInterface function can be called for any interface using the interface's unique identifier – resulting in the same instance of the interface. This is the reflective property. The final property that must be exhibited by COM interfaces is the *transitive* property. This property is closely related to the symmetric property. For example, say we can retrieve interface X from interface Y, and that interface Z can also be retrieved from interface X, then we can also retrieve interface Z from interface Y. Figure 3-2 shows this transitive property of COM interfaces.

A COM class is called a *co-class*. Co-classes allow the language-independent definition of COM-based object-orientated classes. These classes are nothing more than the implementation of COM interfaces. Since co-classes are language-independent, we can define them using any programming language supporting the COM framework (C/C++/Visual Basic/etc).

3.1.2 GUIDs and IIDs

As mentioned earlier, each COM component can be accessed using one or more interfaces. Each interface associated with a component is uniquely identified via interface IDs (IIDs). These identifiers, called *Globally Unique Identifiers* (*GUIDs*), are unique 128-bit values used by the QueryInterface function to access the interface of a COM object. Globally Unique Identifiers are called *Interface IDs* when defining COM interfaces. COM objects and interfaces are assigned their own GUIDs for identification at runtime. COM classes, types and interfaces are listed in the Windows registry (a database storing settings and properties of the Microsoft Windows operation system and its applications). The GUIDs for COM classes are stored under the `HKEY_CLASSES_ROOT\CLSID` hive key (the registry is divided into a number of sections called *hives*). COM interfaces are stored under the `HKEY_CLASSES_ROOT\interface` key. The Component Object Model makes use of the registry to locate local libraries for each of the COM objects.

Globally Unique Identifiers can be generated using Microsoft's 'guidgen.exe' application (there are also websites that can be used for this purpose).

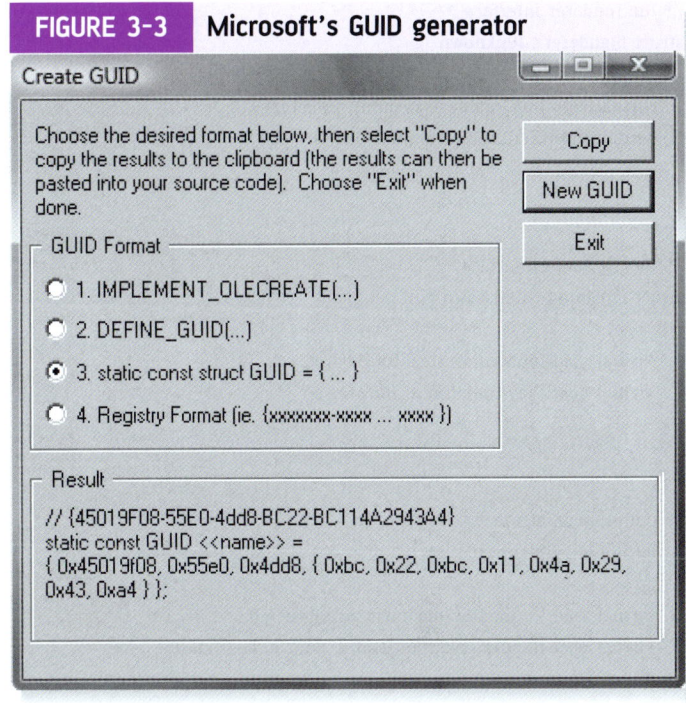

FIGURE 3-3   Microsoft's GUID generator

Create GUID

Choose the desired format below, then select "Copy" to copy the results to the clipboard (the results can then be pasted into your source code). Choose "Exit" when done.

Copy

New GUID

Exit

GUID Format

○ 1. IMPLEMENT_OLECREATE(...)

○ 2. DEFINE_GUID(...)

◉ 3. static const struct GUID = { ... }

○ 4. Registry Format (ie. {xxxxxxxx-xxxx ... xxxx })

Result

```
// {45019F08-55E0-4dd8-BC22-BC114A2943A4}
static const GUID <<name>> =
{ 0x45019f08, 0x55e0, 0x4dd8, { 0xbc, 0x22, 0xbc, 0x11, 0x4a, 0x29,
0x43, 0xa4 } };
```

This application, shown in Figure 3-3, allows us to select the type of ID we want to generate.

The generated IID can be used in our application program to reference COM objects and their interfaces. The ≪name≫ tag in the generated result is replaced by the name chosen for the GUID in our application. The IID for the GUID, `OurVeryOwnGUID`, can be specified as follows:

```
// {45019F08-55E0-4dd8-BC22-BC114A2943A4}
static const OurVeryOwnGUID =
{ 0x45019f08, 0x55e0, 0x4dd8,
{ 0xbc, 0x22, 0xbc, 0x11, 0x4a, 0x29, 0x43, 0xa4 } };
```

We provide other programmers with these generated GUIDs so that they can work with our defined COM objects. New interface IDs must thus be generated whenever a new COM object and its related interfaces are created. Similarly, when using previously specified COM objects and interfaces we only need the IIDs to create them.

3.1.3 Defining a COM Object

The goal for Chapter 3 is to get some idea of what the Component Object Model is all about. We will rarely be required to create a COM object from scratch, rather only using existing ones. However, the discussion so far only really scratched the surface of what COM is all about. The following basic COM example deals with COM objects, their relationship with interfaces as well as the implementation of these interfaces.

The COM object depicted in Figure 3-1 and 3-2 has four interfaces: IRenderer, I3DSound, IInput, and INetworking. We can implement these interfaces in the following manner (notice how each interface is derived from the IUnknown class):

3

```
/* the renderer interface */
struct IRenderer : IUnknown
{
    virtual void InitGraphicsSystem(int renderer) = 0;
    virtual inter SetDisplaySize(int x, int y) = 0;
    ...
}

/* the 3D audio interface */
struct I3DSound : IUnknown
{
    virtual void InitSoundSystem(int device) = 0;
    virtual bool PlayAudio(int x, int y) = 0;
    ...
}

/* the input interface */
struct IInput : IUnknown
{
    virtual void InitInputSystem(int controller) = 0;
    virtual bool HandleStickInput(float x, float y, float z)= 0;
    ...
}

/* the network interface */
struct INetworking : IUnknown
{
    virtual void InitNetworkingSystem(int nic) = 0;
    virtual bool Ping(int ip)= 0;
    ...
}
```

With the interfaces declared, we move on to create the COM class. This class provides an implementation for each of the IUnknown interface functions as well as the above declared COM interfaces (note the public inheritance of IRenderer, I3DSound, IInput and INetworking):

```
class GameEngine: public IRenderer,I3DSound,IInput,INetworking
{
private:
    /* declare all the private types */

public:

    /* implement IUnknown's QueryInterface function */
    virtual HRESULT __stdcall QueryInterface(const IID& iid,
                                            (void **) storage)
    {
        /* the actual implementation — must be reflective,
           transitive and symmetric */
    }
```

```
/* implement IUnknown's Addref function */
virtual ULONG __stdcall Addref()
{
        /* the actual implementation − increase the interface
           reference count for each call */
}

/* implement IUnknown's Release function */
virtual ULONG __stdcall Release()
{
        /* the actual implementation − decrease the interface
           reference count for each call */
}

/* implement IRenderer's virtual functions */
virtual void InitGraphicsSystem(int renderer)
{
        /* implementation */
}
virtual inter SetDisplaySize(int x, int y)
{
        /* implementation */
}

/* implement I3DSound's virtual functions */
virtual void InitSoundSystem(int device)
{
        /* implementation */
}
virtual bool PlayAudio(int x, int y)
{
        /* implementation */
}

/* implement IInput's virtual functions */
virtual void InitInputSystem(int controller)
{
        /* implementation */
}
virtual bool HandleStickInput(float x, float y, float z)
{
        /* implementation */
}

/* implement INetworking's virtual functions */
virtual void InitNetworkingSystem(int nic)
{
        /* implementation */
}
```

```
virtual bool Ping(int ip)
{
     /* implementation */
}
};
```

As can be seen from the above example, COM development has the creation of virtual interfaces and their subsequent implementation at its core. As mentioned, COM objects are registered in the Windows registry upon creation. A generic way to create COM objects is thus still required. The simplest way of doing this is to define a `CoCreateInstance` or `ComCreate` function. These functions can then be used to create the `IUnknown` interface of the COM object by accessing a DLL containing the COM implementation.

The following section looks at the creation of a COM object and a number of interfaces in detail. The given program basically implements a COM object along with three interfaces: `IFunctionOne`, `IFunctionTwo`, and `IFunctionThree`. It also implements the `IUnknown` interface functions – `QueryInterface`, `Release`, and `AddRef`.

3.1.4 A Comprehensive COM Program

We start by including the objbase.h header file. This header declares a number of COM functions and constants required by even the most minimal COM implementations:

```
#include <objbase.h>
```

The next step is to use a GUID generator to generate GUIDs for each of the interfaces making up the COM object. We generate three GUIDs for each of the interfaces (`IFunctionOne`, `IFunctionTwo`, and `IFunctionThree`) using a generator like the one shown in Figure 3-3. These GUIDs are declared as global constants:

```
// {C2F7148C-6EA5-41b4-9FB6-B4BBA4C0488F}
const GUID GUID_IFunctionOne =
{ 0xc2f7148c, 0x6ea5, 0x41b4,
{ 0x9f, 0xb6, 0xb4, 0xbb, 0xa4, 0xc0, 0x48, 0x8f } };

// {D7974908-331E-4f7c-BAB8-6711A9D1C0CC}
const GUID GUID_IFunctionTwo =
{ 0xd7974908, 0x331e, 0x4f7c,
{ 0xba, 0xb8, 0x67, 0x11, 0xa9, 0xd1, 0xc0, 0xcc } };

// {83926E15-FDF5-4fd0-B26D-A9F6E428B7A8}
const GUID GUID_IFunctionThree =
{ 0x83926e15, 0xfdf5, 0x4fd0,
{ 0xb2, 0x6d, 0xa9, 0xf6, 0xe4, 0x28, 0xb7, 0xa8 } };
```

We can now define the interfaces with each interface containing only one virtual function:

```
/* the IFunctionOne interface */
interface IFunctionOne: IUnknown
```

```
{
    virtual void __stdcall functionOne(void) = 0;
}

/* the IFunctionTwo interface */
interface IFunctionTwo: IUnknown
{
    virtual void __stdcall functionTwo(void) = 0;
}

/* the IFunctionThree interface */
interface IFunctionThree: IUnknown
{
    virtual void __stdcall functionThree(void) = 0;
}
```

With the interfaces declared, we can create the COM object class. This class provides an implementation for each of the IUnknown interface functions as well as the above defined COM interfaces. Each of the COM interfaces are implemented to return a message after successfully being called. The class starts by declaring a constructor and a destructor. A *constructor* is similar to any member function, in fact, it is nothing else than a member function with the same name as the class. The only difference between a normal member function and a constructor is that a constructor is invoked every time an object of the class is created. Also, a constructor isn't assigned a return type and there is no restriction on the functionality of a constructor. A program may also have more than one constructor. Once we deallocate the class object, the object's destructor is called. A *destructor* is a constructor's exact opposite and it is called each time an object is deallocated. We denote a member function as a destructor by preceding the function name with a tilde '~'.

```
class COMObject: public IFunctionOne, IFunctionTwo,
                        IFunctionThree
{
public:
    /* the COM object constructor */
    COMObject() : ref_count() {}

    /* the COM object destructor */
    ~COMObject() {}

private:

    /* declare IUnknown's functions */
    virtual HRESULT __stdcall QueryInterface(const IID &iid,
                                              (void **)storage);
    virtual ULONG __stdcall Addref();
    virtual ULONG __stdcall Release();

    /* the reference counter */
    int reference_counter;
};
```

3

We can now fully implement the three virtual IUnknown functions. The implementation given here is fairly generic and can typically be reused with slight modifications to the requested interfaces when creating other COM object programs. The first function, QueryInterface, retrieves a reference to some interface implemented by a COM component. This function returns a pointer to the specified interface by taking an interface identifier and the address of a pointer to the variable (storing the returned pointer) as parameters. QueryInterface mainly casts the IUnknown pointer to the interface requested and it can be implemented in the following manner:

```
HRESULT _stdcall COMObject::QueryInterface(const IID &iid,
                                            (void **)storage)
{
    /* start by calling the IUnknown base interface with
        IDD_IUnknown, the ID of the IUnknown interface */
    if(iid == IID_IUnknown)
    {
        /* cast the 'this' pointer to the IUnknown interface
            requested */
        *storage = (IUnknown*)this;
    }

    /* the IFunctionOne interface has been requested */
    if(iid == GUID_IFunctionOne)
    {
        /* cast the 'this' pointer to the IFunctionOne
            interface requested */
        *storage = (IFunctionOne*)this;
    }

    /* the IFunctionTwo interface has been requested */
    else if(iid == GUID_IFunctionTwo)
    {
        /* cast the 'this' pointer to the IFunctionTwo
            interface requested */
        *storage = (IFunctionTwo*)this;
    }

    /* the IFunctionThree interface has been requested */
    else if(iid == GUID_IFunctionThree)
    {
        /* cast the 'this' pointer to the IFunctionThree
            interface requested */
        *storage = (IFunctionThree*)this;
    }

    /* the requested interface could not be found */
    else
    {
        *storage = NULL;
```

```
    /* QueryInterface should return the error
       E_NOINTERFACE if it fails */
    return(E_NOINTERFACE);
    }


    /* cast the pointer to IUnknown, subsequently calling the
       AddRef function so that the reference count can be
       incremented */
    ((IUnknown*)(*storage))->AddRef();
    /* QueryInterface should return NOERROR if it succeeds */
    return(NOERROR);
}
```

The AddRef function simply increments the nominal reference count associated with each interface. Note that this function returns an unsigned long value. However, this value is not required and should not be depended on in any way – it is returned solely for debugging purposes:

```
ULONG _stdcall COMObject::AddRef()
{
    /* increment the reference count */
    reference_counter = reference_counter + 1;
    /* return this counter for debugging purposes */
    return(reference_counter);
}
```

The final IUnknown function, Release, also returns an unsigned long value for the sake of debugging. This function furthermore checks for a reference count set to zero – an illegal situation that arises when one additional call is made to Release than to AddRef (leading to an invalid interface pointer). The Release function, responsible for decrementing the reference count, can be implemented as follows:

```
ULONG _stdcall COMObject::Release()
{
    /* decrement the reference count */
    reference_counter = reference_counter - 1;

    /* check whether the counter isn't '0' */
    if(reference_counter == 0)
    {
        /* the interface pointer is now invalid, so destroy it */
        delete this;
        return 0;
    }

    else
        /* return this counter for debugging purposes */
        return(reference_counter);
}
```

We can now implement the CoCreateInstance function. This function will be used to create a COM object instance. The object instance can be created using a pointer to any of the following interfaces: IFunctionOne, IFunctionTwo, or IFunctionThree:

```
IUnknown *CoCreateInstance()
{
    /* create the COM object using a pointer to any of our
       interfaces − used IFunctionOne in this case*/
    IUnknown *comObj = (IFunctionOne *)new(COMObject);

    /* increment the reference count */
    comObj->AddRef();

    /* return the create COM object */
    return(comObj);
}
```

The above defined COMObject member functions can be called from other member functions or from an application's main or WinMain function. For example, in a main function, we start by creating the main COM object using the CoCreateInstance function as follows:

```
IUnknown *mainCOMObject = CoCreateInstance();
```

This COM object can now be used to query for interfaces and to call the other member functions, for example, we can query for the IFunctionThree interface via the following call to the QueryInterface function:

```
mainCOMObject->QueryInterface(GUID_IFunctionThree,
                              (void **)&pInterfaceThree);
```

Using the same COM object, we can also query for the IFunctionOne and IFunctionTwo interfaces in exactly the same way:

```
mainCOMObject->QueryInterface(GUID_IFunctionOne,
                              (void **)&pInterfaceOne);

mainCOMObject->QueryInterface(GUID_IFunctionTwo,
                              (void **)&pInterfaceOne);
```

A NULL pointer to the IFunctionThree interface, pInterfaceThree, has to be initialized for use in the QueryInterface call:

```
IFunctionThree *pInterfaceThree = NULL;
```

The same holds true for both the IFunctionOne and IFunctionTwo interfaces:

```
IFunctionOne *pInterfaceOne = NULL;
IFunctionTwo *pInterfaceTwo = NULL;
```

We can now release the interfaces (assuming they are no longer needed by our application). This is done via a call to the Release member function:

```
pInterfaceOne->Release();
pInterfaceTwo->Release();
pInterfaceThree->Release();
```

The COM object itself should also be released during the cleanup done at some stage prior to program termination:

```
mainCOMObject->Release();
```

3.2 DIRECTX AND THE COMPONENT OBJECT MODEL

Chapter 2 dealt with DirectX 10 on an introductory level. We will now build on this and the previous coverage of COM to see how this API and Component Object Model are connected. DirectX is, at its most basic level, comprised of a number of COM objects. These COM objects are the DirectX Dynamic Link Libraries loaded upon execution of a DirectX program. The application will query a number of interfaces, invoking their member functions to perform some task once the DLLs are loaded into memory.

One will seldom access COM objects directly when working with DirectX due to the majority of COM objects being wrapped as DirectX function calls. These functions have a 'black box' approach to COM, hiding the developer from the finer intricacies related to the COM implementation. Specifically, it is the DirectX libraries (containing the COM wrappers) that allow us to create COM objects using DirectX function calls, thus illuminating the need for calling the CoCreateInstance function, for example. The libraries which we will use most include d3dx10.lib for Direct3D 10, dinput8.lib and dinput.lib for DirectInput, dsound.lib for DirectSound, xinput.lib for XInput and x3daudio.lib for the X3DAudio API.

When we say that COM objects are 'wrapped', it does not mean that they are contained within the DirectX libraries. A *wrapper* is basically an interface between a caller and the hidden code, allowing a level of emulation, compatibility and to prevent the calling function from accessing a certain level of functionality (the reverse might also be true). The COM objects are contained within the DirectX DLLs, and the DirectX libraries only control the loading of these DLLs. Calling a DirectX COM object results in the generation of an interface pointer. This interface pointer can now be used for subsequent DirectX function calls.

A DirectX function call indirectly creates a COM object, returning the interface of the object. This is done by passing the address of an interface pointer to the DirectX function. For example, the code fragment below calls the CreateDepthStencilView ID3D10Device interface function to create a depth stencil view (see Chapter 11 for a discussion of stencils) – don't be concerned with the purpose of this function, just notice the last parameter receiving the address of the ID3D10DepthStencilView interface pointer.

When creating an interface (ID3D10Device and ID3D10DepthStencilView in this case), we start by declaring a pointer to the interface:

```
ID3D10Device* pID3D10Device;
ID3D10DepthStencilView* pDepthStencilView;

pID3D10Device->CreateDepthStencilView(
                    pDepthStencilBuffer
                    &depthstencilviewDescription,
                    &pDepthStencilView);
```

3.2.1 DirectX's HRESULT Values

Numerous DirectX functions return a 32-bit integer labeled HRESULT, an integer inherited from the Component Object Model (all COM functions return this value). HRESULT is in essence a structure storing information about an operation's execution. For example, HRESULT is mostly used to indicate whether a function failed or succeeded. Although this result handle is generally used to return error information, specifically a zero for a successful function return and a non-zero value in the event of an error, it also contains additional information related to the specific failure or success. For example, the following incomplete code fragment creates an interface to a Direct3D 10 hardware device and swap chain (see Chapter 4): following the D3D10CreateDeviceAndSwapChain function call, we can check the returned HRESULT value for any execution failures:

```
HRESULT hresult_ = D3D10CreateDeviceAndSwapChain(...);
```

If D3D10CreateDeviceAndSwapChain fails, exit with the returned HRESULT value:

```
if(FAILED(hresult_))
    return hresult_;
```

We can alternatively check for a specific success or failure code (instead of validating the returned HRESULT value against all possible error codes via the FAILED macro). For example, success codes are prefixed by an 's' character with an 'E' preceding failure codes. Two common codes are S_OK and E_FAIL, denoting success and failure, in that order. Using these error codes directly, as shown below, are generally dangerous due to the possibility of a COM function returning a different success or failure code. For example, say hresult_ contains the error E_NOTIMPL, indicating failure due to a non-implemented method, then the following check will be completely ineffective and the error will go unhandled:

```
if(hresult_ == E_FAIL)
{
    cout << "the function failed...";
    return 0;
}
```

3.2.2 DirectX Interface Creation and Queries

COM objects are, as discussed, collections of interfaces. These interfaces can in turn be described as function pointers. Thus, when creating a COM object, and receiving an interface pointer, we basically have a virtual function table, or *vtable*, pointer. A *virtual function table* is a mechanism used by object-orientated programming languages to facilitate run-time method/function binding. Run-time method binding, or *polymorphism*, is encountered when we have two or more functions with exactly the same name but different parameters. The word *polymorphism* comes from the Greek word for 'many shapes' and it is used quite frequently to describe an object that adapts itself to the nature of other objects.

Consider the following function prototypes, each with a different signature, signifying three overloaded functions:

```
int OverloadedFunc(int)
int OverloadedFunc(int, int)
int OverloadedFunc(int, long)
```

The OverloadedFunc method is overloaded three times, with its parameters determining the specific function that is to be called. The third OverloadedFunc will be called, for example, when we invoke OverloadedFunc with int and long as parameter types. Polymorphism thus implies the use of a general interface to manipulate a variety of specialized object types – a programming language concept supported by the virtual function table mechanism.

To understand virtual function tables, consider the following example. Say we have a C++ program with the following inheritance hierarchy: a super-class, Bot, and two subclasses, FieldSoldier and HelicopterPilot. Furthermore, say the Bot class has a virtual function labeled attack (without providing any implementation); then one of its subclasses can provide an implementation suited to their own usage requirements. For example, the FieldSoldier class can implement the attack function to fire an M16 machine gun or to throw a grenade. The HelicopterPilot class can in turn implement this pure virtual function to attack a target using the helicopter's rockets, for example. The run-time environment is tasked with determining the specific attack function to invoke when it is called via a pointer to the Bot class. This is called *dynamic dispatch* and a vtable is used to facilitate this.

The vtable contains the addresses of an object's dynamically bound functions. A function's address is fetched from the vtable when it is called. Vtables are shared between objects belonging to the same class. Objects belonging to a subclass are allocated vtables with identical layouts. Hence, when a function's address is fetched from one of these vtables, then the function corresponding to the object class is returned. The most common method for implementing vtables is to create one of each class, and then to add a virtual table pointer to the vtable for each base class. The compiler will commonly generate some initialization code hidden in the constructor of each class. This code is then used to set the vpointer of the class – the address of the related vtable. This vtable architecture is illustrated in Figure 3-4.

Every COM object has a virtual function table storing a list of pointers to the functions exposed by the object. A COM interface pointer points to one of the pointers stored in the vtable – a pointer to the function being called. Vtables are hidden from the programmer by the C++ programming language; however, an additional level of indirection referencing to the vtable is required when using the Component Object Model with the C programming language.

When working with COM we only need to create a COM object and retrieve its interface pointer. Using this interface pointer, we can make calls to its functions. Interfaces making up a COM object are represented using function pointers, in essence vtables, which allow us to make calls to a function.

FIGURE 3-4   Vtable architecture

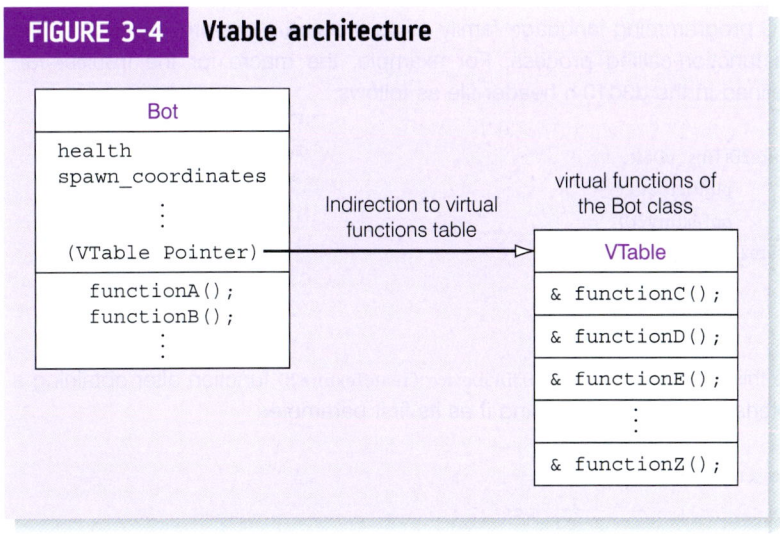

To use any Direct3D, DirectInput, DirectSound, or DirectX API interface, we must ensure that the DirectX run-time COM objects and DLLs are properly loaded and registered. The DirectX SDK installation is responsible for this setup. We must also include the appropriate libraries so that the called wrapper functions can be linked into the application. Finally, we need to ensure that the appropriate header files (d3d10.h, dsound.h, dinput.h, etc.) are included in the application program as required. This allows the application program access to required header information, data types, functions, structures, and prototypes.

Any DirectX call has the following form:

```
interfacePointer->DirectXFunctionName(parameters);
```

This can be illustrated by going back to section 3.2's CreateDepthStencilView function:

```
/* the interface pointer */
ID3D10Device* pID3D10Device;

/* calling the DirectX function */
pID3D10Device->CreateDepthStencilView(/*...parameters...*/);
```

We can also access other interfaces from a retrieved interface by using the QueryInterface COM function.

When a pointer to an interface is no longer needed, it should be released and set to 'NULL' (just to be safe). It is also good practice to verify that a pointer is no longer active before releasing it:

```
/* cleanup */
if(pID3D10Device != NULL)
{
    pID3D10Device->Release();
    pID3D10Device = NULL;
}
```

The methods of DirectX COM interfaces can be accessed using macros. A *macro* is a rule controlling the mapping of an input sequence to a specific output sequence based on some predefined pattern or rule. Macros are set in the C programming language family using the #define pre-processor directive. These macros simplify the function-calling process. For example, the macro for the ID3D10Device:: CreateTexture2D function is defined in the d3d10.h header file as follows:

```
#define ID3D10Device_CreateTexture2D(This, pDesc,
                            pInitialData,
                            ppTexture2D)
    ((This)->lpVtbl->CreateTexture2D(This, pDesc,
                            pInitialData,
                            ppTexture2D))
```

We can now directly use this macro to call the ID3D10Device::CreateTexture2D function after obtaining a pointer to the ID3D10Device interface (pID3D) and passing it as its first parameter:

```
HRESULT hresult_ = ID3D10Device_CreateTexture2D(
                pID3D,
                const D3D10_TEXTURE2D_DESC *pDesc,
```

```
                const D3D10_SUBRESOURCE_DATA *pInitialData,
                ID3D10Texture2D **ppTexture2D);
```

This `CreateTexture2D` function can also be called without use of its macro (the approach we will be taking throughout most of the book):

```
ID3D10Device* g_id3dDevice;

g_id3dDevice->CreateTexture2D (
                const D3D10_TEXTURE2D_DESC *pDesc,
                const D3D10_SUBRESOURCE_DATA *pInitialData,
                ID3D10Texture2D **ppTexture2D);
```

3.3   SUMMARY

This chapter covered the core Component Object Model technology which has had a profound influence on DirectX's overall design and subsequent implementation. The chapter started by considering the Component Object Model as an object-oriented programming model used for inter-object-process interaction, highlighting its purpose as a platform for software componentry.

Building on this, we described COM objects as either one or more classes implementing a series of interfaces, with each interface being a collection of functions. We subsequently discussed the standard `IUnknown` interface and its three functions (`QueryInterface`, `Release`, and `AddRef`), which all COM components are required to implement. Following this, we looked at the unique identification of interfaces associated with components via the use of GUIDs and IIDs, subsequently working through a COM example dealing with COM objects, their relationship with interfaces as well as the implementation of these interfaces.

The remainder of the chapter focused on the relationship between COM and the DirectX API, showing that COM objects are indirectly created by DirectX function calls (with each DirectX function call returning an interface of the created object).

At this point, we have dealt with most introductory material and concepts. The next chapter moves on to window creation and control, also providing a detailed look at the graphics pipeline architecture and the various stages of the rendering process.

3.4   FURTHER READING

There are several good books focusing on Microsoft's Component Object Model and its extension COM+. One such a book is *Essential COM by Don Box* (ISBN: 0201634465). *Inside Com by Dale Rogerson* (ISBN: 1572313498) and *Developer's Workshop to COM and ATL 3.0 by Andrew Troelsen* (ISBN: 1556227043) also deal with COM in detail. COM is officially documented in Microsoft's MSDN libraries complementing the Visual Studio IDE. This documentation can alternatively be accessed from Microsoft's msdn2.microsoft.com website.

3.5   EXERCISES

1   Explain the purpose of the COM `QueryInterface` function in detail.

2   What is the relationship between COM and the .NET framework?

3   Describe the basic implementation of a COM object by specifically referring to COM interfaces.

4   Discuss the purpose of each function defined by the IUnknown interface.

5   Why must COM interfaces be reflective, transitive, and symmetric?

6   What is the purpose of generated IIDs?

7   Create a generic COM interface, IRenderer, containing the virtual function void printStdOutput(void).

8   With the interfaces declared, what is the purpose of a COM object class?

9   Why is it necessary for both the AddRef and Release functions to return an unsigned long value?

10 Explain the purpose of the CoCreateInstance function.

11 Describe shortly how DirectX and COM fit together.

12 What happens when an application queries a number of interfaces?

13 Explain the concept of wrapping COM objects as DirectX libraries.

14 What is a vtable?

15 Using a retrieved interface, how can we access other interfaces?

16 Describe two methods for accessing DirectX COM interfaces.

CHAPTER 4

Window Creation and Control

LEARNING OBJECTIVES

In this chapter you will learn about:

- The graphics system
- Input devices
- Output devices
- The frame buffer
- The elements of a 3D environment
- The graphics pipeline architecture
- Vertex processing
- Clipping and culling
- Rasterization and fragment processing
- Programmable pipelines
- The Direct3D 10 processing pipeline
- The input-assembler stage
- The vertex-shader stage
- The geometry-shader stage
- The stream-output stage
- The pixel-shader stage
- The output-merger stage
- The OpenGL processing pipeline
- Evaluators and display lists
- The primitive assembly and rasterizer
- Pixel processing
- The fragment processor
- The OpenGL, GLUT, and DirectX programming interface
- Window creation and control
- Setting up a window and the main message loop
- Initializing Direct3D and generating output
- Setting up a window (GLUT), the main message loop and initializing OpenGL

INTRODUCTION

Chapter 4 focuses on window creation and control. The chapter starts off by presenting the concept of a graphics system, subsequently investigating the five elements making up such a system. Following this, the image formation process is considered in terms of the elements constituting a 3D environment. The graphics pipeline architecture, including its processing units and the various stages of the rendering process are also discussed in detail. The chapter concludes with examples illustrating window creation and control using OpenGL/GLUT and DirectX.

4

4.1   THE GRAPHICS SYSTEM

The term 'graphics system' formally describes any computing workstation with the ability to generate two- and/or three-dimensional images. Such a system is generally composed of at least five elements: an input device, an output device, a frame buffer, memory (both random access and permanent) and a central processing unit (cpu). Each of these elements must either exist or be emulated for a computer graphics system to be fully functional. Examples of graphics systems range from handheld devices and personal computers to groups of interconnected computers used for parallel rendering. Figure 4-1 gives the high-level representation of a general-purpose graphics system.

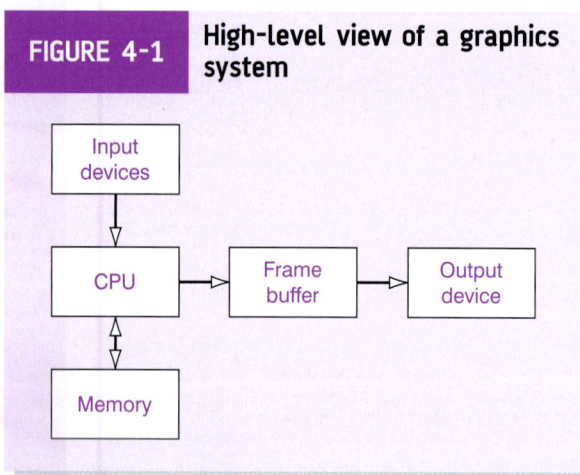

FIGURE 4-1   High-level view of a graphics system

4.1.1 Input Devices

Any system capable of producing graphical images must also be programmable and controllable. General input control is achieved by means of a keyboard coupled with a mouse and/or other pointing device. Graphic artists and animators also make frequent use of graphics tablets due to the high level of precision offered by these devices.

Input devices can be characterised as either *physical* or *logical*. An input device, as a physical device, consists of numerous low-level electronic and mechanical components attributing to the device's functionality. The understanding of these physical components is not required from a programming perspective. We rather consider input devices as logical devices. The properties of logical devices are specified, monitored, and controlled by a high-level application interface. Interaction between a physical device and application layer is accomplished through a series of commands, translated via a device driver to signals understood by the specific device. By dealing with physical devices in a logical way, we are able to write generic applications that will function properly regardless of low-level device specifics.

Considering an input device from a physical perspective reveals certain characteristics pertaining to the intended use of the device. These characteristics lead to one device being more suitable for a specific task than another. Input devices depend on physical gestures such as the movement of a mouse to position an on-screen pointer or the press of a button for the execution of some action. We primarily deal with only two input device classes: keyboard devices and pointing devices. Devices such as game controllers are simply a combination of these two classes. Image and video input devices, such as image scanners and webcams, make up the visual input device class.

Input is communicated to the application program in the form of a measure and trigger. The *measure* of a device is the actual data or signal sent to the application program. The *trigger* is the device's physical input mechanism that generates the data which is sent to the application program. For example, the measure of a mouse consists of a coordinate position with the trigger being one of the mouse buttons. We can obtain the measure of a device using any of the following input methods: request mode, sample mode, or event mode.

4

- Using *request mode*, the application program waits for the measure of a device until it is triggered. An example of this is standard command line input where the application requests some text input from the user, indefinitely waiting for the user to enter a series of characters from the keyboard and only continuing once the Return or Enter key is pressed. This form of input is commonly used in computer games – for example, allowing a player to enter a name next to a high score, to specify some character attribute, or to enter a cheat code. The data being entered are stored in some buffer, allowing unlimited modification of the entered data until the trigger is pressed. Figure 4-2 illustrates this form of input.

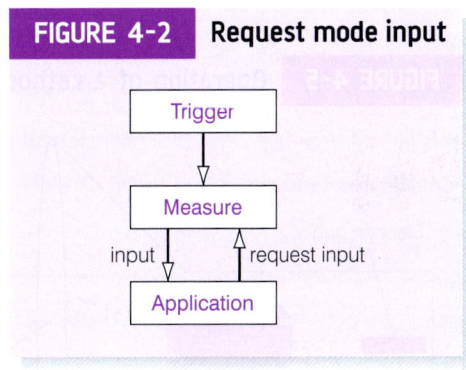

FIGURE 4-2   **Request mode input**

- *Sample mode* is used in situations where real-time input is necessary. This form of input doesn't make use of a trigger, for example, when entering text the entered characters are immediately read from the keyboard buffer and processed. Computer games use sample mode input to control the in-game camera, the character's position/movement, etc. Figure 4-3 depicts sample mode input.

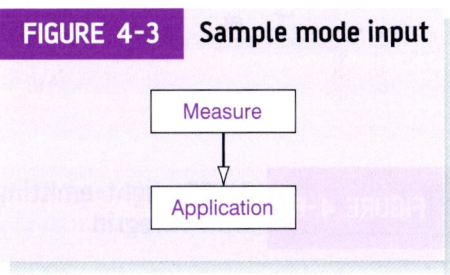

FIGURE 4-3   **Sample mode input**

Both sample mode and request mode necessitate the identification of devices intended for input. This makes it difficult to implement these two methods in a game environment due to the vast array of devices that can be used at any given moment. For this reason we now investigate event mode input and the use of callbacks.

- *Event mode* input is, as the name suggests, based on the generation of events. An event is generated every time an input device is triggered, causing the measure associated with the event to be placed in a buffer referred to as an event queue. The front of this event queue is examined by the application program; if there isn't an event in the queue, the application has to wait for an event to occur. A *callback function* (basically a software routine that is passed as an argument) can also be associated with any event type. For example, a callback associated with some event stored in the event queue can be executed when the event queue is polled or queried by the application program. Figure 4-4 shows one possible arrangement for event mode input.

4

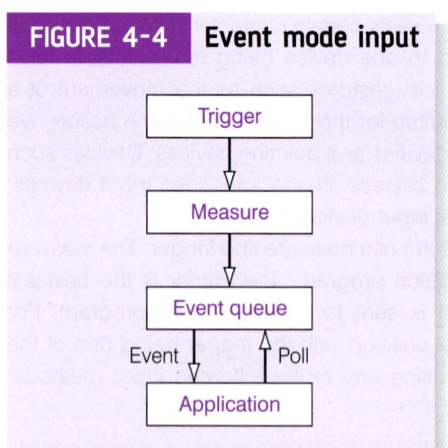

FIGURE 4-4 **Event mode input**

Trigger

Measure

Event queue

Event / Poll

Application

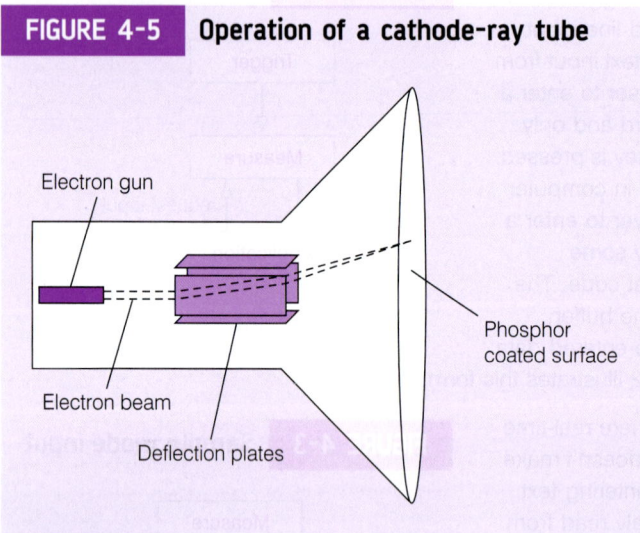

FIGURE 4-5 **Operation of a cathode-ray tube**

Electron gun

Electron beam

Deflection plates

Phosphor coated surface

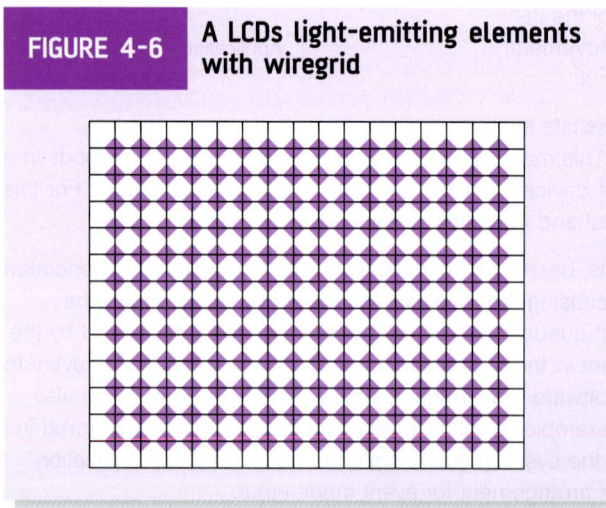

FIGURE 4-6 **A LCDs light-emitting elements with wiregrid**

4.1.2 Output Devices

Cathode-ray tube (CRT) monitors have, until recently, been the norm. These monitors consist of a simple electron gun 'shooting' electrons at a phosphor coated surface. Light is subsequently emitted where an electron collides with this surface. The exact coordinates of collision are controlled by an x and y deflection plate (also sometimes called a *deflection coil*). A digital-to-analog converter transforms the output produced by the computer's video adapter to voltages over the deflection plates. The electron beam is thus deflected or bent depending on the magnitude of these voltages. Figure 4-5 illustrates the operation of a cathode-ray tube.

CRT monitors are assembled from a large number of fragile and environmentally unfriendly components and are quickly being replaced by liquid crystal display (LCD) monitors (also known as flat-panel displays). Liquid crystal displays are less bulky, substantially lighter and have a much lower energy consumption rate than their CRT counterparts. LCD monitors feature a two-dimensional grid consisting of several light-emitting elements. These elements, commonly diodes or liquid crystals, are in turn arranged on a plate covered by a horizontal grid at the front and a vertical grid at the back. A pixel (one picture element or dot on the monitor) will be activated (thus emitting light) when an electrical signal is simultaneously sent to both the horizontal and vertical wires covering it. Figure 4-6 illustrates this basic flat-panel technology.

Earlier CRT displays are *vector*-based and render an image by tracing lines from one point to another. A line is drawn in accordance with electrons striking the phosphor coated surface. When a new line needs to be drawn, electron emissions are stopped with the electron gun being repositioned before it is activated again. This entire

FIGURE 4-7   (a) Image of two cups of tea (b) A close-up showing individual pixels

4

process requires a very high refresh rate to prevent the previously drawn line from fading before subsequent lines have been drawn. These displays are excellent for the rendering of smooth outlines without today's problem of pixilation where the edges of an object often suffer from noticeable artefacts as shown in Figure 4-7(b). An oscilloscope is an example of a device using a vector-based display. The main reason for replacing vector-based displays with raster technology is their limited shading and color support (due to the extremely high refresh rate required to keep an image up-to-date).

Raster technology allows for the generation of extremely high-quality images with the only drawback being the aforementioned presence of artefacts at the edges of objects. A *raster*-based image is produced as an array consisting of a series of picture elements known as *pixels*. A pixel is the smallest abstraction of any image, for example, the pixels of a standard television screen can be red, green, or blue with the intensity of every pixel controlled by a brightness and contrast or saturation value. The quality of a raster image is controlled by the resolution and color depth of the image. The image *resolution* is a factor of the number of pixels on the horizontal and vertical axes. Color *depth* is in turn the number of colors that can possibly be displayed by a pixel. For example, if an image is represented using an 8-bit color buffer, then the maximum number of colors supported by that pixel would be 256. Nearly all displays used today support a color depth of 24 bits – thus allowing the display of over 16 million colors (16 777 216 colors). The higher the resolution of the image, the higher the quality; for example, an image rendered at 300 by 400 pixels contains 120.000 pixels and would have a much higher level of pixilation (appearing much more blocky) than an image rendered at 1280 by 1024 pixels (displayed using 1 310 720 pixels). When considering Figures 4-7(a) and 4-7(b), we can see how Figure 4-7(a) is constructed through the shading of pixels by zooming into a section of it (shown in Figure 4-7(b)). Scaling the image in Figure 4-7 to a higher resolution leads to a clear loss in quality.

4.1.3 Frame Buffer

The *frame buffer*, typically used to store the color information of individual pixels, is one of the most important components of any graphics system. The frame buffer is directly responsible for image detail, a concept based on color depth and resolution. *Color depth*, specified by the depth of the frame buffer's color buffer, is defined as the number of bits available for the representation of each pixel. A 16-bit frame buffer allows for the display of 2^{16} (65 536) different colors. True-color is represented by 24, or more, bits per pixel – resulting in more than 16 million colors. The *resolution* of a frame buffer is determined by the number of pixels arranged in a row-by-column manner. For example, a video resolution of 1024 by 768 pixels consist of 1024 pixels arranged horizontally with 768 pixels vertically, resulting in a total of 786 432 pixels. The only limiting factor to a frame buffer's maximum resolution and color depth is the amount of memory available to it.

4

A frame buffer is constructed out of a series of high-speed memory chips allowing for the fast redisplay of its contents. Access to the frame buffer is generally provided through the direct mapping of memory to the CPU or, these days, to the GPU (graphics processing unit). It is also possible to simulate a frame buffer in software (thus mapping to the CPU). Software frame buffers are called *virtual frame buffers* and are found on many Linux and UNIX implementations (for example, running X without a hardware-based frame buffer). The first commercial frame buffer was released by Evans & Sutherland in 1974 and was capable of handling resolutions of up to 512×512 pixels, supporting a greyscale buffer depth of 8-bits. These early frame buffers rarely held more than the color information of a pixel array.

The modern-day frame buffer has been extended to include several additional buffers. One such a buffer, namely the *depth buffer*, is used to store pixel depth data. Depth data, or *z*-values, are crucial in situations where one object is rendered in front of another. Only the object closest to the viewer, determined by looking at each object's pixel depth data, is rendered. Another buffer closely related to the depth buffer is the *stencil buffer*. This buffer is used to limit the render area of a scene (called stencilling) by enabling or disabling drawing to a specific pixel. The depth– and stencil buffer are extensively used in the generation of real-time shadows and are fully discussed in Chapter 11.

Other buffers incorporated into the frame buffer include:

- the *accumulation buffer* (used to combine multiple images and for the anti-aliasing of images)

- *color indices* (a buffer that indexes various colors using a palette as opposed to shades of red, green and blue)

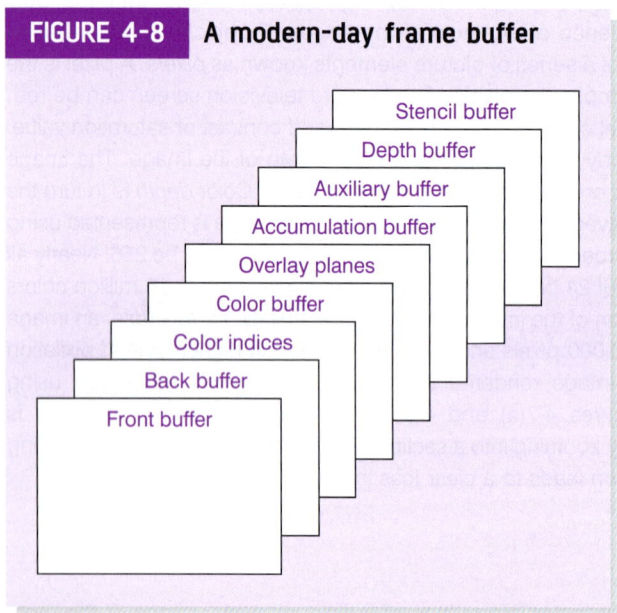

FIGURE 4-8   A modern-day frame buffer

Stencil buffer
Depth buffer
Auxiliary buffer
Accumulation buffer
Overlay planes
Color buffer
Color indices
Back buffer
Front buffer

- *overlay planes* (a buffer located on top of the frame buffer and used for the storage of rendered images without affecting the frame buffer's current pixel values)

- *auxiliary buffers* (buffers used for the storage of additional color data, serving as an extension to the color buffer)

- the *front and back buffer* (the front buffer stores the pixel values visible to the user with the values of the back buffer set to become that of the front buffer).

These buffers, as combined into a frame buffer, are shown in Figure 4-8.

4.2   ELEMENTS OF A 3D ENVIRONMENT

Any three-dimensional environment, at its most basic level, consists of at least a viewer, one light source and a number of objects. These objects can absorb or reflect light emitted from a light source depending on the reflecting object's material properties. Light will thus only be 'visible' when illuminated surfaces have the ability to reflect or absorb said light.

When talking about material properties, we are not concerned with physics or the material sciences as in real life; rather, material properties are primarily built around rules determining the amount of scattering or reflection of incident (incoming) light. Some surfaces, like a mirror, might reflect an incoming ray of light perfectly (hence appear shiny) while a carpet might reflect light in so many directions that it appears matte. OpenGL and Direct3D allow us to specify the material properties of a surface as ambient, diffuse, specular or transparent. *Ambient reflection* occurs whenever light emitted from a source is reflected so much that its origin is impossible to determine. Ambient light is characterized as *omnidirectional* (light radiated uniformly in all directions, or more commonly, light scattered uniformly in all directions). Thus, some of the light hitting a surface is absorbed while the rest is reflected – resulting in ambient reflection. *Specular reflection* occurs whenever light from a single incoming direction is reflected at a single outgoing direction. The amount of shininess exhibited by the object is called the object's *specularity* and is governed by a *shininess* coefficient. The bigger this coefficient, the closer we are to a perfect mirror. Formally, values ranging from 100 to 500 represent most metallic surfaces while smaller values represent materials with broader highlights such as plastic and wood. Contrasting specular reflection, *diffuse reflection* occurs when incoming light is scattered in random directions. The main contributing factor to this form of reflection is an uneven or rough surface. A diffuse surface appears identical regardless of the viewer's respective position.

The interaction between objects and one or more viewers are of crucial importance to the image-formation process. We define objects using primitives such as points, lines and polygons. These primitives are bound to a location using some positioning system such as the Cartesian coordinate system discussed in Chapter 7. Images and scenes are formed by grouping and representing these objects as a unit and it is the viewer that is responsible for the image formation. How precisely the scene is formed depends on the location of the viewer or camera. For example, Figure 4-9 shows an object viewed from two different locations along with the resultant images produced from each perspective.

Objects and viewers exist in a three-dimensional environment with the generated images and scenes being purely two-dimensional in nature. We can define an additional viewer for the object shown in Figure 4-9, namely the reader of this text. This viewer is able to see much more than a side view. The entire object and the two viewers are clearly visible from the reader's perspective.

FIGURE 4-9   **Viewing an object from different locations**

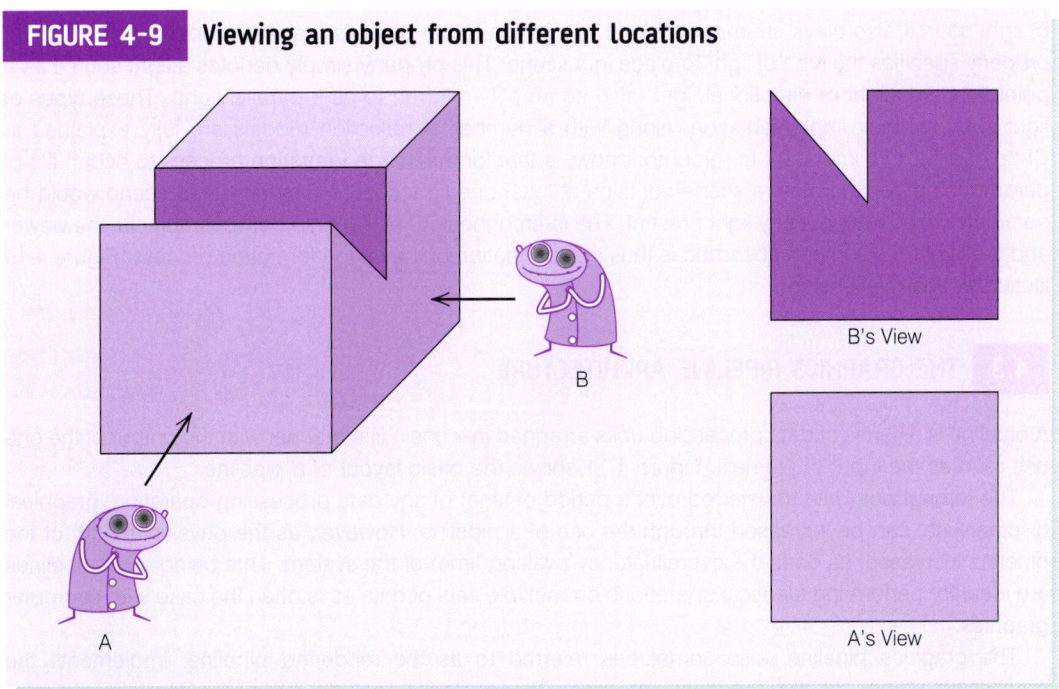

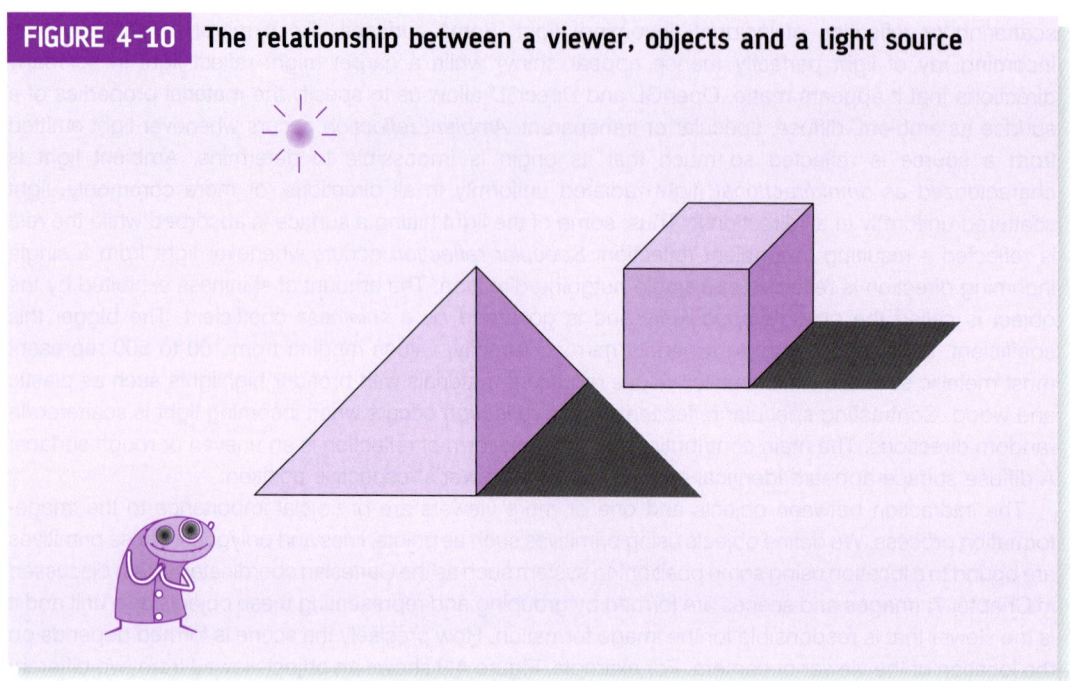

FIGURE 4-10 The relationship between a viewer, objects and a light source

Light can be emitted through either self-emission or reflection. When looking at a light bulb it is obvious that we are dealing with self-emission (although a light bulb can also reflect light from its surrounding environment). Light sources are categorized by their light-emitting direction and the energy emitted at each wavelength (determining the color of the light). We have already mentioned material properties and the effect they have on the way that light is absorbed or reflected by an object. The type of light source also plays an important part in addition to the object's material properties. A *light type property* specifies the type of light to place in a scene. This property simply denotes a light source as a point light, spotlight or directional light (also commonly referred to as a parallel light). These types of light sources, their implementation, along with a number of reflection models are fully explained in Chapter 9. What's important to remember now, is that for the image formation process to occur, it's of paramount importance that a scene contains at least one light source. The rendered scene would be completely black without any light present. The interconnected relationship between objects, the viewer and the light reflected and absorbed is thus the foundation of the image formation process. Figure 4-10 illustrates this relationship.

4.3   THE GRAPHICS PIPELINE ARCHITECTURE

A pipeline is a series of data processing units arranged in a chain like manner with the output of the one unit read as the input of the next. Figure 4-11 shows the basic layout of a pipeline.

The throughput (data transferred over a period of time) of any data processing operation, graphical or otherwise, can be increased through the use of a pipeline. However, as the physical length of the pipeline increases, so does the overall latency (waiting time) of the system. That being said, pipelines are ideal for performing identical operations on multiple sets of data as is often the case with computer graphics.

The graphics pipeline, also sometimes referred to as the rendering pipeline, implements the processing stages of the rendering process. These stages include vertex processing, clipping,

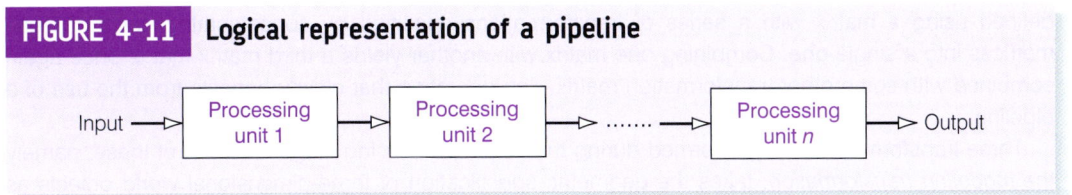

FIGURE 4-11   Logical representation of a pipeline

rasterization, and fragment processing. The purpose of the graphics pipeline is to process a scene consisting of objects, light sources and a camera, converting it to a two-dimensional image (pixel elements) via these four rendering stages. The output of the graphics pipeline is the final image displayed on the monitor or screen. The four rendering stages are illustrated in Figure 4-12 and discussed in detail below.

In summary we can describe the graphics pipeline as an overall process responsible for transforming some object representation from local coordinate space, to world space, view space, screen space and finally display space. These various coordinate spaces are fully discussed in Chapter 7 but for now it's sufficient to consider the *local coordinate space* as the definition used to describe the objects of a scene as specified in our program's source code. The *world space* can be described as a coordinate space where we have a reference to the viewer's position with lighting added to our scene. *View space* is where our scene's objects are culled and clipped to determine whether an object is visible based on the position of the viewer or camera. *Screen space* is where hidden surface removal, shading and rasterization occur and it is the final stage before we enter the *display space* where the produced pixel elements are displayed via some output device. We will now look at the various stages of the graphics pipeline in detail.

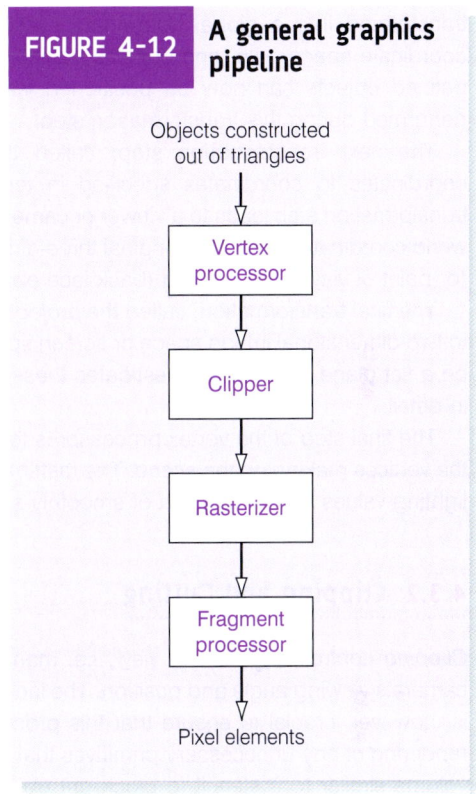

FIGURE 4-12   A general graphics pipeline

4.3.1 Vertex Processing

The first processing unit of the graphics pipeline is the vertex processor. This processor is responsible for performing all geometric transformations (fully discussed in Chapter 7) and the computation of color values of every vertex or point making up an object.

Geometric transformations (such as translations and rotations) simply means the process of converting the current spatial representation of an object to a different coordinate system. For example, a geometric transformation is required to represent an object, originally defined in terms of world coordinates (coordinates specified by the programmer for object representation), in terms of display coordinates (the coordinate system used by the graphics display). Each geometric transformation is defined using a matrix with a series of transformations specified by concatenating each of these matrices into a single one. Combining one matrix with another yields a third matrix that is once again combined with some other transformation matrix – an operation that clearly benefits from the use of a pipeline.

Three transformations are performed during the vertex processing stage. The first of these, namely the *modeling transformation*, takes the geometric specification of three-dimensional world objects as input. Every object, originally defined in local coordinate space, is subsequently transformed to use world-space coordinates. Each object's independent local coordinate system has now been transformed into a global coordinate system. This provides all the objects with a shared global coordinate space – i.e. one object's position can be described in terms of another's and these user defined objects can now be positioned within the same scene. All translations and rotations are performed during this transformation step.

The next transformation step, called the *viewing transformation*, transforms all world-space coordinates to coordinates specified in terms of a viewer's position and viewing direction. This transformation step leads to a viewer or camera that can be moved and rotated to any position within the world coordinate space. The original three-dimensional scene is displayed from this viewer's perspective (or point of view). Both culling (back-face elimination) and clipping are carried out in view space.

The final transformation, called the *projection transformation*, transforms the view space coordinates to two-dimensional image space or screen space so that the three-dimensional scene can be displayed on a flat plane. Chapter 7 investigates these various transformations and coordinate system changes in detail.

The final step of the vertex processor is to assign colors, per-vertex lighting and shading to each of the vertices making up the scene. The rasterization stage discussed below interpolates these per-vertex lighting values for the creation of smoothly shaded lighting ranges between vertices.

4.3.2 Clipping and Culling

Clipping controls the field of view, i.e. managing the percentage of the world visible based on the camera's viewing angle and position. The lack of clipping doesn't hinder the image formation process; it is, however, crucial to ensure that this process is performed in a timely manner as it eliminates the rendering of any unnecessary primitives that would not be visible to the viewer or camera. We define a volume similar to a stencil to block out objects not visible to the viewer. All objects and portions of objects falling outside this stencil or volume do not appear in the final image.

Clipping, unlike vertex processing, should be done on a primitive-by-primitive rather than a vertex-by-vertex basis. To accomplish this, sets of vertices are assembled into primitives, such as polygons and lines based on the implementation of some clipping algorithm such as the Cohen-Sutherland or Liang-Barsky line clipping algorithms or the Sutherland-Hodgman polygon clipping algorithm. An example illustrating the importance of clipping would be to consider a scene from a computer game consisting of numerous buildings, cars, pedestrians, shops, etc. Each of these elements are physical models stored in memory, requiring a lot of processing time for shading, texturing, animation, etc. If the scene's viewer or camera has a viewing angle of 110 degrees, then we needn't render any of the models or meshes located outside this viewing area – thus saving a lot of rendering time in the process.

Culling, or back-face elimination, is the process where polygons or surfaces pointing away from the camera or viewer are not rendered. For example, when a building is viewed directly from the front, then the three sides hidden from the viewer are not drawn (shown in Figure 4-13). This process, just like clipping, improves the rendering speed of a scene by reducing the number of polygons or surfaces that needs to be rendered without affecting the visual output. Chapter 12 deals with both clipping and culling in detail.

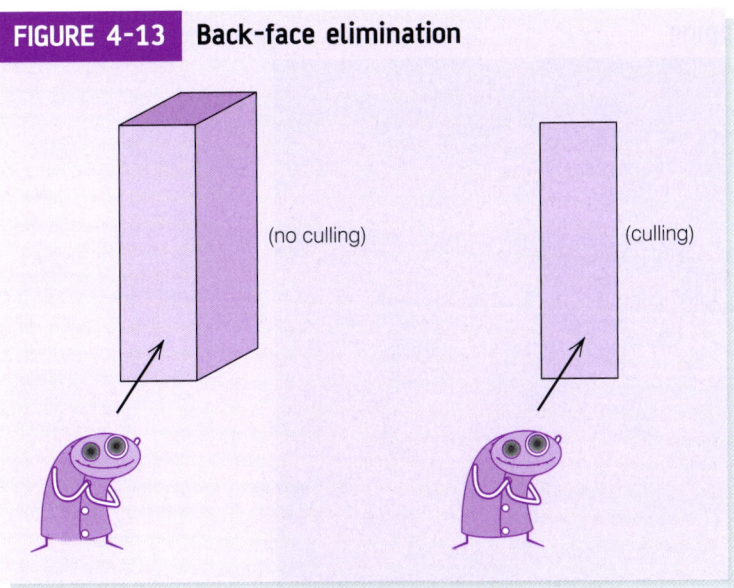

FIGURE 4-13   Back-face elimination

(no culling)

(culling)

4

4.3.3 Rasterization and Fragment Processing

The *rasterization,* or scan conversion process, converts the primitives produced by the clipper (consisting of vertices) to pixels for representation in the frame buffer and for subsequent output to a monitor. For example, a solid rectangle consisting of four vertices are transformed to two-dimensional pixels or points in the frame buffer, with these two-dimensional pixels being colored and shaded as appropriate. The result of the rasterization process is a series of fragments for each of these primitives. A *fragment* is nothing more than a pixel with additional information about its color, position, and depth. The fragment's depth information is used to determine whether a particular pixel lies behind any of the other rasterized pixels. The matching pixel in the frame buffer is updated with the information carried by this fragment. This process of updating the pixels in the frame buffer with the fragments generated by the rasterizer is called *fragment processing*. The color of fragments are manipulated using techniques such as texture mapping, bump mapping, texture filtering, environmental mapping, blending, per-fragment lighting, etc. These rendering techniques are discussed later on in the textbook.

4.3.4 Programmable Pipelines

Today's graphics cards all have pipelines built into their graphics processing units. The operations that could be performed by earlier graphics cards were standardized by the device manufacturer with only a number of parameters and properties available for modification. Modern graphics cards allow for not only the modification of a large number of parameters, but also for complete control over the vertex and fragment processors. These programmable vertex and fragment processors enable the real-time rendering of various advanced techniques only previously achievable using large rendering farms or not even possible in real-time at all. Bump mapping (used for adding depth to pixels and thus creating a lighting-dependent bumpiness to a texture mapped surface) and environmental mapping (used for the generation of reflections by changing the texture coordinates based on the position of the camera) are just two examples of techniques only possible offline in the past, but that have become commonplace in the games of today. Figure 4-14 shows a bump mapped surface with Figure 4-15 showing the application of environmental mapping to simulate reflections on water.

We will now look at both Direct3D 10's and OpenGL's programmable pipelines to fully understand the implication and use of programmable pipelines for the generation of advanced real-time graphical effects.

4

FIGURE 4-14   **Bump mapping**

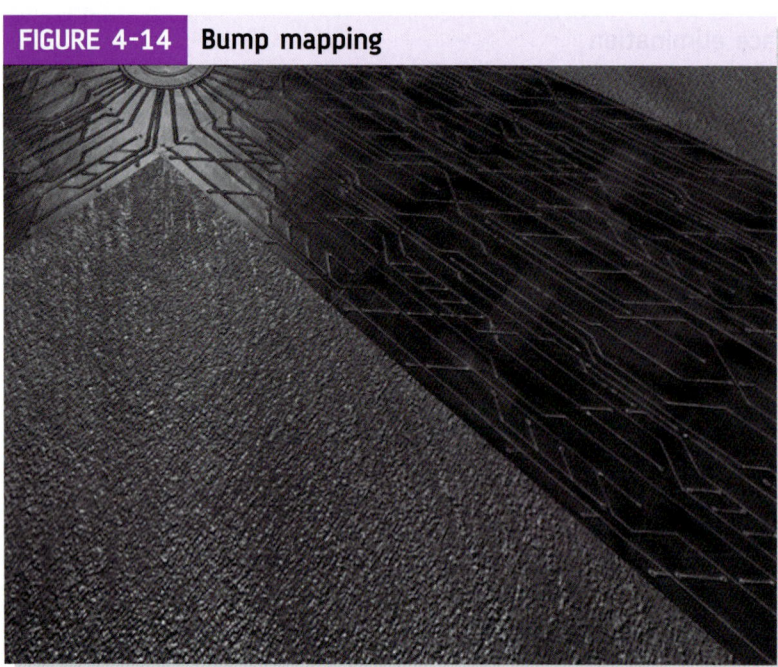

FIGURE 4-15   **Reflections on water using environmental mapping**

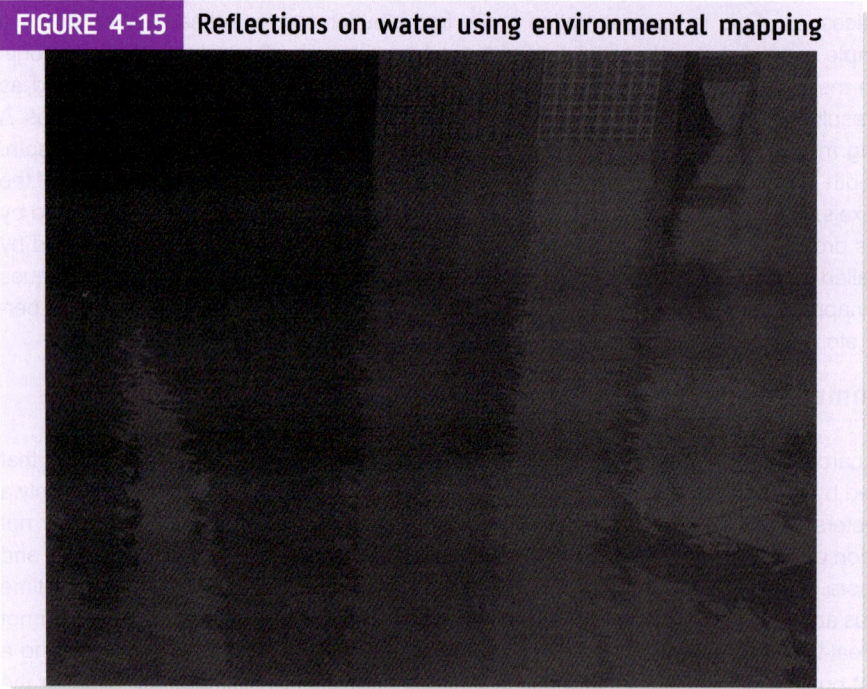

4.3.4.1 The Direct3D 10 Processing Pipeline   Each stage of the Direct3D 10 processing pipeline is configurable using the standard Direct3D application programming interface. The vertex shader, geometry shader, and pixel shader are programmable using either Microsoft's proprietary High Level Shader Language (HLSL) or NVIDIA's C for Graphics (Cg). Each of these programmable processing units, including the pipeline processing states is discussed below. Figure 4-16 illustrates the Direct3D 10 pipeline architecture.

The Input-Assembler Stage The first stage of the programmable pipeline, namely the *input-assembler stage*, is responsible for propagating geometric input data consisting of points, lines and polygons to the rest of the pipeline. This pipeline stage assembles the input data into primitives; following this it forwards these assembled primitives to the next stage in the pipeline. For example, when data are received from a buffer resource, they contain information about a vertex in three-dimensional space, the winding direction used for determining the vertex assembly order (either clockwise or counter-clockwise), and an identifier specifying the first vertex in a sequence of vertices. This information allows the input assembler to create primitive types supported by Direct3D (listed in Chapter 6). Figure 4-17 illustrates how this information is used to create a supported primitive type.

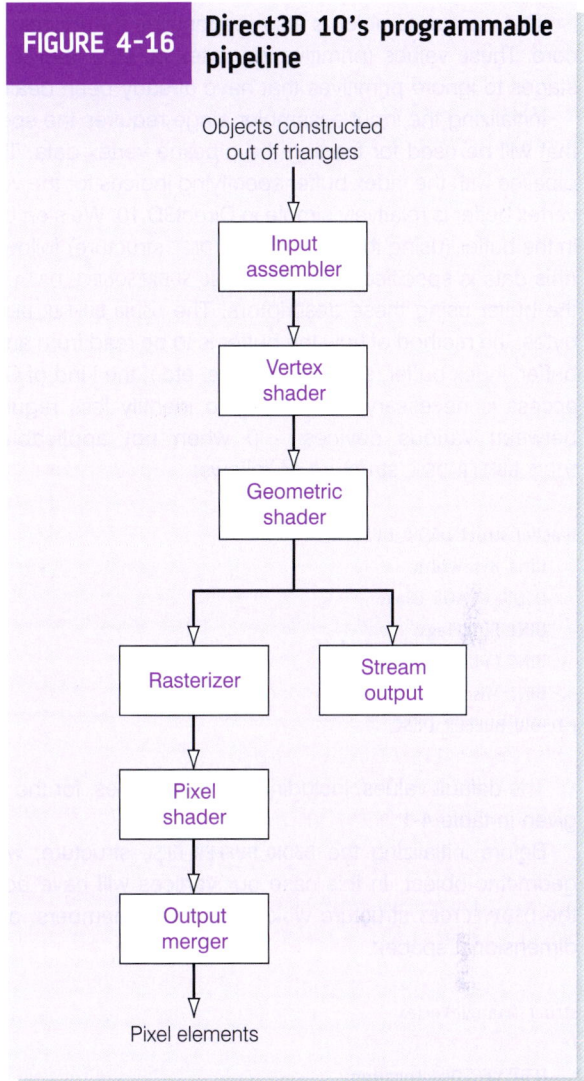

FIGURE 4-16 Direct3D 10's programmable pipeline

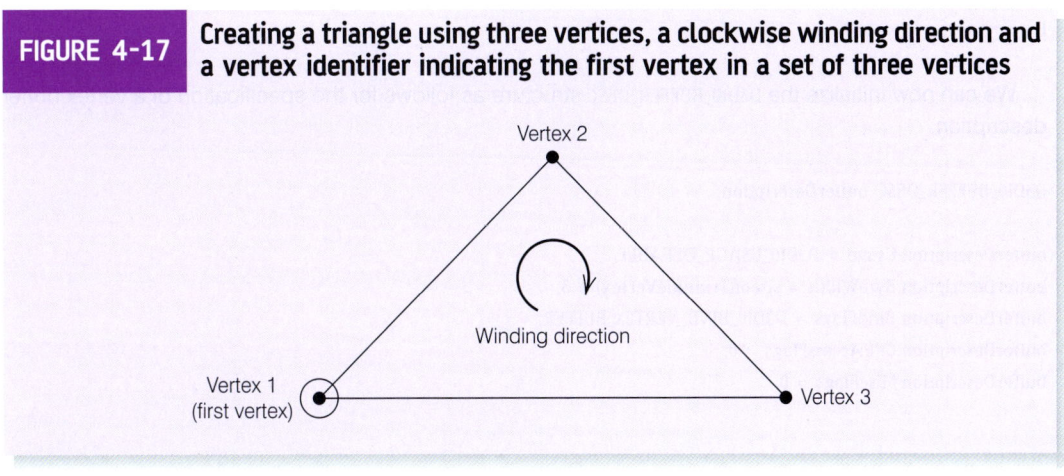

FIGURE 4-17 Creating a triangle using three vertices, a clockwise winding direction and a vertex identifier indicating the first vertex in a set of three vertices

The input assembler is also responsible for attaching *Shader System Values* for use by the shader core. These values (primitive id, vertex id, etc.) lead to faster execution times by allowing the shader stages to ignore primitives that have already been dealt with.

Initializing the input-assembler stage requires the specification of a vertex and optional index buffer that will be used for feeding the pipeline vertex data. The vertex buffer feeds the vertex data into the pipeline with the index buffer specifying indices for the vertex data stored in the vertex buffer. Creating a vertex buffer is relatively simple in Direct3D 10. We start by specifying the type of data that can be stored in the buffer (using the D3D10_BUFFER_DESC structure) followed by reading data into the buffer to initialize it (this data is specified using the D3D10_SUBRESOURCE_DATA structure). Once this is done we simply create the buffer using these descriptors. The D3D10_BUFFER_DESC structure describes the size of the buffer in bytes, the method of how the buffer is to be read from and written to, the nature of the buffer (as a vertex buffer, index buffer, shader resource, etc.), the kind of CPU access allowed (write, read, or 0 if no CPU access is necessary) and a flag to identify less regularly used options (such as resource sharing between various devices – 0 when not applicable). The D3D10.h header file specifies the D3D10_BUFFER_DESC structure as follows:

```
typedef struct D3D10_BUFFER_DESC {
    UINT ByteWidth;
    D3D10_USAGE Usage;
    UINT BindFlags;
    UINT CPUAccessFlags;
    UINT MiscFlags;
} D3D10_BUFFER_DESC;
```

The default values, including the alternatives, for the members of the D3D10_BUFFER_DESC structure are given in table 4-1.

Before initializing the D3D10_BUFFER_DESC structure, we first have to specify the vertices for some geometric object. In this case our vertices will have both a spatial location and a color value (using the D3DXVECTOR3 structure which has three members, an *x*-, *y*- and *z*-coordinate of a vector in three-dimensional space):

```
struct TriangleVertex
{
    D3DXVECTOR3 Location;
    D3DXVECTOR3 Color;
};
```

We can now initialize the D3D10_BUFFER_DESC structure as follows for the specification of a vertex buffer description:

```
D3D10_BUFFER_DESC bufferDescription;

bufferDescription.Usage = D3D10_USAGE_DEFAULT;
bufferDescription.ByteWidth = sizeof(TriangleVertex) * 3;
bufferDescription.BindFlags = D3D10_BIND_VERTEX_BUFFER;
bufferDescription.CPUAccessFlags = 0;
bufferDescription.MiscFlags = 0;
```

TABLE 4-1	Describing a buffer resource using the D3D10_BUFFER_DESC structure
Members	**Flags**
ByteWidth	Any number, for example: 64
Usage	D3D10_USAGE_DEFAULT (won't be read or written to by the CPU that often) D3D10_USAGE_IMMUTABLE (can't be written to by the CPU at all) D3D10_USAGE_DYNAMIC (buffer will be written to by the CPU at least once per frame) D3D10_USAGE_STAGING (read from and write to the GPU)
BindFlags	D3D10_BIND_VERTEX_BUFFER (specify the resource as a vertex buffer) D3D10_BIND_INDEX_BUFFER (specify the resource as an index buffer) D3D10_BIND_CONSTANT_BUFFER (specify the resource as a constant buffer which can only be updated completely, not partially, and which has a limit on the buffer's byte size) D3D10_BIND_SHADER_RESOURCE (specify the buffer as a shader resource) D3D10_BIND_STREAM_OUTPUT (specify the resource as an output buffer for the stream output stage discussed below) D3D10_BIND_RENDER_TARGET (specify the resource as a render target – dealt with later on in the book) D3D10_BIND_DEPTH_STENCIL (specify the resource as a depth stencil buffer – discussed in Chapter 11)
CPUAccessFlags	D3D10_CPU_ACCESS_READ (the buffer's contents can be read by the CPU) D3D10_CPU_ACCESS_WRITE (the CPU can change the buffer's contents directly instead of using the UpdateSubresource ID3D10Device interface)
MiscFlags	D3D10_RESOURCE_MISC_GENERATE_MIPS (species the creation of mipmaps for some texture resource using the GenerateMips ID3D10Device interface) D3D10_RESOURCE_MISC_SHARED (enables resource sharing between various devices) D3D10_RESOURCE_MISC_TEXTURECUBE (specifies the creation of a cube texture – a three-dimensional texture in the shape of a cube constructed from six textures stored in a 2D texture array)

4

Following this we create the vertex buffer using previously specified vertex data. The first step of this process is to specify an array of vertex data elements:

```
TriangleVertex array_of_vertex_data [] =
{
    D3DXVECTOR3( 0.0f, 1.0f, 1.0f ),
    D3DXVECTOR3( 0.0f, 0.0f, 0.5f ),
    D3DXVECTOR3( 1.0f, -1.0f, 1.0f ),
    D3DXVECTOR3( 1.0f, 0.0f, 0.0f ),
    D3DXVECTOR3( -1.0f, -1.0f, 1.0f ),
    D3DXVECTOR3( 0.0f, 1.0f, 0.0f ),
};
```

Next we have to initialize the D3D10_SUBRESOURCE_DATA structure. This data structure initializes a subresource using predefined data. A *subresource* is a portion of a resource that links back to the original resource data but with additional information about the resource so that the pipeline can easily access the data contained within this resource. The D3D10_SUBRESOURCE_DATA structure has three members, namely, a pointer to the data used for initializing the sub-resource, a value used for specifying the memory pitch in bytes required for two- and three-dimensional texture resources (discussed in Chapter 8) and the memory slice pitch associated with three-dimensional texture resources (also discussed in Chapter 8). The D3D10.h header file specifies this structure as follows:

```
typedef struct D3D10_SUBRESOURCE_DATA {
    const void *pSysMem;
    UINT SysMemPitch;
    UINT SysMemSlicePitch;
} D3D10_SUBRESOURCE_DATA;
```

We initialize the D3D10_SUBRESOURCE_DATA structure using the previously defined array of vertex data elements:

```
D3D10_SUBRESOURCE_DATA subresourceData;

subresourceData.pSysMem = array_of_vertex_data;
subresourceData.SysMemPitch = 0;
subresourceData.SysMemSlicePitch = 0;
```

The final step is to create the vertex buffer. We use the CreateBuffer ID3D10Device interface to do this. This interface takes three parameters, the first being a pointer to the previously defined D3D10_BUFFER_DESC structure, the second a pointer to the D3D10_SUBRESOURCE_DATA structure, and the third being the address of a pointer to the ID3D10Buffer interface used for controlling our buffer resource (be it either a vertex or index buffer). The CreateBuffer ID3D10Device interface is declared as follows in the D3D10.h header:

```
HRESULT CreateBuffer(
    const D3D10_BUFFER_DESC *pDesc,
    const D3D10_SUBRESOURCE_DATA *pInitialData,
    ID3D10Buffer **ppBuffer
);
```

We can now call the CreateBuffer ID3D10Device interface to create the vertex buffer:

```
ID3D10Device* g_id3dDevice;
ID3D10Buffer* vertexBuffer[2] = {NULL, NULL};


g_id3dDevice->CreateBuffer(&bufferDescription,
                            &subresourceData,
                            &vertexBuffer[0]);
```

Defining an index buffer is comparable to the creation of a vertex buffer, with the only difference being the specification of the D3D10_BUFFER_DESC structure's BindFlags member, for example:

4

```
D3D10_BUFFER_DESC indexBufferDescription;

indexBufferDescription.Usage = D3D10_USAGE_DEFAULT;
indexBufferDescription.ByteWidth = sizeof(TriangleVertex) * 3;
indexBufferDescription.BindFlags = D3D10_BIND_INDEX_BUFFER;
indexBufferDescription.CPUAccessFlags = 0;
indexBufferDescription.MiscFlags = 0;
```

We also have to specify an array containing index data. This array will be used to initialize the D3D10_SUBRESOURCE_DATA structure:

```
UINT array_of_index_data [] = {0, 1, 2, 3, 4};

D3D10_SUBRESOURCE_DATA indexSubresourceData;

indexSubresourceData.pSysMem = array_of_index_data;
indexSubresourceData.SysMemPitch = 0;
indexSubresourceData.SysMemSlicePitch = 0;
```

The index buffer is created using the CreateBuffer ID3D10Device interface:

```
ID3D10Buffer* indexBuffer = NULL;

g_id3dDevice->CreateBuffer(&indexBufferDescription,
                            &indexSubresourceData,
                            &indexBuffer);
```

With the input buffers specified and properly initialized, we create the *input-layout object* which will be used to control how vertex data are fed into the input-assembler stage (by directly describing the input-buffer data). The type of the input vertex data is identified and checked against shader parameter types ensuring both type compatibility and that the needed shader data are actually stored in the buffer. Shader data are looked at in more detail during Chapter 6. We create the input-layout object using the CreateInputLayout ID3D10Device interface via the specification of five parameters. The first parameter is an array of the input-assembler stage input data type described using the D3D10_INPUT_ELEMENT_DESC structure. The D3D10_INPUT_ELEMENT_DESC structure is defined as follows in the D3D10.h header file:

```
typedef struct D3D10_INPUT_ELEMENT_DESC {
    LPCSTR SemanticName;
    UINT SemanticIndex;
    DXGI_FORMAT Format;
```

```
    UINT InputSlot;
    UINT AlignedByteOffset;
    D3D10_INPUT_CLASSIFICATION InputSlotClass;
    UINT InstanceDataStepRate;
} D3D10_INPUT_ELEMENT_DESC;
```

This structure gives a description of each input assembler stage element, specifically:

- the High Level Shader Language (HLSL) semantic name of the element

- the element's semantic index used when more than one element with the same semantic name exists

- the element's data type

- an integer value used for specifying the input-assembler's input slot (described below)

- the byte offset used to set the location of the element in the input slot (counting in bytes from the beginning of the input slot)

- the input data class (either vertex data using the D3D10_INPUT_CLASSIFICATION enumeration with the constant set to either D3D10_INPUT_PER_VERTEX_DATA for per-vertex input data, or D3D10_INPUT_PER_INSTANCE_DATA for per-instance input data)

- the data step rate controlling the number of instances of one element to draw (using the per-instance input data) before moving on to the next buffer element – must be set 0 for elements containing per-vertex data.

Using the D3D10_INPUT_ELEMENT_DESC structure, we can specify a vertex buffer containing two vertex-data elements as follows:

```
D3D10_INPUT_ELEMENT_DESC input_layout_description[] =
{
    {
        L"POSITION",
        0,
        DXGI_FORMAT_R32G32B32_UINT,
        0,
        0,
        D3D10_INPUT_PER_VERTEX_DATA,
        0
    },

    {
        L"COLOR",
        0,
        DXGI_FORMAT_R32G32B32_UINT,
        1,
        6,
        D3D10_INPUT_PER_VERTEX_DATA,
        0
    },
};
```

Data are fed into the input-assembler stage through a number of units referred to as *input slots*. Each of these input-assembler input slots, shown in Figure 4-18, are used as storage for a vertex buffer, thus storing input data.

The second parameter of the CreateInputLayout ID3D10Device interface is an integer value specifying the number of input-data types making up the input-elements array. The third parameter is a pointer to the compiled shader code (discussed in Chapter 6) with the fourth parameter specifying the byte size of this compiled shader code. The final parameter is a pointer to the input-layout object that will be used as output. This CreateInputLayout ID3D10Device interface is defined as follows in the D3D10.h header file:

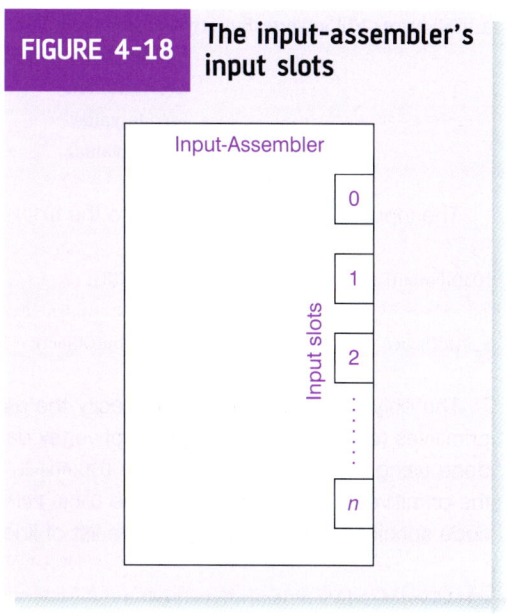

FIGURE 4-18   **The input-assembler's input slots**

```
HRESULT CreateInputLayout (
    const D3D10_INPUT_ELEMENT_DESC  *pInputElementDescs,
    UINT NumElements,
    const void *pShaderBytecodeWithInputSignature,
    SIZE_T BytecodeLength,
    ID3D10InputLayout **ppInputLayout);
```

We can now bind this newly created input-layout object to the input-assembler stage, after which we can call the *draw functions*. This object binding is done using the IASetVertexBuffers and IASetInputLayout ID3D10Device interfaces. The IASetVertexBuffers interface binds a vertex buffer array to the input-assembler stage by specifying the input slot, the total number of buffers in the vertex buffer array, a pointer to the vertex buffer array, a pointer to an array containing values indicating the byte size of elements to be read from the vertex buffer (referred to as stride values) and a pointer to an array containing so called offset values (with one offset value representing the number of bytes to be read from the first element stored in the vertex buffer to the element being accessed). This IASetVertexBuffers ID3D10Device interface is defined as follows in the D3D10.h header file:

```
void IASetVertexBuffers(
    UINT StartSlot,
    UINT NumBuffers,
    ID3D10Buffer *const *ppVertexBuffers,
    const UINT *pStrides,
    const UINT *pOffsets);
```

The IASetInputLayout interface, taking a pointer to the input-layout object, is responsible for binding this object to the input-assembler stage. The following code sample illustrates this process:

```
UINT start_input_slot = 0;
UINT number_buffers_in_array = 1;
UINT offset_value = 0;
UINT stride_value = sizeof (TriangleVertex);
```

```
g_id3dDevice->IASetVertexBuffers(start_input_slot,
                                 number_buffers_in_array,
                                 &vertexBuffer,
                                 &stride_value,
                                 &offset_value);
```

The input-layout takes a pointer to the ID3D10Device object:

```
ID3D10InputLayout* inputLayoutObject = NULL;
```

```
g_id3dDevice->IASetInputLayout(inputLayoutObject);
```

The only remaining step is to specify the assembling of vertices into primitives and to send these primitives (controlling the rendering of vertex data to the screen) to the next step of the pipeline. This is done using the IASetPrimitiveTopology ID3D10Device interface. This interface takes one parameter, namely the primitive type specified using the D3D10_PRIMITIVE_TOPOLOGY enumerator. For example, the following code specifies the primitive type as a list of lines:

```
g_id3dDevice->IASetPrimitiveTopology(
                D3D10_PRIMITIVE_TOPOLOGY_LINELIST);
```

Table 4-2 lists possible primitive types (dealt with in more detail during Chapter 6):

We can now draw these pipeline-bound primitives using various ID3D10Device functions such as Draw, DrawAuto, DrawIndexed, DrawInstanced and DrawIndexedInstanced.

TABLE 4-2   **Specifying a primitive type using the D3D10_PRIMITIVE_TOPOLOGY enumerator**

Constant	Description
D3D10_PRIMITIVE_TOPOLOGY_UNDEFINED	A primitive topology is not specified for the input-assembler stage.
D3D10_PRIMITIVE_TOPOLOGY_LINELIST	The vertex data are interpreted as a list of lines.
D3D10_PRIMITIVE_TOPOLOGY_LINELIST_ADJ	The vertex data are interpreted as a list of lines with adjacency data.
D3D10_PRIMITIVE_TOPOLOGY_LINESTRIP	The vertex data are interpreted as a line strip.
D3D10_PRIMITIVE_TOPOLOGY_LINESTRIP_ADJ	The vertex data are interpreted as a line strip with adjacency data.
D3D10_PRIMITIVE_TOPOLOGY_POINTLIST	The vertex data are interpreted as a list of points.
D3D10_PRIMITIVE_TOPOLOGY_TRIANGLELIST	The vertex data are interpreted as a list of triangles.
D3D10_PRIMITIVE_TOPOLOGY_TRIANGLELIST_ADJ	The vertex data are interpreted as a list of triangles with adjacency data.
D3D10_PRIMITIVE_TOPOLOGY_TRIANGLESTRIP	The vertex data are interpreted as a triangle strip.
D3D10_PRIMITIVE_TOPOLOGY_TRIANGLESTRIP_ADJ	The vertex data are interpreted as a triangle strip with adjacency data.

The Vertex-Shader Stage Per-vertex operations are performed during this pipeline processing stage. Examples of such operations include per-vertex lighting, texture sampling operations, and geometric transformations. Per-vertex lighting allows us to specify distinct light sources, including the interaction of these light sources with adjacent surfaces. These interactions and reflections are considered on a per-vertex basis with the lighting values between vertices being approximated. This stage takes one vertex as input, modifies it according to some predefined operation and outputs it for further processing. There might also be cases where no vertex processing is required, leading to the definition of a pass-through vertex shader. This *pass-through vertex shader* forwards the input vertex data to the geometry-shader stage unmodified.

Input vertex data generally consist of anything from one to sixteen 32-bit vectors made up of one to four elements each. The input assembler basically feeds two data elements into the vertex-shader stage: the vertex ID and the instance ID. These IDs are generated by the graphics hardware and can only be handled during this pipeline stage. We'll look at defining and controlling the vertex shader's operation during Chapter 6.

The Geometry-Shader Stage Primitives such as vertices, lines, and polygons are processed during this pipeline stage. The geometry-shader stage takes these primitives as input, and processes them based on some programmatically defined algorithm, forwarding these newly modified or, in some cases, newly generated primitives to either the stream-output stage or rasterizer stage. The geometry-shader stage takes full primitives as input, for example; lines consisting of two vertices, quads constructed out of four vertices, etc. This is in contrast with vertex shaders which only accept a single vertex as input.

One useful feature of the geometry shader is its ability to handle edge-adjacent primitives. For example, say we have a quad as input, then the vertex data of all primitives adjacent to the quad can also be read as input. Figure 4-19 shows such a quad with four adjacent quads.

The geometry shader's generated primitives are returned as an output stream object. This output stream can be declared as a LineStream (creating a line strip output topology), TriangleStream (creating a

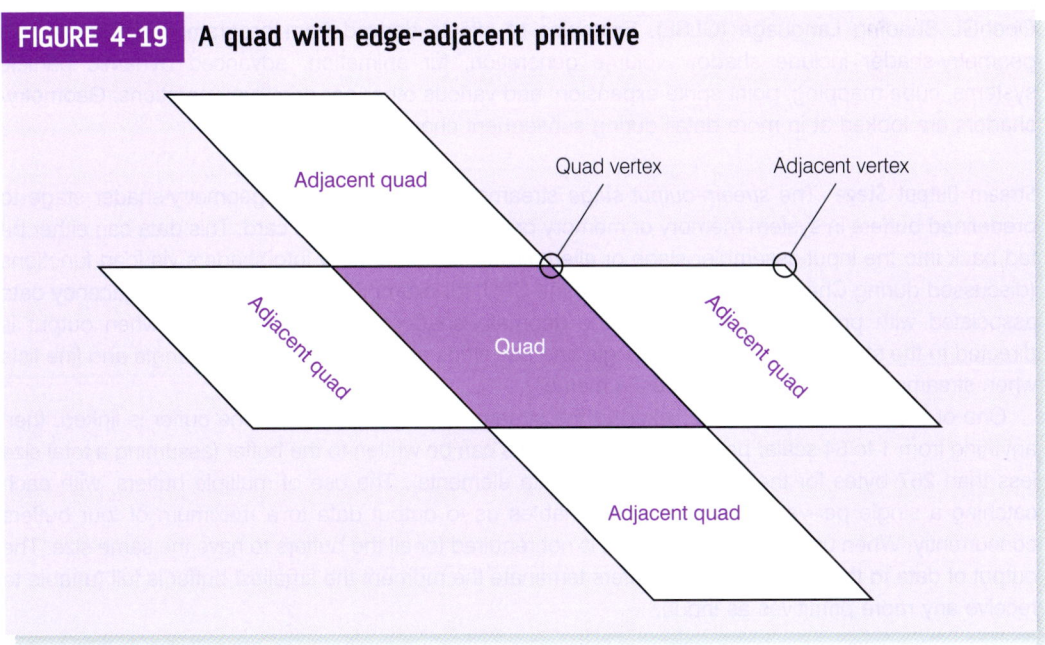

FIGURE 4-19 **A quad with edge-adjacent primitive**

triangle strip output topology), or PointStream (creating a point list output topology) based on the original primitive object type. We create a primitive strip by appending output vertices using the Append interface method. The appending of vertices is necessary since the geometry shader only outputs one vertex data element at a time – requiring this vertex data to be reconstructed into primitives. The RestartStrip method is used to terminate the current primitive strip construction process, signalling the geometry-shader to start the creation of a new primitive strip. The following non-functional code sample shows the creation of a TriangleStream output object via the declaration of a geometry shader.

We start by setting the maximum number of vertices to output using the MaxVertexCount attribute type (causing the geometry shader to terminate once the specified number of vertices has been generated):

[MaxVertexCount(6)]

Next we declare the geometry shader, GS_Sample, to take a triangle strip or triangle list (triangle float4 inputPar[3]) as input, with a TriangleStream object as output (the inout keyword declares the stream object, outputPar, as both an input and output):

```
void GS_Sample(triangle float4 inputPar [3],
              inout TriangleStream<float2> outputPar)
{
    //function body
    //e.g. using Append and RestartStrip:
    outputPar.Append(...);
    outputPar.RestartStrip();
}
```

Modern-day computer games are increasingly making use of geometric shaders, mostly due to the exponential advances being made in graphics hardware and the power given to developers in controlling this hardware at a functional level using shading languages such as HLSL, Cg, and the OpenGL Shading Language (GLSL). Examples of effects derived from programming DirectX 10's geometry-shader include shadow volume generation, fur animation, advanced dynamic particle systems, cube mapping, point sprite expansion, and various other per-primitive operations. Geometry-shaders are looked at in more detail during subsequent chapters.

Stream-Output Stage   The *stream-output stage* streams primitives from the geometry-shader stage to predefined buffers in system memory or memory present on the graphics card. This data can either be fed back into the input-assembler stage or alternatively loaded directly into shaders via load functions (discussed during Chapter 6), or circulated to the CPU, for example (Figure 4-20). The adjacency data associated with primitives outputted by the geometry-shader stage are discarded when output is directed to the stream output stage. Triangle and line strips are also converted to triangle and line lists when streamed to the buffer resources in memory.

One or multiple buffers can be linked to the stream output stage. When one buffer is linked, then anything from 1 to 64 scalar per-vertex data elements can be written to the buffer (assuming a total size less than 257 bytes for the per-vertex output data elements). The use of multiple buffers, with each catching a single per-vertex data element, enables us to output data to a maximum of four buffers concurrently. When using multiple buffers it is not required for all the buffers to have the same size. The output of data to these varying sized buffers terminate the moment the smallest buffer is full (unable to receive any more primitives as input).

FIGURE 4-20 Streaming of data to predefined buffers in system/GPU memory

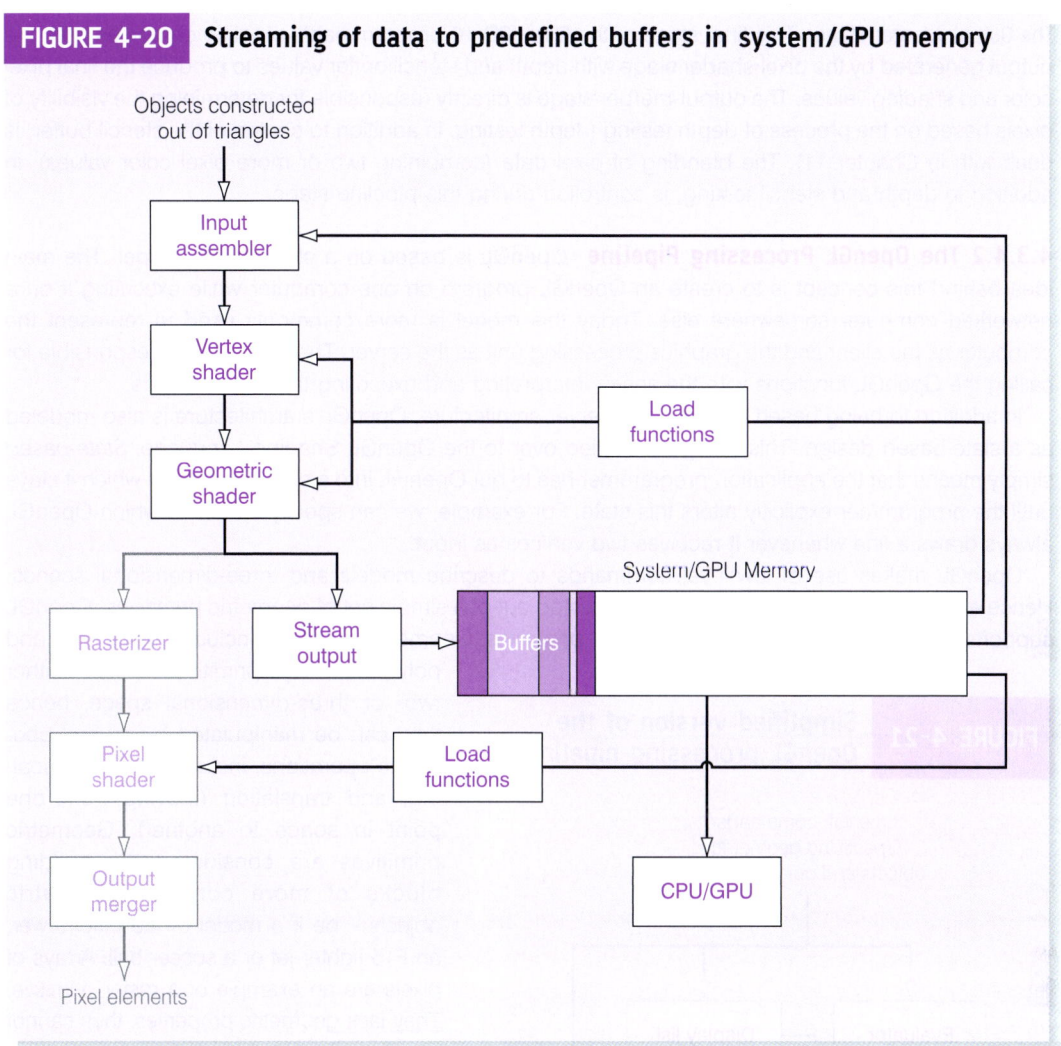

4

The Pixel-Shader Stage The rasterizer stage rasterizes primitives produced by the geometry-shader stage into pixels via the interpolation of vertex values (see section 4.3.3 for further discussion). The shading and color of these pixel values need to be calculated so that each primitive are correctly rendered to the display device. The rasterizer stage calls the pixel-shader stage for the computation of these per-pixel values. Various per-pixel shading techniques such as lighting, fog, bump mapping, shadows, distortion effects, and shading are performed during this stage. In addition to these effect-based per-pixel techniques, the pixel shader is also used for implementing level-of-detail algorithms and during the process of anisotropic filtering crucial for enhancing the image quality of distant located textures.

Programs defining pixel-shader operations are called *shader programs* and can be written in any of the following languages: Assembly, Cg, HLSL, or GLSL. These programs normally take color values, the interpolated per-vertex data produced by the rasterizer stage, and some user defined variables as input, producing the final pixel values that are forwarded to the output-merger stage. Chapter 6 deals with all the issues related to writing and executing pixel shaders using both Microsoft's High Level Shader Language and NVIDIA's Cg.

4

The Output-Merger Stage   This final stage of the Direct3D 10 programmable pipeline combines both the output generated by the pixel-shader stage with depth and stencil buffer values to produce the final pixel color and shading values. The output-merger stage is directly responsible for determining the visibility of pixels based on the process of depth testing (depth testing, in addition to control of the stencil buffer, is dealt with in Chapter 11). The blending of pixel data (combining two or more pixel color values), in addition to depth and stencil testing, is controlled during this pipeline stage.

4.3.4.2 The OpenGL Processing Pipeline   OpenGL is based on a client-server model. The main idea behind this concept is to create an OpenGL program on one computer while executing it on a networked computer somewhere else. Today this model is more commonly used to represent the computer as the client and the graphics processing unit as the server. The client is thus responsible for calling the OpenGL functions with the server interpreting and executing these commands.

In addition to being based on this client-server architecture, OpenGL's architecture is also modeled as a state-based design. This design is carried over to the OpenGL Shading Language. *State-based* simply means that the application programmer has to put OpenGL into a specific state, in which it stays until the programmer explicitly alters this state. For example, we can specify a state in which OpenGL always draws a line whenever it receives two vertices as input.

OpenGL makes use of low-level commands to describe models and three-dimensional scenes. Hence every object imaginable can be constructed out of a simple set of geometric primitives. OpenGL supports both geometric primitives and raster primitives. Geometric primitives include points, lines and polygons. These primitives exists in either two- or three-dimensional space, hence they can be manipulated by several geometric operations, including rotation, scaling, and translation (moving from one point in space to another). Geometric primitives are considered the building blocks of more complex geometric objects – be it a model of the Eiffel tower, an F15 fighter jet or a soccer ball. Arrays of pixels are an example of a raster primitive. They lack geometric properties, thus cannot be manipulated in two- or three-dimensional space.

We will now discuss the primary elements of the OpenGL processing pipeline. This pipeline is mainly responsible for converting vertices into primitives, with these primitives in turn being transformed into fragments and finally pixels. Figure 4-21 shows a simplified version of this pipeline.

Evaluators and Display Lists   The evaluator processing element uses special functions known as evaluators to model curves and surfaces. These functions make use of polynomial mapping to generate vertex, color, texture, and normal coordinates. Evaluators are only used when explicitly

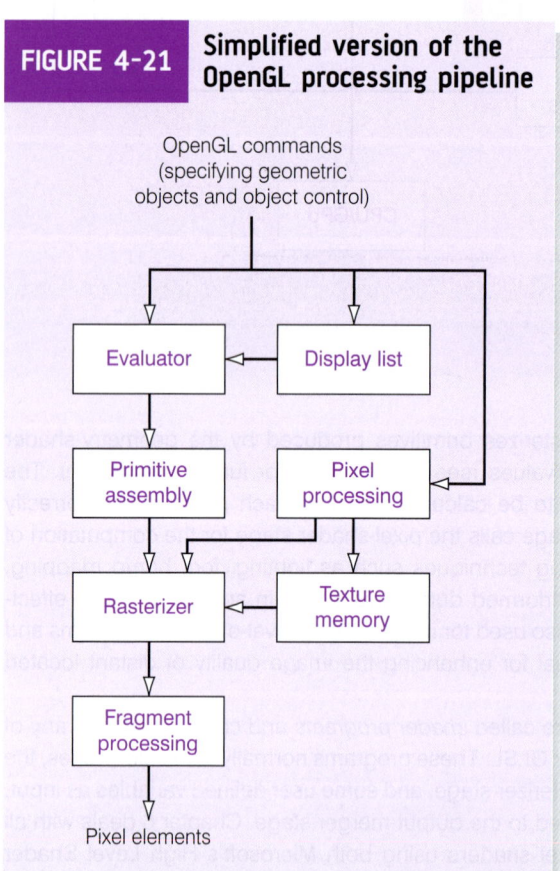

FIGURE 4-21   Simplified version of the OpenGL processing pipeline

OpenGL commands (specifying geometric objects and object control)

Evaluator ← Display list

Primitive assembly   Pixel processing

Rasterizer ← Texture memory

Fragment processing

Pixel elements

| FIGURE 4-22 | Using evaluator functions to generate a uniform B-spline surface |

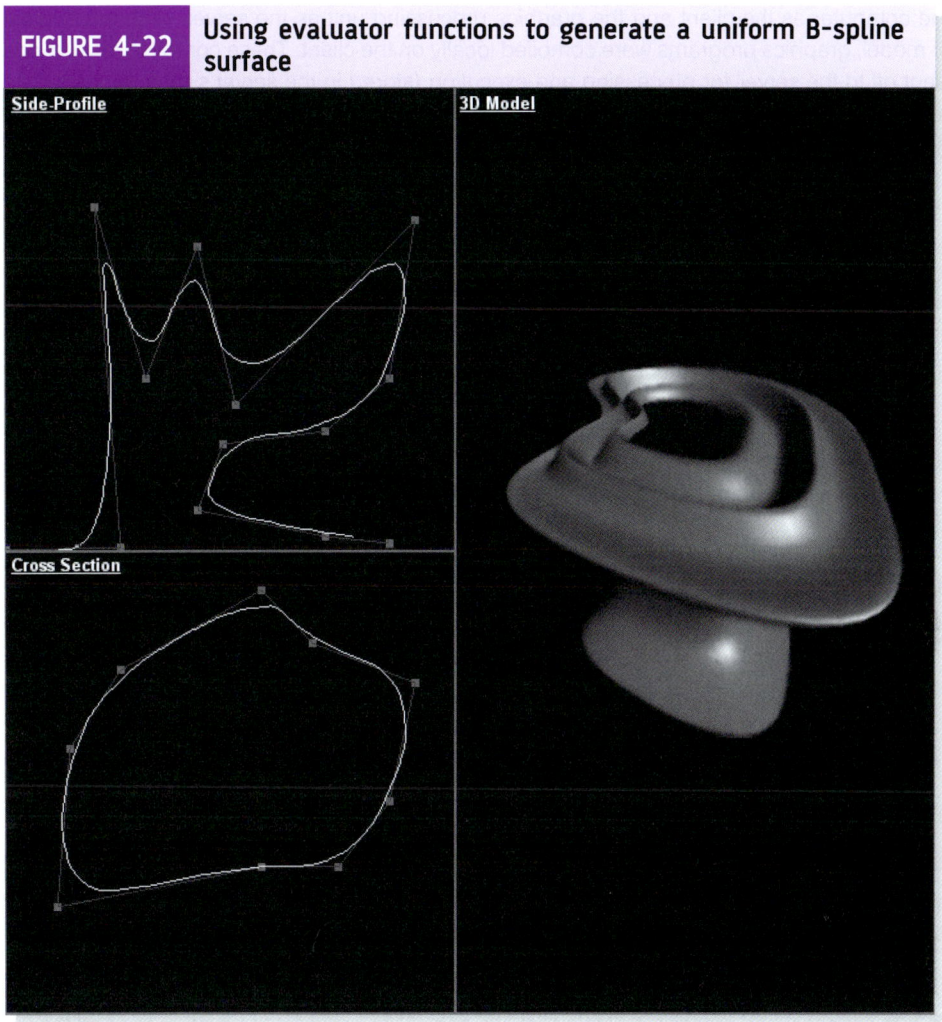

4

invoked by the application programmer. Their generated data elements are then passed on to the other stages of the OpenGL processing pipeline. Geometric transformations, per-pixel operations, lighting calculations, and the rasterization process are not affected by the output of these evaluator functions. Figure 4-22 shows the use of evaluator functions to generate a uniform B-spline surface. A *B-spline surface* is a piecewise polynomial (parametric) curved surface constructed using sweeps. Such a surface is defined using a set of Bezier surface patches. A *Bezier curve* is a polynomial curved surface where the degree of the polynomial is always one less than the number of control points – shown as squares in the side-profile and cross section of Figure 4-22. These curves always conform to the shape of the control point polygon (shown using straight lines connecting the various control points). OpenGL's evaluator functions are thus used to directly render these Bezier patches.

One problem with the use of evaluators is their mathematical intensive nature. This causes a rather big performance bottleneck that are somewhat remedied through the use of display lists. We've already touched on OpenGL's client-server model, including the basic concept of creating an OpenGL program on one computer and then executing it on a networked computer somewhere else. In the early days of computer graphics this was exactly how things were done, where nowadays it is universally common to represent the computer as the client and the graphics processing unit as the server. With the original client-server model, graphics programs were compiled locally on the client. These compiled instructions were then sent off to the server for processing and execution (stored in the server's memory as a data file called a display list).

A *display list* is a set of commands that define primitives or more complex geometric objects. Display lists offer a performance improvement in situations where the same geometric object has to be rendered more than once, hence avoiding the redefinition and reprocessing of a sequence of commands and instructions. OpenGL makes use of display lists to logically order a specific sequence of OpenGL commands for recurrent execution. In practice we'll specify a sequence of function calls in a display list. This list is then stored on the server (the GPU for example) and available for execution via a simple function call from the client. The use of display lists does have certain drawbacks, for example, storing the list on a server (GPU) requires additional memory, and there is of course the overhead of creating and transferring the display list to the server. Nonetheless, display lists provide an elegant way of composing scenes out of independently defined units. The basic routine for defining a display list is outlined below.

We start by defining the display list name and a numeric value that will be used to identify it:

```
#define YOUR_LIST 1
```

Next we create the display list using the glNewList function. This function takes two parameters, namely, the display list name and the display list compilation mode (GL_COMPILE or GL_COMPILE_AND_EXECUTE):

```
glNewList(YOUR_LIST, GL_COMPILE);

glBegin(...);
    //..OpenGL function calls
glEnd();
```

We terminate the list specification using the glEndList function:

```
glEndList();
```

There are two options when creating a display list, we can either program the system to send the list to the server but not execute it (using the GL_COMPILE flag) or we can immediately execute the list as its being constructed (using the GL_COMPILE_AND_EXECUTE flag).

The glCallList function initiates the execution of the list. To execute YOUR_LIST we simply have to call:

```
glCallList(YOUR_LIST);
```

Primitive Assembly and Rasterizer Vertices fed into the OpenGL processing pipeline must be assembled into primitives (such as lines and polygons) before clipping can take place (section 4.3.2) – this process is called the *primitive assembly* of vertices. The primitive assembly consequently outputs a series of primitives that are forwarded to the pipeline's color processing, primitive clipping, and point culling stages (Figure 4-23).

The method at which the primitive assembly operates varies depending on the primitive's type (point, line or polygon). The color values of all vertices entering the primitive assembly are set to the values specified by the *color processor*. Clipping is also performed on all line and polygon primitives during the *primitive clipping stage*. *Point culling* simply discards vertices facing away from the viewer/camera (if enabled).

| FIGURE 4-23 | **The primitive assembly stage with color processing, clipping and culling** |

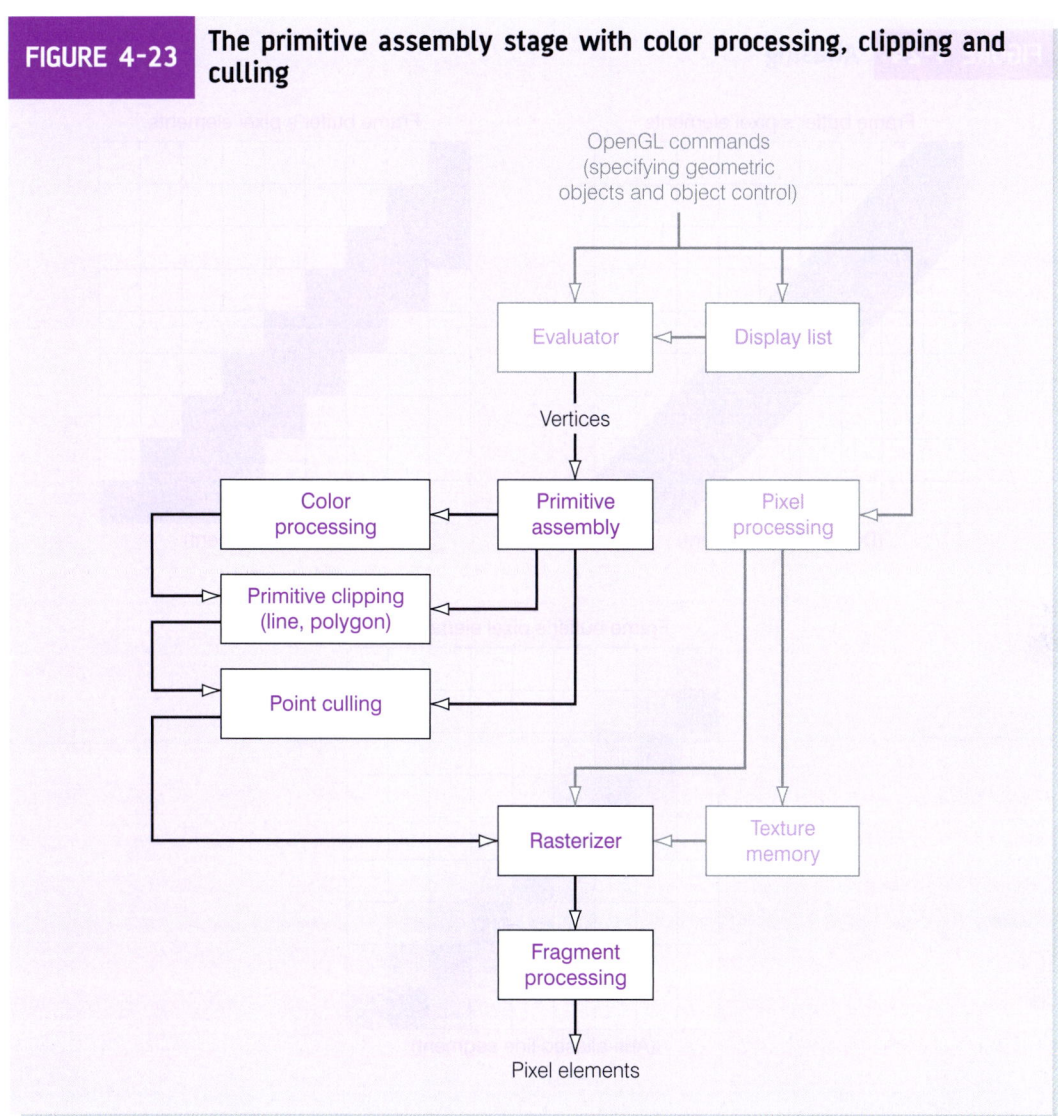

Output generated by the primitive assembly ranges from vertices and lines to polygons. These primitives are rasterized into fragments by the processing pipeline's rasterizer (section 4.3.3).

The process of rasterization is concerned with the generation of fragments. These fragments represent the spatial position and color/shading of pixels in the frame buffer. Fragment color values are obtained from color attributes or by interpolating the color values of vertices. A fragment is two-dimensional in nature and is only concerned with the *x*- and *y*-coordinates of vertices correlating to the pixels in the frame buffer that is to be filled.

One interesting operation performed during the rasterization stage, apart from the calculation of depth and color values, is to determine the angular position of grid units when anti-aliasing is enabled. A *grid unit* contains a primitive defined in terms of window coordinates and *anti-aliasing* is a technique used to reduce image distortion artefacts (jaggedness, known as *aliasing*). Artefacts, present at the edges of line segments and polygons, are the result of the rasterization process. The problem of aliasing is firstly caused by the nature for the frame buffer – specifically, the number of pixels provided

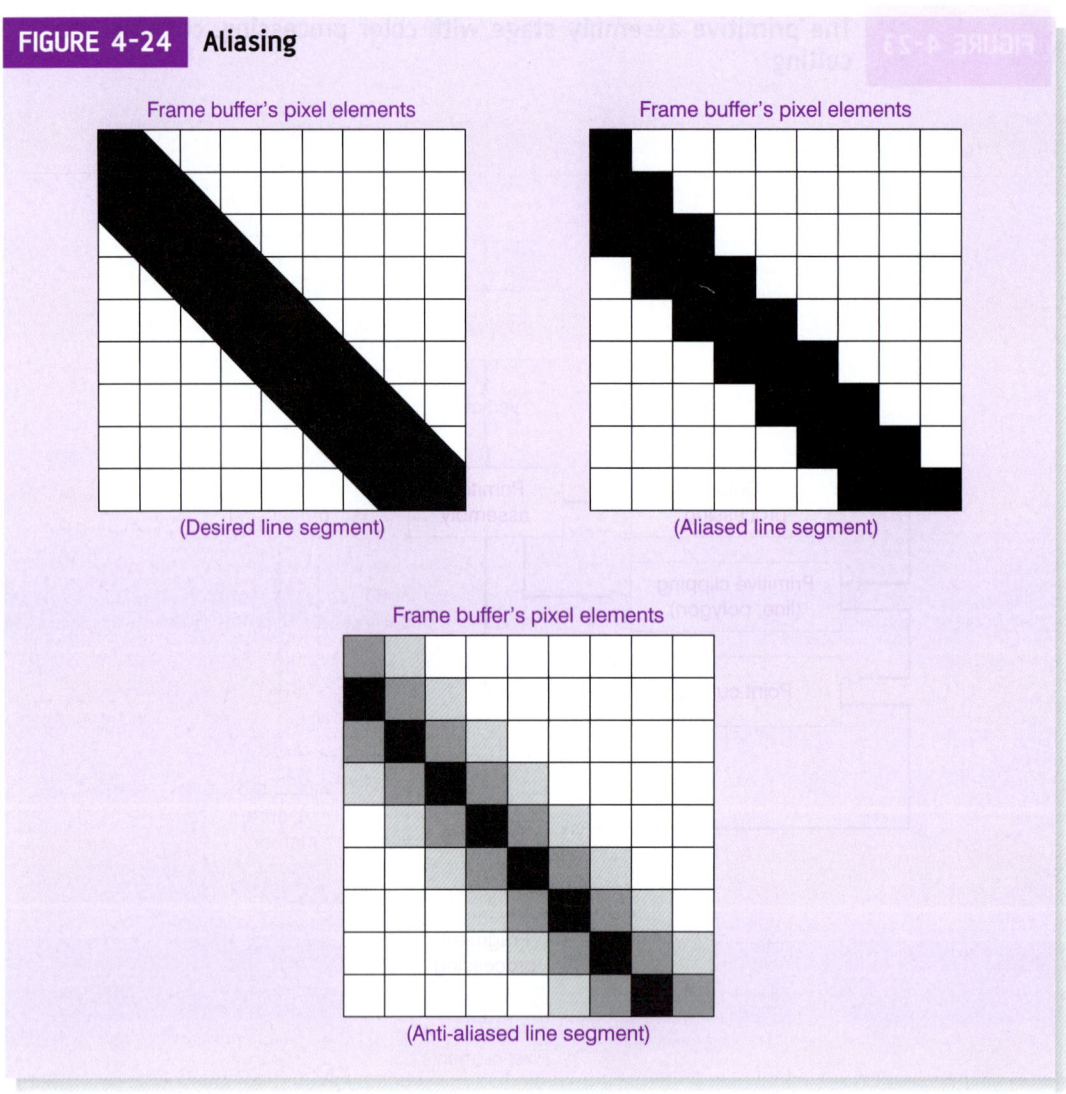

FIGURE 4-24 Aliasing

Frame buffer's pixel elements

(Desired line segment)

Frame buffer's pixel elements

(Aliased line segment)

Frame buffer's pixel elements

(Anti-aliased line segment)

by the frame buffer and the need to approximate a line segment or polygon to this limited number of pixels. The second cause is that the frame buffer's pixel grid is uniform in nature; hence, all pixels are evenly spaced from one another. A diagonal line segment will thus be represented using a fixed number of pixels which will in turn lead to some degree of jaggedness. Figure 4-24 illustrates this problem of aliasing. The frame buffer can only display the 'desired line segment' shown through the use of square pixels. This results in an aliased line segment. The only alternative is to fill pixels based on the percentage of the line crossing it, or, more specifically, to shade these pixels according to this percentage. This method of anti-aliasing is known as *area averaging*.

Pixel Processing The pixel pipeline allows for the transfer of pixel information within the graphics processing unit. Pixel pipelines, consisting of a number of processing units, are generally used for the processing of texture, pixel and geometric data. The first pixel pipeline processing unit, namely, the *unpacker*, converts the user-defined pixel data into OpenGL's internal pixel format. Next these pixels can

FIGURE 4-25 **The OpenGL pixel pipeline (all elements marked with an asterisk)**

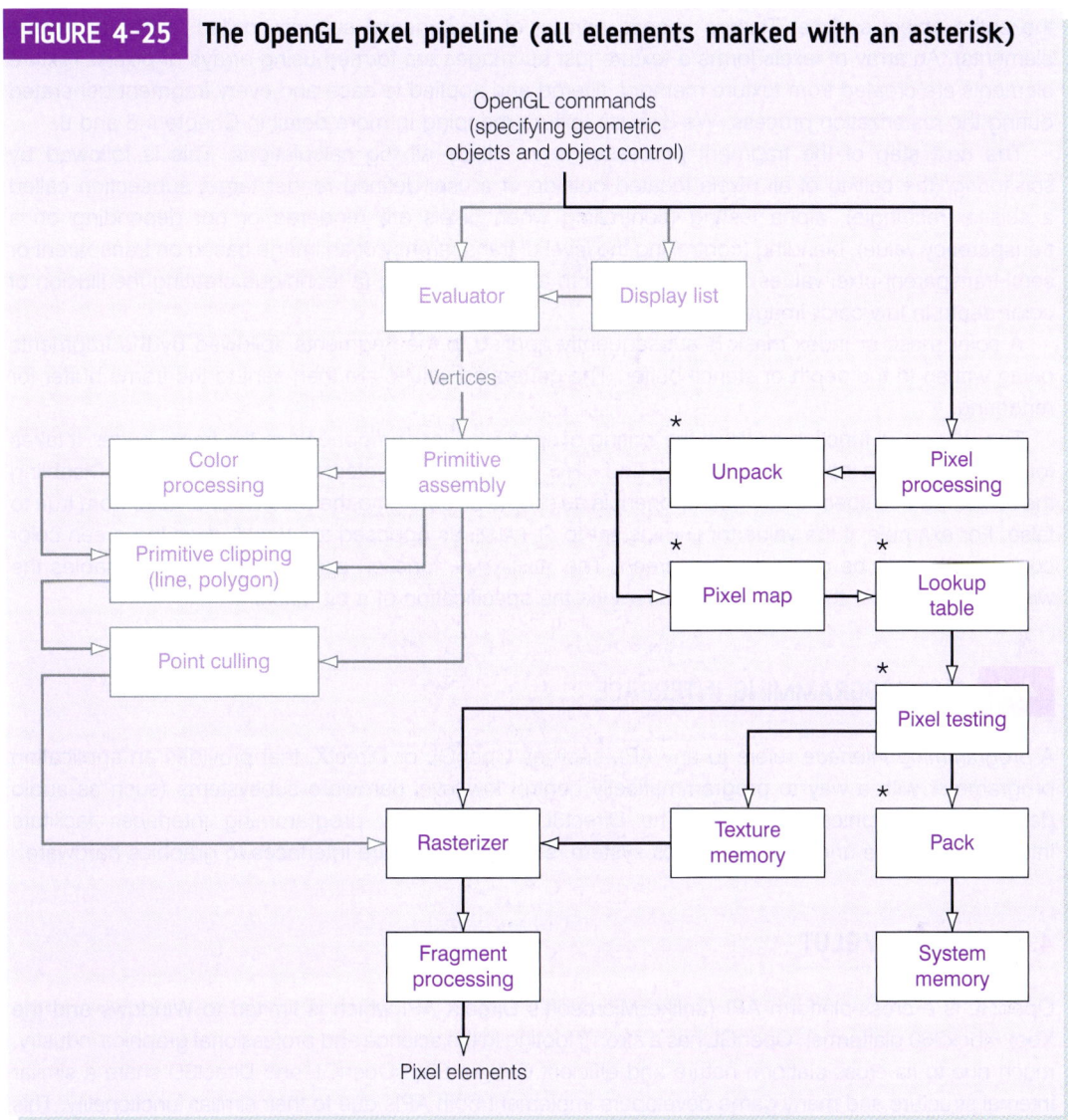

be read, scaled and processed via a *pixel map* (a three-dimensional array of bits arranged as a two-dimensional array of pixels). The *lookup table*, connected to the *pixel map processor,* modifies the logical color values of pixels into physical colors that can be displayed by the monitor. Data is now sent to the *pixel testing unit* which determines the pixels that should be written into the frame buffer. Following this, the pixel pipeline's output is sent to either the texture memory (for use in the texture mapping process) or to the rasterizer. We also have the option of sending the processed pixel data back to the system's memory for further manipulation. If we decide to do that, we must first convert the pixel data (currently in the internal OpenGL format) to a format recognisable by our application program. This is done using the *packer* processing unit. These pixel pipeline processing units are shown in Figure 4-25.

Fragment Processor *Texture mapping* is the process of fitting a texture (photograph or pattern) to a computer-generated geometric object. This texture can be either stretched or tiled to encompass the entire object surface. Texture images consist of fundamental subunits called *texels* (or texture elements). An array of texels forms a texture just as images are formed using arrays of pixels. Texture elements are created from texture memory, filtered and applied to each and every fragment generated during the rasterization process. We discuss texture mapping in more detail in Chapters 6 and 8.

The next step of the fragment processor is to initiate all fog calculations. This is followed by *scissoring* (the culling of all pixels located outside of a user-defined render target subsection called a scissor rectangle), alpha testing (controlling when pixels are rendered or not depending on a transparency value), blending (controlling the level of transparency of an image based on transparent or semi-transparent pixel values), stencil and depth testing, dithering (a technique creating the illusion of color depth in low-color images), etc.

A color mask or index mask is subsequently applied to the fragments, followed by the fragments being written to the depth or stencil buffer. The generated values are then sent to the frame buffer for rendering.

The glColorMask function controls the writing of specific color components to the frame buffer. It takes four parameters as input: red, green, blue and alpha. All these parameters are GLboolean values. Disabling the rendering of a specific color component is as simple as changing the parameter's value from true to false. For example, if the value for green is set to GL_FALSE, as opposed to GL_TRUE, then the green color component won't be drawn to the screen. The glIndexMask function similarly enables or disables the writing of bits within the color-index buffers via the specification of a bit mask.

4.4 THE PROGRAMMING INTERFACE

A *programming interface* refers to any API, such as OpenGL or DirectX, that provides an application programmer with a way to programmatically control low-level hardware subsystems (such as audio devices and graphics hardware). The Direct3D and OpenGL programming interfaces facilitate interaction with the underlying graphics system, serving as software interfaces to graphics hardware.

4.4.1 OpenGL/GLUT

OpenGL is a cross-platform API (unlike Microsoft's DirectX API which is limited to Windows and the Xbox/Xbox360 platforms). OpenGL has a strong footing in the science and professional graphics industry, much due to its cross-platform nature and efficient design. Both OpenGL and Direct3D share a similar internal structure and many game developers implement both APIs due to their similar functionality. This leaves the preference of usage open to the user, with the choice mainly influenced by the user's specific graphics hardware or platform of choice. OpenGL has a far-reaching following and loyal user base and is used throughout the CAD, science, gaming, and information visualization industries.

OpenGL is, as discussed in Chapter 2, only a specification, or a document outlining all its functions, including the actions that should be performed by each of these functions. This OpenGL specification document is then referenced by hardware vendors like NVIDIA and ATI to create OpenGL implementations in the form of libraries. These implementations are subsequently put through rigorous tests to ensure that they comply with the OpenGL specification. The OpenGL specification is periodically updated and/or revised by the OpenGL Architecture Review Board.

The OpenGL programming interface is provided as a library specifying a set of drawing functions and commands. The interoperability between the graphics program, OpenGL, and the graphics system is depicted in Figure 4-26.

We will only interact with the API when writing an OpenGL program. All of OpenGL's rendering functionality is dependent on the level of support offered by the graphics card's manufacturer and is shielded from visibility by the card's device drivers. The OpenGL API is thus responsible for hiding the intricacy of communicating with various graphics accelerators.

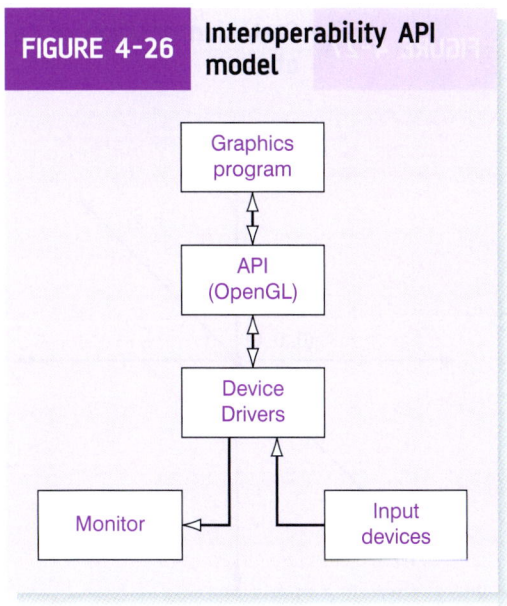

FIGURE 4-26 **Interoperability API model**

All of OpenGL's functions are preceded by the letters 'gl' (e.g. glLineWidth). Similarly, all OpenGL constants are preceded by the characters 'GL_' (e.g. GL_POINTS). OpenGL also has a series of predefined types such as GLint, GLfloat. These types are simply ANSI C implementations of common C/C++ types such as int and float.

The OpenGL library (GL) offers all the functionality needed to define any two– and three-dimensional object or environment conceivable however, additional functions for the specification of common objects are offered by the *OpenGL Utility Library* (GLU). These additional functions include the definition of frequently used objects such as spheres and cylinders. The GLU library is included with all versions of OpenGL.

When calling an OpenGL function, one has the option of specifically setting the number and type of arguments. For example, OpenGL has multiple function definitions for similar operations, such as the drawing of points using the function glVertex3f. Explicitly, this glVertex function call requires three floating point values as parameters (x-, y- and z-coordinates respectively) – specified by the 3f suffix. The meaning of OpenGL functions is always fixed but by changing the suffix of the functions we can custom tailor their usage. For example, changing the previous function to glVertex2i results in a function that draws a two-dimensional point using two integer values, namely, x- and y-coordinates. Thus, the suffix is a two-part clause indicating the number of parameters followed by the type of these parameters.

We also have the option of specifying an array pointer as a type. The glVertex function can be written as glVertex3fv, for example, to facilitate this. The key suffix in this case is the letter 'v'. The code sample below illustrates the specification of a vertex array, vertices, with the values of x, y and z set to 1.0, 1.0 and 2.0, respectively:

```
float vertices[] = {1.0, 1.0, 2.0};
glVertex3fv(vertices);
```

We can just as easily change the same glVertex function to take two integer values as input (x = 1 and y = 2):

```
int vertices[] = {1, 2};
glVertex2iv(vertices);
```

The first block of code draws a point in three-dimensional space (Figure 4-27(a)) with the second drawing one in two-dimensional space (Figure 4-27(b)).

OpenGL is only concerned with graphical elements – ranging from a small set of geometric primitives (points, lines, and polygons) to numerous atmospheric effects such as fog and lightning. OpenGL offers roughly 120 commands, more than enough for the realization of fully interactive three-dimensional applications. However, it is one thing to render an image to a screen: interaction with this image must also be possible. Our OpenGL programs will make use of the OpenGL Utility Toolkit (GLUT) to perform

4

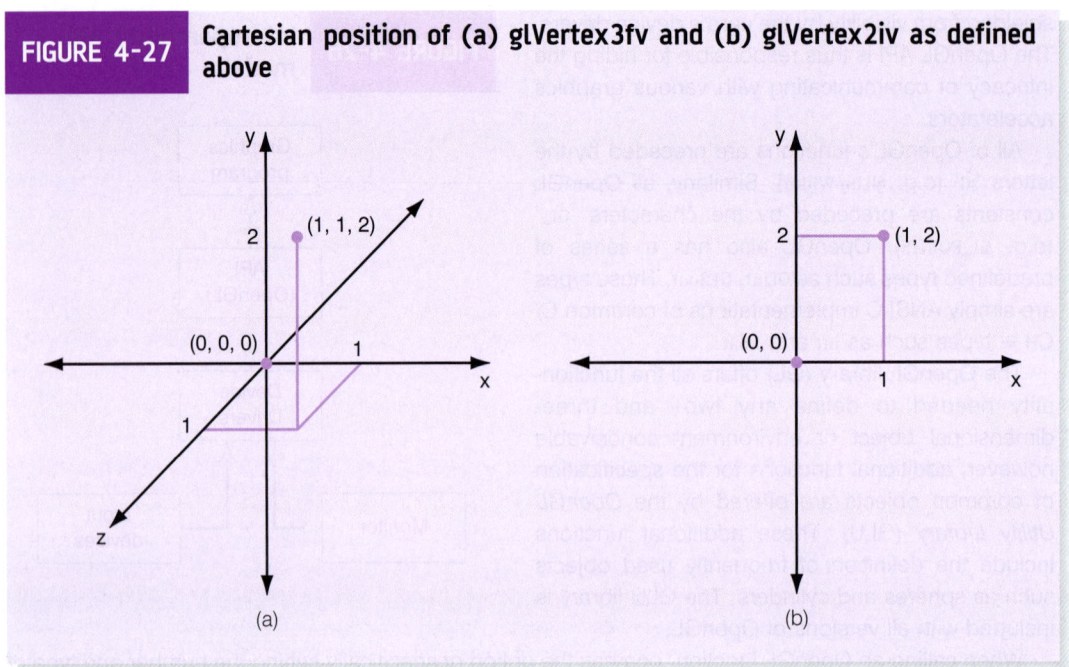

FIGURE 4-27   Cartesian position of (a) glVertex3fv and (b) glVertex2iv as defined above

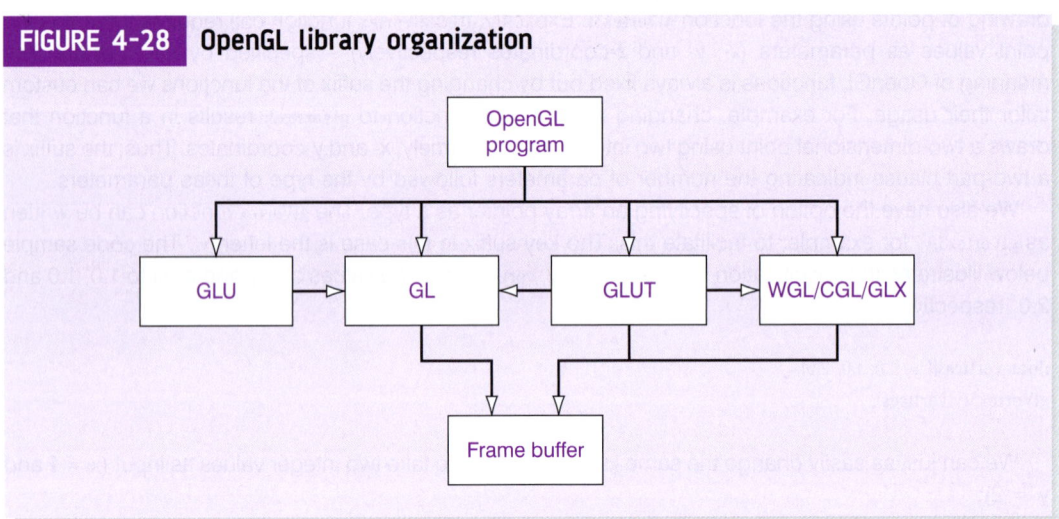

FIGURE 4-28   OpenGL library organization

this system level input control and interaction. GLUT is very powerful yet easy to use and allows both keyboard and mouse input handling. It is also used for window creation and control. GLUT is the work of Mark Kilgard and is a fully cross-platform library, just like OpenGL.

Figure 4-28 shows the organization of and communication between all the libraries needed for creating an interactive OpenGL application. The GLX library (OpenGL Extension to the X Window System) serves as the 'glue' between OpenGL and the X Window System, enabling OpenGL to communicate with the underlying graphics hardware via this Linux and UNIX display protocol. GLX is replaced by the WGL windowing system interface under Microsoft Windows. CGL, an acronym for Core OpenGL, is the MacOS X interface to OpenGL.

4.4.2 DirectX

Microsoft DirectX is, as introduced in Chapter 2, an all encompassing description for a number of game-programming centric APIs. These APIs are also used outside the game development sphere for tasks such as video editing, video playback, input control, 3D rendering and sound and music playback. DirectX is targeted at the Windows and Xbox/Xbox 360 platforms, with DirectX 10, the version covered by this book, completely exclusive to Microsoft Windows Vista. Direct3D allows for the quick rendering of high-quality three-dimensional graphics and is, just like its main competitor OpenGL, used throughout the gaming, animation, science, simulation and CAD industries.

DirectX 10 is currently the latest version of DirectX and is not backwards compatible with older versions of Microsoft Windows. This is mostly due to numerous architectural changes made to the Windows graphics subsystem, especially with the introduction of Windows Vista's Windows Display Driver Model (WDDM) shown in Figure 4-29(b).

The original *Windows Driver Model*, introduced with the release of Windows 98, was primarily based on the rapid advancements made in the field 3D graphics hardware. The *Graphics Device Interface* (GDI) used to be the only way of rendering graphics objects to a computer's monitor since the earliest versions of Windows. The GDI was extensively used, prior to Windows Vista, for the rendering of fonts and primitives (such as lines and polygons). The user system (user32.dll), based on the GDI, is responsible for the rendering of windows, popup menus, etc. Simple two-dimensional games such as Microsoft *Hearts* and *Minesweeper* also make use of the GDI.

The GDI does not make use of 3D acceleration hardware and coexisted with OpenGL and Direct3D prior to Windows Vista's release. Previous versions of Windows thus make use of the GDI to render its two-dimensional graphics. The DirectX runtime is only invoked when hardware accelerated rendering is required, for example, when running a Direct3D-utilizing game or playing back a video. Under Windows XP, this side-by-side arrangement of GDI and Direct3D is known as the *Windows XP Driver Model* – Figure 4-29(a) shows its configuration. With the release of Windows XP, GDI+ deprecated the original GDI system by offering an improved two-dimensional visual experience with advancements such as anti-aliasing, gradient shading, alpha blending, transparency, and floating-point coordinates.

Microsoft re-evaluated the interleaving of GDI and Direct3D with the design of the Windows Vista Display Driver Model. This driver model makes use of Direct3D to render the desktop using 3D acceleration while still facilitating the execution of GDI-based applications by layering them on top of Direct3D. Direct3D is thus the primary way of communicating with the video hardware.

Direct3D 10 represents a major advancement over previous Direct3D APIs, with its most noticeable feature being shader model 4.0. This updated shader model makes use of a new centralized interface,

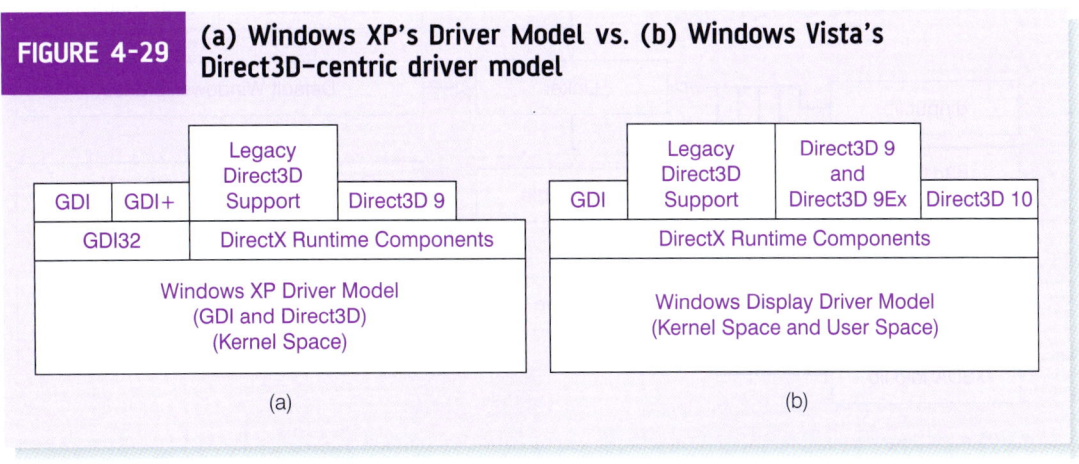

FIGURE 4-29 **(a) Windows XP's Driver Model vs. (b) Windows Vista's Direct3D-centric driver model**

offering unified access to hardware resources via a highly extended shader programming language. Direct3D 10 extends the current processing pipeline by adding the geometric shader stage to the already available pixel and vertex shader stages. This enables much more detailed real-time shader effects by allowing multiple vertices to be fed into (and out of) the pipeline at the same time. Direct3D 10 requires WDDM-compatible device drivers, Windows Vista and Direct3D 10 enabled graphics hardware (such as NVIDIA's Geforce 8 series and ATI's Radeon HD 2000 series) to run.

The DirectX 10 API consists of the following main technologies:

- *DirectX Graphics*:
  - *Direct3D 10*
    — An API for the rendering of two– and three-dimensional graphics.

- *DirectX Audio*:
  - *Cross-Platform Audio Creation Tool (XACT)*
    — A high-level audio library for the playback and recording of digital audio using the Xbox 360's compressed audio format and DirectSound on Windows.
  - *DirectSound*
    — An API for the playback and recording of digital audio.

- *DirectX Input*:
  - *XInput*
    — An API allowing input control using an Xbox 360 Controller connected to a Microsoft Windows based computer.
  - *DirectInput*:
    — An API for input control via input devices such as the mouse, keyboard, or game controllers.

These various API components are linked as libraries during the application's compilation process as depicted in Figure 4-30 (DirectX header files are included as needed in the game's source files with DirectX dlls loaded during runtime).

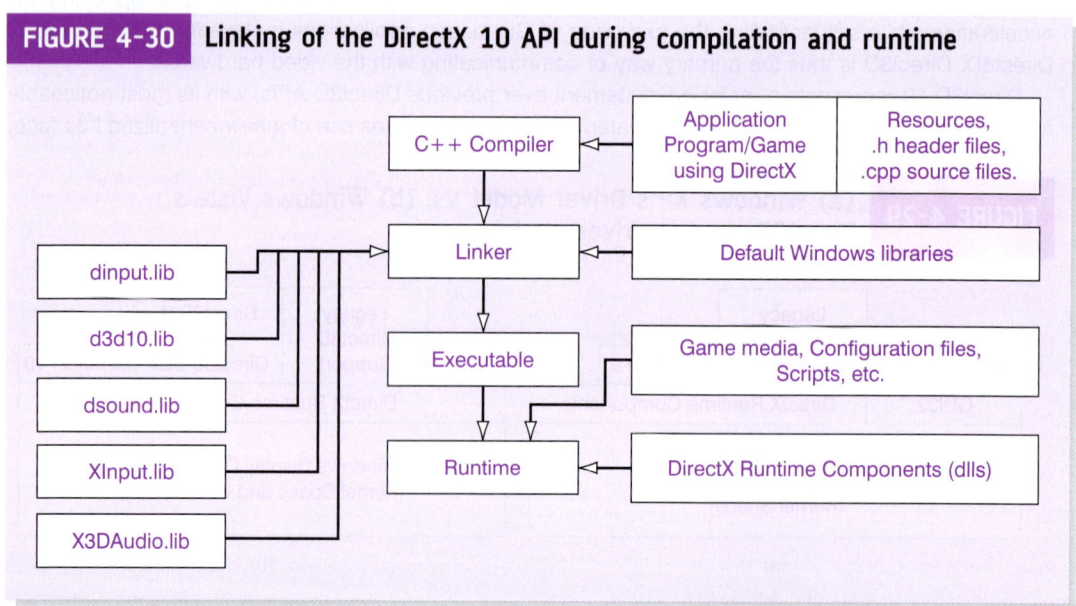

FIGURE 4-30 **Linking of the DirectX 10 API during compilation and runtime**

4.5   WINDOW CREATION AND CONTROL

4.5.1 Setting up a Window and the Main Message Loop

The very first step, before we can even start thinking about initializing any of the DirectX components, is to set up a window. Creating a window using the Win32 API is relatively painless and can be summed up in three steps, namely, registering a window class, creating a window object and handling messages to and from the window. The Win32 API is a grouping of application programming interfaces designed for use by C and C++ programs. This API provides application developers with a direct way of interacting with the underlying Windows operating system.

Registering a window class is done by first specifying the window class information contained within the WNDCLASSEX structure and then calling the RegisterClassEx function. Once a window class is registered, it can be called to create a window. There are various predefined window classes, such as buttons, list boxes, gadgets and so forth. However, most of these classes will often need to be contained within a custom application based on the developer's own windows classes. The WNDCLASSEX structure is defined as follows in the Winuser.h header file (included with windows.h):

```
typedef struct {
    UINT cbSize;
    UINT style;
    WNDPROC lpfnWndProc;
    int cbClsExtra;
    int cbWndExtra;
    HINSTANCE hInstance;
    HICON hIcon;
    HCURSOR hCursor;
    HBRUSH hbrBackground;
    LPCTSTR lpszMenuName;
    LPCTSTR lpszClassName;
    HICON hIconSm;
} WNDCLASSEX, *PWNDCLASSEX;
```

The first member, cbSize, sets the byte size of this structure with the style member setting the class style (the most frequently used style flags for window classes are listed in Table 4-3 and can be combined using the bitwise OR '|' operator). The lpfnWndProc member is a function pointer to the window's message handler, with:

- cbClsExtra specifying the number of extra bytes to allocate to the structure (for the storage of extra class information)

- cbWndExtra specifying the number of extra bytes to allocate to the window instance (for the storage of extra window information)

- hInstance being a handle to the instance of the application

- hIcon setting the main icon by taking a handle to the class icon

- hCursor being a handle specifying the window's cursor

- hbrBackground specifying either a brush or color value for setting the background color of the window

- lpszMenuName taking a pointer to a null-terminated character specifying class menu resource name

TABLE 4-3	Most common window class style flags
Style Flag	**Description**
CS_CLASSDC	Shares one device context among all windows in a class. This prevents deadlock caused when multiple threads try to use a single device context concurrently for the creation of a window.
CS_DBLCLKS	Sends a double-click message event to window's message handler (WndProc) whenever the mouse is double-clicked with its cursor located inside a window owned by the class.
CS_DROPSHADOW	Turns on the drop-shadow effect on a window.
CS_GLOBALCLASS	Sets the window class as an application global class (a public available window class registered by an .exe or .dll).
CS_HREDRAW	Specifies that a window must be redrawn whenever it is moved or horizontally resized.
CS_NOCLOSE	Disables the window menu's 'Close' option.
CS_OWNDC	Allocates a unique device context to each new window created.
CS_VREDRAW	Specifies that a window must be redrawn whenever it is moved or vertically resized.

- lpszClassName specifying the name of the class

- hIconSm specifying the small icon used by the class (if it is NULL, then the value stored in the hIcon member is used).

We create the window using the AdjustWindowRect and CreateWindow functions. The ShowWindow function is called to make the window visible. The AdjustWindowRect function sets the window rectangle's size by taking a pointer to a RECT structure (rectangle in our case specifying the top left (0, 0) and bottom right corners of the window (400, 300)), and the window's style (we will always use the WS_OVERLAPPEDWINDOW style – this window style creates an overlapped window (WS_OVERLAPPED) with a sizing border (WS_THICKFRAME), title bar (WS_CAPTION), a window menu on this title bar (WS_SYSMENU), and a maximize (WS_MAXIMIZEBOX) and minimize box (WS_MINIMIZEBOX). The final parameter of the AdjustWindowRect function takes a Boolean value specifying whether the window has a menu.

The CreateWindow function is declared as follows in the winuser.h header file (included with windows.h):

```
HWND CreateWindow(LPCTSTR lpClassName,
    LPCTSTR lpWindowName,
    DWORD dwStyle,
    int x,
    int y,
    int nWidth,
    int nHeight,
    HWND hWndParent,
    HMENU hMenu,
    HINSTANCE hInstance,
    LPVOID lpParam
);
```

Its first parameter, lpClassName, is a pointer to a null-terminated string (the registered class name) as declared in WNDCLASSEX's lpszClassName member with the second parameter, lpWindowName, being a pointer to a null-terminated string specifying the window name ('Setting up a Window' in our example). The dwStyle parameter specifies the extended window style (we commonly set it to WS_OVERLAPPED-WINDOW, but can vary depending on the desired style). The x, y, nWidth and nHeight parameters control the window's spawning coordinates (initial *x*-coordinate, *y*-coordinate, width and height of the window respectively). The hWndParent parameter takes a handle to the parent/owner window spawning the current window (if applicable, else NULL), hMenu takes a handle to the already defined menu or child-window if applicable (NULL for our purpose). The second last parameter, hInstance, takes a handle to an application instance as value; however, this value is ignored from Windows NT 4 onwards and only provided for backwards compatibility (Windows 95/98/Me). The final parameter, lpParam, takes a pointer to the window-creation data; however, this can always be set to NULL.

Before registering the class or creating the window, we start by including the standard Windows header:

```
#include <windows.h>
```

Next we declare two global variables, g_hInstance and g_hWindow, which will be used during the window creation process:

```
/*
================
Global Variables
================
*/
HINSTANCE    g_hInstance = NULL;
HWND         g_hWindow = NULL;
```

We can now register and create the window class (done inside the InitWindow member function):

```
/*
================
InitWindow
-registers the window class and creates the window
-HRESULT, the result handle, is 0 for a successful return from the function and non-zero in the event of an error
================
*/
HRESULT InitWindow(HINSTANCE hInstance, int nCmdShow)
{
    /* register the window class */
    ///////////////////////////////
    WNDCLASSEX wndcex;
    wndcex.cbSize         = sizeof(WNDCLASSEX);
    wndcex.style          = CS_HREDRAW | CS_VREDRAW;
    wndcex.lpfnWndProc    = WndProc;
    wndcex.cbClsExtra     = 0;
    wndcex.cbWndExtra     = 0;
    wndcex.hInstance      = hInstance;
    wndcex.hIcon          = LoadIcon(hInstance,
                                (LPCTSTR) IDI_PROG4_5_1);
```

4

4

```
wndcex.hCursor           = LoadCursor(NULL, IDC_ARROW);
wndcex.hbrBackground     = (HBRUSH)(1);
wndcex.lpszMenuName      = NULL;
wndcex.lpszClassName     = L"WindowClass";
wndcex.hIconSm           = LoadIcon(wndcex.hInstance,
                                (LPCTSTR) IDI_PROG4_5_1);

//if the window class cannot be registered, return an error
if(!RegisterClassEx(&wndcex))
    return E_FAIL;

/* create the window */
////////////////////////////////

g_hInstance = hInstance;
//create a GDI+ rectangle with x = 0, y = 0, width = 400, //and height = 300
RECT rectangle = {0, 0, 400, 300};

AdjustWindowRect(&rectangle, WS_OVERLAPPEDWINDOW, FALSE);

g_hWindow = CreateWindow(
                L"WindowClass",
                L"Setting up a Window",
                WS_OVERLAPPEDWINDOW,
                CW_USEDEFAULT,
                CW_USEDEFAULT,
                rectangle.right - rectangle.left,
                rectangle.bottom - rectangle.top,
                NULL, NULL, hInstance, NULL);

//return a standard error if the window creation failed
if(!g_hWindow)
    return E_FAIL;

//make the window visible
ShowWindow(g_hWindow, nCmdShow);

//the function has been successful
return S_OK;
}
```

The next step is to create a function, WndProc, for the handling of all messages sent to and from the window. This function, known as an *event handler,* is called by Windows whenever an event occurs that can be handled by our WndProc function. The number of events that can be handled by this callback function depends on the implementation. All the events not handled are simply passed on to Windows. This WndProc function receives messages from the main event loop whenever an event occurs. These events are either generated by the user or Windows and are read into the main event queue, with all messages related to our window being processed by the WndProc function given below (Table 4-4 lists a few message IDs).

The core of the function below is a switch statement that executes some code based on the message ID, msg, of the event generated. The WndProc function given below is only interested in WM_PAINT and WM_DESTROY messages. The WM_PAINT message is sent whenever the window needs to be redrawn

TABLE 4-4	Common message IDs
Message ID	**Description**
WM_ACTIVATE	Message generated the moment a window is activated/brought into focus.
WM_CLOSE	Message generated the moment a window is closed.
WM_CREATE	Message generated when a window is created.
WM_DESTROY	Message generated when a window is about to be destroyed.
WM_KEYDOWN	Message generated when a keyboard key is pressed.
WM_KEYUP	Message generated when a keyboard key is released.
WM_MOUSEMOVE	Message generated when a mouse is moved.
WM_MOVE	Message generated when a window is moved.
WM_PAINT	Message generated when a window needs to be redrawn.
WM_QUIT	Message generated when an application is terminating.
WM_SIZE	Message generated when a window is resized.
WM_TIMER	Message generated whenever a timer event takes place.
WM_USER	Message event allowing the user to send a message.

(when, for example, the window has been moved or resized). The WM_DESTROY message is sent to the window when the window is about to be destroyed (when, for example, the user clicks the 'Close' button). The processing of WM_PAINT calls the BeginPaint, EndPaint function pair. BeginPaint prepares the window specified by its first parameter (a handle to the window) for painting. The second parameter of this function is an address of a PAINTSTRUCT structure that is used for specifying the rectangle to redraw. The PAINTSTRUCT structure is declared as follows in the winuser.h header file:

```
typedef struct tagPAINTSTRUCT {
  HDC  hdc;
  BOOL fErase;
  RECT rcPaint;
  BOOL fRestore;
  BOOL fIncUpdate;
  BYTE rgbReserved[32];
} PAINTSTRUCT, *PPAINTSTRUCT;
```

The first parameter, hdc, is a handle to the display device context used for painting. The fErase parameter is a Boolean value controlling whether the background of the window should be erased before it is repainted, rcPaint is RECT structure with the final three parameters reserved for internal system use.

To close the BeginPaint method, we need to call an EndPaint function. This function signals the end of painting in the specified window by taking two parameters: a handle to the repainted window and a pointer to PAINTSTRUCT structure containing the painting information.

The WM_DESTROY message calls the PostQuitMessage function. This function posts a WM_QUIT, thus signaling the application to terminate. Our WndProc function calls the DefWindowProc function for all other event messages sent to it. This DefWindowProc function simply sends all other unprocessed messages to the default window procedure for default processing. Our example implements the `WndProc` function as follows:

```
/*
================
WndProc
-callback function called whenever an event occurs
 and message is received by the application
-LRESULT stores the result of a message processing operation
-CALLBACK is simply a calling convention for callback
 functions
-WndProc takes four parameters: a handle to the window
 generating the event (hWindow) which is only important when
we have to handle multiple windows with the same window
 class, the message id (msg) and two message parameters
 (wParam and lParam) defining the message
================
*/
LRESULT CALLBACK WndProc(HWND hWindow, UINT msg, WPARAM
                         wParam, LPARAM lParam)
{
    HDC devicecontext;
    PAINTSTRUCT paintstructure;

    switch(msg)
    {
        case WM_PAINT:
            devicecontext = BeginPaint(hWindow,
                                       &paintstructure);
            EndPaint(hWindow, &paintstructure);
            break;

        case WM_DESTROY:
            PostQuitMessage(0);
            break;

        default:
            return DefWindowProc(hWindow, msg, wParam,
                                 lParam);
    }
    return 0;
}
```

The only function still required is one serving as entry point to the application. This function should also, apart from initializing all the variables, execute the message processing loop. The `WinMain` function serves as such an initial entry point for Win32-based applications. The `WINAPI` declarator is a calling convention for all `WinMain` functions. This macro simply forces parameter passing from left to right as opposed to the normal right-to-left order. The `WinMain` function takes four parameters:

1 `hInstance`, which is the application's instance handle generated by Windows (instances allow for the tracking of resources, in `WinMain`'s case this instance is used to track the application)

2 hPrevInstance, which allows for the tracking of a previous application instance (hence the instance of the application that launched the current one – deprecated)

3 lpCmdLine, a null-terminated string allowing the pass of parameters to the program (for example, executing the application as follows: APP.EXE parameter, where 'parameter' is passed as a string and stored in lpCmdLine)

4 nCmdShow, an integer value controlling the manner in which the application launches (it is passed to the application during startup and is in turn sent to the ShowWindow function).

Table 4-5 gives the list of parameters that nCmdShow can be set to.

The WinMain function starts by calling the InitWindow function, thus registering the window class and creating the window. It returns the value zero if the window creation fails. Following this it enters the main message loop by declaring an empty MSG structure, msg. This structure, containing message information from the message queue, sets six members and is declared as follows in the winuser.h header file:

```
typedef struct tagMSG{
    HWND hwnd;
    UINT message;
    WPARAM wParam;
    LPARAM lParam;
    DWORD time;
    POINT pt;
} MSG, *PMSG;
```

Its first member, hwnd, is a handle to the window receiving the message. The second member, message, contains the generated message's identifier, with the next two members, wParam and lParam,

TABLE 4-5	Parameters controlling how the window should be displayed

Parameter	Description
SW_HIDE	Hides the window and focuses another one.
SW_MAXIMIZE	Maximizes the window.
SW_MINIMIZE	Minimizes the window and focuses the second topmost window.
SW_RESTORE	Restores the minimized window.
SW_SHOW	Activates the window and displays it.
SW_SHOWMAXIMIZED	Activates the window and displays it as a maximized window.
SW_SHOWMINIMIZED	Activates the window and displays it as a minimized window.
SW_SHOWMINNOACTIVE	Displays the window as a minimized window without activating it.
SW_SHOWNA	Displays the window without activating it.
SW_SHOWNOACTIVATE	Displays the window using its most recent size and position without activating it.
SW_SHOWNORMAL	Activates the window and displays it. Also restores a minimized or maximized window to its original position.

conveying additional information about the message. The final two members, time and pt, specifies the time and mouse cursor's screen position when the message was generated, respectively.

We now set our WinMain function to listen for any event messages by creating the main event loop. This event loop consists of a while loop that executes as long as the value returned by GetMessage is not equal to zero. The GetMessage function simply fetches the next message from the event queue for processing. This function takes four parameters, the first being the address of the structure, msg, containing the message. The final three parameters are not really important to us and are set to NULL and 0 – for interest's sake, the second parameter is simply a handle to the window whose messages are to be retrieved with the final two parameters taking integer values of the lowest and highest message values to retrieve, respectively.

The next function called, TranslateMessage, generates character messages by translating virtual-key messages. *Virtual-key messages* are generated by the system whenever a key is pressed by the user. These virtual-key messages are simple keycodes identifying the pressed key, but not the key's character value – the TranslateMessage function is thus invoked to translate these virtual-key messages into character values. The DispatchMessage function dispatches the event message to the WndProc function for processing:

```
int WINAPI wWinMain(HINSTANCE hInstance,
                    HINSTANCE hPrevInstance, LPWSTR lpCmdLine,
                    int nCmdShow)
{
    if(FAILED(InitWindow(hInstance, nCmdShow)))
        return 0;

    /* main message loop */
    ///////////////////////////////
    MSG msg = {0};

    while(GetMessage(&msg, NULL, 0, 0))
    {
        TranslateMessage(&msg);
        DispatchMessage(&msg);
    }
    return (int) msg.wParam;
}
```

The above described event loop message processing is illustrated in Figure 4-31.

4.5.2 Initializing Direct3D/OpenGL and Generating Output

The next step is to extend our Win32 program skeleton into a Direct3D 10 application. We start by defining a *swap chain* (used for displaying the contents of a buffer, either the front or back buffer, as rendered to by a device object) and a *device object* (for initializing resources and drawing onto a buffer). The front buffer is the buffer that stores the current displayed image with the back buffer being rendered to by the device object. The contents of a back buffer are set to become that of the front buffer – a process called *double buffering*.

When displaying the contents of the frame buffer, it has to happen at a rate sufficiently fast to prevent the viewer noticing the clearing and redrawing of the scene. When changing or refreshing the frame buffer's contents we generally notice graphic garbage, known as *artifacts*, on the screen. One other

| FIGURE 4-31 | **Event loop message processing** |

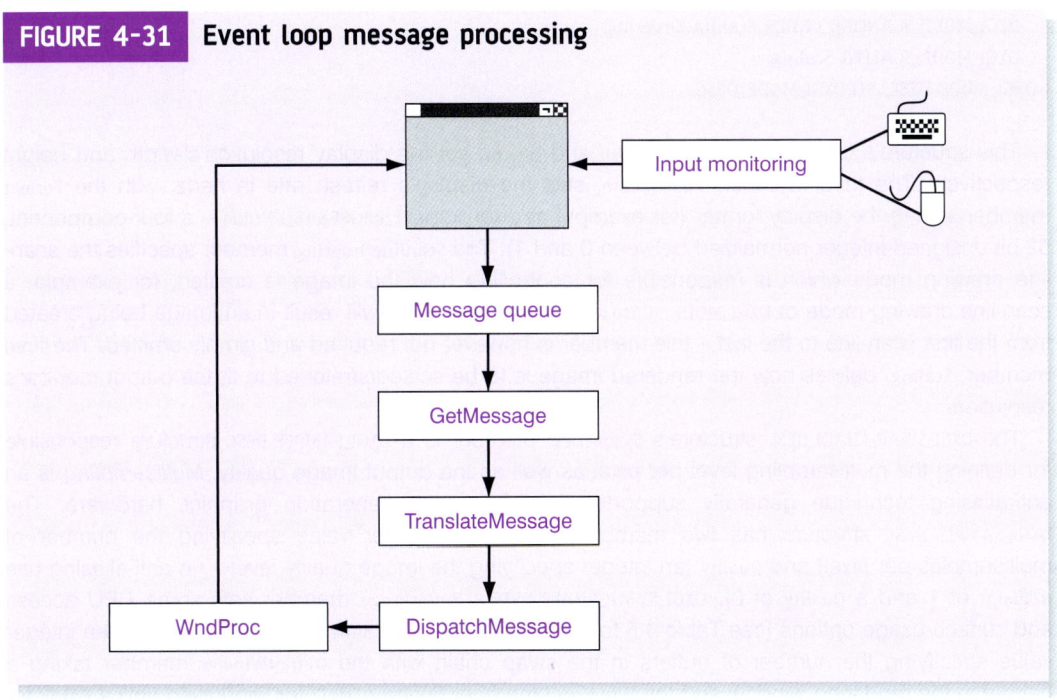

4

problem with this frame buffer refresh is that of a flickering or flashing image. *Double buffering* solves these problems by providing two buffers for display and redraw. The back buffer is used for redrawing the image while the front buffer's concerned with displaying the redrawn image. Thus, we swap these buffers throughout the execution of the program to give the perception of a still image.

A swap chain is created using the DXGI_SWAP_CHAIN_DESC structure. This structure, describing a swap chain, sets eight members and is declared as follows in the DXGI.h header file:

```
typedef struct DXGI_SWAP_CHAIN_DESC {
    DXGI_MODE_DESC BufferDesc;
    DXGI_SAMPLE_DESC SampleDesc;
    DXGI_USAGE BufferUsage;
    UINT BufferCount;
    HWND OutputWindow;
    BOOL Windowed;
    DXGI_SWAP_EFFECT SwapEffect;
    UINT Flags;
} DXGI_SWAP_CHAIN_DESC;
```

The BufferDesc member is a DXGI_MODE_DESC structure describing the display mode. It sets six members and is defined in the DXGI.h header file as follows:

```
typedef struct DXGI_MODE_DESC {
    UINT Width;
    UINT Height;
    DXGI_RATIONAL RefreshRate;
    DXGI_FORMAT Format;
```

DXGI_MODE_SCANLINE_ORDER ScanlineOrdering;
DXGI_MODE_SCALING Scaling;
} DXGI_MODE_DESC, *LPDXGI_MODE_DESC;

This structure's first two members, Width and Height, set the display resolution's width and height respectively. The third member, RefreshRate, sets the display's refresh rate in hertz, with the Format member setting the display format (for example as DXGI_FORMAT_R8G8B8A8_UNORM – a four-component, 32-bit unsigned-integer normalized between 0 and 1). The ScanlineOrdering member specifies the scan-line drawing mode which is responsible for controlling how the image is created, for example, a scan-line drawing mode of DXGI_MODE_SCANLINE_ORDER_PROGRESSIVE will result in an image being created from the first scan-line to the last – this member is however not required and simply omitted. The final member, Scaling, defines how the rendered image is to be scaled/stretched to fit the output monitor's resolution.

The DXGI_SWAP_CHAIN_DESC structure's SampleDesc member is a DXGI_SAMPLE_DESC structure responsible for defining the multisampling level per pixel as well as the output image quality. *Multisampling* is an anti-aliasing technique generally supported by all current generation graphics hardware. The DXGI_SAMPLE_DESC structure has two members, Count (an integer value specifying the number of multisamples per pixel) and Quality (an integer specifying the image quality level – no anti-aliasing has a Count of 1 and a Quality of 0). DXGI_SWAP_CHAIN_DESC's BufferUsage member sets some CPU access and surface usage options (see Table 4-6 for possible flags). The BufferCount member takes an integer value specifying the number of buffers in the swap chain with the OutputWindow member taking a handle to the rendering window and the Windowed member taking a TRUE for windowed and a FALSE for full-screen output. The second last member, SwapEffect, deals with the behaviour of the swap chain based on the constant specified (DXGI_SWAP_EFFECT_DISCARD leaving the behaviour of the swap chain to the display driver and DXGI_SWAP_EFFECT_SEQUENTIAL allowing multiple back buffers). The Flags member specifies whether an image is to be rotated when projected onto the monitor (using the DXGI_SWAP_CHAIN_FLAG_NONPREROTATED flag to disable automatic rotation) and whether to use the desktop resolution or to match the application window when switching to full-screen mode (using the DXGI_SWAP_CHAIN_FLAG_ALLOW_MODE_SWITCH flag to switch the monitor resolution to match the application window's dimensions).

We can now create the render target view (a Direct3D 10 resource that is bound to the graphics pipeline at some specific stage, with the specific stage dependent on the type of the resource view – for example, a render target view which we can render to, a stencil buffer for the masking of pixels, or a texture resource, etc). Following this, the scene's viewport can be initialized and rendered to. For now

TABLE 4-6	Surface and resource creation options
Flags	**Description**
DXGI_USAGE_BACK_BUFFER	Use the resource/surface as the back buffer.
DXGI_USAGE_READ_ONLY	Flag the resource/surface as read-only.
DXGI_USAGE_RENDER_TARGET_OUTPUT	Use the resource/surface as the output device being rendered to (the render target).
DXGI_USAGE_SHADER_INPUT	Use the resource/surface as a shader input.
DXGI_USAGE_SHARED	Share the resource/surface.

we can simply consider a viewport as a sub-window containing our rendered scene; please refer to Chapter 7 for a detailed explanation.

The back buffer of the swap chain is specified as a render target. Direct3D 10 can now render to it. However, before this can be done, we first have to create a render target view. We start by creating an ID3D10Texture2D resource that will serve as a two-dimensional texture surface for the manipulation of the back buffer:

```
ID3D10Texture2D *pBackBufferSurface;
```

Next we obtain the back-buffer object using the GetBuffer IDXGISwapChain interface. GetBuffer takes three parameters. The first is an integer value specifying the buffer to access, the second is the interface type that will be used to manipulate the back buffer (ID3D10Texture2D in our case) and the third is a pointer to the back-buffer interface (pBackBufferSurface).

```
hresult_ = g_pdxl0SwapChain->
          GetBuffer(0, __uuidof(ID3D10Texture2D),
          (LPVOID*)&pBackBufferSurface);
```

If GetBuffer fails, the function exits with the returned HRESULT value:

```
if(FAILED(hresult_))
          return hresult_;
```

We can now create the render target view using CreateRenderTargetView ID3D10Device interface. Before we do this, however, we first have to declare ID3D10RenderTargetView interface responsible for controlling the output of data during rendering:

```
ID3D10RenderTargetView* g_pd3d10RenderTargetView = NULL;
```

This CreateRenderTargetView function takes three parameters: a pointer to the back buffer resource containing the resource data (pBackBufferSurface), a pointer to the D3D10_RENDER_TARGET_VIEW_DESC structure further describing the render target view (set to the default via 'NULL' for now), and the address of a pointer to an ID3D10RenderTargetView object:

```
hresult_ = g_id3dDevice ->
               CreateRenderTargetView(pBackBufferSurface, NULL,
                              &g_pd3d10RenderTargetView);
```

With the render target view created, we can release the resource:

```
pBackBufferSurface->Release();
```

We once again have to check the return value of the CreateRenderTargetView function:

```
if(FAILED(hresult_))
     return hresult_;
```

Next we call the OMSetRenderTargets ID3D10Device interface method to bind the render target view to the pipeline so that the pipeline's output can be written onto the back buffer. The OMSetRenderTargets interface method takes three parameters: the number of render targets to bind to the pipeline, a pointer to the ID3D10RenderTargetView interface and a pointer to the depth stencil view (set to 'NULL' for now):

```
g_id3dDevice -> OMSetRenderTargets(
                    1, &g_pd3d10RenderTargetView, NULL);
```

Following this, an interface to the hardware device and swap chain has to be specified. This interface is created using the D3D10CreateDeviceAndSwapChain function, defined as follows in the D3D10.h header file:

```
HRESULT D3D10CreateDeviceAndSwapChain(
        IDXGIAdapter *pAdapter,
        D3D10_DRIVER_TYPE DriverType,
        HMODULE Software,
        UINT Flags,
        UINT SDKVersion,
        DXGI_SWAP_CHAIN_DESC *pSwapChainDesc,
        IDXGISwapChain **ppSwapChain,
        ID3D10Device **ppDevice
);
```

The first parameter, pAdapter (set to 'NULL' for our purpose), is an IDXGIAdapter interface used for getting graphics hardware specific device information (for example, getting a description of the video adaptor or verifying support for a certain feature). The DriverType parameter is an enumerated type that specifies the device driver's type. For example, setting this parameter to D3D10_DRIVER_TYPE_HARDWARE allows direct access to the system's video hardware (using the ID3D10Device interface). Other options include:

■ D3D10_DRIVER_TYPE_REFERENCE (creates a software driver emulating a hardware interface)

■ D3D10_DRIVER_TYPE_NULL (creates a device that can be manipulated; however, a null device cannot render a scene)

■ D3D10_DRIVER_TYPE_SOFTWARE (reserved for future use).

Our example program declares the driver types as D3D10_DRIVER_TYPE_HARDWARE:

```
D3D10_DRIVER_TYPE g_d3d10driverType = D3D10_DRIVER_TYPE_HARDWARE;
```

The third parameter, Software, takes a handle to the .dll module serving as implementation for a software rasterizer (set to 'NULL' since we're using hardware acceleration). This parameter is followed by an integer flag, Flags, controlling the creation of the device. This parameter can be set to any of the following constants:

■ D3D10_CREATE_DEVICE_SINGLETHREADED (to force single threaded calls to the Direct3D API)

■ D3D10_CREATE_DEVICE_DEBUG (to get additional debug information from Direct3D)

■ D3D10_CREATE_DEVICE_SWITCH_TO_REF (to create both a software and hardware device concurrently to ease debugging)

■ D3D10_CREATE_DEVICE_PREVENT_INTERNAL_THREADING_OPTIMIZATIONS (reserved for future use).

The next parameter, SDKVersion, simply specifies the version of the DirectX software development kit – we always set this parameter to D3D_SDK_VERSION. Next the pSwapChainDesc parameter allows us to specify the swap chain description as specified using the DXGI_SWAP_CHAIN_DESC structure with the ppSwapChain parameter taking a pointer to the IDXGISwapChain interface (responsible for implementing a surface for the storage of rendered data), declared as follows:

```
IDXGISwapChain* g_pdxl0SwapChain = NULL;
```

The final parameter of this D3D10CreateDeviceAndSwapChain function takes the address of a pointer to an ID3D10Device interface (g_id3dDevice) – this interface is responsible for the creation of resources and shaders, the drawing of primitives and the manipulation of system-level values.

We can now almost render some output to the screen; all that remains is the initialization of the viewport using the D3D10_VIEWPORT structure. This structure, including its implementation and binding to the rasterization stage of the pipeline using the RSSetViewports ID3D10Device method, is examined in section 7.4.4.

Reusing the functions from the previous Win32 example, we start by defining an InitD3D10 function (given below) for the creation of a Direct3D 10 device, swap chain and viewport:

```
/*
===============---===
InitD3D10
-create a Direct3D 10 device and swap chain
-HRESULT, the result handle, is 0 for a successful
 return from the function and non-zero in the event of an error
================
*/
HRESULT InitD3D10()
{
    //structure for storing the client area coordinates
    RECT rectangle;
    /* get the coordinates of g_hWindow's client area and
       write them to the RECT structure */
    GetClientRect(g_hWindow, &rectangle);

    /* setup the Direct3D 10 device */
    /////////////////////////////////
    DXGI_SWAP_CHAIN_DESC swapchaindesc;

    //fill the memory block with zeros
    SecureZeroMemory(&swapchaindesc, sizeof(swapchaindesc));

    swapchaindesc.BufferCount = 1;
    swapchaindesc.BufferUsage = DXGI_USAGE_RENDER_TARGET_OUTPUT;
    swapchaindesc.BufferDesc.RefreshRate.Numerator = 60;
    swapchaindesc.BufferDesc.RefreshRate.Denominator = 1;
    swapchaindesc.BufferDesc.Width = rectangle_width;
    swapchaindesc.BufferDesc.Height = rectangle_height;
    swapchaindesc.BufferDesc.Format =DXGI_FORMAT_R8G8B8A8_UNORM;
    swapchaindesc.SampleDesc.Count = 1;
    swapchaindesc.SampleDesc.Quality = 0;
    swapchaindesc.OutputWindow = g_hWindow;
    swapchaindesc.Windowed = TRUE;
```

4

```
                    // create an interface to the hardware device & swap chain
                    HRESULT hresult_ = D3D10CreateDeviceAndSwapChain(
                                             NULL, g_d3d10driverType, NULL,
                                             0, D3D10_SDK_VERSION, &swapchaindesc,
                                             &g_pdxl0SwapChain, &g_id3dDevice);

                    if(FAILED(hresult_))
                      return hresult_;

                    /* create the render target */
                    ////////////////////////////////
                    ID3D10Texture2D *pBackBufferSurface;

                    hresult_ = g_pdxl0SwapChain->
                                 GetBuffer(0, __uuidof(ID3D10Texture2D),
                                           (LPVOID*)&pBackBufferSurface);

                    if(FAILED(hresult_))
                         return hresult_;

                     hresult_ = g_id3dDevice ->
                                 CreateRenderTargetView(pBackBufferSurface, NULL,
                                               &g_pd3d10RenderTargetView);

                    pBackBufferSurface->Release();

                    if(FAILED(hresult_))
                         return hresult_;

                     g_id3dDevice -> OMSetRenderTargets(
                                               1, &g_pd3d10RenderTargetView, NULL);
                    /* calculate the viewport's width and height from the client
                       area coordinates */
                    UINT rectangle_width = rectangle.right - rectangle.left;
                    UINT rectangle_height = rectangle.bottom - rectangle.top;

                    /* define the viewport */
                    ///////////////////////////
                    D3D10_VIEWPORT viewport;
                    viewport.TopLeftX = 0;
                    viewport.TopLeftY = 0;
                    viewport.Width = rectangle_width;
                    viewport.Height = rectangle_height;
                    viewport.MinDepth = 0.0f;
                    viewport.MaxDepth = 1.0f;

                    //bind the viewport to the rasterizer stage of the pipeline
                    g_id3dDevice -> RSSetViewports(1, &viewport);

                    return S_OK;
                }
```

Next we simply have to modify our previously defined message loop (given in wWinMain) so that it doesn't have to wait for the GetMessage function while the event queue is empty. GetMessage only returns when an event message is available, thus causing our program to wait on GetMessage until a message becomes available for processing. By replacing GetMessage with PeekMessage, we effectively eliminate this waiting as the PeekMessage function returns immediately when there aren't any messages in the message queue. This function takes four parameters. The first is a pointer to the msg structure containing the message. Just as with GetMessage, the next three parameters aren't really important to us and are set to NULL and 0 – the second parameter is simply a handle to the window whose messages are to be retrieved with the next two parameters taking integer values of the lowest and highest message values to retrieve respectively. The final parameter controls the message handling method; it can be set to PM_REMOVE for the removal of messages from the message queue after they were processed or PM_NOREMOVE so that messages are not removed after being processed. The types of messages being processed can further be defined via the following constants: PM_QS_INPUT (for the processing of keyboard and mouse input), PM_QS_PAINT (for the processing of painting messages), PM_QS_POSTMESSAGE (for the processing of posted messages) or PM_QS_SENDMESSAGE (for the processing of sent messages). The modified message loop is shown below:

```
/* main message loop */
///////////////////////
MSG msg = {0};

while(WM_QUIT != msg.message)
{
    if(PeekMessage(&msg, NULL, 0, 0, PM_REMOVE))
    {
        TranslateMessage(&msg);
        DispatchMessage(&msg);
    }
    else //if no message is returned, do some rendering
        RenderScene();
}
```

The final step is to actually do some rendering. We start by clearing the back-buffer using the ClearRenderTargetView function. This function takes two parameters, the first being a pointer to the render target declared as follows:

```
ID3D10RenderTargetView* g_pd3d10RenderTargetView = NULL;
```

The second parameter is simply the color we would like to clear the render target with, in our case the color red (as specified using the four-component array ClearBufferColor). With the back buffer filled, we simply have to call the IDXGISwapChain Present function to display it. This function, taking two parameters, sets the swap chain's back buffer as the front buffer, making it visible to the viewer. Both its parameters are integer values, the first specifying the synchronicity at which the rendered image is presented to the viewer (0 for immediate presentation), with the second parameter being set to either 0 to perform the presentation of the rendered image or DXGI_PRESENT_TEST to simply test the swap chain for errors. The following function performs these operations:

```
/*
================
RenderScene
-clears the back buffer using the color red
```

```
-switches the back- and front-buffer, displaying the result
================
*/
void RenderScene()
{
    /* set the clear color - red, green, blue, alpha */
    float ClearBufferColor[4] = {1.0f, 0.0f, 0.0f, 1.0f};

    /* clear the back buffer */
    g_id3dDevice -> ClearRenderTargetView(
                            g_pd3dl0RenderTargetView,
                            ClearBufferColor);

    /* switch the back- and front-buffer and display the
       result */
    g_pdxl0SwapChain->Present(0, 0);
}
```

Before terminating the application, it is always a good idea to free all resources created by it. We create the function, DeviceCleanup, for this specific purpose. This function, listed below, is called just after wWinMain's main message loop terminates (when a WM_QUIT message is sent) and also if the InitD3D10 function returns an error code:

```
/*
================
DeviceCleanup
-clean and release all D3D10 objects created
================
*/
void DeviceCleanup()
{
    /* clean and release ID3D10Device */
    if(g_id3dDevice)
    {
        //restore all default device settings
        g_id3dDevice -> ClearState();
        //release the device
        g_id3dDevice -> Release();
    }

    /* release ID3D10RenderTargetView */
    if(g_pd3dl0RenderTargetView)
        g_pd3dl0RenderTargetView->Release();

    /* release IDXGISwapChain */
    if(g_pdxl0SwapChain)
        g_pdxl0SwapChain->Release();
}
```

Working with OpenGL: Setting up a Window (GLUT), the Main Message Loop and Initializing OpenGL

The following example illustrates the usage of GLUT in setting up a window, the usage of callbacks for the processing of event messages and the swapping of the front and back buffer for rendering to this newly created window.

We begin by including the standard glut header: It imports both the OpenGL (gl.h) and GLU header (glu.h):

```
#include <GL/glut.h> //glut library, it imports gl.h, glu.h
#include <stdlib.h> //for exit call
```

We start by defining the ASCII value for the keyboard's escape character (this value will be used in the keyboard function to terminate the application):

```
#define ESCAPE 27 //define ASCII value for escape keystroke
```

The display function is responsible for rendering the output to the screen. Its first function call, glClearColor, sets the color value to clear the back buffer with. This function takes four parameters, namely the clear color's level of red (0 to 1), level of green (0 to 1), level of blue (0 to 1) and the alpha value controlling the level of transparency (0 to 1). We set this clear color to red by only specifying the red component to its maximum value. Following this we call the glClear function. This function clears the buffers specified by its parameters, in our case we clear both the frame buffer and depth-buffer using the bitwise OR '|' operator. Next we call the glFlush function to ensure that all previously issued commands are completed. We can now swap the front buffer with our red colored back buffer using the glutSwapBuffers function:

```
/*
==================
display()
-Renders output to screen
==================
*/
void display(void)
{
    /* set the clear color - red, green, blue, alpha*/
    glClearColor(1.0, 0.0, 0.0, 0.0);

    /* clear frame buffer and depth-buffer */
    glClear(GL_COLOR_BUFFER_BIT  GL_DEPTH_BUFFER_BIT);

    /* make sure all previously issued commands are
       completed */
    glFlush();

    /* contents of back buffer are set to become that of
       front buffer (double buffering) */
    glutSwapBuffers();
}
```

We now move on to the registering and processing of mouse and keyboard callbacks. The glutMouseFunc routine sets the mouse callback for a window, with the glutKeyboardFunc routine doing the same for keyboard input. The output window stays open until either the escape key or the right mouse button has been pressed, upon which it immediately terminates. In the case of the escape character, the following code segment provides this functionality:

```
if (key == ESCAPE) //escape key handling code
{
    exit(0); //exits the program
}
```

The mouse function's code is similar with the exception of first specifying the right mouse button (GLUT_LEFT_BUTTON specifies the left mouse button) as the event trigger:

```
if (button == GLUT_RIGHT_BUTTON && state == GLUT_DOWN)
{
    exit(0); //exits the program
}
```

We define two functions, keyboard and mouse to provide this functionality:

```
/*
==================
keyboard
-handles keyboard input
==================
*/
void keyboard(unsigned char key, int x, int y)
{
    /* on pressing the escape key the program terminates */
    if (key == ESCAPE) //escape key handling code
    {
        exit(0); //exits the program
    }
}
/*
==================
mouse
-handles mouse input
==================
*/
void mouse(int button, int state, int x, int y)
{
    /* on pressing the right mouse button the program
       terminates */
    if (button == GLUT_RIGHT_BUTTON && state == GLUT_DOWN)
    {
        exit(0); //exits the program
    }
}
```

The main function creates a window and main window frame using GLUT function calls. The sequence at which these functions are called can vary slightly, such as calling glutInitWindowSize before glutInit, however, functions such as glutMainLoop can only be called after the initial GLUT setup has been done. The first function, glutInit, initializes the GLUT library. It takes the command line arguments (passed to the main function at the start of the program's execution) as parameters. Next we set the initial display mode using the glutInitDisplayMode function (we specify its parameters so that double buffering (GLUT_DOUBLE), nonindexed color mode (GLUT_RGB) and the depth buffer (GLUT_DEPTH) are supported). With the display mode set, we can define the dimension of the output window (using glutInitWindowSize), creating the window using the glutCreateWindow function. The callback functions for the current window are now set using the glutMouseFunc and glutKeyboardFunc functions. The glutMainLoop function serves as entry point to the GLUT event processing loop, dealing with any event callback being generated. The glutDisplayFunc function displays the contents of our display function in the newly created window:

```
/*
==================
main
==================
*/
int main(int argc, char** argv)
{
    /* initialize the GLUT library. */
    glutInit(&argc, argv);

    /* set the initial display mode: double buffering and a
       depth buffer. */
    glutInitDisplayMode(GLUT_DOUBLE | GLUT_RGB | GLUT_DEPTH);

    /* set default window size */
    glutInitWindowSize(400, 300);

    /* create a top-level window with a caption */
    glutCreateWindow("Setting up a GLUT/OpenGL Window");

    /* set the mouse callback for the current window */
    glutMouseFunc(mouse);

    /* set the keyboard callback for the current window.*/
    glutKeyboardFunc(keyboard);

    /* display our contents in the window */
    glutDisplayFunc(display);

    /* enter the GLUT event processing loop - will handle
       any callback */
    glutMainLoop();

    return 0;
}
```

4.6 SUMMARY

This chapter presented a number of technical topics pertaining to the graphics system and its underlying hardware components. These topics were covered to ensure a thorough understanding of the rendering process. From a practical perspective, we looked at the OpenGL and DirectX programming interfaces and the process of window creation and control through the setup of a simple window and the specification of a main message loop.

The chapter started by describing each element constituting a general graphics system. We specifically focused on input devices, and their associated input methods, output devices, and related elements influencing image quality as well as the frame buffer used for storing the color information of individual pixels. Next we portrayed three-dimensional environments as a combination of at least a viewer, one light source, and a number of objects, briefly focusing on each of these components.

Following this introduction we considered the graphics pipeline architecture as an overall process responsible for transforming some object representation from local coordinate space, to world space, view space, screen space, and finally display space. We also looked at the various stages of the graphics pipeline in detail. These stages included vertex processing responsible for performing all geometric transformations, clipping for controlling the field of view, culling for back-face elimination, and finally rasterization and fragment processing for converting the primitives produced by the clipper to pixels.

We then investigated the concept of programmable pipelines, specifically looking at both Direct3D 10 and OpenGL to highlight the implication and use of their pipelines for the generation of advanced real-time graphical effects. Dealing with the Direct3D 10 processing pipeline, we started by discussing the input assembler stage responsible for propagating geometric input data to the rest of the pipeline (also discussing the Direct3D 10 code required for the initialization of the input assembler stage). Next we described the vertex-shader stage, geometry-shader stage, the stream-output stage, the pixel-shader stage and the output-merger stage. The OpenGL processing pipeline was in turn discussed in terms of the evaluator processing element, display list processor, primitive assembly, rasterizer, pixel processor, and fragment processor.

The remainder of this chapter dealt with both the Direct3D and OpenGL programming interfaces, their basic library organization, and overall architecture. The chapter concluded with program examples illustrating window creation, the handling of messages sent to and from the window and the initialization of key DirectX and OpenGL components.

The next chapter introduces a variety of commonly used input devices and input classes, explicitly focusing on input and interaction by means of DirectInput and the Xbox 360's XInput API.

4.7 FURTHER READING

A good companion when doing Win32 programming (specifically window creation and control) is Microsoft's official documentation (MSDN libraries) that accompanies the Visual Studio IDE distribution. This documentation is also available from Microsoft's msdn2.microsoft.com website. Similarly, documentation for the DirectX application programming interface is provided with each SDK distribution and available from Microsoft's msdn2.microsoft.com website with the OpenGL reference pages being available from the official OpenGL website (www.opengl.org). The official GLUT documentation is also available from the OpenGL website (http://www.opengl.org/documentation/specs/glut/).

4.8   EXERCISES

1 Briefly describe each element making up a general purpose graphics system.

2 Give an example of a situation where neither request mode nor sample mode input would be appropriate.

3 Explain why event mode input is needed.

4 What is the main reason for replacing vector-based displays with raster technology?

5 How do we deal with the artifacts resulting from raster technology?

6 How does color depth influence image quality?

7 Describe any three buffers constituting a modern frame buffer.

8 What is the purpose of material properties?

9 Explain the relationship between objects, light sources, and a viewer.

10 What is the difference between throughput and overall latency?

11 Shortly describe the purpose of the graphics pipeline.

12 Briefly discuss vertex processing, clipping, rasterization, and fragment processing.

13 Why are programmable pipelines needed?

14 What programming languages can be used to program Direct3D 10's vertex shader, geometry shader and pixel shader?

15 Write a Direct3D 10 program to initialize the input assembler stage using a vertex buffer.

16 Briefly describe each member of the D3D10_BUFFER_DESC structure.

17 What data do we use for initializing the D3D10_SUBRESOURCE_DATA structure?

18 What is the function of the given code sample?

```
g_id3dDevice->CreateBuffer(&bufferDescription,
                           &subresourceData,
                           &vertexBuffer[0]);
```

19 Discuss the difference between the definition of an index buffer and vertex buffer.

20 What is an input-assembler input slot?

21 Discuss the connection between the stream output and geometry-shader stage.

22 What is the purpose of the Output-Merger Stage?

23 What processing unit would the OpenGL processing pipeline utilize when rendering B-spline surfaces?

24 Describe the purpose of the glNewList function in the following sample:

```
glNewList(YOUR_LIST, GL_COMPILE);
    glBegin(...);
        //..OpenGL function calls
    glEnd();
glEndList();
```

25 Vertices fed into the OpenGL processing pipeline must be assembled into primitives, how is this accomplished?

26 Describe two operations performed during the rasterization stage.

27 What is the glColorMask function used for?

28 Briefly describe OpenGL's library organization.

29 What is the main reason for the original Windows Driver Model being replaced by the Windows Display Driver Model (WDDM) in Windows Vista?

30 Write a program, based on the one given in section 4.5.1, that extends this program to spawn an additional child window.

31 How do we specify an interface to the hardware device and swap chain in Direct3D 10?

32 What is the main problem associated with the GetMessage function, and how is it rectified?

CHAPTER 5

Input Control

LEARNING OBJECTIVES

In this chapter you will learn about:

- Input devices
- Six classes of input
- DirectInput
- DirectInput device setup (keyboard, mouse or joystick)
- Creating a DirectInput object
- Creating a DirectInput device
- Setting the data format of a DirectInput device
- Setting the cooperative level of a DirectInput device
- Acquiring a DirectInput device
- Reading data from a DirectInput device
- Buffered and immediate data (keyboard, mouse or joystick)
- Action mapping
- The specification of actions
- Setting up an action map
- Applying an action map to physical devices
- Applying an action map to a device
- Retrieving action map data
- Force feedback
- Setting up a force feedback device
- Using effects
- XInput

INTRODUCTION

Chapter 5 introduces a variety of commonly used input devices and modes of input. The chapter focuses on input and interaction control by means of DirectInput and the Xbox 360's XInput API (DirectX 10). The chapter starts with an introduction to some physical device properties followed by the six classes of logical input devices.

DirectInput device setup, obtaining data from devices, force feedback, and the processing of actions are looked at in detail. The chapter closes with an introduction to the XInput API.

5.1   INPUT DEVICES

This chapter investigates input control using various physical devices (keyboard, mouse and joystick). It also looks at adding application support for Force Feedback capable devices. We start by classifying physical input devices into two primary categories: keyboard devices and pointing devices. *Pointing devices* transmit an onscreen coordinate pair to the computer for interpretation. This coordinate pair denotes a screen position with the pointing device's buttons being a trigger (as discussed in section 4.1.1). Joysticks, game pads, and the mouse can be placed into this category since they all combine the return of coordinate values (to indicate position) with a trigger to signify some action. *Keyboard devices* are all physical devices that generate character codes based on some byte assignment standard, for example, ASCII (the American Standard Code for Information Interchange) assigning a one-byte code to each and every character represented by a keyboard. ASCII is simply a character encoding standard developed in the 1960s and adopted as a standard for the representation of text in input devices, modems, network cards, etc.

The mouse is by far the most popular and commonly used pointing device. Its construction is based on the need for physical gestures such as pointing, clicking, and dragging to manipulate onscreen objects such as menus and dialog boxes. The simplest mouse is generally constructed out of mechanical detectors (rollers) that are rotated by the motion of a slightly protruding ball positioned at the bottom of the device (this ball is located on the top of trackball devices). Rotation of the ball results in the generation of electrical signals based on the measurement of motion in both an x- and a y-direction. More commonly today, these mechanical components are replaced by optical detectors, leading to a higher degree of accuracy and eliminating the build-up of dirt within the device – hence the need for routine cleaning. Trackball devices, popular with portable computers, have also been replaced by motion and pressure sensitive touchpads.

As mentioned, these pointing devices generate two independent values converted by some API, device interface, or user program into positional data that can be interpreted as screen coordinates. This direct approach is, however, rarely used and these two independent values generated by the device are more commonly interpreted by the device driver as velocities. These two velocities are then integrated to yield an x- and y-coordinate value (used to position the mouse cursor) with integration being done at real-time as the mouse is being moved by the user (Figure 5-1). Integration is the mathematical process of calculating some value in relation to another by using a known or available measure and its rate of change with respect to some other quantity such as time.

The main purpose behind using velocities, rather than distance values, lies with the desire to create a variable-sensitivity input device. *Variable sensitivity* refers to slow movements from rest resulting in nominal changes with rapid mouse movements leading to large changes in the cursor's onscreen position. The mouse is referred to as a *relative-positioning* device, meaning that the current cursor position is only dependent on the previous onscreen cursor location, regardless of where the mouse was previously located. For example, using relative-positioning we can move the mouse, pick it up, move it midair without any movement being registered, and put it back on the mousepad where moving it will once again result in repositioning of the onscreen cursor – the cursor is thus not dependent on the actual location of the mouse.

Absolute positioning provides a way of linking onscreen data with the device's physical position. This type of positioning is desirable for drawing and artistic applications as well as touch-sensitive displays where the actual area of selection is an abstraction of the data being presented on the display. For example, using a data tablet and stylus for drawing enables the user to move the stylus on the tablet just

---

FIGURE 5-1   **Integrating velocity values to position the mouse cursor**

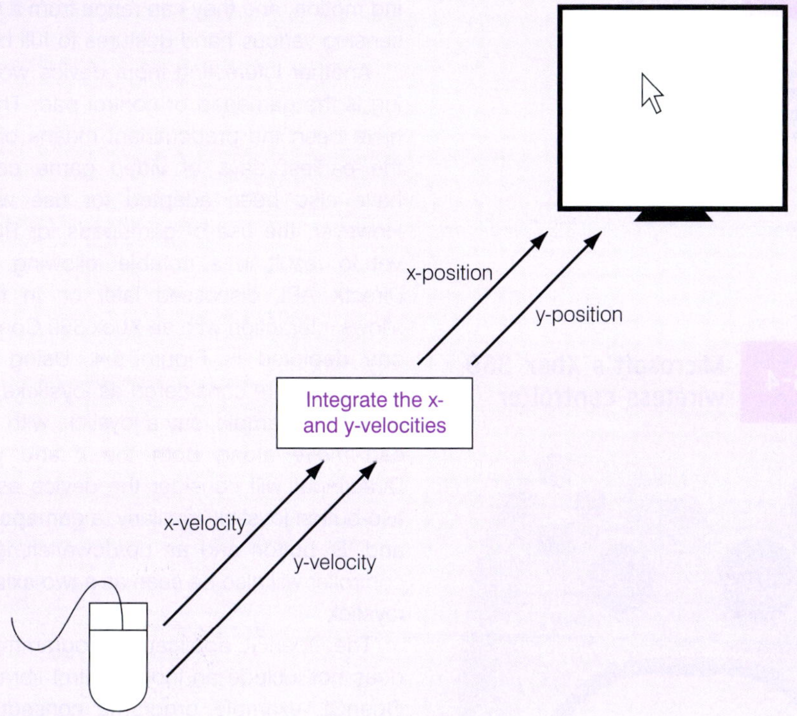

x-position

y-position

Integrate the x-
and y-velocities

x-velocity

y-velocity

---

as he/she would have done using pen and paper – picking up the stylus and repositioning it at a different location will result in the cursor being moved to the part of the screen corresponding to the new absolute position on the tablet.

The joystick is another very important input device, especially to the world of computer gaming and simulations. In its simplest form we interpret the motion of its stick in both an *x* and a *y* direction. These values are then, just as with the mouse, translated into velocities and subsequently integrated into screen coordinates. The joystick is also a variable-sensing device. For example, moving the stick slightly right will lead to a slow change in the cursor's location; however, moving the stick to the far right position will result in rapid cursor relocation.

Most input devices are two-dimensional in nature. These devices are fit for common daily tasks; however, specialized three-dimensional input devices are often needed for virtual reality and engineering applications. An example of such a three-dimensional input device is the spaceball (shown in Figure 5-2). The spaceball, somewhat similar to a joystick, has a vertical stick with a ball at the top. Forces exerted on the ball are measured by pressure sensors, allowing multiple degrees of freedom (commonly six – up/down, left/right, front/back, and three distinct rotations). The data glove (also called a 'wired glove'), shown in Figure 5-3, is another three-dimensional

FIGURE 5-2   **IBM's six-degrees of freedom SpaceBall**

5

FIGURE 5-3   **Essential Reality's P5 glove**

FIGURE 5-4   **Microsoft's Xbox 360 wireless controller**

device finding some application in gaming. These gloves have numerous sensors constantly monitoring motion, and they can range from a simple glove sensing various hand gestures to full body suits.

Another interesting input device worth mentioning is the gamepad or control pad. These devices have been the predominant means of input since the earliest days of video game consoles and have also been adapted for use with the PC. However, the use of gamepads for PC gaming is yet to result in a notable following. The XInput DirectX API, discussed later on in this chapter, allows interaction with an Xbox 360 Controller as the one depicted in Figure 5-4. Using DirectInput, gamepads are considered as joysticks on a logical level. For example, say a joystick, with two buttons, can move along both the x and y axis then DirectInput will consider the device as a two-axis, two-button joystick, similarly, a gamepad with an 'A' and 'B' button and an up/down/left/right direction controller will also be seen as a two-axis, two-button joystick.

The OpenGL application programming interface does not include an input control library. Featured OpenGL example programs consequently make use of the OpenGL Utility Toolkit (GLUT) for system level input control and interaction. There are of course numerous other ways to achieve input interaction; for example, presented OpenGL programs could just as easily, as the case with various presented Direct3D examples, have utilized Microsoft's DirectInput API. However, the presented OpenGL examples implement GLUT for the sake of cross-platform compatibility with the Direct3D examples, already limited to Windows-based platforms, using DirectInput and XInput.

5.2   SIX CLASSES OF INPUT

During Chapter 4 we considered input devices from both a logical and physical perspective. Following this we looked at three types of input, namely, request mode, sample mode, and event mode input (see section 4.1.1). Building on this we can now identify six classes of logical input devices: choice devices, locator devices, pick devices, string devices, stroke devices, and valuators. These classes encapsulate the majority of input forms available for use in interactive application programs.

1   *Choice devices* allow the selection of a separate number of options. A common way to facilitate this form of input is through the use of widgets. A *widget* is a graphical interface element that is interacted with by the user. These widgets make up graphical user interfaces (GUIs) and can be added to a GUI via some widget toolkit. Examples of widgets include text boxes, scrollbars, sliders, and navigation tabs. The concept of a choice device as a widget becomes clear when we consider a drop-down list with several options. This list allows the user to select any of its options, each option performing a specific task.

2 *Locator devices* translate device coordinates to world coordinates for use by the application program. These devices generally take the form of pointing devices such as a mouse or touchpad. Everyday computer games make use of these pointing devices for general input, be it to select menu options or to interact with the game's environment. The device coordinates are, however, commonly translated to screen coordinates, making it the application program's responsibility to translate these screen coordinates to world coordinates.

3 A *picking device* allows a user to click on some element within a scene – the identifier of the element is then returned to the user program. This form of input is crucial for computer games; for example, selecting a unit in a real-time strategy (RTS) or role-playing game (RPG), opening a door in a first-person shooter game or selecting some object in an editor. Picking is performed using a locator device; however, with the locator device's position being given in window coordinates, we have to implement an additional interface to establish the object selected by the user.

4 A *string device* is any logical device that generates ASCII output, sending it to the application program as input. The most common string input device is the QWERTY keyboard. The keyboard still remains the primary method of control despite the large number of specialized input devices targeting the gaming market.

5 *Stroke devices* gather data about a series of positions or actions, temporarily storing them in an array or list. For example, using a locator device (such as a mouse) as a stroke device: pushing down one of the mouse buttons while dragging the mouse cursor across the screen will result in data continuously being read into the array, with this only stopping once the mouse button is released. Stroke devices can be used to select multiple objects on screen, such as selecting numerous units in an RTS game.

6 *Valuators* are the sixth and final input class. They are analog input devices such as dials and switches producing varying levels of input. Some valuators are found on joysticks and gamepads, for example, a lever that can be rotated forwards or backwards to emulate throttle control or an accelerator. Valuators are also incorporated into GUIs via widgets such as slidebars and scrollbars.

All these input classes are supported by both OpenGL/GLUT and DirectInput. However, earlier APIs abided strictly to these classes where modern day APIs are built around the fact that a window system cannot function completely independently from the characteristics of a physical device. The six input classes are thus still useful for illustrating the variety of input that has to be handled by modern-day graphical applications.

5.3 DIRECTINPUT

DirectInput is DirectX's primary input processing API. It provides hardware-independent input control for keyboards, mice, joysticks, gamepads, steering wheels, flight yokes, space balls, paddles, etc. DirectInput's hardware-independent nature can be attributed to the API interfacing directly with the device drivers, thus ensuring a generic way of controlling and communicating with input devices regardless of their physical properties.

DirectInput is thus responsible for the processing of messages sent to and received from physical input devices. Standard Windows mouse and keyboard messages are ignored due to DirectInput's libraries interfacing directly with the device drivers. In addition to this low-level control, DirectInput also provides a facility for communicating with force-feedback enabled devices, including a method, called *action mapping*, which allows the programmer a way of assigning game specific actions to the buttons/axes of input devices. Using action mapping, applications can communicate with an input device without any knowledge about the device type. Apart from these methods, DirectInput allows an application executing in the background to monitor data from input devices, something which isn't possible using standard Windows input events.

Some interesting differences become apparent when using DirectInput as opposed to standard Windows mouse and keyboard messages. The first and most noticeable difference is the lack of any character translation. Character translation is simply the use of one key in combination with another to produce some special character, for example, pressing the 'Shift' key and the '4' key to produce the '$' sign (assuming the use of a US keyboard). DirectInput interprets each key press as a distinct event, hence considering each of the keys in our example as a separate event. DirectInput also allows devices to be used in *exclusive mode*, preventing any other application from receiving any input. Windows has a subsystem for interpreting input device data. This subsystem is bypassed by DirectInput communicating directly with the device drivers, DirectInput thus either allowing Windows to interpret input data or using exclusive mode to suppress all input messages.

DirectInput is made up out of a number of Component Object Model (COM) interfaces. The main interface, IDirectInput8, supported by the DirectInput object, must be created to initialize DirectInput. We also specify a DirectInputDevice object for each of our input devices (each object controlling one input device). This object serves as a data communication channel for each of the input devices. Device object instances are created from the DirectInputDevice object (with the DirectInputDevice object instantiating the IDirectInputDevice8 interface). These instances allow the individual control of device buttons, keys, axes, etc. Figure 5-5 shows the main IDirectInput8 interface with IDirectInputDevice8 interfaces created from the main IDirectInput8 interface. Notice the '8' following the interface names, this number indicates the DirectInput version, in our case DirectInput 8 – DirectInput has not notably been revised since DirectX version 8.

As previously mentioned, DirectInput considers only three device classes, namely, the computer keyboard, mouse, and joystick. All other devices, such as gamepads, paddles, steering wheels, and spaceballs, are considered joystick-like input devices. DirectInput simply creates one or more input objects for the definition of these devices, for example, an input object can be defined to describe a spaceball's rotational or pressure sensors, or similarly, a joystick with both an *x* and *y* axis and one button can be described using three input objects. Input devices with force-feedback capabilities are defined using an object that can communicate in a bidirectional manner (processing both input and output signals).

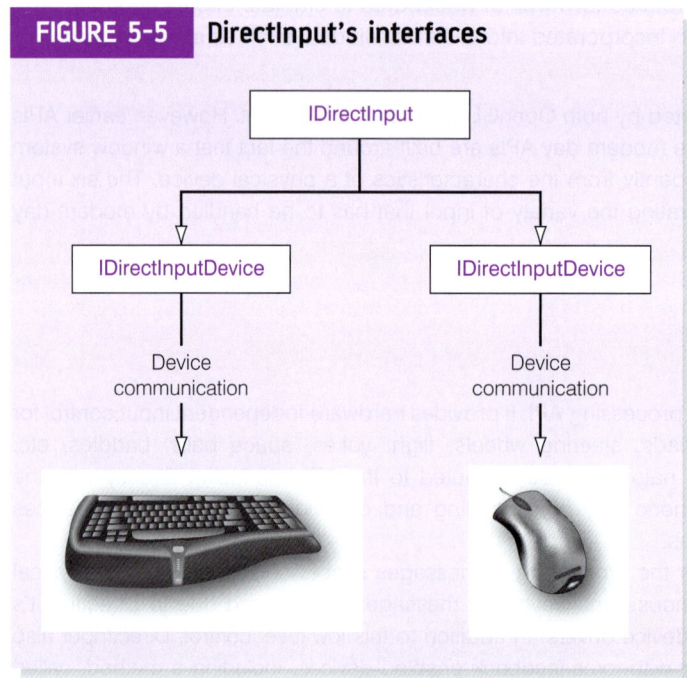

FIGURE 5-5   DirectInput's interfaces

5.3.1 DirectInput Device Setup (Keyboard, Mouse, or Joystick)

Setting up and initializing DirectInput for use is quite an involved process that can be summarized as follows: creating a DirectInput object (the primary DirectInput interface), representing input devices (such as a keyboard, mouse, joystick, etc) using the DirectInputDevice object, and finally creating device object instances for the representation of keys, buttons and so forth found on a DirectInput device object.

The general steps for setting up DirectInput, including connecting to one or more devices, and reading input from at least one device is given here:

1 Create a DirectInput object, using methods of this object to create DirectInputDevice objects and for determining the type of input devices available for use.

2 Enumerate devices using DirectInput. Enumeration simply refers to the process of ascertaining the number and type of input devices present on a system. Each enumerated device has its own unique identifier that is used for representing the device via its DirectInputDevice object.

3 Use the unique identifier obtained during enumeration to create a DirectInputDevice object for each of the devices that will be used.

4 Set the cooperative level of each and every device. The cooperative level controls how the device will be shared amongst applications. Following this we have to specify a data format for the device objects (buttons, triggers, axes, etc.) – we can either use data packets for state data (DirectInput sending us immediate state information) or buffers for event data (DirectInput's buffered data mode being a time-stamped message format).

5 Acquire the device by signalling DirectInput that the program can now read data sent from the device.

6 Receive data from the device(s) during each pass through the message loop. Alternatively, DirectInput can notify the program whenever an event occurs.

7 Process the received data, executing some action based on the result.

8 Shut down DirectInput by releasing all devices when the application program terminates.

Action mapping can be seen as an alternative to the above outlined implementation process. Defining an action map for an input device leaves the device object assignment to DirectInput – hence selecting the most appropriate device for a specific task. For example, setting the primary button on a joystick as a 'fire' button for an FPS game, we can now define an action called BUTTON_ACTION. This action can then be assigned by DirectInput, thus allowing easy configuration for the user.

5.3.1.1 Creating a DirectInput Object
Any DirectInput implementation starts with the creation of a single DirectInput object. This object stays in use until it is released when the application terminates. To create this object we start by creating the main DirectInput COM object interface, IDirectInput8Interface. This interface is created using the DirectInput8Create function – declared in the dinput.h header file as follows:

```
HRESULT DirectInput8Create(
    HINSTANCE hinst,
    DWORD dwVersion,
    REFIID riidltf,
    LPVOID * ppvOut,
    LPUNKNOWN punkOuter
);
```

This function's first parameter, hinst, is the main instance handle of the application; hence the same handle passed to the WinMain function. The next parameter, dwVersion, takes a constant describing the version of DirectInput to use (the default value, indicating the latest version of DirectInput, is the constant DIRECTINPUT_VERSION). The riidltf parameter, specifying the desired interface's unique identifier, sets the version of the interface to either the ANSI or Unicode format – depending on whether Unicode is used by the application (simply set this value to IID_IDirectInput8 which cause ANSI to be selected whenever Unicode isn't available). The second last parameter, ppvOut, is the address of a pointer to a variable storing the interface pointer used for determining whether the function call passed or failed. The final parameter, punkOuter, is simply a COM aggregation of little concern – we will set it to 'NULL' since no aggregation is needed, if aggregation of the interface is needed, the object returned in ppvOut is a pointer to IUnknown.

Creating the DirectInput device object using this DirectInput8Create function is illustrated by the following code sample:

We start by declaring a handle to an instance of the application, g_hInstance, and a HRESULT value that will be used for storing the return value of DirectInput8Create function:

```
HINSTANCE g_hInstance;
HRESULT hresult_;
```

We also have to specify the main DirectInput interface using the LPDIRECTINPUT8 type defined as a pointer to IDirectInput8:

```
LPDIRECTINPUT8 lpdi;
```

Next we can create the main DirectInput object using the DirectInput8Create function:

```
hresult_ = DirectInput8Create(g_hInstance,
                 DIRECTINPUT_VERSION,
                 IID_IDirectInput8,
                 (void**)&lpdi,
                 NULL);
```

The DirectInput8Create function returns a DI_OK value (standing for DirectInput OK) if successful and any of the following DirectInput errors in the event of a failure: DIERR_OUTOFMEMORY (DirectInput could not allocate the requested amount of memory to create the device object), DIERR_INVALIDPARAM (an invalid parameter was passed to the DirectInput subsystem, or the object does not permit the function call in its current state), DIERR_OLDDIRECTINPUTVERSION (a newer version of DirectInput is needed) or DIERR_BETADIRECTINPUTVERSION (when the application is using an unsupported pre-release version of DirectInput). We can check for the returned value using a standard if structure and the FAILED macro:

```
if FAILED(hresult_)
{
      /* take some action because DirectInput object creation
         failed */
}
```

Following the creation of the DirectInput object we move on to create a DirectInput device object, such as a keyboard or mouse object.

5.3.1.2 Creating a DirectInput Device A DirectInput device object, representing an input device, is created so that data can be read from the device. The CreateDevice IDirectInput8 interface method is used for creating and initializing a device instance, for example, providing an interface to a keyboard, mouse, or joystick. This function is declared as follows in the dinput.h header file:

```
HRESULT CreateDevice (
    REFGUID rguid,
    LPDIRECTINPUTDEVICE * lplpDirectInputDevice,
    LPUNKNOWN pUnkOuter
);
```

Its first parameter, rguid, is a reference to the GUID (Globally Unique Identifier) value of the device that has to be created – this value is an input device's unique identifier retrieved using the EnumDevices IDirectInput8 interface method (as an alternative to querying for GUIDs, we can specify default GUID values for common devices, such as GUID_SysKeyboard for keyboard devices and GUID_SysMouse for the mouse). The second parameter, lplpDirectInputDevice, receives a pointer to the new IDirectInputDevice8 Interface (discussed below), with the final parameter, pUnkOuter, a COM aggregation once again of little concern and set to 'NULL'.

The CreateDevice function returns a DI_OK value if successful and any of the following DirectInput errors in the event of a failure:

- DIERR_DEVICENOTREG (the DirectInput device is not registered with the DirectInput subsystem)
- DIERR_INVALIDPARAM (an invalid parameter was passed to the DirectInput subsystem, or the object does not permit the function call in its current state)
- DIERR_NOINTERFACE (the specified interface is not supported by the DirectInput object)
- DIERR_NOTINITIALIZED (the object is not properly initialized) or
- DIERR_OUTOFMEMORY (DirectInput could not allocate the requested amount of memory to create the device object).

Let's say we want to create a keyboard DirectInput device; to accomplish this we start by specifying a variable that will be used for storing a pointer to the IDirectInput8 device interface (previously defined as lpdi). This is done using LPDIRECTINPUTDEVICE8:

```
LPDIRECTINPUTDEVICE8 g_lpInputDevice;
```

The next step is to create and initialize an instance of a device by calling the CreateDevice function:

```
hresult_ = lpdi->CreateDevice(GUID_SysKeyboard,
                    &g_lpInputDevice,
                    NULL);
```

Upon execution, the CreateDevice function will return a pointer to the IDirectInputDevice8 interface, in the event of a failure we must remember to release all devices using the Release function:

```
if FAILED(hresult_)
{
    g_lpInputDevice->Release();
    return FALSE;
}
```

Alternatively we can create a DirectInput mouse device by passing the GUID_SysMouse global variable to the CreateDevice function:

```
hresult_ = lpdi->CreateDevice (GUID_SysMouse,
                               &g_lpInputDevice,
                               NULL);
```

Creating a DirectInput joystick device is considerably more involved than simple mouse or keyboard devices; for instance, we first have to enumerate joystick devices before creating the DirectInput device. Enumerating the joystick (or any other device) allows us to ascertain the number and type of buttons or axes available on the device. DirectX makes use of callback functions for enumeration. This enumeration function is called for every new device; the programmer can then use this data to create a device list by appending the list every time the callback is issued. The IDirectInput8 EnumDevices function, used for enumerating devices, is declared as follows in the dinput.h header file:

```
HRESULT EnumDevices(
    DWORD dwDevType,
    LPDIENUMDEVICESCALLBACK lpCallback,
    LPVOID pvRef,
    DWORD dwFlags
);
```

Its first parameter, dwDevType, specifies the type of device to enumerate/scan for. It can be set to any of the following constants when enumerating for device classes:

■ DI8DEVCLASS_ALL (to enumerate all device classes)

■ DI8DEVCLASS_DEVICE (to enumerate devices not falling into any of the other categories)

■ DI8DEVCLASS_GAMECTRL (to enumerate all game controllers)

■ DI8DEVCLASS_KEYBOARD (to enumerate all keyboard devices – same as using DI8DEVTYPE_KEYBOARD) or

■ DI8DEVCLASS_POINTER (to enumerate all mouse-like input devices).

Alternatively we can enumerate for a specific type of device using any of the following values (only the most popular ones are listed here – there are twelve device types, each having numerous subtypes):

■ DI8DEVTYPE_DEVICE (for devices not fitting into any of the other device categories)

■ DI8DEVTYPE_DRIVING (for steering wheel-type input devices)

■ DI8DEVTYPE_GAMEPAD (for gamepads)

■ DI8DEVTYPE_JOYSTICK (for joystick-like input devices)

■ DI8DEVTYPE_KEYBOARD (for keyboards)

■ DI8DEVTYPE_MOUSE (for mouse or mouse-like input devices).

A device subtype can be specified by using the bitwise OR '|' operator together with a main device type. For example, DI8DEVTYPE_DRIVING can be combined with any of the following subtypes:

■ DI8DEVTYPEDRIVING_COMBINEDPEDALS (used to scan for steering devices relaying information about brake pedal and acceleration values via a single axis)

■ DI8DEVTYPEDRIVING_DUALPEDALS (used to scan for steering devices relaying information about brake pedal and acceleration values via separate axes)

■ DI8DEVTYPEDRIVING_HANDHELD (used to scan for a hand-held steering device).

The DI8DEVTYPE_KEYBOARD flag can similarly be combined with any of the following subtypes:

■ DI8DEVTYPEKEYBOARD_PCXT (for an IBM PC/XT 83-key keyboard)

■ DI8DEVTYPEKEYBOARD_NEC98LAPTOP (for a Japanese NEC PC98 laptop keyboard)

■ DI8DEVTYPEKEYBOARD_PCENH (for a Microsoft Natural or IBM PC Enhanced 101/102-key keyboard).

For mouse-type devices we can specify the following subtypes:

■ DI8DEVTYPEMOUSE_ABSOLUTE (to scan of absolute positioning devices)

■ DI8DEVTYPEMOUSE_TOUCHPAD (to scan for a standard touchpad)

■ DI8DEVTYPEMOUSE_TRACKBALL (to scan for a standard trackball)

■ DI8DEVTYPEMOUSE_TRADITIONAL (to scan for a basic mouse) or

■ DI8DEVTYPEMOUSE_UNKNOWN (when the subtype cannot be determined).

The second parameter of the EnumDevices function, lpCallback, takes a pointer to a callback function that is called for each device detected. The EnumDevices function is internally executed as a loop, continuously calling this callback function for every device found. The second last parameter, pvRef, is a 32-bit pointer to a value passed to the callback each time it is called, with the final parameter, dwFlags, controlling the scope of enumeration (thus the type of devices to scan for). The dwFlags parameter can be set to any of the following constants:

■ DIEDFL_ALLDEVICES (all devices are scanned for)

■ DIEDFL_ATTACHEDONLY (only installed and connected devices are scanned for)

■ DIEDFL_FORCEFEEDBACK (only force-feedback capable devices are scanned for)

■ DIEDFL_INCLUDEALIASES (scan for all devices, including devices serving as aliases for other devices)

■ DIEDFL_INCLUDEHIDDEN (scan for all devices, including hidden devices – a hidden device is a fictitious device created by a device driver for the emulation of certain events), or

■ DIEDFL_INCLUDEPHANTOMS (scan for all devices, including 'phantom' or placeholder devices).

We can now use this EnumDevices function to enumerate all joystick devices present on the system:

```
lpdi->EnumDevices (DI8DEVCLASS_GAMECTRL,
                   EnumJoystickDeviceCallback,
                   NULL,
                   DIEDFL_ATTACHEDONLY)
```

The second parameter, EnumJoystickDeviceCallback, specifies the callback function that is to be called whenever a joystick device is found; creating a device interface to the detected device. This function takes two parameters, the first being a pointer to the DIDEVICEINSTANCE structure sent to the callback for each enumeration (containing information about the device). The DIDEVICEINSTANCE structure, holding information about the device, is briefly shown here:

```
typedef struct DIDEVICEINSTANCE {
    DWORD dwSize;          //size of the structure in bytes
    GUID guidInstance;     //GUID for the device instance
    GUID guidProduct;      //GUID for the device specified by the
                           //manufacturer to identify the product
    DWORD dwDevType;  //device type identifier
    TCHAR tszInstanceName[MAX_PATH];   //generic device name,
                                       //for example: "gamepad 1"
    TCHAR tszProductName[MAX_PATH];    //device product name,
                                       //for example: "Microsoft
                                       //Xbox 360 controller"
    GUID guidFFDriver;     //GUID for the force-feedback driver
    WORD wUsagePage;   //HID usage page code (ignore for now)
    WORD wUsage;         //HID usage code (ignore for now)
} DIDEVICEINSTANCE, *LPDIDEVICEINSTANCE;
```

The second parameter sent to the EnumJoystickDeviceCallback function is the enumeration context (not used at this stage since 'NULL' was passed as the value of EnumDevices's pvRef parameter). We specify this function as follows (the CreateDevice method is called from within this function):

```
BOOL CALLBACK EnumJoystickDeviceCallback (
                        const DIDEVICEINSTANCE* pdeviceInstance,
                        VOID* pdeviceContext)
{
    /* create the device with the guidInstance member
     containing the unique identifier of the device */
    hresult_ = lpdi->CreateDevice (
                        pdeviceInstance->guidInstance,
                        &g_lpInputDevice,
                        NULL);

    /*  if we fail to obtain an interface to the enumerated
        joystick then instruct DirectInput to continue
        enumerating for joystick devices */
    if(FAILED(hresult_))
        return DIENUM_CONTINUE;

    /* else we can stop enumerating devices */
    return DIENUM_STOP;
}
```

We have now created a DirectInput keyboard device, mouse device, and joystick device. However, before we can start using any of these devices we first have to set their data formats.

5.3.1.3 Setting the Data Format of a DirectInput Device   Setting the data format of a device is crucial for the specification of device objects. DirectInput has to know what device objects to use, including specifics about the organization of the input data. The SetDataFormat IDirectInputDevice8 interface function sets the data format of a device. It takes a single parameter, a pointer to a DirectInput data format structure. This structure, describing the format of the data returned by the device, can be specified by the programmer (using the DIDATAFORMAT structure) or via one of the following predefined variables: c_dfDIKeyboard (for a generic keyboard), c_dfDIMouse (for a generic mouse), c_dfDIMouse2 (for a mouse supporting more than four mouse buttons), c_dfDIJoystick (for a generic joystick) or c_dfDIJoystick2 (for a force-feedback capable joystick). The DIDATAFORMAT structure, describing a custom device's data format, is declared as follows in the dinput.h header file:

```
typedef struct DIDATAFORMAT {
    DWORD dwSize;
    DWORD dwObjSize;
    DWORD dwFlags;
    DWORD dwDataSize;
    DWORD dwNumObjs;
    LPDIOBJECTDATAFORMAT rgodf;
} DIDATAFORMAT, *LPDIDATAFORMAT;
```

This data structure specifies how data received from an input device is to be formatted. Its first member, dwSize, sets the size of the DIDATAFORMAT structure in bytes. The second member, dwObjSize, is a bit more complex, setting the size of a DIOBJECTDATAFORMAT structure in bytes. This data structure further describes the device object's data format by specifying four members controlling how an object's data should be reported. The DIOBJECTDATAFORMAT structure, given here, is also declared in the dinput.h header file:

```
typedef struct DIOBJECTDATAFORMAT {
    CONST GUID * pguid;
    DWORD dwOfs;
    DWORD dwType;
    DWORD dwFlags;
} DIOBJECTDATAFORMAT, *LPDIOBJECTDATAFORMAT;
```

The first member of the DIOBJECTDATAFORMAT structure sets the GUID for some device resource such as a button, trigger or axis ('NULL' indicates any resource as acceptable). The second member, dwOfs, sets the allowed offset for a data packet storing the input data received from the input device. The dwType member sets the device type describing the device object, for example, an axis or button – it can be set to any of the following flags:

- DIDFT_ABSAXIS (for an absolute axis object)
- DIDFT_AXIS (for an absolute or relative axis object)
- DIDFT_BUTTON (for a push or toggle button object)
- DIDFT_FFACTUATOR (for a force-feedback capable object)
- DIDFT_FFEFFECTTRIGGER (for a force-feedback effect trigger object)
- DIDFT_POV (for a point-of-view controller object)
- DIDFT_PSHBUTTON (for a push button object)

- DIDFT_RELAXIS (for a relative axis object)

- DIDFT_TGLBUTTON (for a toggle button object) or

- DIDFT_VENDORDEFINED (for some custom, vendor-specific object).

The final member, dwFlags, is set to one of the following flags for the return of some information related to the object:

- DIDOI_ASPECTACCEL (acceleration information is returned by the device)

- DIDOI_ASPECTFORCE (force information is returned by the device)

- DIDOI_ASPECTPOSITION (position information is returned by the device) or

- DIDOI_ASPECTVELOCITY (velocity information is returned by the device).

The third member of the DIDATAFORMAT structure, dwFlags, is concerned with the reporting mode used for the axis of a device (DIDF_ABSAXIS for absolute reporting or DIDF_RELAXIS for relative reporting – reporting is discussed during section 5.3.2). The dwDataSize member sets the size of the data packets, with the dwNumObjs member specifying the number of objects defined in the rgodf array. This final member, rgodf, is an array of DIOBJECTDATAFORMAT structures.

As a note, it's necessary to remember that we won't generally make use of these data structures, rather utilizing one of the predefined data formats such as c_dfDIKeyboard outlined above. The DIDATAFORMAT and DIOBJECTDATAFORMAT structures are only used when defining data formats for non-standard input devices.

Continuing with our keyboard example of section 5.3.1.2: we set its data format using the SetDataFormat IDirectInputDevice8 interface function (via the previously defined LPDIRECTINPUTDEVICE8 type, g_lpInputDevice):

```
hresult_ = g_lpInputDevice->SetDataFormat(&c_dfDIKeyboard);
```

Following this we simply have to check whether this SetDataFormat function call failed; if it did we have to release all devices to deallocate the existing DirectInput object:

```
if FAILED (hresult_)
{
    g_lpInputDevice->Release();
    return FALSE;
}
```

Setting the data format for a mouse device only requires the specification of a different data format structure, c_dfDIMouse or c_dfDIMouse2, as a parameter to the SetDataFormat IDirectInputDevice8 interface function:

```
hresult_ = g_lpInputDevice->SetDataFormat(&c_dfDIMouse);
```

The data format for joystick devices are set in a similar manner, the data format structure in this case being either c_dfDIJoystick or c_dfDIJoystick2 depending on whether the device is force-feedback capable or not:

```
hresult_ = g_lpInputDevice->SetDataFormat(&c_dfDIJoystick);
```

The next step is to define the DirectInput device's cooperative level.

5.3.1.4 Setting the Cooperative Level of a DirectInput Device By setting the cooperation level of a device we are able to control the manner in which this device will share its input with other applications, including the Windows system. This cooperation level is set using the SetCooperativeLevel IDirectInputDevice8 interface method declared as follows in the dinput.h header file:

```
HRESULT SetCooperativeLevel(
    HWND hwnd,
    DWORD dwFlags
);
```

Its first parameter, hwnd, is simply a handle to the window associated with the input device with the second parameter, dwFlags, describing the cooperation level of the device via a combination of the following flags:

- DISCL_BACKGROUND (for using the DirectInput device with an application running in either the background or active in the foreground)

- DISCL_EXCLUSIVE (once the device has been acquired, then no other application can gain exclusive access to it – only non-exclusive access being available)

- DISCL_FOREGROUND (for using the DirectInput device with an application running in the foreground – the device is unacquired when the application window moves to the background)

- DISCL_NONEXCLUSIVE (other applications can gain nonexclusive access to the device, regardless of whether it has been acquired by another application or not) or

- DISCL_NOWINKEY (for disabling the Windows logo key present on most keyboards sold today – this will ensure that the application isn't accidentally exited. This key is also disabled in exclusive mode and the DISCL_NOWINKEY flag is used in combination with DISCL_NONEXCLUSIVE).

The SetCooperativeLevel function returns a DI_OK value if successful and any of the following errors in the event of a failure: E_HANDLE (a standard COM error when an invalid handle was provided as a parameter), DIERR_INVALIDPARAM or DIERR_NOTINITIALIZED.

Cooperation flags are used in specific combinational sets, for example, we have to specify whether the application requires foreground or background access to the input device while at the same time coupling this access type, using the bitwise OR '|' operator, with a flag indicating whether the device will be used in exclusive or non-exclusive mode. As a rule we will generally use the following flag combination (the exception being force-feedback devices): DISCL_BACKGROUND | DISCL_NONEXCLUSIVE.

Keyboard devices are always acquired using non-exclusive mode. This allows Windows to process Windows-specific key combinations such as the 'Ctrl-Alt-Del' or 'Alt-Tab' combinations, even with the application being in focus. Mouse devices can be acquired using exclusive mode; however, this will cause the mouse cursor to disappear (requiring it to be re-rendered by the application itself) due to Windows not gaining any access to mouse messages being generated. Force-feedback-enabled devices must be acquired in exclusive mode; this has to do with the application requiring exclusive access to the device for the force-feedback subsystem to function properly.

Using our previous keyboard device example, we can now set its cooperative level using the SetCooperativeLevel function (with the calling function taking 'HWND hWnd' as a parameter):

```
hresult_ = g_lpInputDevice->
            SetCooperativeLevel(hWnd,
                    DISCL_FOREGROUND |
                    DISCL_NONEXCLUSIVE);
```

We have now defined how our input device, g_lpInputDevice, (a keyboard device) will interact with other DirectInput applications as well as the Windows system. All that remains now is to check whether this SetCooperativeLevel function failed; if it did we would have to release all devices to deallocate the existing DirectInput object:

```
if FAILED (hresult_)
{
    g_lpInputDevice->Release();
    return FALSE;
}
```

Setting the cooperative level of a mouse or joystick device is done as follows – using the DISCL_EXCLUSIVE flag to ensure that only the application will have exclusive access to the device. The DISCL_FOREGROUND flag is also set to ensure that the application does not register any input when another application is in the foreground:

```
hresult_ = g_lpInputDevice->
            SetCooperativeLevel(hWnd,
                        DISCL_FOREGROUND |
                        DISCL_EXCLUSIVE);
```

Joystick devices also require the collection of information pertaining to their capabilities (such as the number of buttons, axes, force-feedback specifications, etc.). This capability information is stored in the DIDEVCAPS structure shown here:

```
typedef struct DIDEVCAPS {
    DWORD dwSize;
    DWORD dwFlags;
    DWORD dwDevType;
    DWORD dwAxes;
    DWORD dwButtons;
    DWORD dwPOVs;
    DWORD dwFFSamplePeriod;
    DWORD dwFFMinTimeResolution;
    DWORD dwFirmwareRevision;
    DWORD dwHardwareRevision;
    DWORD dwFFDriverVersion;
} DIDEVCAPS, *LPDIDEVCAPS;
```

Its first member, dwSize, specifies the size of the structure in bytes with the second member, dwFlags, used for setting some device specific details via a combination of the following flags:

■ DIDC_ALIAS (when the device serves as a clone for another device)

■ DIDC_ATTACHED (when the device is attached to the computer)

■ DIDC_DEADBAND (when *deadband* force-feedback is supported – this is the zone of a joystick or gamepad where no action is generated by device movement)

■ DIDC_EMULATED (when data is coming directly from the input device, not from the kernel driver)

- DIDC_FORCEFEEDBACK (when force-feedback is supported)

- DIDC_FFFADE (when a force-feedback device supports fading effects)

- DIDC_FFATTACK (when a force-feedback device supports a so-called attack parameter)

- DIDC_HIDDEN (when dealing with a fictitious device created by a device driver for the emulation of certain events)

- DIDC_PHANTOM (when it's a phantom/placeholder device without any functionaility)

- DIDC_POLLEDDATAFORMAT and DIDC_POLLEDDEVICE (when the device is not interrupt-driven, rather depending on frequent polling)

- DIDC_POSNEGCOEFFICIENTS (when a device supports both a positive and negative coefficient – for example, a positive value when the axis is in a forward position and a negative value when it is tilted backwards) or

- DIDC_STARTDELAY (when a force-feedback device supports a start delay for one of its effects).

The next parameter, dwDevType, specifies the type of device with dwAxes the number of axes provided by the device and dwButtons the number of buttons present on the device. The dwPOVs member relates the number of point-of-view controllers available and it can be ignored for all intents and purposes. The dwFFSamplePeriod member indicates the time, in milliseconds, between the playback of force commands, while the dwFFMinTimeResolution member gives the time in milliseconds between device resolutions. The final three members hold device-specific information, with dwFirmwareRevision holding the device's firmware details (software that is embedded in a hardware device) revision, dwHardwareRevision storing the hardware revision of the device, and dwFFDriverVersion specifying the device driver version.

This DIDEVCAPS structure is used with the GetCapabilities IDirectInputDevice8 interface method which determines the capabilities of a DirectInput device object. The address of the initialized DIDEVCAPS structure is sent to the GetCapabilities method (in the example below we declared g_deviceCapabilities as a DIDEVCAPS structure, only initializing its dwSize member so we can call the GetCapabilities method using this structure as storage):

```
/* we must initialize this member before calling
   GetCapabilities */
g_deviceCapabilities.dwSize = sizeof (DIDEVCAPS);

hresult_ = g_lpInputDevice ->
                GetCapabilities (&g_deviceCapabilities);
```

Next we have to enumerate the input and output objects present on the joystick device. The EnumObjects IDirectInputDevice8 interface method, shown here as declared in the dinput.h header file, is used to do this:

```
HRESULT EnumObjects (
    LPDIENUMDEVICEOBJECTSCALLBACK lpCallback,
    LPVOID pvRef,
    DWORD dwFlags
);
```

Its first parameter is an address to a callback function, similar to the EnumJoystickDeviceCallback function previously defined, this time dealing with DirectInput device objects. The second parameter, pvRef, is a

32-bit pointer to a value passed to the callback whenever it is called, with the final parameter, dwFlags, controlling the scope of object enumeration; for example, the type of objects to scan for, the most common flags include:

- DIDFT_ABSAXIS (to scan for an absolute axis)

- DIDFT_ALIAS (to scan for controls specified by some usage alias)

- DIDFT_ALL (to scan for all possible objects)

- DIDFT_AXIS (to scan for both relative and absolute axes)

- DIDFT_BUTTON (to scan for either a push or toggle button)

- DIDFT_FFACTUATOR (to scan for objects containing a force-feedback actuator – hence objects supporting force feedback)

- DIDFT_FFEFFECTTRIGGER (to scan for objects that can cause a force-feedback effect)

- DIDFT_NODATA (to scan for objects not generating any data)

- DIDFT_PSHBUTTON (to scan for a push button – a button that reports its state as down when it is being pressed)

- DIDFT_RELAXIS (to scan for a relative axis) or

- DIDFT_TGLBUTTON (to scan for a toggle button – a button that reports its state as down after it was pressed and as up when it is pressed again).

Using this EnumObjects function to enumerate the axis objects found on a joystick device is relatively simple (taking a handle to the main dialog window, 'HWND hWnd', as second parameter):

```
hresult_ = g_lpInputDevice->EnumObjects (
                         EnumDeviceObjectsCallback,
                         (VOID*)hWnd,
                         DIDFT_AXIS );
```

The callback function, specified as the first parameter, sets the user interface elements for detected objects such as discovered buttons and axes – in this case only dealing with axis and slider-like objects (DIDFT_AXIS). This EnumDeviceObjectsCallback callback function takes two parameters (a pointer to the DIDEVICEOBJECTINSTANCE structure sent by the system to the callback for each enumeration, and the enumeration context, pdeviceContext. The DIDEVICEOBJECTINSTANCE structure, containing information about the object, is briefly shown here:

```
typedef struct DIDEVICEOBJECTINSTANCE {
    DWORD dwSize;       //size of the structure in bytes
    GUID guidType;      //GUID identifying the object type (e.g
                        //GUID_RyAxis for rotation about the y-
                        //axis
    DWORD dwOfs;        //offset in the raw data format used by
                        //the device
    DWORD dwType;       //device type describing the object
                        //(axis, button, etc)
```

```
        DWORD dwFlags;      //flags detailing attributes of the
                            //device's data format (e.g.
                            //DIDOI_ASPECTPOSITION for an object
                            //reporting position data)
        TCHAR tszName[MAX_PATH];      //object name (e.g. "Y-Axis")
        DWORD dwFFMaxForce;           //maximum force in Newton that
                                      //can be generated by a force-
                                      //feedback actuator
        DWORD dwFFForceResolution;    //the number of incremental
                                      //units a force can be
                                      //expressed in (ranging from
                                      //zero to maximum force)
        WORD wCollectionNumber;       //HID number the object belongs to
                                      //(ignore for now)
        WORD wDesignatorIndex;        //HID number that can be used to
                                      //obtain additional device
                                      //information (ignore for now)
        WORD wUsagePage;    //HID usage page code (ignore for now)
        WORD wUsage;        // HID usage code (ignore for now)
        DWORD dwDimension;  //HID code representing the units used
                            //for reporting values of the object
                            //(ignore for now)
        WORD wExponent; //an exponential value to combine with an
                        //object's dimension
        WORD wReportId; //reserved for future use
} DIDEVICEOBJECTINSTANCE, *LPDIDEVICEOBJECTINSTANCE;
```

`EnumObjectsCallback` makes use of the DIPROPRANGE structure to set the range of all sliders and axes detected. This range is the maximum and minimum values returned by any of these objects, for example, setting a range of −500 to +500 for the y axis will cause the value of −500 to be returned when the joystick is in its extreme back position and +500 when it is completely forward (with zero when it is in the middle). The DIPROPRANGE structure is declared as follows:

```
typedef struct DIPROPRANGE {
    DIPROPHEADER diph;
    LONG lMin;
    LONG lMax;
} DIPROPRANGE, *LPDIPROPRANGE;
```

The first member is a DIPROPHEADER structure that functions as an overall description for all property structures. This structure, taking four parameters, is in turn declared as:

```
typedef struct DIPROPHEADER {
    DWORD dwSize;
    DWORD dwHeaderSize;
    DWORD dwObj;
    DWORD dwHow;
} DIPROPHEADER, *LPDIPROPHEADER;
```

DIPROPHEADER's first member specifies the size of the DIPROPRANGE structure, its second the size of the DIPROPHEADER structure, with the third member taking an object describing the property being accessed (the device type that describes the object as defined by the DIDEVICEOBJECTINSTANCE structure's dwType member). The final member, dwHow, describes how the dwObj member is to be interpreted, for example:

- DIPH_DEVICE (when no property is to be accessed – thus when dwObj is set to '0')

- DIPH_BYOFFSET (when the dwObj member is an offset of the accessed object's data format)

- DIPH_BYUSAGE (when the dwObj member is a human interface device (HID) usage page – can be ignored) or

- DIPH_BYID (when the dwObj member is an instance identifier – such as when using the DIDEVICEOBJECTINSTANCE structure to describe the device object instance).

The final two members of the DIPROPRANGE structure, lMin and lMax, are used for setting the lower and higher limits of a range respectively.

Once we have defined the device properties (axis range values in this case) using the DIPROPRANGE property structure, we have to set these properties defining device behaviour using the SetProperty IDirectInputDevice8 interface method. This interface method takes two parameters, the GUID of the property to set (with the most common values listed in Table 5-1) and a pointer to the DIPROPHEADER structure storing detailed information about the related property.

The EnumObjectsCallback callback function, as declared in our example program and listed here, contains the definition of the DIPROPRANGE structure's members and the SetProperty function:

```
BOOL CALLBACK EnumObjectsCallback (
            const DIDEVICEOBJECTINSTANCE* pdeviceObjectInstance,
            VOID* pdeviceContext )
{
    HWND hWnd = (HWND)pdeviceContext;

    /* for all the axes and toggle switches returned we can set
       their scaling range with the minimum value = -500 and
       the maximum = 500 */
    DIPROPRANGE dipropRange;
    dipropRange.diph.dwSize = sizeof(DIPROPRANGE);
    dipropRange.diph.dwHeaderSize = sizeof(DIPROPHEADER);
    dipropRange.diph.dwObj = pdeviceObjectInstance->dwType;
    dipropRange.diph.dwHow = DIPH_BYID;
    dipropRange.lMin = -500;
    dipropRange.lMax = +500;

    /* Sets the range of values that can be communicated */
    hresult_ = g_lpInputDevice->SetProperty(DIPROP_RANGE,
                                    &dipropRange.diph);

    /* if we fail to set the device behaviour properties */
    if(FAILED(hresult_))
        return DIENUM_STOP;
}
```

TABLE 5-1	GUID property values to use as the first parameter of the SetProperty IDirectInputDevice8 interface method

Property value	Description
DIPROP_APPDATA	Sets some application-specific value related to some in-game action.
DIPROP_AUTOCENTER	Specifies whether a device is self-centering or not (self-centering devices return to their 'zero' or center position when they are released by the user with non-centering devices not returning to some predefine rest position when released).
DIPROP_AXISMODE	Specifies whether the device will make use of absolute or relative positioning.
DIPROP_BUFFERSIZE	Sets the input buffer size of the device.
DIPROP_CALIBRATION	Property used to enable the calibration of a joystick device.
DIPROP_CALIBRATIONMODE	Specifies whether data should be collected by the device in calibrated or uncalibrated form.
DIPROP_DEADZONE	Sets the dead zone value of a joystick with the value 0 indicating no dead zone and 1000 denoting a dead zone extending over 10 percent of the axial range from the center, for example.
DIPROP_FFGAIN	Specifies the gain of the device. The amount of gain controls whether a force-feedback effect created by a device will be amplified or lessened, for example, a gain value of 7000 will cause all effect forces to be reduced by 30 percent.
DIPROP_PRODUCTNAME	For modifying the product name provided by a device.
DIPROP_RANGE	Sets the range of values that can be communicated by the device as specified via the lmin and lmax members of the DIPROPRANGE structure.

We have so far created the main DirectInput COM object, a DirectInput device, set the data format and specified the cooperation level and device behaviour. The next step is to acquire the device from DirectInput so that data can be retrieved from it.

5.3.1.5 Acquiring the DirectInput Device
Acquiring the DirectInput device is a relatively simple procedure; we merely have to call the Acquire IDirectInputDevice8 interface method. This method doesn't take any parameters:

```
g_lpInputDevice->Acquire ();
```

When acquiring a joystick device we are often interested in its current position or state. We will thus first like to poll it before acquiring the device using the Poll IDirectInputDevice8 interface function. By polling the device, we are able to receive data indicating its current state. The polling function also allows us to update the device state, set notifications, and generate input events (for buffered data). It is called as follows:

```
hresult_ = g_lpInputDevice->Poll ();
```

Next we can acquire the joystick device; however, device acquisition is not permanent and the device might be acquired and released several times, for example, when the application is minimized to the background (causing the device to be released) with focus returned at a later stage (causing Windows to release control of the device and the application to reacquire it). We will thus make use of a simple loop to reacquire the device whenever focus is returned to the application or when access to the device has been lost (scanning for the DIERR_INPUTLOST error):

```
if (FAILED(hresult_))
{
    hresult_ = g_lpInputDevice->Acquire ();

    while(hresult_ == DIERR_INPUTLOST)
        hresult_ = g_lpInputDevice->Acquire ();

    return S_OK;
}
```

Following this device acquisition, DirectInput has access to our previously created input device (keyboard, mouse, or joystick) and we can now start processing device input.

5.3.1.6 Reading Data from a DirectInput Device

With the DirectInput device acquired, we can start reading data from it. The GetDeviceState IDirectInputDevice8 interface function can be used to accomplish this. This function, retrieving immediate data from the device (as opposed to buffered data via the GetDeviceData function), takes two parameters and is declared in the dinput.h header file like so:

```
HRESULT GetDeviceState (
    DWORD cbData,
    LPVOID lpvData
);
```

GetDeviceState's first parameter is the size in bytes of the second parameter, lpvData, the state data structure. This second parameter is an address of the structure used for storing the current state of the device. There are a couple of DirectInput data structures used for the storage of device messages, the most common ones being:

- DIMOUSESTATE (storing a mouse message using the c_dfDIMouse data format)
- DIMOUSESTATE2 (storing a mouse message using the c_dfDIMouse2 data format)
- DIJOYSTATE (storing a standard joystick device message using the c_dfDIJoystick data format)
- DIJOYSTATE2 (storing a force-feedback joystick device message using the c_dfDIJoystick2 data format) with the keyboard structure being a simple array of 256 bytes.

Using the keyboard data format (c_dfDIKeyboard) we only need to use an array of 256 characters as the return data structure. An array works well for the keyboard; however, other devices such as the mouse and joystick require a data structure more suited to their configuration. As mentioned, the DIMOUSESTATE structure is used for the storage of mouse messages using the c_dfDIMouse data format. This structure, supporting devices with up to four buttons, is shown here:

```
typedef struct DIMOUSESTATE {
    LONG lX;
    LONG lY;
```

```
    LONG IZ;
    BYTE rgbButtons[4];
} DIMOUSESTATE, *LPDIMOUSESTATE;
```

The first three members, IX, IY, and IZ, stores information about the *x*-axis, *y*-axis, and *z*-axis (the mouse wheel) respectively, with the final member, rgbButtons, an array representing the mouse buttons (the first element of this array is set when the left mouse button is pressed, the second when the right mouse button is pressed, and the third when the middle mouse button is pressed).

We can alternatively use the DIMOUSESTATE2 structure when supporting pointing devices that have up to eight buttons. It has exactly the same members as DIMOUSESTATE with only the rgbButtons[4] array changed to rgbButtons[8].

When working with joystick devices (all devices that are not a keyboard or a mouse) we use either the DIJOYSTATE or DIJOYSTATE2 structure for the storage of device messages (the device state data). The structure is declared as follows:

```
typedef struct DIJOYSTATE {
    LONG IX;
    LONG IY;
    LONG IZ;
    LONG IRx;
    LONG IRy;
    LONG IRz;
    LONG rglSlider[2];
    DWORD rgdwPOV[4];
    BYTE rgbButtons[32];
} DIJOYSTATE, *LPDIJOYSTATE;
```

The first three members, IX, IY, and IZ, are values corresponding to the *x*-axis (used for left/right movement), *y*-axis (used for forward/backward movement) and *z*-axis (used for throttle control and set to '0' if absent) of the device. The next three members, IRx, IRy, and IRz, represent the rotation of the joystick in each of the axes with the first of these indicating the amount of rotation about the *x*-axis, the second the amount about the *y*-axis, and the third the amount about the *z*-axis. The second last member, rglSlider, deals with slider-like controls such as pedals. The final member, rgbButtons, is an array representing the buttons present on the device (it can handle up to 32 buttons). The DIJOYSTATE2 structure used with force-feedback capable devices has 30 members allowing the description of additional device capabilities such as axial angular velocity, forces, torque, etc.

The GetDeviceState function returns a DI_OK value if successful and any of the following errors when it fails:

■ DIERR_INPUTLOST (when access to the input device has been lost, requiring a reacquisition of the device)

■ DIERR_NOTACQUIRED (when the device has not yet been acquired)

■ E_PENDING (if the device is not currently available, but it will be soon) and

■ DIERR_INVALIDPARAM or DIERR_NOTINITIALIZED as previously described.

We will now use this GetDeviceState function to query the state of our input device, the previously created keyboard device, first creating a buffer for holding the keyboard data and then calling the

`GetDeviceState` function to poll the keyboard:

```
char keybuffer[256];

hresult_ = g_lpInputDevice ->
                    GetDeviceState(sizeof(keybuffer),
                              (LPVOID) & keybuffer);
```

Next we must check the result returned by the function, the most probable reason for a failure being a lost device (indicated by the DIERR_INPUTLOST error code):

```
if FAILED(hresult_)
{
    /*  if GetDeviceState failed because of a lost device,
        reacquire the device here */
    return;
}
```

We now have the keyboard's current state and can proceed to test for specific key presses. These key presses are written to the buffer, each element of this buffer containing one of the keys that were pressed at the time of the keyboard state call. If a buffer element is set to '1' then the key represented by that specific array element was down at the moment of the call. We can check for the specific key pressed by using the DirectInput keyboard state constants used for indexing the buffer data and linking each buffer element to a keyboard key. These keyboard state constants (the most common ones are listed in Table 5-2) correspond to an offset within the 256-byte array, and hence within the keyboard's data packet.

Thus, after polling the keyboard with the GetDeviceState IDirectInputDevice8 interface function, we can check for specific key presses. The only trick to testing whether a key was pressed is to test the 0×80 bit in the 8-bit byte of the key being tested for. Say we want to test whether the spacebar has been pressed, then we can do it directly using a bit test as illustrated here:

```
if(keybuffer[DIK_SPACE] & 0x08)
{
    //the spacebar is pressed
}
else
{
    //the spacebar is not pressed
}
```

Using the bitwise AND operator '&' directly, as in the above sample, is a bit untidy and we would much rather create a macro to test for pressed keys:

```
#define KEYPRESSED(buffer, key) (buffer[key] & 0x80)
```

The following code sample illustrates how we'll go about testing for the left 'Ctrl', right 'Ctrl', left 'Alt' and spacebar using the above defined macro:

```
// check whether the left 'Ctrl' key is pressed
if (KEYPRESSED(keybuffer, DIK_LCONTROL))
{
    //do something
}
```

TABLE 5-2   Keyboard device state constants

Constant	Description
DIK_0 to DIK_9	Keyboard's 0 to 9 keys.
DIK_A to DIK_Z	Keyboard's A to Z keys.
DIK_ADD	The numeric keypad's plus '+' key.
DIK_BACK	Keyboard's Backspace key.
DIK_DELETE	Middle keypad's Delete key.
DIK_DOWN	Arrow keypad's Down key.
DIK_END	Numeric keypad's End key.
DIK_EQUALS	Keyboard's equals '=' key.
DIK_F1 to DIK_F12	Keyboard's function keys F1 to F12.
DIK_HOME	Numeric keypad's Home key.
DIK_INSERT	Middle keypad's Insert key.
DIK_LBRACKET	Keyboard's left bracket.
DIK_LCONTROL	Keyboard's left Ctrl button.
DIK_LEFT	Arrow keypad's Left key.
DIK_LMENU	Keyboard's left Alt button.
DIK_LSHIFT	Keyboard's left Shift button.
DIK_LWIN	Keyboard's Windows logo key.
DIK_MINUS	The numeric keypad's minus '-' key.
DIK_MULTIPLY	Numeric keypad's multiply '*' key.
DIK_NEXT	Middle keypad's Page Down key.
DIK_NUMPAD0 to DIK_NUMPAD9	Numeric keypad's keys 0 to 9.
DIK_NUMPADENTER	Numeric keypad's Enter key.
DIK_PERIOD	Keyboard's period key.
DIK_PRIOR	Middle keypad's Page Up key.
DIK_RBRACKET	Keyboard's right bracket.
DIK_RCONTROL	Keyboard's right Ctrl button.
DIK_RETURN	Keyboard's main Enter key.
DIK_RIGHT	Arrow keypad's Right key.
DIK_RMENU	Keyboard's right Alt button.
DIK_RSHIFT	Keyboard's right Shift button.
DIK_SPACE	Keyboard's spacebar.
DIK_TAB	Keyboard's Tab key.
DIK_UP	Arrow keypad's Up key.

5

```
// check whether the right 'Ctrl' key is pressed
if (KEYPRESSED(keybuffer, DIK_RCONTROL))
{
    //do something
}

// check whether the left 'Alt' key is pressed
if (KEYPRESSED(keybuffer, DIK_LMENU))
{
    //do something
}

// check whether the spacebar is pressed
if (KEYPRESSED(keybuffer, DIK_SPACE))
{
    //do something
}
```

When reading data from mouse devices, we can make use of either the GetDeviceState function to retrieve immediate data or the GetDeviceData function to read buffered data (discussed in section 5.3.2.1). Using the GetDeviceState function, we first have to declare a DIMOUSESTATE structure to hold the mouse data:

```
DIMOUSESTATE mousestructure;
```

Next we call the GetDeviceState function:

```
hresult_ = g_lpInputDevice ->
                GetDeviceState(sizeof(mousestructure),
                                (LPVOID)mousestructure);
```

We now have the mouse's current state and can proceed to test for specific offsets within the mouse device's data structure (DIMOUSESTATE). The following code sample illustrates testing whether the right mouse button or left mouse button has been pressed (remember, this is immediate data, testing for buffered data is a bit more complex and discussed in section 5.3.2):

```
// check whether the left mouse button is pressed
if (mousestructure.rgbButtons[0] & 0x80)
{
    //do something
}

// check whether the right mouse button is pressed
if (mousestructure.rgbButtons[1] & 0x80)
{
    //do something
}
```

Checking for mouse movements (once again using immediate data) is done by accessing the mousestructure structure's first two members. We first declare and initialize two place holders to save the *x* and *y* coordinate to:

```
int position_x = 0;
int position_y = 0;
```

We can now assign the mouse position to these place holders, enabling us to move some onscreen object (which was originally located at (0, 0) :

```
position_x += mousestructure.lX;
position_y += mousestructure.lY;
```

Reading data from a joystick input device is generally accomplished via the GetDeviceState function. The GetDeviceData function can be used as an alternative; however, immediate data as opposed to buffered data are preferred due to the current position of the joystick axes being much more useful to us than their relative movement. Using the GetDeviceState function, we start by declaring a DIJOYSTATE structure that will hold the joystick data:

```
DIJOYSTATE joystickstructure;
```

Following this we call the GetDeviceState function:

```
hresult_ = g_lpInputDevice ->
              GetDeviceState(sizeof(DIJOYSTATE),
                      &joystickstructure);
```

After retrieving all the input needed and finally shutting down the application it is important to close down the entire DirectInput system. This is done by releasing the IDirectInputDevice8 interface, all IDirectInputDevice8 DirectInput devices and the main IDirectInput8 DirectInput object:

```
//unacquire the input device
if(g_lpInputDevice)
  g_lpInputDevice->Unacquire();

//release the input device
if(g_lpInputDevice)
  g_lpInputDevice->Release();

//release the main DirectInput COM object
if(g_lpInputDevice)
  lpdi->Release();
```

The unacquire function, as its name suggests, unacquires a device by releasing access to it, not releasing it, thus allowing the device to be reacquired at a later state.

5.3.2 Device Data

This section presents various methods of obtaining data from input devices, specifically looking at immediate vs. buffered data, as well as polling and event notification used for determining whether any input data is available for processing. DirectInput identifies data retrieved from an input device in one of two ways, either by categorising the data in terms of a specific device object (such as a mouse button or keyboard key) or by using Action Mapping (section 5.3.3).

The most common method of acquiring data from input devices is to use immediate data. *Immediate data* are data representing the present state of an input device; for example, in an FPS computer game we might make use of a mouse in combination with a keyboard to control the player's position and point of view based on the current state of the mouse and keyboard objects. *Buffered data*, serving as a repository of events, would be more suited in situations where we are interested in event sequences such as when we are making use of, say, mouse button clicks to control movement. Buffered data can be considered a collection of recorded events from a specific moment in time to the moment of retrieval.

Polling and event notification are needed for DirectInput devices not generating any interrupts (hardware signals generated due to a change in the state of a hardware device – see Chapter 1). Devices generating hardware interrupts will always signal DirectInput that their state has changed, hence, that new data is available for processing.

Polling is the process of frequently checking whether new input data are available. It can be done by checking the present state of a device object or by examining the contents of an event buffer. We generally poll devices from within the main message loop using the Poll IDirectInputDevice8 interface function just after setting the data format for the device and calling the GetCapabilities IDirectInputDevice8 interface method with its dwFlags member set to the DIDC_POLLEDDATAFORMAT flag. The GetCapabilities method will indicate whether it's necessary to poll the device whenever we require data. *Event notification* is, on the other hand, aimed at applications that remain in an idle state until some form of input is received. DirectInput can be configured to signal an event associated with a device the moment the state of the device is altered.

Another important element of input data is whether they are returned in absolute or relative form. For example, a joystick's axial coordinates can be reported as absolute coordinates when it relates the position of the device in terms of a fixed point (commonly in relation to some centerline or dead zone) with relative coordinates representing the new coordinates of the axis from the previously received device state.

5.3.2.1 Buffered as an alternative to Immediate Keyboard Data

DirectInput uses immediate data by default. Setting the buffer size associated with the device ('0' by default) to any nonzero value designates the use of buffered data. The size of the buffer controls the number of events retrieved during each call, for example, setting the buffer size to '1' leads to the retrieval of one event during each call. The DIPROPDWORD device properties structure, shown here as declared in dinput.h, is used to set the buffer size:

```
typedef struct DIPROPDWORD {
    DIPROPHEADER diph;
    DWORD dwData;
} DIPROPDWORD, *LPDIPROPDWORD;
```

This structure specifies a DIPROPHEADER structure as its first member, with the second member the property value being accessed. We can now use this structure to specify the use of buffered data as follows:

```
DIPROPDWORD dipropdword;

dipropdword.diph.dwSize    = sizeof(DIPROPDWORD);
dipropdword.diph.dwHeaderSize = sizeof(DIPROPHEADER);
```

```
dipropdword.diph.dwObj  = 0;
dipropdword.diph.dwHow = DIPH_DEVICE;
dipropdword.dwData = 8;   //a buffer size of eight elements
```

Using this structure we specify the device behaviour using the SetProperty IDirectInputDevice8 interface method. The method's first parameter is set to the DIPROP_BUFFERSIZE constant (defining the property being set as the input buffer size), with the second taking an address to the DIPROPDWORD property structure:

```
hresult_ = g_lpInputDevice->SetProperty (DIPROP_BUFFERSIZE,
                              &dipropdword.diph);
```

Obtaining buffered data from a keyboard requires the specification of an array of type DIDEVICEOBJECTDATA for storing the retrieved data:

```
/* receives the buffered data */
DIDEVICEOBJECTDATA dideviceobjdata[8];
```

This DIDEVICEOBJECTDATA structure stores buffered device information and is used with both the GetDeviceData and SendDeviceData IDirectInputDevice8 interface functions:

```
typedef struct DIDEVICEOBJECTDATA {
    DWORD dwOfs;
    DWORD dwData;
    DWORD dwTimeStamp;
    DWORD dwSequence;
    UINT_PTR uAppData;
} DIDEVICEOBJECTDATA, *LPDIDEVICEOBJECTDATA;
```

Its first member, dwOfs, is set to a mouse, keyboard, or joystick device state constant depending on the device type being accessed. The device state constants for keyboard devices were listed earlier in Table 5-2. Possible device constants for mouse-like devices are listed in Table 5-3, and joystick device constants are given in Table 5-4.

DIDEVICEOBJECTDATA's second member, dwData, holds the data read from the device. Its third member, dwTimeStamp, gives the time in milliseconds when the input event was generated. The fourth member, dwSequence, is a DirectInput sequence number for the generated event, with the final member holding an application-defined action value assigned using the SetActionMap IDirectInputDevice8 interface function (discussed in section 5.3.3) – this value is ignored when action mapping is not implemented.

Next we can acquire the keyboard device as described in section 5.3.1.5, followed by retrieving buffered data via the GetDeviceData IDirectInputDevice8 interface function. This function takes four parameters:

1 the size of the DIDEVICEOBJECTDATA structure in bytes

2 the array of DIDEVICEOBJECTDATA structures receiving the buffered data (dideviceobjdata)

3 the number of elements in the DIDEVICEOBJECTDATA array

4 a flag specifying the method used to obtain data:

```
DWORD dwNumberElements = 8;   //the buffer size

hresult_ = g_lpInputDevice->GetDeviceData(
                    sizeof(DIDEVICEOBJECTDATA),
                    dideviceobjdata,
                    &dwNumberElements, 0);
```

TABLE 5-3   **Mouse device state constants**

Constant	Description
DIMOFS_BUTTON0	Left mouse button.
DIMOFS_BUTTON1	Right mouse button.
DIMOFS_BUTTON2	Additional button.
DIMOFS_BUTTON3	Additional button.
DIMOFS_BUTTON4	Additional button (only when using DIMOUSESTATE2).
DIMOFS_BUTTON5	Additional button (only when using DIMOUSESTATE2).
DIMOFS_BUTTON6	Additional button (only when using DIMOUSESTATE2).
DIMOFS_BUTTON7	Additional button (only when using DIMOUSESTATE2).
DIMOFS_X	Horizontal mouse movement.
DIMOFS_Y	Vertical mouse movement.
DIMOFS_Z	Diagonal mouse movement

TABLE 5-4   **Joystick device state constants**

Constant	Description
DIJOFS_BUTTON0 to DIJOFS_BUTTON31	Joystick buttons.
DIJOFS_POV(n)	Device point-of-view indicator.
DIJOFS_X	Joystick movement along the x-axis.
DIJOFS_Y	Joystick movement along the y-axis.
DIJOFS_Z	Joystick movement along the z-axis.
DIJOFS_RX	Amount of rotation about the x-axis.
DIJOFS_RY	Amount of rotation about the y-axis.
DIJOFS_RZ	Amount of rotation about the z-axis.
DIJOFS_SLIDER(n)	Device's slider axis.

Each element stored in the dideviceobjdata array represents a state change for one of the keys found on the keyboard device. The DIDEVICEOBJECTDATA structure's dwData member holds this state information, for example, the 0 × 80 bit in the 8-bit byte of the dwData member is set if the key was pressed – hence when the following test is true: 'if ((dwData & 0×80) != 0)'. We determine the key represented by an array element by accessing the DIDEVICEOBJECTDATA structure's dwOfs member. This member holds a keyboard state constant, as listed in Table 5-2.

Input Control **171**

5.3.2.2 Buffered as an Alternative to Immediate Mouse Data Just as with the keyboard device, we set the buffer size associated with the device to a nonzero value to use buffered data:

```
DIPROPDWORD dipropdword;

dipropdword.diph.dwSize  = sizeof(DIPROPDWORD);
dipropdword.diph.dwHeaderSize = sizeof(DIPROPHEADER);
dipropdword.diph.dwObj  = 0;
dipropdword.diph.dwHow = DIPH_DEVICE;
dipropdword.dwData = 12; //a buffer size of twelve elements
```

Next we specify the device behaviour using the SetProperty IDirectInputDevice8 interface method:

```
hresult_ = g_lpInputDevice->SetProperty(DIPROP_BUFFERSIZE,
                            &dipropdword.diph);
```

This is followed by the declaration of a DIDEVICEOBJECTDATA array:

```
/* receives the buffered data */
DIDEVICEOBJECTDATA dideviceobjdata[12];
```

We acquire the mouse device as explained in section 5.3.1.5, once again retrieving buffered data via the GetDeviceData IDirectInputDevice8 interface function as explained previously:

```
DWORD dwNumberElements = 12;    //the buffer size

hresult_ = g_lpInputDevice->GetDeviceData(
                            sizeof(DIDEVICEOBJECTDATA),
                            dideviceobjdata,
                            &dwNumberElements, 0);
```

Each element stored in the DIDEVICEOBJECTDATA array signifies a mouse object state change. For example, moving the mouse horizontally and pressing the left-mouse button will cause an array of two elements to be passed to the GetDeviceData function – one element for the left-mouse button press, and another for the *x*-axis movement. The mouse object corresponding to an array element can be determined by accessing the DIDEVICEOBJECTDATA structure's dwOfs member. This member holds a mouse state constant as listed in Table 5-3. Each of these mouse state constants corresponds to an offset in the previously discussed DIMOUSESTATE rgbButtons array member. For example, both the DIMOFS_BUTTON0 mouse state constant and rgbButtons[0] implies a left-mouse button press. Information regarding changes in the state of a mouse button is, just as with the keyboard device, stored in the DIDEVICEOBJECTDATA structure's dwData member with coordinate values being returned for axes.

5.3.2.3 Buffered as an Alternative to Immediate Joystick Data We once again start by setting the device buffer size to a nonzero value, thus enabling the use of buffered data for input:

```
DIPROPDWORD dipropdword;

dipropdword.diph.dwSize  = sizeof(DIPROPDWORD);
dipropdword.diph.dwHeaderSize = sizeof(DIPROPHEADER);
```

```
dipropdword.diph.dwObj  = 0;
dipropdword.diph.dwHow = DIPH_DEVICE;
dipropdword.dwData = 16; //a buffer size of sixteen elements
```

After initializing the members of the `dipropdword` structure, we can set the device behaviour via the `SetProperty` method:

```
hresult_ = g_lpInputDevice->SetProperty(DIPROP_BUFFERSIZE,
                                    &dipropdword.diph);
```

We can now declare the `DIDEVICEOBJECTDATA` array:

```
/* receives the buffered data */
DIDEVICEOBJECTDATA dideviceobjdata[12];
```

After acquiring the joystick device (see section 5.3.1.5) we can retrieve buffered data from the device by once again using the `GetDeviceData` function:

```
DWORD dwNumberElements = 16;    //the buffer size

hresult_ = g_lpInputDevice->GetDeviceData(
                            sizeof(DIDEVICEOBJECTDATA),
                            dideviceobjdata,
                            &dwNumberElements, 0);
```

Every `DIDEVICEOBJECTDATA` array element denotes a joystick object state change. For example, moving the stick completely forward and pressing the main button causes an array of two elements to be passed to the `GetDeviceData` function – one element for the button press, and another for the y-axis movement. The joystick object represented by one of these array elements can be established by accessing the `DIDEVICEOBJECTDATA` structure's `dwOfs` member. This member holds a joystick state constant as listed in Table 5-4. Each of these joystick state constants matches an offset in the previously discussed `DIJOYSTATE` `rgbButtons` array member. For example, both the `DIJOFS_BUTTON0` joystick state constant and `rgbButtons[0]` signifies the same device button. Device state changes are, just as with the previous devices, stored in the `DIDEVICEOBJECTDATA` structure's `dwData` member. This member stores coordinate values for axes, with the high bit of this member being set for pressed buttons.

5.3.3 Action Mapping

Applications originally hard coded the mapping of certain events to objects of an input device. For example, an FPS computer game could have been programmed to map left and right in-game movement to the left- and right-arrow keys of a keyboard. Furthermore, the responsibility of configuring or choosing the best input device resided with the user.

Action mapping eliminates the need for hard coded event-object mapping by binding events to virtual control objects. For example, an FPS computer game using some designated key to access an in-game menu can set a virtual control, `DIBUTTON_FPS_MENU`, for this specific operation. DirectInput is now used to assign some physical button (a device object) to this virtual control by taking information about the user's preferences, the game's genre and the physical device into account. Action mapping also reduces the complexity of an application's input loop by returning input device data in a device independent form. We will now look at the various steps needed for implementing action mapping.

5.3.3.1 Specifying the Actions
The first task, when specifying an action map, is to define all the game actions. These game actions can either be declared as constants via the C/C++ #define pre-processor directive or as an enumeration. We could, for example, specify the game actions for an FPS computer game via constants as follows:

```
#define INPUT_STRAFE_LEFTRIGHT_AXIS     0
#define INPUT_MOVE_UPDOWN_AXIS          1
#define INPUT_STRAFELEFT                2
#define INPUT_STRAFERIGHT               3
#define INPUT_TURNLEFT                  4
#define INPUT_TURNRIGHT                 5
#define INPUT_MOVEFORWARD               6
#define INPUT_MOVEBACKWARDS             7
#define INPUT_FIREPRIMARY               8
#define INPUT_FIRESECONDARY             9
#define INPUT_SHOWGAMEMENU              10
#define INPUT_EXITGAME                 11
```

These constants can also be written as an enumeration:

```
enum gameActions
{
    INPUT_STRAFE_LEFTRIGHT_AXIS,
    INPUT_MOVE_UPDOWN_AXIS,
    INPUT_STRAFELEFT,
    INPUT_STRAFERIGHT,
    INPUT_TURNLEFT,
    INPUT_TURNRIGHT,
    INPUT_MOVEFORWARD,
    INPUT_MOVEBACKWARDS,
    INPUT_FIREPRIMARY,
    INPUT_FIRESECONDARY,
    INPUT_SHOWGAMEMENU,
    INPUT_EXITGAME
};
```

These game action constants can now be assigned to action mapping constants as explained in the next section.

5.3.3.2 Setting up the Action Map
We now assign each of the previously defined game actions to virtual control/device objects. These virtual controls are constants sorted by genre of applicability. Action mapping defines the following main genres: action, arcade, CAD, control, driving, flight, sport, and strategy. The action genre is divided into the hand-to-hand (DIVIRTUAL_FIGHTING_HAND2HAND), shooting (DIVIRTUAL_FIGHTING_FPS, which we'll primarily be focusing on), and third-person action (DIVIRTUAL_FIGHTING_THIRDPERSON) subgenres. The other genres are also broken down into subgenres, such as the arcade genre being divided into the platform and side-to-side subgenres.

The subgenre controls the number and type of virtual device constants. We will now look at the virtual controls for a classic first-person shooter game (see the DirectX SDK documentation for a list of virtual controls pertaining to each of the other genres). Virtual controls are divided into priority 1 and priority 2

TABLE 5-5	Virtual controls for a FPS game
Priority 1 Controls	**Priority 2 Controls**
DIAXIS_FPS_LOOKUPDOWN	DIAXIS_FPS_SIDESTEP
DIAXIS_FPS_MOVE	DIBUTTON_FPS_BACKWARD_LINK
DIAXIS_FPS_ROTATE	DIBUTTON_FPS_DEVICE
DIBUTTON_FPS_APPLY	DIBUTTON_FPS_DISPLAY
DIBUTTON_FPS_CROUCH	DIBUTTON_FPS_DODGE
DIBUTTON_FPS_FIRE	DIBUTTON_FPS_FIRESECONDARY
DIBUTTON_FPS_JUMP	DIBUTTON_FPS_FORWARD_LINK
DIBUTTON_FPS_MENU	DIBUTTON_FPS_GLANCE_DOWN_LINK
DIBUTTON_FPS_SELECT	DIBUTTON_FPS_GLANCE_UP_LINK
DIBUTTON_FPS_STRAFE	DIBUTTON_FPS_GLANCEL
DIBUTTON_FPS_WEAPONS	DIBUTTON_FPS_GLANCER
	DIBUTTON_FPS_PAUSE
	DIBUTTON_FPS_ROTATE_LEFT_LINK
	DIBUTTON_FPS_ROTATE_RIGHT_LINK
	DIHATSWITCH_FPS_GLANCE

controls. Priority 1 controls represent the smallest number of controls that should be mapped; with priority 2 controls representing less frequently used, optional controls. Controls for the DIVIRTUAL_ FIGHTING_FPS genre are listed in Table 5-5.

The DIACTION structure, shown here, describes the mapping of game actions to virtual controls or device objects, including how the mapping information is to be displayed by specifying the game action, the action-mapping constants or virtual controls, etc:

```
typedef struct DIACTION {
    UINT_PTR uAppData;
    DWORD dwSemantic;
    DWORD dwFlags;
    union {
        LPCTSTR lptszActionName;
        UINT uResIdString;
    };
    GUID guidInstance;
    DWORD dwObjID;
    DWORD dwHow;
} DIACTION, *LPDIACTION;
typedef const DIACTION *LPCDIACTION;
```

Its first member, uAppData, specifies the device object's game action, as returned by the uAppData DIDEVICEOBJECTDATA structure member. The next member, dwSemantic, holds the action-mapping virtual control constant. The dwFlags member, used to request a particular attribute or form of processing, can be set to any of the following flags:

■ DIA_APPFIXED (to indicate that the game action cannot be remapped)

■ DIA_APPMAPPED (to not override the application-defined mapping using the BuildActionMap function)

■ DIA_APPNOMAP (when the current action is not to be mapped)

■ DIA_FORCEFEEDBACK (when the action has to be mapped to a trigger or actuator device) or

■ DIA_NORANGE (when the default range for an axis action is not to be set).

The lptszActionName member is the action's application-defined name used by the ConfigureDevices function, while the uResIdString member represents a resource identifier for the string contained in the lptszActionName member. The guidInstance member represents the instance GUID of the requested device, with the dwObjID member a control identifier used for retrieving both an instance and type of the device object (the DIDFT_GETINSTANCE macro is used for retrieving the object instance with the DIDFT_GetType macro reading the object type). The final member, dwHow, stores a value returned by the BuildActionMap function, signifying the mapping method used for configuring the device. It can contain any of the following constants:

■ DIAH_APPREQUESTED (the application program specified the mapping by setting the device – guidInstance – and device object – dwObjID)

■ DIAH_DEFAULT (DirectInput automatically set the mapping due to the lack of proper mapping data)

■ DIAH_ERROR (an error occurred due to a faulty/invalid mapping)

■ DIAH_HWAPP (the device manufacturer already specified a mapping for the game)

■ DIAH_HWDEFAULT (the device manufacturer already specified a mapping for the game's genre)

■ DIAH_UNMAPPED (there isn't an appropriate device object to map to) or

■ DIAH_USERCONFIG (the user already configured the mapping).

We define an array, gameAction, of type DIACTION for use with the DIACTIONFORMAT structure discussed below. This array sets the game action (as defined using the C/C++ #define directive or an enumeration), the action-mapping constant (as listed in Table 5-5), the dwFlags member used to request a particular attribute or form of processing (it is set to zero) and a simple name for each of the actions:

```
DIACTION gameAction[13] =
{
    /* device input specified by DirectInput, based on genre */
    {INPUT_STRAFE_LEFTRIGHT_AXIS,
     DIAXIS_FPS_SIDESTEP, 0, "Strafe",},
    {INPUT_MOVE_UPDOWN_AXIS, DIAXIS_FPS_MOVE, 0, "Move",},
    {INPUT_SHOWGAMEMENU, DIBUTTON_FPS_MENU, 0, "Show menu",},

    /* standard keyboard mappings */
    {INPUT_STRAFELEFT, DIKEYBOARD_A, 0, "Strafe left",},
    {INPUT_STRAFERIGHT, DIKEYBOARD_B, 0, "Strafe right",},
    {INPUT_TURNLEFT, DIKEYBOARD_LEFT, 0, "Turn left",},
```

```
{INPUT_TURNRIGHT, DIKEYBOARD_RIGHT, 0, "Turn right",},
{INPUT_MOVEFORWARD, DIKEYBOARD_UP, 0, "Move forward",},
{INPUT_MOVEBACKWARDS, DIKEYBOARD_DOWN, 0, "Move back",},
{INPUT_SHOWGAMEMENU, DIKEYBOARD_ESCAPE, DIA_APPFIXED, 0,
 "Show menu",},
{INPUT_EXITGAME, DIKEYBOARD_Q, 0, "Exit game",},

/* standard mouse mappings */
{INPUT_FIREPRIMARY, DIMOUSE_BUTTON0, 0, "Fire primary",},
{INPUT_FIRESECONDARY, DIMOUSE_BUTTON1, 0,"Fire secondary",},
};
```

The final step needed to define the action map is to initialize a DIACTIONFORMAT structure. This structure, used when mapping actions to devices, contains information about the executing application (such as its genre), the game's action/virtual control mappings, the axis scaling, the action map's friendly name, etc. The DIACTIONFORMAT structure is shown here:

```
typedef struct DIACTIONFORMAT {
    DWORD dwSize;
    DWORD dwActionSize;
    DWORD dwDataSize;
    DWORD dwNumActions;
    LPDIACTION rgoAction;
    GUID guidActionMap;
    DWORD dwGenre;
    DWORD dwBufferSize;
    LONG lAxisMin;
    LONG lAxisMax;
    HINSTANCE hInstString;
    FILETIME ftTimeStamp;
    DWORD dwCRC;
    TCHAR tszActionMap[MAX_PATH];
} DIACTIONFORMAT, *LPDIACTIONFORMAT;
```

Its dwSize member is a value specifying the DIACTIONFORMAT structure's size, with the second member, dwActionSize, the DIACTION structure's size in bytes. The next member, dwDataSize, denotes the size of the returned device data (should be equal to: 'sizeof(dwNumActions)*4'). The dwNumActions member is the number of elements in the array of type DIACTION (specifically gameAction as defined previously). The next member, rgoAction, is an address to the DIACTION array (gameAction). The guidActionMap member, a GUID identifier, identifies the action map (g_ApplicationGUID, assigned to guidActionMap in the DIACTIONFORMAT structure initialization below, is specified in the application program for identifying the action map – see Chapter 3 for information about creating COM objects). The seventh member, dwGenre, indicates the application's genre by storing one of the action-mapping constants (for example, DIVIRTUAL_FIGHTING_THIRDPERSON for the third-person action fighting genre). We then have a member, dwBufferSize, indicating the number of input data packets in the buffer of an action-mapped device (this buffer size must be greater than zero to retrieve data using the GetDeviceData function). The next two members, lAxisMin and lAxisMax, hold the minimum and maximum range, respectively, for the returned axis data (set to zero for all other game actions). The hInstString HINSTANCE is a handle to action names in the form of string resources (specified by the uResIdString member of the DIACTION structure), the ftTimeStamp member holds the time when the action map was written to disk, with the dwCRC member containing the cyclic redundancy check for the action map (used by DirectInput when saving a set of action mappings to the hard drive). The final member is a null-terminated string of characters giving the action map's friendly name (it is of the length MAX_PATH).

We can now initialize this DIACTIONFORMAT structure, after which we'll compare it against enumerated input devices to establish the best appropriate matches:

```
DIACTIONFORMAT diactionformat;
diactionformat.dwSize = sizeof(DIACTIONFORMAT);
diactionformat.dwActionSize = sizeof(DIACTION);
diactionformat.dwDataSize = 13 * sizeof(DWORD);
diactionformat.dwNumActions = 13;
diactionformat.rgoAction = gameAction;
diactionformat.guidActionMap = g_ApplicationGUID;
diactionformat.dwGenre = DIVIRTUAL_FIGHTING_FPS;
diactionformat.dwBufferSize = 16;
diactionformat.lAxisMin = −100;
diactionformat.lAxisMax = 100;
diactionformat.tszActionMap = "DI Example";
```

5.3.3.3 Applying an Action Map to Physical Devices
The above specified mapping must now be applied to enumerated (located) input devices. We start this process by enumerating all devices matching the previously defined action map through use of the EnumDevicesBySemantics IDirectInput8 interface function:

```
HRESULT EnumDevicesBySemantics(
    LPCTSTR ptszUserName,
    LPDIACTIONFORMAT lpdiActionFormat,
    LPDIENUMDEVICESBYSEMANTICSCB lpCallback,
    LPVOID pvRef,
    DWORD dwFlags
);
```

This function's first parameter takes a string holding the current user name (used when enumerating devices by giving devices with a user mapping preference over those without). The second parameter, lpdiActionFormat, takes an address to the previously defined DIACTIONFORMAT structure. The next parameter, lpCallback, takes an address to the callback function called for each and every enumerate device, with the second last parameter, pvRef, taking a value that is passed to the callback whenever it is called. The final parameter specifies the scale of the enumeration and can be set to any of the following constants:

- DIEDBSFL_ATTACHEDONLY (to only enumerate installed and attached input devices)

- DIEDBSFL_AVAILABLEDEVICES (to only enumerate installed input devices)

- DIEDBSFL_FORCEFEEDBACK (to only enumerate force feedback-enabled input devices)

- DIEDBSFL_MULTIMICEKEYBOARDS (to only enumerate additional (not primary) keyboard and mouse devices)

- ■ DIEDBSFL_NONGAMINGDEVICES (to only enumerate devices not used for input – such as USB speakers) or

- ■ DIEDBSFL_THISUSER (to only enumerate installed input devices registered for the user as specified by the ptszUserName parameter).

The EnumDevicesBySemantics IDirectInput8 interface function can now be called as follows (its fourth parameter is set to a 'this' pointer pointing to the class object used for the action-mapping functions):

```
hresult_ = lpdi->EnumDevicesBySemantics (NULL,
                                          &diactionformat,
                                          SomeCallbackFunction,
                                          this,
                                          0);
```

SomeCallbackFunction is a user defined callback function that gets called whenever a new device is found on the system. For each device found and enumerated we have to call the BuildActionMap IDirectInputDevice8 interface function. This function retrieves information about the device, creating an action map for it. It takes three parameters:

1 an address to the DIACTIONFORMAT structure

2 a string pointer to the user requesting the mapping – 'NULL' indicates the current user name

3 a flag for controlling the device mapping, specifically, DIDBAM_DEFAULT (all device mappings with the exception of application specific mappings are overridden), DIDBAM_HWDEFAULTS (all device mappings are overridden), DIDBAM_INITIALIZE (all device mappings are overridden) or DIDBAM_PRESERVE (all device mappings are preserved):

```
hresult_ = g_lpInputDevice->BuildActionMap (&diactionformat,
                                            NULL,
                                            DIDBAM_HWDEFAULTS);
```

Following the execution of this function we have successfully mapped the control assignments, as set in the DIACTIONFORMAT structure, to the device objects of the current enumerated input device. The result of this mapping is also returned to this very same DIACTIONFORMAT structure.

5.3.3.4 Applying the Action Map to a Device
The mapping returned via the DIACTIONFORMAT structure can immediately be applied to a device using the SetActionMap IDirectInputDevice8 interface function. Alternatively we can first modify this returned mapping before applying it. This modification is not recommended but can be accomplished by altering the DIACTIONFORMAT structure's data. The SetActionMap function maps the application-defined actions to a device object; it also specifies the device's data format and the buffer size when buffered data are being used. This function takes three parameters:

1 an address to a DIACTIONFORMAT structure storing information pertaining to the action map

2 a string pointer to the user the action map is being set for

3 a flag detailing how the action map is to be applied, specifically, DIDSAM_DEFAULT (the action map is set for the specified user), DIDSAM_FORCESAVE (the action map configuration is always saved to disk) or DIDSAM_NOUSER (reset the device's user ownership):

```
hresult_ = g_lpInputDevice->SetActionMap (&diactionformat,
                                          NULL,
                                          DIDSAM_DEFAULT);
```

5.3.3.5 Retrieving Action Map Data   Retrieving data from action-mapped devices occurs in exactly the same manner as when unmapped buffered input devices are being accessed – via use of the GetDeviceData function. There is, however, a slight difference in the method used when identifying a device object. For example, unmapped input devices make use of the DIDEVICEOBJECTDATA structure's dwOfs member with mapped devices using the uAppData member to set the device object's game action. The following code sample illustrates how data might be retrieved from either a mapped or an unmapped buffered device:

First we poll the device for data:

```
hresult_ = g_lpInputDevice->Poll();
```

Next we retrieve the device data:

```
hresult_ = g_lpInputDevice->GetDeviceData(
                         sizeof(DIDEVICEOBJECTDATA),
                         dideviceobjdata,
                         &dwNumberElements, 0);
```

Following this we can handle the device actions using a standard switch statement:

```
switch(dideviceobjdata.uAppData)
{
    /* call the functions 'MovePlayer' and 'FireWeapon' with
       dwData giving the action associated with the object */
    case INPUT_MOVEFORWARD:
        MovePlayer(dideviceobjdata.dwData);
        break;
    case INPUT_FIREPRIMARY:
        FireWeapon(dideviceobjdata.dwData);
        break;
    case INPUT_SECONDARY:
        FireWeapon(dideviceobjdata.dwData);
        break;

    //etc...

    default:
        break;
}
```

5.3.4 Force Feedback

Force feedback is such a vast topic that discussing it in depth could easily result in an entire book on its own. We will rather focus on force feedback's basic concepts, such as the physics behind it, and setting up a force feedback device.

Force feedback is an all-encompassing term used to describe input devices equipped with actuators, motors and resistance-inducing elements that are used for exerting vibration-based forces.

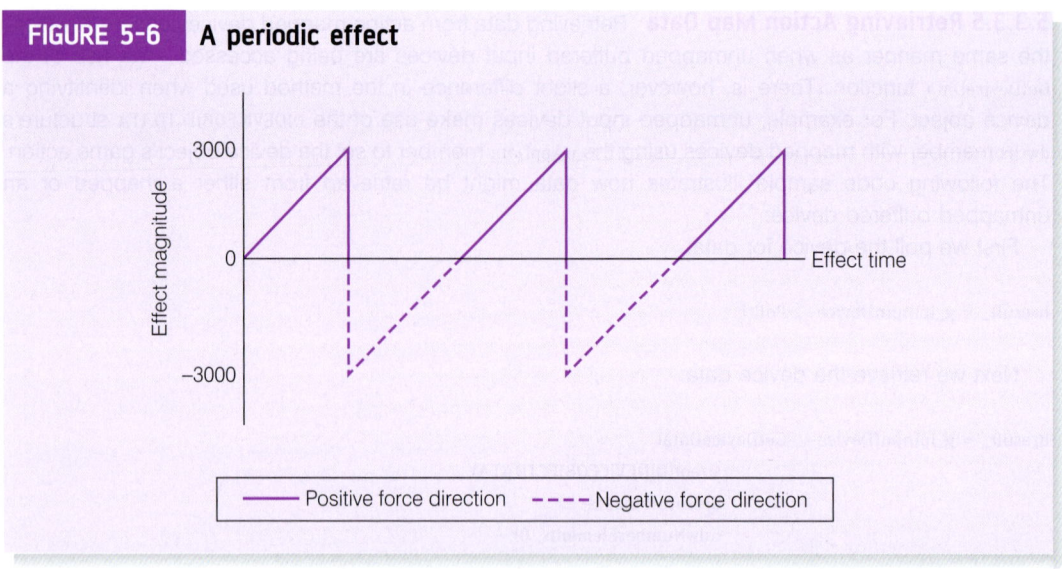

FIGURE 5-6   A periodic effect

The most common force feedback capable devices available today are joysticks and game controllers. Force feedback is also the integral part of creating the 'road feel' for steering wheel devices.

DirectInput allows for the easy generation of the resistance forces applied to the actuators and motors of an input device. Defining these forces is, however, much more complex due to the understanding of physics (mainly spring forces, motion and momentum) needed. DirectInput instances force feedback into effects and forces. An *effect* can be anything from a *ramp force* (a force that steadily rises or lessens in magnitude), a *constant force* (a force that is constant in a particular direction), or a *periodic effect* (a pulsating force mapped to some wave pattern such as a sine wave), to a *conditional effect* (a force that is triggered by a specific motion along one of the axes; condition examples include: friction, spring effects, etc.).

Every force exerted on a device has a magnitude linearly ranging from '0' to '10 000'. Setting the force to '0' results in zero force feedback with '10 000' being the maximum for the specific device. Negative magnitudes simply indicate a force in the opposite direction. Periodic effects hit their maximum force magnitude where the wave pattern peaks with ramp forces requiring a start and end magnitude. A force is a vector, which implies that it has both a magnitude and direction. A force's direction is an indication of the position from where it originates. Figure 5-6 illustrates a periodic effect with a force magnitude of 3000.

A useful way of creating fade effects is to make use of a so-called envelope. An *envelope* specifies an *attack* and a *fade* value. The attack value is the magnitude at the start of the effect, with the fade value representing the fall-off magnitude at the end of the effect. These values are governed by a duration time, for example, the attack value's duration will control the time before the force starts to fade. Setting the attack value to 3000, a fade level of 800, and the basic force magnitude to 2000 results in a force that starts out at 3000, decreases to the basic force magnitude (the *sustain level*), after which it will diminish to the fade level.

5.3.4.1 Setting up a Force Feedback Device

The first step in setting up a force feedback device is to enumerate for capable devices. This process will identify a device GUID which is needed to create and initialize the device instance.

We start by specifying a variable to contain the returned GUID:

```
GUID forceCapableGUID;
```

Scanning for force feedback capable devices works in much the same way as the previous joystick example, we simply have to call the *EnumDevices* function with its first parameter, device type, set to scan for game controllers. This parameter is followed by the enumeration function, the address of the variable storing the returned GUID and the flags DIEDFL_ATTACHEDONLY and DIEDFL_FORCEFEEDBACK specifying that only connected force feedback capable devices should be scanned for:

```
lpdi->EnumDevices (DI8DEVCLASS_GAMECTRL,
                   EnumJoystickDeviceCallback,
                   &forceCapableGUID,
                   DIEDFL_ATTACHEDONLY | DIEDFL_FORCEFEEDBACK)
```

The callback function, EnumJoystickDeviceCallback, as defined in section 5.3.1.2, creates the enumerated DirectInput device. However, the first parameter of the CreateDevice function will now be set to the forceCapableGUID value rather than the guidInstance member as was previously the case (we can, alternatively, still use the guidInstance member to create the device):

```
/* create the device with the forceJoystickGUID value
   containing the unique identifier of the device */
hresult_ = lpdi->CreateDevice(forceCapableGUID,
                   &g_lpInputDevice,
                   NULL);
```

Next we simply have to set the data format and the cooperative level (with exclusive access enabled, using the DISCL_EXCLUSIVE flag, for force feedback to function properly):

```
hresult_ = g_lpInputDevice->SetDataFormat(&c_dfDIJoystick2);

hresult_ = g_lpInputDevice->
           SetCooperativeLevel(hWnd,
                   DISCL_FOREGROUND |
                   DISCL_EXCLUSIVE);
```

Force feedback devices have a feature called *auto centering*. This feature basically emulates physical springs, as present in standard joysticks, through the use of motors. Auto center is enabled by default and must be turned off for force-feedback effects to function without any interference. We make use of the previously discussed DIPROPDWORD device properties structure and the SetProperty function set to the DIPROP_AUTOCENTER property value to do this:

```
DIPROPDWORD dipropdwordac;

dipropdwordac.diph.dwSize        = sizeof(DIPropAutoCenter);
dipropdwordac.diph.dwHeaderSize  = sizeof(DIPROPHEADER);
dipropdwordac.diph.dwObj         = 0;
dipropdwordac.diph.dwHow         = DIPH_DEVICE;
dipropdwordac.dwData             = DIPROPAUTOCENTER_OFF;

hresult_ = g_lpInputDevice->SetProperty (DIPROP_AUTOCENTER,
                                &dipropdwordac.diph);
```

Of course we also have to acquire the device before we can start communicating with it (as described in section 5.3.1.5).

5.3.4.2 Using Effects Once we have enumerated, created and set the properties of a force-feedback device we can determine the effects supported by it. Supported effects are determined through a process known as *effect enumeration*. The IDirectInputDevice8 EnumEffects function, used for enumerating all the effects supported by a force feedback device, is declared as follows in the dinput.h header file:

```
HRESULT EnumEffects (
    LPDIENUMEFFECTSCALLBACK lpCallback,
    LPVOID pvRef,
    DWORD dwEffType
);
```

Its first parameter takes an address of a callback function that is executed for each detected effect. The second parameter, pvRef, is a 32-bit pointer to a value passed to the callback each time it is called. The last parameter, dwEffType, takes a flag indicating the effect types to enumerate (same as the flags stored by the dwEffType member of the DIEffectInfo structure described below).

The form of the abovementioned callback function conforms to that of the DIEnumEffectsCallback DirectInput callback function:

```
BOOL DIEnumEffectsCallback (
    LPCDIEffectInfo pdei,
    LPVOID pvRef
);
```

This callback function's first member takes a DIEffectInfo structure describing the effect. Its second parameter is the GUID value containing information about the device supported effect as returned by the DIEffectInfo structure and subsequently passed to the EnumEffects function. The DIEffectInfo structure, shown here, stores information about the enumerated effect:

```
typedef struct DIEffectInfo {
    DWORD dwSize;
    GUID guid;
    DWORD dwEffType;
    DWORD dwStaticParams;
    DWORD dwDynamicParams;
    TCHAR tszName[MAX_PATH];
} DIEffectInfo, *LPDIEffectInfo;
```

The dwSize member holds the byte size of the DIEffectInfo structure, guid the effect's GUID identifier and dwEffType, information about the effect type. The dwEffType member can be set to any of the following flags:

- DIEFT_ALL (to enumerate all effect types)
- DIEFT_CONDITION (to enumerate only condition effects)
- DIEFT_CONSTANTFORCE (to enumerate only constant force effects)
- DIEFT_CUSTOMFORCE (to enumerate only custom force effects)
- DIEFT_DEADBAND (to enumerate effects supporting deadband)
- DIEFT_FFATTACK (when the attack envelope parameter is supported)
- DIEFT_FFFADE (when the fade parameter is supported)

- DIEFT_HARDWARE (to enumerate only hardware-specific effects)

- DIEFT_PERIODIC (to enumerate only periodic effects)

- DIEFT_POSNEGCOEFFICIENTS (when both positive and negative coefficients are supported for the displacement of axes)

- DIEFT_POSNEGSATURATION (when maximum saturation is supported for both positive and negative forces)

- DIEFT_RAMPFORCE (to enumerate only ramp-force effects)

- DIEFT_SATURATION (when the saturation of condition effects is supported) or

- DIEFT_STARTDELAY (when a delay before playback is supported by an effect).

The third last member, dwStaticParams, describes the parameters supported by the effect. The dwDynamicParams member indicates the parameters of the effect that can be modified while the effect is activated. The final member is a character array storing the effect's name.

We start by enumerating all the effects supported by a device, first declaring a GUID variable, effectGUID, which is passed as second parameter to our callback function, EnumEffectCallback, so that we can store the identifier of the enumerated effect:

```
GUID effectGUID;
hresult_ = g_lpInputDevice->EnumEffects (
                (LPDIENUMEFFECTSCALLBACK) EnumEffectCallback,
                &effectGUID,
                DIEFT_PERIODIC);
```

Our callback function, EnumEffectCallback, has the following form:

```
BOOL CALLBACK EnumEffectCallback ( LPCDIEffectInfo effectInfo,
                                   LPVOID effectIdentifier)
{
    /* access the identifier of the supported effect as stored
       in the second member (guid) of the DIEffectInfo struct */
    *((GUID *)effectIdentifier) = effectInfo->guid;

    /* return after one effect's GUID has been read */
    return DIENUM_STOP;
}
```

Following this effect enumeration, and testing for the enumeration of at least one periodic effect type (as specified using the DIEFT_PERIODIC flag), we can use the effect's GUID to create and initialize the effect object by calling the CreateEffect IDirectInputDevice8 interface function. This function, shown here, takes four parameters:

```
HRESULT CreateEffect(
    REFGUID rguid,
    LPCDIEFFECT lpeff,
    LPDIRECTINPUTEFFECT * ppdeff,
    LPUNKNOWN punkOuter
);
```

Its first parameter is the GUID variable (effectGUID) identifying the effect. There is also a number of predefined effect GUIDs which can be used as alternatives to the GUID obtained from the EnumEffects function, for example: GUID_ConstantForce, GUID_CustomForce, GUID_Damper, GUID_Friction, GUID_Inertia, GUID_RampForce, GUID_SawtoothDown, GUID_SawtoothUp, GUID_Sine, GUID_Spring, GUID_Square and GUID_Triangle. The second parameter, lpeff, can either be set to the DIEFFECT structure, used for specifying the parameters of the effect, or 'NULL' when we wish to create an effect without any parameters. The third parameter, ppdeff, receives a pointer to the IDirectInputEffect interface when an effect instance has been created successfully. The punkOuter parameter is a COM aggregation, once again of little concern – we will set it to 'NULL' since no aggregation of the interface is needed.

Before calling the CreateEffect function, we first have to specify an array holding information about the effect direction (dealing with whether, say, an x-axis decreases or increases from left to right), an array holding information about the axes (assuming a joystick-like input device), a structure for setting the envelope of the effect, a structure for holding information about effect type (a periodic effect in this discussion) and a DIEFFECT structure for setting the effect's parameters.

The arrays holding information about the effect direction and the axes are declared and initialized in the following manner, respectively:

```
LONG lAxesEffectDirection[2] = {0, 0};

DWORD dwAxesInformation[2] = {DIJOFS_X, DIJOFS_Y};
```

Next we declare the structures for the effect envelope, effect type and effect parameters respectively:

```
/* effect envelope */
DIENVELOPE diEffectEnvelope;

/* effect type parameters */
DIPERIODIC diPeriodicEffect;

/* general effect parameters */
DIEFFECT diGeneralEffect;
```

The DIENVELOPE structure, used by the DIEFFECT structure, has five members:

```
typedef struct DIENVELOPE {
    DWORD dwSize;
    DWORD dwAttackLevel;
    DWORD dwAttackTime;
    DWORD dwFadeLevel;
    DWORD dwFadeTime;
} DIENVELOPE, *LPDIENVELOPE;
```

The first member sets the structure's size in bytes, the second the starting amplitude of the envelope ('0' to '10 000'), the third the time before reaching the sustain level and the fourth the ending amplitude of the envelope ('0' to '10 000'). The final parameter sets the time delay before the fade level is reached (as described in section 5.3.1). We can initialize these members for the diEffectEnvelope effect envelope as follows (the effect simulates driving over a small object on a road – shaking the 'steering' slightly, followed by the steering levelling out):

```
diEffectEnvelope.dwSize = sizeof(DIENVELOPE);
diEffectEnvelope.dwAttackLevel = 0;
```

```
diEffectEnvelope.dwAttackTime = (DWORD)(0.8 * DI_SECONDS);
diEffectEnvelope.dwFadeLevel = 0;
diEffectEnvelope.dwFadeTime = (DWORD)(1.5 * DI_SECONDS);
```

The DIPERIODIC structure specifies the parameters for a periodic effect (indicated using the DIEFT_PERIODIC flag):

```
typedef struct DIPERIODIC {
    DWORD dwMagnitude;
    LONG lOffset;
    DWORD dwPhase;
    DWORD dwPeriod;
} DIPERIODIC, *LPDIPERIODIC;
```

Its first member signifies the magnitude of the effect (0 to 10 000); the second is the effect's offset – i.e. the baseline of an applied envelope, with the third member the position in a periodic effect cycle at which playback of the effect begins (0 to 35 999). The final member, dwPeriod, is the effect's period. We set these members in the following manner (creating a maximum-force periodic effect using the DI_FFNOMINALMAX flag, with the period in this case set to one tenth of a second):

```
diPeriodicEffect.dwMagnitude = DI_FFNOMINALMAX;
diPeriodicEffect.lOffset = 0;
diPeriodicEffect.dwPhase = 0;
diPeriodicEffect.dwPeriod = (DWORD)(0.1 * DI_SECONDS);
```

We can now, using the DIEFFECT structure, set up the main effect parameters. This structure is used by the CreateEffect IDirectInputDevice8 interface function. The DIEFFECT structure is declared as follows:

```
typedef struct DIEFFECT {
    DWORD dwSize;
    DWORD dwFlags;
    DWORD dwDuration;
    DWORD dwSamplePeriod;
    DWORD dwGain;
    DWORD dwTriggerButton;
    DWORD dwTriggerRepeatInterval;
    DWORD cAxes;
    LPDWORD rgdwAxes;
    LPLONG rglDirection;
    LPDIENVELOPE lpEnvelope;
    DWORD cbTypeSpecificParams;
    LPVOID lpvTypeSpecificParams;
    DWORD dwStartDelay;
} DIEFFECT, *LPDIEFFECT;
```

The first member is the structure's size in bytes, with the second member being set to a combination of flags pertaining to other members of the effect structure – possible flags include:

- DIEFF_CARTESIAN (the value stored in the rglDirection member is read as Cartesian coordinates)

- DIEFF_OBJECTIDS (the values stored in the dwTriggerButton and rgdwAxes members are read as object identifiers – such as DIDFT_AXIS, DIDFT_FFACTUATOR)

- DIEFF_OBJECTOFFSETS (the values stored in the dwTriggerButton and rgdwAxes members are read as data format offsets)

- DIEFF_POLAR (the value stored in the rglDirection member is read as polar coordinates) and

- DIEFF_SPHERICAL (the value stored in the rglDirection member is read as spherical coordinates).

The next member, dwDuration, sets the effect's total duration, with dwSamplePeriod the period of the playback effect, dwGain the amount of gain determining whether the force-feedback effect created by the device will be amplified or lessened ('0' to '10 000') and dwTriggerButton the button that will trigger the effect. The dwTriggerRepeatInterval member sets the time in microseconds between the end of the previous effect playback and the start of the next in situations where the button that triggered the effect is held down. The next member, cAxes, sets the number of axes associated with the effect. The rgdwAxes member takes a pointer to an array consisting of cAxes elements with each element identifying the axes the effect is to be applied to. The next member, rglDirection, also takes a pointer to an array consisting of cAxes elements, only this time containing coordinates (the coordinate type is specified by the flag DIEFF_CARTESIAN, DIEFF_POLAR, or DIEFF_SPHERICAL). The lpEnvelope member takes a pointer to the DIENVELOPE structure, with cbTypeSpecificParams defining the number of additional bytes used for the effect type's parameters and lpvTypeSpecificParams taking a pointer to one of the type-specific parameters (for DIEFT_CONDITION containing a pointer to an array of type DICONDITION that sets the parameters of a condition, with DIEFT_CUSTOMFORCE requiring a pointer to an array of type DICUSTOMFORCE specifying the parameters of a custom force, DIEFT_PERIODIC requiring a pointer to an array of type DIPERIODIC defining the parameters of a periodic force), DIEFT_CONSTANTFORCE requiring a pointer to an array of type DICONSTANTFORCE holding the parameters of a constant force and DIEFT_RAMPFORCE requiring a pointer to an array of type DIRAMPFORCE defining the parameters of a ramp force. The final member, dwStartDelay, sets the delay time before effect playback.

We can now use this DIEFFECT structure to set the general effect parameters:

```
diGeneralEffect.dwSize = sizeof(DIEFFECT);
diGeneralEffect.dwFlags = DIEFF_OBJECTOFFSETS | DIEFF_POLAR;
diGeneralEffect.dwDuration = (DWORD)(4 * DI_SECONDS);
diGeneralEffect.dwSamplePeriod = 0;
diGeneralEffect.dwGain = DI_FFNOMINALMAX;
diGeneralEffect.dwTriggerButton = DIJOFS_BUTTON0;
diGeneralEffect.dwTriggerRepeatInterval = 0
diGeneralEffect.cAxes = 2;
diGeneralEffect.rgdwAxes = dwAxesInformation;
diGeneralEffect.rglDirection = &lAxesEffectDirection[0];
diGeneralEffect.lpEnvelope = &diEffectEnvelope;
diGeneralEffect.cbTypeSpecificParams = sizeof(diPeriodicEffect);
diGeneralEffect.lpvTypeSpecificParams = &diPeriodicEffect;
diGeneralEffect.dwStartDelay = 0;
```

With all these structures completed we can now call the CreateEffect function to create the effect (the third parameter is set to the g_lpdiEffectInterface effect object declared as the type LPDIRECTINPUTEFFECT – an IDirectInputEffect interface with various member functions used for the management of effects):

```
hresult_ = g_lpInputDevice->CreateEffect(effectGUID,
                                          &diGeneralEffect,
                                          &g_lpdiEffectInterface,
                                          NULL);
```

We can now start or stop this effect using the Start or Stop IDirectInputEffect interface functions respectively. The Start function plays an effect by taking two parameters, the first one specifying the number of times to consecutively play the effect and the second one signaling how the effect should be played (either as DIES_SOLO – all other effects must stop before the current one can play – or as DIES_NODOWNLOAD – specifying that the effect should not be downloaded):

```
/* start the effect, looping it twice and requiring all other
   effects to terminate before playback starts */
g_lpdiEffectInterface->Start(2, 0);
```

The Stop function terminates the effect:

```
g_lpdiEffectInterface->Stop();
```

We can also change an effect as it plays by calling the SetParameters IDirectInputEffect interface function with the newly set parameter. This function takes two parameters, the first a DIEFFECT structure holding the effect data, with the second a flag specifying the portions of the effect information to be set. Legal flags include:

■ DIEP_AXES (cAxes and rgdwAxes hold data)

■ DIEP_DIRECTION (cAxes and rgdwAxes hold data; dwFlags can be set to either DIEFF_POLAR or DIEFF_CARTESIAN)

■ DIEP_DURATION (dwDuration holds data)

■ DIEP_ENVELOPE (lpEnvelope points to a DIENVELOPE structure)

■ DIEP_GAIN (dwGain holds data)

■ DIEP_NODOWNLOAD (do not place the effect on the device, if the effect is on the device, update it to the values specified by SetParameters)

■ DIEP_NORESTART (do not stop and restart the effect when the effect's parameters are being changed)

■ DIEP_SAMPLEPERIOD (dwSamplePeriod holds data)

■ DIEP_START (start/restart the effect after updating its parameters)

■ DIEP_STARTDELAY (dwStartDelay holds data)

■ DIEP_TRIGGERBUTTON (dwTriggerButton holds data)

■ DIEP_TRIGGERREPEATINTERVAL dwTriggerRepeatInterval holds data) or

■ DIEP_TYPESPECIFICPARAMS (lpvTypeSpecificParams and cbTypeSpecificParams hold the address and size of the effect's type-specific data).

For example, setting a new magnitude for a periodic effect can be done as follows:

```
diPeriodicEffect.dwMagnitude = 3000;

g_lpdiEffectInterface->SetParameters (&diGeneralEffect,
                          DIEP_TYPESPECIFICPARAMS);
```

5.4   XINPUT

XInput, introduced with the release of the Xbox 360 gaming console, allows any computer running Windows XP SP1 or later to interface with an Xbox 360 controller. This controller can also be programmed using DirectInput, however, doing so leads to some loss of functionality: for example, no vibration effects are present, and the right and left trigger buttons fail to function separately instead performing as a single button. XInput limits the number of controllers that can be used at any given moment to four (a limit carried over from the Xbox). XInput also doesn't support any keyboard, mouse, or similar input devices. Focusing solely on next generation controllers, XInput supports exactly the same number of buttons and axes as the Xbox 360, namely 10 buttons, 4 axes and an 8-direction pad per controller.

The Xbox 360 controller, as shown previously in Figure 5-4, consists of two analog triggers, two analog sticks coupled with two digital buttons, eight additional digital buttons, two vibration motors, and a four-directional pad. We store the state of these input objects in the XINPUT_GAMEPAD structure with the speeds of the motors defined in the XINPUT_VIBRATION structure.

The XINPUT_GAMEPAD structure is declared as follows in the xinput.h header file:

```
typedef struct _XINPUT_GAMEPAD {
    WORD wButtons;
    BYTE bLeftTrigger;
    BYTE bRightTrigger;
    SHORT sThumbLX;
    SHORT sThumbLY;
    SHORT sThumbRX;
    SHORT sThumbRY;
} XINPUT_GAMEPAD, *PXINPUT_GAMEPAD;
```

The first member, wButtons, is a bitmask (shown below) of all the digital buttons – each button's bit set denotes whether it has been pressed or not:

```
#define XINPUT_GAMEPAD_A                0x1000
#define XINPUT_GAMEPAD_B                0x2000
#define XINPUT_GAMEPAD_X                0x4000
#define XINPUT_GAMEPAD_Y                0x8000
#define XINPUT_GAMEPAD_START            0x00000010
#define XINPUT_GAMEPAD_BACK             0x00000020
#define XINPUT_GAMEPAD_DPAD_UP          0x00000001
#define XINPUT_GAMEPAD_DPAD_DOWN        0x00000002
#define XINPUT_GAMEPAD_DPAD_LEFT        0x00000004
#define XINPUT_GAMEPAD_DPAD_RIGHT       0x00000008
#define XINPUT_GAMEPAD_LEFT_THUMB       0x00000040
#define XINPUT_GAMEPAD_RIGHT_THUMB      0x00000080
#define XINPUT_GAMEPAD_LEFT_SHOULDER    0x0100
#define XINPUT_GAMEPAD_RIGHT_SHOULDER   0x0200
```

The second member, bLeftTrigger, stores the state of the left trigger (0 to 255), with the bRightTrigger member holding the state of the right trigger (0 to 255). The fourth member, sThumbLX, stores the left analog stick's *x*-axis value (-32.768 to 32.767) and sThumbLY, the left analog stick's *y*-axis value (-32.768

to 32.767). The final two members, sThumbRX and sThumbRY, hold the right analog stick's *x*- and *y*-axis values, respectively.

A device state can be retrieved using the XInputGetState function. This function takes two parameters, an index value to the specific controller (ranging from 0 to 3), and a pointer to the XINPUT_STATE structure that holds a controller's state information.

The XINPUT_STATE structure has two members, dwPacketNumber that holds a state packet number indicating whether a controller's state changed, and Gamepad which is a XINPUT_GAMEPAD structure holding the controller's current state.

The XINPUT_VIBRATION structure has two members, wLeftMotorSpeed and wRightMotorSpeed. The first sets the speed of the left motor with the second the right motor (ranging from 0 for no motor use to 65535 for full motor use).

The vibration effects are set by passing this structure to the XInputSetState function. The XInputSetState function takes two parameters: the first's an index value to the specific controller (ranging from 0 to 3) and the second a pointer to the XINPUT_VIBRATION structure.

The following code sample retrieves the state (required for updating game information based on device changes) and sets the vibration effect for an Xbox 360 controller:

```
/* declare the structure holding the controller's state
    information */
XINPUT_STATE xidevState;

/* fill the memory block with zeros */
SecureZeroMemory(&xidevState, sizeof(XINPUT_STATE));

/* retrieve the state of the controller */
DWORD dwState = XInputGetState(0, &xidevState);

/* declare the vibration effect structure */
XINPUT_VIBRATION xidevVibration;

/* fill the memory block with zeros */
SecureZeroMemory(&xidevVibration, sizeof(XINPUT_VIBRATION));

/* set the left and right motor speed */
xidevVibration.wLeftMotorSpeed = 6000;
xidevVibration.wRightMotorSpeed = 19000;

/* set the vibration effects, passing the index of the device
    as '0', hence the first connected XInput device */
XInputSetState(0, & xidevVibration);
```

5.5   SUMMARY

We have now taken our first real look at two of DirectX's core technologies, namely the DirectInput and XInput APIs. The chapter investigated input control through the use of various physical devices, specifically the keyboard, mouse, joystick, and Xbox 360 controller. It started by considering each of these input devices on a physical level, discussing concepts such as relative and absolute positioning.

We then presented six classes of logical input devices to illustrate the variety of input that has to be handled by modern-day graphical applications.

Following this we dealt with DirectInput in depth, specifically the creation of a DirectInput object and device, initialization of the DirectInput device's data format, setting the cooperative level of a device, acquiring the device, and reading data from this DirectInput device. Next we considered various methods of obtaining data from input devices, specifically looking at immediate vs. buffered data, as well as polling and event notification used for determining whether any input data is available for processing. All these topics were discussed with examples pertaining to keyboard, mouse, and joystick devices.

Next we introduced the concept of action mapping, describing the process of defining game actions and subsequently assigning these action constants to virtual control objects. Building on this we looked at applying an action map to physical devices and mapping the application-defined actions to a device object. This section closed by discussing the retrieval of data from action-mapped devices.

Our discussion of DirectInput concluded with an introduction to force-feedback, highlighting its basic principles and the steps required to set up and use a force feedback device. The remainder of the chapter dealt with the XInput API, outlining its initialization and use.

The next chapter deals with rendering, specifically the representation and drawing of geometric primitives and more complex polygonal types. This chapter also offered in depth coverage of Direct3D render states, the DXUT framework, and shaders.

5.6 FURTHER READING

The official DirectInput and XInput documentation is available from Microsoft's msdn2.microsoft.com website. This documentation is also provided with each DirectX SDK distribution.

5.7 EXERCISES

1 Why do variable-sensitivity input devices use velocities rather than distance values?

2 Describe the difference between absolute- and relative-positioning input devices.

3 List a number of modern uses for stroke devices.

4 What is the main functional difference between DirectInput and Windows input events?

5 Briefly explain the purpose of DirectInput's exclusive mode.

6 Why is the IDirectInput8 interface created?

7 How are device object instances created?

8 Give a code sample to create a single DirectInput object. (Hint: start by creating the main DirectInput COM object interface.)

9 Create and initialize an instance of a device by calling the CreateDevice function.

10 Write code to determine the number and type of buttons and axes available on a joystick.

11 Why is it necessary to set the data format of a device?

12 What is the difference between the c_dfDIMouse and c_dfDIMouse2 data format structures?

13 How would we go about setting the cooperative level of any DirectInput device?

14   Describe the purpose of the following code sample:

```
hresult_ = g_lpInputDevice->EnumObjects(
                        EnumDeviceObjectsCallback,
                        (VOID*)hWnd,
                        DIDFT_AXIS);
```

15   When acquiring a joystick device, device acquisition is not permanent and the device might be acquired and released several times. Write a code sample to reacquire a joystick device whenever focus is returned to the application or when access to the device has been lost.

16   With the DirectInput device acquired, describe the process of reading data from it.

17   Under what specific condition will the following if statement be true?

```
if (mousestructure.rgbButtons[0] & 0×80)
{
    //do something
}
```

18   What is the difference between the following two functions: unacquire and release?

19   Explain the difference between buffered and immediate data.

20   What is the purpose of action mapping?

21   Describe the process of specifying an action map.

22   What is a virtual device constant?

23   Give a basic initialization for the DIACTIONFORMAT structure.

24   How is an action map applied to physical devices?

25   Describe the DIEffectInfo structure.

CHAPTER 6

Rendering: Direct3D and OpenGL

LEARNING OBJECTIVES

In this chapter you will learn about:

- Primitives and polygons
- Rendering stroke and raster text
- Drawing primitives and polygons
- Direct3D render states
- The rasterizer state object
- The input-layout state object
- The depth stencil state object
- The blend state object
- The sample state object
- The DXUT framework: simplifying window creation and control
- Shaders
- The hardware graphics pipeline
- The programmable graphics pipeline
- Cg: C for Graphics (Direct3D & OpenGL)
- Cg language profiles
- The Cg compiler
- The Cg runtime
- Initializing Cg
- Creating a vertex program
- Creating a fragment program
- High Level Shader Language (HLSL)
- The HLSL compiler
- Initializing the High Level Shader Language
- Creating HLSL shaders
- Common HLSL data types
- Utilizing a created HLSL effect

INTRODUCTION

Chapter 6 deals with the representation and drawing of geometric primitives (points, line segments, polygons, curves, and surfaces) and more complex polygonal types. It starts off by introducing the reader to primitives as simple geometric elements used in the construction of more complex geometric objects. The storage of geometric data and how Direct3D draws geometry using render states are looked at in detail. Following this is an in-depth analysis of the Direct3D Utility Framework (DXUT) including the usage and application of shaders and effects. The chapter closes with Cg and HLSL shader programming, explaining a number of concepts at hand of code samples and example programs.

6.1   INTRODUCTION: PRIMITIVES AND POLYGONS

Primitives are simple geometric objects or shapes used in the construction of more complex geometric figures. Examples of *geometric primitives* include vertices (points), lines, surfaces, and polygons (such as triangles). Every object imaginable can be either constructed or approximated using this set of primitives.

Direct3D and OpenGL utilize numerous low-level commands and routines for the definition of models and spatial scenes, both APIs supporting a standardized set of geometric primitives. Geometric primitives exist in two- or three-dimensional space and can be manipulated by geometric operations such as rotations, translations and skewing.

A *polygon* (fill area) is a closed surface constructed out of a finite series of line segments. Polygons are primarily used in computer graphics for the approximation of arbitrary surfaces. The most common polygonal type is the triangle, but quadrilaterals are also frequently used. The number of polygons making up an object determines not only its complexity but also the overall performance impact. Two properties must be met to ensure that polygons are rendered correctly: the polygon must be simple and convex.

A polygon is described as *simple* when no two edges of the polygon overlap each other (see Figure 6-1 (a)). A simple polygon has a distinct interior and there isn't any risk of its vertices not rendering properly.

FIGURE 6-1   **(a) Simple Quadrilateral (b) Complex Pentagon**

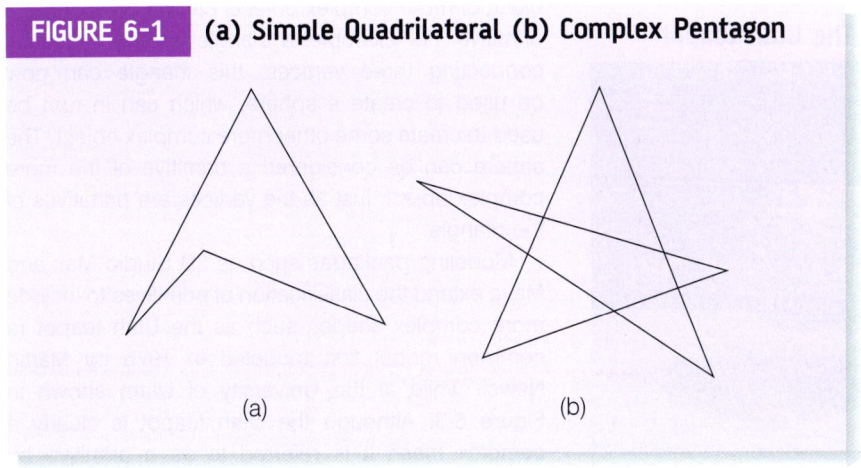

(a)   (b)

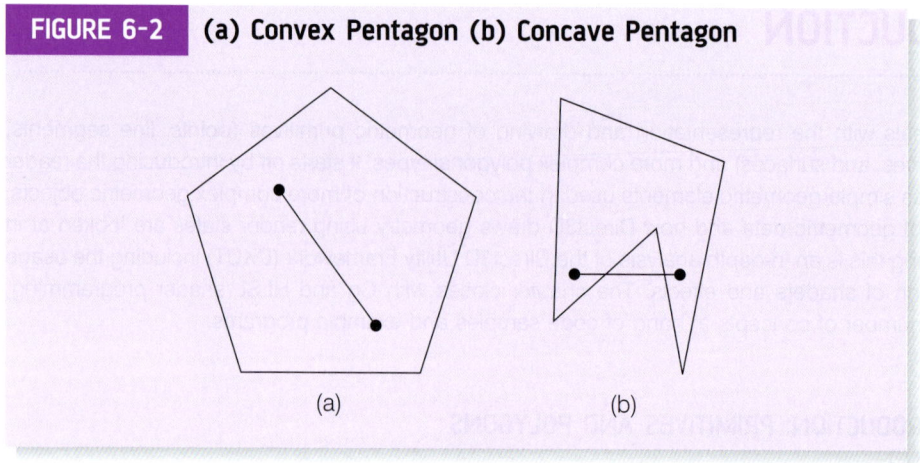

FIGURE 6-2   (a) Convex Pentagon (b) Concave Pentagon

(a)   (b)

6

A polygon can be rendered in one of three ways: in terms of only its edges, only its interior or both its interior and edges. Rendering the interior of a polygon requires some form of filling algorithm and graphics APIs can only guarantee consistent filling for convex polygons. A simple polygon is *convex* when it has no internal angles greater than 180° and if all points on every line segment between two points internal to the polygon are inside the polygon (Figure 6-2). Triangles, rectangles, circles, and spheres are common examples of convex objects. A simple concave polygon is the opposite of a simple convex polygon.

6.1.1 Primitive and Polygon Types

As previously mentioned, primitives are combined to form both 2D and 3D meshes and entities commonly referred to as 'models' – the more complex the object, the greater the number of primitives. We generally work with geometric primitives (points, lines, line segments, planes, and polygons) but can also work with so-called *raster primitives*. An array of pixels is an example of a raster primitive. Raster primitives lack geometric properties, thus cannot be manipulated in two- or three-dimensional space.

FIGURE 6-3   The Utah teapot

Loosely speaking, any object used as the building block of more complex objects can be considered a primitive. For example, a triangle is constructed by connecting three vertices; this triangle can now be used to create a sphere, which can in turn be used to create some other more complex object. The sphere can be considered a primitive of the more complex object, just as the vertices are primitives of the triangle.

Modeling packages such as 3D Studio Max and Maya extend the classification of primitives to include more complex shapes such as the Utah teapot (a common model first modeled in 1975 by Martin Newell while at the University of Utah) shown in Figure 6-3. Although the Utah teapot is clearly a complex mesh it is referred to as a primitive by modeling packages because it has become one of the most commonly distributed 3D objects – being included in AutoCAD, Lightwave 3D, OpenGL, Direct3D, Maya, and 3D Studio Max, and used for numerous self-tests and benchmarks.

The most basic primitive type, which cannot possibly be broken down into anything less complex, is a spatial point or *vertex*. These primitives are, in their most basic form, rendered as single pixels. We normally define these primitives as collections through the use of *point lists*. Figure 6-4(a) shows a series of points.

The next primitive type, known as a *line segment*, is rendered by connecting each successive pair of vertices with a line as illustrated in Figure 6-4(b). We normally make use of line lists to store the vertices in an array followed by a connection between every pair. This primitive type can be used for anything: simulating heavy raining, sparks, a shooting star, etc.

FIGURE 6-4   General geometric types

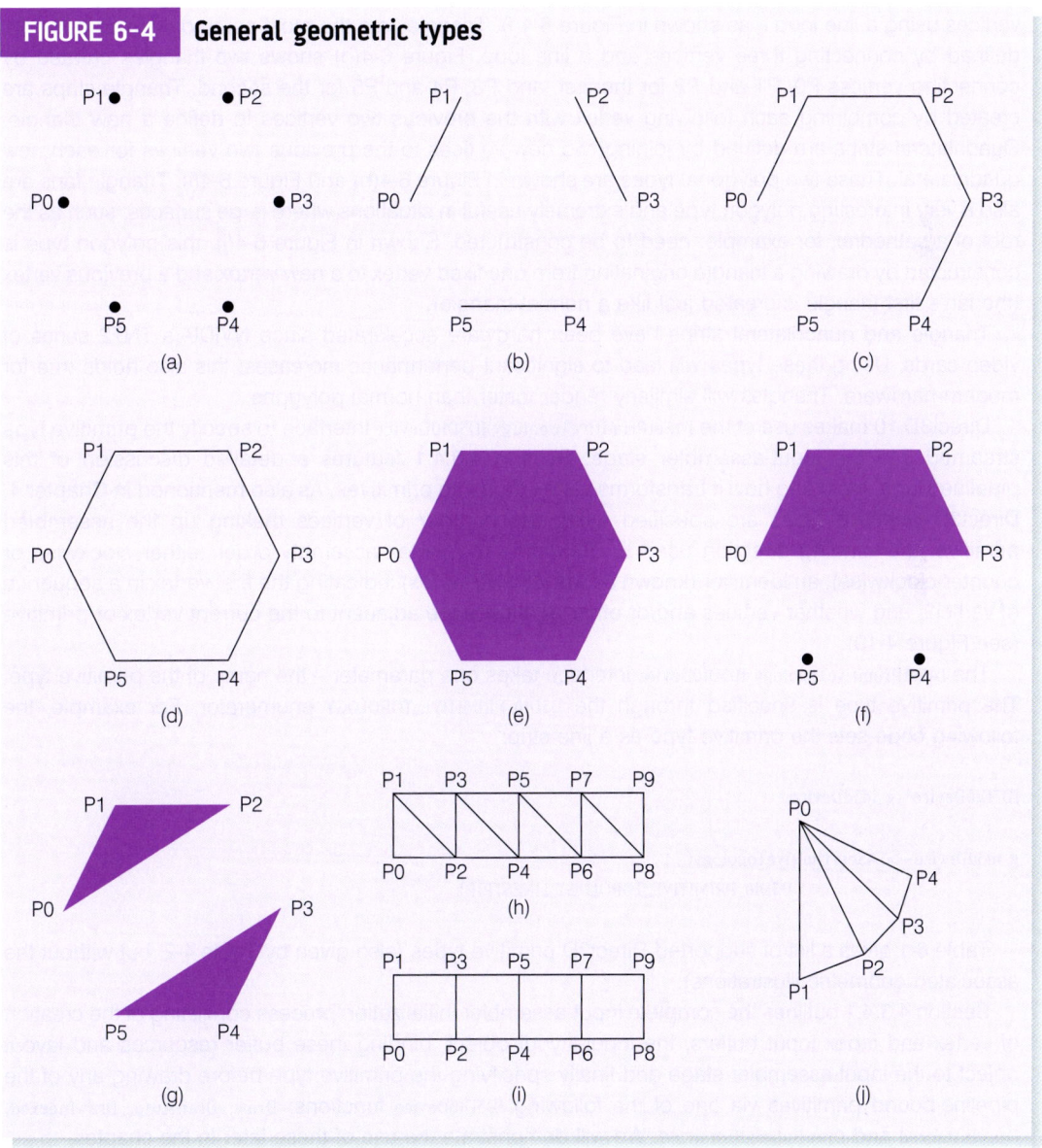

Two extensions of the line segment concept are line strips and line loops. A *line strip* is a series of connected line segments with the first and last vertices not connected – as shown in Figure 6-4(c). Line strips are also called *polylines* and are very suitable for drawing curves. Drawing a series of connected lines and connecting the first and last vertex leads to a closed polygon, also referred to as a *line loop* in its unfilled state. Figure 6-4(d) shows such a primitive.

When we use line segments and/or line strips to map the edges of objects so that the object is completely closed, then we can refer to the object as a polygon. The interior of a polygon is known as its *fill area*, and this area can be filled with any solid color, pattern or texture. In short, the edges of a polygon are defined as a series of vertices connected using line loops. Figure 6-4(e) illustrates a filled polygon constructed by interlinking six vertices using a line loop.

Quadrilaterals, triangles, strips, and fans are examples of polygon types specifically designed to improve rendering performance. Quadrilateral objects are constructed by connecting groups of four vertices using a line loop – as shown in Figure 6-4(f). Triangles are the most commonly used polygon, defined by connecting three vertices and a line loop. Figure 6-4(g) shows two triangles created by connecting vertices P0, P1 and P2 for the first, and P3, P4 and P5 for the second. Triangle strips are created by combining each following vertex with the previous two vertices to define a new triangle. Quadrilateral strips are defined by joining two new vertices to the previous two vertices for each new quadrilateral. These two polygonal types are shown in Figure 6-4(h) and Figure 6-4(i). Triangle fans are also a very interesting polygon type and extremely useful in situations where large surfaces, such as the roof of a cathedral, for example, need to be constructed. Shown in Figure 6-4(j), this polygon type is constructed by drawing a triangle originating from one fixed vertex to a new vertex and a previous vertex (the fan's first triangle is created just like a normal triangle).

Triangle and quadrilateral strips have been hardware accelerated since NVIDIA's TNT2 series of video cards. Using these types will lead to significant performance increases; this also holds true for modern hardware. Triangles will similarly render faster than normal polygons.

Direct3D 10 makes use of the IASetPrimitiveTopology ID3D10Device interface to specify the primitive type streamed into the input-assembler stage. Section 4.3.4.1 features a detailed discussion of this pipeline stage, including how it transforms vertex data into primitives. As also mentioned in Chapter 4, Direct3D primitive types are specified using the number of vertices making up the assembled primitive, the winding direction used to determine the vertex assembly order (either clockwise or counter-clockwise), an identifier (known as the *leading vertex*) indicating the first vertex in a sequence of vertices and whether vertices and/or other primitives are adjacent to the current vertex or primitive (see Figure 4-19).

The IASetPrimitiveTopology ID3D10Device interface takes one parameter – the name of the primitive type. The primitive type is specified through the D3D10_PRIMITIVE_TOPOLOGY enumerator. For example, the following code sets the primitive type as a line strip:

```
ID3D10Device* g_id3dDevice;

g_id3dDevice->IASetPrimitiveTopology(
              D3D10_PRIMITIVE_TOPOLOGY_LINESTRIP);
```

Table 6-1 gives a list of supported Direct3D primitive types (also given by Table 4-2, but without the associated geometric illustrations):

Section 4.3.4.1 outlines the complete input-assembler initialization process consisting of the creation of vertex and index input buffers, the input-layout object, binding these buffer resources and layout object to the input-assembler stage and finally specifying the primitive type before drawing any of the pipeline-bound primitives via one of the following ID3D10Device functions: Draw, DrawAuto, DrawIndexed, DrawInstanced and DrawIndexedInstanced. We will demonstrate the use of these later in the chapter.

TABLE 6-1	Primitive types as specified by the D3D10_PRIMITIVE_TOPOLOGY enumerator
Constant	**Description**
D3D10_PRIMITIVE_TOPOLOGY_UNDEFINED	A primitive topology is not specified for the input-assembler stage.
D3D10_PRIMITIVE_TOPOLOGY_LINELIST	The vertex data are interpreted as a list of lines.
D3D10_PRIMITIVE_TOPOLOGY_LINELIST_ADJ	The vertex data are interpreted as a list of lines with adjacency data.
D3D10_PRIMITIVE_TOPOLOGY_LINESTRIP	The vertex data are interpreted as a line strip.
D3D10_PRIMITIVE_TOPOLOGY_LINESTRIP_ADJ	The vertex data are interpreted as a line strip with adjacency data.

(*Continued*)

TABLE 6-1	Primitive types as specified by the D3D10_PRIMITIVE_TOPOLOGY enumerator *(Continued)*

Constant	Description
D3D10_PRIMITIVE_TOPOLOGY_POINTLIST 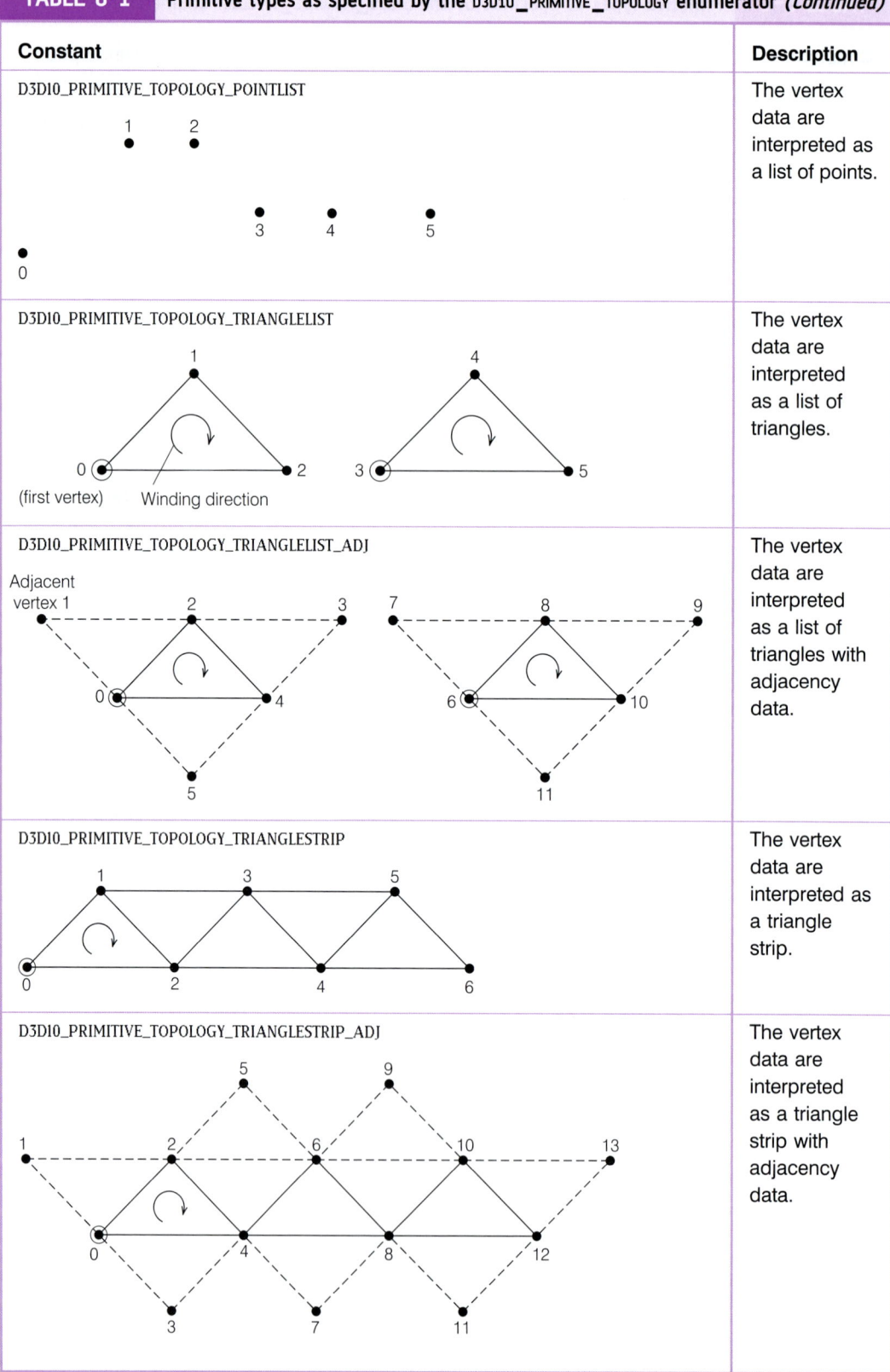	The vertex data are interpreted as a list of points.
D3D10_PRIMITIVE_TOPOLOGY_TRIANGLELIST	The vertex data are interpreted as a list of triangles.
D3D10_PRIMITIVE_TOPOLOGY_TRIANGLELIST_ADJ	The vertex data are interpreted as a list of triangles with adjacency data.
D3D10_PRIMITIVE_TOPOLOGY_TRIANGLESTRIP	The vertex data are interpreted as a triangle strip.
D3D10_PRIMITIVE_TOPOLOGY_TRIANGLESTRIP_ADJ	The vertex data are interpreted as a triangle strip with adjacency data.

Working with OpenGL

To define a geometric object, OpenGL makes use of multiple vertex function calls arranged in sequence (located between a glBegin and glEnd call respectively). For example, to draw the outline of a square using a line loop we can do the following:

```
glBegin(GL_LINE_LOOP);
    glVertex2f(-1.5, -1.5);
    glVertex2f(-1.5, 1.5);
    glVertex2f(1.5, 1.5);
    glVertex2f(1.5, -1.5);
glEnd();
```

This square exists in a two-dimensional area defined between −3 and 3 on the *x*- and *y*-axis respectively. Refer to section 4.4.1 for details about specifying the number and type of arguments of an OpenGL function such as glVertex*.

The glBegin call serves as rendering starting point for a group of primitives. For example, the following call tells OpenGL to render each vertex as a single point:

```
glBegin(GL_POINTS);
```

Now, let's proceed in making our above defined square solid:

```
glBegin(GL_POLYGON);
    glVertex2f(-1.5, -1.5);
    glVertex2f(-1.5, 1.5);
    glVertex2f(1.5, 1.5);
    glVertex2f(1.5, -1.5);
glEnd();
```

By changing glBegin's type specifier, we can change the primitive type being rendered. In our case we only needed to change the GL_LINE_LOOP type specification to GL_POLYGON. All the primitive types supported by OpenGL are listed in Table 6-2.

| TABLE 6-2 | OpenGL primitive types |

OpenGL type specification	Description	Representation
GL_POINTS	Draws individual vertices.	Figure 6-4(a)
GL_LINES	Draws individual lines by connecting each successive pair of vertices with a line.	Figure 6-4(b)
GL_LINE_STRIP	Draws a series of connected lines. The first and last vertices aren't connected.	Figure 6-4(c)
GL_LINE_LOOP	Draws a series of connected lines. The first and last vertices are connected.	Figure 6-4(d)
GL_POLYGON	Draws a closed filled area as specified by a series of vertices.	Figure 6-4(e)

(Continued)

TABLE 6-2	OpenGL primitive types *(Continued)*	
OpenGL type specification	**Description**	**Representation**
GL_QUADS	Special case of a polygon; groups of four vertices are interpreted as a quadrilateral.	Figure 6-4(f)
GL_TRIANGLES	Special case of a polygon; groups of three vertices are interpreted as a triangle.	Figure 6-4(g)
GL_TRIANGLE_STRIP	Combines each vertex with the previous two vertices to define a new triangle.	Figure 6-4(h)
GL_QUAD_STRIP	Combine two new vertices with the previous two vertices to define a new quadrilateral.	Figure 6-4(i)
GL_TRIANGLE_FAN	Draws a triangle originating from one fixed vertex to a new vertex and a previous vertex.	Figure 6-4(j)

6

To render an object we combine the above mentioned type specifications with a series of *attributes*. An attribute is any property governing the rendering of a primitive. Examples of attributes range from color and line thickness to vertex size. We can also consider a texture mapped to a polygon as an attribute of that polygon.

6.1.2 Rendering Stroke and Raster Text

The topic of text rendering is generally divided into two sections, namely, stroke and raster text. *Stroke text* is based on geometric shapes, basically defined through the grouping of curves and lines. For example, we could render the character 'C' using two arches and two line segments at the ends of each curve. Figure 6-5 shows this character constructed out of a bigger curve and a smaller curve, the one fitting within the other with their endpoints connected using line segments.

This character is now defined by closed boundaries and can hence be filled with a color, pattern, or texture. Objects constructed out of geometric primitives have several advantages such as unlimited rotations, translations, and zooming – all without the loss of any detail.

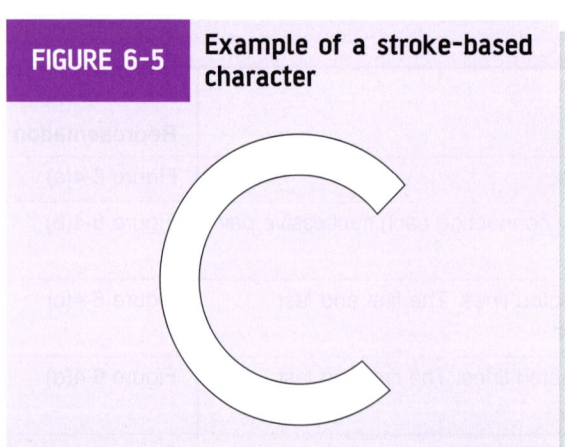

FIGURE 6-5 **Example of a stroke-based character**

Raster text on the other hand doesn't share these advantages. Raster characters are made up of little blocks called bit blocks. These bit blocks can be compared to the output of old dot-matrix printers. Raster text almost always loses quality when scaled because we simply replicate pixels; leading to even larger, blockier characters. Figure 6-6 shows such a raster-based character.

So why use raster text at all? The answer is simple: because it is fast to render and rapidly handled by the frame buffer. Figure 6-7 and 6-8 illustrate the different results from scaling stroke and raster text.

FIGURE 6-6	Example of a raster-based character

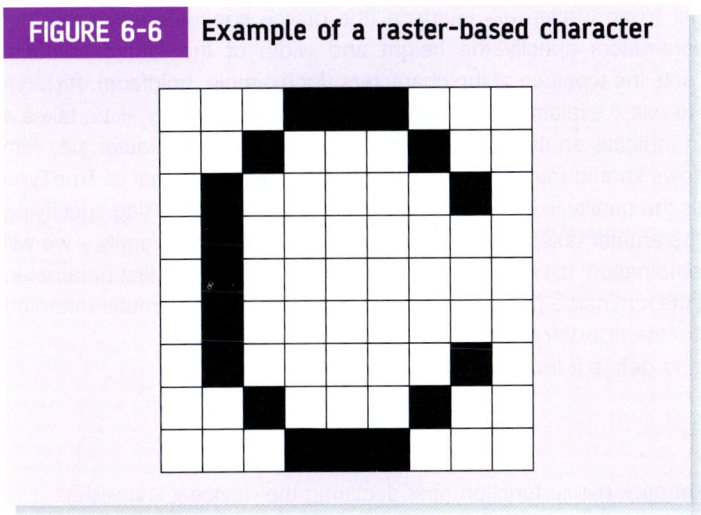

FIGURE 6-7	Scaling stroke-based text

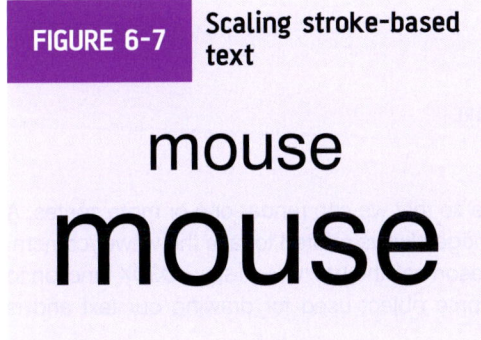

FIGURE 6-8	Scaling raster-based text

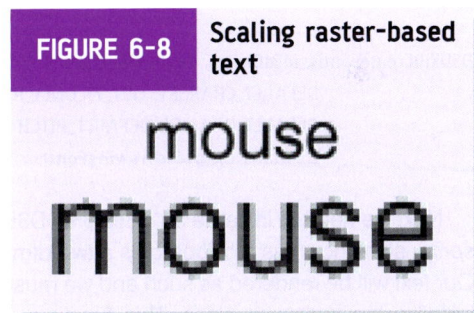

The easiest way to render text in Direct3D 10 is to use the ID3DX10Font Direct3D Extension (D3DX) interface. We obtain this interface by calling either the D3DX10CreateFont or D3DX10CreateFontIndirect function. The D3DX10CreateFont function initializes the ID3DXFont type and is declared as follows in the d3dx10.h header file:

```
HRESULT D3DX10CreateFont(
    ID3D10Device *pDevice,
    INT Height,
    UINT Width,
    UINT Weight,
    UINT MipLevels,
    BOOL Italic,
    UINT CharSet,
    UINT OutputPrecision,
    UINT Quality,
    UINT PitchAndFamily,
    LPCSTR pFaceName,
    LPD3DX10FONT *ppFont
);
```

Its first parameter takes a pointer to an ID3D10Device interface (the device concerned with the font object). The second and third parameters specify the height and width of the font characters, respectively. The Weight parameter sets the typeface of the characters (for example, boldface). MipLevels sets the number of mipmap levels to use – explained in Chapter 8). The next parameter, Italic, takes a Boolean value that is set to true to indicate an italic font. CharSet takes the font's character set, with OutputPrecision specifying how Windows should match the specified font's quality with that of TrueType fonts (the flag OUT_TT_ONLY_PRECIS sets the quality to TrueType, with the OUT_DEFAULT_PRECIS flag specifying default quality). The PitchAndFamily parameter takes an index to the font pitch and font family – we will always set it to the following flag combination: DEFAULT_PITCH | FF_DONTCARE. The second last parameter, pFaceName, takes a string containing the font name (for example 'Ariel'), with the final parameter returning a pointer to the created font object – the ID3DX10Font interface.

The first step in rendering text is to define a font type ID3DXFont:

```
ID3DX10Font* g_pTextDrawingFont = NULL;
```

This font is now passed to the D3DX10CreateFont function (first declaring the device g_id3dDevice):

```
ID3D10Device* g_id3dDevice;

D3DX10CreateFont(g_id3dDevice, 20, 0, FW_BOLD, 1, FALSE,
                 DEFAULT_CHARSET, OUT_TT_ONLY_PRECIS,
                 DEFAULT_QUALITY, DEFAULT_PITCH | FF_DONTCARE,
                 L"Arial", &g_pTextDrawingFont);
```

Next we need to initialize an ID3DXSprite D3DX interface so that we can render one or more sprites. A *sprite*, also known as a *billboard*, is a two-dimensional image always rotated to face the viewer/camera. Our text will be rendered as such and we must for that reason call the D3DX10CreateSprite D3DX function to initialize the ID3DXSprite class. This function creates a sprite object used for drawing our text and is declared as follows in the d3dx10.h header file:

```
HRESULT D3DX10CreateSprite(
    ID3D10Device *pDevice,
    UINT cDeviceBufferSize,
    LPD3DX10SPRITE *ppSprite
);
```

Its first parameter takes a pointer to an ID3D10Device interface (the device concerned with the sprite object), with the second parameter being the vertex buffer's size used for specifying the number of sprites. The third parameter, ppSprite, is an address to the ID3DX10Sprite interface.

We initialize the sprite object as follows (first declaring the sprite g_id3dDevice for the batching of text data):

```
ID3DX10Sprite* g_pTextRenderingSprite = NULL;

D3DX10CreateSprite(g_id3dDevice, MAX_SPRITES,
                   &g_pTextRenderingSprite);
```

DXUT provides a utility class for the rendering of 2D text, namely CDXUTD3D10TextHelper. This utility class allows for the drawing of text through the specification of three parameters, namely, the font created using the D3DX10CreateFont function, the ID3DXSprite class initialized via the D3DX10CreateSprite function and the font height:

```
CDXUTD3D10TextHelper* g_pDXTextHelper =
        new CDXUTD3D10TextHelper(g_pTextDrawingFont,
                            g_pTextRenderingSprite, 20);
```

We can now use the g_pDXTextHelper object to output our text to the screen:

```
/* enter text rendering mode*/
g_pDXTextHelper->Begin();

/* set text rendering position (x, y) */
g_pDXTextHelper->SetInsertionPos(5, 10);

/* set the text color to red */
g_pDXTextHelper->SetForegroundColor(D3DXCOLOR(1.0f, 0.0f,
                            0.0f, 1.0f ));
/* draw the text */
g_pDXTextHelper->DrawTextLine("Just some random text");

/* exit text rendering mode */
g_pDXTextHelper->End();
```

6

Working with OpenGL

OpenGL itself does not offer any functions for the rendering of text; however, the GLUT library gives us access to both raster- and stroke-based text. The glutBitmapCharacter function renders raster characters using OpenGL with the glutStrokeCharacter function handling all stroke-based rendering.

The glutBitmapCharacter function can be used in the following manner (the GLUT_BITMAP_8_BY_13 flag specifies a bitmap character that is 8 by 13 pixels in size):

```
char string[] = "Just some random text";
for(int i = 0; string[i]; i++)
    glutBitmapCharacter(GLUT_BITMAP_8_BY_13, string[i]);
```

Text can be rendered using the glutStrokeCharacter function as follows (the GLUT_STROKE_ROMAN flag sets the font to a Roman-type font):

```
for(int i = 0; string[i]; i++)
    glutStrokeCharacter(GLUT_STROKE_ROMAN, string[i]);
```

6.2   DRAWING: PRIMITIVES AND POLYGONS

Chapter 4 thoroughly discussed the input-assembler stage, the specification and initialization of both index and vertex input buffers, the creation of an input-layout object (for controlling how vertex data is fed into the input-assembler stage) and the binding of the input buffers and input-layout object to the input-assembler stage. We will now build on this discussion by describing how to render these input resources after they have been bound to the pipeline's input-assembler stage.

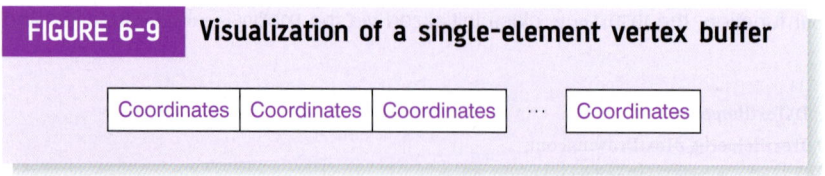

FIGURE 6-9   Visualization of a single-element vertex buffer

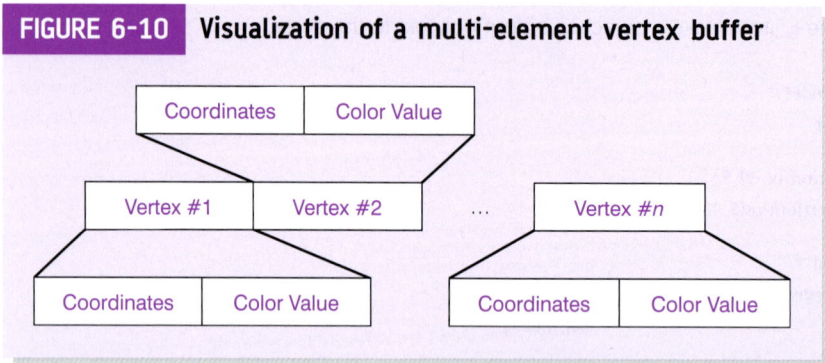

FIGURE 6-10   Visualization of a multi-element vertex buffer

The most basic, yet sensible object to draw is a triangle (a polygon constructed out of three vertices). Triangles represent one of the most useful primitives and allow us to construct more complex objects by grouping any number of them together in some specific pattern.

All Direct3D 10 programs require some sort of data structure for the storage vertex coordinates. These coordinates can be set as either two- or three-dimensional in the form (x, y, z) and must be defined before we can specify anything else. It is thus necessary to create a buffer resource for the storage of vertex coordinates. This buffer resource can be defined as either a vertex or index buffer.

A vertex buffer is basically a grouping of elements, specifically holding the coordinates of vertices. Vertex buffers, in their simplest form, can be visualized as an array of elements as shown in Figure 6-9.

Vertex buffers, as described and implemented in Chapter 4, can also contain multi-element data. For example, we can define a vertex buffer to store the number of vertices, the coordinates of each vertex and a color value for each vertex. This arrangement for such a buffer storing *n* elements is shown in Figure 6-10.

Accessing data from vertex buffers relies on knowledge about the vertex offset (the position of the first vertex's data in bytes from the start of the buffer) and the base vertex location (the position of the first drawn vertex from the buffer's offset in bytes).

To set up a vertex buffer, we start by defining a buffer description (using the D3D10_BUFFER_DESC structure to specify the type of data stored in the buffer), followed by filling the buffer with some initialization data (using the D3D10_SUBRESOURCE_DATA structure). Once this is done we simply create the buffer (by calling the CreateBuffer ID3D10Device). Please see section 4.3.4.1's 'The Input-Assembler Stage' subsection for a full discussion of this process, including examinations of all structures initialized and methods called. To recapitulate, a vertex buffer can be created in the following manner:

We first specify a structure to hold information about our geometric object's vertices:

```
struct TriangleVertex
{
    D3DXVECTOR3 Location;
    D3DXVECTOR3 Color;
};
```

Next we set up the vertex buffer description by initializing the D3D10_BUFFER_DESC structure:

```
D3D10_BUFFER_DESC bufferDescription;

bufferDescription.Usage = D3D10_USAGE_DEFAULT;
bufferDescription.ByteWidth = sizeof(TriangleVertex) * 3;
bufferDescription.BindFlags = D3D10_BIND_VERTEX_BUFFER;
bufferDescription.CPUAccessFlags = 0;
bufferDescription.MiscFlags = 0;
```

Following this we create the vertex buffer using vertex data:

```
TriangleVertex array_of_vertex_data [] =
{
    D3DXVECTOR3( 0.0f, 1.0f, 1.0f ),   //location
    D3DXVECTOR3( 0.0f, 0.0f, 0.5f ),   //color
    D3DXVECTOR3( 1.0f, -1.0f, 1.0f ),  //location
    D3DXVECTOR3( 1.0f, 0.0f, 0.0f ),   //color
    D3DXVECTOR3( -1.0f, -1.0f, 1.0f ), //location
    D3DXVECTOR3( 0.0f, 1.0f, 0.0f ),   //color
};
```

As stated in Chapter 4: 'A subresource is a portion of a resource that links back to the original resource data but with additional information about the resource so that the pipeline can easily access the data contained within this resource'. This subresource description, the D3D10_SUBRESOURCE_DATA structure, is initialized using the previously defined array of vertex data elements:

```
D3D10_SUBRESOURCE_DATA subresourceData;

subresourceData.pSysMem = array_of_vertex_data;
subresourceData.SysMemPitch = 0;
subresourceData.SysMemSlicePitch = 0;
```

We now create the vertex buffer via the CreateBuffer ID3D10Device interface:

```
ID3D10Buffer* vertexBuffer[2] = {NULL, NULL};

g_id3dDevice->CreateBuffer(&bufferDescription,
                &subresourceData,
                &vertexBuffer[0]);
```

Index buffers consist of a set of indices for each vertex data element stored in a vertex buffer. Index buffers are used in combination with either one or multiple vertex buffers, indexing data for processing by the input-assembler stage. An index buffer can be visualized as an array of indices as shown in Figure 6-11.

When accessing an index buffer we need information about the index offset (the position of the first index, in bytes, from the start of the buffer), the start index location (the position of the first

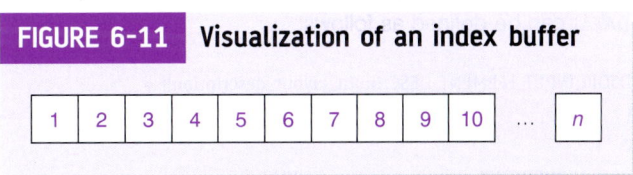

FIGURE 6-11   **Visualization of an index buffer**

| 1 | 2 | 3 | 4 | 5 | 6 | 7 | 8 | 9 | 10 | ... | n |

vertex to be drawn from the buffer's offset in bytes) and the index count specifying the number of indices to draw.

Section 4.3.4.1's 'The Input-Assembler Stage' subsection features a full examination of the process required to set up an index buffer. During that section we illustrated how the definition of an index buffer is comparable to that of a vertex buffer – the only variation being the specification of the D3D10_BUFFER_DESC structure's BindFlags member (it being set to D3D10_BIND_INDEX_BUFFER instead of D3D10_BIND_VERTEX_BUFFER as the case with a vertex buffer). To review, an index buffer is created as follows:

We once again set up the buffer description by initializing the D3D10_BUFFER_DESC structure:

```
D3D10_BUFFER_DESC indexBufferDescription;

indexBufferDescription.Usage = D3D10_USAGE_DEFAULT;
indexBufferDescription.ByteWidth = sizeof(TriangleVertex) * 3;
indexBufferDescription.BindFlags = D3D10_BIND_INDEX_BUFFER;
indexBufferDescription.CPUAccessFlags = 0;
indexBufferDescription.MiscFlags = 0;
```

We also set up an array containing index data (will be used to initialize the D3D10_SUBRESOURCE_DATA structure):

```
UINT array_of_index_data [] = {0, 1, 2, 3, 4};
```

Next we can initialize the subresource description structure using the previously defined index array:

```
D3D10_SUBRESOURCE_DATA indexSubresourceData;

indexSubresourceData.pSysMem = array_of_index_data;
indexSubresourceData.SysMemPitch = 0;
indexSubresourceData.SysMemSlicePitch = 0;
```

The index buffer is created using the CreateBuffer ID3D10Device interface:

```
ID3D10Buffer* indexBuffer = NULL;

g_id3dDevice->CreateBuffer(&indexBufferDescription,
                           &indexSubresourceData,
                           &indexBuffer);
```

Before getting to the rendering phase we still have to create the input-layout object, bind this object and the input buffers to the input assembler stage, and set up the primitive type. Section 4.3.4.1's 'The Input-Assembler Stage' subsection deals with the basic steps outlined below, necessary for setting up the input-assembler stage, in detail.

We create the input-layout object using the CreateInputLayout ID3D10Device interface method that describes the input-buffer data sent to the input-assembler stage.

The first step, when creating this object, is to define an array of the input-assembler stage input data type using the D3D10_INPUT_ELEMENT_DESC structure. This structure describes each element of the input assembler stage. A vertex buffer containing two vertex-data elements (of type D3D10_INPUT_PER_VERTEX_DATA) can be defined as follows:

```
D3D10_INPUT_ELEMENT_DESC input_layout_description[] =
{
    {
        L"POSITION",                //HLSL semantic
```

```
        0,                              //semantic index
        DXGI_FORMAT_R32G32B32_UINT,     //data type
        0,                              //input slot id
        0,                              //offsets between elements
        D3D10_INPUT_PER_VERTEX_DATA,    //data stored in input slot
        0                               //instance specific type
    },

    {
    L"NORMAL",
    0,
    DXGI_FORMAT_R32G32B32_UINT,
    1,
    6,
    D3D10_INPUT_PER_VERTEX_DATA,
    0
    },
};
```

Next we specify an integer type to hold the number of input-data types stored in the above defined input-elements array:

```
int numberOfElements = sizeof(input_layout_description) /
                        sizeof(input_layout_description [0]);
```

The final step, before we can create the input layout object (a vertex layout object in our case), is to determine the vertex-shader input signature. This input signature is needed for the creation of a vertex layout object, as will be illustrated shortly. For now, just know that we must call the GetPassByIndex ID3D10EffectTechnique interface method to acquire an effect pass object representing the first pass of the technique. We also need to call the GetDesc ID3D10EffectTechnique interface function to obtain information about the effect's technique such as the technique's name (can be 'NULL') and its number of passes. In short, an effect can hold several techniques, with each technique containing one or more passes, and every pass containing several pipeline state assignments. Don't worry too much about this now as it all will become clear later on in the chapter, just know that we have to acquire the effect pass object and create a D3D10_PASS_DESC structure to describe the passes contained by an effect technique. We need this structure before calling the CreateInputLayout ID3D10Device interface method to determine the vertex shader's input signature (given by the pIAInputSignature member) and its size in bytes (via the IAInputSignatureSize member).

```
D3D10_PASS_DESC PassDescription;

/* ID3D10EffectTechnique interface */
ID3D10EffectTechnique* g_pd3d10EffectTechnique = NULL;
g_pd3d10EffectTechnique->
        GetPassByIndex(0)->GetDesc(&PassDescription);
```

We can now create the vertex layout object using the CreateInputLayout ID3D10Device interface method as follows:

```
ID3D10InputLayout* inputLayoutObject = NULL;

hresult_ = g_id3dDevice->CreateInputLayout(
            input_layout_description, numberOfElements,
```

```
                    PassDescription.pIAInputSignature,
                    PassDescription.IAInputSignatureSize,
                    &inputLayoutObject);
```

Following this we bind the input-layout object to the input-assembler stage, after which we can call the draw functions. Object binding is done using the IASetVertexBuffers and IASetInputLayout ID3D10Device interfaces. The IASetVertexBuffers interface binds a vertex buffer array to the input-assembler stage with the IASetInputLayout interface binding the input-layout object to the input-assembler stage. The following code sample illustrates this process:

```
UINT  start_input_slot = 0;
UINT  number_buffers_in_array = 1;
UINT  offset_value = 0;
UINT  stride_value = sizeof(TriangleVertex);
g_id3dDevice->IASetVertexBuffers(start_input_slot,
                            number_buffers_in_array,
                            &vertexBuffer,
                            &stride_value,
                            &offset_value);
```

The input-layout takes a pointer to the ID3D10Device object:

```
g_id3dDevice->IASetInputLayout(inputLayoutObject);
```

We finally specify the primitive type as a triangle list:

```
g_id3dDevice->IASetPrimitiveTopology(
                    D3D10_PRIMITIVE_TOPOLOGY_TRIANGLELIST);
```

All resources have now been bound to the pipeline and we can call the Draw ID3D10Device function to perform the actual rendering. We start by clearing the back-buffer using the ClearRenderTargetView ID3D10Device method with a pointer to the render target (in our case the surface being rendered to) declared as follows:

```
ID3D10RenderTargetView* g_pd3d10RenderTargetView = NULL;
```

ClearRenderTargetView's second parameter takes a color to the render target – red in the case of the code sample (as specified using the four-component array ClearBufferColor):

```
/* set the clear color – red, green, blue, alpha*/
float ClearBufferColor[4] = {1.0f, 0.0f, 0.0f, 1.0f};
g_id3dDevice ->ClearRenderTargetView(g_pd3d10RenderTargetView,
                            ClearBufferColor);
```

Next we have to call the GetDesc ID3D10EffectTechnique function on the previously defined technique object that will store the returned D3D10_TECHNIQUE_DESC structure describing the technique:

```
/*  obtain the D3D10_TECHNIQUE_DESC effect-variable
    description */
```

```
D3D10_TECHNIQUE_DESC technique;
g_pd3d10EffectTechnique->GetDesc(&technique);
```

The D3D10_TECHNIQUE_DESC structure is defined as follows:

```
typedef struct D3D10_TECHNIQUE_DESC {
    LPCSTR Name;
    UINT Passes;
    UINT Annotations;
} D3D10_TECHNIQUE_DESC;
```

Its first member holds the name of the effect technique, the second holding the number of passes in the technique, with the third storing the number annotations. For now we are only interested in the number of passes contained by the technique. We draw the triangle by looping over this number of passes, with the GetPassByIndex method being called for each pass, returning the pass object. This pass object is then applied by the effect system binding all related render states and shaders to the graphics pipeline using the Apply ID3D10EffectPass method. This is followed by a call to the Draw ID3D10Device function. This function instructs the GPU to render the contents defined in the vertex buffer based on the specified vertex layout and primitive type. The Draw function's first parameter is the number of vertices to render, with the second parameter indicating the first vertex in this set:

```
/* render by looping over the number of technique passes */
for(int i = 0; i < technique.Passes; ++i)
{
    g_pd3d10EffectTechnique->GetPassByIndex(i)->Apply(0);
    g_pd3d10Device->Draw(3, 0);
}
```

As described in section 4.5.2 we simply call the IDXGISwapChain Present function to display our processed contents:

```
/*  switch the back- and front-buffer and display the
    triangle */
g_pdxl0SwapChain->Present(0,0);
```

Working with OpenGL

OpenGL vertex lists, just as the name suggests, consist of a series of vertex coordinates stored as a list or array. We specify this type by adding a suffix in the form of the letter 'v' to the glVertex* function resulting in a function such as glVertex3fv, for example. The following code sample shows the specification of a vertex list, vertices, with the values of x, y and z set to 1.0, 1.0 and 2.0 respectively for the first index, −1.0, −1.0 and −2.0 for the second, 1.0, 1.0 and 1.0 for the third and 1.0, −1.0 and 1.0 for the fourth:

```
float vertices[4][3] = {{ 1.0,  1.0,  2.0},
                        {-1.0, -1.0, -2.0},
                        { 1.0,  1.0,  1.0},
                        { 1.0, -1.0,  1.0}};
```

Vertex lists reduce the need to redefine vertices. For example, several objects may start at the point (−1.0, 1.0, 1.0) and will each thus require a definition such as the following, leading to the continuous redefinition of a vertex with the coordinates (−1.0, 1.0, 1.0):

```
glBegin(GL_LINE_LOOP);
    glVertex3f(-1.0, 1.0, 1.0);
    ...
glEnd();
```

By using a vertex list we avoid this redefinition and we can specify the vertex to render by referring to its array index in the following manner:

```
glBegin(GL_LINE_LOOP);
    glVertex3fv(vertices[0]); //the (1.0, 1.0, 2.0) vertex
    glVertex3fv(vertices[3]); //the (1.0, -1.0, 1.0) vertex
glEnd();
```

Vertex lists still require several OpenGL function calls when modeling an object. For example, we have a glBegin, a glEnd, a number of calls to glVertex, and normally additional calls for the definition of texture coordinates, normals and/or color values in between.

Vertex arrays, on the other hand, are useful for reducing the number of OpenGL calls needed (such as repeated identical glVertex calls). This is accomplished by passing OpenGL a pointer to the vertex data and then subsequently deciding which of the vertices to render, thus allowing us to group information in a data structure so that objects can be drawn with fewer function calls than by grouping several geVertex and/or glColor calls within a glBegin and glEnd. In addition to vertex arrays there are also color arrays, index arrays, normal arrays, texture coordinate arrays, etc.

To enable a specific type of array we make use of the glEnableClientState function by setting some capability as enabled, possible flags include the following:

- GL_COLOR_ARRAY (enables a color array for writing and use it when calling glDrawArrays or glDrawElements)

- GL_EDGE_FLAG_ARRAY (enables an edge flag array for writing and use it when calling glDrawArrays or glDrawElements)

- GL_INDEX_ARRAY (enables an index array for writing and use it when calling glDrawArrays or glDrawElements)

- GL_NORMAL_ARRAY (enables a normal array for writing and use it when calling glDrawArrays or glDrawElements)

- GL_TEXTURE_COORD_ARRAY (enables a texture coordinate array for writing and use it when calling glDrawArrays or glDrawElements) and

- GL_VERTEX_ARRAY (enables a vertex array for writing and use it when calling glDrawArrays or glDrawElements).

We call this function to enable a vertex array as follows:

```
glEnableClientState(GL_VERTEX_ARRAY);
```

Vertex arrays are declared exactly the same as vertex lists (this set of vertices will be used to create a pyramid as the one shown in Figure 6-12):

```
float pyramidVertices[5][3] = {{ 1.0,  0.0,   1.0},
                               {-1.0,  0.0,   1.0},
                               {-1.0,  0.0,  -1.0},
                               { 1.0,  0.0,  -1.0},
                               { 0.0,  1.0,   0.0}};
```

Next we pass OpenGL a pointer to the vertex data using the `glVertexPointer` function to define an array of vertices. This function takes four parameters: the number of coordinates for each of the vertices, the data type of the coordinates (`GL_FOAT`, `GL_INT`, `GL_SHORT` or `GL_DOUBLE`), the byte offset between successive vertices and a pointer to the vertex array:

```
glVertexPointer(3, GL_FLOAT, 0,
vertices);
```

FIGURE 6-12 **The specified pyramid**

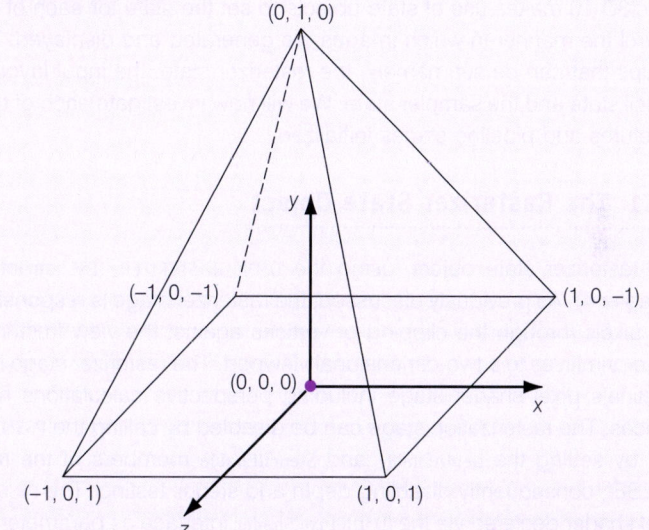

Following this definition we have to provide information about the correlation between the specified vertices and faces of the object we intend to render. Say we are rendering the pyramid in Figure 6-12; then we will have five faces – one for each side as well as the base rectangle. We must thus specify an array to hold the indices for the five faces in this fashion:

```
GLubyte pyramidIndices[16] =
              {0, 1, 2, 3,          //the base rectangle
               0, 3, 4,             //the right triangle
               0, 1, 4,             //the front triangle
               1, 2, 4,             //the left triangle
               2, 3, 4};            //the back triangle
```

This defined pyramid can now be rendered using the `glDrawElements` function. This function, rendering primitives from array data, takes four parameters. The first parameter specifies the primitive type (`GL_POINTS`, `GL_LINE_STRIP`, `GL_LINE_LOOP`, `GL_LINES`, `GL_TRIANGLE_STRIP`, `GL_TRIANGLE_FAN`, `GL_TRIANGLES`, `GL_QUAD_STRIP`, `GL_QUADS` or `GL_POLYGON`). The second parameter sets the number of elements to render and the third the type of the values stored in the indices array (`GL_UNSIGNED_INT`, `GL_UNSIGNED_BYTE` or `GL_UNSIGNED_SHORT`). Since we declared the `pyramidIndices` array as `GLubyte` we must specify this parameter as `GL_UNSIGNED_BYTE`. The final parameter takes a pointer to the array holding the indices.

The glDrawElements function is called for each of the faces to render. The following call renders the base of the pyramid with the four triangles rendered similarly:

glDrawElements(GL_POLYGON, 4, GL_UNSIGNED_BYTE,
                                    &pyramidIndices[0]);

We will thus only have five function calls each and every time the pyramid is drawn.

6.3   DIRECT3D RENDER STATES

Direct3D 10 makes use of state objects to set the state for each of the pipeline stages. Pipeline states control the manner in which images are generated and displayed. There are five possible state object groups that can be set, namely, the rasterizer state, the input-layout state, the blend state, the depth-stencil state and the sampler state. We will now investigate each of these as well as the related Direct3D structures and pipeline stages initialized.

6.3.1 The Rasterizer State Object

The rasterizer state object, using the D3D10_RASTERIZER_DESC structure, initializes the rasterizer stage (Chapter 4). As previously discussed, the rasterizer stage is responsible for the rasterization of primitives into pixels through the clipping of vertices against the view frustum and the subsequent mapping of these primitives to a two-dimensional viewport. The rasterizer stage is also responsible for initializing the pipeline's pixel shader stage including perspective calculations necessary for the transformation of vertices. The rasterization stage can be disabled by calling the PSSetShader ID3D10Device interface function and by setting the DepthEnable and StencilEnable members of the D3D10_DEPTH_STENCIL_DESC structure to 'FALSE', consequently disabling depth and stencil testing. The PSSetShader function takes a pointer to a pixel shader declared via the ID3D10PixelShader interface as parameter. We set this parameter to 'NULL' to indicate that a pixel shader is not bound to the pipeline.

The D3D10_RASTERIZER_DESC render state structure stores data required by the rasterization stage for the conversion of primitives into pixels. This structure sets the application's fill mode behaviour, the culling mode, depth bias, etc. Its use in removing polygons hidden from the viewer (culling) is thoroughly discussed in section 7.3.2.

Once we have declared an ID3D10RasterizerState interface and initialized the members of the D3D10_RASTERIZER_DESC render state structure, we have to create the rasterizer state object using the CreateRasterizerState ID3D10Device interface function. This function takes two parameters, namely, a pointer to the structure describing the rasterizer state (D3D10_RASTERIZER_DESC) and the address of a pointer to the ID3D10RasterizerState rasterizer state interface. The state object controls the behaviour of the rasterizer stage and is created as follows:

ID3D10RasterizerState * generalRasterizerState;
D3D10_RASTERIZER_DESC generalRasterState;

/*...initialize the members of the D3D10_RASTERIZER_DESC
    structure */

g_id3dDevice->CreateRasterizerState(&generalRasterState,
                                    &generalRasterizerState);

With the behaviour of the rasterizer state object defined we can apply this state to the pipeline's rasterizer stage using the RSSetState ID3D10Device function. This function takes one parameter, namely a pointer to the ID3D10RasterizerState rasterizer state interface, and is called:

```
g_id3dDevice->RSSetState(generalRasterizerState);
```

6.3.2 The Input-Layout State Object

The input-layout state object, describing each element of the input-assembler stage via the D3D10_INPUT_ELEMENT_DESC structure, initializes the input-assembler stage by specifying the manner in which input buffer data are read and assembled for use by the subsequent vertex-shader stage (see sections 4.3.4.1 and 6.2). As discussed in Chapter 4, the input-assembler stage is responsible for forwarding geometric input data (vertices, lines, and polygons) to the rest of the pipeline. In short we can summarize the function of this pipeline stage as the assembling of input data such as vertices into primitives (line loops, triangle lists, primitives with adjacency), followed by the forwarding of these assembled primitives to the next stage in the pipeline. The input-assembler stage also attaches system-generated values, called semantics, to the assembled primitives. These attached values are accessed by the shader stages and limit the processing of primitives to only those that have not yet been processed by a previous shader stage.

Following the declaration of an ID3D10InputLayout interface for the input-layout object and the initialization of the D3D10_INPUT_ELEMENT_DESC structure we have to create the input-layout state object using the CreateInputLayout ID3D10Device interface function. Section 6.2 shows this procedure with the process of binding the input-layout object to the input-assembler stage summarized here:

```
ID3D10InputLayout* inputLayoutObject = NULL;
D3D10_INPUT_ELEMENT_DESC input_layout_description;

/*...initialize the members of the D3D10_INPUT_ELEMENT_DESC
   structure */
```

Specify an integer type to hold the number of input-data types:

```
int numberOfElements = sizeof(input_layout_description) /
                    sizeof(input_layout_description [0]);
```

Determine the vertex shader input signature:

```
D3D10_PASS_DESC PassDescription;

/* ID3D10EffectTechnique interface */

ID3D10EffectTechnique* g_pd3d10EffectTechnique = NULL;
g_pd3d10EffectTechnique->
         GetPassByIndex(0)->GetDesc(&PassDescription);
```

Create the input-layout object using the CreateInputLayout ID3D10Device interface method to describe the input-assembler stage's input-buffer data:

```
hresult_ = g_id3dDevice->CreateInputLayout(
             input_layout_description, numberOfElements,
             PassDescription.pIAInputSignature,
             PassDescription.IAInputSignatureSize,
             &inputLayoutObject);
```

This input-layout can now be bound to the input-assembler stage:

```
UINT start_input_slot = 0;
UINT number_buffers_in_array = 1;
UINT offset_value = 0;
UINT stride_value = sizeof(TriangleVertex);

g_id3dDevice->IASetVertexBuffers(start_input_slot,
                                 number_buffers_in_array,
                                 &vertexBuffer,
                                 &stride_value,
                                 &offset_value);

g_id3dDevice->IASetInputLayout(inputLayoutObject);
```

6.3.3 The Depth Stencil State Object

The depth stencil state object controls the initialization of the output-merger stage's depth stencil unit. This state object initializes depth and stencil testing, two operations of crucial importance for effects such as stencil shadow volumes and stencil buffer-based reflections, as detailed in Chapter 11. The output-merger stage is described in Chapter 11 as the final pipeline step responsible for pixel visibility. This pipeline step controls pixel visibility by incorporating pixel shader data with depth and stencil testing results. The stencil buffer controls rendering by enabling or disabling drawing to a specific pixel, with the depth buffer controlling whether a certain pixel's stencil value is increased or decreased based on the result of a depth test (for a detailed explanation, please refer to Chapter 11). The stencil buffer stores a stencil value for each pixel, similarly to the depth buffer storing a depth value for each pixel – both the stencil-buffer and depth-buffer values are required for rejecting or accepting rasterized fragments. The D3D10_DEPTH_STENCIL_DESC structure describes a depth stencil state and is discussed in section 11.2.1.

The depth stencil state is set using the CreateDepthStencilState ID3D10Device interface. This interface, fully described in section 11.1.2, takes a pointer to the depth stencil state description (D3D10_DEPTH_STENCIL_DESC) and the address of the depth stencil state object (ID3D10DepthStencilState) as parameters:

```
D3D10_DEPTH_STENCIL_DESC depthstencilDesc;

/*...initialize the members of the D3D10_DEPTH_STENCIL_DESC
    structure */

ID3D10DepthStencilState * pDepthStencilState;
g_id3dDevice->CreateDepthStencilState (depthstencilDesc,
                                       &pDepthStencilState);
```

6.3.4 The Blend State Object

Blending is the process of altering a pixel's color value based on the color of a previously drawn pixel located at the position where the new pixel is being drawn to. By setting a blend state we are able to control the interaction between previously drawn and overlain pixels. When this blend state is set to default, all newly rendered pixels will overwrite existing ones. Two forms of blending are common in computer graphics. The first, known as *alpha blending*, is a technique that enables a unified level of transparency through objects such as curtains or colored glass. The other, namely *alpha masking*, is, for

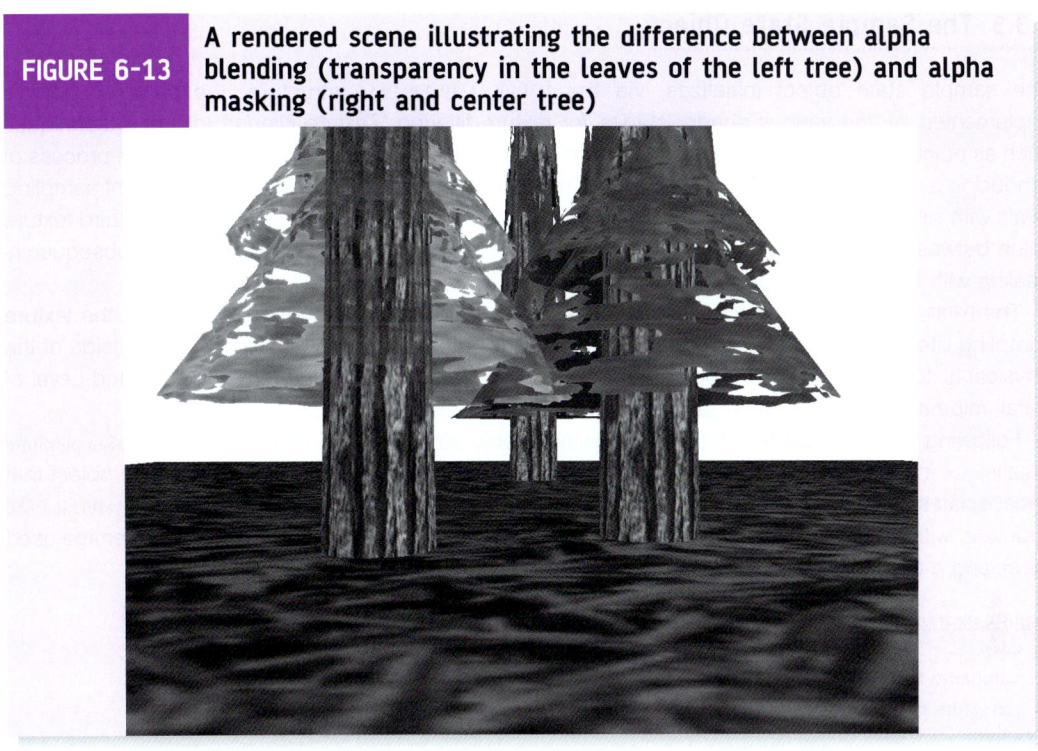

FIGURE 6-13 A rendered scene illustrating the difference between alpha blending (transparency in the leaves of the left tree) and alpha masking (right and center tree)

6

example, what we'll use to see through sections in a staircase's railing. Chapter 10 concentrates on these two techniques; Figure 6-13 illustrates the difference between them.

The blend state initializes the output-merger stage's blending unit with the D3D10_BLEND_DESC structure describing the blend state. Chapter 10 details the use of this structure including the method by which blending combines pixel color values.

We create a blend state object to control the output-merger stage's blending operations using the CreateBlendState ID3D10Device interface function. This function takes two parameters, the first a pointer to the D3D10_BLEND_DESC structure describing the blend state, and the second, address of a pointer to an ID3D10BlendState blend state interface:

```
D3D10_BLEND_DESC blendstateDesc;

/*. . .initialize the members of the D3D10_BLEND_DESC
    structure */

ID3D10BlendState* pBlendState = NULL;

g_id3dDevice->CreateBlendState(&blendstateDesc, &pBlendState);
```

To set the output-merger stage's blend state, we call the OMSetBlendState ID3D10Device interface function. This function, binding the defined blend state object to the output-merger stage, takes three parameters. The first requires a pointer to the ID3D10BlendState blend-state interface, the second an array of blend factors with the third a sample coverage mask. The blending factor enables individual per-pixel control over the blending of new pixels with existing ones. The sample coverage mask controls the sampling of the surface being rendered to. These elements are all explained in Chapter 10; for now we will just initialize the last two parameters using their default values (0xffffffff indicates point sampling):

```
g_id3dDevice->OMSetBlendState(pBlendState, 0, 0xffffffff);
```

6.3.5 The Sample State Object

The sample state object initializes, via the D3D10_SAMPLER_DESC structure, the sampler objects implemented by the various shader stages for texture filtering. *Texture filtering* includes techniques such as point sampling, linear interpolation, and anisotropic filtering. *Texture sampling* is the process of producing a single texture value by combining multiple texels (texture elements/pixels). Point sampling deals with single texels while linear sampling interpolates between two texels to produce a third texture value between the original two. Chapter 8 provides an in-depth coverage of texturing, subsequently dealing with these various forms of sampling.

The D3D10_SAMPLER_DESC structure defines a sampler state, describing elements such as the texture sampling filtering method, the method used for dealing with texture coordinates located outside of the physical texture boundaries (wrapping, mirroring or clamping of the texture, for example) and Level of Detail mipmap settings to name but a few.

Following the initialization of the D3D10_SAMPLER_DESC structure, we can call the CreateSamplerState ID3D10Device interface function. This function, taking two parameters, creates a sampler-state object that encapsulates a texture's sampling information. Its first parameter is a pointer to the D3D10_SAMPLER_DESC structure, with the second the address of a pointer to an ID3D10SamplerState sampler-state interface used for setting a texture's sampling information:

```
D3D10_SAMPLER_DESC samplerstateDesc;

/*. . .initialize the members of the D3D10_SAMPLER_DESC
    structure */

ID3D10SamplerState* pSamplerState = NULL;

g_id3dDevice->CreateSamplerState(&samplerstateDesc,
                        &pSamplerState);
```

With the sampler-state object created, it still has to be initialized. We do this by binding it to the pipeline via any of the following ID3D10Device functions: VSSetSamplers for binding the sampler-state object to the vertex shader pipeline stage, PSSetSamplers for binding the sampler-state object to the pixel shader pipeline stage, or GSSetSamplers for binding the sampler-state object to the geometry shader pipeline stage. Each of these functions takes three parameters: respectively, an integer value serving as index to the array of sample states, the number of samplers in the array, and a pointer to the ID3D10SamplerState array.

6.4   THE DXUT FRAMEWORK

The Direct3D Utility Framework, or DXUT, is a high-level framework built on top of Direct3D. This framework provides a series of functions, callbacks, structures, constants and enumerations to reduce the complexity of low-level Direct3D routines. It encapsulates the Win32 and Direct3D APIs for ease of use, making it easier to create Direct3D applications. To summarize, DXUT allows simplified window creation, and enables rapid Direct3D device setup and initialization as well as the easy handling of Windows messages.

The DXUT framework provides a vast array of functionality, from basic window creation, Direct3D device initialization and the control of these components to more advanced elements such as 3D mesh control, camera control and the creation of graphical user interfaces. We will now look at the most important functional components provided by this framework.

The process of window creation and control using the DXUT framework is relatively simple when compared to the procedure described in Chapter 4. This previous example created a window, using the Win32 API, by registering a window class, creating a window object, and handling messages to and from the window. The DXUT framework simplifies this process in the sense that it is not necessary to register the window class (using the WNDCLASSEX structure) or to create the window using the AdjustWindowRect, CreateWindow and ShowWindow functions. The following series of DXUT function calls manages this entire window creation process:

```
/ * initialize the DXUT framework */
DXUTInit(true, true, NULL);

/* configure mouse cursor settings for full-screen usage */
DXUTSetCursorSettings(true, true);

/* create the application window */
DXUTCreateWindow(L"DXUT Sample", NULL, NULL, NULL, NULL,
                 NULL);
/* create the Direct3D device */
DXUTCreateDevice(true, 800, 600);

/* enter the main DXUT framework render loop */
DXUTMainLoop(NULL);
```

The DXUTInit function initializes DXUT by taking three parameters, namely a Boolean value used for the processing of command-line arguments (with the most common ones listed in Table 6-3), another Boolean parameter controlling whether an error message box is to be displayed whenever an error occurs, and a string value for the specification of additional command-line parameters.

The next called function, DXUTSetCursorSettings, sets the visibility and clipping of the mouse cursor when used in full-screen mode. This function takes two parameters, the first a Boolean value specifying whether the mouse cursor will be visible for a window in full-screen mode (true if yes), and the second, also a Boolean value, defining whether the cursor will be limited from leaving the screen boundaries for a full-screen window (true if yes).

DXUTCreateWindow creates the application window through the initialization of six parameters, namely, a string value defining the window's caption, a HINSTANCE handle to the application instance ('NULL' by default), a HICON handle to the window's icon ('NULL' by default), a HMENU handle to the window's menu resource ('NULL' for no menu) and the upper left x-and y-window coordinates.

We create the actual Direct3D 10 device by calling the DXUTCreateDevice function. Its first parameter takes a Boolean value specifying whether the application will launch in windowed (true) or full-screen mode (false). DXUTCreateDevice's final two parameters set the initial width and height of the back buffer, respectively.

The DXUTMainLoop function enters the main DXUT framework render loop (the main message loop), updating and rendering each frame via callbacks to the application. It takes one parameter, namely a handle to an accelerator table – this parameter is set to 'NULL' when no accelerator table is defined. *Accelerator tables* are created as resources and used for the translation of keyboard messages received from the message queue. One example of a common accelerator is the 'Ctrl+S' key combination used as shortcut for the 'File Save' menu item.

All these functions return the value 'S_OK' if successful. In the event of a failure they return one of the error codes listed in Table 6-4. Calling the DXUTGetExitCode function returns an exit code with '0' indicating successful execution.

In our Chapter 4 example, after registering the window class and creating the window, we entered the main message loop by declaring an empty MSG structure, msg, and passing it as a parameter to the WndProc function. Using DXUT we no longer need to define a MSG structure or WndProc function for the handling of messages sent to and from the window. We will now rather create a series of callback functions, passing each one as a parameter to the appropriate DXUTSetCallback* DXUT function. For example, the following callback function handles all keyboard events:

TABLE 6-3	DXUTInit command-line parameters
Argument	**Description**
—adapter:X	Defines the specific hardware adapter to use.
—automation	Enables user interface navigation via the keyboard (enabled by default)
—constantframetime	Defines a specific time per frame lapse when the desired effect is to render some scene at a FPS value less than real time.
—forceapi:X	Forces the application to use either the Direct3D 9 or Direct3D 10 API.
—forcehal	Forces the use of a HAL device type.
—forcehwvp	Forces the use of hardware vertex processing (not applicable for Direct3D 10 – only supported by the Direct3D 9 API).
—forcepurehwvp	Forces the use of pure hardware vertex processing (not applicable for Direct3D 10 – only supported by the Direct3D 9 API).
—forceref	Forces the use of a reference device type.
—forceswvp	Forces the use of software vertex processing (not applicable for Direct3D 10 – only supported by the Direct3D 9 API).
—forcevsync:X	Specifies whether vertical sync is to be used (X is set to '0' to disable vertical sync).
—fullscreen	Forces the application into full-screen mode on startup.
—height:X	Specifies the default window height.
—noerrormsgboxes	Disables DXUT's error message boxes.
—nostats	Disables the display of statistics such as the current number of frames per second.
—output:X	Forces the use of a specific adapter output (only supported by the Direct3D 10 API).
—quitafterframe:X	Sets an exit frame – i.e. forcing the application to terminate after the specified frame, X, has been rendered.
—startx:#	Sets the x-coordinate of the window's upper left corner when running in windowed mode.
—starty:#	Sets the y-coordinate of the window's upper left corner when running in windowed mode.
—width:X	Specifies the default window width.
—windowed	Forces the application into windowed mode on startup.

6

TABLE 6-4	Error codes returned by DXUT functions
Error code	**Description**
DXUTERR_CREATINGDEVICE	Unable to create a Direct3D device.
DXUTERR_CREATINGDEVICEOBJECTS	A problem has been encountered while creating the Direct3D device objects.
DXUTERR_DEVICEREMOVED	The initialized Direct3D device is no longer accessible.
DXUTERR_MEDIANOTFOUND	The requisite media could not be loaded.
DXUTERR_NOCOMPATIBLEDEVICES	Unable to find any Direct3D capable devices.
DXUTERR_NODIRECT3D	Direct3D could not be initialized.
DXUTERR_NONZEROREFCOUNT	The Direct3D device was not properly released by a previous application.
DXUTERR_RESETTINGDEVICE	Unable to reset the Direct3D device.
DXUTERR_RESETTINGDEVICEOBJECTS	An issue was encountered while resetting the Direct3D device objects.

6

```
void CALLBACK OnKeyPress(UINT nChar, bool bKeyDown,
                    bool bAltDown, void* pUserContext)
{
    /* test whether some key is being pressed */
    if(bKeyDown)
    {
        switch(nChar)
        {
            case VK_TAB: //if 'Tab' is pressed do something
                break;
        }
    }
}
```

This keyboard event callback function, OnKeyPress, is then passed as parameter to the DXUTSetCallbackKeyboard function:

DXUTSetCallbackKeyboard(OnKeyPress, NULL);

This function, initializing the previously defined callback function, takes two parameters, the first being a pointer to a LPDXUTCALLBACKKEYBOARD keyboard event callback function, and the second a pointer to some user-specific variable passed to the callback function – by default set to 'NULL'.

The LPDXUTCALLBACKKEYBOARD DXUT keyboard event callback function is called every time a keyboard event occurs. It is declared as follows in the DXUT.h header file:

```
VOID LPDXUTCALLBACKKEYBOARD(
    UINT nChar,
    bool bKeyDown,
    bool bAltDown,
    void* pUserContext
);
```

TABLE 6-5	Virtual-key codes
Constant	**Description**
VK_LBUTTON	Left mouse button.
VK_RBUTTON	Right mouse button.
VK_BACK	Backspace key.
VK_TAB	Tab key.
VK_RETURN	Enter key.
VK_ESCAPE	Escape key.
VK_UP, VK_DOWN, VK_LEFT, VK_RIGHT	Up, down, left and right keys respectively.
VK_NUMPAD0 to VK_NUMPAD9	Numeric keypad keys '0' to '9'.
VK_F1 to VK_F24	F1 to F24 keys.

6

Its first parameter holds a virtual-key code describing the pressed key (the most commonly used virtual-key codes are given in Table 6-5). The second parameter, bKeyDown, holds the Boolean value 'true' if a key is currently being pressed with the bAltDown parameter set to 'true' if the 'Alt' key is also being pressed. The last parameter, pUserContext, takes a pointer to a user-specific variable passed to the callback function – by default set to 'NULL'.

DXUT provides a number of these so-called application-defined callback functions. The above defined OnKeyPress function is, for example, a LPDXUTCALLBACKKEYBOARD keyboard event callback. These DXUT event callback functions simplify the message-handling process. In addition to a keyboard event callback we also have to define:

- a device acceptable callback function (set using the DXUTSetCallbackD3D10DeviceAcceptable DXUT initialization function)

- a device created callback function (set via DXUTSetCallbackD3D10DeviceCreated)

- a swap chain resized callback function (set using DXUTSetCallbackD3D10SwapChainResized)

- a swap chain release callback function (set via DXUTSetCallbackD3D10SwapChainReleasing)

- a device destroyed callback function (set via DXUTSetCallbackD3D10DeviceDestroyed) and

- a frame render callback function (set through the DXUTSetCallbackD3D10FrameRender DXUT initialization function).

In addition to these callback functions we also need to create a window message callback function dealing with Windows messages (set using DXUTSetCallbackMsgProc), a callback function dealing with frame updates (set by DXUTSetCallbackFrameMove), and a callback function that allows for the change of device settings before the creation of the device (set through the DXUTSetCallbackDeviceChanging DXUT initialization function).

DXUTSetCallbackD3D10DeviceAcceptable initializes the application specific callback function responsible for building an enumerated list of Direct3D 10 capable devices. It takes two parameters, namely, a pointer to a LPDXUTCALLBACKISD3D10DEVICEACCEPTABLE callback function and a pointer to a user-defined variable passed to the callback function – 'NULL' by default.

The LPDXUTCALLBACKISD3D10DEVICEACCEPTABLE callback function returns true for each acceptable Direct3D device. All acceptable Direct3D 10 devices are enumerated into a list by the DXUTSetCallbackD3D10DeviceAcceptable function. DXUT then selects the best rendering device from this list. This callback is declared as follows in the DXUT.h header file:

```
bool LPDXUTCALLBACKISD3D10DEVICEACCEPTABLE(
    UINT Adapter,
    UINT Output,
    D3D10_DRIVER_TYPE DeviceType,
    DXGI_FORMAT BackBufferFormat,
    bool bWindowed,
    void* pUserContext
);
```

Its first parameter, Adapter, holds a value indicating the position of the current Direct3D 10 device in a series of enumerated Direct3D 10 video adapters. The second parameter, Output, holds an index value of the current enumerated video adapter's output (such as a monitor). The DeviceType parameter holds the current Direct3D 10 capable video adaptor's driver type (commonly set to D3D10_DRIVER_TYPE_HARDWARE for a hardware device and D3D10_DRIVER_TYPE_REFERENCE for a reference device). The BackBufferFormat parameter indicates the back buffer format of the Direct3D 10 device (such as a four-component, 64-bit floating-point format). The next parameter takes a Boolean value that is set to 'true' for windowed application and 'false' for those running in full-screen mode. The final parameter, pUserContext, is a pointer to a user-specific variable passed to the callback function – 'NULL' by default unless context information for the callback function is needed.

We create a LPDXUTCALLBACKISD3D10DEVICEACCEPTABLE callback function which is passed as first parameter to the DXUTSetCallbackD3D10DeviceAcceptable DXUT function as follows:

```
/* return 'true' for all acceptable D3D10 devices passed to
   it */
bool CALLBACK OnDeviceAcceptable(UINT Adapter, UINT Output,
                   D3D10_DRIVER_TYPE DeviceType,
                   DXGI_FORMAT BufferFormat,
                   bool bWindowed, void* pUserContext )
{
    return true;
}
DXUTSetCallbackD3D10DeviceAcceptable(OnDeviceAcceptable,NULL);
```

The DXUTSetCallbackD3D10DeviceCreated function sets the created ID3D10Device device. This device interface is used for the rendering of primitives as well as the creation of shaders and resources. The callback is used for the allocation of resources and the initialization of buffers. The DXUTSetCallbackD3D10-DeviceCreated function takes two parameters, namely, a pointer to a LPDXUTCALLBACKD3D10DEVICECREATED callback function and a pointer to a user-define variable passed to the callback function – 'NULL' by default. This function is declared as follows:

```
VOID DXUTSetCallbackD3D10DeviceCreated(
    LPDXUTCALLBACKD3D10DEVICECREATED pCallback,
    void* pUserContext
);
```

The associated LPDXUTCALLBACKD3D10DEVICECREATED callback function is declared as follows:

```
HRESULT LPDXUTCALLBACKD3D10DEVICECREATED(
    ID3D10Device * pd3dDevice,
    CONST DXGI_SURFACE_DESC * pBackBufferSurfaceDesc,
    void* pUserContext
);
```

This resource callback function forwards a pointer to the newly created ID3D10Device interface – the Direct3D 10 device. This pointer, sent to the DXUTSetCallbackD3D10DeviceCreated function, is defined as the first parameter. The second parameter is a DXGI_SURFACE_DESC structure with four members describing the width, height, format, and multisampling parameters of the surface resource respectively. The third parameter, pUserContext, is a pointer to a user-specific variable passed to the callback function – 'NULL' by default unless context information for the callback function is needed.

A LPDXUTCALLBACKD3D10DEVICECREATED callback function can be defined in the following manner:

```
HRESULT CALLBACK OnCreateDevice(ID3D10Device* pd3dDevice,
                    const DXGI_SURFACE_DESC *pBufferSurfaceDesc,
                    void* pUserContext)
{
        /* – set up, create and set the input layout
            – create and set the vertex buffer
            – create and set the index buffer
            – specify the primitive topology
            – load all texture resources
            – initialize the world and view matrices */
}
```

This function is now set using the DXUTSetCallbackD3D10DeviceCreated DXUT initialization function:

```
DXUTSetCallbackD3D10DeviceCreated(OnCreateDevice, NULL);
```

We also have to deal with the callbacks sent to the application whenever the Direct3D 10 swap chain (see section 4.5.2) is resized, this is done using the DXUTSetCallbackD3D10SwapChainResized function. This function has two parameters, the first a pointer to a LPDXUTCALLBACKD3D10SWAPCHAINRESIZED callback function, and the second a pointer to a user-specific variable passed to the callback function – 'NULL' by default.

The LPDXUTCALLBACKD3D10SWAPCHAINRESIZED callback function commonly used to set resources dependent on the back buffer – such as perspective projection matrices based on the field-of-view (see section 7.4.3 and Chapter 7 in general) is declared as follows:

```
HRESULT LPDXUTCALLBACKD3D10SWAPCHAINRESIZED(
    ID3D10Device * pd3dDevice,
    IDXGISwapChain * pSwapChain,
    CONST D3DSURFACE_DESC * pBackBufferSurfaceDesc,
    void* pUserContext
);
```

Its first parameter, pd3dDevice, is a pointer to the newly created Direct3D 10 device (ID3D10Device). The second parameter is a pointer to an IDXGISwapChain interface (see section 4.5.2) with the third holding a pointer to a structure describing the back buffer surface's format. The last parameter, pUserContext, is a pointer to a user-specific variable passed to the callback function.

This LPDXUTCALLBACKD3D10SWAPCHAINRESIZED swap chain resized callback function, passed to DXUTSetCallbackD3D10SwapChainResized, can be defined in the following manner:

```
HRESULT CALLBACK OnSwapChainResize(ID3D10Device* pd3dDevice,
                    IDXGISwapChain *pSwapChain,
                    const DXGI_SURFACE_DESC* pBufferSurfaceDesc,
                    void* pUserContext)
{
    /* – reset the aspect ratio using the back buffer's new
         width and height
       – set the perspective projection matrix using the
         new aspect ratio */
}
```

We set this callback function using DXUTSetCallbackD3D10SwapChainResized:

```
DXUTSetCallbackD3D10SwapChainResized(OnSwapChainResize);
```

All the Direct3D 10 device resources created in the LPDXUTCALLBACKD3D10SWAPCHAINRESIZED callback function must also be released. This is done using a LPDXUTCALLBACKD3D10SWAPCHAINRELEASING callback which is set using the DXUTSetCallbackD3D10SwapChainReleasing swap chain releasing function. This DXUT function takes two parameters, a pointer to a LPDXUTCALLBACKD3D10SWAPCHAINRELEASING callback function and a pointer to a user-specific variable passed to the callback function – 'NULL' by default:

```
HRESULT DXUTSetCallbackD3D10SwapChainReleasing(
    LPDXUTCALLBACKD3D10SWAPCHAINRELEASING pCallback,
    void* pUserContext
);
```

The LPDXUTCALLBACKD3D10SWAPCHAINRELEASING callback function has only one parameter, a pointer to a user-specific variable passed to the callback function when context information for the callback function is needed:

```
VOID LPDXUTCALLBACKD3D10SWAPCHAINRELEASING(
    void* pUserContext
);
```

This LPDXUTCALLBACKD3D10SWAPCHAINRELEASING swap chain releasing callback function, called whenever the swap chain created in OnSwapChainResize is being released can be defined as follows:

```
void CALLBACK OnSwapChainReleasing(void* pUserContext )
{
        /* release all the Direct3D 10 resources created in
           OnSwapChainResize */
}
```

We can now set the OnSwapChainReleasing callback function via the DXUTSetCallbackD3D10SwapChainReleasing DXUT function:

DXUTSetCallbackD3D10SwapChainReleasing(OnSwapChainReleasing);

We also require a callback function to release the Direct3D 10 resources created in the OnCreateDevice callback function. This resource deletion callback, LPDXUTCALLBACKD3D10DEVICEDESTROYED, is executed by the DXUT framework immediately after the Direct3D 10 device has been destroyed. The DXUTSetCallbackD3D10DeviceDestroyed function, with its first parameter taking a pointer to a LPDXUTCALL-BACKD3D10DEVICEDESTROYED function, sets the device destroyed callback. Its second parameter is a pointer to a user-specific variable passed to the callback function whenever context information is needed:

```
VOID DXUTSetCallbackD3D10DeviceDestroyed(
    LPDXUTCALLBACKD3D10DEVICEDESTROYED pCallback,
    void* pUserContext
);
```

The LPDXUTCALLBACKD3D10DEVICEDESTROYED callback function specifies only one parameter, namely a pointer to a user-specific variable for the gathering of context information, pUserContext:

```
VOID LPDXUTCALLBACKD3D10DEVICEDESTROYED(
    void* pUserContext
);
```

A LPDXUTCALLBACKD3D10DEVICEDESTROYED resource deletion callback function can be defined as follows:

```
void CALLBACK OnDeviceDestroy(void* pUserContext)
{
        /* release all the Direct3D 10 resources created in the
          OnCreateDevice callback function */
}
```

This callback function is then subsequently set using the DXUTSetCallbackD3D10DeviceDestroyed DXUT function:

DXUTSetCallbackD3D10DeviceDestroyed(OnDeviceDestroy);

Another significant DXUT callback function is one that deals with frame rendering. This LPDXUTCALLBACKD3D10FRAMERENDER callback function renders a scene using the created Direct3D 10 device by clearing the back buffer and, depth stencil buffer, updating all variable changes per frame, and rendering the geometric objects constituting the scene. This function has four parameters and is declared as follows in the DXUT.h header file:

```
VOID LPDXUTCALLBACKD3D10FRAMERENDER(
    ID3D10Device * pd3dDevice,
    DOUBLE fTime,
    FLOAT fElapsedTime,
    void* pUserContext
);
```

Its first parameter, pd3dDevice, is a pointer to an ID3D10Device interface – the rendering device. The second parameter, fTime, holds the time that has elapsed since initialization of the application with the third parameter, fElapsedTime, holding the time that has passed since the last frame update. Both these time values are given in seconds. The final parameter holds a pointer to the user-specific variable that is passed to the callback function whenever context information is needed. Just as with all the other DXUT callback functions, we will also set this one to 'NULL'.

Such a LPDXUTCALLBACKD3D10FRAMERENDER callback function can be declared as follows:

```
void CALLBACK OnRenderFrame(ID3D10Device* pd3dDevice,
                            double fTime, float fElapsedTime,
                            void* pUserContext)
{
    /* – clear the back buffer using ClearRenderTargetView
       – clear the depth–stencil buffers using
         ClearDepthStencilView
       – update all changed variables
       – render all geometric objects */
}
```

This OnRenderFrame callback function is set by the DXUTSetCallbackD3D10FrameRender function:

```
DXUTSetCallbackD3D10FrameRender(OnRenderFrame);
```

All that remains now is to handle all process messages originating from the DXUT message pump and to set the callback function responsible for doing the frame updates for the scene. We also require a facility that allows us to change the settings of a device before it is created.

Processing messages for the DXUT message pump requires the declaration of a LPDXUTCALL-BACKMSGPROC callback function similar to the previously defined WinProc function. This function takes six parameters. The first is a handle to the window, the second is an integer value identifying the message to process, the third and fourth parameters specify additional message information, with the fifth a Boolean value that controls whether further message processing should be done ('true' preventing further message handling). The final parameter is a pointer to a user-specific variable passed to the callback function whenever context information is needed:

```
LRESULT LPDXUTCALLBACKMSGPROC(
    HWND hWnd,
    UINT uMsg,
    WPARAM wParam,
    LPARAM lParam,
    bool * pbNoFurtherProcessing,
    void* pUserContext
);
```

We can declare a LPDXUTCALLBACKMSGPROC callback function as follows:

```
LRESULT CALLBACK MsgProcCallback(HWND hWnd, UINT uMsg,
                     WPARAM wParam,
                     PARAM lParam,
                     bool* pbNoFurtherProcessing,
                     void* pUserContext)
```

```
{
        /* handle all messages sent to the application */
}
```

The DXUTSetCallbackMsgProc DXUT function sets this window message callback function with its first parameter a pointer to the LPDXUTCALLBACKMSGPROC function and its second a pointer to a user-specific variable passed to the callback function whenever context information is needed:

```
DXUTSetCallbackMsgProc(MsgProcCallback);
```

Frame updates of the scene are done via the LPDXUTCALLBACKFRAMEMOVE callback function. This function takes three parameters, namely, the time that has elapsed since initialization of the application, the time elapsed since the previous frame and a pointer to a user-specific variable passed to the callback function whenever context information is needed:

```
VOID LPDXUTCALLBACKFRAMEMOVE(
    DOUBLE fTime,
    FLOAT fElapsedTime,
    void* pUserContext
);
```

Such a LPDXUTCALLBACKFRAMEMOVE callback function handling updates to a scene can be declared as follows:

```
void CALLBACK OnMoveFrame(double fTime, float fElapsedTime,
                          void* pUserContext)
{
    /* update the scene */
}
```

This callback function is subsequently set using the DXUTSetCallbackFrameMove DXUT function:

```
DXUTSetCallbackFrameMove(OnMoveFrame, NULL);
```

One final callback function is needed for the modification of Direct3D device settings as required. This callback function, LPDXUTCALLBACKMODIFYDEVICESETTINGS, takes a pointer to a DXUTDeviceSettings structure storing the settings of our Direct3D 10 device, and a pointer to a user-specific variable passed to the callback function whenever context information is needed:

```
bool LPDXUTCALLBACKMODIFYDEVICESETTINGS(
    DXUTDeviceSettings * pDeviceSettings,
    void* pUserContext
);
```

An example of a LPDXUTCALLBACKMODIFYDEVICESETTINGS callback function is given here:

```
bool CALLBACK ModDevSettings(DXUTDeviceSettings* pDeviceSettings,
                             void* pUserContext)
```

```
{
        /* allow modification of device settings */
        return true;
}
```

This callback function is called just before the creation of the Direct3D device. It returns a 'true' indicating that DXUT can proceed to create the device, and a 'false' indicating otherwise. The DXUTSetCallbackDeviceChanging function sets this callback function, allowing the application program to modify the device settings as needed. This function takes two parameters, a pointer to a LPDXUTCALLBACKMODIFYDEVICESETTINGS callback function and a pointer to a user-specific variable passed to the callback function whenever context information is needed:

DXUTSetCallbackDeviceChanging(ModDevSettings, NULL);

The functions presented in this section illustrate the fundamentals of the DXUT framework. This framework is useful for experimental applications where the desire is to minimize the amount of time spent on setting up a Direct3D environment. Although the DXUT framework's effectiveness in the simplification of Direct3D API calls cannot be disputed, it must be used with utmost caution as it does impose some level of performance overhead.

6.5   SHADERS

A shader is a grouping of instructions processed by the graphics accelerator to perform some form of special effect or rendering. Chapter 4 presented the concept of programmable pipelines, in particular focusing on the Direct3D 10 and OpenGL processing pipelines. An application program allowing direct interaction with these previously discussed programming pipelines is called a *shader*. These shader programs, written in a shading language such as NVIDIA's Cg or Microsoft's High Level Shader Language, control the movement, composition, form, and appearance of objects through direct manipulation of the graphics processing unit's programmable pipelines.

The instructions listed in a shader program are executed at a specific point in the rendering pipeline – thus leading to user-defined manipulation of vertex or pixel data, for example. More specifically, three types of shader programs can be written: vertex shaders, pixel shaders, and geometry shaders.

1 *Vertex shaders*, operating on vertex data, are executed as part of the graphics pipeline's geometric stage and are used to alter the geometric parameters (shape) of an object. A vertex shader program is fundamental for certain special effects such as grass blowing in the wind where the real time manipulation, transformation and displacement of per-vertex material attributes are necessary. The vertices produced by this shader are forwarded as input to a geometry shader.

2 *Geometry shaders* are executed just prior to the rasterizer and stream output pipeline stages. These shaders group numerous vertices into a geometric object that can be modified by a pixel shader program. Geometry shaders are extremely important in the detection of silhouetted-edges and shadow volume extrusion (Chapter 11). These shaders, performing per-primitive computations, are also vital in the generation of new primitives. The primitives generated by the geometry shader stage are rasterized into fragments during the pipeline's rasterizer stage. These fragments are then sent to the pixel shader as input (Chapter 4).

3 *Pixel shaders*, also known as *fragment shaders* and performing per-pixel processing, operate on the discrete pixels of a primitive, applying some effect to a primitive (such as bump mapping, shadowing, fog) during the pixel shader stage (Chapter 4). Per-pixel lighting and shadowing have greatly contributed to the realism of modern computer games. Examples of effects made

possible through this form of per-pixel processing include texture blending, environmental mapping, normal mapping, real-time shadows (stencil shadow volumes), and reflections.

These three types of shaders are unified by the Direct3D 10 architecture – known as Shader Model 4.0. *Unified shaders* provide the application programmer with a uniform instruction set independent of whether a pixel shader or vertex shader is being implemented. This unified architecture is made possible through Windows Vista's Windows Display Driver Model and the coupled DirectX 10 API. Previous architectures required different instruction sets for both pixel and vertex shaders due to specific hardware architectural requirements. By unifying the independent shader instruction sets, GPU programming has become much more flexible. This unified model also allows workload sharing amongst the various pipeline processors, for example, when the GPU is mainly performing basic geometry rendering with little or no per-pixel processing being done, then the pixel shader can be assigned vertex processing. The first GPU offering support for this unified shader model was NVIDIA's GeForce 8 series – specifically the GeForce 8800 GTX and GTS.

The term used to describe this unified shader architecture, Shader Model 4.0, encapsulates the features offered by the specific shader version in question. For example, Shader Model 3.0 (as supported by Direct3D 9.0c) limits the number of executing instructions to 65,536 while Direct3D 10's Shader Model 4.0 allows for an unlimited number of executing instructions. Shader Model 2.0 (the original Direct3D 9.0 shader specification) limits the number of executing instructions to 32 texture instructions and 64 arithmetic instructions. The version number of instructions is specified in terms of the shader's version number (ps_mainVersion_subVersion for pixel shaders and vs_mainVersion_subVersion for vertex shaders). For example, a vertex shader based on Shader Model 3.0 (DirectX 9.0c) will be declared as vs_3_0, a DirectX 9.0b Shader Model 2.0 pixel shader as ps_2_b, with a Shader Model 4.0 pixel shader declared as ps_4_0. NVIDIA's GeForce FX series of GPUs provide an optimized model for Shader Model 2.0 and we can thus define a vertex shader based on this model as vs_2_a.

The capabilities of shader programs are heavily dependent on the available graphics hardware. Older graphics hardware such as first-generation GPUs (NVIDIA's RIVA TNT2 and ATI's Rage series implementing the DirectX 6 feature set) were only capable of accelerating texture mapping operations as well as the rasterization of certain primitives such as triangles. These GPUs alleviated the CPU from updating individual pixels but vertex transformations such as rotation, translation and scaling (Chapter 7) were still CPU dependent. These GPUs, although slightly configurable, were not programmable.

The second generation of GPUs, introduced in 1999/2000 with the release of NVIDIA's GeForce 256 GPU and also including the GeForce2 and ATI's Radeon 7500, relieved the CPU from 3D vertex transformations and lighting computations. Both the OpenGL and DirectX 7 APIs supported these hardware vertex transformations; however, although highly configurable in the sense of offering support for certain effects such as cube mapping for textures and per-pixel coloring, these GPUs were still not strictly speaking programmable.

The first truly programmable GPUs were NVIDIA's third-generation GeForce3 and GeForce4 Ti, and ATI's Radeon 8500 series. These GPUs offered programmable vertex pipelines, thus allowing an application program to control vertex transformations and lighting. These GPUs also featured a higher level of per-pixel configurability, although not yet offering pixel pipeline programmability. DirectX 8 and the ARB_vertex_program OpenGL extension allowed access to the vertex programmability offered by these GPUs. Pixel shaders could be written using the DirectX 8 pixel shader functionality and numerous OpenGL extensions. These pixel shaders were obviously nothing as powerful as today's pixel shader programs, and were based on configuring the pixel pipeline, rather than freeing the CPU of pixel-shading operations.

Both per-vertex and per-pixel programmability have been available since the release of NVIDIA's GeForce FX and ATI's Radeon 9700 family of GPUs. Application developers were, with the release of these GPUs, for the first time able to assign the GPU for both vertex transformations and pixel operations. With these operations offloaded to the GPU, the CPU is free to perform other calculations. The DirectX 9 API and several OpenGL extensions give access to the pixel and vertex programmability offered by these GPUs. A vertex shader replaces the configurable fixed-function operations performed by the vertex processor with instructions defined by the shader along with a pixel shader executing after the rasterizer stage. This pixel shader takes the fragments processed by the fragment processor/pixel shader stage as input, performing some operation on them. Fragments are processed based on some configurable fixed function in the absence of a pixel shader program.

Table 6-6 highlights some key features introduced with certain milestone GPU releases as well as their respective DirectX and OpenGL version support.

6.5.1 The Hardware Graphics Pipeline Revisited

We previously described a pipeline as a series of parallel stages with each stage processing the output of the previous stage, in turn sending its output to a successive stage, and so forth (see section 4.3). The graphics pipeline consists of a number of stages such as vertex processing, clipping, rasterization, and fragment processing. These stages are responsible for converting some geometrically defined scene into a two-dimensional image (pixel elements) via a number of rendering stages – each physically organized as a pipeline processing unit. We will now revisit our Chapter 4 graphics pipeline architecture discussion, expanding on it by focusing more on the programmable graphics pipeline's physical (hardware-level) organization.

A modern-day GPU is sent a grouping of vertices organized into a geometric primitive such as a sequence of points, lines or a triangle, for example. Each of these vertices has a number of attributes. Attributes can range from the vertex's individual color value, its texture coordinates, a normal vector used during lighting calculations to spatial coordinates used for the positioning of the vertex. A generic graphics hardware pipeline is shown in Figure 6-14.

The vertex transformation stage, as discussed in sections 4.3.1 and 4.3.4.1, performs a series of operations on each of the vertices sent to the GPU for processing. Operations include the transformation of a vertex's coordinate system into one that can be used by the rasterizer, per-vertex lighting, coloring, and the generation of texture coordinates, etc.

The primitive assembly and rasterization stage assembles the vertices being passed from the vertex transformation stage into geometric primitives. The type of assembled primitive (line, polygon, triangle, etc.) depends on the primitive topology data accompanying a set of vertices. Clipping to the visible view frustum (section 4.3.2) is performed during this stage, resulting in the elimination of any unnecessary primitives that would not be visible to the viewer or camera. The rasterization stage also eliminates polygons or surfaces pointing away from the camera or viewer (vertex-by-vertex culling – see section 4.3.2). Following these operations, primitives are rasterized into pixels for representation in the frame buffer (section 4.3.3). Rasterization is performed according to a specific set of rules defined for each of the primitive topologies. The rasterization stage produces a set of pixels, each one mapped to a specific location, as well as a set of fragments (previously defined as a pixel with additional information about its color, position and depth). Building on our previous definition we can now define a fragment as a state necessary for the update of a specific pixel in the frame buffer. During the rasterization process geometric primitives are broken down into pixel-sized fragments. Each fragment holds information about the pixel's location, depth, color, and texture coordinates. This information is then used to update a matching pixel in the frame buffer.

With a primitive successfully rasterized into a series of fragments, we can move on to the fragment processing stage. Fragment processing, as previously explained in Chapter 4, is the process of updating pixels in the frame buffer with the fragments generated during the rasterization stage. The fragment processing unit is responsible for setting the color values of fragments, their texturing as well as the interpolation of fragment parameters. These operations are modified and/or combined for numerous texturing effects such as bump mapping, texture filtering, blending, environmental mapping and so forth. Apart from calculating the fragment's final color value, this pipeline stage can also discard a fragment based on some calculation or predefined parameter, hence resulting in the corresponding frame buffer pixel not being updated.

TABLE 6-6	Features introduced by selected GPUs and DirectX and OpenGL versions	
GPU	**Main feature(s)**	**API support**
— NVIDIA RIVA 128	— Basic vertex acceleration.	DirectX 5, OpenGL 1.0.
— NVIDIA RIVA TNT — NVIDIA RIVA TNT2 — ATI Rage 128	— Multitexturing (applying more than one texture to a polygon, e.g. graffiti art or 'bullet holes' on a textured wall).	DirectX 6, OpenGL 1.1.
— NVIDIA GeForce 256 — NVIDIA GeForce2 — ATI R100 (Radeon 32, 64, 7000 and 7500)	— Hardware transformations, clipping and lighting. — Cube mapping. — Fixed-function vertex processing. — Register combiners.	DirectX 7, OpenGL 1.2 (ATI supporting OpenGL 1.3).
— NVIDIA GeForce3	— Quadtexturing (using four pixel pipelines for the rendering of four independently textured pixels or alternatively two multitextured pixels). — Texture shaders. — Shader Model 1.1. — ARB_vertex_program (OpenGL extension for vertex shaders on both ATI and NVIDIA chipsets).	DirectX 8, OpenGL 1.4.
— NVIDIA GeForce4 Ti — ATI Radeon R200 (Radeon 8500 to 9250)	— Hardware anti-aliasing. — Pixel Shader 1.2, 1.3 or 1.4. — Vertex Shader 1.1. — ATI_fragment_shader (OpenGL extension for fragment shaders on ATI cards only).	DirectX 8.1, OpenGL 1.4.
— NVIDIA GeForce FX — ATI Radeon R300 (Radeon 9500 to 9800 XT and including Radeon X1050)	— Full support for vertex and fragment shader programs. — Floating-point pixel processing. — Shader Model 2.0, 2.0a or 2.0b. — OpenGL Shading Language.	DirectX 9.0b, OpenGL 1.4 (NVIDIA chipsets featured limited support for OpenGL 2.0 with ATI chipsets offering full support).
— NVIDIA GeForce 6 — ATI Radeon R500 (Xbox 360 Xenos, Radeon X1300 to Radeon X1950 XTX)	— Hardware accelerated transparency. — Scalable Link Interface (SLI – parallel graphics processing using two or more graphics accelerators interlinked). — Shader Model 3.0. — OpenGL Shading Language Improved.	DirectX 9.0c, OpenGL 2.0.

(Continued)

GPU	Main feature(s)	API support
— NVIDIA GeForce 7	— High Dynamic Range Lighting.	DirectX 9.0c, OpenGL 2.0.
— NVIDIA GeForce 8 — Radeon R600 (Radeon HD 2400 to Radeon HD 2900 XT)	— Unified Shaders. — Shader Model 4.0.	DirectX 10, OpenGL 2.1.

TABLE 6-6   *(Continued)*

6

FIGURE 6-14   A generic graphics hardware pipeline

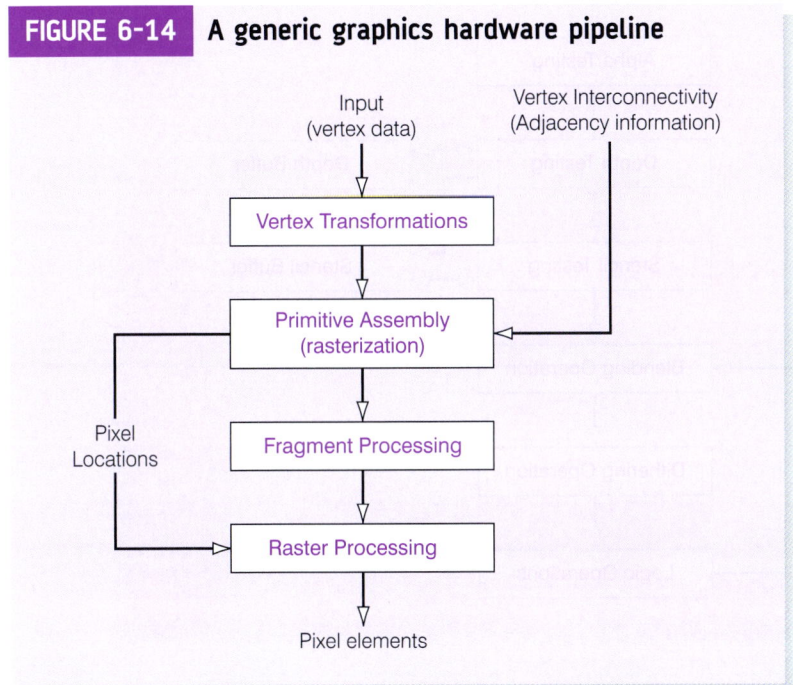

The final number of fragment centric operations, based on the functionality of Direct3D and OpenGL, are performed during the raster processing stage. These operations, such as depth testing (the removal of hidden surfaces), blending, stencil testing for the generation of stencil shadow volumes, and stencil-based reflections, are performed prior to the frame buffer update. A number of tests are conducted during this pipeline stage; for example, a scissor test culls all the fragments located outside a user-specified rectangle positioned within the render target area, with an alpha test determining whether fragments are written to the render target area based on some predefined alpha-test function. A fragment is discarded whenever any of these tests fail. When passing a specific test, one of the pixel's property values (such as depth for depth testing) is updated with that of the fragment. The blending operation stage reads the fragment's color value and combines it with the color value of the matching pixel. We can also dither the color values of fragments and pixels to create the illusion of color depth in low-color images by approximating colors not available in the palette through the diffusion of the available palette's color values. The final operation is to write the new blended/dithered fragment color value out to the appropriate pixel in the frame buffer. This raster processing stage, consisting of a series of pipeline stages (raster operations and tests), is shown in Figure 6-15.

FIGURE 6-15   **Direct3D and OpenGL raster processing operations**

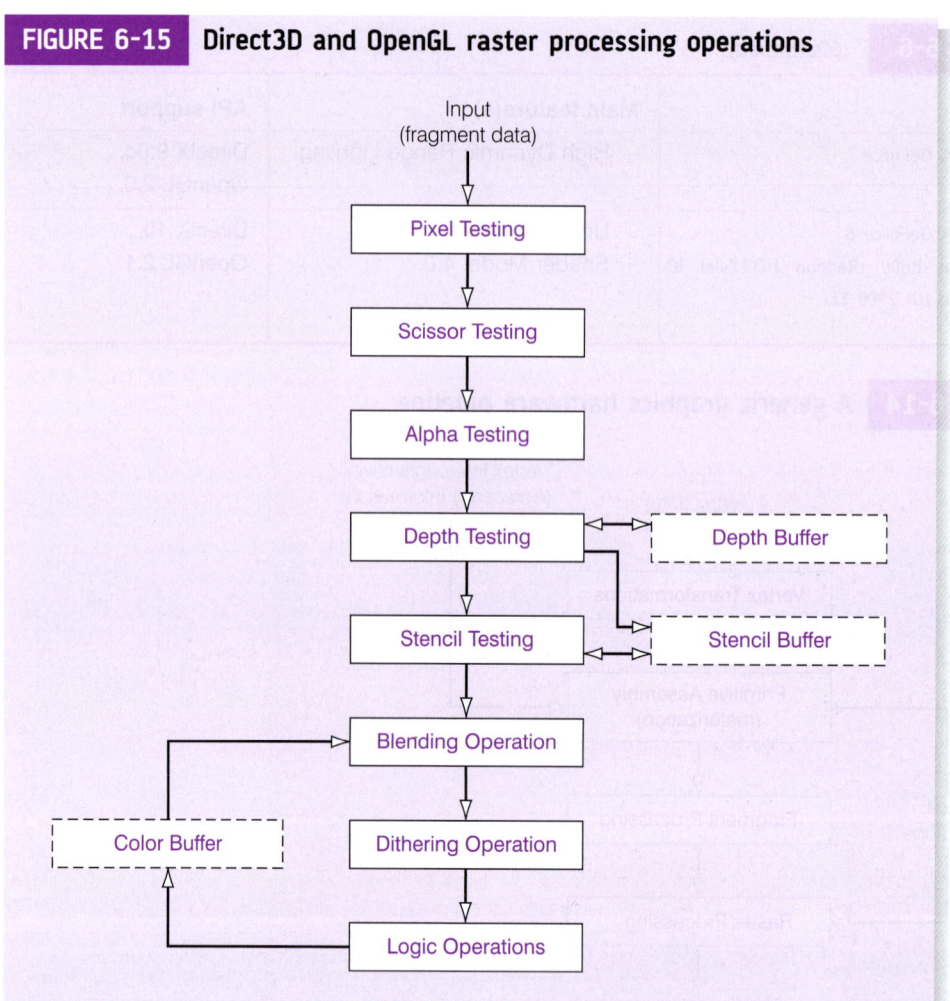

6.5.2 The Programmable Graphics Pipeline Revisited

Section 4.3.4 describes both the Direct3D and OpenGL processing pipelines. We will now build on this discussion by investigating the underlying hardware configuration that makes the pipeline stages of a GPU programmable. Previous generation GPUs have separate vertex and pixel shader processing units. The GeForce 8 GPU does not follow this approach, rather offering eight shader units, with none of them limited to vertex or pixel processing. This architectural change is the product of recognising that the future of GPU design lies with programmable processing. By unifying the shaders we're not just only able to use the same instruction set for both pixel and vertex shaders or to enable workload sharing amongst these pipeline processors, but this new architecture also makes it easier to extend our current shader model with future shader types. As illustrated in Table 6-6, GPU architecture has evolved from supporting configurable vertex and fragment processors, to programmable vertex processors, then fully programmable vertex and fragments processors to the current unified architecture. Extending Figure 6-14, the generic graphics hardware pipeline, we can show both vertex and fragment processing units as simple add-ons to this generic pipeline (Figure 6-16).

FIGURE 6-16 **Example of a hardware programmable graphics pipeline**

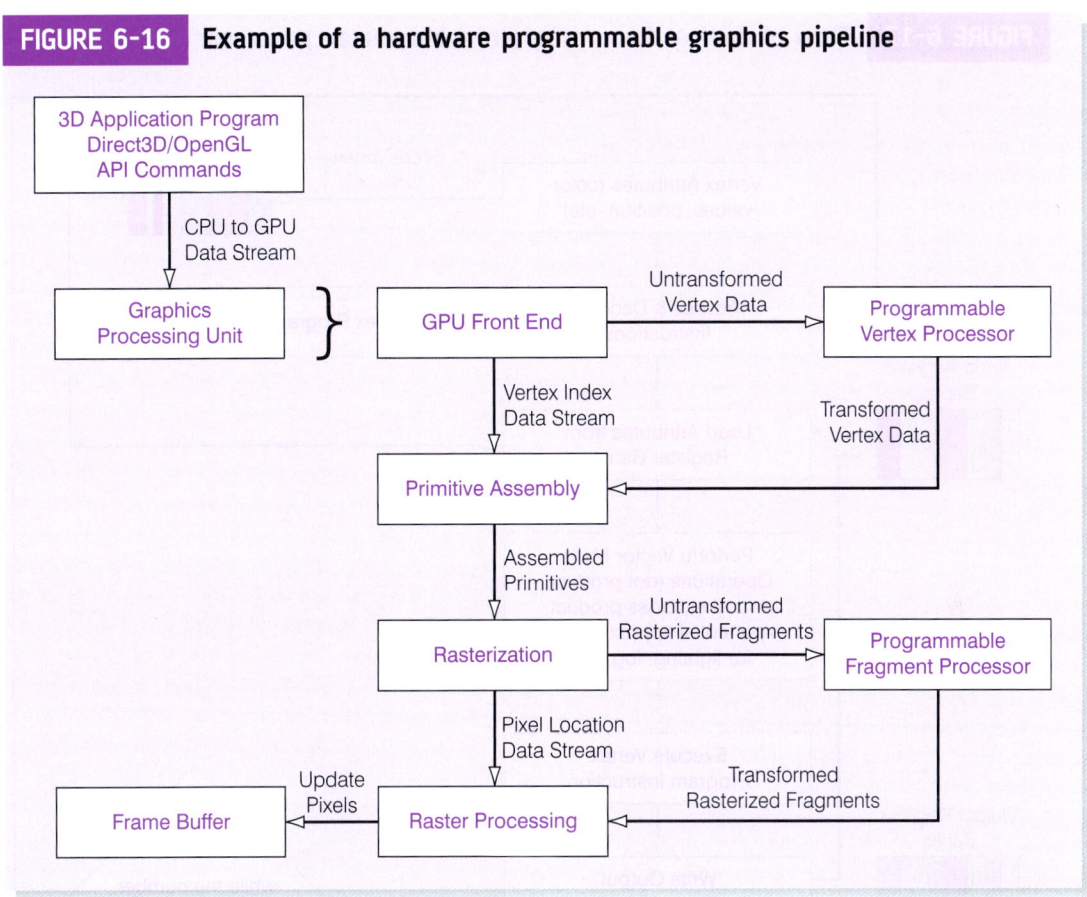

The unified shader architecture considered, vertex and fragment processing can still be broken down into logical programmable units; with a programmable vertex processor, the processing unit responsible for the execution of an HLSL, Cg or GLSL vertex program, and a programmable fragment processor, the processing unit tasked with execution of a HLSL, Cg or GLSL fragment program.

The programmable vertex processor is fed vertex attributes such as coordinates, color values, and depth information. These attributes are stored in the vertex processor's attribute register banks. Vertex shaders actually make use of several registers for the storage of position, data and color data, for example. The vertex program, consisting of a sequence of instructions, is stored in memory. The vertex processor accesses this program, decoding one instruction at a time until the program terminates. Results generated from computations, in essence the transformed vertex data, are stored in the output result registers with intermediate data, still being read by instructions, stored in the temporary register banks. Figure 6-17 shows the classic flow of control for a programmable vertex processor.

Programmable fragment processors are extremely useful for manipulating texture coordinates as well as to set the final color of a pixel. These processors also support several of the vector math operations performed by vertex processors. For example, a fragment processor can be programmed to read the texture coordinates of a textured image and to subsequently perform some operation on these values – returning a filtered sample of the texture. Similar to a vertex processor, fragment processors operate by executing a set of instructions stored in a program file – the fragment program. These instructions are executed until the fragment program terminates (when there aren't any more instructions to fetch). The fragment program reads untransformed interpolated fragments as input, storing these values in input

FIGURE 6-17   **Flow of control for a programmable vertex processor**

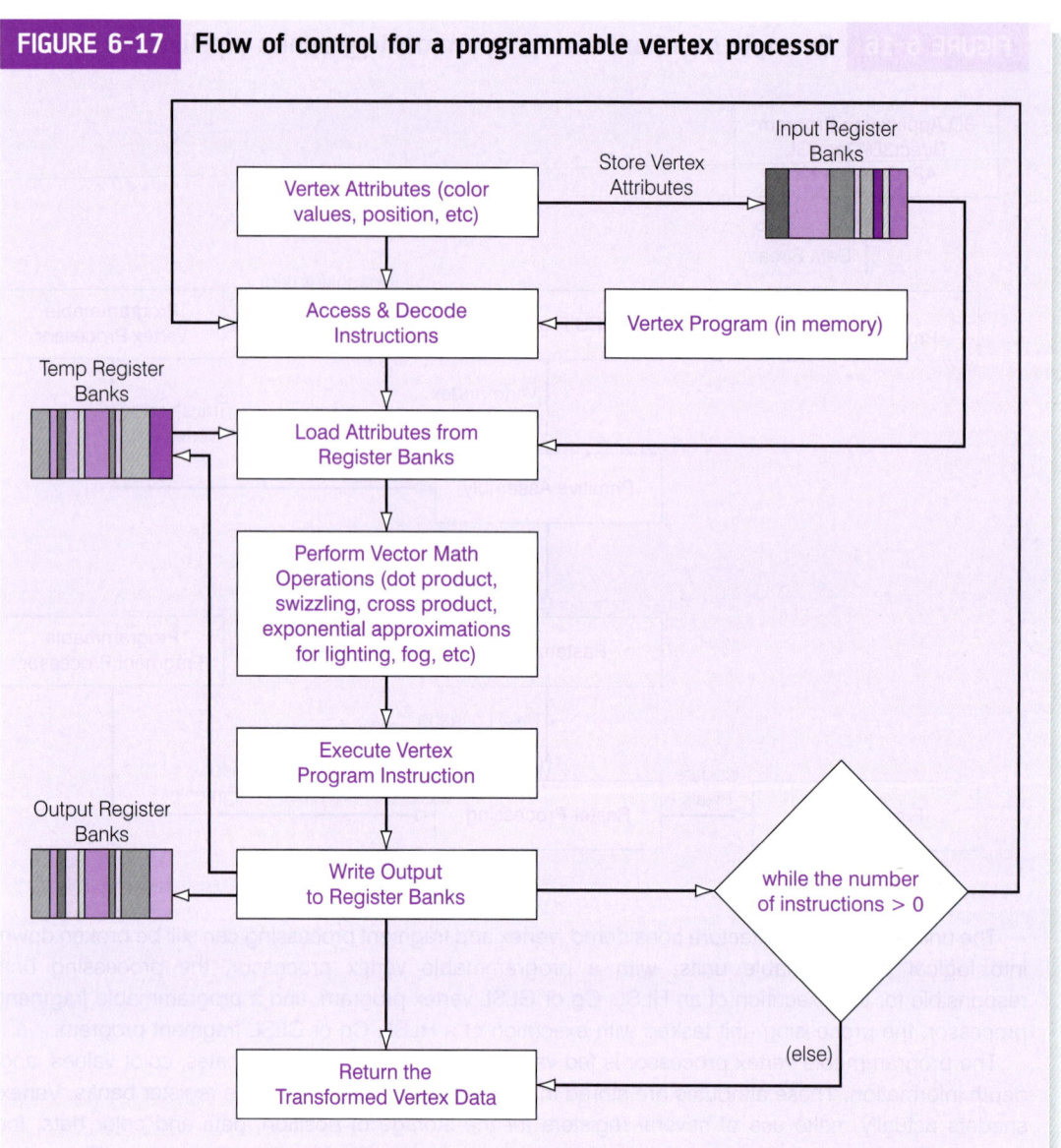

register banks. Results generated from applying the specified instructions on input data are stored in the output registers. Intermediate data, just as with vertex processing, are stored in the temporary register banks. The output values can range from a fragment's new color to a transformed depth value.

As explained in Chapter 8, a texture is nothing more than a two-dimensional array consisting of color values with each of these color values referred to as a texel, or texture element. Each texel, being an element in this color array, is thus assigned a unique address in the texture (simply a column and row value). Fragment processors generally include a *texture fetch instruction*. This instruction is used to compute the address of a texture, fetch texture elements, determine its Level-of-Detail and to perform texture filtering. Examples of texture filtering include nearest-point sampling, linear texture filtering, anisotropic texture filtering, bilinear filtering and filtering via mipmaps (all of these filtering methods are discussed in section 8.2). Figure 6-18 illustrates the flow of control for a typical programmable fragment processor.

FIGURE 6-18 Flow of control for a programmable fragment processor

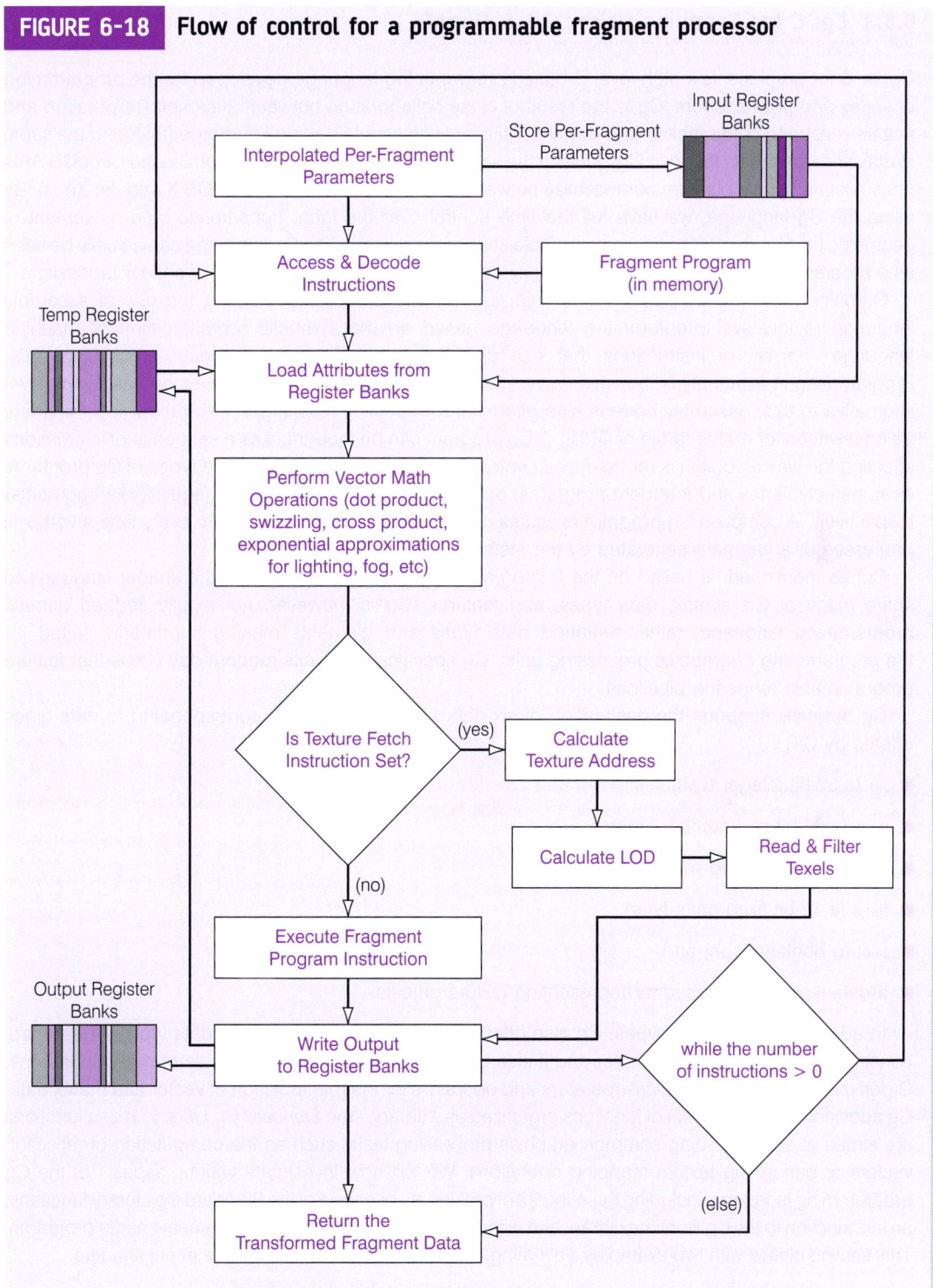

6

6.5.3 Cg: C for Graphics (Direct3D & OpenGL)

Cg, or C for graphics, is a high-level C-based programming language developed for the programming of vertex and pixel shaders. Cg is the result of close collaboration between Microsoft Corporation and NVIDIA – ensuring compatibility with Microsoft's similar High Level Shading Language (featuring the same syntax and constructs found in Cg) while at the same time targeting both the OpenGL and Direct3D APIs (thus ensuring cross-platform compatibility between Linux, Windows, Macintosh OS X and the Xbox). By using the Cg language, we have full real-time control over the form, appearance, and movement of geometric objects rendered via programmable shader processors. The Cg language can actually be seen as a programming platform rather than simply a language for the programming of shader processors.

Graphics hardware can be programmed, just as any processing unit, via the use of assembly language (a low-level programming language based on the symbolic representation of machine language – a set of instructions that can directly be executed by a central processing unit). Programming in assembly is, however, a very tedious exercise and Cg was developed as a high-level alternative to this. Assembly code is also often vendor specific, resulting in several low-level shaders being rewritten for a wide range of GPUs. A Cg program can be thought of as a sequence of instructions affecting the way an object is rendered via control of the graphics hardware. Two types of Cg programs exist, namely vertex and fragment programs, operating on vertices and pixels (specifically fragments) respectively. A compiled Cg program executes on the GPU of a graphics system every time a vertex is processed or a fragment generated by the rasterizer.

Cg, as mentioned, is based on the C programming language. This lends the shader language to share many of C's syntax, data types, and features. Cg is, however, not a fully fledged generic programming language, rather featuring data types and elements making it primarily suited for the programming of graphics processing units. Cg specifically exploits modern-day GPUs that feature programmable rendering pipelines.

Cg basically supports the declaration of six data types (the majority corresponding to data types offered by C/C++):

- int (a 32-bit integer type)

- float (a 32-bit real number type)

- half (a 16-bit floating point type)

- fixed (a 12-bit fixed point type)

- bool (a Boolean type) and

- a data type, sampler, used for representing texture objects.

In addition to these data types, Cg also offers struct, array, vector and matrix data types, flow-control constructs such as loops (for/while) and if/else conditions, function calls, a series of math operations, C-derived arithmetic, and logical operators and operators for the manipulation of vector and matrix data. Cg additionally features a set of functions organized as a library – the *Standard Cg Library*. These functions are aimed at accomplishing common graphics processing tasks such as the computation of reflection vectors or performing texture mapping operations. We will now investigate various aspects of the Cg programming language, including the concept of profiles, an overview of the Standard Cg Library functions, an introduction to the Cg Runtime Library and writing and compiling vertex and fragment shader programs. This section closes with two examples illustrating the use of per-vertex and per-fragment shaders.

6.5.3.1 Cg Language Profiles
Cg programs can run across a wide range of GPUs by being compiled for each of these graphics hardware platforms. The best-suited shader is thus executed based

TABLE 6-7	Supported Cg profiles	
Profile target	**Runtime option**	**Compiler option to specify a profile**
Generic OpenGL vertex programs (advanced level of functionality).	CG_PROFILE_ARBVP1	−profile arbvp1
Generic OpenGL fragment programs (advanced level of functionality).	CG_PROFILE_ARBFP1	−profile arbfp1
GeForce 6 series+ OpenGL vertex programs (advanced level of functionality).	CG_PROFILE_VP40	−profile vp40
GeForce 6 series+ OpenGL fragment programs (advanced level of functionality).	CG_PROFILE_FP40	−profile fp40
GeForce FX series OpenGL vertex programs (average level of functionality).	CG_PROFILE_VP30	−profile vp30
GeForce FX series OpenGL fragment programs (average level of functionality).	CG_PROFILE_FP30	−profile fp30
OpenGL NV2X vertex programs (basic level of functionality).	CG_PROFILE_VP20	−profile vp20
OpenGL NV2X fragment programs (limited level of functionality).	CG_PROFILE_FP20	−profile fp20
DirectX 9 vertex shaders (advanced level of functionality).	CG_PROFILE_VS_2_X CG_PROFILE_VS_2_0	−profile vs_2_x −profile vs_2_0
DirectX 9 pixel shaders (advanced level of functionality).	CG_PROFILE_PS_2_X CG_PROFILE_PS_2_0	−profile ps_2_x −profile ps_2_0
DirectX 8 vertex shaders (basic level of functionality).	CG_PROFILE_VS_1_1	−profile vs_1_1
DirectX 8 pixel shaders (limited level of functionality).	CG_PROFILE_PS_1_3 CG_PROFILE_PS_1_2 CG_PROFILE_PS_1_1	−profile ps_1_3 −profile ps_1_2 −profile ps_1_1

on a predefined hardware profile. For example, there might be two versions of a vertex shader – one utilizing all the features of an advanced GPU with the other catering for more mainstream graphics hardware and supporting a reduced set of features. Cg allows us to specify a different profile for each of these systems – always resulting in the execution of the most powerful shader. Profiles are specified when a Cg program is compiled, with each profile catering for a specific GPU and graphics API by defining a subset of the complete Cg language that can be utilized on the GPU or API in question. Table 6-7 lists the current supported Cg profiles.

Using the data from Table 6-7 we can, for example, compile a Cg source file to a vertex program compatible with the Direct3D Shader Model 2.0 vertex shader specification by invoking the −profile vs_2_0 compiler option when compiling our Cg vertex shader program. This shader will now be limited to Shader Model 2.0's features. Limits are imposed on the number of executable instructions (limited to 256), the number of vector registers for the storage of program parameters, and results, including the statements, data types, data structures and operators allowed. We also have to set the runtime option when creating a context for our Cg program. A *context* can be considered a central grouping for a number of Cg programs and their shared data (section 6.5.3.4).

6.5.3.2 The Cg Compiler

Cg programs have to be compiled into a form that can be executed on a GPU. This compilation process starts with the Cg compiler translating a vertex or fragment shader program into a form readable by the implemented API (OpenGL/Direct3D). This translation of the original Cg program (simply a number of OpenGL or Direct3D commands) can now be sent to either the OpenGL or Direct3D API driver which does the final conversion into instructions that can be processed by the GPU.

Cg supports both static and dynamic compilation. *Static compilation* refers to the situation where the Cg compiler is used to compile a shader program once, eliminating the need to compile it again. When pre-compiling shader programs, we must compile a version of the program for each profile defined. This results in many compiled versions limited to specific profiles, and thus GPU features, supported at the time of compilation.

Static compiling is rarely used and *dynamic compilation,* made possible through the Cg runtime, is a much better alternative for enabling the real-time manipulation of Cg programs and so that Cg programs can be modified to fully utilize the features of the installed GPU. The Cg compiler is integrated into the Cg runtime and all applications using Cg must link to this runtime library. Dynamic compilation is possible because whenever an application calls a Cg runtime routine, the compiler is invoked via the runtime.

The Cg runtime is coupled with two closely mirrored libraries – the CgGL library for use with OpenGL renderers and the CgD3D library for Direct3D-based programs. These libraries set up Cg programs for execution. CgGL executes the OpenGL commands needed to send the Cg program to the OpenGL driver with CgD3D calling the appropriate Direct3D routines to forward the Cg program to the Direct3D driver. CgGL routines start with the prefix 'cgGL' while CgD3D routines are preceded by the string 'cgD3D'.

6.5.3.3 The Cg Runtime

The Cg Runtime is a library that enables either an OpenGL or Direct3D application to create and manage one or more Cg programs. More specifically, the Cg runtime can be considered an API facilitating the linking and compilation of Cg programs at runtime. This library is also used for the creation of shader effects. We will start by discussing the use of this runtime to specify and control Cg programs, also looking at the API-specific runtimes offering additional functions to those provided by the core Cg runtime.

For either OpenGL or Direct3D applications to interface with Cg programs we must compile these programs to an appropriate profile. This profile ensures compatibility between the Cg program and the implemented API as well as the target GPU. We also have to link these Cg programs to the 3D application so that vertex and other data can be transferred back and forth between them. This process, as discussed above, can be performed either at run time (using dynamic compilation) or at compile time (when the application is built into an executable).

The Cg runtime can be separated into three units: a set of functions and routines responsible for the core functionality offered by the runtime, a number of OpenGL-specific functions, and a set of Direct3D-specific functions. The interconnection between the Cg runtime, the OpenGL/Direct3D APIs and 3D application is shown in Figure 6-19.

6.5.3.4 Initializing Cg

The first step when using the Cg runtime is to including the cg.h header file. This header file encapsulates the core Cg runtime functionality:

```
#include <Cg/cg.h>
```

Next we include the OpenGL Cg runtime library (cgGL.h) for OpenGL-based applications or the Direct3D Cg runtime (cgD3D9.h) library for Direct3D:

```
#include <Cg/cgGL.h>
#include <Cg/cgD3D9.h>
```

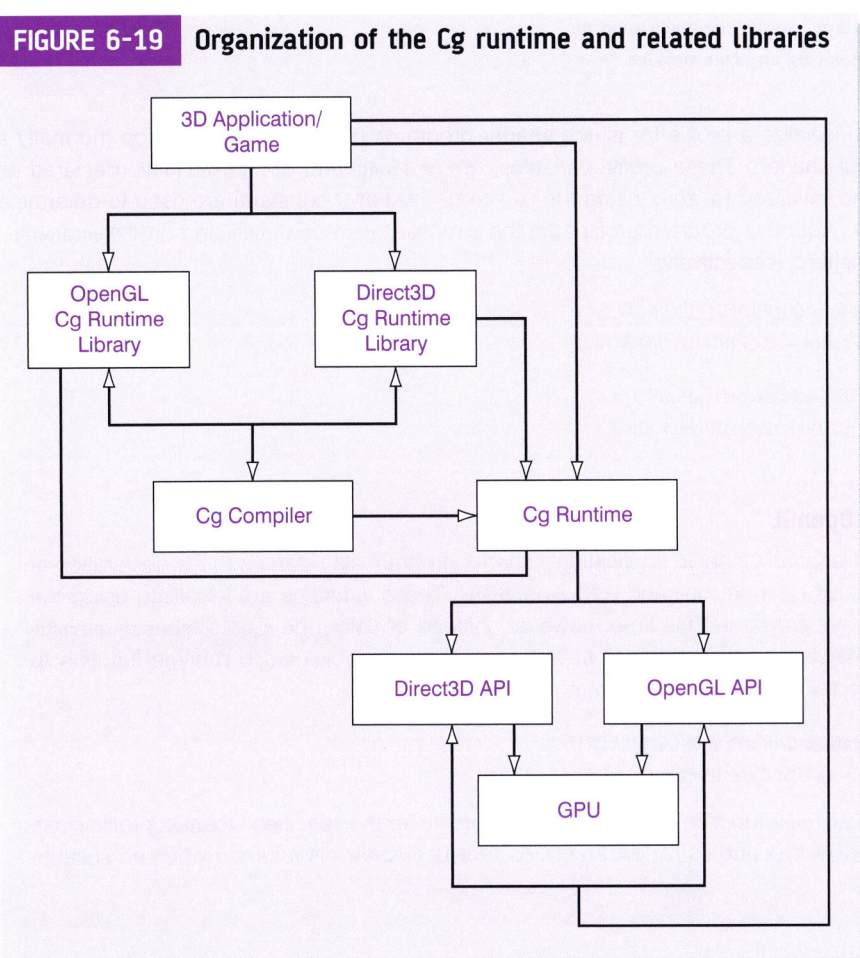

FIGURE 6-19   **Organization of the Cg runtime and related libraries**

6

Direct3D 10 is currently not yet supported by Cg – it being limited to the extended Direct3D 9 shader model 2.x architecture. The core Cg functions, defined with the string 'cg' as prefix, can be called for both Direct3D and OpenGL implementations. The functions from the Direct3D and OpenGL Cg runtimes are, as mentioned in section 6.5.3.2, defined using the 'cgGL' prefix for all versions of OpenGL and 'cgD3D9' for the newest supported Direct3D API. Following the Cg function naming convention, and the fact that functions from the Direct3D 8 Cg runtime use the 'cgD3D8' prefix, one can make the assumption that the Direct3D 10 Cg runtime, when defined, would make use of the prefix 'cgD3D10'. This is of course pure conjecture based solely on past Cg naming conventions.

With the necessary header files included, we have to create a Cg context. This so called context will be used to store all the Cg programs and their data used by the application:

```
CGcontext context = cgCreateContext();
```

It is subsequently important to validate whether this context generation was successful:

```
if(context == 0)
{
```

```
    /* handle the failure, exiting the application for
       example or displaying an error message */
}
```

We also have to initialize a profile for all the shader programs used by the application (normally a vertex and fragment shader). These profile variables, cgVertexProfile and cgFragmentProfile (declared as global variables and initialized to 'zero' using the CG_PROFILE_UNKNOWN constant) are used to determine the latest vertex and fragment program profiles via the cgD3D9GetLatestVertexProfile and cgD3D9GetLatestPixelProfile runtime functions respectively:

```
CGprofile cgVertexProfile = CG_PROFILE_UNKNOWN;
CGprofile cgFragmentProfile = CG_PROFILE_UNKNOWN;

cgVertexProfile = cgD3D9GetLatestVertexProfile();;
cgFragmentProfile = cgD3D9GetLatestPixelProfile();
```

Working with OpenGL

Initializing a profile for an OpenGL application's shader program also starts with the declaration of the profile variables cgVertexProfile and cgFragmentProfile. These variables are initialized using the CG_PROFILE_UNKNOWN constant. This time, however, instead of using the cgD3D9GetLatestPixelProfile and cgD3D9GetLatestVertexProfile functions, we will used the cgGLGetLatestProfile runtime function to determine the vertex and fragment program profiles:

```
cgVertexProfile = cgGLGetLatestProfile(CG_GL_VERTEX);
cgFragmentProfile = cgGLGetLatestProfile(CG_GL_FRAGMENT);
```

The cgGLGetLatestProfile function retrieves the latest profile for the specified OpenGL profile class (in this case CG_GL_VERTEX and CG_GL_FRAGMENT). CG_PROFILE_UNKNOWN is returned when no suitable profile is found.

We should once again do some validation, ensuring the successful execution of these profile determination functions:

```
if ((cgVertexProfile == CG_PROFILE_UNKNOWN) ||
    (cgFragmentProfile == CG_PROFILE_UNKNOWN))
{
    /* handle the failure, exiting the application or
       displaying an error message, for example */
}
```

Working with OpenGL

For OpenGL programs we have to set the optimal vertex and fragment shader program profiles using the cgGLSetOptimalOptions OpenGL Cg runtime function:

```
cgGLSetOptimalOptions(cgVertexProfile);
cgGLSetOptimalOptions(cgFragmentProfile);
```

This is done prior to the shader program source code being read from the user defined '.cg' files.

Shader program source files are saved with the extension '.cg'. These files, defining the actual vertex and fragment manipulation techniques, are loaded into memory using the cgCreateProgramFromFile function:

```
vprogram = cgCreateProgramFromFile(context, CG_SOURCE,
                                    "vlight_vprog.cg",
                                    cgVertexProfile, "main",
                                    0);
fprogram = cgCreateProgramFromFile(context, CG_SOURCE,
                                    "vlight_fprog.cg",
                                    cgFragmentProfile, "main",
                                    0);
```

This function generates new CGprogram objects (vprogram for our vertex shader and fprogram for our fragment shader). These objects are added to the previously defined Cg context, context. cgCreateProgramFromFile takes six parameters. The first is a CGcontext object, the second a Cg enumerator describing the shader file's contents (CG_SOURCE if the program contains Cg source code or CG_OBJECT if the program contains object code – precompiled Cg source code). The third parameter specifies the name of the shader program, followed by the shader program profile and the name of the shader program's entry function. The sixth parameter facilitates the passing of optional compiler options/arguments in the form of NULL-terminated strings.

These newly created CGprogram objects must be validated. A CGprogram handle is returned on success, with a 'NULL' otherwise:

```
if ((vprogram == 0) || (fprogram == 0))
{
    /* retrieve the last error that has occurred */
    CGerror error = cgGetError();

    /* display the error and take some action */
    cout << cgGetErrorString(error) << endl;
    exit(-1);
}
```

The read vertex and fragment programs must be enabled and bound to the 3D application for use. This is a two-function call operation – we first prepare the program for binding using the cgD3D9LoadProgram function followed by a call to the cgD3D9BindProgram function to activate the shader program:

```
/* load and bind the fragment program */
cgD3D9LoadProgram(fprogram, false, 0);
cgD3D9BindProgram(fprogram);

/* load and bind the vertex program */
cgD3D9LoadProgram(vprogram, false, 0);
cgD3D9BindProgram(vprogram);
```

The first parameter of the cgD3D9LoadProgram function is a CGprogram object – the object used to create the shader. The second parameter is set to true or false depending on whether shadowing is required for the program specified in the first parameter. The final parameter allows for the specification of some additional flags passed to Direct3D.

The cgD3D9BindProgram function activates the shader program passed as parameter.

Working with OpenGL

Loading and binding a shader program in OpenGL is similar to Direct3D; however, we must additionally enable the profile corresponding to the shader program using the cgGLEnableProfile function:

```
/* load the vertex program */
cgGLLoadProgram(vprogram);

/* enable the vertex shader's profile within OpenGL */
cgGLEnableProfile(cgVertexProfile);

/* bind the vertex program to the current OpenGL state */
cgGLBindProgram(vprogram);

/* load the fragment program */
cgGLLoadProgram(fprogram);

/* enable the fvertex shader's profile within OpenGL */
cgGLEnableProfile(cgFragmentProfile);

/* bind the fragment program to the current OpenGL state */
cgGLBindProgram(fprogram);
```

The vertex and fragment programs are now bound to the current render state and will be processed until another shader program is bound. These function calls, responsible for the initialization of Cg variables and parameters, can be grouped into a single function, void initCg or something similar, which can be called from the application's entry point – its main function, for example.

On termination of our application we still have to release all acquired Cg resources, specifically the Cg context and all resources allocated for our vertex and fragment programs:

```
/* free all allocated context resources */
cgDestroyContext(context);

/* free shader program resources */
cgDestroyProgram(vprogram);
cgDestroyProgram(fprogram);
```

6.5.3.5 Creating a Vertex Program
We will now present a shader program used for the real-time calculation of vertex lighting (on a textured sphere) updated in accordance with its angle of rotation (shown in Figure 6-20).

As discussed in Chapter 9, lighting calculations can be performed in either object space or view space; other options are also possible although rarely seen. Direct3D and OpenGL, for example, perform their lighting calculations in view space (refer to section 7.4 for more information on coordinate systems). We will now write a vertex program that transforms object space into homogeneous clip-space coordinates (coordinates that are actually viewable for a scene in view space). Following this our vertex program computes the per-vertex light color consisting of an ambient, specular, and diffuse lighting component (for a concise definition of each, see section 4.2).

FIGURE 6-20   **Vertex lighting**

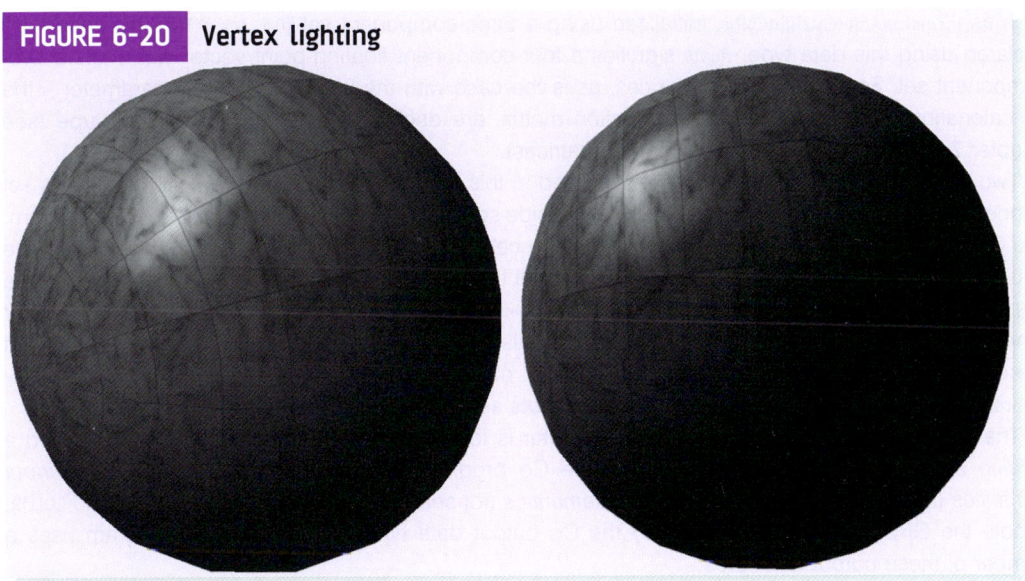

We might be getting ahead of ourselves in the sense that we have not yet discussed lighting or texture mapping – two elements presented in this sample. These elements are, however, not of much concern as our main aim here is to investigate the syntax and structure of a proper Cg program. The real-time lighting calculations done in this sample will be much clearer after dealing with lighting in Chapter 9 and texture mapping in Chapter 8.

The first step when creating a shader program is to specify the name of the entry function, main in our example. The entry function given here is called to compile the shader:

```
void main(
        float4 objectspaceVertexPosition : POSITION,
        float3 objectspaceVertexNormal : NORMAL,
        float2 inputTextureCoordinates : TEXCOORD0,

        out float4 outputVertexPosition : POSITION,
        out float2 outputTextureCoordinates : TEXCOORD0,
        out float4 color : COLOR,
        /* parameters supplied by the application program */

        uniform float3 incomingAmbientLightColor,
        uniform float3 incomingDiffuseLightColor,
        uniform float3 objectspaceLightPosition,
        uniform float3 objectspaceEyePosition,
        uniform float3 materialAmbientReflectance,
        uniform float3 materialDiffuseColor,
        uniform float3 materialSpecularColor,
        uniform float materialShininess,
        uniform float4x4 modelviewProjection
)
```

This entry function specifies a series of parameters declared using various Cg data types. The float scalar data type specifies a single floating point value, such as required by the materialShininess parameter. The float3 data type represents a vector consisting of three floating-point values – parameters such as incomingAmbientLightColor, initialized using a three-component set (0.5, 0.5, 0.5 in this case), are declared using this data type. float4 signifies a four-component floating-point vector with float2 a two-component set. Four-component matrices, as is the case with the modelviewProjection parameter – the concatenation of a modelview and projection matrix, are declared using the float4x4 data type (see Chapter 7 for information on concatenating matrices).

Two Cg qualifiers – uniform and out – are used in this sample program. The uniform modifier is set whenever a parameter is to be initialized by an outside source such as an OpenGL or Direct3D program. The Cg runtime provides API functions that can be called from the application program to specify the values of these parameters. For example, we set all the above defined uniform parameters using the cgGLSetParameter for OpenGL programs, the cgD3D9SetUniform for Direct3D or the cgSetParameter function for either. The cgSetParameterValuefr Cg runtime call can also be used to set numeric parameters. The use of these functions will be explained shortly. The *out* modifier sets the outputVertexPosition, outputTextureCoordinates and color parameters as program outputs sent to the graphics pipeline for processing.

The declaration of an input or output parameter is followed by a colon and an identifier (called a *binding semantic*) responsible for binding the Cg program to the graphics pipeline. These *input semantics* (in the case of inputs) and *output semantics* (for shader outputs), such as POSITION and COLOR, denote the GPU resource that is fed by the Cg output data type. The sample Cg program uses a number of these output structures:

- POSITION (the transformed vertex's clip-space coordinates)

- COLOR (the diffuse vertex color also referred to as the primary vertex color),

- NORMAL (the object space normal) and

- TEXCOORD0 (the texture coordinate set).

These binding semantics are initialized with per-vertex data via appropriate OpenGL or Direct3D commands.

Before continuing with the shader program it is important to take a quick look at some of the basics pertaining to the implementation of a per-vertex lighting model. The per-vertex lighting model presented here is already implemented by OpenGL and Direct3D. We will mimic the lighting model provided by these APIs to a high degree, simplifying it somewhat and overriding the related API version with our implementation. Chapter 9 deals with this model in much more detail. For now, simply consider this basic lighting model as a high-level equation summing an ambient, diffuse, and specular component to calculate the color of an object's surface:

Surface color = ambient lighting term
+ diffuse lighting term
+ specular lighting term.

These lighting components are in turn dependent on the material properties of the surface as well as the color and position of a light source.

Ambient reflection occurs whenever light emitted from a source is reflected so much that its origin is impossible to determine. Ambient light is characterized by being omnidirectional (light radiated uniformly in all directions; more commonly, light scattered uniformly in all directions). Some of the light hitting a surface is absorbed while some is reflected. The ambient reflection coefficient is an indication of the reflected amount and is comprised out of red, blue, and green ambient reflection coefficients collectively. The equation for calculating ambient lighting factors in the material's ambient reflectance and the color of the incoming ambient light is:

Ambient lighting term = material's ambient reflectance
× incoming ambient light color.

Specular reflection occurs when light from a single incoming direction is reflected at a single outgoing direction. The amount of shininess exhibited by the object is called the object's specularity and is governed by a shininess coefficient. The bigger our coefficient, the closer we are to a perfect mirror. Formally, values ranging from 100 to 500 represent most metallic surfaces while smaller values represent materials with broader highlights such as plastic and wood. Specularity is responsible for surface highlights exhibited by shiny objects. For example, a bright red painted piece of metal viewed under a white light has a clearly visible white highlight; this highlight is light reflected in the direction of the viewer. Specularity is thus, unlike diffuse or ambient lighting, dependent on the location of the viewer as well as the color properties of the material, light source and shininess of the surface. The equation for calculating specularity is:

Specular lighting term = material's specular color
                $\times$ color of incoming specular light
                $\times$ *geometryFacingFlag*
                $\times$ (max(normalized surface normal
                 . normalized halfway vector,0))^{shininess}

6

The *geometryFacingFlag* element is a flag ensuring that specular highlights are limited to geometry facing a light source – its value is calculated by taking the dot product between the normalized surface normal and the normalized vector pointing to the light source. If this dot product is greater than zero then the *geometryFacingFlag* element is set to 1, otherwise 0. The normalized halfway vector element is the vector halfway between the normalized vector pointing towards the viewpoint and the normalized vector pointing in the direction of the light source. Specular highlights are prominent when the angle between these two vectors is small. Figure 6-21 shows the vectors used in the calculation of this specular term.

In contrast to specular reflection, diffuse reflections occur when incoming light is reflected in random directions. The main contributing factor to this form of reflection is an uneven or rough surface. A diffuse surface appears identical to all viewers, regardless of their respective positions. Diffuse reflections are

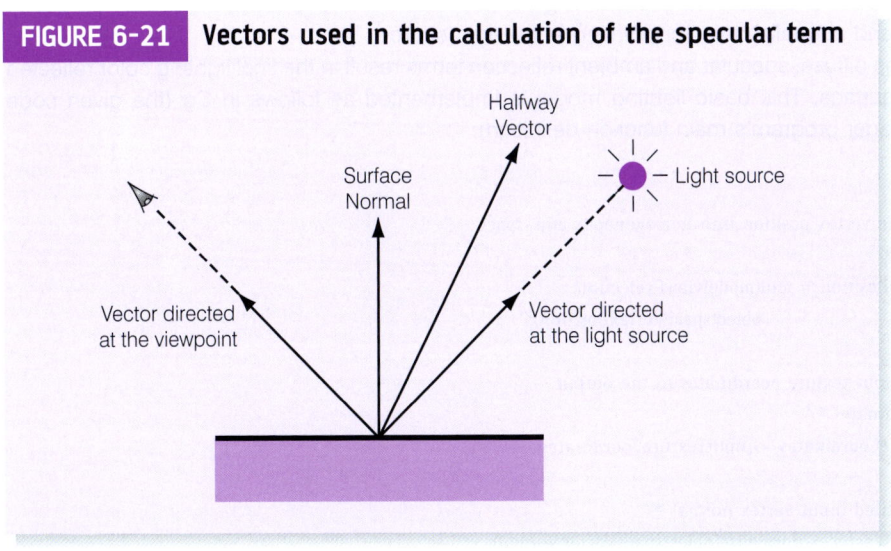

FIGURE 6-21 **Vectors used in the calculation of the specular term**

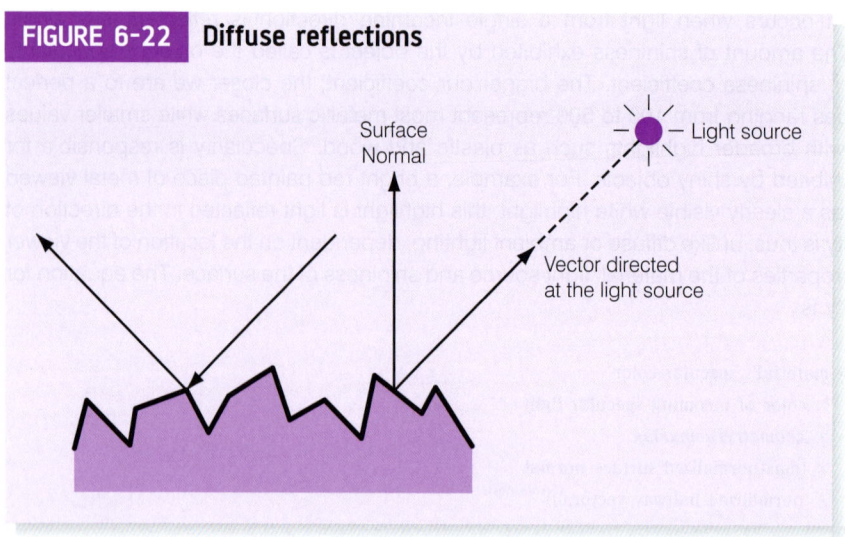

FIGURE 6-22   Diffuse reflections

Surface
Normal

Light source

Vector directed
at the light source

6

common for matte or dull surfaces such as carpets or matte paints as used in home painting. The equation for calculating diffuse lighting is:

Diffuse lighting term = material's diffuse color
$\times$ color of incoming diffuse light
$\times$ max(normalized surface normal
. normalized vector towards light,0)

The dot product between the normalized surface normal and normalized vector pointing towards light source gives the measure of incident light received by the surface – the smaller the angle between these two vectors, the greater the dot product result, and the greater the amount of incident light falling on the surface. The max (normalized surface normal . normalized vector towards light, 0) element in the equation ensures that only surfaces facing a light source reflect some diffuse lighting – surfaces facing away from a light source result in a negative dot product. Figure 6-22 shows a diffuse surface with the normalized surface normal and normalized vector pointing at the light source.

Combining the diffuse, specular and ambient reflection terms result in the final lighting color reflected by an object's surface. This basic lighting model is implemented as follows in Cg (the given code following the shader program's main function definition):

```
{
    /* transform the vertex position into homogeneous clip-space
       coordinates */
    outputVertexPosition = mul(modelviewProjection,
                               objectspaceVertexPosition);

    /* assign the input texture coordinates to the output
       texture coordinates */
    outputTextureCoordinates = inputTextureCoordinates;

    /* store normalized input vertex normal */
    float3 normalVector = normalize(objectspaceVertexNormal);
```

```
    /* store normalized light vector */
    float3 normalizedVectorTowardLightSource =
                    normalize(objectspaceLightPosition −
                            objectspaceVertexPosition.xyz);

    /* calculate the ambient light component */
    float3 ambientTerm = materialAmbientReflectance *
                    incomingAmbientLightColor;

    /* calculate the diffuse light component */
    float diffuseLight = dot(normalVector,
                    normalizedVectorTowardLightSource);
    float3 diffuseTerm = materialDiffuseColor *
                    incomingDiffuseLightColor *
                    diffuseLight;

    /* calculate the specular light component */
    float3 normalizedVectorTowardViewpoint =
                    normalize(objectspaceEyePosition −
                    objectspaceVertexPosition.xyz);
    float3 normalizedHalfwayVector =
                    normalize(normalizedVectorTowardLightSource +
                    normalizedVectorTowardViewpoint);
    float specularLight = pow(max(dot(normalVector,
                    normalizedHalfwayVector), 0), materialShininess);
    float3 specularTerm = materialSpecularColor *
                    incomingDiffuseLightColor * specularLight;

    /* the basic lighting model */
    color.xyz = ambientTerm + diffuseTerm + specularTerm;
}
```

The first step in this vertex program is to calculate the clip-space position as required by the rasterizer. This is mandatory for all Cg vertex programs because these programs will always generate their outputs in clip space coordinates. The POSITION semantic indicates that the vertex program will produce outputs in clip space. We transform the object-space vertex position into homogeneous clip-space coordinates by multiplying it with the concatenated modelview and projection matrices.

Next we assign the input texture coordinates to the output texture coordinates and normalize both the input vertex normal and light vector as required by our light equations. The diffuse calculation, for example, requires this vector from a vertex on the object to the light source. We calculate this vector by starting at the end point, namely the light position objectspaceLightPosition, and subtracting the starting point of the vector – the object space vertex position (objectspaceVertexPosition.xyz). Notice the .xyz syntax following the variable name. This is a Cg feature called *swizzling*. Swizzling is a technique used to reorganize vector elements with the aim of creating a new vector. The 'xyz' letters designate the original vector components to use when creating a new vector – *x* being the first component of the old vector, *y* the second and *z* the third. In this example, .xyz extracts the related vector components from objectspaceVertexPosition, creating a new vector in the process. The object space light position is bound to the vertex shader using the cgSetParameter3f Cg library function:

```
cgSetParameter3f(cgGetNamedParameter(vprogram,
        "objectspaceLightPosition"), 0.0, 10.0, 10.0);
```

The cgSetParameter3f function, setting the value of a uniform scalar or vector parameter, takes four parameters. The first indicates the parameter that will be set, with the rest, the *x*, *y* and *z* floating point values, to set the parameter to. We make use of the cgGetNamedParameter function to determine a program parameter by name. This function's first parameter is the program from which to retrieve the program parameter with its second parameter indicating the name of the program parameter to retrieve.

All vectors have to be normalized using the normalize function declared in the Cg standard library. Normalising a vector ensures consistent lighting; otherwise we will have lighting that is either overly bright or dark. The dot product between two vectors is calculated using the dot Cg library function. We also make use of the max function to clamp dot product results to zero. This clamping function sets all dot product values less than zero to zero, ensuring that the surfaces facing away from the light source are not lit.

The vertex program proceeds to calculate the ambient, diffuse, and specular lighting components in accordance with the presented per-vertex lighting model equations. Calculating the ambient light component requires specification of the material's ambient color, materialAmbientReflectance, and global ambient light color, incomingAmbientLightColor. These two parameters are set in the application program as follows:

```
cgSetParameter3f(cgGetNamedParameter(vprogram,
          "incomingAmbientLightColor"), 0.5, 0.5, 0.5);

cgSetParameter3f(cgGetNamedParameter(vprogram,
          "materialAmbientReflectance"), 0.1, 0.1, 0.1);
```

The diffuse light component calculation makes use of two uniform parameters initialized by the application program: materialDiffuseColor and incomingDiffuseLightColor. These two variables, like the previous two, are initialized using the cgSetParameter3f function:

```
cgSetParameter3f(cgGetNamedParameter(vprogram,
          "materialDiffuseColor"), 0.5, 0.5, 0.5);

cgSetParameter3f(cgGetNamedParameter(vprogram,
          "incomingDiffuseLightColor"), 1.0, 1.0, 1.0);
```

Determining the specular light component, as discussed, involves the definition of four vectors. One of these vectors, the normalized vector pointing to the light source, has already been calculated for the diffuse lighting component and stored in the variable, normalizedVectorTowardLightSource. Calculating the normalized vector pointing to the viewpoint and the vector halfway between this vector and the normalized vector pointing in the direction of the light source is relatively simple. The vector pointing to the viewpoint is calculated by starting at the end point, namely the eye position objectspaceEyePosition, and subtracting the starting point of the vector; the object space vertex position (objectspaceVertexPosition.xyz). The vector halfway between the normalized vector pointing to the viewpoint and the normalized vector pointing in the direction of the light source can be calculated by scaling both the vector pointing to the viewpoint and the vector pointing in the direction of the light source by 0.5 and then combining the result. However, this scaling has no effect as the result is normalized anyway, so we can simply just combine the vector pointing to the viewpoint with the vector pointing in the direction of the light source. The result is saved in the variable, normalizedHalfwayVector. Calculating the specular term is simply an implementation of the specular equation given above. One Cg library function pow is, however, worth some mention. This function takes two parameters, returning the first to the power of the second and is used to calculate the result of the dot product between the normalized surface normal and the normalized halfway vector to the power of the material's shininess value, materialShininess. This shininess factor and object space eye position are set in the shader utilizing OpenGL or Direct3D program as follows:

```
cgSetParameter3f(cgGetNamedParameter(vprogram,
                "objectspaceEyePosition"), 0.0, 2.0, 5.0);

cgSetParameter1f(cgGetNamedParameter(vprogram,
                "materialShininess"), 100.0);
```

We make use of the cgSetParameter1f function because we only need to set the uniform materialShininess parameter to a single value. The final specular term is computed by multiplying the materialSpecularColor and incomingDiffuseLightColor uniform parameters with the calculated specular light component, specularLight. These uniform parameters are initialized by the application program as follows:

```
cgSetParameter3f(cgGetNamedParameter(vprogram,
                "materialSpecularColor"), 1.0, 1.0, 1.0);

cgSetParameter3f(cgGetNamedParameter(vprogram,
                "incomingDiffuseLightColor"), 1.0, 1.0, 1.0);
```

6

The final step of this vertex program combines the ambient, diffuse and specular lighting terms/contributions to obtain the vertex color. This output is assigned to the color output parameter and sent to the graphics pipeline for processing.

6.5.3.6 Creating a Fragment Program
Per-vertex lighting suffers from a certain degree of coarseness attributable to the structure of a 3D model/mesh. Per-vertex lighting calculates the lighting at each vertex making up a triangle. This calculated lighting is then interpolated for each generated triangle fragment, resulting in a somewhat course interpolation for low polygon models. There is thus a correlation between the number of vertices and the quality of the lighting. Another side effect of per-vertex lighting is its inability to factor in specular highlights that are not incident at the vertices of a triangle – thus failing to apply the lighting equation for each and every fragment. The vertex program therefore calculates the lighting at each vertex while the rasterizer interpolates the calculated color for every generated fragment. Per-vertex lighting is thus not suitable for models with few vertices as shown in Figure 6-23.

Per-fragment lighting, more commonly called 'per-pixel lighting', applies the lighting model on each and every fragment as opposed to every vertex as is the case with per-vertex lighting. This results in a lighting color calculation at each pixel – making the quality of the rendered lighting independent from the complexity of the mesh. Figure 6-24

FIGURE 6-23 **Per-vertex lighting on a very low polygon sphere**

FIGURE 6-24 **Per-fragment lighting on a very low polygon sphere**

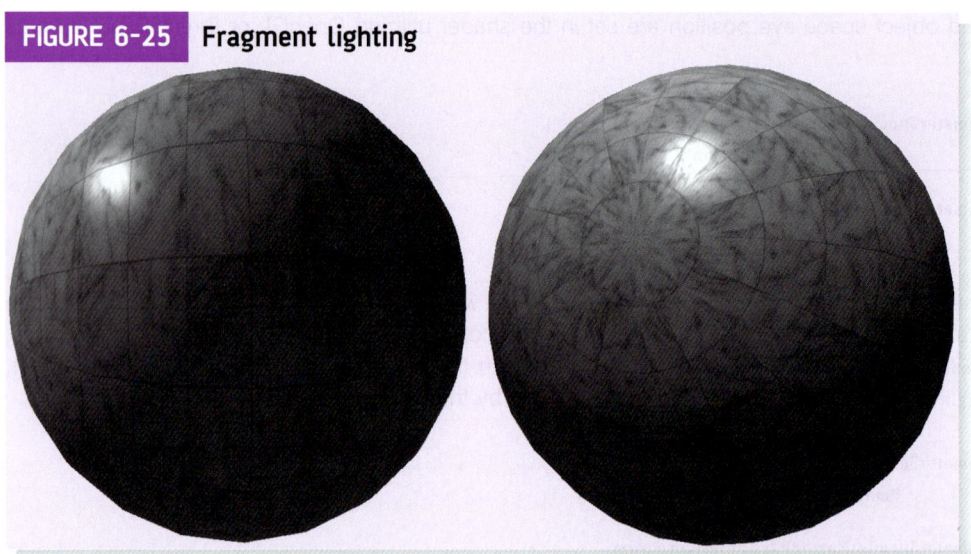

FIGURE 6-25 **Fragment lighting**

shows the same low polygon sphere from before, only this time with the implementation of per-fragment lighting.

We will now present a shader program for the real-time calculation of fragment lighting on a textured sphere updated based on its rotation (shown in Figure 6-25).

This fragment program is strikingly similar to the previously presented vertex program, a similarity that can be attributed to Cg using the same syntax for both fragment and vertex shaders. Despite the syntactic similarity we have considerably more control over the produced image than is the case with the earlier vertex program. Fragment programs are, however, more performance hungry than their vertex counterparts. Performance degradation is mostly due to the number of per-fragment processing calls made by the shader program and the greater number of fragments than vertices present in a frame. A fragment program will thus execute several times more than a vertex program due to this greater number of fragments. This sample also requires a bit more graphics processor functionality than the previous program – at a minimum requiring a GeForce FX- or Radeon 9700-based video card.

We once again start by specifying the name of the entry function, main in our shader program. The entry function given here is called to compile the fragment shader:

```
void main(
        float4 objectspacePosition : TEXCOORD1,
        float3 objectspaceNormal : TEXCOORD2,
        out float4 color : COLOR,
        float2 textureCoordinatesLookup : TEXCOORD0,

        /* parameters supplied by the application program */

        uniform float3 incomingAmbientLightColor,
        uniform float3 incomingDiffuseLightColor,
        uniform float3 objectspaceLightPosition,
        uniform float3 objectspaceEyePosition,
        uniform float3 materialAmbientReflectance,
        uniform float3 materialDiffuseColor,
        uniform float3 materialSpecularColor,
```

```
            uniform float materialShininess,
            uniform sampler2D sphereTexture
)
```

This fragment program is coupled with a vertex program tasked with some simple calculations and the forwarding of data through the pipeline. The vertex program outputs the homogenous clip coordinates, object-space position, and object-space normal in the form of texture coordinate sets. Two texture coordinate sets are sent to the fragment program as input parameters, specifically as the objectspacePosition and objectspaceNormal parameters. The vertex program is given here:

```
void main(
            float4 objectspaceVertexPosition : POSITION,
            float4 objectspaceVertexNormal : NORMAL,
            float2 inputTextureCoordinates : TEXCOORD0,
            out float4 outputVertexPosition : POSITION,
            out float2 outputTextureCoordinates : TEXCOORD0,
            out float3 outputObjectPosition : TEXCOORD1,
            out float3 outputObjectNormal : TEXCOORD2,

            /* parameter supplied by the application program */

            uniform float4x4 modelviewProjection
)
{
    /* transform the vertex position into homogeneous clip-space
        coordinates */
    outputVertexPosition = mul(modelviewProjection,
                                objectspaceVertexPosition);

    /* set the object-space position and object-space normal for
        the fragment program */
    outputObjectPosition = objectspaceVertexPosition.xyz;
    outputObjectNormal = objectspaceVertexNormal;

    /* assign the input texture coordinates to the output
        texture coordinates */
    outputTextureCoordinates = inputTextureCoordinates;
}
```

There aren't any new concepts illustrated by this program except for the concept of various texture coordinate sets, specifically, TEXCOORD0, TEXCOORD1 and TEXCOORD2. We previously only made use of the TEXCOORD0 binding semantic. The number following the TEXCOORD* semantic indicates a different texture coordinate set and can range from one to seven, resulting in TEXCOORD0 to TEXCOORD7.

Returning to the fragment program and its main function's parameters we make use of a new Cg type, namely sampler2D to declare the sphereTexture parameter. A *sampler* is an externally declared object that can be sampled by Cg – in this case a texture. The sampler2D type denotes a typical two-dimensional texture. This texture parameter is used as the tex2D Cg function's first parameter. The tex2D function performs a 2D texture lookup determining the fragment's color (the '2D' suffix indicating the sampling of 2D sampler objects). It takes two parameters, the first being a sampler object and the second a texture coordinate set specifying the location to sample the object at. This function produces sampled data as output which is returned by the fragment program through the `color` variable. The rest of the fragment program (almost identical to the vertex program) is given below:

```
{
    /* store normalized input vertex objectspaceNormal */
    float3 normalVector = normalize(objectspaceNormal);

    /* store normalized light vector */
    float3 normalizedVectorTowardLightSource =
                    normalize(objectspaceLightPosition −
                    objectspacePosition.xyz);

    /* calculate the ambient light component */
    float3 ambientTerm = materialAmbientReflectance *
        incomingAmbientLightColor;

    /* calculate the diffuseTerm light component */
    float diffuseLight = max(dot(normalVector,
                        normalizedVectorTowardLightSource), 0);
    float3 diffuseTerm = materialDiffuseColor *
                        incomingDiffuseLightColor *
                        diffuseLight;

    /* calculate specularTerm light component */
    float3 normalizedVectorTowardViewpoint =
                        normalize(objectspaceEyePosition −
                        objectspacePosition.xyz);
    float3 normalizedHalfwayVector =
                normalize(normalizedVectorTowardLightSource +
                normalizedVectorTowardViewpoint);
    float specularLight = pow(max(dot(normalVector,
                        normalizedHalfwayVector), 0),
                        materialShininess);
    float3 specularTerm = materialSpecularColor *
                        incomingDiffuseLightColor *
                        specularLight;
    /* the basic lighting model */
    color.xyz = ambientTerm + diffuseTerm + specularTerm;

    /* the tex2D() function performs a 2D texture lookup
       determining the fragment's color */
    color = color * tex2D(sphereTexture,
                        textureCoordinatesLookup);
}
```

6.5.4 High Level Shader Language (HLSL)

Microsoft's High Level Shader Language is a proprietary Direct3D shading language analogous to NVIDIA's Cg. The Direct3D 10 High Level Shader Language allows for the creation of three types of shader programs, namely, vertex shaders, geometry shaders and pixel shaders (see section 6.5 for a

FIGURE 6-26   Common shader core architecture

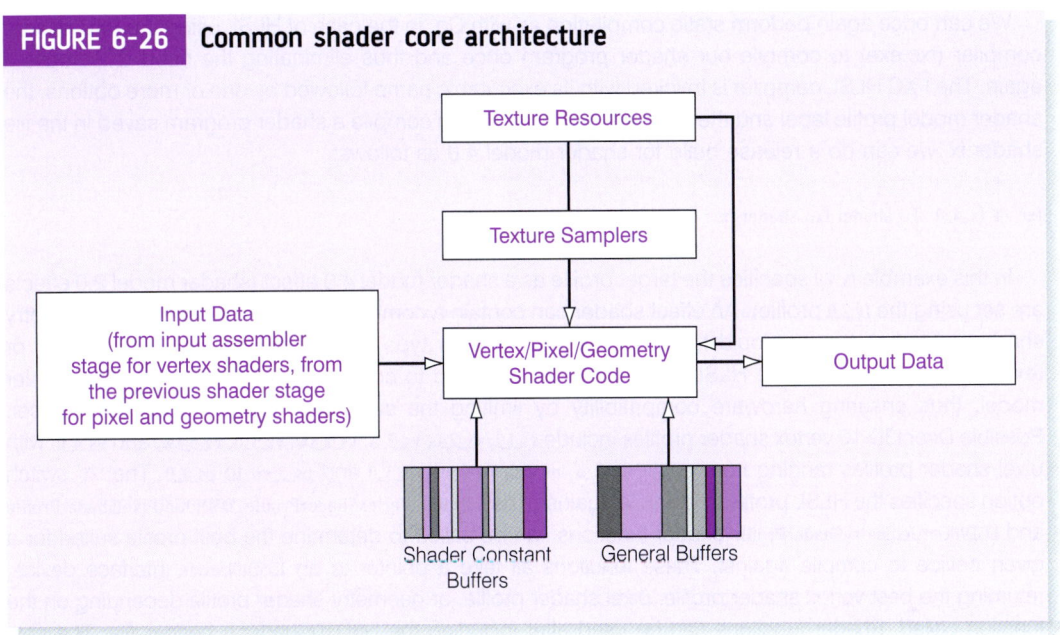

description of each). Similar to Cg, HLSL shaders can be compiled either statically or dynamically, depending on the preference of the developer and intended application for the shader.

As previously mentioned in section 6.5, Direct3D 10 shaders are unified to provide the application programmer with a uniform instruction set independent of whether a pixel, vertex, or geometric shader is being implemented. These different shaders, offering the same core functionality, are implemented by the Shader Model 4.0 common shader core. Building on the core functionality, each shader implementation offers its own unique functionality, such as stencilling done via pixel shaders, or the generation of new primitives and the manipulation of 3D models on a per-primitive basis by a geometric shader. This common shader core data flow is shown in Figure 6-26.

The stages given in the above depicted data-flow model can be summarized as follows:

1 Input data are sent to the vertex, pixel or geometry shader for processing with the vertex shader receiving data from the input assembler stage and the pixel and geometry shaders receiving their input data from the previous shader stage.

2 The shaders can now perform some arithmetic or flow control operation on the read data.
  a Texel data are either directly read without any filtering or sampling using the Load HLSL function or, alternatively, filtered and sampled by binding up to 16 HLSL samplers to the shader.
  b General buffers are also accessed from system memory, allowing the shader program to bind up to 128 texture elements and buffer resources to the shader.
  c Shader constant buffers can also be bound to a shader stage. These buffers are frequently updated by the CPU and are larger in size and layout than the general buffers.

3 The output generated by the shader code is passed to the next stage in the graphics pipeline.

6.5.4.1 The HLSL Compiler   Like Cg programs, HLSL programs have to be compiled into a GPU executable form. Compilation is based on the translation of a vertex, pixel or geometry shader program into a form readable by Direct3D. This translation of the original HLSL program is sent to the Direct3D API driver which converts it to instructions that can be processed by the GPU.

We can once again perform static compilation as with Cg, in the case of HLSL using the FXC shader compiler (fxc.exe) to compile our shader program once and thus eliminating the need to compile it again. The FXC HLSL compiler is invoked with its executable name followed by one or more options, the shader model profile label and the filename. For example, to compile a shader program saved in the file shader.fx, we can do a release build for shader model 4.0 as follows:

```
fxc /T fx_4_0 /Fo shader.fxo shader.fx
```

In this example fx_4.0 specifies the target profile as a shader model 4.0 effect (shader model 2.0 effects are set using the fx_2.0 profile). An effect shader can contain a combination of pixel, vertex and geometry shaders. Alternatively we could have specified the shader type as a vertex shader, pixel shader or texture shader (tx_1.0). These HLSL shader profiles are used to compile a shader to a specific shader model, thus ensuring hardware compatibility by limiting the supported shader model feature set. Possible Direct3D 10 vertex shader profiles include vs_1_1, vs_2_0, vs_2_a, vs_2_sw, vs_3_0, vs_3_sw, and vs_4_0, with pixel shader profiles ranging from ps_2_0, ps_2_a, ps_2_b, ps_2_sw, ps_3_0 and ps_3_sw to ps_4_0. The '/T' switch option specifies the HLSL profile to compile against. The D3D10GetVertexShaderProfile, D3D10GetPixelShaderProfile and D3D10GetGeometryShaderProfile shader functions can be called to determine the best profile suited for a given device to compile against. These functions all take a pointer to an ID3D10Device interface device, returning the best vertex shader profile, pixel shader profile, or geometry shader profile depending on the function called. Shader functions can be used after including the D3D10Shader.h header file. The next switch option, '/Fo', is used to set the output object file name used to store the compiled shader effect.

We can alternatively compile a shader using debug mode. Debug mode is similar to that found in Visual Studio, allowing the generation of debug information and additional processing data that can be used to narrow down errors and possible bottleneck areas. We can compile the shader program saved in the shader.fx file using debug mode in the following manner:

```
fxc /Zi /Od /T fx_4_0 /Fo shader.fxo shader.fx
```

The '/Zi' switch option enables debugging information with the '/Od' switch disabling any code-based optimizations that would normally be performed by the compiler.

6.5.4.2 Initializing the High Level Shader Language

This section focuses on the initialization of the High Level Shader Language so that a Direct3D application program can bind the shader program to the appropriate pipeline stage. The steps of this initialization process are as follows:

1 Compilation of the shader to ensure that the HLSL statements are syntactically correct.

2 Create a vertex, pixel, or geometry shader object.

3 Set the created shader object to bind the shader to the proper pipeline stage.

A shader program is compiled by calling the D3D10CompileShader shader function, declared as follows in the D3D10Shader.h header file:

```
HRESULT D3D10CompileShader(
    LPCSTR pSrcData,
    SIZE_T SrcDataLen,
    LPCSTR pFileName,
    CONST D3D10_SHADER_MACRO *pDefines,
    LPD3D10INCLUDE *pInclude,
    LPCSTR pFunctionName,
```

```
    LPCSTR pProfile,
    UINT Flags,
    ID3D10Blob **ppShader,
    ID3D10Blob **ppErrorMsgs
);
```

Its first parameter, pSrcData, takes a pointer to the string holding the shader source code. The second parameter, SrcDataLen, specifies the size of the pSrcData parameter in bytes with the next parameter, pFileName, the name of the shader program file. The pDefines parameter takes a pointer to a D3D10_SHADER_MACRO shader macro array. This null-terminated array of macro definitions, enabling the application program to define tokens at runtime, is optional and can be set to 'NULL'. A D3D10_SHADER_MACRO macro definition can be specified in the following manner:

```
D3D10_SHADER_MACRO Macro[1] = {"ten", "10"};
```

The D3D10_SHADER_MACRO shader structure has two members, Name and Definition. The Name member holds the macro name and the Definition member the macro definition.

D3D10CompileShader's next parameter, pInclude, takes a pointer to the ID3D10Include interface allowing the opening and closing of included files when loading an effect from memory. For example, a shader program can include a file using the #include directive, and by calling the Close or Open ID3D10Include members we can open this file for reading and subsequently close it when done. Specification of the pInclude parameter is optional and set to 'NULL' when the shader doesn't contain any #include directives. The next parameter, pFunctionName, takes a pointer to a string holding the shader entry point function name indicating the function to begin the shader execution at. The pProfile parameter is used for setting the shader model profile with the Flags parameter setting the shader compile options (possible options are listed in Table 6-8). The first of the final two parameters, ppShader, takes a pointer to an ID3D10Blob interface containing the debug information and compiled shader. A *blob* is a data buffer used for the storage of vertex, adjacency and material data. Blobs also return error/debug messages and object code during the compilation of pixel, vertex and geometry shaders. The last parameter, ppErrorMsgs, also takes a pointer to an ID3D10Blob interface, this time one containing errors and warning messages generated during the compilation process.

Before calling the D3D10CompileShader shader function, we first have to create an ID3D10Blob interface:

```
IPD3D10Blob * pShaderBlob;
```

We can, for instance, compile a vertex shader stored in the file vertex_shader.vsh as follows:

```
D3D10CompileShader(strPath, strlen(strPath),
    "vertex_shader.vsh", NULL, NULL,
    "EffectFunctionName", "vs_4_0",
    D3D10_SHADER_ENABLE_STRICTNESS,
    &pShaderBlob, NULL);
```

The shader function, EffectFunctionName, could have been declared in the shader program like this (taking one input parameter and returning a vertex shader structure. The declaration of shader functions, their basic, vector, texture, struct and matrix data types as well as sampler type syntax are all dealt with in the next section):

```
VS_OUTPUT EffectFunctionName (in float2 vertexPosition : POSITION)
```

TABLE 6-8	HLSL compile options
Compile options	**Description**
D3D10_SHADER_AVOID_FLOW_CONTROL	The HLSL compiler will disable flow control as far possible.
D3D10_SHADER_DEBUG	The HLSL compiler enables the generation of debug information.
D3D10_SHADER_ENABLE_BACKWARDS_COMPATIBILITY	The HLSL compiler will compile older shaders to the shader model 4.0 spec.
D3D10_SHADER_ENABLE_STRICTNESS	The HLSL compiler enables strictness on deprecated shader syntax.
D3D10_SHADER_FORCE_PS_SOFTWARE_NO_OPT	The HLSL compiler will compile a pixel shader to the next best shader profile, enabling debugging and disabling compiler optimizations.
D3D10_SHADER_FORCE_VS_SOFTWARE_NO_OPT	The HLSL compiler will compile a vertex shader to the next best shader profile, enabling debugging and disabling compiler optimizations.
D3D10_SHADER_IEEE_STRICTNESS	The HLSL compiler enables IEEE strictness – thus conforming to a predefined set of standards.
D3D10_SHADER_NO_PRESHADER	The HLSL compiler disables the use of preshaders – an optimization where constant expressions are replaced with references to the GPU's registers and memory addresses.
D3D10_SHADER_OPTIMIZATION_LEVEL0	The HLSL compiler enables level 0 warnings.
D3D10_SHADER_OPTIMIZATION_LEVEL1	The HLSL compiler enables level 1 warnings.
D3D10_SHADER_OPTIMIZATION_LEVEL2	The HLSL compiler enables level 2 warnings.
D3D10_SHADER_OPTIMIZATION_LEVEL3	The HLSL compiler enables level 3 warnings.
D3D10_SHADER_PACK_MATRIX_COLUMN_MAJOR	The HLSL compiler packs the matrices in column-major order – leading to more efficiency since matrix manipulations can be performed via a series of dot-products.
D3D10_SHADER_PACK_MATRIX_ROW_MAJOR	The HLSL compiler packs the matrices in row-major order.
D3D10_SHADER_PARTIAL_PRECISION	The compiler sets all calculations to be done with partial precision which will lead to some performance gains.
D3D10_SHADER_PREFER_FLOW_CONTROL	The HLSL compiler will enable flow control as far possible.
D3D10_SHADER_SKIP_OPTIMIZATION	The HLSL compiler will disable optimizations.
D3D10_SHADER_SKIP_VALIDATION	The HLSL compiler will disable the validation of code against common constraints and capability limits.

A pointer to the compiled shader code is returned via the pShaderBlob ID3D10Blob interface. This pointer is used to create the vertex shader object using the CreateVertexShader function (for this example) or alternatively CreatePixelShader to create a pixel shader object or the CreateGeometryShader ID3D10Device interface function for geometry shaders. The CreateVertexShader function is declared in the D3D10.h header file as follows:

```
HRESULT CreateVertexShader(
    const void *pShaderBytecode,
    SIZE_T BytecodeLength,
    ID3D10VertexShader **ppVertexShader
);
```

Its first parameter, pShaderBytecode, takes a pointer to the compiled shader retrieved using the GetBufferPointer ID3D10Blob interface function. The BytecodeLength parameter takes the size of the compiled shader determined via the GetBufferSize ID3D10Blob interface function. The final parameter, ppVertexShader, is the address of a pointer to an ID3D10VertexShader interface.

The CreateGeometryShader and the CreatePixelShader ID3D10Device interface functions have the same first two parameters as CreateVertexShader. These functions only differ in respect to the last parameter which takes a pointer to an ID3D10PixelShader interface in the case of the CreatePixelShader function and an ID3D10GeometryShader interface for the CreateGeometryShader function.

Continuing with our vertex shader program, before calling the CreateVertexShader function, we specify a shader object by first declaring an ID3D10VertexShader interface:

```
ID3D10VertexShader **ppOurVertexShader;
```

We create the vertex shader object using the CreateVertexShader function (using the previously declared ID3D10Device* interface, g_id3dDevice):

```
hresult_ = g_id3dDevice->CreateVertexShader(
                    (DWORD*)pShaderBlob->GetBufferPointer(),
                    pShaderBlob->GetBufferSize(),
                    &ppOurVertexShader);
```

We must also remember to release the pointer to the compiled shader source:

```
pShaderBlob->Release();
```

The final step requires us to set this newly created shader object to the pipeline stage. To set the vertex shader to the device, we call the VSSetShader ID3D10Device interface function. This function takes one parameter, namely, a pointer to the ID3D10VertexShader vertex shader:

```
g_id3dDevice->VSSetShader(pOurVertexShader);
```

The vertex shader stage is now initialized with the compiled vertex shader code. To initialize the pixel shader stage we need to call the PSSetShader ID3D10Device interface function (using an ID3D10PixelShader interface as parameter). The GSSetShader ID3D10Device interface function is called for setting a geometry shader to a device (using an ID3D10GeometryShader interface as parameter).

6.5.4.3 Creating HLSL Shaders

Pixel, vertex and geometry shaders, as shown in Figure 4-16, each make out a different stage of the Direct3D 10 programmable pipeline. These shaders, operating on input data and sending their results to subsequent pipeline stages, are created in the form of program files that can be compiled and executed on the GPU. To recap, vertex shaders operate on vertex data with pixel shaders reading fragments (pixels) as input and geometry shaders processing primitives as input.

Vertex shaders process a vertex read as input and generates some output in the form of a transformed vertex. Vertex data are passed to the GPU via a vertex buffer (see sections 6.2 and 4.3.4.1). Each vertex element stored in this vertex buffer is then sent to the vertex shader for processing. For example, the following vertex shader function returns its input data as output without doing any processing on it:

```
float4 VertexShader(float4 Position : POSITION) : SV_POSITION
{
    return Position;
}
```

The vertex shader function, labeled VertexShader, with the return type float4 takes a parameter, Position, of type float4 as input – float4 being a four-component HLSL vector type with each of its vector components a floating-point value. As with Cg the declaration of the input and output parameters are followed by a colon and binding semantic to further describe the data type. The input parameter is set to the POSITION semantic (the input vertex's clip-space coordinates) with the output value semantic set to SV_POSITION. Semantics using the 'SV_' prefix are referred to as system-value semantics, meaning they are system-generated values and can be used for both input and output data. The SV_POSITION semantic is, for example, processed during the rasterization stage and in this case used to notify the graphics pipeline that the output data will also be in the form of clip-space coordinates.

We can now create a pixel shader function to take the output produced by the above-defined vertex shader function as input (a float4 type coupled with the SV_POSITION semantic). This pixel shader then returns an output color (red) using the SV_TARGET semantic that denotes the output as a render target format:

```
float4 PixelShader(float4 Position : SV_POSITION) : SV_TARGET
{
    return float4(1.0f, 0.0f, 0.0f, 1.0f); //red
}
```

The next step is to specify an effect technique definition used for setting the previously defined vertex and pixel shaders. Such an effect technique, starting with the syntax, technique10 to label it as a Direct3D 10 technique, is a set of rendering passes. Each rendering pass specifies the shader states used to render the geometry of a scene. An effect is thus a way for Direct3D to organize the states responsible for setting the stages of the graphics pipeline. The technique10 label is followed by the name of the technique, TechniqueName and the name of the rendering pass, P0, containing the callback function(s) (such as SetPixelShader, SetVertexShader, or SetGeometryShader) used to set the device state from an effect. Other states that can be set include the blend state (SetBlendState) and depth stencil state (SetDepthStencilState). We can create the following effect technique for the above-defined vertex and fragment shaders:

```
technique10 TechniqueName
{
    pass P0
    {
        SetGeometryShader(NULL);
```

```
        SetVertexShader(CompileShader(ps_4_0, VertexShader()));
        SetPixelShader(CompileShader(ps_4_0, PixelShader()));
    }
}
```

The SetPixelShader, SetVertexShader and SetGeometryShader functions take a compiled shader as parameter, setting it to the appropriate render state. The geometry shader is in this case set to 'NULL' because it has not yet been defined. The vertex and pixel shaders, as well as the effect technique, are stored in an effect file (using the '.fx' file extension).

Returning to our Direct3D application, all that remains is to create the effect object and technique object that will be used for performing the rendering operation. We call the D3DX10CreateEffectFromFile function to create an effect from the specified effect file. This D3DX function is specified as follows in the D3DX10Effect.h header file:

```
HRESULT D3DX10CreateEffectFromFile(
        LPCTSTR pFileName,
        CONST D3D10_SHADER_MACRO *pDefines,
        ID3D10Include *pInclude,
        LPCSTR pProfile,
        UINT HLSLFlags,
        UINT FXFlags,
        ID3D10Device *pDevice,
        ID3D10EffectPool *pEffectPool,
        ID3DX10ThreadPump *pPump,
        ID3D10Effect **ppEffect,
        ID3D10Blob **ppErrors
);
```

This function's first parameter, pFileName, takes a pointer to a string containing the name of the effect file. The next parameter, pDefines, takes a pointer to a D3D10_SHADER_MACRO shader macro array with the pInclude parameter requiring a pointer to an ID3D10Include include interface, as previously described. The shader profile, as a string value, is set via the pProfile parameter with the HLSL compilation options being set by the HLSLFlags parameter. The sixth parameter, FXFlags, allows us to set the effect compilation options and it can be set to any of the following D3D10_EFFECT constants:

■ D3D10_EFFECT_COMPILE_CHILD_EFFECT (the '.fx' file is compiled as a child effect, thus not initializing any shared data due to all shared values being set in the effect pool)

■ D3D10_EFFECT_COMPILE_ALLOW_SLOW_OPS (compiles the effect file without performance mode) or

■ D3D10_EFFECT_SINGLE_THREADED (the effect thread is not synchronized with other effects in the effect pool).

An *effect pool* facilitates the sharing of variables, textures, and shaders between different effects.

The next parameter, pDevice, takes a pointer to an ID3D10Device interface that will use the resources to create a shader. The pEffectPool parameter takes a pointer to an ID3D10EffectPool effect pool interface signifying the memory pool used for the sharing of variables and resources between effects. The next parameter, pPump, is a pointer to an ID3DX10ThreadPump thread pump interface used for the asynchronous execution of routines; we will generally set this parameter to 'NULL' so that the D3DX10CreateEffectFromFile function completes its operation before returning. The second last parameter, ppEffect, takes the address of the pointer to the ID3D10Effect created effect. The ID3D10Effect interface is responsible for managing the shaders, state objects, and resources constituting the effect. The ppErrors parameter is set to the address of a pointer to an ID3D10Blob interface. This final parameter is used for storing debug and compile-time error information.

We can create the effect using this D3DX10CreateEffectFromFile function in the following manner:

```
ID3D10Effect* g_id3dEffect = NULL;

D3DX10CreateEffectFromFile(L"file_name.fx", NULL, NULL,
                    D3D10_SHADER_ENABLE_BACKWARDS_COMPATIBILITY,
                    0, g_id3dDevice, NULL, NULL, &g_id3dEffect,
                    NULL);
```

Following the effect creation we must obtain the effect technique using the GetTechniqueByName ID3D10Effect interface function. This function takes a string value containing the name of the technique as parameter, returning a pointer to the ID3D10EffectTechnique interface:

```
ID3D10EffectTechnique* g_id3dTechnique = NULL;

g_id3dTechnique = g_id3dEffect->GetTechniqueByName(
                            "TechniqueName");
```

A useful feature of effects is the ability to define multiple passes (subsets of a technique and a render state set – for example 'P0' in the above-shown technique). We can thus define multiple passes to implement multi-pass rendering. To understand multi-pass rendering, consider the following example. Say we have a geometry object with a texture and we decide to render some three-dimensional mesh on top of it, then we can render and texture the geometry in the first pass with the second pass being responsible for rendering the mesh on top of it. By specifying each phase as a render pass we can render both passes simultaneously during the render loop. Techniques are also useful when designing a shader to run across a vast range of hardware; for example, a technique can be specified using a pixel, vertex and geometry shader for the newest DirectX 10 hardware, while another can be specified to limit the implementation to only vertex and pixel shaders so that the program can run on DirectX 9 hardware.

6.5.4.4 Common HLSL Data Types
Just as the case with Cg, HLSL features all the C++ derived scalar types such as bool, int, float, string, double, uint and half (a 16-bit floating point type). Shader Model 4.0 features two additional types derived from the float type, namely, unorm float (a 32-bit unsigned floating point value normalized to the range $[-1, 1]$) and snorm float (a 32-bit unsigned floating point value normalized to the range $[0, 1]$).

Another parallel between Cg and the HLSL is their use of vector and matrix types. Vector types can contain anything from one to four components with matrix types containing up to 16 components. Matrix types are declared using the form ScalartypeRowxColumn, for example, a floating point matrix, fMatrixVar, consisting out of four rows and three columns can be declared as follows:

```
float4x3 fMatrixVar;
```

This matrix variable can be initialized in the following manner:

```
fMatrixVar = {1.5f, 5.5f, 0.1f,
             0.4f, 0.1f, 2.7f,
             0.3f, 2.6f, 0.2f,
             0.9f, 0.5f, 4.2f };
```

Matrix types can also be declared using the following syntax:

```
matrix <scalar type, number of rows, number of columns>
                        MatrixVariableName
```

We can create the same matrix as the fMatrixVar one defined above using this alternate syntax:

```
matrix <float, 4, 3> fMatrixVar = {1.5f, 5.5f, 0.1f,
                        0.4f, 0.1f, 2.7f,
                        0.3f, 2.6f, 0.2f,
                        0.9f, 0.5f, 4.2f };
```

Vector types are declared using the syntax Scalartype VectorVariableName. For example, a floating point vector holding four components can be declared in the following manner:

```
float4 fVectorVar = {1.5f, 1.7f, 0.5f, 1.0f};
```

There is also, as with matrix types, an alternative syntax for the declaration of vector types:

```
vector <vector type, number of components> VectorVariableName
```

We can create the same vector, fVectorVar, using this alternate syntax:

```
vector <float, 4> fVectorVar = {1.5f, 1.7f, 0.5f, 1.0f};
```

HLSL also allows for the definition of structures in the following manner:

```
struct structName
{
    float variable1;
    int variable2;

    float4 fVectorVar = {1.5f, 1.7f, 0.5f, 1.0f};
    matrix <float, 4, 3> fMatrixVar = {1.5f, 5.5f, 0.1f,
                        0.4f, 0.1f, 2.7f,
                        0.3f, 2.6f, 0.2f,
                        0.9f, 0.5f, 4.2f };
                . . .etc
}
```

The HLSL also supports a number of operators identical to those employed by Cg and clearly inherited from the C programming language. The most commonly used ones are listed in Table 6-9.

6.5.4.5 Utilizing a Created HLSL Effect
After compiling and creating an effect by loading the effect file into the effects framework (using the D3DX10CreateEffectFromFile function), we can proceed to initialize a number of effect constants before setting the effect state. Effects that have not yet been compiled will be compiled when they are loaded into the effects framework. Effect constants and variables are first declared in the effect/shader file(s), for example:

```
int numberOfLightSources;
```

TABLE 6-9   HLSL operators

Operator type	Operators	Usage examples

Additive	+, −	int x = 5;
		int y = 7;
		int z = x − y;
		int k = z + y;

Multiplicative	*, %, /	int x = 5;
		int y = 7;
		int z = x * y;
		float k = z / y;
		int l = z % y;

Array selection	[i]	int array[2] = {3,4}; array[0] = 2;

Assignment	+=, =, *=, −=, %=, /=	int x = 5;
		int y = 7;
		int z += 3;

Bitwise	~, &, |,^ ≪, ≫, ≪=, |=, ≫=, &=, ^=	z≫y //shifts the bits of z right y positions (5 ≫ 2 equals 1)

Boolean	||, &&, ?:	bool a = false;
		bool b = true;
		bool c = a && b;

Comparison	==, !=, <, >, <=, >=	if (diffuseLight <= 0) specularLight = 0;

Prefix/postfix incrementing/ decrementing	++, −−	int x = 0;
		x++;
		−−x;

Type cast	(scalar type)	float x = 0.5;
		int y;
		y = (int)x;

Unary	+, −, !	bool a = true; bool b = !a;

float3 incomingAmbientLightColor[3];
float4 incomingDiffuseLightColor[3];
float3 objectspaceLightPosition[3];

float4x4 modelviewProjection;
float4x4 worldviewProjection;

Texture2D meshTexture;

These variables, declared using the HLSL data types, are set by the Direct3D application. We must thus declare variables in our application that will be used to update the shader variables:

```
int numberOfLights;

D3DXVECTOR3 vIncomingAmbientLightColor [3];
D3DXVECTOR4 vIncomingDiffuseLightColor [3];
D3DXVECTOR3 vObjectspaceLightPosition [3];

D3DXMATRIX mWorldviewProjectionMatrix;
D3DXMATRIX mModelviewProjectionMatrix;
```

Before we can set the HLSL variable values using the ID3D10EffectVariable update methods we first have to obtain the effect variables via ID3D10Effect retrieval functions for each of the above defined shader variables (this operation is similar to the retrieval of technique objects in section 6.5.4.3):

```
ID3D10EffectScalarVariable* g_pNumberOfLightSources;
g_pNumberOfLightSources = g_id3dEffect
            ->GetVariableByName("numberOfLightSources")
                            ->AsScalar();

ID3D10EffectVectorVariable* g_pIncomingAmbientLightColor;
g_pIncomingAmbientLightColor = g_id3dEffect
            ->GetVariableByName("incomingAmbientLightColor")
                            ->AsVector();

ID3D10EffectVectorVariable* g_pIncomingDiffuseLightColor;
g_pIncomingDiffuseLightColor = g_id3dEffect
            ->GetVariableByName("incomingDiffuseLightColor")
                            ->AsVector();

ID3D10EffectVectorVariable* g_pObjectspaceLightPosition;
g_pObjectspaceLightPosition = g_id3dEffect
            ->GetVariableByName("objectspaceLightPosition")
                            ->AsVector();

ID3D10EffectMatrixVariable* g_pWorldviewProjectionMatrix;
g_pWorldviewProjectionMatrix = g_id3dEffect
            ->GetVariableByName("worldviewProjection")
                            ->AsMatrix();

ID3D10EffectMatrixVariable* g_pModelviewProjectionMatrix;
g_pModelviewProjectionMatrix = g_id3dEffect
            ->GetVariableByName("modelviewProjection")
                            ->AsMatrix();

ID3D10EffectShaderResourceVariable* g_pMeshTexture;
g_pMeshTexture = g_id3dEffect
                ->GetVariableByName("meshTexture")
                            ->AsShaderResource();
```

The GetVariableByName ID3D10Effect interface function takes a string value containing the name of the variable declared in the shader/effect program as parameter, returning a pointer to the ID3D10EffectVariable interface. The AsVector ID3D10EffectVariable interface function casts this returned ID3D10EffectVariable interface to an ID3D10EffectVectorVariable interface so that we can access the vector type. The AsScalar interface function casts the returned interface to an ID3D10EffectScalarVariable interface used for accessing a scalar variable with the AsMatrix function casting it to an ID3D10EffectMatrixVariable interface so that we can read the shader variable as a matrix type.

Other frequently used ID3D10EffectVariable interface casting methods include:

- AsBlend (casts to an ID3D10EffectBlendVariable interface used for accessing blend-state variables)

- AsDepthStencil (casts to an ID3D10EffectDepthStencilVariable interface used for accessing depth stencil variables)

- AsRasterizer (casts to an ID3D10EffectRasterizerVariable interface used for accessing rasterizer-state variables)

- AsShader (casts to an ID3D10EffectShaderVariable interface used for accessing shader variables)

- AsShaderResource (casts to an ID3D10EffectShaderResourceVariable interface used for accessing shader-resource variables) and

- AsString (casts to an ID3D10EffectStringVariable interface used for accessing string variables).

We can now set the values of the shader/effect variables using the following ID3D10EffectVariable, ID3D10EffectVectorVariable, ID3D10EffectMatrixVariable and ID3D10EffectScalarVariable methods:

- SetRawValue for generic array items

- SetFloatVectorArray for four-component vector arrays containing floating point elements

- SetBoolVectorArray for four-component vector arrays containing Boolean elements

- SetIntVector for four-component vectors containing integer elements

- SetIntVectorArray for four-component vector arrays containing integer elements

- SetMatrix for a floating-point matrix

- SetMatrixArray for an array of floating-point matrices

- SetFloat for normal floating-point variables and

- SetInt for integer variables:

```
g_pNumberOfLightSources->SetInt(numberOfLights);

g_pIncomingAmbientLightColor
                ->SetRawValue(vIncomingAmbientLightColor, 0,
                        sizeof(D3DXVECTOR3) * 3);

g_pIncomingDiffuseLightColor->SetFloatVectorArray(
                (float*)vIncomingDiffuseLightColor,
                0, 3);

g_pObjectspaceLightPosition->SetFloatVectorArray(
                (float*)vObjectspaceLightPosition,
                0, 3);

g_pWorldviewProjectionMatrix->SetMatrix(
                (float*)&mWorldviewProjectionMatrix));

g_pModelviewProjectionMatrix->SetMatrix(
                (float*)&mModelviewProjectionMatrix));
```

The SetInt ID3D10EffectScalarVariable function takes a pointer to an integer variable as parameter. The SetRawValue ID3D10EffectVariable function has three parameters, the first taking a pointer to the variable being set, the second specifying the offset in bytes from the beginning of the input data being set and the third the number of bytes to set from the offset value. The ID3D10EffectVectorVariable SetFloatVectorArray method also takes three parameters as input, namely, a pointer to the first element of a vector array, the vector offset from the start of the array to the first vector that is to be set, and the number of array elements, in that order. The SetMatrix ID3D10EffectMatrixVariable interface function sets a floating-point matrix and is passed a pointer to the first element of a matrix as parameter.

That is it, the values declared in the shader program are now set and can be changed during each rendering pass. The final step is to set the effect state within the device itself. This is done by invoking the effect state from within the render loop by selecting a technique and subsequently setting the state for each of the passes. The code performing this task, given here, is fully explained in section 6.2.

We start by calling the GetDesc ID3D10EffectTechnique function on the previously defined technique object which is used for storing the returned D3D10_TECHNIQUE_DESC structure, i.e. the structure describing the technique:

```
ID3D10EffectTechnique* g_pd3d10EffectTechnique = NULL;

/*   obtain the D3D10_TECHNIQUE_DESC effect-variable
     description */
D3D10_TECHNIQUE_DESC technique;
g_pd3d10EffectTechnique->GetDesc(&technique);
```

The GetPassByIndex ID3D10EffectTechnique interface method is now called to acquire an effect pass object representing the first pass of the technique:

```
/* apply the effect state by looping over the number of
   technique passes */
for(int i = 0; i < technique.Passes; ++i)
{
    g_pd3d10EffectTechnique->GetPassByIndex(i)->Apply(0);
    . . .etc
}
```

We will continue our discussion of the High Level Shader Language throughout many of the examples to follow, such as those dealing with High Dynamic Range lighting, stencil shadow volumes, bump mapping, cube mapping (illustrating geometric shaders), adding specular highlights to objects, and so forth. We will similarly continue our discussion of the Cg shader language in subsequent chapters.

6.6   SUMMARY

In this chapter we started by introducing primitives such as vertices, lines, surfaces, and polygons as simple geometric elements used in the construction of more complex geometric objects. We subsequently discussed each of the main primitive and polygon types, as supported by Direct3D and OpenGL, followed by the rendering of stroke- and raster-based text. Building on this, we focused on the drawing of primitives and polygons using both Direct3D and OpenGL.

Next we considered a number of Direct3D render states, specifically how Direct3D 10 makes use of state objects to set the state for each of the pipeline stages, thus in turn controlling the manner in which images are generated and displayed. We specifically investigated five possible state object groups: the rasterizer state, the input-layout state, the blend state, the depth stencil state and the sampler state including a number of associated Direct3D structures and pipeline stages.

Following this we looked at the Direct3D Utility Framework, or DXUT, providing a vast array of functionality, from basic window creation, Direct3D device initialization and the control of these components, to more advanced elements such as 3D mesh control, camera control, and the creation of graphical user interfaces. The process of window creation and control using the DXUT framework was subsequently compared to the native win32/Direct3D procedure described in Chapter 4.

The remainder of the chapter focused on shader programming, starting with an introduction to vertex, pixel and geometry shaders. This introduction also outlined the relation between graphics hardware advancements and the capabilities of shader programs. We then revisited the hardware graphics pipeline, expanding on our previous discussion by focusing more on the programmable graphics pipeline's physical organization. Following this discussion we also built on our previous discussion of the programmable graphics pipeline by investigating the underlying hardware configuration that makes the pipeline stages of a GPU programmable. Next we discussed the Cg high-level programming language, developed for the programming of vertex and pixel shaders, in detail. Our primary focus was on concepts such as Cg language profiles, the Cg compiler, the Cg runtime, and the initialization of Cg for both Direct3D and OpenGL. This section closed with two examples detailing the use of Cg to create both a vertex and fragment program for the real-time calculation of per-vertex and per-pixel lighting, respectively.

The chapter concluded with a discussion of Microsoft's High Level Shader Language, a proprietary Direct3D shading language analogous to NVIDIA's Cg, used for the creation of three types of shader programs: vertex shaders, geometry shaders and pixel shaders. This discussion looked at elements such as the HLSL compiler, a number of HLSL data types, initialization of the High Level Shader Language, creation of HLSL shaders and the utilization of a created HLSL effect.

The next chapter deals with viewing and transformations, specifically describing the mathematical representation of objects in a three-dimensional environment and defining the virtual camera model essential for perspective and orthographic projections. Furthermore, Chapter 7 focuses on the mechanisms used for changing coordinate systems, including various transformation techniques such as rotation, translation and scaling.

6.7   FURTHER READING

A great textbook dealing with shader programming is *The Cg Tutorial: The Definitive Guide to Programmable Real-Time Graphics by Randima Fernando and Mark J. Kilgard* (ISBN: 0321194969). *GPU Gems 2: Programming Techniques for High-Performance Graphics and General-Purpose Computation by Matt Pharr and Randima Fernando* (ISBN: 0321335597), and *GPU Gems 3 by Hubert Nguyen* (ISBN: 0321515269) also serve as great books for all the latest graphics processing unit programming techniques.

Once again, documentation for the DirectX application programming interface is provided with each SDK distribution and available from Microsoft's msdn2.microsoft.com website with the OpenGL reference pages being available from the official OpenGL website (www.opengl.org).

6.8   EXERCISES

1   When can a polygon be classified as convex and under what conditions is it considered concave?

2   Why would the use of triangle and quadrilateral strips lead to significant performance increases when compared to the use of arbitrary polygon types?

3   Briefly describe the difference between a D3D10_PRIMITIVE_TOPOLOGY_TRIANGLELIST and a D3D10_PRIMITIVE_TOPOLOGY_TRIANGLELIST_ADJ primitive type as specified by the D3D10_PRIMITIVE_TOPOLOGY enumerator.

4   Write a simple OpenGL program to render any raster-based text string.

5   Write a Direct3D program using the ID3DX10Font Direct3D Extension (D3DX) interface to render the string 'Hello World!'.

6   Explain the process of accessing data from Direct3D vertex buffers.

7   Why do we initialize the subresource description structure?

8   What is the GetDesc ID3D10EffectTechnique function used for?

9   Explain the purpose of OpenGL vertex lists.

10 Describe the purpose of the following code sample:

```
glDrawElements(GL_POLYGON, 4, GL_UNSIGNED_BYTE,
               &pyramidIndices[0]);
```

11 What is the depth stencil state Direct3D object used for?

12 Give a code snippet that creates a blend state object.

13 Write a program that creates a window using the DXUT framework.

14 Briefly highlight the main differences between a vertex, pixel and geometry shader.

15 Explain the primary advantages of the unified shader architecture.

16 Shortly describe each of the Direct3D and OpenGL raster processing operations.

17 Compare the flow of control for a programmable vertex processor with that of a programmable fragment processor.

18 Why would one rather program graphics hardware using a high-level language such as Cg or the HLSL as opposed to using assembly language?

19 What is a Cg language profile?

20 Shortly describe the organization of the Cg runtime and related libraries.

21 Modify the vertex program in section 6.5.3.5 to generate blue per-vertex lighting instead of its standard white.

22 Modify the fragment program in section 6.5.3.6 to generate red per-fragment lighting instead of its standard white.

23 Briefly describe the HLSL common shader core architecture.

24 What is the purpose of the D3D10CompileShader and CreateVertexShader shader functions?

25   Why do we specify effect technique definitions?

26 Describe the purpose of the following code sample:

```
ID3D10EffectVectorVariable* g_pIncomingAmbientLightColor;
g_pIncomingAmbientLightColor = g_id3dEffect
        ->GetVariableByName("incomingAmbientLightColor")
                            ->AsVector();
```

CHAPTER 7

Viewing and Transformations

LEARNING OBJECTIVES

In this chapter you will learn about:

- 3D Cartesian coordinate systems
- The synthetic-camera model
- The viewing system
- The view volume
- Culling
- Clipping
- Changing coordinate systems
- Viewing transformations
- The modeling/world transformation
- The projection transformation
- The viewport transformation
- Spatial transformations
- Translation
- Rotation
- Scaling
- Drawing a triangle without any transformations
- Drawing a triangle translated
- Drawing a triangle rotated
- Drawing a triangle scaled

INTRODUCTION

Chapter 7 describes the mathematical representation of objects in a three-dimensional environment. It includes the definition of the virtual camera model essential for perspective and orthographic projections. Furthermore, Chapter 7 focuses on the mechanisms used for changing coordinate systems, including various transformation techniques such as rotation, translation, and scaling. The chapter concludes with a number of examples implementing the presented theory.

7.1   3D CARTESIAN COORDINATE SYSTEMS

The field of mathematics identifies several coordinate systems, each allowing the representation of arbitrary points in space. However, the field of computer graphics relies heavily on vector calculations and matrix transformations. These calculations, along with the Cartesian coordinate system, are based on numbers indicating distances. The Cartesian coordinate system is consequently the most fundamental system for the unique identification of arbitrary points in space. This section investigates two kinds of Cartesian coordinate systems: two- and three-dimensional.

A two-dimensional Cartesian coordinate system consists of an origin intersected by two axes perpendicular to each other. The vertical axis is known as the *y*-axis and the horizontal axis, the *x*-axis. Figure 7-1 illustrates such a coordinate system. The coordinates of a vertex are written in the form (*x, y*) – specified by an *abscissa* (*x*-coordinate), and *ordinate* (*y*-coordinate).

The three-dimensional Cartesian coordinate system provides an additional dimension for spatial measurement by means of a diagonal *z*-axis (Figure 7-2). Vertex coordinates are written in the form (*x, y, z*), with *xy*-, *xz*-, and *yz*-planes dividing the coordinate space into eight areas (Figure 7-3).

Original graphics systems required the implicit specification of objects in terms of display device coordinates. This created numerous porting complexities. Not only did we need to define vertices in terms of physical screen pixel coordinates, but object distances also had to be scaled accurately. Although based on Cartesian coordinates, these systems didn't have great practical value. The introduction of *device independent graphics* afforded developers freedom from these device specific details.

Device independent coordinate systems function on the principle of translating between *world* and *device* or *screen coordinates* (the coordinate system used by the graphics display). World coordinates are user-defined and application specific. The graphics system is responsible for converting between world and screen coordinates. This ensures

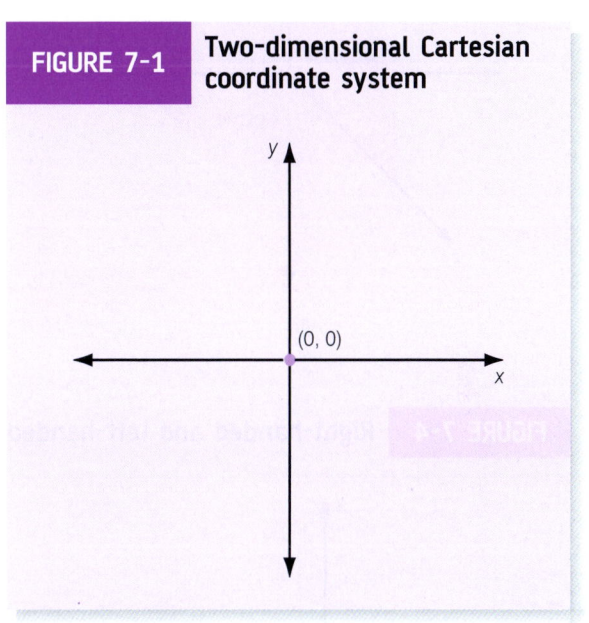

FIGURE 7-1   **Two-dimensional Cartesian coordinate system**

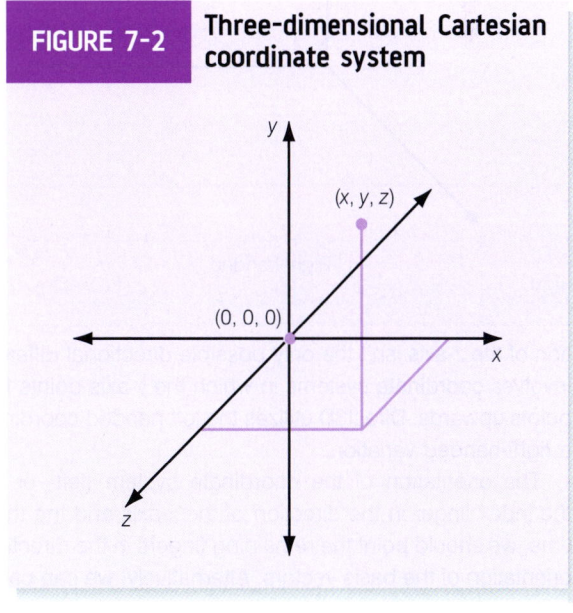

FIGURE 7-2   **Three-dimensional Cartesian coordinate system**

7

FIGURE 7-3	Three-dimensional Cartesian coordinate planes

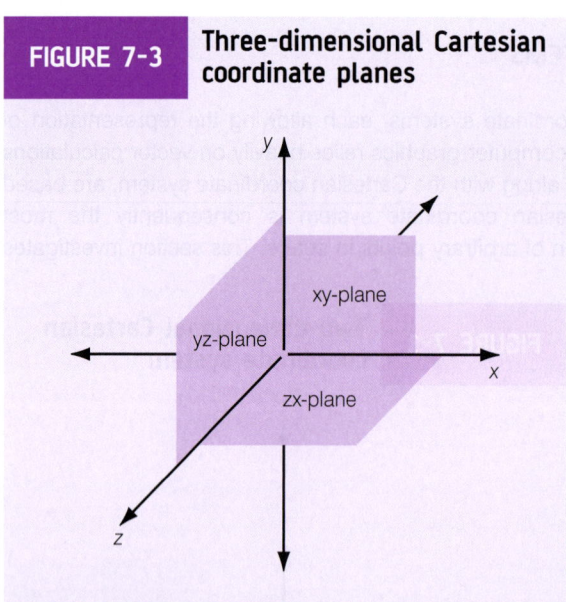

consistency across numerous hardware devices. When talking about transformations we are simply referring to the process of switching between different coordinate systems. Coordinate system changes are represented by matrices, with a *transformation matrix* representing a series of translations, rotations and/or scaling operations.

Graphics systems are primarily based on either the left-handed or right-handed Cartesian coordinate system. The pointing direction of the positive z-axis is the only variation between these two coordinate systems. The *left-handed* coordinate system's z-axis points away from the viewer, with this axis pointing towards the viewer for the *right-handed* coordinate system. Figure 7-4 illustrates the aforementioned directional difference. However, the orienta-

FIGURE 7-4	Right-handed and left-handed Cartesian coordinate systems

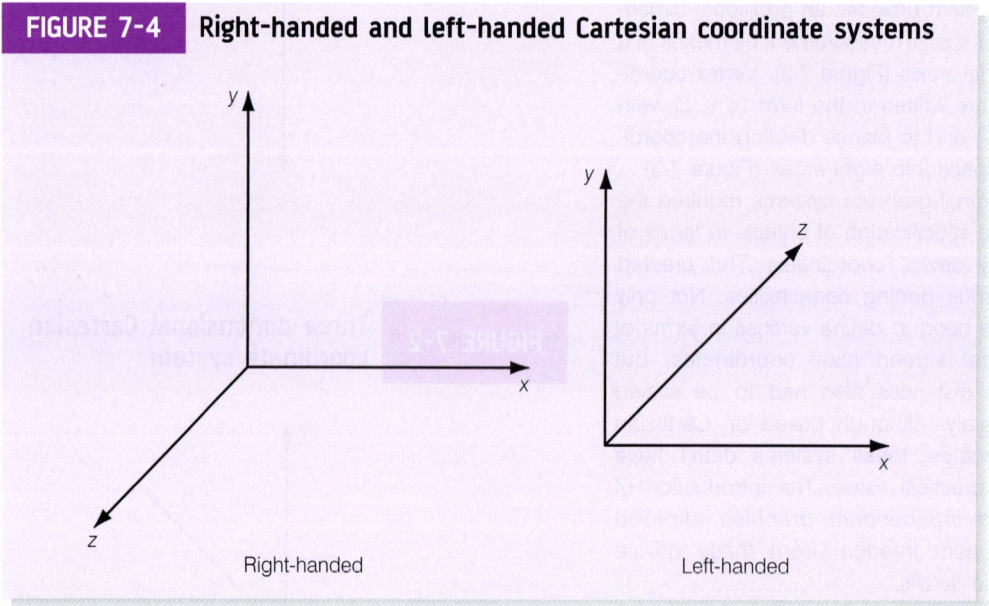

tion of the z-axis isn't the only possible directional difference. Another frequently encountered variation involves coordinate systems in which the y-axis points towards or away from the viewer and the z-axis points upwards. Direct3D utilizes the left-handed coordinate system by default, with OpenGL employing a right-handed variation.

The orientation of the coordinate system (left- or right-handed) can be calculated by pointing the index finger in the direction of the x-axis and the thumb in the direction of the z-axis. At the same time, we should point the remaining fingers in the direction of the y-axis. This allows us to determine the orientation of the basis vectors. Alternatively, we can calculate the determinant of the matrix defined by the set of basis vectors. A positive determinant identifies a right-handed coordinate system, with a negative determinant identifying a left-handed coordinate system. Please refer to the linear algebra appendix for more information regarding the calculation of determinants.

7.2 THE SYNTHETIC-CAMERA MODEL

The Synthetic-Camera Model is an optical imaging paradigm for three-dimensional computer graphics. This paradigm is based on the *pinhole camera model* where image formation is a simple process based on a film plane located at a distance, *s*, from an opening (the *pinhole*). The pinhole allows only a single ray of light to enter. If the pinhole is located exactly at the origin of our three-dimensional Cartesian coordinate system, then we can calculate where a certain image would be rendered on the *film plane*. Figure 7-5 illustrates such a pinhole camera oriented along the *x*-axis.

The image rendered on the film plane is called the *projection* of an object in space with the *field of view* (FOV) controlling the largest possible object fully viewable on the film plane. Computer graphics are based on the principle of infinite *depth of field*. Depth of field determines the number of objects in the field of view that are in focus.

The synthetic camera model adds several principles to the pinhole camera model for the representation of artificial images. Firstly, it stresses the independence between objects and the viewer. Additionally, it introduces a second projection plane called the *virtual image plane*, which is located in front of the lens. With the pinhole camera model, images are rendered upside down. This is in contrast with the synthetic camera model, which eliminates the flipping of images. Figure 7-6 illustrates image formation using the virtual image plane.

FIGURE 7-5 **Pinhole camera model**

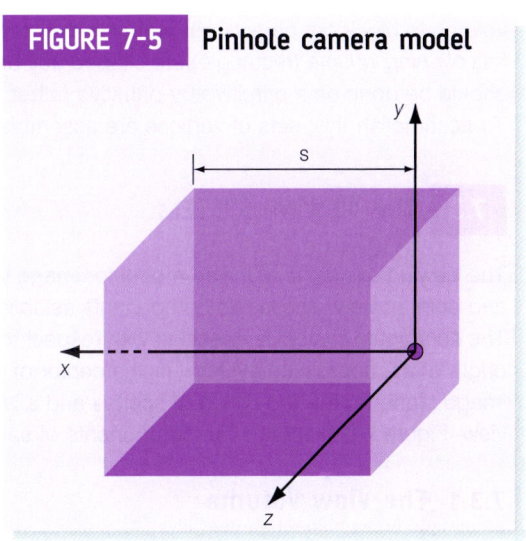

FIGURE 7-6 **Rendering an image on the virtual image plane**

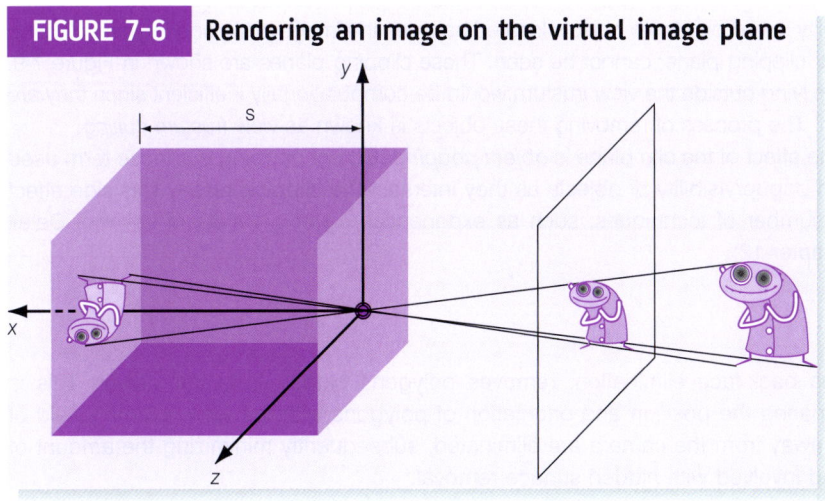

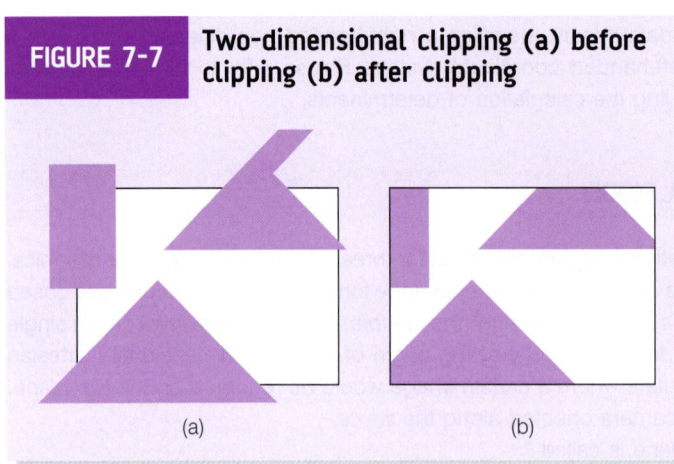

FIGURE 7-7   Two-dimensional clipping (a) before clipping (b) after clipping

(a)   (b)

The rays originating from the image and terminating at the film plane are called *projectors*. These projectors enter the camera through the *center of projection* (COP).

The virtual image plane is also responsible for controlling the clipping of observed objects. Clipping allows us to set up the field of view. For example, changing our field of view from 90 degrees to 20 degrees will create the effect of zooming into an object. We define a clipping volume to block out objects not visible to the viewer. All objects and portions of objects falling outside this *clipping volume* (rectangle) are clipped out, and thus do not appear in the viewable image. Clipping should be done on a primitive-by-primitive rather than a vertex-by-vertex basis, as shown in Figure 7-7. To accomplish this, sets of vertices are assembled into primitives, such as polygons and lines.

7.3   THE VIEWING SYSTEM

The viewing system is a unified model for image visualization and consists of a view coordinate system and point of view. These two components establish the viewer's position in terms of world coordinates. The coordinate system is specified with respect to this point of view. The *point of view* can either be the origin of the coordinate system, or the center of projection. The viewing system must also contain an image plane for the projection of scenes and a *view frustum/volume* for the specification of the field of view. Figure 7-8 illustrates the components of such a viewing system.

7.3.1 The View Volume

The view frustum/volume is a semi-infinite, truncated pyramid defined by an image plane window and a near and far clipping plane. These clipping planes are positioned perpendicular to the viewing direction and determine the visibility cut-off points. All objects located between the image plane and the near clipping plane, or beyond the far clipping plane, cannot be seen. These clipping planes are shown in Figure 7-9. The rendering of objects lying outside the view frustum would be computationally inefficient since they are not visible to begin with. The process of removing these objects is known as *view frustum culling*.

One quite visible side effect of the clip plane is *object popping*. Object popping is a loose term used to describe the sudden popup/visibility of objects as they intersect the clipping plane. This side effect can be masked by a number of techniques, such as exponential fog or a variety of Level of Detail algorithms (refer to Chapter 12).

7.3.2 Culling

Culling, also known as back-face elimination, removes polygons hidden from the viewer. This is accomplished by comparing the position and orientation of polygons with the view volume's field of view. Polygons facing away from the camera are eliminated, subsequently minimizing the amount of computational overhead involved with hidden surface removal.

A culling test is based on a simple vector calculation, namely, the dot product between the polygon's normal and the line-of-sight vector (the vector from the center of projection to the polygon). If the result of the dot product is positive then we can flag the polygon as visible (with its normal facing towards the viewer). On average, nearly 50 percent of polygons are back-facing. This stresses the importance of performing a culling test prior to the application of any hidden-surface removal algorithm.

To enable culling in Direct3D we create a D3D10_RASTERIZER_DESC render state structure with its CullMode value set to D3D10_CULL_NONE if we want to render all faces, D3D10_CULL_FRONT for the culling of all front-facing polygons, or D3D10_CULL_BACK to cull all back-facing polygons. This render state structure is passed as a parameter to the CreateRasterizerState method, with the second

FIGURE 7-8   **The viewing system**

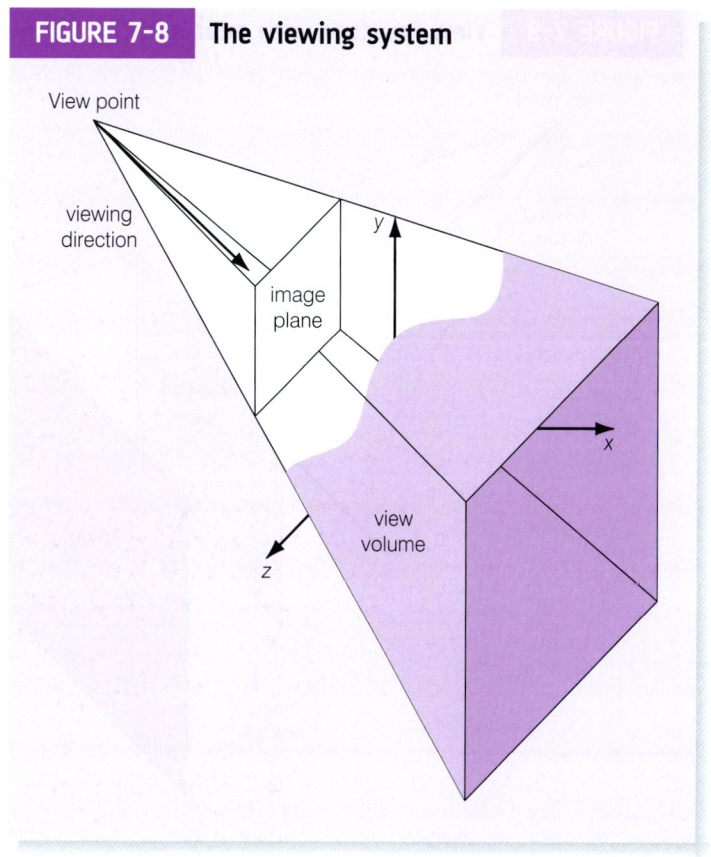

parameter, the ID3D10RasterizerState interface, containing behavioural information about the rasterizer stage. The ID3D10RasterizerState interface and D3D10_RASTERIZER_DESC render state structure are subsequently declared as:

```
ID3D10RasterizerState * generalRasterizerState;
D3D10_RASTERIZER_DESC generalRasterState;
```

Next we initialize the members of the D3D10_RASTERIZER_DESC structure:

```
generalRasterState.FillMode = D3D10_FILL_WIREFRAME;
generalRasterState.CullMode = D3D10_CULL_FRONT;
generalRasterState.FrontCounterClockwise = true;
generalRasterState.DepthBias = false;
generalRasterState.DepthBiasClamp = 0;
generalRasterState.SlopeScaledDepthBias = 0;
generalRasterState.DepthClipEnable = true;
generalRasterState.ScissorEnable = true;
generalRasterState.MultisampleEnable = false;
generalRasterState.AntialiasedLineEnable = false;
```

The FillMode member sets the polygon's rendering mode to either wire-frame (D3D10_FILL_WIREFRAME) or solid (D3D10_FILL_SOLID). The FrontCounterClockwise member specifies whether the polygons will be rendered

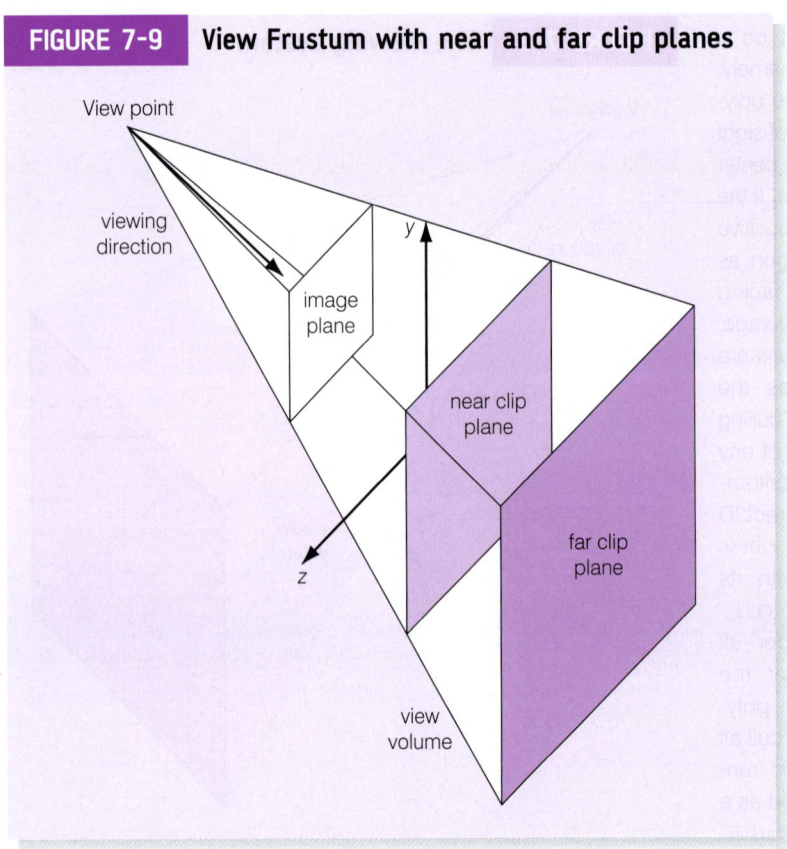

FIGURE 7-9   **View Frustum with near and far clip planes**

as front-facing (true) or back-facing (false). DepthBias controls the depth value added to a particular pixel with DepthBiasClamp setting the maximum pixel bias and SlopeScaledDepthBias the pixel's slope scalar. DepthClipEnable determines whether distance based clipping is enabled (true) or disabled (false) with ScissorEnable setting the scissor rectangle and MultisampleEnable setting multisample antialiasing. The final member, AntialiasedLineEnable, sets line-based antialiasing (if multisampling isn't selected).

And finally we create the rasterizer state object:

```
(D3DDevice)->CreateRasterizerState(&generalRasterState,
                          &generalRasterizerState);
```

All that remains now is to set the device like this:

```
(D3DDevice)->RSSetState(generalRasterizerState);
```

Working with OpenGL

The glCullFace function enables back-face elimination using the GL_BACK flag and front-face elimination using the GL_FRONT flag. Before, however, calling this function, we first need to specify our polygons as either front-facing (GL_CCW) or back-facing (GL_CW) using the glFrontFace function.

Usage example:

```
glFrontFace(GL_CCW);
glCullFace(GL_BACK);
```

Occlusion culling is another frequently used culling operation for determining the parts of objects obscured by other objects and thus hidden from the viewer. The *painter's algorithm* is the most common occlusion algorithm. This algorithm is based on the concept of 'painting' the most distant polygons first, followed by the progressive addition of polygons as the viewer is approached. Polygons are thus sorted and drawn from back to front. *Z* buffering, sometimes referred to as depth buffering, stores the depth values for each pixel being drawn and it is the most widespread occlusion culling technique, enabling the masking of pixels with depth values less than that of the pixel being rendered. Section 12.2 describes the mathematics behind these hidden-surface removal algorithms in detail.

7.3.3 Clipping

Section 7.2 introduced clipping as an optimization operation responsible for the display of only visible objects. Clipping takes place in either the image space, object space or in both. *Image space clipping* is pixel-based and occurs during the rasterization phase. It defines a clipping filter operating on a pixel-by-pixel basis, determining whether a particular pixel lies within the specified viewport or not. Although image space clipping works extremely well for pixel elements, it is highly inefficient for large polygon-based objects. *Object space clipping* is plane-based in object space and boundary-based in screen space. When working in the object space, we have to convert our view space boundaries to an object space clipping plane, subsequently testing for the visibility of vertices inside this clipping plane. We can alternatively clip against screen boundaries while in screen space by flagging the intersection of objects with planes adjacent to the *x*-, *y*- and *z*-axes. Section 12.3 presents several clipping algorithms and techniques such as simple line clipping, Liang-Barsky clipping, Cohen-Sutherland clipping, the clipping of polygons and three-dimensional clipping.

7.4 CHANGING COORDINATE SYSTEMS

It's often necessary to define geometry in terms of a coordinate system innately fitting the representation of a model. Such a coordinate system is referred to as the *object* or *model frame* (also known as *model space*) where vertices are defined relative to the modeling coordinate system's origin. This model frame must be converted to the *world frame* (all vertices are defined relative to a mutual origin) for proper model representation. Once we've converted the model frame to the world frame we still have no idea how these models would appear to the camera. To accomplish this we need to change the coordinate system from the world frame to the *camera* or *view frame* with the viewer at the origin of the camera's lens looking in the positive *z* direction. This switch in coordinate systems is accomplished with the world and view matrices via the viewing transformation for Direct3D and the model-view matrix for OpenGL. Figure 7-10 illustrates the world and model frame.

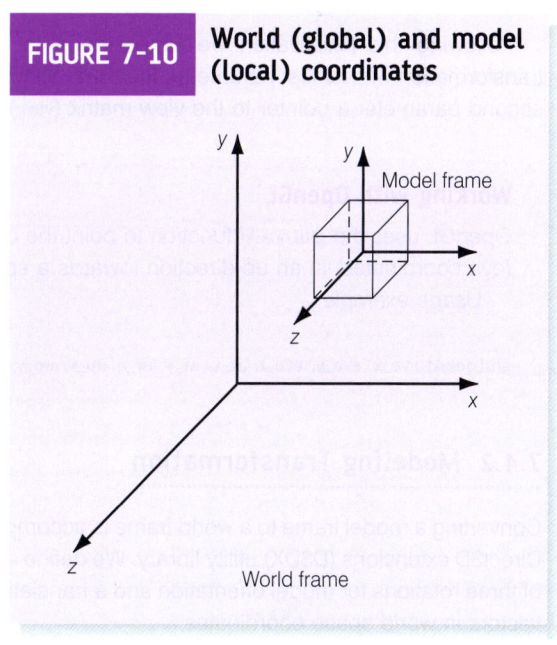

FIGURE 7-10 **World (global) and model (local) coordinates**

7.4.1 Viewing Transformation

A camera's position is specified through the center of projection, the camera's orientation about the center of projection's origin, the focal length determining the size of the rendered image and the height and width of the film plane. The viewer's orientation and position are specified through a series of transformations. These transformations convert object coordinates defining object vertices to object coordinates with their origin at the center of projection.

Direct3D creates a view matrix (*view transformation*) using the camera's location and look-at point. A camera located at the center of projection (*eye coordinates*) is pointed in an 'up' direction towards a specific 'at' location.

The D3DXVECTOR3 structure is used to denote the coordinates of a vector in three-dimensional space. The first parameter represents the *x*-coordinate, the second the *y*-coordinate and the third the *z*-coordinate:

```
D3DXVECTOR3 eye(4,6,6);
D3DXVECTOR3 at(0,0,0);
D3DXVECTOR3 up(0,1,0);
```

Having defined these camera coordinates we need to define the view matrix. It is this view matrix that converts object coordinates to center of projection object coordinates. A view matrix can be created with either the D3DXMatrixLookAtLH (for a left-handed look-at matrix) or the D3DXMatrixLookAtRH (for a right-handed look-at matrix) helper function. The D3DXMATRIX structure stores the result of this operation and it must be declared before the D3DXMatrixLookAtLH helper function can be called:

```
D3DXMATRIX view;
```

The right-handed look-at matrix is initialized with the previously declared D3DXMATRIX structure, the eye coordinates defining the center of projection, the look-at point and the up-direction:

```
D3DXMatrixLookAtRH(&view, &eye, &at, &up);
```

Following this initialization we simply need to call the SetTransform callback function to set the transformation with its first parameter, the D3DTS_VIEW constant, specifying a view transformation and the second parameter a pointer to the view matrix (view).

Working with OpenGL

OpenGL uses the gluLookAt function to point the camera from a certain center of projection point (eye coordinates) in an up-direction towards a specific look-at point:
  Usage example:

```
gluLookAt(eye_x, eye_y, eye_z, at_x, at_y, at_z, up_x, up_y, up_z);
```

7.4.2 Modeling Transformation

Converting a model frame to a world frame is accomplished through the helper functions included in the Direct3D extensions (D3DX) utility library. We define a world matrix (*world transformation*) comprised out of three rotations for model orientation and a translation operation to reposition the model frame's basis vectors in world space coordinates.

We start by defining a matrix, TempRotationMatrix, for the temporary storage of our rotation operations and FinRotationMatrix for the final rotation matrix:

```
D3DXMATRIX TempRotationMatrix;
D3DXMATRIX FinRotationMatrix;
```

D3DXMATRIX* pTranslateMatrix is our initialized translation matrix with the mod_xCoord, mod_yCoord and mod_zCoord variables containing the model's world coordinates.

Next we apply the translation to the object's world position with the function D3DXMatrixTranslation, creating the translation matrix and D3DXMatrixIdentity specifying an identity matrix:

```
D3DXMatrixTranslation(pTranslateMatrix, mod_xCoord, mod_yCoord,
                    mod_zCoord);
D3DXMatrixIdentity(&FinRotationMatrix);
```

Following this, we apply our axial rotations to the world matrix, first by rotating about the *x*-axis, then the *y*-axis and finally the *z*-axis.

Define a matrix that rotates around the *x*-axis:

```
D3DXMatrixRotationX(&MatTemp, model_rotateAngleX);
```

Combine the matrix product:

```
D3DXMatrixMultiply(&FinRotationMatrix, &FinRotationMatrix,
                &TempRotationMatrix);
```

Define a matrix that rotates around the *y*-axis:

```
D3DXMatrixRotationY(&TempRotationMatrix, model_rotateAngleY);
```

Combine the matrix product:

```
D3DXMatrixMultiply(&FinRotationMatrix, & FinRotationMatrix,
                &TempRotationMatrix);
```

Define a matrix that rotates around the *z*-axis:

```
D3DXMatrixRotationZ(&TempRotationMatrix, model_rotateAngleZ);
```

Combine the matrix product:

```
D3DXMatrixMultiply(&FinRotationMatrix, &FinRotationMatrix,
                &TempRotationMatrix);
```

And finally, to complete the world matrix, apply the above calculated final rotation matrix to our initialized translation matrix by determining the product of the two matrices:

```
D3DXMatrixMultiply(pTranslateMatrix, &FinRotationMatrix,
                pTranslateMatrix);
```

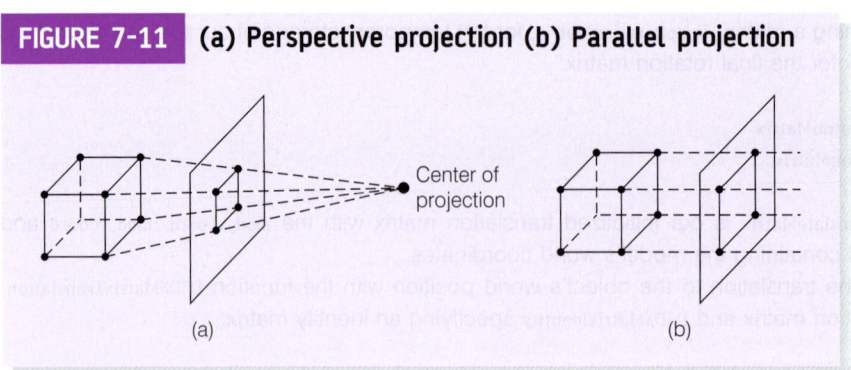

FIGURE 7-11   (a) Perspective projection (b) Parallel projection

(a)   (b)

Center of projection

With the world transformation matrix defined, we simply need to call the SetTransform callback function to set it. This function takes the transformation type that should be applied to the matrix and the transformation matrix itself as parameters. The first parameter, determining the transformation type, must be set to the D3DTS_WORLDMATRIX macro.

7.4.3 Projection Transformation

Any image or scene rendered with a computer (on a flat surface) is strictly speaking two-dimensional in nature. The interpretation of these images is thus a matter of perspective and visualization. Computer graphics utilize a specific class of projections known as planar geometric projections. Perspective and parallel projections form part of this projection class and are illustrated in Figure 7-11.

Once we've converted from model space to world space via the world transformation matrix and from world space to view space using the view transformation matrix, we need to translate these view space coordinates to projection space using the *projection transformation*.

Perspective projections are based on the concept of *foreshortening*. Foreshortening refers to the decreasing size of objects as their distance from the center of projection increases. This foreshortening effect enables the perception of three-dimensional depth on a two-dimensional surface.

A parallel or orthographic projection is based on the notion of parallel projectors with the center of projection replaced by a *direction of projection*. Parallel projection is achieved by moving the camera infinitely far from the viewing plane. However, the term 'infinite' clearly indicates computational difficulty and when implementing this type of projection we simply start with projectors parallel to one of the axes. In a practical sense we simply perform an orthographic projection transformation operation, converting the viewing frustum's truncated pyramid shape into a cubic shape. The viewing frustum's origin is also moved to the center of the camera position. We use the default truncated pyramid shape of the viewing frustum for perspective viewing, while converting it to a cubic shape for parallel projections.

To set up a standard perspective projection in Direct3D we can use one of six D3DX utility functions, the most common being the D3DXMatrixPerspectiveLH function. This function defines a left-handed perspective projection matrix, with the first parameter a pointer to a D3DXMATRIX structure storing the result of the operation, the second the near-view plane's width, and the third this view plane's height. The final two parameters are respectively the z-values of the near and far view-planes. Alternative functions include:

- D3DXMatrixPerspectiveRH (for a right-handed perspective projection matrix),

- D3DXMatrixPerspectiveFovLH (for a left-handed perspective projection matrix based on a field of view and aspect ratio)

- D3DXMatrixPerspectiveFovRH (for a right-handed perspective projection matrix based on a field of view and aspect ratio)

- D3DXMatrixPerspectiveOffCenterLH (for a custom left-handed perspective projection matrix) and

- D3DXMatrixPerspectiveOffCenterRH (for a custom right-handed perspective projection matrix).

Let's look at the conversion from a perspective to an orthographic projection. First we define the distance between the center of projection and the origin of the view transformation space as *S*. The projection matrix is subsequently defined as:

$$\begin{bmatrix} 1 & 0 & 0 & 0 \\ 0 & 1 & 0 & 0 \\ 0 & 0 & 1 & 1/S \\ 0 & 0 & 0 & 1 \end{bmatrix}$$

Next we move the camera to the origin (−*S* units via the *z* axis) with the following translation matrix:

$$\begin{bmatrix} 1 & 0 & 0 & 0 \\ 0 & 1 & 0 & 0 \\ 0 & 0 & 1 & 0 \\ 0 & 0 & -S & 1 \end{bmatrix}$$

Finally we multiply these two matrices to give us the final projection matrix:

$$\begin{bmatrix} 1 & 0 & 0 & 0 \\ 0 & 1 & 0 & 0 \\ 0 & 0 & 1 & 1/S \\ 0 & 0 & -S & 0 \end{bmatrix}$$

This perspective projection transformation only considers the camera's distance to the near clipping plane, not dealing with the field of view and depth comparisons at all. The following matrix resolves these issues:

$$\begin{bmatrix} W & 0 & 0 & 0 \\ 0 & H & 0 & 0 \\ 0 & 0 & S & 1 \\ 0 & 0 & -SZn & 0 \end{bmatrix} \text{with}: W = \frac{2(Z_n)}{(ViewportWidth)}, H = \frac{2(Z_n)}{(ViewportHeight)}, S = \frac{Z_f}{Zf - Zn}$$

W and *H* represent the *x*- and *y*-scaling coefficients for a scene's objects. These scaling coefficients control the size of objects based on their distance from the center of projection to the near clipping plane with *ViewportWidth* and *ViewportHeight* representing the viewport's width and height respectively. A *viewport* is a window located inside a viewing volume. An application is not limited to one viewport and each viewport can have its own input handling and menu system. Z_n is the position (*z* value) of the near clipping plane.

To set up a projection matrix we first need to define the distance to the near (near_planeDistance) and far (far_planeDistance) clipping planes, including the horizontal (viewport_width) and vertical (viewport_height) viewport dimensions. We can then use these values to initialize our perspective projection matrix:

```
float W = ((2*near_planeDistance)/(viewport_width));
float H = ((2*far_planeDistance)/(viewport_height));
float S = far_planeDistance/(far_planeDistance −
        near_planeDistance);
```

Next we define the perspective projection matrix, perspective, using the D3DXMATRIX data structure. Following this, we fill a memory block with zeros using the SecureZeroMemory function. This function takes a pointer to the starting address of the memory block as its first parameter and the size of the memory block to fill with zeros as its second parameter:

```
D3DXMATRIX perspective;
SecureZeroMemory(&ret, sizeof(ret));
```

With all the variables and parameters set, we can initialize the perspective projection matrix:

```
perspective(0, 0) = W;
perspective(1, 1)  = H;
perspective(2, 2) = S;
perspective(3, 2) = -S*planeDistance;
perspective(2, 3) = 1;
```

Now, with the orthographic perspective projection matrix initialized, we simply need to call the SetTranform callback function to set it. The first parameter must be set to the D3DTS_PROJECTION constant, indicating the transformation matrix as a projection transformation matrix.

Alternatively, we can build a left-handed orthogonal projection matrix using the D3DXMatrixOrthoLH function. The first parameter of this function is a pointer to a D3DXMATRIX structure storing the result of the operation; the second, the view volume's width; the third, this view volume's height. The final two parameters are respectively the z-values of the near and far view-planes.

Working with OpenGL

The default matrix mode in OpenGL is the model-view matrix and we alter this matrix by switching modes with the glMatrixMode function. The projection matrix (GL_PROJECTION) controls the 'type' of camera, with the model-view matrix (GL_MODELVIEW) the camera location. The model-view matrix converts the coordinates of objects from the model frame to the camera frame. These are the standard matrices provided by OpenGL.

Specification of the model-view and projection matrices is part of the graphics pipeline architecture. This architecture depends on the multiplication of a series of transformation matrices. The concatenation of transformation matrices produces the correct image of a primitive. The model-view and projection matrices are initially set to identity matrices. In OpenGL we modify the identity matrix via a series of transformations. The first matrix we apply our operations to is the projection matrix, after setting the matrix mode to the projection matrix we switch back to the model-view matrix. The typical routine is:

```
glMatrixMode(GL_PROJECTION);
glLoadIdentity();
glFrustum(vert_left, vert_right, horiz_bottom, horiz_top,
          near_depth, far_depth);
```

This glFrustum function multiplies the current matrix (the identity matrix in this case) and the perspective matrix, with:

- vert_left, the left vertical clipping plane coordinate.

- vert_right, the right vertical clipping plane coordinate.

- horiz_bottom, the bottom vertical clipping plane coordinate.

- `horiz_top`, the top horizontal clipping plane coordinate.

- `near_depth`, the distance to near-depth clipping plane.

- `far_depth`, the distance to far-depth clipping plane.

The `gluPerspective` utility function specifies a perspective projection matrix via an up-direction angle, the aspect ratio of the projection plane and the near and far clipping planes. The typical routine is:

```
glMatrixMode(GL_PROJECTION);
glLoadIdentity();
gluPerspective(up_direction, aspect_ratio, near_depth,
        far_depth);
```

The specification of an orthographic projection is also much less complicated than the conversion process required by Direct3D. We simply use the `glOrtho` function to multiply the current matrix with an orthographic matrix, specifying the coordinates for the `left` and `right` vertical clipping planes, the coordinates for the `bottom` and `top` horizontal clipping planes and the distances to the `near` and `far` clipping planes.

Usage example:

```
glOrtho(left, right, bottom, top, near, far);
```

7.4.4 Viewport Transformation

In section 7.3.3 we defined a viewport as a window located inside a viewing volume. A viewport takes up the entire viewing volume by default and is formally defined as a two-dimensional projection rectangle with its position (lower left corner for OpenGL and upper left corner for Direct3D) specified by a set of coordinates and its width and height denoted in pixels.

The primary purpose of a viewport is to preserve the aspect ratio of a rendered image. We already talked about the independence of objects, the viewer and the hardware representation of images, including how this independence can cause undesirable effects if the view volume's aspect ratio doesn't correspond to that of the output device. The aspect ratio is preserved when the clipping rectangle has exactly the same height and width as the display window. By creating a viewport we avoid image distortion with the additional benefit of generating a theoretically unlimited number of 'mini' viewing volumes, each with its own input control and interface. Figure 7-12 depicts an aspect ratio mismatch and the subsequent result of using a viewport.

FIGURE 7-12 **(a) Aspect ratio mismatch (b) Mapping to a viewport**

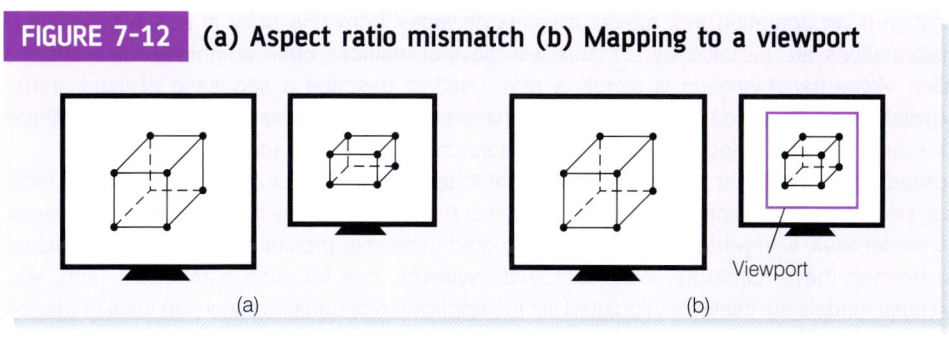

Viewport

(a)   (b)

The dimensions of a viewport are defined by means of the D3D10_VIEWPORT structure. This structure takes the following values, in the order presented, as parameters: the x-coordinate of the top left-hand side of the viewport, the y-coordinate of the top left-hand side of the viewport, the viewport's width, its height, its minimum depth (between 0 and 1) and finally the maximum depth of the viewport (also between 0 and 1). For standard Direct3D games we define the first four parameters as (0, 0, res_x, res_y, 0.0, 1.0), with res_x and res_y the user's monitor resolution. If you set both the minimum and maximum depth values to 0, then all objects will be rendered to the foreground. Similarly, setting both these depth values to 1 result in images rendered to the background. These depth values indicate the depth-ranges into which the scene will be rendered.

Following the definition of a viewport, we need to bind it to the rasterization stage of the pipeline using the RSSetViewports ID3D10Device method. This method simply takes the number of viewports to bind as its first parameter (maximum 16) and a pointer to the D3D10_VIEWPORT structure as its second.

The following code segment creates a viewport of 1024 by 768 pixels:

```
D3D10_VIEWPORT viewport[1];
viewport[1].TopLeftX = 0;
viewport[1].TopLeftY = 0;
viewport[1].Width = 1024.0f;
viewport[1].Height = 768.0f;
viewport[1].MinZ = 0;
viewport[1].MaxZ = 1;

D3DDevice->RSSetViewports(1, viewport);
```

Working with OpenGL

OpenGL uses the glViewport function to set up a viewport, with the first two parameters the lower-left corner of the viewport rectangle in pixels, and the last two, the width and height of the viewport respectively.

Usage example:

```
glViewport(x-coord, y-coord, width, height);
```

7.5   SPATIAL TRANSFORMATIONS

In this section we focus on three-dimensional transformations such as rotation, scaling, and translation. A transformation is an operation that moves a vertex or vector from one point in space to another. These transformations are denoted by a matrix with several matrices often combined for a custom transformation. *Affine transformation* is simply a term used to describe a sequence of linear transformations (rotation, scaling, etc.) followed by a translation operation. A *linear transformation* or *linear map* is a function that maps objects (vertices and vectors) from one vector space to another.

As discussed in section 7.4, it is fitting and practical to specify models or objects in their own local coordinate system. This local coordinate system, or object frame, is generally based on some reference point in the model itself, with additional polygons adjoined in relative proximity to this point. Complex models will normally have numerous local coordinate systems, one for each component (arm, leg, torso, etc). These models are easily manipulated via the application of transformations to local reference

TABLE 7-1	Affine transformations in matrix notation
Transformation	**Matrix notation**
Translation of vertex **K** with vector **S**	**K' = K + S**
Scaling of vertex **K** with scaling matrix **Q**	**K' = QK**
Rotation of vertex **K** with rotation matrix **P**	**K' = PK**

points and to the model's local coordinate system. Local coordinate systems can also be brought into the world and camera frame through previously discussed world and view matrices, etc.

Say we have a vertex **K**. We can then translate this vertex by adding a translation vector **S** to it. We can also scale or rotate this vertex by multiplying it with an appropriate scaling (**Q**) or rotation matrix (**P**). Table 7-1 illustrates these affine transformations in matrix notation.

Homogenous coordinates allow for the easy representation of affine transformations via four-dimensional column matrices. Without this coordinate representation we'll have many references to and from one point in space. For example, say we have a vector from the point (1, 3, 3) to (2, 7, 3), then this vector is the same as the vector from the point (0, 0, 0) to (1, 4, 0). The only way to distinguish these two vectors from one another is to fix one of their ends to one of their coordinate points. The four-dimensional homogenous column matrices represent both the coordinate points and the vectors in three dimensions.

Using homogenous coordinates, we are able to represent the vertex A(x, y, z) as A(b · X, b · Y, b · Z, b) with $b \neq 0$. The Cartesian coordinates of this vertex, **A**, is specified as:

$$x = X/b$$
$$y = Y/b$$
$$z = Z/b$$

Assigning the value of 1 to b results in the following column matrix representation for **A**:

$$A = \begin{bmatrix} x \\ y \\ z \\ 1 \end{bmatrix}$$

Most of the transformations used in computer graphics are affine and represented in homogenous coordinates. The combinational usage of these transformations is an integral part of computer animation and motion. A model, for example, undergoes a series of rotations and translations when animated just as we make use of a translation matrix (rather than simple vector addition) for the viewer's spatial navigation and movement. We will now look at several transformation operations from a mathematical and practical implementation perspective.

7.5.1 Translation

A translation operation shifts vertices and vectors in a specific direction by some distance as illustrated in Figure 7-13. We can either specify a displacement vector or a translation matrix to denote a translation. However, moving from one spatial point to another via a displacement distance does not integrate nicely with our other transformation column matrices. The definition of a translation matrix is thus required.

FIGURE 7-13   **Translation operation**

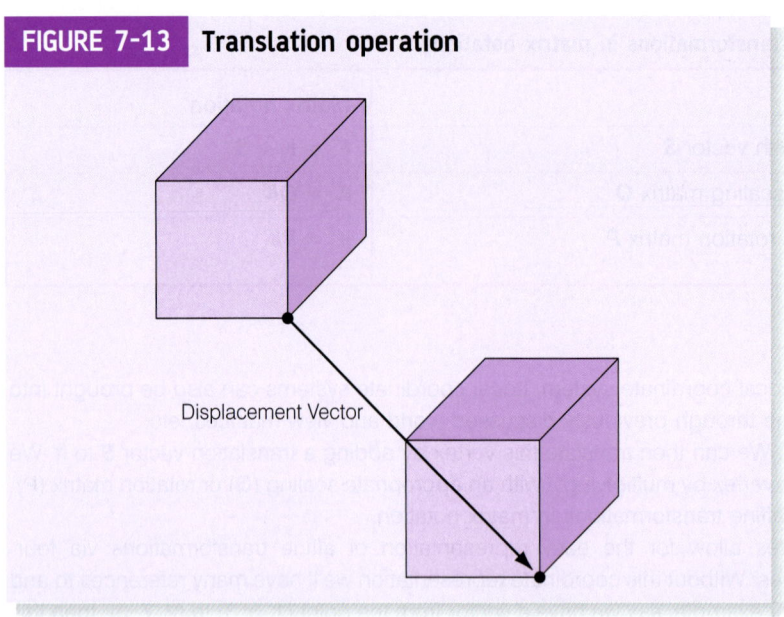

Displacement Vector

Translation of vertex **K** using the displacement vector **S** results in a new point, **K'**, displaced by the distance and direction as denoted by **S** (matrix notation given in Table 7-1). The homogenous coordinates of these vertices and vectors are:

$$K' = \begin{bmatrix} x' \\ y' \\ z' \\ 1 \end{bmatrix}, \quad K = \begin{bmatrix} x \\ y \\ z \\ 1 \end{bmatrix}, \quad S = \begin{bmatrix} \alpha_x \\ \alpha_y \\ \alpha_z \\ 0 \end{bmatrix}, \quad \text{with } \alpha_k \text{ the displacement factor's } k \text{ component.}$$

and these equations can be written component based as:

$$x = \alpha_x - x',$$
$$y = \alpha_y - y',$$
$$z = \alpha_z - z'.$$

Homogenous coordinates allow us to define translation as a matrix multiplication operation. With the above displacement vector operation replaced, we are able to specify a consistent affine transformation system entirely based on matrix multiplications. Using a translation matrix, we can displace vertex **K** by multiplying it with the following matrix, the translation matrix **T**:

$$T = \begin{bmatrix} 1 & 0 & 0 & \alpha_x \\ 0 & 1 & 0 & \alpha_y \\ 0 & 0 & 0 & \alpha_z \\ 0 & 0 & 0 & 1 \end{bmatrix}$$

The complete translation (K'=TK) in matrix notation is:

$$\begin{bmatrix} x' \\ y' \\ z' \\ 1 \end{bmatrix} = \begin{bmatrix} 1 & 0 & 0 & \alpha_x \\ 0 & 1 & 0 & \alpha_y \\ 0 & 0 & 1 & \alpha_z \\ 0 & 0 & 0 & 1 \end{bmatrix} \begin{bmatrix} x \\ y \\ z \\ 1 \end{bmatrix}$$

The displacement coordinates $(\alpha_x, \alpha_y, \alpha_z)$ are applied to each vertex of the object being translated, with the transformation subsequently represented by the following three equations:

$$x' = x + \alpha_x,$$
$$y' = y + \alpha_y,$$
$$z' = z + \alpha_z.$$

It is sometimes necessary to find the inverse of the transformation matrix. This is easily calculated by observing that if we translated a vertex by the vector **V**, we can return to the original position by translating the vertex with the vector $-$**V**. Via this method we obtain the inverse as:

$$T^{-1} = \begin{bmatrix} 1 & 0 & 0 & -\alpha_x \\ 0 & 1 & 0 & -\alpha_y \\ 0 & 0 & 1 & -\alpha_z \\ 0 & 0 & 0 & 1 \end{bmatrix}$$

Defining a translation matrix in Direct3D can be done either manually or by use of the D3DX utility library function, D3DXMatrixTranslation.

Assuming we have three variables (x, y and z) and we want to translate to this coordinate, then we begin by declaring a translation matrix via the D3DXMATRIX structure:

```
D3DXMATRIX translate;
```

Next we create an identity matrix using the D3DX D3DXMatrixIdentity function, followed by the specification of our translation matrix, translate:

```
D3DXMatrixIdentity(&translate);
translate(6, 3) = x;
translate(6, 4) = y;
translate(6, 5) = z;
```

Using the D3DXMatrixTranslation utility function is much more common than the method given in the above example. This function returns a pointer to a D3DXMATRIX structure containing the translated matrix. The first parameter of the D3DXMatrixTranslation function is a pointer to the D3DXMATRIX structure (the resultant translation matrix). The function's next three parameters are the transformation's coordinate offsets x, y and z respectively.

Working with OpenGL

To define a translation matrix we can use either the glTranslatef() or glTranslated() function. These functions multiply the translation matrix with the current matrix on the stack, effectively moving the coordinate system to a new point (x, y, z).

Usage examples:

```
glTranslatef(x, y, z); //expecting floating values
glTranslated(x, y, z); //expecting integer values
```

7.5.2 Rotation

Rotation is one of the more difficult transformation operations due to the large number of parameters involved. It is further complicated by either being about the coordinate axes or about some arbitrary

FIGURE 7-14   **A point with the coordinate (x, y) is rotated about the origin, β degrees**

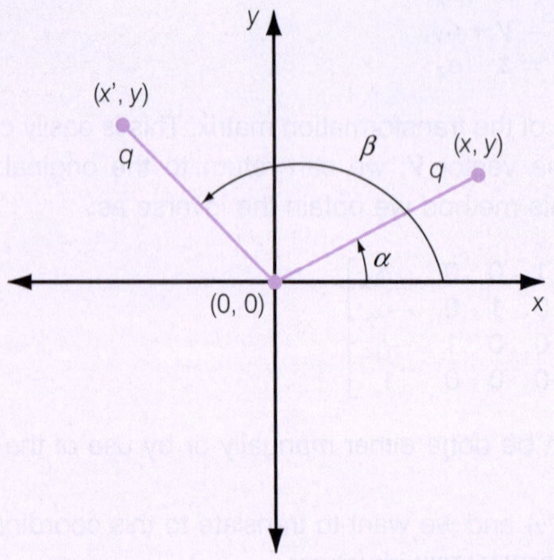

point. The principles of two-dimensional rotation form the basis for more complex rotations and Figure 7-14 illustrates the rotation of a point about the origin.

To obtain the matrix for the rotation illustrated in Figure 7-14, we start by writing (x, y) and (x', y') in polar form:

$$x = q\cos\alpha,\ y = q\sin\alpha,$$
$$x' = q\cos\beta,\ y' = q\sin\beta.$$

Next we make use of trigonometric identities to expand these polar equations:

$$x' = x\cos(\beta - \alpha) - y\sin(\beta - \alpha),$$
$$y' = x\sin(\beta - \alpha) + y\cos(\beta - \alpha).$$

Finally we substitute $(\beta - \alpha)$ with θ, writing the above two equations in matrix form:

$$\begin{bmatrix} x' \\ y' \end{bmatrix} = \begin{bmatrix} \cos\theta & -\sin\theta \\ \sin\theta & \cos\theta \end{bmatrix} \begin{bmatrix} x \\ y \end{bmatrix},$$

with $\begin{bmatrix} \cos\theta & -\sin\theta \\ \sin\theta & \cos\theta \end{bmatrix}$ the two-dimensional rotation matrix about the x-axis; Figure 7-15 illustrates two-dimensional rotation about an arbitrary point.

Two-dimensional rotation corresponds to three-dimensional rotation about the z-axis. No z-values exist in two-dimensional rotation, with z-values remaining constant for three-dimensional rotation about the z-axis.

The definition of a frame independent three-dimensional rotation matrix requires three components: a rotation angle, a fixed point of rotation and a rotation vector. The rotation angle determines the clockwise angle at which to rotate, the fixed point serves as the origin of rotation and the rotation vector is the line about which the object is rotated. We will now discuss three-dimensional rotation about the coordinate axes followed by the examination of rotation about an arbitrary fixed point.

7.5.2.1 Rotation About the Coordinate Axes   This form of rotation occurs at the three-dimensional Cartesian coordinate system's origin. Different rotation matrices are derived for each of the three coordinate axes based on the results obtained from the previously discussed two-dimensional rotation operation. We already noted the correlation between two-dimensional rotation and three-dimensional rotation about the z-axis. However, to write out a three-dimensional rotation matrix we make use of a 4×4 matrix explicitly leaving the fourth component of the representation unchanged:

$$M = \begin{bmatrix} \omega_{11} & \omega_{12} & \omega_{13} & \omega_{14} \\ \omega_{21} & \omega_{22} & \omega_{23} & \omega_{24} \\ \omega_{31} & \omega_{32} & \omega_{33} & \omega_{34} \\ 0 & 0 & 0 & 1 \end{bmatrix},$$ with each of the twelve ω values changeable.

FIGURE 7-15   **Two-dimensional rotation about point p**

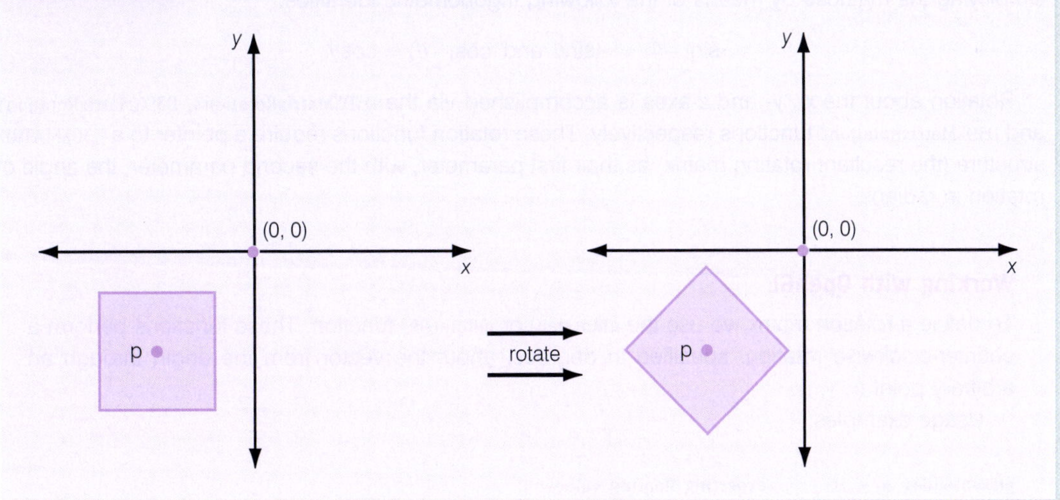

Rotation about the z-axis by an angle θ is given by the following three equations:

$$x' = x\cos(\theta) - y\sin(\theta),$$
$$y' = x\sin(\theta) + y\cos(\theta),$$
$$z' = z.$$

Next we write these equations in matrix form:

$$\begin{bmatrix} x' \\ y' \\ z' \end{bmatrix} = \begin{bmatrix} \cos\theta & -\sin\theta & 0 & 0 \\ \sin\theta & \cos\theta & 0 & 0 \\ 0 & 0 & 1 & 0 \\ 0 & 0 & 0 & 1 \end{bmatrix} \begin{bmatrix} x \\ y \\ z \end{bmatrix},$$

with $Rz = \begin{bmatrix} \cos\theta & -\sin\theta & 0 & 0 \\ \sin\theta & \cos\theta & 0 & 0 \\ 0 & 0 & 1 & 0 \\ 0 & 0 & 0 & 1 \end{bmatrix}$, the two-dimensional rotation matrix about the z-axis.

Rotation about the x- and y-axes is derived in a similar manner, with rotation about the x-axis implying rotation in a plane where x-values remain constant and y-values remaining unchanged for y-axis rotation. The transformation matrices for rotation about the x- and y-axes are respectively:

$$Rx = \begin{bmatrix} 1 & 0 & 0 & 0 \\ 0 & \cos\theta & -\sin\theta & 0 \\ 0 & \sin\theta & \cos\theta & 0 \\ 0 & 0 & 0 & 1 \end{bmatrix},$$

$$Ry = \begin{bmatrix} \cos\theta & 0 & \sin\theta & 0 \\ 0 & 1 & 0 & 0 \\ -\sin\theta & 0 & \cos\theta & 0 \\ 0 & 0 & 0 & 1 \end{bmatrix}.$$

We simply rotate at a counter-clockwise angle $(-\theta)$ to find the inverse of these rotation matrices, simplifying the matrices by means of the following trigonometric identities:

$$\sin(-\theta) = -\sin\theta \text{ and } \cos(-\theta) = \cos\theta.$$

Rotation about the *x*-, *y*- and *z*-axes is accomplished via the D3DXMatrixRotationX, D3DXMatrixRotationY and D3DXMatrixRotationZ functions respectively. These rotation functions require a pointer to a D3DXMATRIX structure (the resultant rotation matrix) as their first parameter, with the second parameter, the angle of rotation in radians.

Working with OpenGL

To define a rotation matrix we use the glRotatef() or glRotated() function. These functions perform a counter-clockwise rotation, specified in degrees, about the vector from the origin through an arbitrary point (x, y, z).
   Usage examples:

```
glRotatef(deg, x, y, z);    //expecting floating values
glRotated(deg, x, y, z);    //expecting integer values
```

7.5.2.2 Rotation About an Arbitrary Fixed Point
In our previous discussion we considered rotation about a fixed point at the coordinate system's origin. We will now examine rotation about the object's center, while still rotating the object about a coordinate axis.
   Say we want to rotate any arbitrary object at its center about the *x*-axis: this object center becomes the fixed point of rotation. In our previous example this fixed point was the Cartesian coordinate system's origin and we simply applied the appropriate rotation matrix corresponding to the axis of rotation; however, this isn't possible for an arbitrary point in space. To apply the appropriate rotation matrix we first need to move the object to the coordinate system's origin, apply the rotation matrix, and translate it back to its original fixed point of rotation. Figure 7-16 illustrates this process.
   The rotation of any object, with its fixed point at some arbitrary location (*x, y, z*), is given by the following net transformation matrices for rotation about the *x*-, *y*- and *z*-axes respectively:

$$\begin{bmatrix} 1 & 0 & 0 & -x \\ 0 & 1 & 0 & -y \\ 0 & 0 & 1 & -z \\ 0 & 0 & 0 & 1 \end{bmatrix} \begin{bmatrix} 1 & 0 & 0 & 0 \\ 0 & \cos\theta & -\sin\theta & 0 \\ 0 & \sin\theta & \cos\theta & 0 \\ 0 & 0 & 0 & 1 \end{bmatrix} \begin{bmatrix} 1 & 0 & 0 & x \\ 0 & 1 & 0 & y \\ 0 & 0 & 1 & z \\ 0 & 0 & 0 & 1 \end{bmatrix},$$

$$\begin{bmatrix} 1 & 0 & 0 & -x \\ 0 & 1 & 0 & -y \\ 0 & 0 & 1 & -z \\ 0 & 0 & 0 & 1 \end{bmatrix} \begin{bmatrix} \cos\theta & 0 & \sin\theta & 0 \\ 0 & 1 & 0 & 0 \\ -\sin\theta & 0 & \cos\theta & 0 \\ 0 & 0 & 0 & 1 \end{bmatrix} \begin{bmatrix} 1 & 0 & 0 & x \\ 0 & 1 & 0 & y \\ 0 & 0 & 1 & z \\ 0 & 0 & 0 & 1 \end{bmatrix},$$

$$\begin{bmatrix} 1 & 0 & 0 & -x \\ 0 & 1 & 0 & -y \\ 0 & 0 & 1 & -z \\ 0 & 0 & 0 & 1 \end{bmatrix} \begin{bmatrix} \cos\theta & -\sin\theta & 0 & 0 \\ \sin\theta & \cos\theta & 0 & 0 \\ 0 & 0 & 1 & 0 \\ 0 & 0 & 0 & 1 \end{bmatrix} \begin{bmatrix} 1 & 0 & 0 & x \\ 0 & 1 & 0 & y \\ 0 & 0 & 1 & z \\ 0 & 0 & 0 & 1 \end{bmatrix}.$$

Direct3D provides the D3DXMatrixRotationAxis function for the specification of rotation about some arbitrary axis. This function takes three parameters, the first being a pointer to the D3DXMATRIX structure for storage of the rotation result, the second a pointer to an arbitrary axis (specified via the D3DXVECTOR3

FIGURE 7-16	Transformation sequence required for rotation about an arbitrary fixed point

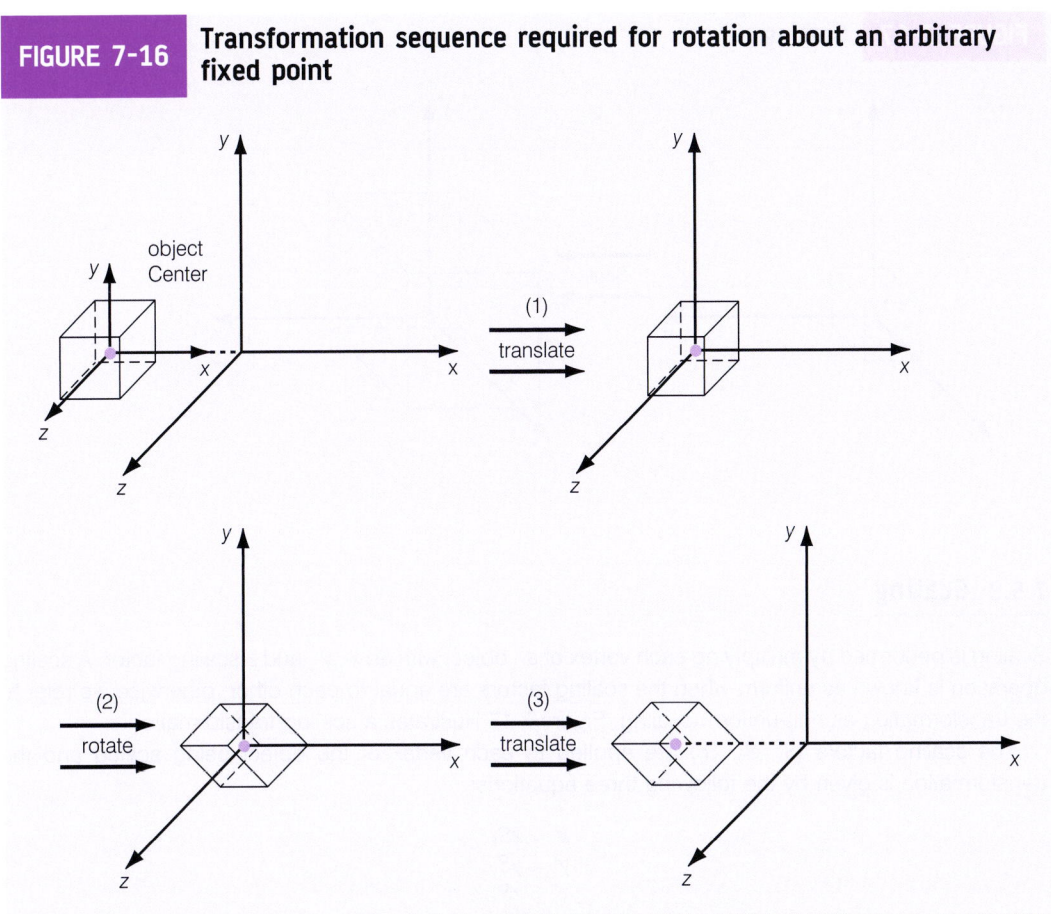

structure), and the third, the angle of rotation in radians. For rotation about some arbitrary fixed point we simply implement the axes-based rotation functions introduced in the previous section coupled with a translation to and from the global origin via the D3DXMatrixTranslation function.

Working with OpenGL

The following series of OpenGL functions enable the rotation of an object about a line located from the origin to some arbitrary point (x_2, y_2, z_2). This object has the fixed point: (x_1, y_1, z_1).

We start by switching to the model-view matrix and loading the identity matrix:

```
glMatrixMode(GL_MODELVIEW);
glLoadIdentity();
```

Following this we translate the object's local coordinate system to a new point (x_1, y_1, z_1), rotating it at some specified angle (deg), and finally moving it back to its original fixed point:

```
glTranslatef(x₁, y₁, z₁);
glRotatef(deg, x₂, y₂, z₂);
glTranslatef(-x₁, -y₁, -z₁);
```

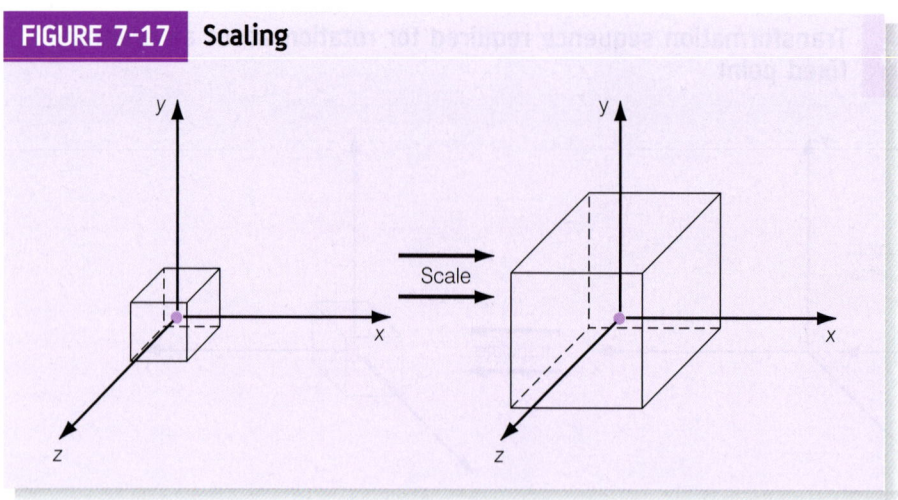

FIGURE 7-17   Scaling

7.5.3 Scaling

Scaling is performed by multiplying each vertex of an object with an x-, y-, and z-scaling factor. A scaling operation is known as uniform when the scaling factors are equal to each other; otherwise we refer to the transformation as non-uniform scaling. Figure 7-17 illustrates a scaling transformation.

The scaling factors (S_x, S_y, S_z) are applied to each vertex of the object being scaled and the transformation is given by the following three equations:

$$x' = xS_x,$$
$$y' = yS_y,$$
$$z' = zS_z.$$

These equations can be written in matrix form as:

$$\begin{bmatrix} x' \\ y' \\ z' \end{bmatrix} = \begin{bmatrix} S_x & 0 & 0 & 0 \\ 0 & S_y & 0 & 0 \\ 0 & 0 & S_z & 0 \\ 0 & 0 & 0 & 1 \end{bmatrix} \begin{bmatrix} x \\ y \\ z \end{bmatrix},$$

with $\begin{bmatrix} S_x & 0 & 0 & 0 \\ 0 & S_y & 0 & 0 \\ 0 & 0 & S_z & 0 \\ 0 & 0 & 0 & 1 \end{bmatrix}$, the scaling matrix.

The inverse of the scaling matrix is found by substituting the scaling factors with their reciprocals, resulting in the following matrix:

$$\begin{bmatrix} \dfrac{1}{S_x} & 0 & 0 & 0 \\ 0 & \dfrac{1}{S_y} & 0 & 0 \\ 0 & 0 & \dfrac{1}{S_z} & 0 \\ 0 & 0 & 0 & 1 \end{bmatrix}.$$

The D3DXMatrixScaling utility function enables scaling along the *x*-, *y*- and *z*-axes. This function takes four parameters with the first, a pointer to the D3DXMATRIX structure, storing the result of the operation. The final three parameters are the scaling factors along the x-, y- and z-axes.

Working with OpenGL

We define a scaling matrix using either the glScaled() or glScalef() function. These functions scale a geometric object along the x-, y- and z-axes.

Usage examples:

```
glScalef(x, y, z);    //expecting floating values
glScaled(x, y, z);    //expecting integer values
```

7.6   EXAMPLES

We now present four programs illustrating the above-discussed concepts. The complete source code of the first program is listed, combining the concepts dealt with in previous chapters with those presented here.

7.6.1 Rendering a triangle without any transformations

The following code renders a two-dimensional red triangle like the one shown and is used as a basis for our translation examples. We start by including the standard DirectX 10 headers:

```
#include <windows.h>
#include <d3d10.h>
#include <d3dx10.h>
```

We also create a structure for storing our triangle's vertex coordinates:

```
struct TriangleVertex
{
    D3DXVECTOR3 Coordinate;
};
```

Following this we initialize our instance handle (g_hInstance), the handle to the window (g_hWindow), the DirectX 10 device driver type (g_dxl0DriverType), and the ID3D10Device interface, g_pd3d10Device, used for DrawPrimitive-based rendering. As explained in Chapters 4 and 6, we also have to set the IDXGISwapChain, ID3D10RenderTargetView, ID3D10Effect, ID3D10EffectTechnique, ID3D10InputLayout and ID3D10Buffer interfaces:

```
HWND              g_hWindow = NULL;
HINSTANCE         g_hInstance = NULL;
D3D10_DRIVER_TYPE  g_dxl0DriverType = D3D10_DRIVER_TYPE_NULL;
ID3D10Device*     g_pd3d10Device = NULL;
IDXGISwapChain*   g_pdxl0SwapChain = NULL;
ID3D10EffectTechnique*   g_pd3d10EffectTechnique = NULL;
ID3D10Buffer*         g_pd3d10VertexBuffer = NULL;
```

```
ID3D10InputLayout*          g_pd3d10InputVertexLayout = NULL;
ID3D10Effect*               g_pd3d10Effect = NULL;
ID3D10RenderTargetView*     g_pd3d10RenderTargetView = NULL;
```

Next we declare our function prototypes:

```
HRESULT                 InitDevice();
LRESULT CALLBACK        WndProc(HWND, UINT, WPARAM, LPARAM);
HRESULT                 InitWindow(HINSTANCE hInstance,
                                   int nCmdShow);
void                    DrawTriangle();
void                    Clean();
```

Just as in our previous examples, we initialize the message processing loop elements and the idle time required for the rendering of our triangle via winMain, the entry point of our application:

```
int WINAPI winMain(HINSTANCE hInstance, HINSTANCE
                   hPrevInstance, LPWSTR lpCmdLine,
                   int nCmdShow)
{
    if((FAILED(InitDevice()))||(FAILED(InitWindow(hInstance,
            nCmdShow))))
    {
        Clean(); //do device cleanup - freeing resources
        return 0;
    }
    MSG msg = {0};

    while(WM_QUIT != msg.message)
    {
        if(PeekMessage(&msg, NULL, 0, 0, PM_REMOVE))
        {
            TranslateMessage(&msg);
            DispatchMessage(&msg);
        }
        else
        {
            DrawTriangle(); //render our triangle
        }
    }
    Clean();
    return (int)msg.wParam;
}
```

With the application's entry point declared we need to register the class and create the output window as detailed in Chapter 4:

```
HRESULT InitWindow(HINSTANCE hInstance, int nCmdShow)
{
```

```
/* register the window class */
//////////////////////////////
WNDCLASSEX wndcex;

wndcex.cbSize           = sizeof(WNDCLASSEX);
wndcex.style            = CS_HREDRAW | CS_VREDRAW;
wndcex.lpfnWndProc      = WndProc;
wndcex.cbClsExtra       = 0;
wndcex.cbWndExtra       = 0;
wndcex.hInstance        = hInstance;
wndcex.hIcon            = LoadIcon(hInstance,
                                (LPCTSTR) IDI_PROG7_6_1);
wndcex.hCursor          = LoadCursor(NULL, IDC_ARROW);
wndcex.hbrBackground    = (HBRUSH)(COLOR_WINDOW+1);
wndcex.lpszMenuName     = NULL;
wndcex.lpszClassName    = L"StaticTriangle";
wndcex.hIconSm          = LoadIcon(wndcex.hInstance,
                                (LPCTSTR) IDI_PROG7_6_1);

if(!RegisterClassEx(&wndcex))
    return E_FAIL;

/* create the window */
//////////////////////////////
g_hInstance = hInstance;

RECT rectangle = {0, 0, 800, 600};
AdjustWindowRect(&rectangle, WS_OVERLAPPEDWINDOW, FALSE);

g_hWindow = CreateWindow(
            L"StaticTriangle",
            L"Rendering a triangle without any transformations",
            WS_OVERLAPPEDWINDOW,
            CW_USEDEFAULT, CW_USEDEFAULT,
            rectangle.right - rectangle.left,
            rectangle.bottom - rectangle.top,
            NULL, NULL, hInstance, NULL);
if(!g_hWindow)
    return E_FAIL;

ShowWindow(g_hWindow, nCmdShow);

return S_OK;
}
```

Next we create the Direct3D device and swap chain as presented in Chapter 4. Following this InitDevice function declaration, we set up our WndProc callback:

```
HRESULT InitDevice()
{
    HRESULT hresult_ = S_OK;
```

```
/* setup client rectangle width and height */
/////////////////////////////////////////
RECT rectangle;
GetClientRect( g_hWindow, &rectangle );

int rectangle_width = rectangle.right - rectangle.left;

int rectangle_height = rectangle.bottom - rectangle.top;

int deviceFlags = 0;

/* specify D3D10 drivers to use */
/////////////////////////////////
D3D10_DRIVER_TYPE d3d10drivers[] =
{
    D3D10_DRIVER_TYPE_HARDWARE,
    D3D10_DRIVER_TYPE_REFERENCE,
};

int numberDrivers =
            sizeof(d3d10drivers)/sizeof(d3d10drivers[0]);

/* create the swap chain */
////////////////////////////
DXGI_SWAP_CHAIN_DESC swapchain;
SecureZeroMemory(&swapchain, sizeof(swapchain));

swapchain.BufferCount = 1;
swapchain.BufferDesc.Width = rectangle_width;
swapchain.BufferDesc.Height = rectangle_height;
swapchain.BufferDesc.Format = DXGI_FORMAT_R8G8B8A8_UNORM;
swapchain.BufferDesc.RefreshRate.Numerator = 30;
swapchain.BufferDesc.RefreshRate.Denominator = 1;
swapchain.BufferUsage = DXGI_USAGE_RENDER_TARGET_OUTPUT;
swapchain.OutputWindow = g_hWindow;
swapchain.SampleDesc.Count = 1;
swapchain.SampleDesc.Quality = 0;
swapchain.Windowed = TRUE;

for(int d3d10DriverCount = 0; d3d10DriverCount <
    numberDrivers; d3d10DriverCount++)
{
    g_dxl0DriverType = d3d10drivers[d3d10DriverCount];
    hresult_           = D3D10CreateDeviceAndSwapChain(
                    NULL, g_dxl0DriverType, NULL,
                    deviceFlags, D3D10_SDK_VERSION,
                    &swapchain, &g_pdxl0SwapChain,
                    &g_pd3d10Device);

    if(SUCCEEDED(hresult_))
        break;
}
```

```
if(FAILED(hresult_))
    return hresult_;

/* specify the render target view */
/////////////////////////////////////
ID3D10Texture2D *pBuffer;
hresult_ = g_pdxl0SwapChain->
        GetBuffer(NULL, __uuidof(ID3D10Texture2D),
                    (LPVOID*)&pBuffer);
if(FAILED(hresult_))
    return hresult_;

hresult_ = g_pd3d10Device->
        CreateRenderTargetView(pBuffer, NULL,
                            &g_pd3d10RenderTargetView);

pBuffer->Release();

if(FAILED(hresult_))
    return hresult_;

g_pd3d10Device->OMSetRenderTargets(1,
                &g_pd3d10RenderTargetView, NULL);

/* create the viewport */
////////////////////////////
D3D10_VIEWPORT viewport;
viewport.TopLeftX    = 0;
viewport.TopLeftY    = 0;
viewport.Width       = rectangle_width;
viewport.Height      = rectangle_height;
viewport.MinDepth    = 0.0f;
viewport.MaxDepth    = 1.0f;

g_pd3d10Device->RSSetViewports(1, &viewport);

/* load the effect file specifying our triangle's color*/
/////////////////////////////////////////////////////////////
hresult_ = D3DX10CreateEffectFromFile(
                    L"effect.fx", NULL, NULL,
                    D3D10_SHADER_ENABLE_STRICTNESS, 0,
                    g_pd3d10Device, NULL, NULL, &g_pd3d10Effect,
                    NULL);

/* if the effect file is missing */
///////////////////////////////////////
if(FAILED(hresult_))
{
    return hresult_;
}
```

7

```
/* set the effect technique and input layout */
////////////////////////////
g_pd3d10EffectTechnique = g_pd3d10Effect->
                         GetTechniqueByName("Triangle");

D3D10_INPUT_ELEMENT_DESC inputlayout[] =
{
    {"POSITION", 0, DXGI_FORMAT_R32G32B32_FLOAT, 0, 0,
     D3D10_INPUT_PER_VERTEX_DATA, 0},
};

int numberOfElements = sizeof(inputlayout) /
                         sizeof(inputlayout[0]);

D3D10_PASS_DESC PassDescription;
g_pd3d10EffectTechnique->
        GetPassByIndex(0)->GetDesc(&PassDescription);

hresult_ = g_pd3d10Device->CreateInputLayout(
                         inputlayout, numberOfElements,
                         PassDescription.pIAInputSignature,
                         PassDescription.IAInputSignatureSize,
                         &g_pd3d10InputVertexLayout);

if(FAILED(hresult_))
    return hresult_;

g_pd3d10Device->IASetInputLayout(
                         g_pd3d10InputVertexLayout);
/* specify our triangle's vertices */
////////////////////////////////////
TriangleVertex vertices[] =
{
    D3DXVECTOR3(0.0f, 1.0f, 1.0f),
    D3DXVECTOR3(1.0f, -1.0f, 1.0f),
    D3DXVECTOR3(-1.0f, -1.0f, 1.0f),
};

/* setup the buffer resource */
///////////////////////////////////
D3D10_BUFFER_DESC bufferdesc;

bufferdesc.Usage          = D3D10_USAGE_DEFAULT;
bufferdesc.BindFlags      = D3D10_BIND_VERTEX_BUFFER;
bufferdesc.CPUAccessFlags = 0;
bufferdesc.MiscFlags      = 0;
bufferdesc.ByteWidth      = sizeof(TriangleVertex)*3;
```

```
/* initialize resource */
////////////////////////////
D3D10_SUBRESOURCE_DATA ResourceData;
ResourceData.pSysMem = vertices;

hresult_ = g_pd3d10Device->CreateBuffer(&bufferdesc,
                                &ResourceData,
                                &g_pd3d10VertexBuffer);

if(FAILED(hresult_))
    return hresult_;

/* setup the vertex buffer */
////////////////////////////
int elementstride = sizeof(TriangleVertex);

int bufferoffset = 0;
g_pd3d10Device->IASetVertexBuffers(
                        0, 1, &g_pd3d10VertexBuffer,
                        &elementstride, &bufferoffset);
/* bind the primitive type and data order information to a
    triangle list */
g_pd3d10Device->IASetPrimitiveTopology(
                    D3D10_PRIMITIVE_TOPOLOGY_TRIANGLELIST);

return S_OK;
}

LRESULT CALLBACK WndProc(HWND hWindow, UINT msg, WPARAM
            wParam, LPARAM lParam)
{
    HDC devicecontext;
    PAINTSTRUCT paintstructure;

    switch(msg)
    {
        case WM_DESTROY:
            PostQuitMessage(0);
            break;

        case WM_PAINT:
            devicecontext = BeginPaint (hWindow,
                                &paintstructure);
            EndPaint(hWindow, &paintstructure);
            break;

        default:
            return DefWindowProc(hWindow, message, wParam,
                            lParam);
    }
    return 0;
}
```

7

The second to last function, Clean(), checks whether an object has been created, and if it has, it deallocates it, freeing the resources:

```
void Clean()
{
    if(g_pd3d10Device)
        g_pd3d10Device->ClearState();

    if(g_pd3d10InputVertexLayout)
        g_pd3d10InputVertexLayout->Release();

    if(g_pd3d10VertexBuffer)
        g_pd3d10VertexBuffer->Release();

    if(g_pd3d10RenderTargetView)
        g_pd3d10RenderTargetView->Release();

    if(g_pd3d10Effect)
        g_pd3d10Effect->Release();

    if(g_pd3d10Device)
        g_pd3d10Device->Release();

    if(g_pdxl0SwapChain)
        g_pdxl0SwapChain->Release();
}
```

The DrawTriangle function does the actual triangle rendering. We start by clearing the back buffer using the ClearRenderTargetView method.

```
void DrawTriangle()
{
    /* start by clearing the back-buffer */
    float ClearBufferColor[4] = {0.0f, 0.125f, 0.3f, 1.0f};
    g_pd3d10Device->ClearRenderTargetView(
                        g_pd3d10RenderTargetView,
                        ClearBufferColor);

    /* obtain the D3D10_TECHNIQUE_DESC effect-variable
        description */
    D3D10_TECHNIQUE_DESC technique;
    g_pd3d10EffectTechnique->GetDesc(&technique);

    /* render by looping over the number of technique passes */
    for(int i = 0; i < technique.Passes; ++i)
    {
        g_pd3d10EffectTechnique->GetPassByIndex(i)->Apply(0);
        g_pd3d10Device->Draw(3, 0);
    }
```

```
/* switch the back- and front-buffer and display the
triangle */
g_pdx10SwapChain->Present(0,0);
}
```

As mentioned, this sample makes use of DirectX's effect system, with the FX file's pixel shader returning the color of the triangle. The file, effect.fx, defines the following pixel shader:

```
float4 PixelShader( float4 Pos : SV_POSITION ) : SV_Target
{
    return float4(1.0f, 0.0f, 0.0f, 1.0f); //red
}

technique10 Triangle
{
    pass P0
    {
        SetGeometryShader( NULL );
        SetPixelShader(CompileShader(ps_4_0, PixelShader()));
    }
}
```

7.6.2 **Rendering a triangle translated**

We will now modify the above example to translate our triangle along the positive *x*-axis, starting with the initialization of our world, view, and projection matrix. Before initializing these matrices, however, we first need to declare them and their access interfaces:

```
D3DXMATRIX        g_WorldMatrix;
D3DXMATRIX        g_ViewMatrix;
D3DXMATRIX        g_ProjectionMatrix;
ID3D10EffectMatrixVariable* g_pd3d10EffectWorldMatrix = NULL;
ID3D10EffectMatrixVariable* g_pd3d10EffectViewMatrix = NULL;
ID3D10EffectMatrixVariable* g_pd3d10EffectProjectMatrix = NULL;
```

The following code is inserted just above the InitDevice function's return call:

```
/* initialize the world matrix to an identity matrix */
//////////////////////////////////////////////////////
D3DXMatrixIdentity(&g_WorldMatrix);

/* set the view matrix */
//////////////////////////////////////////////////////
D3DXVECTOR3 EyeCoord( 0.0f, 1.0f, -10.0f);
```

```
D3DXVECTOR3 LookAt(0.0f, 1.0f,  0.0f);
D3DXVECTOR3 UpDir(0.0f, 1.0f,  0.0f);
D3DXMatrixLookAtLH(&g_ViewMatrix, &EyeCoord, &LookAt, &UpDir);

/* set the left-handed perspective projection */
//////////////////////////////////////////////////
D3DXMatrixPerspectiveFovLH(&g_ProjectionMatrix,
                           (float)D3DX_PI*0.25f,
                           rectangle_width/rectangle_height,
                           0.1f, 100.0f);
```

Next we declare a translation matrix via the D3DXMATRIX structure, followed by the initialization of the translation matrix using the D3DXMatrixTranslation function (setting the *x*-component of the translation to eight units). Once this is done, we apply the above-calculated translation matrix to our word matrix via the D3DXMatrixMultiply function. Before rendering the triangle, we have to call the SetMatrix method so that the GPU can read our matrices:

```
void DrawTriangle()
{
    /* declare translation matrix */
    D3DXMATRIX translationMatrix;

    /* initialize the translation matrix */
    D3DXMatrixTranslation(&translationMatrix, 8.0f,0.0f, 0.0f);

    /* apply the translation matrix to our world matrix */
    D3DXMatrixMultiply(&g_WorldMatrix, &g_WorldMatrix,
                       &translationMatrix);

    /* clear the back-buffer */
    float ClearBufferColor[4] = {0.0f, 0.125f, 0.3f, 1.0f};
    g_pd3d10Device->ClearRenderTargetView(g_pd3d10RenderTargetView,
                                          ClearBufferColor);

    /* update the world, view, and projection matrices */
    //////////////////////////////////////////////////
    g_pd3d10EffectWorldMatrix->
            SetMatrix((float*)& g_WorldMatrix);

    g_pd3d10EffectViewMatrix->
            SetMatrix((float*)& g_ViewMatrix);

    g_pd3d10EffectWorldMatrix->
            SetMatrix( (float*)& g_ProjectionMatrix);

    /* obtain the D3D10_TECHNIQUE_DESC effect-variable
       description */
    D3D10_TECHNIQUE_DESC technique;
    g_pd3d10EffectTechnique->GetDesc(&technique);
```

```
/* render by looping over the number of technique passes */
for(int i = 0; i < technique.Passes; ++i)
{
    g_pd3d10EffectTechnique->GetPassByIndex(i)->Apply(0);
    g_pd3d10Device->Draw(3, 0);
}

/* switch the back- and front-buffer and display the
    triangle */
g_pdxl0SwapChain->Present(0,0);
}
```

7.6.3 Rendering a triangle rotated

This example illustrates a 90-degree rotation about the z-axis. Similar to the above example, we start with the declaration and initialization of the world, view, and projection matrices (with associated access interfaces):

```
D3DXMATRIX      g_WorldMatrix;
D3DXMATRIX      g_ViewMatrix;
D3DXMATRIX      g_ProjectionMatrix;
ID3D10EffectMatrixVariable* g_pd3d10EffectWorldMatrix = NULL;
ID3D10EffectMatrixVariable* g_pd3d10EffectViewMatrix = NULL;
ID3D10EffectMatrixVariable* g_pd3d10EffectProjectMatrix= NULL;
```

Exactly as we did in example 7.6.2, we insert the following code just above the InitDevice function's return call:

```
/* initialize the world matrix to an identity matrix */
//////////////////////////////////////////////////////
D3DXMatrixIdentity(&g_WorldMatrix);

/* set the view matrix */
//////////////////////////////////////////////////////
D3DXVECTOR3 EyeCoord( 0.0f, 1.0f, -10.0f);
D3DXVECTOR3 LookAt(0.0f, 1.0f, 0.0f);
D3DXVECTOR3 UpDir(0.0f, 1.0f, 0.0f);
D3DXMatrixLookAtLH(&g_ViewMatrix, &EyeCoord, &LookAt, &UpDir);

/* set the left-handed perspective projection */
//////////////////////////////////////////////////////
D3DXMatrixPerspectiveFovLH(&g_ProjectionMatrix,
                    (float)D3DX_PI*0.25f,
                    rectangle_width/rectangle_height,
                    0.1f, 100.0f);
```

Next we declare a rotation matrix via the D3DXMATRIX structure, followed by its initialization using the D3DXMatrixRotationZ function. Once this is done, we apply the above-calculated rotation matrix to the world matrix via the D3DXMatrixMultiply function. Before rendering the triangle, we have to call the SetMatrix method so that the GPU can read our matrices:

```
void DrawTriangle()
{
    /* declare the rotation matrix */
    D3DXMATRIX rotationMatrix;

    /* initialize the rotation matrix (rotate 1.57 radians) */
    D3DXMatrixRotationZ(&rotationMatrix, 1.57f);

    /* apply the rotation matrix to the world matrix */
    D3DXMatrixMultiply(&g_WorldMatrix, &g_WorldMatrix,
                       &rotationMatrix);

    /* clear the back-buffer */
    float ClearBufferColor[4] = {0.0f, 0.125f, 0.3f, 1.0f};
    g_pd3d10Device->ClearRenderTargetView(g_pd3d10RenderTargetView,
                                          ClearBufferColor);

    /* update the world, view, and projection matrices */
    //////////////////////////////////////////////////////
    g_pd3d10EffectWorldMatrix->
            SetMatrix((float*)&g_WorldMatrix);

    g_pd3d10EffectViewMatrix->
            SetMatrix((float*)&g_ViewMatrix);

    g_pd3d10EffectWorldMatrix->
            SetMatrix( (float*)&g_ProjectionMatrix);

    /* obtain the D3D10_TECHNIQUE_DESC effect-variable
       description */
    D3D10_TECHNIQUE_DESC technique;
    g_pd3d10EffectTechnique->GetDesc(&technique);

    /* render by looping over the number of technique passes */
    for(int i = 0; i < technique.Passes; ++i)
    {
        g_pd3d10EffectTechnique->GetPassByIndex(i)->Apply(0);
        g_pd3d10Device->Draw(3, 0);
    }

    /* switch the back- and front-buffer and display the
       triangle */
    g_pdxl0SwapChain->Present(0,0);
}
```

7.6.4 Rendering a scaled triangle

Our final example demonstrates 50 percent scaling. The declaration and initialization of the world, view and projection matrices, including the code added to the InitDevice function, are identical to the previous two examples.

We define a scaling matrix using the D3DXMATRIX structure, initializing it via the D3DXMatrixScaling function. In a similar way to the above examples, we apply this scaling matrix to the world matrix via the D3DXMatrixMultiply function, finally updating the world, view and projection matrices using the SetMatrix method:

```
void DrawTriangle()
{
    /* declare the scaling matrix */
    D3DXMATRIX scalingMatrix;

    /* initialize the scaling matrix (50% original size) */
    D3DXMatrixScaling(&scalingMatrix, 0.5f, 0.5f, 0.5f);
    /* apply the scaling matrix to the world matrix */
    D3DXMatrixMultiply(&g_WorldMatrix, &g_WorldMatrix,
                        &scalingMatrix);

    /* clear the back-buffer */
    float ClearBufferColor[4] = {0.0f, 0.125f, 0.3f, 1.0f};
    g_pd3d10Device->ClearRenderTargetView(
                        g_pd3d10RenderTargetView,
                        ClearBufferColor);

    /* update the world, view, and projection matrices */
    /////////////////////////////////////////////////////
    g_pd3d10EffectWorldMatrix->
            SetMatrix((float*)&g_WorldMatrix);

    g_pd3d10EffectViewMatrix->
            SetMatrix((float*)&g_ViewMatrix);

    g_pd3d10EffectWorldMatrix->
            SetMatrix( (float*)&g_ProjectionMatrix);

    /* obtain the D3D10_TECHNIQUE_DESC effect-variable
        description */
    D3D10_TECHNIQUE_DESC technique;
    g_pd3d10EffectTechnique->GetDesc(&technique);

    /* render by looping over the number of technique passes */
    for(int i = 0; i < technique.Passes; ++i)
    {
        g_pd3d10EffectTechnique->GetPassByIndex(i)->Apply(0);
        g_pd3d10Device->Draw(3, 0);
```

```
    }
    /* switch the back- and front-buffer and display the
       triangle */
    g_pdxl0SwapChain->Present(0,0);
}
```

Working with OpenGL: Translation, Rotation and Scaling

The following example combines translation, rotation, and scaling operations.

We begin by including the standard glut header, it imports both gl.h and glu.h:

```
#include <GL/glut.h>
```

Next we define the drawTriangle function, subsequently specifying our triangle via a list of vertices:

```
void drawTriangle()
{
    /* sets color to red */
    glColor3f(1.0,0.0,0.0);
    /* glBegin composes the group of vertices below as a
       polygon */
    glBegin(GL_POLYGON);
        glVertex3f(0.0, -10.0, -6.0); //x = 0, y = -10, z = -6
        glVertex3f(-10.0, 0.0, 6.0); //x = -10, y = 0, z = 6
        glVertex3f(10.0, 0.0, 6.0); //x = 10, y = 0, z = 6
    /* glEnd indicates the end of the rendering group */
    glEnd();
}
```

Our next function, constructTriangles, executes a series of transformations, rendering the triangle in the middle of the viewport rotated towards the viewer. This function also scales the triangle to 50 percent, its original size.

```
void constructTriangles()
{
    /* -90 degree rotation about the x-axis (90 degree
       clockwise) */
    glRotatef(-90.0, 1.0, 0.0, 0.0);
    /* translate 30 units along the y-axis */
    glTranslatef(0,30,0);
    /* -180 degree rotation about the x-axis (180 degree
       clockwise) */
    glRotatef(-180.0,1.0,0.0,0.0);
    /* reduce the triangle's size by 50% */
    glScalef(0.5,0.5,0.5);
    /* apply the above translations to the drawTriangle
       function */
```

```
        drawTriangle();
}
```

The display function is responsible for rendering the output to the screen:

```
void display(void)
{
    /* clear frame buffer and z-buffer */
    glClear(GL_COLOR_BUFFER_BIT | GL_DEPTH_BUFFER_BIT);
    /* move to the center of the screen */
    glLoadIdentity();

    /* call our triangle drawing function */
    constructTriangles();

    /* make sure all previously issued commands have
        completed */
    glFlush();
     /* switch the back- and front-buffer and display the
        triangle */
    glutSwapBuffers();
}
```

A GLUT callback is generated via the glutReshapeFunc function whenever we resize the output window. This callback is handled by our reshape function, ensuring a correctly rendered viewport, regardless of the window's size or shape. It works by clearing and redrawing the screen following each resize:

```
void reshape(int w, int h)
{
    /* sets the viewport */
    glViewport(0, 0, (GLsizei) w, (GLsizei) h);

    /* sets the Projection matrix as the current matrix */
    glMatrixMode(GL_PROJECTION);
    /* move to the center of the screen */
    glLoadIdentity();

    /* initializes the  perspective projection matrix */
    gluPerspective(45, (double)w / (double)h, 0.05, 100);

    /* sets the Modelview matrix as the current matrix */
    glMatrixMode(GL_MODELVIEW);
}
```

Finally, the main function, is called by the system as the application's entry point:

```
int main(int argc, char** argv)
{
```

```
      /* initialize the GLUT library. */
      glutInit(&argc, argv);
      /* sets the initial display mode:
         double buffering and a depth buffer. */
      glutInitDisplayMode(GLUT_DOUBLE|GLUT_RGB|GLUT_DEPTH);
      /* sets default window size */
      glutInitWindowSize(800, 600);
      /* creates a top-level window with a caption */
      glutCreateWindow("OpenGL: Translation, Rotation, and
                        Scaling");
      /* reshape callback */
      glutReshapeFunc(reshape);
      /* displays the triangle in the viewport */
      glutDisplayFunc(display);
      /* enables hidden-surface removal */
      glEnable(GL_DEPTH_TEST);
      /* the GLUT event processing loop */
      glutMainLoop();
      return 0;
}
```

7.7   SUMMARY

We can now create arbitrary, modifiable objects in three-dimensional space. Coupling the rendering topics of Chapter 6 and 7 with Chapter 5's input control provides a complete toolset for the creation of interactive three-dimensional applications.

We started by looking at the foundation for object representation, namely two- and three-dimensional Cartesian coordinate systems. Following this we dealt with the concept of device independent graphics. We also learned about the synthetic-camera model, the concept of depth-of-field, the film plane, projectors and the virtual image plane. We subsequently focused on the viewing system, culling, clipping and the change of coordinate system frames by means of viewing, modeling, projection, and viewport transformations. The remainder of the chapter focused on various spatial transformations, such as rotation about the coordinate axes and arbitrary fixed points, translation and scaling.

At this point, we have examined the main functional units of both OpenGL and DirectX. The rest of the book delves into more advanced rendering techniques, such as texturing methods, lighting and reflection models, shaders, special effects, stencil shadow volumes, hidden surface removal, clipping, Level of Detail algorithms, polygonal meshes, artificial intelligence and physics modeling.

7.8   FURTHER READING

There are several excellent books dealing with linear algebra, matrix manipulations, vector space and linear transformations. One such a book is *Linear Algebra and Its Applications* by David C. Lay (ISBN: 0321287134). *Linear Algebra with Applications* by Steven J. Leon (ISBN: 0130337811) balances mathematical theory with application to present the topic of linear algebra in a visual manner.

7.9 EXERCISES

1 Explain the relationship between projectors and the center of projection.

2 Discuss the rationale behind the change of coordinate systems.

3 Consider the following code sample:

```
D3DXMATRIX matrixTranslate;
D3DXMatrixRotationZ(&matrixTranslate, -0.78f);
D3DXMatrixRotationY(&matrixTranslate, 0.78f);
D3DXMatrixScaling(&matrixTranslate, 0.5f, 0.5f, 0.5f);
D3DXMatrixTranslation(&matrixTranslate,-1.0f,2.0f,1.0f);
```

Illustrate, using a three-dimensional Cartesian coordinate system, the combined effect of these transformations on a cube located at the origin.

4 Describe the purpose of the virtual image plane.

5 Rotation about the z-axis is given by the following matrix:

$$R_z = \begin{bmatrix} \cos\theta & -\sin\theta & 0 & 0 \\ \sin\theta & \cos\theta & 0 & 0 \\ 0 & 0 & 1 & 0 \\ 0 & 0 & 0 & 1 \end{bmatrix}$$

If we want to rotate an object about its center, (x^P, y^P), via the z-axis, and the transformation matrix is calculated by first translating the object back to the origin, rotating it about the z-axis, and moving it back to its fixed point, what is the concatenated matrix, M, for this operation?

6 What is the purpose of the D3D10_RASTERIZER_DESC render state structure?

7 Draw a comparison between perspective and parallel projections, also listing some of their uses in computer games.

8 What Direct3D function combines a matrix product?

9 Discuss the purpose of a viewport, and, using Direct3D 10, define a viewport of 1280 by 1024 pixels.

10 List two diverse approaches for producing an orthographic projection.

11 What is the purpose of the SetMatrix method?

12 Compare back-face elimination to occlusion culling.

13 What does the D3DTS_VIEW constant specify?

14 Using Direct3D, create and set a vertex buffer for a 10 by 10 triangle.

15 Specify a view matrix with an eye coordinate of (0, 1, 1), a look at point of (0, 1, 0) and an 'up' direction of (0, 1, 1).

16 Set a left-handed perspective projection matrix based on an arbitrary field of view and 600 by 400 pixel aspect ratio.

17 Write either an OpenGL or Direct3D program that creates a floor with some randomly placed spheres – resulting in a scene similar to the one depicted here:

18 Extend the program written for exercise 17 to include input control – thus allowing arbitrary movement and rotation of the camera within the scene.

19 Briefly describe how the camera can be prevented from flying through the spheres.

CHAPTER 8

Color and Texture Mapping

LEARNING OBJECTIVES

In this chapter you will learn about:

- Color
- Texturing
- Texture filtering
- Mipmapping
- Nearest point interpolation
- Bilinear filtering
- Trilinear filtering
- Anisotropic filtering
- Basic texture mapping
- Bump mapping
- Cube mapping (environmental mapping)

INTRODUCTION

Chapter 8 presents a number of techniques used for adding detail to geometric objects. It starts by presenting theory related to color perception, subsequently discussing a number of color models and the application of color in both Direct3D and OpenGL programs. Following this, it provides in-depth coverage of texturing, including a number of texture filtering techniques such as mipmapping, nearest point interpolation, and trilinear filtering. The chapter concludes with a detailed discussion of two frequently utilized texturing techniques: bump mapping and cube mapping. Bump mapping is discussed at hand of a High Level Shade Language (HLSL) implementation with cube mapping being illustrated via both an HLSL and a Cg implementation.

8.1 COLOR

Visible light can be defined as a wavelength function ranged from 350 to 780 nm (nano meter). While there aren't clearly defined wavelength limits separating different colors, we can roughly define color ranges starting at black with a wavelength of 350 nm. Black goes over into violet at about 380 nm. Different shades of violet can be observed from 380 to about 450 nm. Violet turns into blue at about 450 nm which becomes green at roughly 495 nm. The color green (ranged from 495 to 570 nm) goes over into yellow (570 to 590 nm) which subsequently becomes orange (590 to 630 nm). The final visible color, red, spans from about 630 to 760 nm. Figure 8-1 shows the shades of these visible light spectrum colors.

The representation of color in display devices (using a red, green, and blue component) can directly be linked to the human perception of it. The human brain only picks up three color values at any given moment (as opposed to the complete color distribution outlined above). These three values, called *tri-stimulus values,* are the result of the human visual system's color cones. Color cones reduce any perceived color range to three distinct values. The significance of this reduction to computer graphics is that any color can be reproduced using three color elements, namely, a red, green, and blue component.

Computers make use of the red–green–blue (RGB) color model. This is an *additive color model* where perceived colors are formed by overlapping the primary red, green, and blue colors (see Figure 8-2). The additive color model thus adds light to a black surface through the combination of varying shades of red, green, and blue.

8

FIGURE 8-1   **The visible light spectrum's color distribution**

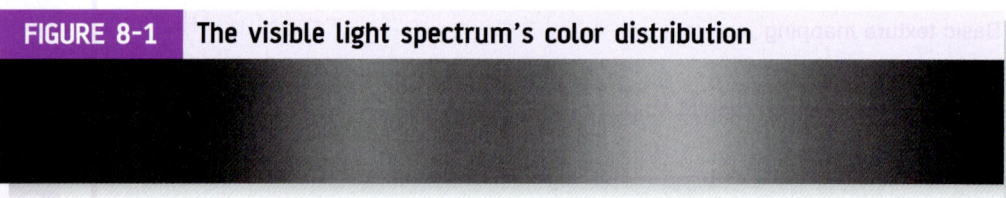

FIGURE 8-2   **The additive color model**

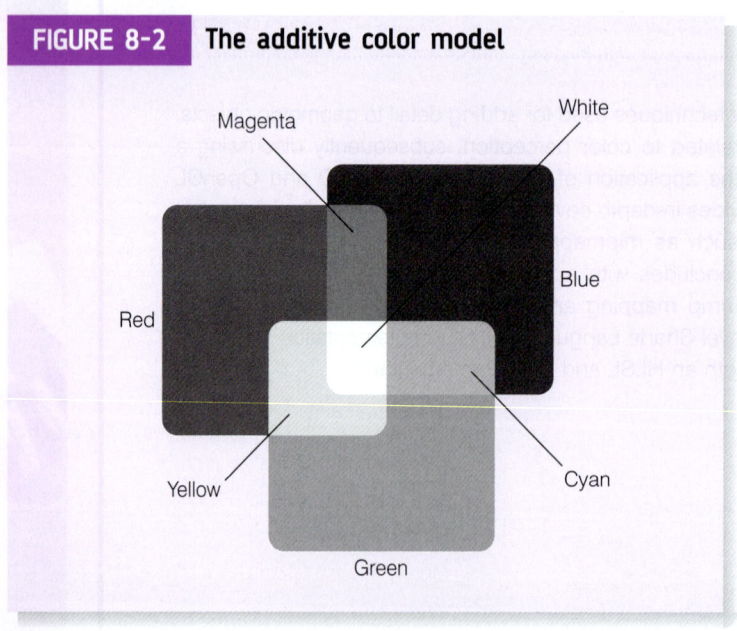

Another commonly used color model is the cyan–magenta–yellow (CMY) model, also called the *subtractive color model*. The use of this color model can be observed with printing or painting where a white surface generally serves as background. The perceived colors are formed by overlapping the complementary colors cyan, magenta, and yellow (see Figure 8-3). The process is called subtractive due to the surface absorbing all incoming light except for that of the resulting color. For example, if a white light strikes a surface, then a green color will be observed if all other wavelengths with the exception of the 495 to 570 nm wavelength is absorbed by the surface.

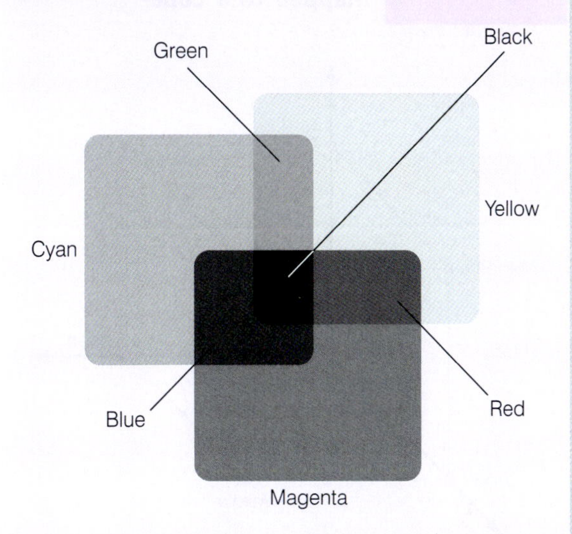

The color value at any specific point can be expressed in terms of a three-component vector. Numerous color intensities/shades can be described by additively combining various intensities of red, green, and blue. The general equation for additive color is defined as follows (r, g and b are weights representing the intensity of each color component):

FIGURE 8-3   **The subtractive color model**

Color = (r x Red) + (g x Green) + (b x Blue)

The physical construction of a monitor is amenable to the use of a three-component vector for the description of a single color element. This is due to monitors grouping their light-emitting elements (phosphors in CRTs and light-emitting elements such as diodes for other displays such as LCDs) in triangular sets known as *triads*. Each triad consists of a red, green, and blue pixel. Colors on a monitor are thus not produced by mixing the red, green, and blue component specified by the color vector but rather by placing the light-emitting elements in close proximity with each other and then setting each of these triads to one of the colors specified by the vector. The human eye interprets these three values as one due to the color elements being positioned so close to each other.

The additive color model describes a color in terms of red, green, and blue intensity. This intensity varies from minimum, indicating absence of the specific primary color (resulting in black), to maximum for full intensity. White is produced when the intensity of the red, green, and blue primary colors have all been set to their maximum. OpenGL and Direct3D both set color intensities using the range 0.0 (minimum) to 1.0 (maximum). For example, full-intensity blue is represented by the vector (0.0, 0.0, 1.0). Many drawing applications also make use of intensities ranging from 0 to 255. Full-intensity blue is represented as (0, 0, 255) in this context. Hexadecimal values can also represent color ranges (as the convention with web colors).

Working in *true-color* (a representation of red–green–blue color values using 24 bits per pixel), we can specify a cube by viewing color as a specific point in three-dimensional space. This cube is defined via a coordinate system analogous to the three primary colors with the intensity of a color represented by the distance from the origin to any other location within the cube – the color vector. Figure 8-4 shows such a color cube with the maximum value of each primary color normalized to 1.

The red–green–blue color cube suffers for perceptual nonlinearality. What that means is that there is not necessarily any correlation between the distances in the color cube and the perceived color.

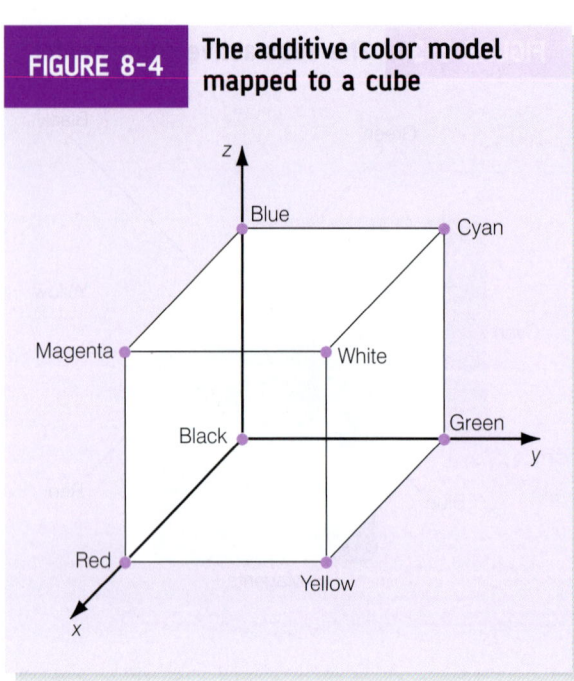

FIGURE 8-4 **The additive color model mapped to a cube**

Hence, a slight distance increase might result in no perceived color change in one part of the cube with a noticeable change at another region.

Describing a color using a red, green, and blue component is somewhat troublesome since humans rather use terms such as 'blood red' or 'royal blue' to express colors. Calculating the red, green, and blue values to produce a 'blood red' color, for example, isn't intuitive since these three color components need to be tweaked separately and by different amounts. The Hue, Saturation and Value (HSV) single hexcone model offers a more intuitive interface for the selection of colors.

The hexcone model presents a hexagonal cone for the representation of the color space. Using a hexagonal cone, also referred to as a *hexcone*, leads to a greater level of perceptual linearity. The manner in which we thus think of color is akin to the way in which color values are described using this model. That said, the HSV model still suffers from perceptual nonlinearality; specifically, linear changes to the hue of a color value results in nonlinear perceptual changes for the observer.

The HSV single hexcone model is based on polar coordinates to describe Saturation and Value with degrees for Hue rather than Cartesian coordinates (as is the case with the red–green–blue cube model). Hue is defined in terms of degrees and ranges from 0° to 360°. *Hue* is the aspect by which we differentiate between different colors, for example red from yellow or blue from purple. *Value* is a parameter that allows us to tell apart light colors from dark ones; increasing the value parameter increases the lightness of a color until the color completely saturates to white. *Saturation* is the scale by which the richness or quality of a color is controlled. The higher the saturation, the more vivid the produced colors, while the less the saturation, the more grey the specific color. Figure 8-5 shows a hexcone color space.

Graphics accelerators commonly employed today all support 24 bits per pixel for the storage of color information. This equates to 8 bits for each of the red, green, and blue color elements, resulting in 256 color intensities for each primary color. There are thus 16 777 216 (2^{24}) distinct colors that can be displayed using this array of 24 bits per pixel.

In Direct3D we can either set the color value of a vertex directly or through the use of an effect program. The direct approach, as discussed in Chapter 6, relies on the specification of a structure to hold information about our geometric object's vertices. For example:

```
struct TriangleVertex
{
    D3DXVECTOR3 Location;
    D3DXVECTOR3 Color;
};
```

FIGURE 8-5	A hexcone color solid

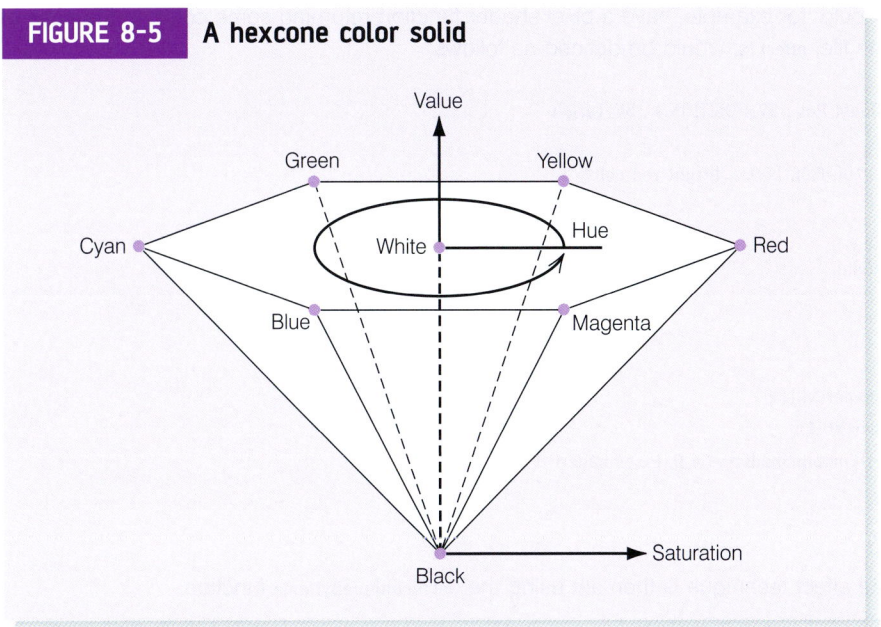

We also have to create a vertex buffer to assign color values to each of the vertices – hence, for a triangle object we will have three vertices, each assigned a specific color value:

```
TriangleVertex array_of_vertex_data [] =
{
    D3DXVECTOR3( 0.0f, 1.0f, 1.0f ),    //location
    D3DXVECTOR3( 0.0f, 0.0f, 0.5f ),    //dark blue color
    D3DXVECTOR3( 1.0f, −1.0f, 1.0f ),   //location
    D3DXVECTOR3( 1.0f, 0.0f, 0.0f ),    //bright red color
    D3DXVECTOR3( −1.0f, −1.0f, 1.0f ),  //location
    D3DXVECTOR3( 0.0f, 1.0f, 0.0f ),    //bright green color
};
```

Using this vertex data we initialize the D3D10_SUBRESOURCE_DATA structure using the data array, also creating a vertex buffer using the CreateBuffer ID3D10Device interface. Once this is done we create the input-layout object using the CreateInputLayout ID3D10Device interface method and binding it to the input-assembler stage via the IASetVertexBuffers and IASetInputLayout ID3D10Device interfaces. Following this we simply have to set the primitive type and call the Draw ID3D10Device function to do the actual rendering (please refer to section 6.2 for a detailed discussion of this process).

We can also load an effect file to specify an object's color using D3DX10CreateEffectFromFile function (see section 6.5.4.3). The following code snippet loading an effect is taken from example 7.6.1:

```
hresult_ =    D3DX10CreateEffectFromFile(
                  L"effect.fx", NULL, NULL,
                  D3D10_SHADER_ENABLE_STRICTNESS, 0,
                  g_pd3d10Device, NULL, NULL, &g_pd3d10Effect,
                  NULL);
```

8

The effect file could, for example, have a pixel shader function returning some color. In the case of our discussion, the file, effect.fx, would be defined as follows:

```
float4 PixelShader( float4 Pos : SV_POSITION ) : SV_Target
{
    return float4(1.0f, 0.0f, 0.0f, 1.0f); //bright red color
}


technique10 TriangleColor
{
    pass P0
    {
        SetGeometryShader(NULL);
        SetVertexShader(NULL);
        SetPixelShader(CompileShader(ps_4_0, PixelShader()));
    }
}
```

The appropriate effect technique is then set using the GetTechniqueByName function:

```
g_pd3d10EffectTechnique = g_pd3d10Effect->
                        GetTechniqueByName("TriangleColor");
```

The final step is to apply the defined pixel shader to the rendered object as explained in Chapters 6 and 7:

```
/* obtain the D3D10_TECHNIQUE_DESC effect-variable
   description */
D3D10_TECHNIQUE_DESC technique;
g_pd3d10EffectTechnique->GetDesc(&technique);

/* render by looping over the number of technique passes */
for(int i = 0; i < technique.Passes; ++i)
{
    g_pd3d10EffectTechnique->GetPassByIndex(i)->Apply(0);
    g_pd3d10Device->Draw(3, 0);
}
```

Working with OpenGL

Using OpenGL we set the color state using the function glColor** – mostly used in the form glColor3f. This function specifies the red, green, and blue color components by setting the color value of each parameter to a floating-point value ranging from 0 to 1. For example, to set the color state to red we will issue the following function call:

```
glColor3f(1.0, 0.0, 0.0);
```

OpenGL is as previously mentioned state-based, meaning that the programmer has to specifically put it into a state, in which the API stays until the programmer explicitly alters the state.

An example of this is when we specify OpenGL to draw lines which results in a line being drawn whenever two vertices are defined. Color is no exception to this. The above-listed call will set the current OpenGL drawing color to red, and every object will be drawn using this color until the color is changed by another glColor function call. The following function, taken from section 7.6.4, illustrates this by setting the drawing color to red and then composing a group of vertices into a triangle:

```
void drawTriangle()
{
    /* set the drawing color to red */
    glColor3f(1.0,0.0,0.0);
    /* glBegin composes the group of vertices below as a
       triangle */
    glBegin(GL_TRIANGLE);
        glVertex3f(0.0, -10.0, -6.0);
        glVertex3f(-10.0, 0.0, 6.0);
        glVertex3f(10.0, 0.0, 6.0);
    /* glEnd indicates the end of the rendering group */
    glEnd();
}
```

We also frequently add another component to specify color, resulting in glColor calls such as:

```
glColor4f(1.0, 0.0, 0.0, 1.0);
```

The fourth value in this call is an alpha color component used for setting the opacity of an object when blending is enabled. This alpha value ranges from 0.0 for fully transparent objects to 1.0 for fully opaque ones.

8.2   TEXTURING

Texture mapping is an easy way of adding realism to a computer generated object. The texture (be it a tile-able photograph or complex pattern) is mapped (fitted) to the computer generated object, either stretched or tiled to encompass the entire object area. Figure 8-6 shows a texture mapped sphere; notice the hard shadows on the unmapped sphere (a) and how these shadows seem natural once the object has been textured (b). By adding a texture to the sphere we are able to portray it as a planet or moon – no longer just as an arbitrarily shaded object.

Textures consist of a number of fundamental subunits called texels or texture elements (which can be considered the pixels of a texture). Arrays of texels make up a texture just as images are created using arrays of pixels. Textures can be one, two or three dimensional in nature (sometimes even four dimensional) with two-dimensional textures being the most common of all these. A one-dimensional texture is simply an array of texture elements (as shown in Figure 8-7). Each texture element is addressable using a vector/texture coordinate – x in Figure 8-7. These one-dimensional textures are normally used for the creation of simple patterns that can be mapped to a line-based geometric object such as a curve.

FIGURE 8-6   Texture mapping (a) before (b) after

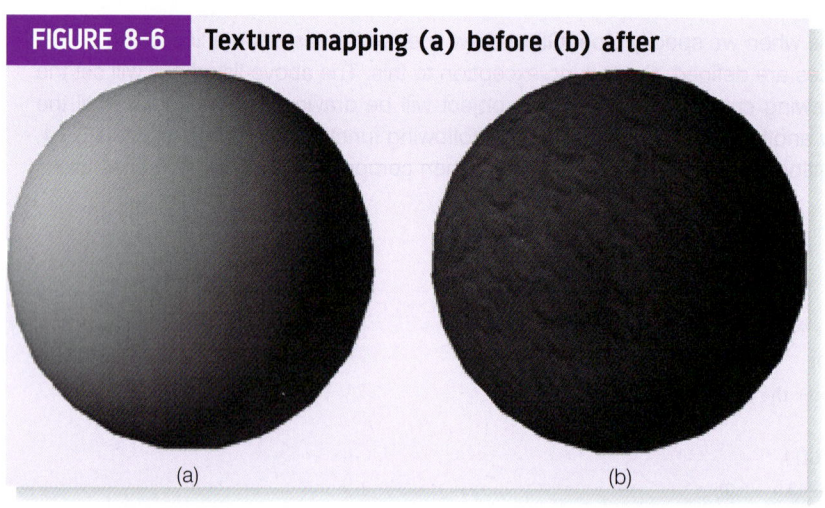

(a)   (b)

FIGURE 8-7   Representation of a one-dimensional texture

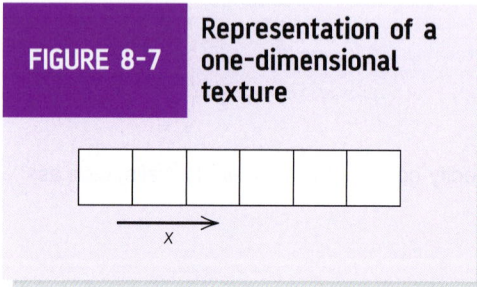

FIGURE 8-8   Representation of a two-dimensional texture

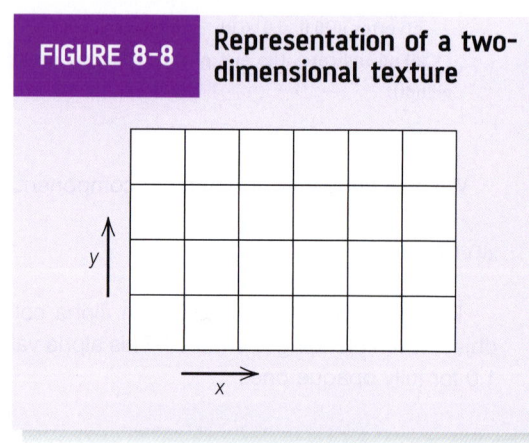

8

FIGURE 8-9   Representation of a three-dimensional texture

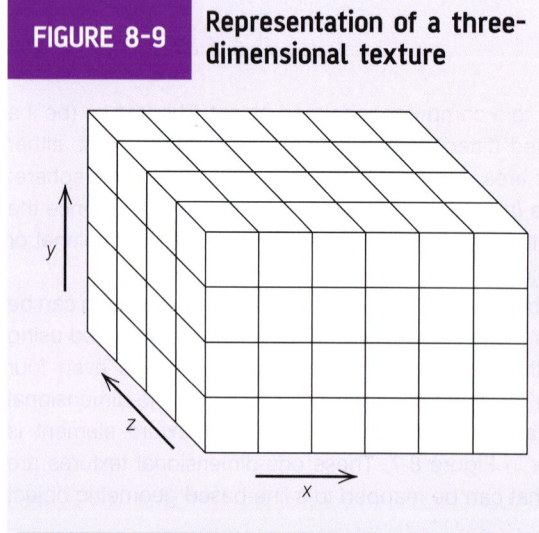

Two-dimensional textures are represented using a two-dimensional array with each texture element addressable via an x and y vector. These textures are the type that we will be working with; even our depth and normal maps used during bump mapping are represented using these two-dimensional bitmap arrays. Figure 8-8 shows the layout for a 4×6 texture.

Volumetric textures, also called three-dimensional textures, are another interesting texture resource type. These textures, represented as three-dimensional volumes, are useful for describing solid material blocks from which arbitrary objects can be shaped. Figure 8-9 shows an interpretation of such a texture with a texel being addressable via x, y and z vectors.

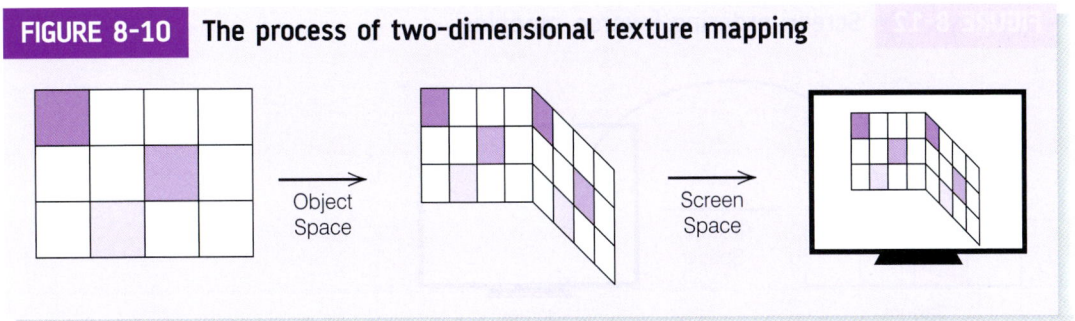

FIGURE 8-10   **The process of two-dimensional texture mapping**

Object Space

Screen Space

Texture mapping is based on the mani-pulation of individual fragments during the graphics pipeline's fragment processing stage. The method used to perform the actual texture mapping at application level depends mainly on the level of quality required. The most common method maps a two-dimensional texture resource onto the surface of an object. This texture mapping process starts out in two-dimensional texture space and moves to three-dimensional object space where the texture is mapped onto the object – a process known as *surface parameterization*. A projection transforma-tion, as described in Chapter 7, is then used to move from object space to screen space. Figure 8-10 illustrates this process.

Textures are loaded into system memory as arrays with coordinates, called *texture*

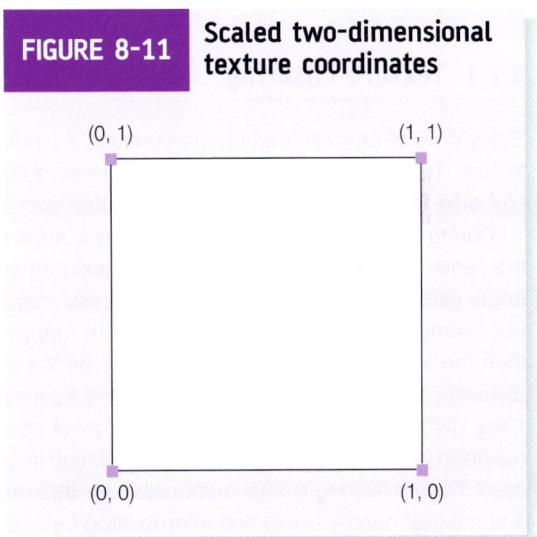

FIGURE 8-11   **Scaled two-dimensional texture coordinates**

(0, 1)   (1, 1)

(0, 0)   (1, 0)

coordinates. These coordinates allow us to address and access the individual texel elements making up the array. Texture coordinates are generally scaled to range over the interval (0, 1) as shown in Figure 8-11.

Two-dimensional textures can be described using the notation $T(u, v)$ with u and v the texture coordinates uniquely defined for each vertex on a given surface. The process of texture mapping is thus concerned with aligning each texel's texture space coordinates with a vertex on the surface of an object.

Matching texture space coordinates with object vertices can be done using a number of techniques, the most common two being texture ordering (also referred to as forward mapping) and the screen ordering (inverse mapping) algorithm. The s*creen ordering algorithm* starts in screen space and uses an inverse mapping to find a pixel's pre-image in texture space. A *pre-image* is the area of the texture calculated in terms of texture coordinates that will contribute to the individual color of a pixel. The u and v texture coordinates are thus determined for each pixel with the color value at that texture location assigned to the pixel. Figure 8-12 shows this inverse mapping process.

The *texture ordering* algorithm generates a quadrilateral from a texture element in texture space and maps this quad to the object in screen space. This technique was illustrated in Figure 8-10 and can be summarized as the stretching of a texture to fit the surface of an object.

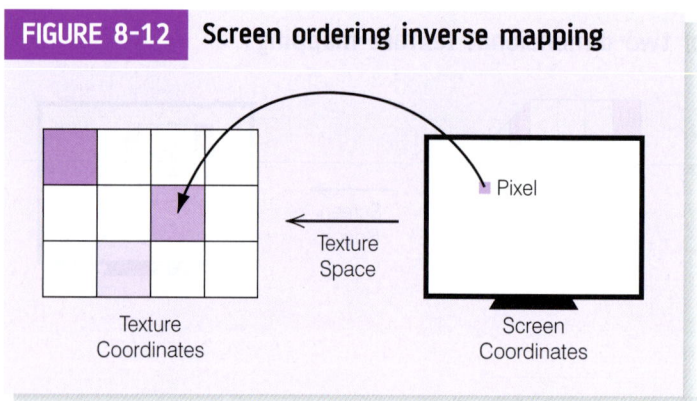

FIGURE 8-12   Screen ordering inverse mapping

Texture Space

Texture Coordinates

Pixel

Screen Coordinates

8.2.1 Texture Filtering

Every pixel of an onscreen image contains an independently controlled color value obtained from the texture. Texture filtering, also called 'texture smoothing', controls the way in which pixels are colored by blending the color values of adjacent texture elements.

During the texturing process a mapping is done to determine the location, in texture space, matching the center of each individual pixel. Since textured surfaces are often curved or rotated at some arbitrary angle (with regard to the point of view) a pixel might not perfectly map to an individual texture element. For example, say we have a square texture mapped to an object of exactly the same size and shape; then the size of one screen pixel will only be the same as the size of one texel at a particular viewing distance. Texels will appear larger than the screen pixels when we move closer to the object. Further away distances will in turn result in one pixel covering multiple texels. This mapping 'misalignment' results in jagged, blurry, shimmering, or aliased images and a different type of filtering is needed in each case. *Texture filtering* is thus responsible for determining the most accurate color of a pixel by sampling a number of nearby texels and interpolating between these values. Examples of texture filtering include nearest-point sampling, linear texture filtering, anisotropic texture filtering, bilinear filtering, trilinear filtering, and filtering via mipmaps. We will now look at each of these techniques in detail.

8.2.1.1 Mipmapping
A *mipmap* is a series of pre-filtered texture images of varying resolution. Mipmaps are created by progressively lowering the resolution of the main texture. When using mipmaps, Direct3D or OpenGL automatically maps a suitable texture, based on size in pixels, to the object being mapped. Thus, the closer the object to the viewer, the higher the resolution of the mipmap image. Mipmaps are represented in memory as a sequence of attached images with the high-resolution 'source' texture at the start of this sequence. The next texture in this sequence is smaller by a power of two. For example, if the main texture has a resolution of 512×512 pixels, then the next one will be 256×256, followed by one of 128×128 pixels, with the smallest texture set to 64×64 pixels (image resolution can be reduced even further, down to a single pixel, resulting in the add-on of the following chain: 32×32, 16×16, 8×8, 4×4, 2×2 and 1×1). Figure 8-13 shows a texture chain starting with a 256×256 source texture and ending with a 64×64 image.

Each texture shown in Figure 8-13 has a maximum viewing distance for which it will be displayed. For example, say this texture is used as a poster on a wall: when the viewer is standing far away from it, the 64×64 resolution texture will be displayed, and the highest resolution texture is shown when the viewer is very close to the object. The resolution of each mipmap texture is referred to as a 'mipmap level'. These mipmap levels are linked to the distance from the textured object, with mipmap level 0 indicating

FIGURE 8-13   **Mipmap image storage**

8

textures closest to the viewer. Mipmaps improve the quality of textured objects and they also decrease the amount of time required to render a scene, however, large amounts of texture memory is generally required for their implementation.

FIGURE 8-14   **A misaligned point sample and texture elements**

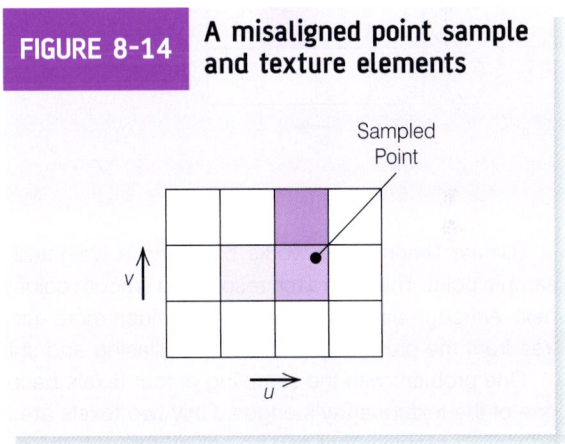

8.2.1.2 Nearest Point Interpolation The point matching the center of a texture element is rarely obtained when texture coordinates are mapped to a two-dimensional array of texels (shown in Figure 8-14).

Nearest point interpolation is used to approximate this point by using the color value of the texel closest to the sampled point. This texture filtering method has the best performance but poorest overall result of all the sampling/filtering techniques. Nearest point interpolation, sometimes called 'nearest point sampling', results in blocky looking textures on closely zoomed objects and shimmering aliased artifacts when the textured object is located relatively far from the viewer. Nearest neighbor interpolation selects color values from a textured surface by sampling the color of the texel closest to the mapped texture coordinates. The worst results are generated by this filtering method when a texture is sampled at the boundary between two texels. Figure 8-15 illustrates the artifacts generated when implementing nearest point sampling without taking care not to sample textures at texel boundaries.

We can also combine nearest point interpolation with mipmapping to produce fewer artifacts by selecting the most appropriate mipmap level and then to sample the color of the texel closest to the

FIGURE 8-15 **Artifacts generated as an effect of nearest point sampling**

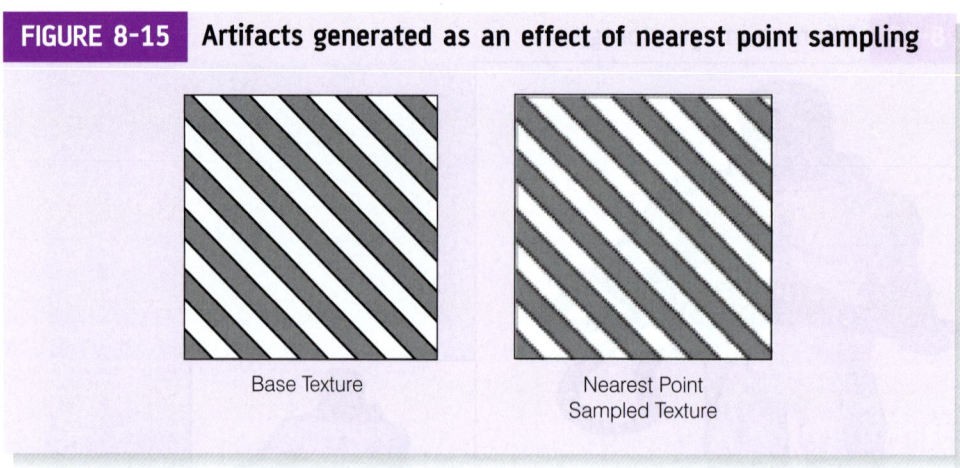

Base Texture

Nearest Point
Sampled Texture

FIGURE 8-16 **A misaligned point sample with 'X' indicating a texel used for bilinear filtering**

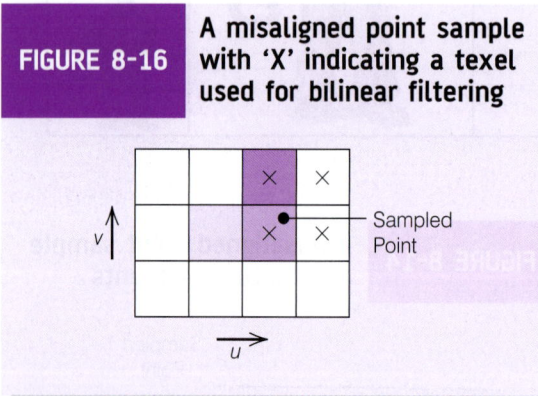

mapped texture coordinates. This results in more accurate sampling due to a higher correlation between the size of one pixel and that of one texture element.

8.2.1.3 Bilinear Filtering *Bilinear filtering* builds on the concept of nearest point interpolation by sampling not just one but four texture elements when texture coordinates are mapped to a two-dimensional array of texels (shown in Figure 8-16). Bilinear filtering is nearly always combined with mipmapping, resulting in a noticeable quality switch whenever one mipmap level changes to another.

Bilinear filtering thus works by taking a weighted average of the group of texels surrounding the sample point. This approach results in a smooth color gradient transition from one texture element to the next. Although bilinear interpolation is much more accurate than nearest point interpolation, it is still not free from the previously encountered aliasing and shimmering issues.

One problem with the sampling of four texels becomes apparent when a sample point is located at one of the texture array's edges. Only two texels are available for bilinear interpolation at one of these edges – a problem that can be solved through the addition of a texel wide border.

8.2.1.4 Trilinear Filtering Bilinear filtering does not perform any interpolation between mipmaps, resulting in noticeable quality changes where the graphics system switches between mipmap levels. *Trilinear filtering* solves this quality issue by extending the previous technique to perform a texture lookup coupled with a bilinear filtering operation for the two bordering mipmap images, one for the higher resolution texture, and the other for the lower resolution one. The results obtained from this filtering are then interpolated to give a smooth quality falloff as distance from the viewer increases.

Trilinear filtering is far from perfect and suffers from the assumption that pixels will always map to square texture areas. For example, when a texture is orientated at a relative steep angle with regard to the point of view, then a pixel will map to an elongated quadrilateral – thus mapping to two or more texels along the breadth of the quad (resulting in 'texture smears') and to a smaller number of texels than it should along its length (resulting in detail falloff since color information is lost).

8.2.1.5 Anisotropic Filtering

Anisotropy is a distortion visible in the texels of a textured object when the object is rotated at a specific angle to the point of view. This distortion is due to the elongation and deformation of a pixel's shape when it is mapped to texels from a distorted primitive using the screen ordering algorithm. Figure 8-17 shows a trilinear mipmapped scene with Figure 8-18 showing the same scene, only this time making use of anisotropic texture filtering – notice the much more blurry appearance of the distant textures in the first image.

Bilinear and trilinear filtering are only capable of sampling equally sided rectangles from textures and are only accurate in situations where the texture's normal vector is perpendicular to the viewer (shown in Figure 8-19). The textures of objects consequently turn blurry when viewed at slanting angles with the texture pattern often diminishing into the distance.

Anisotropic texture filtering deals with this blurriness by sampling texture elements using a quadrilateral modified according to the viewing angle. A single pixel, as mentioned, could encompass more texel elements in one direction, such as along the *x*-axis, than in another, for instance along the *z*-axis. By using a modifiable quadrilateral for the sampling of texels, we are able to maintain proper perspective and precision when mapping a texture

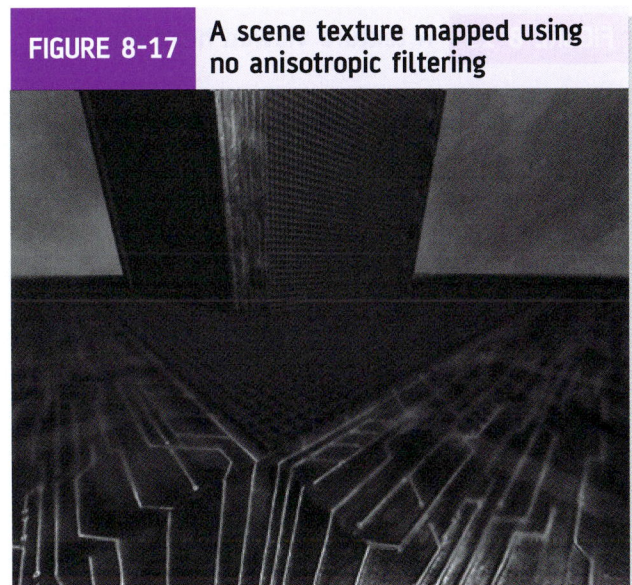

FIGURE 8-17 A scene texture mapped using no anisotropic filtering

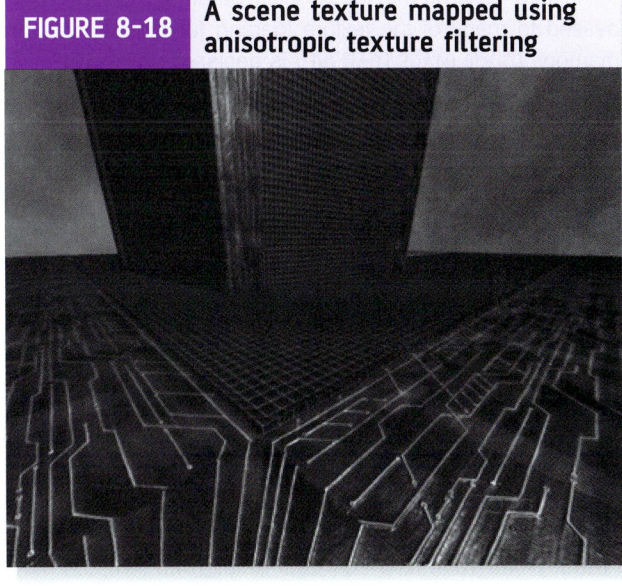

FIGURE 8-18 A scene texture mapped using anisotropic texture filtering

to an object. Anisotropic filtering is not limited to quad-shaped texture sampling patterns and can also use rectangular and parallelogram-shaped ones – each sampling pattern's shape modified in proportion to the orientation and stretching of the texture.

8.2.2 Basic Texture Mapping

We will now look at texture mapping from an implementation perspective, in essence the implementation steps required to project a two-dimensional bitmap array onto a three-dimensional geometric object.

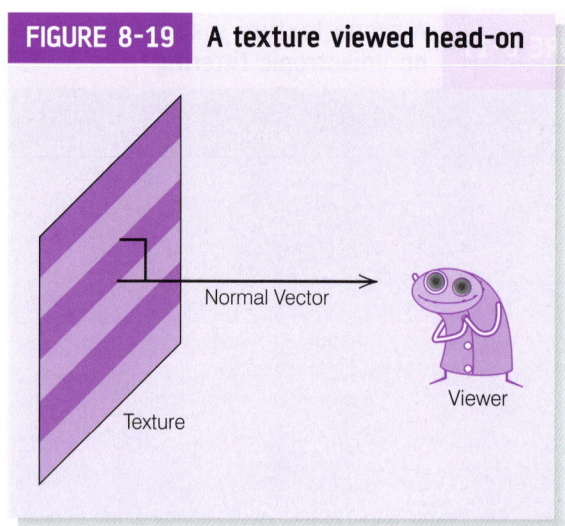

FIGURE 8-19   A texture viewed head-on

Normal Vector

Viewer

Texture

The first step is to load a two-dimensional texture array into memory. This is the texture map, a properly scaled image created using a drawing package such as Adobe Photoshop, for example. We make use of the D3DX10CreateTextureFromFile texturing function to create a texture resource from an image file. This function is declared in the d3dx10.h header file as follows:

```
HRESULT D3DX10CreateTextureFromFile(
    ID3D10Device *pDevice,
    LPCTSTR pSrcFile,
    D3DX10_IMAGE_LOAD_INFO *pLoadInfo,
    ID3DX10ThreadPump *pPump,
    ID3D10Resource **ppTexture
);
```

Its first parameter, pDevice, takes a pointer to an ID3D10Device interface that will apply the texture resource during rendering. The second parameter, pSrcFile, takes a pointer to a string containing the texture filename with the pLoadInfo parameter set to a D3DX10_IMAGE_LOAD_INFO structure. This structure, passed to many of the texture loading functions, alters properties of the image as it is loaded into memory. D3DX10_IMAGE_LOAD_INFO is declared as follows:

```
typedef struct D3DX10_IMAGE_LOAD_INFO {
    UINT Width;
    UINT Height;
    UINT Depth;
    UINT FirstMipLevel;
    UINT MipLevels;
    D3D10_USAGE Usage;
    UINT BindFlags;
    UINT CpuAccessFlags;
    UINT MiscFlags;
    DXGI_FORMAT Format;
    UINT Filter;
    UINT MipFilter;
    D3DX10_IMAGE_INFO *pSrcInfo;
} D3DX10_IMAGE_LOAD_INFO, *LPD3DX10_IMAGE_LOAD_INFO;
```

Its first two members, Width and Height, specify the width and height of the loaded texture, respectively. The loaded texture is scaled according to these target values. The next member, Depth, allows the texture's depth information to be modified and is only applicable to three-dimensional textures. The FirstMipLevel member specifies the highest resolution mipmap level to use for the loaded texture. The next member, MipLevels, sets the maximum number of mipmaps that will be associated with the texture. The Usage member is in turn responsible for controlling the manner in which the texture resource is used and it can be set to any of the D3D10_USAGE flags (D3D10_USAGE_DEFAULT to allow read and write access by the GPU, D3D10_USAGE_IMMUTABLE to allow read access to the resource, D3D10_USAGE_DYNAMIC for resources that can be read by the GPU and written to by the CPU and

D3D10_USAGE_STAGING for resources supporting the copy of data from the GPU to CPU). Next, the BindFlags member controls the manner in which the texture resource will be bound to the pipeline (D3D10_BIND_SHADER_RESOURCE to use the resource as a shader resource, D3D10_BIND_RENDER_TARGET to use the resource as a render target, or D3D10_BIND_DEPTH_STENCIL to use the resource as a depth-stencil buffer). We set CPU access permissions for the texture resources using the CpuAccessFlags member (D3D10_CPU_ACCESS_WRITE when the CPU is allowed to change the resource, or D3D10_CPU_ACCESS_READ when the CPU can only read from the resource). The MiscFlags member allows us to set a number of miscellaneous options for the texture resource, specifically using the flag D3D10_RESOURCE_MISC_GENER-ATE_MIPS to generate mipmaps for the resource, D3D10_RESOURCE_MISC_SHARED to enable sharing of resource data between a number of Direct3D devices, and D3D10_RESOURCE_MISC_TEXTURECUBE to create a texture cube (six textures arranged in the form of a cube). The Format member specifies the format of the texture after being loaded into memory with the Filter member specifying a texture filtering method (D3DX10_FILTER_POINT for point sampling, D3DX10_FILTER_LINEAR for bilinear filtering, D3DX10_FILTER_NONE for no filtering, etc.). The second last member, MipFilter, also deals with texture filtering and can be set to the same flags as those given for the Format member with the addition of D3DX10_FILTER_TRIANGLE which filters the texture so that every pixel in the source image is factored in equally when creating a destination image. The final member, pSrcInfo, contains a description of the original texture.

The D3DX10CreateTextureFromFile function's fourth parameter, pPump, is a pointer to an ID3DX10ThreadPump thread pump interface used for the asynchronous execution of routines; we will generally set this parameter to 'NULL' so that the D3DX10CreateTextureFromFile function completes its operation before returning. The final parameter, ppTexture, is used for returning the address of a pointer to the texture resource. This parameter must be declared as an ID3D10Resource interface. We can thus, using this function, load a texture into memory as follows (the pLoadInfo and pPump parameters are both set to 'NULL'):

```
/* declare the ID3D10Resource and ID3D10Device interfaces */
ID3D10Resource *g_id3dResource;
ID3D10Device *g_id3dDevice;

/* load the texture from file */
hresult_ = D3DX10CreateTextureFromFile(g_id3dDevice,
                                       L"texture_filename.dss",
                                       NULL,
                                       NULL,
                                       &g_id3dResource);
```

It is good programming practice to check for any error values returned by the D3DX10CreateTexture-FromFile function call:

```
if FAILED(hresult_)
{
        /* take some action because texture resource creation
          failed */
}
```

With the texture map loaded into memory and the associated texture resource created, we have to link a shader resource view to it. The shader resource view will allow a shader program to read data from the texture resource. The first step is to create a D3D10_TEXTURE2D_DESC structure that will be used to

8

describe our two-dimensional texture resource. This structure is declared as follows in the d3d10.h header file:

```
typedef struct D3D10_TEXTURE2D_DESC {
    UINT Width;
    UINT Height;
    UINT MipLevels;
    UINT ArraySize;
    DXGI_FORMAT Format;
    DXGI_SAMPLE_DESC SampleDesc;
    D3D10_USAGE Usage;
    UINT BindFlags;
    UINT CPUAccessFlags;
    UINT MiscFlags;
} D3D10_TEXTURE2D_DESC;
```

It's first two members, Width and Height, set the width and height of the 2D texture resource in terms of texels. The third member, MipLevels, sets the maximum number of mipmaps that will be associated with the texture resource (set it to 0 for the maximum possible number of mipmap levels or to 1 for no mipmapping). The ArraySize member specifies the number of textures in the texture array with the Format member specifying the texel format (for example DXGI_FORMAT_R32G32B32A32_FLOAT for a four-component 128-bit floating-point format). The next member, SampleDesc, is a DXGI_SAMPLE_DESC structure defining the multisampling parameters for the texture resource. Multisampling, as previously mentioned, is an anti-aliasing technique supported by all current generation graphics hardware. The DXGI_SAMPLE_DESC structure has two members, Count (an integer value specifying the number of multisamples per pixel) and Quality (an integer specifying the image quality level - no anti-aliasing has a count of 1 and a quality of 0). The Usage member is in turn responsible for controlling the manner in which the texture resource is used. It can be set to any of the D3D10_USAGE flags (as defined for the D3DX10_IMAGE_LOAD_INFO structure's Usage member). The BindFlags member controls the manner in which the texture resource is bound to the pipeline (its flags are identical to that of the D3DX10_IMAGE_LOAD_INFO structure's BindFlags member). We also, as with the D3DX10_IMAGE_LOAD_INFO structure, set CPU access permissions using the CpuAccessFlags member. The final member, MiscFlags, allows us to set a number of miscellaneous options for the texture resource (it also takes the same flags as the D3DX10_IMAGE_LOAD_INFO structure's MiscFlags member).

We get the properties of the texture resource by calling the GetDesc ID3D10Texture2D interface function with a pointer to the D3D10_TEXTURE2D_DESC texture resource description. The ID3D10Texture2D interface is responsible for managing the texel data of a two-dimensional texture:

```
/* define the 2D texture resource description structure */
D3D10_TEXTURE2D_DESC textureDescription;

/* declare the ID3D10Texture2D interface */
ID3D10Texture2D *g_id3dTextureResource;

/* get the texture resource properties */
g_id3dTextureResource->GetDesc(&textureDescription);
```

Next we describe the shader resource view using the D3D10_SHADER_RESOURCE_VIEW_DESC structure. A view is simply a format-centric way of thinking about data stored in a resource; for instance, controlling how these data are accessed and written. Texture resources are accessed using a view – the view

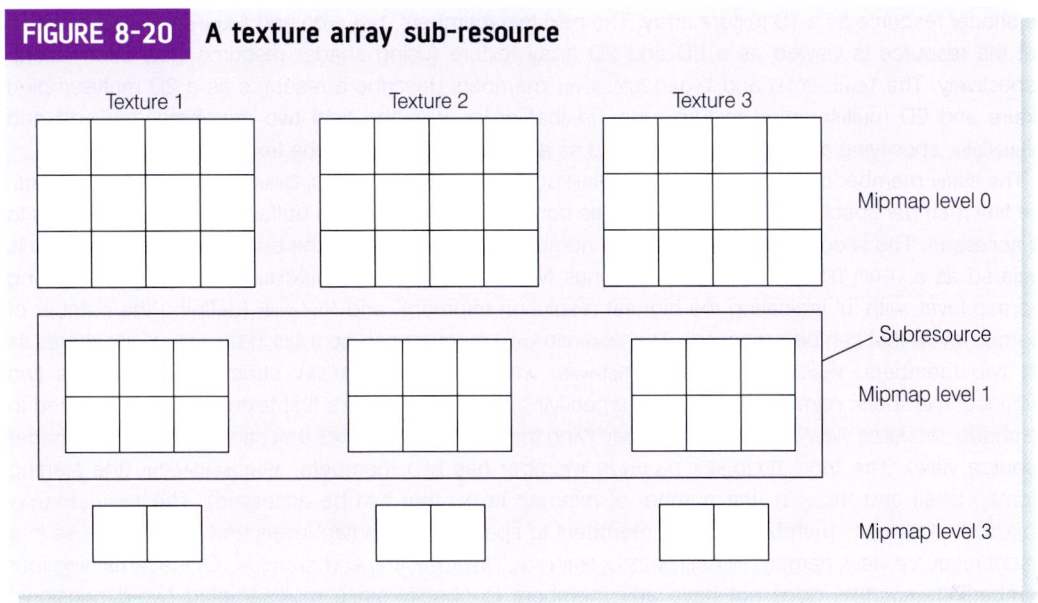

FIGURE 8-20   **A texture array sub-resource**

Texture 1   Texture 2   Texture 3

Mipmap level 0

Subresource

Mipmap level 1

Mipmap level 3

simply being a means of interpreting the texture resource stored in memory. A view is generally used to access an array of subresources (a mipmap-level and texture combination, i.e. an array segment at a particular mipmap level). For example, a texture array consists of several textures; each of these assigned a number of mipmap levels. A subresource can be considered a selection of all the textures on one mipmap level (as illustrated in Figure 8-20) or a single mipmap level for single textures.

The D3D10_SHADER_RESOURCE_VIEW_DESC structure, used for describing a shader resource view (in turn used for binding a resource to a shader stage), is declared as follows in the d3d10shader.h header file:

```
typedef struct D3D10_SHADER_RESOURCE_VIEW_DESC {
    DXGI_FORMAT Format;
    D3D10_SRV_DIMENSION ViewDimension;
    union {
        D3D10_BUFFER_SRV Buffer;
        D3D10_TEX1D_SRV Texture1D;
        D3D10_TEX1D_ARRAY_SRV Texture1DArray;
        D3D10_TEX2D_SRV Texture2D;
        D3D10_TEX2D_ARRAY_SRV Texture2DArray;
        D3D10_TEX2DMS_SRV Texture2DMS;
        D3D10_TEX2DMS_ARRAY_SRV Texture2DMSArray;
        D3D10_TEX3D_SRV Texture3D;
        D3D10_TEXCUBE_SRV TextureCube;
    };
} D3D10_SHADER_RESOURCE_VIEW_DESC;
```

Its first member, Format, describes the viewing format (can be set to a constant such as DXGI_FORMAT_R10G10B10A2_UINT, representing a 32-bit, four-component unsigned-integer format). The next member, ViewDimension, is the view's resource type. This member must be set to the same type as that of the defined resource (D3D10_SRV_DIMENSION_TEXTURE2D for a 2D texture, D3D10_SRV_DIMENSION_TEXTURE2DARRAY for a 2D texture array, etc). The Buffer member describes the shader resource as a buffer resource using a shader resource view. Texture1D describes the shader resource as a 1D texture with Texture1DArray specifying the shader resource as a 1D texture array. The next two members, Texture2D and Texture2DArray, are set so that the resource is viewed as a 2D and 2D array texture (using shader resource view information), respectively. The Texture2DMS and Texture2DMSArray members describe a resource as a 2D multisampled texture and 2D multisampled texture array, in that order, with the final two members, Texture3D and TextureCube, specifying a resource to be viewed as a 3D texture and 3D cube texture correspondingly.

The Buffer member of structure type D3D10_BUFFER_SRV has two members, ElementOffset and ElementWidth. The first member specifies the number of bytes from the beginning of the buffer to the element that is to be accessed. The second member gives the number of bytes stored in the buffer elements. Texture1D is declared as a D3D10_TEX1D_SRV structure and has two members: MostDetailedMip (specifying the starting mipmap level, with '0' indicating the highest resolution mipmap), and MipLevels (defining the number of mipmap levels that can be accessed). The Texture1DArray member of type D3D10_TEX1D_ARRAY_SRV shares its first two members, MostDetailedMip and MipLevels, with the D3D10_TEX1D_SRV structure. It also has two additional members, namely FirstArraySlice (specifying the texture array's first texture that will be used in the shader resource view), and ArraySize (specifying the number of textures that can be used in the shader resource view). The D3D10_TEX2D_SRV Texture2D member has two members: MostDetailedMip (the starting mipmap level) and MipLevels (the number of mipmap levels that can be accessed). The Texture2DArray D3D10_TEX2D_ARRAY_SRV member has four members to specify the mipmap levels and textures to use in a shader resource view, namely, MostDetailedMip, MipLevels, FirstArraySlice, and ArraySize. Of the remaining four members, Texture2DMS does not have any members to specify since multisampled two-dimensional textures contain only one subresource. The Texture2DMSArray member of type D3D10_TEX2DMS_ARRAY_SRV has two members, FirstArraySlice and ArraySize – both with the same function as their previously discussed counterparts. Both the D3D10_TEX3D_SRV Texture3D and D3D10_TEXCUBE_SRV TextureCube members can be set using the MostDetailedMip and MipLevels members.

We describe the texture shader resource view using this D3D10_SHADER_RESOURCE_VIEW_DESC structure in the following manner:

```
/* define the shader-resource view description structure */
D3D10_SHADER_RESOURCE_VIEW_DESC shaderResourceViewDescription;

/* fill the shader-resource memory block with zeros */
ZeroMemory(&shaderResourceViewDescription,
            sizeof(shaderResourceViewDescription));

/* set shaderResourceViewDescription's Format member */
shaderResourceViewDescription.Format = textureDescription.Format;

/* set shaderResourceViewDescription's ViewDimension member */
shaderResourceViewDescription.ViewDimension =
                    D3D10_SRV_DIMENSION_TEXTURE2D;

/* set the resource type as a 2D texture (Texture2D),
    subsequently setting this type's members */
shaderResourceViewDescription.Texture2D.MostDetailedMip =
                            textureDescription.MipLevels;
shaderResourceViewDescription.Texture2D.MipLevels =
                            textureDescription.MipLevels;
```

The shader resource view is now associated with the created texture resource. We now call the CreateShaderResourceView ID3D10Device interface function to create a shader resource view that will be used to access data in the created resource. This function is declared as follows in the d3d10.h header file:

```
HRESULT CreateShaderResourceView(
    ID3D10Resource *pResource,
    const D3D10_SHADER_RESOURCE_VIEW_DESC *pDesc,
    ID3D10ShaderResourceView **ppSRView
);
```

Its first parameter, pResource, is a pointer to either a buffer resource such as a vertex buffer, index buffer, shader constant buffer, or, alternatively, a texture resource (as in our case). The second parameter, pDesc, takes a pointer to the shader resource view description structure, D3D10_SHADER_RESOURCE_VIEW_DESC. Its last parameter, ppSRView, takes the address of a pointer to the shader resource view interface, ID3D10ShaderResourceView; dealing with how the resource is to be accessed by the shader. The following code sample creates a shader resource view so that the texture resource can be accessed:

```
/* declare the ID3D10ShaderResourceView interface */
ID3D10ShaderResourceView* g_pTextureResourceView;
/* create the shader resource view so that the resource data
    can be read */
hresult_ = g_id3dDevice->CreateShaderResourceView
                        (g_id3dTextureResource,
                         &shaderResourceViewDescription,
                         &g_pTextureResourceView);
```

The texture image is now loaded into memory and ready to be mapped to any arbitrary geometric object. The next step in the texture mapping process is to specify the texture coordinates for each of the object's vertices. As mentioned, texture coordinates are always normalized to range from 0 to 1 with the top left corner of the texture mapped to the coordinates (0,0) and its bottom right corner mapped to the coordinates (1,1). This precise mapping is, however, not always necessary and the texture can be stretched to fit the entire geometric object – although such an approach will normally result in a distorted looking exterior.

Say we are texturing the following cube:

Then we have to apply our texture image to six distinct faces. This process involves changing the object's vertex structure to include texture coordinates, then updating the input layout to incorporate these coordinates:

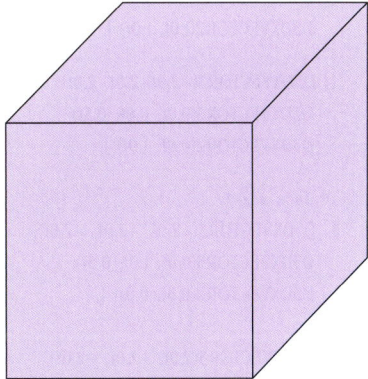

```
struct CubeVertex
{
    D3DXVECTOR3 Location;
    D3DXVECTOR3 Color;
    D3DXVECTOR2 TextureCoordinate; /* add texture coordinate
                            member */
};
```

```
D3D10_INPUT_ELEMENT_DESC input_layout_description[] =
{
    {
        L"POSITION", 0, DXGI_FORMAT_R32G32B32_UINT, 0, 0,
        D3D10_INPUT_PER_VERTEX_DATA, 0
    },

    {
        L"COLOR", 0, DXGI_FORMAT_R32G32B32_UINT, 1, 6,
        D3D10_INPUT_PER_VERTEX_DATA, 0
    },

    /* add description for the texture coordinates */
    {
        L"TEXTURE0", 0, DXGI_FORMAT_R32G32_FLOAT, 0, 6,
        D3D10_INPUT_PER_VERTEX_DATA, 0
    },
};
```

Next we add texture coordinates to the vertices defining our object, in this case a six sided cube defined by the vertex buffer array_of_vertex_data. Every vertex of this cube is assigned one of the following coordinates based on its position: (0,0), (0,1), (1,0) or (1,1):

```
CubeVertex array_of_vertex_data [] =
{
    /* face # 1 */
    {  D3DXVECTOR3(-2.0f, 2.0f, -2.0f),     //vertex coordinate
       D3DXVECTOR3(0.0f, 0.0f, 0.5f),       //color
       D3DXVECTOR2(0.0f, 0.0f) },           //texture coordinate

    {  D3DXVECTOR3(2.0f, 2.0f, -2.0f),      //vertex coordinate
       D3DXVECTOR3(0.0f, 0.0f, 0.5f),       //color
       D3DXVECTOR2(1.0f, 0.0f) },           //texture coordinate

    {  D3DXVECTOR3(2.0f, 2.0f, 2.0f),       //vertex coordinate
       D3DXVECTOR3(0.0f, 0.0f, 0.5f),       //color
       D3DXVECTOR2(1.0f, 1.0f) },           //texture coordinate

    {  D3DXVECTOR3(-2.0f, 2.0f, 2.0f),      //vertex coordinate
       D3DXVECTOR3(0.0f, 0.0f, 0.5f),       //color
       D3DXVECTOR2(0.0f, 1.0f) },           //texture coordinate

    /* face # 2 */
    {  D3DXVECTOR3(-2.0f, -2.0f, -2.0f),    //vertex coordinate
       D3DXVECTOR3(0.0f, 1.0f, 0.5f),       //color
       D3DXVECTOR2(0.0f, 0.0f) },           //texture coordinate

    {  D3DXVECTOR3(2.0f, -2.0f, -2.0f),     //vertex coordinate
       D3DXVECTOR3(0.0f, 1.0f, 0.5f),       //color
       D3DXVECTOR2(1.0f, 0.0f) },           //texture coordinate
```

8

```
    { D3DXVECTOR3(2.0f, -2.0f, 2.0f),       //vertex coordinate
      D3DXVECTOR3(0.0f, 1.0f, 0.5f),        //color
      D3DXVECTOR2(1.0f, 1.0f) },            //texture coordinate

    { D3DXVECTOR3(-2.0f, -2.0f, 2.0f),      //vertex coordinate
      D3DXVECTOR3(0.0f, 1.0f, 0.5f),        //color
      D3DXVECTOR2(0.0f, 1.0f) },            //texture coordinate

    /* face # 3 */
    { D3DXVECTOR3(-2.0f, -2.0f, 2.0f),      //vertex coordinate
      D3DXVECTOR3(0.5f, 1.0f, 0.5f),        //color
      D3DXVECTOR2(0.0f, 0.0f) },            //texture coordinate

    { D3DXVECTOR3(-2.0f, -2.0f, -2.0f),     //vertex coordinate
      D3DXVECTOR3(0.5f, 1.0f, 0.5f),        //color
      D3DXVECTOR2(1.0f, 0.0f) },            //texture coordinate

    { D3DXVECTOR3(-2.0f, 2.0f, -2.0f),      //vertex coordinate
      D3DXVECTOR3(0.5f, 1.0f, 0.5f),        //color
      D3DXVECTOR2(1.0f, 1.0f) },            //texture coordinate

    { D3DXVECTOR3(-2.0f, 2.0f, 2.0f),       //vertex coordinate
      D3DXVECTOR3(0.5f, 1.0f, 0.5f),        //color
      D3DXVECTOR2(0.0f, 1.0f) },            //texture coordinate

    //...and similarly for the remaining 3 faces
};
```

8

We also need to set up a vertex shader input structure that will receive data from the input assembler stage, but more on this when applying the texture:

```
struct VERTEXSHADER_INPUT
{
    float4 Loc : POSITION;
    float2 Tex : TEXCOORD;
};
```

Before the texture object can be used by the shader, we first need to set the texturing effect. This is done by retrieving a pointer to the Texture2D variable, textureVar, declared in the shader program:

```
/*  declare the ID3D10Effect interface responsible for managing
    the shaders, state objects and resources constituting the effect */
ID3D10Effect* g_id3dEffect = NULL;

/* declare the ID3D10EffectShaderResourceVariable interface
    responsible for accessing the shader resource variables */
ID3D10EffectShaderResourceVariable* g_pTexture;

g_pTexture = g_id3dEffect->GetVariableByName("textureVar")
                                        ->AsShaderResource();
```

The GetVariableByName ID3D10Effect interface function takes a string value containing the name of the variable declared in the shader/effect program as parameter, returning a pointer to the ID3D10EffectVariable interface. The AsShaderResource ID3D10EffectVariable function casts the returned interface to an ID3D10EffectShaderResourceVariable interface that is used for accessing the shader-resource variable.

Next we can set this retrieved resource pointer using the SetResource ID3D10EffectShaderResourceVariable function. Its parameter must be set to the declared ID3D10ShaderResourceView shader resource interface, g_pTextureResourceView:

```
g_pTexture->SetResource(g_pTextureResourceView);
```

The texture can now be used by the shader. All that remains is to simply set the effect state within the device itself. This is done by invoking the effect state from within the render loop by selecting the appropriate technique and subsequently setting the state for each of the passes.

We start by calling the GetDesc ID3D10EffectTechnique function on the previously defined technique object which is used for storing the returned D3D10_TECHNIQUE_DESC structure, i.e. the structure describing the technique:

```
ID3D10EffectTechnique* g_pd3d10EffectTechnique = NULL;

/*  obtain the D3D10_TECHNIQUE_DESC effect-variable
    description */
D3D10_TECHNIQUE_DESC technique;
g_pd3d10EffectTechnique->GetDesc(&technique);
```

The GetPassByIndex ID3D10EffectTechnique interface method is now called to acquire an effect pass object representing the first pass of the technique:

```
/* apply the effect state by looping over the number of
   technique passes */
for(int i = 0; i < technique.Passes; ++i)
{
    g_pd3d10EffectTechnique->GetPassByIndex(i)->Apply(0);
    //...draw the cube
}
```

The actual texturing of the cube is done using a shader program. We will first define a pixel shader to perform the texel lookup, returning the sampled color value:

```
float4 PixelShader(PIXELSHADER_INPUT inputcoords) : SV_Target
{
    return textureVar.Sample(samplingMethod,
                        inputcoords.Tex)*objectColor;
}
```

The textureVar Texture2D constant buffer variable stores the texture passed to the shader program. Specifically, this texture is passed to the shader the moment the texture resource view, g_pTextureResource-View, is bound to the textureVar shader variable. The variable objectColor is simply the object material's ambient color. The pixel shader multiplies the returned sampled color (using Sample to perform a texture lookup of the texture image) with the object material color, objectColor, returning the final color of the pixel. The object will be fully textured once all the texels have been sampled and the final pixel color returned.

Our pixel shader makes use of the Sample HLSL texture object type. This object type samples a texture using two parameters, a sampler type, samplingMethod, defining the texture lookup method and a floating-point value, location, specifying the sampling coordinates – in this case the texture coordinates previously specified and accessed via inputcoords.Tex. The texture object type has the following syntax:

returnValue <T>.Sample(sampler s, float location)

The sampler type is a pseudo-register for both pixel and vertex shaders that is used to identify the sampling stage. What this means is that there are a number of shader sampling registers with one of these sampling units corresponding to a texture sampling stage. We can thus read the same number of texture surfaces as there is sampling stage registers using a single shader pass.

In the case of our pixel shader we define a sampler specifying the manner in which the texture will be sampled using the SamplerState type. This structure defines the texture filtering method as linear mipmapping (MIN_MAG_MIP_LINEAR) and the texture coordinates u and v, to repeat the sampling on every integer junction via the address wrap constant, wrap:

```
SamplerState samplingMethod
{
    Filter = MIN_MAG_MIP_LINEAR;
    AddressU = Wrap;
    AddressV = Wrap;
};
```

The input texture coordinates and vertex coordinates of the object are passed to the vertex shader, VertexShader. This shader then outputs these coordinates to the hardware where the pixel shader, PixelShader, is then able to subsequently read them from. The vertex shader is defined as follows:

```
PIXELSHADER_INPUT VertexShader(VERTEXSHADER_INPUT
                    coordsInput)
{
    PIXELSHADER_INPUT coordsOutput = (PIXELSHADER_INPUT)0;
    coordsOutput.Loc = mul(coordsInput.Loc, World);
    coordsOutput.Loc = mul(coordsInput.Loc,
    modelviewProjection);
    coordsOutput.Tex = coordsInput.Tex;

    return coordsOutput;
}
```

The pixel shader input structure receiving the texture coordinates from the graphics pipeline, are defined as follows:

```
struct PIXELSHADER_INPUT
{
    float4 Loc : SV_POSITION;
    float2 Tex : TEXCOORD0;
};
```

A number of other shader variables are also defined in this program, for example the uniform float4x4 modelviewProjection and worldviewProjection matrices used for performing transformations on the cube's vertex coordinates. These variables, declared using the HLSL data types, are set by the Direct3D application. Chapter 6 deals with this process in more detail. Example 8.2.2, available from the book's website, gives the complete source code for mapping a texture to a cube.

Working with OpenGL

We start by defining a structure to store our texture image data:

```
/* structure for storing the image data */
struct Image
{
unsigned long size_x;
unsigned long size_y;
char *data;
};
```

OpenGL doesn't provide any API functions for the loading of textures into memory, we must thus write our own.

The function, imageLoader is responsible for the physical texture loading (supporting only bitmap files – image files using the *.bmp file extension) and the related storage of the file in the Image structure; it performs the said file operations using standard C++ I/O (input/output) functions:

```
/*
==================
imageLoader
-loads our bitmap data into the Image struct
==================
*/
int imageLoader(const char *filename, Image *image)
{
    FILE *file;

    unsigned long size;
    unsigned long i;
    unsigned short int planes;
    unsigned short int bpp;

    char temp;
    char finalName[80];

    glTexCoord2f(1.0, 0.0);
    strcpy(finalName, "");

    strcat(finalName, filename);
    if ((file = fopen(finalName, "rb"))==NULL)
    {
        printf("File Not Found : %s\n",finalName);
        return 0;
    }
```

```
fseek(file, 18, SEEK_CUR);

glTexCoord2f(1.0, 0.0);

if ((i = fread(&image->size_x, 4, 1, file)) != 1)
{
    printf("Error reading width from %s.\n", finalName);
    return 0;
}

if ((i = fread(&image->size_y, 4, 1, file)) != 1)
{
    printf("Error reading height from %s.\n", finalName);
    return 0;
}

size = image->size_x * image->size_y * 3;
if ((fread(&planes, 2, 1, file)) != 1)
{
    printf("Error reading planes from %s.\n", finalName);
    return 0;
}

if (planes != 1)
{
    printf("Planes from %s is not 1: %u\n", finalName, planes);
    return 0;
}

if ((i = fread(&bpp, 2, 1, file)) != 1)
{
    printf("Error reading bpp from %s.\n", finalName);
    return 0;
}
if (bpp != 24)
{
    printf("Bpp from %s is not 24:%u\n", finalName, bpp);
    return 0;
}

fseek(file, 24, SEEK_CUR);

image->data = (char *) malloc(size);

if (image->data == NULL)
{
    printf("Error allocating memory for color-corrected
            image data");
    return 0;
}
if ((i = fread(image->data, size, 1, file)) != 1)
{
```

8

```
        printf("Error reading image data from %s.\n",
               finalName);
        return 0;
    }
    for (i=0; i<size; i+=3)
    {
        temp = image->data[i];
        image->data[i] = image->data[i+2];
        image->data[i+2] = temp;
    }
    return 1;
}
```

The textureLoader function converts the loaded bitmap image into a texture data form readable by OpenGL:

```
/*
==================
textureLoader
-physically loads the BMPs by calling the imageLoader
 function
-converts the loaded images into texture data
==================
*/
void textureLoader()
{
    /* set the pixel storage */
    glPixelStorei(GL_UNPACK_ALIGNMENT, 1);

    for(int k=0; k < textureCount; k++)
    {
        if(!imageLoader(textureFilenames[k],
                       &myTextureData[k]))
            exit(1);

        /* generate texture names */
        glGenTextures(1, &theTexture[k]);
        /* create a named texture and bind it to a texture
           target */
        glBindTexture(GL_TEXTURE_2D, theTexture[k]);

        /* set the texture parameters */
        glTexParameterf(GL_TEXTURE_2D, GL_TEXTURE_WRAP_S,
                        GL_REPEAT);
        glTexParameterf(GL_TEXTURE_2D, GL_TEXTURE_WRAP_T,
                        GL_REPEAT);
        glTexParameteri(GL_TEXTURE_2D, GL_TEXTURE_MAG_FILTER,
                        GL_LINEAR);
        glTexParameteri(GL_TEXTURE_2D, GL_TEXTURE_MIN_FILTER,
                        GL_LINEAR_MIPMAP_NEAREST);
```

```
        /* build and load a set of mipmaps*/
        gluBuild2DMipmaps(GL_TEXTURE_2D, 3,
                          myTextureData[k].size_x,
                          myTextureData[k].size_y, GL_RGB,
                          GL_UNSIGNED_BYTE,
                          myTextureData[k].data);
    }
}
```

The manner by which data is arranged and represented in system memory differs from one type of processor to another. An example of this is the storage of a multi byte data type such as a floating point number; one processor will differ from another with regards to defining the most significant byte for this value. Thus, the storage of a bitmap image as an array consisting of multiple bits might not correlate on all computers. Such a system-dependent issue obviously has the potential for causing havoc with our OpenGL programs.

The glPixelStorei routine called by the textureLoader function is OpenGL's solution to the significant byte problem. It allows the program to specify the packing and unpacking of data - specifically setting the pixel storage mode. In our case we set the start of each pixel row in memory to one byte alignment by using the GL_UNPACK_ALIGNMENT symbolic constant and a '1' for the second parameter:

```
glPixelStorei(GL_UNPACK_ALIGNMENT, 1);
```

By using this same symbolic constant for the first parameter and the value '2' for the second, we set the rows to be aligned to even-numbered bytes. Similarly, setting the second parameter to the value '4' indicates word alignment, with an '8' denoting rows starting on double-word boundaries. Additionally there are numerous other constants that can be substituted for the first glPixelStore parameter, for example: GL_PACK_SWAP_BYTES, GL_PACK_ALIGNMENT, GL_PACK_ROW_LENGTH, and GL_PACK_SKIP_PIXELS (none of which are regularly used).

The glGenTextures function, called right after glPixelStorei and imageLoader, deals primarily with the generation of texture names. The call to glBindTexture creates a two-dimensional texture object. A texture object allows for the creation of objects consisting of a texture array and numerous texture parameters controlling the mapping of a texture to a surface. Each time glBindTexture is called, a new texture image with related parameters are defined. Calling glBindTexture with an existing texture name causes a switch to the specified texture object – the object that will be mapped to a surface. For example:

```
/* easy indexing for texture array */
#define CEMENT 0
/* binds the texture stored in array position '0' to the
   texture target */
glBindTexture(GL_TEXTURE_2D, theTexture[CEMENT]);
```

Texture parameters are specified using the glTexParameterf function. This function has the following form:

```
glTexParameterf(GLenum target, GLenum param, TYPE value);
```

The texture parameter, param, is set to value for a texture of type target. The target parameter can be set to either GL_TEXTURE_1D or GL_TEXTURE_2D, indicating a one- or two-dimensional texture respectively. The name of the texture parameter, param, can be set to GL_TEXTURE_MIN_FILTER (specifying the filtering method when the texture must be minimized to fit a specific primitive), GL_TEXTURE_MAG_FILTER (specifying the filtering method when the texture must be maximized to fit a specific primitive), GL_TEXTURE_WRAP_S (specifying the wrapping of textures to cover an object) or GL_TEXTURE_WRAP_T (specifying the clamping of textures to some boundary value).

To avoid graphical artifacts (graphic garbage generated during the synthesis of an image), we create a series of pre-filtered texture maps of varying resolution, called mipmaps. When using mipmaps, OpenGL automatically maps a suitable texture, based on its size (in pixels) to the object being textured. We make use of the gluBuild2DMipmaps function to build our series of mipmap images. It is of the form:

```
gluBuild2DMipmaps(GLenum target, GLint iformat, GLint width,
                  Glint height, GLenum format, GLenum type,
                  void *data);
```

The target texture, target, must be set to GL_TEXTURE_2D. The number of color components in our texture is specified by the iformat parameter (it can be set to the following values: '1', '2', '3' or '4'). The width and height parameters represent our texture's width and height, respectively. The format of the pixel data, specified by the format parameter, is normally set to GL_RGB but we also make regular use of the GL_RGBA constant when specifying textures with an alpha component for transparency. gluBuild2DMipmaps's second last parameter, type, sets the data type for the pointer to the image data, data. As a rule we can nearly always set it to GL_UNSIGNED_BYTE but there are also other options such as GL_BITMAP, GL_INT, or GL_UNSIGNED_SHORT. An alternative to using gluBuild2DMipmaps is to simply call the glTexImage2D function – it has exactly the same parameters as gluBuild2DMipmaps.

With the basic texturing constructs in place we can now do the actual texture mapping, a process that basically comes down to the definition of texture coordinates.

OpenGL "marks" an object's surface with the given texture coordinates by assigning texture coordinates to the related vertices. This is done by specifying the texture coordinates via the glTexCoord2f function for each of the object's vertices. A sequence of these calls can be seen in the following function, boxCreator, creating four sides of a three-dimensional box:

```
/*
==================
boxCreator
–creates the sides of a 3D box
==================
*/
void boxCreator()
{
    /* bind a texture to a texture target */
    glBindTexture(GL_TEXTURE_2D, theTexture[CEMENT]);

    /* right–front */
    glBegin(GL_QUADS);
        /* set the texture coordinates for the given vertex*/
        glTexCoord2f(0.0,0.0);
        glVertex3f(-1,-1,1);
```

```
        glTexCoord2f(0.0,1.0);
        glVertex3f(-1,0.25,1);

        glTexCoord2f(1.0,1.0);
        glVertex3f(1,0.25,1);

        glTexCoord2f(1.0,0.0);
        glVertex3f(1,-1,1);
    glEnd();

    /* right-back */
    glBegin(GL_QUADS);
        glTexCoord2f(0.0,0.0);
        glVertex3f(1,-1,-1);

        glTexCoord2f(0.0,1.0);
        glVertex3f(1,0.25,-1);

        glTexCoord2f(1.0,1.0);
        glVertex3f(1,0.25,1);

        glTexCoord2f(1.0,0.0);
        glVertex3f(1,-1,1);
    glEnd();

    /* left-back */
    glBegin(GL_QUADS);
        glTexCoord2f(0.0,0.0);
        glVertex3f(-1,-1,-1);

        glTexCoord2f(0.0,1.0);
        glVertex3f(-1,0.25,-1);

        glTexCoord2f(1.0,1.0);
        glVertex3f(1,0.25,-1);

        glTexCoord2f(1.0,0.0);
        glVertex3f(1,-1,-1);
    glEnd();

    /* left-front */
    glBegin(GL_QUADS);
        glTexCoord2f(0.0,0.0);
        glVertex3f(-1,-1,-1);

        glTexCoord2f(0.0,1.0);
        glVertex3f(-1,0.25,-1);

        glTexCoord2f(1.0,1.0);
        glVertex3f(-1,0.25,1);
```

```
        glTexCoord2f(1.0,0.0);
        glVertex3f(-1,-1,1);
    glEnd();
}
```

The geometric object is textured the moment all the coordinates are mapped, assuming the OpenGL texturing feature has been activated via the glEnable function call:

```
/* enable the OpenGL texturing feature */
glEnable(GL_TEXTURE_2D);
```

The object textured using the above listed code is shown in Figure 8-21.

FIGURE 8-21   **The textured object**

8.2.3 Bump Mapping

There are a number of techniques combining lighting calculations with texture surface normal perturbations to create more realistic looking object surfaces. *Bump mapping* is one such technique. It can actually be described more as a lighting technique than a pure variation of texture mapping due to its simulation of lighting interactions with bumpy surfaces. We will, however, discuss it here due to its close relation with texture mapping. *Bump mapping* can thus be described as a form of texture mapping incorporating light reflection to simulate real-world surfaces where the unevenness of a surface influences the reflection of light. Bump mapping combines per-pixel lighting calculations with the normals calculated at each pixel of a surface. Figure 8-22 shows a bump mapped surface.

Most real-world surfaces aren't 100 percent smooth; however, the variations in their surface textures are too small to reproduce using conventional geometry. Even if we could manage to reproduce this detail using a 3D mesh, then the mesh would be so complex that it would be close to impossible to display at real time – especially if every object in a scene had to be represented using such a high-

FIGURE 8-22   **Bump mapping**

8

polygon mesh. Bump mapping allows us to represent these detailed surface variations using a normal texture and normal map. Bump mapped surfaces also reflect the lighting applied to it in real time, thus causing the surface to change its appearance in relation to the angle of reflection. Bump mapping thus allows a higher level of visual detail, lower polygon models since textures can now contain more depth information and thus result in the same visual quality as that achieved via high polygon meshes and the reuse of 3D models. For example, we can now reuse a model of a door by simply applying different bump maps to it – for one instance texturing it as a wooden door while for another texturing it with a rusted metal looking bump map.

Standard textures are simply two-dimensional arrays containing red, green, blue, and sometimes alpha color values. Textures can, however, be used to store additional data that can be read by shader programs. For example, a shader program can perform some arbitrary operation on the results obtained from a texture lookup, thus executing some action based on additional data received.

Surface variations are commonly represented using a series of normals. These normal vectors are stored in an additional type of texture called a *normal map*. Normal maps don't contain any color information, rather replacing this information with the surface normal data – three-component directional vectors pointing away from the texture surface (normalized between the range -1 and 1). Normal maps are thus saved using conventional image formats such as .bmp, .jpg, .tga, etc.

Normal maps are typically generated from height fields. A height field image is simply a version of the texture where the elevation of texels is encoded using different levels of darkness. For example, say we have a grate/grill as the one shown in Figure 8-23(a), then we can use a drawing package such as Adobe Photoshop coupled with a height map plug-in to generate the appropriate height field as shown in Figure 8-23(b).

The darker the area represented by a height map, the lower the corresponding texture area. Lighter regions will be rendered as protruding. This height field can be converted into a normal map using NVIDIA's Adobe Photoshop Normal Map plug-in. This plug-in creates normal maps from height maps. The generated normal maps can then subsequently be used for per pixel rendering. An alternative to this plug-in is to use the GIMP normal map plug-in (a plug-in for the GNU Image Manipulation Program).

FIGURE 8-23   Creating a height map (b) from a typical standard texture (a)

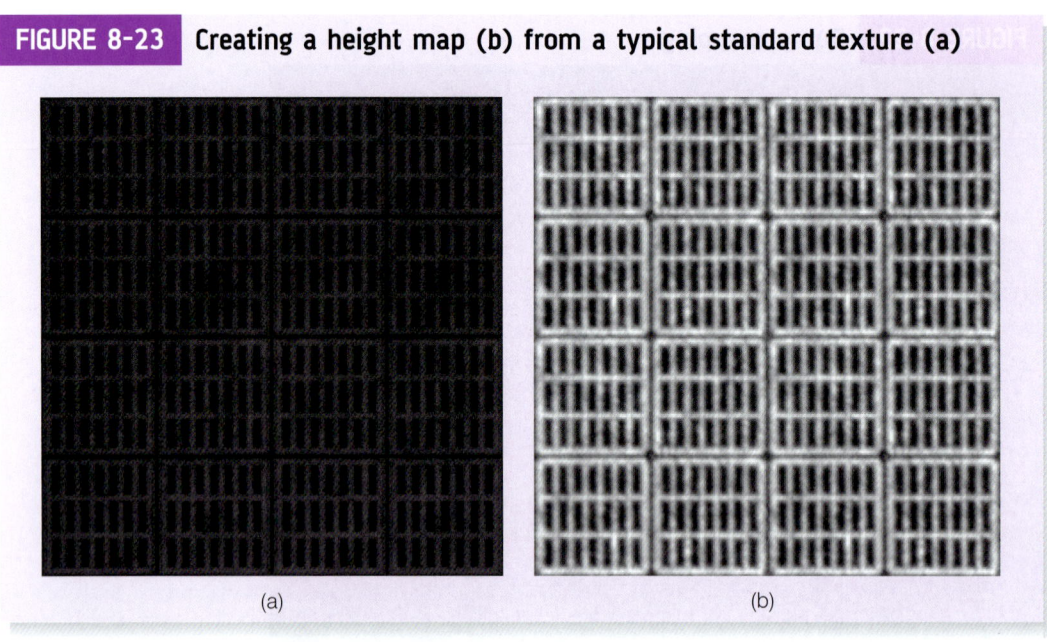

(a)   (b)

FIGURE 8-24   (a) Normal map of the grate/grill texture (b) Normal map applied to a quad

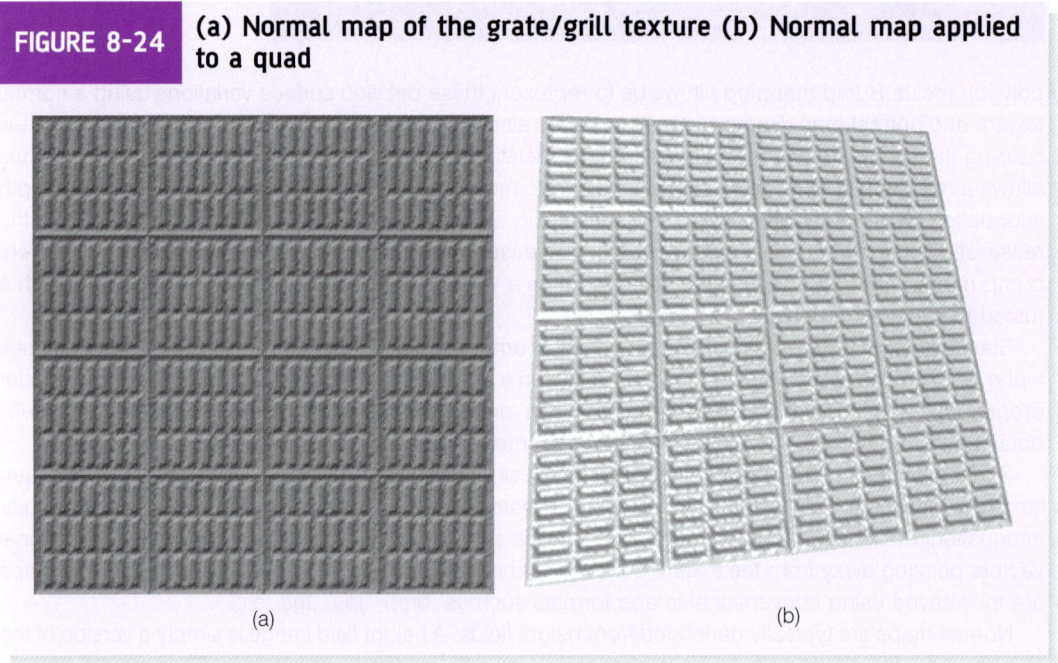

(a)   (b)

The generated normal map for the texture, shown in Figure 8-21, is given by Figure 8-24 (a) with the mapping of this texture to a quadrilateral given by Figure 8-24(b).

Figure 8-25 shows this normal map combined with the original texture and mapped to the Utah teapot mesh.

8.2.3.1 Implementing Bump Mapping

We will now implement bump mapping using the High Level Shader Language. The utilized normal map is encoded with a red, green, and blue component – each

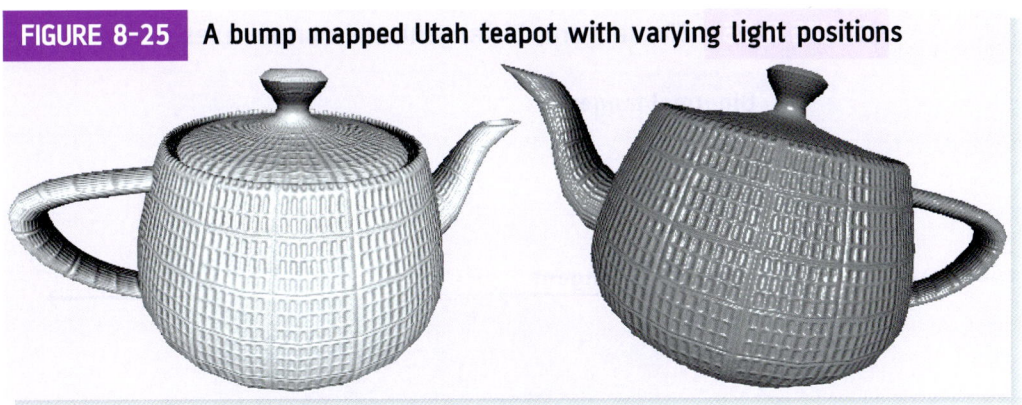

FIGURE 8-25 **A bump mapped Utah teapot with varying light positions**

corresponding to x-, y- and z-coordinates respectively. The red component denotes the normal vector's x-coordinate (the color intensity giving an indication of the vector's x-component magnitude), with the green component signifying the y-direction, and the blue component specifying the z-direction (full-intensity blue indicating a normal vector pointing up and away from the surface).

Bump mapping, at the highest level, is based on the principle of mapping both the normal map and standard texture to some arbitrary object. This process is done in so-called tangent space, the space relative to the texture surface, which is also responsible for controlling related texture-light interactions. *Tangent space* (also referred to as texture space) is defined using a tangent, binormal-tangent and normal axis. Figure 8-26 shows a texture with each of these axes at its vertex coordinates.

The tangent vector can be considered the x-axis, the binormal-tangent the y-axis, and the normal vector pointing straight out of the page as the z-axis. Each texture vertex is assigned its own coordinate space, namely a tangent or texture space. The tangent (T), binormal-tangent (B) and normal (N) vectors are used to create a *TBN matrix*:

$$TBN = \begin{bmatrix} Tx & Bx & Nx \\ Ty & By & Ny \\ Tz & Bz & Nz \end{bmatrix}$$

This matrix is used to transform the texture coordinates defined in texture space to points in object space. Light is defined in world space, so we will conversely have to transform light coordinates to world space, then to object space, and then to texture space using the TBN matrix. We also need to calculate the dot product between the surface normal and light vector to get the desired bump mapped result. This surface normal is defined in texture space and the light vector is defined in object space. We must thus either transform the light vector into texture space by multiplying it with the TBN matrix, or we should transform all the normal map surface normals into object space – the least desirable option of the two.

Before looking at the HLSL implementation (the Cg version of this HLSL program is nearly identical), we can summarize the process of bump mapping as follows:

1 Determine the inverse TBN matrix. This is required because the TBN matrix translates coordinates from texture space to object space and we need to convert the light vector from object space to texture space.

2 Calculate the light vector.

3 Transform the light vector from object space to texture space by multiplying it with the TBN matrix.

4 Read the normal vector at the specific pixel.

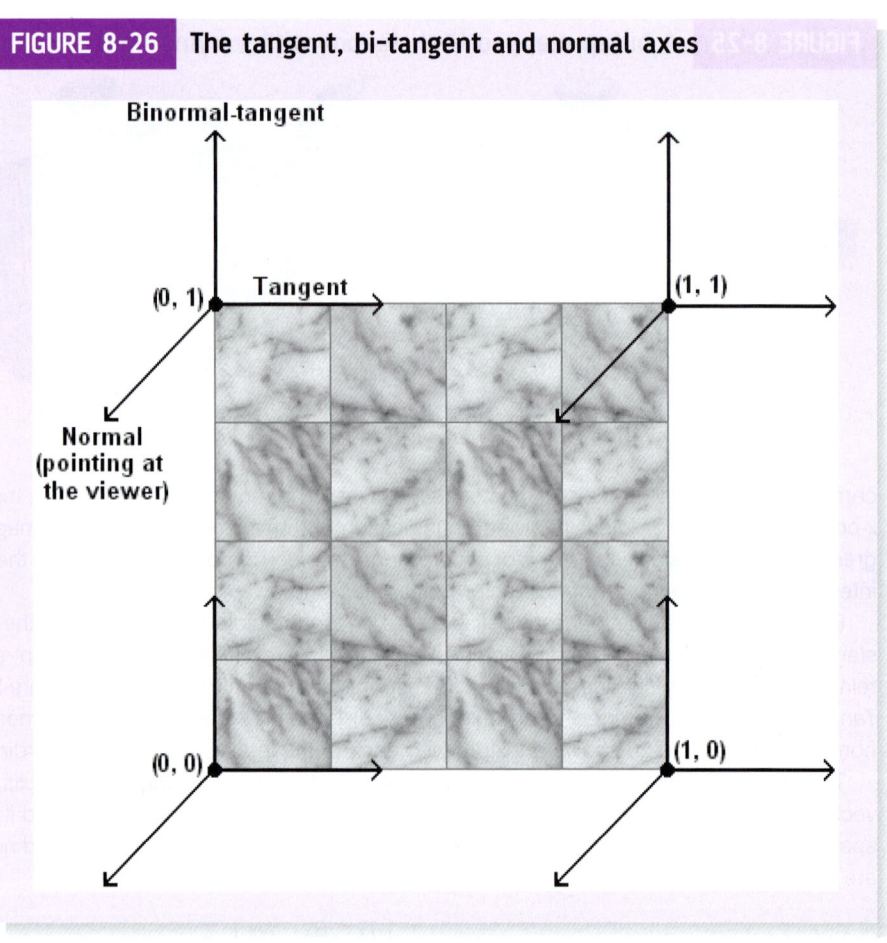

FIGURE 8-26   The tangent, bi-tangent and normal axes

5 Calculate the dot product between the light vector and normal vector.

6 Multiply the result from step 5 with the color of the light and that of the surface material (this is the final diffuse light color).

7 Repeat the previous six steps for each and every pixel of the textured surface.

We start by declaring the world view projection matrix, the world matrix, and the inverse transposed world matrix, followed by the object space light position, also allocating storage for the normal map and standard texture:

```
/* world view projection matrix — the concatenation of a
    modelview and projection matrix */
float4x4 modelviewProjection;

/* world matrix for representation of the object */
float4x4 worldProjection;

/* inverse transposed world view projection matrix */
float4x4 transposedModelviewProjection;
```

```
/* object space light position */
float4 lightPosition;

/* declare the texture variables of type: 2D texture arrays */
Texture2D standardTexture;
Texture2D normalMappedTexture;
```

The next step is to create a texture sampler for both the standard and normal mapped texture. Both samplers, specifying the manner in which the texture will be sampled, are initialized to use linear filtering. The sampler2D type is used in texture lookups, in this case taking the value stored in the TEXUNIT0 register and assigning it to StandardTextureSampler and NormalmapTextureSampler:

```
/* create a texture sampler for the diffuse texture */
sampler2D StandardTextureSampler: TEXUNIT0 = sampler_state
{
    Texture = (standardTexture);
    MIPFILTER = LINEAR;
    MAGFILTER = LINEAR;
    MINFILTER = LINEAR;
};

/* create a texture sampler for the normal map texture */
sampler2D NormalmapTextureSampler: TEXUNIT1 = sampler_state
{
    Texture = (normalMappedTexture);
    MIPFILTER = LINEAR;
    MAGFILTER = LINEAR;
    MINFILTER = LINEAR;
};
```

We will now specify a structure to hold our texture vertex information as received from the Direct3D application:

```
/* vertex structure */
struct vertexStruct
{
    float4 pos: POSITION0;
    float2 texture: TEXCOORD0;
    float3 normal: NORMAL;
    float3 binormal_tangent: BINORMAL;
    float3 tangent: TANGENT;
};
```

We also define a structure that will be used when data are sent from the vertex shader to the pixel shader:

```
/* pixel shader input structure */
struct pixelShaderStruct
{

    float4 pos: POSITION0;
    float2 texture: TEXCOORD0;
    float2 texture2: TEXCOORD1;
```

```
float3 lightVector: TEXCOORD2;
float lightingAttenuation: TEXCOORD3;
};
```

The final structure, outputStruct, is used to store the final pixel color. This is the color returned by the pixel shader and subsequently shown on the screen:

```
/* pixel shader output structure */
struct outputStruct
{
    float4 outputColor : COLOR0;
};
```

We now define the vertex and pixel shader responsible for the actual bump mapping procedure.

The vertex shader starts by translating the input coordinates to object space by multiplying the position of the input vertices with the world view projection matrix. This matrix is simply the concatenation of a modelview and projection matrices. The resultant world space position is sent as output to the pixelShaderStruct. It then calculates the world space vertex position by multiplying the input vertex coordinates with the world matrix. Following this we calculate the object space light direction, lightDirection, as well as the TBN matrix, TBNMatrix. The final vertex shader operations set up a number of members for the pixel shader, these include the light vector, lighting attenuation and the texture coordinates. *Attenuation* is the reduction in intensity of reflected light as the distance between a light source and a reflecting surface increases (see Chapter 9 for a full discussion). The distance HLSL intrinsic function returns the distance between the light position in object space and the vertex position.

```
/* vertex shader */
void VertexShaderFunc(vertexStruct IN, pixelShaderStruct OUT)
{
    /* translate the input position to object space */
    OUT.pos = mul(IN.pos, ModelviewProjection);

    /* calculate the world space vertex position */
    float4 positionWorldSpace = mul(IN.pos, WorldProjection);

    /* calculate the object-space light direction */
    float3 lightDirection = normalize(lightPos -
                                  positionWorldSpace);

    /* calculate the TBN matrix */
    float3x3 TBNMatrix = float3x3(IN.tangent,
                              IN.binormal_tangent,
                              IN.normal);

    /* calculate the light vector */
    OUT.lightVector = mul(TBNMatrix, lightDirection);

    /* calculate the attenuation falloff */
    OUT.lightingAttenuation = 1 / (1 +
                          (0.01 * distance(lightPos.xyz,
                          positionWorldSpace)));

    /* output the texture coordinates */
    OUT.texture = IN.texture;
    OUT.texture2 = IN.texture;
}
```

The pixel shader calculates the color of each pixel based on the normals obtained from the uncompressed normal map and the influence of the incoming light on these normals. Its first call uses the tex2D function to perform a 2D texture lookup. This lookup determines the fragment's color (the '2D' suffix indicating the sampling of 2D sampler objects). It takes two parameters; the first being the standard texture sampler object, StandardTextureSampler, and the second a texture coordinate set specifying the location to sample the object at. Following the texture lookup we need to uncompress the normal map so that we can access its normal data. We then normalize the light vector, calculate the diffuse output color, and multiply our previous attenuation factor with these values to produce the final pixel color – in essence a bump mapped pixel. One new intrinsic HLSL function used during the calculation of the diffuse light component is saturate. This function clamps any value between '0' and '1'. So, after calculating the dot product between the normalized light vector and the normal map's normal, we use this function to clamp the result within the range of '0' to '1'.

```
/* pixel shader */
void PixelShaderFunc(pixelShaderStruct IN, outputStruct OUT)
{
    /* performs a 2D texture lookup determining the
       fragment's color */
    float4 outputColor = tex2D(StandardTextureSampler,
                              IN.texture);

    /* uncompress the normal map so that we can access its
       normal data */
    float3 normalmapNormal = 2.0f *
                              tex2D(NormalmapTextureSampler,
                              IN.texture2).rgb – 1.0f;

    /* normalize the light vector */
    float3 normalizedLight = normalize(IN.lightVector);

    /* calculate the diffuseTerm light component */
    float diffuseTerm = saturate(dot(normalmapNormal,
                              normalizedLight));

    /* calculate the final pixel color */
    OUT.outputColor = outputColor * diffuseTerm *
                      IN.lightingAttenuation;
}
```

The next step is to specify the effect technique definition that will set the previously defined vertex and pixel shaders. This effect technique has one rendering pass, P0. This rendering pass specifies the shader states used to perform the bump mapping operation. It is defined as follows:

```
technique10 BumpMapping
{
    pass P0
    {
        SetGeometryShader(NULL);
        SetVertexShader(CompileShader(ps_4_0, VertexShaderFunc()));
        SetPixelShader(CompileShader(ps_4_0, PixelShaderFunc()));
    }
}
```

| FIGURE 8-27 | An environmentally mapped model and scene (the most basic form of environmental mapping results in a chrome-like appearance) |

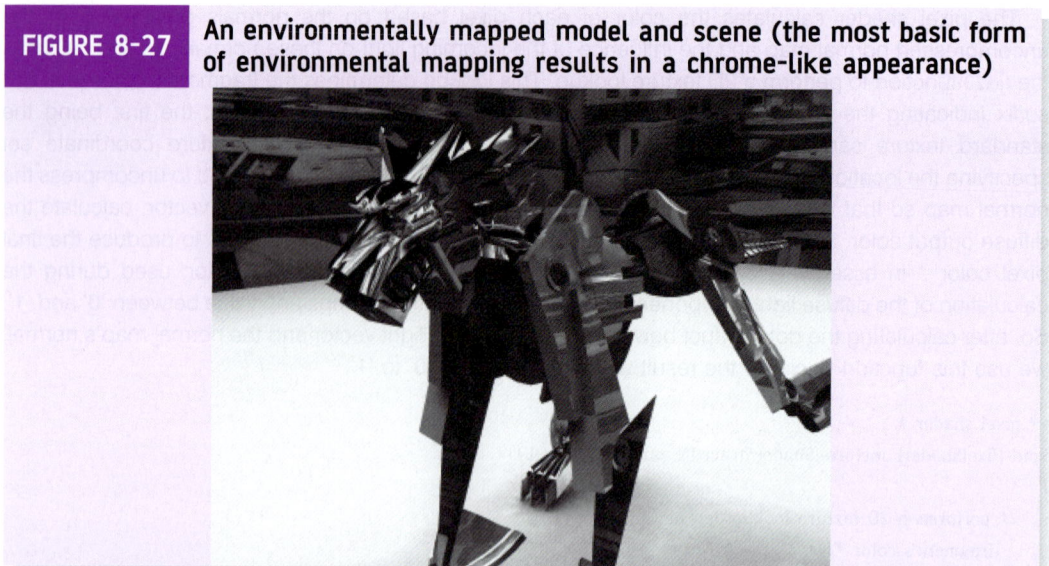

8.2.4 Cube Mapping

Cube mapping, also called *environmental mapping* or sometimes *reflection mapping*, allows us to simulate complex reflections by mapping real-time computed texture images to the surface of an object. Each texture image used for environmental mapping stores a 'snapshot' image of the environment surrounding the mapped object. These snapshot images are then mapped to a geometric object to simulate the object reflecting its surrounding environment. An environment map can be considered an omnidirectional image. Figure 8-27 shows an environmentally mapped object placed within a scene that also makes use of standard environmental mapping to reflect objects in the scene from its 'mirror-like walls'.

Cube mapping is a type of texturing where six environmental maps are arranged as if they were faces of a cube (Figure 8-28). Images are combined in this manner so that an environment can be reflected in an omnidirectional fashion.

Cube maps are accessed using a three-dimensional texture coordinate set, specifically a 3D directional vector. We create cube maps by placing a camera at the object's center and taking 90 degree field-of-view 'snapshots' of the environment in each direction of the cube (i.e. along the axes of the Cartesian coordinate system), thus along each of the following: the positive *x-axis*, the negative *x-axis*, the positive *y-axis*, the negative *y-axis*, the positive *z-axis* and the negative *z-axis*.

8.2.4.1 Implementing Cube Mapping
Cube mapping was, before the advent of shaders, typically implemented in a manual fashion. The conventional process is to acquire snapshots of the environment in each direction of the cube and subsequently set each of these snapshots as the render target (thus rendering the scene for each side surface of the cube). This approach is rather tedious and implementing cube mapping via a vertex and/or pixel shader program greatly improves performance by decreasing the number of rendering passes (one pass is required for each face of the cube when implementing the technique manually). The Cg example, given after the HLSL geometry shader implementation, illustrates a vertex/pixel shader approach that can be used with OpenGL programs (or even Direct3D programs not making use of the High Level Shader Language). Direct3D 10 combines an HLSL geometry shader with render target arrays to improve the performance of cube mapping.

FIGURE 8-28   **A cube map consisting of six texture images**

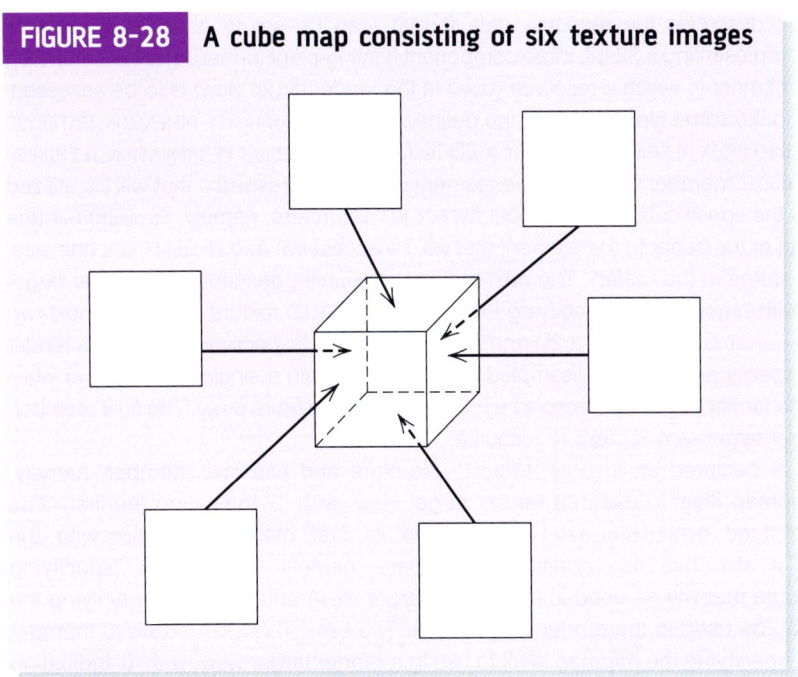

Geometry shaders are executed just prior to the rasterizer and stream output pipeline stages. As previously mentioned, these shaders (executing for each primitive) group numerous vertices into a geometric object – thus generating new primitives that can be modified by a pixel shader program. The primitives generated by the geometry shader stage are rasterized into fragments during the pipeline's rasterizer stage.

We will use a geometry shader coupled with a render target array consisting of six elements (each element representing a cube face) to render onto several render targets at the same time. The geometry shader outputs primitives, assigning each output primitive to one of the elements in the render target array.

The D3D10_RENDER_TARGET_VIEW_DESC structure is used to describe the render target view (specifically the manner in which a render target resource is interpreted by the pipeline). This structure is defined as follows in the d3d10.h header file:

```
typedef struct D3D10_RENDER_TARGET_VIEW_DESC {
    DXGI_FORMAT Format;
    D3D10_RTV_DIMENSION ViewDimension;
    union {
        D3D10_BUFFER_RTV Buffer;
        D3D10_TEX1D_RTV Texture1D;
        D3D10_TEX1D_ARRAY_RTV Texture1DArray;
        D3D10_TEX2D_RTV Texture2D;
        D3D10_TEX2D_ARRAY_RTV Texture2DArray;
        D3D10_TEX2DMS_RTV Texture2DMS;
        D3D10_TEX2DMS_ARRAY_RTV Texture2DMSArray;
        D3D10_TEX3D_RTV Texture3D;
    };
} D3D10_RENDER_TARGET_VIEW_DESC;
```

Its first member, Format, describes the resource data format (can be set to a constant such as DXGI_FORMAT_RIIGIIBI0_FLOAT, representing a 32-bit, three-component floating-point format). The next member, ViewDimension, specifies the manner in which a resource (used in the render-target view) is to be accessed. This member must be set to the same type as that of the defined resource (D3DI0_RTV_DIMENSION_TEXTURE2D for a 2D texture, D3DI0_RTV_DIMENSION_TEXTURE2DARRAY for a 2D texture array, D3DI0_RTV_DIMENSION_TEXTURE3D for a 3D texture, etc). The Buffer member describes the elements in a buffer resource that will be utilized in a render target view via the specification of two D3DI0_BUFFER_RTV members, namely, ElementOffset (the offset, in byte, from the start of the buffer to the element that will be accessed) and ElementWidth (the size, in bytes, of each element stored in the buffer). The next member, TextureID, describes the render target resource as a 1D texture with TextureIDArray specifying the resource as a 1D texture array. The next two members, Texture2D and Texture2DArray, specify a 2D and 2D array texture, respectively, to use as a render target. Texture2DMS doesn't specify anything (multisampled 3D textures contain a single subresource) while Texture2DMSArray specifies the render target resources as a multisampled 2D texture array. The final member, Texture3D, specifies the render target as a 3D texture resource.

The TextureID member is declared as a D3DI0_TEXID_RTV structure and has one member, namely, MipSlice (specifying the mipmap level to use in a render target view, with '0' indicating the first). The TextureIDArray member of type D3DI0_TEXID_ARRAY_RTV shares its first member, MipSlice with the D3DI0_TEXID_RTV structure. It also has two additional members, namely FirstArraySlice (specifying the texture array's first texture that will be used in the render target view) and ArraySize (specifying the number of textures that can be used in the render target view). The D3DI0_TEX2D_RTV Texture2D member has one member, MipSlice, specifying the mipmap level to use in a render target view, with '0' indicating the first. The Texture2DArray D3DI0_TEX2D_ARRAY_RTV member has three members to specify the mipmap levels and textures to use in a render target view: MipSlice, FirstArraySlice, and ArraySize. Of the remaining three members, Texture2DMS does not have any members to specify since multisampled two-dimensional textures contain only one subresource. The Texture2DMSArray member of type D3DI0_TEX2D_ARRAY_RTV has two members – FirstArraySlice and ArraySize – both with the same function as their previously discussed counterparts. The final member, Texture3D, of type D3DI0_TEX3D_RTV, has the following members: MipSlice (specifying the mipmap level to use in a render target view, with '0' indicating the first), FirstWSlice (defining the first depth level that will be used by the render target view), and WSize (specifying the number of depth levels).

We can now define a six-faced render target view using this D3DI0_RENDER_TARGET_VIEW_DESC structure as follows:

```
/* define the render target view description structure */
D3DI0_RENDER_TARGET_VIEW_DESC renderTargetViewDescription;
/* set renderTargetViewDescription's Format member */
renderTargetViewDescription.Format = textureDescription.Format;

/* set renderTargetViewDescription's ViewDimension member */
renderTargetViewDescription.ViewDimension =
                    D3DI0_RTV_DIMENSION_TEXTURE2DARRAY;

/* set the resource type as a 2-D texture array
   (Texture2DArray), subsequently setting its members to
   represent an array of 6 render targets (one for each face of
   the cube) */
renderTargetViewDescription.Texture2DArray.MipSlice = 0;
renderTargetViewDescription.Texture2DArray.FirstArraySlice    = 0;
renderTargetViewDescription.Texture2DArray.ArraySize = 6;
```

We now call the CreateRenderTargetView ID3D10Device interface function to create a render target view that will be used to access data in the defined resource. This function is declared as follows in the d3d10.h header file:

```
HRESULT CreateRenderTargetView(
    ID3D10Resource *pResource,
    const D3D10_RENDER_TARGET_VIEW_DESC *pDesc,
    ID3D10RenderTargetView **ppRTView
);
```

Its first parameter, pResource, is a pointer to either a buffer resource (such as a vertex buffer, index buffer or a shader constant buffer) or alternatively a texture resource (as in our case). The second parameter, pDesc, takes a pointer to the render target view description structure, D3D10_RENDER_TARGET_VIEW_DESC. Its last parameter, ppSRView, takes the address of a pointer to the render target view interface, ID3D10RenderTargetView; dealing with how the pipeline outputs data during the rendering process. The following code sample creates a render target view so that the cube texture can be rendered:

```
/* declare a 2-D texture interface to manage texel data */
ID3D10Texture2D* g_pEnvironmentalMap;

/* declare a ID3D10RenderTargetView interface */
ID3D10RenderTargetView* g_pEnvironmentalMapRenderTargetView;

/* create the render target resource view */
hresult_ = g_id3dDevice-> CreateRenderTargetView
                        (g_pEnvironmentalMap,
                        &renderTargetViewDescription,
                        &g_pEnvironmentalMapRenderTargetView);
```

The six faces of the cube are rendered at the same time by setting the render target view as active when rendering onto the cube map. This is done by calling the OMSetRenderTargets ID3D10Device interface function. This function binds the render target view to the pipeline so that the pipeline's output can be written onto the back buffer. The OMSetRenderTargets interface method takes three parameters, namely, the number of render targets to bind to the pipeline, a pointer to the ID3D10RenderTargetView interface and a pointer to the depth stencil view:

```
/* define an array of render target views */
ID3D10RenderTargetView* arrayRenderTargetViews[1] =
                    {g_pEnvironmentalMapRenderTargetView};

/* define a depth stencil view for controlling the texture
   resource utilized during the depth stencil test –
   specifically the Depth stencil view of the environment map
   for all six faces */
ID3D10DepthStencilView* pDepthStencilView;

g_id3dDevice->OMSetRenderTargets(
                    sizeof(arrayRenderTargetViews)/
                    sizeof(arrayRenderTargetViews[0]),
                    arrayRenderTargetViews,
                    pDepthStencilView);
```

8

We render the scene onto the current render target by first clearing the render target, then clearing the depth stencil buffer, followed by setting up the appropriate matrices and drawing the actual object that is to be cube mapped. The scene is then rendered onto the cube texture (by first saving the old viewport and then specifying the new viewport for rendering to the cube map and computing the view matrices used for this rendering – the eye coordinates are set at the center of the cube mapped object after we have combined the six different view directions to obtain the final view matrix). Following this, we render one cube face at a time, restoring the saved viewport and rendering the final reflective scene.

The actual cube mapping is done via a geometry shader. This geometry shader is used to output each primitive to every render target – six in total. The cube mapping effect also uses a vertex shader to transform vertex coordinates from object space to world space (as required for the geometry shader to function). We will now look at this vertex shader used for propagating texture coordinates from the application program to the geometric shader.

The first step is to declare a vertex shader storage structure to store the world position, normals for each cube surface and texture coordinates:

```
struct VERTEXSHADER_CUBEMAP
{
    float4 Loc : POSITION;
    float2 Tex : TEXCOORD0;
    float3 Normals[6] : SIXNORMS;
};
```

Next we define the vertex shader to transform vertex coordinates from object space to world space, returning these translated coordinates and forwarding the texture coordinates:

```
VS_OUTPUT_CUBEMAP CubemapVertexShader(float4 Loc: POSITION,
                            float3 Normal : NORMAL,
                            float2 Tex : TEXCOORD)
{
    /* declare a VERTEXSHADER_CUBEMAP structure */
    VERTEXSHADER_CUBEMAP output;

    /* transform vertex positions from object space to world
       space */
    output.Loc = mul(Loc, worldProjection);

    /* pass the texture coordinates to the geometric shader */
    output.Tex = Tex;

    return output;
}
```

Our geometric shader processes each primitive produced by the above-defined vertex shader. It does this by looping through all the cube faces/cube maps and for each face, looping an additional three times to create the vertices making up a triangle. The geometric shader calculates the position of the output vertices used by the rasterizer to rasterize the triangle – i.e. assigns a primitive to each distinct render target in the render target array. The geometric shader also transforms the world space vertices using view transformations for every render target view per iteration.

Specifying the geometric shader, we start by creating a structure to store the projection coordinates, texture coordinates, and render target array index used for controlling the render target to which a primitive is written (using the SV_RenderTargetArrayIndex HLSL semantic):

```
struct GEOMETRYSHADER_CUBEMAP
{
    /* projection coordinates */
    float4 Loc : SV_POSITION;

    /* texture coordinates */
    float2 Tex : TEXCOORD0;

    /* the index specifying the render target to which the
       primitive is written */
    int RenderTargetArrayIndex : SV_RenderTargetArrayIndex;
};
```

Following this structure we create the actual geometry shader:

```
/* declare a view matrix for the cube map */
matrix g_mCubemapViewMatrix[6];

/* declare a projection matrix for the cube map */
matrix projectionMatrix : PROJECTION;

/*the geometry shader */
[maxvertexcount(24)]
CubemapGeometryShader(
            triangle VERTEXSHADER_CUBEMAP Input[3],
            inout TriangleStream<GEOMETRYSHADER_CUBEMAP> GS_Output)
{
    for(int i = 1; i <= 7; i++)
    {
        /* declare a GEOMETRYSHADER_CUBEMAP structure */
        GEOMETRYSHADER_CUBEMAP output;

        /* set the render target array's index */
        output.RenderTargetArrayIndex = i;

        /* compute the screen vertex & texture coordinates */
        for(int j = 1; j <= 4; i++)
        {
            output.Loc = mul(Input[j].Loc,g_mCubemapViewMatrix[i]);
            output.Loc = mul(output.Loc, projectionMatrix);
            output.Tex = Input[j].Tex;
            GS_Output.Append(output);
        }
        GS_Output.RestartStrip();
    }
}
```

The first parameter, `maxvertexcount`, is set to 24 – hence limiting the maximum number of vertices that the shader can output at a time to this value. Two interesting HLSL stream object functions are used, namely `Append` and `RestartStrip`. `Append` adds geometry shader data to an output stream by appending them to the data already in the output stream. `RestartStrip` terminates the current primitive strip, in this case a triangle strip, signalling the start of a new strip. This geometry shader writes one triangle to each render target texture (the six faces of the cube) in one rendering pass.

Following this geometry shader definition we create a pixel shader to retrieve and apply the environmentally mapped texture to the 3D model.

The first step is to define the sampling method which will control the texture lookup method:

```
SamplerState samplingMethod
{
    Filter = MIN_MAG_MIP_LINEAR;
    AddressU = Wrap;
    AddressV = Wrap;
};
```

We define the pixel shader, retrieving and applying the environmental texture to the object, as follows:

```
/* declared 2-D texture variable */
Texture2D g_texture;

float4 CubemapPixelShader(GEOMETRYSHADER_CUBEMAP inputcoords):
                                        SV_Target
{
    /* samples a texture using the specified texture lookup
       method and a floating-point value, inputcoords.Tex,
       specifying the sampling coordinates */
    return g_texture.Sample(samplingMethod,
                        inputcoords.Tex);
}
```

We can now specify the effect technique that will set the previously defined vertex, pixel and geometry shaders. This effect technique has one rendering pass, namely P0:

```
technique10 RenderCubemap
{
    pass p0
    {
        SetVertexShader(CompileShader(vs_4_0,
                    CubemapVertexShader()));
        SetGeometryShader(CompileShader(gs_4_0,
                        CubemapGeometryShader()));
        SetPixelShader(CompileShader(ps_4_0,
                    CubemapPixelShader()));
    }
};
```

The final step is to calculate and render the reflecting mesh. In short, to accomplish this, we basically have to write shaders to approximate the Fresnel reflection function (see Chapter 9) and chromatic dispersion so that the object color is blended with reflections from the cube map. This is, however, outside the scope of the current chapter and only after thoroughly discussing lighting in the next chapter will be returning to this cube mapping example.

Working with Cg

We now present a much simpler method to implement environmental mapping – this time using NVIDIA's Cg as our shading language. This implementation makes use of the reflect Standard Library Function. It takes an incident vector – a light ray as first parameter, and a surface normal as second parameter, returning the reflected vector. The reflected vector has the same magnitude as the incident ray.

A vertex shader program is used to perform the per-vertex environmental mapping reflection calculations.

The first step is to specify the name of the vertex program's entry function, main_vertex in our example:

```
void main_vertex(
        float4 objectspaceVertexPosition : POSITION,
        float3 objectspaceVertexNormal : NORMAL,
        float2 inputTextureCoordinates : TEXCOORD0,

        out float4 outputVertexPosition : POSITION,
        out float2 outputTextureCoordinates : TEXCOORD0,
        out float3 reflectionVector : TEXCOORD1,

        /* parameters supplied by the application program */

        uniform float3 pointOfView,
        uniform float4x4 modelToWorldTransformation,
        uniform float4x4 modelviewProjection
)
{
```

We start by calculating the clip-space position as mandatory for all Cg vertex programs:

```
/* transform the vertex position into homogeneous clip-
    space coordinates */
outputVertexPosition = mul(modelviewProjection,
                        objectspaceVertexPosition);
```

Next we assign the input texture coordinates to the output texture coordinates:

```
/* assign the input texture coordinates to the output
    texture coordinates */
outputTextureCoordinates = inputTextureCoordinates;
```

Environmental maps are defined in terms of world space coordinates. We must thus transform the normal and vertex position from object space to world space by multiplying both of them with the modelToWorldTransformation matrix. This transformation is required since we wish to calculate the reflection vector in terms of world space coordinates. This transformation is done as follows:

```
/* transform the vertex position and normal to world space
coordinates */
float3 worldspaceVertexPosition =
                        mul(modelToWorldTransformation,
                            objectspaceVertexPosition);
float3 worldspaceVertexNormal =
                        mul(modelToWorldTransformation,
                            objectspaceVertexNormal);

/* normalize the vertex normal */
worldspaceVertexNormal =
                normalize(worldspaceVertexNormal);
```

The final operation is to calculate both the incident and reflection vectors. The incident vector is the vector traced from the point of view to the vertex. The incident vector is calculated using simple subtraction:

```
/* calculate the incident light vector */
float3 incidentVector = worldspaceVertexPosition −
                            pointOfView;
```

Using the incident and vertex normal, we can calculate the reflected world-space vector:

```
/* calculate the reflection vector */
float3 reflectionVector = reflect(incidentVector,
                            worldspaceVertexNormal);
}
```

We now define a fragment shader program that uses this reflection vector to retrieve a cube map texture – the environmental map.

The first step is to specify the name of the fragment program's entry function, main_fragment in our example:

```
void main_fragment(
        float3 reflectionVector : TEXCOORD0,
        float2 inputTextureCoordinates : TEXCOORDI,

        out float4 outputColor : COLOR,

        /* parameter supplied by the application program */

        uniform samplerCUBE environmentMap

)
{
```

The fragment program uses the interpolated reflection vector to determine the environment map's reflected color. We use the texCUBE texture lookup function to do this. This function takes two parameters, a cube map and a three component texture coordinate set – the reflection vector:

```
/* obtain the reflected color */
float 4 reflectionColor = texCUBE(environmentMap,
                        reflectionVector);
```

Assigning this reflection color to an object will result in a completely reflective mirror-like appearance:

```
/* set the reflected color */
color = reflectionColor;
```

We could extend this program to do a texture lookup of the object's current color, blending the sampled texture color with the reflection color – thus resulting in a much more realistic- looking object (due to no material being a perfect reflector). This program will be extended in this fashion after our discussion of reflectivity in the next chapter.

8

8.3   SUMMARY

In this chapter we started by looking at the concept of color as an abstraction of visible light, subsequently linking the representation of color in display devices to the human perception of it. We presented two commonly used color models – the additive and subtractive color models – further extending the additive model by mapping it to a cube and hexcone color solid. Following this we investigated the practical application of color to geometric objects using both Direct3D and OpenGL.

Next we introduced texture mapping as an easy way of adding realism to computer-generated objects, focusing on concepts such as texture elements, texel arrays, the process of two-dimensional texture mapping, and the matching of texture space coordinates with object vertices. Building on this we discussed a number of texture filtering techniques, specifically mipmapping, nearest point interpolation, bilinear filtering, trilinear filtering, and anisotropic filtering.

We then investigated texture mapping from an implementation perspective, in essence focusing on the steps required to project a two-dimensional bitmap array onto a three-dimensional geometric object. This section presented texture mapping from both a Direct3D and OpenGL perspective.

Following this we discussed bump mapping as a form of texture mapping incorporating light reflection to simulate real-world surfaces where the unevenness of a surface influences the reflection of light. We subsequently implemented bump mapping using the High Level Shader Language, discussing concepts such as tangent space and the creation of a TBN matrix used to transform the texture coordinates defined in texture space to points in object space.

In the remainder of the chapter we focused on cube mapping, also called environmental mapping or sometimes reflection mapping, allowing us to simulate complex reflections by mapping real-time computed texture images to the surface of an object. The implementation of cube mapping was illustrated using both a HLSL geometry shader and Cg example.

The next chapter deals with lighting in detail, discussing a number of light source types and reflection models such as the empirical Phong model and ambient, specular and diffuse reflection. Following this discussion, the chapter investigates the computation of vectors and normal vectors (an integral part of lighting in computer graphics). Chapter 9 features a number of examples focusing on the creation and interaction of light sources, also discussing advanced techniques like High Dynamic Range lighting.

8.4   FURTHER READING

The paper titled 'Texture and Reflection in Computer Generated Images' by Jim Blinn and Martin Newell, published in *Communications of the ACM* (1976) first dealt with environmental mapping. The idea of storing environmental maps as cube maps was first presented in Ned Greene's paper titled 'Environment Mapping and Other Applications of World Projections' published in *IEEE Computer Graphics and Applications* (1986).

The book *Texturing and Modeling: A Procedural Approach* (*third edition*) by David S. Eberly, F. Kenton Musgrave, Darwyn Peachey, Ken Perlin and Steven Worley (ISBN: 1558608486) discuss a great number of procedural texturing and modeling techniques.

Aliasing is also dealt with in a number of books and papers. F.C. Crow's original paper titled 'A Comparison of Antialiasing Techniques' published in *IEEE Computer Graphics and Applications* (1981) analyzed the aliasing problem in depth.

Books dealing with shader programming, such as *The Cg Tutorial: The Definitive Guide to Programmable Real-Time Graphics by Randima Fernando and Mark J. Kilgard* (ISBN: 0321194969); *GPU Gems 2: Programming Techniques for High-Performance Graphics and General-Purpose Computation* by Matt Pharr and Randima Fernando (ISBN: 0321335597) and *GPU Gems 3 by* Hubert Nguyen (ISBN: 0321515269) also deal with texture mapping, filtering, bump mapping, cube mapping, and various other mapping techniques in detail.

8.5   EXERCISES

1 Briefly outline the primary differences between the subtractive and additive color models.

2 What does it mean when we say the red–green–blue color cube suffers from perceptual non-linearality?

3 Why is the single hexcone model based on polar coordinates?

4 Modify the program given in section 8.1 to render a blue pyramid instead of a red triangle.

5 Explain how the glColor3f function is used to set an OpenGL program's state.

6 What is the main difference between a three-dimensional and two-dimensional texture?

7 Briefly explain the process of two-dimensional texture mapping.

8 What is the purpose of a pre-image?

9 Describe each of the following filtering techniques: nearest-point sampling, linear texture filtering, anisotropic texture filtering, bilinear filtering, trilinear filtering, and filtering via mipmaps.

10 Write a Direct3D program that renders a texture mapped cube of dimension similar to the one shown in Figure 8-21.

11 Why do we need to create a shader resource view when texture mapping an object in Direct3D?

12 Before the texture object can be used by the shader, we first need to set the texturing effect – explain how this is done.

13 What is the glPixelStorei OpenGL routine used for?

14 Explain the relationship between the tangent vector, the binormal-tangent and the normal vector of a bump mapped texture surface.

15 Briefly describe the process of bump mapping.

16 Extend the cube mapping Cg example to do a texture lookup of the object's current color, blending the sampled texture color with the reflection color – thus resulting in a much more realistic-looking object.

8

CHAPTER 9

Lighting

LEARNING OBJECTIVES

In this chapter you will learn about:

- Light sources
- Point lights
- Spotlights
- Ambient lights
- Parallel lights
- Emissive light
- Reflection models
- The ambient reflection model
- The specular reflection model
- The diffuse reflection model
- The Phong reflection model
- Vectors
- Vector length
- Vector addition (head-to-tail rule)
- Scalar multiplication
- Calculating a cross product (normal vectors)
- Unit vectors
- Direct3D extension vector functions
- Implementing local illumination
- Reflection and refraction
- High Dynamic Range (HDR) lighting

INTRODUCTION

The chapter starts with an analysis of various light sources (point lights, spotlights, ambient lights, and parallel lights) followed by a discussion of different reflection models such as the empirical Phong model and the ambient, specular, and diffuse reflection models. Following this discussion, the chapter investigates the computation of vectors and normal vectors (an integral part of lighting in computer graphics), the implementation of local illumination and High Dynamic Range lighting. The chapter also extends the environmental mapping example presented in Chapter 8 to factor in the Fresnel effect phenomenon and chromatic dispersion.

9.1 LIGHT SOURCES

Most of the examples and sample programs presented so far implemented basic lighting – resulting in dull, flat-looking object surfaces. Texture mapping helped to enhance the overall appearance of an object but failed to convey any real sense of depth. For example, when looking at the two flat objects in Figure 9-1(a), it is clear that the three-dimensional nature of the scene, a wall positioned perpendicular on a floor, is not being conveyed properly. Figure 9-1(b) shows this same scene illuminated by a properly defined light source.

   This lack of depth is the result of uniform lighting, i.e. the equal illumination of all surfaces. Figure 9-2(a) shows a uniform lit sphere and Figure 9-2(b) the same sphere with basic lighting enabled. The shaded sphere is the result of graduations in the sphere's color based on the color of the light source. In this case the color grey is incrementally decreased from dark grey to white.

FIGURE 9-1 (a) Two rendered rectangles, the one representing a floor, the other a facing wall (b) The same rectangles with lighting enabled

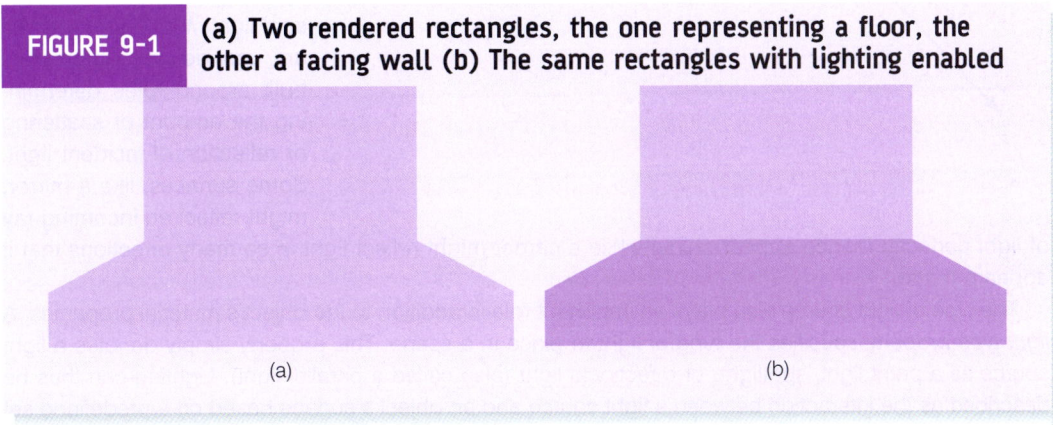

(a)   (b)

FIGURE 9-2 (a) A uniformly lit sphere and (b) a properly lit and shaded sphere

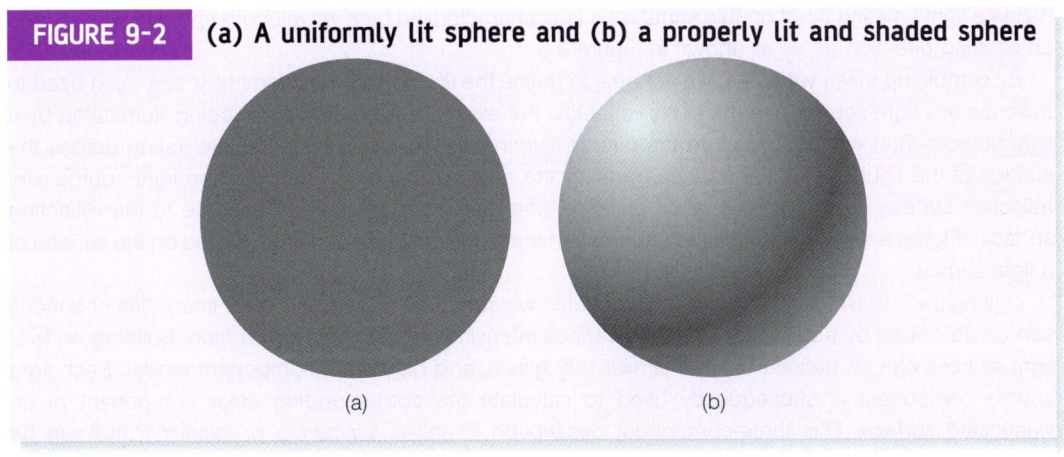

(a)   (b)

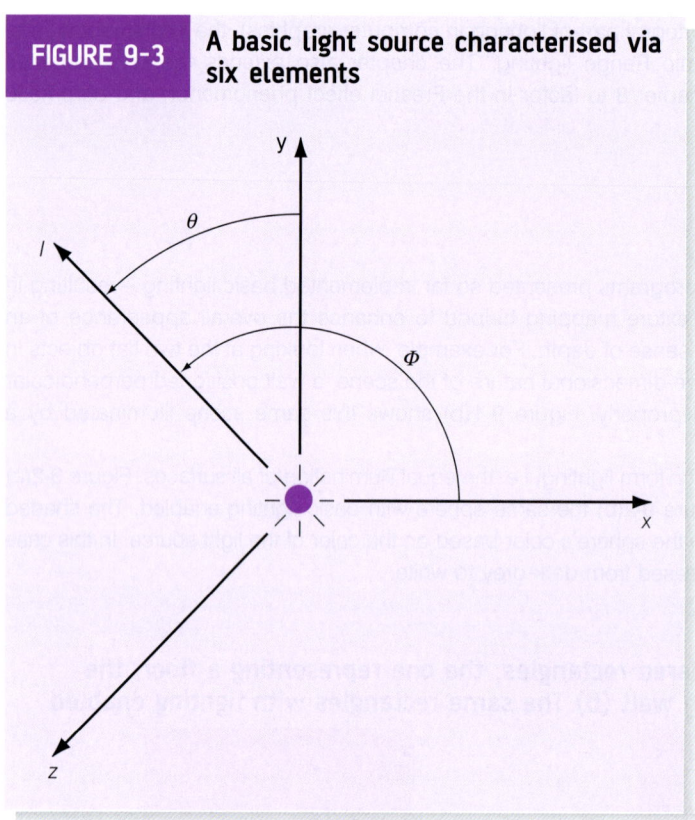

FIGURE 9-3 A basic light source characterised via six elements

Light can be emitted through either self-emission or reflection. When looking at a light bulb it is obvious that we are predominantly dealing with self-emission. Light sources are categorized by their light emitting direction and the energy emitted at each wavelength – determining the color of the light.

As also mentioned previously, objects can absorb or reflect light emitted from a light source depending on the reflecting object's material properties. Light will thus only be 'visible' when illuminated surfaces have the ability to reflect or absorb the said light. *Material properties* are user-defined parameters built around rules determining the amount of scattering or reflection of incident light. Some surfaces, like a mirror, might reflect an incoming ray of light perfectly (hence appear shiny) while a carpet might reflect light in so many directions that it appears matte.

The type of light source also plays an important role in addition to the object's material properties. A *light type property* specifies the type of light to place in a scene. This property simply denotes a light source as a point light, spotlight, or directional light (also called a parallel light). Lighting can thus be described as the interaction between a light source and an object's surface based on a predefined set of material properties. We will focus on each of these light source types in subsequent subsections.

A light source can be considered a geometric object, i.e. a simple light emitting surface. We can define a light emitting point on this surface (*x, y, z*) characterized by a wavelength energy value (*λ*) and an emitting direction (*θ, ϕ*) as shown in Figure 9-3.

By combining these variables, we are able to define the *illumination function I* (*x, y, z, θ, ϕ, λ*) used to describe any light source in terms of six variables. For example, say a surface is being illuminated by a light source; then we can calculate the overall illumination on this surface by integrating across the surface of the light source – thus incorporating the effect of the angle between the light source and reflection surface as well as the falloff distance (the distance from the light source to the reflecting surface). Figure 9-4 shows two distinct illumination functions for a pair of points located on the surface of a light source.

Linking back to Chapter 8's discussion of color, we stated that numerous color intensities or shades can be described by additively combining various intensities of red, green, and blue. Building on this, light sources can be defined using a similar red, green, and blue color component model. Each light source component is subsequently used to calculate the corresponding color component of an illuminated surface. This three-component description is called *luminance* or *intensity*, and can be written using standard matrix notation with each component representing the intensity of the red, green, or blue color component of the light source:

$$I = \begin{bmatrix} I_r \\ I_g \\ I_b \end{bmatrix}.$$

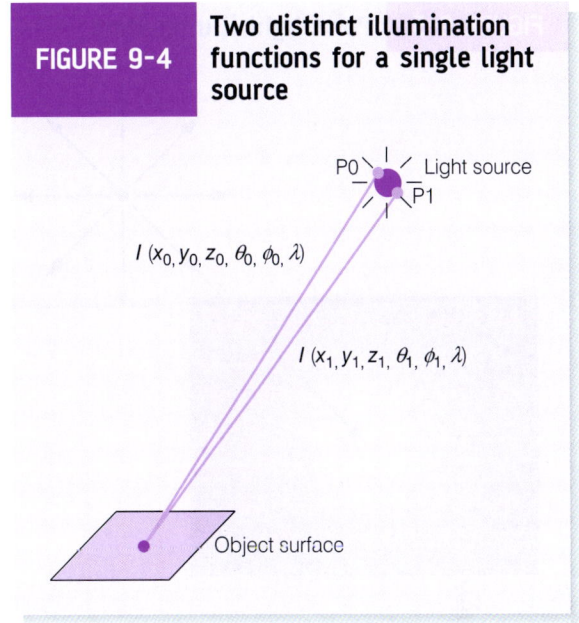

FIGURE 9-4 **Two distinct illumination functions for a single light source**

Furthermore, the overall lighting effect can be characterized by a lighting model. A *lighting model* defines light-object interactions based on the type of light source and the material properties of the object. There are a number of commonly implemented lighting models and we will discuss several of these in section 9.2. For now, it's just important to note that the basic graphics pipeline is constrained to the use of just one lighting model, the *fixed-function lighting model.* This lighting model is basically an extended version of the Phong lighting model (see section 9.2.4 for a discussion of this). The dawn of shader programming allows for full programmability of the graphics pipeline, thus facilitating the implementation of custom user-specified lighting models such as Lambertian lighting, anisotropic lighting, Fresnel lighting, and Blinn lighting (Lambert's law and everything related to it is dealt with in section 9.2.3).

9.1.1 Point Lights

A *point light* emits light uniformly in 360 degrees. Point lights have fixed color and position values and are omnidirectional in nature. The objects illuminated by this light type appear either oversaturated (overly bright with a high contrast) or too dark – a side effect easily corrected through the addition of ambient lights. The primary factor influencing brightness is the distance between the illuminated surface and the point light. Point lights are the easiest of all light types to implement, resulting in their widespread use regardless of their unrealistic simulation of real-life light sources. Figure 9-5 illustrates the effect of a point light illuminating a surface.

Using the previously discussed luminance function, we can define a point light located at point P_1 as follows:

$$I(P_1) = \begin{bmatrix} I_r(P_1) \\ I_g(P_1) \\ I_b(P_1) \end{bmatrix}.$$

Using this luminance function, we can calculate the level of illumination at a specific point, k, on a surface by multiplying the intensity of the light with the inverse square distance between the light source and illuminated surface:

$$I(k,P_1) = \begin{bmatrix} I_r(P_1) \\ I_g(P_1) \\ I_b(P_1) \end{bmatrix} * \frac{1}{|k - P_1|^2}.$$

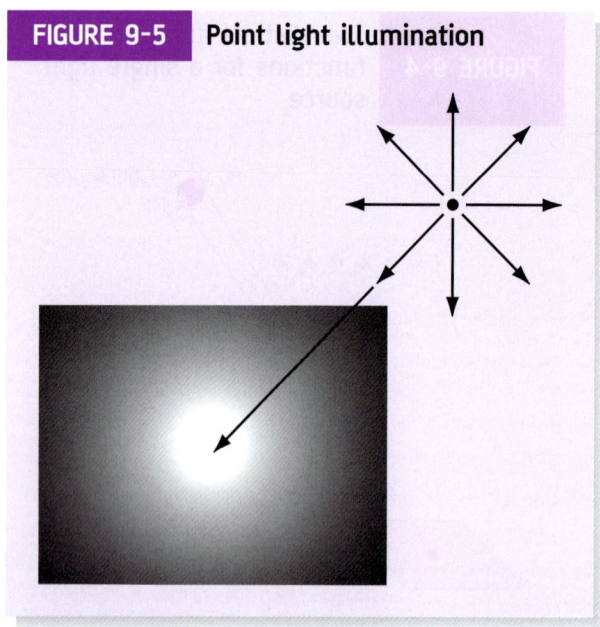

FIGURE 9-5 Point light illumination

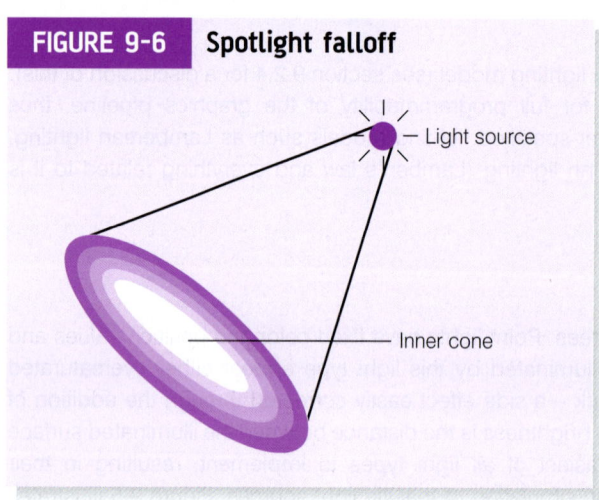

FIGURE 9-6 Spotlight falloff

- Light source

- Inner cone

9.1.2 Spotlights

Spotlights are specified by a color, spatial position and some specific direction and range in which light is emitted. A spotlight is basically a point light with its emitting light constrained within an angle range. This range is defined using two cones: a bright inner cone, and an encircling outer cone. The inner cone has a high intensity (correlating to the user-defined luminescence of the light source), with the outer cone used for fading or attenuating the light source's intensity in an outwards direction. This gradual reduction of light intensity is referred to as *falloff*. Falloff governs the decrease in light intensity from the inner cone to the outer cone and a falloff value of 1.0 generally denotes an evenly distributed light intensity decrease. Figure 9-6 illustrates this diminishing property.

The intensity of a spotlight can be calculated by considering the angle between the direction of the light source and a vector to the point being illuminated. The simplest way of formulating this intensity is to calculate the cosine, to the power of *e*, of the direction angle:

$$I = \cos^e \theta, \text{ with e representing exponential falloff.}$$

We can also calculate the dot product of the spotlight's direction vector and the vector to the point being illuminated. This calculation results in the cosine of the angle between these two vectors (shown in Figure 9-7):

$$\cos \theta = (spotlightDirectionVector) \bullet (vectorToSurface).$$

9.1.3 Ambient Lights

Ambient lighting provides a uniform level of illumination throughout a scene. Numerous large light sources are generally positioned in such a way as to scatter emitted light in all directions, thus making it impossible to determine the original position of the light source. Even though ambient light hitting a

FIGURE 9-7
FIGURE 9-7 The relationship between the direction vector and the vector to the point being illuminated

Light source

Direction vector

θ

Vector to the point being illuminated

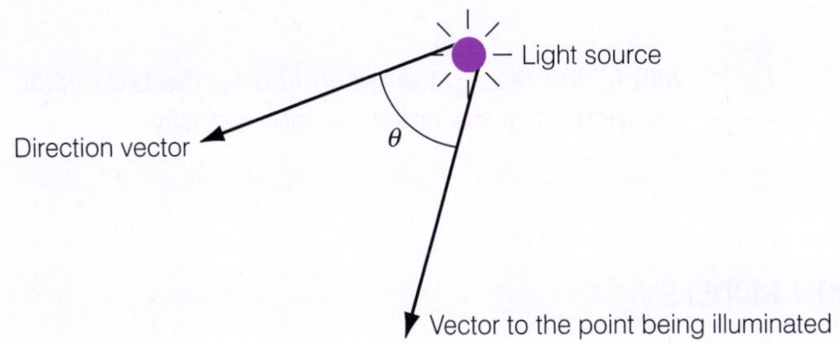

surface is scattered equally in all directions, we can still determine the ambient intensity at each point on the surface.

This type of illumination has a luminance, I, which is the same for all points in the scene; with the manner of reflection being completely dependent on the material properties of a surface:

$$I_A = \begin{bmatrix} I_{Ar} \\ I_{Ag} \\ I_{Ab} \end{bmatrix},$$ with I_{Ar} the red, I_{Ag} the green and I_{Ab} the blue color component of the ambient light intensity.

9.1.4 Parallel Lights

A *parallel* or *directional light* illuminates objects through a series of parallel light rays. These light sources can be considered as point lights located a significant distance from the surface of an object. Moving from one closely located object to another has little influence on the direction at which light hits the object. Sunlight can be considered a parallel light source due to it illuminating closely located objects at the same angle. Thus, the vector to the point being illuminated does not change a great deal when moving from one object to the next. We also use this direction vector to describe the light source. Figure 9-8 illustrates a parallel light source.

Parallel lights do not exhibit attenuation or range properties, consequently not requiring any calculations dealing with illumination effects such as falloff. They are thus excellent light sources when computational overhead is being considered.

FIGURE 9-8 A parallel light

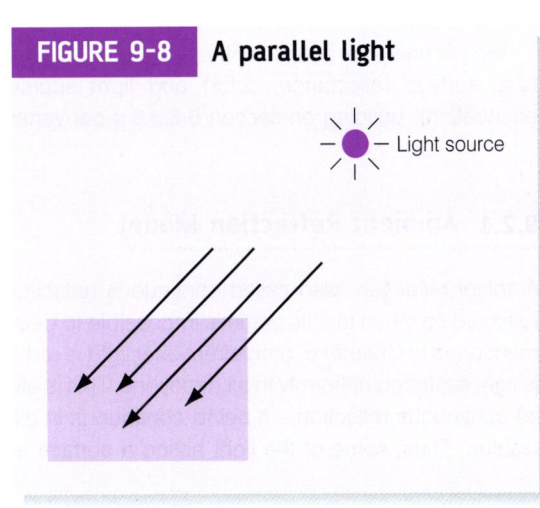

Light source

9.1.5 Emissive Light

Emissive light is radiated (can be considered self-reflecting) light originating from an object's surface. This type of light blends with our other light types, resulting in a surface smoothly colored through the combination of all global light color components.

An object colored using emissive light appears flat and unshaded; this is due to emissive reflection not considering vertex normals or 'incoming' light direction. We can describe emissive lighting using a three-component intensity function:

$$I_E = \begin{bmatrix} I_{Er} \\ I_{Eg} \\ I_{Eb} \end{bmatrix},$$ with I_{Er} the red, I_{Eg} the green and I_{Eb} the blue color component of the emissive light intensity.

9.2 REFLECTION MODELS

A surface is only visible when it has the ability to reflect or absorb light. This ability is the result of the surface's material properties, i.e. rules determining the amount of scattering and/or reflection of incident light. We can specify material properties for any surface, the most common types being the Phong reflection model, ambient reflection, diffuse reflection, specular reflection, and transparency. We can also specify our own per-vertex or per-pixel reflection models via either Cg or HLSL shaders as discussed in section 6.5.3.5.

Chapter 6 described the basic lighting model as a high-level equation summing an ambient, diffuse and specular component to calculate the color of an object's surface:

```
Surface color =  ambient lighting term
               + diffuse lighting term
               + specular lighting term.
```

This surface color is actually equal to the overall amount of light present in a scene, commonly called global illumination and extended to include an emissive lighting term, resulting in the following lighting model equation used to simulate a wide range of lighting conditions:

```
Global illumination =  ambient lighting term
                     + diffuse lighting term
                     + specular lighting term
                     + emissive lighting term.
```

We will now look at each of these lighting/reflectance components as functions of material properties (e.g. surface reflectance, color) and light source properties (e.g. light direction, color, position, attenuation); building on section 6.5.3.5's per-vertex lighting model discussion.

9.2.1 Ambient Reflection Model

Ambient reflection, also called continuous reflection, occurs whenever light emitted from a source is reflected so much that its origin is impossible to determine. Ambient light is omnidirectional in nature. As mentioned in Chapter 6, omnidirectional light is radiated uniformly in all directions, or more commonly, it is light scattered uniformly in all directions. This is also the reason for ambient reflection being described as continuous reflection – it being continuous in all directions, affecting the entire surface in an equal fashion. Thus, some of the light hitting a surface is absorbed while the rest is reflected – resulting in ambient reflection. Also, every point in a scene receives the same amount of ambient lighting, with only the reflection of this light varying. Figure 9-9 illustrates this concept.

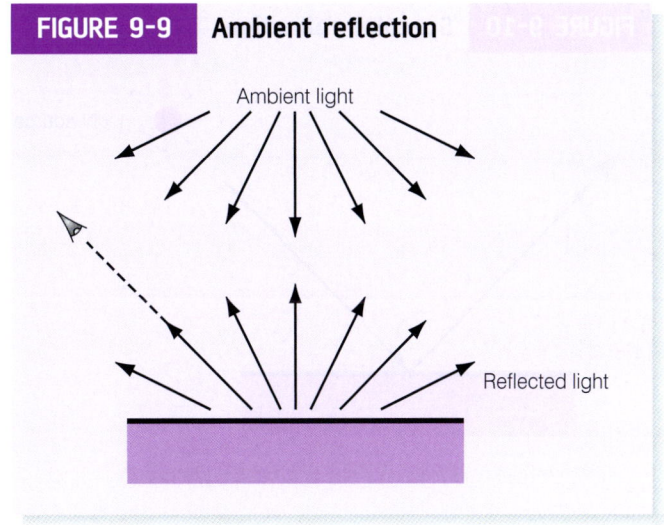

FIGURE 9-9   **Ambient reflection**

Ambient light

Reflected light

The problem with ambient reflection is that illuminated objects appear rather flat and unshaded; Figures 9.1(a) and 9.2(a) show the classic appearance of ambient lit surfaces. This 'flatness' is the result of ambient lighting not factoring in vertex normals or the direction, position, range, and additional light source properties such as attenuation or falloff. Ambient reflection is thus the most computationally efficient of all the reflection models.

The ambient reflection coefficient is an indication of the reflected amount and is comprised out of red, blue, and green ambient reflection coefficients collectively. The equation for calculating ambient lighting factors in the material's ambient reflectance and the color of the incoming ambient light:

Ambient lighting term = material's ambient reflectance
x incoming ambient light color.

We can also define the intensity of ambient reflection using the ambient luminance function (I_A), the incoming ambient light color (I) and the material's ambient reflectance consisting of three reflection coefficients – R_{Ar}, R_{Ag} and R_{Ab}, representing the red, green, and blue ambient reflection coefficients, respectively:

$$\begin{bmatrix} I_{Ar} \\ I_{Ag} \\ I_{Ab} \end{bmatrix} = \begin{bmatrix} R_{Ar} \\ R_{Ag} \\ R_{Ab} \end{bmatrix} * \begin{bmatrix} I_r \\ I_g \\ I_b \end{bmatrix}.$$

9.2.2 Specular Reflection Model

Specular reflection occurs whenever light, from a single incoming direction, is reflected at a single outgoing direction. Specular reflection is characterized by bright highlights on the surface of an object reflected in the direction of the view vector. This concept is illustrated in Figure 9-10.

We previously defined the amount of shininess exhibited by an object as specularity, subsequently attributing the level of specular reflection to a user definable value, namely, the shininess coefficient. The bigger this coefficient, the smoother the object's surface and the closer we are to a perfect mirror. For example, values ranging from 100 to 500 represent most metallic surfaces while smaller values represent materials with broader highlights such as plastic and wood. Figure 9-11 shows several spheres with specular highlights.

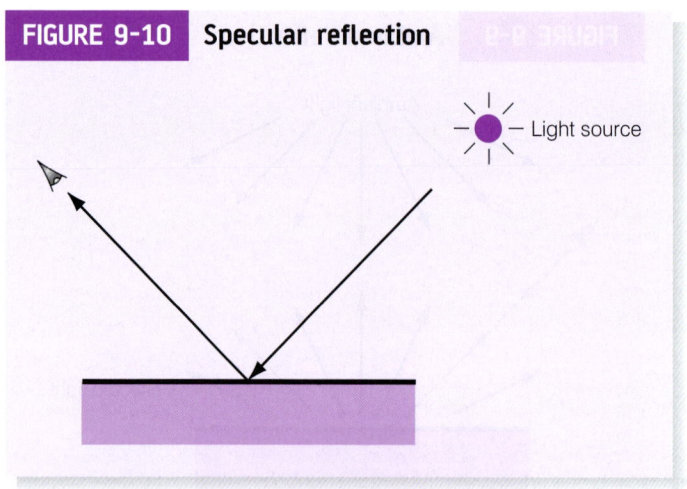

FIGURE 9-10   Specular reflection

FIGURE 9-11   Examples of specular highlights

To calculate specular reflection we need information about both the incoming light direction and location of the viewer as well as the color properties of the material, light source and shininess of the surface. As presented in Chapter 6, the equation for calculating specularity is:

Specular lighting term = material's specular color
            x color of incoming specular light
            x *geometryFacingFlag*
            x (*max*(normalized surface normal
            • normalized halfway vector,0))^{shininess}

As given in Chapter 6, the geometryFacingFlag element is a flag ensuring that specular highlights are limited to geometry facing a light source – its value is calculated by taking the dot product between the

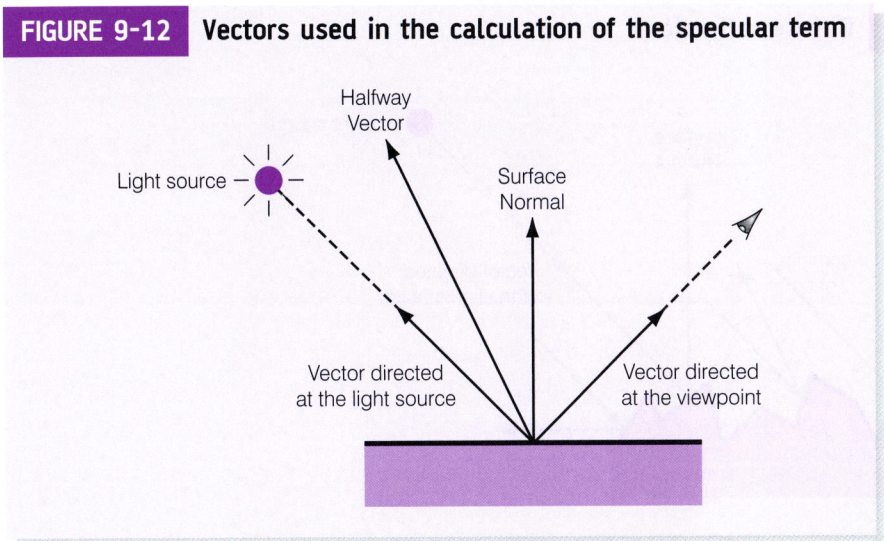

FIGURE 9-12   **Vectors used in the calculation of the specular term**

normalized surface normal and the normalized vector pointing to the light source, if this dot product is greater than zero then the geometryFacingFlag element is set to 1, otherwise 0. The normalized halfway vector element is the vector halfway between the normalized vector pointing towards the viewpoint and the normalized vector pointing in the direction of the light source. Specular highlights are prominent when the angle between these two vectors is small. Figure 9-12, like Figure 6.21, shows the vectors used in the calculation of this specular term.

Alternatively we can define the intensity of specular reflection using the specular luminance function (I_S); the angle between the reflection vector (the direction of a perfectly reflected ray) and the vector directed at the viewpoint; the intensity of the specular light, I; the shininess coefficient, α, and R_s; the fraction of the incoming specular light being reflected:

$$\begin{bmatrix} I_{Sr} \\ I_{Sg} \\ I_{Sb} \end{bmatrix} = \begin{bmatrix} R_{Sr} \\ R_{Sg} \\ R_{Sb} \end{bmatrix} \begin{bmatrix} I_r \\ I_g \\ I_b \end{bmatrix} \cos^{\alpha}\phi.$$

9.2.3 Diffuse Reflection Model

Diffuse reflections occur when incoming light is reflected in arbitrary directions. The main contributing factor to this form of reflection is an uneven or rough surface. A diffuse surface appears identical to all viewers, regardless of their respective point of view. This type of reflection is common for matte or uneven surfaces (such as carpets or brushed metal) and is used for shading surfaces in such a way as to convey a sense of depth.

Diffuse reflection is a function of the incoming light direction and surface normal, in other words, the reflection of incoming light is dependent on the surface roughness and incoming light angle. The equation for calculating diffuse lighting is:

Diffuse lighting term = material's diffuse color

           x color of incoming diffuse light

           x max(normalized surface normal

           • normalized vector towards light,0)

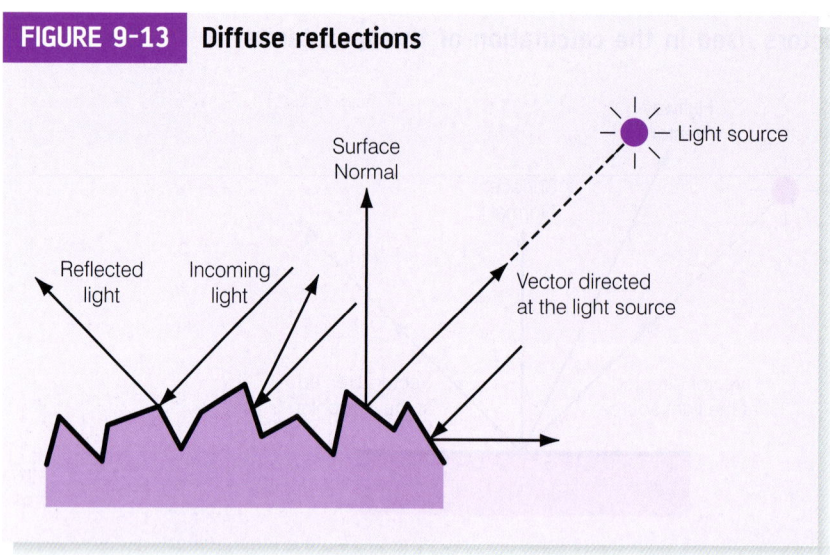

FIGURE 9-13 **Diffuse reflections**

As presented in Chapter 6, the dot product between the normalized surface normal and normalized vector pointing towards the light source gives the measure of incident light received by the surface – the smaller the angle between these two vectors, the greater the dot product result, and the greater the amount of incident light falling on the surface. The max (normalized surface normal. normalized vector towards light, 0) element in the equation ensures that only surfaces facing a light source reflect some diffuse lighting – surfaces facing away from a light source result in a negative dot product. Figure 9-13 shows a diffuse surface with the normalized surface normal and normalized vector pointing at the light source.

We can also define *perfect diffuse* surfaces, i.e. surfaces reflecting light in no particular direction. These surfaces, also called *Lambertian surfaces*, are generally so rough that it is mathematically impossible to determine a preferred angle of reflection. Also, Lambertian light has a consistent intensity regardless of the distance between the reflecting surface and light source.

Perfect diffuse reflection can be modeled using *Lambert's cosine law*. This law states that the reflection or radiance observed from a perfect diffuse surface is directly relative to the cosine of the angle between the vector directed at the light source and the surface normal:

$R_D \propto \cos\phi$, where R_D is the diffuse reflection and ϕ is the angle between the vector directed at the light source and the surface normal.

In common English, Lambert's law simply states that a perfectly diffuse surface always reflects the same amount of light, regardless of the viewing angle. For example, say a surface is being illuminated using a parallel light source, when this light is positioned perpendicular to the surface; the surface will appear brightly lit. Placing this light source at, say, a 135° angle will result in a more dimly lit surface due to the light rays covering a larger surface area. Figure 9-14 illustrates Lambert's cosine law.

9.2.4 The Phong Reflection Model

The *Phong reflection model*, also loosely called Phong shading, was developed in 1973 by Bui Tuong Phong (the late computer graphics researcher and pioneer) and later extended to include a halfway vector in the calculation of the specular term by Jim Blinn. The Phong model is an illumination model

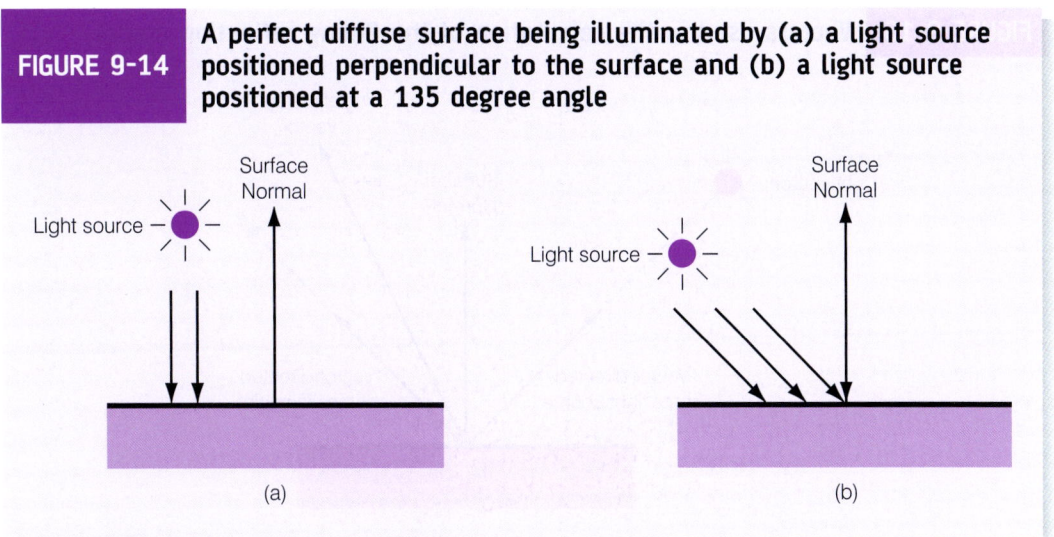

FIGURE 9-14   A perfect diffuse surface being illuminated by (a) a light source positioned perpendicular to the surface and (b) a light source positioned at a 135 degree angle

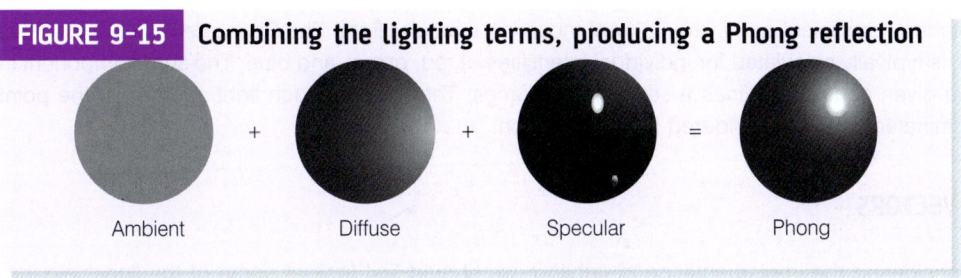

FIGURE 9-15   Combining the lighting terms, producing a Phong reflection

Ambient   Diffuse   Specular   Phong

that controls the shading of individual pixels; it is computationally efficient and leads to realistic looking reflections. Phong's goal was to create realistic looking objects in as close to real time as possible.

The Phong reflection model basically combines ambient, specular and diffuse lighting components to closely approximate real world reflections. This concept is shown in Figure 9-15.

We can consequently write the combination of these lighting terms as:

$$I = Ia + Id + Is.$$

Mathematically, the Phong reflection model considers reflected light as a function of the cosine between the surface normal and the incoming light direction. More precisely, the color value of a point on the surface being illuminated is a function of four vectors, as shown in Figure 9-16: the normal vector at this point, the vector directed at the viewpoint, a vector directed at the light source, and the reflection vector (indicating the direction of a perfectly reflected ray).

The following equation can be used to calculate the Phong reflection of a point on the surface of an object:

$$Phong\ reflection = k_a i_a + \sum (k_d (L \cdot N) i_d + k_s (R \cdot V)^\alpha i_s)$$

with k_a the material's ambient reflectance, i_a the color of incoming ambient light, k_d the material's diffuse reflectance, L the vector directed at light source, N the surface normal, i_d the color of incoming diffuse

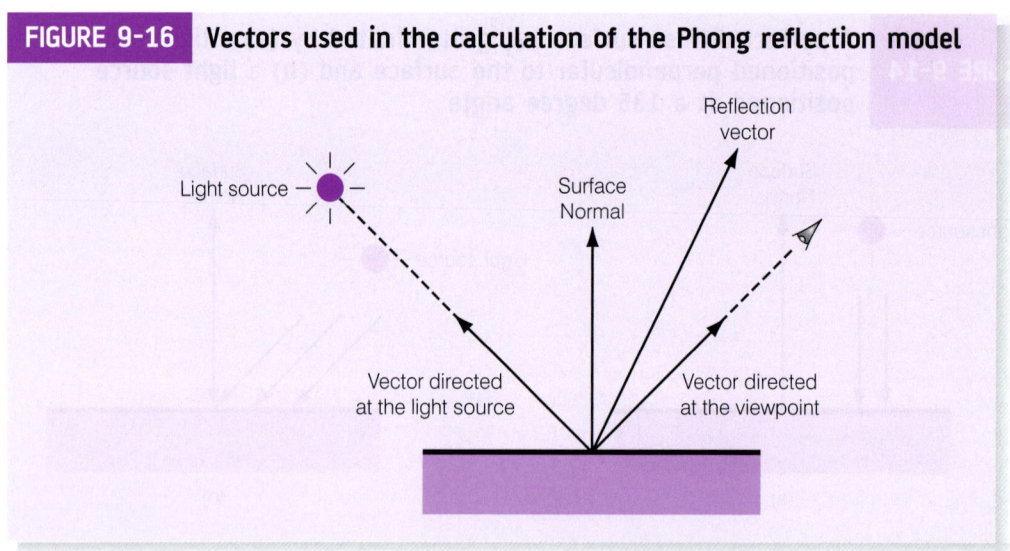

FIGURE 9-16 **Vectors used in the calculation of the Phong reflection model**

light, k_s the material's specular reflectance, R the reflection vector, V the vector directed at the viewpoint, α the shininess coefficient and i_s the color of incoming specular light. The Phong reflection, using this equation, is typically calculated for individual intensities of red, green, and blue. The sum component in the above given equation defines a set of light sources. The effect of each light source, on the point being illuminated, is thus considered by the equation.

9.3   VECTORS

Before considering the implementation of lighting, we should first look at some of the linear algebra required for the representation of light. Determining the lighting of a scene entails the calculation of vectors, dot products, and cross products. A *vector* can be represented as a line/entity with both a magnitude and direction. A line/entity lacking direction but with a magnitude is known as a *scalar*. We first investigated vectors, matrices, and scalars in Chapter 7. A daily example of a vector is the acceleration of a car from a static to moving state. The car accelerates at a specified magnitude and in a specific direction. An example of a scalar might be the car's speed at one specific instance or the distance travelled over a five minute period.

In three-dimensional space, as discussed in Chapter 7, a vector consists of an x, y, and z component. For example, the vector **K** consists of three scalar components, namely, Kx, Ky and Kz:

$$\mathbf{K} = (Kx, Ky, Kz)$$

Vectors are usually written in boldface but can also be represented with a line positioned on top of its alphabetical character. Scalars are commonly written in italics.

9.3.1 Vector Length

To determine the length of a vector (often referred to as its magnitude, i.e. the distance from the vector's 'tail' to its 'head'), we calculate the square root of the sum of the squares of its scalar components:

$$|\mathbf{M}| = \sqrt{(Mx^2 + My^2 + Mz^2)}$$

This result is crucial for the calculation of the dot product. The *dot product* is an easy way to determine the angle between two vectors. For example, the dot product between two vectors, **A** and **B** is denoted as $A \cdot B$ and can be calculated by multiplying the magnitude of the two vectors with the cosine of the angle between them:

$$A \cdot B = |A||B|COS(\theta)$$

Thus, in the above given formula, θ is the angle between the vectors **A** and **B** with $|A|$ and $|B|$ the length of the vectors **A** and **B**, respectively. Figure 9-17 gives a graphical representation of these vectors as well as the angle between them.

9.3.2 Vector Addition (Head-to-Tail Rule)

We use vector addition to create a third, composite vector. This process involves summing the related scalar components of two successive vectors (hence the *head-to-tail* rule). For example, if we have two vectors, **K** and **L**, then we can define a third vector, **M**, their resultant, by summing the scalars of vector **K** and **L** in the following manner (graphically illustrated in Figure 9-18):

$$
\begin{aligned}
\mathbf{M} &= \mathbf{K} + \mathbf{L} \\
&= (Kx + Lx, Ky + Ly, Kz + Lz) \\
&= (Mx, My, Mz).
\end{aligned}
$$

FIGURE 9-17   Vectors and angle necessary for the calculation of a dot product

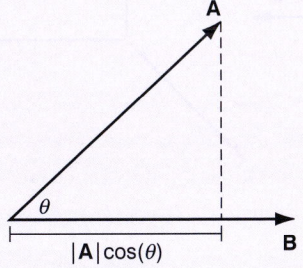

FIGURE 9-18   The head-to-tail rule, creating a third composite vector

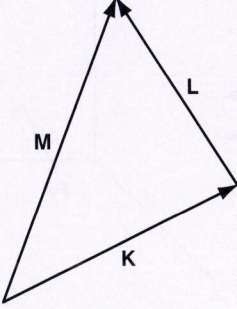

9.3.3 Scalar Multiplication

We can multiply a vector with a scalar to change its magnitude or direction. For example, vector **M** can be multiplied by the value 2 to produce a vector twice the magnitude of the original (Figure 9-19):

$$\mathbf{M} = (2)(Mx, My, Mz)$$
$$= ((2)Mx, (2)My, (2)Mz)$$
$$= 2\mathbf{M}.$$

Similarly, multiplying vector **M** with a negative value produces a vector pointing in the opposite direction of the original (Figure 9-20):

$$\mathbf{M} = (-1)(Mx, My, Mz)$$
$$= ((-1)Mx, (-1)My, (-1)Mz)$$
$$= -\mathbf{M}.$$

FIGURE 9-19 | Increasing the magnitude of a vector by multiplying it with a scalar greater than 1

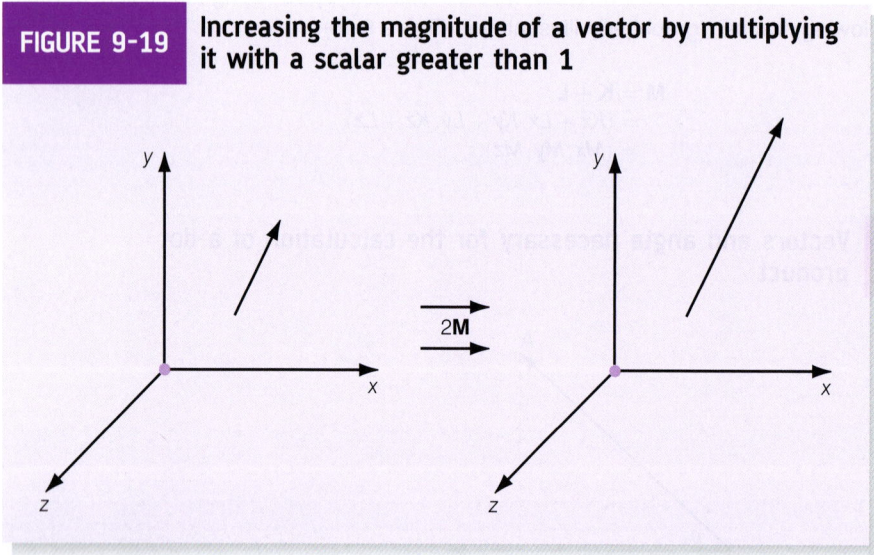

FIGURE 9-20 | Changing the direction of a vector by multiplying it with a negative scalar

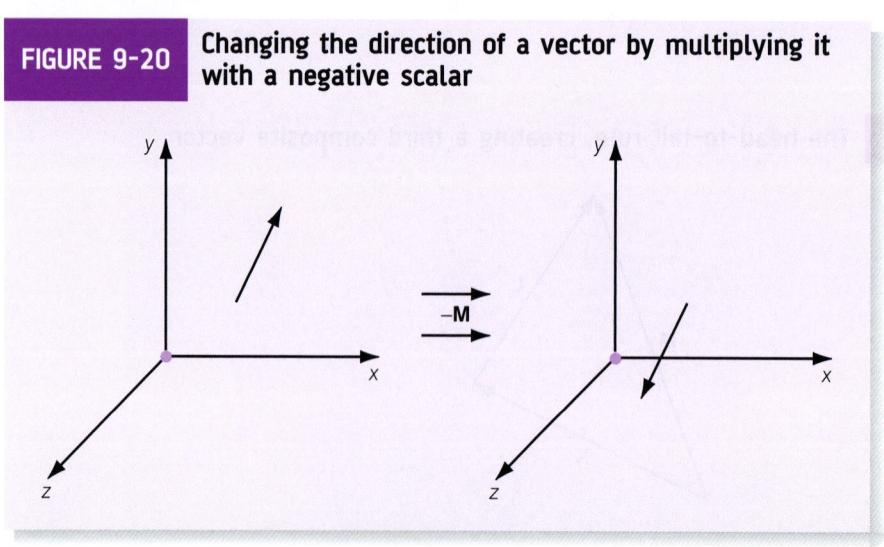

9.3.4 Cross Product (Normal Vectors)

Normal vectors are used to indicate the orientation of a surface with respect to a light source or camera position. A surface with its normal vector facing away from a light source will not be visible to the viewer (unless illuminated by reflected light). These vectors are thus a very important element of lighting. To calculate the normal vector of a polygonal surface, we need three surface vertices. These three vertices are used to define two vectors. The surface normal, **N**, can then be determined by calculating the cross product of these two vectors, **K** and **L**, for example (illustrated in Figure 9-21):

$$\mathbf{N} = \mathbf{K} \times \mathbf{L}$$

The cross product, denoted **K** × **L**, is a vector perpendicular to both the vectors **L** and **K**. We generally calculate the cross product by multiplying the magnitude of the two vectors with the sine of the angle between them:

$$\mathbf{K} \times \mathbf{L} = |\mathbf{K}||\mathbf{L}|\operatorname{Sin} \theta$$

Algebraically we'll calculate the cross product **C**, for example, as:

$$\begin{aligned}\mathbf{C} &= \mathbf{K} \times \mathbf{M} \\ &= (KyMz - KzMy)i + (KzMx - KxMz)j + (KxMy - KyMx)k\end{aligned}$$

with i, j and k representing the x, y and z axes, respectively.

9.3.5 Unit Vectors

We previously defined the length of a vector as the distance from its 'tail' to its 'head'. A vector of length 1 is called a normalized or *unit vector*. We use normalized vectors because we are mostly interested in the orientation of entities, and comparing the orientation of one entity to that of another requires vectors of equal size. A vector is normalized by dividing its three-dimensional components with its length. For example, the unit vector **U** can be calculated by dividing vector **A** with its length, |**A**| (shown in Figure 9-22).

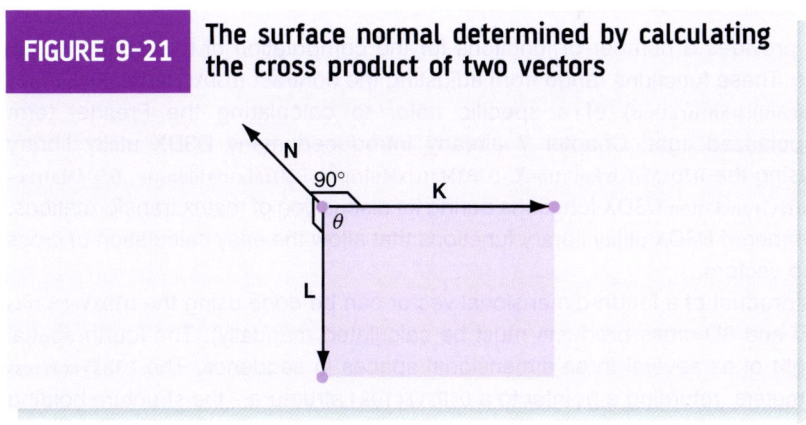

FIGURE 9-21 The surface normal determined by calculating the cross product of two vectors

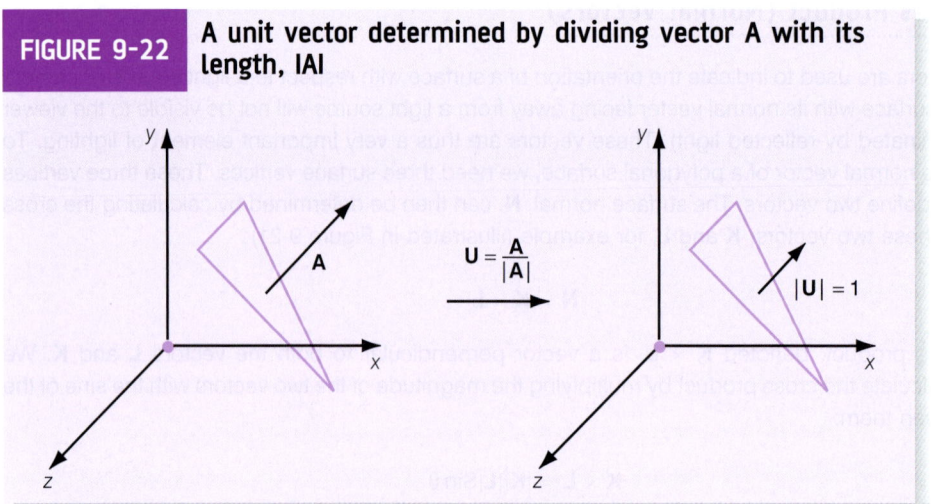

FIGURE 9-22 **A unit vector determined by dividing vector A with its length, IAI**

Vector **A** is defined as a three-dimensional vector with each of its components a scalar:

$$\mathbf{A} = (Ax, Ay, Az)$$

The magnitude of this vector is defined as:

$$|\mathbf{A}| = \sqrt{(Ax)^2 + (Ay)^2 + (Az)^2}$$

The normalized vector **U** is calculated as follows:

$$\mathbf{U} = \frac{\mathbf{A}}{|\mathbf{A}|}$$

9.3.6 Direct3D Extension Vector Functions

The D3DX utility library provides a number of functions for the computation of three-dimensional mathematical operations. These functions range from adjusting the contrast (D3DXColorAdjustContrast) or saturation (D3DXColorAdjustSaturation) of a specific color to calculating the Fresnel term (D3DXFresnelTerm) for unpolarized light. Chapter 7 already introduced many D3DX utility library functions, for instance using the D3DXMatrixRotationX, D3DXMatrixMultiply, D3DXMatrixIdentity, D3DXMatrix-PerspectiveLH, and D3DXMatrixTranslation D3DX functions during its discussion of matrix transformations. We will now look at a number of D3DX utility library functions that allow the easy calculation of cross products and normalized vectors.

Calculating the cross product of a fourth-dimensional vector can be done using the D3DXVec4Cross D3DX math function (2D and 3D cross products must be calculated manually). The fourth spatial dimension can be thought of as several three-dimensional spaces in sequence. The D3DXVec4Cross function takes four parameters, returning a pointer to a D3DXVECTOR4 structure – the structure holding the calculated cross product. The D3DXVec4Cross function is declared as follows in the d3dx10math.h header:

```
D3DXVECTOR4 * D3DXVec4Cross (
    D3DXVECTOR4 *pOut,
    CONST D3DXVECTOR4 *pV1,
    CONST D3DXVECTOR4 *pV2,
    CONST D3DXVECTOR4 *pV3
);
```

Its first parameter, pOut, is a pointer to a D3DXVECTOR4 structure that will store the calculated cross product. The next three parameters each take a pointer to a D3DXVECTOR4 structure describing one of the vectors in 4D space. This 4D structure, declared in the d3dx10math.h header, takes four parameters, namely, the x, y, z and w components of a vector:

```
typedef struct D3DXVECTOR4 {
    FLOAT x;
    FLOAT y;
    FLOAT z;
    FLOAT w;
} D3DXVECTOR4, *LPD3DXVECTOR4;
```

Normalising a 2D, 3D, or 4D vector is also straightforward through use of the D3DXVec2Normalize, D3DXVec3Normalize, or D3DXVec4Normalize D3DX math functions, respectively.

The D3DXVec2Normalize function, declared as follows in d3dx10math.h header, takes two parameters, namely, a pointer to a D3DXVECTOR2 structure that will store the normalized vector and pV, a pointer to a D3DXVECTOR2 structure holding the vector to normalize:

```
D3DXVECTOR2 * D3DXVec2Normalize (
    D3DXVECTOR2 *pOut,
    CONST D3DXVECTOR2 *pV
);
```

The D3DXVECTOR2 D3DX structure describes a two-dimensional vector via two parameters, the x- and y-component of the vector, in that order.

Normalising a 3D vector is accomplished via the D3DXVec3Normalize function. This function, just as its 2D counterpart, takes two parameters; the first, pOut, a pointer to a D3DXVECTOR3 structure that will store the normalized vector and the second, pV, a pointer to a D3DXVECTOR3 structure containing the vector to normalize:

```
D3DXVECTOR3 * D3DXVec3Normalize (
    D3DXVECTOR3 *pOut,
    CONST D3DXVECTOR3 *pV
);
```

The D3DXVECTOR3 structure, declared in the d3dx10math.h header, is used to define a three-dimensional vector using its x-, y- and z-component:

```
typedef struct D3DXVECTOR3 {
    FLOAT x;
```

```
    FLOAT y;
    FLOAT z;
} D3DXVECTOR3, *LPD3DXVECTOR3;
```

We can also normalize a 4D vector using the D3DXVec4Normalize function. This D3DX math function is declared as follows:

```
D3DXVECTOR4 * D3DXVec4Normalize (
    D3DXVECTOR4 *pOut,
    CONST D3DXVECTOR4 *pV
) ;
```

Its first parameter, pOut, is a pointer to a D3DXVECTOR4 structure that is used for storing the normalized vector. The second parameter, pV, is a pointer to a D3DXVECTOR4 structure with the 4D components of the vector to normalize.

There are also several other D3DX vector functions, for example, the D3DXVec2TransformNormal function can be used to transform a 2D vector by some predefined matrix, and a Hermite spline interpolation can be performed using the D3DXVec3Hermite function. D3DX math functions will, however, mostly be used for matrix calculations as seen in Chapter 7, with vector and normal calculations being done either in a shader program or manually by the programmer.

9.4 IMPLEMENTING LOCAL ILLUMINATION

Local illumination, unlike global illumination, only considers the interaction between a light source and object. For example, when lighting a series of cubes, each cube is lit independently from the others. Thus, even though one cube might be blocking light from another, it is never considered by the local illumination model. This model is shown in Figure 9-23.

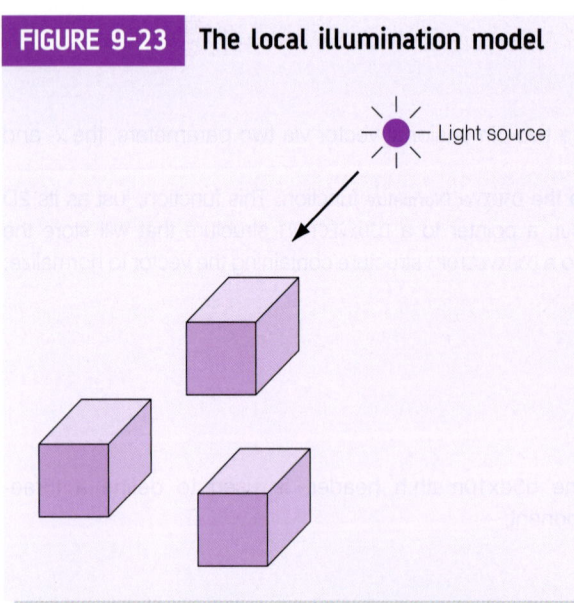

FIGURE 9-23 **The local illumination model**

Light source

Global illumination on the other hand incorporates this "blocked-out light" via the implementation of a ray tracing algorithm, for example. Ray tracing follows the light (via vectors) from the source to object surfaces, rendering objects and effects based on the subsequent object-light interaction. We will not be looking at global illumination as it falls outside the scope of interactive graphics, rather belonging to the field of photo realistic rendering. Its overall effect can, however, be simulated through the use of a number of shadowing algorithms, as will be discussed in Chapter 11. Figure 9-24 shows global illumination where one object blocks light from reaching other objects.

We will now implement local illumination using the diffuse reflection model, resulting in a uniformly lit scene. The amount of reflection is calculated using Lambert's law – hence by considering the cosine of the angle between the vector directed at the light source and the surface normal (Figure 9-25). We can determine the angle, θ, by calculating the dot product of these two vectors.

The rendered scene, comprised of several cubes, two parallel light sources and using Lambertian light, will thus have a consistent intensity regardless of the distance between the reflecting surface and light source (as shown in Figure 9-26).

Our example (program 9.1 on the book's website) implements an HLSL pixel shader to calculate the lighting effect on each pixel in our scene. The

FIGURE 9-24   **The global illumination model**

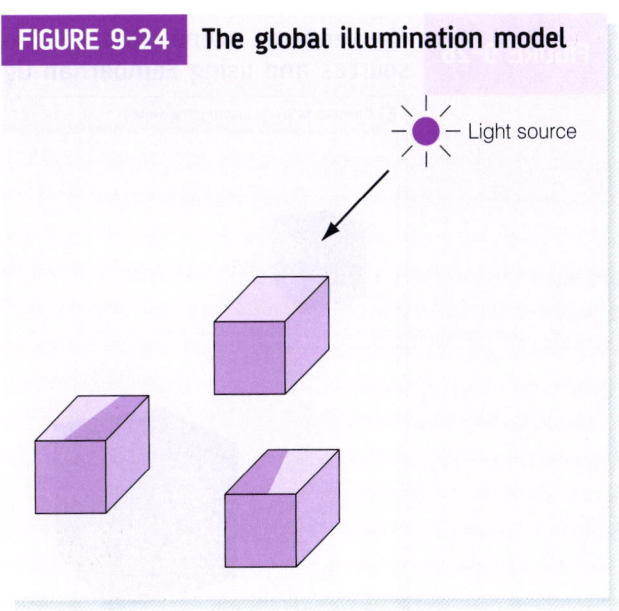

FIGURE 9-25   **The projected light calculated by considering the cosine of the angle between the vector directed at the light source and the surface normal**

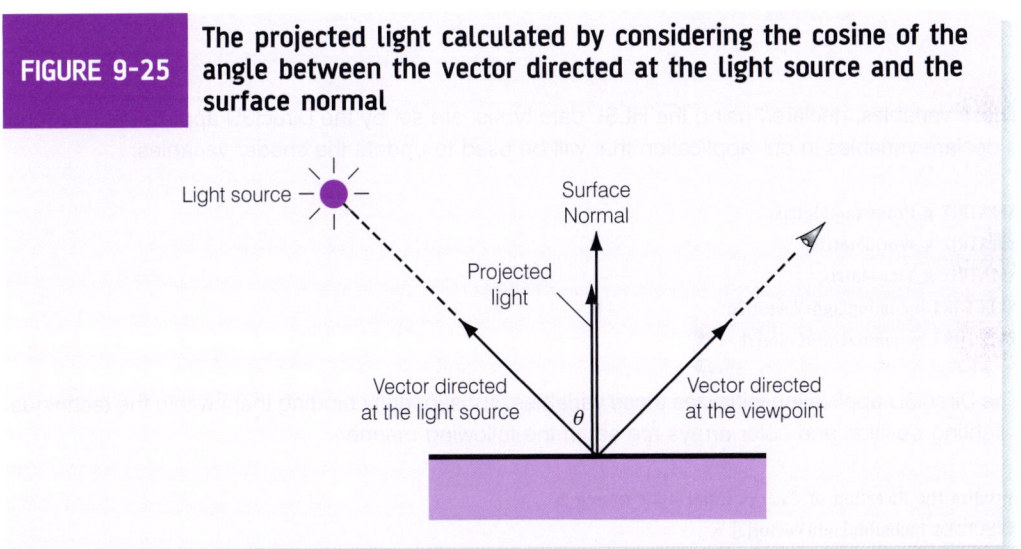

shader's effect file starts with a declaration of the projection, world and view matrices, followed by a floating point array storing the incoming light vector of each light source, and another floating point array holding the color of each light:

```
matrix ProjectionMatrix;

matrix WorldMatrix;
matrix ViewMatrix;

float4 LightDirection[2];
float4 LightColor[2];
```

FIGURE 9-26	The rendered scene; comprised of three cubes, two parallel light sources and using Lambertian light

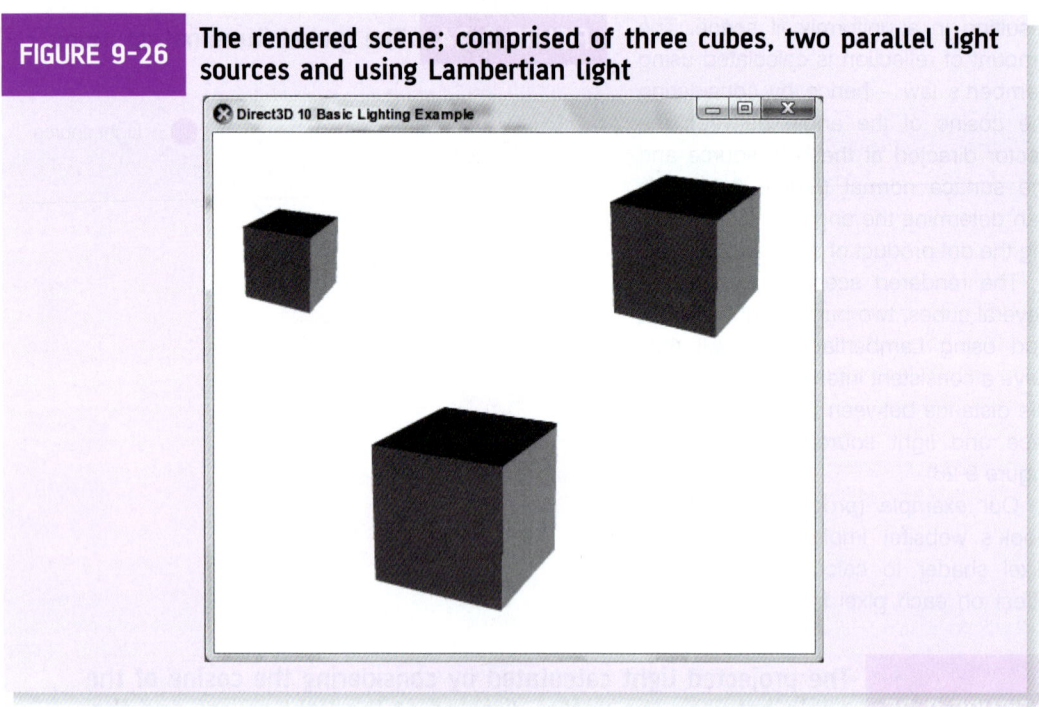

These variables, declared using the HLSL data types, are set by the Direct3D application. We must thus declare variables in our application that will be used to update the shader variables:

```
D3DXMATRIX g_ProjectionMatrix;
D3DXMATRIX g_WorldMatrix;
D3DXMATRIX g_ViewMatrix;
D3DXVECTOR4 IncomingLightVector[2];
D3DXVECTOR4 IncomingLightColor[2];
```

The Direct3D application initializes these variables, subsequently binding them within the technique. The lighting position and color arrays are set in the following manner:

```
/* initialize the direction of each parallel light source */
D3DXVECTOR4 IncomingLightVector[2] =
{
    //the spatial position of the first light source
    D3DXVECTOR4(1.0f, 0.5f, 0.5f, 1.0f),
    //the spatial position of the second light source
    D3DXVECTOR4(0.0f, 0.0f, 1.0f, 1.0f)
};

/* specify the color of each parallel light source */
D3DXVECTOR4 IncomingLightColor[2] =
{
    //bright red
    D3DXVECTOR4(1.0f, 0.0f, 0.0f, 1.0f),
```

```
//deep orange
D3DXVECTOR4(1.0f, 0.5f, 0.0f, 1.0f)
};
```

As detailed in Chapter 7, the g_WorldMatrix variable is initialized to an identity matrix using the D3DXMatrixIdentity D3DX math function, the g_ViewMatrix variable via the D3DXMatrixLookAtLH D3DX function, and the g_ProjectionMatrix variable using the D3DXMatrixPerspectiveFovLH D3DX function:

```
/* initialize the world matrix */
D3DXMatrixIdentity (&g_WorldMatrix) ;

/* initialize the view matrix */
D3DXVECTOR3 EyeCoord ( 0.0f, 1.0f, –10.0f) ;
D3DXVECTOR3 LookAt (0.0f, 1.0f, 0.0f) ;
D3DXVECTOR3 UpDir (0.0f, 1.0f, 0.0f) ;
D3DXMatrixLookAtLH(&g_ViewMatrix, &EyeCoord, &LookAt, &UpDir);

/* set the left–handed perspective projection */
D3DXMatrixPerspectiveFovLH(&g_ProjectionMatrix,
                           (float)D3DX_PI*0.25f,
                           rectangle_width/rectangle_height,
                           0.1f, 100.0f);
```

Before we can set the HLSL variable values using the ID3D10EffectVariable update methods we first have to obtain the effect variables via ID3D10Effect retrieval functions for each of the above defined shader variables:

```
/* obtain the ProjectionMatrix shader variable */
ID3D10EffectMatrixVariable* g_pd3d10ProjMatrixVar = NULL;
g_pd3d10ProjMatrixVar = g_pd3d10Effect
            ->GetVariableByName("ProjectionMatrix")
                                    ->AsMatrix();

/* obtain the WorldMatrix shader variable */
ID3D10EffectMatrixVariable* g_pd3d10WorldMatrixVar = NULL;
g_pd3d10WorldMatrixVar = g_pd3d10Effect
            ->GetVariableByName ("WorldMatrix") ->AsMatrix();

/* obtain the ViewMatrix shader variable */
ID3D10EffectMatrixVariable* g_pd3d10ViewMatrixVar = NULL;
g_pd3d10ViewMatrixVar = g_pd3d10Effect
            ->GetVariableByName ("ViewMatrix") ->AsMatrix();

/* obtain the LightDirection shader variable */
ID3D10EffectVectorVariable* g_pd3d10LightDirectionVectorVar = NULL;
g_pd3d10LightDirectionVectorVar = g_pd3d10Effect
            ->GetVariableByName("LightDirection")
                                    ->AsVector();
```

9

```
/* obtain the LightColor shader variable */
ID3D10EffectVectorVariable* g_pd3d10LightColorVectorVar = NULL;

g_pd3d10LightColorVectorVar = g_pd3d10Effect
              ->GetVariableByName("LightColor")->AsVector();
```

To recap, the GetVariableByName ID3D10Effect interface function takes a string value containing the name of the variable declared in the shader/effect program as parameter, returning a pointer to the ID3D10EffectVariable interface. The AsVector ID3D10EffectVariable interface function casts this returned ID3D10EffectVariable interface to an ID3D10EffectVectorVariable interface so that we can access the vector type. The AsMatrix function casts the returned ID3D10EffectVariable interface to an ID3D10EffectMatrixVariable interface used for reading the shader variable as a matrix type.

Next our Direct3D program sets the values of the shader/effect variables using the SetMatrix ID3D10EffectMatrixVariable interface for all floating-point matrices and the SetFloatVectorArray ID3D10Effect-VectorVariable interface for our four-component floating point vector arrays:

```
g_pd3d10ProjMatrixVar->SetMatrix((float*)&g_ProjectionMatrix);
g_pd3d10WorldMatrixVar->SetMatrix((float*)&g_WorldMatrix);
g_pd3d10ViewMatrixVar->SetMatrix((float*)&g_ViewMatrix);

g_pd3d10LightDirectionVectorVar
      ->SetFloatVectorArray((float*)IncomingLightVector, 0, 2);
g_pd3d10LightColorVectorVar
      ->SetFloatVectorArray((float*)IncomingLightColor, 0, 2);
```

The values declared in the shader program are now set and can be changed during each rendering pass.

Returning to our shader program, we declare two structures for the storage of received vertex data and returned pixel data, respectively:

```
struct VERTEXSHADER_INPUT
{
    float4 Loc : POSITION;
    float3 Norm : NORMAL;
};

struct PIXELSHADER_INPUT
{
    float4 Loc : SV_POSITION;
    float3 Norm : TEXCOORD0;
};
```

The first structure, VERTEXSHADER_INPUT, holds our texture vertex information as received from the Direct3D application and is used to pass input data to a vertex shader that transforms the input vertex position, defined in object space, to projection space. This is done by multiplying the input vertex position, IN.Loc, with a world matrix, thus transforming it from object space to world space. The next transformation multiplies this transformed vertex position, output.Loc, with a view matrix, resulting in a world space to view space transformation. The final transformation takes this view space vertex position and multiplies it with a projection matrix to transform the vertex from view space to projection space. Our vertex shader also transforms the input vertex normal to world space, finally returning the transformed vertex data via the PIXELSHADER_INPUT structure:

```
PIXELSHADER_INPUT LightingVertexShader(VERTEXSHADER_INPUT IN)
{
    PIXELSHADER_INPUT output = (PIXELSHADER_INPUT)0;

    output.Loc = mul(IN.Loc, WorldMatrix);
    output.Loc = mul(output.Loc, ViewMatrix);
    output.Loc = mul(output.Loc, ProjectionMatrix);

    output.Norm = mul(IN.Norm, WorldMatrix);

    return output;
}
```

We determine the diffuse lighting on each pixel via a pixel shader. In short, the dot product of the incoming light vector and the surface normal is calculated, with the overall lighting effect determined by multiplying the dot product result with the color of each light source. All these calculated values are then summed to determine the overall pixel color:

```
/* pixel shader */
float4 LightingPixelShader(PIXELSHADER_INPUT IN) : SV_Target
{
    float4 finalPixelColor = 0;
    float4 dotPixelColor = 0;

    /* calculate the overall lighting by multiplying the dot product result of the incoming light vector and the
       surface normal with the color of each light source */
    for(int i = 0; i < 2; i++)
    {
        dotPixelColor = dot((float3)LightDirection[i],
                            IN.Norm);
        finalPixelColor += saturate(dotPixelColor *
                                    LightColor[i]);
    }

    /* return the overall pixel color */
    return finalPixelColor;
}
```

The final step is to create the effect technique definition. This effect technique has one rendering pass, P0, specifying the shader states used to perform the lighting operation. It is defined as follows:

```
technique10 LightScene
{
    pass P0
    {
        SetGeometryShader(NULL);
```

```
            SetVertexShader(CompileShader(ps_4_0,
                            LightingVertexShader()));
        SetPixelShader(CompileShader(ps_4_0,
                            LightingPixelShader()));
    }
}
```

Returning to our Direct3D application, all that remains is to create the effect object and technique object that will be used to perform the lighting operation. We can create the effect using this D3DX10CreateEffectFromFile function in the following manner:

```
ID3D10Device* g_pd3d10Device = NULL;
ID3D10Effect* g_pd3d10Effect = NULL;

D3DX10CreateEffectFromFile(
        L"file_name.fx", NULL, NULL,
        D3D10_SHADER_ENABLE_BACKWARDS_COMPATIBILITY,
        0, g_pd3d10Device, NULL, NULL,
        &g_pd3d10Effect, NULL, NULL);
```

Following the effect creation we must obtain the effect technique using the GetTechniqueByName ID3D10Effect interface function. This function takes a string value containing the name of the technique as parameter, returning a pointer to the ID3D10EffectTechnique interface:

```
ID3D10EffectTechnique* g_id3dTechnique = NULL;
g_id3dTechnique = g_id3dEffect->GetTechniqueByName(
                            "LightScene");
```

Working with OpenGL

Using OpenGL we set the lighting state using the routine:

```
glEnable(GL_LIGHTING);
```

Calling glDisable(GL_LIGHTING) disables all lighting, resulting in a pitch-black scene.

OpenGL lighting requires the initialization of a light source position, orientation, type, and color. A diffuse yellow light source positioned at the coordinates (20, 20, −20) can be specified as follows:

```
glEnable(GL_LIGHT1);
GLfloat diffuse_light_color[] = {1.0f, 1.0f, 0.0f};
GLfloat diffuse_light_position[] = {20.0f, 20.0f, −20.0f,
                            1.0f};
glLightfv(GL_LIGHT1, GL_DIFFUSE, diffuse_light_color);
glLightfv(GL_LIGHT1, GL_POSITION, diffuse_light_position);
```

OpenGL utilizes a logical numbering scheme in the form of 'GL_LIGHTx', to identify light sources. Thus, by using this numbering scheme, we can clearly indicate the light source being initialized. If our scene had an additional light source, then the definition of that source could start with the routine glEnable(GL_LIGHT2), for example.

The above defined diffuse_light_position variable takes four parameters. Its first three parameters are just the light's *x*, *y* and *z* coordinates, respectively. The fourth parameter indicates whether the light source is to be considered directional (0.0f) or not (1.0f).

The glLightfv function sets the properties of a light source via three parameters. Its first parameter specifies the light source being initialized. The second parameter specifies the property type being set with the third parameter defining this property. Legal flags for the second parameter include:

- GL_AMBIENT (sets the type of light to ambient with the third parameter specifying the color intensity in red–green–blue–alpha components)

- GL_DIFFUSE (sets the type of light to diffuse with the third parameter specifying the color intensity)

- GL_SPECULAR (sets the type of light to specular with the third parameter specifying the color intensity)

- GL_POSITION (sets the light position via the third parameter)

- GL_SPOT_DIRECTION (sets the direction of the light via the third parameter)

- GL_SPOT_EXPONENT (sets the intensity distribution of the light with the third parameter specifying this value ranging from 0 to 128)

- GL_SPOT_CUTOFF (sets the maximum spread angle of a light source with the third parameter specifying this angle ranging from 0 to 90 degrees).

You can also set the light attenuation factors to GL_CONSTANT_ATTENUATION, GL_LINEAR_ATTENUA-TION, or GL_QUADRATIC_ATTENUATION.

We also have to initialize the preferred shading model and calculate the normal vectors for each of our surfaces. OpenGL programs use the glNormal3f routine to set the normal vector of a surface. This function takes three parameters, namely, the *x*, *y* and *z* coordinates of the normal vector. Our shading model is set to smooth with the following routine:

```
glShadeModel(GL_SMOOTH);
```

Smooth shading results in the gradual shading of objects; setting this model to flat shading (using the GL_FLAT flag) leads to much harsher visible changes in the shading of objects.

This pretty much sums up OpenGL lighting. We will now implement basic lighting by creating a floor with some placed spheres – all illuminated using a static yellow light. This example also illustrates variation in shading. The spheres are rendered using GLU Quadrics. *GLU Quadrics* are a set of frequently used, predefined, relatively complex geometric objects ranging from cylinders and spheres to discs. The following sequence of Quadric function calls generate a sphere:

```
GLUquadricObj*  q = gluNewQuadric();
gluQuadricDrawStyle(q, GLU_FILL);
/* affects the overall shading, either flat or smooth */
gluQuadricNormals(q, GLU_SMOOTH);
/* sets texturing of the quadric as enabled or disabled */
gluQuadricTexture(q, GL_FALSE);
gluSphere(q, 1.0, 20, 16);
```

FIGURE 9-27 **The rendered scene; comprised of three spheres and one ambient light source**

The gluSphere function draws a sphere of a specified radius centered at its origin. It is constructed out of a series of longitudinal and latitudinal slices that can be set to wide or narrow depending on the required smoothness of the sphere. This function is specified as follows:

gluSphere(quadric object, sphere's radius, longitude subdivisions, latitude subdivisions);

Before drawing the sphere, we first need to specify a new quadric object, GLUquadricObj, via the gluNewQuadric function. We refer back to this quadric object whenever calling the quadric's rendering and/or property functions.

The draw style of the quadric, specified using the gluQuadricDrawStyle function, can be defined as a set of lines (GLU_LINE), a set of points (GLU_POINT) or a solid object (GLU_FILL). There is also additional support for the drawing of silhouette-like surfaces (GLU_SILHOUETTE).

The quadric's shading is controlled by the gluQuadricNormals function, it can be set to either smooth (GL_SMOOTH) or flat (GL_FLAT) depending on the desired outcome. The gluQuadricTexture function specifies whether texturing of the object is enabled or not.

The following OpenGL sample (full source given as program 9.2 on the book's website) combines all these concepts to render the scene shown in Figure 9-27:

```
/*
=================================================== ====
display
-renders the scene
=================================================== ====
*/
void display(void)
{
    /* clear frame buffer and z-buffer – thus clearing the screen */
    glClear(GL_COLOR_BUFFER_BIT | GL_DEPTH_BUFFER_BIT);
    /* move to the center of the screen */
    glLoadIdentity();
```

```
/* enable lighting — without it the entire scene appears dark */
glEnable(GL_LIGHTING);


/* activate light x (GL_LIGHTx) in the evaluation of
   the lighting equation
   – can be any # but logical numbering helps . . .*/
glEnable(GL_LIGHT1);
/* specify the color of the light (yellow) */
GLfloat diffuse_light_color[] = {1.0f, 1.0f, 0.0f};
/* specify the position of the light */
GLfloat diffuse_light_position[] = {20.0, 20.0, –20.0, 1.0};


/* set the light source parameters */
glLightfv(GL_LIGHT1, GL_DIFFUSE, diffuse_light_color);
/* set the light source position */
glLightfv(GL_LIGHT1,GL_POSITION,diffuse_light_position);


/* rotate camera 120 degrees about the y–axis */
glRotatef(120, 0.0, 1.0, 0.0);
/* translate the camera –1 units (down) on y–axis */
glTranslatef(0, –1, 0);


/* define the floor */

glBegin(GL_QUADS);
     /* specify the floor's normal */
     glNormal3f(0, 1, 0);
     /* specify the floor's vertices */
     glVertex3f(–20.0, 0.0, –20.0);
     glVertex3f(–20.0, 0.0, 20.0);
     glVertex3f(20.0, 0.0, 20.0);
     glVertex3f(20.0, 0.0, –20.0);
glEnd();


/* place the spheres – each glTranslatef call setups a
   sphere at a different position */

/* position the camera */
glRotatef(135, 0.0, 1.0, 0.0);
/* smooth shaded far right sphere */
//////////////////////////////////
glTranslatef(–9, 1, –1);
/* create the quadrics object */
GLUquadricObj*  q = gluNewQuadric();
/* set the quadric's draw style */
gluQuadricDrawStyle(q, GLU_FILL);
/* set the shading as smooth */
gluQuadricNormals(q, GLU_SMOOTH);
```

```
/* disable texturing of the quadric */
gluQuadricTexture(q, GL_FALSE);
gluSphere(q, 1.0, 20, 16);

/* flat shaded middle sphere */
/////////////////////////////
glTranslatef(-1, 1, 4);
GLUquadricObj*  r = gluNewQuadric();
gluQuadricDrawStyle(r, GLU_FILL);
gluQuadricNormals(r, GLU_FLAT);
gluQuadricTexture(r, GL_FALSE);
gluSphere(r, 2.0, 20, 16);

/* smooth shaded far left sphere */
///////////////////////////////////
glTranslatef(1, 0, 5);
GLUquadricObj*  s = gluNewQuadric();
gluQuadricDrawStyle(s, GLU_FILL);
gluQuadricNormals(s, GLU_SMOOTH);
gluQuadricTexture(s, GL_FALSE);
gluSphere(s, 2.0, 20, 16);

/* make sure all previously issued commands are completed */
glFlush();

/* contents of back buffer are set to become that of
    front buffer */
glutSwapBuffers();
}
```

9.5 REFLECTION AND REFRACTION

The basic reflective environmental mapping presented in Chapter 8 didn't factor in the phenomenon known as the Fresnel effect nor the chromatic dispersion effect. The *Fresnel effect* combines reflection and refraction; i.e. it allows us to simulate the accurate reflection off and refraction through a surface using a number of Fresnel equations. *Chromatic dispersion* extends the basic refraction model to consider the wavelength of the incoming light, that is, to recognise that certain light colors are refracted more than others. Specifically, the higher the wavelength of the color, the more is it refracted. For example, green has a wavelength ranging from 495–570nm with orange ranging from 590 to 630nm. The color orange will thus refract more than green due to its higher wavelength.

We now present the physics and implementation of refractive environmental mapping, followed by a discussion of the Fresnel effect and chromatic dispersion. This section features a number of shader programs illustrating refraction, the Fresnel effect and chromatic dispersion resulting in an object's color being blended with reflections from its cube map. It concludes by extending Chapter 8's cube mapping example to appear more lifelike.

9.5.1 Refraction

With the cube mapping technique discussed in Chapter 8, we are able to simulate basic environmental reflections. Environmental mapping, as it was presented, results in the chrome-like appearance of objects, (see Figure 8.25). The main reason for this chrome-like appearance is our technique's failure to blend an object's color with the reflections from the cube map – in short, a failure to consider the effect of refraction. Our previous model will now be extended to incorporate refraction.

Refraction is the change in direction of a light ray due to a variance in material density (for example, a light wave travelling from air into water). This directional change is the result of a light ray's speed. For example, light travels faster in air than in water – hence, light travels more slowly in denser materials causing a change in direction where the light enters this material. Figure 9-28 shows the refraction of light rays in water.

Snell's Law, also known as Descartes' law, is used to calculate the degree of refraction at the boundary of a lower- and higher density material. This law describes the correlation between the incoming light direction and the amount of refraction based on the index of refraction for each material. The *index of refraction* is simply a measure based on the manner in which the material affects the speed of light – the higher the index of refraction, the slower the speed of light. Common indices of refraction are 1.0 for a vacuum, 1.0003 for air, 1.333 for water and 1.5 for glass. Snell's Law (illustrated in Figure 9-29) can be mathematically expressed as follows:

$n_1 Sin\, \theta_1 = n_2 Sin\, \theta_2$, with n_1 the refraction index of the lower density material, n_2 the refraction index of the higher density material, θ_1 the incident angle and θ_2 the angle of refraction.

Adding refraction to an environmental map involves tracing each incident ray from the point of view to the surface of the object. In the case of reflection, this ray bounces off the surface of the object while changing direction inside the object in the case of refraction. The shader implementation for refraction is thus very similar to the environmental mapping implementation of section 8.2.4.1.

When implementing refraction, we'll only consider one refraction ray per incoming ray of light as opposed to multiple refractions (as the case with real life where refraction also occurs at the exit boundary of the object). We will thus only be simulating refraction to a

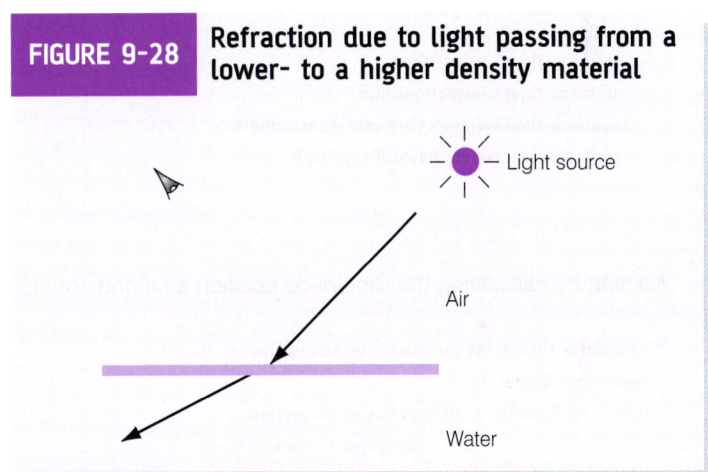

FIGURE 9-28 **Refraction due to light passing from a lower- to a higher density material**

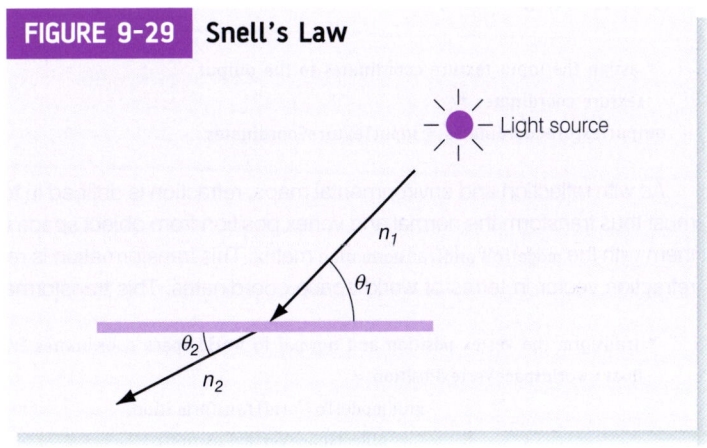

FIGURE 9-29 **Snell's Law**

certain degree; however, refraction is so complex that the human eye will experience significant difficulty in identifying minor faults with the resulting rendering.

We now present a Cg implementation for refraction. The HLSL version of this Cg program is practically identical and won't be duplicated here for that reason. This sample utilizes the Cg refract Standard Library Function to calculate the refraction vector (identical to the DirectX HLSL refract intrinsic function). It takes an incident vector – a light ray as first parameter, and a surface normal as second parameter. Its third parameter is the index of refraction – the ratio of indices of refraction of the two materials. It returns the refraction vector. The refracted vector has the same magnitude as the incident ray.

A vertex shader program is used to perform the per-vertex refraction calculations.

The first step is to specify the name of the vertex program's entry function, main_vertex in our example:

```
void main_vertex(
          float4 objectspaceVertexPosition : POSITION,
          float3 objectspaceVertexNormal : NORMAL,
          float2 inputTextureCoordinates : TEXCOORD0,

          out float4 outputVertexPosition : POSITION,
          out float2 outputTextureCoordinates : TEXCOORD0,
          out float3 refractionVector : TEXCOORD1,

          /* parameters supplied by the application program */

          uniform float3 pointOfView,
          uniform float3 refractionRatio
          uniform float4x4 modelToWorldTransformation,
          uniform float4x4 modelviewProjection
)
{
```

We start by calculating the clip-space position as mandatory for all Cg vertex programs:

```
/* transform the vertex position into homogeneous clip-
   space coordinates */
outputVertexPosition = mul(modelviewProjection,
                      objectspaceVertexPosition);
```

Next we assign the input texture coordinates to the output texture coordinates:

```
/* assign the input texture coordinates to the output
   texture coordinates */
outputTextureCoordinates = inputTextureCoordinates;
```

As with reflection and environmental maps, refraction is defined in terms of world space coordinates. We must thus transform the normal and vertex position from object space to world space by multiplying both of them with the modelToWorldTransformation matrix. This transformation is required since we wish to calculate the refraction vector in terms of world space coordinates. This transformation is done as follows:

```
/* transform the vertex position and normal to world space coordinates */
   float3 worldspaceVertexPosition =
                   mul(modelToWorldTransformation,
                   objectspaceVertexPosition);
```

```
float3 worldspaceVertexNormal =
                        mul(modelToWorldTransformation,
                            objectspaceVertexNormal);

/* normalize the vertex normal */
worldspaceVertexNormal =
                        normalize(worldspaceVertexNormal);
```

The final operation is to calculate both the incident and refraction vectors. The incident vector is the vector traced from the point of view to the vertex. The incident vector is calculated using simple subtraction:

```
/* calculate the incident light vector */
float3 incidentVector = worldspaceVertexPosition − pointOfView;
```

Using the ratio of refraction and the incident and vertex normal, we can calculate the refracted world-space vector:

```
/* calculate the refraction vector */
float3 refractionVector = refract(incidentVector,
                                  worldspaceVertexNormal,
                                  refractionRatio);
}
```

We now define a fragment shader program that uses this refraction vector to retrieve a cube map texture – the environmental map. This time we extend our fragment shader from section 8.2.4.1 to mix the environment map lookup result with the object's texture color. This is done by performing a texture lookup of the object's current color, blending the sampled texture color with the refraction color – thus resulting in a much more realistic-looking object (due to no material being a perfect refractor). Our original Cg environmental mapping example can be extended in a similar fashion, in its case blending the sampled texture color with the reflection color instead of the refraction color.

The first step is to specify the name of the fragment program's entry function, main_fragment in our example:

```
void main_fragment(
        float3 refractionVector : TEXCOORD0,
        float2 inputTextureCoordinates : TEXCOORD1,

        out float4 outputColor : COLOR,

        /* parameter supplied by the application program */

        uniform samplerCUBE environmentMap,
        uniform sampler2D lookupTextureColor,
)
{
```

The fragment program uses the interpolated refraction vector to determine the environment map's refracted color. We use the texCUBE texture lookup function to do this. This function takes two parameters: a cube map, and a three-component texture coordinate set – the refraction vector:

```
/* obtain the refracted color */
float4 refractionColor = texCUBE(environmentMap,
                                 refractionVector);
```

Next we perform a texture color lookup using the tex2D function:

```
float4 textureColor = tex2D(lookupTextureColor,
                            inputTextureCoordinates);
```

Following this, we blend the sampled texture color with the refraction color using the lerp function. This function performs a linear interpolation, computing the average of two color samples. Its first two parameters are the color vectors to average, with its third parameter controlling the amount of averaging, for example, a weight of '0.5' resulting in uniform averaging. Setting this weight to '0' results in no reflection or refraction. Conversely, setting the weight to '1' will lead to the program not considering the texture color, thus producing a completely reflective or refractive object:

```
float4 blendedColor = lerp(textureColor,
                           refractionColor, 0.5);
```

We finally assign this linearly interpolated blended color to the output color:

```
/* set the refracted color */
color = blendedColor;
}
```

9.5.2 Reflection and Refraction Extended

The implementation of reflection was previously discussed during Chapter 8's bump mapping and cube mapping examples. We will now extend our previous implementation using a number of advancements to improve the overall reflection effect, thus resulting in more realistic and lifelike images.

To recap, reflection is the change in direction of a light ray where the light ray is reflected back into the originating material upon contact with the surface of another material. Perfect reflection is characterized by the angle of incidence, θ_1, being equal to the angle of reflection, θ_2. Figure 9-30 shows the perfect reflection of light.

We can subsequently compute the reflection vector, R, by taking the incident vector, I, and subtracting two times the surface normal, N, multiplied by the dot product between the surface normal and the incident light:

$$R = I - 2N(N \cdot I).$$

Cg and HLSL, as mentioned, utilize the refract Standard Library Function to calculate the refraction vector. This function takes an incident vector – a light ray as first parameter, and a surface normal as second parameter, subsequently returning the reflection vector of the incident ray.

We previously defined the Fresnel effect as a series of equations combining reflection and refraction to accurately simulate the reflection off and refraction through a surface. These equations are used to determine the amount of light reflected and refracted; however, using these equations directly is a bit

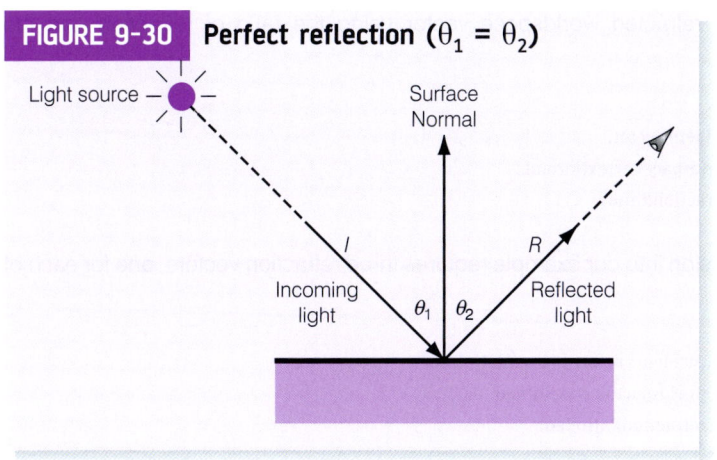

FIGURE 9-30 Perfect reflection ($\theta_1 = \theta_2$)

Light source

Surface Normal

I

R

Incoming light

Reflected light

θ_1 θ_2

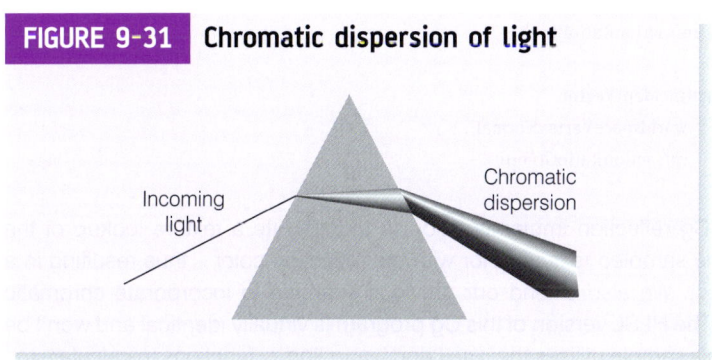

FIGURE 9-31 Chromatic dispersion of light

Incoming light

Chromatic dispersion

excessive and we will instead approximate the Fresnel equations into the following equation that can easily be incorporated into our programs:

```
FresnelReflectionCoefficient = 0.183673 + 0.816327 *
                    pow(1.0 - dot(incidentVector,
                    worldspaceVertexNormal), 5.0);
```

This equation is based on the principle of Fresnel reflection; namely, that when the incident vector is parallel to the surface normal, then the majority of light is refracted with the reflection coefficient approaching '0'. As the angle between the incident vector and surface normal increases, so does the amount of light reflected. This Fresnel reflection coefficient is used in the calculation of the final color contribution resulting from both reflection and refraction. The Fresnel reflection coefficient is simply used as the lerp function's weight.

We previously defined chromatic dispersion as an extension to the basic lighting model that deals with the fact that certain light colors are refracted more than others. Chromatic dispersion models the refraction of red, green, and blue light. We can thus extend the single refracted ray lookup (as done previously) by using these refracted light rays for our environmental map lookup. Adding chromatic dispersion to our current reflection and refraction models result in the rainbow-like refraction of light – as is the case with the dispersion of a light beam in a prism (Figure 9-31).

We previously calculated the refracted worldspace vector using the ratio of refraction and the incident and vertex normal:

```
/* calculate the refraction vector */
float3 refractionVector = refract(incidentVector,
                                  worldspaceVertexNormal,
                                  refractionRatio);
```

Incorporating chromatic dispersion into our example requires three refraction vectors, one for each of the primary colors:

```
float3 refractionVectorRed = refract(incidentVector,
                                     worldspaceVertexNormal,
                                     refractionRatioRed);

float3 refractionVectorBlue = refract(incidentVector,
                                      worldspaceVertexNormal,
                                      refractionRatioBlue);

float3 refractionVectorGreen = refract(incidentVector,
                                       worldspaceVertexNormal,
                                       refractionRatioGreen);
```

We now extend our previous Cg reflection implementation to incorporate a texture lookup of the object's current color, blending the sampled texture color with the reflection color – thus resulting in a much more realistic looking object. We also extend our previous example to incorporate chromatic dispersion and the Fresnel effect. The HLSL version of this Cg program is virtually identical and won't be duplicated here for that reason. This sample utilizes the reflect and refract library functions to calculate the reflection vector and refraction vectors, respectively.

A vertex shader program is used to calculate the reflection vector together with the chromatic dispersion vectors and the Fresnel reflection coefficient, which will be sent to a fragment shader.

The first step is to specify the name of the vertex program's entry function, main_vertex in our example:

```
void main_vertex(
        float4 objectspaceVertexPosition : POSITION,
        float3 objectspaceVertexNormal : NORMAL,
        float2 inputTextureCoordinates : TEXCOORD0,

        out float fresnelReflectionCoefficient : COLOR,
        out float4 outputVertexPosition : POSITION,
        out float3 reflectionVector : TEXCOORD0,
        out float3 refractionVectorRed : TEXCOORDI,
        out float3 refractionVectorBlue : TEXCOORD2,
        out float3 refractionVectorGreen : TEXCOORD3,

        /* parameters supplied by the application program */

        uniform float3 pointOfView,
        uniform float4x4 modelToWorldTransformation,
```

```
                uniform float4x4 modelviewProjection,
                uniform float3 refractionRatioRed,
                uniform float3 refractionRatioBlue,
                uniform float3 refractionRatioGreen
)
{
```

We start by calculating the clip-space position:

```
/* transform the vertex position into homogeneous clip-
    space coordinates */
    outputVertexPosition = mul(modelviewProjection,
                                objectspaceVertexPosition);
```

Next we assign the input texture coordinates to the output texture coordinates:

```
/* assign the input texture coordinates to the output
    texture coordinates */
    outputTextureCoordinates = inputTextureCoordinates;
```

Reflection and environmental maps are defined in terms of world space coordinates. We must thus, as discussed previously, transform the normal and vertex position from object space to world space by multiplying both of them with the modelToWorldTransformation matrix. This transformation is required since we wish to calculate the reflection vector in terms of world space coordinates. This transformation is done as follows:

```
/* transform the vertex position and normal to world space
    coordinates */
    float3 worldspaceVertexPosition =
                        mul(modelToWorldTransformation,
                            objectspaceVertexPosition);
    float3 worldspaceVertexNormal =
                        mul(modelToWorldTransformation,
                            objectspaceVertexNormal);

/* normalize the vertex normal */
worldspaceVertexNormal = normalize(worldspaceVertexNormal);
```

The final operation is to calculate both the incident and reflection vectors. The incident vector is the vector traced from the point of view to the vertex. The incident vector is calculated using simple subtraction:

```
/* calculate the incident light vector */
float3 incidentVector = worldspaceVertexPosition − pointOfView;
```

Using the incident and vertex normal, we can calculate the reflected worldspace vector:

```
/* calculate the reflection vector */
float3 reflectionVector = reflect(incidentVector,
                                    worldspaceVertexNormal);

/* normalize the incident Vector */
incidentVector = normalize(incidentVector);
```

The next step is to calculate the Fresnel reflection coefficient via our previously listed approximation:

```
fresnelReflectionCoefficient = 0.183673 + 0.816327 *
                                pow(1.0 - dot(incidentVector,
                                worldspaceVertexNormal), 5.0);
```

We lastly calculate the chromatic dispersion refraction vectors (one for each of the primary colors):

```
float3 refractionVectorRed = refract(incidentVector,
                                    worldspaceVertexNormal,
                                    refractionRatioRed);
float3 refractionVectorBlue = refract(incidentVector,
                                    worldspaceVertexNormal,
                                    refractionRatioBlue);

float3 refractionVectorGreen = refract(incidentVector,
                                    worldspaceVertexNormal,
                                    refractionRatioGreen);
}
```

We now define a fragment shader program that uses the calculated Fresnel reflection coefficient, reflection vector, and refraction vectors to retrieve a cube map texture – the environmental map. Our shader also mixes the environment map lookup result with the object's texture color. This is done via a texture lookup of the object's current color and the blending of this sampled texture color with the reflection and refraction colors – thus resulting in a highly accurate lighting model.

The first step is to specify the name of the fragment program's entry function, main_fragment in our example:

```
void main_fragment(
        float3 reflectionVector : TEXCOORD0,
        out float3 refractionVectorRed : TEXCOORD1,
        out float3 refractionVectorBlue : TEXCOORD2,
        out float3 refractionVectorGreen : TEXCOORD3,
        float fresnelReflectionCoefficient: COLOR,

        out float4 outputColor : COLOR,

        /* parameter supplied by the application program */

        uniform samplerCUBE environmentMap
)
{
```

The fragment program uses the interpolated reflection and refraction vectors to determine the environment map's reflected color. We use the texCUBE texture lookup function to do this. This function takes two parameters; a cube map and a three component texture coordinate set – the reflection vector:

```
/* obtain the reflection color */
float4 reflectionColor = texCUBE(environmentMap,
                                 reflectionVector);


/* obtain the refraction color */
float4 refractionColor.r = texCUBE(environmentMap,
                                   refractionVectorRed).r;


float4 refractionColor.b = texCUBE(environmentMap,
                                   refractionVectorBlue).b;


float4 refractionColor.g = texCUBE(environmentMap,
                                   refractionVectorGreen).g;
```

Following this, we blend the sampled refraction texture color with the reflection color using the lerp function (its weight set to the calculated Fresnel reflection coefficient):

```
float4 blendedColor = lerp(textureColor,
                           reflectionColor,
                           fresnelReflectionCoefficient);
```

We finally assign this linearly interpolated blended color to the output color:

```
/* set the blended color */
color = blendedColor;
}
```

9.6 HIGH DYNAMIC RANGE (HDR) LIGHTING

High Dynamic Range (HDR) lighting, also known as High Dynamic Range Rendering (HDRR), is the rendering of lighting using more than 256 color shades for each of the primary colors, namely, the red, green, and blue components. Thus, we can now use 16 to 32-bit colors per RGB channel as opposed to the normal 8 – eliminating luminance and pixel intensity being clamped to a [0, 1] range. This allows for the display of light sources over 100 000 times brighter than normally possible.

HDR's wide color range leads to the effect of bright lights appearing overly bright, with dark areas looking even darker at the same time. HDR lighting results in the full visibility of both very dark and fully lit areas; this is unlike normal lighting, or *Low Dynamic Range lighting*, where details are hidden in dark scenes when contrasted by a fully lit area. Using this form of lighting generally leads to a more vibrant looking scene. Figure 9-32 shows an example of HDR from Valve Software's *Half-Life 2: Lost Coast* technology showcase.

HDR lighting generally makes use of two techniques: tone mapping and the bloom effect. *Tone mapping* is used to approximate real-world luminance with an extremely high dynamic range to a computer monitor with a limited range of luminance values. The *bloom effect* basically blends light

FIGURE 9-32   **High dynamic range lighting**

9

sources beyond their natural edges – causing the edges of a bright light source to overlap nearby geometry, thus creating the illusion of an even brighter light.

Floating-point textures are normally used for the storage of HDR lighting color information (this color data can also be encoded using integer textures as discussed in the DirectX 10 SDK's 'HDRFormats10' sample). The main reason for using floating-point textures is due to the pixel shader clamping integer textures to the range [0, 1]. Floating-point textures are not clamped at all and can thus contain a wide range of values.

The following steps outline the process of rendering a scene using HDR lighting:

1 Load the HDR floating-point values into a buffer (a floating-point render target).

2 Apply the bloom effect.
   a Down-sample the buffer to $\frac{1}{4}$ its original size. This is required so that the bloom effect is only ranged from edge pixels to neighbouring ones.
   b Blur the image both vertically and horizontally (thus averaging the pixels and consequently creating the bloom effect by bleeding color from edge to neighboring pixels).

3 Combine the blurred and original texture.

4 Tone map the composed texture.

We start by reading the red, green, and blue (RGB) components of our HDR floating-point texture – such as images stored in the radiance HDR ('.hdr' or '.pic') file format. This image will be used to texture a simple quadrilateral. This quadrilateral will in turn be illuminated using High Dynamic Range lighting. The RGB components of our HDR floating-point texture are stored as an array of floating-point values. These RGB floating-point values are in turn set to a floating-point render target.

Our first HLSL shader is used to down-sample the floating-point render target to $\frac{1}{4}$ its original size. The process basically involves rendering the original floating-point render target to another one $\frac{1}{4}$ the original's size. We start by declaring the pixel offset as used in our vertex shader, also declaring a structure for the storage of vertex data:

```
/* pixel offset = 1 / 1280 and 1 / 1024
float2 GlobalPixelOffset = float2(0.00078125, 0.000976562);


struct PIXELSHADER_INPUT
{
    float4 Loc:  POSITION;
    float2 Texture:  TEXCOORD0;
};
```

Our vertex shader starts by transforming the input vertex position, defined in object space, to projection space. This is done by multiplying the input vertex position, IN.Loc, with a world matrix, thus transforming it from object space to world space. The next transformation multiplies this transformed vertex position, output.Loc, with a view matrix, resulting in a world space to view space transformation. The final transformation takes this view space vertex position and multiplies it with a projection matrix to transform the vertex from view space to projection space. The shader's final routine outputs the texture coordinates:

```
/* vertex shader */
PIXELSHADER_INPUT DownSamplerVertexShader(
                            float3 IN: POSITION,
                            float2 IN_TEXTURE: TEXCOORD0)
{
    PIXELSHADER_INPUT output;

    /* transforms the input vertex position */
    output.Loc = mul(IN.Loc, WorldMatrix);
    output.Loc = mul(output.Loc, ViewMatrix);
    output.Loc = mul(output.Loc, ProjectionMatrix);

    output.Texture = IN_TEXTURE + (GlobalPixelOffset * 0.5);

    return output;
}
```

In the case of our pixel shader we define a sampler specifying the manner in which the texture will be sampled. We simply assign the original render target texture to a new one:

```
texture sampledTexture;

SamplerState samplingMethod
{
    Texture = sampledTexture;
};
```

We return the RGB components of our HDR values only if they are in fact HDR values, thus ignoring all Low Dynamic Range lighting values – the function OnlyHDR, used by the pixel shader, is declared as follows:

```
float4 OnlyHDR(float4 color)
{
```

```
    if(color.r > 1.0f)
    {
      if(color.g > 1.0f)
      {
        if(color.b > 1.0f)
        {
            return color;
        }
      }
    }
    else
        float4 new_color = {0.0f, 0.0f, 0.0f, 0.0f};

    return new_color;
}
```

The pixel shader performs a texture color lookup using the tex2D function, subsequently rendering this texture onto the resized render target, finally outputting the RGB components of our HDR values only if they are in fact HDR values:

```
float4 DownSamplerPixelShader(float2 IN_TEXTURE: TEXCOORD0) : COLOR0
{
    float4 color = tex2D(samplingMethod, inTex);

    float4 sampledColor = OnlyHDR(color);

    return sampledColor;
}
```

Following this we need to blur the image both vertically and horizontally (thus averaging the pixels and consequently creating the bloom effect by bleeding color from edge- to neighbouring pixels). This is done using a simple Gaussian effect – its effect shown in Figure 9-33.

We start by declaring a sampler assigning the original render target texture to a new one:

```
texture blurredTexture;

SamplerState blurredSampler
{
    Texture = blurredTexture;
};
```

We also declare a texture sampler for the original non-blurred texture:

```
Texture2D originalTexture;
```

| FIGURE 9-33 | (b) Gaussian blur of (a), a simple image |

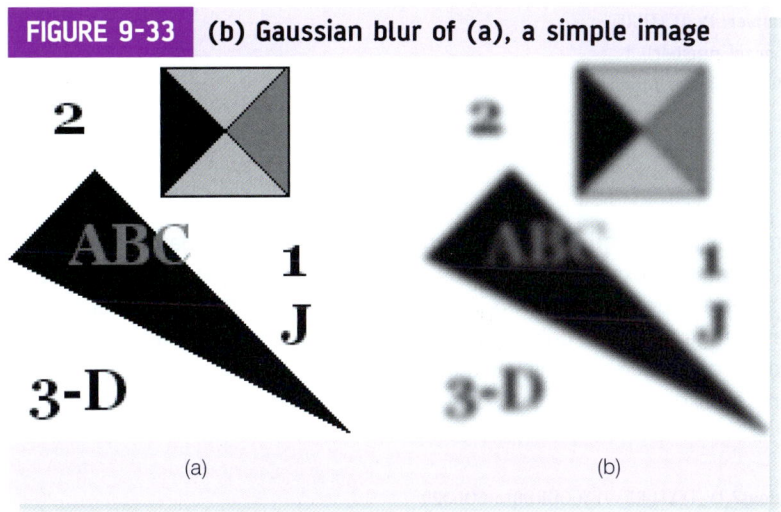

(a)   (b)

```
SamplerState originalSampler
{
    Texture = originalTexture;
};
```

Next we define a pixel shader to do the actual Gaussian blur. The XOffset variable is the texel width and the XOffset variable the texel height. For example, an image of 256 by 512 pixels will have an XOffset of 0.00390625 and a YOffset of 0.001953195:

```
float4 GaussianBlurPixelShader(float2 IN_TEXTURE: IN_TEXTURE) : COLOR0
{
    float4 color = tex2D(blurredSampler, IN_TEXTURE);

    /* sample eight pixels at each side */
    for(int pixel_number = 1; pixel_number <= 9; pixel_number++)
    {
        /* blur in the x-axis direction */
        color += tex2D(blurredSampler, IN_TEXTURE +
                    (XOffset* pixel_number)) *
                    GaussianWeights[pixel_number];

        color += tex2D(blurredSampler, IN_TEXTURE -
                    (XOffset * pixel_number)) *
                    GaussianWeights[pixel_number];

        /* blur in the y-axis direction */
        color += tex2D(blurredSampler, IN_TEXTURE +
                    (YOffset * pixel_number)) *
                    GaussianWeights[pixel_number];
```

9

```
        color += tex2D(blurredSampler, IN_TEXTURE −
                       (YOffset * pixel_number)) *
                       GaussianWeights[pixel_number];
    }
    return color;
}
```

The final pixel shader combines the blurred and original textures, applying a tone mapping operation to the result. It starts by performing two texture color lookups using declared samplers for both, one for the original, originalSampler, and another for the blurred image, blurredSampler. It then performs a linear interpolation, computing the average of the two color samples. Following this, we calculate the distance of the current pixel to the center of the screen. This value to the power of 3.8 is then multiplied by the linearly interpolated color and an exposure value, the subsequent result to the power of 0.5 being our final HDR pixel color:

```
float4 ToneMappingPixelShader(float2 IN_TEXTURE: TEXCOORD0) : COLOR0
{
    float4 nonBlurredTexture = tex2D(originalSampler,
                                     IN_TEXTURE);

    float4 gaussianTexture = tex2D(blurredSampler,
                                   IN_TEXTURE);

    float4 color = lerp(nonBlurredTexture, gaussianTexture,
                        0.5f);

    float pixelDistance  = 1 − dot(IN_TEXTURE − 0.5f,
                                   IN_TEXTURE − 0.5f);

    color = pow(color * pow(pixelDistance, 3.8) * exposure,
                0.5);
    return color;
}
```

Using an exposure ranging from '0.0' to '1.5' will generally result in an underexposed image with an exposure of '2.0' to '4.0' resulting in a properly exposed image. Increasing the exposure even more will lead to an overexposed image.

9.7   SUMMARY

This chapter covered lighting in detail, starting with a discussion of light source types, and reflection models, and building up to the implementation of local illumination and advanced rendering techniques such as chromatic dispersion, reflection, refraction, and High Dynamic Range lighting.

A number of light sources were introduced at hand of the role they play in the creation of properly lit and shaded objects. Building on this we presented the illumination function as a way to describe any light source in terms of six variables. We also discussed how a lighting model can be used to define light-object interactions based on the type of light source and the material properties of the object.

We subsequently investigated a number of light source types, specifically looking at point lights as light sources emitting light uniformly in 360 degrees, spotlights as point lights emitting light within an angle range, ambient lighting as a way to provide a uniform level of illumination throughout a scene, parallel lights as sources illuminating objects through a number of parallel light rays, and emissive light as self-reflecting light originating from an object's surface.

Following this we looked at several reflection models, namely, the ambient reflection model, the specular reflection model, diffuse reflection and the Phong reflection model. We specifically investigated these reflection models as functions of material properties (e.g. surface reflectance, color) and light source properties (e.g. light direction, color, position, attenuation).

Next we looked at the linear algebra required for the representation of light, specifically focusing on the calculation of vector lengths, vector addition to create a composite vector, scalar multiplication to change the magnitude or direction of a vector, normal vectors as used to indicate the orientation of a surface with respect to a light source or camera position, dot products and cross products. We also considered a number of D3DX utility library functions for the computation of cross products, normal vectors, etc.

Building on this we implemented local illumination using the diffuse reflection model and Lambertian light. The Direct3D 10 example utilized an HLSL pixel shader to calculate the per-pixel lighting with standard OpenGL routines being used for the OpenGL example.

We then investigated reflection and refraction in great detail, in essence focusing on the physics and implementation of refractive environmental mapping, followed by a discussion of Snell's law, the Fresnel effect and chromatic dispersion resulting in an object's color being blended with reflections from its cube map. This section featured a number of shader programs illustrating discussed concepts.

The chapter concluded with a discussion of High Dynamic Range lighting as an alternative to normal lighting. We specifically outlined the general HDR rendering process followed by an HLSL implementation example.

The next chapter deals with two techniques crucial for atmospheric perspective and realism – blending (transparency) and fog.

9.8 FURTHER READING

The book *Mathematics for 3D Game Programming and Computer Graphics* (second edition) *by Eric Lengyel* (ISBN: 1584502770) contains a good chapter on lighting models in general. *The OpenGL Programming Guide: The Official Guide to Learning OpenGL by the OpenGL Architecture Review Board, Dave Shreiner, Mason Woo, Jackie Neider and Tom Davis, (sixth edition)* (ISBN: 0321481003) is an excellent resource for more information about OpenGL's fixed-function lighting model.

For more information on the Phong lighting model see B.T. Phong's paper *Illumination for Computer Generated Scenes* published in *Communications of the ACM* (1975). Also, for an additional discussion of the Fresnel effect, see Matthias Wloka's 2002 paper *Fresnel Reflection* published online as an NVIDIA white paper.

9.9 EXERCISES

1 Briefly describe the concept of self-emission and the basic factors controlling the absorption and reflection of light.

2 What is the purpose of a so-called 'light type property' and lighting models in general?

3 Differentiate between fixed-function lighting and lighting models such as Lambertian lighting, anisotropic lighting, Fresnel lighting, and Blinn lighting.

4 Define a point light using a luminance function.

5 How do we calculate the intensity of a spotlight?

6 Compare parallel light sources to ambient lighting.

7 What information is required to calculate the specular highlight on an object?

8 Briefly highlight the differences between the diffuse and ambient reflection models.

9 How is the Phong reflection of a point on the surface of an object calculated?

10 Describe the purpose of the following code sample:

```
for(int i = 0; i < 2; i++)
{
    dotPixelColor = dot((float3)LightDirection[i],
                    IN.Norm);
    finalPixelColor += saturate(dotPixelColor *
                        LightColor[i]);
}
```

11 What is the difference between local and global illumination?

12 Describe Lambert's law.

13 Why would one want to add the Fresnel effect or chromatic dispersion to a basic reflective environmental mapping implementation?

14 What is the implication of Snell's Law?

15 Describe the process of adding refraction to an environmental map.

16 When implementing refraction, why is it only necessary to consider one refraction ray per incoming ray of light as opposed to multiple refractions?

17 Using the ratio of refraction and the incident and vertex normal, how can we calculate the refracted world-space vector?

18 What Cg/HLSL function can be used to blend a sampled texture color with a refraction color?

19 Explain the process of incorporating chromatic dispersion into a standard shader-based reflection implementation.

20 Briefly describe the process of rendering a scene using HDR lighting.

CHAPTER 10

Alpha Blending and Fog

LEARNING OBJECTIVES

In this chapter you will learn about:

- Alpha blending
- Implementing blending
- Implementing blending using shaders
- Alpha testing
- Fog
- The physics of fog
- Implementing fog

INTRODUCTION

Chapter 10 concentrates on two techniques crucial for atmospheric perspective and realism – blending (transparency) and fog.

10.1 ALPHA BLENDING

Alpha blending is a technique used to render the transparent and/or semi-transparent areas in textures. During some of our previous examples we talked about alpha channels. To recap, an alpha channel can be considered a fourth color component, i.e. an add-on to our current red–green–blue (RGB) color model controlling the transparency of a pixel. The alpha channel, just like the RGB color components, stores an 8-bit value ranging from '0' to '255' ('0' indicating full transparency and '255' a solid area). Figure 10-1 shows a number of partially transparent cloths rendered with alpha blending enabled.

FIGURE 10-1 **Alpha blending of four textured cloths**

Alpha blending works by merging the per-pixel color of one texture with that of another – specifically by combining the color of an alpha-enabled texture with a texture already present at the corresponding screen location. The alpha blending equation calculates the final blended color by adding the overlaid pixel color, *overlaidPixelColor* (which has some specific alpha percentage, *alphaPercentage)* to the pixel color of the opaque surface, *originalPixelColor,* with the alpha percentage being subtracted from its opaque solid color:

$$BlendedColor = overlaidPixelColor(alphaPercentage)$$
$$+ originalPixelColor(1.0f - alphaPercentage).$$

The *opacity* of a surface controls the amount of light that can pass through it. A fully opaque object, thus a surface with an opacity of '1', is completely impenetrable to light. Transparent surfaces have an opacity of '1' minus its degree of transparency.

Opacity is added to an object during the fragment processing stage where the color of a pixel in the frame buffer is blended with the color of a fragment. Alpha values control the amount of per-pixel blending. For example, if the following arrays represent two independent pixels that are to be blended:

```
overlaidPixelColor = {Redl, Greenl, Bluel, Alphal};
backgroundPixelColor = {Red2, Green2, Blue2, Alpha2};
```

then the final composed pixel color can be written as:

```
composedPixelColor = {(Redl)(overlaid_Red_Blending_Factor) +
                      (Red2)(background_Red_Blending_Factor),
                      (Greenl)(overlaid_Green_Blending_Factor) +
```

(Green2)(background_Green_Blending_Factor),
(Blue1)(overlaid_Blue_Blending_Factor) +
(Blue2)(background_Blue_Blending_Factor),
(Alpha1)(overlaid_Alpha_Blending_Factor) +
(Alpha2)(background_Alpha_Blending_Factor)};

Our previous texture mapping examples all made use of the bitmap image format (.bmp). This format generally doesn't support transparency, hence, it can only be used for alpha masking and blending through a series of texturing hacks, for example, storing two separate images and executing the blending operation twice. Since the introduction of Windows XP a 32-bit enabled bitmap format is supported (allowing for transparency via an alpha channel). However, its use isn't widespread since the format does not natively support any form of texture compression.

The Truevision TGA (.tga) image format offers a solution to the bitmap file format's lack of compression, transparency, and limited use. It was one of the first formats to support truecolor (millions of colors) and is a 32-bit image format with support for transparency and RLE (run-length encoding) compression. Our code to load textures must thus handle both 24-bit opaque (solid) and 32-bit transparent images. Apart from this, the OpenGL and Direct3D code used to load and initialize textures remains exactly the same, regardless of this additional alpha component.

Any paint program, such as Adobe Photoshop or The GIMP, allows for the addition of transparency to a texture image. This is generally accomplished via some 'color to alpha' operation. For example, the texture shown in Figure 10-2(a) is fully opaque without any alpha values specified. This texture's white-colored pixels are subsequently set to transparent, resulting in the image shown in Figure 10-2(b).

FIGURE 10-2   **(a) An opaque texture with (b) a transparency component added to it**

(a)   (b)

10.1.1 Implementing Blending

Implementing alpha blending in Direct3D 10 is done via the API's Blend State. The Blend State initializes the blending unit of the output-merger stage. This unit controls the blending operation. As discussed in Chapter 4, the output-merger stage is directly responsible for determining the visibility of pixels based on the process of depth testing, stencil testing, and the blending of pixel data (combining two or more pixel color values). The blending process is outlined in Figure 10-3.

The first step is to create the blend state object using ID3D10BlendState:

ID3D10BlendState* g_pBlendStateInterface = NULL;

This blend state interface is required by the CreateBlendState ID3D10Device function – the function creating the encapsulated blend state object as required by the output-merger stage. The CreateBlendState ID3D10Device function is declared as follows in the d3d10.h header file:

HRESULT CreateBlendState(
    const D3D10_BLEND_DESC *pBlendStateDesc,
    ID3D10BlendState **ppBlendState
);

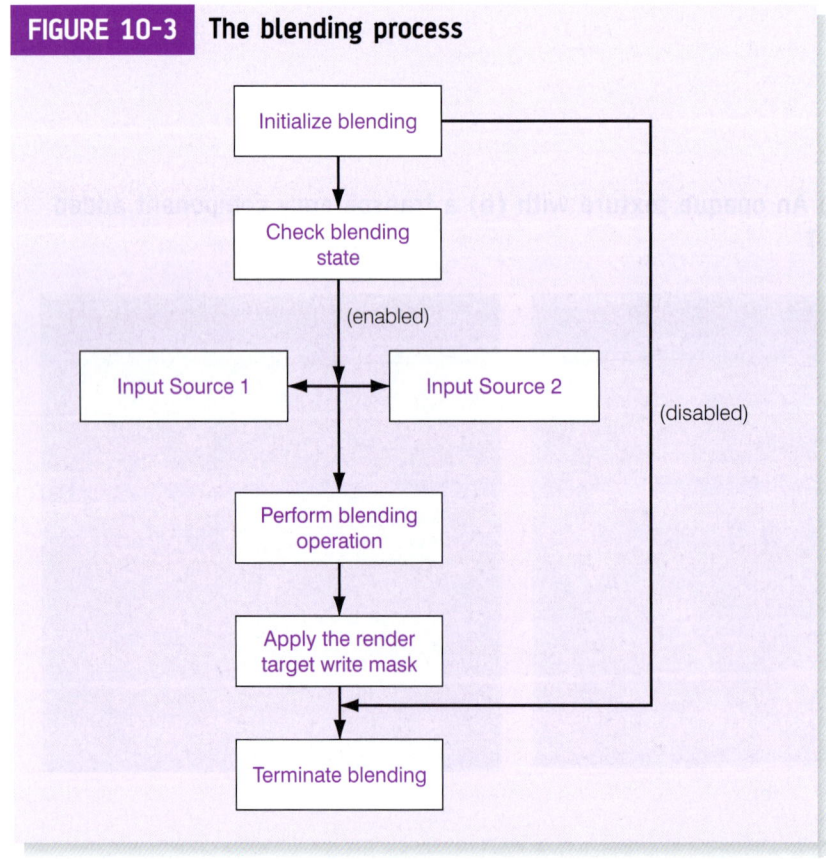

FIGURE 10-3 **The blending process**

Its first parameter, pBlendStateDesc, is a pointer to the D3D10_BLEND_DESC structure with its second parameter, ppBlendState, the address of the pointer to the ID3D10BlendState object. The D3D10_BLEND_DESC blend description structure, used for describing the blend state, is declared as follows:

```
typedef struct D3D10_BLEND_DESC {
    BOOL AlphaToCoverageEnable;
    BOOL BlendEnable[8];
    D3D10_BLEND SrcBlend;
    D3D10_BLEND DestBlend;
    D3D10_BLEND_OP BlendOp;
    D3D10_BLEND SrcBlendAlpha;
    D3D10_BLEND DestBlendAlpha;
    D3D10_BLEND_OP BlendOpAlpha;
    UINT8 RenderTargetWriteMask[8];
} D3D10_BLEND_DESC;
```

Its first member, AlphaToCoverageEnable, takes a Boolean value controlling whether the alpha-to-coverage multisampling technique should be used. *Alpha-to-coverage* is a technique often used in scenes composed of several overlapping polygons where it would be CPU-expensive to sort these polygons back to front. The technique reads the alpha component of a color value produced by a pixel shader, using it to create a coverage mask consisting of a number of multisamples. This coverage mask is then used to update corresponding output-merger stage render target samples.

The BlendEnable member is simply a Boolean array enabling or disabling blending for each of the eight render-targets that can be set to the output-merger stage. The next two members, SrcBlend and DestBlend (of the type D3D10_BLEND) set the first and second RGB data source, respectively. The D3D10_BLEND enumeration type provides a number of blending and pre-blending options (given in Table 10-1).

The D3D10_BLEND_DESC structure's fifth member, BlendOp, of the type D3D10_BLEND_OP, defines the manner in which the RGB data sources are to be combined. This is done using one of the following D3D10_BLEND_OP constants:

- D3D10_BLEND_OP_ADD (simply add the two sources together)

- D3D10_BLEND_OP_SUBTRACT (subtract the overlaid source from the background/destination source)

- D3D10_BLEND_OP_REV_SUBTRACT (subtract the background source from the overlaid source)

- D3D10_BLEND_OP_MIN (determine the minimum between the two sources) or

- D3D10_BLEND_OP_MAX (determine the maximum between the two sources).

D3D10_BLEND_DESC's next two members, SrcBlendAlpha and DestBlendAlpha, set the first and second alpha data source, respectively. The second last member, BlendOpAlpha, of the type D3D10_BLEND_OP, defines the manner in which the alpha data sources are to be combined. The RenderTargetWriteMask member is simply a pixel write mask controlling whether the red (D3D10_COLOR_WRITE_ENABLE_RED), green (D3D10_COLOR_WRITE_ENABLE_GREEN), blue (D3D10_COLOR_WRITE_ENABLE_BLUE), alpha (D3D10_COLOR_WRITE_ENABLE_ALPHA), or all (D3D10_COLOR_WRITE_ENABLE_ALL) render-target pixel color components are writeable during the blending operation.

Following the creation of the blend state object using ID3D10BlendState, we can enable alpha blending using the D3D10_BLEND_DESC structure and the CreateBlendState ID3D10Device interface function:

```
ID3D10Device* g_id3dDevice;
```

10

TABLE 10-1	Possible D3D10__BLEND blend options
Constants	**Description**
D3D10_BLEND_ZERO	Set the data source to the color black.
D3D10_BLEND_ONE	Set the data source to the color white.
D3D10_BLEND_SRC_COLOR	Set the data source to the color retrieved from a pixel shader.
D3D10_BLEND_INV_SRC_COLOR	Set the data source to the color retrieved from a pixel shader, with the pre-blending operation inverting this RGB color data.
D3D10_BLEND_SRC_ALPHA	Set the data source to the alpha channel retrieved from a pixel shader.
D3D10_BLEND_INV_SRC_ALPHA	Set the data source to the alpha channel retrieved from a pixel shader, with the pre-blending operation inverting the alpha data.
D3D10_BLEND_DEST_ALPHA	Set the data source to the alpha channel retrieved from a render-target.
D3D10_BLEND_INV_DEST_ALPHA	Set the data source to the alpha channel retrieved from a render-target, with the pre-blending operation inverting the alpha data.
D3D10_BLEND_DEST_COLOR	Set the data source to the color retrieved from a render-target.
D3D10_BLEND_INV_DEST_COLOR	Set the data source to the color retrieved from a render-target, with the pre-blending operation inverting the alpha data.
D3D10_BLEND_SRC_ALPHA_SAT	Set the data source to the alpha channel retrieved from a pixel shader, with the pre-blending operation clamping this data to the range [0, 1].
D3D10_BLEND_BLEND_FACTOR	Set the data source to the blend factor as specified using the OMSetBlendState ID3D10Device interface.
D3D10_BLEND_INV_BLEND_FACTOR	Set the data source to the blend factor as specified using the OMSetBlendState ID3D10Device interface, with the pre-blending operation inverting the blend factor.
D3D10_BLEND_SRC1_COLOR	Use two pixel shader outputs to provide color data to the input source, as with dual-source color blending. *Dual-source color blending* enables the use of two pixel shader outputs in parallel. These outputs are then read as the blending operation's inputs.
D3D10_BLEND_INV_SRC1_COLOR	Use two pixel shader outputs to provide color data to the input source, as with dual-source color blending. The pre-blending operation inverts the RGB color data.
D3D10_BLEND_SRC1_ALPHA	Use two pixel shader outputs to provide alpha data to the input source, as with dual-source color blending.
D3D10_BLEND_INV_SRC1_ALPHA	Use two pixel shader outputs to provide alpha data to the input source, as with dual-source color blending. The pre-blending operation inverts the alpha data.

10

```
/* define the blend state description structure */
D3D10_BLEND_DESC blendStateDesc;
/* fill a memory block with zeros using the SecureZeroMemory function */
SecureZeroMemory(&blendStateDesc, sizeof(D3D10_BLEND_DESC));

/* not using alpha-to-coverage */
blendStateDesc.AlphaToCoverageEnable = FALSE;
/* enable blending */
blendStateDesc.BlendEnable[0] = TRUE;

/* set the blend options */
blendStateDesc.SrcBlend = D3D10_BLEND_SRC_ALPHA;
blendStateDesc.DestBlend = D3D10_BLEND_DEST_COLOR;
blendStateDesc.BlendOp = D3D10_BLEND_OP_ADD;
blendStateDesc.SrcBlendAlpha = D3D10_BLEND_OP_ADD;
blendStateDesc.DstBlendAlpha = D3D10_BLEND_OP_ADD;

/* set the blending operation */
blendStateDesc.BlendOpAlpha = D3D10_BLEND_OP_ADD;

/*set all render-target pixel color components as writeable*/
blendStateDesc.RenderTargetWriteMask[0] =
                         D3D10_COLOR_WRITE_ENABLE_ALL;

/*create the blend state object */
g_id3dDevice -> CreateBlendState(&blendStateDesc,
                       &g_pBlendStateInterface));
```

10

Next we have to bind the created blend state object to the output-merger stage. This is done using the OMSetBlendState ID3D10Device interface function. OMSetBlendState is declared as follows in the d3d10.h header file:

```
void OMSetBlendState(
    ID3D10BlendState *pBlendState,
    const FLOAT BlendFactor[4],
    UINT SampleMask
);
```

Its first parameter, pBlendState, is a pointer to the ID3D10BlendState blend state interface. The BlendFactor parameter takes an array of RGBA blend factors specified by the D3D10_BLEND enumerator – providing per-pixel control over the blending of new and existing pixel color values. The final parameter, SampleMask, determines the render-target samples to update (use its default 'Oxffffffff' value for point sampling).

Binding the created blend state object to the output-merger stage can thus be done as follows:

```
/* bind the blend state to the output-merger stage */
g_id3dDevice -> OMSetBlendState(g_pBlendStateInterface, 0,
                       0xffffffff);
```

Working with OpenGL

Using OpenGL we set the blending state using the routine:

glEnable(GL_BLEND);

With the blend state set, we basically have to specify the source and destination blending factors using the glBlendFunc function. This function takes two parameters, the first being a constant specifying the computation of the red, green, blue, and alpha source blending factors with the second, a constant specifying the computation of the red, green, blue and alpha destination blending factors. The source factors, or fragment color values, are combined with the destination color values stored in the frame buffer. The most common source and destination factors are given in Table 10-2.

TABLE 10-2 Common OpenGL blending options

Constants	Description
GL_ZERO	Set either the source or destination to the color black.
GL_ONE	Set either the source or destination to the color white.
GL_DST_COLOR	Set the source to the destination color retrieved.
GL_DST_ALPHA	Set the source or destination to the destination alpha retrieved.
GL_ONE_MINUS_DST_ALPHA	Set the source or destination to one minus the destination alpha retrieved.
GL_ONE_MINUS_DST_COLOR	Set the source color to one minus the destination color retrieved.
GL_ONE_MINUS_SRC_ALPHA	Set the source or destination to one minus the source alpha retrieved.
GL_ONE_MINUS_SRC_COLOR	Set the destination color to one minus the source color retrieved.
GL_SRC_ALPHA	Set the source or destination to the source alpha retrieved.
GL_SRC_COLOR	Set the destination to the source color retrieved.

There is one more detail to consider when combining transparent and solid surfaces, namely, hidden-surface removal. Hidden-surface removal eliminates polygons hidden from the viewer by not passing these polygons to the rasterization stage – resulting in their exclusion. In short, when enabling blending, we have to disable hidden-surface removal because solid geometry located behind translucent geometry must be rendered for the composition of these objects to be possible.

There is luckily an easy way around this problem without the need to disable hidden-surface removal. We simply use the glDepthMask function to disable writing to the depth buffer (using the flag GL_FALSE). Disabling depth buffer writing will allow us to layer a translucent object over a solid one with the position of the solid object in relation to the translucent one not being registered.

The following code fragment enables basic OpenGL blending:

```
/* enable OpenGL blending */
glEnable(GL_BLEND);

/* define the blending operation */
glBlendFunc(GL_SRC_ALPHA, GL_ONE_MINUS_SRC_ALPHA);

/* bind some texture for blending */
glBindTexture(GL_TEXTURE_2D, someTexture[BLENDINGTEXTURE]);

/* enable hidden-surface removal */
glEnable(GL_DEPTH_TEST);

/*draw some geometric object to blend */
...

/* disable OpenGL blending */
glDisable(GL_BLEND);
```

10.1.2 Implementing Blending using Shaders

Blending can also be performed using pixel and vertex shaders; specifically, textures are combined via fragment program operations and subsequently written to the frame buffer. Shaders also allow significantly more control over the blending operation, leading to a vast array of advanced blending effects.

Working with the High Level Shader Language, we can set up the blending states directly by first declaring a structure in our FX file to enable and configure the blending operation:

```
BlendState EnableBlending
{
    BlendEnable[0] = TRUE;
    SrcBlend = SRC_ALPHA;
    DestBlend = ONE;
    BlendOp = ADD;
    SrcBlendAlpha = ZERO;
    DestBlendAlpha = ZERO;
    BlendOpAlpha = ADD;
    RenderTargetWriteMask[0] = 0xffffffff;
};
```

This blend state structure, declared using the BlendState constant, enables blending for the first render target. It then sets up blending to modify the color of the pixel being rendered to the framebuffer based on the following process:

1 Multiply the EnableBlending structure's SrcBlend factor with the source color (the pixel color of the object being drawn over the existing one).

2 Multiply the destination color (the color of a pixel already drawn in the framebuffer) with the EnableBlending structure's DestBlend factor.

3 The blend operation, as defined by the EnableBlending structure's BlendOp member, is now performed on these values.

This process can be summarized as the ADD blending operation between the source RGB color component multiplied by the source alpha (the pixel alpha of the object being drawn over the existing one) and the destination RGB color component multiplied by the color white (1,1,1,1).

The final step is to create the effect technique definition. This effect technique has one rendering pass, P0, specifying the shader states and a SetBlendState routine, analogous to the OMSetBlendState ID3D10Device interface function, to set the blend state of the output-merger stage. It is defined as follows:

```
technique10 Blending
{
   pass P0
    {
        /* the specified shader states */
        SetGeometryShader(CompileShader(ps_4_0,
                          SomeGeometryShader()));
        SetVertexShader(CompileShader(ps_4_0,
                          SomeVertexShader()));
        SetPixelShader(CompileShader(ps_4_0,
                          SomePixelShader()));

        /* set the blend state */
        SetBlendState(EnableBlending, float4(0.0f,0.0f,0.0f,0.0f),
                  0xFFFFFFFF);
    }
}
```

It is also a good idea to declare a structure that can be called by another effect technique definition to disable the blending operation:

```
BlendState DisableBlending
{
    BlendEnable[0] = FALSE;
};
```

Working with Cg

We now present a low-level blending implementation – this time using NVIDIA's Cg as our shading language. Two images can be blended using a very simple fragment shading program.

The first step is to specify the name of the fragment program's entry function, main_fragment in our example:

```
void main_fragment(
        float4 objectspaceVertexPosition : POSITION,
        float4 objectspaceVertexNormal : NORMAL,
        float2 inputTextureCoordinates : TEXCOORD0,
```

```
        out float4 outputColor : COLOR,

        /* parameter supplied by the application program */

        uniform sampler2D textureOne,
        uniform sampler2D textureTwo
)
{
```

The fragment program uses the tex2D texture lookup function to determine the fragment's color. It takes two parameters; the first being a sampler object and the second a texture coordinate set specifying the location to sample the object at:

```
/* the tex2D() function performs a 2D texture lookup determining the fragment's color */
float4 fragmentOne;
float4 fragmentTwo;

fragmentOne = tex2D(textureOne, inputTextureCoordinates);
fragmentTwo = tex2D(textureTwo, inputTextureCoordinates);
```

These fragment colors can now be combined through a simple lerp operation, blending the source image with the destination image:

```
outputColor = lerp(fragmentOne, fragmentTwo, 0.5);
```

We can also, for example, compose two images using the following equation:

```
outputColor = (fragmentOne) + ((1.0f − fragmentOne.w) *
            fragmentTwo));
```

The ".w" position element (part of the position set x, y, z, w and similar to the color set r, g, b, a) is used to access the fourth component of a vector, in this case the alpha value of the color stored in either the fragmentOne or fragmentTwo variables.

Numerous other blending operations are possible, with the only constraint being the desired effect. For example, we can implement our own hidden-surface removal algorithm by rendering one image only when it's not in front of another:

```
outputColor = fragmentOne * (1.0f − fragmentTwo.w);
```

10.1.3 Alpha Testing

Alpha testing is a technique that controls whether pixels are written to the render-target. Each pixel of a texture image is either rendered or discarded based on its alpha value. Thus, the pixel is only written to the render-target if its alpha value is more than 0.5, for example. Alpha testing is much simpler to implement than blending as it doesn't require the initialization of an alpha blend state. Its effect is, however, slightly different.

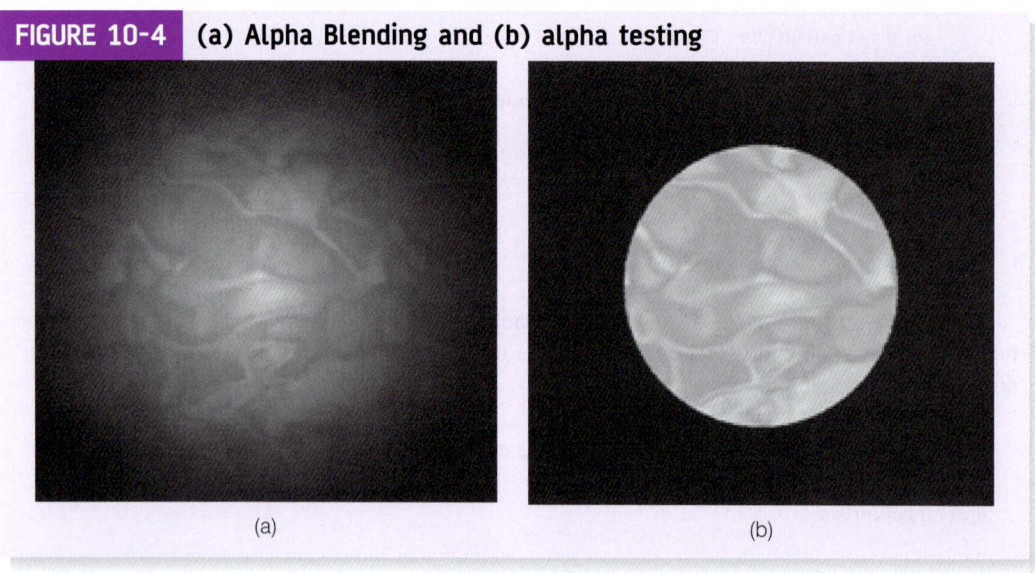

FIGURE 10-4   **(a) Alpha Blending and (b) alpha testing**

(a)   (b)

Alpha testing is, for example, what we will use to simulate the see-through sections in a staircase's railing (due to the technique simply not rendering alpha value pixels). Blending, on the other hand, enables a unified level of transparency through objects such as curtains or colored glass by blending the alpha value pixels with the pixels in the frame buffer. Figure 10-4(a) illustrates blending, with Figure 10-4(b) alpha testing. Both images are created using a transparent black texture rendered in front of a pearl-like textured bright background. The alpha blended image is created by merging the per-pixel color of one texture with that of another – specifically by combining the color of the alpha-enabled black texture with a texture already present at the related screen location. The alpha tested image is formed by the OpenGL or Direct3D device discarding all alpha pixels, and thus only rendering the pixels with an alpha value greater than '0.4'.

Alpha testing can be implemented via a simple HLSL pixel shader configured to discard all pixels with an alpha value less than '0.4'. The Cg version of this HLSL program is practically identical and won't be duplicated here for that reason.

We start by declaring two structures for the storage of received vertex data and returned pixel data, respectively:

```
struct VERTEXSHADER_INPUT
{
    float4 Loc : POSITION;
    float2 texture: TEXCOORD0;
};

struct PIXELSHADER_INPUT
{
    float4 Loc : SV_POSITION;
    float2 texture: TEXCOORD0;
};
```

The first structure, VERTEXSHADER_INPUT, stores the vertex information as received from the Direct3D application. This structure is used to pass input data to a vertex shader responsible for transforming the input vertex position, defined in object space, to projection space. This process starts with the multiplication of the input vertex position, IN.Loc, and a world matrix, thus resulting in a transformation from object space to world space. The next transformation multiplies this transformed vertex position, output.Loc, with a view matrix, resulting in a world space to view space transformation. The final transformation takes this view space vertex position and multiplies it with a projection matrix to transform the vertex from view space to projection space (please see section 10.2.2 for the declaration and initialization of these projection matrices):

```
/* vertex shader */
PIXELSHADER_INPUT AlphaTestVertexShader(VERTEXSHADER_INPUT IN)
{
    PIXELSHADER_INPUT output = (PIXELSHADER_INPUT)0;

    output.Loc = mul(IN.Loc, WorldMatrix);
    output.Loc = mul(output.Loc, ViewMatrix);
    output.Loc = mul(output.Loc, ProjectionMatrix);

    /* pass on the texture coordinates */
    output.texture = IN.texture;

    return output;
}
```

In the case of our pixel shader we define a sampler specifying the manner in which the color of the alpha-enabled texture is to be sampled using the SamplerState type. This structure defines the texture filtering method as linear mipmapping (MIN_MAG_MIP_LINEAR) with the texture coordinates u and v, clamped to the range [0, 1]:

```
SamplerState samplingMethod
{
    Filter = MIN_MAG_MIP_LINEAR;
    AddressU = Clamp;
    AddressV = Clamp;
};
```

We also declare a texture variable that will be used during the sampling operation:

```
Texture2D sampledTexture;
```

The pixel shader starts by calculating the color of the fragment by sampling the texture using HLSL's Sample method. The alpha component of this sampled color is then tested using a standard if statement. The pixel is discarded (via the discard function) if its alpha value is less than '0.4':

```
/* pixel shader */
float4 AlphaTestingPixelShader(PIXELSHADER_INPUT IN): SV_Target
{
    float4 color = sampledTexture.Sample(samplingMethod,
                                IN.texture);
    /* if the pixel's alpha value < 0.4, discard it */
```

```
if(color.a < 0.4)
    discard;

return color;
}
```

The effect technique definition of the alpha testing shader program is similar to that of the fog example which will be given in section 10.2.2 – the only difference being the vertex and pixel shader function names.

Working with OpenGL

Performing per-vertex alpha testing in OpenGL (without the use of shaders) is a relatively simple operation. We start by enabling the alpha testing state using the GL_ALPHA_TEST flag:

```
glEnable(GL_ALPHA_TEST);
```

With the alpha testing state enabled, we basically have to specify the alpha testing function (i.e. a rule for the rendering of our transparent object) using the glAlphaFunc routine. This routine takes two parameters, the first specifying the alpha channel comparison function and the second an alpha reference value ('0' representing the minimum alpha value and '1' the highest). The comparison function specifies the conditions under which transparent pixels are drawn. Thus, only if the incoming alpha pixel passes a certain condition is it rendered. For example, the following routine will render all fragments with an alpha value greater than '0.4':

```
glAlphaFunc(GL_GREATER, 0.4);
```

Legal alpha channel comparison functions are given in Table 10-3.

TABLE 10-3 Alpha comparison functions

Alpha comparison function	Description
GL_NEVER	Pixel is never drawn.
GL_GREATER	Pixel is drawn if the incoming alpha value is greater than the reference value.
GL_LESS	Pixel is drawn if the incoming alpha value is less than the reference value.
GL_EQUAL	Pixel is drawn if the incoming alpha value is equal to the reference value.
GL_NOTEQUAL	Pixel is drawn if the incoming alpha value is not equal to the reference value.
GL_GEQUAL	Pixel is drawn if the incoming alpha value is greater than or equal to the reference value.
GL_ALWAYS	Pixel is always drawn.
GL_LEQUAL	Pixel is drawn if the incoming alpha value is less than or equal to the reference value.

The following code fragment enables basic OpenGL alpha testing:

```
/* enable OpenGL alpha testing */
glEnable(GL_ALPHA_TEST);

/* set the alpha testing function – the fragment is drawn if
   its alpha value is > "0.4" */
glAlphaFunc(GL_GREATER, 0.4);

/* bind some texture for blending */
glBindTexture(GL_TEXTURE_2D, someTexture[BLENDINGTEXTURE]);

/* enable hidden-surface removal */
glEnable(GL_DEPTH_TEST);

/*draw some geometric object to blend */
...

/* disable OpenGL alpha testing */
glDisable(GL_ALPHA_TEST);
```

10.2 FOG

Fog can be described as dense vapour of condensed particles reducing visibility to less than a kilometre. Figure 10-5 shows the most common form of fog, a low altitude cloud, engulfing the Golden Gate Bridge.

10

FIGURE 10-5 **The Golden Gate Bridge engulfed in Fog**

FIGURE 10-6   **A basic scene without any fog**

FIGURE 10-7   **A basic scene with linear fog enabled**

Fog is used for countless environmental effects, its implementation specifically adding to the mood of outdoor environments while at the same time improving rendering performance when combined with the culling of fully obscured objects. In Figure 10-6 we have an image of a shadow casted by a tall building; this same shadow is shown in Figure 10-7 with a degree of fog added. These two images show how we can make use of fog to simulate the natural dissipation of shadows as they fall further from the source – a process known as atmospheric perspective.

Fog is thus frequently used in computer games for the simulation of atmospheric effects such as mist, smoke, and water vapor. It contributes heavily to the general sense of depth via manipulation of the color values of geometric objects based on the object's distance from the viewer. Hence, the implementation of fog can be described as the blending of some pre-defined fog color with the color values of objects, with

FIGURE 10-8	Adding linear fog to a scene

the amount of blending being based on the object's distance from the point-of-view. Blending is controlled using a linear, exponential, or Gaussian equation. Varying these equations results in blending factor changes. The *blending factor* is just a way for us to measure exactly how much a certain color value will be blended with the fog color at a given time. For example, linear fog (as shown in Figure 10-8) will 'dense up' at a constant rate as an object's distance from the viewer increases. Exponential fog will, on the other hand, increase much more rapidly after a specific distance from the viewer.

10.2.1 The Physics of Fog

Fog particles, such as smoke and condensed vapor, scatter and absorb light travelling from one point to another. Scattered light can either be directed at or away from the viewer, resulting in a cloudy white color for water vapor and a greyish color for smog due to the higher light absorption rate of smoke particles (depending on its thickness).

The calculation of fog, as previously mentioned, is based on a distance function – specifically, either a linear (fog increases linearly from the point of view to an end point) or exponential function (fog intensifies exponentially from the point-of-view to an end point). Figure 10-9 shows fog density as a factor of fog intensity and distance. *Fog intensity* is the amount of scattered and/or absorbed light; the greater this scattering or absorption, the thicker the fog. *Fog distance* can be described as the distance from some point to the viewer; the greater this distance, the greater the amount of fog visible.

The color of a fog fragment, C_f, can be expressed as a function of absorption and scattering. This premise is based on the assumption that the intensity of light traveling through a number of particles, such as smoke and condensed vapor, is reduced at a constant rate. We must, however, also factor in the possibility that scattered light will be scattered again by other particles, thus possibly

10

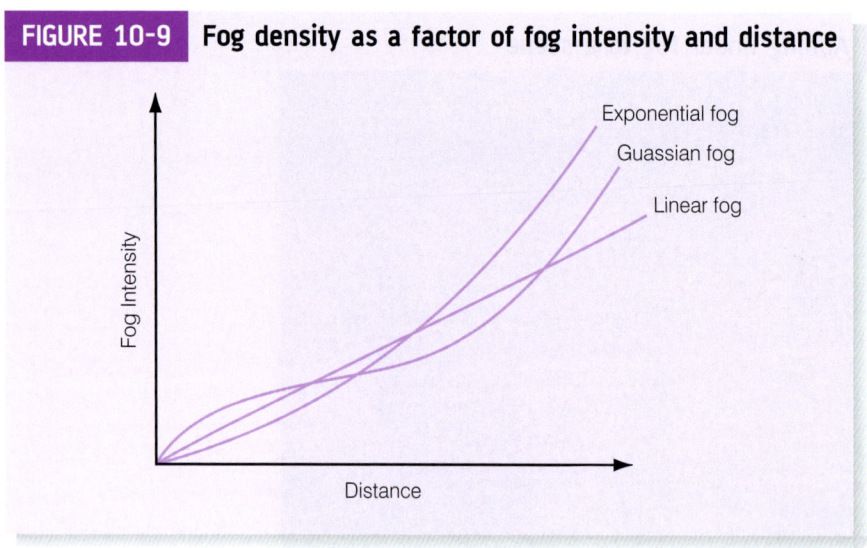

FIGURE 10-9   **Fog density as a factor of fog intensity and distance**

converging at a later stage to reach the viewer. We can now express the color of a fog fragment, C_f, as:

$$C_f = \textit{color of the pixel being rendered}$$
$$- (\textit{color intensity resulting from the absorbed light})$$
$$- (\textit{color intensity resulting from the scattered light})$$
$$+ (\textit{color intensity resulting from the converging light}).$$

This expression can be simplified by rewriting the color intensity, resulting from the absorbed and scattered light, as a scale factor greater than zero and less than one. This simplification is based on the premise that the amount of light absorbed and scattered will always be less than the original light intensity, thus, the original color of the pixel being rendered.

The color of a fog fragment, C_f, can now be computed by multiplying a fog factor, f, with the color of the pixel being rendered, C_p, added to the fog color, C_f, multiplied by '1' minus the fog factor, $1{-}f$. This results in a blending equation where the light intensity at the fragment being rendered equals the original light intensity at the viewer minus the fog factor (f) increased by some fog color fraction, $1{-}f$:

$$C_f = (C_p)(f) + (C_f)(1-f)$$

The fog factor, as mentioned previously, can be expressed using an exponential, linear, or Gaussian function. *Linear fog* is a factor of the depth or distance from the viewer to the pixel or vertex being rendered and the start and end distances at which the fog effect starts and ends, respectively:

$$f = \frac{endPosition - depth}{endPosition - startPosition}.$$

Exponential fog is expressed using the mathematical constant, e (≈ 2.71828), the distance from the viewer to the pixel or vertex being rendered and an arbitrary fog density ranging from 0.0 to 1.0:

$$f = \frac{1}{e^{(depth)(fogDensity)}}.$$

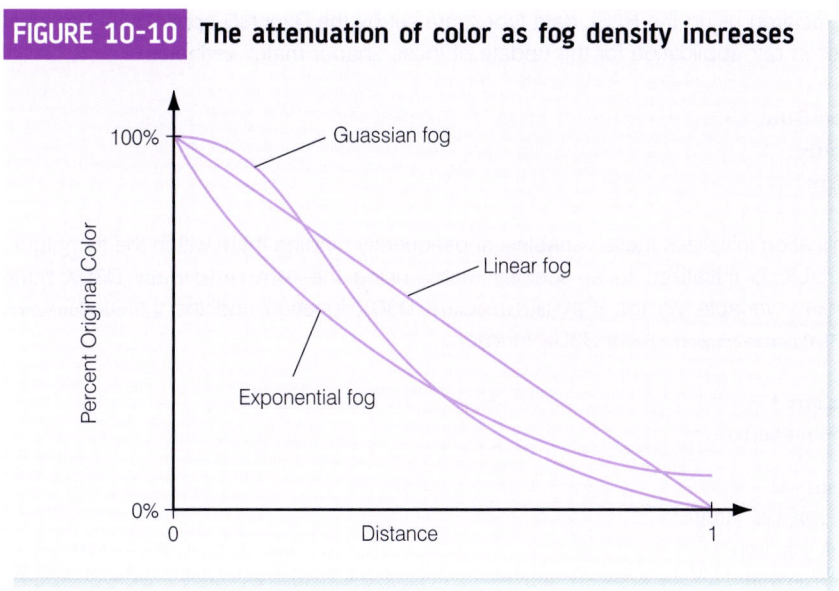

FIGURE 10-10 The attenuation of color as fog density increases

Gaussian fog is easily defined by taking our previous exponential fog equation and squaring the distance from the viewer to the pixel or vertex being rendered multiplied by an arbitrary fog density:

$$f = \frac{1}{e^{((depth)(fogDensity))^2}}.$$

Figure 10-10 illustrates the effect of fog density on the original color of the pixel being rendered.

10

10.2.2 Implementing Fog

Implementing fog in a Direct3D 10 environment requires emulation of Direct3D 9's fixed function pipeline via use of an HLSL vertex and pixel shader. The implementation is relatively simple with a pre-calculated fog factor determining the amount of fog obscuring a particular pixel.

The shader's effect file starts with a declaration of the projection, world and view matrices:

```
matrix ProjectionMatrix;

matrix WorldMatrix;
matrix ViewMatrix;
```

It also declares constants for use during the calculation of the fog factors:

```
int userSpecifiedFogMode;
float fogDensity;
float4 fogColor;
float fogStartPosition;
float fogEndPosition;
```

These variables, declared using the HLSL data types, are set by the Direct3D application. We must thus declare variables in our application for the update of these shader matrix variables:

```
D3DXMATRIX g_ProjectionMatrix;
D3DXMATRIX g_WorldMatrix;
D3DXMATRIX g_ViewMatrix;
```

The Direct3D application initializes these variables, subsequently binding them within the technique. The g_WorldMatrix variable is initialized to an identity matrix using the D3DXMatrixIdentity D3DX math function, the g_ViewMatrix variable via the D3DXMatrixLookAtLH D3DX function and the g_ProjectionMatrix variable using the D3DXMatrixPerspectiveFovLH D3DX function:

```
/* initialize the world matrix */
D3DXMatrixIdentity(&g_WorldMatrix);

/* initialize the view matrix */
D3DXVECTOR3 EyeCoord( 0.0f, 1.0f, -10.0f);
D3DXVECTOR3 LookAt(0.0f, 1.0f, 0.0f);
D3DXVECTOR3 UpDir(0.0f, 1.0f, 0.0f);
D3DXMatrixLookAtLH(&g_ViewMatrix, &EyeCoord, &LookAt, &UpDir);

/* set the left-handed perspective projection */
D3DXMatrixPerspectiveFovLH(&g_ProjectionMatrix,
                    (float)D3DX_PI*0.25f,
                    rectangle_width/rectangle_height,
                    0.1f, 100.0f);
```

Before we can set the HLSL variable values using the ID3D10EffectVariable update methods, we first have to obtain the effect variables for each of the above defined shader variables (using ID3D10Effect retrieval functions):

```
ID3D10Effect* g_pd3d10Effect = NULL;

/* obtain the ProjectionMatrix shader variable */
ID3D10EffectMatrixVariable* g_pd3d10ProjMatrixVar = NULL;
g_pd3d10ProjMatrixVar = g_pd3d10Effect
            ->GetVariableByName("ProjectionMatrix")
                            ->AsMatrix();

/* obtain the WorldMatrix shader variable */
ID3D10EffectMatrixVariable* g_pd3d10WorldMatrixVar = NULL;
g_pd3d10WorldMatrixVar = g_pd3d10Effect
            ->GetVariableByName("WorldMatrix")->AsMatrix();

/* obtain the ViewMatrix shader variable */
ID3D10EffectMatrixVariable* g_pd3d10ViewMatrixVar = NULL;
g_pd3d10ViewMatrixVar = g_pd3d10Effect
            ->GetVariableByName("ViewMatrix")->AsMatrix();
```

10

```
/* obtain the userSpecifiedFogMode shader variable */
ID3D10EffectScalarVariable* g_pUserSpecifiedFogMode = NULL;
g_pUserSpecifiedFogMode = g_pd3d10Effect
    ->GetVariableByName("userSpecifiedFogMode")->AsScalar();


/* obtain the fogDensity shader variable */
ID3D10EffectScalarVariable* g_pFogDensity = NULL;
g_pFogDensity = g_pd3d10Effect
        ->GetVariableByName("fogDensity")->AsScalar();


/* obtain the fogColor shader variable */
ID3D10EffectScalarVariable* g_pFogColor = NULL;
g_pFogColor = g_pd3d10Effect
        ->GetVariableByName("fogColor")->AsScalar();


/* obtain the fogStartPosition shader variable */
ID3D10EffectScalarVariable* g_pFogStartPosition = NULL;
g_pFogStartPosition = g_pd3d10Effect
        ->GetVariableByName("fogStartPosition")->AsScalar();


/* obtain the fogEndPosition shader variable */
ID3D10EffectScalarVariable* g_pFogEndPosition = NULL;
g_pFogEndPosition = g_pd3d10Effect
        ->GetVariableByName("fogEndPosition")->AsScalar();
```

Setting the fog factor constants are done in the following manner:

```
g_pFogStartPosition->SetFloat(20.0f);
g_pFogEndPosition->SetFloat(40.0f);
g_pFogDensity->SetFloat(0.08f);


/* specify linear fog as explained below */
g_pUserSpecifiedFogMode->SetInt(1);


/* specify the fog color as yellowish-mustard */
D3DXVECTOR4 vFogColorVector(1.0,0.7,0.1,1);
g_pFogColor->SetFloatVector((float*)&vFogColorVector);
```

The values declared in the shader program are now set and can be changed during each rendering pass.

Returning to our shader program, we declare two structures for the storage of received vertex data and returned pixel data, respectively:

```
struct VERTEXSHADER_INPUT
{
    float4 Loc : POSITION;
    float2 texture: TEXCOORD0;
    float fogDistance : FOGDISTANCE;
```

10

```
};
struct PIXELSHADER_INPUT
{
    float4 Loc : SV_POSITION;
    float2 texture: TEXCOORD0;
    float fogDistance : FOGDISTANCE;
};
```

The first structure, VERTEXSHADER_INPUT, holds our vertex information as received from the Direct3D application and is used to pass input data to a vertex shader that transforms the input vertex position, defined in object space, to projection space. This is done by multiplying the input vertex position, IN.Loc, with a world matrix, thus transforming it from object space to world space. The next transformation multiplies this transformed vertex position, output.Loc, with a view matrix, resulting in a world space to view space transformation. The final transformation takes this view space vertex position and multiplies it with a projection matrix to transform the vertex from view space to projection space. The vertex shader also calculates the distance for each vertex of a triangle – these distances are then interpolated, as a fog distance, and forwarded to the pixel shader:

```
/* vertex shader */
PIXELSHADER_INPUT FogVertexShader(VERTEXSHADER_INPUT IN)
{
    PIXELSHADER_INPUT output = (PIXELSHADER_INPUT)0;

    output.Loc = mul(IN.Loc, WorldMatrix);

    /* calculate the camera position */
    float4 cameraPosition = mul(output.Loc, ViewMatrix);

    output.Loc = mul(output.Loc, ViewMatrix);
    output.Loc = mul(output.Loc, ProjectionMatrix);

    /* calculate the fog distance */
    output.fogDistance = cameraPosition.z;

    return output;
}
```

In the case of our pixel shader we define a sampler specifying the manner in which the fogged object's texture color will be sampled using the SamplerState type. This structure defines the texture filtering method as linear mipmapping (MIN_MAG_MIP_LINEAR) with the texture coordinates *u* and *v*, clamped to the range [0, 1]:

```
SamplerState samplingMethod
{
    Filter = MIN_MAG_MIP_LINEAR;
    AddressU = Clamp;
    AddressV = Clamp;
};
```

We also declare a texture variable that will be used during the sampling operation:

```
Texture2D sampledTexture;
```

The pixel shader starts by calculating the fog factor based on the fog distance received from the vertex shader. The fog factor correlating to the user-specified fog mode is computed. For example, if the user specified the integer variable, userSpecifiedFogMode, as '1' (as for our example), then the linear fog factor will be computed. With the fog factor determined, the program calculates the color of the fragment that is to be blended with the fog color by sampling the texture using HLSL's Sample method.

```
/* pixel shader */
float4 FogPixelShader(PIXELSHADER_INPUT IN) : SV_Target
{
    /* the fog factor */
    float fogFactor = 0;

    /* calculate the fog factor based on the fog distance
       received from the vertex shader */

    /* linear fog */
    if(userSpecifiedFogMode == 1)
    {
        fogFactor = (fogEndPosition - IN.fogDistance)/
                    (fogEndPosition - fogStartPosition);
    }

    /* exponential fog */
    else if(userSpecifiedFogMode == 1) //exponential fog
    {
        fogFactor = 1.0/exp(IN.fogDistance*fogDensity);
    }

    /* Gaussian fog */
    else if(userSpecifiedFogMode == 3)
    {
        fogFactor = 1.0/exp(pow(IN.fogDistance*fogDensity,
                            2));
    }

    /* calculate the fragment color */
    float4 fragmentColor = sampledTexture.Sample(samplingMethod,
                            IN.texture);

    /* determine the final pixel color by blending the
       original texture color and fog color */
    float4 blendedColor = (1.0 - fogFactor)*fogColor
                        + (fogFactor*fragmentColor);

    return blendedColor;
}
```

10

The final step is to specify the effect technique definition that will set the previously defined vertex and pixel shaders:

```
technique10 AddFog
{
    pass P0
    {
        SetGeometryShader(NULL);
        SetVertexShader(CompileShader(ps_4_0, VertexShaderFunc()));
        SetPixelShader(CompileShader(ps_4_0, PixelShaderFunc()));
    }
}
```

Working with Cg

Instead of calculating the fog distance using the planar eye distance (cameraPosition.z), we can also use the HLSL or Cg length function to return the floating-point Euclidean eye distance. The Cg program given here will use this approach.

We start with a vertex program that computes the fog distance. This value, used in the calculation of the fog factor, is the distance from the fogged fragment to the camera position calculated using the length function and camera position:

```
/* vertex shader */
void main_vertex(
            float4 objectspaceVertexPosition : POSITION,
            float2 inputTextureCoordinates : TEXCOORD0,
            float4 inputColor: COLOR,

            out float4 outputVertexPosition : POSITION,
            out float2 outputTextureCoordinates : TEXCOORD0,
            out float4 outputColor : COLOR,
            out float fogDistance : TEXCOORD1,

            /* parameters supplied by the application program */

            uniform float4x4 modelviewMatrix,
            uniform float4x4 modelviewProjection
)
{
```

We start by calculating the clip-space position:

```
/* transform the vertex position into homogeneous clip-
   space coordinates */
outputVertexPosition = mul(modelviewProjection,
                        objectspaceVertexPosition);
```

We also calculate the camera position:

```
float3 cameraPosition = mul(modelviewMatrix,
                            objectspaceVertexPosition).xyz;
```

Next we assign the input texture coordinates to the output texture coordinates:

```
/* assign the input texture coordinates to the output
   texture coordinates */
outputTextureCoordinates = inputTextureCoordinates;
```

The input color value is also assigned to the output color value:

```
/* assign the input color to the output color */
outputColor = inputColor;
```

The fog distance, used in the calculation of the fragment shader's fog factor, is the length of the cameraPosition vector:

```
/* calculate the fog distance */
fogDistance = length(cameraPosition);
}
```

The fragment shader starts by calculating the fog factor based on the received fog distance. It subsequently multiplies this received distance with the user specified fog density, calculating the fog factor by taking the base 2 exponential (2^x) of this computed value using the Cg exp2 intrinsic function. Following this the program calculates the color of the fragment that is to be blended with the fog color by sampling the texture using Cg's text2D method. The fragment shader blends a sampled texture color with the user defined fog color to determine the refraction color using the lerp function:

```
void main_fragment(
        float2 inputTextureCoordinates : TEXCOORD0,
        float3 fogDistance : TEXCOORD1,
        float4 color : COLOR,

        out float4 outputColor : COLOR,

        /* parameter supplied by the application program */

        uniform float fogColor,
        uniform sampler2D sampledTexture,
        uniform float fogDensity
)
{
```

The fog factor is calculated by multiplying the received fog distance with the fog density and then computing the base 2 exponential of this value negated:

```
float fogFactor = exp2(-1.0f*fogDistance*fogDensity);
```

Next we perform a texture color lookup using the tex2D function:

```
/* obtain the fragment color */
float4 fragmentColor = tex2D(sampledTexture,
                inputTextureCoordinates);
```

The sampled fragment color is now combined with the vertex program's interpolated color:

```
float4 finalColor = color*fragmentColor;
```

Following this, we blend the sampled texture color with the fog color using the lerp function. The weight of this function is set to the fog factor:

```
float4 blendedColor = lerp(finalColor,
                fogColor, fogFactor);
```

We finally assign this linearly interpolated blended color to the output color:

```
color = blendedColor;
}
```

Working with OpenGL

Enabling per-vertex fog in OpenGL without the use of shaders is really easy. OpenGL offers support for Gaussian (GL_EXP2), exponential (GL_EXP) and linear fog (GL_LINEAR).

Our basic routine for defining and enabling fog will typically look something like this:

```
/* specify the fog color – RGBA*/
GLfloat fogColor[] = {0.8, 0.8, 0.8, 1.0};

/* enable OpenGL fog – similar to enabling lighting or
   blending */
glEnable(GL_FOG);

/* set the fog mode to linear */
glFogf(GL_FOG_MODE, GL_LINEAR);

/* set the fog density */
glFogf(GL_FOG_DENSITY, 0.2);

/* set the fog color */
glFogfv(GL_FOG_COLOR, fogColor);
```

The glFog* function sets a number of fog parameters. It can take floating-point, integer, or array data. For example, the specification:

```
glFogf(GLenum par, GLfloat value)
```

sets any of the following parameters: GL_FOG_COLOR, GL_FOG_DENSITY, GL_FOG_END, GL_FOG_INDEX, GL_FOG_MODE, or GL_FOG_START to a floating-point value passed as second parameter.

10.3 SUMMARY

Chapter 10 started by discussing alpha blending as a technique for merging the per-pixel color of one texture with that of another – specifically by combining the color of an alpha-enabled texture with a texture already present at the corresponding screen location. Following this we looked at the alpha blending equation and the addition of transparency to a texture image.

Next we focused on the implementation of alpha blending using Direct3D 10's Blend State and basic OpenGL blending operations – both API approaches dealing with the specification of source and destination blending factors. We subsequently extended this discussion to focus on the implementation of blending using Cg and HLSL pixel and vertex shaders.

We then investigated alpha testing as a technique to control whether pixels are written to the render target, in essence highlighting the differences between alpha blending and alpha testing. We subsequently implemented alpha testing via a simple HLSL pixel shader with the presented OpenGL example performing per-vertex alpha testing.

The remainder of the chapter focused on the physics and implementation of atmospheric fog. The HLSL fog implementation emulated Direct3D 9's fixed function pipeline using HLSL vertex and pixel shaders with the Cg example calculating the fog distance by means of the Euclidean eye distance as opposed to the planar eye distance.

The next chapter takes a detailed look at a number of shadow-generating algorithms, particularly focusing on the rendering of shadows by means of stencil shadow volumes.

10.4 FURTHER READING

A great paper dealing with variable fog density is *'Fast Multi-Layer Fog'* by Justin Legakis published in *ACM SIGGRAPH 98 Conference Abstracts and Applications*. The paper *'Advanced Real-Time Rendering in 3D Graphics and Games: Real-Time Atmospheric Effects in Games'* by Carsten Wenzel (SIGGRAPH Proceedings 2006) deals with a number of atmospheric effects such as volumetric fog and the advanced topic of global volumetric fog for alpha transparent objects.

For additional foundational information on alpha blending and compositing in general, see Thomas Porter and Tom Duff's paper *'Compositing Digital Images'* published in *Communications of the ACM* (1984).

10.5 EXERCISES

1 Explain how we go about calculating the final blended color of an image.

2 How is opacity added to an object?

3 Briefly describe the implementation of alpha blending using Direct3D 10's Blend State.

4 Describe the purpose of the following:

```
blendStateDesc.SrcBlend = D3D10_BLEND_SRC_ALPHA;
blendStateDesc.DestBlend = D3D10_BLEND_DEST_COLOR;
```

10

```
blendStateDesc.BlendOp = D3D10_BLEND_OP_ADD;
blendStateDesc.SrcBlendAlpha = D3D10_BLEND_OP_ADD;
blendStateDesc.DstBlendAlpha = D3D10_BLEND_OP_ADD;
```

5 How is the blend state bound to the output-merger stage?

6 Write HLSL code to perform blending using pixel and vertex shaders.

7 What is the purpose of the '.w' position element in the following code sample:

```
outputColor = (fragmentOne) + ((1.0f - fragmentOne.w) *
              fragmentTwo));
```

8 Compare alpha testing to alpha blending.

9 Differentiate between linear, exponential or Gaussian fog.

10 How can the color of a fog fragment be computed?

11 Extend sample program 9.1 to include linear fog.

CHAPTER 11

Shadows

LEARNING OBJECTIVES

In this chapter you will learn about:

- Shadow rendering algorithms
- Blinn's shadow polygons
- Scan-line polygon projection
- Shadow mapping
- Shadow volumes
- Depth-pass testing
- Depth-fail testing
- Soft-edged shadows using penumbra wedges
- The stencil buffer
- Enabling depth stencil testing
- Implementing stencil shadow volumes

INTRODUCTION

Chapter 11 investigates a number of shadow-generating algorithms, particularly focusing on the rendering of shadows by means of stencil shadow volumes and depth stencil testing.

11.1   SHADOW RENDERING ALGORITHMS

Real-time shadow generation contributes heavily towards the realism and ambience of any scene being rendered. Research dealing with the calculation of shadows has been conducted since the late 1960s and has picked up great momentum with the evolution of high-end dedicated graphics hardware. Shadows are produced by opaque or semi-opaque objects obstructing light from reaching other objects or surfaces. A *shadow* is a two-dimensional projection of at least one object onto another object or surface. The size of a shadow is dependent on the angle between the light vector and light-blocking object. The intensity of a shadow is in turn influenced by the opacity of the light-blocking object. An opaque object is completely impenetrable to light and will thus cast a darker shadow than a semi-opaque object. The number of light sources will also affect the number of shadows in a scene; with the darkness of a shadow intensifying where multiple shadows overlap. Figure 11-1 illustrates shadow generation, specifically the implementation of stencil shadow volumes – a popular shadow rendering technique.

The drive towards realism has led to the development of many shadowing algorithms. Some of these algorithms, like shadow mapping and shadow volumes, are more successful than others. The success of an algorithm is dependent on the balance between speed and realism and techniques like shadow mapping and stencil shadow volumes are particularly amenable to hardware implementation – thus freeing the CPU of a substantial processing burden and making the real-time rendering of shadows feasible.

Looking at shadows from a foundational perspective reveals them as a product of an environment's lighting. Shadows can have either hard or soft edges. This is dependent on the type of light source used and the distance between the light source and object. In the case of soft shadows we differentiate between an umbra and penumbra. The darkest area of a shadow, receiving no light at all, is referred to as the *umbra* with the *penumbra*, receiving a small amount of light, indicating the partially shadowed edge. Figure 11-2 illustrates a shadow's umbra and penumbra.

It should be noted that there is always a gradual intensity transformation from the umbra to penumbra. However, the fading of the shadow (as its distance from the casting object increases) need not necessarily be gradual. Point lights will, for example, produce non-fading hard-edged shadows, with

11

FIGURE 11-1   **Example of stencil shadowing — note the overlapping shadows in the first image**

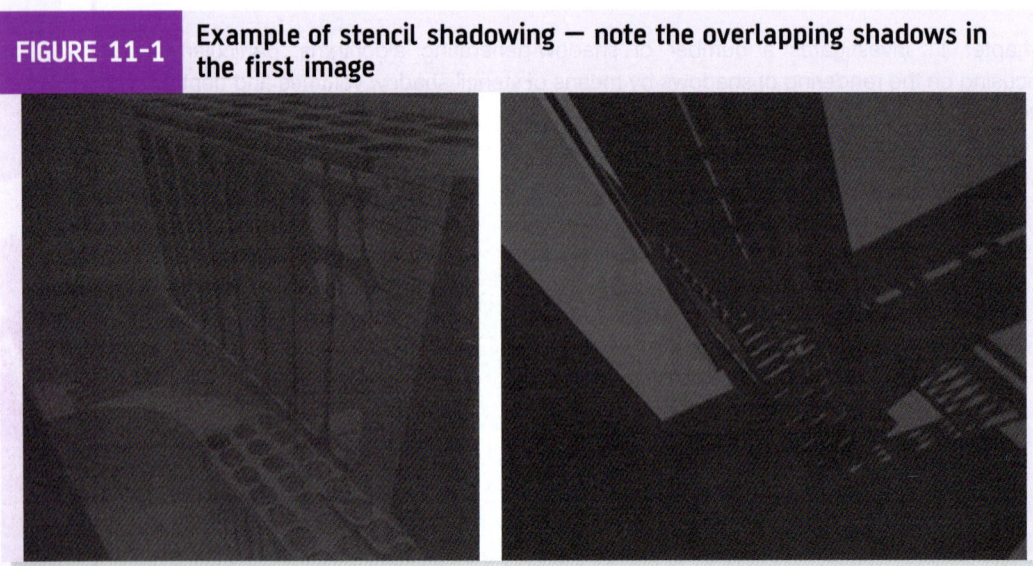

ambient light sources producing soft-edged shadows fading into the distance. The area of a light source also affects the gradual softening of shadows. The larger the light source's area, the more quickly the shadow grades off. Figure 11-3 shows the difference between shadows produced by point and ambient light sources.

We will now investigate several shadowing algorithms, including the fundamentals of shadow volumes and shadow mapping. The first two algorithms, Blinn's shadow polygons and scan-line polygon projection, are historic in nature. We describe these algorithms here not only for the sake of completeness but also since some of the elements introduced by them form the basis of general shadow computation. These first two techniques aren't suited for real-time implementations; however, more recent algorithms such as stencil shadow volumes and hardware shadow mapping remedy this situation by emphasizing the balance between processor efficiency and realism.

In foresight it is necessary to note that shadowing remains one of the most processor intensive tasks and despite each technique's limitations, it is important to consider each algorithm with its intended application area in mind.

11.1.1 Blinn's Shadow Polygons

An extremely easy to use shadow generation technique was described by James Blinn in 1988. This method simply calculates the projection of an object on some base-plane. In short, a shadow cast by a point light and a polygon onto another polygon can be rendered by projecting the first polygon onto the plane of the second polygon. The point light is in this case at the center of

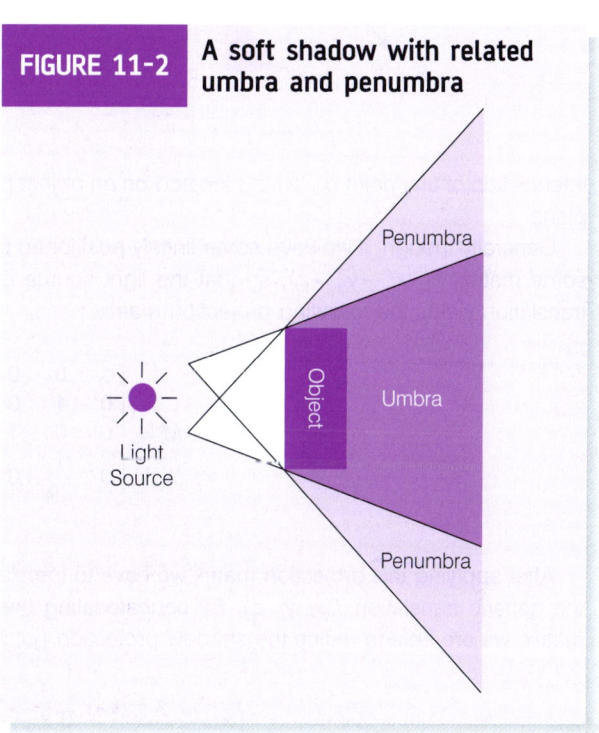

FIGURE 11-2 **A soft shadow with related umbra and penumbra**

11

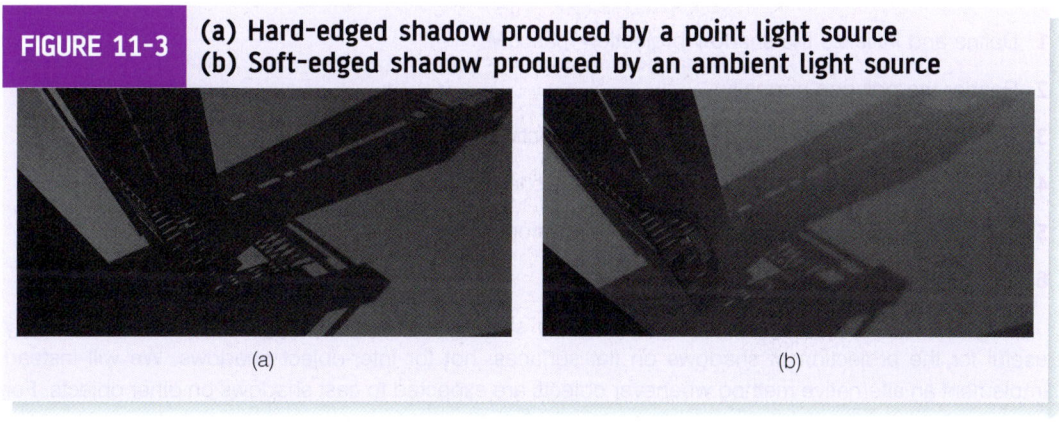

FIGURE 11-3 **(a) Hard-edged shadow produced by a point light source**
(b) Soft-edged shadow produced by an ambient light source

(a)   (b)

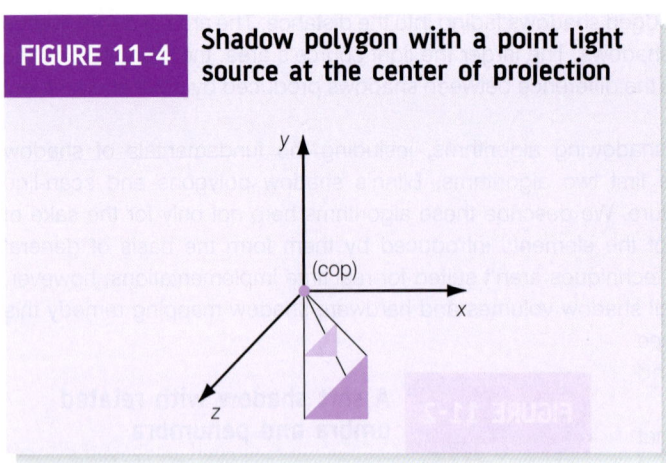

Shadow polygon with a point light source at the center of projection

projection and the resulting shadow is referred to as a *shadow polygon*. Figure 11-4 illustrates the projection of a shadow polygon (onto the *xy*-plane) with the light source located at the center of projection.

During Chapter 9 we explored the local illumination approximation stating that if we have an infinitely positioned point light source, then we can consider its light rays as parallel. These rays, emanating from a light source located at the point (x_l, y_l, z_l), will cast a shadow at the point (x_s, y_s, z_s) based on the intersection of any point (x_o, y_o, z_o) located on an object positioned between the light source and some plane.

Generally though, if we have some finitely positioned point light, then we can translate the scene by some matrix, $T(-x_l, -y_l, -z_l)$, so that the light source is positioned at the center of projection. This translation yields the following projection matrix:

$$M = \begin{bmatrix} 1 & 0 & 0 & 0 \\ 0 & 1 & 0 & 0 \\ 0 & 0 & 1 & 0 \\ 0 & \dfrac{1}{-y_l} & 0 & 0 \end{bmatrix}.$$

After applying this projection matrix we have to translate the scene back to its original position with the generic translation $T(x_l, y_l, z_l)$. By concatenating the two translation matrices with the projection matrix, we are able to define the shadow projection (x_s, y_s, z_s) of the original point (x_o, y_o, z_o) as:

$$\left(x_l - \frac{x - x_l}{(y - y_l)/y_l}, 0, z_l - \frac{z - z_l}{(y - y_l)/y_l} \right).$$

The following steps outline the process of creating a shadow polygon:

1 Define and initialize the shadow projection matrix **M**.

2 Render the polygon normally.

3 Translate the light to the origin (center of projection).

4 Calculate the projection of the object with the shadow projection matrix.

5 Translate everything back to their original positions.

6 Render the shadow polygon.

Blinn's method is often utilized to render the shadows of single polygons. It is, however, only useful for the projection of shadows on flat surfaces, not for inter-object shadows. We will instead implement an alternative method whenever objects are expected to cast shadows on other objects. For example, we could create a relatively uncomplicated shadow algorithm by modifying one of Chapter 12's hidden surface removal algorithms. The premise behind our modification would be that shadows are in fact areas hidden from light sources.

11.1.2 Scan-Line Polygon Projection

A quite complex, and now mostly redundant shadow algorithm was introduced by Arthur Appel in 1968 and further developed by Jack Bouknight and Karl Kelley in 1970. This algorithm, commonly known as *scan-line polygon projection*, adds shadow generation to scan-line rendering. A *scan-line algorithm* operates on a row-by-row basis, as opposed to a pixel-by-pixel or polygon-by-polygon basis. A *scan-line* itself is a single line or row composed of a series of successive pixels stored in an array or list. The overall image is rendered as a result of the consecutive downwards repositioning of the scan-line. To enable both pre-rendered and real-time shadow generation via scan-line algorithms, it is necessary to append the original algorithm with a pre-processing stage. This pre-processing stage builds up a secondary data structure linking all the polygons that will cast a shadow on some other polygon.

The scan-line projection algorithm has an additional stage where all the polygons of a scene are projected onto a sphere centered at the light source (the center of projection). This allows for the identification of all polygons casting shadows on other polygons. It is important to remember that, in a scene with k polygons, one will have at most $k(k - 1)$ shadows – the detection and elimination of polygon groups not interacting are thus of crucial importance. With all the shadow casting polygons linked in a secondary data structure, we can now project the edges of these polygons onto polygons intersecting the scan-line. A pixel's color value is modified wherever the scan-line traverses one of these shadow edges. Hence, the light source (at the center of projection) and shadow polygon cast a shadow onto the polygon intersected by the scan-line. The following cases denote whether a given pixel is in shadow or not:

1 The scan-line algorithm continues normally if no shadow casting polygon for the given pixel exists.

2 Decrease the brightness of the scan-line segment's pixels if a shadow casting polygon fully overlaps the intersected polygon.

3 If a shadow casting polygon partially overlaps the intersected polygon, subdivide the intersecting scan-line segment recursively until condition 1 or 2 is reached.

Scan-line polygon projection only allows for the generation of hard-edged shadows via point light sources. Figure 11-5 illustrates the above-described process.

11.1.3 Shadow Mapping

Lance Williams introduced the concept of shadow mapping in 1978. His primary aim was the rendering of shadows on curved surfaces. *Shadow mapping* adds shadows to a scene by testing whether a particular pixel is hidden from a light source. It does this by first constructing a separate shadow

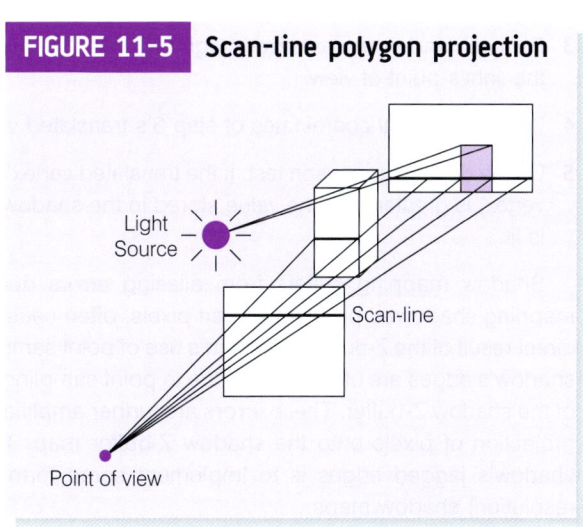

FIGURE 11-5 **Scan-line polygon projection**

Light Source

Scan-line

Point of view

Z-buffer for every light source and then storing the depth information of a scene in this buffer with the light source as view point. This depth information leads to a *depth image* or *shadow map* consisting of all the polygons not hidden from the light source. Hidden pixels are discovered through a comparison with this depth image. The shadow map partitions a light's view volume into shadowed and non-shadowed regions and we store this depth buffer image (shadow map) as a texture in the 3D accelerator's texture unit. This texture is subsequently projected onto an area and/or object(s) for the shadow effect.

Although the shadow map is now stored in the display adaptor's texture memory, it must still be updated every time changes are made to the scene's light sources, geometry or object positions. However, no updating of the shadow map is required when altering the camera's point of view. We will typically partition the scene when implementing shadow maps, thus limiting the time it takes to update the depth image.

The final step of the algorithm is to render the scene via a Z-buffer algorithm. More specifically, if a pixel is not hidden from the light source then the related vertex is translated from the view point's screen space to light space (screen space with the light at the center of projection). After all the vertices of an object have been translated, we have the object's spatial location from the light source's point of view.

The *x*- and *y*-coordinates of a translated vertex are used to index the shadow Z-buffer. Its *z*-component is used during the depth comparison test. This test simply compares a vertex's depth value to the corresponding value stored in the shadow map, determining whether the specific vertex will be shadowed or not. More explicitly, the vertex is in shadow if its depth value is greater than the value stored in the shadow map. For all other cases we can say that the vertex is closer to the light source than another arbitrary shadow casting surface and will thus be rendered without a shadow. Figure 11-6 shows a 3D object and its resulting shadow map.

Shadow mapping can be implemented as either a single- or a multi-pass algorithm. That is, if a fragment shader is used to render shadows by performing the depth comparison test, then we will not require additional passes to produce the shadow maps. However, if we do not make use of programmable shaders (such as NVIDIA's Cg or DirectX's High Level Shader Language) then we won't have access to predefined lighting models (lit or shadowed) and will consequently have to implement an additional shadow map generation pass for each light source. In more complete terms, we can outline the dual-pass shadow mapping process as follows:

1 Create the shadow map by rendering the Z-buffer with regard to the light's point of view.

2 Draw the scene from the viewer's point of view.

3 For each and every rasterized fragment, calculate the fragment's coordinate position with regard to the light's point of view.

4 Use the *x*- and *y*-coordinates of step 3's translated vertex to index the shadow Z-buffer.

5 Do the depth comparison test. If the translated vertex's depth value (the z-value of step 3's translated vertex) is greater than the value stored in the shadow Z-buffer, then the fragment is shadowed, or it is lit.

Shadow mapping suffers from aliasing errors due to the use of a projection transformation mapping shadowed pixels to screen pixels, often causing changes in a pixel's screen size. This is a direct result of the Z-buffer algorithm's use of point sampling, as discussed in Chapter 6. The rendered shadow's edges are often jagged due to point sampling errors occurring during the calculation phase of the shadow Z-buffer. These errors are further amplified when accessing the shadow Z-buffer for the projection of pixels onto the shadow Z-buffer map. The only way of minimizing the visibility of a shadow's jagged edges is to implement some form of pre-filtering and to use very large (high resolution) shadow maps.

FIGURE 11-6 (a) Object as seen from the light's point of view (b) Object's depth map from the light's point of view (c) Shadow polygon rendered via the horizontal projection of the depth map

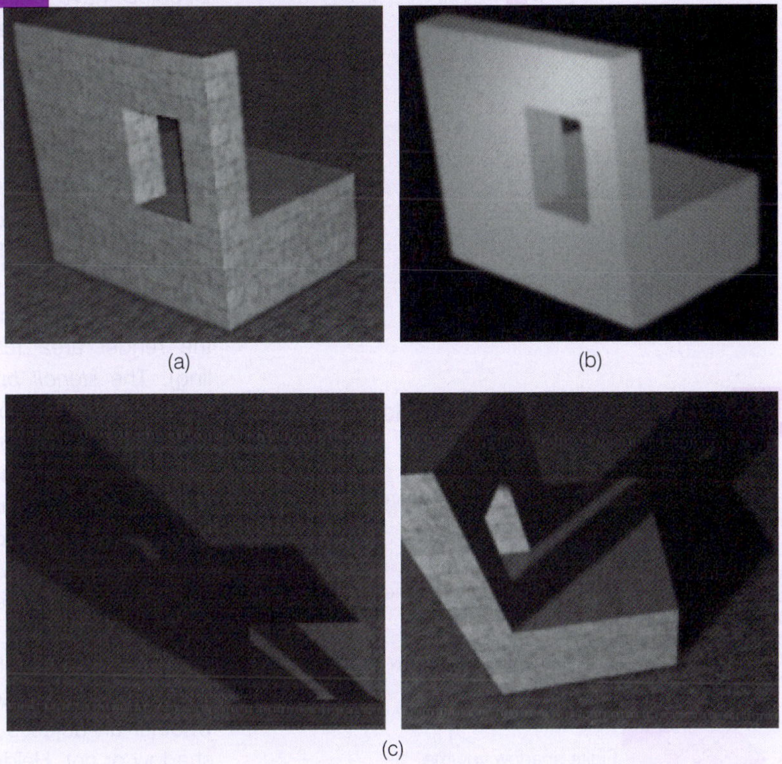

(a)

(b)

(c)

11.1.4 Shadow Volumes

A *shadow volume* is a volumetric area defined by light rays extending outwards about the silhouette edge of an object. All the objects positioned within a shadow volume are hidden from the light source and are thus in either full or partial shadow. The contour of an object's surface is defined as a *silhouette edge* when the normal vector of the surface is perpendicular to the view vector. A silhouette edge can more generally be considered as an outline or edge separating a front- and back-facing surface. The shape of the shadow volume is determined by the shape of the object's silhouette edge and a shadow volume is made up of so-called 'invisible' shadow polygons. We refer to these shadow polygons as 'invisible' since they are never rendered and only used to determine the shadowed areas. Shadow volumes are theoretically infinite volumes produced by polygons; however, for practical usability we intersect an infinite shadow volume with the view volume to produce a finite front- and back-capped shadow volume. Figure 11-7 shows the silhouette edge of a cube with Figure 11-8 illustrating the capping of a semi-infinite shadow volume.

The original shadow volume concept was introduced by Frank Crow in 1977. Crow defined a shadow volume as three-dimensional area occluding objects and surfaces from a light source. This original approach has since been extended to incorporate the generation of soft-edged shadows, including revision of the algorithm to utilize modern-day 3D acceleration capabilities. The advent of dedicated 3D

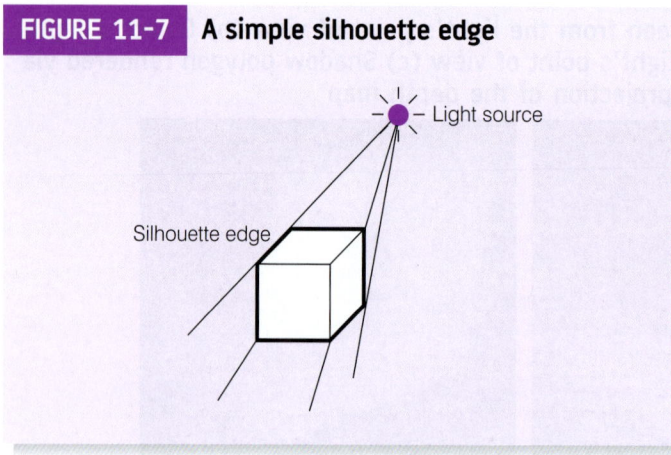

FIGURE 11-7   A simple silhouette edge

Light source

Silhouette edge

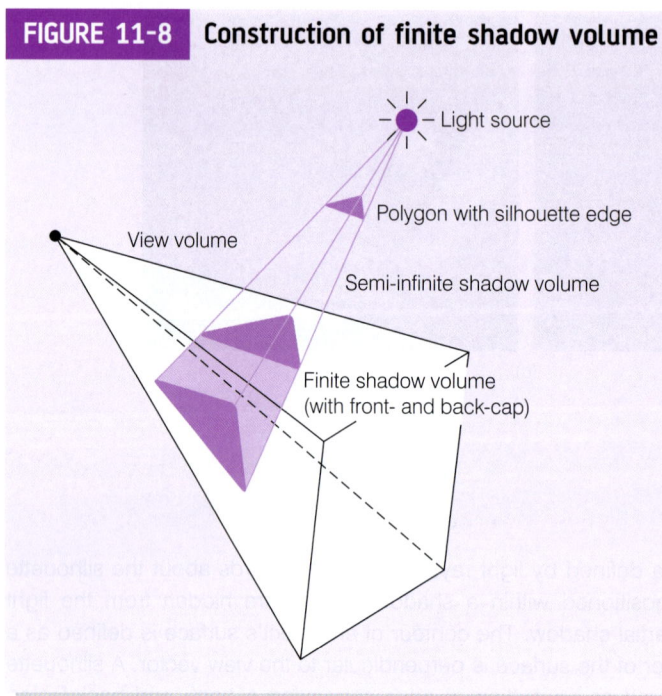

FIGURE 11-8   Construction of finite shadow volume

Light source

Polygon with silhouette edge

View volume

Semi-infinite shadow volume

Finite shadow volume
(with front- and back-cap)

acceleration hardware and the direct control of this hardware via APIs such as OpenGL and Direct3D have significantly contributed to the use of shadow volumes in modern computer games such as id Software's *Doom 3* and Bioware's *Neverwinter Nights*. The first feasible real-time shadow volume algorithm was introduced by Tim Heidmann in 1991. His algorithm made use of the 3D accelerator's stencil buffer – effectively limiting the render area (called stencilling). The *stencil buffer* controls rendering by enabling or disabling drawing to a specific pixel. Heidmann discovered that the stencil buffer could be used to count the number of front- and back-facing shadows in front of an object if we rendered the shadow surfaces in two passes. By counting these shadow surfaces we are able to determine whether an object's surface is in shadow or not. Heidmann's technique became known as the *depth-pass* stencil mask generation algorithm.

The general Heidmann stencil shadow volume process is summarized by the following phases:

1   Assume the scene is entirely shadowed.

2   Render the shadowed scene.

3   Calculate the shadowed scene's depth information.

4   Use this depth information to define a mask via the stencil buffer to indicate the lit areas.

5   Assume the scene is entirely lit.

6   Render the lit scene, applying the stencil buffer mask to cast the shadows.

There are two variations to the depth-pass technique, namely, depth-fail and exclusive-or. All shadow volume algorithms follow the above described shadow generation process and differ only in their approach of calculating the stencil mask. The depth-pass and depth-fail stencil shadow volume algorithms are described in detail below.

11.1.4.1 Depth-pass Shadow volume algorithms operate on a per-pixel basis, performing a shadow test for every pixel in the frame buffer. As discussed in Chapter 4, we refer to all the data needed for the rendering of a pixel (stored in the frame buffer) as a fragment. Our algorithms will thus focus on all rasterized fragments to determine whether a specific fragment is in shadow or not. In more complete terms, we can write the above-outlined stencil shadow volume process as follows:

1 For each rasterized fragment, render the fragment using ambient lighting, updating the Z-buffer after each fragment has been rendered.

2 Now we have to compute which fragments are in shadow. We once again look at each rasterized fragment, rendering the fragment as lit if not shadowed.

We can use the depth-pass method to test whether a fragment is in shadow or not. This method computes the fragments in shadow by generating a stencil mask. Using the stencil buffer, we count the number of front- and back-facing shadows in front of an object by rendering the front- and back-faces of the shadow surfaces in two passes. By counting these shadow surfaces we are able to determine whether an object's surface is in shadow or not. If there are more front-facing shadow surfaces than back-facing ones, then we can conclude that a shadow is projected onto an object. The following process is used to compute the number of fragments in shadow:

1 For each rasterized fragment, render the fragment using ambient lighting, updating the Z-buffer after each fragment has been rendered.

2 Determine the silhouette edges of a shadow casting object. Following this the shadow volume polygons (shadow surfaces) are calculated (from the light source using the silhouette edges of the shadow casting object). These two steps are performed for each shadow casting object.

3 Now deal with the front- and back-facing shadow surfaces with regard to the point of view, *incrementing* the stencil buffer value for each front facing shadow surface if the depth-test *passes* (depth-pass using the Z-buffer) – counting the shadows in front of the object. Following the test for front-facing shadow surfaces, we focus on each back-facing shadow surface with regard to the view point – *decrementing* the stencil buffer value if the depth-test for a specific shadow surface *passes*.

Following the above process, we simply have to check the stencil buffer value for each fragment to identify the fragments in shadow. If a fragment's stencil buffer value is greater than zero then we need not draw this fragment during the second rendering pass – hence causing the fragment to be in shadow. Figure 11-9 illustrates the above described process.

The described depth-pass process is extremely efficient; however, certain issues become apparent upon implementation. The most common problem occurs whenever the point of view (camera or viewer) is positioned within a shadow volume. This leads to visibility of the shadow's back-face. The depth-test will pass in this case, causing the stencil buffer value to be decremented, thus becoming -1 due to a back-face being visible prior to any front-facing shadow surfaces. This problem is referred to as *stencil counting inversion* and it can be resolved by capping the front of the shadow volume. Alternatively we can initialize the stencil buffer to 2^{K-1}, with K the precision of the stencil buffer. These approaches are, however, less than efficient and the depth-fail technique is generally implemented as an alternative.

11.1.4.2 Depth-fail The depth-pass approach computes the stencil buffer values by incrementing for front- and decrementing for back-facing shadow surfaces. The depth-fail approach modifies this calculation process (originally counting from the point of view) by counting from infinity. So, by reversing the depth and counting the shadow surfaces behind an object instead of those in front of it, we no longer face the *stencil counting inversion* issue. The only general issue with this approach is that we

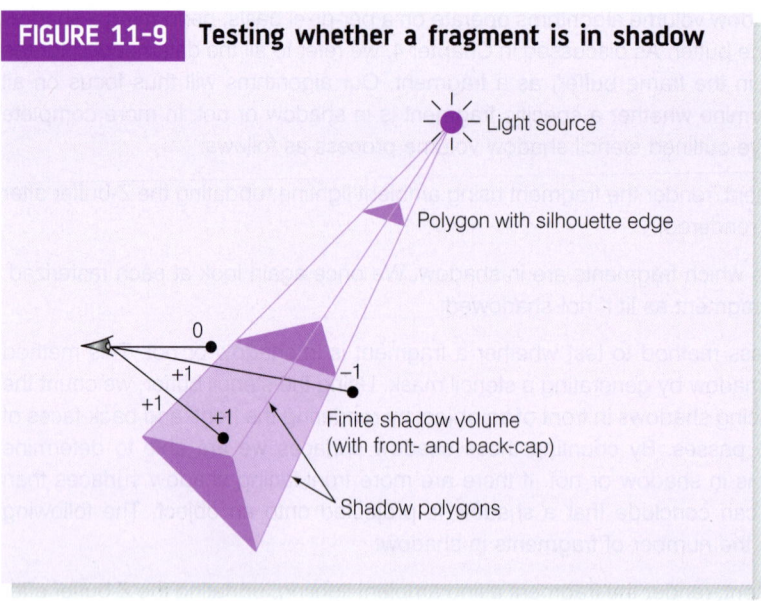

FIGURE 11-9   **Testing whether a fragment is in shadow**

Light source

Polygon with silhouette edge

0

+1

+1   +1   −1

Finite shadow volume
(with front- and back-cap)

Shadow polygons

must cap the end of the shadow volume to avoid the condition where shadows point to infinity. The following process is used to compute the number of fragments in shadow:

1 For each rasterized fragment, render the fragments using ambient lighting, updating the Z-buffer after each fragment has been rendered.

2 Determine the silhouette edges of a shadow casting object. Following this the shadow volume polygons (shadow surfaces) are calculated (from the light source using the silhouette edges of the shadow casting object). These two steps are performed for each shadow casting object.

3 Now deal with the front- and back-facing shadow surfaces with regard to the point of view, *decrementing* the stencil buffer value for each front-facing shadow surface if the depth-test *fails* (depth-fail using the Z-buffer). Following the test for front-facing shadow surfaces, we focus on each back-facing shadow surface with regard to the view point – *incrementing* the stencil buffer value if the depth-test for a specific shadow surface *fails*.

Although the depth-fail method effectively avoids the stencil counting inversion issue it still requires the additional back-capping of shadow volumes. This results in some extra rasterization time which can lead to considerable performance slowdowns under certain conditions. It is thus in some cases more advantageous to use the depth-pass method while explicitly dealing with the cases where the point of view is located within a shadow volume. It is also often possible to increase the performance of a stencil shadow volume implementation by utilizing some hardware extension such as NVIDIA's *depth bounds test* that enables the culling of shadow volume sections not affecting the visible area.

11.1.4.3 Soft-edged Shadows using Penumbra Wedges
Implementation of the above discussed shadow volume techniques always results in pixel-accurate hard-edged shadows. Soft-edged shadows can be simulated through the construction of several shadow volumes by translating the original light source to various positions close to that of the original. Following this we simply have to combine the resulting shadows. The problem with this approach is rendering performance due to shadow volume construction taking up a substantial amount of processor time. One solution is the calculation of *penumbra wedges* as proposed by Tomas Akenine-Möller and Ulf Assarsson. A so-called penumbra

wedge is defined in place of a shadow polygon for each silhouette edge of an object – combining a series of these penumbra wedges results in the creation of a soft-edged shadow.

The penumbra wedge algorithm calculates the amount of light that reaches a certain point p. This amount of light intensity ranges from '0' to '1'. When the light intensity is '0' we can define the point p as fully shadowed or conversely as fully lit with a light intensity of '1'. For all other values we can define point p located within the penumbra region. The light intensity inside the penumbra region is calculated using a signed 16-bit buffer. This light intensity buffer is simply a high precision stencil buffer. The lower the number of bits used for the buffer, the higher the implementation's performance and the lower the number of shades in the penumbra region. The varying shade levels in the penumbra region are created by multiplying each light intensity value stored in this buffer with some value s. This value is normally chosen as '255' since color buffers allow for 8-bits per component, leading to at least '256' on-screen penumbra wedges. The following process is used for calculation of the penumbra wedges (illustrated in Figure 11-10):

1 Initialize the light intensity buffer to '255' – indicating that the viewer is now positioned outside of the shadow volume.

2 Draw the scene using both specular and diffuse lighting.

3 Draw the penumbra wedges using the following algorithm:
   a For some light ray, compute the entry and exit points on the outside penumbra wedge. This must be done for each and every visible fragment. The entry point is defined by an x- and y-coordinate, with the corresponding z-value stored in the Z-buffer.
   b Transform this point to world space coordinates.
   c Test whether the point is located within the penumbra region.
      i If the point is located within the penumbra region, compute the light intensity of this point and the entry point, scaling the light intensity by subtracting the computed light intensity of the point located within the wedge from the entry point and multiplying this result by '255'.
      ii Add the above calculated light intensity to the light intensity buffer.

4 Add ambient lighting to the rendered scene.

11

FIGURE 11-10 **Locating a point within the penumbra region**

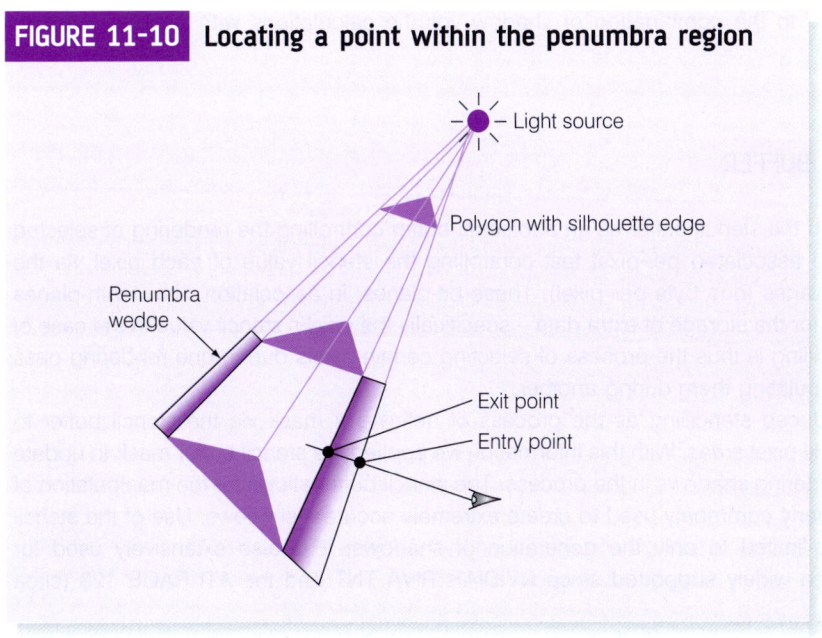

- Light source
- Polygon with silhouette edge
- Penumbra wedge
- Exit point
- Entry point

The possibility of overlapping penumbra wedges exists in situations where the volume is entered more than once. Such cases result in negative light intensity values, thus requiring the clamping of the values stored in the light intensity buffer to the range [0, 255]. It is also possible to leave the volume more than once whenever the viewer is located within the volume. By setting the maximum possible light intensity value to '255', we effectively avoid higher light intensities than that of the areas outside the volume – which clearly isn't possible.

Akenine-Möller and Assarsson's penumbra wedges algorithm can be implemented using either OpenGL or Direct3D. The main problem is the large vertex and pixel shader programs required, making true real-time performance only achievable on extremely high-end hardware. The following steps outline a hardware-accelerated implementation of the penumbra wedge algorithm:

1 Render the scene using either OpenGL or Direct3D.

2 Implement the wedge rasterization, initializing the Z-buffer prior to rasterization.

3 Rasterize the front-facing triangles of the penumbra wedges – the entry point's plane is now identified.

4 Identify the exit point by calculating the ray's intersection with the back facing planes and picking the one closest to the ray.

5 Specify the point in world space coordinates via a transformation based on the Z-value.

6 Determine whether this point falls within a penumbra wedge or not by substituting the point's coordinates into the plane equations:
   a If the point falls within a wedge, calculate the intersection distances from the point to the planes.

Brotman and Badler developed a similar algorithm for the generation of soft-edged shadows (adding penumbras to hard-edged shadows). They proposed the use of an enhanced Z-buffer algorithm, thus retaining the benefits inherent to the Z-buffer rendering approach. They extended the Z-buffer to represent a pixel location as a record of five fields. During the shadow polygon rendering phase, these pixel records are modified based on whether a point is lit or not. The penumbras are created by representing a distributed light source as a series of point light sources. This approach is processor intensive due to the combination of shadow volume calculations with Z-buffer memory access costs.

11.2 THE STENCIL BUFFER

We have already defined the stencil buffer as an additional buffer controlling the rendering of selected pixels. *Stencilling* is the associated per-pixel test controlling the stencil value of each pixel via the addition of several bit-planes (one byte per pixel). These bit-planes, in association with depth-planes and color-planes, allow for the storage of extra data – specifically the pixel's stencil value in the case of the stencil buffer. Stencilling is thus the process of selecting certain pixels during one rendering pass and subsequently manipulating them during another.

Section 11.1.4 introduced stencilling as the process of defining a mask via the stencil buffer to indicate shadowed and lit pixel areas. With this information we applied the stencil buffer mask to update all the lit pixels, thus rendering shadows in the process. The stencil buffer allows for the manipulation of individual pixels, a property commonly used to create extremely accurate shadows. Use of the stencil buffer is, however, not limited to only the generation of shadows; it is also extensively used for reflections and has been widely supported since NVIDIA's RIVA TNT and the ATI RAGE 128 (circa 1998).

It is important to note the close relation between the stencil buffer and depth buffer. Firstly, these two buffers are located in physical proximity to each other (both commonly share the same physical area in the graphics hardware's memory). Secondly, the depth buffer is required to control whether a certain pixel's stencil value is increased or decreased based on the result of a depth test (pass/fail). The stencil buffer stores a stencil value for each pixel, similarly to the depth buffer storing the depth value of every pixel – both the stencil buffer and depth buffer values are required for rejecting or accepting rasterized fragments.

11.2.1 Enabling Depth Stencil Testing

Before initializing the stencil buffer it is important to set the format of the depth stencil to DXGI_FORMAT_D24_UNORM_S8_UINT (previously D3DFMT_S8D24 in DirectX 9). This DirectX Graphics Infra-structure (DXGI) component is responsible for defining the memory layout of each pixel making up an image. DXGI_FORMAT_D24_UNORM_S8_UINT is simply a DXGI enumeration type required by the DXUTDevice-Settings DXUT structure. As previously discussed, DXUT simplifies the creation of a Direct3D device, the specification of windows and the handling of Windows messages. We set the AutoDepthStencilFormat member of the DXUTDeviceSettings structure as follows:

```
DXUTDeviceSettings* pDXUTDeviceSettings;

pDXUTDeviceSettings-> d3d10.AutoDepthStencilFormat =
                        DXGI_FORMAT_D24_UNORM_S8_UINT;
```

It is customary to clear the stencil buffer at the start of the rendering process. This is accomplished via the ClearDepthStencilView ID3D10Device (pID3D10Device) interface. ClearDepthStencilView clears the depth stencil using four parameters. Its first parameter is a pointer to the depth stencil we wish to clear, the second is a clear flag indicating the parts of the buffer to clear (D3D10_CLEAR_STENCIL for the stencil buffer and D3D10_CLEAR_DEPTH for the depth buffer), the third is the value we are clearing the depth buffer with (any value between '0' and '1') with the fourth parameter the value to clear the stencil buffer with. To initialize the first parameter (the depth stencil to be cleared), we simply call the DXUTGetD3D10DepthStencilView interface, resulting in a pointer to the ID3D10DepthStencilView interface for the current Direct3D 10 device:

```
ID3D10DepthStencilView* pDepthStencilView =
                        DXUTGetD3D10DepthStencilView();

pID3D10Device->ClearDepthStencilView(pDepthStencilView,
                        D3D10_CLEAR_STENCIL,
                        1.0, 0);
```

In addition to clearing the stencil buffer, we also have to clear the depth buffer. The exact same process is used with ClearDepthStencilView's second parameter being set to D3D10_CLEAR_DEPTH:

```
pID3D10Device->ClearDepthStencilView(pDepthStencilView,
                        D3D10_CLEAR_DEPTH,
                        1.0, 0);
```

The depth test's result is also needed in addition to that of the stencil test. As previously mentioned, the depth test result is required for controlling whether a certain pixel's stencil value is increased or decreased. If the depth test passes then the tested pixel's depth value is overwritten by that of the incoming fragment. Both the depth test and stencil test results are combined for certain effects. The stencil test can simply fail, requiring no additional information, however, when the stencil test passes then the depth test can either fail or pass.

We can enable or disable both depth testing and stencil testing via the first (DepthEnable) and fourth (StencilEnable) parameters of Direct3D 10's D3D10_DEPTH_STENCIL_DESC structure. Furthermore, this structure allows us to specify the depth write mask controlling the area of the depth stencil buffer that can be modified by depth data (DepthWriteMask), the depth function for comparing depth data against current depth data (DepthFunc), the stencil read mask specifying the area of the depth stencil buffer for the reading of stencil data (StencilReadMask), the stencil write mask identifying the writeable depth stencil buffer area (StencilWriteMask) and the stencil operations for both front-facing (FrontFace) and back-facing pixels (BackFace). These stencil testing operations (defined using the D3D10_DEPTH_STENCILOP_DESC structure) include the states when stencil testing fails; stencil testing passes and depth testing fails; or both stencil testing and depth testing passes.

The D3D10_DEPTH_STENCIL_DESC and D3D10_DEPTH_STENCILOP_DESC structures are defined as follows in the d3d10.h header file:

```
typedef struct D3D10_DEPTH_STENCIL_DESC {
    BOOL DepthEnable;
    D3D10_DEPTH_WRITE_MASK DepthWriteMask;
    D3D10_COMPARISON_FUNC DepthFunc;
    BOOL StencilEnable;
    UINT8 StencilReadMask;
    UINT8 StencilWriteMask;
    D3D10_DEPTH_STENCILOP_DESC FrontFace;
    D3D10_DEPTH_STENCILOP_DESC BackFace;
} D3D10_DEPTH_STENCIL_DESC;

typedef struct D3D10_DEPTH_STENCILOP_DESC {
    D3D10_STENCIL_OP StencilFailOp;
    D3D10_STENCIL_OP StencilDepthFailOp;
    D3D10_STENCIL_OP StencilPassOp;
    D3D10_COMPARISON_FUNC StencilFunc;
} D3D10_DEPTH_STENCILOP_DESC;
```

The default values, including the alternatives, for the members of the D3D10_DEPTH_STENCIL_DESC structure are given in Table 11–1.

Table 11-2 lists the D3D10_DEPTH_STENCILOP_DESC structure's possible stencil operations. These operations can be specified depending on the outcome of the stencil test. The D3D10_DEPTH_STENCILOP_DESC structure is a member of depth stencil description which is specified using the D3D10_DEPTH_STENCIL_DESC structure.

A depth stencil state (depthstencilDesc), specifying the details of the depth and stencil testing operations, is defined by first initializing the depth testing members, namely, DepthEnable, DepthWriteMask and DepthFunc:

```
D3D10_DEPTH_STENCIL_DESC depthstencilDesc;

depthstencilDesc.DepthEnable = true;
depthstencilDesc.DepthWriteMask = D3D10_DEPTH_WRITE_MASK_ALL;
depthstencilDesc.DepthFunc = D3D10_COMPARISON_LESS;
```

11

TABLE 11-1	Default and alternative depth stencil states
Depth stencil state	***Default*** **Alternative**
DepthEnable	TRUE FALSE
DepthWriteMask	*D3D10_DEPTH_WRITE_MASK_ALL* (enables writing to the depth stencil buffer) D3D10_DEPTH_WRITE_MASK_ZERO (disables writing to the depth stencil buffer)
DepthFunc	*D3D10_COMPARISON_LESS* (the test passes if the new data $<$ existing data) D3D10_COMPARISON_NEVER (no depth test is performed) D3D10_COMPARISON_EQUAL (the depth test passes if the new data $==$ existing data) D3D10_COMPARISON_LESS_EQUAL (the depth test passes if new data $<=$ existing data) D3D10_COMPARISON_GREATER (the depth test passes if new data $>$ existing data) D3D10_COMPARISON_NOT_EQUAL (the depth test passes if new data $!=$ existing data) D3D10_COMPARISON_GREATER_EQUAL (the depth test passes if new data $>=$ existing data) D3D10_COMPARISON_ALWAYS (the depth test is always performed and always passes)
StencilEnable	FALSE TRUE
StencilReadMask	*D3D10_DEFAULT_STENCIL_READ_MASK*
StencilWriteMask	*D3D10_DEFAULT_STENCIL_WRITE_MASK*

TABLE 11-2	Possible stencil operations
Stencil operation	**Description**
D3D10_STENCIL_OP_KEEP	Do not modify the existing stencil buffer data.
D3D10_STENCIL_OP_ZERO	Reset the stencil buffer data to zero.
D3D10_STENCIL_OP_REPLACE	Set the stencil buffer data to a reference value.
D3D10_STENCIL_OP_INCR_SAT	Increment the stored stencil buffer value by 1 (won't exceed the maximum clamped value).
D3D10_STENCIL_OP_DECR_SAT	Decrement the stored stencil buffer value by 1 (won't decrease below 0).
D3D10_STENCIL_OP_INVERT	Do a bitwise invert of the sorted stencil buffer data.
D3D10_STENCIL_OP_INCR	Increment the stored stencil buffer value by 1 (wrapping the result if required).
D3D10_STENCIL_OP_DECR	Decrement the stored stencil buffer value by 1 (wrapping the result if required).

11

Following the above initialization, the members required by the stencil test (StencilEnable, StencilReadMask and StencilWriteMask) must be initialized:

```
depthstencilDesc.StencilEnable = true;
depthstencilDesc.StencilReadMask = 0xFFFFFFFF;
depthstencilDesc.StencilWriteMask = 0xFFFFFFFF;
```

Next we have to setup the stencil operations for both back-facing and front-facing pixels via the D3D10_DEPTH_STENCILOP_DESC structure's members. For example, if StencilFailOp is set to D3D10_STENCIL_OP_KEEP and the stencil test fails then the current stencil buffer value is saved. Similarly, if StencilDepthFailOp is set to D3D10_STENCIL_OP_DECR with a failing stencil test, then the stencil buffer value is decremented by 1. Alternatively, the passing functions such as StencilPassOp only perform a stencil buffer operation on a passing stencil test and can have a different result depending on whether a pixel is back-facing or front-facing:

```
depthstencilDesc.BackFace.StencilFailOp = D3D10_STENCIL_OP_KEEP;
depthstencilDesc.BackFace.StencilDepthFailOp = D3D10_STENCIL_OP_DECR;
depthstencilDesc.BackFace.StencilPassOp = D3D10_STENCIL_OP_KEEP;
depthstencilDesc.BackFace.StencilFunc = D3D10_COMPARISON_ALWAYS;

depthstencilDesc.FrontFace.StencilFailOp = D3D10_STENCIL_OP_KEEP;
depthstencilDesc.FrontFace.StencilDepthFailOp = D3D10_STENCIL_OP_INCR;
depthstencilDesc.FrontFace.StencilPassOp = D3D10_STENCIL_OP_KEEP;
depthstencilDesc.FrontFace.StencilFunc = D3D10_COMPARISON_ALWAYS;
```

Now we simply have to set the depth stencil state to encapsulate all the above defined information for the pipeline stage determining the visible pixels. We do this using the CreateDepthStencilState ID3D10Device interface. This interface takes two parameters, the first a pointer to the depth stencil state description (D3D10_DEPTH_STENCIL_DESC) structure and the second, the address of the depth stencil state object (ID3D10DepthStencilState):

```
ID3D10Device * pID3D10Device;
ID3D10DepthStencilState * pDepthStencilState;

pID3D10Device->CreateDepthStencilState (depthstencilDesc,
                                        &pDepthStencilState);
```

With the depth stencil state set, we still have to create a depth stencil buffer resource. This can be accomplished using a texture resource. During Chapter 8 we described texture resources as structured collections of data – specifically texture data. We also discussed how these structured data collections, as opposed to buffers, allow for the filtering of textures via texture samplers; with the exact filtering method determined by the texture resource type. Specifically, to create a depth stencil buffer we require a texture resource (defined using the ID3D10Texture2D interface) consisting of a two-dimensional grid of texture elements (specified via the D3D10_TEXTURE2D_DESC structure describing a two-dimensional texture resource):

```
ID3D10Texture2D* pDepthStencilBuffer = NULL;
D3D10_TEXTURE2D_DESC depthResource;
```

The members of the texture resource (D3D10_TEXTURE2D_DESC) are initialized as follows, with the BindFlags member set to the D3D10_BIND_DEPTH_STENCIL enumeration to identify the texture resource as a depth stencil buffer (refer to Chapter 8 for a description of the D3D10_TEXTURE2D_DESC structure and each of its members):

```
depthResource.Width = backBufferSurfaceDescription.Width;
depthResource.Height = backBufferSurfaceDescription.Height;
depthResource.MipLevels = 1;
depthResource.ArraySize = 1;
depthResource.Format = pDeviceSettings -> d3d10.AutoDepthStencilFormat;
depthResource.SampleDesc.Count = 1;
depthResource.SampleDesc.Quality = 0;
depthResource.Usage = D3D10_USAGE_DEFAULT;
depthResource.BindFlags = D3D10_BIND_DEPTH_STENCIL;
depthResource.CPUAccessFlags = 0;
depthResource.MiscFlags = 0;
```

The ID3D10Device method, CreateTexture2D, is used to create a two-dimensional array – the depth stencil buffer. This method takes three parameters with the first parameter a pointer to the above defined two-dimensional texture resource structure (D3D10_TEXTURE2D_DESC), the second a pointer to a texture subresource ('NULL' in our case) and the third the address of a pointer to the specified texture (pDepthStencilBuffer):

```
pID3D10Device->CreateTexture2D(&depthResource, NULL,
                    &pDepthStencilBuffer);
```

The final step in configuring depth and stencil functionality is to bind the previously defined depth and stencil data to the output-merger stage. The *output-merger* stage is the final pipeline step dealing with pixel visibility. This step controls pixel visibility by incorporating pixel shader data with depth and stencil testing results. We start by binding the depth stencil state, pDepthStencilState, to the output-merger stage using the OMSetDepthStencilState method. This method takes two parameters with the first being a pointer to the depth stencil state interface (pDepthStencilState). This depth stencil state interface was previously created using the CreateDepthStencilState ID3D10Device interface. The second parameter, an unsigned integer, is the reference value we are doing the depth stencil test against:

```
pID3D10Device->OMSetDepthStencilState(pDepthStencilBuffer, 1);
```

Next the view mechanism is used to describe how the depth stencil resource will be handled (viewed) by the pipeline. In this case we use a depth stencil view, thus defining the resource as a depth stencil. The D3D10_DEPTH_STENCIL_VIEW_DESC structure, given here, is used for this purpose and is contained within the d3d10.h header file:

```
typedef struct D3D10_DEPTH_STENCIL_VIEW_DESC {
    DXGI_FORMAT Format;
    D3D10_DSV_DIMENSION ViewDimension;
    union
    {
        D3D10_TEX1D_DSV Texture1D;
        D3D10_TEX1D_ARRAY_DSV Texture1DArray;
```

11

```
        D3D10_TEX2D_DSV Texture2D;
        D3D10_TEX2D_ARRAY_DSV Texture2DArray;
        D3D10_TEX2DMS_DSV Texture2DMS;
        D3D10_TEX2DMS_ARRAY_DSV Texture2DMSArray;
    };
} D3D10_DEPTH_STENCIL_VIEW_DESC;
```

The first member, Format, controls the data resource interpretation and it can range from a typeless, unsigned-integer or signed-integer to floating-point format. The given code example uses the DXGI_FORMAT_D32_FLOAT format (a 32-bit floating-point format). The second member, ViewDimension, is used to determine the depth stencil access method. This member is set to the D3D10_DSV_DIMENSION_TEXTURE2D constant, indicating the depth stencil resources access type as a two-dimensional texture (due to the depth stencil resource being defined as a two-dimensional texture resource). Alternative constants include:

■ D3D10_DSV_DIMENSION_TEXTURE1D (for a one-dimensional depth stencil resource)

■ D3D10_DSV_DIMENSION_TEXTURE1DARRAY (for accessing the depth stencil resource as an array consisting of one-dimensional textures)

■ D3D10_DSV_DIMENSION_TEXTURE2DARRAY (for accessing the depth stencil resources as an array consisting of two-dimensional textures)

■ D3D10_DSV_DIMENSION_TEXTURE2DMS (for a two-dimensional depth stencil resource with multisampling support)

■ D3D10_DSV_DIMENSION_TEXTURE2DMSARRAY (for accessing the depth stencil resources as an array consisting of two-dimensional textures with multisampling support) and

■ D3D10_DSV_DIMENSION_UNKNOWN (for depth stencil resources where the access method is to be determined dynamically during depth stencil view creation).

Only one member contained within the union is to be initialized. Texture1D is initialized by setting the D3D10_TEX1D_DSV structure's MipSlice member to an integer value when a one-dimensional texture is required as a depth stencil view ('0' indicates the first mipmap level in the depth stencil view). Texture1DArray specifies the texture and related mipmap level when a one-dimensional texture array is required as a depth stencil view. This member is of the type D3D10_TEX1D_ARRAY_DSV and requires the initialization of three members, namely, MipSlice (the depth stencil view's mipmap level, with '0' indicating the first mipmap level in the depth stencil view), FirstArraySlice (the texture, stored in the array, to use in the depth stencil view) and ArraySize (the number of textures, stored in the array, to use in the depth stencil view). Similarly, Texture2D is initialized by setting the D3D10_TEX2D_DSV structure's MipSlice member to an integer value when a two-dimensional texture is required as a depth stencil view ('0' indicates the first mipmap level in the depth stencil view). Texture2DArray specifies the texture and related mipmap level when a two-dimensional texture array is required as a depth stencil view. This member is of the type D3D10_TEX2D_ARRAY_DSV, and just as with Texture1DArray requires the initialization of three members, namely, MipSlice (the depth stencil view's mipmap level, with '0' indicating the first mipmap level in the depth stencil view), FirstArraySlice (the texture, stored in the array, to use in the depth stencil view) and ArraySize (the number of textures, stored in the array, to use in the depth stencil view). The final two members, Texture2DMS and Texture2DMSArray, are initialized when using a multisampled two-dimensional texture and a multisampled two-dimensional texture array as a depth stencil respectively. The

D3D10_TEX2DMS_DSV structure's UnusedField_NothingToDefine member can be initialized to any integer value with the D3D10_TEX2DMS_ARRAY_DSV structure having two members, namely, FirstArraySlice (the texture, stored in the array, to use in the depth stencil view) and ArraySize (the number of textures, stored in the array, to use in the depth stencil view). The following code sample defines the depth stencil resource as a view:

```
D3D10_DEPTH_STENCIL_VIEW_DESC depthstencilviewDescription;

depthstencilviewDescription.Format = DXGI_FORMAT_D32_FLOAT;
depthstencilviewDescription.ResourceType = D3D10_RESOURCE_TEXTURE2D;

depthstencilviewDescription.Texture2D.FirstArraySlice = 0;
depthstencilviewDescription.Texture2D.ArraySize = 1;
depthstencilviewDescription.Texture2D.MipSlice = 0;
```

Following this, we simply have to create and bind the depth stencil view to the output-merger stage using the CreateDepthStencilView and OMSetRenderTargets ID3D10Device interfaces. The CreateDepthStencilView method, creating the depth stencil view, takes three parameters:

1 a pointer to an ID3D10Texture2D object (pDepthStencilBuffer) used for storing the resource data

2 a pointer to the D3D10_DEPTH_STENCIL_VIEW_DESC structure and

3 the address of a pointer to an ID3D10DepthStencilView interface (pDepthStencilView) used for controlling the texture resource utilized during the depth stencil test:

```
ID3D10DepthStencilView* pDepthStencilView;

pID3D10Device->CreateDepthStencilView(
                    pDepthStencilBuffer
                    &depthstencilviewDescription,
                    &pDepthStencilView);
```

The OMSetRenderTargets method binds this depth stencil view to the output-merger stage. It takes three parameters, with the first identifying the number of render targets, the second a pointer to a render target view array, and the third a pointer to the ID3D10DepthStencilView interface. A render target is written to by the output-merger stage, containing the pixel color information:

```
ID3D10RenderTargetView* pRenderTargetView;

pID3D10Device->OMSetRenderTargets(1, &pRenderTargetView,
                    &pDepthStencilView);
```

The OMSetDepthStencilState ID3D10Device interface is used to update the depth stencil state. This update is performed by setting the output-merger stage's depth stencil state. The OMSetDepthStencilState method

11

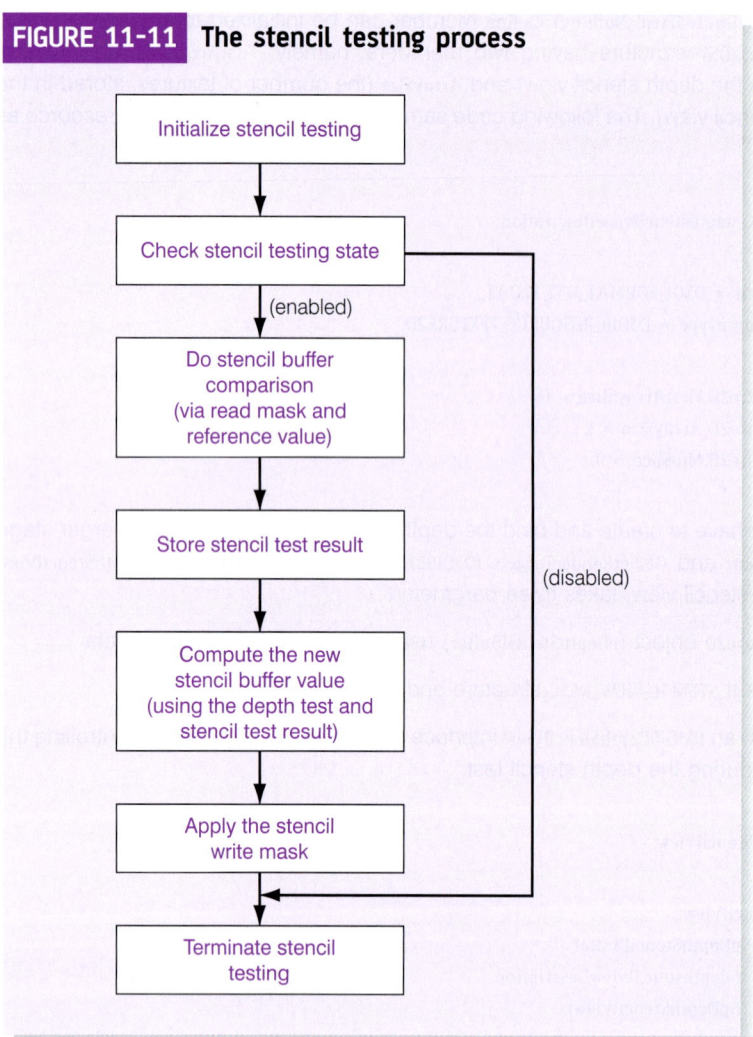

FIGURE 11-11 **The stencil testing process**

takes two parameters with the first parameter a pointer to an `ID3D10DepthStencilState` interface (`pDepthStencilState`) and the second the reference value we are doing the depth stencil test against:

```
pID3D10Device->OMSetDepthStencilState(pDepthStencilState, 0);
```

As an alternative to the above described process, we can initialize the depth and stencil states using the DirectX FX system. The FX system also allows us to view the contents of a stencil buffer, something not possible via the Direct3D 10 API. The final chapter's stencil shadow volume implementation makes use of FX techniques to set the stencil and depth testing states as well as to do the physical stencil rendering. It is, however, important to remember that the depth stencil testing process is always conducted in the same manner, regardless of the implementation details. This complete depth testing process (used to determine the pixels positioned closest to the camera) and stencil testing process (controlling, via a mask, which pixels to update) are outlined in Figure 11-11 and Figure 11-12 respectively.

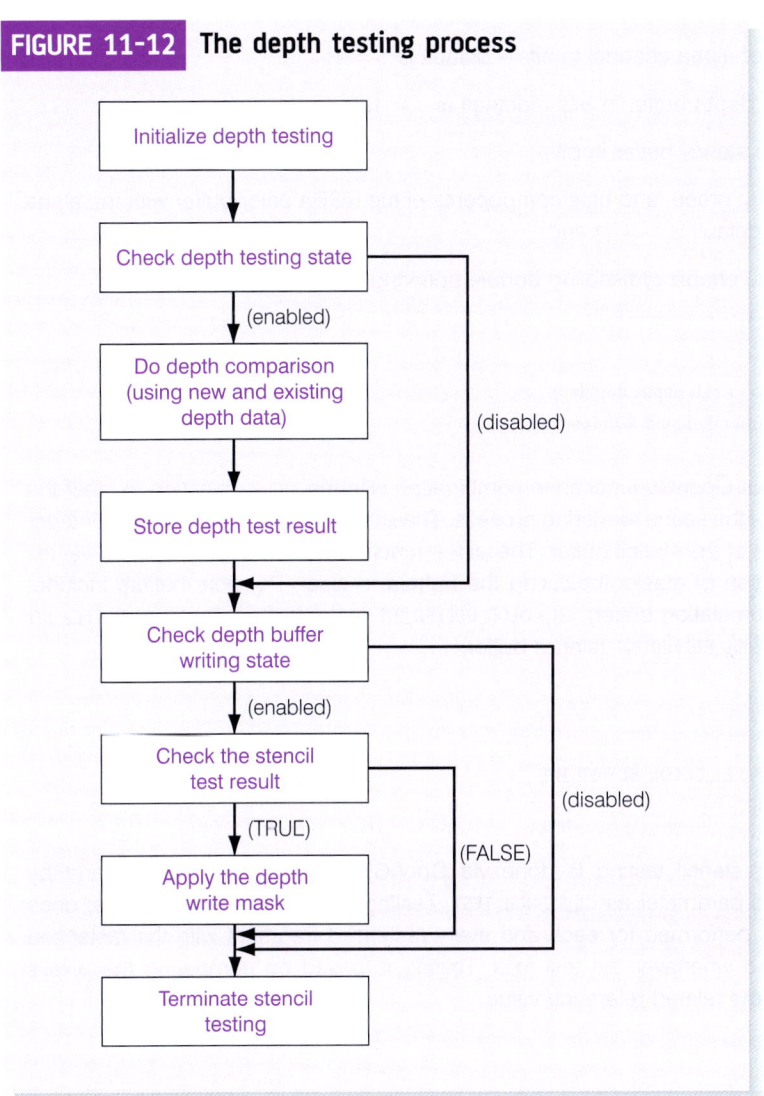

FIGURE 11-12 The depth testing process

Working with OpenGL

The easiest way of enabling stencilling in OpenGL is to use the GLUT functions glutInitDisplayString and glutCreateWindow to create a window supporting stencil buffering. An alternative to these GLUT functions would be to use the ChoosePixelFormat OpenGL function. This function requires two parameters: the device context to the best pixel format matching the specified pixel format and the specified pixel format (cStencilBits) respectively.

The glutInitDisplayString function sets the initial display mode by combining comparators with capability names. Some valid comparators include equal (=), not equal (!=), greater than (>), less than (<), greater than or equal (>=) and less than or equal (<=). The capability descriptions are used for specifying the frame buffer configuration. Examples of commonly used capability descriptors include:

- alpha (color precision of alpha channel in bits – default is $>= 1$)

- depth (precision of the depth buffer in bits – default is $>= 12$)

- stencil (precision of the stencil buffer in bits)

- rgb (precision of the red, green, and blue components of the RGBA color buffer with the alpha component set to 0 - default is $>= 1$) and

- double (a Boolean value enabling/disabling double buffering - default is $==1$).

Usage example:

```
glutInitDisplayString("stencil>=1 rgb depth double");
glutCreateWindow("Stencil Buffer Enabled Window");
```

We use the glClearStencil OpenGL function in combination with the glClear function to clear the stencil buffer at the start of the scene rendering process. The glClearStencil function takes an integer specifying the clear value of the stencil buffer. The glClear function clears buffers to preset values using a logical combination of masks indicating the buffers to clear. Possible buffers include: GL_ACCUM_BUFFER_BIT (accumulation buffer), GL_COLOR_BUFFER_BIT (color buffer), GL_DEPTH_BUFFER_BIT (depth buffer) and GL_STENCIL_BUFFER_BIT (stencil buffer).

Usage example:

```
glClearStencil(0);
glClear(GL_DEPTH_BUFFER_BIT | GL_COLOR_BUFFER_BIT |
        GL_STENCIL_BUFFER_BIT);
```

Enabling or disabling stencil testing is done via OpenGL's glEnable function call and by specifying the associated parameter as GL_STENCIL_TEST. Testing is quite a simple process; once enabled, a stencil test is performed for each and every rasterized fragment with the rasterized fragment being discarded whenever the test fails. Testing is based on comparing the pixel's stencil buffer value to some related reference value.

Usage example:

```
glEnable(GL_STENCIL_TEST);
glDisable(GL_STENCIL_TEST);
```

The glStencilFunc function sets the function and reference values for stencil testing. This method takes three parameters, the first being one of the following test comparison functions:

GL_ALWAYS:	Always passes.
GL_EQUAL:	Passes if (the reference value for the stencil test AND the stencil comparison bit mask) = (the corresponding stencil value stored in the stencil buffer AND the stencil comparison bit mask).
GL_GEQUAL:	Passes if (the reference value for the stencil test AND the stencil comparison bit mask) $>=$ (the corresponding stencil value stored in the stencil buffer AND the stencil comparison bit mask).

GL_GREATER:	Passes if (the reference value for the stencil test AND the stencil comparison bit mask) > (the corresponding stencil value stored in the stencil buffer AND the stencil comparison bit mask).
GL_LEQUAL:	Passes if the (reference value for the stencil test AND the stencil comparison bit mask) <= (the corresponding stencil value stored in the stencil buffer AND the stencil comparison bit mask).
GL_LESS:	Passes if (the reference value for the stencil test AND the stencil comparison bit mask) < (the corresponding stencil value stored in the stencil buffer AND the stencil comparison bit mask).
GL_NEVER:	Always fails.
GL_NOTEQUAL:	Passes if (the reference value for the stencil test AND the stencil comparison bit mask) / (the corresponding stencil value stored in the stencil buffer AND the stencil comparison bit mask).

These stencil test comparison functions control the comparison between the stencil buffer value and associated reference value. The second and third parameters specify the stencil test reference value (originally '0') and the stencil comparison bit mask (with every element initially set to '1') respectively.

Usage example:

```
glStencilFunc(GL_ALWAYS, 1, 1);
```

When dealing with a depth test result (required for increasing or decreasing some pixel's stencil value), we often want to specify some operation based on the result of the depth test and stencil test – stencil fail, stencil pass and depth fail, or stencil pass and depth pass. We make use of the glStencilOp and glStencilMask functions to do this. The glStencilOp function specifies the action to take based on the result of both the stencil test and depth test. It takes three parameters: the first specifying the action when the stencil test fails, the second the action to take when the stencil test passes and the depth test fails, with the final parameter defining the action when both the stencil test and depth test passes. Possible actions include any of the following:

GL_KEEP:	Specifies that the stored stencil buffer value will be used.
GL_ZERO:	Resets the stencil buffer value to zero.
GL_REPLACE:	Replaces the stencil buffer value with the reference value used in the glStencilFunc function.
GL_INCR:	Increments the stored stencil buffer value (won't exceed the maximum clamped value).
GL_DECR:	Decrements the stored stencil buffer value (won't decrease below '0').
GL_INVERT:	Does a bitwise invert of the sorted stencil buffer value.

The stencil write mask (using the glStencilMask function) enables the writing of bits to the stencil planes. It takes one parameter, namely a mask identifying the writable and write-protected bits. Writable bits are identified by setting the mask value to '1' with write-protected bits identified using a mask value of '0'.

11

Usage example:

```
glStencilOp(GL_KEEP, GL_DECR, GL_INCR);
glStencilMask(1);
```

11.3 IMPLEMENTING STENCIL SHADOW VOLUMES

The first step of a shadow volume implementation is to construct the shadow volume itself. This process starts with the calculation of silhouette edges followed by the generation of the shadow volume geometry. We use a shader to calculate the silhouette edges of an object with respect to a light source (we could alternatively calculate these edges on the CPU). The given geometry shader calculates the silhouette edges by determining the normal of each triangle face followed by the normals of the adjacent triangles. Thus, if the current triangle normal is facing the light source, with the adjacent triangle normal facing away, then we can flag their shared edge as a silhouette.

Our shader program starts with the declaration of three structures for the storage of vertex and normal coordinate parameters.

```
struct VERTEXSHADER_INPUT
{
    float4 Loc : POSITION;
    float3 Norm : NORMAL;
};


struct PIXELSHADER_OUTPUT
{
    float4 Loc : SV_POSITION;
};


struct GEOMETRYSHADER_INPUT
{
    float4 Loc: POSITION;
    float3 Norm : NORMAL;
};
```

The first structure, VERTEXSHADER_INPUT, holds our vertex information as received from the Direct3D application and is used to pass input data to a vertex shader that transforms the input vertex position to clip space as discussed in previous chapters. It also transforms the input vertex normal to world space, finally returning the transformed vertex data via the GEOMETRYSHADER_INPUT structure:

```
/* vertex shader for sending the vertex data to the shadow
   volume geometry shader */
GEOMETRYSHADER_INPUT ShadowVertexShader(VERTEXSHADER_INPUT IN)
{
    GEOMETRYSHADER_INPUT output = (GEOMETRYSHADER_INPUT)0;

    /* transforms the input vertex position to world space */
    output.Loc = mul(float4(IN.Loc,1), WorldMatrix);
```

```
/* transforms the input vertex normal to world space */
output.Norm = mul(IN.Norm, (float3x3)WorldMatrix);

    return output;
}
```

Next we write a geometry shader to determine an object's silhouette edges using groups of vertices, each group consisting of two shared vertices and one adjacent vertex. This shader function also receives an un-normalized triangle normal (normal) as input; returning a TriangleStream containing the extruded shadow volume as a series of triangles. The shader starts by calculating the light vector pointing from the triangle towards the light source. This is followed by the calculation of the dot product between the triangle normal and the light vector, this dot product value is greater than '0' for triangles facing towards the light source. Following the initialization of the shadow volume extrusion amount, shadowExtrusionAmount, and bias, shadowExtrusionBias (for extending the shadow volume silhouette edges) we iterate through the adjacent triangles, calculating the silhouette edges and extruding the volumes out of the determined silhouettes. The geometry shader's final operation is to create the front- and back-cap of the newly defined shadow volume. Before listing this shader we need to look at a new input primitive type, triangleadj. This newly supported geometry shader type flags every other vertex as an adjacent vertex, in other words simplifying the work required to find the silhouette edges:

```
[maxvertexcount(18)]
void SilhouetteEdgeAndVolumeGS(
        triangleadj GEOMETRYSHADER_INPUT vertex[6],
        float3 normal,
        inout TriangleStream<PIXELSHADER_INPUT> ExtrudedVolume)
{
    /* determine the light vector from the triangle to light
       source — see program 17.1 on the book's website */
    float lightVector = LightPosition — In[0].Loc;
    /* calculate the triangle normal */
    float triangleNormal = cross(In[2].Loc — In[0].Loc,
                                 In[4].Loc — In[0].Loc);

    /* calculate the dot product between the triangle normal
       and the light vector — if this value (the length of
       triangleNormal projected onto the lightVector) is
       greater than '0' then the triangle is facing the light
    */
    float3 projectionLength = dot(triangleNormal,
                                  lightVector);


PIXELSHADER_OUTPUT Output;

/* set the amount and bias to extrude the shadow
   volume from the silhouette edge */
float shadowExtrusionAmount = 119.9f;
float shadowExtrusionBias = 0.1f;
```

11

```
/* iterate through the adjacent triangles — where:
   - vertex[0], vertex[1] and vertex[6] are adjacent
   - vertex[2], vertex[3] and vertex[4] are adjacent
   - vertex[4], vertex[5] and vertex[0] are adjacent */
for(int i = 0; i < 6; i += 2)
{
    /* calculate the adjacency triangle normal */
    float triangleNormal = cross(vertex[i].Loc —
                                 vertex[i+1].Loc,
                                 vertex[i+2].Loc —
                                 vertex[i+1].Loc);

    /* calculate the silhouette edges and extrude for
       triangles facing the light source */
    if(projectionLength > 0.0f)
    {
        float3 silhouette[4];

        /* extrude the silhouette edges */
        /////////////////////////////////////
        silhouette[0]= vertex[i].Loc + shadowExtrusionBias*
                       normalize(vertex[i].Loc — LightPosition);

        silhouette[1]= vertex[i].Loc + shadowExtrusionAmount*
                       normalize(vertex[i].Loc — LightPosition);

        silhouette[2]= vertex[i+2].Loc + shadowExtrusionBias*
                       normalize(vertex[i+2].pos — LightPosition);

        silhouette[3]= vertex[i+2].Loc + shadowExtrusionAmount *
                       normalize(vertex[i+2].Loc — LightPosition);

        /* create two new triangles for the extruded silhouette */
        Output.Loc=mul(float4(silhouette[v],1),ViewMatrix);

        //append shader-output data to an existing stream
        TriangleStream.Append(Output);
    }

//end the current-primitive strip and start a new one
TriangleStream.RestartStrip();
}
    /* create the front- and back-cap for the newly created
       triangles */

    //start with the nearest cap
    for(int k = 0; k < 6; k += 2)
    {
```

```
float3 nearCapPosition = vertex[k].Loc +
                         shadowExtrusionBias *
                         normalize(vertex[k].Loc –
                         LightPosition);


    Output.Loc = mul(float4(nearCapPosition,1), ViewMatrix);
    TriangleStream.Append(Output);
}
TriangleStream.RestartStrip();


//now calculate the furthest cap
for(int k = 4; k >= 0; k –= 2)
{
    float3 farCapPosition = vertex[k].Loc +
                         shadowExtrusionAmount *
                         normalize(vertex[k].Loc –
                         LightPosition);


    Output.Loc = mul(float4(farCapPosition,1), ViewMatrix);
    TriangleStream.Append(Output);
}
TriangleStream.RestartStrip();
}
```

We can test whether a fragment is in shadow or not using either the previously discussed depth-fail or depth-pass technique. The chosen depth stencil test can be implemented using native Direct3D 10 structures and functions as listed in section 11.2.1. The final step is to render the scene, resulting in the update of the pixels located inside the shadow volume and thus leading to the generation of shadowed regions. Program 17.1, available on the book's website, features a complete Direct3D 10 stencil shadow volume implementation.

11

Working with OpenGL

We initiate shadow rendering, following construction of the shadow volume, by clearing the depth, stencil and color buffers; in the process initializing the depth buffer with the initial pixel depth matching the scene's viewable surfaces. To implement the basic shadow volume testing algorithm, as described in section 11.1.4, the scene must first be rendered fully lit:

```
glEnable(GL_LIGHTING);
glEnable(GL_LIGHT0);
```

Following this, depth testing is enabled with the depth function, glDepthFunc, set to GL_LEQUAL and the depth mask, glDepthMask, set to enable writing to the depth buffer. The glDepthFunc takes one parameter, namely a depth comparison function specifying the conditions under which to draw a pixel:

GL_ALWAYS: Always passes.

GL_EQUAL: Passes if the incoming depth value == depth value stored in the depth buffer.

GL_GEQUAL: Passes if the incoming depth value >= depth value stored in the depth buffer.

GL_GREATER: Passes if the incoming depth value > depth value stored in the depth buffer.

GL_LEQUAL: Passes if the incoming depth value <= depth value stored in the depth buffer.

GL_LESS: Passes if the incoming depth value < depth value stored in the depth buffer.

GL_NEVER: Always fails.

GL_NOTEQUAL: Passes if the incoming depth value ⊨ depth value stored in the depth buffer.

Usage example:

```
glEnable(GL_DEPTH_TEST);
glDepthFunc(GL_LEQUAL);
glDepthMask(GL_TRUE);
```

Before rendering the illuminated scene it is also important to disable stencil testing while at the same time clearing the stencil buffer using the glClearStencil function in combination with the glClear function as previously discussed:

```
glClearStencil(0);
glClear(GL_DEPTH_BUFFER_BIT | GL_COLOR_BUFFER_BIT |
        GL_STENCIL_BUFFER_BIT);
```

The next step, following the rendering of the non-shadowed scene, is to identify all the pixels located inside a shadow volume by physically rendering the shadow volume and implementing depth buffering as defined in the previous step. We start by disabling the lighting and similarly to the previous step, enabling depth testing using the glDepthFunc function (only this time disabling depth buffer writing so that the constructed shadow volumes are not rendered to the screen and thus not visible to the viewer):

```
glDisable(GL_LIGHTING);
glEnable(GL_DEPTH_TEST);
glDepthFunc(GL_LESS);
glDepthMask(GL_FALSE);
```

Stencil testing can now be enabled, followed by glStencilFunc's comparison function being set to GL_ALWAYS with its stencil test reference value and the stencil comparison bit mask both set to '0':

```
glEnable(GL_STENCIL_TEST);
glStencilFunc(GL_ALWAYS, 0, 0);
```

The stencil write mask (using the glStencilMask function) is initialized as follows, always writing the least significant stencil bit in the stencil planes:

```
glStencilMask(1);
```

With the stencil write mask defined, we simply have to define the stencil operation so that the stencil bit are inverted whenever the depth test passes:

```
glStencilOp(GL_KEEP, GL_KEEP, GL_INVERT);
```

Both the front- and back-facing polygons located within the stencil shadow volume boundary can now be rendered. This step allows us to identify all the shadowed (stencil bit equals '1') and lit pixels (stencil bit equals '0') when the point of view is located outside of the shadow volume. For situations where the point of view is located within the shadow volume, a stencil bit equalling '1' indicates a lit pixel with a '0' indicating a pixel located inside the shadow volume.

With all the pixels located inside and outside the shadow volume identified, we simply redraw the complete scene with stencil testing set to update the pixels located inside the shadow volume. The first step of this final stage is to enable lighting, with the exception of the shadow casting light source:

```
glEnable(GL_LIGHTING);
glDisable(GL_LIGHT0);
```

Depth testing is enabled with the depth function, glDepthFunc, set to GL_EQUAL (only the fragments with depth values equalling the depth values from the first step are updated) and the depth mask, glDepthMask, set to disable depth buffer writing:

```
glEnable(GL_DEPTH_TEST);
glDepthFunc(GL_EQUAL);
glDepthMask(GL_FALSE);
```

Following this, the stencil test is enabled with the stencil function set to update all the pixels with a stencil bit value of '1':

```
glEnable(GL_STENCIL_TEST);
glStencilFunc(GL_EQUAL, 1, 1);
```

The glStencilOp function specifies the action to take based on the result of both the stencil test and depth test, in this case we set it to use the stored stencil buffer value when the stencil test fails, when the stencil test passes and the depth test fails and when both the stencil test and depth test passes. However, as defined in the previous step, the glStencilOp function only accepts pixels with a stencil bit value of '1':

```
glStencilOp(GL_KEEP, GL_KEEP, GL_KEEP);
```

The final step is to render the scene, resulting in the update of the pixels located inside the shadow volume, thus leading to the generation of shadowed regions.

The above outlined stencilling process makes use of an invert stencilling operation. This allows accurate counting of shadowed and lit pixels. However, the invert stencilling operation is two-part and requires polygon boundary reduction (the shadow volume is only considered with regard to its shadow polygon borders). Most real-word stencil shadow volume applications (as described in section 11.1.4) will rather deal with both front- and back-facing shadow surfaces by incrementing or decrementing the stencil buffer value for these shadow surfaces based on the result of a depth test. Section 11.1.4 describes two such processes, namely depth-passing and depth-failing. Depth-pass counting is implemented by first disabling lighting to save processing time (since lighting isn't required), following this we enable depth testing with the depth function set to pass for all incoming depth values smaller than the depth value stored in the depth buffer (GL_LESS):

```
glDisable(GL_LIGHTING);
glEnable(GL_DEPTH_TEST);
glDepthFunc(GL_LESS);
```

Next, writing into the depth buffer is disabled by setting the glDepthMask flag to GL_FALSE:

```
glDepthMask(GL_FALSE);
```

Following this we clear the stencil write mask, enable face culling and specify the culling of all back-facing surfaces (thus incrementing for all front-facing surfaces):

```
glStencilMask( 0);
glEnable(GL_CULL_FACE);
glCullFace(GL_BACK);
```

We can now implement the depth-pass operation using the glStencilOp function by incrementing the stored stencil buffer value for all actions where both the stencil test and the depth test passes while keeping the original buffer value for actions where the stencil test fails or where the stencil test passes and the depth test fails:

```
glStencilOp(GL_KEEP, GL_KEEP, GL_INCR);
```

Next we simply have to extend and render the shadow volume for all the polygons within the scene:

```
for (int i = 1; i <= totalNumberOfPolygons; i++)
{
    drawShadowVolume(i);
}
```

The final phase is to decrement for all back-facing surfaces, thus culling all front-facing surfaces using the glCullFace function:

```
glCullFace(GL_FRONT);
```

Following this we have to implement the depth-pass operation for these back faces using the glStencilOp function. This is done by decrementing the stored stencil buffer value for all actions where both the stencil test and the depth test passes:

```
glStencilOp(GL_KEEP, GL_KEEP, GL_DECR);
```

We can now extend and render the shadow volume for all the back-facing polygons within the scene:

```
for (int i = 1; I <= totalNumberOfPolygons; i++)
{
    drawShadowVolume(i);
}
```

11.4 SUMMARY

In this chapter we focused on the fundamentals of real-time shadow generation and its contribution to the realism and ambience of rendered environments. We started by defining a shadow as the two-dimensional projection of at least one object onto another object or surface, subsequently looking at the physical properties of shadows and the technique of shadow casting in general.

Following this introduction we investigated a number of shadowing algorithms, specifically Blinn's shadow polygons, scan-line polygon projection, shadow mapping and stencil shadow volumes. Our discussion of Blinn's shadow polygons revealed them to be an extremely easy-to-use shadow generation technique often utilized to render the shadows of single polygons on flat surfaces. We also considered the quite complex, and now mostly redundant scan-line polygon projection algorithm historically used for the generation of hard-edged shadows.

Next we discussed the fundamentals of shadow mapping and stencil shadow volumes, our shadow mapping discussion highlighting the general dual-pass shadow mapping technique. The shadow volume section presented the theory behind the construction of finite shadow volumes as well as the stencilling process, differentiating between the depth-pass and depth-fail methods used to test whether a fragment is in shadow or not. We also briefly touched on the generation of soft-edged shadows using penumbra wedges.

The remainder of the chapter focused on the stencil buffer as an additional buffer controlling the rendering of selected pixels as well as the per-pixel test known as stencilling. The stencil and depth testing process was looked at in detail – both from a Direct3D 10 and OpenGL perspective. The chapter concluded with a shadow volume implementation, highlighting the shadow volume construction process and calculation of silhouette edges.

The next chapter deals with the construction and efficient rendering of large environments using height maps for terrain creation, hidden surface removal for determining the parts of objects hidden from the viewer and subsequently removing these areas from the rendering process, clipping as an optimization operation for the display of only visible objects, and Level of Detail algorithms for the dynamic control of an object's polygonal complexity.

11

11.5 FURTHER READING

A great paper dealing with the stencil buffer is '*Improving Shadows and Reflections via the Stencil Buffer*' *by Mark J. Kilgard* published as an NVIDIA white paper (1999). Another NVIDIA white paper titled '*Hardware Shadow Mapping*' *by Cass Everitt, Ashu Rege and Cem Cebenoyan* (2001) thoroughly discusses the implementation of hardware accelerated shadow mapping. Other groundbreaking papers focusing on shadow volumes include Crow's original titled *'Shadow Algorithms for Computer Graphics'* published in the 1977 SIGGRAPH Proceedings; Heidmann's *'Real Shadows Real Time'* published in 1991 (IRIS Universe, 18, 28–31) as well as Everitt and Kilgard's 2002 NVIDIA white paper *Practical and Robust Stenciled Shadow Volumes for Hardware-Accelerated Rendering.*

For more information on Blinn shadow polygons, see Jim Blinn's paper *'Me and My (Fake) Shadow'* published in IEEE Computer Graphics and Applications(1988). Also, for an additional discussion of scan-line polygon projection, see Bouknight and Kelly's 1970 paper *'An Algorithm for Producing Half-tone Computer Graphics Presentations with Shadows and Moveable Light Sources* published in the Proceedings of the AFIPS Spring Joint Computer Conference.

Tomas Akenine-Möller and Ulf Assarsson's paper, *'Approximate Soft Shadows on Arbitrary Surfaces using Penumbra Wedges'* published in the Proceedings of the 13th Eurographics Workshop on Rendering (2002) details a soft shadow algorithm extended from the classical shadow volume algorithm.

11.6   EXERCISES

1   Briefly outline how we might control the size and intensity of a shadow.

2   Briefly differentiate between the umbra and penumbra of a shadow.

3   List the inherent benefits and drawbacks when casting a shadow by simply calculating the projection of an object on some base-plane.

4   How can the projection of a shadow casting polygon be calculated?

5   Explain the process of scan-line polygon projection.

6   What is the purpose of the display adaptor's texture memory when implementing shadow mapping?

7   Briefly describe the shadow mapping algorithm.

8   What advantages does the stencil shadow volume technique have over basic shadow mapping?

9   What is a silhouette edge and how is it calculated?

10   Why is it necessary to calculate a shadowed scene's depth information?

11   Compare the depth-fail and depth-pass stencil buffer implementations, listing the benefits and drawbacks inherent to each.

12   Describe the purpose of the stencil buffer with regard to the stencil testing process.

13   What is the purpose of the following code sample:

```
pID3D10Device->ClearDepthStencilView(pDepthStencilView,
                     D3D10_CLEAR_DEPTH,
                     1.0, 0);
```

14   Give a code snippet to clear the stencil buffer.

15   How are the details of the depth and stencil testing operations specified?

16 Briefly describe the purpose of the D3D10_DEPTH_STENCIL_VIEW_DESC structure.

17 Explain what is meant by the phrase 'invert stencilling operation'.

18 What does the dot product between a triangle normal and light vector tell us when extruding a shadow volume from a silhouette edge?

19 Why is the triangleadj input primitive type useful when finding silhouette edges?

11

CHAPTER 12

Height Maps, Hidden Surface Removal, Clipping and Level of Detail Algorithms

LEARNING OBJECTIVES

In this chapter you will learn about:

- Height maps
- Creating and rendering a height map
- Hidden surface removal
- The Z-buffer algorithm
- The painter's algorithm
- Clipping
- Two-dimensional line clipping
- Cohen-Sutherland clipping
- Liang-Barsky clipping
- The clipping of polygons
- Three-dimensional clipping
- Level of Detail (LOD) algorithms

INTRODUCTION

Chapter 12 deals with the construction and optimal rendering of large environments. We will specifically focus on height maps for terrain creation, culling and hidden surface removal, clipping algorithms and Level of Detail algorithms as a way to control geometric complexity.

12.1 HEIGHT MAPS

Height maps, also called height fields, are predominantly used in computer games for realistic terrain generation. A height map is stored as a two-dimensional array consisting of x- and z-values. Each x- and z-coordinate is assigned a certain value (a y-coordinate) representing the height of a specific point on a 3D surface. Height maps can thus be described as simple two-dimensional arrays containing height values, sampled at evenly spaced intervals. This concept is illustrated in Figure 12-1.

The area between the various interconnected y-coordinates, or heights, is smoothly interpolated, giving the illusion of mountainous terrain, for example.

To create a height map we can either define a two-dimensional array representing the height of the surface in terms of x- and z-coordinates or we can make use of a greyscale image (as with our bump mapping example in Chapter 8) where the elevation levels of the field are encoded using different levels of darkness. The darker the area represented by a height map, the lower the corresponding mesh height. Lighter regions will be rendered as protruding. Figure 12-2(a) shows a greyscale image with black representing minimum height and white representing maximum height. The related height map mesh is given in Figure 12-2(b).

Height maps, as a function of x- and z-coordinates, can be represented using the following equation:

$$height(y) = func(x, z).$$

This equation is of course only relevant for one height value at a time and can easily be written to represent an entire height field based on the spacing between specified height values:

$height(y_{kl}) = func[(x_0 + k(\Delta x)),(z_0 + l(\Delta z)]$, with Δx and Δz the respective distance between the height measurements in the x and z directions and k and l ranging from '0' to the width and breadth of the mesh, correspondingly.

FIGURE 12-1 **A height map – there is exactly one height for each z- and x-coordinate**

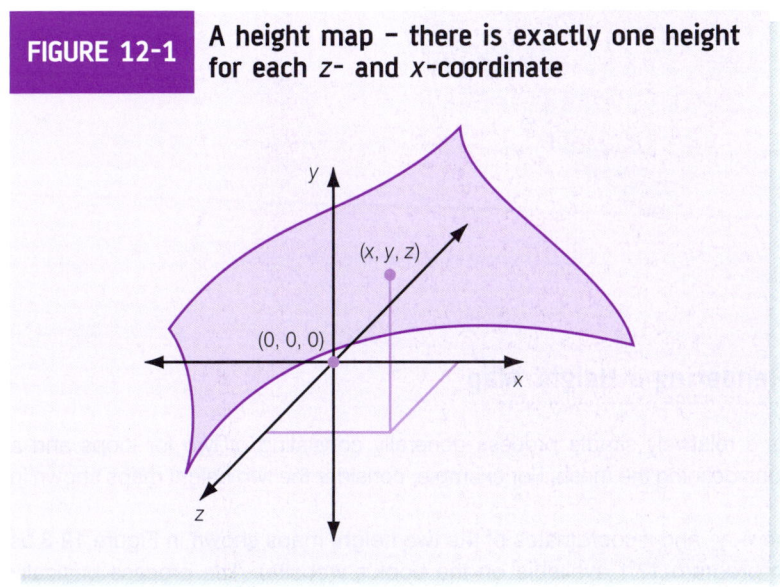

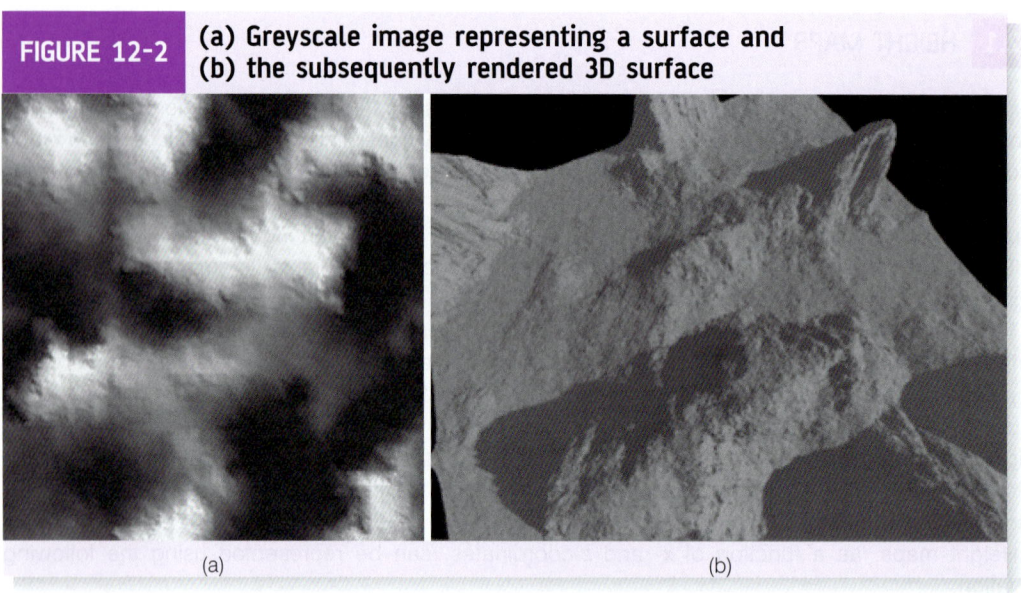

FIGURE 12-2 | (a) Greyscale image representing a surface and (b) the subsequently rendered 3D surface

(a)   (b)

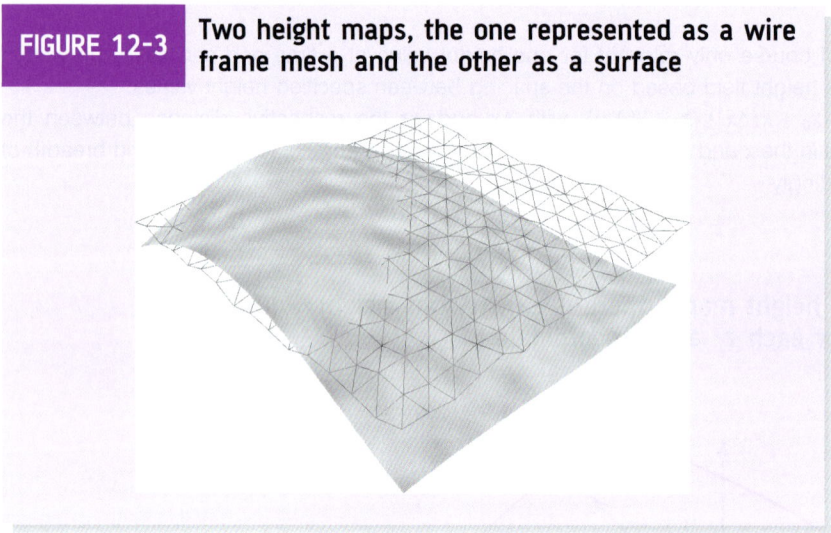

FIGURE 12-3 | Two height maps, the one represented as a wire frame mesh and the other as a surface

12.1.1 Creating and Rendering a Height Map

Generating a height map is a relatively simple process generally consisting of two for loops and a number of vertex specifications defining the mesh. For example, consider the two height maps shown in Figure 12-3.

We can easily specify the x-, y- and z-coordinates of the two height maps shown in Figure 12-3 as outlined below (taken from program 12.1 available on the book's website). The process basically starts with the declaration of a global variable, g_mapDimension, specifying the mesh width and breadth and two 2D arrays, wireframeHeightMap and surfaceHeightMap, for the storage of height data:

```
/* specify the width and breadth of the height maps */
const int g_mapDimension = 16;

/* the height map used for the rendering of the wire frame
   mesh */
float wireframeHeightMap[g_mapDimension][g_mapDimension];

/* the height map used for the rendering of the surface mesh*/
float surfaceHeightMap[g_mapDimension][g_mapDimension];
```

Next we define a generic function that returns a random double value between the provided bounds. This function is called to set up the wire frame height map mesh:

```
double GetRandomDouble(double low, double high)
{
    return ((double)rand()/(RAND_MAX+1.0))*(high - low) + low;
}
```

The data values of both surfaces are generated using the two for loops given here:

```
for (int i = 0; i < g_mapDimension; i++)
{
    for (int j = 0; j < g_mapDimension; j++)
    {
        /* create the randomly protruded wire frame mesh with
           heights ranging from 0.0 to 0.1 */
        wireframeHeightMap[i][j] = GetRandomDouble(0.0, 0.1);

        /* create the surface mesh using a scaled sine
           function */
        surfaceHeightMap[i][j] = sin(0.25 * (sqrt((double)(i) *
                                (double)(i) + ((double)j) *
                                (double)(j)))) / 4.0;
    }
}
```

With the surface data generated, we can now render each mesh using either OpenGL or Direct3D function calls. The coordinates of each point on the mesh are simply assigned to the x-, y- and z-components of the D3DXVECTOR3 vector structure in the case of a Direct3D program or to the glVertex3f function call in the case of OpenGL.

For example, we assign the surface mesh's generated height values as x-, y- and z-components to the D3DXVECTOR3 vector structure by iterating through these values:

```
/* initialize some variables used during the iteration */
double mapWidth = 2.0;
double mapLength  = 2.0;
```

12

```
double mapWidthStep = mapWidth / g_mapDimension;
double mapLengthStep = mapLength  / g_mapDimension;

double mapStartXPos = 0 - (mapWidth/2.0);
double mapStartZPos  = 0 - (mapLength /2.0);

double currentXPos = 0.0;
double currentZPos = 0.0;

currentZPos = mapStartZPos ;
currentXPos = mapStartXPos;

/* specify the height map vertices by iterating through the
   height values */
for (int i = 0; i < g_mapDimension - 1; i++)
{
    currentZPos = mapStartZPos ;

    for (int j = 0; j < g_mapDimension - 1; j++)
    {
      D3DXVECTOR3(currentXPos,
                       surfaceHeightMap[i][j],
                       currentZPos);

      D3DXVECTOR3(currentXPos + mapWidthStep,
                       surfaceHeightMap[i+1][j],
                       currentZPos);

      D3DXVECTOR3(currentXPos,
                       surfaceHeightMap[i][j+1],
                       currentZPos + mapLengthStep);

      D3DXVECTOR3(currentXPos + mapWidthStep,
                       surfaceHeightMap[i+1][j],
                       currentZPos);

      D3DXVECTOR3(currentXPos + mapWidthStep,
                       surfaceHeightMap[i+1][j+1],
                       currentZPos + mapLengthStep);

      D3DXVECTOR3(currentXPos,
                       surfaceHeightMap[i][j+1],
                       currentZPos + mapLengthStep);

      /* draw the above assigned vertices */
      . . .

      currentZPos += mapLengthStep;
    }

    currentXPos += mapWidthStep;
}
```

Working with OpenGL

Specifying the vertices of our solid mesh using OpenGL is similar to the previous Direct3D example – we simply replace the D3DXVECTOR3 structure with glVertex3f function calls grouped between a glBegin and glEnd:

```
/* initialize some variables used during the iteration */
double mapWidth = 2.0;
double mapLength  = 2.0;

double mapWidthStep = mapWidth / g_mapDimension;
double mapLengthStep = mapLength  / g_mapDimension;

double mapStartXPos = 0 - (mapWidth/2.0);
double mapStartZPos = 0 - (mapLength /2.0);

double currentXPos = 0.0;
double currentZPos = 0.0;

currentZPos = mapStartZPos ;
currentXPos = mapStartXPos;

/* specify the height map vertices by iterating through the
   height values */
for (int i = 0; i < g_mapDimension - 1; i++)
{
currentZPos = mapStartZPos ;

   for (int j = 0; j < g_mapDimension - 1; j++)
   {
     glBegin(GL_TRIANGLES);
         glVertex3f (currentXPos,
                  surfaceHeightMap[i][j],
                  currentZPos);

         glVertex3f (currentXPos + mapWidthStep,
                  surfaceHeightMap[i+1][j],
                  currentZPos);

         glVertex3f (currentXPos,
                  surfaceHeightMap[i][j+1],
                  currentZPos + mapLengthStep);

         glVertex3f (currentXPos + mapWidthStep,
                  surfaceHeightMap[i+1][j],
                  currentZPos);

         glVertex3f (currentXPos + mapWidthStep,
                  surfaceHeightMap[i+1][j+1],
                  currentZPos + mapLengthStep);
```

```
            glVertex3f (currentXPos,
                        surfaceHeightMap[i][j+1],
                        currentZPos + mapLengthStep);
        glEnd();

        currentZPos += mapLengthStep;
    }

    currentXPos += mapWidthStep;
}
```

Iterating through and assigning the generated height values of the wire frame surface to D3DXVECTOR3 vector structures are done in a similar fashion:

```
/* specify the height map vertices by iterating through the
   height values */
for (int i = 0; i < g_mapDimension - 1; i++)
{
  currentZPos = mapStartZPos ;

  for (int j = 0; j < g_mapDimension - 1; j++)
  {
    D3DXVECTOR3(currentXPos,
                wireframeHeightMap[i][j],
                currentZPos);

    D3DXVECTOR3(currentXPos + mapWidthStep,
                wireframeHeightMap[i+1][j],
                currentZPos);

    D3DXVECTOR3(currentXPos,
                wireframeHeightMap[i][j+1],
                currentZPos + mapLengthStep);

    D3DXVECTOR3(currentXPos + mapWidthStep,
                wireframeHeightMap[i+1][j],
                currentZPos);

    D3DXVECTOR3(currentXPos + mapWidthStep,
                wireframeHeightMap[i+1][j+1],
                currentZPos + mapLengthStep);

    D3DXVECTOR3(currentXPos,
                wireframeHeightMap[i][j+1],
                currentZPos + mapLengthStep);
```

```
    /* draw the above assigned vertices */
    ...

    currentZPos += mapLengthStep;
}

currentXPos += mapWidthStep;
}
```

Working with OpenGL

Specifying the vertices of our wire frame mesh using OpenGL is nearly identical to the process described in the previous Direct3D example. As before, we simply replace the D3DXVECTOR3 structure with glVertex3f function calls grouped between a glBegin and glEnd. The only difference is the primitive type specification. The solid surface is rendered using the GL_TRIANGLES type specification while the wire frame surface is rendered using the GL_LINE_LOOP type specification (refer to 6.1.1 for a detailed explanation of each):

```
/* specify the height map vertices by iterating through the
    height values */
for (int i = 0; i < g_mapDimension - 1; i++)
{
    currentZPos = mapStartZPos ;

    for (int j = 0; j < g_mapDimension - 1; j++)
    {
      glBegin(GL_LINE_LOOP);
          glVertex3f (currentXPos,
                      wireframeHeightMap[i][j],
                      currentZPos);

          glVertex3f (currentXPos + mapWidthStep,
                      wireframeHeightMap[i+1][j],
                      currentZPos);

          glVertex3f (currentXPos,
                      wireframeHeightMap[i][j+1],
                      currentZPos + mapLengthStep);

          glVertex3f (currentXPos + mapWidthStep,
                      wireframeHeightMap[i+1][j],
                      currentZPos);

          glVertex3f (currentXPos + mapWidthStep,
                      wireframeHeightMap[i+1][j+1],
                      currentZPos + mapLengthStep);
```

12

```
            glVertex3f (currentXPos,
                        wireframeHeightMap[i][j+1],
                        currentZPos + mapLengthStep);
    glEnd();

    currentZPos += mapLengthStep;
    }

    currentXPos += mapWidthStep;
}
```

Rendering the vertices of our Direct3D meshes involves specifying the primitive type for the solid surface mesh as a triangle strip using the D3D10_PRIMITIVE_TOPOLOGY_TRIANGLESTRIP constant or as a triangle list using the D3D10_PRIMITIVE_TOPOLOGY_TRIANGLELIST constant. The wire frame mesh can in turn be rendered using the D3D10_PRIMITIVE_TOPOLOGY_LINESTRIP primitive topology, for example. Primitive types are specified via the D3D10_PRIMITIVE_TOPOLOGY enumerator as explained in Chapter 6.

We will now look at another height map data generation example (program 12.2 on the book's website) dealing with the creation of a simple "hat" function as shown in Figure 12-4.

The height map shown in Figure 12-4 is stored in a 24 × 24 two-dimensional array, map:

```
float map[24][24];
```

We use the function SetupHeights to generate the various coordinate values (it basically samples a simple mathematical 'hat' function at evenly spaced intervals):

```
void SetupHeights()
{
    /* initialize some variables – the hat functions starts at
       the point (–6, 0, –6) */
    double hatStartXPos = –6.0;
```

12

FIGURE 12-4   A height map representing a hat function

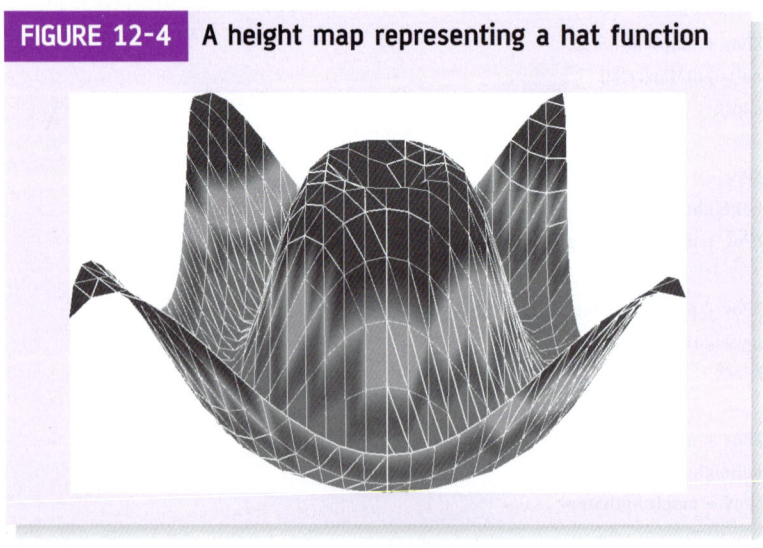

```
double hatStartZPos = -6.0;
double currentXPos = -6.0;
double currentZPos = -6.0;

/* sample the mathematical "hat" function at regular
   intervals - "24" is our height map's dimension */
for (int i = 0; i < 24; i++)
{
   currentZPos = hatStartZPos;
   for (int j = 0; j < 24; j++)
   {
      /* value generation function */
      map[i][j] = sin(sqrt((currentXPos)*( currentXPos) +
                      (currentZPos)*(currentZPos))) / 2.0;

      /* increase the height of the mesh with 12 units
         divided by the height map's dimension */
      currentZPos += 12.0 / 24;
   }

   currentXPos += 12.0 / 24;
}
}
```

Using the above data generated, we can now specify the vertices of our mesh, the x-, y- and z-coordinates of each point making up the mathematical hat function by iterating through the generated height values:

```
/* specify the height map vertices by iterating through the
   generated height values, "24" is the height map dimension */
for(i = 0; i < 24; i++)
{
   for(j = 0; j < 24; j++)
   {
      D3DXVECTOR3((i+1)/scale - 1.0,
                  map[i+1][j],
                  j/scale - 1.0);

      D3DXVECTOR3((i)/scale - 1.0,
                  map[i][j],
                  j/scale - 1.0);

      D3DXVECTOR3((i+1)/scale - 1.0,
                  map[i+1][j+1],
                  (j+1)/scale - 1.0);

      D3DXVECTOR3((i)/scale - 1.0,
                  map[i][j+1],
                  (j+1)/scale - 1.0);
```

12

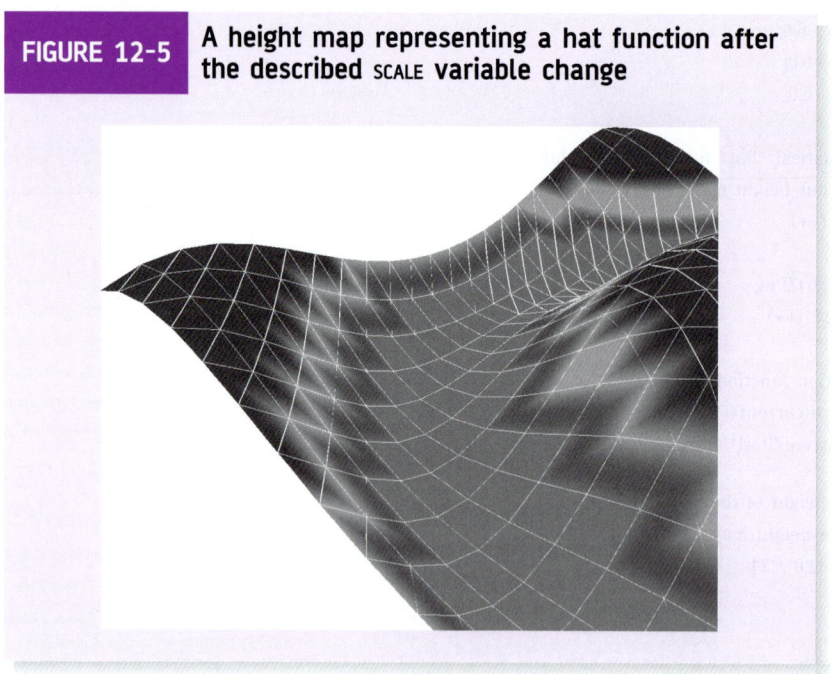

```
/* draw the above assigned vertices */
   ...


   }
}
```

The scale variable is a floating-point value set to the map dimension, '24', divided by '2.0'. Dividing the map dimension by '6.0' results in the output shown in Figure 12-5. The scale variable is used to control the width (x-coordinates) and breadth (z-coordinates) of the height map.

The height map vertices are rendered following the input-assembler initialization process. To recap, this process includes specification of vertex and index input buffers, creation of the input-layout object, binding of these buffer resources and layout object to the input-assembler stage and finally specification of the primitive type followed by the drawing of the pipeline-bound primitives via the Draw ID3D10Device function. This process is fully discussed in section 4.3.4.1 and Chapter 6.

Working with OpenGL

Drawing the vertices of our mesh using OpenGL is similar to the Direct3D example given above – we simply replace the D3DXVECTOR3 structure with glVertex3f function calls:

```
/* specify the height map vertices by iterating through the
   height values – "24" is the dimension of our height map*/
for(i = 0; i < 24; i++)
{
    for(j = 0; j < 24; j++)
```

12

```
    {
        glBegin(GL_LINE_LOOP);
            glVertex3f ((i+1)/scale - 1.0,
                        map[i+1][j],
                        j/scale - 1.0);

            glVertex3f ((i)/scale - 1.0,
                        map[i][j],
                        j/scale - 1.0);

            glVertex3f ((i+1)/scale - 1.0,
                        map[i+1][j+1],
                        (j+1)/scale - 1.0);

            glVertex3f ((i)/scale - 1.0,
                        map[i][j+1],
                        (j+1)/scale - 1.0);
        glEnd();
    }
}
```

12.2 HIDDEN SURFACE REMOVAL

The importance of culling in the removal of polygons hidden from the viewer was previously discussed in Chapter 7. We described culling as the process of comparing the position and orientation of polygons against the view volume's field of view, with polygons facing away from the camera being eliminated. This elimination minimized the amount of computational overhead involved with hidden surface removal.

Culling, to recap, is basically a test determining the visibility of an object, and based on this test the object can be removed if not visible – a process known as *hidden surface removal*. A culling test is based on a simple vector calculation, specifically, the dot product between a polygon's normal and the line-of-sight vector (the vector from the center of projection to the polygon). If the result of the dot product is positive then we can flag the polygon as visible (with its normal facing towards the viewer). On average, nearly 50 percent of polygons are back-facing, stressing the importance of performing a culling test prior to the application of any hidden-surface removal algorithm. We will now recap the process of enabling culling before continuing our discussion of hidden surface removal techniques.

Enabling culling in Direct3D requires the creation of a D3D10_RASTERIZER_DESC render state structure. The CullMode value of this structure is set to either D3D10_CULL_NONE to render all faces, D3D10_CULL_FRONT to cull all front-facing polygons or D3D10_CULL_BACK for the culling of all back-facing polygons. The D3D10_-RASTERIZER_DESC render state structure is passed as a parameter to the CreateRasterizerState method. The CreateRasterizerState method's second parameter, the ID3D10RasterizerState interface, contains behavioral information pertaining to the rasterizer stage. The ID3D10RasterizerState interface and D3D10_RASTERIZER_DESC render state structure are subsequently declared as:

```
ID3D10RasterizerState * generalRasterizerState;
D3D10_RASTERIZER_DESC generalRasterState;
```

12

The members of the D3D10_RASTERIZER_DESC structure are initialized as follows:

generalRasterState.FillMode = D3D10_FILL_WIREFRAME;
generalRasterState.CullMode = D3D10_CULL_FRONT;
generalRasterState.FrontCounterClockwise = true;
generalRasterState.DepthBias = false;
generalRasterState.DepthBiasClamp = 0;
generalRasterState.SlopeScaledDepthBias = 0;
generalRasterState.DepthClipEnable = true;
generalRasterState.ScissorEnable = true;
generalRasterState.MultisampleEnable = false;
generalRasterState.AntialiasedLineEnable = false;

To review, the FillMode member sets the polygon's rendering mode to either wireframe (D3D10_FILL_WIREFRAME) or solid (D3D10_FILL_SOLID). The FrontCounterClockwise member specifies whether the polygons will be rendered as front-facing (true) or back-facing (false). DepthBias controls the depth value added to a particular pixel with DepthBiasClamp setting the maximum pixel bias and SlopeScaledDepthBias the pixel's slope scalar (depth bias and slope scalars are fully explained in Chapter 6). DepthClipEnable determines whether distance-based clipping is enabled (true) or disabled (false) with ScissorEnable setting the scissor rectangle and MultisampleEnable setting multisample antialiasing. The final member, AntialiasedLineEnable, sets line-based antialiasing (if multisampling isn't selected).

Following this we create the rasterizer state object:

(D3DDevice)->CreateRasterizerState(&generalRasterState,
                                   &generalRasterizerState);

The final step is to set the device:

(D3DDevice)->RSSetState(generalRasterizerState);

Working with OpenGL

As described in Chapter 7, we use the glCullFace function to enable back-face elimination via the GL_BACK flag or front-face elimination using the GL_FRONT flag. Before, however, calling this function, we first have to specify our polygons as either front-facing (GL_CCW) or back-facing (GL_CW). This is done using the glFrontFace function (the given call specifies our polygons as front-facing):

glFrontFace(GL_CCW);

Following this, we can enable back-face elimination using the following OpenGL function call:

glCullFace(GL_BACK);

Consider the objects shown in Figure 12-6; object B is partially obscured by both object A and object C while object A is partially blocked by object C. The hidden areas of triangle A and rectangle B can be eliminated from the drawing process without any change to the final rendered image. This is a very simple *hidden surface removal problem* – determining the parts of objects hidden from the viewer and subsequently removing these areas from the rendering process. Determining the surfaces or parts of surfaces hidden from the viewpoint can be done using a number of techniques or algorithms. This section investigates two commonly used algorithms, the z-buffer and painter's algorithm, highlighting the benefits and drawbacks of each.

There are two main hidden surface removal algorithm classes, namely, object space algorithms and image space algorithms. *Object space algorithms* work by ordering the surfaces of objects prior to the rendering phase – thus ensuring that objects are ordered such as to give the correct image. For example, we can order the objects in Figure 12-6 so that they are drawn from back to front, thus starting with object B, followed by object A and then finally object C. The back-facing surfaces are thus 'painted over' with the front surfaces, producing the correct image.

Image space algorithms are based on the determination of pixel positions. A projector originating from the center of projection is 'shot' through all the object surfaces in the scene. The position of intersection is subsequently used to determine the distance of an object from the viewer. For example, Figure 12-7 shows a center of projection, a projector and three objects. Using the projector intersection values, the rectangle is flagged closest to the viewer.

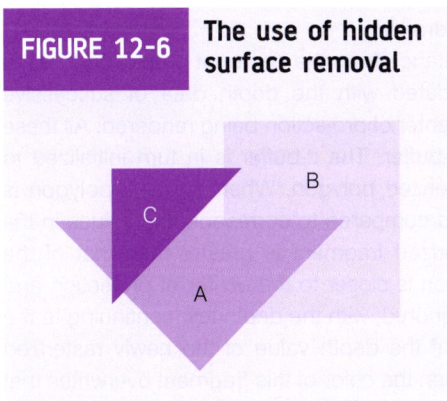

FIGURE 12-6 | **The use of hidden surface removal**

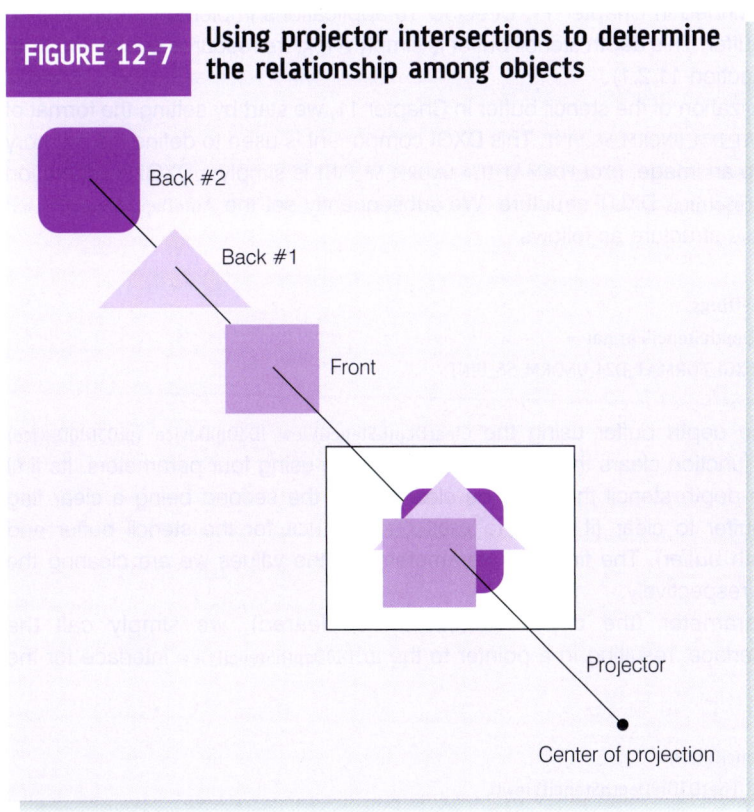

FIGURE 12-7 | **Using projector intersections to determine the relationship among objects**

Back #2

Back #1

Front

Projector

Center of projection

12

12.2.1 The Z-Buffer Algorithm

The most common hidden surface removal algorithm is called the *z-buffer algorithm*. This image space algorithm was developed in 1975 by Edwin Catmull, current president of Walt Disney and Pixar Animation Studios. Z-buffering, sometimes referred to as depth-buffering, stores the depth values for each pixel being drawn in the frame buffer's depth buffer. This stored depth data, or *z*-values, are then used by the algorithm to determine the pixels that should be drawn. Only the pixels closest to the viewer, determined by looking at each pixel's depth data, are rendered. Hence, the depth value of each pixel is compared to that of a selected pixel, and if the selected pixel is further from the center of projection than the pixel in the depth buffer, then the selected pixel is not drawn.

The *z*-buffer algorithm works by keeping track of the distance from the center of projection to each rasterized polygon. This information is continuously updated with the depth data of successive rasterized polygons, with only the polygons closest to the center of projection being rendered. All these distances, or depth values, are stored in the depth- or z-buffer. The z-buffer is in turn initialized to the distance from the center of projection to the first rasterized polygon. When the next polygon is rasterized, the depth of each of its pixels is determined and compared to corresponding values in the depth buffer. Thus, if the depth value of the newly rasterized fragment is greater than that of the corresponding fragment, then the original rasterized polygon is closer to the center of projection and viewer. The color of this newly rasterized fragment is then ignored, with the depth test continuing to the next pixel of the rasterized polygon. On the other hand, if the depth value of the newly rasterized fragment is less than the value stored in the depth buffer, then the color of this fragment overwrites that of the stored fragment.

Z-buffering is performed during the rasterization stage and is integrated into most GPUs, thus hardware accelerated. As described in Chapter 11, Direct3D 10 applications implement depth testing natively via the depth stencil buffer. This depth stencil buffer is simply a texture resource containing both stencil and depth data (see section 11.2.1).

As discussed with the initialization of the stencil buffer in Chapter 11, we start by setting the format of the depth stencil to DXGI_FORMAT_D24_UNORM_S8_UINT. This DXGI component is used to define the memory layout of each pixel making up an image. DXGI_FORMAT_D24_UNORM_S8_UINT is simply a DXGI enumeration type required by the DXUTDeviceSettings DXUT structure. We subsequently set the AutoDepthStencilFormat member of the DXUTDeviceSettings structure as follows:

```
DXUTDeviceSettings* pDXUTDeviceSettings;
pDXUTDeviceSettings->d3d10.AutoDepthStencilFormat =
                    DXGI_FORMAT_D24_UNORM_S8_UINT;
```

Next we have to clear the depth buffer using the ClearDepthStencilView ID3D10Device (pID3D10Device) interface. To summarize, this function clears the depth stencil resource using four parameters. Its first parameter is a pointer to the depth stencil that is to be cleared with the second being a clear flag indicating the parts of the buffer to clear (it is set to D3D10_CLEAR_STENCIL for the stencil buffer and D3D10_CLEAR_DEPTH for the depth buffer). The final two parameters are the values we are clearing the depth and stencil buffer with, respectively.

To initialize the first parameter (the depth stencil to be cleared), we simply call the DXUTGetD3D10DepthStencilView interface, resulting in a pointer to the ID3D10DepthStencilView interface for the current Direct3D 10 device:

```
ID3D10DepthStencilView* pDepthStencilView =
                    DXUTGetD3D10DepthStencilView();
```

The depth buffer is cleared with ClearDepthStencilView's second parameter set to D3D10_CLEAR_DEPTH:

```
pID3D10Device->ClearDepthStencilView(pDepthStencilView,
                         D3D10_CLEAR_DEPTH,1.0,0);
```

As mentioned, the depth test result is required for controlling whether a certain pixel is rendered or discarded. If the depth test passes then the tested pixel's depth value is overwritten by that of the incoming fragment. We enable depth testing by setting the first parameter, DepthEnable, of Direct3D 10's D3D10_DEPTH_STENCIL_DESC structure to true. The D3D10_DEPTH_STENCIL_DESC structure describes the depth stencil state, thus controlling the manner in which the depth test is performed. This structure and its members are fully discussed in section 11.2.1. D3D10_DEPTH_STENCIL_DESC's default member values (including alternatives) are listed in Table 11.1.

A depth stencil state, specifying the details of the depth and stencil testing operations, is defined by first initializing the D3D10_DEPTH_STENCIL_DESC structure's depth testing members, namely, DepthEnable, DepthWriteMask, and DepthFunc:

```
D3D10_DEPTH_STENCIL_DESC depthstencilDesc;

/* enable depth testing */
depthstencilDesc.DepthEnable = true;

/* enable writing to the depth stencil buffer */
depthstencilDesc.DepthWriteMask = D3D10_DEPTH_WRITE_MASK_ALL;

/* the test passes if the new data < existing data */
depthstencilDesc.DepthFunc = D3D10_COMPARISON_LESS;
```

Next we disable stencil testing, thus not requiring initialization of the stencil test parameters (StencilEnable, StencilReadMask and StencilWriteMask):

```
/* disable stencil testing */
depthstencilDesc.StencilEnable = false;
```

Now we simply have to set the depth stencil state for the output-merger stage to perform the depth test. This is done via the CreateDepthStencilState ID3D10Device interface. This interface takes two parameters, the first being a pointer to the depth stencil state description, D3D10_DEPTH_STENCIL_DESC, and the second, the address of the depth stencil state object, ID3D10DepthStencilState:

```
ID3D10Device* pID3D10Device;

ID3D10DepthStencilState* pDepthStencilState;
pID3D10Device->CreateDepthStencilState(depthstencilDesc,
                         &pDepthStencilState);
```

With the depth stencil state set, we still have to create a depth stencil buffer resource using a texture resource. As previously described, to create a depth stencil buffer we require a texture resource (defined using the ID3D10Texture2D interface) consisting of a two-dimensional grid of texture elements (specified via the D3D10_TEXTURE2D_DESC structure):

```
ID3D10Texture2D* pDepthStencilBuffer = NULL;
D3D10_TEXTURE2D_DESC depthResource;
```

12

The texture resource is initialized as a depth stencil buffer with its BindFlags member set to the D3D10_BIND_DEPTH_STENCIL enumeration (refer to section 8.2.2 for a full description of the D3D10_TEXTURE2D _DESC structure and each of its members):

```
/* set the width and height of the 2D texture resource in
    terms of texels */
depthResource.Width = backBufferSurfaceDescription.Width;
depthResource.Height = backBufferSurfaceDescription.Height;

/* set the maximum number of mipmaps that will be associated
    with the texture resource */
depthResource.MipLevels = 1;

/* specify the number of textures in the texture array */
depthResource.ArraySize = 1;

/* specify the texel format */
depthResource.Format = pDeviceSettings ->
                            d3d10.AutoDepthStencilFormat;

/* specify the number of multisamples per pixel */
depthResource.SampleDesc.Count = 1;

/* specify the image quality level */
depthResource.SampleDesc.Quality = 0;

/* control the manner in which the texture resource is used –
    D3D10_USAGE_DEFAULT allows read & write access by the GPU*/
depthResource.Usage = D3D10_USAGE_DEFAULT;

/* control the manner in which the texture resource is bound to
    the pipeline – D3D10_BIND_DEPTH_STENCIL specifies the
    resource as a depth stencil buffer */
depthResource.BindFlags = D3D10_BIND_DEPTH_STENCIL;

/* no need to set CPU access permissions */
depthResource.CPUAccessFlags = 0;

/* no need to set any miscellaneous options */
depthResource.MiscFlags = 0;
```

Following the initialization of D3D10_TEXTURE2D_DESC structure members, we use the CreateTexture2D ID3D10Device method to create a two-dimensional texture array: the depth stencil buffer, also called the depth stencil resource. The CreateTexture2D function takes three parameters, the first being a pointer to the above defined two-dimensional texture resource structure, D3D10_TEXTURE2D_DESC; the second a pointer to a texture subresource ('NULL' in our case); and the third the address of a pointer to the previously specified depth stencil state object, pDepthStencilBuffer:

```
pID3D10Device->CreateTexture2D(&depthResource,
    NULL,
    &pDepthStencilBuffer);
```

The final step in configuring depth testing is to bind the previously defined depth data to the output-merger stage. The output-merger stage, as previously described, is the final pipeline step that controls pixel visibility by incorporating pixel shader data with depth and stencil testing results (see Chapter 4 and Chapter 11).

We start by binding the depth stencil state, pDepthStencilState, to the output-merger stage using the OMSetDepthStencilState method. As discussed in Chapter 11, this method takes two parameters with the first being a pointer to the depth stencil state interface, pDepthStencilState, previously created using the CreateDepthStencilState ID3D10Device interface. The second parameter, an unsigned integer, is the reference value we are doing the depth test against:

```
pID3D10Device->OMSetDepthStencilState(pDepthStencilBuffer, 1);
```

Next we have to bind the depth stencil resource via a view – a mechanism used to describe how the depth stencil resource will be handled (viewed) by the pipeline. The D3D10_DEPTH_STENCIL_VIEW_DESC structure, described in section 11.2.1, is used for this purpose. The following code sample illustrates the definition of a depth stencil resource view using this structure:

```
D3D10_DEPTH_STENCIL_VIEW_DESC depthstencilviewDescription;

/* interpret the data in the resource as 32-bit floating-point
    values */
depthstencilviewDescription.Format = DXGI_FORMAT_D32_FLOAT;

/* specify the resource as a 2D texture */
depthstencilviewDescription.ResourceType = D3D10_RESOURCE_TEXTURE2D;

/* specify the texture, stored in the array, to use in the
    depth stencil view */
depthstencilviewDescription.Texture2D.FirstArraySlice = 0;

/* specify the number of textures, stored in the array, to use
    in the depth stencil view */
depthstencilviewDescription.Texture2D.ArraySize = 1;

/* set the depth stencil view's mipmap level to 0 – the 1st
    mipmap level in the depth stencil view */
depthstencilviewDescription.Texture2D.MipSlice = 0;
```

Following this, we simply have to create and bind the depth stencil view to the output-merger stage using the CreateDepthStencilView and OMSetRenderTargets ID3D10Device interfaces, respectively. As discussed in Chapter 11, the CreateDepthStencilView method, creating the depth stencil view, takes three parameters, namely a pointer to an ID3D10Texture2D object (pDepthStencilBuffer) used for storing the resource data, a pointer to the D3D10_DEPTH_STENCIL_VIEW_DESC structure, and the address of a pointer to an ID3D10DepthStencilView interface (pDepthStencilView) used for controlling the texture resource utilized during the depth stencil test:

```
ID3D10DepthStencilView* pDepthStencilView;

pID3D10Device->CreateDepthStencilView(pDepthStencilBuffer
                        &depthstencilviewDescription,
                        &pDepthStencilView);
```

12

The `OMSetRenderTargets` method binds this depth stencil view to the output-merger stage. It takes three parameters, with the first identifying the number of render targets (in this case only '1'), the second a pointer to a render target view array, `pRenderTargetView`, and the third a pointer to the `ID3D10DepthStencilView` interface, `pDepthStencilView`. A render target is written to by the output-merger stage containing the pixel color information:

```
ID3D10RenderTargetView* pRenderTargetView;

pID3D10Device->OMSetRenderTargets(
                   1, &pRenderTargetView, pDepthStencilView);
```

Working with OpenGL

Enabling hidden surface removal via the z-buffer algorithm in OpenGL is a simple process consisting of one GLUT and two OpenGL function calls. We start by enabling the depth buffer for the storage of z-values by adding the flag, `GLUT_DEPTH` to the `glutInitDisplayMode` display initialization function as described in Chapter 2:

```
glutInitDisplayMode(GLUT_DOUBLE | GLUT_RGB | GLUT_DEPTH);
```

The z-buffer algorithm is now enabled via the `GL_DEPTH_TEST` flag:

```
glEnable(GL_DEPTH_TEST);
```

The depth buffer must be cleared to preset values whenever the screen is to be redrawn. This is done via the `glClear` function. The buffers to clear are passed to this function as a logical combination of masks. Possible buffers include:

- GL_ACCUM_BUFFER_BIT (accumulation buffer)
- GL_COLOR_BUFFER_BIT (color buffer)
- GL_DEPTH_BUFFER_BIT (depth buffer) and
- GL_STENCIL_BUFFER_BIT (stencil buffer).

We will, for example, clear the frame- and depth buffer using the following routine:

```
glClear(GL_COLOR_BUFFER_BIT | GL_DEPTH_BUFFER_BIT);
```

The two main advantages of the z-buffer algorithm are its support for dynamic scenes and native implementation of the algorithm in graphics hardware as well as the Direct3D and OpenGL APIs. Performance of the z-buffer algorithm is also directly proportional to the number of generated fragments. Another advantage is the algorithm's compatibility with pipeline architectures where it can process the rasterized pixels of polygons as they are passed through the graphics pipeline. The only real disadvantage to using z-buffering is the additional required storage of 2 to 4 bytes per rasterized fragment.

12.2.2 **The Painter's Algorithm**

The previous section highlighted the ease of use and efficiency of the z-buffer image space algorithm. Object space algorithms, although not as widely used nor hardware accelerated as the z-buffer image space algorithm, can be useful in reducing the number of polygons rendered by considering them on an object-by-object rather than primitive-by-primitive basis. Object space algorithms, as previously mentioned, work by ordering the surfaces of objects prior to the rendering phase. The simplest of these sorting algorithms is known as the painter's algorithm.

The *painter's algorithm* orders polygons based on their distance from the viewer. This distance is calculated from the polygon's centroid to the point of view. A *centroid* of a geometric object is the intersection of all the lines dividing it into equal parts. The centroid of an object can be considered its center of mass. Figure 12-8 shows the centroid of a triangle.

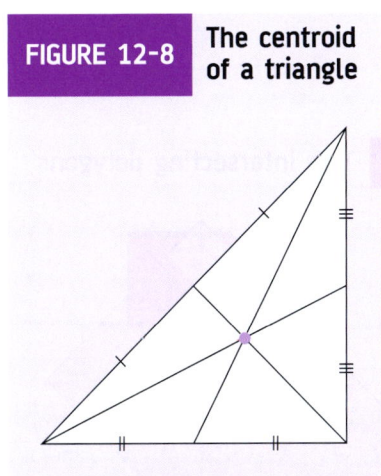

| FIGURE 12-8 | The centroid of a triangle |

The name of this simple object space algorithm comes from the way a painter might draw a scene. The painter could draw the distant objects of a scene first, covering the parts of these objects not visible to the viewer with closer objects, and finally adding the objects nearest to the viewer. Applying this painting approach to computer graphics results in the complete back-to-front rendering of polygons. The painter's algorithm sorts all the polygons in a scene using the depth data of each, subsequently painting them in this order. For example, consider the two polygons shown in Figure 12-9(a) – using the painter's algorithm we will render polygon A completely, with the nearer polygon, polygon B, covering the part of polygon A not visible to the viewer, resulting in the image shown in Figure 12-9(b).

It is also possible to draw the objects of a scene in a front-to-back manner, resulting in the *reverse painter's algorithm*.

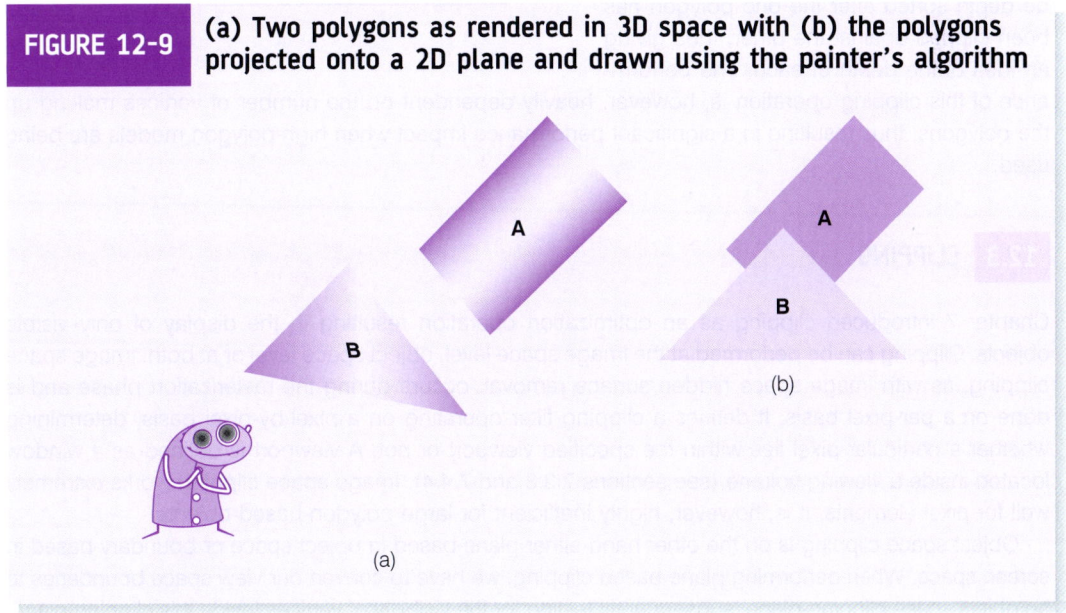

| FIGURE 12-9 | (a) Two polygons as rendered in 3D space with (b) the polygons projected onto a 2D plane and drawn using the painter's algorithm |

This variant algorithm deals with the performance overhead of the painter's algorithm by enforcing a precondition stating that no polygon can be rendered over any previously drawn polygons. Using this approach we are able to limit the number of polygons rendered due to only the visible parts of partially hidden objects being drawn. For example, using the reverse painter's algorithm for the two polygons shown in Figure 12-9(a), we start by rendering polygon B completely, with only the visible areas of the more distant polygon, polygon A, subsequently being drawn.

There is one serious flaw in the painter's hidden surface removal algorithm – the overlapping of three or more polygons can cause it to fail. For example, polygons A, B and C in Figure 12-10 overlap in a cyclic clockwise direction, making it impossible to discern the polygons closest to the point of view. The only real solution to this problem is to divide at least one of the polygons into two parts, thus in this way finding the drawing order.

Another problem is encountered when two or more polygons intersect each other. For example, the intersecting cube and pyramid shown in Figure 12-11 can only be depth sorted after the one polygon has been clipped against the other, thus giving an idea of the depth of each. The performance of this clipping operation is, however, heavily dependent on the number of vertices making up the polygons, thus resulting in a significant performance impact when high-polygon models are being used.

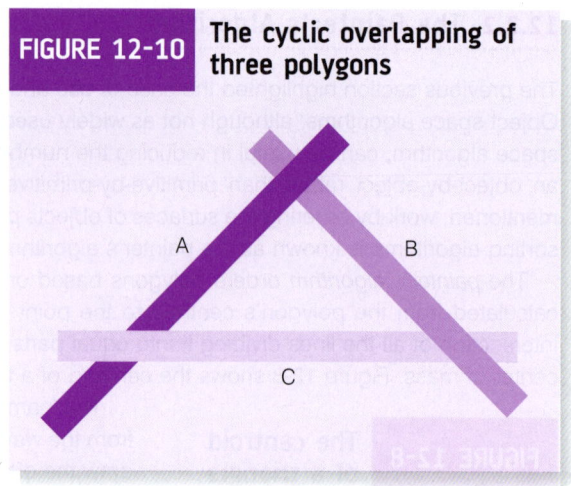

| FIGURE 12-10 | The cyclic overlapping of three polygons |

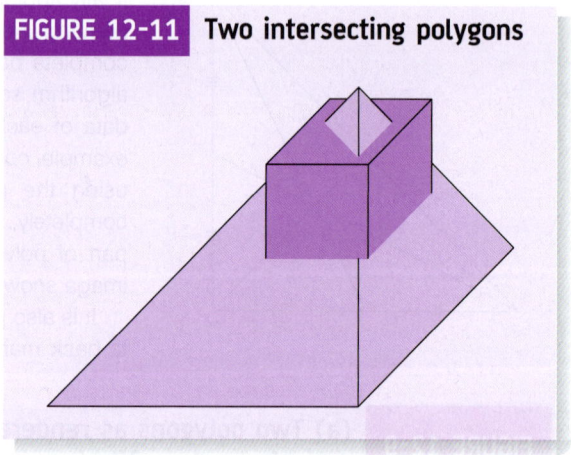

| FIGURE 12-11 | Two intersecting polygons |

12.3   CLIPPING

Chapter 7 introduced clipping as an optimization operation resulting in the display of only visible objects. Clipping can be performed at the image space level, object space level or at both. Image space clipping, as with image space hidden surface removal, occurs during the rasterization phase and is done on a per-pixel basis. It defines a clipping filter operating on a pixel-by-pixel basis, determining whether a particular pixel lies within the specified viewport or not. A viewport is defined as a window located inside a viewing volume (see sections 7.3.3 and 7.4.4). Image space clipping works extremely well for pixel elements. It is, however, highly inefficient for large polygon-based objects.

Object space clipping is on the other hand either plane-based in object space or boundary-based in screen space. When performing plane-based clipping, we have to convert our view space boundaries to an object space clipping-plane, subsequently testing for the visibility of vertices inside this clipping-plane.

12

FIGURE 12-12 Two-dimensional clipping (a) before clipping (b) after clipping

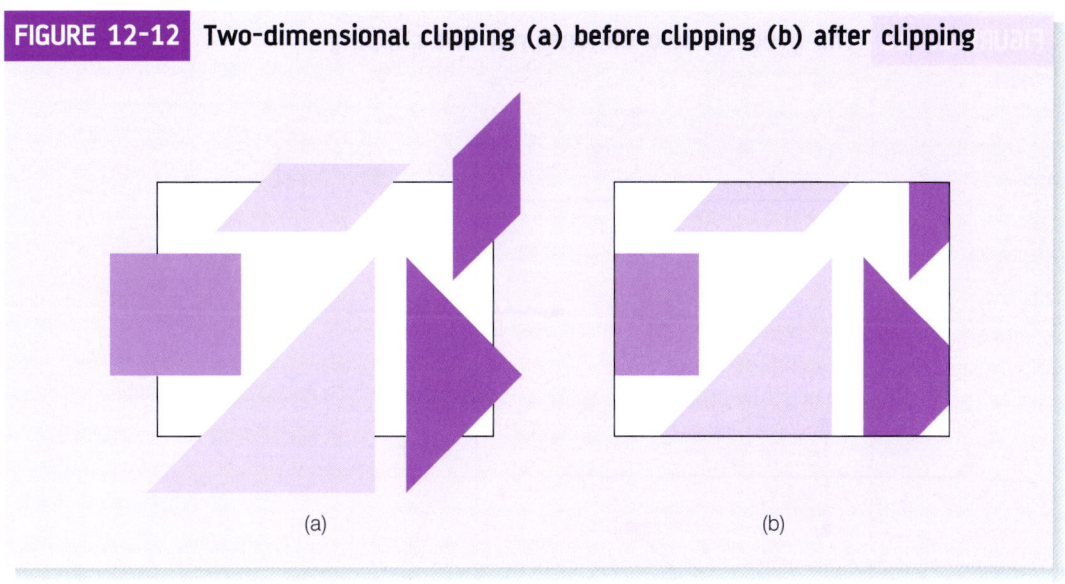

(a)   (b)

Boundary-based clipping clips against screen boundaries while in screen space by flagging the intersection of objects with planes adjacent to the *x-*, *y-* and *z*-axes.

As discussed in Chapter 7, the virtual image plane is commonly used to control the clipping of objects. A programmatically defined clipping volume blocks out objects not visible to the viewer. All objects and portions of objects falling outside this clipping volume or clipping rectangle are clipped out and thus do not appear in the viewable image. Clipping via a clipping volume is normally done on a primitive-by-primitive rather than a vertex-by-vertex basis, as shown in Figure 12-12.

We will now investigate several clipping algorithms and techniques such as simple two-dimensional line clipping, Liang-Barsky clipping, Cohen-Sutherland clipping, the clipping of polygons, and three-dimensional clipping.

12.3.1 Two-Dimensional Line Clipping

Two-dimensional line clipping or line-segment clipping determines the primitives, or sections of primitives, visible to the viewer. All lines located within the predefined view volume pass the clipping test and are sent to the rasterizer for display. Primitives not located within the view volume are culled or eliminated. The lines, or primitives, partially located within the view volume are clipped so that only their visible sections are sent to the rasterizer for display.

Consider the general two-dimensional line clipping problem illustrated in Figure 12-13. This figure illustrates the following four possible clipping situations:

A The line is completely visible within the predefined view volume, thus passing the clipping test.

B The line is completely outside the predefined view volume and can be eliminated from the drawing process.

C The line extends from outside the clipping region, enters the view volume and exits it again at another point. Lines like these must be clipped at both ends of the view volume.

D The line segment is only partially within the predefined view volume. Its section outside of the clipping region must thus be clipped.

12

12

FIGURE 12-13   **The need for two-dimensional line clipping**

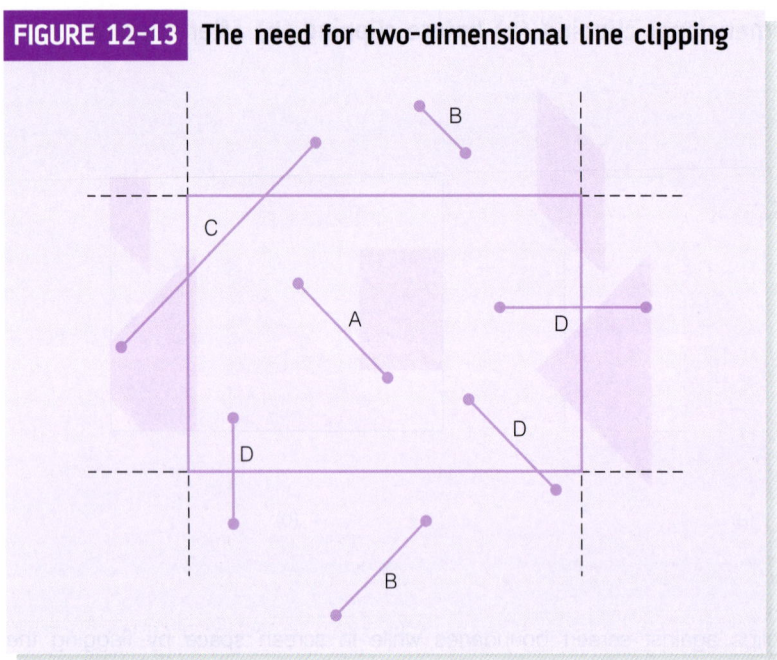

There are several line clipping algorithms, such as the Cohen-Sutherland clipping algorithm, Liang-Barsky clipping, and Cyrus-Beck clipping. We will specifically focus on the first two in later sections, for now only considering the basic mathematical theory behind the general line clipping process.

The core issue with clipping algorithms is determining the intersection of two lines. For example, consider line C shown in Figure 12-13. This line extends from one point in 2D space (x_1, y_1) to another (x_2, y_2), intersecting a rectangle defined by four points (r_1, r_1), (r_2, r_2), (r_3, r_3) and (r_4, r_4) with a line connecting each adjacent pair. We can assume that this rectangle will be intersected at no less than one of its edges, meaning that all view volume intersections will occur at either a vertical or horizontal edge. The clipping process determines these intersections and can be described by the following three steps:

1   Take the input coordinates of a line, (x_1, y_1) and (x_2, y_2), as input.

2   Read the coordinates of the clipping rectangle.

3   Generate the clipped line coordinates, (x_1', y_1') and (x_2', y_2'), by comparing the input values of the line to the coordinates of the clipping region.

Say we have two line segments, P_1 from the point (x_1, y_1) to (x_2, y_2) and P_2 from (x_3, y_3) to the point (x_4, y_4), and that we would like to calculate the point of their intersection as shown in Figure 12-14.

Determining the intersection as illustrated in Figure 12-14 is really simple, all we have to do is find the point where $P_1 = P_2$. We start by calculating the slope of both lines:

$$m_{P_1} = \frac{(y_2 - y_1)}{(x_2 - x_1)}$$

$$m_{P_2} = \frac{(y_4 - y_3)}{(x_4 - x_2)}$$

FIGURE 12-14 **Two intersecting line segments**

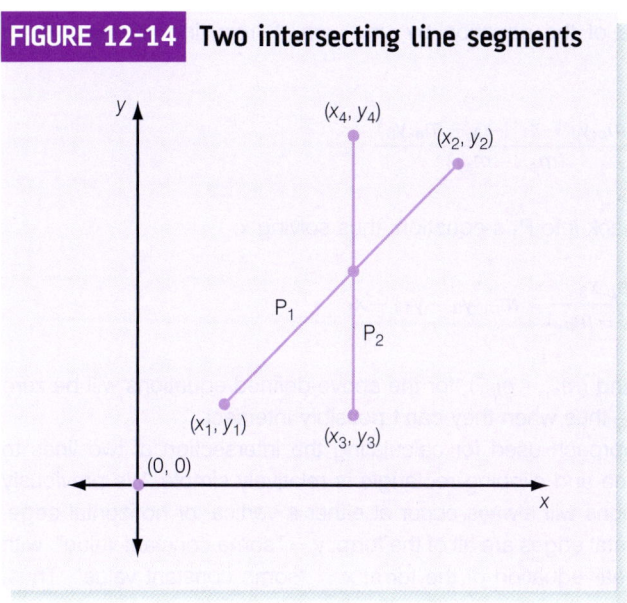

Using a linear equation ($y = mx + b$) in its point-slope form, $y - y_1 = m(x - x_1)$, with m the slope of the line and (x_1, y_1) any point on the line, we can represent each straight line in terms of Cartesian coordinates:

$$\text{Equation for } P_1: (x - x_1) = m_{P_1}(y - y_1)$$

$$\text{Equation for } P_2: (x - x_3) = m_{P_2}(y - y_3)$$

To find the point of intersection we need to determine x and y. The simplest approach is to find x in terms of y for P_1's equation, substituting it into P_2's equation.

Equation for P_1 written as x in terms of y:

$$x = m_{P_1}(y - y_1) + x_1$$

We can now substitute x in P_2's equation with $x = m_{P_1}(y - y_1) + x_1$:

$$m_{P_1}(y - y_1) + x_1 - x_3 = m_{P_2}(y - y_3)$$

The point of intersection is thus where:

$$m_{P_2}(y - y_3) + x_3 = m_{P_1}(y - y_1) + x_1$$

Next we can simplify the equation:

$$m_{P_1}y - m_{P_1}y_1 + x_1 - x_3 = m_{P_2}y - m_{P_2}y_3$$

This is followed by the grouping of terms:

$$m_{P_1}y - m_{P_2}y = m_{P_1}y_1 - x_1 + x_3 + m_{P_2}y_3$$

The terms on the left can now be rewritten as:

$$y(m_{P_1} - m_{P_2}) = m_{P_1}y_1 - x_1 + x_3 + m_{P_2}y_3$$

12

The final step is to divide both sides of the equation by $(m_{p_1} - m_{p_2})$, resulting in the point of intersection's y-coordinate:

$$y = \frac{(m_{p_1}y_1 - x_1 + x_3 + m_{p_2}y_3)}{(m_{p_1} - m_{p_2})}$$

We can now substitute this equation back into P_1's equation, thus solving x:

$$x = \frac{m_{p_1}x_3}{(m_{p_2} - m_{p_1})} + m_{p_1}(y_3 - y_1) + x_1$$

Note: the denominators, $(m_{p_2} - m_{p_1})$ and $(m_{p_1} - m_{p_2})$, for the above-defined equations will be zero when the lines are parallel to each other – thus when they can't possibly intersect.

Extending this basic mathematical approach used for calculating the intersection of two lines to determine the point of intersection of a line and clipping rectangle is relatively simple. We previously mentioned that clipping volume intersections will always occur at either a vertical or horizontal edge. Furthermore, the clipping volume's horizontal edges are all of the form: $y =$ "some constant value", with the vertical edges being defined by a linear equation of the form: $x =$ "some constant value". Thus, calculating the point of intersection of a line and the edge of a clipping rectangle is simply a matter of substitution. For example, consider the above-defined line segments P_1 clipped against the view volume in Figure 12-15.

The clipped line coordinates, (x_1', y_1') and (x_2', y_2'), can be computed by substituting the line equation of the vertical or horizontal line into the point-slope form of the intersecting line. Thus, when calculating the point of intersection on the vertical line segment, we already have the x-coordinate of intersection and simply have to substitute this value ($x = 5$ in this case) into the line equation for P_1 to determine the point of intersection's y-coordinate. Similarly, to calculate the point of intersection on the horizontal line, we already have the y-coordinate ($y = 8$ in Figure 12-15) and we simply have to substitute it into the point-slope equation of the intersecting line to get the second point of intersection's x-coordinate.

FIGURE 12-15 **Intersection of a line segment and clipping rectangle**

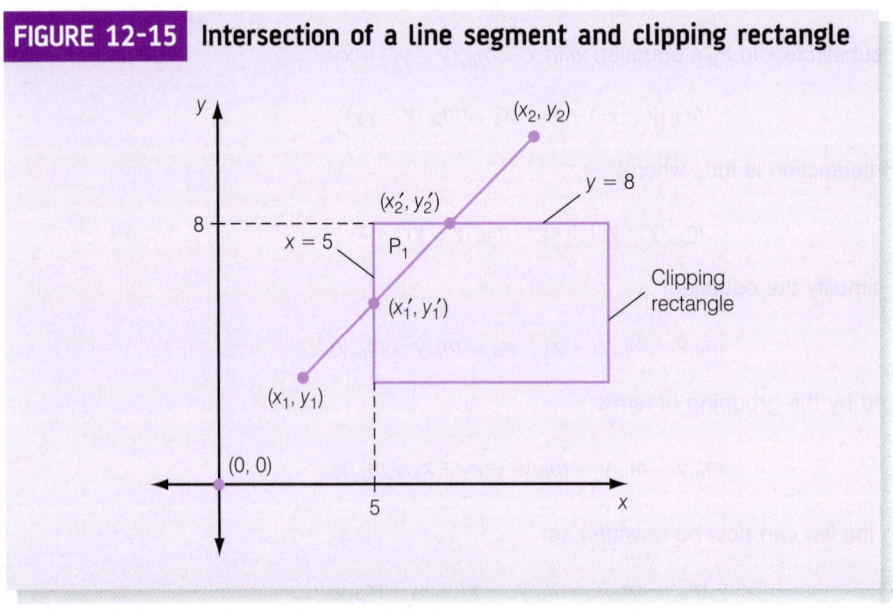

FIGURE 12-16	The nine Cohen-Sutherland clipping regions, each assigned a unique outcode

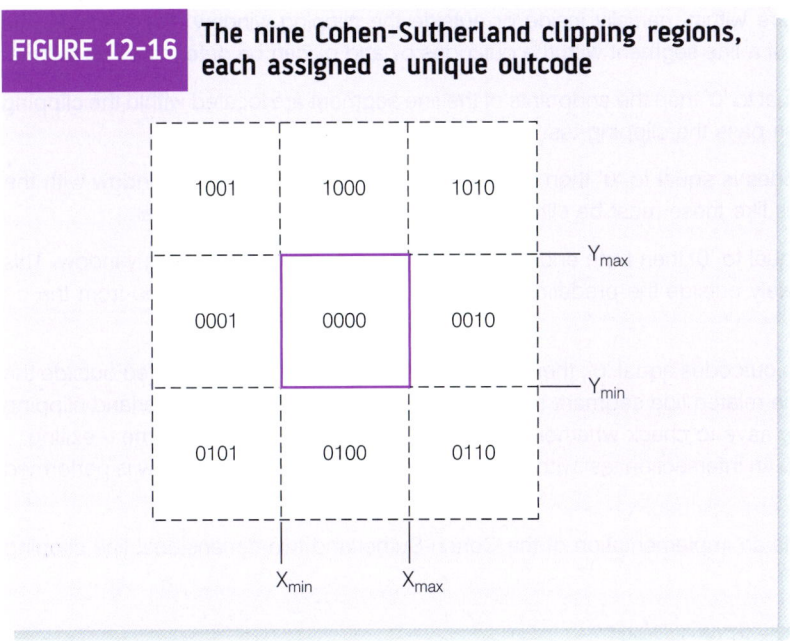

12.3.1.1 Cohen-Sutherland Clipping

Our previous approach to computing the intersection of a line segment and clipping rectangle requires a number of floating-point divisions. One floating-point division is specifically required for each intersection, thus resulting in a significant performance overhead in situations where a great number of lines are being clipped. The Cohen-Sutherland algorithm substitutes these floating-point divisions with bit operations and floating-point subtractions, leading to an overall performance gain when compared to the traditional approach.

The *Cohen-Sutherland* two-dimensional line clipping algorithm can be considered a brute-force approach to the clipping problem. The algorithm basically divides the clipping region into a number of sections (specifically nine regions), each with its own unique 4-bit binary number, called an *outcode*. These regions, shown in Figure 12-16, are then used for relatively fast end-point determination.

The nine regions in Figure 12-16 are assigned an outcode in the form $a_0a_1a_2a_3$ based on the following algorithm:

- If (x, y) is a point in any of the Cohen-Sutherland clipping regions, then:

  a The leftmost outcode bit, a_0, is set to '1' if y is greater than Y_{max}.

  b The leftmost outcode bit, a_0, is set to '0' if y is less than or equal to Y_{max}.

  c The next outcode bit, a_1, is set to '1' if y is smaller than Y_{min}.

  d The a_1 outcode bit is set to '0' if y is greater than or equal to Y_{min}.

  e The a_2 outcode bit is set to '1' if x is greater than X_{max}.

  f The a_2 outcode bit is set to '0' if x is less than or equal to X_{max}.

  g The rightmost outcode bit, a_3, is set to '1' if x is smaller than X_{min}.

  h The rightmost outcode bit, a_3, is set to '0' if x is greater than or equal to X_{min}.

We can thus calculate the outcodes for each endpoint of a line segment located within one or spanning across multiple Cohen-Sutherland clipping regions. And we can, based on these outcodes, determine whether these endpoints are within, partially inside or outside the clipping window. For example, the position of each endpoint of a line segment with the outcodes o_1 and o_2 can be determined as follows:

- If both o_1 and o_2 are equal to '0' then the endpoints of the line segment are located within the clipping window. Lines like these pass the clipping test and are sent to the rasterizer.

- If only one of the outcodes is equal to '0' then that endpoint is inside the clipping window with the other one outside. Lines like these must be clipped before being sent to the rasterizer.

- If neither o_1 nor o_2 is equal to '0' then both endpoints are located outside the clipping window. This line segment is completely outside the predefined view volume and can be eliminated from the drawing process.

- If the bitwise AND of the outcodes equal '0', then we know that the endpoints are located outside the clipping window with the related line segment spanning across multiple Cohen-Sutherland clipping regions. In this case we have to check whether the line actually enters the view volume – exiting it again at another point. An intersection test with one of the sides of the clipping window is performed to determine this.

The following function is an implementation of the Cohen-Sutherland two-dimensional line clipping algorithm:

```
/* this function clips a line using its two endpoint
    coordinates (x1, y1) & (x2, y2) */
int CohenSutherlandClip(float &x1, float &y1, float &x2,
                        float &y2)
{
    /* global variables specifying the clipping codes */
    #define CLIPPING_REGION_OUTCODE      0x0000 //binary: 0000
    #define TOP_CENTER_OUTCODE           0x0008 //binary: 1000
    #define BOTTOM_CENTER_OUTCODE        0x0004 //binary: 0100
    #define MIDDLE_RIGHT_OUTCODE         0x0002 //binary: 0010
    #define MIDDLE_LEFT_OUTCODE          0x0001 //binary: 0001
    #define TOP_RIGHT_OUTCODE            0x000a //binary: 1010
    #define BOTTOM_RIGHT_OUTCODE         0x0006 //binary: 0110
    #define TOP_LEFT_OUTCODE             0x0009 //binary: 1001
    #define BOTTOM_LEFT_OUTCODE          0x0005 //binary: 0101


    /* assign the received endpoint coordinates local
        coordinates */

    float x1_clipping_coordinate = x1;
    float y1_clipping_coordinate = y1;
    float x2_clipping_coordinate = x2;
    float y2_clipping_coordinate = y2;
    /* specify the clipping rectangle borders.
        – the clipping edges are given the same names as those
          shown in Figure 12.16  */
    float x_min = 0;
    float x_max = SCREEN_WIDTH;
    float y_min = 0;
    float y_max = SCREEN_HEIGHT;
```

```
float line_segment_endpoint1 = 0;
float line_segment_endpoint2 = 0;

/* use the bitwise inclusive OR and assign operator "|="
   to assign outcodes to each of the line segment
   endpoints */

/* determine the outcode of the first endpoint */
//////////////////////////////////////////////////
if (x1 < x_min)
    line_segment_endpoint1 |= MIDDLE_LEFT_OUTCODE;

else
    if (x1 > x_max)
        line_segment_endpoint1 |= MIDDLE_RIGHT_OUTCODE;

if (y1 < y_min)
    line_segment_endpoint1 |= TOP_CENTER_OUTCODE;
else
    if (y1 > y_max)
        line_segment_endpoint1 |= BOTTOM_CENTER_OUTCODE;

/* determine the outcode of the second endpoint */
//////////////////////////////////////////////////
if (x2 < x_min)
    line_segment_endpoint2 |= MIDDLE_LEFT_OUTCODE;
else
    if (x2 > x_max)
        line_segment_endpoint2 |= MIDDLE_RIGHT_OUTCODE;

if (y2 < y_min)
    line_segment_endpoint2 |= TOP_CENTER_OUTCODE;
else
    if (y2 > y_max)
        line_segment_endpoint2 |= BOTTOM_CENTER_OUTCODE;

/* both endpoints will be equal to "0" if the line is
   completely visible */
if (line_segment_endpoint1==0&& line_segment_endpoint2==0)
    return 0;

/* clip the line for the first endpoint using the defined
   clipping window and determined outcode */
//////////////////////////////////////////////////
switch(line_segment_endpoint1)
{
    /* the endpoint is located within the clipping
       window */
    case CLIPPING_REGION_OUTCODE:
    break;

    /* the endpoint is located within the bottom-center
       clipping region */
```

```
  case BOTTOM_CENTER_OUTCODE:
  {
      int m = (x2 - x1)/(y2 - y1);
      x1_clipping_coordinate = x1+0.5+(y_max - y1)*m;
      y1_clipping_coordinate = y_max;
  }
  break;

  /* the endpoint is located within the top-center
     clipping region */
  case TOP_CENTER_OUTCODE:
  {
      int m = (x2 - x1)/(y2 - y1);

      x1_clipping_coordinate = x1+0.5+(y_min - y1)*m;
      y1_clipping_coordinate = y_min;
  }
  break;

  /* the endpoint is located within the middle-right
     clipping region */
  case MIDDLE_RIGHT_OUTCODE:
  {
      int m = (y2 - y1)/(x2 - x1);

      y1_clipping_coordinate = y1+0.5+(x_max - x1)*m;
      x1_clipping_coordinate = x_max;
  }
  break;

  /* the endpoint is located within the middle-left
     clipping region */
  case MIDDLE_LEFT_OUTCODE:
  {
      int m = (y2 - y1)/(x2 - x1);

      y1_clipping_coordinate = y1+0.5+(x_min - x1)*m;
      x1_clipping_coordinate = x_min;
  }
  break;

  /* the endpoint is located within the bottom-right
     clipping region, requiring the computation of two
     intersections */
  case BOTTOM_RIGHT_OUTCODE:
  {
      int m = (x2 - x1)/(y2 - y1);

      /* calculate the bottom horizontal line
         intersection*/
```

12

```
        xl_clipping_coordinate = xl+0.5+(y_max - yl)*m;
        yl_clipping_coordinate = y_max;


        /* the horizontal line intersection is tested
        for validity, if it passes then we can
        calculate the right vertical line
        intersection */
        if (xl_clipping_coordinate > x_max ||
            xl_clipping_coordinate < x_min)
        {
        int m2 = (y2 - yl)/(x2 - xl);

            yl_clipping_coordinate = yl + 0.5 +
                                  (x_max - xl)*m2;
            xl_clipping_coordinate = x_max;
        }
    }
    break;


    /* the endpoint is located within the top-right
       clipping region, requiring the computation of two
       intersections */
    case TOP_RIGHT_OUTCODE:
    {
        int m = (x2 - xl)/(y2 - yl);

        /* calculate the top horizontal line
           intersection*/
        xl_clipping_coordinate = xl + 0.5 +
                                  (y_min - yl) * m;
        yl_clipping_coordinate = y_min;

        /* the horizontal line intersection is tested
           for validity, if it passes then we can
           calculate the right vertical line
           intersection */
        if (xl_clipping_coordinate > x_max ||
            xl_clipping_coordinate < x_min)
        {
            int m2 = (y2 - yl)/(x2 - xl);

            yl_clipping_coordinate = yl + 0.5 +
                                  (x_max - xl)*m2;
            xl_clipping_coordinate = x_max;
        }
    }
    break;
```

12

```
/* the endpoint is located within the bottom-left
   clipping region, requiring the computation of two
   intersections */
case BOTTOM_LEFT_OUTCODE:
{
     int m = (x2 - x1)/(y2 - y1);

     /* calculate the bottom horizontal line
        Intersection */
     xl_clipping_coordinate = x1+0.5+(y_max - y1)*m;
     yl_clipping_coordinate = y_max;

     /* the horizontal line intersection is tested
        for validity, if it passes then we can
        calculate the left vertical line
        intersection */
     if (xl_clipping_coordinate > x_max ||
        xl_clipping_coordinate < x_min)
     {
          int m2 = (y2 - y1)/(x2 - x1);

          yl_clipping_coordinate = y1 + 0.5 +
                               (x_min - x1)*m2;
          xl_clipping_coordinate = x_min;
     }
break;

/* the endpoint is located within the top-left
   clipping region, requiring the computation of two
   intersections */
case TOP_LEFT_OUTCODE:
{
     int m = (x2 - x1)/(y2 - y1);

     /* calculate the top horizontal line
        intersection*/
     xl_clipping_coordinate = x1+0.5+(y_min - y1)*m;
     yl_clipping_coordinate = y_min;

     /* the horizontal line intersection is tested
        for validity, if it passes then we can
        calculate the left vertical line
        intersection */
     if (xl_clipping_coordinate > x_max ||
        xl_clipping_coordinate < x_min)
     {
          int m2 = (y2 - y1)/(x2 - x1);

          yl_clipping_coordinate = y1 + 0.5 +
                               (x_min - x1)*m2;
```

12

```
                xl_clipping_coordinate = x_min;
        }
    }
    break;

    default:break;
}

/* clip the line for the second endpoint using the
defined clipping window and determined outcode */
/////////////////////////////////////////////////////
switch(line_segment_endpoint2)
{
    /* the endpoint is located within the clipping
        window */
    case CLIPPING_REGION_OUTCODE:
    break;

    /* the endpoint is located within the bottom-center
        clipping region */
    case BOTTOM_CENTER_OUTCODE:
    {
        int n = (xl - x2)/(yl - y2);

        x2_clipping_coordinate = x2+0.5+(y_max - y2)*n;
        y2_clipping_coordinate = y_max;
    }
    break;

    /* the endpoint is located within the top-center
        clipping region */
    case TOP_CENTER_OUTCODE:
    {
        int n = (xl - x2)/(yl - y2);

        x2_clipping_coordinate = x2+0.5+(y_min - y2)*n;
        y2_clipping_coordinate = y_min;
    }
    break;

    /* the endpoint is located within the middle-right
        clipping region */
    case MIDDLE_RIGHT_OUTCODE:
    {
        int n = (yl - y2)/(xl - x2);

        y2_clipping_coordinate = y2+0.5+(x_max - x2)*n;
        x2_clipping_coordinate = x_max;
    }
    break;
```

12

```
/* the endpoint is located within the middle-left
   clipping region */
case MIDDLE_LEFT_OUTCODE:
{
    int n = (y1 - y2)/(x1 - x2);

    y2_clipping_coordinate = y2+0.5+(x_min - x2)*n;
    x2_clipping_coordinate = x_min;
}
break;

/* the endpoint is located within the bottom-right
   clipping region, requiring the computation of two
   intersections */
case BOTTOM_RIGHT_OUTCODE:
{
    int n = (x1 - x2)/(y1 - y2);

    /* calculate the bottom horizontal line
       intersection*/
    x2_clipping_coordinate = x2+0.5+(y_max - y2)*n;
    y2_clipping_coordinate = y_max;
    /* the horizontal line intersection is tested
       for validity, if it passes then we can
       calculate the right vertical line
       intersection */
    if (x2_clipping_coordinate < x_min ||
        x2_clipping_coordinate > x_max)
    {
        int n2 = (y1 - y2)/(x1 - x2);

        y2_clipping_coordinate = y2 + 0.5 +
                                 (x_max - x2)*n2;
        x2_clipping_coordinate = x_max;
    }
}
break;

/* the endpoint is located within the top-right
   clipping region, requiring the computation of two
   intersections */
case TOP_RIGHT_OUTCODE:
{
    int n = (x1 - x2)/(y1 - y2);

    /* calculate the top horizontal line
       intersection*/
    x2_clipping_coordinate = x2+0.5+(y_min - y2)*n;
    y2_clipping_coordinate = y_min;
```

12

```
    /* the horizontal line intersection is tested
       for validity, if it passes then we can
       calculate the right vertical line
       intersection */
  if (x2_clipping_coordinate < x_min ||
     x2_clipping_coordinate > x_max)
  {
         int n2 = (y1 − y2)/(x1 − x2);

         y2_clipping_coordinate = y2 + 0.5 +
                                    (x_max − x2)*n2;
         x2_clipping_coordinate = x_max;
  }
}
break;

/* the endpoint is located within the bottom−left
   clipping region, requiring the computation of two
   intersections */
case BOTTOM_LEFT_OUTCODE:
{
     int n = (x1 − x2)/(y1 − y2);

     /* calculate the bottom horizontal line
        intersection*/
    x2_clipping_coordinate = x2+0.5+(y_max − y2)*n;
    y2_clipping_coordinate = y_max;

     /* the horizontal line intersection is tested
        for validity, if it passes then we can
        calculate the left vertical line
        intersection */
  if (x2_clipping_coordinate < x_min ||
     x2_clipping_coordinate > x_max)
  {
         int n2 = (y1 − y2)/(x1 − x2);

         y2_clipping_coordinate = y2 + 0.5 +
                                    (x_min − x2)*n2;
         x2_clipping_coordinate = x_min;
  }
}
break;

/* the endpoint is located within the top−left
   clipping region, requiring the computation of two
   intersections */
case TOP_LEFT_OUTCODE:
{
     int n = (x1 − x2)/(y1 − y2);
```

12

```
/* calculate the top horizontal line
    intersection*/
x2_clipping_coordinate = x2+0.5+(y_min – y2)*n;
y2_clipping_coordinate = y_min;

    /* the horizontal line intersection is tested
        for validity, if it passes then we can
        calculate the left vertical line
        intersection */
    if (x2_clipping_coordinate < x_min ||
        x2_clipping_coordinate > x_max)
    {
        int n2 = (y1 – y2)/(x1 – x2);

        y2_clipping_coordinate = y2 + 0.5 +
                                 (x_min – x2)*n2;
        x2_clipping_coordinate = x_min;

    }
}
break;

default:break;
}

/* return the clipping coordinates to the address
    variables */
x1 = x1_clipping_coordinate;
y1 = y1_clipping_coordinate;
x2 = x2_clipping_coordinate;
y2 = y2_clipping_coordinate'

return 1;
}
```

12.3.1.2 Introduction to Liang-Barsky Clipping

The *Liang-Barsky* two-dimensional line clipping algorithm uses the parametric form of a line and the clipping window to determine the clipping coordinates of lines intersecting the clipping volume. This algorithm is significantly more efficient than Cohen-Sutherland clipping.

A parametric equation is basically a line equation where arbitrary values are used to determine the value of a point in space. For example, a circle centered at the origin with the radius r is commonly represented by the following formula:

$$x^2 + y^2 = r^2$$

This same circle can be represented using the following parametric equations (the arbitrary values, t in the equations, are used to determine the value of a point in space):

$$x = r \cos(t)$$
$$y = r \sin(t)$$

To understand Liang-Barsky clipping, consider a line segment consisting of two endpoints, $E_1 = (x_1, y_1)$ and $E_2 = (x_2, y_2)$. These endpoints can now be used to specify the following parametric line:

$$E(t) = E_1(1 - t) + E_2 t$$

The above given parametric line equation is expressed in matrix form and can easily be written in scalar form:

$$x(t) = x_1(1 - t) + x_2 t$$
$$y(t) = y_1(1 - t) + y_2 t$$

Using these equations, we can define endpoint E_1 at $t = 0$ and endpoint E_2 at $t = 1$. All values of t greater than '0' and less than '1' result in points on the line segment. Values of t less than '0' yield points past E_1 leading to negative infinity, with values for t greater than '1' resulting in points beyond E_2 going off into infinity.

The line segments shown in Figure 12-17 are located inside, partially inside or completely outside the predefined clipping window. Now, consider line segment C extending from outside the clipping region, entering the view volume and exiting it again at another point. This line segment intersects both the sides and extended sides of the clipping window resulting in a total of four intersections. The shown intersections correspond to arbitrary parametric values, t_1, t_2, t_3 and t_4 with these values constrained within the range (0, 1). The parametric value, t_4, is thus less than '1' with t_3 less than t_4, t_2 less than t_3 and t_1 the smallest of them all but still bigger than '0'.

Line segment B, shown in Figure 12-18, also has four intersections; however, it only intersects the extended sides of the clipping window. This can be determined by considering the order of intersections: the parametric value, t_4, is less than '1' with t_2 less than t_4, t_3 less than t_2 and t_1 the smallest of them all but still bigger than '0'. The shown line segment thus intersects the left and right sides of the window without intersecting either the top or bottom. The clipping volume is hence never intersected and the line segment can be discarded from the clipping process.

FIGURE 12-17	Several line segments and a clipping window, with t representing the arbitrary values of each parametric line

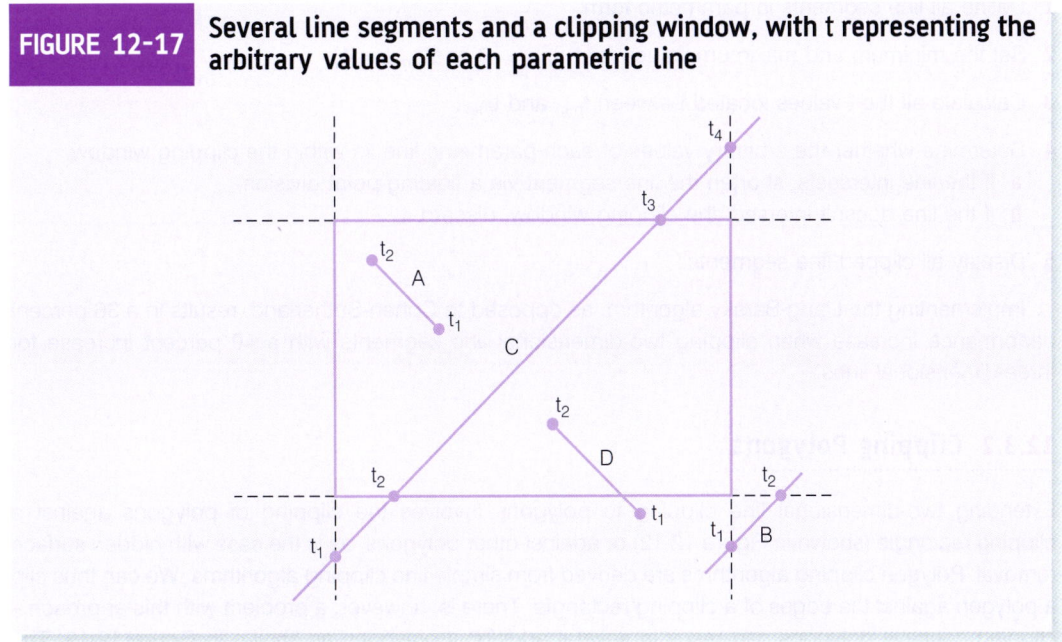

FIGURE 12-18	**A line segments and clipping window, with _t_ representing the arbitrary values of the parametric line**

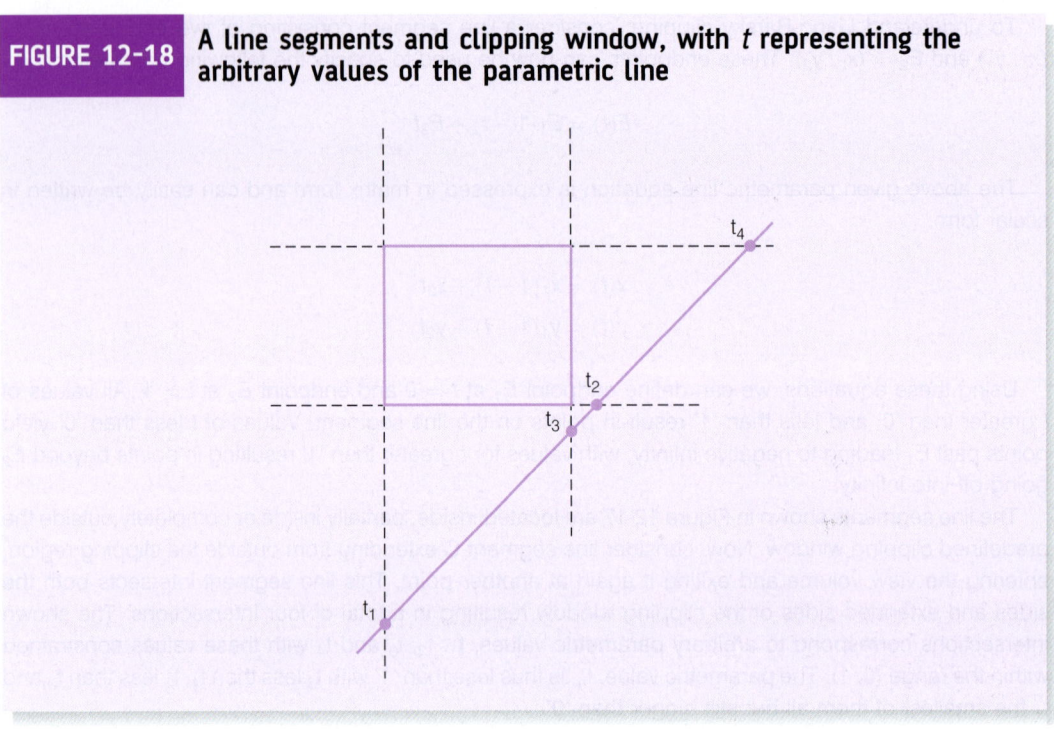

Rejecting line segments not intersecting the clipping window is thus the primary aim of the Liang-Barsky clipping algorithm. This algorithm also reduces the number of floating-point divisions needed by using the parametric form of lines to determine the clipping volume intersections. Floating-point divisions are only done when a line has to be clipped.

To summarize, the Liang-Barsky clipping algorithm consists of the following steps:

1 Define all line segments in parametric form.

2 Set the minimum and maximum values for t ($t_{min} = 0$ and $t_{max} = 1$).

3 Calculate all the t values located between t_{min} and t_{max}.

4 Determine whether the arbitrary values of each parametric line lie within the clipping window.
   a If the line intersects, shorten the line segment via a floating-point division.
   b If the line doesn't intersect the clipping window, discard it.

5 Display all clipped line segments.

Implementing the Liang-Barsky algorithm, as opposed to Cohen-Sutherland, results in a 36 percent performance increase when clipping two-dimensional line segments with a 40 percent increase for three-dimensional lines.

12.3.2 Clipping Polygons

Extending two-dimensional line clipping to polygons involves the clipping of polygons against a clipping rectangle (shown in Figure 12-12) or against other polygons, as is the case with hidden surface removal. Polygon clipping algorithms are derived from simple line clipping algorithms. We can thus clip a polygon against the edges of a clipping rectangle. There is, however, a problem with this approach – clipping concave polygons can result in several additional polygons as shown in Figure 12-19. The

FIGURE 12-19 **The clipping of (a) one big concave polygon resulting in (b) three independent polygons**

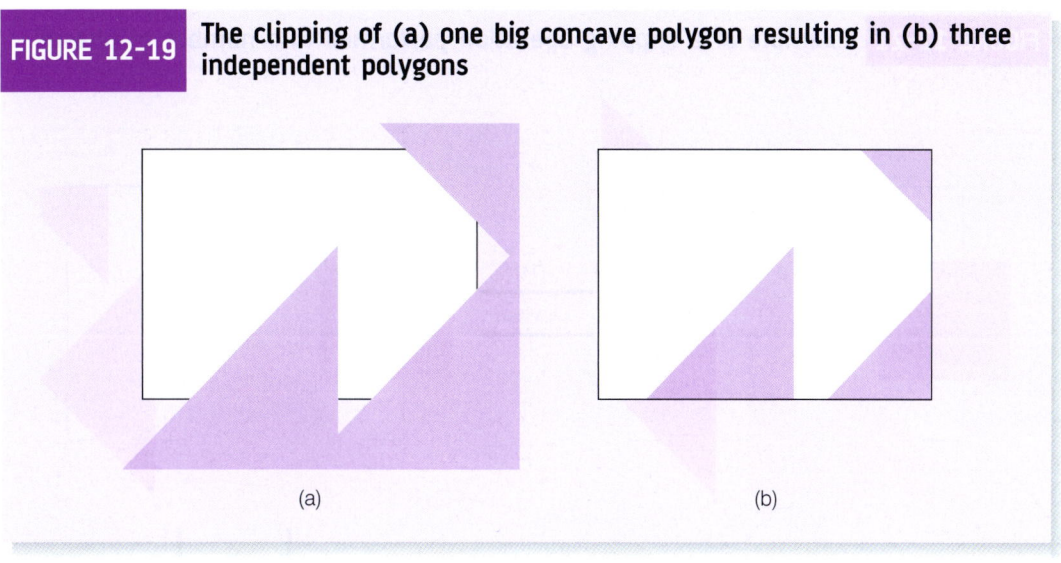

(a)   (b)

FIGURE 12-20 **The tessellation of a concave polygon into a number of convex polygons**

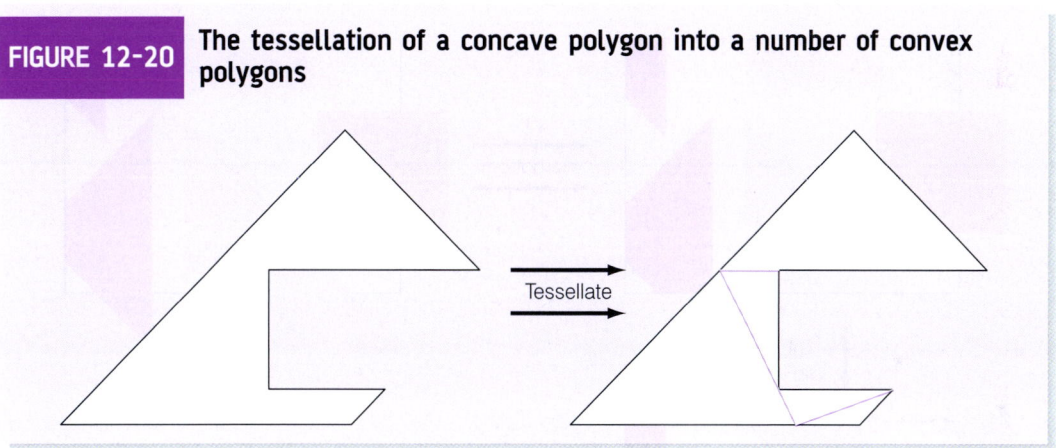

Tessellate

illustrated problem is not encountered when working with convex polygons. The only solution to this problem is to consider the clipped region as a single polygon or to tessellate (divide) the polygon into a number of convex polygons (shown in Figure 12-20). This could nevertheless lead to other problems and the use of concave polygons is thus, for this reason, prohibited by a number of graphics systems.

The previously discussed Cohen-Sutherland and Liang-Barsky clipping algorithms can be adapted for use with polygons. These algorithms, as with line segments, clip polygons in accordance with the edges of the clipping window. The clipping operation is actually performed in four phases: one phase checking for intersections with the top edge of the clipping window, another checking for right edge intersections, a clipper dealing with bottom edge intersections and the final clipper checking for left edge intersections. These clipping operations are performed in sequence as shown in Figure 12-21.

12.3.3 Three-Dimensional Clipping

Three-dimensional objects are clipped against a bounding volume as opposed to a clipping rectangle. Specifically, when clipping in 3D space we need to consider the intersections of lines and planes or

FIGURE 12-21   **Example of a clipping operation performed in a number of phases**

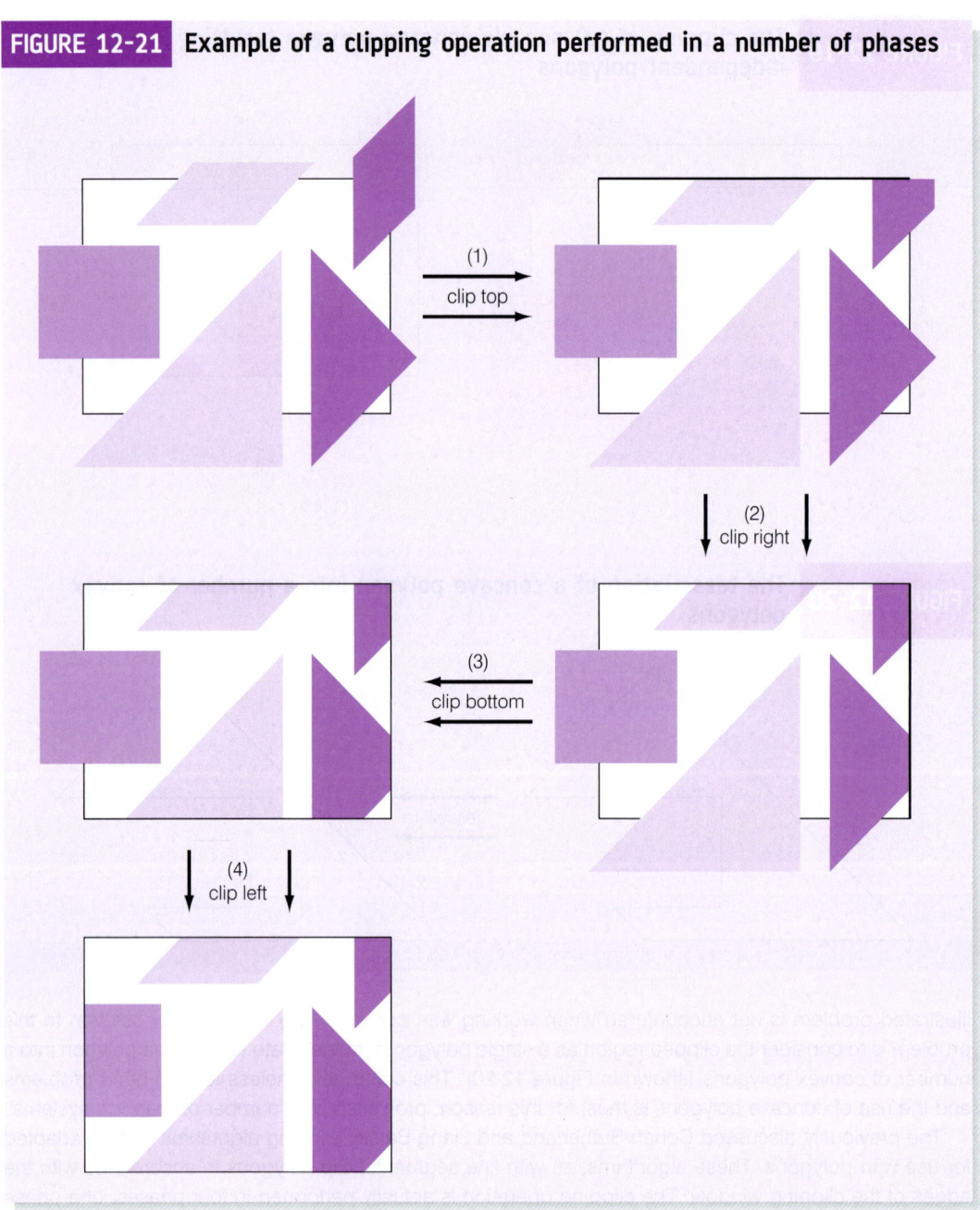

polygons and planes as opposed to the clipping of lines against lines, which is the case with 2D space. A simple technique often employed to reject objects completely outside the clipping volume and to accept objects entirely inside it is to create a bounding sphere for the object and to subsequently test its edges against that of the view volume.

A *bounding volume*, or bounding box, is simply a volume containing a geometric object. These cubic volumes are specified using the minimum and maximum x-, y- and z-values of the contained geometric object. Figure 12-22 shows a 3D mesh and its bounding box.

FIGURE 12-22 **The Utah Teapot and its bounding volume**

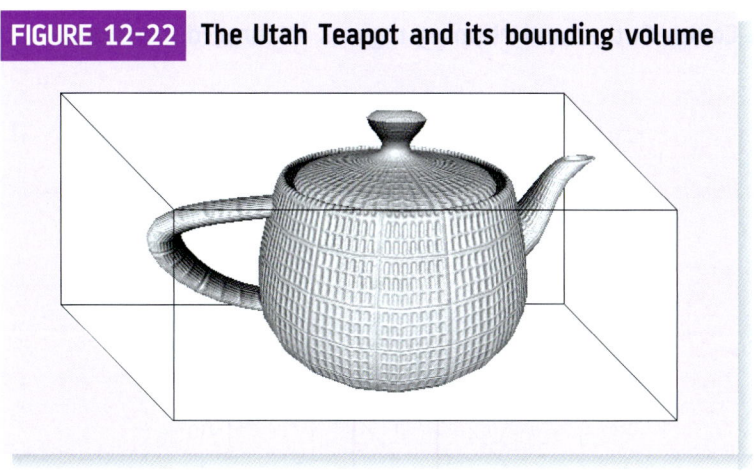

FIGURE 12-23 **Clipping of a line against a clipping volume**

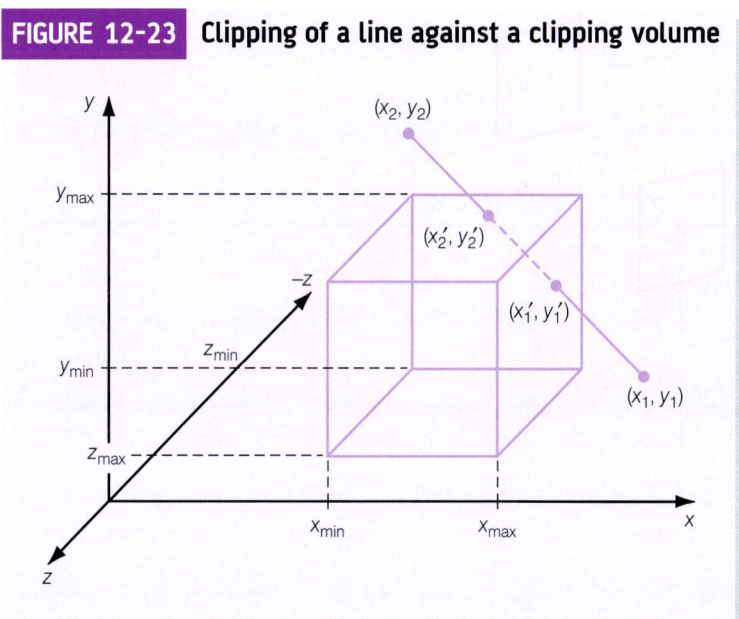

A cubic clipping volume, as an extension of the bounding box concept, is defined with its x-, y- and z-coordinates ranging from some minimum to maximum value as shown in Figure 12-23.

The Cohen-Sutherland line clipping algorithm can be extended for use in three dimensions by substituting the 4-bit outcodes with 6-bit ones. The extra two bits are used to indicate whether a point is located in front or behind the clipping volume. The algorithm, as with 2D clipping, divides the clipping region into nine sections used for fast end-point determination.

Each Cohen-Sutherland clipping region is assigned an outcode in the form $b_0b_1a_0a_1a_2a_3$ based on the following algorithm (as shown in Figure 12-24):

■ If (x, y, z) is a point in any of the Cohen-Sutherland clipping regions, then:

    a The leftmost outcode bit, b_0, is set to '1' if z is greater than Z_{max}; thus if the point is located in front of the clipping volume.

12

FIGURE 12-24 | The nine Cohen-Sutherland clipping regions in three-dimensional space

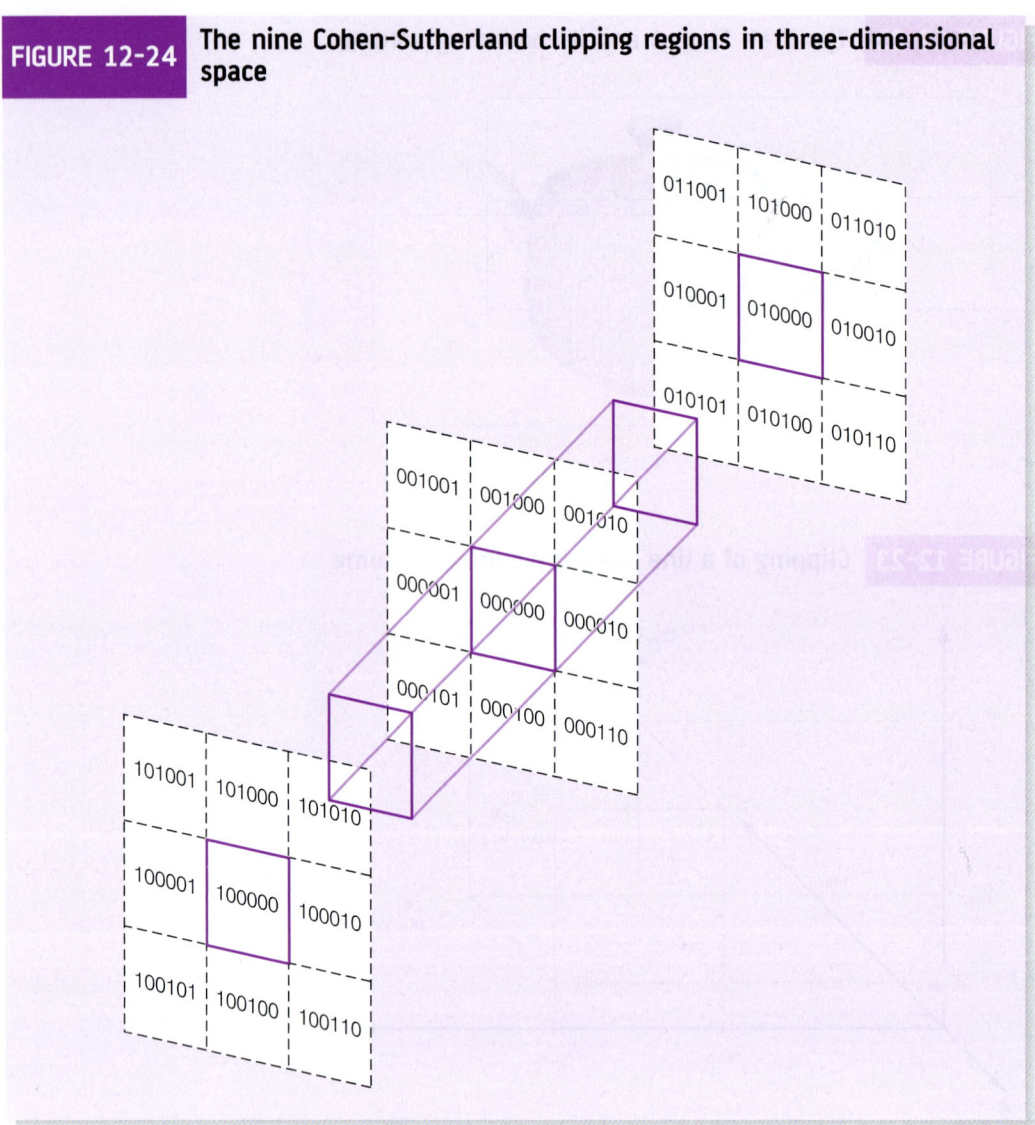

b The leftmost outcode bit, b_0, is set to '0' if z is less than or equal to Z_{max}.

c The next outcode bit, b_1, is set to '1' if z is smaller than Z_{min}; thus if the point is located in the back of the clipping volume.

d The b_1 outcode bit is set to '0' if z is greater than or equal to Z_{min}.

e The outcode bit, a_0, is set to '1' if y is greater than Y_{max}.

f The outcode bit, a_0, is set to '0' if y is less than or equal to Y_{max}.

g The outcode bit, a_1, is set to '1' if y is smaller than Y_{min}.

h The a_1 outcode bit is set to '0' if y is greater than or equal to Y_{min}.

i The a_2 outcode bit is set to '1' if x is greater than X_{max}.

j The a_2 outcode bit is set to '0' if x is less than or equal to X_{max}.

k The rightmost outcode bit, a_3, is set to '1' if x is smaller than X_{min}.

l The rightmost outcode bit, a_3, is set to '0' if x is greater than or equal to X_{min}.

FIGURE 12-25 **A line-plane intersection with related line segment endpoints and surface normal**

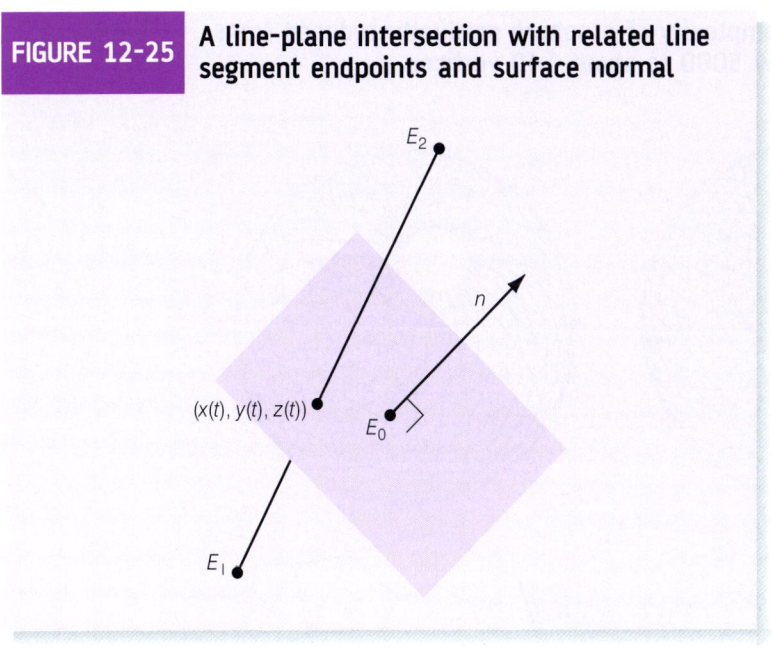

Extending the Liang-Barsky algorithm to 3D space simply requires the addition of the following equation:

$$z(t) = z_1(1-t) + z_2 t$$

The above equation is combined with the previously defined Liang-Barsky parametric line equations to produce a scalar set that can be used to represent, in parametric form, a three-dimensional line segment:

$$x(t) = x_1(1-t) + x_2 t$$
$$y(t) = y_1(1-t) + y_2 t$$
$$z(t) = z_1(1-t) + z_2 t$$

Calculating a line-plane or polygon-plane intersection requires us to solve the above three equations for t corresponding to the point of intersection where n is the normal to the plane and E_0 is a point on the plane (Figure 12-25 shows a line-plane intersection with related line segment endpoints and surface normal):

$$t = \frac{n \cdot (E_0 - E_1)}{n \cdot (E_2 - E_1)}$$

12.4   INTRODUCTION TO LEVEL OF DETAIL (LOD) ALGORITHMS

Level of Detail algorithms are concerned with the complexity of geometric objects; basically decreasing an object's mesh complexity (the number of polygons) as the distance between the object and the viewer increases. The main reason for using these algorithms is to increase the efficiency of a rendering operation by lessening the workload on the graphics system. The resulting quality tradeoff is justified due to the consequential performance increase and the decrease in object detail often going unseen by

12

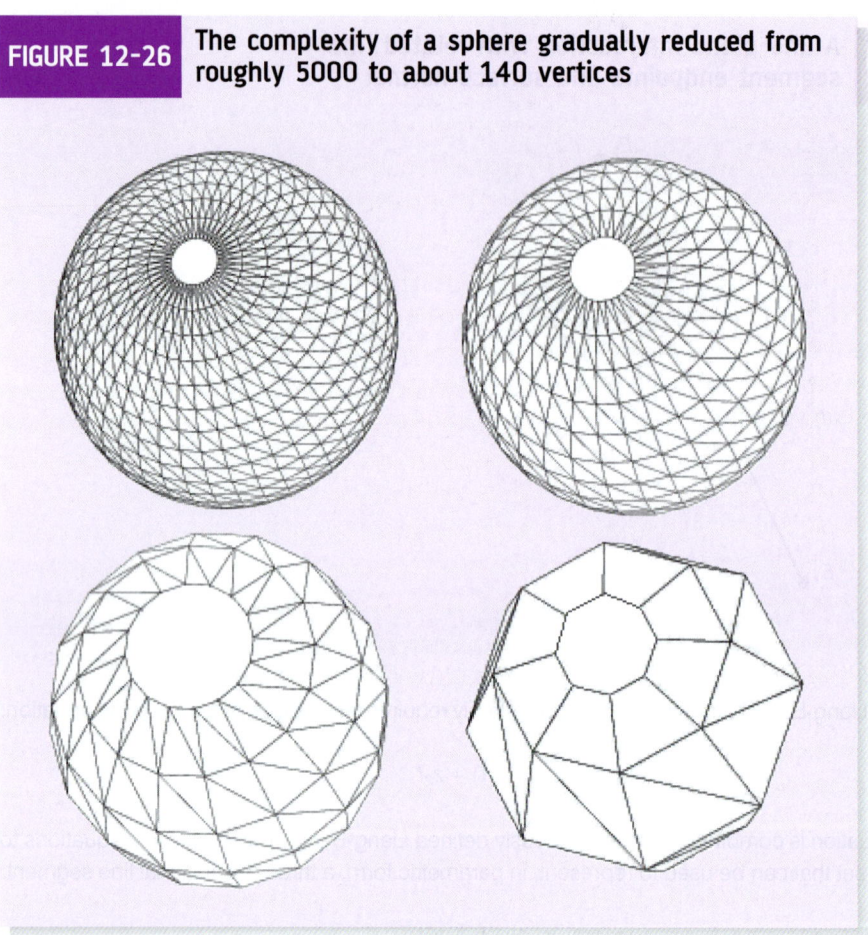

FIGURE 12-26 The complexity of a sphere gradually reduced from roughly 5000 to about 140 vertices

the viewer. Figure 12-26 shows a sphere with its mesh complexity gradually reduced through the application of a Level of Detail (LOD) algorithm.

LOD algorithms are generally divided into two groups, namely top-down and bottom-up algorithms. A *top-down LOD* algorithm will, for example, start off with two triangles or one quadrilateral, subsequently dividing it (progressively adding vertices) until the desired resolution is reached. A bottom-up LOD algorithm starts with a complete complex mesh and functions by progressively removing vertices (thus reducing complexity) until the target resolution is reached.

LOD algorithms can also be described as uniform or view-dependent. *Uniform LOD algorithms* are applied on all geometric objects regardless of the viewer-object distance with *view-dependent algorithms* varying the LOD with regard to the view direction, distance and region of the mesh contained within the view frustum.

Although LOD algorithms are generally applied to geometric objects and textures (as is the case with mipmapping), they are also extensively used to speed up terrain rendering. There are commonly two main terrain representations when using LOD algorithms, namely, representing the terrain via a number of regular grids or using a triangulated irregular network. Using *regular grids*, shown in Figure 12-27, results in an easy to store, easy to manipulate data structure (such as a two-dimensional array) best suited for real-time viewing algorithms. This data structure is, however, less storage efficient (size wise) than a triangulated irregular network.

FIGURE 12-27 **A regular grid LOD terrain representation**

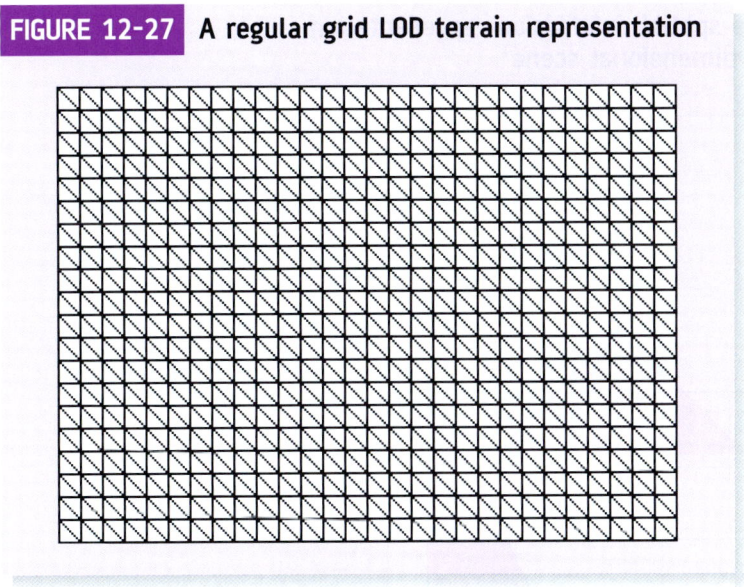

FIGURE 12-28 **A triangulated irregular network LOD terrain representation**

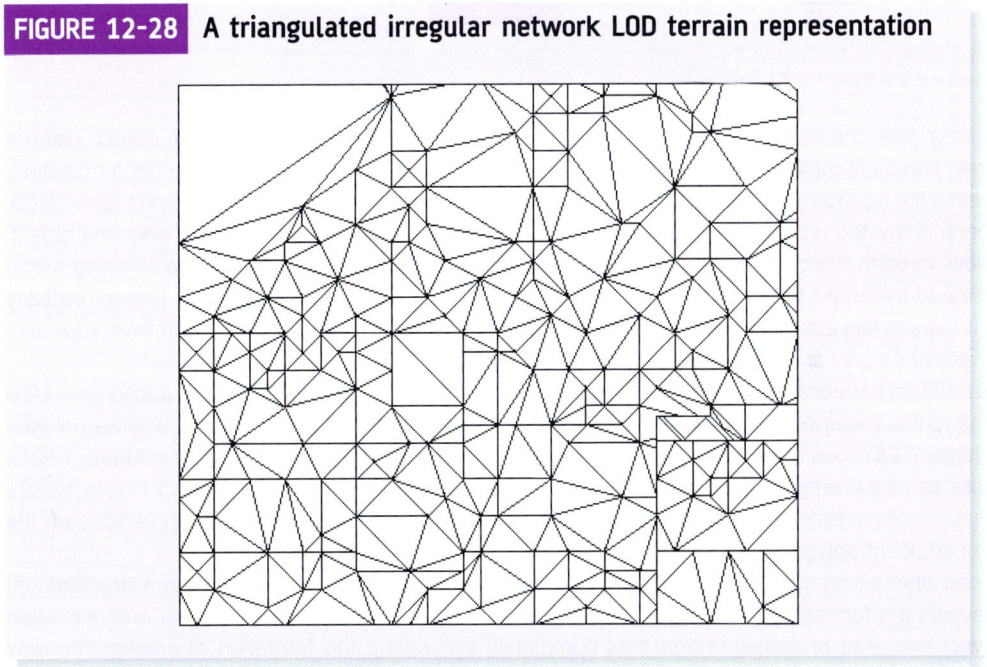

12

A *triangulated irregular network* (shown in Figure 12-28), compared to a regular grid, uses significantly less polygons to approximate an area and can be used to model any arbitrary object. It is, however, difficult to perform view-frustum culling, terrain following, collision detection and dynamic deformation due to the irregular nature of this terrain representation.

Regular grid LOD algorithms are based on the creation and manipulation of quad-trees or binary-trees. A *quad-tree* is a type of spatial subdivision tree data structure where each node is assigned a

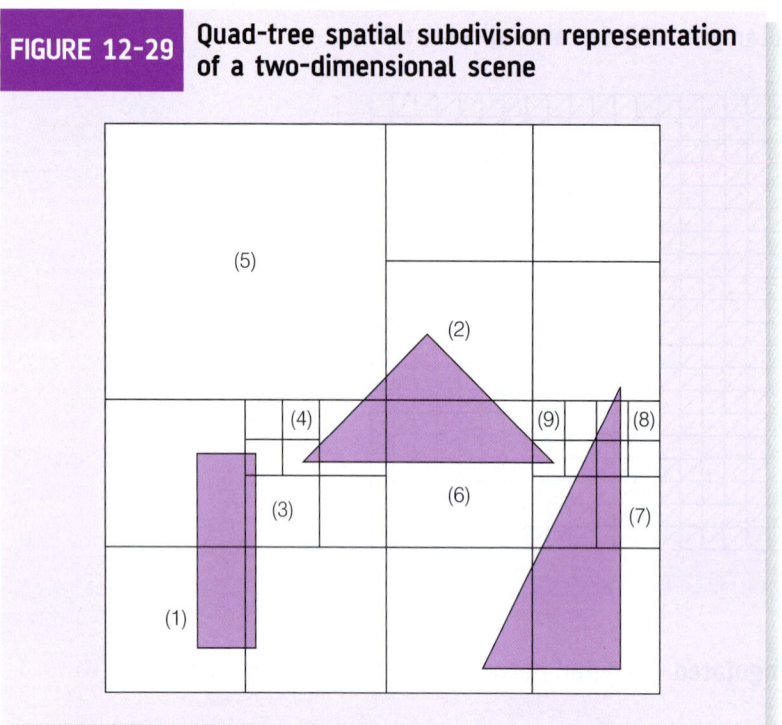

FIGURE 12-29 **Quad-tree spatial subdivision representation of a two-dimensional scene**

maximum of four children. A scene (such as the map of an FPS game) or geometric object, using a quad-tree, can be recursively subdivided into quadrants, thus resulting in its cell-based decomposition.

Consider the top-down view of a scene consisting of two triangles and a rectangle given in Figure 12-29. This scene is divided down to the Level of Detail where each quad-tree cell contains only one object, thus allowing us to describe the world object space and the relationship among objects using a tree (as illustrated by Figure 12-30). This relationship is subsequently used for fast visibility testing. Visibility testing is used to flag the objects visible by the viewer, allowing us to discard those hidden from view or to render distant objects at a lower resolution.

One problem frequently encountered when partitioning a mesh using quad-trees and applying an LOD algorithm to it is the appearance of cracks. *Cracks*, or open untextured spaces, occur when a polygon from a higher LOD does not share a vertex with an adjacent lower LOD polygon (shown in Figure 12-31).

Cracks can be corrected or avoided by forcing a crack into a T-junction (shown in Figure 12-32), rendering a triangle to fill or "plug" the crack or by ensuring the existence of common vertices on the edges of adjacent polygons.

We can alternatively subdivide the terrain using *bin-trees*, or binary triangle trees (a tree structure that easily avoids the formation of cracks). The triangles of a bin-tree are never more than one resolution level away from that of its neighbors, thus completely eliminating the formation of cracks. The only difference between quad-trees and bin-trees is the splitting technique – quad-trees being based on quad splitting with bin-trees making use of triangle splitting (illustrated in Figure 12-33).

Finally, when implementing an LOD algorithm, it is important to specify the type of memory management needed. For example, an *out-of-core algorithm* will load the required objects from some dataset outside memory, thus minimizing the amount of video memory required. Also, a general problem with LOD algorithms is that of *object popping* – the sudden appearance of an object as the viewer moves from one LOD range to another. We can achieve the smooth transition between LOD levels through techniques such as alpha blending and tile paging. *Tile paging* is a technique used to

12

FIGURE 12-30	The tree structure of the quad-tree spatial subdivision representation given in Figure 12-29

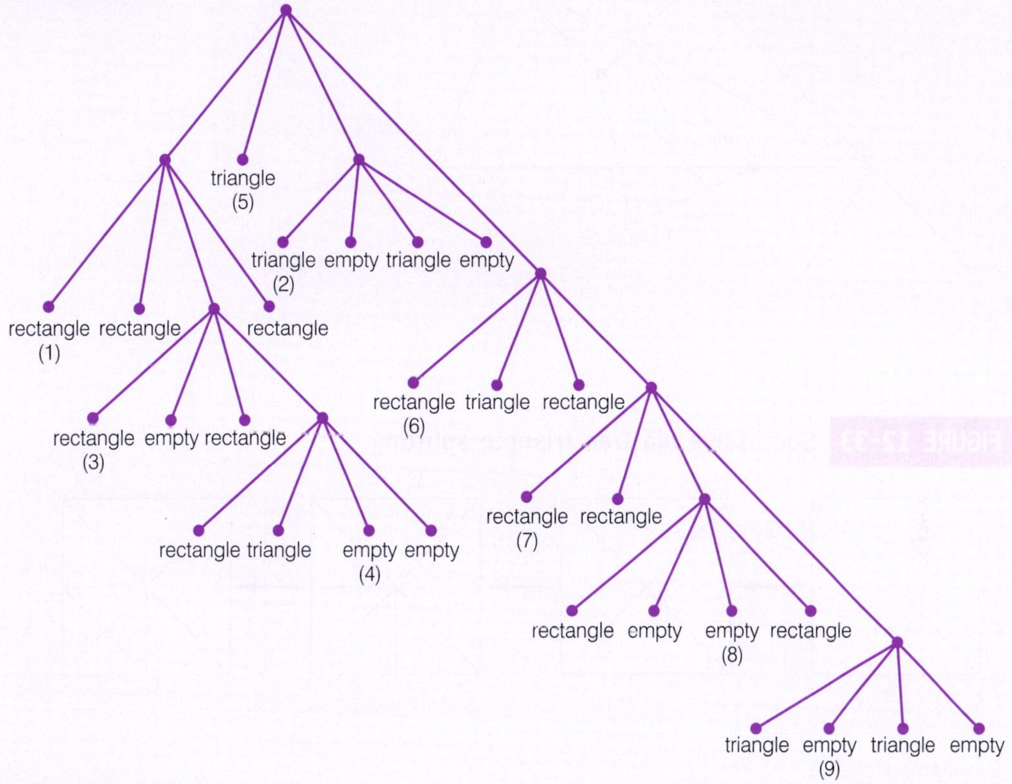

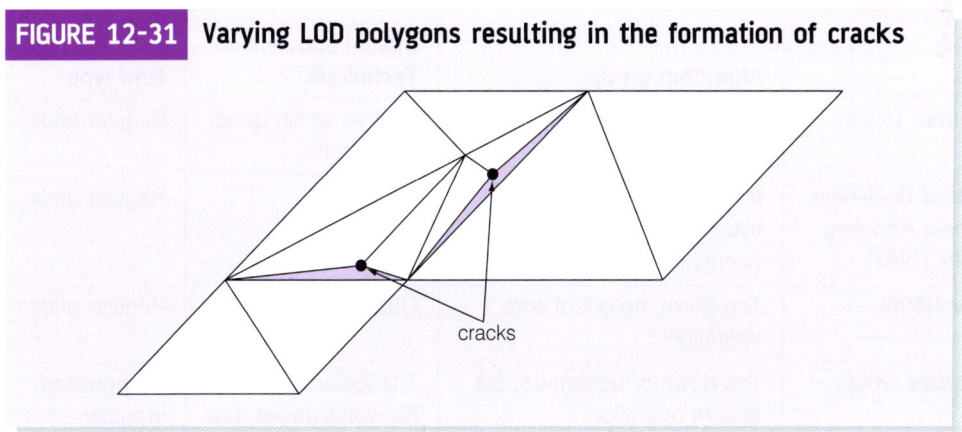

FIGURE 12-31	Varying LOD polygons resulting in the formation of cracks

preload tiles or a specific LOD polygon when a boundary is reached – thus swapping out portions of the terrain based on the camera position.

A number of LOD algorithms have been developed over the years, each with its own advantages, disadvantages, and field of application. The discussion of these algorithms is outside the scope of this book but several major terrain LOD algorithms are briefly listed and described in Table 12-1.

FIGURE 12-32 Forcing cracks into T-junctions

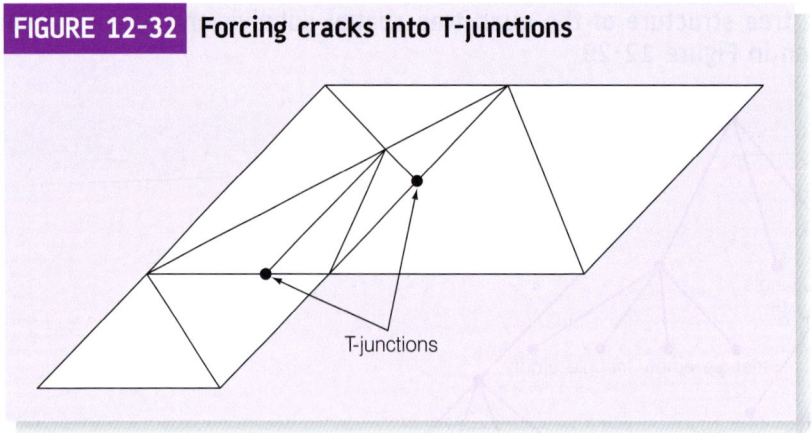

T-junctions

FIGURE 12-33 Successive bin-tree triangle-splitting

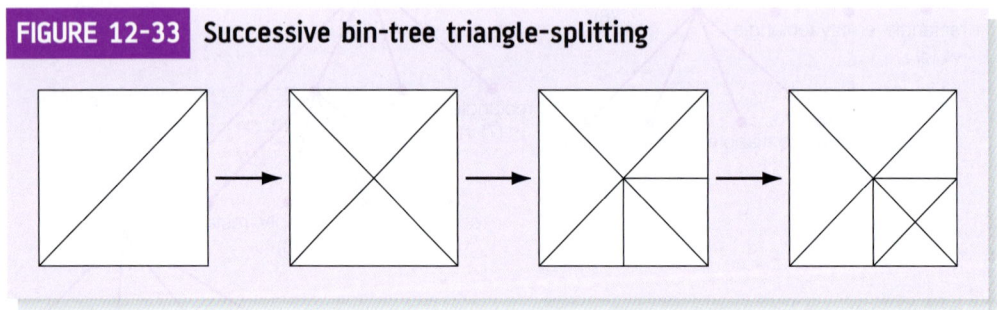

TABLE 12-1 Summary of LOD algorithms

Name	Algorithm group	Spatial subdivision Technique	Grid type
Lindstrom (1996)	Bottom-up, no out of core operation.	Bin-tree within quad-tree blocks.	Regular grids.
ROAM or Real-Time Optimally Adapting Meshes (1997)	Bottom-up and top-down hybrid, no out of core operation.	Bin-tree.	Regular grids.
Rötter (1998)	Top-down, no out of core operation.	Quad-tree.	Regular grids.
DeFloriani (2000)	Top-down or bottom-up, out of core operation.	Triangular Irregular Networks based data structure.	Triangulated irregular network.
Lindstrom and Pascucci (2001)	Top-down, out of core operation.	Bin-tree.	Regular grids.

12.5   SUMMARY

In this chapter we started by looking at height maps as two-dimensional arrays consisting of *x*- and *z*-values, each assigned a certain value (a *y*-coordinate) representing the height of a specific point on a 3D surface. This discussion was supplemented with implementation examples focusing on the creation and rendering of various height maps.

Next we discussed the theoretical and practical implementation of culling and hidden surface removal, specifically focusing on determining the parts of objects hidden from the viewer and subsequently removing these areas from the rendering process using hidden surface removal algorithms. Two hidden surface removal algorithms were investigated, namely, the z-buffer algorithm and the painter's algorithm.

Following this we investigated clipping as an optimization operation resulting in the display of only visible objects. Two-dimensional line clipping (Liang-Barsky clipping and Cohen-Sutherland clipping), as well as the clipping of polygons and three-dimensional clipping via bounding volumes, were also dealt with in detail.

The remainder of the chapter considered Level of Detail algorithms from a foundational perspective, in essence highlighting the difference between several algorithms at hand of whether it's a top-down or bottom-up algorithm, whether the algorithm is uniform or view-dependent, the spatial subdivision technique, the type of memory management needed, and the main terrain representation associated with it.

The next chapter deals with the representation of polygonal meshes as well as the specification of relationships among various parts of a mesh using joints. A number of animation techniques focusing on the animation of rigid bodies, particles, articulated objects, and so forth are also considered.

12.6   FURTHER READING

For more information on Level of Detail algorithms, refer to the paper '*Smooth View-Dependent Level-of-Detail Control and its Application to Terrain Rendering,*' by Hugues Hoppe published in the *IEEE Proceedings of Visualization* (1998). The paper titled '*Visualization of Large Terrains Made Easy,*' by, Lindstrom and Pascucci published in IEEE *Proceedings of Visualization* (2001) deals in detail with large-scale terrain visualization. A great reference on the ROAM Level of Detail algorithm is Mark Duchaineua, Murry Wolinsky and Divid Sigeti's paper '*ROAMing Terrain: Real-Time Optimally Adapting Meshes*' published in *IEEE Proceedings of Visualization* (1997).

For additional information on polygon clipping and hidden surface removal, refer to the following sources: '*Sketchpad, A Man-Machine Graphical Communication System,*' published in *Proceedings of the SHARE Design Automation Workshop DAC'64 by; Sutherland* (1964); 1. Sutherland and G Hodgeman's paper *Reentrant Polygon Clipping* published in the Communications of the ACM (1974); and Sutherland, R. Sproull and R. Schumacker's paper '*A Characterisation of Ten Hidden-Surface Algorithms*' (*Computer Surveys,* 1974). Liang-Barsky clipping was originally discussed in the paper '*A New Concept and Method for Line Clipping*' by Y. Liang and B. Barsky published in the *ACM Transactions of Graphics* (1984).

12

12.7   EXERCISES

1 Explain how height maps can be used for realistic terrain generation.

2 What does the equation *height* (*y*) = *func* (*x*, *z*) represent?

3 Compare the process of culling to hidden surface removal in general.

4 Describe the purpose of the D3D10_RASTERIZER_DESC render state structure as part of the culling process.

5 What is the hidden surface removal problem?

6 Describe the two main hidden surface removal algorithm classes.

7 Outline the z-buffer algorithm's implementation steps.

8 How does the painter's algorithm compare to the z-buffer algorithm?

9 Explain the process of two-dimensional line clipping.

10 Briefly describe the Cohen-Sutherland two-dimensional line clipping algorithm.

11 What is the primary aim of the Liang-Barsky clipping algorithm?

12 How can two-dimensional line clipping be extended for the clipping of polygons?

13 What is a cubic clipping volume?

14 Describe the problem frequently encountered when partitioning a mesh using quad-trees while applying an LOD algorithm to it.

15 What is an out-of-core LOD algorithm?

CHAPTER 13

Polygonal Meshes and Animation

LEARNING OBJECTIVES

In this chapter you will learn about:

- Polygonal meshes
- Representing a mesh
- Connecting rigid parts of objects using joints
- Computer animation techniques
- The animation of rigid bodies
- The animation of particles
- Animation via the laws of physics
- Animation of articulated objects
- The behavioural animation of objects
- Loading and rendering meshes in Direct3D 10

INTRODUCTION

Chapter 13 deals with polygonal meshes by focusing on their internal and three-dimensional representation. It also investigates the specification of relationships among the various components of a mesh via the use of joints. A number of game-centric animation techniques focusing on the animation of rigid bodies, particles, articulated objects, and so forth are also considered.

13.1 POLYGONAL MESHES

We have so far created geometry by defining each vertex constituting an object manually. For instance, when defining a triangle we had to hard-code its vertex coordinates as part of our application's source code. This method is very rudimentary and becomes impractical when representing anything more complex than a cube or pyramid. As such, game artists and animators use high-end 3D modeling packages to visually create complex meshes for import into games.

A *polygon mesh*, or *3D model*, is a set of vertices connected in such a way as to define a polyhedral object. A *polyhedron*, shown in Figure 13-1, is an arbitrary geometric object consisting of flat faces and straight lines. Figure 13-2 shows a complex high-polygon mesh built using simple geometric primitives.

| FIGURE 13-1 | A dodecahedron (a polyhedron with 12 faces) |

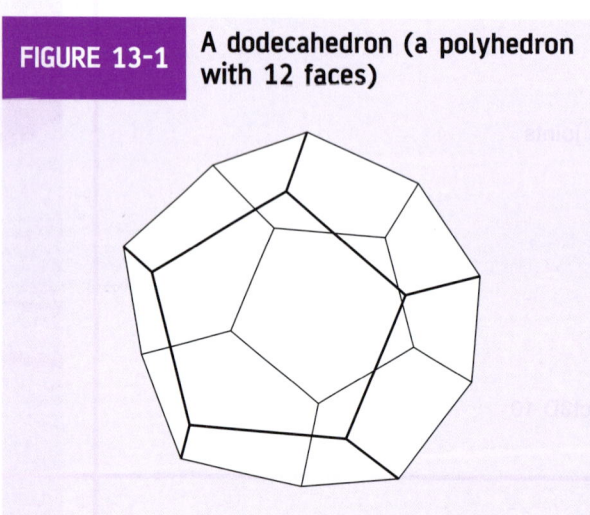

Meshes are usually constructed using a number of triangles or quadrilaterals. Using these polygon types simplifies the model's data structure storage requirements as well as the implementation of LOD algorithms. Common applications for polygonal meshes in gaming include the modeling of complex architecture such as arches, buildings and bridges, vehicles, in-game characters, items, and weapons to name but a few.

Apart from consisting of a set of interconnected vertices, meshes almost always contain additional data generated using the modeling software such as surface normals, material properties, pixel color information, and texture coordinates.

| FIGURE 13-2 | A high polygon mesh representing an in-game character |

We will now investigate a number of mesh creation and implementation strategies, specifically focusing on the representation of polygonal meshes, the creation of hierarchical relationships among geometric objects, the concept of connecting rigid parts of objects using joints and finally manipulating these joints for the purpose of animating the object.

13.1.1 Representing a Mesh

Two issues become apparent when attempting to create a structure for the storage of a geometric mesh. The first issue relates to the internal representation of the model itself with the second issue pertaining to the representation of models in three-dimensional space. Neither OpenGL nor Direct3D place any limitations on the construction of more complex objects via the interconnection of numerous primitives – the constraint being only hardware-based (the higher the number of polygons, the greater the strain on the GPU and memory).

The simplest way of representing a mesh in 3D space is to view it as an *entity*. We can thus define a scene as a set of entities, for example, each object constituting the scene shown in Figure 13-3 and Figure 13-4 exist independently from each other.

Looking at the scene in Figure 13-4, we can either consider it as a single rigid mesh in its entirety or as a collection of independent meshes. For example, the pillars and cubes appear as a single object but are in fact created by generating the cubes before rendering the pillars (as can be seen in Figure 13-3).

All the objects shown in the previous two images have a certain spatial position and orientation – the cylinders and cubes are, for example, all rotated parallel to the *y*-axis. Rotating an entity at a specific angle, for instance, results in an orientation change for that object without the rest of the scene being affected or keeping track of this change.

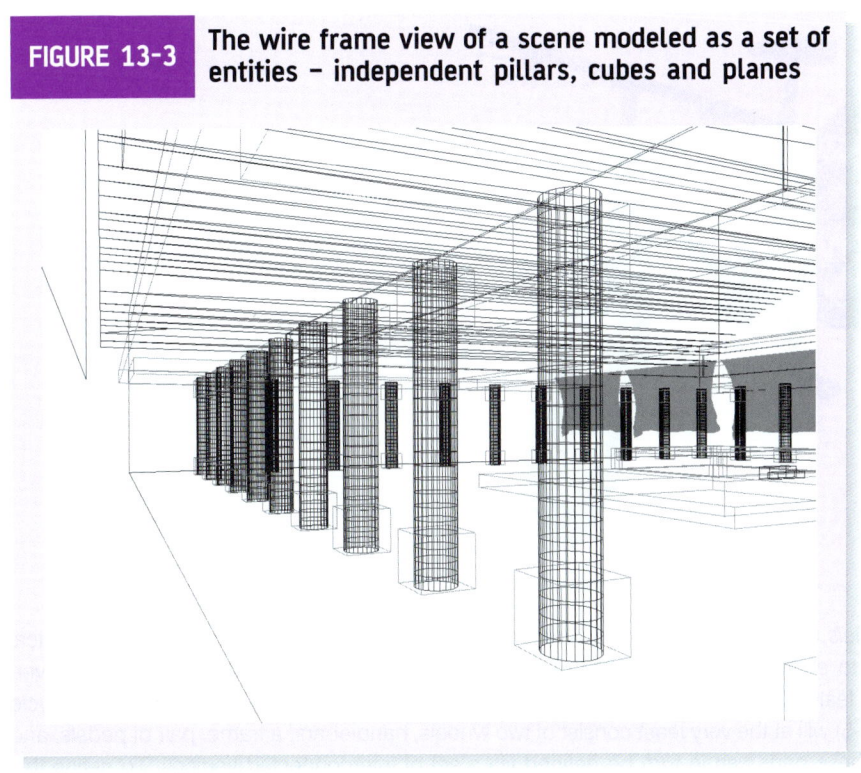

FIGURE 13-3 The wire frame view of a scene modeled as a set of entities – independent pillars, cubes and planes

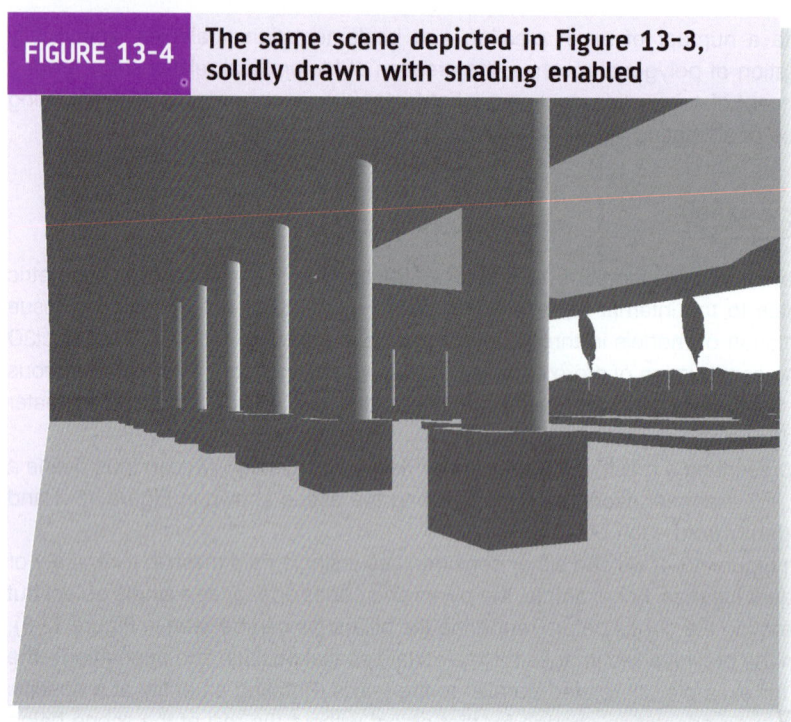

FIGURE 13-4 The same scene depicted in Figure 13-3, solidly drawn with shading enabled

FIGURE 13-5 A mountain bike mesh from Rockstar North's game *Grand Theft Auto: San Andreas*

Hierarchical models can be used as an alternative to entities when representing meshes. Hierarchical models are similar to entity-based models and are also defined using a collection of parts; however, hierarchical models feature an added relationship among these parts. For example, a model of a bicycle (shown in Figure 13-5) will at the very least consist of two wheels, handlebars, a frame, pair of pedals, and a saddle. Each of these parts can in turn be defined via a set of interconnected vertices. To define this model as a hierarchical mesh, we will simply need to specify a relationship between its various components.

This hierarchical model can be animated by noting the interrelationship between its various parts – i.e. we can define the animation of our model in such a way so that the front wheel turns whenever the handlebar is rotated. Also, when the hierarchical model's front wheel is translated in an upwards direction, for example, the rest of the model will follow.

Animating our mountain bike mesh is quite easy. The movement of the bike can be simulated by rotating both the pedals and wheels in either a clockwise or counter-clockwise direction. In addition, rotation of the handlebars can be used to horizontally rotate the front wheel, thus simulating the steering mechanism of a real-life bicycle. We can now basically define the distance travelled by the bike by noting that one complete 360-degree wheel rotation equates to a distance of $2\pi r$, with r the radius of a wheel. This distance can subsequently be used to translate the entire hierarchical model in accordance with the rotation angle of the wheels.

When modeling a complex mesh via a set of entities, we can construct and animate it using a series of function calls, each generating and transforming a part of the model. For example, to create the mesh shown in Figure 13-5 using entities we will have a function to define a wheel, the handlebars, the saddle, the bicycle frame and the pair of pedals. These functions can now be grouped together to define the entire model, each being passed parameters such as the translation distance and angle of rotation:

```
void AnimateHierarchicalBike(spatialPosition,
                             distanceTravelled,
                             handlebarRotation,
                             wheelRotation)
{
    float spatialPosition_ = spatialPosition;
    float distanceTravelled_ = distanceTravelled;
    float handlebarRotation_ = handlebarRotation;
    float wheelRotation_ = wheelRotation;

    /* construct and animate the mesh */
    RenderFrontWheel(spatialPosition_, wheelRotation_);
    RenderRearWheel(spatialPosition_, wheelRotation_);

    RenderBikeFrame(spatialPosition_ + distanceTravelled_);
    RenderBikeSaddle(spatialPosition_ + distanceTravelled_);

    RenderHandlebars(spatialPosition_ + distanceTravelled_,
                     handlebarRotation_);
    RenderPedals(spatialPosition_ + distanceTravelled_,
                 wheelRotation_);
}
```

This approach is clearly far from optimal and fails to establish any relationship among the various parts (although the objects would seem interconnected to the person viewing at the animation). Representing inter-object relationships visually and programmatically is relatively easy and done via tree-based data structures. For example, we can represent the relationship among the components of our mountain bike model using a tree as shown in Figure 13-6. This tree uses the bike frame as root node and the handlebars, rear wheel, saddle and pedals as its children nodes. The front wheel is

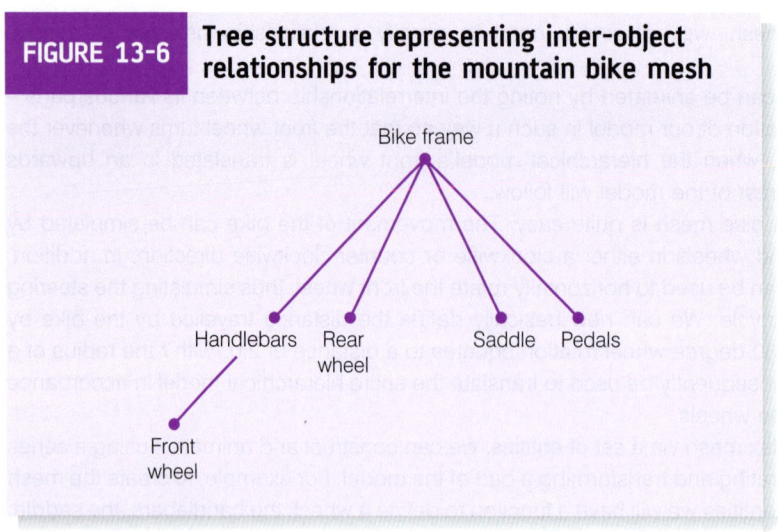

FIGURE 13-6   **Tree structure representing inter-object relationships for the mountain bike mesh**

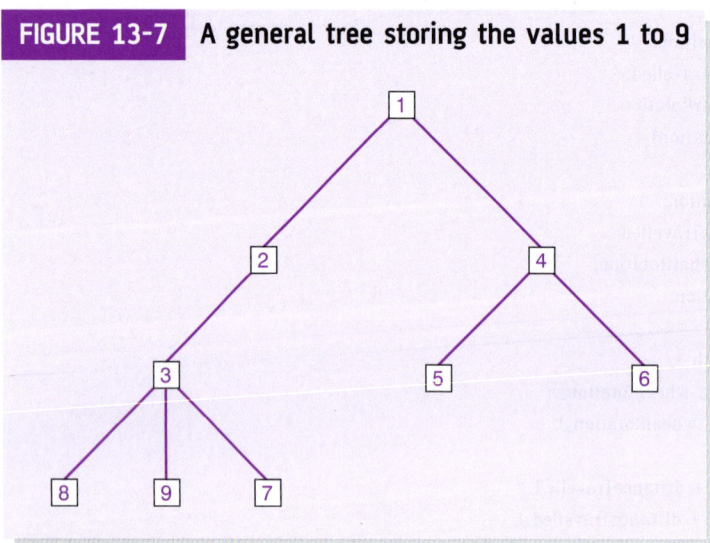

FIGURE 13-7   **A general tree storing the values 1 to 9**

directly dependant on the rotation about the *y*-axis of the handlebars and thus added as the handlebar node's child.

We can thus, using the depicted relationships, say that if the bike frame is translated then all the other parts must also be translated, and if one of the wheels is rotated perpendicular to the *zx*-plane, then the bike frame with all other interconnected node elements must also be translated along the related plane.

Designing a generic tree container is really straightforward, but before presenting a basic tree implementation it is perhaps a good idea to quickly review some tree basics.

A *tree structure* is a set of nodes linked together to form a branching pattern. Each of these nodes is used as a storage container, with additional nodes being connected to preceding ones. If a node doesn't have any nodes beneath it, it is called a 'leaf node', with interior nodes called 'branch nodes'. The first node of a tree is called the root node. Figure 13-7 shows a general tree with its nodes storing the numbers '1' to '9'.

The elements stored in the above given tree can be accessed or traversed in one of three ways. The first method of traversal, *pre-order traversal*, starts at the root node, subsequently visiting each higher-level node before visiting its children. Pre-order traversal for the above given tree will visit the nodes in the following order: *1–2–3–8–9–7–4–5–6*. This traversal method is most commonly encountered in computer gaming and is also used in skeletal animation. *Post-order traversal* is the exact opposite of the previous technique. It starts at the leaf nodes followed by the higher-level nodes: *8–9–7–3–5–6–2–4–1*. The third traversal technique called *level-order traversal,* starts at the root node, visiting all its child nodes, then the nodes below them and so forth: *1–2–4–3–5–6–8–9–7*.

The simplest way of implementing a tree is to use either a list or vector for the storage of nodes. A *list*, or doubly-linked list, data structure consists of successive nodes, with each node providing data fields and reference links to the previous and subsequent nodes. A *vector* can be considered a dynamic array with the ability to automatically resize itself whenever an object is inserted or removed from it.

We can manually implement a list or vector data structure; however, the performance of manual implementations will rarely measure up to that of the vector and list containers provided by the *Standard Template Library* (STL). The STL is a software library included as part of the C++ Standard Library. The list and vector containers can be accessed by a C/C++ program after being included:

```
#include <list.h>
#include <vector.h>
```

Creating a generic tree structure requires the definition of a container for the storage of node elements. Apart from that we only have to add elements to this container in a specific way, for example, the following code sample illustrates how ten elements may be added to a tree in a pre-order fashion:

```
/* specify the tree storage container */
struct Tree
{
    T element;
    Vector<Tree> nodes;
};

/* variable used for storing the users input */
int input = 0;

/* recursively called function used for loading elements into
   the tree */
void AddElement(Stream& input, Tree &tree)
{
    cout << "Please enter a numeric value:" << endl;
    cin >> input;

    input >> tree.element;

    for(int i = 0; i < 10; i ++)
    {
        AddElement(input, tree.nodes[i]);
    }
}
```

13

Traversing this tree and accessing its elements in a pre-order fashion can be done as follows:

```
/* counter variable */
int numberChildNodes;

/* recursively called function used for traversing the tree
   and accessing its elements */
void ReadElement(Stream& output, Tree &tree)
{
    output << tree.element;

    numberChildNodes = tree.nodes.size();

    for(int i = 0; i < numberChildNodes; i ++)
    {
        ReadElement(ouput, tree.nodes[i]);
    }
}
```

The above given scheme can be considered a brute force approach for the creation of a tree container and more advanced approaches are generally followed when implementing a tree structure intended for extensive use. The main problem actually lies with the use of a vector for the storage of nodes. This is due to vectors only effectively using about 75 to 80 percent of the memory allocated to them. One solution to this problem is to replace the vector container with four structure pointers, one for the higher-level parent nodes, two for the children nodes and one for the leaf nodes:

```
/* specify the tree storage container */
struct Tree
{
    T element;

    /* higher-level parent nodes */
    Tree* parentNode;

    /* children nodes */
    Tree* previousChildNode;
    Tree* nextChildNode;

    /* lead nodes */
    Tree* leafNode;
};
```

The most common method of representing a mesh hierarchy is to use a basic *left-child*, *right-sibling* tree structure coupled with a traversal algorithm. This type of tree is created with all its nodes linked from left to right, with subsequent child nodes linked in a similar fashion. Figure 13-8 shows a basic tree structure and its left-child, right-sibling representation.

Looking at the left-child, right-sibling representation in the above figure we see that it is necessary to store pointers to both the child and sibling nodes (nodes on the same level as the

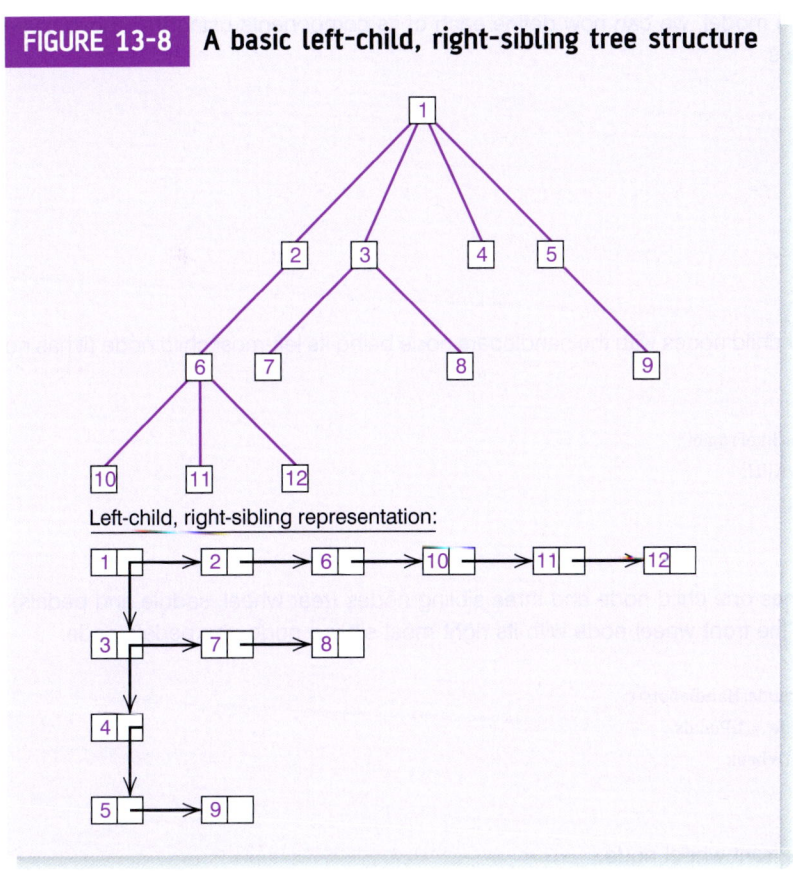

FIGURE 13-8 **A basic left-child, right-sibling tree structure**

Left-child, right-sibling representation:

current node). When working with models we'll also store a 4 × 4 homogenous coordinate matrix for multiplication with the model's model-view matrix and a pointer to the model's rendering function:

```
/* specify the tree-node storage container */
struct TreeNode
{
    /* model's rendering function */
    void* renderingFunc();

    /* pointer to the right-most sibling node */
    TreeNode* rightmostSiblingNode;

    /* pointer to the next child node */
    TreeNode* childNode;

    /* homogeneous coordinate matrix */
    float* modelviewMatrix[16];
};
```

13

Returning to our bicycle model, we can now define each of its components using the above given TreeNode structure as follows:

```
TreeNode FrontWheel;
TreeNode Handlebars;
TreeNode Frame;
TreeNode Pedals;
TreeNode Saddle;
```

The bike frame has four child nodes with the handlebars node being its left-most child node (it has no sibling nodes):

```
Frame.renderingFunc = RenderBikeFrame();
Frame.rightmostSiblingNode = NULL;
Frame.childNode = &Handlebars;
```

The handlebars node has one child node and three sibling nodes (rear wheel, saddle and pedals). Its left-most child node is the front wheel node with its right most sibling node, the pedals node:

```
Handlebars.renderingFunc = RenderHandlebars();
Handlebars.rightmostSiblingNode = &Pedals;
Handlebars.childNode = &FrontWheel;
```

Next we can define the front wheel node:

```
FrontWheel.renderingFunc = RenderWheel();
FrontWheel.rightmostSiblingNode = NULL;
FrontWheel.childNode = NULL;
```

The rear wheel, saddle and pedals (none of them containing any child nodes) can be initialized as follows:

```
RearWheel.renderingFunc = RenderWheel();
RearWheel.rightmostSiblingNode = &Pedals;
RearWheel.childNode = NULL;

Saddle.renderingFunc = RenderSaddle();
Saddle.rightmostSiblingNode = &Pedals;
Saddle.childNode = NULL;

Pedals.renderingFunc = RenderPedals();
Pedals.rightmostSiblingNode = NULL;
Pedals.childNode = NULL;
```

13

Furthermore, the homogenous coordinate matrix for each mesh component has to be initialized to the model view matrix before any transformation operation can be performed (see Chapter 7):

```
FrontWheel.modelviewMatrix = g_ViewMatrix;
Handlebars.modelviewMatrix = g_ViewMatrix;
Frame.modelviewMatrix = g_ViewMatrix;
Pedals.modelviewMatrix = g_ViewMatrix;
Saddle.modelviewMatrix = g_ViewMatrix;
```

We can now translate, rotate or scale each of these components using the techniques described in Chapter 7. For example, the handlebars (or theoretically any of the other components) can be rotated 90 degrees about the y-axis as outlined below.

We start by declaring and initializing the world, view, and projection matrices (with associated access interfaces):

```
D3DXMATRIX g_WorldMatrix;
D3DXMATRIX g_ViewMatrix;
D3DXMATRIX g_ProjectionMatrix;
ID3D10EffectMatrixVariable* g_pd3d10EffectWorldMatrix = NULL;
ID3D10EffectMatrixVariable* g_pd3d10EffectViewMatrix = NULL;
ID3D10EffectMatrixVariable* g_pd3d10EffectProjectMatrix= NULL;
```

Next we initialize the world matrix to an identity matrix:

```
D3DXMatrixIdentity(&g_WorldMatrix);
```

We also set the view matrix as a left-handed, look-at matrix using the D3DXMatrixLookAtLH D3DX math function:

```
D3DXVECTOR3 EyeCoord( 0.0f, 1.0f, −10.0f);
D3DXVECTOR3 LookAt(0.0f, 1.0f, 0.0f);
D3DXVECTOR3 UpDir(0.0f, 1.0f, 0.0f);
D3DXMatrixLookAtLH(&g_ViewMatrix, &EyeCoord, &LookAt, &UpDir);
```

As is customary for all 3D programs and introduced in Chapter 7, we also have to define a perspective projection matrix:

```
D3DXMatrixPerspectiveFovLH(&g_ProjectionMatrix,
                    (float)D3DX_PI*0.25f,
                    rectangle_width/rectangle_height, 0.1f, 100.0f);
```

Next we declare a rotation matrix via the D3DXMATRIX structure, followed by its initialization using the D3DXMatrixRotationY function. Once this is done, we apply the above-calculated rotation matrix to the world matrix via the D3DXMatrixMultiply function. Before rendering the handlebars, we have to call the SetMatrix method so that the GPU can read our matrices:

```
/* declare the rotation matrix */
D3DXMATRIX rotationMatrix;

/* initialize the rotation matrix (rotate 1.57 radians) */
D3DXMatrixRotationY(&rotationMatrix, 1.57f);

/* apply the rotation matrix to the world matrix */
D3DXMatrixMultiply(&g_WorldMatrix, &g_WorldMatrix,
                &rotationMatrix);
/* update the world, view, and projection matrices */
/////////////////////////////////////////////////////
g_pd3dl0EffectWorldMatrix->
                SetMatrix((float*)&g_WorldMatrix);

g_pd3dl0EffectViewMatrix->
                SetMatrix((float*)&g_ViewMatrix);

g_pd3dl0EffectWorldMatrix->
                SetMatrix((float*)&g_ProjectionMatrix);

/* render the previously defined handlebars rotated */
g_pd3dl0Device->Draw(3, 0);

/* switch the back- and front-buffer and display the mesh */
g_pdxl0SwapChain->Present(0,0);
```

Working with OpenGL

To rotate the handlebars 90 degrees about the y-axis we start by setting the matrix mode, loading the identity matrix and specifying a perspective projection matrix via an up-direction angle. Following this we set the aspect ratio of the projection plane and the near and far clipping planes (see Chapter 7):

```
glMatrixMode(GL_PROJECTION);
glLoadIdentity(); //move to the center of the screen
gluPerspective(upDirection, aspectRatio, nearDepth,
            farDepth);
```

Following this we specify the handlebars rotation:

```
/* -90 degree rotation about the y-axis (90-deg clockwise) */
glRotatef(-90.0, 0.0, 1.0, 0.0);
```

Next we set the object's homogenous coordinate matrix to the model view matrix using the glGetFloatv function:

```
glGetFloatv(GL_MODELVIEW_MATRIX, Handlebars.modelviewMatrix);
```

The above specified rotation can subsequently be applied to the handlebars drawing function by calling it after the glGetFloatv function.

13.1.2 Connecting Rigid Parts of Objects Using Joints

The handlebars–front wheel interconnection presented in the previous section illustrates the need for a relationship among the various parts of a mesh. This relationship does not only make sense from a logical perspective but is crucial for the realistic and efficient animation of meshes. One mechanism used to model this relationship is joint angles.

A *joint angle* determines the manner in which the attached mesh component is positioned with respect to the mesh object at the other end of the joint. Thus, rotating the bike mesh's handlebars about its vertical axis at some specific angle, θ, will also cause the attached front wheel to rotate at this exact same angle.

Now, consider the structure shown in Figure 13-9. This structure consists of three parts: a base rectangle, a pyramid affixed to it through a joint, and, finally, a rectangle attached to the pyramid (also via a joint). Each of these parts, through the use of joints, can be animated in an incremental fashion. The cube can, for instance, be defined as the base of our mesh with all other objects subsequently attached to it in a hierarchical manner. For our example we constrain rotation of the cube to the *y*-axis. The rotation of the pyramid and rectangle is also constrained to the *y*-axis.

Defining objects incrementally (as in the example above) results in a hierarchical animation model. Rotation of the base object (the cube) will result in the rotation of all other objects affixed to it (the pyramid and rectangle). A similar rotation applied to next object (the pyramid) will only affect the objects subsequently added to it (the rectangle in this case), not the base object, and so forth. Figure 13-10 illustrates the relationships among the parts shown in Figure 13-9 as a tree.

The position and orientation of mesh components are thus controlled by a number of joint angles. We can in turn animate an object by specifying a moment and a number of degrees of freedom for each joint.

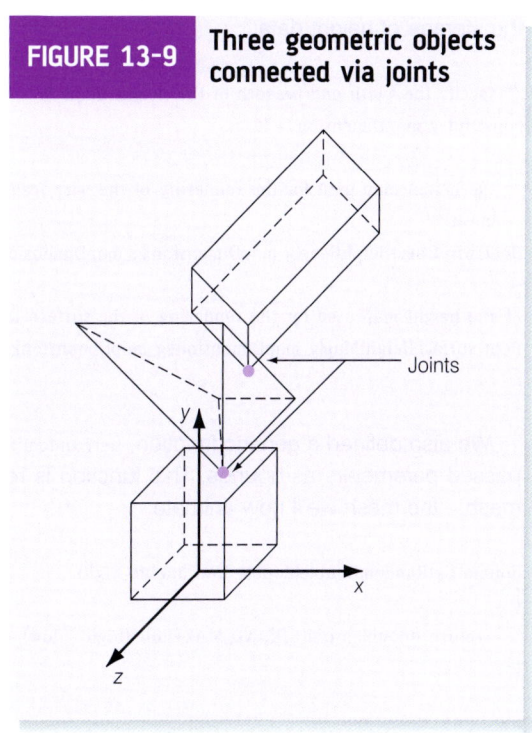

FIGURE 13-9 **Three geometric objects connected via joints**

13

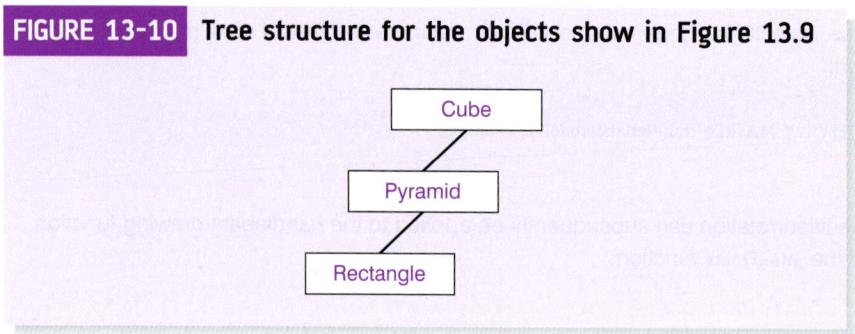

FIGURE 13-10   **Tree structure for the objects show in Figure 13.9**

13.2   ANIMATION

Computer games draw heavily on animation – simply put, without animation most games will not be worth playing. Animation in games can include any motion such as flowing water, bubbling lava or a character running across the screen (which is simply a series of polygons or triangles manipulated and translated in real-time, as discussed in the previous section). Despite offering the possibility of user interaction, all our programs have so far been static. User interaction doesn't count towards animation because the output does not change until the screen is cleared and redrawn.

Returning to the height maps shown in Figure 12.3, we will now animate the wire frame mesh to simulate the movement of water and lava. To recap, in section 12.1.1 we generated the surface data for each mesh as given here. We basically started by declaring a global variable, g_mapDimension, for specifying the mesh width and breadth and two 2D arrays, wireframeHeightMap and surfaceHeightMap, for the storage of height data:

```
/* specify the width and breadth of the height maps */
const int g_mapDimension = 16;

/* the height map used for the rendering of the wire frame
    mesh */
float wireframeHeightMap[g_mapDimension][g_mapDimension];

/* the height map used for the rendering of the surface mesh*/
float surfaceHeightMap[g_mapDimension][g_mapDimension];
```

We also defined a generic function, GetRandomDouble, returning a random double value by using the passed parameters as bounds. This function is responsible for setting up the wire frame height map mesh – the mesh we'll now animate:

```
double GetRandomDouble(double low, double high)
{
    return ((double)rand()/(RAND_MAX+1.0))*(high - low) + low;
}
```

Finally, we generated the data values of both surfaces using two for loops:

```
for (int i = 0; i < g_mapDimension; i++)
{
    for (int j = 0; j < g_mapDimension; j++)
    {
        /* create the randomly protruded wire frame mesh with
           heights ranging from 0.0 to 0.1 */
        wireframeHeightMap[i][j] = GetRandomDouble(0.0, 0.1);

        /* create the surface mesh using a scaled sine
           function */
        surfaceHeightMap[i][j] = sin(0.25 * (sqrt((double)(i) *
                                    (double)(i) + ((double)j) *
                                    (double)(j)))) / 4.0;
    }
}
```

Animating the wire frame mesh requires real-time modification of the mesh's generated height map data as stored in the array, wireframeHeightMap. The simplest technique would be to replace the original elements with an entirely newly generated set; however, doing so will result in erratic movements – definitely not anything like the fluid movement of water or lava. So, we firstly need to create a temporary 2D array for the storage of newly generated height map data:

```
/* a temporary height map used for animation calculations */
float tempHeightMap[g_mapDimension][g_mapDimension];
```

For this example we consider flow speed as the only difference between water and lava:

```
/* the water animation is quick */
if(WATER)
    duration = 50;

/* the lava animation is slow */
if(LAVA)
    duration = 400;
```

The animation is performed similar to the original data generation process outlined above – once again using two for loops. We start by declaring a simple integer counter, durationCounter, which will be used to control the animation speed:

```
int durationCounter = 0;
```

Next we generate random x- and y-values for the temporary height map using the GetRandomDouble function. This is done for as long as the specified duration isn't greater than the durationCounter variable; the wireframe height map, wireframeHeightMap, is updated the moment this happens. The update

13

operation adds the difference between the newly generated height map data and the previous iteration's wire frame height map data divided by the specified duration to the wireframeHeightMap array:

```
if(duration <= durationCounter)
{
    for (int y = 0; y < g_mapDimension; y++)
    {
        for(int x = 0; x < g_mapDimension; x++)
        {
            tempHeightMap[x][y] = getRandomDouble(0.0, 0.1);
        }
    }
    durationCounter = 0;
}
else
{
    for (int y = 0; y < g_mapDimension; y++)
    {
        for(int x = 0; x < g_mapDimension; x++)
        {
            wireframeHeightMap[x][y] +=
                        (tempHeightMap[x][y] -
                        wireframeHeightMap[x][y])/duration;
        }
    }
    durationCounter++;
}
```

We make use of an idle callback, as discussed previously, when animating something. This idle callback allows for the incremental (or random) background modification of parameters used in the rendering of the animated object. The front buffer stores the current displayed image with the back buffer being rendered to by the device object. The modified version of the object is thus rendered onto the back buffer. The contents of the front buffer are subsequently replaced by that of the back buffer – a process at the core of animation and called double buffering (see Chapter 4).

13.2.1 Introduction to Computer Animation Techniques

A number of computer animation techniques exist, each technique category describing a programming technique and the type of objects best suited for achieving the desired animation:

1 Animation of rigid bodies.

2 Animation of particles.

3 Animation via the laws of physics.

4 Animation of articulated objects (bipeds and quadrupeds).

5 Animation of objects according to their behaviour.

Rigid body animation is the most common animation technique used in computer gaming today. This is the kind of animation we have touched on so far – using transformations to translate geometric objects.

Particle animation is the individual animation of groups of primitives or numerous objects used for the simulation of some physical phenomenon such as smoke, dust, cloud formations, sparks, etc.

Animating objects via the use of Newton's laws results in extremely realistic motion. This form of animation is frequently seen in games using advanced physics engines such as the *Havok* physics engine (used by games such as *Half Life 2, BioShock* and *Halo* 3).

The animation of *articulated objects* includes all geometric objects representing bipeds and/or quadrupeds (humans and animals). This form of animation is one of the most difficult due to the high degree of complex transformations needed to simulate natural movement associated with humans and animals.

Animating objects according to their behavior combines a number of rules pertaining to the known movement of an object for the simulation of complex movement patterns. One example of this form of animation is a school of fish – each fish moves individually and in relation to the position of the other fish around it.

13.2.1.1 Animation of Rigid Bodies
Rigid body animation is the simplest and most frequently encountered form of computer animation. A common example is simply translating an object from one spatial position to another – in that way creating the illusion of a smoothly moving object. One traditional requirement for this type of animation is for the scene to be rendered at roughly 15 frames per second or faster (hence 15 images per second for a hand-drawn animation). Animating objects via this technique often requires frame rates of 15 frames per second or higher to maintain the illusion of smooth motion.

The moving height map example given in section 13.2 is thus an example of rigid body animation. We will now discuss the most commonly encountered form of rigid body animation, namely, keyframing.

Keyframing involves the specification of a hierarchical system where the starting and ending points (called frames) of an animation is defined. The frames amid these two points are then filled with in-between frames, a technique called *tweening*, to give the illusion of smooth motion from the first image into the second. Figure 13-11 illustrates this concept where the left-most triangle is the starting point and the right-most the ending point.

Keyframing is not only used for the simulation of motion, but also for the morphing of one shape into another or for transforming one object color to another. Color transformation is performed by specifying a starting keyframe with the original object color and an ending keyframe – with the in-between frames using colors that will result in a smooth transformation. *Keyframe-morphing* is based on the specification of start and end shapes, with the starting point containing the original object and the ending point the transformed one. For example, morphing a cube into a triangle can be done by selecting one point on the cube and moving it towards the cube's diagonal as shown in Figure 13-12.

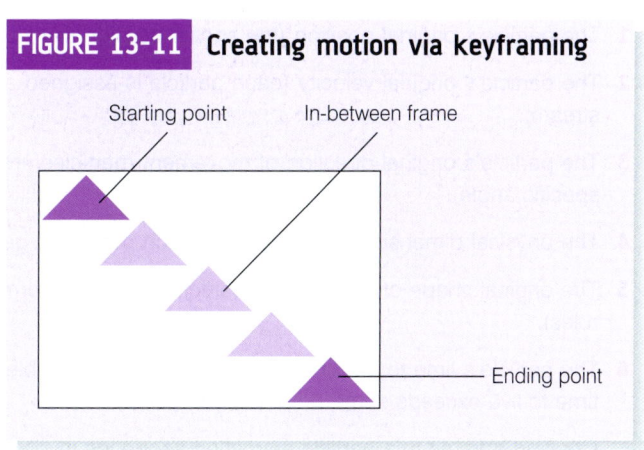

FIGURE 13-11 **Creating motion via keyframing**

Starting point   In-between frame

Ending point

13

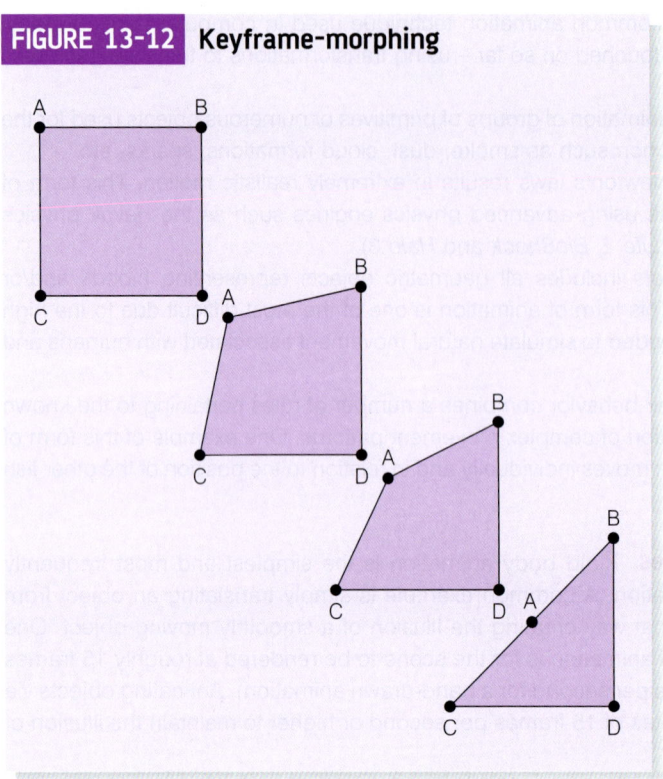

FIGURE 13-12   Keyframe-morphing

13.2.1.2 Animation of Particles Particle animation is based on the scripting and subsequent translation of a large group of objects – either particles (pixel sized units) or objects (mesh-based units). Simulating the movement of these objects requires the modeling of real-life phenomena such as cloud movement, sparks emanating from cutting a piece of metal using an angle grinder, dust resulting from wind blowing over a dry area, etc. For example, the movement of a waterfall depicted using numerous particles can be simulated as shown in Figure 13-13.

Particle scripting controls each of the following properties:

1   The particle's original position (the spatial position the particle is injected at).

2   The particle's original velocity (each particle is assigned a speed when injected into the particle stream).

3   The particle's original direction of movement (particles are injected into the particle stream at a specific angle).

4   The physical dimension of the particle (each particle is generated with a specific size).

5   The original shape of the particle (particles can be deformed based on the application of certain rules).

6   The particle's time to live or the amount of time it is visible (the particle is destroyed the moment its time to live exceeds some predefined threshold).

Creating a frame in a particle animation sequence involves the generation of a number of particles followed by the initialization of each particle's attributes. Next we simply have to check whether any

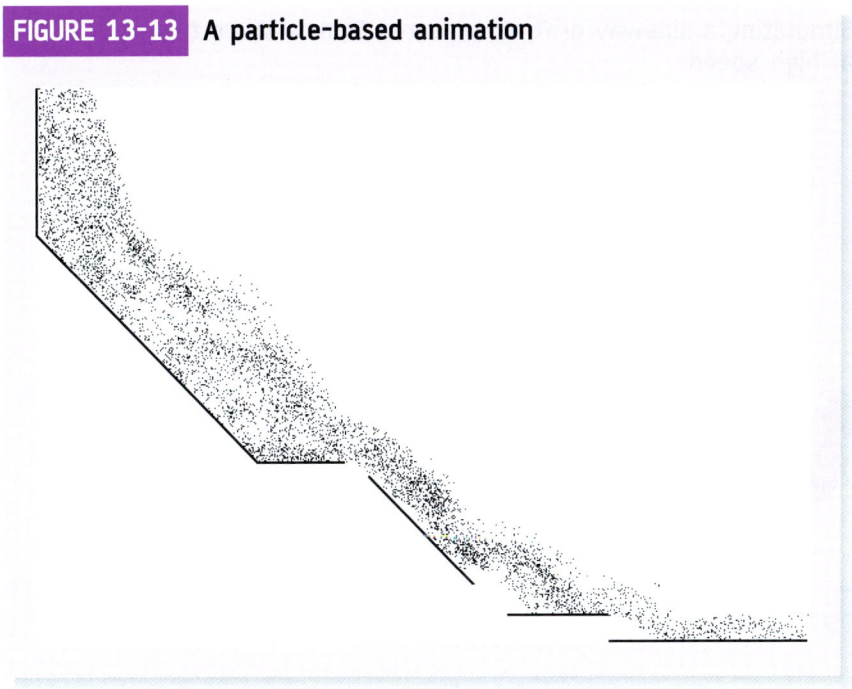

FIGURE 13-13   A particle-based animation

particles have exceeded their lifetime, subsequently destroying those that have. Each particle can now be moved and rendered according to the particle script. Chapter 14 has an entire section dedicated to the creation and animation of particle systems.

13.2.1.3 Animation via the Laws of Physics

Computer animation can be scripted to simulate a high degree of realism; however, the simulation of motion without factoring in the effect of object masses, friction, momentum, and forces will always seem what they are – scripted. By modeling motion through the laws of physics, we can simulate the movement, interaction and deformation of objects automatically. For example, Figure 13-14 shows a vehicle with a velocity and acceleration vector. Both vectors are initially in the same direction but the velocity vector changes as the vehicle is rotated, resulting in a sideways drift.

In Chapter 14 we will look at the modeling of physics in games, for example, incorporating the laws of physics and kinematics with the modeling of gravity, friction and collisions.

13.2.1.4 Animation of Articulated Objects

The animation of geometric objects representing bipeds and/or quadrupeds, as previously mentioned, is an extremely difficult form of animation due to the great number of complex transformations needed for the simulation of natural movement associated with humans and animals. These objects are represented using articulated meshes.

An *articulated mesh* is simply a number of rigid objects connected to each other via a series of joints allowing the different parts to be translated and/or rotated as presented in section 13.1.2.

For example, consider the arm shown in Figure 13-15. This arm is modeled using three joints (representing the shoulder, elbow and wrist) and two rigid links (representing the upper arm and lower arm). This structure is shown as a hierarchy of nodes in Figure 13-16.

The movement of the arm illustrated can be limited to the xy-plane to simplify our discussion. We can now, for example, specify a scripting curve to rotate the shoulder joint in this plane. A *scripting curve* specifies a sequence of transformations as a function of time. This script allows us the freedom of

13

FIGURE 13-14 Simulating a sideway drift as expected from a sharp turn at high speed

assigning numerous characteristics to each structure link. Hence, we can define an inheritance hierarchy where rotation about the shoulder joint also results in an elbow and wrist rotation, etc. An animation is thus scripted for each joint, starting at the top of the hierarchy and traversing to the final joint, in this case the wrist joint. Figure 13-17 illustrates the application of a script mimicking the movement of a sine wave – the only rotation in this case is about the upper shoulder joint.

13.2.1.5 Behavioural Animation of Objects
Objects can be animated by simulating their known behaviour through the definition of a behavioural model, for example, to simulate the flocking of birds, the swarming of bees, or the movement of a school of fish. The simplest behavioural model will require us to specify a set of rules for each fish or bee in relation to the position of the other fish or bees around it.

Craig Reynolds developed a behavioural animation model in 1987 to describe the flocking of birds as well as the swarming of fish. This model expressed flocking as a twofold process, namely, a wish of

FIGURE 13-15 **An arm modeled using two links connecting three joints**

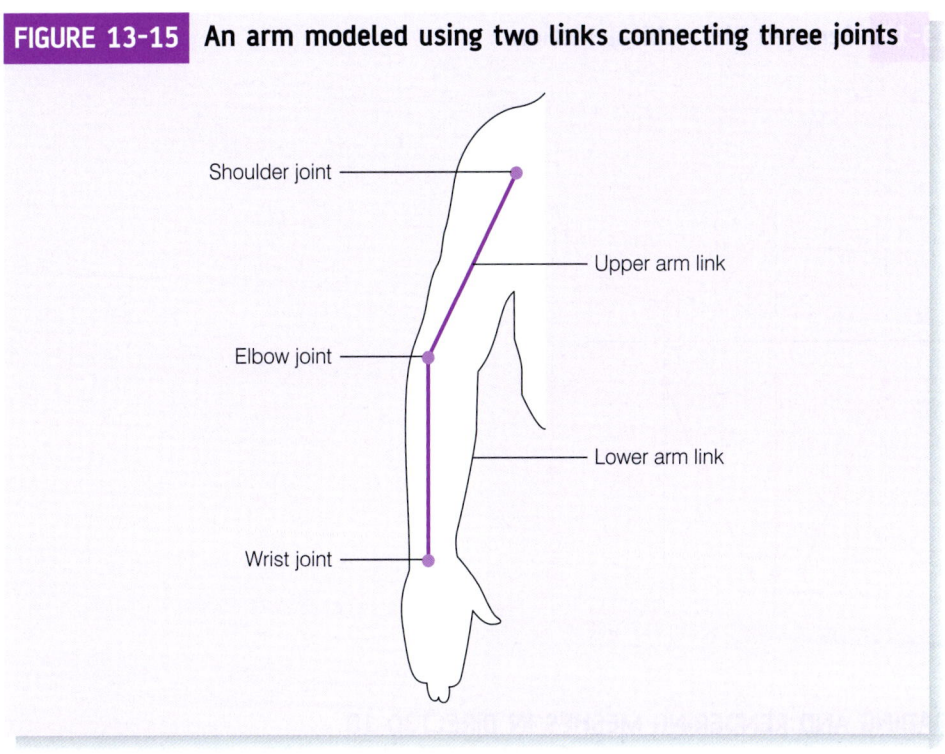

FIGURE 13-16 **A hierarchical representation of the arm shown in Figure 13.15**

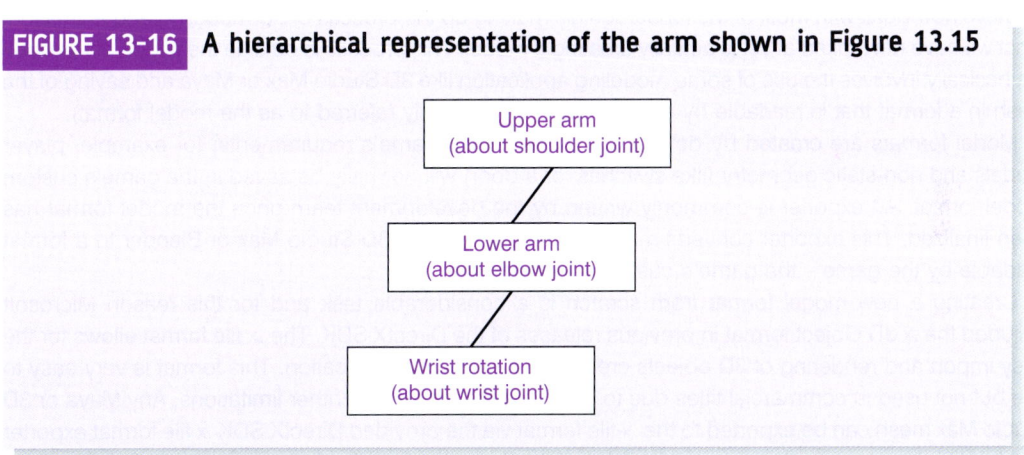

13

each flock member to stay close to each other while at the same time actively avoiding collisions. The *Reynolds behavioural model* is based on the following three rules:

1 Avoid collisions with nearby flock/swarm members.

2 Match the speed of nearby flock/swarm members.

3 Stay close to nearby flock/swarm members.

It is thus relatively simple to create quite complex swarm simulation by scripting these three rules for each of the objects constituting a flock or swarm.

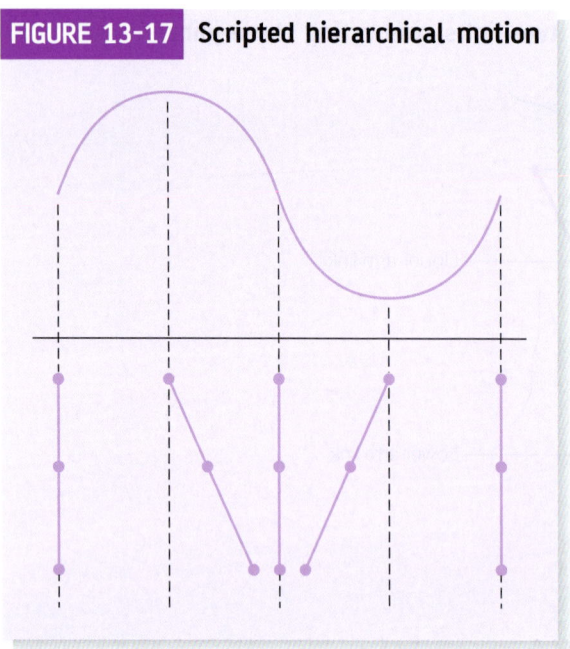

FIGURE 13-17   **Scripted hierarchical motion**

13.3   LOADING AND RENDERING MESHES IN DIRECT3D 10

We have now dealt with most of the fundamentals making up the process of 3D modeling and animation. What we have not looked at yet is actually creating a model. This process is outside the scope of the book but basically involves the use of some modeling application like 3D Studio Max or Maya and saving of the mesh in a format that is readable by our application (commonly referred to as the model format).

Model formats are created by developers to meet their game's requirements; for example, player models and non-static geometry (like switches, or a door) will normally be saved in the game's custom model format. An exporter is commonly written by the development team once the model format has been finalized. This exporter converts meshes created in Maya, 3D Studio Max or Blender to a format readable by the game – the game's custom model format.

Creating a new model format from scratch is a considerable task and for this reason Microsoft included the .x 3D Object format in previous releases of the DirectX SDK. The .x file format allows for the easy import and rendering of 3D objects created in a modeling application. This format is very easy to use but not used in commercial titles due to performance issues and other limitations. Any Maya or 3D Studio Max mesh can be exported to the .x file format via the provided DirectX SDK .x file format exporter plugins (third-party exporters are also freely available from the net). Once the mesh has been converted to the .x format, it can be loaded into the application for display.

Support for the .x file format is, as mentioned, extremely limited in DirectX 10, with the new SDK samples instead using the DXUT Mesh format (.sdkmesh) and associated loader functions. An exporter (meshconvert. exe – stored under "SDKpath" \Utilities\Bin\x86) is provided for converting from .x to this new file format.

Once we have a mesh in the .sdkmesh model format we can import it. The first step requires the creation of a mesh object using the CDXUTSDKMesh class declared in the sdkmesh.h header file:

```
CDXUTSDKMesh g_MeshObject;
```

We can now read the .sdkmesh file into memory using the Create CDXUTSDKMesh function. This function requires a pointer to the Direct3D 10 device (the ID3D10Device interface) as its first parameter, the name of the .sdkmesh file as its second parameter and lastly two Boolean parameters, the first being optimization related and the second dealing with the creation of adjacency indices (the mesh is loaded just after definition of the input layout object):

```
/* declare the Direct3D 10 device */
ID3D10Device* g_id3dDevice;

/* load the mesh */
g_MeshObject.Create(g_id3dDevice,
                    "ourMesh.sdkmesh",
                    false, true);
```

The textures, normals and vertices of the mesh, including the Direct3D vertex and index buffers are now contained in the CDXUTSDKMesh object. The mesh can be rendered using the Render CDXUTSDKMesh function (after binding the input-layout object to the input-assembler stage via the IASetInputLayout ID3D10Device interface). The CDXUTSDKMesh Render function takes three parameters, namely, the Direct3D 10 device and the effect and technique used to render the mesh (a pixel and vertex shader is needed to calculate the texture color of the mesh):

```
/* render the mesh */
g_MeshObject.Render(g_id3dDevice,
                    g_pd3d10EffectTechnique,
                    g_pTexture);
```

The Render function's second parameter, g_pd3d10EffectTechnique, is declared and initialized as follows:

```
ID3D10Effect* g_id3dEffect = NULL;
ID3D10EffectTechnique* g_pd3d10EffectTechnique = NULL;
g_pd3d10EffectTechnique = g_id3dEffect->
                    GetTechniqueByName("RenderMesh");
```

The RenderMesh shader technique is defined in our program's shader file as previously discussed:

```
technique10 RenderMesh
{
    pass P0
    {
        SetGeometryShader(NULL);
        SetVertexShader(CompileShader(ps_4_0, VertexShader()));
        SetPixelShader(CompileShader(ps_4_0, PixelShader()));
    }
}
```

As can be seen from the above technique definition, we need to declare a vertex and pixel shader. The input texture coordinates and vertex coordinates of the mesh are passed to the vertex shader, VertexShader. This shader then outputs these coordinates to the hardware where the pixel shader is then able to subsequently read them from. The vertex shader is defined as follows:

```
PIXELSHADER_INPUT VertexShader(VERTEXSHADER_INPUT
                    coordsInput)
```

13

```
    {
        PIXELSHADER_INPUT coordsOutput = (PIXELSHADER_INPUT)0;
        coordsOutput.Loc = mul(coordsInput.Loc, World);
        coordsOutput.Loc = mul(coordsInput.Loc,
                                modelviewProjection);
        coordsOutput.Tex = coordsInput.Tex;

        return coordsOutput;
    }
```

The pixel shader input structure receiving the texture coordinates from the graphics pipeline, is defined as follows:

```
struct PIXELSHADER_INPUT
{
    float4 Loc : SV_POSITION;
    float2 Tex : TEXCOORD0;
};
```

A number of other shader variables are also defined in this vertex program, for example the uniform float4x4 modelviewProjection and worldviewProjection matrices used for performing transformations on the cube's vertex coordinates. These variables, declared using the HLSL data types, are set by the Direct3D application. Chapter 6 deals with this process in more detail.

Next we define a pixel shader to perform the texel lookup, returning the sampled color value:

```
float4 PixelShader(PIXELSHADER_INPUT inputcoords) : SV_Target
{
    return textureVar.Sample(samplingMethod,
                             inputcoords.Tex)*objectColor;
}
```

As discussed in previous chapters, our pixel shader uses a sampler specifying the manner in which the texture will be sampled using the SamplerState type. This structure defines the texture filtering method as linear mipmapping (MIN_MAG_MIP_LINEAR) and the texture coordinates u and v, to repeat the sampling on every integer junction via the address wrap constant, wrap:

```
SamplerState samplingMethod
{
    Filter = MIN_MAG_MIP_LINEAR;
    AddressU = Wrap;
    AddressV = Wrap;
};
```

Before the texture object can be used by our program, we first need to set the texturing effect. This is done by retrieving a pointer to the Texture2D variable, textureVar, declared in the shader program (g_pTexture is the Render function's third parameter):

```
ID3D10EffectShaderResourceVariable* g_pTexture;

g_pTexture = g_id3dEffect->GetVariableByName("textureVar")
                          ->AsShaderResource();
```

Following all this we must remember to destroy the mesh object after releasing the DirectX resources. We do this by calling the `CDXUTSDKMesh Destroy` function:

`g_MeshObject.Destroy();`

13.4 SUMMARY

The chapter started by looking at polygonal meshes as arbitrary geometric objects consisting of flat faces and straight lines. Following this it investigated a number of mesh creation and implementation strategies, specifically focusing on the representation of polygonal meshes, the creation of hierarchical relationships among geometric objects, the concept of connecting rigid parts of objects using joints and finally manipulating these joints for the purpose of animating the object.

We saw that the simplest way of representing a mesh was to view it as an entity and that an object could be constructed as a single rigid mesh or as a collection of independent meshes. Following this we considered hierarchical models as an alternative to entities. We then discussed the animation of hierarchical models using a series of function calls, each generating and transforming a part of the model. This was followed by the representation of models using tree-based data structures.

Next we introduced the concept of joint angles as a way to determine the manner in which an attached mesh component is positioned with respect to the mesh object at the other end of the joint.

The remainder of the chapter focused on computer animation, in essence presenting the topic in a hands-on fashion by animating a wireframe mesh to simulate the movement of water and lava. Building on this we considered a number of computer animation techniques dealing with the animation of rigid bodies, particles, animation via the laws of physics, the animation of articulated objects, and the animation of objects according to their behaviour. The chapter concluded with the loading and rendering of meshes in Direct3D 10.

The next chapter deals with the implementation of basic physics as required by games. Elements focused on include the laws of physics, particle systems and the modeling of gravity, friction, and collisions.

13.5 FURTHER READING

For more information on the animation of articulated objects, refer to the excellent book *Advanced Animation and Rendering Techniques by Alan Watt and M. Watt* [ISBN: 0201544121]. The paper titled '*Flocks, Herds, and Schools: A Distributed Behavioural Model' by Craig Reynolds* published in the *SIGGRAPH '87 Conference Proceedings* presents an animation model for the simulation of a flock of birds, a herd of land animals or a school of fish. The animation of rigid bodies is very nicely presented in James Hahn's paper '*Realistic Animation of Rigid Bodies*' published in *Communications of the ACM* (1988). For additional information on keyframe animation, refer to *Game Programming Gems edited by Mark DeLoura* [ISBN: 1584500492].

13.6 EXERCISES

1 Why are meshes constructed using basic polygon types?

2 Name the two issues that become apparent when attempting to create a structure for the storage of a geometric mesh.

3 Compare the benefits of using heuristic models as opposed to entity models.

4 Briefly describe the advantages of representing models using tree-based data structures as opposed to a set of entities.

5 What is the most common method of representing a mesh hierarchy?

6 Describe how we might go about connecting rigid parts of objects using joints.

7 Briefly describe keyframe animation and the animation of articulated objects.

8 Extend program 9.1 to load the mesh "EvilDrone.sdkmesh" available from the book's website.

13

CHAPTER 14

Physics Modeling

LEARNING OBJECTIVES

In this chapter you will learn about:

- The fundamentals of physics
- Time
- Position
- Mass and weight
- Velocity
- Acceleration
- Force
- Momentum
- Physics modeling and implementation
- Linear momentum
- Gravitational pull
- Trajectory paths
- Friction
- Object collisions
- Implementing a particle system

INTRODUCTION

Chapter 14 presents the foundational principles and implementation of basic physics as required by games. Elements focused on, from both a theoretical and practical perspective, include the laws of physics and the modeling and implementation of gravity, friction, trajectory paths, momentum, acceleration, force and collisions. The chapter concludes with the implementation of a physics-based particle system.

14.1   FUNDAMENTALS OF PHYSICS

Video games originally featured a very small amount of physics simulation, with games like *Breakout* (released by Atari in 1976) incorporating a limited degree of collision detection and response to simulate the destruction of bricks upon collision with a ball, as well as the bouncing of this ball upon impact with the movable paddle (shown in Figure 14-1).

During the 1990s, concepts such as gravity and the fundamental laws of physics were steadily finding their way into games. It wasn't, however, until the release of games like *Valve Software's Half Life 2* that true physics simulation really contributed to the overall game play experience. *Half Life 2* included numerous physics-based puzzles where the player, for example, had to use gravity by removing bricks from one end of a pulley system to lower the other end, etc. Physics has thus found its way into games for the realistic simulation of object-player interaction as well as for the animation of objects based on exerted forces and environmental resistance.

One interesting development in the world of physics is dedicated Physics Processing Units or PPUs. These dedicated physics microcontrollers act in much the same way as GPUs, in this case relieving the CPU of all physics and math calculations. AGEIA is the primary company currently doing work on Physics Processing Units and invented the *PhysX* (shown in Figure 14-2) – a PPU that accelerates

FIGURE 14-1	A Breakout clone (source code available on the book's website)

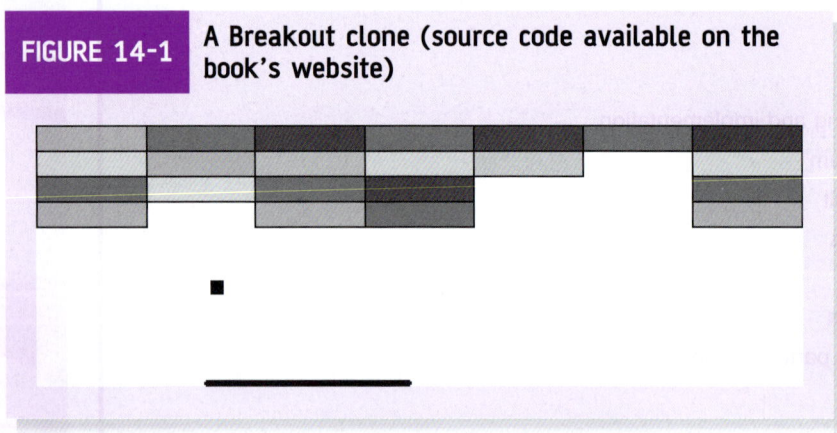

FIGURE 14-2	Asus-based AGEIA's PhysX PPU card

physics calculations by offloading them from the CPU to PPU. This PPU is limited to acceleration of AGEIA's own physics engine – the PhysX SDK.

NVIDIA and ATI compete against the PhysX PPU by accelerating the Havok FX SDK (a specialized version of the Havok physics engine used in Half Life 2) to utilize the GPUs in ATI and NVIDIA video cards for physics simulations.

Most physics simulations are based on *Newton's laws of motion* – three laws describing the relationship between the forces influencing a rigid body and the resulting motion of this body. The performance of a physics simulation is heavily dependant on the number of bodies being simulated with the exact modeling of these laws requiring a lot of processing power that can result in even the most powerful computers grinding to a halt. Newton's laws of motion can be summarized as follows:

1 The first law: law of inertia:
   - A body in motion will remain in motion unless a net force is exerted upon it.

2 The second law: law of acceleration:
   - The net force of a particle is the rate of change of its linear momentum.
   - Momentum is the mass of the body multiplied by its velocity.
     - The force on a body is thus its mass multiplied by its acceleration ($F=m.a$).

3 The third law: law of reciprocal actions:
   - To every action there is an equal and opposite reaction.

Computer games will rarely implement physics or Newton's laws of motion down to the letter. Doing so will leave little if any processing power for the game's AI, networking, game loop, etc. We will thus rather outline the physics needed and simulate the required effects as close to real life as possible, hence creating an extremely close approximation but using a lot of optimizations and assumptions to simplify the original laws of motion.

We will now cover some fundamental concepts of physics before moving on to actual physics modeling and simulation.

14.1.1 Time

Time is perhaps the most critical part of any simulation – an abstract concept spanning science, philosophy and art. Time in the real word is, of course, a basic concept and a core element of the human intellectual structure. In physics, time is considered a *fundamental quantity* meaning that it can't be defined in terms of other quantities such as force or momentum because these concepts are already defined in terms of time.

When designing an algorithm for use in a simple game (such as the *Breakout* example previously discussed) it is more common to define time around the game's frame rate than in terms of seconds, minutes, hours, and so forth. For most of these games, one frame is normally taken as one second or one time-step. More advanced games, such as 3D first-person shooters, require a real time system operating independently from the game's frame rate. Using real time (seconds) as opposed to virtual time (frames) is required when modeling movement and forces without the end result being unrealistically influenced by changes in the game's frame rate.

14.1.2 Position

As mentioned in Chapter 7, the Cartesian coordinate system is the most fundamental system for the unique identification of arbitrary points in space. Each point in 3D space can be identified in terms of an x-, y- and z-coordinate – the point's spatial position (shown in Figure 14-3).

Calculating the spatial position of a real-world object is slightly more involved than the simple specification of a point. For instance, an irregular object like a sword can not merely be described using

14

a randomly assigned position or coordinate set. There is, however, a single point that can be used to describe the object's spatial position, namely, the object's center of mass (also known as the object's balancing point). For example, the balancing point of a sword (thus its center) is shown in Figure 14-4. This point can now be used to denote the position of the object in three-dimensional space.

When defining the position of an irregular object, we will rarely go through the trouble of calculating its center of mass. The most general approach involves the specification of a bounding volume. A bounding volume, as described in Chapter 12, is a volume enclosing a geometric object. Bounding volumes are specified using the minimum and maximum x-, y- and z-values of the contained object with the center of the volume used to represent the center of the contained object – thus the object's spatial position. Physics calculations based on this presumed center will generally be correct due to the mass of most objects being at their centers. However, calculations will be far from correct for objects with an alternatively located center of mass. The most common solution to this problem is to assign a weight to each vertex making up the object and to subsequently calculate the object's actual center of mass.

14.1.3 Mass and Weight

Mass is a fundamental concept describing an object's atomic mass or the amount of matter used to make up an object. The physical concept of mass must not be confused with the weight of an object. *Weight* is directly proportional to the amount of gravitational pull exerted upon the mass of an object, for example, a person might weigh 80 kilograms on earth but will only weigh about 14 kilograms on the moon. The mass of this person will however remain constant.

Mass is measured in kilograms (kg) while weight, synonymous to force, is measured in Newton (N). Mass in computer games is a much more abstract concept and normally represented in arbitrary terms. For example, a crate might be assigned a mass of 10 mass units. The crate's mass can now be compared to another object in the game, like a bridge with a mass of 5000 mass units. Mass in computer games is thus described in terms of one object compared to another.

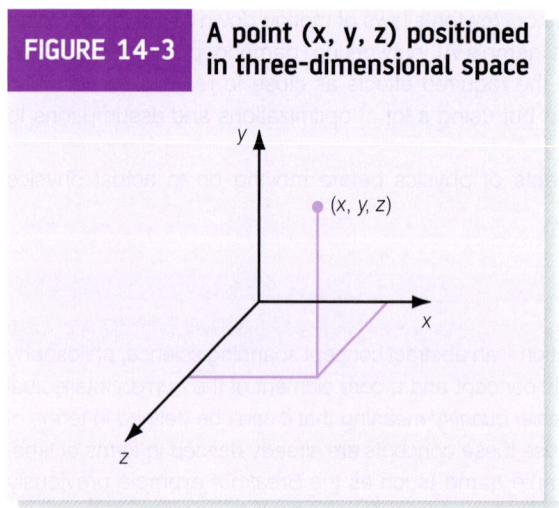

FIGURE 14-3 **A point (x, y, z) positioned in three-dimensional space**

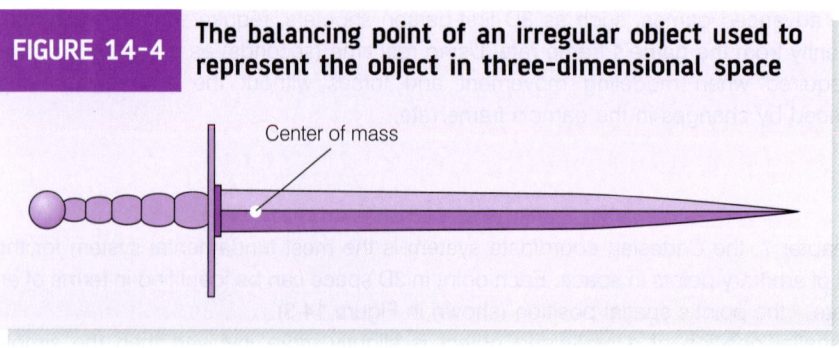

FIGURE 14-4 **The balancing point of an irregular object used to represent the object in three-dimensional space**

Center of mass

14.1.4 Velocity

Velocity can be described as the rate of change of an object's position. Velocity, measured in meters per second (m/s), has both magnitude (speed) and direction, and is thus described as a vector quantity. We use the following formula to mathematically describe velocity (**v**):

$v = \frac{ds}{dt}$, with ds denoting the change in position and dt denoting the change in time.

Using this formula first presented as part of the school physics curriculum is really easy. For example, say we have travelled a total distance of 300 kilometres in 2 hours then we can calculate our average speed as follows:

$$
\begin{aligned}
v &= \frac{ds}{dt} \\
&= \frac{300km}{2h} \\
&= 150km/h
\end{aligned}
$$

Velocity in computer gaming is, as with mass, an arbitrary concept. Also, calculating the velocity of an object is dependent on whether the physics engine uses the game's frame rate or a real-time system. Using the frame rate is no problem as long as it remains constant, for example, a game running at 60 frames per second spends a total of $1/60^{th}$ of a second per frame. This virtual time unit can now be combined with the number of pixels translated. So, the velocity of an object being moved 2 pixels per frame in some arbitrary direction can be written as:

$$
\begin{aligned}
v &= \frac{2Pixels}{\frac{1}{60}Seconds} \\
&= 120 \; pixels/s
\end{aligned}
$$

The above described approach works fairly well for puzzle and platform games but is not frequently seen in first-person shooters or real time strategy games. The main reason for this is the fluctuating frame rates encountered with these high-end processor intensive games – a stand alone timing class is much more reliable and thus commonplace.

We can now combine velocity with an object's original position to determine its new position. The basic formula given here can thus be used to determine the translation of an object based on its velocity:

$Pos_{new} = Pos_{old} + v \times t$, where v is the velocity of the object and t the duration of movement.

14

14.1.5 Acceleration

Acceleration is the rate of change of velocity. Acceleration, measured in meters per second² (m/s²), has both magnitude and direction, and is thus also described as a vector quantity. We use the following formula to mathematically describe acceleration (**a**):

$a = \frac{dv}{dt}$, with dv denoting the change in velocity (final velocity − initial velocity) and dt denoting the change in time.

Using this formula is also very easy; for example, say we are traveling at 1200 m/s and at some point we increase our speed to 1600 m/s which takes 12 seconds in total, then we can calculate our acceleration as follows:

$$a = \frac{dv}{dt}$$
$$= \frac{(1600 - 1200)m/s}{12s}$$
$$= 33m/s^2$$

We can now combine acceleration with an object's original velocity to determine its new velocity. The basic formula given here can be used to determine the new velocity of an object based on its acceleration: $V_{new} = V_{old} + a \times t$, with V_{new} the new velocity of the object, V_{old} the old velocity, a the acceleration of the object and t the duration of acceleration.

The new position of an object at some specific time can in turn be calculated by adding its original position to its initial velocity multiplied by the duration of the movement plus the time integral of the velocity (one half the acceleration times the duration squared): $s_t = s_0 + (v_0 \times t) + (\frac{1}{2} \times a \times t^2)$ where s_t is the new position of the object, s_0 the original position, v_0 its initial velocity, t the duration of acceleration and a the acceleration of the object.

We can now adopt this formula for the calculation of an object's position in 3D space. For example, say we have an object at the coordinates (100, 0, 0) with an initial velocity of 120 pixels/s and an acceleration of 6 pixels/s^2, then we can calculate the position of the object after some specified amount of time using the following equation:

$$s_t = 100 + (120 \; pixels/s \times t) + \left(\frac{1}{2} \times 6pixels/s^2 \times t^2 \right)$$

We can model one-dimensional acceleration in C++ by simply adding the predetermined acceleration of the object to the object's current velocity every time the object is translated a single frame – of course assuming linear acceleration (such as the acceleration experienced by a falling object), for example:

```
float objectAcceleration = 4.0;
float objectVelocity  = 0.0;
float objectPosition = 0.0;

/* set the current velocity of the object each time it is
   translated */
objectVelocity = objectVelocity + objectAcceleration;

/* calculate the current position of the object */
objectPosition = objectPosition + objectVelocity;
```

Acceleration is used in computer games to accurately simulate motion, and without it we'll rarely have a true 'sense of mass'.

14.1.6 Force

Force is the physical action exerted upon an object to accelerate it. There is thus a relationship between the mass of the object, the force exerted upon it and the resulting acceleration; and according to

Newton's second law of motion, we can calculate the force (**F**) on a body by multiplying its mass (*m*) with its acceleration (*a*), resulting in the following equation:

$$F = m \times a.$$

Looking at the given equation we can express acceleration as the force exerted upon the object divided by the mass of the object:

$$a = \frac{F}{m}.$$

Force is measured in Newtons (N), with one Newton being equal to one kilogram-meter per second squared (kgm/s^2).

To fully grasp the concept of force, consider the object shown in Figure 14-5; it has a mass of 100 kilograms with an acceleration of 9.80665 m/s^2. This acceleration (standard gravity) is exerted upon the object by the earth's gravitational field. We can thus calculate the gravitational force on this object as follows:

$$
\begin{aligned}
F_{gravity} &= m \times a \\
&= 100kg \times 9.80665m/s^2 \\
&= 980.665N
\end{aligned}
$$

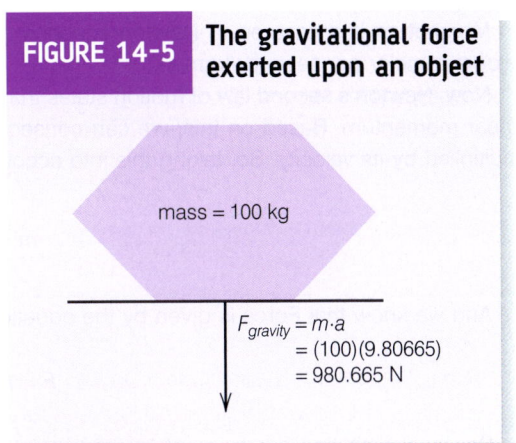

FIGURE 14-5 The gravitational force exerted upon an object

mass = 100 kg

$$
\begin{aligned}
F_{gravity} &= m \cdot a \\
&= (100)(9.80665) \\
&= 980.665 \text{ N}
\end{aligned}
$$

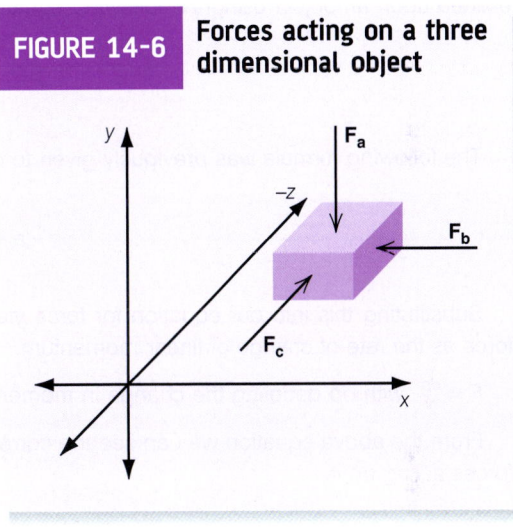

FIGURE 14-6 Forces acting on a three dimensional object

Moving this object in the y-direction will require a force greater than the one exerted by the planet (980.665N), thus a force greater than the one giving the object weight.

Objects in 3D games, unlike the above given one-dimensional example, experience forces in three directions, namely, as x-, y- and z-force components. A three-dimensional force can hence be decomposed into these three components, with each component independently calculated and then finally summed together. For example, three forces; **F$_a$**, **F$_b$** and **F$_c$** are applied to the object shown in Figure 14-6.

We can now find the resultant vector by summing the scalars of vector **F$_a$**, **F$_b$** and **F$_c$** in the following manner:

$$
\begin{aligned}
\mathbf{F}_{final} &= \mathbf{F_a} + \mathbf{F_b} + \mathbf{F_c} \\
&= (F_a x + F_b x + F_c x,\ F_a y + F_b y + F_c y,\ F_a z + F_b z + F_c z) \\
&= (F_{final} x, F_{final} y, F_{final} z).
\end{aligned}
$$

14

14.1.7 Momentum

Momentum is the product of mass and velocity, i.e. a property inherent to objects in motion. We use the following formula to mathematically describe momentum (**P**):

$P = m \times v$, where *m* is the mass of the object and *v* its velocity.

Momentum is measured in Newton seconds (Ns), with one Newton second being equal to one kilogram-meter per second (kgm/s).

Now, Newton's second law of motion states that the net force of a particle is the rate of change of its linear momentum. Based on this, we can consequently describe momentum as the mass of a body multiplied by its velocity. So, taking this into account, we can rewrite our equation for momentum as:

$$m = \frac{P}{v}.$$

And we know that Force is given by the equation:

$$F = m \times a.$$

So, by substituting our momentum formula into the equation for force, we can calculate the force exerted upon an object using the following equation:

$$F = \frac{p \times a}{v}.$$

The following formula was previously given to describe acceleration (**a**):

$$a = \frac{dv}{dt}$$

Substituting this into our equation for force yields the Newton's second law of motion describing force as the rate of change of linear momentum:

$F = \frac{dp}{dt}$, with dp denoting the change in momentum and dt the change in time.

From the above equation we can see the correlation between the momentum of an object and the forces acting on it.

14.2   PHYSICS MODELING AND IMPLEMENTATION

Simulating Newtonian physics through the use of quantities such as mass, acceleration, velocity, friction, momentum, and force allows for the prediction of object behaviour under certain conditions. For example, through physics modeling we can simulate the expected behaviour of several stacked barrels falling over or even an explosion ripping through a bunker complex.

Physics modeling is generally implemented as part of a physics engine. Physics engines are classified into two classes: real-time engines such as the Havok physics engine and high-precision physics engines such as those used by scientists. *Real-time physics engines* 'approximate' physics modeling to balance computational accuracy with the speed of the simulation. *Scientific physics engines* are employed by organizations like NASA and universities for various simulations, for example, Figure 14-7 shows the computational fluid dynamics model used for simulating the air flow around a space shuttle during atmospheric re-entry.

The shown computational fluid dynamics model requires an incredible amount of processing power to simulate. This is mostly due to the use of numerical methods and advanced algorithms when analyzing the flow of particles – each particle is assigned a force vector which are then combined across the entire region to illustrate the resulting particle flow.

When adding Newtonian physics to a game we must always keep processing constraints in mind. Our biggest problem is not performing the physics calculations but dealing with a fluctuating frame rate and rounding errors that can result in unrealistic motion. On the other hand, increasing data precision will solve the problem of rounding errors but with a significant impact on CPU usage.

We will now model Newtonian physics by looking at the conservation and transfer of momentum as well as the modeling of gravitational pull, trajectories, friction, and object collision.

| **FIGURE 14-7** | **Simulated air flow around a space shuttle during atmospheric re-entry** |

14.2.1 Linear Momentum

Action-oriented games without collisions would simply not work. Whether it's a projectile fired from a weapon striking a monster, a car skidding across the Daytona Speedway or the player activating a switch; without the ability to simulate one object striking another we would simply not 'have game.'

At the core of collision simulation is the conservation and transfer of momentum. The *conservation of momentum* is described as a rule of nature stating that if we have a closed system of objects, without any external interaction, then the total momentum of this system will remain constant. This rule links back to Newton's first law of motion: that is, a body in motion will remain in motion unless a net force is exerted upon it. Building on this, Newton's third law of motion states that for every action there is an equal and opposite reaction – a law that can be proven by considering the conservation of momentum.

To understand conservation of momentum, consider a game of squash in a perfect world where no energy is lost when the ball hits the squash court's wall (in the real word energy will be released in the form of sound, heat and deformation the moment the ball hits the wall, thus resulting in a slower velocity (and less momentum) after the collision than before). However, in a perfect world we don't consider loss in momentum and the velocity of the ball remains the same after the collision than as before.

The *transfer of momentum* describes the situation where a collision occurs and momentum is transferred from the one object to the other. Thus, the loss of momentum at the one side must equal the momentum gained at the other (assuming conservation of kinetic energy as well as momentum before and after the collision). This concept is described mathematically as follows:

$$\triangle p_{object1} = - \triangle p_{object2},$$ where $\triangle p$ is the change in momentum of each object.

A well-known example demonstrating the conservation and transfer of momentum is Newton's cradle – a device consisting of five (or more) pendulums neighbouring one another. Figure 14-8 shows Newton's cradle, when the midair pendulum is released, it will collide with the left-most static pendulum. On impact, energy is transferred from one pendulum to the other until the right-most pendulum is

14

pushed outwards by the transferred force. The motion will eventually cease due to a continuous energy loss (mostly released as sound energy i.e. 'clacking' sounds).

To fully understand perfect collisions and the conservation of momentum, consider the two objects shown in Figure 14-9.

Both objects have a mass ($m_{object1}$ and $m_{object2}$) and initial velocity ($v_{initial1}$ and $v_{initial2}$). After collision each will have a new velocity – two unknown values at this stage (v_{after1} and v_{after2}). Using these variables we can now describe the conservation of momentum mathematically using the following equation:

$$m_{object1} \times v_{initial1} + m_{object2} \times v_{initial2} = m_{object1} \times v_{after1} + m_{object2} \times v_{after2}$$

One problem with this equation is that we normally wish to calculate each object's vector velocity after the collision, something which is impossible because we'll always end up with two unknowns. For example, say object 1 has a mass of 250kg and an initial velocity of 1200m/s while object 2 has a mass of 300kg and an initial velocity of 2400m/s, then by substituting these values in the above equation, we get:

$$250kg \times 1200m/s + 300kg \times 2400m/s = 250kg \times v_{after1} + 300kg \times v_{after2}$$

FIGURE 14-8   **Newton's cradle used for demonstrating the conservation/ transfer of momentum and energy**

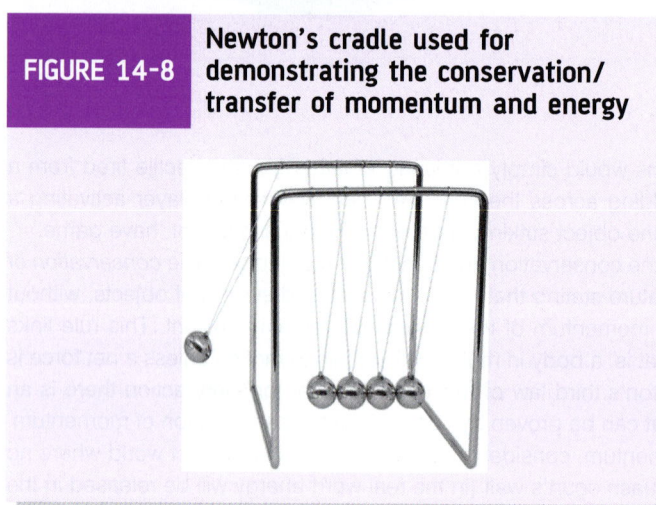

The only logical approach is to combine this equation with something we already know, in this case the conservation of energy, specifically the *conservation of kinetic energy*.

Kinetic energy is energy stored in a moving object, or more specifically, the mechanical work needed to accelerate this object from rest to its current state. *Mechanical work* is the total amount of energy transferred to an object through the application of force. The simplest way of calculating work, measured in joules (J), is to use the following formula:

FIGURE 14-9   **Collision and the transfer of momentum**

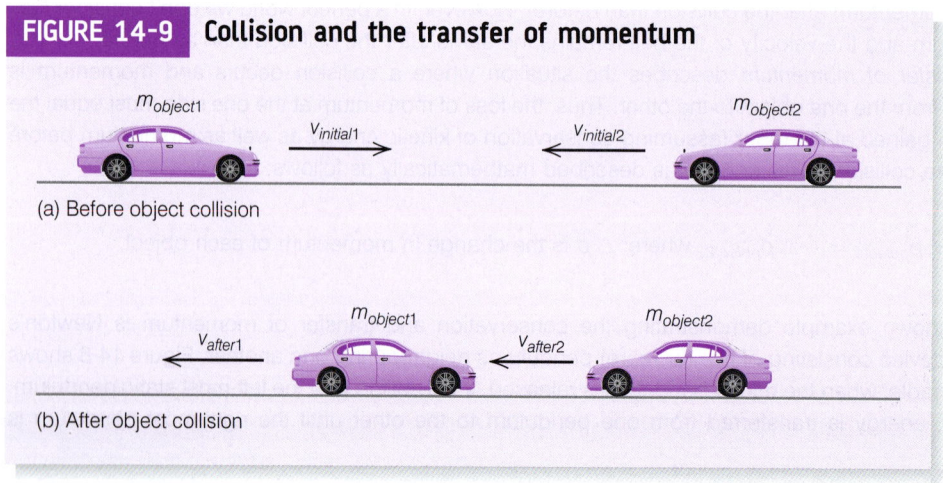

$m_{object1}$ $v_{initial1}$ $v_{initial2}$ $m_{object2}$

(a) Before object collision

v_{after1} $m_{object1}$ v_{after2} $m_{object2}$

(b) After object collision

$W = Fd$, where F is the force exerted on the object and d the distance travelled by the object.

This formula can also be written as:

$W = \frac{1}{2}mv^2$, with m the mass of the object and v its velocity.

Applying external work to an object causes a change in its kinetic energy. For example, say an object has an initial kinetic energy of $E_{k\_initial}$ and some force is applied to it resulting in a new kinetic energy, E_{k_final}, then we can represent the relation between work and kinetic energy as follows:

$$W = \Delta E_k$$
$$= E_{k\_final} - E_{k\_initial}$$

Kinetic energy (E_k) is the ability to do work and can easily be calculated using the following equation:

$E_k = \frac{1}{2}mv^2$, with m the mass of the object in kilograms and v its velocity in meters per second.

Kinetic energy, akin to work, is measured in joules (J), with one joule being equal to one kilogram-meter squared per second squared (kgm^2/s^2). This energy remains constant before and after a collision – a condition described as the *conservation of kinetic energy*. In the real world, energy will of course be lost in the form of sound, heat and deformation; however, this is only something that will be considered for the implementation of a scientific physics engine. Using this conservation property we can now describe the total kinetic energy before and after a collision via the following equation:

$$\frac{1}{2}m_{object1} \times v_{initial1}^2 + \frac{1}{2}m_{object2} \times v_{initial2}^2 = \frac{1}{2}m_{object1} \times v_{after1}^2 + \frac{1}{2}m_{object2} \times v_{after2}^2$$

We can now use this equation in combination with the previous listed one describing the conservation of momentum to solve the given example's two unknown velocities following the collision:

$$250kg \times 1200m/s + 300kg \times 2400m/s = 250kg \times v_{after1} + 300kg \times v_{after2}$$

$$\frac{1}{2}(250kg)(1200m/s)^2 + \frac{1}{2}(300kg)(2400m/s)^2 = \frac{1}{2}(250kg)v_{after1}^2 + \frac{1}{2}(300kg)v_{after2}^2$$

The simplest approach would be to write V_{after1} in terms of V_{after2} for the second equation, substituting it into the first equation and solving V_{after2}.

Section 14.2.5 extends this discussion by looking at the simulation of bouncing objects and inter-object collision detection and response.

14.2.2 Gravitational Pull

When looking at any early 1990s side-scrolling game, such as *Super Mario World* or *Commander Keen*, one can quickly see the effect of gravity on the player. For example, jumping vertically into the air is quickly followed by the game character returning to its previous position. This is an early example of gravity in games with modern games modeling gravity much more closely.

Gravity is the natural phenomenon where objects attract each other due to each object being surrounded by a gravitational field. This field, interpreted as an attractive power, exerts a pulling force on all surrounding objects, as shown in Figure 14-10.

Each of the two objects shown in Figure 14-10 will experience the effect of gravity, with the exact gravitational force between the two objects given by the following equation:

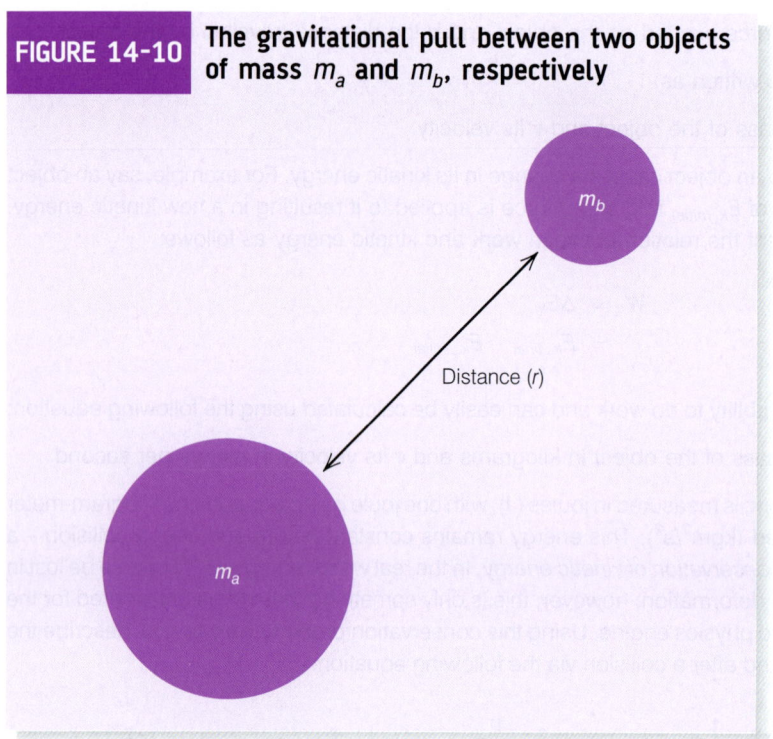

FIGURE 14-10 | The gravitational pull between two objects of mass m_a and m_b, respectively

$F = \frac{G \times m_a \times m_b}{r^2}$, where G is the universal gravitational constant (equal to $6.67 \times 10^{-11} \text{Nm}^2/\text{kg}^2$), m_a the mass of the one object and m_b the mass of the other, with r the distance in meters between the two objects.

Simulating gravity in games does not generally require advanced calculations that involve the universal gravitational constant or the exact mass of an object. For example, when modeling gravity for an object being dropped to the ground, we can start with the assumption that the acceleration of this object will be 9.8m/s² regardless of its mass (standard acceleration due to the earth's gravitational field). We can now define the velocity and position of this object as follows:

$$V_{new} = V_{old} + (9.8)t$$
$$Pos_{new} = Pos_{old} + (V_{old} \times t) + \left(\frac{1}{2} \times a \times t^2 \right),$$
$$= Pos_{old} + (V_{old} \times t) + \left(\frac{1}{2} \times 9.8m/s^2 \times t^2 \right)$$

Now, let's assume a crate is dropped at an initial velocity of 0 m/s from a position located at coordinates (0, 17, 0) as shown in Figure 14-11.

Substituting these values into the above given equations yields the following equations (assuming the coordinate y = 17 equates to a virtual height of 17 meters):

$$V_{new} = 0m/s + (9.8)t$$
$$= 9.8t$$
$$Pos_{new} = 17m + (0m/s \times t) + \left(\frac{1}{2} \times 9.8m/s^2 \times t^2 \right),$$
$$= 17m + \left(\frac{1}{2} \times 9.8m/s^2 \times t^2 \right)$$

FIGURE 14-11	Gravitational attraction of an object towards the zx-plane

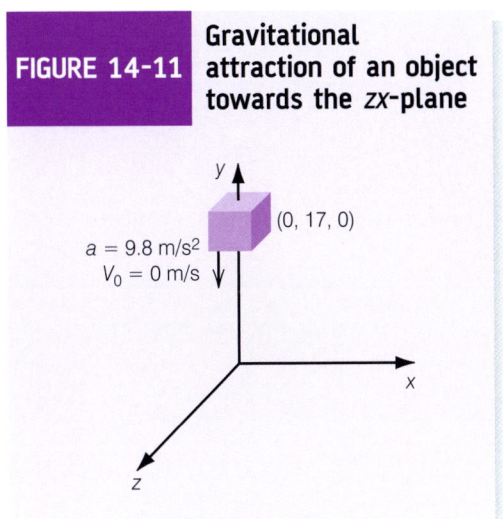

FIGURE 14-12	Gravitational attraction of an object thrown in the x-direction

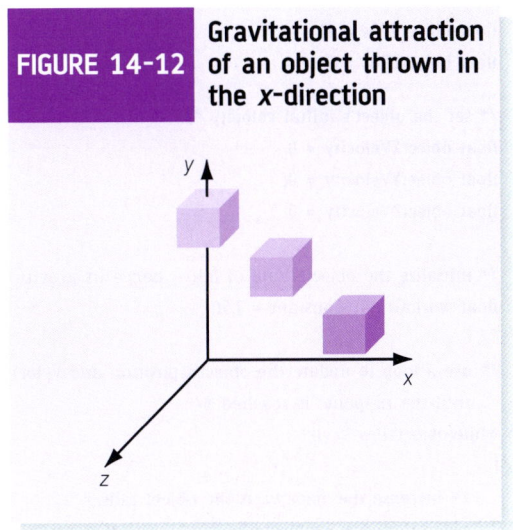

We can now implement these equations in the following manner – thus simulating gravity:

```
/* initialize the object's initial position */
float objectXPos = 0;
float objectYPos = 17;
float objectZPos = 0;


/* set the object's initial velocity */
float objectXVelocity = 0;
float objectYVelocity = 0;
float objectZVelocity = 0;


/* initialize the object's rate of fall – hence its gravity */
float worldGravityConstant = 1.5f;


/* use a loop to update the object's position and velocity
   until the zx-plane is reached */
while(objectYPos > 0)
{
    /* increase the velocity as the object falls */
    objectYVelocity = objectYVelocity + worldGravityConstant;

    /* calculate the object's new position */
    objectYPos = objectYPos + objectYVelocity;
}
```

This object will only fall in a straight vertical line, by incrementally adjusting its x-coordinate in the loop, for example, we can simulate a curved falling trajectory as shown in Figure 14-12.

We can now modify the above listed code snipped to simulate a curved falling trajectory as follows:

```
/* initialize the object's initial position */
float objectXPos = 0;
```

```
float objectYPos = 17;
float objectZPos = 0;

/* set the object's initial velocity */
float objectXVelocity = 0;
float objectYVelocity = 0;
float objectZVelocity = 0;

/* initialize the object's rate of fall – hence its gravity */
float worldGravityConstant = 1.5f;

/* use a loop to update the object's position and velocity
   until the zx–plane is reached */
while(objectYPos > 0)
{
    /* increase the velocity as the object falls */
    objectYVelocity = objectYVelocity + worldGravityConstant;

    /* calculate the object's new y–position */
    objectYPos = objectYPos + objectYVelocity;

    /* calculate the object's new x–position by adding a
       constant x velocity */
    objectXPos = objectXPos + 3;
}
```

14.2.3 Trajectory Paths

Without accurate projectile simulation, we would not be able to model bomb drops from aeroplanes, a kickoff in a football game, or the trajectory of a baseball after being hit by a batter. Figure 14-13 shows the trajectory path of a ball being kicked in the positive *x*-direction.

Trajectory can be described as the path or course travelled by an object. Calculating this path often requires the consideration of gravitational forces, aerodynamic factors, wind shear, etc. For most game-based implementations we'll assume uniform gravity while negating wind and other aerodynamic factors. For example, to model the trajectory path shown in Figure 14-13 we can define the ball's initial velocity in terms of an *x*- and *y*-component as follows (with θ the inclination angle):

$$V_x = V_{initial} \times \cos\theta$$
$$V_y = V_{initial} \times \sin\theta$$

We can also assume that V_y will equal '0' at the apex of the arch (the maximum height reached by the projectile).

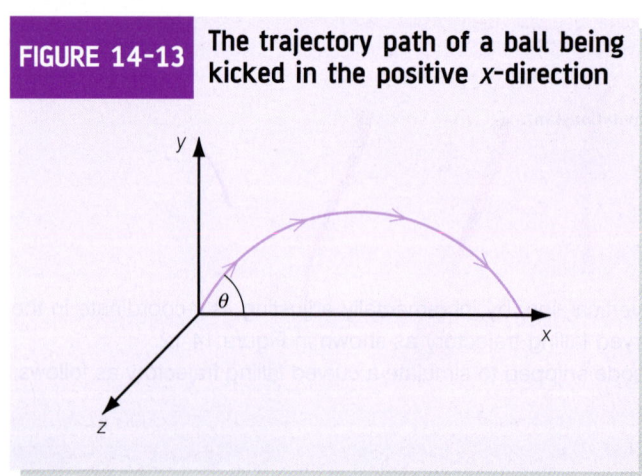

FIGURE 14-13   **The trajectory path of a ball being kicked in the positive *x*-direction**

Modeling a trajectory path involves applying a constant velocity along the *x*-axis (in the case of the above shown path) as well as the effect of gravity in the direction of the negative *y*-axis. We also factor in air resistance without needlessly complicating our simulation. The following code sample simulates a trajectory path as illustrated in Figure 14-13:

```
/* initialize the object's initial position */
float objectXPos = 0;
float objectYPos = 0;
float objectZPos = 0;

/* set the object's initial velocity */
float objectXVelocity = 0;
float objectYVelocity = 0;
float objectZVelocity = 0;

/* initialize the object's rate of fall - hence its gravity */
float worldGravityConstant = 1.5f;

/* set the inclination angle to 45 degrees in radians */
float initialAngle = 0.79

/* set the air resistance that will be factored in to simulate
   the deceleration of the projectile */
float airResistance = 0.01f;

/* calculate the velocity's x- and y-component */
objectXVelocity = objectXVelocity*cos(initialAngle);
objectYVelocity = objectYVelocity*sin(initialAngle);

/* use a loop to update the object's position and velocity
   until the zx-plane is reached */
while(objectYPos > 0)
{
    /* update the object's velocity */
    objectYVelocity = objectYVelocity + worldGravityConstant;
    objectXVelocity = objectXVelocity - airResistance;

    /* calculate the object's new y-position */
    objectYPos = objectYPos + objectYVelocity;

    /* calculate the object's new x-position */
    objectXPos = objectXPos + objectXVelocity;
}
```

14.2.4 Friction

Friction, stemming from electromagnetic forces between atomic particles, is an energy consuming force between two objects in contact. The most common form of friction is known as Coulomb friction.

14

Coulomb friction is an approximation stating that the maximum force exerted by friction (F_f) is always less than or equal to the direct normal force (F_n) between two objects multiplied by the material's friction coefficient (μ):

$$F_f \leq F_n \times \mu$$

The *normal force* (shown in Figure 14-14) is a force component perpendicular to the surface of contact with the coefficient of friction an empirically determined constant that varies depending on the type of material surface and whether the surface is perfectly clean, etc.

Table 14-1 gives some of the most common friction coefficients; also note that friction varies depending on whether an object is static or in motion.

We generally calculate the force required to move a static object via the following equation:

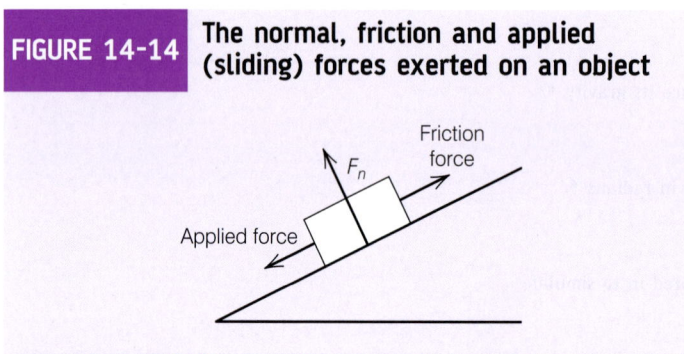

FIGURE 14-14	The normal, friction and applied (sliding) forces exerted on an object

$F_f = m \times g \times \mu_{static}$, where m is the mass of the object, g the gravitational constant ($9.8m/s^2$) and μ the material's static friction co-efficient.

The object will only move once a force greater than F_f is applied to it, after which its friction coefficient normally decreases. For example, consider an aluminum object

TABLE 14-1	Common coefficients of friction

Material	Static	In motion (kinetic)
Aluminum on aluminum	1.05 – 1.35	1.4
Aluminum on steel	0.61	0.47
Copper on cast iron	1.05	0.29
Copper on steel	0.53	0.36
Glass on glass	0.9 – 1.0	0.4
Glass on nickel	0.78	0.56
Leather on wood (along the grain)	0.61	0.52
Nickel on nickel	0.7 – 1.1	0.53
Nylon on nylon	0.15 – 0.25	
Steel on steel (high level hardness)	0.78	0.42
Steel on steel (relative hardness)	0.74	0.57
Wood on wood (against the grain)	0.54	0.32
Wood on wood (along the grain)	0.62	0.48

weighing 90 kilograms placed on a flat polished steel surface – we can calculate the maximum force exerted by friction as follows:

$$F_f = m \times g \times \mu_{static}$$
$$= 90kg \times 9.8m/s^2 \times 0.61$$
$$= 538.02N$$

We will thus require a force of at least 538.03N to move this object, once it is in motion we can recalculate its frictional force using aluminum on steel's kinetic friction coefficient:

$$F_f = m \times g \times \mu_{kinetic}$$
$$= 90kg \times 9.8m/s^2 \times 0.47$$
$$= 414.54N$$

Friction on a flat plane can be modeled just like air resistance (which is in fact a form of friction):

```
/* initialize the object's initial position */
float objectXPos = 0;
float objectYPos = 0;
float objectZPos = 0;

/* set the object's initial velocity */
float objectXVelocity = 15;
float objectYVelocity = 0;
float objectZVelocity = 0;

/* set the friction value */
float friction = 1.5f

/* use a loop to update the object's position and velocity
   until the object's speed reaches zero */
while(objectXVelocity > 0)
{
    /* update the object's velocity */
    objectXVelocity = objectXVelocity - friction;

    /* calculate the object's new x-position */
    objectXPos = objectXPos + objectXVelocity;
}
```

14

14.2.5 Introduction to Object Collisions

Let's start with a two dimensional 'asteroid field' from Atari's 1979 cult-hit, *Asteroids*. This game, as shown in Figure 14-15, is heavily dependent on object collisions such as asteroids colliding with other asteroids, alien spaceships or with the player's ship.

The game *Asteroids* illustrates the basic problem of collision detection and response in one of the simplest forms possible. Before, however, discussing object-to-object collision response as encountered in *Asteroids*, let's return to the *Breakout* example given in section 14.1.

FIGURE 14-15   **Screenshot of Atari's arcade game Asteroids**

FIGURE 14-16   **A ball always reflects at an angle equal and opposite to its initial incoming angle**

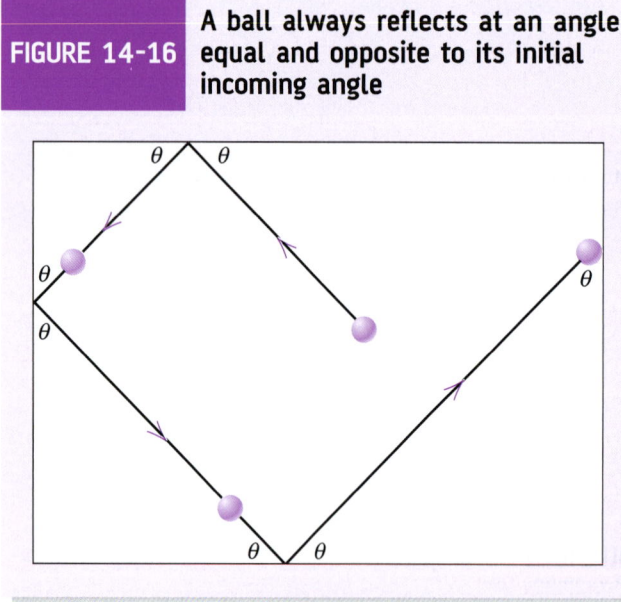

The game *Breakout* features a ball that can either bounce from the boundaries of the game window or movable paddle while also destroying bricks upon collision. Bouncing the ball off the screen boundaries requires very basic collision detection mainly because we already know where the boundaries of the screen are while at the same time only considering collisions with two horizontal and two vertical edges. Also, an object such as the ball in *Breakout* will always reflect at an angle equal and opposite to its initial incoming angle (illustrated in Figure 14-16).

Now, considering the shown image; it can be deduced that when the ball hits either vertical edge, then its direction can be changed by reversing the *x*-component of its velocity. Similarly, reversing the *y*-component of the ball's velocity upon collision with one of the horizontal edges will result in a perfect direction change:

```
/* initialize the object's initial position */
float objectXPos = 5;
```

```
float objectYPos = 2;
float objectZPos = 0;

/* set the object's initial velocity */
float objectXVelocity = 15;
float objectYVelocity = 20;
float objectZVelocity = 0;

/* update the object's velocity due to a vertical collision */
if(objectXPos > LEFT_EDGE || objectXPos < RIGHT_EDGE)
{

    /* update the object's velocity */
    objectXVelocity = -objectXVelocity;
    /* calculate the object's new x-position */
    objectXPos = objectXPos + objectXVelocity;
}
/*update the object's velocity due to a horizontal collision*/
if(objectYPos > BOTTOM_EDGE || objectYPos < TOP_EDGE)
{
    /* update the object's velocity */
    objectYVelocity = -objectYVelocity;

    /* calculate the object's new y-position */
    objectYPos = objectYPos + objectYVelocity;
}
```

This technique can now be extended to simulate one object bouncing off another. The simplest approach would be to test for horizontal and vertical collisions with the sides of a bounding volume. For example, consider the screenshot of the *Asteroids* clone in Figure 14-17 where the bounding volume of each object is shown (these volumes are specified using the contained object's minimum and maximum *x*- and *y*-values).

We can implement this approach in much the same way as with our horizontal and vertical screen boundary collision example – for instance, when we have a ball bouncing off objects as shown in Figure 14-18, then we can change its direction by reversing the *x*-component of its velocity when it hits a vertical edge of another object. Similarly, reversing the *y*-component of the ball's velocity upon collision with one of the horizontal edges will result in a perfect direction change.

The above given object collision approach works extremely well for horizontal and vertical surfaces, but in nearly all action-oriented games written today we'll need to calculate vector reflections for arbitrarily rotated surfaces. For example, consider the object shown in Figure 14-19. This object has several flat planes, with each of these positioned at an arbitrary angle.

The core of collision detection, when dealing with arbitrarily positioned faces, is vector calculations; specifically the calculation of a reflection vector when we have an initial vector direction and a normal to the plane. We've already looked at vector and normal calculations during the chapter on lighting and will now look at an example to illustrate vector-based object reflections for arbitrarily rotated surfaces.

Figure 14-20 illustrates our vector reflection problem; showing an incoming vector **I**, the surface normal **N** and the unknown reflection vector **R**.

We use vector addition to create a third, composite vector. This process involves summing the related scalar components of two successive vectors (using the head-to-tail rule). In Figure 14-20 we

14

FIGURE 14-17 Using bounding boxes to simulate inter-object collisions

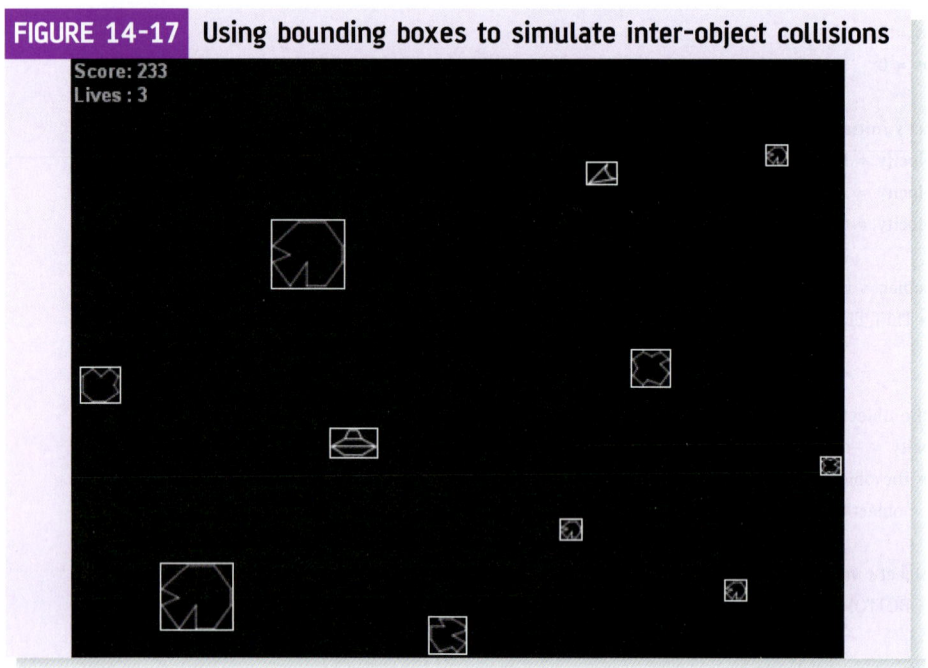

FIGURE 14-18 Inter-object collisions – the same rules hold true as with screen boundary collisions

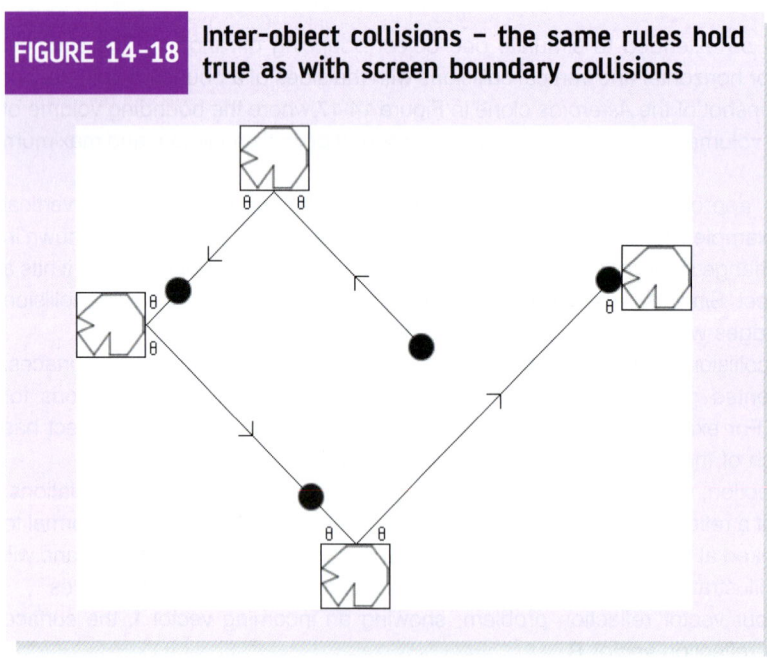

14

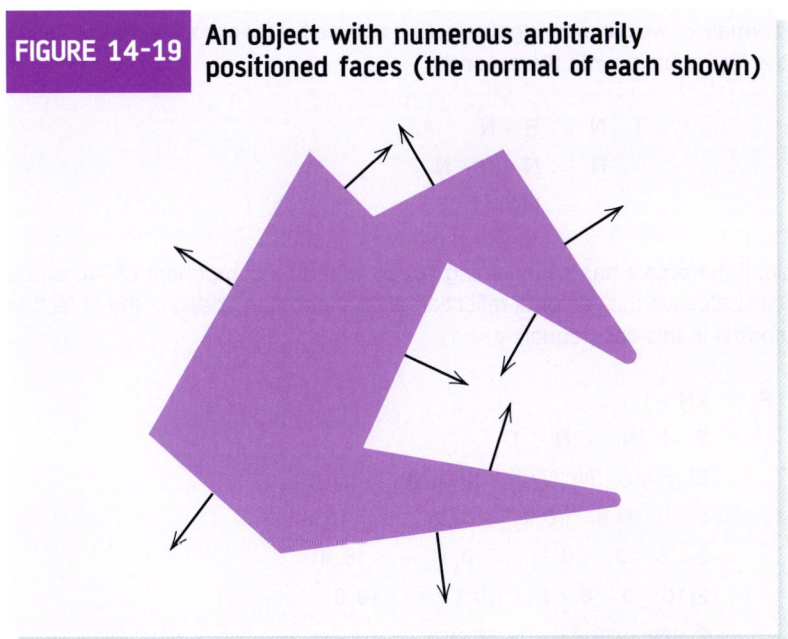

FIGURE 14-19   An object with numerous arbitrarily positioned faces (the normal of each shown)

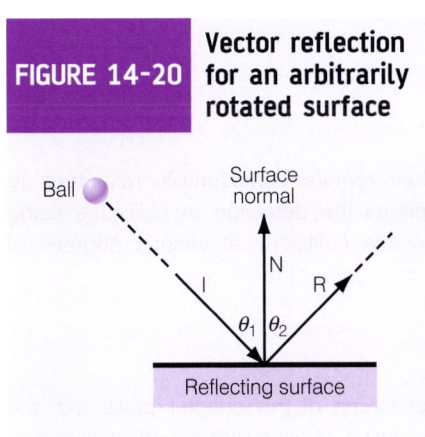

FIGURE 14-20   Vector reflection for an arbitrarily rotated surface

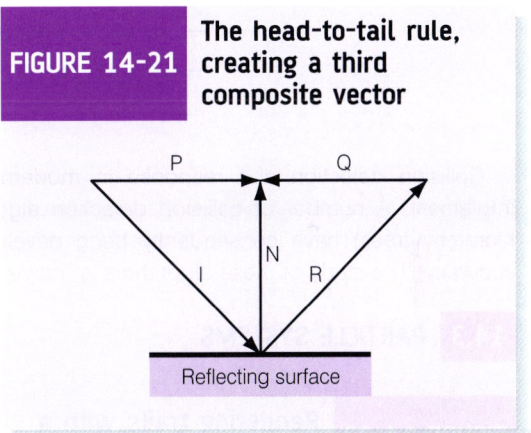

FIGURE 14-21   The head-to-tail rule, creating a third composite vector

have three vectors, namely, **I**, **N** and **R**; using these vectors we define a third and forth vector, **P** and **Q** (the resultant of **I** and **N** and **R** and **N** respectively) by summing the scalars of vector **I** and **N** and **R** and **N** in the following manner (graphically illustrated in Figure 14-21):

$$\mathbf{P} = \mathbf{I} + \mathbf{N}$$
$$= (Ix + Nx, Iy + Ny, Iz + Nz)$$
$$= (Px, Py, Pz).$$
$$\mathbf{Q} = \mathbf{R} + \mathbf{N}$$
$$= (Rx + Nx, Ry + Ny, Rz + Nz)$$
$$= (Qx, Qy, Qz).$$

14

Using the above given information, we can now algebraically calculate the reflection vector by stating that $\mathbf{P} \cdot \mathbf{Q}$ and substituting the first equation into the second:

$$
\begin{aligned}
\mathbf{I} + \mathbf{N} &= \mathbf{R} + \mathbf{N} \\
\mathbf{R} &= \mathbf{N} + (\mathbf{I} + \mathbf{N}) \\
&= 2\mathbf{N} + 1
\end{aligned}
$$

Returning to our example, if the object has an incoming speed with an x-component of −16 and a y-component of 8 then we can calculate the vector of reflection (thus the exiting speed of the object) in the following manner (the normal in this case equals y = 1):

$$
\begin{aligned}
\mathbf{R} &= 2\mathbf{N} + \mathbf{I} \\
&= 2(-\mathbf{I} \cdot |\mathbf{N}|) \times |\mathbf{N}| + \mathbf{I} \\
&= 2[(Ix, Iy) \cdot |(Nx, Ny)|] \times |(Nx, Ny)| + (Ix, Iy) \\
&= 2[-(-16, 8) \cdot |(0, 1)|] \times |(0, 1)| + (-16, 8) \\
&= 2[(16, -8) \cdot |(0, 1)|] \times |(0, 1)| + (-16, 8) \\
&= 2(16 \times 0 - 8 \times 1) \times |(0, 1)| + (-16, 8) \\
&= 2(-8) \times |(0, 1)| + (-16, 8) \\
&= -16 \times (0, -1) + (-16, 8) \\
&= (0, 16) + (-16, 8) \\
&= (0 - 16, 16 + 8) \\
&= (-16, 24).
\end{aligned}
$$

Collision detection and response in modern games often require considerable resources to implement. A number of collision detection algorithms (such as the detection of collisions using hierarchy trees) have consequently been developed to simulate collisions at various degrees of accuracy. The study of these algorithms is, however, beyond the scope of this book.

14.3 PARTICLE SYSTEMS

FIGURE 14-22 Rendering trails with a particle system

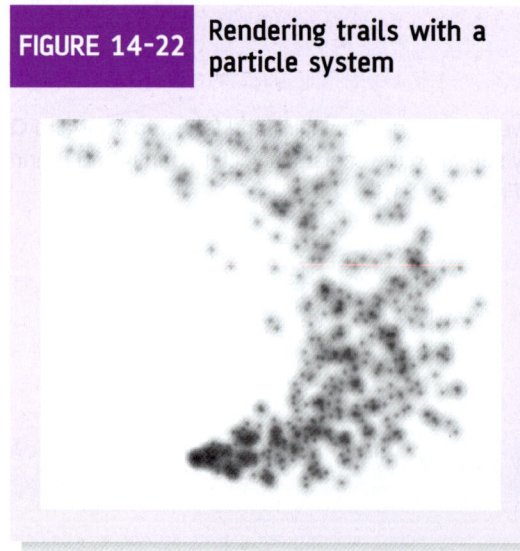

The final theme of this chapter deals with the implementation of a physics-based particle system. A *particle system* is a graphics subsystem used to simulate certain natural phenomena such as fire, smoke, sparks, explosions, dust, magic spells, trail effects (Figure 14-22), etc.

Particle systems are usually implemented using three stages, namely, the setup stage, the simulation stage, and the rendering stage.

■ The *setup stage* involves specification of the particle system's spatial position and area of constraint – parameters controlled by the *emitter*. The emitter also controls the particle creation rate, that is, the rate at which new particles are injected into the system. Each particle has a specific time to live, after which it is destroyed.

FIGURE 14-23 **Particles being generated over time**

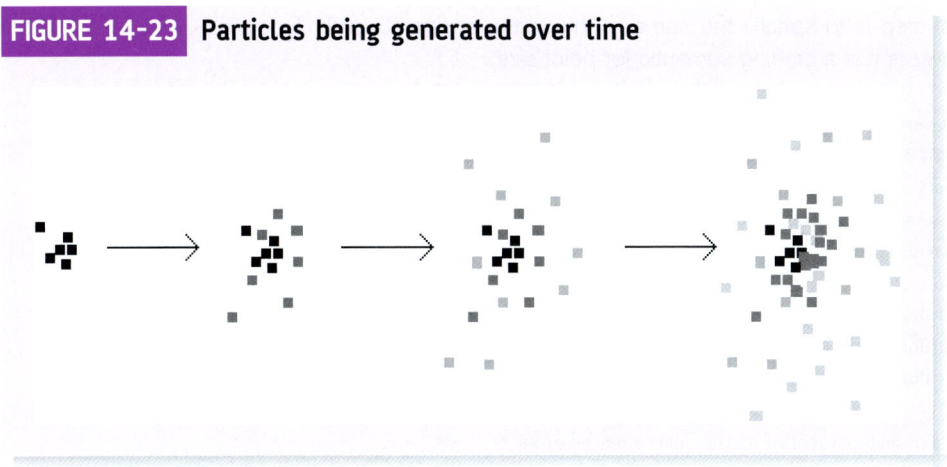

- The *simulation stage* takes care of particle rendering rates, particle spawning position (mostly randomized between some minimum and maximum coordinate range), particle properties (such as particle color, velocity) and positioning of the emitter. This stage also keeps track of each particle to check whether a specific particle has exceeded its lifetime. Each particle has an initial velocity and is translated based on some sort of physics model or simply by adding velocity to its current spatial position. Collision detection is also possible at this stage but rarely implemented.

- Following the simulation state, each particle is *rendered* as either a colored point, polygon or as a mesh. Figure 14-23 shows the generation of particles over time.

Particle systems based on the rules of physics use the following standard equations to calculate each particle's velocity and position (see section 14.1):

$$V_{new} \; = \; V_{old} + a \times t$$
$$Pos_{new} \; = \; Pos_{old} + (V_{old} \times t) + \left(\frac{1}{2} \times a \times t^2\right),$$

The above-given equations factor in the initial motion of the particle, its trajectory and the overall effect of gravity where Pos_{new} is the particle's final position, Pos_{old} its initial position, V_{new} its final velocity, V_{old} its initial velocity, a the particle's acceleration, and t the change in time. Using these equations we start by initializing each particle's initial position and velocity. These values will be assigned to a particle when it is generated by the emitter.

Implementing a particle system in C++ is quite a tedious task due to the necessary creation of a data structure for the storage of particle data (particle state, spawning coordinates and velocity, current velocity and position, rendering color, etc). We also need member functions for the setup, initialization, generation, and rendering as well as the cleanup of particles the moment their time to live expires. Using shaders on the other hand allow us to create a particle system within minutes – as illustrated by the vertex and fragment shader-based particle system example given in the following section.

14.3.1 Implementing a Particle System

We now present the Cg implementation of a particle system. The HLSL version is once again practically identical and won't be duplicated here for that reason.

14

The first step is to specify the name of the vertex program's entry function, particle _vertex in our example (PSIZ is just a binding semantic for point size):

```
void particle_vertex(
            float4 initialParticleVelocity : TEXCOORD0,
            float4 particleAcceleration : TEXCOORDl,
            float4 initialParticlePosition : POSITION,
            float  particleCreationTime : TEXCOORD2,

            out float  outputParticleSize : PSIZ,
            out float4 outputParticleColor : COLOR,
            out float4 outputParticlePosition : POSITION,

            /* parameters supplied by the application program */

            uniform float4x4 totalRunningTime,
            uniform float4x4 modelToWorldTransformation,
            uniform float4x4 modelviewProjection
)
{
```

We start by calculating the particle's current position by first computing its total amount of time active (the particle's time of creation is subtracted from the total time the simulation has been running – as sent from the application to the shader):

```
/* calculate the amount of time the particle has been
    active */
float particleTime = totalRunningTime –
                particleCreationTime;
```

The particle's spatial position is calculated using the standard physics equation:

$$Pos_{new} = Pos_{old} + (v_{old} \times t) + \left(\frac{1}{2} \times a \times t^2\right):$$

```
float4 finalParticlePosition = initialParticlePosition +
                initialParticleVelocity*particleTime +
                (0.5f)*particleAcceleration*
                pow(particleTime, 2);
```

Next we calculate the clip-space position as mandatory for all Cg vertex programs:

```
/* transform the vertex position into homogeneous clip–
    space coordinates */
outputParticlePosition = mul(modelviewProjection,
                finalParticlePosition);
```

14

All that remains now, before we set the particle's width and height, is to initialize its color:

```
/* set the particle color to green */
outputParticleColor = (0, 0.5, 0, 1);
```

The final operation is to set the particle's width and height:

```
/* set the particle's size */
float3 outputParticleSize = 0.5;
}
```

We now define a fragment shader function, particle_fragment, that simply returns a texture coordinate set as a color:

```
void particle_fragment(
        float4 inputParticleColor : TEXCOORD0,

        out float4 color : COLOR
)
{
    /* set the color */
    return color;
}
```

The above given implementation will generate particles as shown in Figure 14-22. On the C++ side of things we'll have to initialize the number of particles, create a list of particle start times, spawn particles on a semi-random fashion and destroy particles whenever their time limit is exceeded:

```
/* start by limiting the number of particles at any given time
   to 600 */
#define TOTAL_NUMBER_PARTICLES 600
/* set the maximum time to live */
#define TTL 30;

/* create a structure to store the particle states */
typedef struct Particle
{
    float initialParticlePosition_[3];
    float initialParticleVelocity_[3];
    float particleAcceleration_;
    float particleTime_;
    bool isAlive;
} Particle;

/* store the particle data in a struct-array */
Particle particleStartData[TOTAL_NUMBER_PARTICLES];
```

14

```
/* return a random double within the passed range */
double GetRandomDouble(double low, double high)
{
    return ((double)rand()/(RAND_MAX+1.0))*(high - low) + low;
}


/* function to initialize and reset the particles */
void InitParticleSystem()
{
    /* initialize each particle */
    for(int i = 0; i < TOTAL_NUMBER_PARTICLES; i++)
    {
        /* set the initial starting position (x, y, z) */
        particleStartData[i].initialParticlePosition_[0] = 0.0;
        particleStartData[i].initialParticlePosition_[1] = 0.0;
        particleStartData[i].initialParticlePosition_[2] = 0.0;

        /* set the initial velocity (x, y, z) */
        particleStartData[i].initialParticleVelocity_[0] = 0.0;
        particleStartData[i].initialParticleVelocity_[1] = 0.0
        particleStartData[i].initialParticleVelocity_[2] = 0.0;

        /* set the gravity acceleration */
        particleStartData[i].particleAcceleration_ = -9.8;

        /* start the particles at a random time */
        particleStartData[i].particleTime_ =
                            GetRandomDouble(0, 5);

        /* activate particles */
        particleStartData[i].isAlive = false;
    }
}
/* function to spawn particles */
void spawnParticles()
{
    /* spawn particles */
    for(int j = 0; j < TOTAL_NUMBER_PARTICLES; j++)
    {
      if((particleStartData[j].isAlive == false) &&
        (particleStartData[j].particleTime_ < TTL))
      {
        /* change the particle velocity (x, y, z) */
        particleStartData[j].initialParticleVelocity_[0] =
                            GetRandomDouble(-1,1);

        particleStartData[j].initialParticleVelocity_[1] =
                            GetRandomDouble(-0.5, 0.5);
```

14

```
                particleStartData[j].initialParticleVelocity_[2] =
                                GetRandomDouble(0, 2.5);


            /* flag the particle as active */
            particleStartData[j].isAlive = true;
        }
    }
}


/* function to decrease a particle's time to live */
void decreaseParticleTTL()
{
    /* destroy particles */
    for(int k = 0; k < TOTAL_NUMBER_PARTICLES; k++)
    {
        if((particleStartData[k].isAlive == true) &&
           (particleStartData[k].particleTime_ < TTL))
        {
            /* flag the particle as inactive */
            particleStartData[k].isAlive = false;

            /* increase the particle's time alive */
            particleStartData[k].particleTime_ += 0.01;
        }
    }
}
```

We can now combine the above given functions with the featured vertex and fragment shader to render live particles as shown in Figure 14-22.

As a final thought it is necessary to note that particle systems can be created using several 3D modeling packages such as Maya and 3D Studio Max. This allows easy specification and modification of particle system behaviour – all in real time.

14.4 SUMMARY

The chapter started by investigating the fundamentals of physics with an introduction highlighting Newton's laws of motion and the contribution of physics to the overall game play experience. Core physics concepts discussed include time as a fundamental quantity, determining the spatial position of irregular objects, mass as a fundamental concept describing an object's atomic mass or the amount of matter used to make up an object, velocity as the rate of change of an object's position, acceleration as the rate of change of velocity, force as the physical action exerted upon an object to accelerate it, and momentum as a property inherent to objects in motion.

Following this we investigated the simulation of Newtonian physics through concepts such as mass, acceleration, velocity, friction, momentum, and force, in essence focusing on the importance of these concepts for the prediction of object behaviour. We specifically considered the conservation and transfer of momentum as well as the modeling of gravitational pull, trajectories, friction, and object collision and response – each topic discussed from both a theoretical and practical perspective. The remainder of the chapter focused on the implementation of a physics-based particle system.

14

The next chapter serves as an introduction to the field of game artificial intelligence. It focuses on the history of AI in games, basic AI techniques such as pre-programming and scripting, AI modeling using finite state automata, the simulation of autonomous behaviour by means of memory and planning as well as a number of pathfinding algorithms and advanced AI techniques such as neural networks, expert systems and genetic algorithms.

14.5   FURTHER READING

For more information on particle systems, see Jeff Lander's article *'The Ocean Spray in Your Face'* available from www.gdmag.com. W.T. Reeves' paper, titled *'Particle Systems: A Technique for Modeling a Class of Fuzzy Objects'* and published in *Computer Graphics* makes for an excellent resource on particle systems and the modeling of objects such as fire, clouds, and water. The paper *'Physics in Computer Games'* by Chris Hecker, published in *Communications of the ACM*, makes for an interesting read on physical simulation in games as well as concepts such as contact detection and force computation.

14.6   EXERCISES

1   What are the main factors affecting the performance of a physics simulation?

2   How can the spatial position of an irregular object be determined?

3   When doing physics calculations, when is it appropriate to use the game's frame rate?

4   Describe the following formula: $Pos_{new} = Pos_{old} + v \times t$,

5   Discuss the purpose of the following code sample:

```
float objectAcceleration = 4.0;
float objectVelocity = 0.0;
float objectPosition = 0.0;

objectVelocity = objectVelocity + objectAcceleration;
objectPosition = objectPosition + objectVelocity;
```

6   What is the correlation between exerted force and friction?

7   Describe momentum in terms of Newton's second law of motion.

8   Write a program to simulate the trajectory path of a projectile fired at an inclination angle of 60 degrees – the projectile exits a cannon with a velocity of 450km/h (make sure to factor in air resistance and the effect of gravity).

9   Write a *Breakout* clone with basic collision detection and response as discussed in section 14.2.5.

10   How is a particle's spatial position calculated?

11   Briefly describe each of the stages associated with the implementation of particle systems.

14

CHAPTER 15

Artificial Intelligence

LEARNING OBJECTIVES

In this chapter you will learn about:

- History of AI in games
- Pre-programmed AI
- Scripting
- Modeling AI by means of finite state machines
- Autonomous behaviour: memory and planning
- Pathfinding
- The A* algorithm
- Depth-first search
- Breadth-first search
- Waypoint pathfinding
- More advanced AI: neural networks, expert systems and genetic algorithms

INTRODUCTION

Chapter 15 serves as an introduction to the field of game artificial intelligence (AI) by dealing with techniques pertaining to the realistic behaviour of computer controlled characters. It covers AI in a bottom-up fashion by presenting the history of AI in games, basic AI techniques such as pre-programming and scripting, AI modeling using finite state automata, and the simulation of autonomous behaviour by means of memory and planning. The chapter also presents a number of pathfinding algorithms and advanced AI techniques such as neural networks, expert systems and genetic algorithms.

15.1 HISTORY OF AI IN GAMES

Artificial intelligence (AI) is the design and application of methods modeled after the behaviour of humans and/or animals to solve complicated problems. More formally, AI can be defined as the design and application of intelligent agents. An *intelligent agent* is a piece of software that intelligently supports the actions of a user. These agents are used to monitor and intelligently act upon certain triggers present in an environment. So what is *intelligence*? It is a collection of logic, mathematics, probability, and memory, all applied in an interconnected manner that maximizes the chances of a successful outcome.

AI in games is a variation of the above-described technique to bring to 'life' non-player characters, thus creating the illusion of a lifelike computer controlled player that is plotting, thinking and planning as a human would. Game AI differs substantially from theoretical academic AI in the sense that, even though numerous techniques exist, there is no right or wrong way of doing something – the end result is what matters. For example, if a non-player character or 'bot' (an abbreviation for the word robot) is indistinguishable from a real-life opponent then the AI of that character can be described as ideal.

The first games featuring computer controlled opponents started surfacing in the early 1970s – the non-player character movement in these games was based on predetermined patterns and rules as opposed to intelligent path finding and decision making. These primitive algorithms soon evolved to include distinct movement patterns based on the player's input and actions as seen in Taito's *Space Invaders* and Namco's *Galaxian* released in 1979 (a screenshot of which is shown in Figure 15-1).

Real-time strategy games like *Dune II* (Figure 15-2) released by Westwood Studios in 1992 and first-person shooters such as id Software's *Wolfenstein 3D* and *Doom* (Figure 1-6) pushed game AI to new levels – especially the fields of path-finding and real-time decision making. The enemies in these games initiate an attack the moment the player enters their field of view, also pursuing the player when an attempt is made to flee.

The next big step in game AI came with the release of id Software's *Quake II* (1997) where enemies appeared much more intelligent due to improved chasing capabilities as well as the ability to duck and avoid an approaching projectile such as a missile launched by the player. These non-player characters were still not autonomous enough to emulate human characteristics and could thus not be used as a substitute for a human player. The first game to feature convincing bots or non-player characters was Epic's first-person shooter *Unreal*, released in 1998. Unreal's path finding is based on the placement of waypoints. These waypoints serve as markers for bots to find their way around an environment,

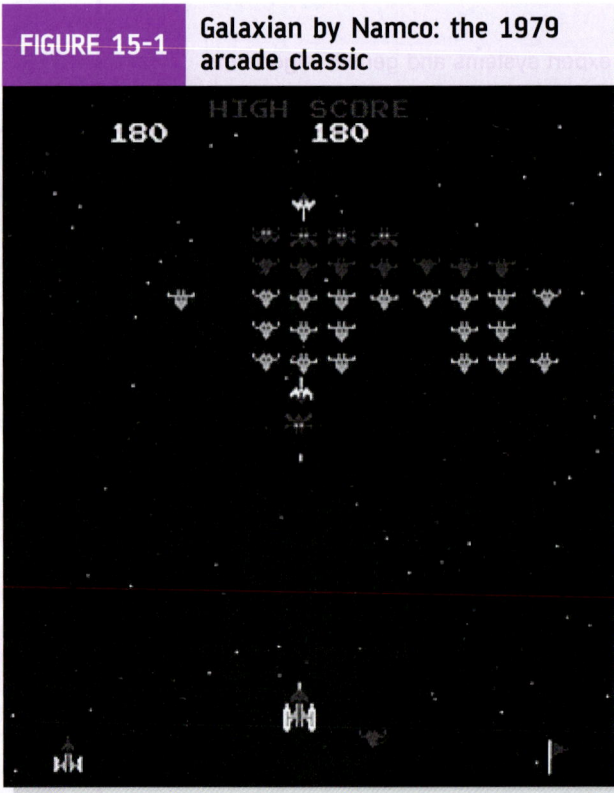

FIGURE 15-1 Galaxian by Namco: the 1979 arcade classic

for example, specific items such as health boosters or weapons can be retrieved by placing waypoints at the spawn locations of these objects.

Jan van Waveren developed the first ever commercial artificial player based on completely automated path finding – a bot operating independently of any navigational aids such as waypoints or any form of human intervention. His bot technology formed a critical part of id Software's game *Quake III Arena* (Figure 15-3) released at the end of 1999. In van Waveren's own words: 'The bot uses a volume (area) based representation of the 3D game environment, which serves as a backbone for the bot's cognitive world model. Together with a high performance path finding solution this cognitive model makes the bot rather resource efficient ... the *Quake III* Arena bot is supposed to act like a human player in the virtual world of the game. The bot replaces the need for other people to connect to the game. Just like a player can play the game with multiple other people the game can be played with one or more bots.'

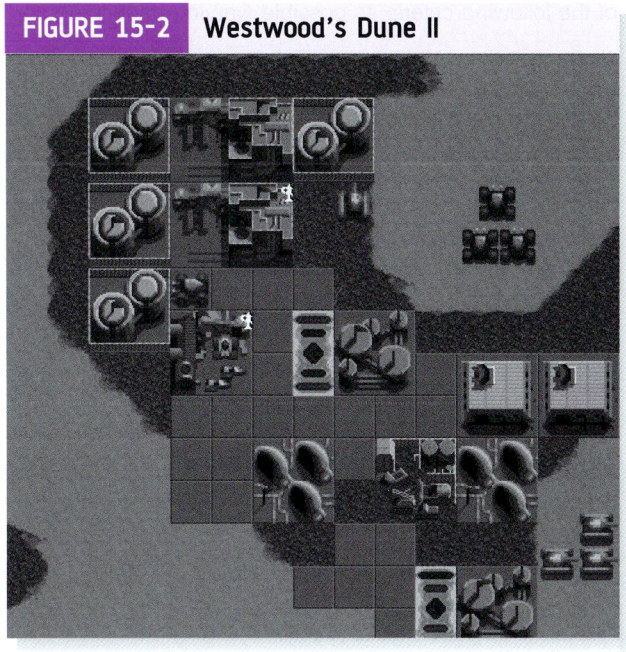

FIGURE 15-2   **Westwood's Dune II**

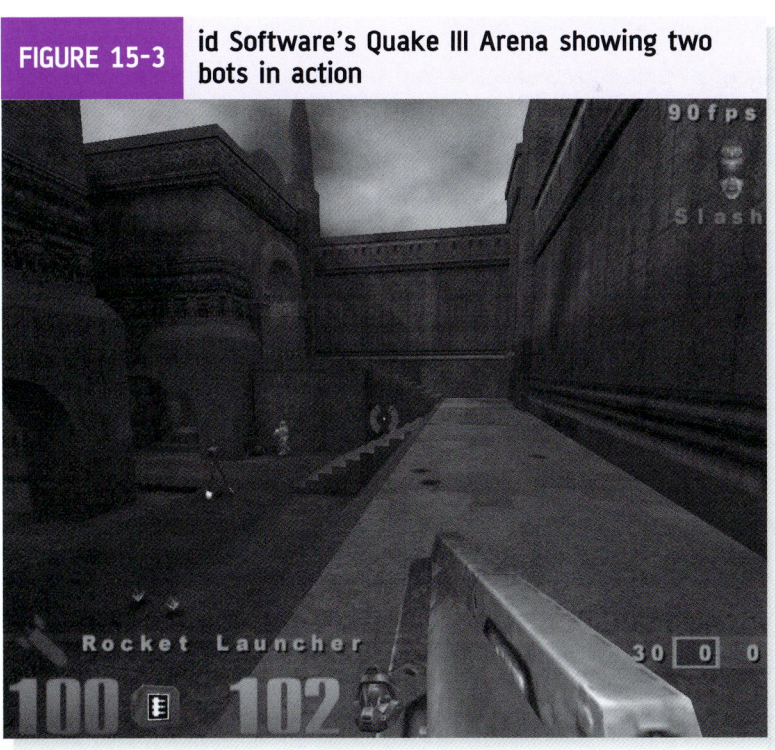

FIGURE 15-3   **id Software's Quake III Arena showing two bots in action**

15

Following *Quake III*, games like Valve's *Half-Life 2* and Crytek's *Far Cry* featured very advanced AI where non-player characters would adapt their playing style to that of the player while at the same time using a variety of known military strategies against the player.

Developers implementing AI as showcased by the games released today, attempt to meet as many of the following criteria as possible (varying depending on the type of game and its genre):

1 Cognitive model based non-player character AI (no way-point system).

2 'Intelligent' non-combat (allies) and combat (enemies) non-player character interaction.

3 Interactive communication system, for example, the player can instruct an ally to help out in a fight or to defend some other location.

4 Non-player characters make automatic decision to fight, dodge, flee, hide, burrow, etc. based on player resistance, for example, enemies can make decision to fall back to regroup if resistance is overwhelming.

15.2 PRE-PROGRAMMED AI

Pre-programmed or *deterministic AI* is the simplest form of AI found in games. Such algorithms add predetermined behaviour to an object and are characterized as minimal goal algorithms. For example, an object can move from one position to another based on some randomly calculated velocity (the only goal here is to move in a pre-defined path as shown in Figure 15-4):

```
/* initialize the object's initial position */
float objectXPos = 5;
float objectYPos = 2;

/* set the object's initial velocity */
float objectXVelocity = 0;
float objectYVelocity = 0;
```

FIGURE 15-4   Basic pre-programmed AI in action

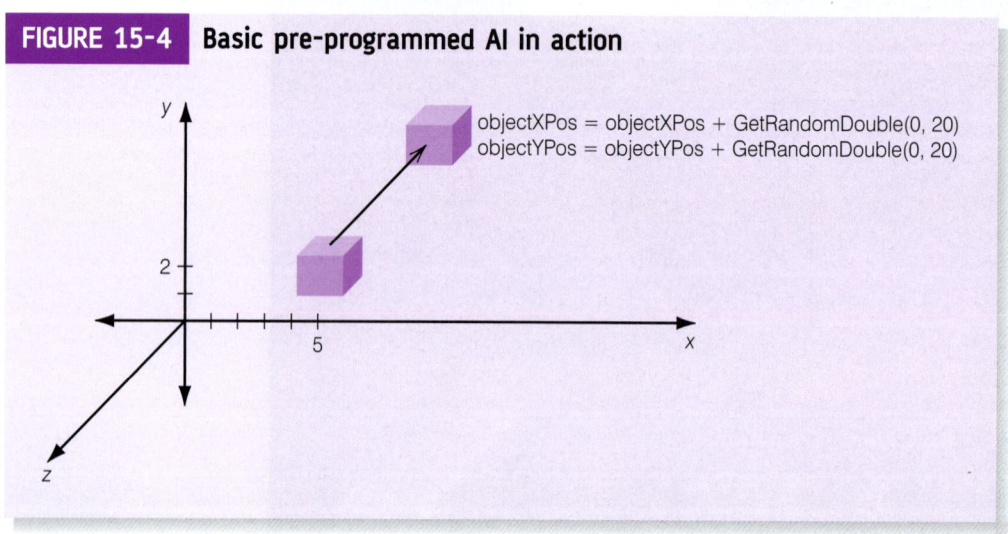

```
objectXPos = objectXPos + GetRandomDouble(0, 20)
objectYPos = objectYPos + GetRandomDouble(0, 20)
```

```
/* return a random double within the passed range */
double GetRandomDouble(double low, double high)
{
    return ((double)rand()/(RAND_MAX+1.0))*(high - low) + low;
}


/* move the object using a randomly generated velocity */
void MoveObjectAI()
{
    /* generate a random x & y velocity */
    objectXVelocity = GetRandomDouble(0, 20);
    objectYVelocity = GetRandomDouble(0, 20);

    /* calculate the object's new x-position */
    objectXPos = objectXPos + objectXVelocity;

    /* calculate the object's new y-position */
    objectYPos = objectYPos + objectYVelocity;
}
```

The AI presented here is highly predictable and one can easily extend it by randomly changing the object's movement direction in addition to its velocity (illustrated in Figure 15-5):

```
/* initialize the object's initial position */
float objectXPos = 5;
float objectYPos = 2;

/* set the object's initial velocity */
float objectXVelocity = 0;
float objectYVelocity = 0;
```

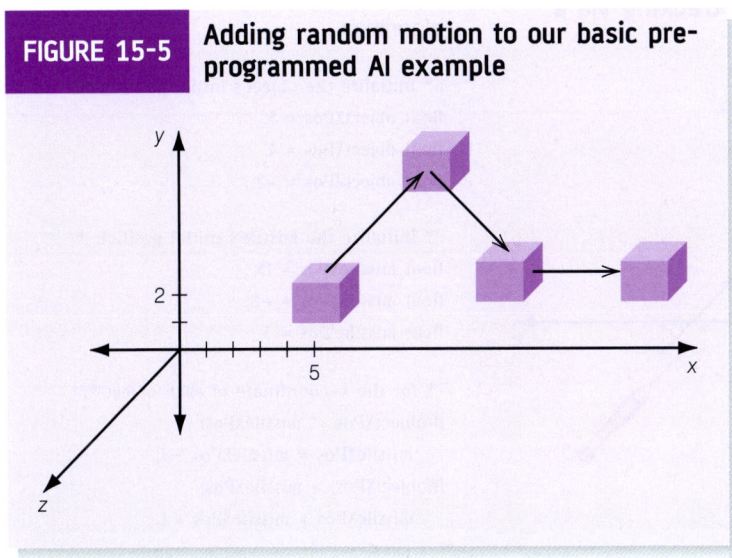

FIGURE 15-5   **Adding random motion to our basic pre-programmed AI example**

```
/* return a random double within the passed range */
double GetRandomDouble(double low, double high)
{
    return ((double)rand()/(RAND_MAX+1.0))*(high - low) + low;
}


/* move the object according to a randomly generated direction
   and velocity */
void MoveObjectAI()
{
    /* generate a random x & y position */
    objectXPos = objectXPos + GetRandomDouble(0, 20);
    objectYPos = objectYPos + GetRandomDouble(0, 20);

    /* generate a random x & y velocity */
    objectXVelocity = GetRandomDouble(0, 20);
    objectYVelocity = GetRandomDouble(0, 20);

    /* calculate the object's new x-position */
    objectXPos = objectXPos + objectXVelocity;

    /* calculate the object's new y-position */
    objectYPos = objectYPos + objectYVelocity;
}
```

The next progression in basic deterministic AI is path-tracking. *Path-tracking* involves tracing the path represented by a vector from some specific point in space (representing a projectile, for example) to another point or object (perhaps the target). Basic path-tracking is illustrated in Figure 15-6.

The vector between the projectile and object shown in the given figure actively changes whenever the position of the object is changed, thus, the missile will always follow or track the object in a straight trajectory. The following code snippet illustrates such a basic path-tracking algorithm:

FIGURE 15-6 Basic path-tracking via a vector

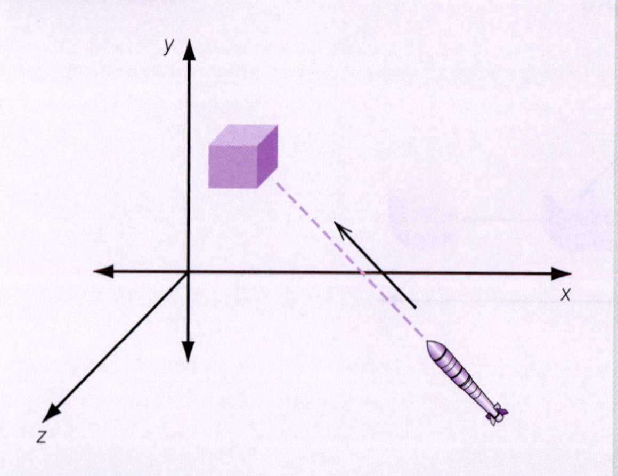

```
/* initialize the object's initial position */
float objectXPos = 5;
float objectYPos = 4;
float objectZPos = -2;

/* initialize the missile's initial position */
float missileXPos = 15;
float missileYPos = -8;
float missileZPos = 3;

/* for the x-coordinate of each object */
if(objectXPos < missileXPos)
    missileXPos = missileXPos - 1;
if(objectXPos > missileXPos)
    missileXPos = missileXPos + 1;
```

```
/* for the y-coordinate of each object */
if(objectYPos < missileYPos)
    missileYPos = missileYPos - 1;
if(objectYPos > missileYPos)
    missileYPos = missileYPos + 1;


/* for the z-coordinate of each object */
if(objectZPos < missileZPos)
    missileZPos = missileZPos - 1;
if(objectZPos > missileZPos)
    missileZPos = missileZPos + 1;
```

Straight line tracking such as this is very effective but not that realistic. A missile immediately changing direction in an angular fashion to match the position of its target without any consideration for the laws of physics is far from realistic. This precise tracking does not take into account varying velocity of the missile or the effect of the missile's acceleration to produce a curved trajectory as seen in real-life. A more intuitive path-tracking method is to calculate the velocity vector of the projectile and to add the size of this vector to the current velocity of the missile:

```
/* initialize the object's initial position */
float objectXPos = 5;
float objectYPos = 4;
float objectZPos = -2;


/* initialize the missile's initial position */
float missileXPos = 15;
float missileYPos = -8;
float missileZPos = 3;


/* set the missile's initial velocity */
float missileXVelocity = 2;
float missileYVelocity = 8;
float missileZVelocity = 3;


/* function to calculate the length of a vector */
float VectorLength(int x, int y, int z)
{
    /* use the sqrt function to calculate the length */
    float vectorLength = sqrt(x*x + y*y + z*z);
    return vectorLength;
}


/* calculate the vector from the missile to the object */
float vectorX = objectXPos - missileXPos;
float vectorY = objectYPos - missileYPos;
float vectorZ = objectZPos - missileZPos;


/* calculate the length of the vector */
float vecLength = VectorLength(vectorX, vectorY, vectorZ);
```

15

```
/* normalize the vector*/
vectorX = vectorX/vecLength;
vectorY = vectorY/vecLength;
vectorZ = vectorZ/vecLength;

/* add the velocity vector to the missile's current velocity*/
missileXVelocity = missileXVelocity + vectorX;
missileYVelocity = missileYVelocity + vectorY;
missileZVelocity = missileZVelocity + vectorZ;

/* calculate the missile's new position */
missileXPos = missileXPos + missileXVelocity;
missileYPos = missileYPos + missileYVelocity;
missileZPos = missileZPos + missileZVelocity;
```

Our tracking algorithm is still too precise, that is, the trajectory between the missile and object is always a 100 percent straight line. This is a problem often encountered in first-person shooters where 100 percent accuracy isn't realistic from a human's perspective. For example, a bot that never misses is no fun to play against and will only frustrate the player. The simplest way of dealing with this problem is to include random noise when calculating the missile's velocity:

```
/* return a random double within the passed range */
double GetRandomDouble(double low, double high)
{
     return ((double)rand()/(RAND_MAX+1.0))*(high – low) + low;
}

/* add some random noise to the velocity of the missile */
missileXVelocity = missileXVelocity + GetRandomDouble(–1, 1);
missileYVelocity = missileYVelocity + GetRandomDouble(–1, 1);
missileZVelocity = missileZVelocity + GetRandomDouble(–1, 1);
```

Using the above-given tracking algorithm will result in relatively realistic path tracing with the missile staying close to the direct path between itself and its target while at the same time giving the impression that it is actually 'seeking' its target as a heat seeking missile would. From this discussing it is thus clear that game AI differs substantially from classic AI with regard to game AI's use of 'hacks' and 'cheats' for it to seem more 'real'.

15

15.3 SCRIPTING

Pre-programmed AI is great for adding basic predetermined behaviour to an object, but the associated randomness doesn't serve us well in situations where an object is required to perform a specific sequence of tasks or steps. For instance, a bot might be required to patrol an area between two points; using deterministic AI we can place two objects at the ends of this path with the bot doing simple path-tracing between them. This works well but becomes tedious and computationally intensive when numerous paths need to be traced or when additional tasks such as the activation of a switch are required. For example, a deterministic algorithm would not be able to cope with a complicated sequence of steps such as the ones given here:

1 If the player is within MAX_ATTACK_DISTANCE:
   a Break into room through air vent.
   b Attack player using a combination of the following:
      i Throw foreign objects such as barrels at the player.
      ii Use projectile-based weaponry.
      iii Use melee weapons after launching at player.
   c Fight, dodge, flee, hide, or burrow based on player resistance.

2 If the player is not within MAX_ATTACK_DISTANCE:
   a Wait.

This is the reason for *scripted AI*; it provides us with a convenient and accurate way of controlling the behaviour of non-player characters. Returning to our example where a bot was tasked with patrolling an area between two points, we can now script its actions using the following scripted sequence:

1 Move forward.

2 If END_OF_BRIDGE is reached, stop.
   a Turn around (180-degree rotation).
   b Move forward.
   c If START_OF_BRIDGE is reached, stop.
      i Turn around (180-degree rotation)

Each of these steps can subsequently be represented in C++ as follows:

```
#define MOVE_FORWARD 1
#define STOP 2
#define TURN_AROUND 3

/* use a simple array to store the movement pattern − called a
   pattern script */
int patternScript[7] = {MOVE_FORWARD,
                        STOP,
                        TURN_AROUND,
                        MOVE_FORWARD,
                        STOP};
/* process the above defined script by assigning an action to
   each movement */
switch(/* switch on one of the instructions */)
{
    case MOVE_FORWARD:
    {
        /* code to move the bot forward */
    }
    break;

    case STOP:
    {
        /* code to stop the bot from moving */
```

15

```
    }
    break;

    case TURN_AROUND:
    {
        /* code to rotate the bot 180 degrees — either
            clockwise or counter clockwise depending on the
            implementation */
    }
    break;
}
```

This is of course just a simple pseudo-code example illustrating how we might define a pattern 'language' using the #define pre-processor directive and a data structure to hold the sequence script (an array in this case). Real-world action scripting will normally consist of a pattern engine reading various patterns based on whether any preconditions (such as a bot reaching a door) are met. For example, if a walking pattern is being executed for a bot and this bot reaches a wall, then another pattern will be loaded from the pattern database. The same holds true for nearly all fighting games released during the 1990s. One such a game heavily utilizing patterns was *Mortal Kombat* first released by Midway in 1992. *Mortal Kombat* (and all similar fighting games of the time) recorded various fighting patterns, with each pattern played back according to the user's input. For example, performing an uppercut or jump kick without being at a proper position for the move to work resulted in your opponent either moving away or blocking your attack.

Basic patterns, no matter how effective, are still deterministic in nature, and as such may appear novel at first only to become repetitive after a while. One solution to this problem is to mix patterns with production rules (or conditional logic) as done in *Mortal Kombat;* that is, to consider both the outside game-world factors and the actions performed by the human player.

15.4   MODELING AI BY MEANS OF FINITE STATE MACHINES

Chapter 1 depicted the transition between the various states of a game loop using a simplified *finite state machine* (FSM), also commonly called a *finite state automaton*. These state machines are nothing more than models depicting a system's various states as well as the transition between these states. States are used to represent goals with transition conditions and actions controlling state changes. For example, a simple electrical switch will have at least two states – open and closed. The FSM for such a switch is given in Figure 15-7.

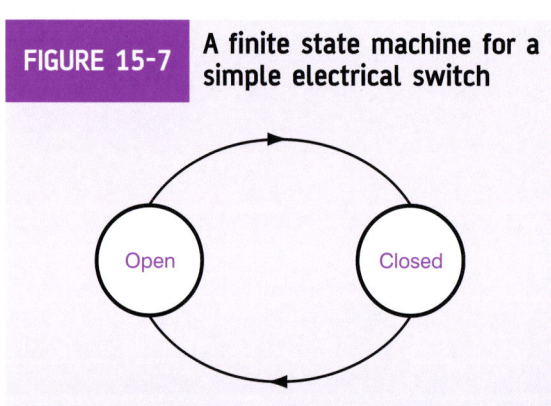

FIGURE 15-7 **A finite state machine for a simple electrical switch**

Using FSMs, we can model the actions of AI controlled computer opponents through a number of states. For example, advanced bots, such as those found in modern games, can literally have hundreds of states. That said, a basic bot can seem quite lifelike when modeled as an FSM consisting of only three states, specifically an attack, hide, and collect state. The finite state machine of such a bot is given in Figure 15-8.

Considering the above-given FSA diagrams, we can start to appreciate their use in the modeling of behaviour and thinking – two core aspects of 'intelligent' game AI.

These state machines are thus extremely useful when modeling the behaviour and think process of a computer controlled opponent.

As an example of developing an FSA for a bot, as found in common first-person shooter games such as *Quake III* and *Unreal Tournament*, we can start with a number of master states as listed here:

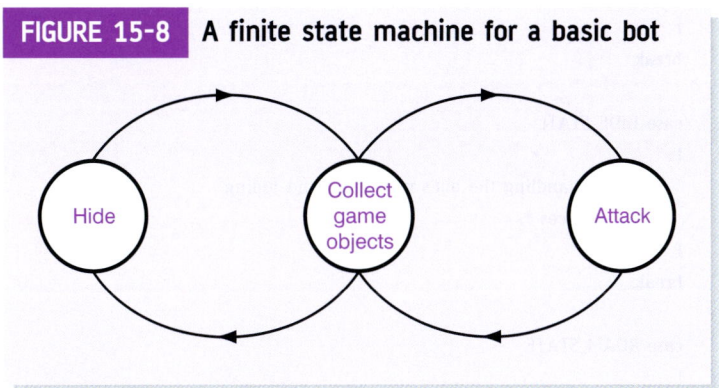

FIGURE 15-8 **A finite state machine for a basic bot**

1 Attack the player and other bots in sight.

2 Hide when under heavy attack.

3 Roam the game level if no target in sight.

4 Collect game items like health boosters, weapons, and armor.

5 Select an attack pattern based on the movement of the player.

6 Stop the current action.

Each of these states can subsequently be divided into substates, for example, the attack state can be branched into a number of states dealing with weapon selection and attack patterns. A substate simply represents an additional phase to a stage. An AI system based on the above listed states can be implemented in the following manner:

```
/* define the main states */
#define ATTACK_STATE;           0
#define HIDE_STATE;             1
#define ROAM_STATE              2
#define COLLECT_ITEMS_STATE     3
#define ATTACK_PATTERN_STATE    4
#define STOP_STATE              5

/* variable to hold the bot state */
int botState;

/* the state can either be set randomly, based on a trigger
   event or using a script — we'll use random selection for
   the time being */
botState = rand()%6;

/* process the bot's current state */
switch(botState)
{
    case ATTACK_STATE:
    {
        /* code handling the bot's attack sequence */
```

15

```
        }
        break;

        case HIDE_STATE:
        {
            /* code handling the bot's retreating and hiding
                sequences */
        }
        break;

        case ROAM_STATE:
        {
            /* code enabling the bot to move around the map */
        }
        break;

        case COLLECT_ITEMS_STATE:
        {
            /* code enabling the bot to pick up objects */
        }
        break;

        case ATTACK_PATTERN_STATE:
        {
            /* analyse the player's movements and execute a fitting
                counter-attack pattern */
        }
        break;

        case STOP_STATE:
        {
            /* force the bot into an idle state */
        }
        break;

        default: break;
}
```

Finite state machines are of course just a tool and numerous other tools can be used to model a computer controlled component's line of thinking. FSMs are, however, very easy to use – a fact that makes them the AI programmer's 'weapon of choice' when designing AI subsystems and bots.

15

15.5 AUTONOMOUS BEHAVIOUR: MEMORY AND PLANNING

Up to this point we have not really dealt with any real AI. Granted, pre-programmed AI and scripting are great ways to create seemingly intelligent opponents but a truly intelligent opponent must have the ability to learn, remember, and adapt in much the same way as expected from a human being. A human

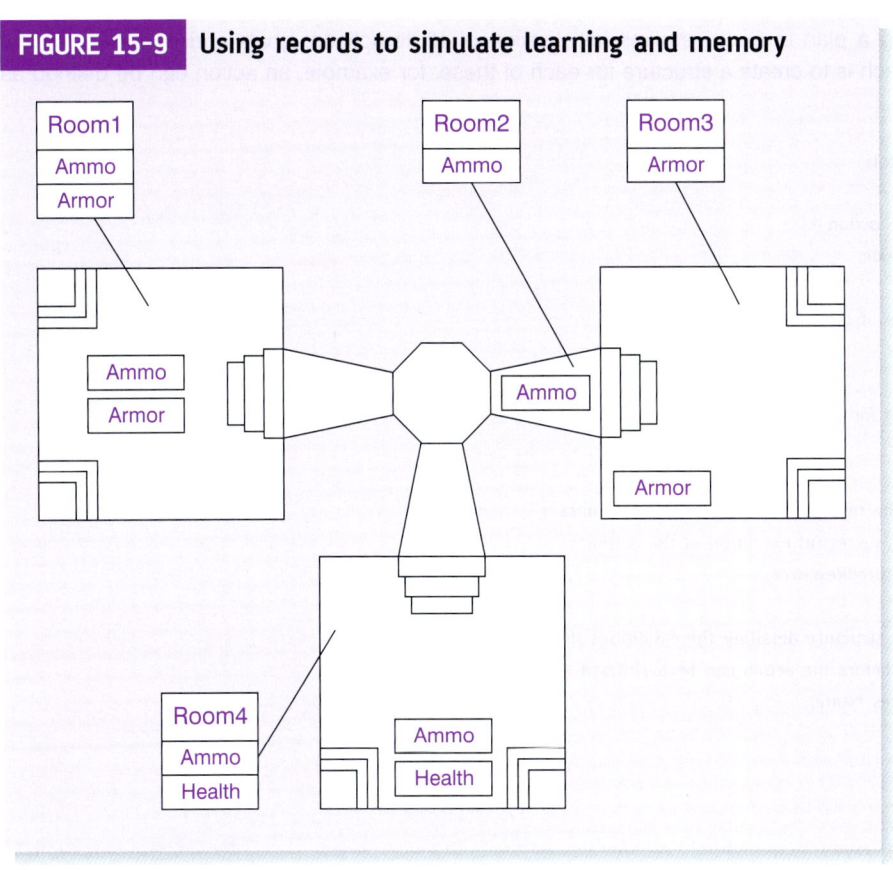

FIGURE 15-9 Using records to simulate learning and memory

player's ability to learn allows him or her to remember where the best items and traps are located, for example. We humans also have the ability to anticipate actions based on previously observed ones. For example, we will quickly change our targeting when players continuously crouch to avoid missiles fired at them. Adding this form of reasoning to a computer controlled opponent isn't as difficult as it seems.

The simplest solution to the memory problem involves creating tables with information about the items stored at a specific location. These tables can then be updated by the bot on an area-by-area basis. For example, when a bot enters an area to find a large amount of ammunition then we can store that information in a table or record, with the bot accessing this information at a later stage when low on ammunition. Thus, by implementing such a simple scheme our game will have learning AI (at least with regard to memory). Figure 15-9 illustrates such a scheme where the game level is divided into a number of sections with a record for each.

Records can also contain additional information such as player movement and attack patterns, player weapon preferences, etc. Using this information, the bot can adjust its playing style by selecting a different attack or movement pattern from the pattern database. There is thus no limit to the kind of information that can be stored in records.

The next step towards the goal of creating more realistic AI is to implement planning and decision trees. *Planning* is used to solve problems where a series of actions must be performed to reach some goal. An *action* is a specific step performed towards the successful completion of a goal. Actions are in turn governed by *conditionals*, i.e. states that must be reached before a particular action can be executed.

Implementing a plan in C++ requires initialisation of all its actions, goals and conditionals. The simplest approach is to create a structure for each of these, for example, an action can be defined as follows:

```
typedef struct Action
{
    /* name of the action */
    string actionName;

    /* class or type of the action */
    int actionType;

    /* time allowed for execution of the action */
    int actionTime;

    /* pointer to the resources structure – possible data
        required for successful execution of the action */
    Resources *requiredResources;

    /* pointer to a structure detailing the conditions that must
        be satisfied before the action can be performed */
    ConditionalStates *state;

    //...etc

} Action;
```

A structure for our AI goals can be defined in a similar fashion:

```
typedef struct Goal
{
    /* name of the goal, for example: "attack player" */
    string goalName;

    /* class or type of the goal */
    int goalType;

    /* time allowed for execution of the goal */
    int goalTime;

    //...etc
} Goal;
```

15

These structures are of course only abstract representations of what might be needed for the implementation of a planning algorithm. Also, this hard-coded approach focusing on the implementation of actions, goals and the overall plan was extremely popular in the early 1990s. However, elegance, being an ever-present requirement in modern game design, forced developers to improve the previous approach by means of production rules and decision trees.

A *production rule* is in essence a conditional if-statement. For example, if we have an event dependent on the outcome of a certain condition then a simple if-then-else test can be used to assert this precondition:

```
if(playerHealth > 0)
{
    AttackPlayer();
}
else
    TakeItems();
```

A *decision tree* is on the other hand a basic tree structure consisting of nodes representing either production rules or actions. Decision trees are normally populated using data read in from a file and are thus not hard-coded. These trees are extremely useful for implicitly representing a plan. Figure 15-10 shows a decision tree for a basic first-person shooter bot.

A decision tree can contain any number of Boolean operators with each node of the tree implemented as follows:

```
typedef struct DecisionTree
{
    /* when using Boolean operators − AND/OR/NOT */
    bool booleanOperator;

    /* when using standard comparisons − >/</==/!= */
    int comparisonOp;

    /* the first antecedent (input1, input3, input5, etc) */
    int antecedent1;

    /* the second antecedent (input2, input4, input6, etc) */
    int antecedent2;
```

FIGURE 15-10   **A generic decision tree**

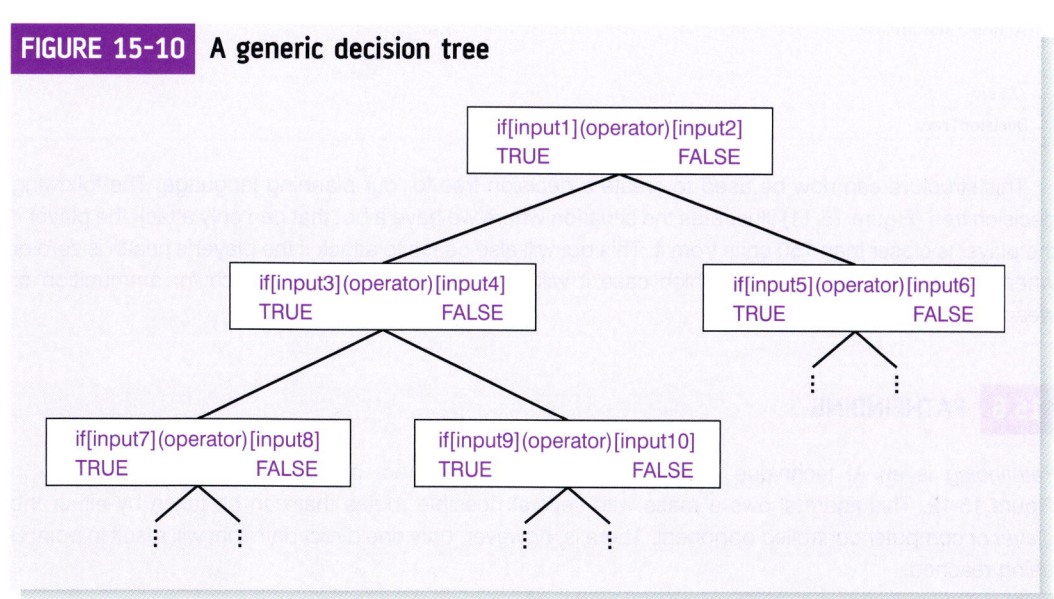

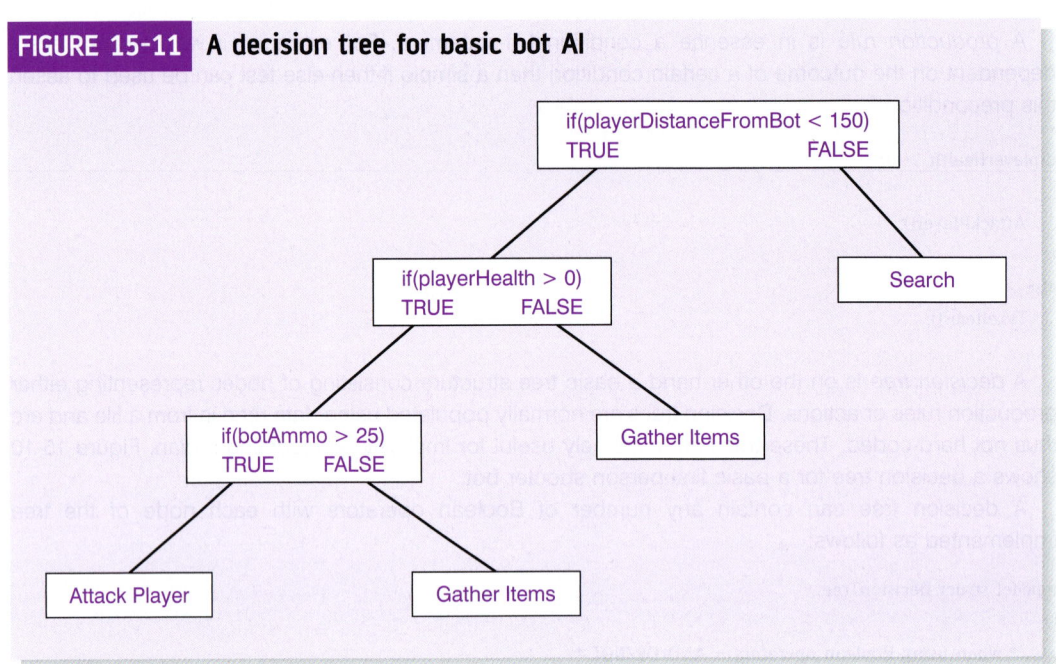

FIGURE 15-11   A decision tree for basic bot AI

```
/* follow the left branch if false */
DecisionTree *decisionTreeLeftBranch;

/* follow the right branch if true */
DecisionTree *decisionTreeRightBranch;

/* a pointer to the previously defined Action struct for
   both true and false outcomes */
Action *actionTrue;
Action *actionFalse;

//...etc
} DecisionTree;
```

This structure can now be used to create a decision tree for our planning language. The following decision tree (Figure 15-11) illustrates the situation where we have a bot that can only attack the player if the player is closer than 150 units from it. This bot will also cease to attack if the player's health is zero or when it runs out of ammo – in which case it will break off the attack to search for ammunition or weapons.

15.6 PATHFINDING

Pathfinding is an AI technique used to determine a route from point A to point B, as shown in Figure 15-12. This figure shows a maze with several possible routes that can be taken by either the player or computer controlled opponent. There is, however, only one direct path that will result in point B being reached.

If obstacle avoidance wasn't a primary concern, we could simply have calculated a vector from the start point to end point. For example, Figure 15-13 shows two points (A and B) in three-dimensional space with the AI technique of vectoring being used to determine the path.

Vectoring is an extremely useful technique that forms the basis of many pathfinding algorithms; however, more robust algorithms are needed when calculating paths around obstacles, for example, navigating through a first-person shooter map or around buildings and elevated terrain in a real-time strategy game. The type of algorithm used is in turn dependent on the unique challenges posed by the environment being navigated. A real-time strategy game will require an algorithm that can deal with larger, open areas (not to mention the large number of units moving around simultaneously) with first-person shooters on the other hand focusing more on enclosed spaces and fewer units.

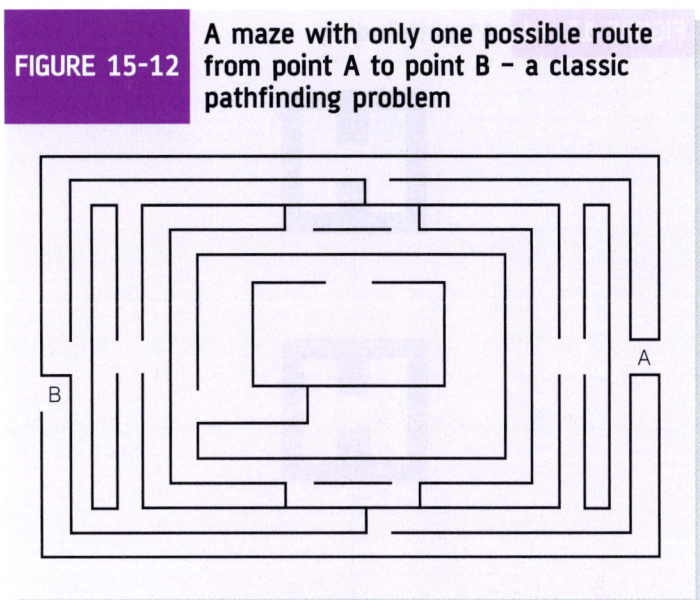

| FIGURE 15-12 | **A maze with only one possible route from point A to point B – a classic pathfinding problem** |

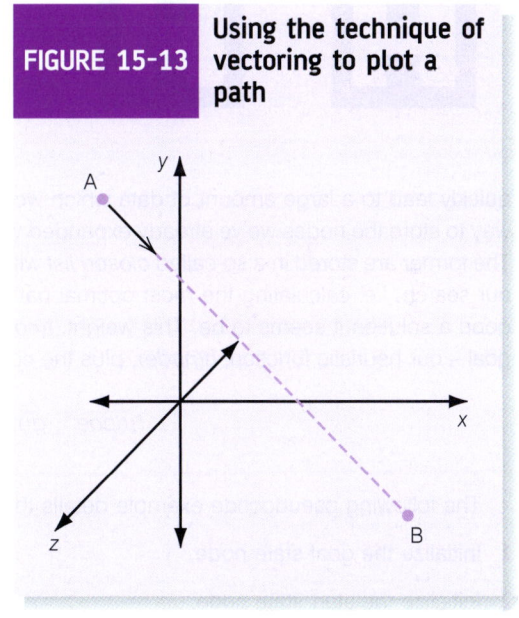

| FIGURE 15-13 | **Using the technique of vectoring to plot a path** |

15.6.1 The A* Algorithm

The *A* algorithm* (pronounced 'A star') is one of the most commonly used path finding algorithms. It is basically a tree-based search algorithm that calculates the path from one node to some pre-specified goal node. Without going too deeply into the heuristics driving this algorithm, simply consider it as a basic tree structure coupled with a heuristic function to select a path through this tree. The tree is constructed by dividing the game map into several tiles, with each tile representing a tree node. The A* algorithm starts at the root node, progressively writing the nodes to a list in order of accessibility. Written nodes are each assigned a heuristic which is used to sort them in a manner that should reveal the optimal route to the goal node – i.e. the algorithm continuously extends the path by moving to the node that seems to be closest to the goal. The A* algorithm will thus not only find the path, but it will find the shortest path if it exists.

When implementing the A* algorithm, we start with the goal node while generating the tree in a downwards fashion depending on the number of moves available. For example, Figure 15-14 shows a

FIGURE 15-14 **A* pathfinding**

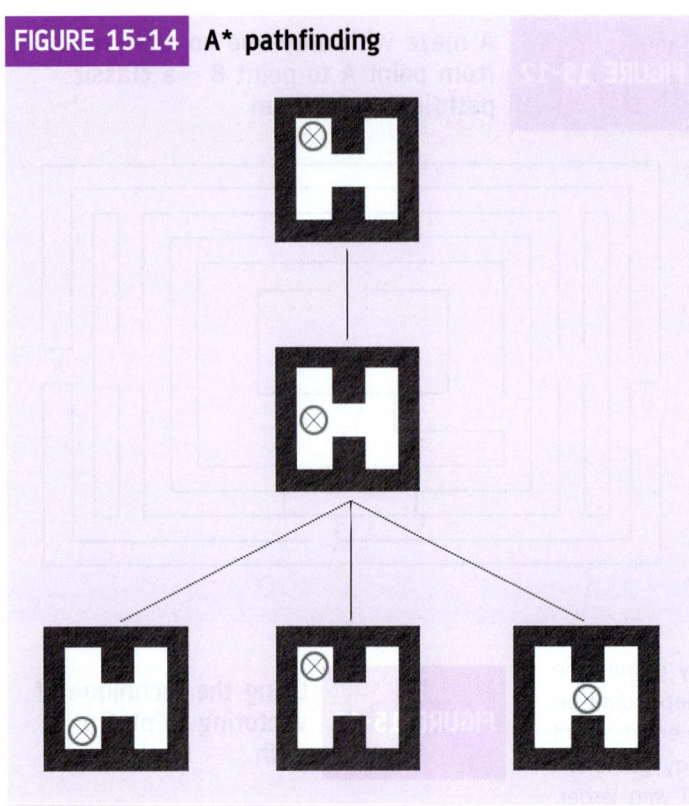

basic two-dimensional map with walls and an 'H'-shaped room. The computer controlled opponent shown here can only move one tile down during the first step, at the next level of the tree it can move either back to its original position, down or right.

The algorithm operates according to the following question: how many moves are possible from the current state? Hence, if we started at the top left position, as the case in Figure 15-14, and our goal state was the top right position then an A* algorithm will move our bot one position down, two right and finally one up – giving us the most optimal path between these two points.

It is clear from the above given example that the blind generation of nodes will quickly lead to a large amount of data which would be extremely difficult to process. We thus need a way to store the nodes we've already expanded while at the same time storing those not yet expanded. The former are stored in a so-called *closed list* with the latter in an *open list*. These lists allow us to focus our search, i.e. calculating the most optimal path by assigning a weight to each node based on how good a solution it seems to be. This weight, *f(node)*, is the traversal cost from the current node to the goal – our heuristic function, *h(node)*, plus the cost of the path so far leading up to the node, *g(node)*:

$$f(node = g(node) + h(node)).$$

The following pseudocode example details the A* algorithm's basic operation:

1 Initialize the goal state node.

2 Initialize the start state node.

3 Add the start state node to the open list.

4 While the open list has items in it:
   a Determine the node with the lowest *f(node)* weight and initialize it as the current node – this node is removed from the open list.
   b Generate all the nodes possible from the current node.
   c For each of these generated nodes:
      i Calculate the cost of the generated node by taking the cost of the current node plus the cost to go from the generated node to the current node.

    ii Search for the next generated node on the open list.
        — If the weight of the current generated node is as good as or better than this located node, then disregard the found node and continue.
    iii Search for the next generated node on the closed list.
        — If the weight of the current generated node is as good as or better than this located node, then disregard the found node and continue.
    iv Remove all instances of the generated node from the open and closed list.
    v Set the generated node as a child node of the current node.
    vi Calculate the traversal cost from the current node to the goal and add the generated node to the open list.
  d Add the current node to the closed list

In addition to the A* algorithm, other implementations such as breadth-first search (a special case of A* where *h(node)* is always '0') and depth-first search can also be employed to find the path from one point to another. We will now briefly look at each of these algorithms before looking at waypoint pathfinding.

15.6.2 Depth-First Search

Depth-first search is a commonly used search algorithm that follows each path to its greatest depth before moving on to the next. This algorithm is extremely rudimentary when compared to A*; for example, it needs a stopping limit to halt the search if a goal isn't found in say the first 200 nodes. Depth-first search is an example of brute-force search/exhaustive search, that is, all nodes are traversed until the goal node is found.

Depth-first search uses a method called *chronological backtracking* to move back up the search tree once a dead end has been found. Chronological backtracking is basic backtracking to undo choices in reverse order of the time the traversals were originally made. Figure 15-15 illustrates the order in which nodes will be traversed when using depth-first search (the node numbers correlate to the visiting order).

The following pseudocode example details the depth-first search algorithm's basic operation:

1 Start at the given node (initially at root):
  a Mark it as visited.

2 For all the vertices adjacent to the initial node:
  a If the vertex is unvisited:
    i Recursively jump to step 1 with this node as input.

15.6.3 Breadth-First Search

Breadth-first search is an alternative to the depth-first search pathfinding algorithm that traverses a tree by breadth rather than depth. The algorithm terminates the moment the goal state is reached and is much more efficient than depth-first search where the tree

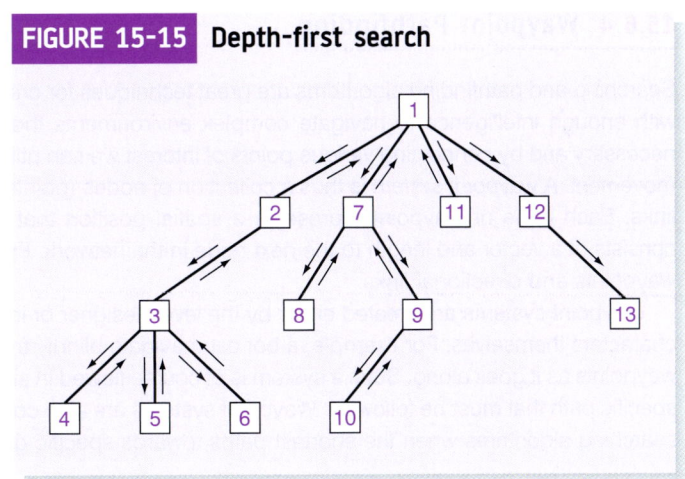

FIGURE 15-15 Depth-first search

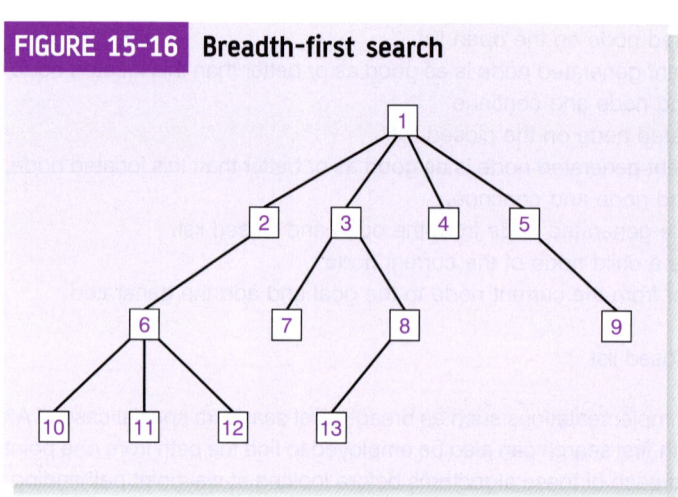

FIGURE 15-16 Breadth-first search

has very deep paths and particularly where the goal node is in a shallower part of the tree. That said, depth-first search is simpler to implement and requires less memory space because it only needs to store information about the path actually being explored.

This search basically spreads out in several directions at the same time, visiting all the nodes on one level of the tree, then the next level and so forth. The main problem when using it for pathfinding is that it doesn't focus on the goal, only searching for it, after which its position can be used to calculate the actual path. Figure 15-16 illustrates the order in which nodes will be traversed when using breadth-first search (the node numbers correlate to the visiting order).

The following pseudocode example details the depth-first search algorithm's basic operation:

1 Start at the given node (initially at root):
   a Mark it as visited.
   b Add it to a queue.

2 While the queue isn't empty:
   a Access the node at the beginning of the cue:
      i If this node is the goal node, quit and return this result.
      ii Otherwise add all the subsequent unmarked child nodes of this node to the end of the queue.

3 If the queue is empty then no path has been found.

4 Jump to step 2 and repeat.

15.6.4 Waypoint Pathfinding

Searching and pathfinding algorithms are great techniques for creating computer controlled opponents with enough intelligence to navigate complex environments themselves. This isn't, however, always necessary and by connecting various points of interest we can utilize vectoring to produce accurate bot movement. A *waypoint system* is thus a collection of nodes (points of interest) connected via directional links. Each node or waypoint represents a spatial position that can be visited. Each directional link consists of a vector and length to the next node in the network. Figure 15-17 shows a map with various waypoints and directional links.

Waypoint systems are created either by the level designer or in real-time by the computer controlled characters themselves. For example, a bot can navigate blindly from some starting position, 'dropping' waypoints as it goes along. Such a system is of course flawed in situations where we want to predefine a specific path that must be followed. Waypoint systems are also combined with the previously discussed searching algorithms when the shortest paths towards specific goals are important.

15

FIGURE 15-17	A waypoint-based pathfinding network

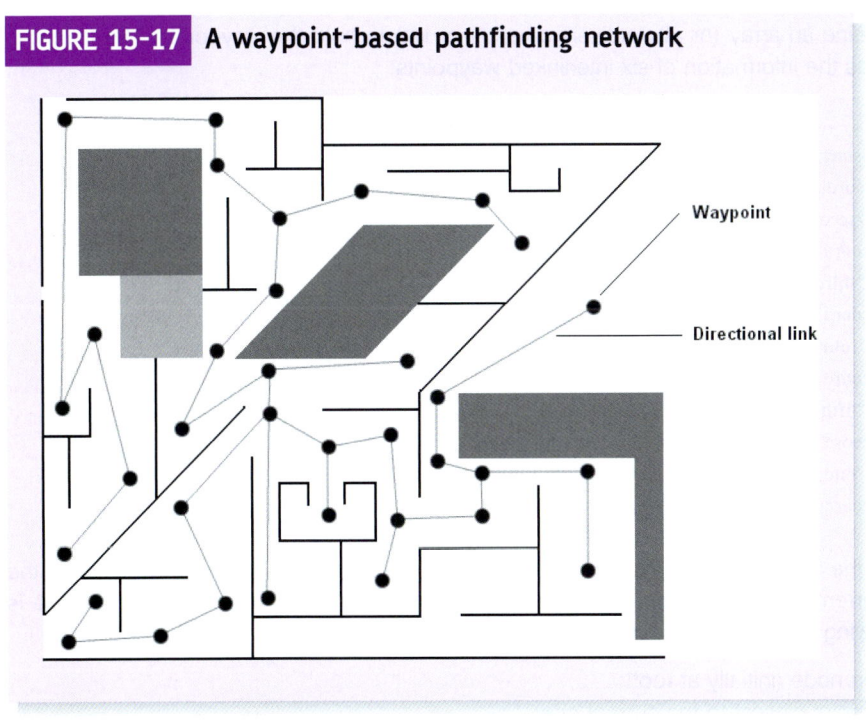

The implementation of a waypoint system is a twofold process where we have to define a routine that will enable the bot to follow a path and a storage structure for the actual network. The following structure can be used to store information about the actual path being followed:

```
typedef struct Waypoint
{
    /* number to identify the waypoint */
    int waypointId;

    /* description of the waypoint */
    string waypointDescription;

    /* waypoint's x-, y- and z-coordinates */
    float waypointXCoord;
    float waypointYCoord;
    float waypointZCoord;

    /* length from the current waypoint to the next */
    float distanceToNext;

    /* pointer to the next waypoint – NULL if none */
    Waypoint *nextWaypoint;

    /* pointer to the previous waypoint – NULL if none */
    Waypoint *previousWaypoint;
}
```

15

We can now define an array (or alternatively a vector or list) to hold the waypoints. The following Waypoint array stores the information of six interlinked waypoints:

```
Waypoint nodes[6] =
              {{1, "start_node", x_coord1, y_coord1,
                z_coord1, distance1, &nodes[1], NULL},
               {2, "second_node", x_coord2, y_coord2,
                z_coord2, distance2, &nodes[2], &nodes[1]},
               {3, "third_node", x_coord3, y_coord3,
                z_coord3, distance3, &nodes[3], &nodes[2]},
               {4, "fourth_node", x_coord4, y_coord4,
                z_coord4, distance4, &nodes[4], &nodes[3]},
               {5, "fifth_node", x_coord5, y_coord5,
                z_coord5, distance5, &nodes[5], &nodes[4]},
               {6, "end_node", x_coord6, y_coord6,
                z_coord6, distance6, NULL, &nodes[5]}};
```

Finally, moving the bot from one waypoint to the next is extremely easy – we simply calculate the vector from the current waypoint to the next, moving the bot along this path until the goal node is reached. The following pseudocode example details this basic operation:

1 Start at the given node (initially at root):
   a Find the waypoint closest to the current one:
      i Calculate and normalize the trajectory vector to this waypoint.
      ii Follow the calculated path until the next waypoint is reached.
   b Update the current node.

2 Jump to step 1 and repeat until the final goal node is reached.

15.7 INTRODUCTION TO MORE ADVANCED AI: NEURAL NETWORKS, EXPERT SYSTEMS AND GENETIC ALGORITHMS

The field of artificial intelligence is of course about much more than just pathfinding, planning, and production rules and with the aim of true intelligence driving research, modeling the human brain and thinking process seems like the most obvious step to achieve this goal. An artificial neural network is such a model of the human brain.

A *neural network* is a mathematical model based on human brain cells or neurons. An average human being can have anything from 10 to 100 billion neurons, each of these responsible for the manner in which information is processed. Biological *neurons* are cells that process and forward information to other neurons. These cells (consisting of a soma, body, axon, and dendrites) are found in the brain, spinal cord, and peripheral nerves. The *soma* is responsible for all information processing, with the *axon* forwarding information to *dendrites* which are in turn responsible for feeding the processed information to other neurons. Figure 15-18 illustrates the basic structure of a biological neuron.

A neural network consists of several connected artificial neurons (nodes) tasked with the parallel processing of information. The network adapts its structure based on the flow of information from node to node – this change in structure occurs during the learning phase. Neural networks consist of numerous processing nodes interconnected by means of signal channels. The number of nodes and the manner in which nodes are connected control the learning ability and functionality of the network.

15

Learning is, as mentioned, implemented through the reconfiguration of the synaptic connections between the nodes with the rate of learning controlled by the learning strategy employed. Figure 15-19 illustrates the structure of a typical neural network.

Neural networks are extremely useful when applied to solve particularly complex problems without clearly defined algorithmic solutions. For example, one area where neural networks have surpassed all other methods is in the field of object and image recognition. For instance, a neural net can be trained to recognise certain hand gestures which in turn can be used to change TV channels or to interact with a game. Bots on the other hand can be trained via these networks while exposed to the game world – thus making decisions based on gathered information, such as adapting to the player's game style or improved skill with ease.

Another technique often employed to facilitate the storage of and access to human expertise, accumulated through training, is that of *expert systems* (also called

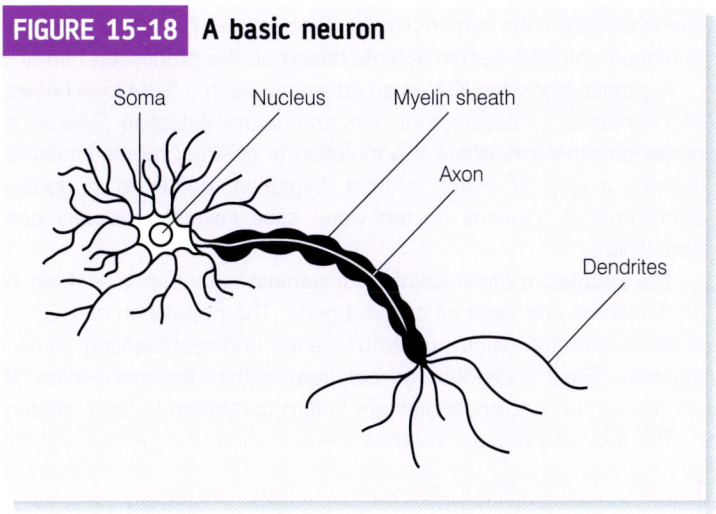

FIGURE 15-18   **A basic neuron**

Soma   Nucleus   Myelin sheath

Axon

Dendrites

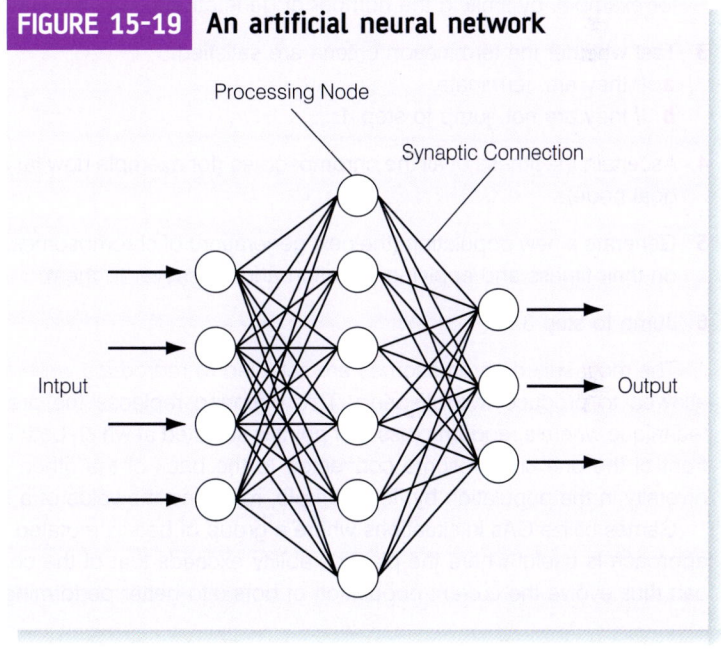

FIGURE 15-19   **An artificial neural network**

Processing Node

Synaptic Connection

Intput

Output

'knowledge systems'). An expert system is based on three concepts, namely, the knowledge of facts, data about the relationship among these facts and a method to store and access this data. An expert system is created by extracting facts from human knowledge, such as routines, historic events, relationships, and transforming these data so that they can be used to influence the reasoning of a computer controlled opponent, for example.

The most basic expert system is defined by a set of production rules which is in turn used to analyse information. This mathematical analysis yields a recommendation with regards to the course of action that should be taken by the user or bot.

Expert systems can, for example, be used in games to implement the reasoning of computer controlled opponents. When used in such a way the knowledge system can be defined to extract and

15

store facts about the human players. Production rules (simple if-conditionals) can subsequently be used to reason and take certain actions based on the processed human knowledge.

A *genetic algorithm* (GA) is an advanced search technique based on the principles of genetics such as inheritance, crossover, mutation, and natural selection. GAs are extremely useful in the optimization of search problems where a population of abstract representations of possible solutions are evolved towards a goal or better solution. Evolution, occurring in generational cycles, starts with several approximated solutions (in the worst case several randomly generated solutions) making up the population.

The simplest representation of a genetic algorithm is a string of bits, with the string known as a *chromosome* and each bit called a *gene*. The population of a GA consists of several chromosomes – each constructed using numerous genes and representing some aspect of the individual's genetic makeup. Each individual (a solution) within the population is represented by one of these chromosomes. Chromosomes are in turn combined to form *creatures*.

The following process outlines the execution of a genetic algorithm:

1 Start by generating a population of chromosomes.

2 Define some termination or goal criteria which can be used to terminate the algorithm when satisfied, for example, by limiting the number of generations.

3 Test whether the termination criteria are satisfied:
   a If they are, terminate.
   b If they are not, jump to step 4.

4 Ascertain the fitness of all the chromosomes (for example how far a specific node is located from the goal node).

5 Generate a new population (the next generation) of chromosomes by selecting chromosomes based on their fitness and applying mutation and crossover to them.

6 Jump to step 3.

The most suited chromosomes are selected to reproduce while each pair of chromosomes is only allowed to produce two offspring. This offspring replaces the previous generation. *Crossover* is a technique where a random crossover point is selected at which both chromosomes will be split, with the front of the one chromosome connected to the back of the other, and vice versa. *Mutation* sustains diversity in the population by, for example, reversing the value of a bit in a chromosome.

Games utilize GAs in situations where a group of bots is mutated into a slightly different group. This approach is useful where the player's ability exceeds that of the computer controlled opponents. We can thus evolve the current population of bots into better performing ones.

15.8 SUMMARY

In this chapter we started by describing artificial intelligence as the design and application of methods modeled after the behaviour of humans and/or animals to solve complicated problems. Intelligence was subsequently defined as a collection of logic, mathematics and memory; all applied in an interconnected manner to maximize the probability of a successful outcome. We also looked at the history of AI in games, specifically focusing on the main AI-centric advancements made over the past couple of years.

Next we discussed the theory and implementation of a number of basic AI techniques, specifically, pre-programming and scripting at hand of tracking algorithms, action modeling of AI controlled computer opponents through a number of states, and the simulation of autonomous behaviour by means of memory and planning via the implementation of production rules and decision trees.

Building on this we discussed pathfinding in detail, focusing on a number of algorithms for the creation of computer controlled opponents with enough intelligence to navigate complex environments themselves. Algorithms presented include the A* algorithm, depth-first search, breadth-first search and waypoint pathfinding.

The remainder of the chapter investigated more advanced AI approaches, specifically focusing on neural networks for solving particularly complex problems lacking clearly defined algorithmic solutions, expert systems as a way of adding reasoning to computer controlled opponents and genetic algorithms as advanced search techniques based on the principles of genetics.

The next chapter deals with audio playback and control using the DirectSound, XACT and XAudio2 audio APIs.

15.9 FURTHER READING

For more on FSAs, refer to the books *Modeling Software with Finite State Machines: A Practical Approach by F. Wagner et al.* (ISBN: 0849380863) and *Synthesis of Finite State Machines: Functional Optimization by Timothy Kam et al.* (ISBN: 0792398424).

The books *AI for Games and Animation by John David Funge* (ISBN: 1568811039) and *Principles of Artificial Intelligence by Nils Nilsson* (ISBN: 0934613109) are two great sources for more information on artificial intelligence algorithms and approaches. Another great book covering a range of AI techniques is Ben Coppin's *Artificial Intelligence Illuminated* (ISBN: 0763732303).

15.10 EXERCISES

1 Briefly describe the process of tracing a path from one point in space to another.

2 Write a sample program that implements basic path-tracking.

3 Describe the benefits inherent to the use of scripted AI.

4 Discuss how we might go about modeling the actions of AI controlled computer opponents.

5 Briefly explain the use of records for the simulation of learning and memory.

6 What is the purpose of decision trees?

7 Discuss the A* algorithm's basic operation.

8 Compare depth-first search to breadth-first search.

9 What does each node of a waypoint system represent?

10 Describe the implementation of a waypoint system.

11 How can a bot be moved from one waypoint to the next?

12 How can games utilize neural networks, genetic algorithms and expert systems?

15

CHAPTER 16

Audio

LEARNING OBJECTIVES

In this chapter you will learn about:

- The fundamentals of sound
- DirectX Audio
- DirectSound
- XACT
- XAudio2

INTRODUCTION

Chapter 16 presents audio playback and control using the DirectSound, XACT and XAudio2 DirectX APIs.

16.1 INTRODUCTION TO SOUND

Sound, on a physical level, is the propagation of potential and kinetic energy waves. Potential or stored energy is released in the form of kinetic energy (including other forms of energy) to affect the states of other objects. Kinetic energy, as discussed in Chapter 14, is energy stored in a moving object. A *sound wave* (vibration that travels through some medium) is described by means of its frequency, wavelength, period, direction, speed, and amplitude. We will now briefly discuss each of these properties.

FIGURE 16-1	Three sound waves with varying frequencies

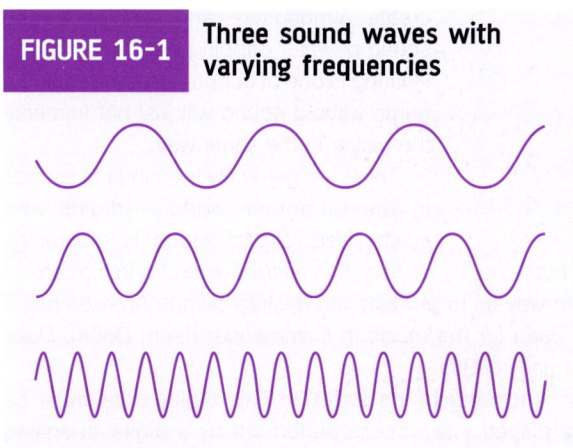

Frequency is a measure of repeated occurrences over some period of time, for example, Figure 16-1 shows three sound waves with the top one having the lowest frequency. Frequency is measured in Hertz (Hz), with one Hertz equalling one repeat per second.

Wavelength is the distance between two repeating points of a sound wave (Figure 16-2). Frequencies ranging from 20Hz to about 20 000Hz are audible to the human ear. The wavelengths corresponding to these frequencies range from 17 metres to about 17 millimetres.

FIGURE 16-2	The wavelength of a sine wave

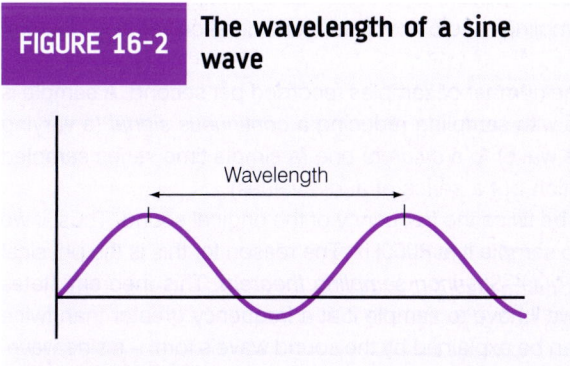

The *amplitude* of a sound wave is its magnitude of oscillation (the wave's variation in time) – i.e. the maximum variation in the wave during one wave cycle (Figure 16-3). Amplitude, as a measure, controls the loudness of a sound and can be used to refer to either the oscillation magnitude of the sound wave or the displacement of the diaphragm of a speaker.

The *speed of sound* expresses the distance travelled by a sound wave over a period of time. This velocity is dependent on the medium of propagation; for example, the speed of sound in dry air at 21 degrees Celsius is 344m/s (1238km/h or 768mph) and 1478m/s under water. Speed is combined with the direction of the sound wave to form a velocity vector.

Sound is thus mechanical energy in the form of a wave emitted from a vibrating source (Figure 16-4). This wave moves through a medium such as air or water (via molecular collisions), with the density of the medium controlling the

FIGURE 16-3	The amplitude of a sound wave

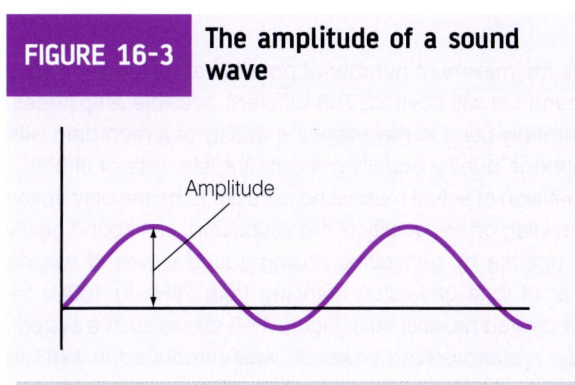

16

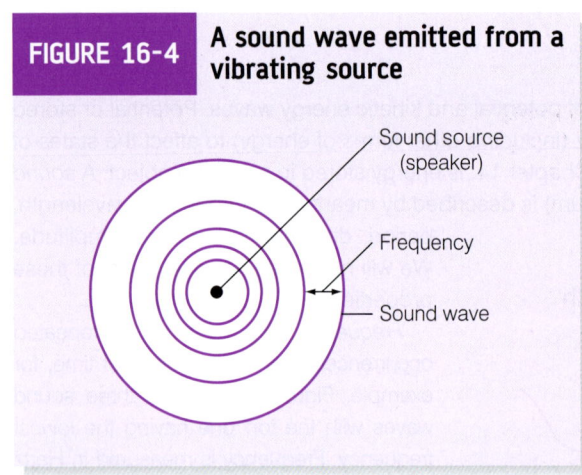

FIGURE 16-4 **A sound wave emitted from a vibrating source**

Sound source (speaker)

Frequency

Sound wave

velocity of the wave – the higher the material density, the greater the velocity of the sound wave.

Sound and music in games form a crucial part of the overall gaming experience. Sounds can, for example, be used to alert the player of certain hazards such as another player or bot approaching or to create atmosphere and ambience (the sound of water dripping or lava bubbling). Hearing is one of our primary senses and a game without sound will just not immerse the player in the same way.

There are generally two kinds of sounds in the computer world – digital and synthesized. *Digital* sound is recordings in the form of wave files, mp3s or oggs; to name but a few file formats. *Synthesized* sound is in turn based on hardware generated tones arranged in such a way as to produce the desired output. An example of synthesized sound include the MIDI file format used for the music in *Commander Keen*, *Doom*, *Duke Nukem* and most other games of the 1980s and early 1990s.

Digital sound is, as the name suggests, an encoding of 1's and 0's. This digital data must be converted into analog form before they can be played – a process performed by a digital-to-analog converter (generally a hardware processor located on the soundcard). On the other hand, recording audio requires the conversion of an analog sound wave into a digital data stream – done using an analog-to-digital converter. Recording or sampling audio involves consideration of two factors: amplitude and frequency.

Frequency controls the sampling rate – i.e. the number of samples recorded per second. A sample is simply a sound value at a specific point in time with sampling reducing a *continuous signal* (a varying signal expressed as a function – such as a sine wave) to a *discrete* one (a simple time series sampled from a continuous-time signal – it is not a function but a series of audio values).

The sample rate of a recording must at least be twice the frequency of the original sound. Thus, if we have a sound wave of 4000Hz then we'll have to sample it at 8000Hz. The reason for this is the physical nature of sound waves as governed by the *Nyquist–Shannon sampling theorem*. This theorem states that, in order to perfectly reconstruct a signal, we'll have to sample it at a frequency greater than twice the peak frequency of the original signal. This can be explained by the sound wave's form – a sine wave. A sine wave has both an upwards and downwards crest per cycle, and sampling this wave requires differentiation between these two crests – hence the use of a sample rate that is twice the frequency of the sine wave.

The *amplitude sampling resolution* represents the maximum number of possible amplitudes or wave variations per sample. For instance, an 8-bit sound file will have 32 768 different possible amplitudes. The number of bits streamed per second is commonly used to represent the quality of a recording with near CD quality being 192kbit/second and telephone quality equalling a data transfer rate of 8kbit/s.

Synthesized sound, as a mathematical representation of actual musical notes, used to be the only option for the playback of audio on computers and, depending on the quality of the soundcard, can sound nearly as good as its digital counterpart. Synthesizers operate by generating analog sound waves of varying frequency, for example, we can define a number of tone generators (ranging from 20Hz to 100Hz for instance) and trigger each of these to produce the desired musical note. Figure 16-5 shows such a system.

MIDI (*Musical Instrument Digital Interface*), as a standardized protocol, was introduced in 1983 to enable communication between digital equipment, electronic instruments (such as keyboards) and

16

FIGURE 16-5	A basic synthesizer

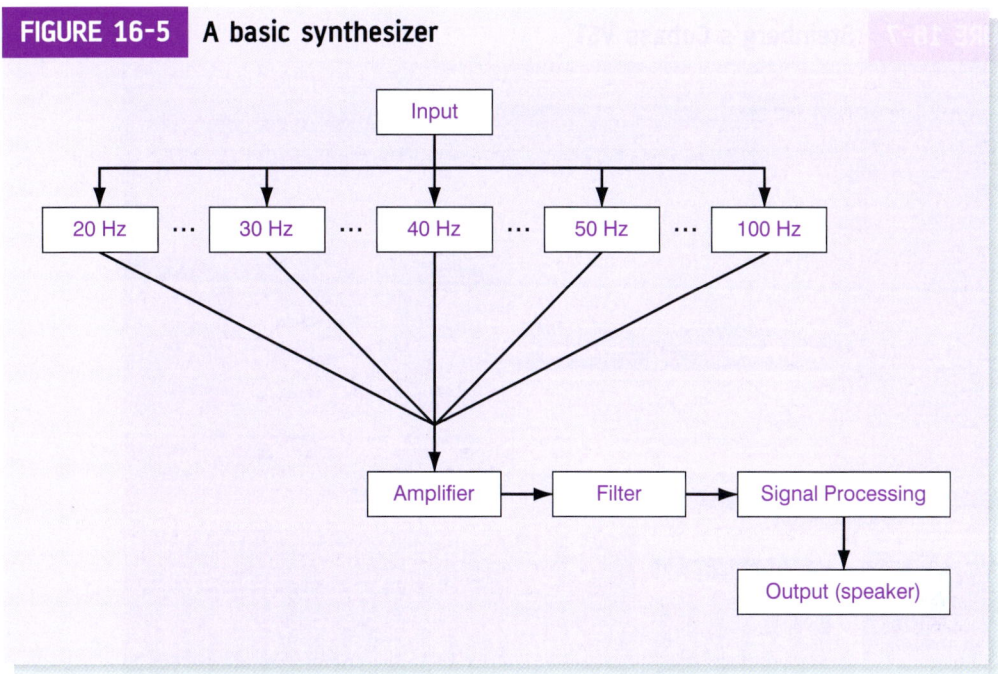

computers. This protocol can be considered a musical 'language' that describes musical notes in terms of pitch, tempo, volume, vibrato (a recurrent change in pitch), cues and panning ('moving' a sound from one speaker to another in a stereo sound field). Furthermore, a MIDI file contains several channels, each representing a different musical instrument (piano, guitar, drums, bass, trumpet, etc). The actual sound synthesis is left to the soundcard.

A *soundcard* (Figure 16-6) is an add-on card that enables the input and output of audio. These cards consist of at least one sound chip (an integrated circuit that produces sound), one or more digital-to-analog converters (to convert binary data to analog signals for digital sound reproduction) and sometimes a wave table for wave table synthesis. Soundcards are also commonly integrated on PC motherboards or used in 'outboard' form as USB devices.

Wave table synthesis combines digital recording with audio synthesis. The sampled digital audio contained within the soundcard's wave table is processed by its digital signal processor or DSP. The DSP allows the playback of these samples at any amplitude and frequency. Wave table synthesis was introduced during the early 1990s in higher-end soundcards like Creative Labs' Sound Blaster AWE-32 to improve the playback of synthesized sound (heavily used in

FIGURE 16-6	A Creative Labs Sound Blaster X-Fi

16

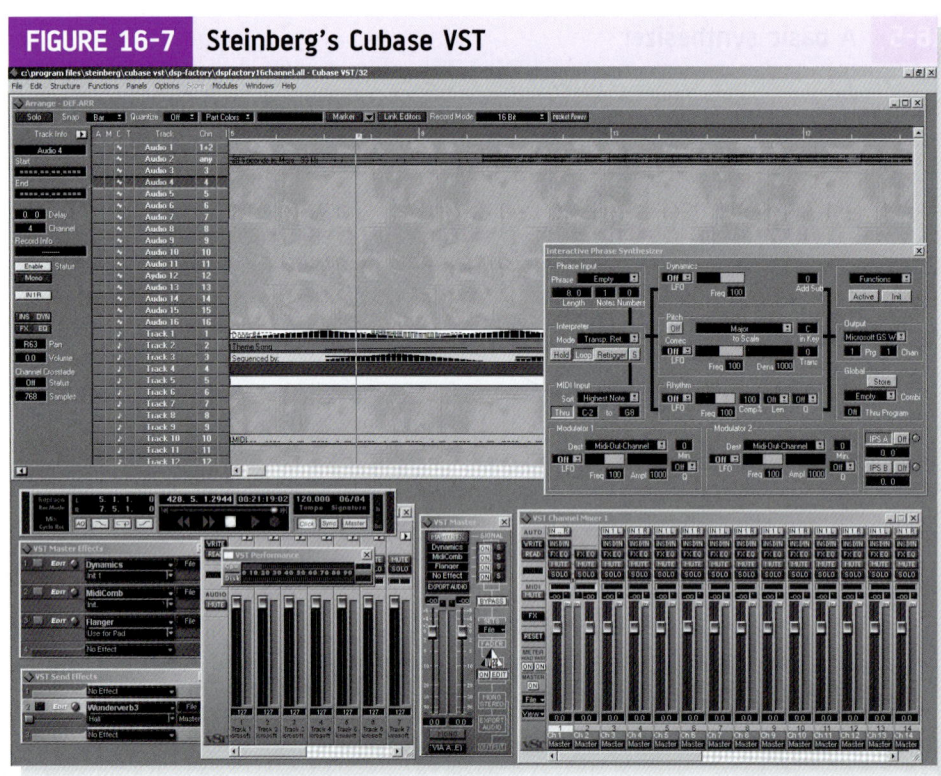

FIGURE 16-7   Steinberg's Cubase VST

games at the time). This technology was further extended with the release of the Sound Blaster AWE-64 in 1996 where the DSP created a mathematical model of any instrument (called wave guide synthesis) – resulting in near life-like synthesised playback.

Modern games rarely utilize synthesized sound but it is still worth a look due to the widespread use of music sequencers (such as Steinberg's *Cubase* and Digidesign's *Pro Tools*). These digital audio editing applications, used throughout the professional music world, allow for the creation and editing of MIDI files, the programming of drums or the composition, for example, of an entire musical score. Applications like these are frequently used in film music production, post production and film scoring. For example, Trent Reznor from *Nine Inch Nails* released 'The Hand That Feeds' from the *With Teeth* album in *GarageBand* 2.0 format, with the track 'Only' from the same album released in GarageBand 2.0, *Ableton Live*, Pro Tools and Sony *ACID* formats. Both Ableton Live and Sony ACID are loop-based music sequencers. Figure 16-7 shows Cubase VST v5.1 in action.

An application can only produce audio if a direct interface between itself and the soundcard drivers is provided. This interface allows for the passing of sound data to and the receiving of audio data from the soundcard. Additional tasks such as mixing and effect processing are also needed. Prior to the release of Windows 95, developers had to utilize third-party sound libraries like the *Miles Sound System* or the *Diamondware Sound Toolkit* to provide them with such an interface. These libraries were rather expensive and many developers implemented their own, giving rise to significant soundcard compatibility issues. It wasn't until the release of the DirectX API that developers were provided with a powerful direct interface to the soundcard drivers. Cross-platform alternatives to DirectSound and XAudio also exist. One such a library, *OpenAL*, was originally developed by Loki Software to aid in the

16

porting of Windows games to Linux. The OpenAL library is now largely maintained by Creative Labs and Apple.

We will now look at the libraries constituting DirectX Audio in detail.

16.2   DIRECTX AUDIO

DirectX Audio is a collective term used to describe a number of DirectX audio libraries, specifically: X3DAudio, Microsoft Cross-Platform Audio Creation Tool (XACT), XAudio2 and DirectSound.

The XACT, as listed in Chapter 2, is a high-level audio library and engine for the playback and recording of digital audio using the Xbox 360's compressed audio format (XAudio) and DirectSound on Windows. It also features the XACT Audio Creation Tool that arranges audio files into so called wave banks (a single audio file made up of multiple audio files). XACT supports 5.1 surround sound configurations. *X3DAudio* is simply a 3D sound spatialization helper library for Windows and the Xbox.

DirectSound is, as discussed in Chapter 2, an API for the playback and recording of digital audio – allowing a single audio playback/recoding implementation regardless of the audio hardware being used. Following the architectural changes in Windows Vista, DirectSound no longer has direct communication with the underlying hardware, rather using an emulation layer. There is thus no longer any DirectSound hardware acceleration. DirectSound3D, as an extension of the DirectSound API that facilitates the playback of 3D audio, has been integrated into the DirectSound API for the DirectX 10 SDK release.

DirectSound is set to be replaced by XAudio2, a cross-platform, low-level API to be used in unison with Windows XP, Windows Vista and the Xbox 360 gaming console. Microsoft describes XAudio2 as an API providing 'a signal processing and mixing foundation for games similar to its predecessors, DirectSound and XAudio. For Windows game developers, XAudio2 is the long-awaited replacement for DirectSound. For Xbox 360 developers, it is an enhanced version of the previous XAudio API, addressing several outstanding issues and feature requests.' XAudio2 has only been released as a beta version at the time of writing and it should officially be released in mid 2008.

16.2.1 DirectSound

The DirectSound API was last revised with the release of DirectX 8.0, with only some performance improvements made for the DirectX 9.0c release. The DirectSound library consists of three modules: the run-time dynamic link libraries (dsound,.dll and dsound3d.dll), a compile-time library (dsound.lib), and the DirectSound header (dsound.h). DirectSound allows for the simultaneous playback and manipulation of multiple wave sound files (.wav), the recording of audio, dynamic control over the addition of audio effects such as distortion and echo.

DirectSound, similar to DirectInput, requires the creation of a main COM (Component Object Model) object from which all the other interfaces are requested. DirectSound consequently consists of a number of COM interfaces. The main interface, IDirectSound8, is responsible for initializing the DirectSound environment and for creating sound buffer objects. We also specify an IDirectSoundBuffer8 object to manage these created sound buffers. The IDirectSoundCapture8 interface is used to create sound capture buffers to facilitate recording of audio from an external device such as a keyboard or microphone. Sometimes it will be necessary to send control messages to the soundcard via notification events; IDirectSoundNotify8 is used for this purpose. There are, in addition to these interfaces, several other which can be used based on the complexity of the implemented sound system. Examples include IDirectSoundFXDistortion8, IDirectSoundFXWavesReverb8, IDirectSoundCaptureFXNoiseSuppress8 and IDirectSoundFull-Duplex8. Figure 16-8 shows the main IDirectSound8 interface with additionally created IDirectSoundBuffer8, IDirectSoundNotify8 and IDirectSoundCapture8 interfaces.

16

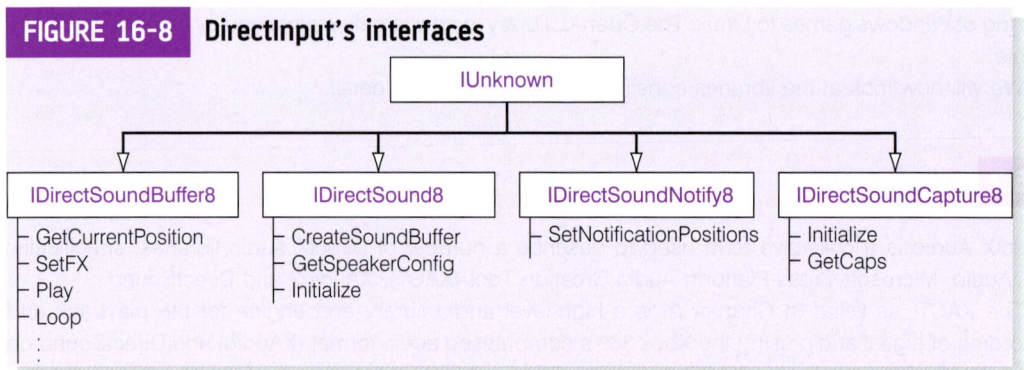

FIGURE 16-8 **DirectInput's interfaces**

The general steps for setting up and playing audio via the DirectSound API are as follows:

1 Create a DirectSound IDirectSound8 interface object via the DirectSoundCreate8 function – this object represents the default playback device.

2 Call the CreateSoundBuffer IDirectSound8 interface function to create a sound buffer which will be used for the storage and management of sound data.

3 Access the wave data (stored in an audio file) and write it to the private sound buffer.

4 Call the Lock IDirectSoundBuffer8 interface function to prepare a secondary buffer for the write operation.

5 Call the Unlock IDirectSoundBuffer8 interface function to transfer the audio data from the private buffer to the initialized secondary buffer.

6 Play the audio clip via the Play IDirectSoundBuffer8 interface function and, if playback is set to loop, then we can stop it using the Stop IDirectSoundBuffer8 interface function.

DirectSound plays audio via four playback objects, namely, a device object, primary buffer object, secondary buffer object, and an effect object. A device object (IDirectSound8) must be created for each DirectSound application – the first step of any DirectSound implementation. This object is used to create and control sound buffers. A secondary buffer object (IDirectSoundBuffer8, IDirectSound3DBuffer8 or IDirectSoundNotify8) must be created for each sound that is to be played. Sounds waiting to be played are thus stored in these buffers. The sounds stored in the secondary buffers are loaded into the primary buffer when played. One primary buffer object (IDirectSoundBuffer or IDirectSound3DListener8) is created per application. This buffer combines and plays audio loaded from secondary buffers. Effect objects (IDirectSoundFXChorus8, IDirectSoundFXFlanger8, etc.) are in turn used for the transformation of sound clips stored in the secondary buffers.

The main DirectSound object symbolizes the soundcard. When the system has more than one soundcard, we often have to enumerate the different devices; however, games will only play sounds through the user's default device – hence negating the need for enumeration. That said, many game setup programs give the user the option of choosing the best device to use, an option that requires device enumeration. Enumeration basically tells us which devices are available, in the process giving us the GUID of each.

Enumerating sound devices requires a basic callback function (to be called for each device found). The signature of this callback function must match that of the DSEnumCallback function. This function is a standard DirectSound callback function that enumerates all the DirectSound drivers and it is called by the system for each DirectSoundEnumerate or DirectSoundCaptureEnumerate function call. The DSEnumCallback function is defined as follows in the dsound.h header file:

```
BOOL CALLBACK DSEnumCallback(
    LPGUID lpGuid,
    LPCSTR lpcstrDescription,
    LPCSTR lpcstrModule,
    LPVOID lpContext
);
```

The first parameter, lpGuid, is the GUID identifying the audio device being enumerated – it is set to 'NULL' for the default sound device and is passed to the DirectSoundCaptureCreate8 or DirectSoundCreate8 functions when creating the main DirectSound IDirectSound8 interface object. The next parameter, lpcstrDescription, is a pointer to a string containing the description of the sound device with the lpcstrModule parameter a pointer to a string holding the name of the device's DirectSound driver. The final parameter, lpContext, is a pointer to application specific data. This data is used as DirectSoundEnumerate and DirectSoundCaptureEnumerate's second and fourth parameter, respectively. We specify the callback function as follows (this function will later be called by the DirectSoundEnumerate function):

```
BOOL CALLBACK DirectSoundEnumCallback(LPGUID lpGuid,
                                      LPCTSTR lpszDesc,
                                      LPCTSTR lpszDrvName,
                                      LPVOID lpContext)
{
    /* counter for traversing the sound drivers */
    int driverCounter = 0;

    /* a GUID array with storage space for 10 sound drivers*/
    GUID driverGUIDs[10];

    /* a temporary buffer */
    GUID* pTempGUIDs = NULL;

    /* enumerate a device if it is not NULL, i.e. if it is
       not the primary sound driver */
    if(lpGuid != NULL)
    {
        /* we only have storage space for 10 drivers */
        if(driverCounter >= 10 )
            return true;
        pTempGUIDs = &driverGUIDs[driverCounter++];

        /* copy the GUID identifying the audio device being
           enumerated (lpGuid) to the pTempGUIDs buffer for
           the number of bytes specified by sizeof(GUID) */
        memcpy(pTempGUIDs, lpGuid, sizeof(GUID));
    }

    /* deallocate the memory block */
    free(pTempGUIDs);

    return true;
}
```

16

The DirectSoundEnumerate function enumerates all DirectSound drivers present on the system and is declared as follows in the dsound.h header file:

```
HRESULT DirectSoundEnumerate(
    LPDSENUMCALLBACK lpDSEnumCallback,
    LPVOID lpContext
);
```

Its first parameter, lpDSEnumCallback, is a pointer to the callback function with its second parameter a pointer to application specific data sent to the callback. We can enumerate the sound devices via this function as follows:

```
HRESULT hresult_ = DirectSoundEnumerate(
                (LPDSENUMCALLBACK)DirectSoundEnumCallback,
                (void)*theContext);
```

We can create and initialize the DirectSound device object via the DirectSoundCreate8 function. This function is declared in the dsound.h header file:

```
HRESULT DirectSoundCreate8(
    LPCGUID lpcGuidDevice,
    LPDIRECTSOUND8 * ppDS8,
    LPUNKNOWN pUnkOuter
);
```

Its lpcGuidDevice parameter is the address of the GUID identifying the audio device ('NULL' for the default audio device or the GUID returned by the DirectSoundEnumerate function). This parameter can also be set to DSDEVID_DefaultPlayback (equivalent to using 'NULL' – playback via the default audio device) or DSDEVID_DefaultVoicePlayback (the default voice playback device). The ppDS8 parameter is a pointer to the IDirectSound8 interface object, with the pUnkOuter parameter a COM aggregation, as discussed in Chapter 5, which must be set to 'NULL' (COM aggregation is not supported).

The following code sample illustrates the creation and initialization of the default DirectSound device object:

```
/* define a IDirectSound8 interface which will be used to
   create the buffer objects */
LPDIRECTSOUND8 lpDirectSound; //pointer to the DirectSound obj
hresult_ = DirectSoundCreate8(NULL, &lpDirectSound, NULL);
```

We can check for the returned value using a standard if structure and the FAILED macro – the success value DS_OK should be returned. Our device object creation failed whenever the DSERR_ALLOCATED, DSERR_NODRIVER, DSERR_INVALIDPARAM, DSERR_NOAGGREGATION, or DSERR_OUTOFMEMORY value is returned:

```
if FAILED(hresult_)
{
    /* take some action because DirectSound object creation
       failed */
}
```

16

It is also very important to release the DirectSound device object during the shutdown stage of our application:

```
lpDirectSound->Release();
```

Following the DirectSound object creation, we must set the cooperative level of the device. *Cooperative levels* ensure timely and correct device accesses. We need to enforce proper device communication because of all the numerous applications that can simultaneously interact with a device driver. The DirectSound cooperative levels limit the degree to which a device can be accessed.

There are three DirectSound cooperative levels: normal cooperation, priority cooperation, and write-primary cooperation.

- *Normal cooperation* (DSSCL_NORMAL) limits the functionality of the application to the playback of audio. The application will not be able to modify the primary sound buffer's format or write to it. The primary buffer will be limited to 8-bit stereo with a 22kHz buffer format. This cooperative level is generally used when multiple applications need access to a single device.

- *Priority cooperation* (DSSCL_PRIORITY) enables first access to all the hardware including the ability to change mixer settings and to modify the primary sound buffer's format. We will mostly use this cooperative level to enable the playback of 16-bit audio files as common for modern games.

- The *write-primary cooperative level* (DSSCL_WRITEPRIMARY) gives total control over the device. For example, using this level, we can not only access the sound hardware directly but we can also write directly to the primary buffer. This mode is useful when writing a sound mixer or standalone sound engine.

The SetCooperativeLevel IDirectSound8 interface function sets the application's cooperative level, it is declared as follows in the dsound.h header file:

```
HRESULT SetCooperativeLevel(
    HWND hwnd,
    DWORD dwLevel
);
```

Its first parameter, hwnd, is simply a handle to the application window with the second parameter, dwLevel, describing the cooperation level of the device via a combination of the following flags:

- DISCL_NORMAL (for normal cooperation where resource-sharing is required)

- DISCL_EXCLUSIVE (for priority cooperation and exclusive control)

- DSSCL_PRIORITY (for priority cooperation) or

- DSSCL_WRITEPRIMARY (sets the write-primary cooperative level for complete control of the primary buffer).

We can now set its cooperative level using the SetCooperativeLevel function (with the calling function taking 'HWND hWnd' as a parameter):

```
hresult_ = lpDirectSound->
            SetCooperativeLevel(hWnd,
                    DSSCL_NORMAL);
```

16

We can also check the returned value using a standard if structure and the FAILED macro – the success value DS_OK should be returned. Our device object creation failed whenever the DSERR_ALLOCATED, DSERR_NODRIVER, DSERR_INVALIDPARAM, DSERR_NOAGGREGATION or DSERR_OUTOFMEMORY value is returned:

All that remains now is to check whether this SetCooperativeLevel function failed; if it did we have to release all devices to deallocate the existing DirectSound object:

```
if FAILED(hresult_)
{
    lpDirectSound->Release();
    return FALSE;
}
```

The created DirectSound object has its own primary buffer. The only situation where we are required to setup our own primary buffer is when the cooperation level is set to the highest priority. We are, however, required to set up secondary buffers for the storage of sounds waiting to be played.

The CreateSoundBuffer IDirectSound8 interface function, declared as follows in the dsound.h header file, is called to create a sound buffer:

```
HRESULT CreateSoundBuffer(
    LPCDSBUFFERDESC pcDSBufferDesc,
    LPDIRECTSOUNDBUFFER * ppdirectSoundBufferuffer,
    LPUNKNOWN pUnkOuter
);
```

This function's first parameter, pcDSBufferDesc, is the address of the DirectSound buffer description structure. This buffer, of the type DSBUFFERDESC, specifies the properties of the buffer object. The second parameter, ppdirectSoundBuffer, is a pointer to the sound buffer (the IDirectSoundBuffer interface object) with the pUnkOuter parameter the COM aggregation (always 'NULL').

The DSBUFFERDESC structure, describing the buffer object, is declared as follows:

```
typedef struct DSBUFFERDESC {
    DWORD dwSize;
    DWORD dwFlags;
    DWORD dwBufferBytes;
    DWORD dwReserved;
    LPWAVEFORMATEX lpwfxFormat;
    GUID guid3DAlgorithm;
} DSBUFFERDESC;
```

Its first member describes the size of the structure in bytes. The second member, dwFlags, is a control flag detailing the capabilities of the sound buffer (the most common flags are listed in Table 16-1). The dwBufferBytes member is the sound buffer's size in bytes with the dwReserved member unused (always set to '0'). The second last member, lpwfxFormat, is the address of a WAVEFORMATEX or WAVEFORMATEXTENSIBLE structure containing a description of the sound stored in the buffer. The final member, guid3DAlgorithm, is a unique identifier of the preferred speaker virtualization algorithm to use when DirectSound3D hardware emulation is enabled – must be set to DS3DALG_DEFAULT when the dwFlags member is set to DSBCAPS_CTRL3D (alternative values are listed in Table 16-2).

16

TABLE 16-1	The most common DirectSound secondary buffer creation flags

Flag	Description
DSBCAPS_CTRL3D	Gives the buffer 3D control capabilities.
DSBCAPS_CTRLFREQUENCY	Enables frequency control.
DSBCAPS_CTRLFX	Adds support for effect processing.
DSBCAPS_CTRLPAN	Enables pan control.
DSBCAPS_CTRLVOLUME	Adds volume control to the buffer.
DSBCAPS_GLOBALFOCUS	Sets the buffer as a global sound buffer – the application continues playing sound even if focus is switched to another application also using DirectSound.
DSBCAPS_LOCHARDWARE	Enables hardware mixing for the buffer.
DSBCAPS_LOCSOFTWARE	Forces the buffer to be created in software memory and to use software mixing.
DSBCAPS_PRIMARYBUFFER	Flags the buffer as a primary buffer.
DSBCAPS_STATIC	Forces the buffer to be created in the sound card's memory.

TABLE 16-2	Unique identifiers of the two-speaker virtualization algorithm

Value	Description
DS3DALG_DEFAULT	DirectSound uses the default algorithm.
DS3DALG_HRTF_FULL	A high quality 3D sound algorithm is used.
DS3DALG_HRTF_LIGHT	An efficient 3D sound algorithm is used.
DS3DALG_NO_VIRTUALIZATION	The 3D audio is mapped to the normal left and right speaker configuration – for example, a sound positioned 90 degrees to the right will only play on the right speaker.

Returning to the DSBUFFERDESC structure's lpwfxFormat member – the address of a WAVEFORMATEX structure containing a description of the sound loaded in the buffer. This structure must be set up as part of the DSBUFFERDESC structure and is declared as follows in the mmreg.h header file:

```
typedef struct WAVEFORMATEX {
    WORD wFormatTag;
    WORD nChannels;
    DWORD nSamplesPerSec;
    DWORD nAvgBytesPerSec;
    WORD nBlockAlign;
    WORD wBitsPerSample;
    WORD cbSize;
} WAVEFORMATEX;
```

16

The first member of the WAVEFORMATEX structure sets the waveform-audio format type (we'll always set this member to WAVE_FORMAT_PCM). The second member, nChannels, sets the number of audio channels – one for mono and two for stereo. The nSamplesPerSec member sets the playback sample rate in Hz (44.1kHz for example). The fourth member, nAvgBytesPerSec, is concerned with the average data transfer rate, in bytes per second. The nBlockAlign member is the block alignment of the data – it is calculated by multiplying the value stored in the nChannels member with the bytes per sample. The second last member, wBitsPerSample, is the number of bits per sample with the cbSize member the size in bytes of additional format information related to non-PCM (wave) formats – we'll always set it to '0' for .wav files.

We can now use the CreateSoundBuffer IDirectSound8 interface function and above described structures to create a secondary sound buffer:

```
HRESULT CreateSoundBuffer(LPDIRECTSOUND8 lpDirectSound,
                          LPDIRECTSOUNDBUFFER8* ppDirectSoundBuffer)
{
    /* declare the WAVEFORMATEX structure which will be used to
       hold the format description */
    WAVEFORMATEX pcmWaveFormat;

    /* declare the DirectSound buffer description structure*/
    DSBUFFERDESC dsBufferDescStruct;

    /* a pointer to the DirectSound buffer */
    LPDIRECTSOUNDBUFFER pdirectSoundBuffer = NULL;

    /* initialize the members of the WAVEFORMATEX structure*/
    memset(&pcmWaveFormat, 0, sizeof(WAVEFORMATEX));
    pcmWaveFormat.wFormatTag = WAVE_FORMAT_PCM;
    pcmWaveFormat.nSamplesPerSec = 22050;
    pcmWaveFormat.nChannels = 2;
    pcmWaveFormat.wBitsPerSample = 16;
    pcmWaveFormat.nBlockAlign = 4;
    pcmWaveFormat.nAvgBytesPerSec = pcmWaveFormat.nSamplesPerSec *
                                    pcmWaveFormat.nBlockAlign;

    /* initialize the members of the DSBUFFERDESC structure*/
    memset(&dsBufferDescStruct, 0, sizeof(DSBUFFERDESC));
    dsBufferDescStruct.dwSize = sizeof(DSBUFFERDESC);
    dsBufferDescStruct.dwFlags = DSBCAPS_CTRLPAN |
                                 DSBCAPS_CTRLVOLUME |
                                 DSBCAPS_CTRLFREQUENCY;
    dsBufferDescStruct.dwBufferBytes = 44100; //2 seconds at
                                              //22050 Hz
    dsBufferDescStruct.lppcmWaveFormatFormat= &pcmWaveFormat;

    /* create the secondary buffer */
    HRESULT hresult_ = lpDirectSound
                       ->CreateSoundBuffer(&dsBufferDescStruct,
                                           &pdirectSoundBuffer,
                                           NULL);
```

16

```
    if(FAILED(hresult_))
    {
        /* error */
        pdirectSoundBuffer->Release();
    }
    else
    {
        /* the IDirectSoundBuffer8 interface to return */
        hresult_ = pdirectSoundBuffer
                    ->QueryInterface(IID_IDirectSoundBuffer8,
                                    (LPVOID*)ppDirectSoundBuffer);
        pdirectSoundBuffer->Release();
    }
    return hresult_;
}
```

With the secondary buffer created and passed to the direct sound buffer, we only have to write the audio data (that should be played) to it. The created secondary buffer can be reused for different sounds; however, most DirectSound application will write to a secondary buffer only once. Sound is loaded into the buffer during a three-phase process:

1 Lock the buffer so that data can be written to it.

2 Write the sound data to the buffer.

3 Unlock (release) the buffer.

The buffer is locked and prepared for a data write via the Lock IDirectSoundBuffer8 interface function. The prototype of this function is declared in the dsound.h header:

```
HRESULT Lock(
    DWORD dwOffset,
    DWORD dwBytes,
    LPVOID * ppvAudioPtrl,
    LPDWORD pdwAudioBytesl,
    LPVOID * ppvAudioPtr2,
    LPDWORD pdwAudioBytes2,
    DWORD dwFlags
);
```

The dwOffset parameter sets the write cursor's offset, in bytes – i.e. the position from the start of the buffer where the lock should begin. The dwBytes parameter is the size, in bytes, of the buffer to lock with the ppvAudioPtrl parameter a pointer to a variable storing the pointer to the start of the lock. The next parameter, pdwAudioBytesl, is a pointer to the variable receiving the specified number of bytes at ppvAudioPtrl. The fifth parameter, ppvAudioPtr2, holds a pointer to a variable storing the pointer to the second part of the lock, with pdwAudioBytes2 a pointer to the variable receiving the specified number of bytes at ppvAudioPtr2. The final parameter, dwFlags, details how the buffer should be locked, either entirely (DSBLOCK_ENTIREBUFFER) or from the write cursor (DSBLOCK_FROMWRITECURSOR).

16

Some of the audio data are written to the first pointer with the rest to the second. Upon completion of this write process, we can release the locked buffer by means of the Unlock IDirectSoundBuffer8 interface function. This function is declared as follows:

```
HRESULT Unlock(
    LPVOID pvAudioPtrl,
    DWORD dwAudioBytesl,
    LPVOID pvAudioPtr2,
    DWORD dwAudioBytes2
);
```

Its first parameter, pvAudioPtrl, is a pointer to a variable storing the pointer to the start of the lock (as retrieved by Lock) with its second parameter, dwAudioBytesl, the number of bytes written at pvAudioPtrl. Similarly, pvAudioPtr2 is a pointer to a variable storing the pointer to the second part of the lock with dwAudioBytes2 the number of bytes written at pvAudioPtr2.

The following code sample illustrates the loading of data into a secondary buffer:

```
/* pointer to the DirectSound buffer */
LPDIRECTSOUNDBUFFER pdirectSoundBuffer;

/* pointers to retrieve buffer memory */
UCHAR * audioPointerl;
UCHAR * audioPointer2;

/* length of each buffer segment */
int audioLengthl;
int audioLength2;

/* lock the buffer */
hresult_ = pdirectSoundBuffer->Lock(0,
                        1000,
                        (void **) &&audioPointerl,
                        &audioLengthl,
                        (void **) &&audioPointer2,
                        audioLength2,
                        DSBLOCK_ENTIREBUFFER);

/* test whether the Lock call succeeded */
if(FAILED(hresult_))
{
     /* error */
}
/* write into the buffer, pAudioData is a pointer to the audio
    file */
memcpy(audioLengthl, pAudioData, audioLengthl);

/* after writing to the buffer, unlock it */
hresult_ = pdirectSoundBuffer->Unlock(audioPointerl,
                        audioLengthl,
                        audioPointer2,
                        audioLength2);
```

TABLE 16-3	Flags specifying the playback of a buffer
Flag	**Description**
DSBPLAY_LOCHARDWARE	Only valid for buffers created with the DSBCAPS_LOCDEFER flag – plays the audio in hardware buffer mode.
DSBPLAY_LOOPING	After the file has finished playing, replay it from the start.
DSBPLAY_LOCSOFTWARE	Only valid for buffers created with the DSBCAPS_LOCDEFER flag – plays the audio in software buffer mode.
DSBPLAY_TERMINATEBY_PRIORITY	Only valid for buffers created with the DSBCAPS_LOCDEFER flag – terminates a current playing nonlooping buffer to play the new buffer. The buffer with the lowest priority (as set by the dwPriority parameter) is terminated.
DSBPLAY_TERMINATEBY_TIME	Only valid for buffers created with the DSBCAPS_LOCDEFER flag – terminates a current playing nonlooping buffer to play the new buffer. The buffer with the least amount of playtime left is terminated.

The next step is to actually play the buffer. This is done by calling the Play IDirectSoundBuffer8 interface function. This function is declared as follows in the dsound.h header file:

```
HRESULT Play(
    DWORD dwReservedl,
    DWORD dwPriority,
    DWORD dwFlags
);
```

The first parameter is reserved and thus always set to '0' with the second, dwPriority, controlling the priority of the playback – the buffer must be created with the DSBCAPS_LOCDEFER flag for this to work, else this parameter must be set to '0'. The final parameter, dwFlags, controls the buffer playback. The most common flags are listed in Table 16-3.

The following code snippet will play a sound sample over and over:

```
/* set the position of the play cursor */
pdirectSoundBuffer->SetCurrentPosition(0);

/* play the sound */
hresult_ = pdirectSoundBuffer->Play(0, 0, DSBPLAY_LOOPING);

/* test whether the play operation failed */
if(FAILED(hresult_))
{
    /* error */
}
```

16

We might also want to stop a sound before it has finished playing. The Stop IDirectSoundBuffer8 interface function can be used to do this:

```
/* stop the sound */
hresult_ = pdirectSoundBuffer->Stop();

/* test whether the stop operation failed */
if(FAILED(hresult_))
{
    /* error */
}
```

Games also need control over the volume of sounds; for example, the sound of footsteps far away should not be audible and their volume should increase linearly as they near the player. Volume is controlled via the SetVolume IDirectSoundBuffer8 interface function. This function takes one parameter – the attenuation in hundredths of a decibel. Setting the volume to '0' will result in maximum volume (no attenuation). An attenuation of -5000 will in turn set the attenuation to -50 decibels with a value of $-10\,000$ setting the attenuation to -100 decibels, resulting in complete silence:

```
/* set the audio to 50% full volume */
hresult_ = pdirectSoundBuffer->SetVolume(DSVOLUME_TO_DB(50));
```

Another useful feature is the ability to get the current volume or attenuation of the sound. The GetVolume IDirectSoundBuffer8 interface function can be used for this purpose. It takes one parameter, the address of the variable to receive this attenuation:

```
/* the variable to receive the attenuation */
long volume;

/* get the attenuation of the sound */
hresult_ = pdirectSoundBuffer->GetVolume(&volume);
```

We also have to test both the GetVolume and SetVolume operations for failure.

The next step is actually loading sound files from disk. DirectSound unfortunately lacks a native audio file loader and we will thus have to write our own conforming to the audio format being used (such as .wav, .mp3, and.ogg). This sounds easier than it is – audio files are very complex and the code for such a file loader will easily take up several pages with the related discussion more than half a chapter. Many audio file loaders are available on the internet and we will be making use of DirectSound's Sample Utility Framework classes for the loading and playback of .wav files (via the DXUTsound.cpp file). The sample utility classes, included with the DirectX SDK, provide basic functionality for the SDK samples.

We will now look at loading wav data into our created buffer. The .wav format is a Windows audio format based on Electronic Arts' original .IFF or *Interchange File Format*. A .wav file is an audio file where the sound data are encoded in a basic header/data structure. Reading one of these files requires a lot of header parsing and the subsequent extraction of audio data – a process requiring a significant amount of code. The CWaveFile sample class (provided as part of the DirectSound sample utility classes) is used for reading audio data from and/or writing sound data to wav files. It is declared as follows in the SDKwavefile.h header:

```
class CWaveFile
{
public:
```

```
    WAVEFORMATEX*        m_pwfx;            //pointer to WAVEFORMATEX structure
    HMMIO                m_hmmio;           //MM I/O handle for the WAVE
    MMCKINFO             m_ck;              //multimedia RIFF chunk
    MMCKINFO             m_ckRiff;          //use in opening a WAVE file
    DWORD                m_dwSize;          //the size of the wave file
    MMIOINFO             m_mmioinfoOut;
    DWORD                m_dwFlags;
    BOOL                 m_bIsReadingFromMemory;
    BYTE*                m_pbData;
    BYTE*                m_pbDataCur;
    ULONG                m_ulDataSize;
    CHAR*                m_pResourceBuffer;
protected:
    HRESULT ReadMMIO();
    HRESULT WriteMMIO(WAVEFORMATEX *pwfxDest);

public:
    CWaveFile();
    ~CWaveFile();

    HRESULT Open(LPWSTR strFileName, WAVEFORMATEX* pwfx,
                 DWORD dwFlags);
    HRESULT OpenFromMemory(BYTE* pbData, ULONG ulDataSize,
                           WAVEFORMATEX* pwfx, DWORD dwFlags);
    HRESULT Close();

    HRESULT Read(BYTE* pBuffer, DWORD dwSizeToRead,
                 DWORD* pdwSizeRead);
    HRESULT Write(UINT nSizeToWrite, BYTE* pbData,
                  UINT* pnSizeWrote);

    DWORD GetSize();
    HRESULT ResetFile();
    WAVEFORMATEX* GetFormat() {return m_pwfx;};
};
```

A number of member functions are of importance to us: the Close function is used to close a file whenever data have been written to it; the Open function opens a file for either reading or writing (its strFileName parameter being the wave file's name, with the pwfx parameter ignored when reading a file and set to the format of the data to write if capturing data, while the dwFlags parameter must be set to WAVEFILE_READ to read from a file, or to WAVEFILE_WRITE to write to it). Another useful function is the Read method. This function parses data from the audio file, copying it to a specified buffer address – its dwSizeToRead parameter sets the write pointer position to the number of bytes specified. The ResetFile method is used to reset the audio file to the beginning of the data chunk with the Write function used for writing data from the buffer to a file. It is also useful to determine the format of the waveform as described via the WAVEFORMATEX structure – we can call the GetFormat function to access these data.

The following function uses the CWaveFile helper class to open a wave file:

```
VOID OpenWavFile(TCHAR* waveFileName)
{
```

16

```
/* declare the CWaveFile object */
CWaveFile waveFileObj;

/* variable to hold the retrieved samples per second */
DWORD dwSampleRate = 0;

/* a buffer to hold the wave file name */
TCHAR tempFileName[MAX_PATH];

/* the amount of data read from the wav file */
DWORD dwWaveDataSize;

HRESULT hresult_;

/* access and load the wave file into memory */
if(FAILED(hresult_ = waveFileObj.Open(wavFileName, NULL,
                                WAVEFILE_READ)))
{
    /* the load call failed */
    cout << "error opening file:" << hresult_;
    waveFileObj.Close();
}
else
{
    /* the load call succeeded — we can now load this audio
       file into the previously created secondary buffer,
       specifically passing a variable storing the pointer
       to the start of the lock and the size of the locked
       buffer as parameters */
    hresult_ = waveFileObj.Read((BYTE*)audioPointer1,
                            audioLength1,
                            &dwWaveDataSize);

    /* some examples of other operations that can be
       performed on the open file */
    ////////////////////////////////

    /* copy the received wave file name */
    StringCchCopy(tempFileName, MAX_PATH, wavFileName);

    /* determine the wave file's sample rate */
    if(waveFileObj.m_pwfx)
        dwSampleRate = waveFileObj.m_pwfx->nSamplesPerSec;

    /* close the open file */
    waveFileObj.Close();
}
}
```

We can now simply call this function with the name of the wave file to open and load into the secondary buffer:

```
OpenWavFile("test.wav");
```

With the wave data loaded into the secondary buffer, we can play it using the Play IDirectSoundBuffer8 interface function as previously explained.

16.2.2 XACT

XACT is more than just an audio API, it is a complete high-level engine and library for the authoring and playback of audio via XAudio exclusive to the Xbox, DirectSound for older versions of Windows and the session-based audio stack in Windows Vista. XACT also features a helper library for 3D audio spatialization, namely, X3DAudio.

XACT supports the following file formats: .wav, .aiff and .xma. It also has support for 5.1 surround sound as well as the grouping and queuing of sounds in so called wave and sound banks, respectively. The terminology used by the XACT library and documentation is outlined in Table 16-4.

The XACT Audio Creation Tool shown in Figure 16-9, shipped with the DirectX SDK, arranges audio files into so-called wave banks. It is typically used to construct and organize the data files needed for the

TABLE 16-4	XACT terminology
XACT terminology	**Description**
Sound banks	A collection of sounds and cues arranged by the sound designer. Sound banks don't contain any wave data and are rather used to control the playback of wave data. Each sound bank is stored in a file with the extension '.xsb'.
Wave banks	A collection of waves grouped into a file by the sound designer. Each wave bank is stored in a file with the extension '.xwb'.
Global settings	A way to define rules for the control of sounds.
Waves	The raw audio data stored in a .wav or .aiff sound file.
Sounds	Sounds, as located in a sound bank, defining the playback of waves.
Track	A collection of events making up a sound.
Event	The action to perform on a sound, for example, a play event or volume change event.
Cue	A trigger for an event.
Categories	The grouping of various sounds to control their properties in a unified manner; for example, several sounds can be assigned to a category where they all have the same pitch, volume, etc.
DSPs	Effect path presets that allow the modification of sound parameters such as pitch and/or volume changes.
Compression presets	Presets allowing certain compression techniques to be applied to the data in the wave banks.

16

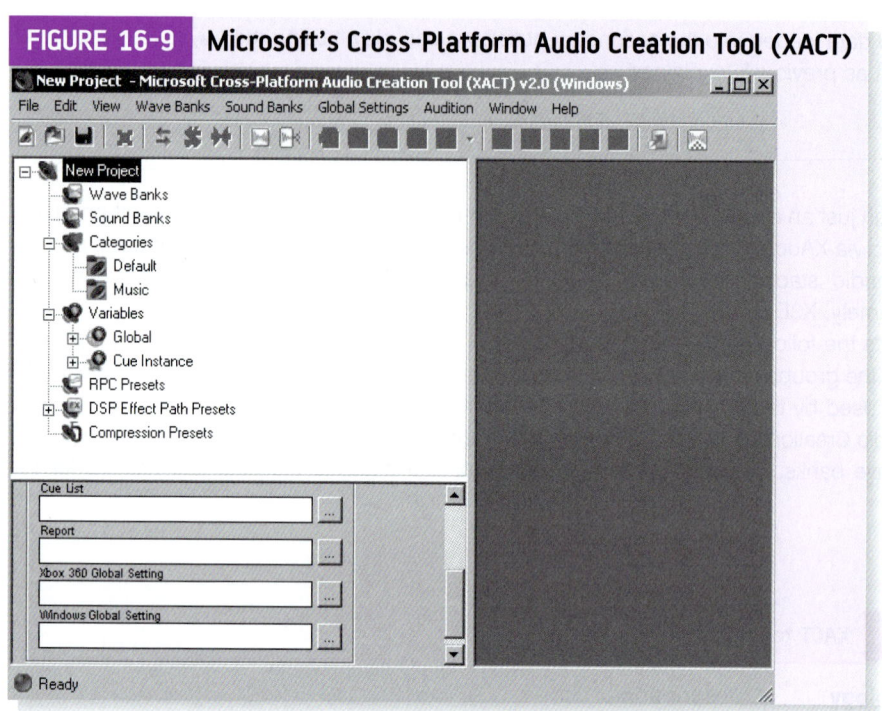

FIGURE 16-9   Microsoft's Cross-Platform Audio Creation Tool (XACT)

integration of the XACT audio resources. The XACT Audio Creation Tool has the ability to dynamically modify the sounds of a running game. It is also used for the creation of sound banks, wave banks, cues, etc.

The XACT-created wave, sound, and cue data can now be integrated into an application. We will, however, focus on the XACT core library for the lower level audio playback and authoring without use of the XACT Audio Creation Tool.

The general steps for setting up and playing audio via the XACT API are:

1   Initialize the XACT sound engine.

2   Initialize an IXACTWave interface by first reading the .wave file into memory and then initializing the WAVEBANKENTRY XACT wave bank structure.

3   Create an IXACTWave interface with the loaded wave data. This is done via the PrepareInMemoryWave IXACTEngine interface function.

4   Play the wave file using the Play IXACTWave interface function.

5   When finished using, destroy the IXACTEngine interface.

The XACT sound engine is initialized via the Initialize IXACTEngine interface function. This function is declared as follows in the xact.h header file:

16

```
HRESULT Initialize(
    const XACT_RUNTIME_PARAMETERS *pParams
);
```

This function takes a pointer to an XACT_RUNTIME_PARAMETERS structure as parameter. The XACT_RUNTIME_PARAMETERS is in turn declared as follows:

```
typedef struct XACT_RUNTIME_PARAMETERS {
    DWORD lookAheadTime;
    void *pGlobalSettingsBuffer;
    DWORD globalSettingsBufferSize;
    DWORD globalSettingsFlags;
    DWORD globalSettingsAllocAttributes;
    XACT_FILEIO_CALLBACKS fileIOCallbacks;
    XACT_NOTIFICATION_CALLBACK fnNotificationCallback;
    PWSTR pRendererID;
} XACT_RUNTIME_PARAMETERS, *LPXACT_RUNTIME_PARAMETERS;
typedef const XACT_RUNTIME_PARAMETERS*LPCXACT_RUNTIME_PARAMETERS;
```

Its first member describes the look-ahead time in milliseconds – i.e. the amount of milliseconds the XACT audio engine will look ahead when calculating the point at which to play another sound. The second member, pGlobalSettingsBuffer, is a buffer containing the file data generated during the XACT project creation stage. The globalSettingsBufferSize is the size of the buffer containing the file data with the globalSettingsFlags member controlling how the XACT file should be handled by the audio engine (can be set to '0' or to XACT_FLAG_API_CREATE_MANAGEDATA when the buffer pointed to by the pGlobalSettingsBuffer member should be freed following initialization). The next member, globalSettingsAllocAttributes, sets some attributes of the buffer pointed to by the pGlobalSettingsBuffer member – this member is only relevant when working with the Xbox 360 and can thus be ignored for Windows-based applications. The next two members, fileIOCallbacks and fnNotificationCallback, set the file I/O callbacks and the callback that receives notifications, respectively. The final member, pRendererID, is the ID of the audio device that should be connected to. This ID is contained within the XACT_RENDERER_DETAILS structure declared as follows in the xact.h header file:

```
typedef struct XACT_RENDERER_DETAILS {
    WCHAR rendererID[XACT_RENDERER_ID_LENGTH];
    WCHAR displayName[XACT_RENDERER_NAME_LENGTH];
    BOOL defaultDevice;
} XACT_RENDERER_DETAILS, *LPXACT_RENDERER_DETAILS;
```

The XACT_RENDERER_DETAILS structure holds the id of the audio device (rendererID), the name of the device (displayName) and a Boolean value indicating whether it is the default device (defaultDevice).

We start the XACT initialization process by querying the audio device that should be used and connected to by declaring a XACT_RENDERER_DETAILS structure and calling the GetRendererDetails IXACTEngine interface function (it takes two parameters, the index of the device to retrieve information from and a pointer to a XACT_RENDERER_DETAILS structure). This is followed by the initialization of the XACT_RUNTIME_-PARAMETERS structure's members and initialization of the XACT sound engine via the Initialize IXACTEngine interface function:

```
/* declare an XACT engine object */
IXACTEngine* ppXACTEngineObj = NULL;
```

16

```
/* declare a XACT_RENDERER_DETAILS structure to hold the id of
   the audio device, etc */
XACT_RENDERER_DETAILS deviceDetails = {0};
hresult_ = (*ppXACTEngineObj)
                      ->GetRendererDetails(0, &deviceDetails);

/* setup required members of the XACT_RUNTIME_PARAMETERS
   structure*/
XACT_RUNTIME_PARAMETERS xactRuntimeParams = {0};

xactRuntimeParams.fnNotificationCallback = NULL;
xactRuntimeParams.lookAheadTime =XACT_ENGINE_LOOKAHEAD_DEFAULT;
xactRuntimeParams.pRendererID = rendererDetails.rendererID;

/* initialize the XACT engine */
hresult_ = (*ppXACTEngineObj)->Initialize(&xactRuntimeParams);
```

We can now load the .wav file into memory followed by initialization of the WAVEBANKENTRY XACT wave bank structure – two steps required during the IXACTWave interface setup stage.

The WAVEBANKENTRY structure must be initialized when loading PCM/wave audio data into memory. This structure describes an XACT wave bank and is declared in the xact2wb.h header file:

```
typedef struct WAVEBANKENTRY {
    union {
      struct {
          DWORD dwFlags : 4;
          DWORD Duration : 28;
      };
      DWORD dwFlagsAndDuration;
    };
    WAVEBANKMINIWAVEFORMAT Format;
    WAVEBANKREGION PlayRegion;
    WAVEBANKSAMPLEREGION LoopRegion;
} WAVEBANKENTRY, *LPWAVEBANKENTRY;
```

The first member, dwFlags, controls some of the wave bank's properties, for instance, setting it to the value WAVEBANKENTRY_FLAGS_LOOPCACHE indicates that the wave is used by at least one looping sound – we'll always set this one to '0'. The Duration member contains the length or duration of the wave in sample units, for example, the duration of a 20- second-long wave sampled at 24Khz would be 480 000. The dwFlagsAndDuration value is used to represent both the dwFlags and Duration members. The final three members are all structures describing the wave format (Format), the area within the wave data fragment containing the wave bank entry (PlayRegion) and region of the wave data to loop (LoopRegion). The structure types of these members are defined in the xact2wb.h header file:

```
typedef union WAVEBANKMINIWAVEFORMAT {
    struct {
        DWORD wFormatTag : 1;
        DWORD nChannels : 3;
        DWORD nSamplesPerSec : 27;
```

```
        DWORD wBitsPerSample : 1;
    };
    DWORD dwValue;
} WAVEBANKMINIWAVEFORMAT, *LPWAVEBANKMINIWAVEFORMAT;

typedef struct WAVEBANKREGION {
    DWORD dwOffset;
    DWORD dwLength;
} WAVEBANKREGION, *LPWAVEBANKREGION;

typedef struct WAVEBANKSAMPLEREGION {
    DWORD dwStartSample;
    DWORD dwTotalSamples;
} WAVEBANKSAMPLEREGION, *LPWAVEBANKSAMPLEREGION;
```

The first structure, WAVEBANKMINIWAVEFORMAT, has five members, the first specifying the format of the wave file (WAVEBANKMINIFORMAT_TAG_PCM for PCM wave files or WAVEBANKMINIFORMAT_TAG_XMA for Microsoft's .xma file format). Its second member, nChannels, represents the number of audio channels in the wave file – 1 to 16. The nSamplesPerSec member contains the wave file's sample rate with the wBitsPerSample member holding the wave file's bit depth and it can be set to either 8-bit (WAVEBANKMINIFORMAT_BITDEPTH_8) or 16-bit (WAVEBANKMINIFORMAT_BITDEPTH_16). The final member, dwValue, is unused.

The next structure, WAVEBANKREGION, has two members, the first (dwOffset) setting the wave bank region information in bytes and the second (dwLength) setting the region length. The WAVEBANKSAMPLEREGION structure's first parameter, dwStartSample, specifies the start sample for the wave bank region and the second, dwTotalSamples, the wave bank region's length in terms of samples.

We can now load a wave file into memory by first opening the file (using the Win32 platform SDK CreateFile function – its parameters are as follows: the name of the object to create or open, access to the object such as read or write, sharing properties of the file, security attributes, action to take on files that exist, file attributes such as whether the file should be hidden, encrypted, archived, etc., and a handle to a template file):

```
/* open the audio file – the returned handle is used to access
    the file */
HANDLE fileHandle = CreateFile("one.wav", GENERIC_READ, 0,
                            NULL, OPEN_EXISTING, 0, 0);

/* handle the event where the file has not been found */
if(fileHandle == INVALID_HANDLE_VALUE)
    cout << "file not found" << endl;
```

Following this, we initialize the members of the WAVEBANKENTRY structure:

```
/* calculate the total number of bytes for initialization of
    the dwLength member (audio file's length in seconds * its
    sample rate * number of channels * its bitrate) */
DWORD dwWaveBankRegionLength = 5 * 44100 * 1 * 16 / 8;

/* initialize the members of the WAVEBANKENTRY structure */
WAVEBANKENTRY waveBankEntry;
```

16

```
waveBankEntry.Format.wFormatTag = WAVEBANKMINIFORMAT_TAG_PCM;
waveBankEntry.Format.wBitsPerSample = WAVEBANKMINIFORMAT_BITDEPTH_16;
waveBankEntry.Format.nChannels = 1;

//channels * (bitrate / 8)
waveBankEntry.Format.wBlockAlign = 1 * (16 / 8);
waveBankEntry.Format.nSamplesPerSec = 44100;

//file duration in seconds * sample rate
waveBankEntry.Duration = 5 * 44100;
waveBankEntry.LoopRegion.dwStartSample = 0;
waveBankEntry.LoopRegion.dwTotalSamples = 0;
waveBankEntry.PlayRegion.dwOffset = 0;
waveBankEntry.PlayRegion.dwLength = dwWaveBankRegionLength;
waveBankEntry.dwFlags = 0;
```

Next we can read the wave data from the file into a buffer (using the Win32 platform SDK ReadFile function – its parameters are as follows: a handle to the file being read, a pointer to the buffer receiving the data, number of bytes to read, a pointer to the variable receiving the number of bytes read with its last parameter set to 'NULL'):

```
/* define a buffer to hold the wave data */
BYTE* pwaveBuffer = new BYTE[dwWaveBankRegionLength];

/* variable receiving the number of bytes read */
DWORD dwNumberBytesRead = 0;

/* read the audio data from a file, first skipping the
   'format' section in the wave file and then loading it into
   our defined wave data buffer */
ReadFile(fileHandle, pwaveBuffer, 44, &dwNumberBytesRead,
        NULL );
/* read the wave data into a buffer */
ReadFile(fileHandle, pwaveBuffer, dwWaveBankRegionLength,
        &dwNumberBytesRead, NULL);
```

An in-memory IXACTWave object can now be created using this data. We use the PrepareInMemoryWave IXACTEngine interface function for this purpose. This function is declared as follows in the xact.h header file:

```
HRESULT PrepareInMemoryWave(
    DWORD dwFlags,
    WAVEBANKENTRY entry,
    DWORD *pdwSeekTable,
    BYTE *pbWaveData,
    DWORD dwPlayOffset,
    XACTLOOPCOUNT nLoopCount,
    IXACTWave **ppWave
);
```

16

Its first parameter, dwFlags, controls wave properties such as whether the wave data are passed in as samples (XACT_FLAG_UNITS_SAMPLES) or measured in milliseconds (XACT_FLAG_UNITS_MS). The entry parameter is the WAVEBANKENTRY structure describing the loop region, format and play region of the loaded wave with the pdwSeekTable parameter a pointer to a seek table only valid for .xma files and pbWaveData a pointer to the wave data. The dwPlayOffset parameter is the offset in milliseconds or in samples to position the play cursor at (hence the position to start the wave at) with the nLoopCount parameter the wave's loop count. The final parameter, ppWave, is a pointer to the IXACTWave object.

Creating an in-memory IXACTWave object using the data loaded into memory requires only a single call to the PrepareInMemoryWave function:

```
/* declare the IXACTWave object */
IXACTWave* pXACTWaveObj = NULL;

hresult_ = ppXACTEngineObj
                   ->PrepareInMemoryWave(XACT_FLAG_UNITS_MS,
                         waveBankEntry,
                         NULL,
                         &pwaveBuffer,
                         0, 0,
                         &pXACTWaveObj);
```

The final step is to play the in-memory wave file using the Play IXACTWave interface function:

```
pXACTWaveObj->Play();
```

After we have finished using the IXACTEngine interface, we need to deallocate the IXACTEngine object:

```
ppXACTEngineObj->ShutDown();
ppXACTEngineObj->Release();
```

16.2.3 XAudio2

XAudio2 is a new, still underdevelopment (at the time of writing) cross-platform, low-level audio API for unified code development under Windows XP, Windows Vista and the Xbox 360 gaming console. XAudio2 serves as replacement of DirectSound and as an extended version of the XAudio API for Xbox 360 development. All code developed using the XAudio2 API is exactly the same for both the Xbox and Windows platforms – thus resulting in a 'write once, compile twice' implementation.

The general steps for setting up and playing audio via the XAudio2 API are as follows:

1 Initialize the XAudio2 sound engine.

2 Create a mastering voice to control the mixing format of all audio played by the application.

3 Load the wave file to play.

4 Create a source voice and load the audio data into it.

5 Play the source voice.

6 Cleanup the source voice and all associated data.

7 When finished using, release the XAudio2 engine.

16

The XAudio2 sound engine is initialized via the XAudio2Create function. This function creates a XAudio2 object, returning an IXAudio2 interface pointer which is used to manage the sound engine's state, processing, etc. The XAudio2Create function is declared as follows in the xaudio2.h header file:

```
HRESULT XAudio2Create(
    IXAudio2 **ppXAudio2,
    UINT32 Flags,
    IXAudio2EngineCallback *pCallback,
    XAUDIO2_PROCESSOR XAudio2Processor
);
```

Its first parameter, ppXAudio2, holds the returned IXAudio2 object pointer. The second parameter, Flags, is used to control the behaviour of the XAudio2 engine (can currently only be set to XAUDIO2_DEBUG_ENGINE to initialize the debug version of the XAudio2 engine). The pCallback parameter is a pointer to an IXAudio2EngineCallback object responsible for notifying the client whenever a certain XAudio2 engine event occurs. The final parameter, XAudio2Processor, is an enumeration value controlling CPU utilization (for instance, XAUDIO2_MAX_PROCESSOR to utilize the maximum number of processors, or XAUDIO2_DEFAULT_PROCESSOR for the default).

XAudio2 initialization starts with declaration of the IXAudio2 interface object followed by a XAudio2Create function call:

```
/* declare an IXAudio2 interface object */
IXAudio2* pXAudio2Obj = NULL;

/* create a XAudio2 object, saving the returned IXAudio2
   interface object in the pXAudio2Obj variable */
hresult_ = XAudio2Create(&pXAudio2Obj, XAUDIO2_DEBUG_ENGINE,
                    NULL, XAUDIO2_DEFAULT_PROCESSOR);

/* test whether the XAudio2 object creation failed */
if(FAILED(hresult_))
{
    /* error handling code */
}
```

We create and configure a so-called mastering voice using the CreateMasteringVoice IXAudio2 function:

```
HRESULT CreateMasteringVoice(
    IXAudio2MasteringVoice **ppMasteringVoice,
    UINT32 InputChannels,
    UINT32 InputSampleRate,
    UINT32 Flags,
    UINT32 uDeviceIndex,
    const XAUDIO2_EFFECT_CHAIN *pEffectChain
);
```

16

Its first parameter holds the returned IXAudio2MasteringVoice object pointer. This IXAudio2MasteringVoice interface is, for instance, used to set the overall playback volume, or the volume per channel, etc. The next parameter, InputChannels, is the sound clip's number of audio channels with the InputSampleRate parameter, the clip's sample rate. The Flags parameter is always set to '0' with uDeviceIndex an index specifying the output device. The final parameter, pEffectChain, details the effects applied to the sound – commonly set to 'NULL'.

To create a mastering voice, we start by declaring an IXAudio2MasteringVoice interface object followed by a CreateMasteringVoice function call:

```
/* declare an IXAudio2MasteringVoice interface object */
IXAudio2MasteringVoice* pMasteringVoiceObj = NULL;

/* create a mastering voice */
hresult_ = pXAudio2Obj
           ->CreateMasteringVoice(&pMasteringVoiceObj,
                          XAUDIO2_DEFAULT_CHANNELS,
                          XAUDIO2_DEFAULT_SAMPLERATE,
                          0, 0, NULL);

/* test whether the mastering voice creation failed */
if(FAILED(hresult_))
{
    /* error handling code */
}
```

Next we read a wave file into memory using the CWaveFile utility class as previously discussed. Following this we have to create a source voice via the IXAudio2SourceVoice interface and CreateSourceVoice IXAudio2 function. The prototype of this function is declared in the xaudio2.h header file:

```
HRESULT CreateSourceVoice(
    IXAudio2SourceVoice **ppSourceVoice,
    const WAVEFORMATEX *pSourceFormat,
    UINT32 Flags,
    float MaxFrequencyRatio,
    IXAudio2VoiceCallback *pCallback,
    const XAUDIO2_VOICE_SENDS *pSendList,
    const XAUDIO2_EFFECT_CHAIN *pEffectChain
);
```

Its first parameter, ppSourceVoice, is a pointer to an IXAudio2SourceVoice interface object responsible for voice filter parameters, voice frequency adjustments, voice looping, etc. The pSourceFormat parameter is a pointer to a WAVEFORMATEX structure containing a description of the sound stored in a buffer, with the Flags parameter controlling the behaviour of the source voice (XAUDIO2_VOICE_NOPITCH to disable pitch control, XAUDIO2_VOICE_USEFILTER to enable a voice filtering effect, or XAUDIO2_VOICE_MUSIC to use the voice for background music). The MaxFrequencyRatio parameter sets the maximum possible voice frequency ratio. The optional pCallback parameter is a pointer to an IXAudio2VoiceCallback object responsible for notifying the client whenever a certain voice event occurs (such as when the end of the audio buffer has been reached). The next two parameters are also optional, the first describing a set of so called destination voices with the second describing the effects to apply to the sound.

16

The source voice is created in the following manner:

```
/* while reading a wave file into memory declare the
   WAVEFORMATEX structure which will be used to hold the
   format description */
WAVEFORMATEX pcmWaveFormat;

/* declare an IXAudio2SourceVoice interface object */
IXAudio2SourceVoice* pSourceVoiceObj;

hresult_ = pXAudio2Obj
             ->CreateSourceVoice(&pSourceVoiceObj,
                         pcmWaveFormat, 0,
                         XAUDIO2_DEFAULT_FREQ_RATIO,
                         NULL, NULL, NULL);
```

Before actually playing the file we need to write the audio data to the source voice. This process starts with the creation and initialization of an XAUDIO2_BUFFER structure declared in the xaudio2.h header:

```
typedef struct XAUDIO2_BUFFER {
    UINT32 Flags;
    UINT32 AudioBytes;
    const BYTE *pAudioData;
    UINT32 PlayBegin;
    UINT32 PlayLength;
    UINT32 LoopBegin;
    UINT32 LoopLength;
    UINT32 LoopCount;
    void *pContext;
} XAUDIO2_BUFFER;
```

The Flags member can be set to either '0' or XAUDIO2_END_OF_STREAM to suppress debug information output. The AudioBytes member is the size of the audio clip in bytes with the pAudioData member being a pointer to the audio data. The PlayBegin member is the index of the first sample that should be played with the PlayLength member specifying the length of the region to play. The next member, LoopBegin, is the first sample that should be looped with the LoopLength member specifying the length of this loop region and LoopCount the number of times to loop. The final member, pContext, is simply a context value that can be passed to the client whenever a callback event occurs.

The following code snippet illustrates the submission of wave data by means of the XAUDIO2_BUFFER structure:

```
/* declare the XAUDIO2_BUFFER structure */
XAUDIO2_BUFFER xaudio2Buffer;

/* pwaveBuffer is the previously defined buffer holding the
   wave data */
xaudio2Buffer.pAudioData = pwaveBuffer;

xaudio2Buffer.Flags = XAUDIO2_END_OF_STREAM;
```

16

```
/* dwWaveBankRegionLength is the size of pwaveBuffer */
xaudio2Buffer.AudioBytes = dwWaveBankRegionLength;
```

With the `XAUDIO2_BUFFER` structure initialized we simply have to submit this buffer data to the source voice using the `SubmitSourceBuffer` `IXAudio2SourceVoice` function:

```
hresult_ = pSourceVoiceObj ->SubmitSourceBuffer(&xaudio2Buffer);

/* test whether the wave data submission failed */
if(FAILED(hresult_))
{
    pSourceVoiceObj->DestroyVoice();
}
```

Following this, the source voice can be played using the `Start` `IXAudio2Voice` function (its first parameter is simply a flag that can be set to force the playback of a pending effect with its second parameter defining the function as part of an operation set – i.e. a group of operations applied simultaneously):

```
hresult_ = pSourceVoiceObj->Start(0, XAUDIO2_COMMIT_NOW);
```

After we have finished using the `IXAudio2SourceVoice` interface object, we need to deallocate it:

```
pSourceVoiceObj->DestroyVoice();
```

We also have to release the `IXAudio2` interface object:

```
pXAudio2Obj->Release();
```

16.3 SUMMARY

The chapter investigated audio playback and control through the use of a soundcard or similar sound output device. It started by considering sound as the propagation of potential and kinetic energy waves, subsequently discussing concepts such as frequency, wavelength, period, direction, speed, and amplitude. Following this we compared digital and synthesized sound, focusing on a number of factors involved with the sampling of audio.

Next we dealt with DirectSound in depth, specifically creating a DirectSound object, creating a sound buffer for the storage and management of sound data, setting the cooperative level of a device, loading wave data, buffer setup and initialization, and the playback of audio files.

Building on this we presented XACT as a complete high-level engine and library for the authoring and playback of audio. We discussed initialization of the XACT sound engine, initialization of its structures for the storage, and playback of wave files, reading wave data from a file into a buffer and the playback of this wave data.

Our discussion of DirectX Audio concluded with the XAudio2 API. We specifically discussed initialization of the XAudio2 sound engine, the creation of a mastering voice to control the mixing format of all audio played by the application, the specification of a source voice and the loading and playback of wave data.

16

The next chapter combines the knowledge and several of the techniques presented throughout the book. It starts by outlining the general design of a game engine followed by the implementation of both an interactive DirectX 10 and OpenGL environment.

16.4 FURTHER READING

The official DirectSound, XACT and XAudio2 documentation is available from Microsoft's msdn2.microsoft.com website. This documentation is also provided with each DirectX SDK distribution.

16.5 EXERCISES

1 Briefly explain the physics of sound.

2 Explain each of the following sound wave properties: frequency, wavelength, period, direction, speed and amplitude.

3 Compare digital to synthesized sound.

4 Why is the Nyquist–Shannon sampling theorem important?

5 What is the purpose of a digital signal processor?

6 When is an IDirectSoundBuffer8 object specified?

7 Following the DirectSound object creation, we must set the cooperative level of the device, why is this important?

8 Describe the purpose of the following code sample:

```
hresult_ = pdirectSoundBuffer
        ->QueryInterface(IID_IDirectSoundBuffer8,
                    (LPVOID*)ppDirectSoundBuffer);
```

9 Write code to load data into a DirectInput secondary buffer.

10 Give a basic initialization for the XACT_RUNTIME_PARAMETERS structure.

11 Describe the WAVEBANKENTRY structure.

12 Write code to read wave data from a file into a buffer.

13 Briefly describe each of the steps for setting up and playing audio via the XAudio2 API.

14 Describe the purpose of the following code sample:

```
hresult_ = pXAudio2Obj
        ->CreateSourceVoice(&pSourceVoiceObj,
                    pcmWaveFormat, 0,
                    XAUDIO2_DEFAULT_FREQ_RATIO,
                    NULL, NULL, NULL);
```

16

CHAPTER 17

Creating an Interactive 3D Environment

LEARNING OBJECTIVES

In this chapter you will learn about:

- Game engine architecture
- Game initialization and shutdown
- The game loop
- Creating an interactive DirectX 10 3D environment
- Creating an interactive OpenGL 3D environment

INTRODUCTION

Chapter 17 combines the knowledge and several of the techniques presented throughout the book. It starts by outlining the general design of a game engine. Focus then shifts to the implementation of two interactive environments, the first a DirectX 10 3D environment featuring mesh-loading, texture mapping, a movable light source, a GUI and stencil shadow volumes with the second an OpenGL implementation featuring blending, alpha masking, physics-based animation (four cloths blowing in the wind), texture mapping, lighting and menu interaction.

17.1 GAME ENGINE ARCHITECTURE

We will now combine the knowledge and techniques presented throughout the book to develop a 3D immersive environment – i.e. a basic 3D renderer. A game engine is the central unit of any computer game and it can be described as a collection of technologies such as a sound engine, AI subsystem, physics engine, networking subsystem, 3D renderer, and input control system. The number of subsystems provided is highly dependent on the developer's requirements and the implementation platform of choice.

Game engines, built upon various APIs such as DirectX and OpenGL, are normally designed with software componentry in mind. This allows for decomposition of the engine, resulting in numerous functional units. By designing component-based engines, we are able to replace provided technologies with other third-party or in-house developed units as needed. For example, a game engine's renderer, physics engine or sound system can easily be replaced by an improved or alternate version in a plug-and-play fashion.

The term 'game engine' existed for some time, but only became truly common in the mid-1990s when developers started licensing the core code of other games for their own titles. This reuse led to the development of high-end commercial game engines and middleware providing game developers with a number of game creation tools and technical components – i.e. accelerating the game development process. The following list gives some idea of what might be supported by a commercially targeted game engine (taken from the *RelentENGINE* technical specifications document):

1 3D engine
   - Direct3D 10 renderer for Microsoft Windows-based systems
   - OpenGL renderer for MacOS X, Linux, Unix, etc
   - HLSL and Cg shader support
   - Normal mapping
   - Environmental mapping
   - Displacement mapping
   - High Dynamic Range lighting
   - Depth-of-field
   - Motion blur
   - Bloom and sobel effects (for older hardware support)
   - Rome algorithmic based Level Of Detail automatic adaptation system
   - Dynamic lighting and shadowing
   - Soft shadows
   - Specular reflections with specular bump maps
   - Reflective water (with refraction)
   - Highly efficient occlusion culling
   - Dynamically deformable and destroyable geometry
   - Cg rendered moving grass, trees, fur, hair, etc.
   - Advanced Particle System: model and sprite based (snow, smoke, sparks, rain, ice storms, fire storms, volumetric clouds, weather system, etc.)
   - NPC Material Interaction System (vehicle sliding on ice, etc.)

2 AI subsystem
   - Cognitive model-based NPC (non-player character, i.e. computer, controlled) AI (no way-point system)
   - Intelligent non-combat and combat NPC interaction
   - Conversation system

- NPCs make decision to fight, dodge, flee, hide, burrow, etc. based on player resistance
- NPCs fall back to regroup if resistance is overwhelming

3 Sound engine
- Stereo, 5.1 surround sound, quadraphonic sound, 3D spatialization
- Ogg and ADPCM decompression
- Real-time audio file stitching (Ogg and Wave)
- Distant variant distortion
- Material-based distortion (e.g. under water distortion of helicopter hovering overhead)
- Environmental DSP

4 Physics engine
- Realistic object interaction based on Newton's laws
- Particle system inherits from physics engine
- NPCs interact with objects realistically
- All objects react based on force exerted and environmental resistance

5 Networking system
- Up to 64-player LAN and 32-player internet support
- High-latency, high-packet loss optimizations
- Predictive collision detection performance enhancement

6 Development
- In-game level and terrain editor
- Exporters (meshes, brushes, etc)
- C++ written code compiled to modular design
- Event debugger and monitoring tools built into engine
- Shader editor

Creating a game engine supporting all the above-listed elements takes a lot of time, money, skilled developers and support infrastructure; however, most of the listed features can be added to an engine framework in a pluggable fashion. Hence, designing and implementing a basic first-person shooter game engine can be done by one programmer, with time the only limit with regard to the amount of supported features. It is thus of critical importance to have a well-defined architecture, without which the source code of an engine would not be extendible, maintainable or easily understandable.

We can divide the source code of a game into two units, namely, the game-engine code and the game-specific code.

- The *game-specific code* deals exclusively with in-game play elements, for instance, the behaviour of non-player characters, mission-based events and logic, and the main menu. Game-specific code is not intended for future reuse and thus excluded from the game engine code.

- *Game-engine code* forms the core of the entire game implementation with the game-specific code being executed on top of it. The game engine is separate from the game being developed in the sense that it provides all the technological components without any hard coded information about the actual gameplay.

Game-specific and engine-specific code are commonly compiled to dynamic-link libraries for easy distribution, modification and updating.

Game-engine code and game-specific code can be designed and integrated using one of the following architectures: ad-hoc, modular, or the directed acyclic graph architecture (DAG).

17

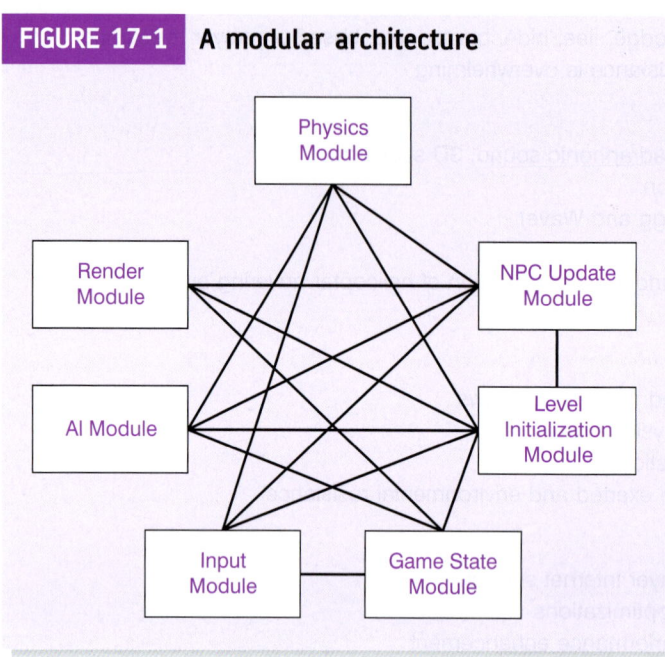

FIGURE 17-1   A modular architecture

- *Ad-hoc architecture* is a code base developed without any specific direction or logical organization; for example, a developer would simply add features to a game engine on an 'as-needed' basis. This form of code organization leads to very tight coupling (a high level of dependency) between the game-specific and game-engine code – something that is acceptable with small game projects such as mobile and casual games.

- *Modular architecture* organizes the code base into modules or libraries with a module consisting of numerous functions available for use by other modules or libraries. Using this design, we are able to add and change modules as needed. Middleware such as a third-party physics engine can also easily be integrated into a modular designed code base. Modular organization results in moderate coupling between the various code components; however, one must take care to limit inter-module communication to avoid a situation where every module is communicating with every other module – leading to a tighter level of coupling. Figure 17-1 illustrates the modular organization of a code base.

- A *directed acyclic graph architecture* is a modular architecture where the inter-module dependencies are strictly regulated. A direct acyclic graph (DAG) is a directed graph without any directed cycles. What this means is that for every node in the graph, there should not be any circular dependencies. For example, if the input module depicted in Figure 17-1 depends on the game state module, then the game state module cannot depend on any of the other modules that depend on the input module. The directed acyclic graph architecture is thus used to create a hierarchical design where some modules are classified on a higher level than others. This hierarchical structure, shown in Figure 17-2, ensures relative loose coupling.

FIGURE 17-2   A directed acyclic graph architecture

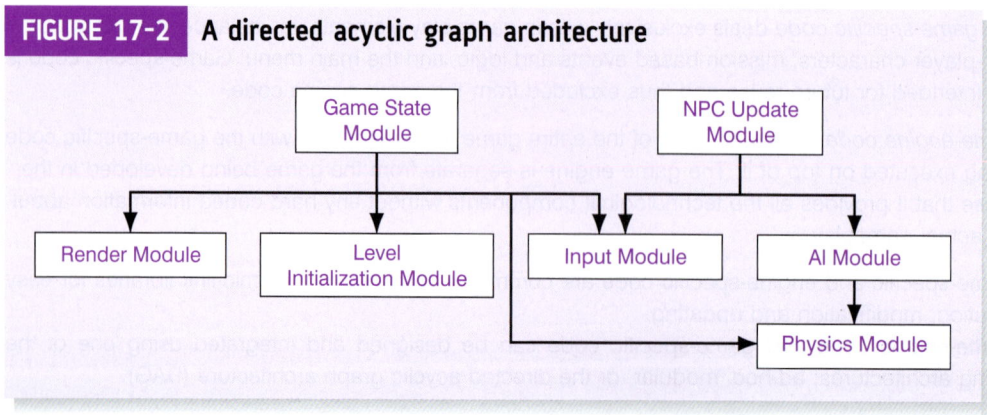

Other architectures also exist, each providing a different level of coupling and inter-module communication with the choice in architecture varying from application to application.

Once we have chosen the preferred overall architecture, we have to summarize all possible states our game will go through from initialization to shutdown. Possible states (with associated events) are listed here:

1 Initialization.

2 Enter the main game loop:
   a Additional initialization and memory allocation.
   b Load intro video.
   c Initialize and display in-game menu:
      i Event monitoring.
     ii Process user input.
   d Start game.
   e In-game loop:
      i Input monitoring.
     ii Execution of artificial intelligence (AI)
     iii Execution of physics routines.
     iv Sound and music output.
     v Execution of game logic.
     vi Rendering of the scene based on the input from the user and other subsystems.
     vii Display synchronization.
     viii Update game state.
   f Exit the game and return to the in-game menu.

3 Shutdown of the game if the user wishes to terminate the program.

We will now investigate these states in more detail.

17.1.1 Initialization and Shutdown

The first step invoked whenever a game is executed, is initialization. This step deals with resource and device acquisition, memory allocation, initialization of the game's GUI, and loading of art assets such as an intro video from file. The first initialization phase is commonly referred to as the 'front-end initialization step' to distinguish it from the level and actual game play initialization phases. Front-end initialization occurs prior to the game loop and is required for setting up the environment by assigning resources and loading game data and assets:

```
void FrontEndInit()
{
    AcquireResources();
    AllocMem();
    LoadAssets();
    InitGUI();
    LoadPlayerPreferences();
}
```

All devices and resources are released and final program cleanup is done during the exit state. The exit state has to release all resources and devices acquired, memory allocated and data loaded in the reverse order of the initial front-end acquisition:

```
void Cleanup()
{
    SavePlayerPreferences();
    ShutdownGUI();
    ShutdownAssetAccess();
    FreeMem();
    ReleaseResources();
}
```

It is essential to recognize the importance of error handling in the above listed initialization and shutdown functions, especially due to the loading of files or acquisition of resources that might not exist or that might be locked by another program.

17.1.2 The Game Loop

The game loop allows uninterrupted execution of the game. It enables us to execute a series of tasks such as input monitoring, execution of artificial intelligence and physics routines, sound and music processing, execution of game logic, display synchronization and so forth for every frame rendered. All these tasks are processed on a per-frame basis, thus resulting in a living world where everything happens in a seemingly concurrent manner, especially so where the computer game runs at 40 frames per second or more. A game running at 60 frames per second will result in the tasks for one frame being executed in less than 16.7 milliseconds. We will now look at the core tasks performed by a game loop.

The first task performed by any modern day game loop is timing. *Timing* allows a game to execute at a speed independent of the frame rate or processor's clock speed. Computer games developed during the 1970s and 1980s executed the maximum number of tasks possible for each frame cycle. This caused considerable variation in game speed whenever the user's hardware changed, for instance, a game running fine on an Intel 80286 would be impossible to play on an Intel 80486 due to the 486's overall faster execution speed.

Each frame update reflects changes made since the previous frame and the computations performed during the game loop will be used to update all the necessary game entities accordingly. The game clock operates by using the time elapsed since the last completely executed game loop as the time measure for the current frame calculation. Timing also updates the game clock to match the actual hardware clock.

Most games released today make use of *variable frame timing*. What this means is that the game's frame rate can vary depending on scene complexity, the user's hardware capabilities, etc., with these changes not affecting timing-based calculations. Thus, a game might operate at 60 frames per second (16.6ms for a complete frame calculation) where the number of polygons, light sources and in-game entities are kept to a minimum. This frame rate could on the other hand drop to 20 frames per second (50ms computation time) when rendering more computationally intensive scenes. The variable frame timing approach works extremely well for games targeting different platforms and hardware configurations. This is due to computations using the actual time duration of each frame as opposed to the actual frame rate.

Another key element of any game is the processing of player input, as detailed in Chapter 5. The main goal here is to minimize the amount of time taken to process an input event from the moment of occurrence up to the instant where the game can react to it – the smaller this reaction time, the more responsive the input and the more immersive the game. We can minimize this time by processing input at the beginning of the game loop. Networking can also be considered a form of input due to messages being received for processing.

Other tasks performed during the game loop include the execution of AI code so that NPCs can decide where to go next or what action to take, object updates, the execution of game code and scripts, the execution of physics code to ensure correct inter-object and object-entity interaction, updating the camera according to player input, animating objects and updating particle effects, etc. Collision detection (determining whether two entities have collided) and response (processing the collision and updating the health and position, for example, of related entities) is also a critical part of the game loop. Once all these tasks have successfully been executed, we can render the frame to the screen. The overall structure of a game loop is discussed in section 1.1.2, with a typical game loop looking something like this:

```
while(!ExitGame())
{
    UpdateTiming();
    InputHandling();
    UpdateNetworking();
    ExecuteScripts();
    UpdateAI();
    UpdatePhysics();
    UpdateSound();
    UpdateEntities();
    UpdateCamera();
    CollisionDetection();
    CollisionResponse();
    RenderFrame();
    UpdateGameState();
}
```

We can often improve performance by decoupling the game loop's rendering step from all the other update tasks. This will result in the rendering phase updating at a much higher rate than the other steps; however, all this will accomplish is several duplicate frames for each slower update. This situation is avoided by interpolating all the spatial values based on their previous coordinates and velocities, a process resulting in a higher frame rate. The following code sample illustrates the possible structure of a decoupled game loop:

```
while(!ExitGame())
{
    UpdateTiming();
    InputHandling();

    if(UpdateWorld())
    {
        UpdateNetworking();
        ExecuteScripts();
        UpdateAI();
        UpdatePhysics();
        UpdateSound();
```

17

```
    UpdateEntities();
    UpdateCamera();
    CollisionDetection();
    CollisionResponse();
}

InterpolateObjectStates();
RenderFrame();
UpdateGameState();
}
```

There are also numerous other miscellaneous tasks that can be performed during the game loop. Tasks such as network processing are on the other hand not needed for single player game modes and should be removed from the game loop to improve performance. The easiest way of doing this is to add a check at the start of the function, for example, the `UpdateNetworking` function could have a simple if statement returning '0' when network play isn't enabled.

We will now look at two game implementations. The first is a DirectX 10 3D environment featuring mesh-loading, texture mapping, a movable light source, a GUI (one button for switching to full-screen mode) and stencil shadow volumes. The second is an OpenGL implementation featuring blending, alpha masking, physics-based animation (four cloths blowing in the wind), texture mapping, lighting and menu interaction. The OpenGL implementation also introduces OpenGL extensions in the form of volumetric fog. Both environments allow for full control of the camera – hence, the ability to move around freely. The core sections of each program are discussed here with the complete source code available on the book's website.

17.2 CREATING AN INTERACTIVE DIRECTX 10 3D ENVIRONMENT

The DirectX 10 sample (shown in Figure 17-3) allows for basic input control in the form of a user-movable light source, first-person camera and mesh. It simply loads two meshes – one for the scene (the room) and one for the movable object (the drone). These meshes are provided as part of the DirectX software development kit – the drone was originally released as part of XNA in the .x file format and converted to the .sdkmesh format via the MeshConvert utility located in the DX10 SDK's '…\Utilities\Bin\x86' directory.

We start by declaring a structure to hold the coordinates and color of the light source:

```
struct LightingProperties
{
    D3DXVECTOR3 Position;
    D3DXVECTOR4 Color;

    LightingProperties() {}

    LightingProperties(D3DXVECTOR3 Position,
                       D3DXVECTOR4 Color)

    {
        Position = Position_;
        Color = Color_;
    }
};
```

17

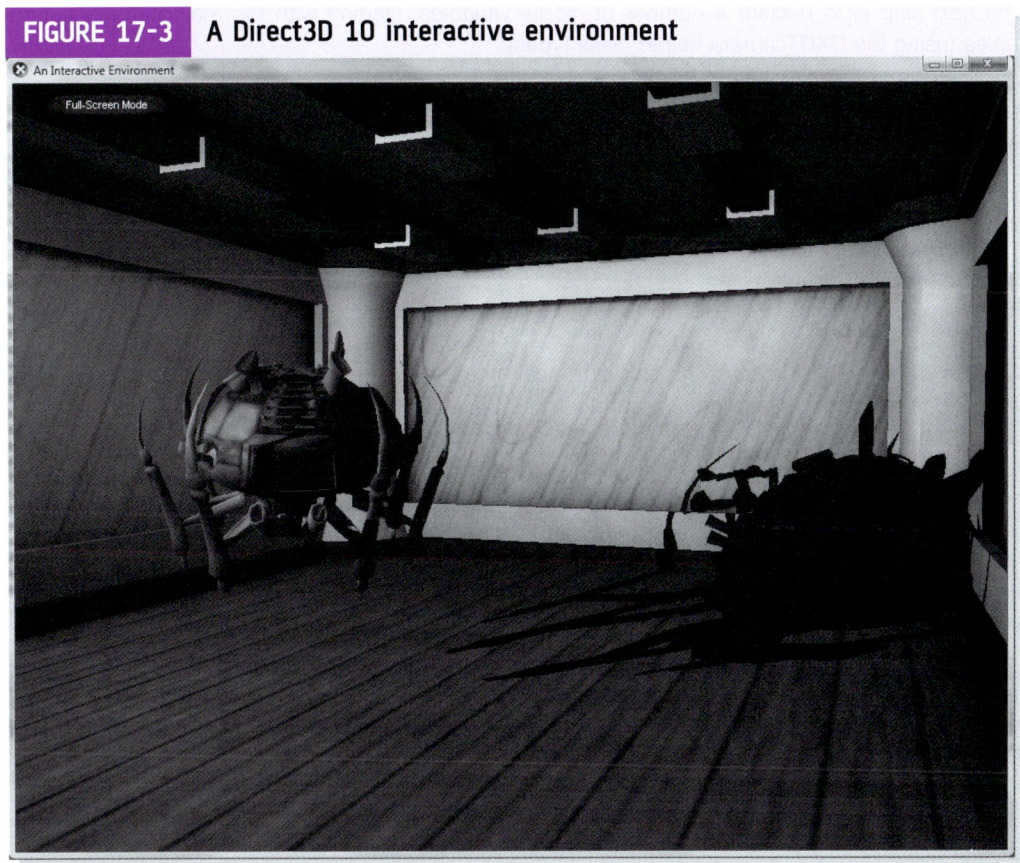

FIGURE 17-3 **A Direct3D 10 interactive environment**

Next we set up the spatial position and color of the light source using this structure:

```
LightingProperties g_SetupLights = LightingProperties(
                    D3DXVECTOR3(-4.0f,  2.0f,  -4.0f),
                    D3DXVECTOR4(10.0f,  10.0f,  10.0f,  1.0f));
```

We also have to declare a structure to store the position, color and world transformation matrix of the light source. This structure will be used to setup and translate the light source in 3D space using the previously declared g_SetupLight data:

```
struct LightData
{
    D3DXVECTOR3 m_LightPosition;
    D3DXVECTOR4 m_LightColor;
    D3DXMATRIX m_WorldTransformationMatrix;
};
```

This structure is used for the declaration of a LightData object that will store the data of each light source:

```
LightData g_LightObjectData;
```

17

The next step is to declare a number of global variables, starting with the main camera control variables (using the DXUTcamera helper class types):

```
//first-person perspective model view camera
CFirstPersonCamera g_FPSModelViewCamera;

//camera for controlling the 3D mesh movement
CModelViewerCamera g_MeshControlCamera;

//camera for controlling light movement
CModelViewerCamera g_LightControlCamera;
```

We also declare two matrices, the first is to scale the object mesh (drone) and the second is for scaling and translating the map mesh (room):

```
D3DXMATRIX g_MeshScalingMatrix;
D3DXMATRIX g_BackgroundWorldMeshMatrix;
```

Next we declare a D3DXVECTOR4 that will be used to set the scene's ambient lighting color:

```
D3DXVECTOR4 AmbientLighting(0.1f, 0.1f, 0.1f, 1.0f);
```

Input control is linked to three mouse buttons, with the left mouse button controlling rotation of the viewer's camera, the middle mouse button controlling rotation of the light source, and the right mouse button controlling the drone's rotation:

```
//true when the left mouse button is pressed
bool g_bLeftMBPressed = false;

//true when the right mouse button is pressed
bool g_bRightMBPressed = false;

//true when the middle mouse button is pressed
bool g_bMiddleMBPressed = false;
```

We also have to declare a number of Direct3D 10 resources as discussed in previous chapters:

```
/* a mesh object used to read the background .sdkmesh files
   into memory */
CDXUTSDKMesh g_GameLevelMesh10;

/* a mesh object used to read the movable .sdkmesh file into
   memory */
CDXUTSDKMesh g_MeshObject;

//interface for implementing a rendering effect
ID3D10Effect* g_pID3D10Effect = NULL;

//interface managing a vertex buffer resource
ID3D10Buffer* g_pID3D10VertexBuffer = NULL;

//interface for a vertex input layout object
ID3D10InputLayout* g_pID3D10VertexLayout = NULL;
```

```
/* ID3DlOEffectTechnique interfaces */
ID3DlOEffectTechnique* g_pID3DlOEffectRenderTextured = NULL;
ID3DlOEffectTechnique* g_pID3DlOEffectRenderLit = NULL;
ID3DlOEffectTechnique* g_pID3DlOEffectRenderAmbient = NULL;
ID3DlOEffectTechnique* g_pID3DlOEffectRenderShadow = NULL;

/* ID3DlOEffectMatrixVariable interfaces for reading shader
   variables as matrix types */

//projection matrix
ID3DlOEffectMatrixVariable* g_pd3dlOProjMatrixVar = NULL;

//view matrix
ID3DlOEffectMatrixVariable* g_pd3dlOViewMatrixVar = NULL;

//world matrix
ID3DlOEffectMatrixVariable* g_pd3dlOWorldMatrixVar = NULL;

/* ID3DlOEffectShaderResourceVariable interface for accessing
   shader-resource variables */
ID3DlOEffectShaderResourceVariable* g_pd3dlODiffuseTexture = NULL;

/* ID3DlOEffectVectorVariable interfaces for accessing shader
   variables as vector types */

ID3DlOEffectVectorVariable* g_pd3dlOLightPositionVectorVar = NULL;
ID3DlOEffectVectorVariable* g_pd3dlOLightColorVectorVar = NULL;
ID3DlOEffectVectorVariable* g_pd3dlOAmbientLightingVectorVar = NULL;
ID3DlOEffectVectorVariable* g_pd3dlOShadowColorVectorVar = NULL;

/* ID3DlOEffectScalarVariable interfaces for accessing scalar
   shader-resource variables */
ID3DlOEffectScalarVariable* g_pd3dlOExtrudeShadowAmountScalarVar = NULL;

ID3DlOEffectScalarVariable* g_pd3dlOExtrudeShadowBiasScalarVar = NULL;
```

With all the global variables set, we can now define the entry point of the application – wWinMain. This function initializes the message processing loop elements and the idle time required for the rendering of our scene:

```
int WINAPI wWinMain(HINSTANCE hInstance, HINSTANCE
                    hPrevInstance, LPWSTR lpCmdLine,
                    int nCmdShow)
{
   /* set DXUT callbacks */
   ///////////////////////////

   /* set a callback function to change the device settings
      prior to device creation */
   DXUTSetCallbackDeviceChanging(SetD3DlODeviceSettings);
```

17

```
//set the main message callback function
DXUTSetCallbackMsgProc(MsgProc);

//set the mouse event callback function
DXUTSetCallbackMouse(MouseEventProcessing);

//set the frame update callback function
DXUTSetCallbackFrameMove(HandleSceneFrameUpdates);

/* set the callback creating the Direct3D 10 resources not
   dependent on the back buffer */
DXUTSetCallbackD3D10DeviceCreated(OnD3D10CreateDevice);

/* set the callback creating the Direct3D 10 resources
    dependent on the back buffer */
DXUTSetCallbackD3D10SwapChainResized(OnD3D10SwapChainResized);

/* set the callback function releasing resources created
   by the OnD3D10ResizedSwapChain function */
DXUTSetCallbackD3D10SwapChainReleasing(ReleaseSwapChain);

/* set the callback function releasing resources created
   by the OnD3D10CreateDevice function */
DXUTSetCallbackD3D10DeviceDestroyed(OnD3D10DestroyDevice);

/* set the callback function rendering the scene on a per-
   frame basis */
DXUTSetCallbackD3D10FrameRender(RenderFrame);

//initialize the application
Initialize();

/* initialize DXUT: parses for command line arguments,
shows a message box on errors */
DXUTInit(true, true, NULL);

/* properties of the mouse cursor in full-screen mode (show
   it & prevent it from exiting the screen boundaries) */
DXUTSetCursorSettings(true, true);

//create an application window with the specified caption
DXUTCreateWindow(L"An Interactive Environment");

/* create a Direct3D 10 device with an initial width and
   height */
DXUTCreateDevice(true, 1024, 768);

//enter the main DXUT execution loop
DXUTMainLoop();

return DXUTGetExitCode();
}
```

17

In the above-given wWinMain function, we make calls to various callback functions. The first, MsgProc (passed as parameter to the DXUTSetCallbackMsgProc DXUT initialization function) handles all application messages. This callback function is called whenever an event occurs and it is declared as follows:

```
LRESULT CALLBACK MsgProc(HWND hWnd, UINT uMsg, WPARAM wParam,
                         LPARAM lParam,
                         bool* pbNoFurtherProcessing,
                         void* pUserContext)
{
    /* first let the dialogs handle all generated messages
       before passing on the remaining messages — see full
       program source code for details */

    /* all remaining messages (user input) should be passed to
       the camera */
    g_FPSModelViewCamera.HandleMessages(hWnd, uMsg, wParam, lParam);
    g_MeshControlCamera.HandleMessages(hWnd, uMsg, wParam, lParam);
    g_LightControlCamera.HandleMessages(hWnd, uMsg, wParam, lParam);
    return 0;
}
```

The DXUTSetCallbackDeviceChanging DXUT function sets a callback function responsible for changing the device settings prior to device creation. The SetD3D10DeviceSettings callback function is passed as parameter and used for this purpose (specifying how to create the D3D10 device):

```
bool CALLBACK SetD3D10DeviceSettings(
                         DXUTDeviceSettings* pDeviceSettings,
                         void* pUserContext)
{
    /* the DXGI_FORMAT_D24_UNORM_S8_UINT format supports
       stencilling */
    pDeviceSettings->d3d10.AutoDepthStencilFormat =
                         DXGI_FORMAT_D24_UNORM_S8_UINT;

    return true;
}
```

The mouse event callback function, MouseEventProcessing, processing all mouse input, is subsequently set in the wWinMain function via the DXUTSetCallbackMouse DXUT function:

```
void CALLBACK MouseEventProcessing(bool bLeftButtonDown,
                         bool bRightButtonDown,
                         bool bMiddleButtonDown,
                         bool bSideButton1Down,
                         bool bSideButton2Down,
                         int nMouseWheelDelta,
                         int xPos, int yPos,
                         void* pUserContext)
```

17

```
    {
        /* flags indicating the mouse buttons pressed */
        bool bOldLeftButtonDown = g_bLeftMBPressed;
        bool bOldRightButtonDown = g_bRightMBPressed;
        bool bOldMiddleButtonDown = g_bMiddleMBPressed;

        //is the left mouse button down?
        g_bLeftMBPressed = bLeftButtonDown;
        //is the middle mouse button down?
        g_bMiddleMBPressed = bMiddleButtonDown;
        //is the right mouse button down?
        g_bRightMBPressed = bRightButtonDown;

        //move the mesh if the right mouse button is down
        if(bOldRightButtonDown && !g_bRightMBPressed)
        {
            g_MeshControlCamera.SetEnablePositionMovement(false);
        }
        else
            if(!bOldRightButtonDown && g_bRightMBPressed)
            {
                g_MeshControlCamera.SetEnablePositionMovement(true);
                g_FPSModelViewCamera.SetEnablePositionMovement(false);
            }

        //rotate the player camera if the left mouse button is down
        if(bOldLeftButtonDown && !g_bLeftMBPressed)
            g_FPSModelViewCamera.SetEnablePositionMovement(false);
        else
            if(!bOldLeftButtonDown && g_bLeftMBPressed)
                g_FPSModelViewCamera.SetEnablePositionMovement(true);

        //move the light source if the middle mouse button is down
        if(bOldMiddleButtonDown && !g_bMiddleMBPressed)
        {
            g_LightControlCamera.SetEnablePositionMovement(false);
        }
        else
            if(!bOldMiddleButtonDown && g_bMiddleMBPressed)
            {
                g_LightControlCamera.SetEnablePositionMovement(true);
                g_FPSModelViewCamera.SetEnablePositionMovement(false);
            }

        /* move the player camera if none of the mouse buttons are
           held down */
        if(!g_bRightMBPressed && !g_bMiddleMBPressed &&
           !g_bLeftMBPressed)
            g_FPSModelViewCamera.SetEnablePositionMovement(true);
    }
```

17

The frame update callback function, HandleSceneFrameUpdates, processing each scene update, is set by the DXUTSetCallbackFrameMove DXUT function and defined as follows:

```
void CALLBACK HandleSceneFrameUpdates(double time,
                                      float timePassed,
                                      void* context)
{
    /* update the view matrix based on user input and elapsed
       time */
    g_FPSModelViewCamera.FrameMove(timePassed);
    g_MeshControlCamera.FrameMove(timePassed);
    g_LightControlCamera.FrameMove(timePassed);
}
```

The callback function creating the Direct3D 10 resources not dependent on the back buffer, OnD3D10CreateDevice, is set via the DXUTSetCallbackD3D10DeviceCreated DXUT function and defined as follows:

```
HRESULT CALLBACK OnD3D10CreateDevice(ID3D10Device* pd3dDevice,
                const DXGI_SURFACE_DESC *pBackBufferSurfaceDesc,
                void* pUserContext)
{
    //the effect file
    WCHAR effectName[MAX_PATH];

    //read and compile the effect
    DXUTFindDXSDKMediaFileCch(effectName, MAX_PATH,
                              L"MainFX10.fx");
    //create an effect from the file
    D3DX10CreateEffectFromFile(effectName, NULL, NULL, "fx_4_0",
                               D3D10_SHADER_ENABLE_STRICTNESS,
                               0, pd3dDevice, NULL, NULL,
                               &g_pID3D10Effect, NULL, NULL);

    /* get the technique handles by name from the MainFX10.fx
       file */
    g_pID3D10EffectRenderTextured = g_pID3D10Effect->
            GetTechniqueByName("RenderTextured");
    g_pID3D10EffectRenderLit = g_pID3D10Effect->
            GetTechniqueByName("RenderLitEnvironment");
    g_pID3D10EffectRenderAmbient = g_pID3D10Effect->
            GetTechniqueByName("RenderWithAmbientLighting");
    g_pID3D10EffectRenderShadow = g_pID3D10Effect->
            GetTechniqueByName("RenderSceneWithShadow");

    /* create the input-assembler stage's single element
       description */
    const D3D10_INPUT_ELEMENT_DESC vertex_input_layout[] =
    {
        {"POSITION", 0, DXGI_FORMAT_R32G32B32_FLOAT, 0, 0,
```

17

```
                 D3D10_INPUT_PER_VERTEX_DATA, 0),
             {"TEXTURE", 0, DXGI_FORMAT_R32G32_FLOAT, 0, 24,
                 D3D10_INPUT_PER_VERTEX_DATA, 0),
             {"NORMAL", 0, DXGI_FORMAT_R32G32B32_FLOAT, 0, 12,
                 D3D10_INPUT_PER_VERTEX_DATA, 0),
       };
       //structure to describe each effect pass
       D3D10_PASS_DESC EffectPassDescription;

       //get the effect pass to render the scene lit
       g_pID3D10EffectRenderLit->GetPassByIndex(0)
                                   ->GetDesc(&EffectPassDescription);

       //create an input-layout object
       pd3dDevice->CreateInputLayout(vertex_input_layout, 3,
                       EffectPassDescription.pIAInputSignature,
                       EffectPassDescription.IAInputSignatureSize,
                       &g_pID3D10VertexLayout);

       /* load the mesh representing the environment/game map as
          well as the character mesh */
       g_GameLevelMesh10.Create(pd3dDevice,
                           L"\\blackholeroom.sdkmesh",
                           false, true);
       g_MeshObject.Create(pd3dDevice, L"\\EvilDrone.sdkmesh",
                       false, true);

       //get the effect variables by name (from MainFX10.fx)
       g_pd3d10ProjMatrixVar = g_pID3D10Effect->
             GetVariableByName("ProjectionMatrix")->AsMatrix();
       g_pd3d10ViewMatrixVar = g_pID3D10Effect->
             GetVariableByName("ViewMatrix")->AsMatrix();
       g_pd3d10WorldMatrixVar = g_pID3D10Effect->
             GetVariableByName("WorldMatrix")->AsMatrix();
       g_pd3d10DiffuseTexture = g_pID3D10Effect->
             GetVariableByName("DiffuseTexture")->AsShaderResource();
       g_pd3d10LightPositionVectorVar = g_pID3D10Effect->
             GetVariableByName("LightPosition")->AsVector();
       g_pd3d10LightColorVectorVar = g_pID3D10Effect->
             GetVariableByName("LightColor")->AsVector();
       g_pd3d10AmbientLightingVectorVar = g_pID3D10Effect->
             GetVariableByName("AmbientLighting")->AsVector();
       g_pd3d10ShadowColorVectorVar = g_pID3D10Effect->
             GetVariableByName("ShadowColor")->AsVector();
       g_pd3d10ExtrudeShadowAmountScalarVar  = g_pID3D10Effect->
             GetVariableByName("ShadowExtrusionAmount")->AsScalar();
       g_pd3d10ExtrudeShadowBiasScalarVar = g_pID3D10Effect->
             GetVariableByName("ShadowExtrusionBias")->AsScalar();

       /* set the camera at the center of projection (eye) pointed
          towards the"at" location */
```

17

```
        D3DXVECTOR3 eye(0.0f, 3.0f, -8.0f);
        D3DXVECTOR3 at(0.0f, 3.1f, 0.0f);
        g_FPSModelViewCamera.SetViewParams(&eye, &at);
        g_LightControlCamera.SetViewParams(&eye, &at);
        g_MeshControlCamera.SetViewParams(&eye, &at);

        return S_OK;
}
```

The callback function creating the Direct3D 10 resources dependent on the back buffer, OnD3D10SwapChainResized, is set using the DXUTSetCallbackD3D10SwapChainResized DXUT function. This function, called for each swap chain resize, is given here:

```
HRESULT CALLBACK OnD3D10SwapChainResized(
                        ID3D10Device* pd3dDevice,
                        IDXGISwapChain *pSwapChain,
                        DXGI_SURFACE_DESC* pBackBufferSurfaceDesc,
                        void* pUserContext)
{
    //calculate aspect ratio
    float WidthHeightRatio = pBackBufferSurfaceDesc->
                Width/(FLOAT)pBackBufferSurfaceDesc->Height;

    /* called the moment the Direct3D 10 swap chain is about to
       be resized or created */
    g_DXUTDialogResourceManager.OnD3D10ResizedSwapChain(
                        pd3dDevice, pBackBufferSurfaceDesc);

    //set the camera's projection parameters
    g_FPSModelViewCamera.SetProjParams(D3DX_PI/4,
                                WidthHeightRatio,
                                0.1f, 500.0f);
    g_MeshControlCamera.SetWindow(pBackBufferSurfaceDesc ->Width,
                        pBackBufferSurfaceDesc->Height);
    g_LightControlCamera.SetWindow(pBackBufferSurfaceDesc ->Width,
                        pBackBufferSurfaceDesc->Height);

    return S_OK;
}
```

The resources created in these OnD3D10ResizedSwapChain and OnD3D10CreateDevice functions are subsequently released by the ReleaseSwapChain and OnD3D10DestroyDevice callback functions (set in wWinMain using the DXUTSetCallbackD3D10SwapChainReleasing and DXUTSetCallbackD3D10DeviceDestroyed DXUT functions, respectively). See the full source code available on the book's website for the related definitions.

We set the callback function rendering the scene on a per-frame basis by means of the DXUTSetCallbackD3D10FrameRender DXUT initialization function. This callback, RenderFrame, renders the complete frame (all the meshes, shadows, lights, etc). The RenderFrame function is given here:

```
void CALLBACK RenderFrame(ID3D10Device* pd3dDevice,
                double fTime, float fElapsedTime,
                void* pUserContext)
```

17

```
{
    //set the clear color to black
    float RenderTargetClearColor[4] = {0.0, 0.0, 0.0, 0.0};

    //clear the render target
    ID3D10RenderTargetView* pRenderTargetView =
                            DXUTGetD3D10RenderTargetView();
    pd3dDevice->ClearRenderTargetView(pRenderTargetView,
                            RenderTargetClearColor);

    //clear the stencil buffer
    ID3D10DepthStencilView* pDepthStencilView =
                            DXUTGetD3D10DepthStencilView();
    pd3dDevice->ClearDepthStencilView(pDepthStencilView,
                            D3D10_CLEAR_DEPTH,
                            1.0f, 0);

    //bind the input-layout object to the input-assembler stage
    pd3dDevice->IASetInputLayout(g_pID3D10VertexLayout);

    //draw the scene with ambient lighting
    g_pd3d10AmbientLightingVectorVar
            ->SetFloatVector((float*)&AmbientLighting);
    RenderScene(pd3dDevice, g_pID3D10EffectRenderAmbient,
                false);

    /* set the amount and bias to extrude the shadow volume
       from the silhouette edge */
    g_pd3d10ExtrudeShadowAmountScalarVar ->SetFloat(120.0f - 0.1f);
    g_pd3d10ExtrudeShadowBiasScalarVar->SetFloat(0.1f);

    /* set up the light */
    D3DXVECTOR4 LightVector(g_LightObjectData.m_LightPosition.x,
                            g_LightObjectData.m_LightPosition.y,
                            g_LightObjectData.m_LightPosition.z,
                            1.0f);

    D3DXVec4Transform(&LightVector, &LightVector,
                    g_LightControlCamera.GetWorldMatrix());
    g_pd3d10LightPositionVectorVar
            ->SetFloatVector((float*)&LightVector);
    g_pd3d10LightColorVectorVar->SetFloatVector(
                ((float*)g_LightObjectData.m_LightColor);

    /*for the light source, render the resulting shadow*/
    //////////////////////////////////////////////////////

    //clear the stencil buffer
    pd3dDevice->ClearDepthStencilView(pDepthStencilView,
                            D3D10_CLEAR_STENCIL, 1.0, 0);
```

17

```
    //prepare to render the shadow volume
    ID3D10EffectTechnique* pEffectTechnique =
                                g_pID3D10EffectRenderShadow;
    pEffectTechnique = g_pID3D10EffectRenderShadow;

    //render the actual shadow
    RenderScene(pd3dDevice, pEffectTechnique, true);

    //render the scene with normal lighting
    RenderScene(pd3dDevice, g_pID3D10EffectRenderLit, false);

    /* code to render the GUI – the"Full-Screen Mode" button
       – see full program source code for details */

    DXUT_EndPerfEvent();
}
```

The `RenderFrame` function calls the `RenderScene` function when drawing the scene with ambient lighting (without shadows), when rendering the drone's shadow and when rendering the final lit and shadowed scene. The `RenderScene` function renders the map/level mesh, the drone character and the shadow. It is also responsible for calculating the view matrices:

```
void RenderScene(ID3D10Device* pd3dDevice,
                ID3D10EffectTechnique* pEffectTechnique,
                bool renderShadowVol)
{
    //setup the view matrices
    D3DXMATRIX ProjectionMatrix;
    D3DXMATRIX ViewMatrix;
    D3DXMATRIX ViewProjectionMatrix;
    D3DXMATRIX WorldMatrix;
    D3DXMATRIX WorldViewProjectionMatrix;

    //calculate the projection matrix
    ProjectionMatrix = *g_FPSModelViewCamera.GetProjMatrix();
    //calculate the view matrix
    ViewMatrix = *g_FPSModelViewCamera.GetViewMatrix();

    //calculate and set the view project matrix
    ViewProjectionMatrix = ViewMatrix * ProjectionMatrix;
    g_pd3d10ViewMatrixVar->SetMatrix( (float*)&ViewProjectionMatrix);

    /* render the mesh representing the map/level */
    if(!renderShadowVol)
    {
        //calculate and set the world view projection matrix
        WorldViewProjectionMatrix = g_BackgroundWorldMeshMatrix*
                                ViewMatrix *
                                ProjectionMatrix;
```

17

```
        g_pd3d10ProjMatrixVar->SetMatrix(
                              (float*)&WorldViewProjectionMatrix);
        g_pd3d10WorldMatrixVar->SetMatrix(
                              (float*)&g_BackgroundWorldMeshMatrix);

        //render the map mesh
        g_GameLevelMesh10.Render(pd3dDevice, pEffectTechnique,
                              g_pd3d10DiffuseTexture);
    }

    /* render the mesh representing the object/character */
    //////////////////////////////////////////////////////

    //calculate the world matrix
    WorldMatrix = g_MeshScalingMatrix *
                    *g_MeshControlCamera.GetWorldMatrix();
    //calculate the world view projection matrix
    WorldViewProjectionMatrix = WorldMatrix * ViewMatrix *
                              ProjectionMatrix;
    //set the world and world view project matrices
    g_pd3d10ProjMatrixVar->SetMatrix(
                              (float*)&WorldViewProjectionMatrix);
    g_pd3d10WorldMatrixVar->SetMatrix((float*)&WorldMatrix);

    //render the character mesh and the shadow
    if(renderShadowVol)
      g_MeshObject.RenderAdjacent(pd3dDevice,
                              pEffectTechnique,
                              g_pd3d10DiffuseTexture);
    else
      g_MeshObject.Render(pd3dDevice, pEffectTechnique,
                          g_pd3d10DiffuseTexture);
}
```

That's pretty much it – all that remains now is to initialize the application. This is done in wWinMain via a call to our own Initialize function:

```
void Initialize()
{
    /* init the application HUD (the"Full-Screen Mode"
       button) – see full program source code for details */

    //init the light
    g_LightObjectData.m_LightPosition = g_SetupLights.Position;
    g_LightObjectData.m_LightColor = g_SetupLights.Color;

    //initialize the cameras
    g_FPSModelViewCamera.SetRotateButtons(true, false, false);
    g_MeshControlCamera.SetButtonMasks(MOUSE_RIGHT_BUTTON,0,0);
    g_LightControlCamera.SetButtonMasks(MOUSE_MIDDLE_BUTTON,0,0);
```

17

```
/* scale and translate the environment's map mesh */
/////////////////////////////////////////////////

//the translation matrix
D3DXMATRIX mapTranslationMatrix;

//create the translation matrix
D3DXMatrixTranslation(&g_BackgroundWorldMeshMatrix,0.0f,
                 1.0f, 0.0f);
D3DXMatrixTranslation(&mapTranslationMatrix, 1.0f, 1.0f,
                 0.0f);

//create an identity matrix
D3DXMatrixIdentity(&g_MeshScalingMatrix);
}
```

The main application code has now been discussed. For the related shader code, please see the full program source code available on the book's companion website. The HLSL code basically consists of lighting, texturing and shadow volume calculations – as presented in previous chapters.

17.3 CREATING AN INTERACTIVE OPENGL 3D ENVIRONMENT

The OpenGL sample is shown in Figure 17-4. The user can easily navigate the scene from a first-person perspective with the added option of changing various settings in real time. These settings are listed in Figure 17-5 and accessible by clicking the right mouse button. Similar to the DirectX sample, we navigate the scene using the keyboard's arrow keys to control the horizontal camera movement. The 'w' and 's' keys are mapped for control of the camera's vertical position.

The program starts by defining the ASCII codes for the various control keys:

```
#define ESCAPE 27
#define UP_ARROW 72
#define DOWN_ARROW 80
#define LEFT_ARROW 75
#define RIGHT_ARROW 77
```

We also set the light's vertical and horizontal angles:

```
#define LIGHTDIR_H 100.0
#define LIGHTDIR_V 60.0
```

Next we declare a number of global variables, starting with the main camera control variables (its initial 'spawn' position) and the initial y-axis rotation of the camera:

```
double g_curX = 21, g_curY = -1.5, g_curZ = 29;
double g_angle = 120;
```

We also create a global cloth instance:

```
Cloth *clothInstance = new Cloth();
```

17

FIGURE 17-4   **An OpenGL interactive environment**

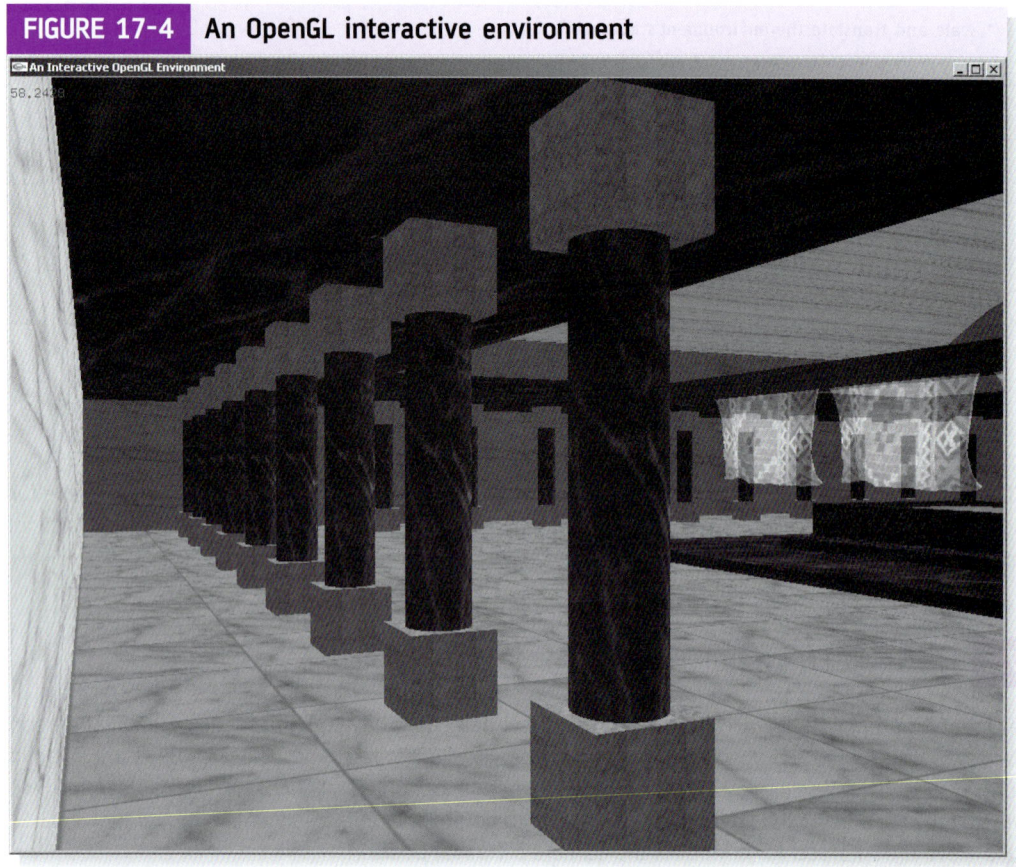

FIGURE 17-5   **Our program's settings**

Draw Wireframe
Draw Wireframe with Normals
Lighting On (Smooth Shading)
Lighting On (Flat Shading)
Lighting Off
Textures On
Textures Off
Fullscreen
Blow Wind
Stop Wind
Pool Transparency Off
Pool Transparency On
Quit

The cloth simulation is basically a physics implementation illustrating numerous physics concepts such as spring damping factors and spring forces. The cloth simulation's code is contained in the file 'ClothSimulation.cpp' (available on the book's companion website) with the DrawCloth function performing the actual rendering. We will now look at the core of our OpenGL example.

The first defined function, SetupLights, specifies our scene's light properties:

```
void SetupLights()
{
    //ambient RGBA reflectance of the material
    float materialAmbience[] = {0.5, 0.5, 0.5, 1.0};
    //ambient RGBA intensity of entire scene
    float sceneAmbience[] = {0.7, 0.7, 0.7, 1.0};
```

```
      /* specify lighting model parameters
        - GL_LIGHT_MODEL_AMBIENT: specify ambient RGBA intensity
          of entire scene */
      glLightModelfv(GL_LIGHT_MODEL_AMBIENT, sceneAmbience);

      /* specify material parameters for lighting model
        - GL_FRONT_AND_BACK: front and back faces are being
                              updated
        - GL_AMBIENT: update all the ambient faces */
      glMaterialfv(GL_FRONT_AND_BACK, GL_AMBIENT,
                  materialAmbience);
}
```

The next set of functions are used not only during initialization of the scene but also whenever the user chooses to deactivate or enable some feature such as texture mapping, lighting, or the wind effect to animate the cloths:

```
//enables texturing
void SetModeTextured()
{
    glEnable(GL_TEXTURE_2D);
}
//disables lighting
void SetLightsOff()
{
    glDisable(GL_LIGHTING);
}
//enables lighting
void SetLightsOn()
{
    glEnable(GL_LIGHTING);
}
//enables smooth shading
void SetSmoothShading()
{
    glEnable(GL_LIGHTING);
    glShadeModel(GL_SMOOTH);
}
//enables flat shading
void SetFlatShading()
{
    glEnable(GL_LIGHTING);
    glShadeModel(GL_FLAT);
}

//activates the GL_LIGHT0 light source
void ActivateLight()
{
    glEnable(GL_LIGHT0);
}
```

17

The light source position is set using the SetupLightDirection function:

```
void SetupLightDirection()
{
    float lightDirection[] = (sin(g_lightAngle) * LIGHTDIR_H,
                              LIGHTDIR_V, cos(g_lightAngle) *
                              LIGHTDIR_H, 0.0);
    glLightfv(GL_LIGHT0, GL_POSITION, lightDirection);
}
```

We also need a function that will allow us to switch from a perspective to orthographic projection. This function is used to render the frames per second text information on screen – the scene is rendered in perspective projection and the text in orthographic projection mode:

```
void SwitchToOrtho()
{
    //specify the projection matrix as the current matrix
    glMatrixMode(GL_PROJECTION);

    //push current matrix stack down by one
    glPushMatrix();

    //move to the center of the screen
    glLoadIdentity();

    //define a 2-D orthographic projection matrix
    gluOrtho2D(0, 1024, 0, 768);

    //scale along the x, y, and z-axes
    glScalef(1, -1, 1);
    /* traverse along the x, y and z-axis: move -'768' units
       (down) on y-axis */
    glTranslatef(0, -1.0*768, 0);

    //specify the modelview matrix as the current matrix
    glMatrixMode(GL_MODELVIEW);

    //move to the center of the screen
    glLoadIdentity();
}
```

With this function defined, we also need one to switch back from orthographic projection to perspective projection mode:

```
void SwitchFromOrtho()
{
    //specify the projection matrix as the current matrix
    glMatrixMode(GL_PROJECTION);

    //pop current matrix stack
    glPopMatrix();
```

```
    //specify the modelview matrix as the current matrix
    glMatrixMode(GL_MODELVIEW);
}
```

All the code specifying the scene's geometry is contained within the file 'Geometry.h' available on the book's website. This file also includes the standard texturing code. The Display function calls these 'world drawing routines' and is also responsible for rendering the frames per second text:

```
void Display(void)
{
    /* clear frame buffer and z-buffer – thus clearing the
       screen */
    glClear(GL_COLOR_BUFFER_BIT | GL_DEPTH_BUFFER_BIT);

    //move to the center of the screen
    glLoadIdentity();
    /* switch to orthographic projection, we are currently in
       perspective projection, the text has to be rendered in
       orthographic projection mode */
    SwitchToOrtho();

    //set text color to white
    glColor3f(1.0,1.0,1.0);

    //set the font rendering position to (0, 20)
    glRasterPos2i(0, 20);

    /* draw the frames per second to the screen */
    /////////////////////////////////////////////

    stringstream ss;
    //temp calculated in the"Idle" function
    ss << temp;
    string s = ss.str();

    //render the FPS raster characters
    for(int i = 0; s[i]; i++)
        glutBitmapCharacter(GLUT_BITMAP_8_BY_13, s[i]);

    //switch back to perspective projection
    SwitchFromOrtho();

    //push current matrix stack down by one
    glPushMatrix();

    //set the modelview matrix as the current matrix
    glMatrixMode(GL_MODELVIEW);

    //rotate camera 'g_angle' degrees about the y-axis
    glRotatef(g_angle, 0.0, 1.0, 0.0);

    /* translate (move) camera to the initial"spawn" position,
       thereafter moving the camera to the updated position as
       calculated by InputKeyPressed */
```

17

```
        glTranslatef(g_curX, g_curY, g_curZ);

        //init the light source position
        SetupLightDirection();

        /* world drawing routines as defined in geometry.h */
        /////////////////////////////////////////////////////
        DrawMainBottomFloor();
        ConstructPillarArchitecture();
        ConstructOuterWalls();
        ConstructInnerPedestal();
        ConstructTerraces();
        ConstructTerraceRailing();
        ConstructPersianRoof();
        ConstructRoofWalls();
        ConstructRoofWallWindow();
        ConstructPool();
        ConstructPoolSteps();
        ConstructSupportBeam();
        DrawPoolBottomFog();
        DrawPoolWater();

        /* disable culling — only facing triangles of the cloth are
           visible if not disabled */
        glDisable(GL_CULL_FACE);

        //initialize the cloth
        clothInstance->DrawCloth();

        /* enable culling (remove all the faces pointing away from
           the viewer) */
        glEnable(GL_CULL_FACE);

        //pop current matrix stack
        glPopMatrix();

        /* contents of back buffer are set to become that of front
           buffer (double buffering)*/
        glutSwapBuffers();

        glFlush();
}
```

As with all our previous OpenGL examples, we need a function to correctly adjust the aspect ratio of our window in the event of a resize:

```
void Reshape(int w, int h)
{
        /* set the viewport with the first two parameters the
           lower-left corner of the viewport rectangle, in pixels
           and the last two, the width and height of the viewport*/
        glViewport(0, 0, (GLsizei) w, (GLsizei) h);
```

```
//set the projection matrix as the current matrix
glMatrixMode(GL_PROJECTION);

//move to the center of the screen
glLoadIdentity();
/* set the perspective projection matrix:
    – the first parameter specifies the field of view (fov)
      in degrees (in the y–direction)
    – the second parameter is the aspect ratio determining
      the fov (in the x–direction)
    – the third parameter is the distance from the viewer to
      the near clipping plane
    – the final parameter is the distance from the viewer to
      the far clipping plane */
gluPerspective(45, (GLdouble)w / (GLdouble)h, 0.05, 100);

//set the modelview matrix as the current matrix
glMatrixMode(GL_MODELVIEW);
}
```

The next function, MyInit, handles the basic initialization and setup of the OpenGL parameters – in the process enabling all the necessary tests like hidden surface removal and culling while also performing tasks such as the setup and initialization of fog, lighting and texturing via calls to the previously defined functions:

```
void MyInit(void)
{
    //start by clearing the color buffers with black
    glClearColor(0.0, 0.0, 0.0, 0.0);

    //set smooth shading as our default
    SetSmoothShading();

    //enable hidden–surface removal
    glEnable(GL_DEPTH_TEST);

    //enable culling
    glEnable(GL_CULL_FACE);

    //call the texture loader from Geometry.h
    TextureLoader();

    //enable normalization
    glEnable(GL_NORMALIZE);

    /* specify the front– and back–facing polygons
        –counter clockwise polygons are front–facing (GL_CCW)
        –clockwise polygons are back–facing (GL_CW) */
    glFrontFace(GL_CCW);
```

17

```
//specify whether front- or back-faces are to be culled
glCullFace(GL_BACK);

/* initialize the volumetric fog - defined in
    "VolumetricFog.h" */
InitializeVolumetricFogExtension();

/* set the fog parameters */
/////////////////////////////

//fog fade is linear
glFogi(GL_FOG_MODE, GL_LINEAR);

//set the fog color
glFogfv(GL_FOG_COLOR, fog_color);

//set the fog start position (least dense)
glFogf(GL_FOG_START, 0.0f);

// set the fog end position (most dense)
glFogf(GL_FOG_END, 1.0f);

//per-pixel fog calculation
glHint(GL_FOG_HINT, GL_NICEST);

//set fog based on vertex coordinates(hence volumetric fog)
glFogi(GL_FOG_COORDINATE_SOURCE_EXT,GL_FOG_COORDINATE_EXT);

//activate the defined light source
ActivateLight();

//setup the light source
SetupLights();

//enable lighting
SetLightsOn();

//enable texturing
SetModeTextured();
}
```

In the above-listed function we have made a call to a method enabling volumetric fog – fog specified as a volume. To explain this function we first have to look at OpenGL extensions. The OpenGL API has undergone several updates and changes throughout its existence. It started with IrisGL (SGI's early proprietary graphics API) and running right through from OpenGL 1.0 to OpenGL 1.5 and now OpenGL 2.1, the seventh update since OpenGL version 1.0. New specifications were added during each version update, making more and more operations, routines and effects possible. For example, a 3D graphics card's packaging will state the supported OpenGL specification – the OpenGL version supported by the card gives an indication of its capabilities.

OpenGL extensions provide a way to extend the existing standard OpenGL specification. Graphics card manufacturers and other involved partners can add additional features to their graphics hardware and then provide a way to access these added features through OpenGL extensions. Only features

17

TABLE 17-1	Identifying OpenGL extensions
ID	**Description**
ARB	Extensions widely used and thus approved by the Architectural Review Board
EXT	Extensions approved by numerous OpenGL vendors
INTEL	Intel specialized extensions
HP	Hewlett Packard specialized extensions
SUN	Sun Microsystems specialized extensions
WIN	Microsoft specialized extensions
SGI	Silicon Graphics specialized extensions
SGIX	Experimental Silicon Graphics specialized extensions
NV	NVIDIA specialized extensions
ATI	ATI specialized extensions
ATIX	Experimental ATI specialized extensions (not in final state and subject to change)
S3	S3 graphics specialized extensions
IBM	International Business Machines specialized extensions
KTX	Kinetix specialized extensions

generally supported by the majority of graphics hardware end up in the ARB OpenGL specification while card specific features are accessed through the vendor specified extensions.

A large number of manufacturers and parties are involved in the specification of extensions and it is for this reason necessary to incorporate the id of the responsible party into the extension name. For example, the 'EXT' in glFogCoordfEXT indicates that the extension was established by numerous OpenGL vendors. Table 17-1 gives a list of these ids. One can also visit http://oss.sgi.com/projects/ogl-sample/registry/ for a complete list of OpenGL extensions.

Having, say, an 'NV' specialized extension doesn't mean other manufacturers can't make use of it. It simply means that the extension is specialized and may not be available on all hardware. For example, an ATI Radeon will support the extensions GL_NV_texgen_reflection, GL_HP_occlusion_test and GL_S3_S3TC – none of which were specified by ATI.

In our program we make use of glFogCoordfExt – the fog coordinate extension. Unlike normal fog, which is based on eye distance (linear or exponential), the volumetric fog extension is based on fog coordinates. This extension replaces the distance component of normal fog with vertex coordinates defining the start- and endpoint of the fog. The swimming pool in the middle of our scene utilizes volumetric fog to create a murky-watery-depth illusion.

In the file 'VolumetricFog.h', we initialize the volumetric fog extension by assigning the address of the specific video card's volumetric fog extension to the glFogCoordfEXT variable:

```
/* value taken from the glext.h header file
    -PFNGLFOGCOORDFEXTPROC takes a floating point value
    -initialize glFogCoordfEXT to NULL */
PFNGLFOGCOORDFEXTPROC glFogCoordfEXT = NULL;
```

```
//specify the fog color
GLfloat fogColor[4] = {0.0, 0.5, 0.9f, 1.0f};

//function called by MyInit to initialize volumetric fog
void InitializeVolumetricFogExtension()
{
    /* assign glFogCoordfEXT the address of the specific video
       card's volumetric fog extension
       -this routine enables volumetric fog
       Note: this will generate an error if volumetric fog
       isn't supported */
    glFogCoordfEXT = (PFNGLFOGCOORDFEXTPROC)
                          wglGetProcAddress("glFogCoordfEXT");
}
```

The wglGetProcAddress routine is used to enable OpenGL extensions on a Microsoft Windows platform. When working in Linux/UNIX, we can access the extensions in a more intuitive way by linking directly with the OpenGL extension functions. The wglGetProcAddress("glFogCoordfEXT") routine queries the address of the video card's volumetric fog extension. Using this returned address, we can call the extension function – as shown in the InitializeVolumetricFogExtension function.

The DrawPoolBottomFog function in the file 'Geometry.h' illustrates the usage of the defined glFogCoordfEXT parameter. Here we want a completely 'foggy' pool floor using the specified fog color. To facilitate this, we set the glFogCoordfEXT parameter for each vertex to '1.0'. The glFogCoordfEXT calls in the DrawPool function are responsible for the fading fog noticed on the sides of the pool. Here we set the fog intensity at the bottom two coordinates to '1.0', with the intensity at the top two coordinates set to '0.0'.

Returning to our core program source file, 'main.cpp', we have a function responsible for the vertical translation of the camera – a task performed by modifying the global position variables (g_curX, g_curZ and g_angle) whenever one of the arrow keys is pressed (GLUT_KEY_UP, GLUT_KEY_DOWN, GLUT_KEY_LEFT or GLUT_KEY_RIGHT). These variables are either incremented or decremented depending on the user input. The player movement is processed by the InputKeyPressed function. The first-person view camera position is subsequently updated in the Display function. We define this InputKeyPressed function, controlling the player's horizontal movement (forward, backward, left and right), as follows:

```
void InputKeyPressed(int key, int x, int y)
{
    //switch control structure
    switch(key)
    {
        //when the keyboard's up-arrow is pressed
        case GLUT_KEY_UP:
        {
            double rads = g_angle / 180.0L * PI;
            /* the smaller the number divided by, the faster
               the camera's forward motion */
            double dx = -sin(rads) / 1.5;
            double dz = cos(rads) / 1.5;

            g_curX += dx;
            g_curZ += dz;
        }
        break;
```

```
    // when the back-arrow is pressed
    case GLUT_KEY_DOWN:
    {
        double rads = g_angle / 180.0L * PI;

        /* the smaller the number divided by, the faster the
           backward motion */
        double dx = -sin(rads) / 3.0;
        double dz = cos(rads) / 3.0;

        g_curX -= dx;
        g_curZ -= dz;
    }
    break;

    //when the right-arrow is pressed
    case GLUT_KEY_RIGHT:
        g_angle += 5;
    break;

    //when the left-arrow is pressed
    case GLUT_KEY_LEFT:
        g_angle -= 5;
    break;

    //for all other keys pressed
    default:break;
    }
    //set the current window for redisplay
    glutPostRedisplay();
}
```

Vertical movement of the camera is performed by the Keys function (this function also tests whether the 'q' key has been pressed – subsequently causing the application to terminate if true):

```
void Keys(unsigned char key, int x, int y)
{
    //exit the program
    if(key == 'q' || key == 'Q')
    {
        exit(-1);
    }
    //move vertically up
    if(key == 'w' || key == 'W')
        g_curY -= 2;

    //move vertically down
    if(key == 's' || key == 'S')
        g_curY += 2;
}
```

17

Our next function, Idle, is used for the animation of our scene – it is a callback function setting all the states on a per-frame basis (for example, disabling texture mapping if selected):

```
void Idle()
{
    /* set the initial wind force */
    clothInstance->wind = 0.4;
    clothInstance->clothPhysics();
    clothInstance->initUnitForce();

    /* calculate the frames per second rendered */
    /////////////////////////////////////////////
    g_frames++;
    float time = glutGet(GLUT_ELAPSED_TIME);
    if (time - g_timeZero > 1000)
    {
        temp = (g_frames*1000/(time-g_timeZero));
        glRasterPos2i(3, 20);
        g_timeZero = time;
        g_frames = 0;
    }
    //set the current window for redisplay
    glutPostRedisplay();

    //draw wireframe or wireframe with normals
    if(SELECT == 1 || SELECT == 2)
    {
        SetLightsOff();
        glDisable(GL_TEXTURE_2D);
    }

    //lighting on + smooth shading
    if(SELECT == 3)
    {
        SetSmoothShading();
        ActivateLight();
        SetupLights();
        SetLightsOn();
    }

    //lighting on + flat shading
    if(SELECT == 4)
    {
        SetFlatShading();
        ActivateLight();
        SetupLights();
        SetLightsOn();
    }

    //lighting off
    if(SELECT == 5)
    {
```

17

```
                SetLightsOff();
        }

        //textures on
        if(SELECT == 6)
        {
                SetModeTextured();
        }

        //textures off
        if(SELECT == 7)
        {
                glDisable(GL_TEXTURE_2D);
        }

        //switch to full screen mode
        if(SELECT == 8)
        {
                glutFullScreen();
        }

        //activate the wind
        if(SELECT == 9)
        {
                clothInstance->wind = 2.9;
                clothInstance->clothPhysics();
                clothInstance->initUnitForce();
        }

        //stop the wind
        if(SELECT == 10)
        {
                clothInstance->wind = 0.0;
                clothInstance->clothPhysics();
                clothInstance->initUnitForce();
        }
}
```

The SELECT variable in the above-listed function is assigned values based on the menu item selected. For example, if the user chooses to disable texture mapping then SELECT will be set to the integer value '7' – a value assigned using a simple switch statement in the function ControlMenu:

```
void ControlMenu(int x)
{
    /* basic switch control structure, sets the global SELECT
       variable for switching between the different rendering
       modes */
    switch(x)
    {
```

17

```
            case 1: SELECT = 1; break;
            case 2: SELECT = 2; break;
            case 3: SELECT = 3; break;
            case 4: SELECT = 4; break;
            case 5: SELECT = 5; break;
            case 6: SELECT = 6; break;
            case 7: SELECT = 7; break;
            case 8: SELECT = 8; break;
            case 9: SELECT = 9; break;
            case 10: SELECT = 10; break;
            case 11: SELECT = 11; break;
            case 12: SELECT = 12; break;
            case 13: exit(0);
    }

    //set the current window for redisplay
    glutPostRedisplay();
}
```

This ControlMenu function is in turn called by the Menu function (responsible for creating and controlling the popup menu):

```
void Menu()
{
    //create a new pop-up menu
    glutCreateMenu(ControlMenu);

    //add menu entries
    glutAddMenuEntry("Draw Wireframe",1);
    glutAddMenuEntry("Draw Wireframe with Normals",2);
    glutAddMenuEntry("Lighting On (Smooth Shading)",3);
    glutAddMenuEntry("Lighting On (Flat Shading)",4);
    glutAddMenuEntry("Lighting Off",5);
    glutAddMenuEntry("Textures On",6);
    glutAddMenuEntry("Textures Off",7);
    glutAddMenuEntry("Fullscreen",8);
    glutAddMenuEntry("Blow Wind",9);
    glutAddMenuEntry("Stop Wind",10);
    glutAddMenuEntry("Pool Transparency Off", 11);
    glutAddMenuEntry("Pool Transparency On", 12);
    glutAddMenuEntry("Quit",13);

    //attach the right mouse button for menu selection
    glutAttachMenu(GLUT_RIGHT_BUTTON);
}
```

The last bit of code is the entry point of the application; it sets all the callback functions and enters the GLUT event processing loop to handle all the callback events as discussed in Chapter 2:

```
int main(int argc, char** argv)
{
```

```
//initialize the GLUT library
glutInit(&argc, argv);
/* set initial display mode: double buffering, depth
   buffer, alpha masking */
glutInitDisplayMode(GLUT_DOUBLE|GLUT_RGBA|GLUT_DEPTH|
                    GLUT_ALPHA);
//set default window size
glutInitWindowSize(1024, 768);

//create a top-level window with a caption
glutCreateWindow("An Interactive OpenGL Environment");

//reshape callback for the current window
glutReshapeFunc(Reshape);

//display the rendered frame
glutDisplayFunc(Display);

//set special keys callback for movement control
glutSpecialFunc(InputKeyPressed);

//key handling
glutKeyboardFunc(Keys);

/* set the global Idle callback for background
   processing/animation */
glutIdleFunc(Idle);

//cloth setup
clothInstance->particleSetup();
clothInstance->clothPhysics();

//call the Menu function
Menu();

//call the MyInit function
MyInit();

/* enter the GLUT event processing loop - will handle any
   callback */
glutMainLoop();

return 0;
}
```

17.4 SUMMARY

In this chapter, we started by looking at game engine architecture in general, highlighting the importance of software componentry, and the difference between game-engine code and game-specific code. Following this we focused on a number of game engine architectures, specifically ad-hoc, modular, and the directed acyclic graphs architecture (DAG).

17

Next we considered the first step invoked whenever a game is executed, namely initialization. Initialization was described as the stage responsible for resource and device acquisition, memory allocation, setup of the game's GUI, loading of art assets, etc. Following front-end initialization, we discussed the exit state and the game loop for the uninterrupted execution of a game.

The remainder of the chapter dealt with the implementation of two 3D environments. Our first implementation was a DirectX 10 based implementation featuring mesh-loading, texture mapping, a movable light source and object mesh, a GUI and stencil shadow volumes, with the second an OpenGL implementation featuring blending, alpha masking, physics-based animation, texture mapping, lighting, and menu interaction. The OpenGL implementation also introduced the concept of OpenGL extensions in the form of volumetric fog. Both environments allowed for full control of the camera.

17.5   FURTHER READING

As previously listed, Steve Rabin's *Introduction to Game Development* [ISBN: 1584503777] and Jonathan S. Harbour's *Game Programming All in One* [ISBN: 1598632892] are two excellent resources on the theory and practice of game development, design and production. The *Game Programming Gems* series by Charles River Media contain a great number of articles dealing with topics such as general programming, mathematics and physics, graphics, artificial intelligence, networking, and audio.

17.6   EXERCISES

1 Briefly describe what is meant by software componentry.

2 Compare game-engine code to game-specific code.

3 Why must one take care to limit inter-module communication when designing a modular game engine?

4 Explain the benefits inherent to loose coupling.

5 Draw a UML diagram of a basic game loop.

6 What is meant by variable frame timing?

7 Why is it a good idea to decouple the game loop's rendering step from all the other update tasks?

8 Write code to scale a mesh.

9 Describe the purpose of the following code sample:

```
g_FPSModelViewCamera.SetProjParams(D3DX_PI/4,
                    WidthHeightRatio,
                    0.1f, 500.0f);
g_MeshControlCamera.SetWindow(pBackBufferSurfaceDesc ->Width,
                    pBackBufferSurfaceDesc->Height);
g_LightControlCamera.SetWindow(pBackBufferSurfaceDesc->Width,
                    pBackBufferSurfaceDesc->Height);
```

10 Explain how either sample program can be extended to include collision detection – i.e. collision detection for the whole scene, to keep a viewer from walking through walls.

BIBLIOGRAPHY

Akeley K. (1993) Reality Engine Graphics. *Proceedings of SIGGRAPH 93.* New York: ACM.

Akeley K. and Jermoluk T. (1988) High Performance Polygon Rendering. *Computer Graphics,* 22(4).

Akenine-Möller T. and Assarsson U. (2002) Approximate Soft Shadows on Arbitrary Surfaces using Penumbra Wedges. *Proceedings of the 13th Eurographics Workshop on Rendering.* Aire-la-Ville: Eurographics Association.

Angel E. (1990) *Computer Graphics.* Reading, MA: Addison-Wesley.

Angel E. (2006) *Interactive Computer Graphics* (fourth edition). Boston, MA: Addison-Wesley.

Appel A. (1968) Some Techniques for Machine Rendering of Solids. *AFIPS Conference Proceedings,* 32.

Arvo J. and Kirk D. (1987) Fast Ray Tracing by Ray Classification. *Computer Graphics,* 21(4).

Arvo J. (ed.) (1991) *Graphics Gems II.* Academic Press.

Atherton P., Weiler K. and Greenberg D. (1978) Polygon Shadow Generation. *Computer Graphics,* 12(3).

Banchoff T. and Werner J. (1983) *Linear Algebra through Geometry.* New York: Springer-Verlag.

Barr A. (1984) Global and Local Deformations of Solid Primitives. *Computer Graphics,* 18(3).

Bartels R., Beatty J. and Barsky B. (1987) *An Introduction to Splines for Use in Computer Graphics and Geometric Modelling.* San Francisco, CA: Morgan Kaufmann.

Bartels R., Beatty J. and Barsky B. (1988) *Splines for Use in Computer Graphics and Geometric Modeling.* San Mateo, CA: Morgan Kaufmann.

Bier E. and Sloan K. (1986) Thow-part Texture Mapping. *IEEE Computer Graphics and Applications,* 6(9).

Beck K. and Andres C. (2004) *Extreme Programming Explained: Embrace Change.* Boston, MA: Addison-Wesley.

Blinn J. (1977) Models of Light Reflection for Computer Synthesized Pictures. *Computer Graphics,* 11(2).

Blinn J. (1978) Simulation of Wrinkled Surfaces. *Computer Graphics,* 12(3).

Blinn J. (1988) Me and My (Fake) Shadow. *IEEE Computer Graphics and Applications,* 8(1).

Blinn J. and Newell M. (1976) Texture and Reflection in Computer Generated Images. *Communications of the ACM,* 19(10).

Blinn J. (1977) Models of Light Reflection for Computer-Synthesized Pictures. *Computer Graphics,* 11(2).

Borges C. (1991) Trichromatic Approximations for Computer Graphics Illumination Models. *Computer Graphics,* 25(4).

Bouknight W. and Kelly K. (1970) An Algorithm for Producing Half-tone Computer Graphics Presentations with Shadows and Moveable Light Sources. *Proceedings of the AFIPS, Spring Joint Computer Conference,* 36.

Bowyer A. and Woodwark J. (1983) *A Programmer's Geometry.* London: Butterworth.

Box D. (1998) *Essential COM.* Reading, MA: Addison-Wesley.

Bresenham J. (1963) Algorithm for Computer Control of Digital Plotter. *IBM Systems Journal,* 4(1).

Bresenham J. (1987) Ambiguities in Incremental Line Rastering. *IEEE Computer Graphics and Applications,* 7(5).

Brotman L. and Badler N. (1984) Generating Soft Shadows with a Depth Buffer Algorithm. *IEEE Computer Graphics and Applications,* 4(10).

Cabral B., Max N. and Springmeyer R. (1987) Bidirectional Reflection Functions from Surface Bump Maps. *Computer Graphics,* 21(4).

Carlbom I. and Paciorek J. (1978) Planar Geometric Projection and Viewing Transformations. *Computing Surveys,* 10(4).

Carpenter L. (1984) The A-buffer, an Antialiased Hidden Surface Method. *Computer Graphics,* 18(3).

Castleman, K. (1996) *Digital Image Processing.* Englewood Cliffs, NJ: Prentice Hall.

Catmull E. (1978) A Hidden Surface Algorithm with Anti-aliasing. *Computer Graphics,* 12(3).

Cohen J., Lin M., Manocha D. and Pongami M. (1995) I-COLLIDE: An Interactive and Exact Collision Detection System for Large Scale Environments. *Proceedings of the 1995 Symposium on Interactive 3D Graphics.* New York: ACM.

Cohen M. (1992) Interactive Spacetime Control for Animation. *1992 SIGGRAPH Proceedings.* New York: ACM.

Cook R. and Torrance K. (1982) A Reflectance Model for Computer Graphics. *Computer Graphics,* 15(3).

Coppin B. (2004) *Artificial Intelligence Illuminated.* Sudbury, MA: Jones & Bartlett.

Crow F. (1977) Shadow Algorithms for Computer Graphics. *SIGGRAPH Proceedings 1977.* New York: ACM.

Crow F. (1981) A Comparison of Antialiasing Techniques. *IEEE Computer Graphics and Applications,* 1(1).

Crossno P. and Angel E. (1997) Isosurface Extraction Using Particle Systems. *Proceedings of the 8th IEEE Visualization Conference.* Available at: http://ieeexplore.ieee.org/xpls/abs_all.jsp?arnumber=663930.

DeLoura M. (ed.) (2000) *Game Programming Gems.* Hingham, MA: Charles River Media.

DeRose T. (1988) A Coordinate Free Approach to Geometric Programming. *1988 SIGGRAPH Course Notes.* New York: ACM.

Drebin R., Carpenter L. and Hanrahan P. (1988) Volume Rendering. *Computer Graphics*, 22(4).

Duchaineua M., Wolinsky M. and Sigeti D. (1997) ROAMing Terrain: Real-time Optimally Adapting Meshes. *IEEE Proceedings of Visualization 1997*.

Eberly D. (2001) *3D Game Engine Design*. San Francisco, CA: Morgan Kaufman.

Eberly D., Musgrave D., Peachey D., Perlin K. and Worley S. (2002) *Texturing and Modeling, A Procedural Approach* (third edition). San Francisco, CA: Morgan Kaufman.

Enderle G., Kansy K., Pfaff G. (1984) *Computer Graphics Programming: GKS – The Graphics Standard*. Berlin and Heidelberg: Springer-Verlag.

Everitt C. and Kilgard M. (2002) *Practical and Robust Stenciled Shadow Volumes for Hardware-Accelerated Rendering*. *NVIDIA* white paper published online at http://developer.nvidia.com/object/robust_shadow_volumes.html.

Everitt C., Rege A. and Cebenoyan C. (2001) *Hardware Shadow Mapping*. NVIDIA white paper published online at http://developer.nvidia.com/object/hwshadowmap_paper.html.

Farin G. (1988) *Curves and Surfaces for Computer Aided Geometric Design*. New York: Academic Press.

Faux I. and Pratt M. (1980) *Computational Geometry for Design and Manufacturing*. Chichester: Halsted Press.

Fernando R. (2004) *GPU Gems: Programming Techniques, Tips, and Tricks for Real-Time Graphics*. Reading, MA: Addison-Wesley.

Fernando R. and Kilgard M. (2003) *The Cg Tutorial: The Definitive Guide to Programmable Real-Time Graphics*. Boston, MA: Addison-Wesley.

Flynt J. and Salem O. (2004) *Software Engineering for Game Developers*. Boston, MA: Course Technology PTR.

Foley J., van Dam A., Feiner S. and Hughes J. (1990) *Computer Graphics* (second edition). Reading, MA: Addison-Wesley.

Fosner R. (1996) *OpenGL Programming for Windows 95 and Windows NT*. Reading, MA: Addison-Wesley.

Fowler M., Beck K., Brant J., Opdyke W. and Roberts D. (1999) *Refactoring: Improving the Design of Existing Code*. Reading, MA: Addison-Wesley.

Fuchs H., Kedem Z. and Naylor B. (1980) On Visible Surface Generation by A Priori Tree Structures. *SIGGRAPH Proceedings 80*. New York: ACM.

Funge J. (1999) *AI for Computer Games and Animation: A Cognitive Modeling Approach*. Natick, MA: AK Peters.

Gallagar R. (1995) *Computer Visualization: Graphics Techniques for Scientific and Engineering Analysis*. Boca Raton, FL: CRC Press.

Glassner A. (ed.) (1990) *Graphics Gems I*. Boston, MA: Academic Press.

Greene N. (1986) Environment Mapping and Other Applications of World Projections. *IEEE Computer Graphics and Applications*, 6(11).

Goral C, Torrance D., Greenberg D. and Battaile B. (1984) Modeling the Interaction of Light Between Diffuse Surfaces. *Computer Graphics*, 18(3).

Gouraud H. (1971) Computer Display of Curved Surfaces. *IEEE Transactions on Computers,* 20(6).

Gray K. (2003) *The Microsoft DirectX 9 Programmable Graphics Pipeline*. Redmond, WA: Microsoft Press.

Hahn J. (1988) Realistic Animation of Rigid Bodies. *Communications of the ACM*, 22(4).

Hall R. (1989) *Illumination and Color in Computer Generated Imagery*. New York: Springer-Verlag.

Halliday D., Resnick R. and Walker J. (2007) *Fundamentals of Physics Extended*. New York: Wiley.

Harbour J.S. (2004) *Game Programming All in One* (second edition). Boston, MA: Thomson Course Technology.

Hearn D. and Baker M. (2004) *Computer Graphics* (third edition). Englewood, NJ: Prentice Hall.

Heckbert P. and Hanraham P. (1984) Beam Tracing Polygonal Objects. *Computer Graphics*, 18(3).

Heckbert P. (1986) Survey of Texture Mapping. *IEEE Computer Graphics and Applications*, 6(11).

Heckbert P. (ed.) (1994) *Graphics Gems IV*. Boston, MA: Academic Press.

Hecker C. (2000) Physics in Computer Games. *Communications of the ACM*, 43(7).

Heidmann T. (1991) Real Shadows Real Time. *IRIS Universe*, 18.

Hill F. (2001) *Computer Graphics* (second edition). Englewood Cliffs, NJ: Prentice Hall.

Hopgood F., Duce D., Gallop A. and Sutcliffe D. (1983) *Introduction to the Graphical Kernel System: GKS*. London: Academic Press.

Hoppe H. (1996) Progressive Meshes. *1996 SIGGRAPH Proceedings*. New York: ACM.

Hoppe H. (1998) Smooth View-Dependent Level-of-Detail Control and its Application to Terrain Rendering. *IEEE Proceedings of Visualization*, 98.

Hubbard P. (1996) Interactive Collision Detection. *IEEE Transactions on Visualization and Computer Graphics,* 1(3).

Jacobson I., Booch G. and Rumbaugh J. (1999) *The Unified Software Development Process*. Reading, MA: Addison-Wesley.

Kajiya J. (1986) The Rendering Equation. *1986 SIGGRAPH Proceedings*. New York: ACM.

Kam T., Villa T., Brayton R. and Sangiovanni-Vincentelli A. (1996) *Synthesis of Finite State Machines: Functional Optimization*. Boston, MA: Kluwer Academic Publishers.

Kilgard M. (1994a) An OpenGL Toolkit. *The X Journal,* November/December.

Kilgard M. (1994b) OpenGL and X, Part 3: Integrated OpenGL with Motif. *The X Journal,* July/August.

Kilgard M. (1996a) *OpenGL Programming for the X Windows System*. Reading, MA: Addison-Wesley.

Kilgard M. (1996b) *The OpenGL Utility Toolkit (GLUT) Programming Interface*. Published online by Silicon Graphics at www.opengl.org/resources/libraries/glut/glut-3.spec.pdf.

Kilgard M. (1999) *Improving Shadows and Reflections via the Stencil Buffer*. Published online by NVIDIA at http://developer.nvidia.com/object/stencil_Buffer_Tutorial.html.

Kirk D. (ed.) (1992) *Graphics Gems III*. Boston, MA: Academic Press.

Kruchten P. (2003) *The Rational Unified Process: An Introduction*. Boston, MA: Addison-Wesley.

Lane J. and Riesenfeld R. (1980) A Theoretical Development for the Computer Generation and Display of Piecewise Polynomial Surfaces. *IEEE Transactions on Pattern Analysis and Machine Intelligence*, 2(1).

Landes J. (1998) *The Ocean Spray in Your Face*. From www .gdmag.com, July.

Lane J., Carpenter L., Whitted T. and Blinn J. (1980) Scan Line Methods for Displaying Parametrically Defined Surfaces. *Communications of the ACM*, 23(1).

Lasseter J. (1987) Principles of traditional Animation Applied to 3D Computer Animation. *Computer Graphics*, 21(4).

Lay D. (2005) *Linear Algebra and Its Applications* (third edition). New York: Addison-Wesley.

Legakis J. (1998) Fast Multi-Layer Fog. *ACM SIGGRAPH 98 Conference Abstracts and Applications*. New York: ACM.

Lengyel E. (2003) *Mathematics for 3D Game Programming and Computer Graphics* (second edition). Hingham, MA: Charles River Media.

Leon S. (2006) *Linear Algebra with Applications*. Upper Saddle River, NJ: Prentice Hall.

Levoy M. (1988) Display of Surface from Volume Data. *IEEE Computer Graphics and Applications*, 8(3).

Levoy M. and Hanrahan P. (1996) Light Field Rendering. *1996 SIGGRAPH Proceedings*. New York: ACM.

Liang Y. and Barsky B. (1984) A New Concept and Method for Line Clipping. *ACM Transactions on Graphics*, 3(1).

Lindstrom P. and Pascucci V. (2001) Visualization of Large Terrains Made Easy. *IEEE Proceedings of Visualization 2001*.

Linholm E., Kilgard M. and Morelton H. (2001) A User-Programmable Vertex Engine. *SIGGRAPH Proceedings 2001*. New York: ACM.

Lorsensen W. and Cline H. (1987) Marching Cubes: A High Resolution 3D Surface Construction Algorithm. *Computer Graphics*, 21(4).

Magnenat-Thalmann N. and Thalman D. (1985) *Computer Animation: Theory and Practice*. New York: Springer-Verlag.

Max N. and Troutman R. (1993) Optimal Hemi-Cube Sampling. *Proceeding of the Fourth Eurographics Workshop on Rendering*. Aire-la-Ville: Eurographics Association.

Maxwell E. (1951) *General Homogeneous Coordinates in Space of Three Dimensions*. Cambridge: Cambridge University Press.

McReynolds T. and Blythe D. (1997) *Programming with OpenGL: Advanced Rendering*. From: www.opengl.org/resources/ code/samples/advanced/advanced97/notes/

Miamo J. (1999) *Compressed Image File Formats*. New York: ACM Press.

Microsoft. DirectX 10 SDK Documentation. Available from msdn2 .microsoft.com/en-us/library/aa139763.aspx.

Microsoft. Platform SDK C++ Documentation. Available from msdn2. microsoft.com/en-us/library/52csφ5fz.aspx

Miller G. and Hoffman C. (1984) Illumination and Reflection Maps: Simulated Objects in Simulated and Real Environments. *1984 SIGGRAPH Course Notes*. New York: ACM.

Möller T. and Haines E. (2002) *Real-Time Rendering* (second edition). Natick, MA: A K Peters.

Montrym J., Baum D., Dignam D. and Migdal C. (1997) InfiniteReality: A Real-Time Graphics System. *Computer Graphics*, 31(3).

Moore M. and Wilhelms J. (1988) Collision Detection and Response for Computer Animation. *Computer Graphics*, 22(4).

Munsell A. (1946) *A Color Notation*. Baltimore, MD: Munsell Color Co.

Murray J. and van Ryper W. (1994) *Encyclopaedia of Graphics File Formats*. Sebastapol, CA: O'Reilly and Associates.

Newman W. and Sproull R. (1973) *Principles of Interactive Computer Graphics*. New York: McGraw-Hill.

Nguyen H. (2007) *GPU Gems 3*. Reading, MA: Addison-Wesley.

Nielsen J. (1994) *Usability Engineering*. Boston, MA: Academic Press.

Nilsson N. (1986) *Principles of Artificial Intelligence*. Palo Alto, CA: Morgan Kaufmann.

Nishita T. and Nakamae E. (1985) Continuous Tone Representation of 3D Objects Taking Account of Shadows and Interreflection. *Computer Graphics*, 19(3).

Novins K., Sillion F. and Greenberg D. (1990) An Efficient Method for Volume Rendering using Perspective Projections. *Computer Graphics*, 24(5).

OpenGL Architecture Review Board, Shreines D., Woo M., Neider J., and Davis T. (2007) *OpenGL Programming Guide: The Official Guide to Learning OpenGL, Version 2.1* (sixth edition). Reading, MA: Addison-Wesley.

OpenGL Architecture Review Board et al. (2005) *OpenGL Programming Guide, Version 2* (fifth edition). Boston, MA: Addison-Wesley.

OpenGL Architecture Review Board and Shreines D. (2004) *OpenGL(R) Reference Manual: The Official Reference Document to OpenGL, Version 1.4* (fourth edition). Boston, MA: Addison-Wesley.

Paeth A. (ed.) (1995) *Graphics Gems V*. Boston, MA: Academic Press.

Pavlidis T. (1995) *Interactive Computer Graphics in X*. Boston, MA: PWS Publishing.

Peachey D. (1985) Solid Texturing of Complex Surfaces. *Computer Graphics*, 19(3).

Peercy M., Airey J. and Cabral B. (1997) Efficient Bump Mapping Hardware. *1997 SIGGRAPH Proceedings*. New York: ACM.

Pharr M. and Fernando R. (2005) *GPU Gems 2: Programming Techniques for High-Performance Graphics and General-Purpose Computation*. Reading, MA: Addison-Wesley.

Phillips C. and Badler N. (1991) Interactive Behaviour for Bipedal Articulated Figures. *Computer Graphics*, 25(4).

Phong B. (1975) Illumination for Computer-Generated Pictures. *Communications of the ACM*, 18(6).

Piegl L. (1993) *Fundamental Developments of Computer-Aided Geometric Modelling*. New York: Academic Press.

Pilone D. and Pitman N. (2005) *UML 2.0 in a Nutshell*. Sebastapor, CA: O'Reilly.

Porter T. and Duff T. (1984) Compositing Digital Images. *Communications of the ACM*, 18(3).

Rabin S. (ed.) (2005) *Introduction to Game Development*. Hingham, MA: Charles River Media.

Rector B. and Newcomer J. (1997) *Win32 Programming*. Reading, MA: Addison-Wesley.

Reeves W. (1983) Particle Systems – a Technique for Modelling a Class of Fuzzy Objects. *Computer Graphics*, 17(3).

Reeves W. and Blau R. (1985) Approximate and Probabilistic Algorithms for Shading and Rendering Structured Particle Systems. *Computer Graphics*, 19(3).

Reeves W., Salesin D. and Cook R. (1987) Rendering Anti-aliased Shadows with Depth Maps. *Computer Graphics*, 21(4).

Reynolds C. (1987) Flocks, Herds, and Schools: A Distributed Behavioural Model. *Computer Graphics*, 21(4).

Riesenfeld R. (1987) Homogeneous Coordinates and Projective Planes in Computer Graphics. *IEEE Computer Graphics and Applications*, 1(1).

Rogers D. (1985) *Procedural Elements for Computer Graphics* (second edition). New York: McGraw-Hill.

Rogers D. and Adams J. (1990) Mathematical Elements for Computer Graphics. New York: McGraw-Hill.

Rogerson D. (1997) *Inside Com*. Redmond, WA: Microsoft Press.

Rossignac J. and Requicha A. (1986) Depth Buffering Display Techniques for Constructive Solid Geometry. *IEEE Computer Graphics and Applications*, 6(9).

Royce W. (1970) Managing the Development of Large Software Systems. *IEEE WESCON 26*.

Rubin S. and Whitted T. (1980) A 3D Representation for Fast Rendering of Complex Schemes. *Computer Graphics*, 14.

Schaufler G. and Sturzlinger W. (1996) A 3D Image Cache for Virtual Reality. *Proceedings of the 1996 Eurographics*. Aire-la-Ville: Eurographics Association.

Schlick C. (1993) A Customizable Reflectance Model for Everyday Rendering. *Fourth Eurographics Workshop on Rendering*. Aire-la-Ville: Eurographics Associations.

Schumaker R., Brand B., Guilliland M. and Sharp W. (1969) *Applying Computer Generated Images to Visual Simulation*. US Airforce Human Resources Lab Technical Report: AFHRL-Tr-69.

Segal M. and Akeley K. (1992) *The OpenGL Graphics System: A Specification* (version 1.0). Silicon Graphics.

Seitz S. and Dyer C. (1996) View Morphing. *1996 SIGGRAPH Proceedings*. New York: ACM.

Shade J., Gortler S., He L. and Szeliski R. (1998) Layered Depth Images. *1998 SIGGRAPH Proceedings*. New York: ACM.

Shade J., Lischinski D., Salesin D., DeRose T. and Snyder J. (1996) Hierarchical Image Caching for Accelerated Walk-throughs of Complex Environments. *1996 SIGGRAPH Proceedings*. New York: ACM.

Shirley P. (2002) *Fundamentals of Computer Graphics*. Natick, WA: AK Peters.

Sillion F. and Puech C. (1989) A General Two-Pass Method Integrating Specular and Diffuse Reflection. *Computer Graphics*, 22(3).

Smith A. (1978) Color Gamut Transformation Pairs. *Computer Graphics*, 12.

Snyder J. (1992) *Generative Modelling for Computer Graphics*. London: Academic Press.

Snyder J. (1998) Visibility Sorting and Compositing without Splitting for Image Layer Decomposition. *1998 SIGGRAPH Proceedings*. New York: ACM.

Stallings W. (2000) *Operating Systems: Internals and Design Principles* (fourth edition). Upper Saddle River, NJ: Prentice Hall.

Stallings W. (2002) *Computer Organization and Architecture* (sixth edition). Upper Saddle River, NJ: Prentice Hall.

Stam J. and Loop C. (2003) Quad/Triangle Subdivision. *Computer Graphics Forum*, 22(1).

Stang G. (1993) *Introduction to Linear Algebra*. Wellesley, MA: Wellesley-Cambridge Press.

Sutherland I. (1964) Sketchpad, A Man-Machine Graphical Communication System. *Proceedings of the SHARE Design Automation Workshop DAC '64*. New York: ACM.

Sutherland I. and Hodgman G. (1974) Reentrant Polygon Clipping. *Communications of the ACM*, 17(1).

Sutherland I., Sproull R. and Schumacher R. (1974) A Characterization of Ten Hidden-Surface Algorithms. *Computer Surveys*, 6(1).

Swanson R. and Thayer L. (1986) A Fast Shaded-Polygon Renderer. *Computer Graphics*, 20(4).

Torrance K. and Sparrow E. (1967) Theory for Off-Specular Reflection from Roughened Surfaces. *Journal of the Optical Society of America*, 57(9).

Troelsen A. (2000) *Developer's Workshop to COM and ATL 3.0*. Piano, TX: Wordware Publishing.

Upstill S. (1989) *The RenderMan Companion: A Programmer's Guide to Realistic Computer Graphics*. Reading, MA: Addison-Wesley.

Wagner F., Schmuki R., Wagner T. and Wolstenholme P. (2006) *Modeling Software with Finite State Machines: A Practical Approach*. Boca-Raton, FL: Auerbach.

Walter B., Hubbard P., Shirley P. and Greenberg D. (1997) Global Illumination using Local Linear Density Estimation. *ACM Transactions on Graphics*, 16(3).

Warn D. (1983) Lighting Controls for Synthetic Images. *Computer Graphics*, 17(3).

Warren J. and Weimer H. (2003) *Subdivision Methods for Geometric Design*. San Francisco, CA: Morgan Kaufmann.

Warren J. and Schaefer S. (2004) A Factored Approach to Subdivision Surfaces. *IEEE Computer Graphics and Applications*, 24(3).

Warnock J. (1969) *A Hidden-Surface Algorithm for Computer Generated Half-Tone Pictures*. University of Utah Computer Science Department Technical Report: 4-15, NTIS AD-753 671.

Watt A. (2000) *3D Computer Graphics* (third edition). Reading, MA: Addison-Wesley.

Watt A. and Watt M. (1992) *Advanced Animation and Rendering Techniques*. Workingham: Addison-Wesley.

Weiler K. and Atherton P. (1977) Hidden Surface Removal using Polygonal Area Sorting. *Computer Graphics*, 11(2).

Wenzel C. (2006) Advanced Real-time Rendering in 3D Graphics and Games: Real-time Atmospheric Effects in Games. *SIGGRAPH Proceedings 2006*. New York: ACM.

Whitted J. (1980) An Improved Illumination Model for Shaded Display. *Communications of the ACM*, 23(6).

Williams L. (1978) Casting Curved Shadows on Curved Surfaces. *Computer Graphics*, 12(3).

Williams L. and Chen S. (1993) View Interpolation for Image Synthesis. *1993 SIGGRAPH Proceedings*. New York: ACM.

Witkin A. and Heckbert P. (1994) Using Particles to Sample and Control Implicit Surfaces. *Computer Graphics*, 28(3).

Witkin A. (ed.) (1994) An Introduction to Physically Based Modeling. *SIGGRAPH Proceedings 94*. New York: ACM.

Wloka M. (2002) *Fresnel Reflection*. Published online by NVIDIA at: http://developer.nvidia.com/object/fresnel_wp.html.

Wolfram S. (1991) *Mathematica*. New York: Addison-Wesley.

Wyszecki G. and Stiles W. (1982) *Color Science*. New York: Wiley.

Young D. (1994) *The X Window System: Programming and Applications with XT, OSF/Motif*. Englewood, NJ: Prentice Hall PTR.

INDEX

3D
Cartesian coordinate systems *see* coordinate system, Cartesian
environment
creating 623–58
elements 90–2
Studio Max 30–1, 194, 534

A* algorithm 583–5
Ableton Live 596
abscissa 269
absolute positioning *see* positioning, absolute
acceleration 543–4
accelerator tables 217
accumulation buffer *see* buffer, accumulation
ACID 596
action Mapping 172–9
applying 177–8
retrieving 179
setting 173–7
specifying 173
additive color model *see* color model, additive
addressing
real mode 15
virtual mode 15
Adobe Photoshop 30–1, 339, 405
affine transformation *see* transformation, affine
aggregate 28
see also class diagrams, associations
Agile Software Development *see* extreme programming
AI *see* Artificial Intelligence
aliasing 111–2, 320, 436
anti- 111–2, 117, 128
alpha
blending 117, 214, 404–17, 508
masking 214–5, 405, 657
testing 114, 413–7
version *see* version, alpha
alpha-to-coverage 407
ambient lights *see* light, ambient
ambient reflection model *see* reflection, ambient
AmigaOS 14

amplitude 184, 593–5
sampling resolution 594
analysis and design 19
animation 526–34
articulated objects, of 531–2
behavioural 532–3
particle 530–1
physics, via the Laws 531
rigid bodies, of 529–30
anisotropic filtering *see* texture filtering, anisotropic
anisotropy 321
anti-aliasing *see* aliasing, anti-
API *see* Application Programming Interfaces
Apple II 5–6
Plus 6
Applesoft 6
Application Programming Interfaces 38–9
ARB *see* OpenGL, Architecture Review Board
arcade systems 2
architecture design document *see* design document, architecture
area averaging 112
articulated mesh *see* mesh, articulated
artifacts 126, 319
Artificial Intelligence 567–91
history in games 568–70
modeling, by means of finite state machines 576–8
pre-programmed 570–4
scripted 575
scripting 574–6
assembly 28
see also class, base
association name 26
see also class diagrams, associations
Asteroids 555–7
Atari ST 6–8
atmospheric perspective 418
attack 180
see also Force, feedback
attenuation 344
attribute functions *see* function, attribute
audio 592–621
auto centering 181
see also force, feedback

automated testing *see* testing, automated
autonomous behaviour *see* memory and planning
auxiliary buffer *see* buffer, auxiliary
axon 588

back buffer *see* buffer, back
base class *see* class, base
Beck, Kent 21–2
behavioural animation of objects *see* animation, behavioural
beta version *see* version, beta
Bezier curve 109
bilinear filtering *see* texture filtering, bilinear
billboard *see* sprite
binding semantic 244, 258
bin-trees *see* tree, binary triangle
BioShock 529
blackbox 38
blender 30, 534
blend state object 214–5
blending
factor 215, 410, 419
implementing 406–13
Blinn's shadow polygons 433–5
blitters 8
blob 255
bloom effect *see* effect, bloom
bottom-half interrupts *see* interrupts, bottom-half
Bouknight, Jack 435
bounding
box *see* bounding, volume
volume 501–2, 503, 542, 557
breadth-first search *see* search, breadth-first
breakout 5, 540, 555–6
B-spline surface 109
buffer
accumulation 90, 452, 482
auxiliary 90
back 48, 90, 528
depth 90, 214, 443
frame 86, 89–90, 95, 114
front 48, 90, 126–7, 528
stencil 90, 128, 214, 438–9, 442–54

buffered data 168–72
  see also DirectInput;
    immediate data
bump mapping see mapping, bump
business
  case 18
  modeling 19

C for Graphics 236–52
  compiler 238
  context 239, 241–2
  initializing 238–42
  language profiles 236–8
  runtime 238–9
callback
  creation and registration 45
  function 45
  global 45
  menu 45, 50
  window 45
camera
  frame see frame, camera
  model
    pinhole 271
    synthetic- 271–2
Carmack, John 6
Cartesian coordinate system
    see coordinate system,
    Cartesian
Catacomb 3D 7
center of projection 272–3, 276, 278–9
centroid 483
Cg see C for Graphics
change control 20
  see also rational unified process
choice devices see device, choice
chromatic dispersion 386, 391–4
chromosome 590
chronological backtracking 585
class
  base 27–8, 81
  co- 70
  derived 27
  diagrams 23–8
    aggregation 27–8
    associations 25–6
    generalizations 27
    instance 28
    interfaces 28
client-server model 41, 108, 110
clipping 94, 110, 272–5, 484–505
  Cohen-Sutherland 489–98, 500, 503
  image space 275, 484
  Liang-Barsky 498–500, 505
  object space 275, 484
  polygon 500–501
  primitive 110
  three-Dimensional 501–505
  two-Dimensional 485–500
  volume 38–9, 272, 485, 499, 503–4

closed
  beta see version, closed beta
  list 584–5
co-class see class, co-
Cohen-Sutherland Clipping see clipping,
    Cohen-Sutherland
code
  game-engine 625
  game-specific 625
color 310–315
  depth 89
  hue 312–3
  indices 90
  model
    additive 310–12, 356
    frame see frame, model
    hexcone 312–3, 355, 356
    subtractive 311, 355
  processor 110
  saturation 312–13
  true- 311
  value 204, 312–13, 603
COM see Component Object Model
  aggregation 148
  object and interfaces 69–79
Commander Keen 549, 594
Commodore 64 6
communication 22–4
  see also extreme programming
compilation
  dynamic 238
  static 238
complex polygon see polygon, complex
Component Object Model 68–83, 146, 597
component-based architecture 20
  see also rational unified process
composition 28
  see also class diagrams, aggregation
computer animation techniques 528–34
concave polygon see polygon, concave
conditional effect see effect, conditional
conditionals 579–80, 590
  see also autonomous behaviour
configuration and change
    management 19
console systems 2
constant force see force, constant
construction phase 18–9
  see also rational unified process
constructor 75, 81
content elements 19
continuous
  integration 21
    see also extreme programming
  signal see sound, continuous signal
control functions see function, control
convex polygon see polygon, convex
cooperative
  levels
    normal 601

  priority 601
  write-primary 601
multitasking see multitasking,
    cooperative
coordinate
  space
    global 94
    local 93–4
    world 93–4
  system
    Cartesian 269–71, 541
    changing 275–82
    left-handed 270
    right-handed 270–1
coordinates
  device 145, 269
  eye 276, 350
  homogenous 283–4
  screen 269
  texture 317–20, 327–8
  world 93, 145, 269
COP see center of projection
Coulomb friction see friction, Coulomb
courage 22
  see also extreme programming
CPU-bound processes see processes,
    CPU-bound
cracks 508
creatures 590
cross product 373–5
  see also vectors
crossover 590
Cross-Platform Audio Creation
    see XACT
Crow, Frank 437
Cubase 596
cube mapping see mapping, cube
culling 94, 272–5, 475
  occlusion 275
  point 110
  view frustum 272
Cunningham, Ward 21
customer feedback 22

DAG see game engine architecture,
    directed acyclic graph
data design document see design
    document, data
DDE see Dynamic Data Exchange
deadlock 14
decision tree see tree, decision
deflection coil 88
dendrites 588
deployment 19
  see also rational unified process
depth
  -fail 439–40
  -first search see search, depth-first
  -pass 438–40, 457, 460
  buffer see buffer, depth

image 436
of field 271
stencil
    state object 214
    testing, enabling 443–54
derived class *see* class, derived
design 17
document
    architecture 17
    data 17
    game 2
    interface 17
    procedural 17
destructor 75
deterministic AI *see* Artificial Intelligence,
        pre-programmed
device
    choice 144
    coordinates *see* coordinates,
        device
    independent graphics 269
    keyboard 142
    locator 145
    measure 87
    object 126
    picking 145
    string 144–5
    stroke 145
    trigger 87
    valuators 145
Diamondware Sound Toolkit 596
diffuse reflection model,
        see reflection, diffuse
digital sound *see* sound, digital
Direct3D
    10 processing pipeline 96–108
    extension vector functions 374–6
    generating output 126–34
    initialization 126–34
    render states 212–6
    utility framework *see* DXUT framework
    see also DirectX, graphics
DirectAnimation 54
DirectDraw 53
DirectInput 145–87
device
    acquiring 161–2
    capturing data 168–72
    cooperative level 155–61
    creating 149–52
    data format 153–4
    reading data 162–7
    setup 147–67
object, creating 147–8
direction of projection 278
directional lighting *see* light,
        directional
DirectMusic 54
DirectPlay 54
DirectShow 54

DirectSound 53, 79, 118, 597–611
DirectSound3D 54, 597, 602
DirectX
    audio 53, 118, 597–621
    foundation classes 52–65
    graphics 53, 118
    input 54, 118
    interface creation 80–3
    media 54
    networking 54
    programming interface 117–8
    queries 80–3
discriminator 27
display list 110
dithering 114
Donkey Kong 5
Doom 6–8, 438, 568, 594
Doom3 40, 438
    engine 9
dot product 371
    see also vectors
double buffering 126–7
draw functions *see* function, draw
Dune II 568, 569
Dungeon Master 6
Dungeons & Dragons Online 4
DxDiag 54
DXUT framework 216–27
Dynamic Data Exchange 68
dynamic dispatch 81

effect
    bloom 395–6, 398
    conditional 180
    enumeration 182–3
    Fresnel 386, 390
    periodic 180, 183–5, 187
    pool 259
    see also Cg; force, feedback; HLSL;
        shaders
elaboration phase 18
    see also rational unified process
emissive light *see* light, emissive
emitter 560–1
entity 515
    see also mesh
envelope 180, 184–5
    see also force, feedback
environment discipline 20
    see also rational unified process
environmental mapping *see* mapping,
        environmental
evaluators 108
event
    -driven 9, 48
    processing 45
    handler 122
    loop 9–10, 51, 56, 62, 122, 126
    mode *see* mode, event

evolutionary design 21
    see also extreme programming
exclusive mode 146, 155
    non- 155
    see also DirectInput
expert systems 589–90
extreme programming 3, 21–23
eye coordinates *see* coordinates, eye

fade 180, 182, 184, 650
    see also attack; envelope; fog;
        force, feedback
falloff 362
    see also light
Far Cry 570
field of view 94, 271–2, 568
fixed-function lighting model 361
fill area 196
    see also polygon
film plane 271–2, 276
finite state
    automaton *see* finite state, machine
    machine 12, 576
flow-driven 9
fog 417–29
    distance 419
    implementing 421–9
    intensity 419
    physics of 419–21
font rendering functions *see* function,
        font rendering
force 544–5
    constant 180
    feedback 179–87
        device setup 180–1
        effect 180
        effects, using 182–7
    normal 554
    ramp 180
foreshortening 278
FOV *see* field of view
fragment 95
    processing 95, 229
    processor 113–4, 233
    program, creating 249–52
frame
    buffer *see* buffer, frame
    camera 280, 283
    model 275–6, 280
    object 282
    view 275
    world 275–6
frequency 593–4
    see also sound
Fresnel effect *see* effect, Fresnel
friction 553–5
    Coulomb 554
friction 184, 539, 553–5
front buffer *see* buffer, front
FSA *see* finite state automaton

FSM *see* finite state machine
function 10
   attribute 38
   control 39
   draw 103
   font rendering 46
   initialization 46
   input 39
   menu creation and control 46
   model rendering 46
   primitive 38
   query 39
   state retrieval 47
   transformation 39
   viewing 38
   window color-map manipulation 47
   window creation and control 48
functional testing *see* testing,
        functional
fundamental quantity 541
FX Composer 31

GA *see* Genetic Algorithm
Galaxian 568
game
   design document *see* design
        document, game
   development 2–15
      elements of 8–12
      history of 4–8
      techniques and methodologies
        15–23
      tools 29–34
   engine architecture 624–7
      ad-hoc 626
      directed acyclic graph 625–6
      modular 626
   loop 9–12, 628–30
   states 627–30
      initialization 627–8
      shutdown 627–8
GarageBand 596
Gates, Bill 7
GDI *see* Graphics Device Interface
general availability release 4
generalization *see* class diagrams,
        generalizations
   see also inheritance
genetic algorithm 590
geometric transformation *see*
        transformation, geometric
geometry
   -shader 96, 106, 227, 347, 350, 454
   stage 105–6, 216, 347
GIMP 30, 33, 339, 405
global
   callback *see* callback, global
   coordinate space *see* coordinate
      space, global
   illumination *see* illumination, global

globally unique identifiers 70–1
GLU *see* OpenGL, Utility Library
   quadrics 383
GLUT *see* OpenGL, Utility Toolkit
gold *see* version, gold
Golden Gate Bridge 417
graphics
   device interface, 117
   pipeline architecture 92–114
   system 86–90, 269–70
gravitational pull 549–52
gravity 549
grid unit 111
GUIDs *see* Globally Unique
      Identifiers
Guildwars 4

Half-Life 8
Half-Life2 529, 540–1, 570
   Lost Coast 395
Halo 3 529
handheld devices 2, 86
Hardware Graphics Pipeline 229–32
   see also programmable, graphics
      pipeline
Havok 529, 541, 546
HDR *see* light, high dynamic range
head-to-tail rule *see* vector, addition
Hearts 117
Heidmann, Tim 438
height maps 464–75
hexcone color model *see* color
      model, hexcone
hidden surface removal 475–84
   problem 476
hierarchical models, 516
high dynamic range rendering
      see light, high dynamic range
high level shader language
      252–65, 411, 436
   compiler 253–4
   data types 260–1
   effects, utilizing 261–5
   initialization 254–7
   shaders, creating 258–60
HLSL *see* high level shader
      language
homogenous coordinates *see*
      coordinates, homogenous
Hovertank 3D 7
HRESULT 80
hue *see* color, hue

I/O-bound processes *see* processes,
      I/O-bound
IDE *see* integrated development
      environment
IFF *see* interchange file format
IIDs *see* interface IDs
   see also GUIDs

illumination
   function 360
   global 364, 376
   local 376–86
image space
   algorithms *see* space, image
   clipping *see* clipping, Image space
immediate data 162–8
   see also buffered data; DirectInput
implementation 17
   see also waterfall model
implementation discipline 19
   see also rational unified process
implementation iteration 21
   see also extreme programming
inception phase 18
   see also rational unified process
index of refraction 387–8
inheritance 24, 27, 69, 72, 81
initialization functions
      see function, initialization
input
   -assembler stage 97–8,
      101–3, 196, 213–4
   -layout (state) object 213–4
   classes 144–5
   devices 86–7, 142–4
   functions *see* function, input
   logical 86
   physical 86
   slots 103
installation and maintenance 17
   see also waterfall model
instance diagrams *see* class diagrams,
      instance
integer 6
   see also Applesoft
integrated development environment 33
integration 17
   see also waterfall model
intelligence 568
intelligent agent 568
interchange file format 608
interfaces *see* class diagrams, interfaces
interface design document *see* design
      document, interface
interface IDs 70
interrupt handlers 9
interrupts
   bottom-half 9
   top-half 9
iterative software development
      see rational unified process

Jefferies, Ron 21
joint
   angle 525
   rigid parts of objects, connecting
      525–6
Judgement Day 7

Kelley, Karl 435
kernel 12–3, 15
    hybrid 12–3
    micro 13
    monolithic 12–3
keyboard devices *see* device,
        keyboard
keyframing 529
Khronos Group 40
    see also ARB
Kilgard, Mark 116
kinetic energy 548–9, 593
    conservation of 547–9

Lambert's cosine law 368
Lambertian surfaces 368
leading vertex *see* vertex, leading
left-child, right-sibling tree *see* tree, left-
        child, right-sibling
level of detail 505–10
    top-down 506
    Uniform 506
    view-dependent 506
Liang-Barsky clipping *see* clipping,
        Liang-Barsky
light
    ambient 91, 244, 362–3
        see also reflection, ambient
    directional 92, 363
    emissive 363–4
    high dynamic range 395–400
    intensity *see* falloff
    low dynamic range 395, 397
    model 361
    omnidirectional *see* light, ambient
    parallel *see* light, directional
    point 361
    sources 359–64
    spot 362
    type property 92, 360
line
    loop 196
    segment 195
    strip 104–5, 106, 196, 197
linear
    momentum *see* momentum, linear
    transformation *see* transformation,
        linear
Linux 12, 14–5, 116, 597, 624, 652
local coordinate space
        see coordinate space, local
local illumination, *see* illumination, local
locator devices *see* device, locator
LOD *see* level of detail
logical input device *see* input, logical
lookup table 113
loop 10
low dynamic range lighting *see* light, low
        dynamic range
luminance 360, 363

Mac OS X 14
macro 82
main message loop 119–26
mainstream production 2
management of requirements 20
    see also rational unified process
mapping
    bump 95, 338–46
    cube 346–55
    environmental *see* mapping, cube
    reflection *see* mapping, cube
    shadow 435–7
    texture 113, 315–55
mass 542
material properties 90–1, 360, 364
Maya 30, 194, 534, 565
measure *see* device, measure
memory *see* planning
    action 579
menu callback *see* callback, menu
menu creation and control functions
        see function, menu creation
        and control
Mesa 41
mesh
    articulated 531
    loading and rendering 534–7
    polygonal 514–26
    representation 515–525
MIDI *see* Musical Instrument
        Digital Interface
Miles Sound System 596
milestone 2–3
Minesweeper 117
Minix 13
    see also kernel, micro
mipmapping *see* texture filtering, mipmap
mode
    event 87
    request 87
    sample 87
model
    rendering functions *see* function,
        model rendering
    space *see* space, model
modeling transformation
        see transformation, modeling
momentum 545–6
    conservation of 547–9
    linear 547–9
    transfer of 547–8
Mortal Kombat 576
MS-DOS 7
MUDs *see* multi-user dungeons
multiplicity 25–6
    see also class diagrams,
        associations
multiprocessing 13
multiprocessor 13
multiprogramming 13–4

multisampling 128, 324
    see also anti-aliasing
multitasking 13–5
    cooperative 14
    pre-emptive 14
multithreading 13
multi-user dungeons 4
musical instrument digital
        interface 594–5
mutation 590

nearest point interpolation
        see texture filtering,
        nearest point
neural network 588–9
neurons 588
Nine Inch Nails 596
non-exclusive mode *see* exclusive
        mode, non-
normal cooperation *see* cooperative
        levels, normal
normal force *see* force, normal
normal map 33, 316, 339–45
NVPerfKit 31
Nyquist–Shannon sampling theorem 594

object
    -orientated operating system
        design 15
    collisions 555–60
    frame *see* frame, object
    linking and embedding 68
    popping 272, 508
    space
        clipping see clipping, object space
occlusion culling *see* culling, occlusion
OLE *see* object, linking and
        embedding
omnidirectional light *see* light,
        omnidirectional
opacity 404, 432
Open Graphics Library *see* OpenGL
open
    beta *see* version, open beta
    list 584–5
    see also pathfinding
OpenAL 596–7
OpenGL 40–4
    Architecture Review Board 40, 114
    extensions 228, 650–2
    generating output 135–7
    initialization 135–7
    processing pipeline 108–14
    programming interface 114–6
    Utility Library 115
    Utility Toolkit 44–52, 115–6, 144
operating system architecture 12–5
ordinate 269
out modifier 244
    see also shaders

outcode 489
out-of-core algorithm 508
output
    -merger stage 107–8, 447, 449,
        479, 481–2
    devices 88–9
    semantics 244
overlay planes 90
OXO 4

Pac-Man 5
pages 15
    see also addressing, virtual mode
Painter's Algorithm 275, 483–4
    reverse 483
pair programming 21–2
    see also extreme programming
parallel lights see light, parallel
particle system 560–5
    implementing 561–5
    setup stage 560
    simulation stage 561
pathfinding 582–8
    see also A* Algorithm; search,
        breadth-first; search, depth-first
path-tracking 572–3
PC game see personal computer game
penumbra 432
    wedges 440–2
    see also umbra
PerfHUD 31
performance counters 31
periodic effect see effect, periodic
personal computer game 5
Peter Molyneux's Populous 6
Phong Reflection Model see reflection,
    Phong model
physical input device see input,
    physical
Physics
    fundamentals of 540–6
    implementation see physics,
        modeling
    modeling 546–60
PhysX 540–41
picking device see device, picking
pinhole Camera Model see camera
    model, pinhole
pixel 89
    -shader stage 107
    map 113
        processor 113
        processing 112–3
    shaders 62, 227–8
    testing unit 113
planning 578–82
plug-in 31, 33, 339
point
    culling see culling, point
    lights see light, point

lists 195
of view 272
polling 9, 161, 168
    see also interrupt handlers
polygon 193–212
    clipping see clipping, polygon
    complex 193
    concave 194, 500–1
    convex 194, 501
    drawing 203–12
    mesh see mesh, polygonal
    shadow see shadow, polygon
    types 194–200, 514
polyhedron 514
polylines 196
polymorphism 80–1
Pong 5
PONG 4–5
pool effect see effect, pool
portable gaming systems 2
position 541–2
positioning
    absolute 142
    relative- 142
pre
    -alpha see version, pre-alpha
    -emptive multitasking
        see multitasking, pre-emptive
    -image 317
    -processor 42
    -production 2
    -programmed AI see Artificial
        Intelligence, pre-programmed
primitive 193–212
    assembly and rasterizer 110–2, 229
    assembly see primitive, assembly
        and rasterizer
    attributes 200
    clipping stage see clipping, primitive
    drawing 203–12
    functions see function, primitive
    geometric 41, 108, 115, 193–200,
        229, 514
    raster 108, 194
    types 194–200
priority cooperation see cooperative
    levels, priority
Pro Tools 596
procedural design document see design
    document, procedural
process 9
    scheduler 9
    see also threads
processes
    CPU-bound 14
    I/O-bound 14
production rule 576, 581, 589–90
programmable
    graphics pipeline 232–5
    pipelines 95–114

programming interface 114–8
progressive chain 19
project management 2, 19
    see also rational unified process
projection 271
    transformation see transformation,
        projection
projectors 272, 278

Q3Radiant 30
quadrics see GLU, quadrics
quad-tree see tree, quad-
Quake 6, 40
Quake 3 30, 569–70
Quake II 568
Quake III Arena see Quake 3
query functions see function, query

ramp force see force, ramp
rasterization 95, 111, 212, 229
    see also fragment, processing
raster text see text, raster
rasterizer state object 212–3
rational method compiler 18
rational unified process 17–21
real-time physics engines 546
    see also physics modeling
refactoring 22
    see also extreme programming
reference counting 70
    see also COM
reflection 386–395
    ambient 91, 244, 246, 364–5
    diffuse 91, 245, 367–8, 376
    mapping see mapping, reflection
    models 364–70
    perfect diffuse 368
        see also Lambert's cosine law
    Phong model 368–70
    specular 91, 245, 365–7
reflective 70
    see also COM; transitive; symmetric
refraction 387–90
regular grids 506
    see also level of detail
relative-positioning see positioning,
    relative
release candidate see version, release
    candidate
RelentENGINE 624
rendered 561
    see also particle system
RenderWare 9
request mode see mode, request
requirements analysis and
    specification 16
    see also waterfall model
requirements management 19
    see also rational unified process
resolution 89

respect 22
  see also extreme programming
reverse painter's algorithm *see* Painter's
      Algorithm, reverse
Reynolds behavioural model 533
right-handed coordinate system *see*
      coordinate system,
      right-handed
role names 26
  see also class diagrams, associations
roles 19
  see also rational unified process
Romero, John 6
rotation 285–90
  about an arbitrary fixed point 288–90
  about the coordinate axes 286–8
run-time dynamic linking 68

sample mode *see* mode, sample
sample state object 216
sampler 251
saturation *see* color, saturation
scalar multiplication 372
  see also vectors
scaling 290–1
scan-line
  algorithm 435
  polygon projection 435–7
scissoring 114
screen
  coordinates *see* coordinates, screen
  ordering algorithm 317, 321
  screen space *see* space, screen
scripted AI *see* Artificial Intelligence,
      scripted
scripting *see* Artificial Intelligence, scripting
search
  breadth-first 585–6, 591
  depth-first 585–6, 591
sequential software development
      see waterfall model
shader(s) 227–65
  model 228, 237, 253–4, 260
  pass-through vertex 105
  programs 107, 227–8, 238, 240, 252
  system values 98
  see also C for Graphics; high level
      shader language; pixel,
      shaders; vertex, shaders;
      unified shaders
shadow(s) 431–61
  map 436
  mapping *see* mapping, shadow
  polygon *see* Blinn's shadow polygons
  rendering algorithms 432–42
  soft-edged 440–2
  volumes 437–42
    see also stencil, shadow
      volumes

shininess 91, 245, 248, 365
silhouette edge 437
simple DirectMedia Layer 38
simplicity 22
  see also extreme programming
soft-edged shadows *see* shadows,
      soft-edged
software
  componentry 68, 624
  engineering 2, 8, 16, 20–1, 23
  quality 20
    see also rational unified process
  regression 4
Solaris 40
soma 588
sound 593–7
  continuous signal 594
  digital 594–5
  speed of 593
  synthesized 594
  wave 593–4
  see also audio; DirectSound; XACT;
      XAudio
soundcard 7, 594–8
space
  image 94, 477
    see also clipping, Image space;
        z-buffer algorithm
  model 275, 278
  see also frame, model
  object 247, 317, 341, 344, 380, 477, 483
    see also clipping, object space;
        Painter's Algorithm
  screen 93, 275, 317
    see also transformation, projection
  tangent 341
  texture 317–8, 341
  view 93
  world 93, 341
    see also transformation, world
specular reflection model
      see reflection, specular
specularity 91, 245, 365–6
speed of sound *see* sound, speed of
spotlights *see* light, spot
sprite 202
standard Cg Library 236
  see also C for Graphics
starting condition 10–1
state
  -based 41, 108
    see also OpenGL, processing
        pipeline
  retrieval functions *see* function, state
      retrieval
stencil
  buffer *see* buffer, stencil
  counting inversion 439–40
  shadow volumes 432, 454–61

stencilling 90, 438, 442, 451, 459
STL *see* standard template library
stream-output stage 85, 105–6
string device *see* device, string
stroke
  devices *see* device, stroke
  text *see* text, stroke
subresource 100, 205–6, 267, 325
subtractive color model *see*
      color model, subtractive
Super Mario World 549
sustain level 180
  see also force, feedback
swap chain 58, 126–9
swizzling 247
symmetric 70
  see also COM; reflective; transitive
synthesized sound *see* sound,
      synthesized
synthetic-camera model *see* camera
      model, synthetic-
syntax highlighting 33
system feedback 22
  see also extreme programming

tangent space *see* space, tangent
tasks 19
  see also rational unified process
TBN matrix 341, 344
team feedback 22
  see also extreme programming
Tennis for Two 4
text
  raster 200–3
  stroke 200–3
test cases 3
  see also testing, unit
testing
  automated 4, 22
  discipline 19
  functional 3–4, 22
  unit 3, 19, 22
texels 114, 216, 234, 253, 315–21, 339
texture
  coordinates *see* coordinates, texture
  fetch instruction 234
  filtering 216, 234, 318–21
    anisotropic 321
    bilinear 320
    mipmap 318–9
    nearest point 319–21
    trilinear 320–1
  mapping *see* mapping, texture
  ordering 317
  sampling 216
texturing *see* mapping, texture
threads 9, 13
three-dimensional clipping *see* clipping,
      three-dimensional

tile paging 508
time 541
timing 628
t-junction 508
top-down LOD *see* level of detail,
    top-down
top-half interrupts *see* interrupts, top-half
trajectory 552
    paths 552–3
transform and lighting 8
transformation
    affine 282–4
    functions *see* function, transformation
    geometric 93, 109
    linear 282
    matrix 270
    modeling 94, 276–8
    projection 94, 278–81, 317, 436
    spatial 282–91
    view 276, 278–9, 350
    viewport 281–2
    world *see* transformation, modeling
transition phase 18–9
    see also rational unified process
transitive 70
    see also COM; reflective; symmetric
translation 283–5
traversal
    level-order 519
    post-order 519
    pre-order 519
tree
    binary triangle 508
    decision 579–82
    left-child, right-sibling 520
    quad- 507–8
    structure 508, 518–20
triads 311
triangle
    rendering rotated 301–2
    rendering scaled 303–6
    rendering translated 299–301
    rendering without any transformations
        291–9
triangulated irregular network 506–7
    see also Level of Detail
trigger *see* device, trigger
    function 9
    see also measure
trilinear filtering *see* texture filtering,
        trilinear
tri-stimulus values 310
tweening 529
two-dimensional line clipping *see*
        clipping, two-dimensional

umbra 432
    see also penumbra

UML *see* Unified Modeling Language
Unified Modeling Language 17, 23–9
unified shaders 228
uniform LOD algorithms
        see level of detail, uniform
unit
    testing *see* testing, unit
    vectors *see* vectors, unit
UNIX 12, 15, 38, 40, 44–5, 116
unpacker 112
Unreal 8, 40, 568
Unreal Engine 3 40
Unreal Tournament 577
use case model 18

valuators *see* device, valuators
variable
    frame timing 628
    sensitivity 142
vector(s) 370–6
    addition 371
    length 370–1
    unit 373–4
velocity 543
version
    alpha 3
    beta 3
    closed beta 3
    gold 4
    open beta 3
    pre-alpha 3
    release candidate 3, 18, 19
vertex 195
    -shader stage 105, 213
    leading 196
    processing 93–4, 228–9
    program, creating 242–9
    shaders 105, 227, 233, 258
video game 2, 5–6, 15, 144, 540
view
    -dependent LOD algorithms *see* level
        of detail, view-dependent
    frame *see* frame, view
    frustum 212, 229, 272, 506
        culling *see* culling, view frustum
    space *see* space, view
    transformation *see*
        transformation, view
    volume 272, 280–1
viewing function *see* function,
        viewing
viewing
    system 272–5
    transformation see transformation,
        view
viewport 58, 129, 212
    transformation *see* transformation,
        viewport

virtual
    -key messages 126
    frame buffers 90
    function table 80–1
    image plane 271–2, 485
    memory 15
visual software modeling 20
vtable *see* virtual, function table

waterfall model 15–7
wave table synthesis 595
wavelength 92, 310–1, 360, 386, 593
waypoint
    pathfinding 586–8
    system 586–7
weight *see* mass
widget 144–5
Williams, Lance 435
Windows 95 7, 14, 121, 596
window
    color-map manipulation functions *see*
        function, color-map
        manipulation
    creation and control 85–138, 119–37
        functions *see* function, window
            creation and control
    setup 119–126
Windows Driver Model 117
Windows XP Driver Model 117
With Teeth 596
Wolfenstein 3D 7, 568
work product 19
    see also rational unified process
World of Warcraft 4
world
    coordinate space *see* coordinate
        space, world
    coordinates *see* coordinates, world
    frame *see* frame, world
    space *see* space, world
    transformation *see* transformation,
        modeling
wrapper 79, 82
    see also COM
write-primary cooperative level *see*
        cooperative levels, write-
        primary

X3DAudio 79, 597, 611
XACT 53, 118, 597, 611–7
XAudio2 617–21
Xbox 360 52–4, 117–8, 144, 188–9,
        613, 617
XInput 118, 188–9

z-buffer algorithm 478–82
    see also hidden surface removal;
        shadow, mapping